Oracle8*i* Web Development

Oracle8*i* Web Development

Bradley D. Brown

Osborne/McGraw-Hill

Berkeley New York St. Louis San Francisco
Auckland Bogotá Hamburg London Madrid
Mexico City Milan Montreal New Delhi Panama City
Paris São Paulo Singapore Sydney Tokyo Toronto

Osborne/**McGraw-Hill**
2600 Tenth Street
Berkeley, California 94710
U.S.A.

For information on translations or book distributors outside the U.S.A., or to arrange bulk purchase discounts for sales promotions, premiums, or fund-raisers, please contact Osborne/**McGraw-Hill** at the above address.

Oracle8*i* Web Development

234567890 DOC DOC 019876543210

ISBN 0-07-212242-0

Publisher
Brandon A. Nordin

Associate Publisher and Editor-in-Chief
Scott Rogers

Acquisitions Editor
Jeremy Judson

Project Editor
Cynthia Douglas

Acquisitions Coordinator
Monika Faltiss

Technical Editor
Dan Wittry

Copy Editor
Dennis Weaver

Proofreaders
Pat Mannion
Mike McGee

Indexer
Valerie Robbins

Computer Designers
Gary Corrigan
Elizabeth Jang
Roberta Steele

Illustrators
Robert Hansen
Brian Wells
Beth Young

Series Designer
Jani Beckwith

This book was composed with Corel VENTURA ™ Publisher.

To my wife, Kristen

The one I love, who makes me a better man, makes me complete, and helps me to be the best I can possibly be—I wouldn't be half the person I am without her. She has taught me more about myself than anyone ever, and edified my ability to be patient. She is my soulmate and life partner. She taught me when to stop and realize that there is always tomorrow. She helps me to put life into perspective and helps me to use all of my talents (as defined in the Bible). Kristen puts balance in my life and helps me to keep life in the non-urgent important box (as defined by Steven Covey) rather than the urgent important side of life—she helps me to eliminate crisis from our lives. She has not only given me my children, but she had them—a task I certainly could not bear. She always does the hard things! Kristen always helps me understand what I need to participate in and supports me 110 percent. She completes me and makes me the best person I can possibly be. She helped me finish college in three and a half years, she helped me choose my first job, supported me when we lived in my hometown, and understood and supported me when it came to moving to New York or Chicago for my career. She has always supported my career over her own, all the way. Kristen supported my dream to start my own company and then to move to Colorado (I've dreamt of living in Colorado since I visited when I was 10 years old). She supports me every day in every way. Not only did she support my dream to write one book, but also supported every moment of the second book. I know she is always there for me. Our relationship grows every day; we are better friends every day, and we are best friends now. I love Kristen because she thinks a lot like me. She knows that if you do good things for others, good things will happen to you. She supports our children in every way—when they hurt, she hurts. She lives her life for others. When I say the wrong thing, she knows what I mean. I want nothing but the best for everyone I know and so does she. Kristen and I are very much alike, but she thinks more with her heart, and I tend to think with my head. She is a person of feelings—I'm an ESTJ (Meyers-Briggs), and she's an ESFJ. I'm strong on the thinking side, and she's strong on the feeling side. She completes me. Behind every good man there is a great woman, and Kristen is the woman behind this man! Kristen, thank you for completing me and making me a better man!

About the Author

Bradley D. Brown is president of TUSC (The Ultimate Software Consultants), a 1997 and 1998 Inc. 500 full-service consulting company specializing in Oracle with offices in Chicago, Denver, and Detroit. Brad has been working with management information systems for more than 17 years, including the last 12 with a focus on Oracle. He is recognized worldwide as a leading Oracle author. In June of 1998, Brown co-wrote *Oracle Application Server Web Toolkit Reference* with Richard J. Niemic and Joeseph C. Trezzo as part of the Oracle Press Tips & Techniques series TUSC is writing for Osborne/McGraw-Hill.

Contents at a Glance

PART I
Getting Prepared

PART II
Core Concepts

Contents

PART II
Core Concepts

PART III

Oracle Tools

PART IV
Other Cartridge Options

PART V
Miscellaneous

PART VI
Appendix

Foreword

By Randy Baker, Vice President of Oracle Support Services, Oracle Corporation

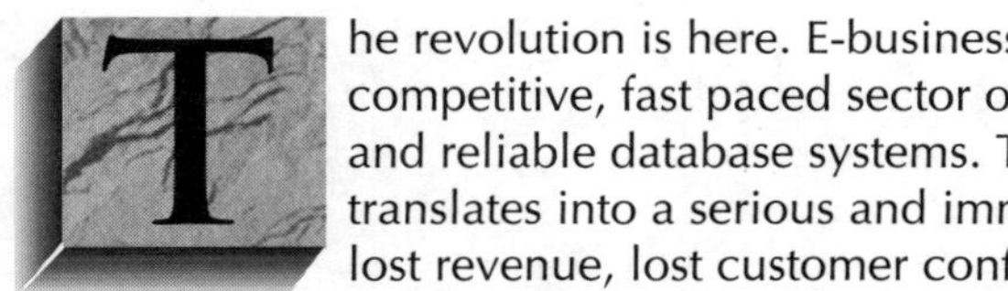

The revolution is here. E-business has evolved into a highly competitive, fast paced sector of the economy that counts on fast and reliable database systems. To e-business customers, downtime translates into a serious and immediately measurable impact of lost revenue, lost customer confidence, customer defections, and adverse media attention. At Oracle Support Services, we actively assist and support our customers as they develop and implement e-business solutions. We gain special insight ourselves because we are evolving at the same time into an e-business model for Oracle Corporation.

I can't begin to tell you the importance I put on Web-based support. With our MetaLink Web-based service, we can provide the customer with immediate access to timely information on Oracle products and services, as well as solutions to difficult problems. With our latest version of MetaLink (MetaLink 2.0), we will truly conduct business with our customers online! In addition to technical libraries and forums, file access, knowledge base search, and bug search, our customers customize the information they receive, manage MetaLink access, update contract information, and query, create, and update Technical Assistance Requests (TARs) online.

As we move into the year 2000, I am excited about Oracle Support's move to use our own Customer Relationship Management (CRM) software. For many years, Oracle Support developed our own tools and systems to run our business. With the release of CRM, we have the privilege of being among the first to put our support business on the intranet—and gain all the productivity that one, worldwide system affords.

And so, it is my pleasure to introduce *Oracle8*i *Web Development,* by Brad Brown. With this book, it is my hope that you will get the information you need to develop effective Web-based solutions for your, and our, customers in the 21st century.

I will recommend this book to our Web developers within Oracle Corporation, and I highly recommend it to you.

Acknowledgments

My life is filled with many great people. My children are a huge part of my life—I learn so much from them. My son, Austin, is now 12 years old and about one inch from growing taller than me. He has grown from a small child into a small man of considerable wisdom. Austin has incredible common sense and tireless imagination and creativity. He is an amazing young man who cares very much for other people. Austin is confident in his own abilities, which makes me proud. I have so enjoyed the opportunity to have him as a part of my life. Amazingly, we only have about six more years with Austin before he goes away to college. I know that we will be best of friends forever. Watch for Austin on the big screen some day; he's an incredible actor.

My daughter, Paige is 9 years old. Paige is an absolutely brilliant child, smarter than almost everyone I know. Not only is she incredibly smart and brilliant with a keen common sense, she is an incredible athlete. She won the state championship in the breaststroke this summer. She's extremely modest and would be very upset if anyone knew she was a state champion, so please don't say anything to her about it. She's the most amazing and fascinating child you will ever meet. Paige will give 110 percent of herself; she is always there for everyone. While I was working on this book, she actually typed for me while I was driving her to a friend's house. I am extremely fortunate to have such special children. I could not have written this book without their love and support.

Even though my name is on the front of this book, a large group of people contributed to the project. Specifically, the people mentioned here, who wrote entire chapters or made significant contributions to chapters. The following people wrote entire chapters start to finish (if there is not a company name, the authors are employed at TUSC):

Randy Swanson (Chapter 1), Larrel "Scotty" Scott (Chapter 3), Venkat Devraj, Raymond James Consulting (Chapter 7), Jason Bennett, Oracle (Chapter 13), Chris Piacesi, Jeff Fagan, and Jason Bennett, all from Oracle (Chapter 16), Patrick Fagan, Corporate Express (Chapter 19), Jean Kuzniar (Chapter 22), Robert Taylor (Chapter 25) and Steve Hamilton (Appendix A).

The following people contributed significant portions of these chapters:

Ellen Robinson, Dot to Dot Communications (Introduction) Dave Fornalsky, Jack Wachtler, Dianna Anderson, Brian Anderson (Chapter 3), Matt Malcheski (Chapter 6), Felix Lacap (Chapter 10), Vince Vazquez (Chapter 11), Mark Reidel (Chapter 12), Matt Malcheski (Chapters 15, 23, and 24), Dan Wittry (Chapter 24), and Karen Callaghan (Chapter 26).

When it came time to perform the technical reviews, Dan Wittry stepped up to the plate when I asked for an interim technical reviewer. Dan quickly realized the value of reading the book from start to finish, but also made personal sacrifices to do so. Thank you so much, Dan, for performing such a fine technical review of this book. Dan was not alone in his technical review efforts. Robin Fingerson performed technical reviews on numerous chapters. Mark Pelzel, Don Tornquist, and Brett Feldmann each reviewed a chapter or two as well.

A special thanks goes out to my review team. Jennifer Galloway provided countless hours of reviews at every stage of the book. Her spirit and determination to make it all flow made such a difference in the quality of this book.

My executive assistants, Kathy Sumpter and Lynn Agans, also provided numerous edits, standardizations and reviews in this process and of course, they also kept me pointing in the right direction each day.

Of course, all the people at Oracle Press made writing this book a pleasure as well: Scott Rogers, Associate Publisher and Editor-in-Chief, who has an amazing way of creating book ideas and making them a reality. Jeremy Judson, the acquisitions editor; Monika Faltiss, Jeremy's acquisitions coordinator; Cynthia Douglas, the project editor; Dennis Weaver, the copy editor; Pat Mannion and Mike McGee, the proofreaders; and Valerie Robbins, the indexer.

Everyone at TUSC has contributed to this book in some way, shape, or form. Whether directly or indirectly, each person has played a role in the completion of this book.

My partners Joe Trezzo and Rich Niemiec are two of the greatest guys in the world. I've been exceptionally fortunate to have met up with them many years ago. For three partners to stick together through thick and thin for more than 11 years is pretty amazing. I owe this to their dedication to life and making the world a better place for us all. It's also amazing that three entrepreneurs spending as much time as we have on the business have such unbelievable partners in life—the same partners since before we started the business—our first partners ever. Thank you to Lori Trezzo and Regina Niemiec for everything you have done as well. TUSC is a team effort all the way!

I would like to specifically thank Bill Lewkow for his dedication to keeping the Denver ship afloat and pressing forward while I was writing this book. Bill does such an incredible job of managing the day-to-day business. Thank you Bill.

Also, special thanks to all my associate partners, who held down the fort while I wrote this book: Tony Catalano, Dave Kaufman, Burk Sherva, Jake Van der Vort, and Dave Ventura.

I would also like to thank Dave Ventura for getting me into this crazy Web world to begin with. TUSC was asked to speak at a Society for Information Management (SIM) to debate with Richard Finklestein as to whether client/server was dead. Dave felt I was in the best position to participate in this great geek debate. I was to argue that client/server was alive and kicking. After a considerable amount of research while preparing for this debate, I quickly realized that even though client/server was not dead, it was soon to be. In fact, my recommendation was that the early adopters within the group better get going. It was that spark that ignited my curiosity and got me fired up about the Web and the possibilities that lay therein. I have never once looked back—I just kept digging. I'm still at the point where the more I learn, the less I feel like I know. I'm really excited that Dave is now getting into the world of the Web himself. Thank you Dave!

All of the fine employees and friends that work at TUSC: Lynn Agans, Brian Anderson, Dianna Anderson, Joel Anonick, Diane Ansah, Kamila Bajaria, Dean Bouchard, Greg Bogode, Mike Butler, Karen Callaghan, Pat Callahan, Alain Campos, Tony Catalano, Holly Clawson, Judy Corley, Janet Dahmen, Jennifer Deletzke, Susan DiFabio, Doug Dikun, Deb Dudek, Barb Dully, Brett Feldmann, Robin Fingerson, David Fornalsky, Jennifer Galloway, Craig Gauthier, Deb Gollnick, Chelsea Graylin, Mark Greenhalgh, John Gregory, Steve Hamilton, Scott Heaton, Mike Holder, Leslie Hutchings, Mohammad Jamal, Dave Kaufman, Lori Kelley, Prabhjot Khurana, Andrea Kummer, Jean Kuzniar, Felix Lacap, Lynn Lafleur, Ron Lemanske, Bill Lewkow, Larry Linnemeyer, Antonia Lopez, Matt Malcheski, Dan Martino, Sean McGuire, James Michel, Paul Murray, Kent Nichols, Rich Niemiec, Mike O'Mara, Mark Pelzel, Allen Peterson, Dennis Pieniazek, Nadica Podgurski, Amy Prevatt, Heidi Ratini, Bob Reczek, Sheila Reiter, Mark Riedel, Kathleen Rinker, Chris Rizzo, Nancy Robbins, Kim Ross, Chad Scott, Larrel Scott, Kevin Sheahan, Burk Sherva, Avi Smith, Rick Snyder, Tim Somero, Chi Son, Jack Stein, Randy Swanson, Linda Talacki, Jennifer Taylor, Bob Taylor, Chris Thoman, Cheryl Thomas, John Thompson, Don Tornquist, Joe Tseng, Jake Van der Vort,

Vince Vazquez, Dave Ventura, Jon Vincenzo, Jack Wachtler, Aisha Walls, Jim Walsh, Kim Washington, Chuck Wisely, Dan Wittry, Tom Wood, and Bob Yingst.

The following thoughts and comments are from some of the TUSC people who contributed to this book:

Dan Wittry: "In the past three and a half years I have accomplished so much (successful consulting engagements, building a house, running a half-marathon, doing black-moguls on a snowboard, etc.). I feel I am in a position to help others, albeit maybe only in small ways.

"I know I'm still young, but I've reached the age when people feel mortal. I guess deep inside, helping with this book is my way to help society be a better place by passing along the knowledge others have put between my ears. When others use our experiences to get their products or projects to market faster and with higher quality, then I guess the little pain I felt while rearranging my schedule for a few months is all worth it. If this book is Brad's 'baby,' then I feel like the next-door neighbor who changed a few diapers in its infancy."

Karen Callaghan: "The book offers insider information on OAS topics in greater detail than found anywhere else and in a consolidated format. The information in the book offers readers knowledge that can only be gained from knowing and working with the OAS product from its earliest version to present. Anyone who wants to work with OAS or would like to improve upon their existing knowledge of programming in an Oracle /OAS environment will stand to benefit and add to their arsenal of Web development knowledge."

Jennifer Galloway: "I have been presented a phenomenal opportunity in my career to be offered the experience to edit three books by three incredible men. Through each book, I have acquired the pleasure of working and becoming acquainted with men who possess morals, standards, and ethics that I thought had become extinct.

"I have witnessed the intricacies of publishing, the hours of purple ink, the ten reasons never to write a book (Rich Niemiec) and the sweet aroma of success. Working on the Oracle Press series has been a lifetime experience."

Felix Lacap: "Writing takes inspiration, preparation, and perspiration, with lots of imagination. Writing a chapter under a time schedule requires focus, stamina, and patience—and more importantly, reaching inside your 'bag of tricks,' i.e., drawing heavily from your experience. With my years at TUSC, I have accumulated a good amount of experience working with Oracle products and the Web technology. This is in part due to my assignment at Argonne National Laboratory Advanced Photo Source (ANLAPS), which provided me the opportunity to work on a variety of challenging and interesting projects. Thank you Brad Brown (TUSC), Joe Trezzo (TUSC), Rich Niemiec (TUSC), Burk Sherva (TUSC), Tony Catalano (TUSC), Marcia Wood (ANLAPS), and Steve Leatherman (ANLAPS)."

David M. Fornalsky: "I was very excited when Brad contacted me and asked if I'd like to contribute to the Design section of his book. I was nervous as well, since I'd never done any 'formal' writing. It was much more difficult than I thought it would be, and I complement the partners on their efforts for writing these books for TUSC. My hope is that what I've written will indeed help people to design better Web pages."

Larrel (Scotty) Scott: "I really am grateful that Brad asked me to help with his book. It is very exciting to help build something that will help so many people. I learned a lot writing my chapter and really hope that those who read the book find it useful. It is overwhelming to see how much work it is to write a book. It is even more impressive how so many people have worked together to get this book finished. Again, I feel very lucky to have had the chance to help."

Matthew Malcheski: " Writing is not for the faint of heart. It is a long arduous task. However, once completed, a relief not known to many overtakes you and fills you with a sense of accomplishment."

Kathy Sumpter: "Although my contribution to the book was minimal, it was a pleasure to be part of the process. It was exciting to follow the development of the book as it progressed. What started out as a collection of 1,000+ emails that needed to be organized soon migrated to chapter outlines and drafts that were then molded and transformed into the next bestseller. Deadlines were tight, as the entire book was to be written in a short timeframe, but Brad's knowledge, focus, dedication, and enthusiasm made my small part in the process a piece of cake. It was a great learning experience."

A special thank you to my family for putting up with my dream to write a second book and for understanding who I am. Thank you Kristen, for always being there. Thank you Austin, for understanding why I brought my laptop to swim meets. Thank you Paige, for typing part of Chapter 26 in the car when I was under deadline. Thank you family!

Where would I be without my all family? J. Birney and Julie Brown, Howard and Cordilia Miles, Mike and Michele Scanlon, Tom and Pam McCallum, Wes and Carol Haas, Brian and Patty Haas, Steve and Kristene Haas, and so many more. Your love and support is unconditional and sincerely appreciated.

A great number of people contributed to this book by the questions they asked about my first book, by being a customer, or just being a friend. These people include my customers: Ellen Robinson and Ellen Hahn, Marcia Wood and Steve Leatherman, Dave Mason, Matt Schroeder and Bryon Osborne, Natalie Webb, Danny Lee and John Halgren, Dave Leonard, Pat Fagan and Monty Sooter, Bill Gilbert, Brian Symmonds, Al Gonzales, Mike Harp and Matt Kramer, Michael Wickham, Tim Drouillard, Kent Loundré, Dan Ebert, Sherry Heindenreich and Todd Deshon, Maureen Sielaff, Ken Hamermesh, Stan Rasor, Jeff Manning, Jay Drager, Mike Beaudoin and William Brown, Dave Maney, Scott Lawrence and Corey Belt, Tim Bay and Mark Jesski, Tom Sheridan and Frank Ress, Mike Jones and Hector Martinez, Ron Rose, Terri Miller, Byron Ferguson, Penny Berg, Gary Johnson, Pete Baker and Mary McGee, Patrick Holmes, Mia Lund, Scott Barbarick and Bill Stauffer.

My college friends and those who I vacation with every year on Table Rock Lake: Frank and Kathy Huschitt, Dave and Cindy Litcherman, Rich and Gina Fritz, Tim and Mary Walsh, and Jim and Mary Hooper.

If I left out your name, you're in my heart and thoughts. Thank you for buying a copy of this book.

Introduction

In an era with an explosive growth in Internet technology and its applications, it is difficult—if not impossible—to predict where these advances will take us. However, one thing is for certain: companies are realizing that for their business to grow, the Internet is the place to be. If you are not concerned about what the Internet is going to do to your business, you should be. The Internet is changing the world.

Oracle and the Internet

For those companies looking to expand their business applications to the Internet, Oracle delivers unprecedented power and performance. With today's dynamic workgroup and line-of-business environments, Oracle includes a fully integrated set of easy-to-use management tools, full distribution, replication, and integrated Web features. Replication and distributed data-access features enable users to share relational data across applications and servers. The built-in Web capabilities enable complete intranet-computing solutions. This book will explore practical and useful ways to build Internet applications using Oracle and the Oracle Application Server (OAS).

OAS 4.0.8 has extended the Java envelope for OAS with EJB 1.0, JServlet 2.1a, Enterprise CORBA Objects for Java (ECO4J), and JavaServer Pages (Web release with 4.0.8.1). OAS 4.0.8.2 will be released roughly when this book hits the book stores and will include Java Server pages (packaged with media), improved 8i interoperability (ORB, EJB, and 8i Libraries), robust OTS environment (OCI), persistent session state, IIOP/SSL server gated crypto, OMB - auto-invocation of OAS components, and an XML Parser will be available. OAS-Lite is also promised about the same time as 4.0.8.2, which will include a single process Servlet/PLSQL with no-knobs and a small footprint. It is based on the new OAS 4.1 infrastructure and includes OMB - Message Broker integrated with OAS, more XML integration and more infrastructure improvements: component architecture, availability, performance, and JTS OCI Driver. OAS 4.1 is scheduled to be released around March of 2000 and will include Java and component support, advanced EJB/J2EE spec compliance, interop with 8.2 OiD, ESM (Security), naming, tools, single sign-on and so forth, all single points of failure will be removed, enhanced XML support, complete administration through OEM, next level of performance, scalability, reliability, and QoS.

A fair amount of confusion still resides about Oracle8i and how it relates to OAS. Some wonder if OAS is unnecessary if you have 8i, and others have heard that 8i includes a Web server of its own. Let me assure you that OAS is not going away. It is, in fact, very complimentary to Oracle8i. The OAS isn't distributed with the Oracle8i product; that is the purpose of OAS-Lite. So even when Oracle8i includes the Web server, there are many situations where you would still want to use OAS. One example is if you're serving up CORBA objects in languages other than Java. OAS and Oracle8i will remain two distinct products.

There are still things I'd like to see in Oracle's future for the OAS product. For example, better packaging. Shouldn't all the "Web Development" products (for example, WebDB, OAS, Oracle8i, and WebAlchemy) be bundled together? It's simply too confusing now. Back in August of 1999, Oracle released their dotcom suite, which simplified the package to a degree, so I am optimistic that this will continue to improve over time. I also think that Oracle needs to figure out an overall Web strategy. There are too many "languages" now. You have the Web Publishing Assistant language; WebDB has the <ORACLE> tag in its "Dynamic Pages;" there is the PL/SQL toolkit; LiveHTML uses Perl as its language; Java is everywhere.

What ever happened to iFS? To refresh your memory, iFS is a new component of Oracle8i. It's scheduled to be released in version 8.1.6. iFS stands for Internet File System. iFS allows a user to use a file system for functionality and ease-of-use, but the data is stored in the Oracle8i database. This is great for consolidating the data (documents) for management and for ease of integrated searching. One of the main features of iFS is the ability to store a document in one format (i.e., MWord) and then view it in a different format (HTML). This is called rendering a document. iFS will support some default rendering (for example, HTML) and it will have APIs, so you can develop your own document rendering. So iFS will be production with 8.1.6 (the next release Oracle8i), but at the current time version 8.1.6 has no scheduled release date... yet.

If you're looking for confidence from others that Oracle is the right solution for your company, consider the fact that on TheStreet.com's Internet Sector Index—13 of the 15 companies on its E-Commerce Index use Oracle. From Amazon to Yahoo!, when it comes to operating the most profitable, highest-volume businesses on the Web, the "dotcom"s turn to Oracle to meet the system demands of serving millions of customers online 24 hours a day. Similarly, TheStreet.com's E-Commerce Index (Ticker symbol: ICX) is an equal-weighted measure of 15 prominent e-commerce players generating all or a significant portion of their revenue from commerce conducted over the Internet. The Index lists Amazon.com, Ameritrade, Beyond.com, BroadVision, CDnow/N2K, Cyberian Outpost, Digital River, eBay, E4L, Egghead.com, E*Trade Group, Onsale, Peapod, Preview Travel, and Ubid.

Excite@Home has more than 20 million registered users, Excite has built a customized system that personalizes each individual's visit to its site. Each time a member returns to the site or changes his or her profile, that information is retrieved from and rewritten to an Oracle database. By providing non-stop, reliable service to thousands of concurrent customers 24 hours a day, Excite has been able to achieve its impressive growth and retention rates. "When the competition is just a click away, performance is critical," said Andy Halliday, Vice President and General Manager of Commerce at Exite@Home. "Oracle-based solutions have made it possible for Excite to offer the kind of experience that persuades customers to dwell on a page longer, resulting in a higher retention rate."

Robert Petrossian, Vice President of Engineering at Onsale, Inc., said: "We chose Oracle to power our Web site because of Oracle's proven track record in supporting thousands of concurrent users. We chose Oracle as a technology partner because they offered us a scalable platform for e-business." Onsale buys merchandise directly from manufacturers and then acts as a clearinghouse for a wide variety of computer products, consumer electronics, sporting goods, and vacation packages—conducting live, interactive auctions over the Internet. An Oracle database is used to store product information, orders, unique customer profiles, and statistical logging of transaction information. That information then flows into a second database running Oracle Financials, which issues invoices, records purchase orders, and registers items in rehouse inventory. The continuous flow of information between the auction-management systems and the Oracle applications provide customers with 24-hour access to order status and billing information. With this solution, users can view the time and date when their credit card was charged, when the order was transmitted to the warehouse, and when their order was shipped.

"When the choice is e-business or out of business, the most successful companies on the Net rely on Oracle," said Mark Jarvis, Senior Vice President of Worldwide Marketing at Oracle. "Business at Web speed requires lightning-fast response and superior levels of service, reliability, and scalability. Oracle provides the architecture of choice for companies in the rapidly growing, increasingly competitive Internet sector."

No matter what your business is, you must understand the pervasiveness of e-commerce technology and the changes required to your business model. According to the GartnerGroup, failure to plan for these changes will reduce competitiveness by between 15 and 30 percent through 2001, and for five percent of enterprise, the loss of competitiveness will lead to business failure by year-end 2001!

Bradley D. Brown

Let's back up just a bit and talk about how I got to where I am today. As a child, I was an inventor, but I also liked to keep busy. I have never required much sleep. As a kid, I invented many things that already had been invented, such as my voice-activated tape recorder. I bought a barbecue grill rotisserie motor and rigged it to the TV in my bedroom so that I had remote control TV. I am from a small town, Princeton, Illinois and I'm proud of it! My grandparents live in Princeton—it was great to have them around. They helped me buy my first car when I was 15—a midnight blue Dodge Charger—by doubling every dollar I earned. When I was in eighth grade, they took me to Europe, and what a great experience that was. When I was about 12 or 13, I won the Duncan YoYo contest when they came, to town and I secretly hoped to be "discovered." I can relate to the movie *Doc Hollywood* a bit.

When I was in high school, during the summers I had three jobs at one time. I detassled corn from sunup until about 1 p.m., then I worked at the local paint store, and I mowed lawns after that. The inventor in me didn't stop as an adult. I drove Kristen crazy with this—at least until I "invented" TUSC. In 1985 I invented what I called "Comradio." The Internet as we know it now was not available, and I couldn't even imagine how we would physically wire the world together. My concept involved broadcasting digital data to the world and using software to screen and collect information that interested each person. Basically, a personalized communication channel, communication radio or Comradio. When the Internet first gained popularity, a company developed a site called Crayon (CReAte Your Own Newspaper). Pointcast instilled a similar approach. Today, my.yahoo.com is identical to my Comradio concept.

In a small town you have your basic sports, which I certainly didn't overachieve in. In my freshman year in high school, my next-door neighbor and science teacher, John Young, got me interested in computers. John also taught Electronics, which I took. We built a HealthKit computer. It was literally a kit containing a circuit board, resisters, and transistors. We built the computer and then turn it on. It worked! We then learned to program the computer. I learned the BASIC language, and my excitement for computers began. We later purchased one of the first Apple II computers—we didn't even have to build it! During my junior year in high school, I went to the state wrestling meet (Champaign, Illinois) and saw an Interdac computer in a store window. When I got back from the meet, I wrote out an envelope with a letter to Interdac requesting the computer I saw in the window. I planned to save my money and when I had enough, I'd send off for the computer. My mom saw the envelope on my desk, sealed it and mailed it for me. When I got home, I asked my mom what happened to the envelope, and she said she mailed it and asked what it was for anyway. The computer came COD and I instantly owed my parents $400. I loved that computer—all 8K of RAM and cassette tape drive (the *only* storage) of it. The "PC" connected to a TV for the monitor, which had a resolution of about 30 characters and 17 lines. The programming language was BASIC (and Assembler). I wrote games on it like Human Cannonball and Horse Races. I later sold several games to Interdac while I was in college. I actually closed the deal while I was on spring break in Florida.

In college, I had to do a sales presentation for my speech class. My sales presentation covered how anyone could have a well-paying ($10-$20 per hour) summer job. I spoke about contract detassling and actually convinced about ten people to move to my hometown for the summer, live in a hotel, and perform contract detassling. However, I met my wife, Kristen, that year. Because she graduated from college that semester, I decided to live with her parents in the Chicago area for the summer.

Kristen's dad, Wes, helped me find a consulting job at Econ Labs in Joliet, Illinois. I spent the summer writing various programs to handle their plant overtime rules and regulations. I learned a lot about unions and their rules, too. Kristen continued her search for her first "real" job. About a week after I found my job at Econ Labs, Kristen got a job at State Farm as an underwriter in Bloomington (where we went to college). We got engaged. I went to summer school at night at Joliet Junior College. I went back to school in Bloomington in the fall. The next summer Kristen and I got married, and I took 12 hours in summer school. We took our honeymoon between the pre-session and summer session. I was almost finished with college in three years plus summer school. Kristen and I started a "computer company" with another couple and a sales person. I was in charge of software development (Vice President, in fact), and my partner was in charge of hardware sales. We sold one of the first luggable computers, the Kaypro. We wrote a lot of software and did some consulting, too. My last semester at Illinois State University was spent in the work/study program.

When I graduated from college, it was time to find a "real" job. I got a job in Princeton (my hometown) at Pioneer Hybrid International—a seed company (for farmers). It was a fun job and a great company with great people. I had to go to Des Moines for training because I.T. did not exist in Illinois, it was just me. Pioneer put us up in apartments in a not-so-nice neighborhood. Kristen was scared the whole time we lived there. I ended up asking the President of Pioneer Data Systems if Kristen could have a job organizing the library or something. We stayed in Des Moines for about two months and then moved to Princeton. We bought a house right away. I was only 21. People would come to the door and ask if my mom was home. A couple times she was there, too! In 1985, we decided that bigger city life was for us and for my career. I had an offer in New York City, which we considered. I also had an offer in Chicago at the Midwest Stock Exchange (MSE), now the Chicago Stock Exchange (CSE), which we decided was a better fit for both of us. I developed back-office accounting applications for the floor brokers and worked on a shared tenant telecommunications application. My job gave me the opportunity to make sales calls to AT&T. Austin was born in 1987.

In 1988, I went to work for Oracle in their Chicago consulting group, where I met Joe Trezzo and Rich Niemiec. They started working there a week after I did. It was a wild but fun ride. The three of us started TUSC in 1988, and it's been nothing but fun ever since.

Paige was born in 1990, and we moved to Denver in 1994. I got into the Web heavily in early 1996. I wrote my first book, and it was published in 1998. Here we are today, continuing to develop and deploy Internet applications—inventing every day!

I love my life, and I try to live every day to its fullest. I enjoy taking calculated risks. I love hockey, water skiing, and snow skiing. I've been working on my private pilot's license in between books, but took time off to write this one. I try to do everything with passion. I am energized by people and working with them.

This book is the result of about 1,500 emails I have received since my first book was published. My goal is to addresses Web development questions raised in those emails, and any that you may have as well.

The Web, Your Business, and You

According to Harry S. Dent, Jr., in his book *Roaring 2000s,* we are moving into the Internet age full of prosperity and will witness a strong spending wave until about mid 2009 when the Dow hits 20,500! I think Harry is right! Harry was right when he previously predicted that the Dow would hit 10,000—everyone thought he was way off then.

It will not be long before nearly everyone will be connected to the Internet, which will dramatically change the world. We will be connected with cell phones to PDAs from wireless communication to fiber in the home. Are you too late? Is your idea too late? Is it too late for your business to succeed on the Web? Not by any stretch of the imagination! In fact, read the *Innovator's Dilemma* by Clayton Christensen, which talks about how you don't necessarily want to be the first, but you don't want to be too late either. For example, Crayon was the first information collection site, and they are not around today. There are many more similar examples. We're still *very* early in this Internet game. Then again, look at bluemountain.com which came up with simple concept of providing free greeting cards on the Internet. It is about to be sold for about $1.5 billion!

What's the number-one complaint you hear from your family about the Web? It's a waste of time? It's too slow? I can never find what I'm looking for? The search engines are still *way* behind the curve. How do you find what you're *really* looking for on the Web? There are a ton of search engines, as described in Appendix A. Some people prefer Dogpile, others like Google, some still use Yahoo!—the list goes on and on. There is a good article by The Associated Press on how "search engines lag behind Net expansion." It contains an amazing graphic that covers several Internet search engines and the percentage of the searchable Web they cover. The highest percentage was, surprisingly, Northern Light, which covers 16 percent of the Web. The more commonly used search engines, AltaVista, HotBot, Microsoft, Infoseek, Google, Yahoo!, Excite, and Lycos reported percentages of 15.5, 11.3, 8.5, 8.0, 7.8, 7.4, 5.6, and 2.5! The article talked about how the Internet search engines are not keeping pace with the explosive growth of the Web. The most comprehensive engine, Northern Light, only covers about one-sixth of the Internet pages that search engines can reach. That is down from one-third for the best engine a year and a half ago. In fact, in a prior study, HotBot led with 34 percent coverage and was down to 11 percent this year. The study also found that, on average, it takes more than six months for a new Web page to make it into a search engine's listings.

If you're planning to build a dotcom or e-business from the ground up, there are two aspects to the process that you must consider: business and technical. You've got to get through the business aspects before you can begin the technical.

If you have an existing company into which you plan to introduce e-business, the GartnerGroup breaks e-business into five critical actions that maximize opportunities and reduce the risks involved for your company. They are defined as e-vision, e-management, e-competition, e-plans and e-review. I highly recommend reading about their strategies for existing businesses.

To begin the process, you first need a concept. If you're reading this book, you may already have a concept in mind. In fact, many people establish an idea by seeing a gap in an existing business or service. Many entrepreneurs search the world for a gap they can fill. The idea phase should encompass not only the concept, but objectives and strategies as well. Are you selling a product or other people's products? What kind of volume do you project? How much time will you invest in maintaining and supporting your dotcom? These are just a few of the questions you must address in the concept phase. You also want to set the key goals of the planning process.

The most effective approach to moving from concept to venture is what we refer to as building the "no brainer" plan. In other words, customers, investors, and employees who learn about the concept will agree that your concept is a "no brainer"—there is a clear, unmet and large customer need and a clear path to making the idea into a viable business. It must be obvious how you will accomplish making your idea a reality. It is best if your concept is easy to explain. Do you remember the letter that Mark Twain wrote in which he implied that if he had more time, he would have written a shorter letter? Isn't that the truth? It takes a lot of time to make the complex sound simple. Take the time to turn your concept into something you can explain easily.

The first step in building a compelling, no-brainer case for your idea is to start with the customer and build the *customer case*. To do so effectively, you need to spend time validating (defining the value proposition) why a customer would want your services. In other words, the customer is going to love this... why? Be sure to include cost and timesaving. The customer really needs to love your product relative to its costs. Is this a new product or service venture? If it is, you need to focus on using technology to drive real business process innovation in the industry, not just on providing another way to do the same things. On the other hand, are any behavior changes involved with using the product or service? Remember that required behavioral changes are difficult to justify.

After building the customer case, it's time to insure there is a real business or profit opportunity by understanding and building the *business case*. Your work here should be focused on understanding the size of the market, potential competitors, and the general profit potential of the business. You need to research the size of the market. Make a stab at defining your revenue model (for example, subscription, licensing, advertising, commerce, and so forth) and pricing your service; try to understand the costs of your business; and then determine at what share of the market can you make "good" money. If you determine that you need a market share greater than 15-20 percent, *beware!* In fact, even 5 percent of entire market is extremely difficult to achieve. Most sophisticated investors are looking for markets bigger than $10 billion (this is the low bar), so if you plan to take on venture capital, be prepared. Another critical area for you to address while building the business case—and certainly in the business plan—is your plan for building the management team. Unless you're exceptionally well connected, you can't do this alone. Now is the time to consider your strengths and weaknesses and how they will affect the success of starting a new venture. What is the likelihood of attracting other talented people to this venture? What will be your approach to do so?

Once you have built a "no-brainer" customer and business case for your idea, you can develop your business plan. Your business plan is a very important component for your success. It represents your "road map" toward a successful venture. We won't get into the details of the business plan, as there are numerous resources available to assist with this. Just remember this is the presentation you'll be taking to potential investors to finance your dotcom. If you are a non-business person, you may even want to consider a business advisor or consultant to work with on your business plan.

You may want to sit down before you read this next section. It can take up to eight months (working on it nearly full time) or longer to gather enough information to write a complete business plan. If you already have all the information you need from your own experience and you can just sit down and write (without researching every detail), this will probably be much shorter. It's unlikely that you can really build a compelling, investor-ready plan without time spent on research, personal interviews, and so forth. Unless you've raised some "friends and family" money in this stage (and if you have, you probably will not be paying yourself with it), you must be able to live without income during this phase. It's difficult, if not impossible, to effectively accomplish this work while retaining other full-time employment. If you are not fully immersed, it will not be a comprehensive plan. Depending on your situation, this may be too "high-risk" for you.

Marketing will be covered in your business plan, but let's address a few key marketing areas. Make sure your marketing analysis is comprehensive and thorough. You have to know the market you are about to enter. Set specific goals and develop strategies on how to reach those goals. Determine how you will advertise and promote your dotcom. Success or failure of any business often hinges on marketing. The investors will all ask you how you plan to penetrate the market you're going after. To create a consumer-based brand name in the dotcom space in today's market will cost far in excess of $20 million.

It is quickly becoming apparent that it is not enough to have a good URL name or a good "location." The most successful Web sites are using traditional advertising (for example, radio, print, mailers, and press releases) to brand their URLs and names. There are a lot of places on the Web where you can buy books, but people think Amazon when buying books (and now other stuff) because they gotten significant "mindshare." The Web is already too big and unwieldy for you to be able to assume customers will find a site—it increasingly requires traditional advertising to create name recognition so people will actively point to a site. Do you even see a banner ad or do you simply ignore them as I do? A study was performed where the Continue button was placed into a *huge* flashing banner ad. The number-one complaint of the application was that people could not find the Continue button—what does that tell you?

Your business plan must include a well-thought-out timeline for launching and growing the venture. This timeline will include your plans and milestones for developing the product. For example, Month One might include storyboarding the entire application (see Chapter 3 of this book). Month Two would be used to determine functionality within the release of your prototype (document management, profiling, and so forth). You would determine the components that can be purchased versus built. During Month Two, you might select a team for design, development, graphics, and so forth. You would develop a detailed product schedule for your first release of the "real thing." You would also develop a high-level project schedule for future releases.

In Month Two, you would focus on negotiating with hardware (see Chapter 1) and software vendors and also complete and approve the design of your dotcom. Month Three would encompass development completion including unit testing and complete system testing of the prototype. You would release your prototype in Month Four and your "real" version in Month Six.

Don't forget about methodology. Cover your storyboard design, design with transactive content and the Five Cs of Design: Cool, Content, Context, Contact, and Control. Review your technical architecture, including the open architecture (CORBA, Unix, and TCP/IP). Explain why your choice is scalable, reliable, and recoverable—and why these features are important. Illustrate how it is a proven technology and how it is portable across platforms. Demonstrate that it has high availability, which is where an Oracle solution really comes into play. Chapter 3 covers Web application design tips and techniques.

You also must realize that your system is going to go down at times. Chapter 7 discusses how to position yourself as a 24x7 shop. How are you going to handle this when your site is down (planned or unplanned)? If you're using cookies to keep track of your users, you can track who attempted to come to your site while it was down and send them a message. For example, if you visit Amazon's site when they are down, you'll receive an email identical to the following:

> Dear Friend:
>
> We're sorry that our store was closed when you visited earlier today. We hope that you weren't inconvenienced. We're now open for business, and hope you'll come back soon.
>
> Best regards,
> Your friends at Amazon.com
> http://www.amazon.com

Pretty nice touch, isn't it?

Review the software you will use for your dotcom. For example, Oracle 8i RDBMS, Oracle Application Server, Java (Chapter 19) and PL/SQL (Chapter 14), XML (Chapter 13), and SQL*Net, SSL (Chapter 15), and the Apache Web Listener (Chapter 8). Be prepared to address questions on why you have chosen this particular software. Expound on Oracle 8i and include information on Oracle iFS, Java VM in the Database, Seamless interactions (Java-SQL-PL/SQL), SQLJ—Embedded SQL in Java, enhanced JDBC Drivers, Web monitoring, partitioning and unlimited database size.

Show the N-Tier Architecture of your dotcom. This basic drawing will bring together the technical architecture in an easy to understand way for your potential investors.

Examine the browser you will use and what it encompasses. As an example, HTML (Chapter 11) and JavaScript (Chapter 12), cookies used to store encrypted user ID, limited plug-ins (for example, Adobe Acrobat Reader), limited Java, and XML later. Explain why your choice is bandwidth friendly and why this is important.

For example, your site will have a dialup focus, small graphics and low color requirement.

Next you need to discuss hardware (Chapter 1)—what you will use initially (for example, Intel Multiprocessor Pentium), and the long-term solution (for example, Sun, Solaris 2.6+). Demonstrate how you will scale up your hardware and how quickly and easily that can be done.

Review where your site will be hosted and why. For example, if you host your site at an ASP, it's close to the backbone (so it's fast), you have 24x7 system support, mission-critical redundancy, and backup and recovery capabilities.

Address whether you will buy or build your dotcom solutions. I suggest building *only if* there is nothing available to buy or no reasonably priced solution. With the numerous products available on the market today, you should be able to buy most, if not all, of the software for your site. Your job will be to put it all together.

Few enterprises are equipped to support all e-commerce business solutions; therefore, GartnerGroup recommends that you outsource what you cannot perform internally. They have identified Web-based e-commerce services that can be considered for outsourcing. Enterprises considering e-commerce may decide to outsource certain functions because they lack core competencies in these areas. For enterprises evaluating outsourcing, GartnerGroup identified and defined six Web-enabled e-commerce services, as well as vendors, offering specific software or outsourcing support. The decision to outsource should be made with the in-house IS department, and costs and requirements should be clearly defined. Some commerce service providers will offer all six functions, while others specialize in one. GartnerGroup's six outsourcing categories are hosting, e-mail, transaction/payment processing, distribution/order fulfillment, customer service, and support and security. GartnerGroup states the bottom line as follows: "Enterprises looking at outsourcing part of their e-commerce functions will benefit from reallocating critical company resources back into core competencies. Outsourcing specific e-commerce functions is often the best choice for an Internet presence when e-commerce solutions are not core competencies."

Be prepared to discuss the people who will make up your Project Team and their roles—technical architects, design team, graphic artist, developer, content provider (users), testing team (users), project management, and database administrator, for example. This topic is also discussed in Chapter 3.

Present your team development tools, such as Oracle Application Server and the Java, PL/SQL, Perl (Chapter 20) or LiveHTML (Chapter 21) Cartridge, Oracle Designer (Chapter 16) for CASE/Modeling, Macromedia Dreamweaver (Chapter 23) for HTML Development, Tool for Oracle Application Developers (TOAD) or another PL/SQL editor, WebAlchemy (Chapter 6) for converting HTML to PL/SQL, WebTrends (Chapter 26) for site analysis, and Oracle Reports (Chapter 18) as your Reporting Tool. How does Oracle Developer Forms (Chapter 17) fit into your architecture?

Review the site security and what it entails (Chapter 15). For example, SSL, application authentication, domain and IP restriction, basic and digest authentication, and database user authentication. Be prepared to discuss the firewall security as well.

By the way, early on in this business planning process, even when your idea is on the cocktail napkin, it's a good idea to select a domain name, determining whether it's available and then registering it. If you have ideas about the name, you will want to register it before too much time passes.

Now, let's talk money! Once you have your business plan information in place, you can start thinking about financing, a critical phase of building your dotcom. You must have the financial backing for your dotcom or it will never make it off the ground. We're not talking about a few thousand dollars, or even a few hundred thousand dollars. The financial backing you're looking for runs into the millions—yes, millions—of dollars.

Where are you going to get millions of dollars? How do you find the right people to talk to? How do you determine who to talk to and what to talk about? There are several components you must have in place before you can even begin the financing stage. You cannot even talk to potential investors or venture capital people without an executive summary from your business plan, a presentation, and a financial plan, and so forth. Money that you hope to raise to prove your concept (prove your initial customer case) is called seed or early stage money. If you have a proven concept and you are looking for additional funds to launch your business, that money is called first round financing. Later rounds of financing are used to grow the business. Venture capital firms often prefer to provide financing for a particular stage of the business (for example, early stage or later stage only), so you will need to align your search with the type of funds you are looking for. If the investment you're looking for is less than $1 million, "Angel Investors" tend to look for investments of this size.

Many books and resources will define the various "stages" of a venture (e.g., seed, early stage, xyz stage, late stage, and pre-IPO stage). In general, you are probably at the seed stage (or, most probably, friends and family pre-seed stage) if you're starting from an idea on a cocktail napkin or have a basic prototype, and need money to:

1. Do the research
2. Fly around to talk with customers
3. Hire some consultants to help in various areas
4. Continue developing the customer/business cases

You might need $100,000 (or more if you need to spend money on technology) to just see if there is even a business for your solution.

If you've done all the work on your business plan as previously discussed, you'll probably next need money to "prove the concept," which means actually getting the product or service developed and building a small team of business and technical people to get real customers. People today are typically raising $1 million to $1.5 million to move through the "prove the concept" phase. How much you raise, of course, depends on how much money it really takes (the driver for something more than this amount of money would be expensive technology; the business costs are fairly defined). And, one can only raise this amount of money if there appears to be a large market opportunity. This is where the greatest risk is involved for investors, but if it is successful, this is where the greatest amount of financial value (and personal reward) is created.

In fact, GartnerGroup recently confirmed these numbers when they announced that the average cost of developing and launching an enterprise Web e-commerce site is $1 million. They also mentioned that the cost will increase by 25 percent annually during the next two years, according to a new research study. Another interesting point in this report talked about how 79 percent of the cost was labor-related while 10 percent was spent on software and 11 percent on hardware. The report also identifies three cost categories that will emerge based on function. These include:

- $300,000 to $1 million to "Get on the Map." The site is adequate, but it is functionally behind most industry participants.
- $1 million to $5 million to "Run with the Pack." The site is functionally equivalent to most industry participants.
- $5 million to $20 million to achieve "Market Differentiator." The site raises the industry competitive bar and changes the nature of online competition.

There is a lot of jargon and characterizations of investor types for various stages. This stage is where the term "Angel" comes in. Angels are unlikely to invest the entire $1 million+ amount, but a group of Angels might. An Angel can be a successful entrepreneur who has made a bunch of money and wants to get involved directly with new companies as opposed to a person who gives their money to a venture capital and remains a passive investor. An Angel is really any high net worth individual who is a sophisticated investor and recognizes all the risks at this stage.

The other type of investor would be a seed/early stage venture capitalist. This would mean that the venture capital fund has specifically set a strategy around taking this type of risk, working with companies in this stage, and with its partners. By the way, this would be called the venture capital's "sweet spot" (the stage, and then other descriptors around the type of companies in which that venture capital invests). Given the amount of risk at this stage (if you cannot prove the concept, you lose the entire investment) and the amount of support the entrepreneur requires (patient investors, investors with experience in the space with contacts, knowledge, ideas, and so forth.), this is not a good time to take more money from friends and family.

Finding investors to talk with should start (and hopefully finish) within the entrepreneur's own "six degrees of separation." In other words—contacts are key! It is extremely rare to have much success by simply shipping a business plan around without direct exposure to the investor(s) receiving it (unless the entrepreneur has a notable reputation). There are just too many opportunities being presented at the present time. If an entrepreneur is "light here" with their own contacts, we'd suggest convincing a service professional (lawyer, accountant, business consultant, and so on) to support you and asking them to use their contacts. This usually means their calling on your behalf or sending a plan directly to the targeted investors. This really is tough if the entrepreneur is a real techie without any business contacts. There are people who will take a percentage and do fundraising. This certainly is an option if someone needs it, but it is often difficult to find someone you can trust and work with well.

When you meet with investors, you need to have the most comprehensive plan possible. You can capture the key elements in an executive summary and a presentation, but you should be prepared with the finished plan to "close" the investment deal. The business plan will provide additional information and your overall thinking. For example, relative to the product development cycle, your product rollout needs to be addressed. A project kickoff plan must be in place. Will you have more than one project phase or version? Will you have new versions every quarter? Every six months?

Once an investor has "bought into your concept" it's time to have him buy into the company. The central discussion regarding an investor's investment will be around what is called a "pre-money valuation" of the company. A pre-money valuation of your venture is defined as what the value of your venture is immediately prior to accepting a round of financing. Believe it or not, with a solid customer and business case, a good business plan, and a few key members of the management team at least identified, your venture already has a value, and this valuation will be heavily negotiated during the financing process. The valuation ultimately determines the percentage of the company an investor receives in return for the money invested, which ultimately determines the investor's return on that investment some time in the future (usually when the venture is sold or does an IPO). It is important to understand what drives valuations and then determine where this venture fits within these parameters. The valuation process is as much art as science, and you would be well advised to get some good support here. Nevertheless, there are probably very good ranges one can expect if a venture breaks into the professional investment range at all. Basically, investors at each stage are looking for a return commensurate with their risk. This is *after* the investor determines that if the venture successfully penetrates the market (this is where the risk is calculated), there is really a market large enough to be worthwhile. The investor at this stage probably needs to see a potential for the venture to be "worth" hundreds of millions of dollars over the next three to five years.

For example, an investor willing to invest $1 million in an early stage might desire a future return of $10 million (10 times the original investment, or 10x). If the $1 million is the only sum of money ever needed, and if the venture "harvested" $100 million, the investor would have assumed 10 percent of the company to achieve its goals. Usually, the venture will need additional investors in later stages, so what drives the investor's goals (the initial portion of the company you give away) will also include a calculation for future "dilution." For example, if after the $1 million is spent, and another round of $10 million is needed, those investors may require 30 percent of the company beyond the dilution of the initial investors (as well as the founder and employees.) In the simple example of the initial investor having 10 percent, this stake would be diluted to 7 percent, and now the venture would have to harvest at $142 million to return at 10x. All these type of projections are what goes on in the initial valuation (and all subsequent valuations) and this is what ends up leading to seed companies "giving away" anywhere from 30 to 60 percent of their companies in the first round of financing.

In addition to negotiating pre-money valuations, there are several other terms the entrepreneur must be aware of and negotiate in any financing, for example, board participation, employee stock option pools, and so on. There are several other areas to take into consideration under the business aspect umbrella. When can or should you go public? When should you think about a CEO to take the business to the next level? Where do you fit into your organization—CEO? CIO? Idea dreamer?

If you are a pure techie with hopes of successfully emerging from the seed stage with a viable business, you will need a CEO with a business and probably sales and marketing background. At any stage, there needs to be a combination of business and technical expertise to handle the scale of the business at that size. If you are a techie, you will play a key role just as the business members, but *no one* does it on their own. Whether you become Vice President of Development, CTO, or CIO probably depends most on your business acumen and leadership skills. But you will always be the "evangelist." You have to be able to convince people to "sign-up" with your idea and work *very* hard to contribute to the success of the venture.

Now that your financing is in place, your business plan is on track, you can delve into the technical side of building your dotcom. We techies like to dive right to this stage, don't we? Some of the initial legwork was already completed in the business planning stage such as selecting applications, determining goals, resource costing and choosing the right tools.

Even though you came up with a basic design concept to present to your investors, you need to get down to the nuts and bolts of designing your site. Truly great Web applications are designed to be practical. That means they are well planned, easy to use, easy to maintain, intuitive, open (support most browsers without plug-ins), relevant, and addictive. Make sure you employ Netiquette in your design, including avoiding having too much information on your home page and being sure to send users only what they need. Remember the features you can use and limitations you have in regards to software and hardware.

Prototyping and testing are important components of the design phase and were included in your methodology for that reason. Your prototype lays the groundwork for later versions. Testing will uncover the positive and negative aspects of your site before you "go live."

Once your design is finished, you can move onto installation (Chapter 2) and configuration (Chapter 4). Make sure your architecture components are in place, configure your hardware, and install and configure your software—Oracle Application Server. Security and logging should be addressed, as well as establishing virtual hosts. Remember the optional software, such as Oracle Designer and Developer. Will you include WebDB (Chapter 5) in your application development?

Next, we move into the development phase. The tools you need are HTML and JavaScript for client-side development, PL/SQL and Perl for server-side development (both CGI and cartridges). Most projects will usually include a combination of PL/SQL and Perl. File system operations must be developed either against the Web server or against the data server. Address cookies and ports/security issues. Database authentication needs to be performed and a locking method chosen. This is a good time to develop a library of routines including a generic error routine. If you write your documentation in Word, create bookmarks for context sensitive positions and save the document as HTML, and you can use this for your on-line documentation. Use the Listener logs to track usage (Chapter 26), do research, and perform market analysis.

Your next step is testing, debugging (Chapter 25), and tuning (Chapter 4). Remember that your site requires more testing than standard business applications and must encompass back-end (server) code testing, browser (client) variations, network issues, and security and hackers. Things to consider during your testing are browsers supported, network and modem speeds, and reliance upon Java, JavaScript, and cookies since client [PC] configurations may have these "turned-off."

When tuning for throughput, be sure to address the following areas:

- Balance processing between client and server
- Offload FTP, mail and database services to other servers
- Generate static HTML for standard reports using UTL_FILE and DBMS_JOBS
- Regularly check to make sure the site is up
- Tune cartridge instance parameter accordingly
- Use Net.Medic to analyze your network

Don't forget application tuning of SQL queries, PL/SQL and PL/SQL packages, CGI, Perl, and other dynamic programs. And last but not least, tune the graphics. For example, reduce the color count, use thumbnails when possible, and so on.

Now you're ready to implement your site. Remember, you only have one chance to make a first impression. Jazz up your site. Check your use of animated images, sound, and so on. It's easy to refine your application once it's been implemented, but it is considerably less costly (about 1,000 times less expensive, in fact) to make the modifications to a design document. Address all the aspects of security, from protection from physical tampering and environmental disasters to network firewalls to proxy servers. I highly recommend that you develop a written security policy.

Once up and running, your Web Listener log files, along with data you store about your dotcom users and customers, can also provide you with some useful marketing analysis information. You should be able to pull the following information from your site, as discussed further in Chapter 26:

- **Demographics** gender, race, age, education, home value, family size, income
- **Psychographics** self-concept, attitude, interests, opinion, beliefs, preferences, personality traits
- **Clickographics** attention span, focus, appetite, impulsiveness, judgment, analytical skills
- **Communigraphics** communication skills, cooperation, participation

The use of this information will result in predictive marketing, which will then increase page hits and sales, decrease sales costs, and so on.

It's important to determine the steps you will use to implement application changes. You should also define a policy on change control. This is something you'll use again and again in the future, so it's best to take care of it now. There's no need to keep reinventing the wheel, and you will ensure uniformity for future changes.

The last item under the support and maintenance umbrella is determining the methods of contacting your Help Desk. Will customers e-mail, phone, or fax in their problems—or will they have all three options? Determine the turn-around time for each method and establish policies.

Your final step in this process is planning for the future. What will the future bring? Faster networks and cheaper and cheaper memory, to name a few things. However, technology is changing so quickly that it's hard to predict what lies 10, 25, or 50 years down the road. What you really need to focus on is Web site development. Where are you today? Where do you want to go? What do you need to be aware of?

Three key areas I suggest you take into consideration for your future planning decisions are

1. The future of the dotcom is transactive content as defined by Forrester Reports.
2. Web sites will need to incorporate interpersonal skills.
3. Thin-client computing is around to stay.

Building a dotcom from the ground up is very similar to opening up a retail store. The business plan must be developed, marketing analysis performed, financing obtained, employees hired, and so on. The major difference is the end result—an actual storefront as opposed to a virtual storefront.

Here's one last thought, borrowed respectfully from Ralph Waldo Emerson, I'd like to leave with you before you begin this process. Do not go where the path may lead, go instead where there is no path and leave a trail.

Audience

This book is written for individuals like you and businesses that are looking for a comprehensive, cost-effective Internet development environment that easily accommodates deploying applications on the Web. You should be familiar with Oracle, the Internet architecture, and should have some experience on how the Application Server works. For extreme beginners, a perfect pre-requisite to this book would be my first book, *Oracle Application Server Web Toolkit Reference* (Oracle Press, 1998).

How the Book Is Organized

This book is packed with practical and usable tips and techniques on topics that you, as a Web developer, might encounter. Not only are the topics identified, but solutions are provided along with code when applicable. This book will save you time, effort, and frustration while developing and deploying applications on the Web using the Oracle Application Server.

We start our journey with a look at the foundation. In Chapter 1, "Hardware Considerations" you will explore the hardware parameters affected in building an internet application. You will also learn how to select a vendor and choose an operating system. Sizing the box and determining available patches is also explained.

Chapter 2, "Installation" provides step-by-step instructions on installing Internet applications using Oracle and the Oracle Application Server. From reviewing the system requirements to correcting ORA-600 errors, this chapter will walk you through installation. You will learn how to determine how buggy the Beta is, how to change the NT service startup order, and how to load OAS and the database on the same machine. An overview of WebTrends Log Analyzer, Symantec Visual Page, OpenConnect's WebConnect, Vital Sign's Net Medic, Eventus' CONTROL, and Fujitsu's COBOL Cartridge is provided.

Chapter 3, "Designing the Site" discusses Web site design from the ground up. You will learn how to design your Web team and what roles each member will play. Maximizing the 5 C's to get the most bangs for your buck is explained. This chapter covers how to plan your design and then flow with that design to make your site uniform and aesthetically pleasing. You will also learn nuts and bolts of information, such as developing coding standards, using JavaScript, and organizing your directories. This chapter concludes with thinking thin-client.

Chapter 4, "OAS Configuration and Tuning" teaches you how to configure the Oracle Application Server. You will learn how to stop Web server processes on demand, how to move OAS from one machine to another, and how to manager SQL*Net connections. Re-installation issues, mapping multiple hosts, and linking databases are covered. You will be able to configure an automatic start-up, set up SSL start to finish, and set up the Java cartridge. You will also learn how to evaluate your Y2K compliance and what to do when you receive the infamous Internal Error.

Chapter 5, "WebDB" examines why you should consider using WebDB. A look at primary functionality, backing up to the installation, and using the toolbar will be offered. We will cover how to help yourself and review some frequently asked WebDB questions. We will show you how to browse the database and administer WebDB. The chapter concludes with how to build sites.

Chapter 6, "Oracle Extras" contains instructions for utilizing the tools offered by Oracle. You will establish a Web Development Toolkit and create one of your own. You will learn about using WebAlchemy, generating graphs using OWA_CHART, and using the Web Publishing Assistant. Want to learn how to configure SQL*Net and configure and use SQL*Plus? You will find it in this chapter. Discover how to make the most of Oracle File Packager and how to use Oracle's Enterprise Manager. The final topic covered in this chapter is using Oracle's GUI PL/SQL Editor – Procedure Builder.

If you are interested in learning more about support, then Chapter 7, "24x7 Uptime" is for you. This chapter discusses the importance of having support 24 hours a day, 7 days a week.

Chapter 8, "HTTP Listeners" examines using the Oracle listener. You will learn how to configure IIS, Netscape FastTrack, Netscape Enterprise, or Apache Listener with OAS and how to unregister IIS, Netscape FastTrack, Netscape Enterprise, or Apache from OAS. In addition, this chapter covers turning file caching off, guarding your base domain name, and monitoring your site for crashes. You will also learn troubleshooting why you cannot access the node manager and copying a listener from another server.

Chapter 9, "Oracle8i Built-In Packages" discusses the built-in packages as an important components of any Web development project using Oracle. You will learn messaging with dbms_alert, executing DDL with dbms_ddl, and writing Output with dbms_output. In Chapter 9, how to queue with dbms_job, set Session Properties with dbms_session, and execute Dynamic SQL Using dbms_sql will be covered. Discover how to make the most of dbms_utility and how to make Accessing Operating System Files with utl_file.

Chapters 10 through 15 contains core concept information about the Oracle Application Server. Chapter 10, "Differences Among the Various Oracle Web Server Versions" examines what's new in OAS 4.0. Chapter 11, "HTML Development" details writing HTML, using HTML tables, creating forms, and more. Chapter 12, "JavaScript Development" compares JavaScript to PL/SQL and teaches you how to incorporate JavaScript in your applications. Chapter 13, "XML" covers everything from the basic rules of XML to examining the Oracle XML SQL Utility. Chapter 14, "PL/SQL Cartridge" is a comprehensive guide to using this cartridge. Chapter 15, "Security" takes a look at security issues.

Chapters 16 through 18 examine the Oracle tools Designer WebServer Generator, Developer—Oracle Forms for the Web, and Developer—Oracle Reports for the Web. You will learn how to install, configure, and utilize these tools.

Chapters 19 through 22 discuss other cartridge options. Java, Perl, Live HTML, and Oracle Commerce Server (OCS) are reviewed and instructions given on installing, configuring, and so forth.

Chapters 23 through 26 cover miscellaneous topics such as utilities to help Web development (Chapter 23), troubleshooting (Chapter 24), debugging your code (Chapter 25), and logging and site analysis (Chapter 26).

Appendix A contains site information you may need throughout the application process.

Book Conventions

The following conventions are used in this book to help you, the reader:

- **Boldface** is used for user input.
- *Italics* is used to emphasize and to highlight important terms.
- Keys or Keypresses are formatted in small caps (ESC). Keypress combinations are separated with a hyphen (ALT-F). Sequences of keypress combinations are separated by a comma (ALT-F,O).
- Numbered lists indicate step-by-step instructions.

PART I

Getting Prepared

CHAPTER 1

Hardware Considerations

ith the exploding growth of the Internet, choosing the right hardware for a Web-based application is critical to a successful deployment. The hardware you choose will need to balance cost, reliability, service support, uptime, and performance requirements with the capability to scale with your user-base.

Even though many factors must be considered when choosing hardware, this chapter will focus on the following areas:

- Selecting a vendor
- Sizing the Web server and related hardware
- Choosing an operating system
- Researching available patches

Selecting a Vendor

The first step in selecting your hardware is choosing your vendor. Many factors should be considered as part of this decision. Your choice should be based on the combination of these factors and the production environment where your system will operate.

Support Priority

One often overlooked consideration when selecting hardware is how widely the platform is supported. There is no single answer—for example, when Oracle Oracle8i Server began shipping, it shipped for Sun Sparc Solaris first. However, when Oracle Developer 6.0 Server began shipping, it shipped for Windows NT first. Groups of products tend to ship earlier on certain platforms, and some products are not available on all platforms.

The first platform Oracle currently releases software for depends on the product. Developer tools, as an example, tend to ship for Windows clients first, but new versions of Oracle Server products tend to ship first for Sun Sparc Solaris and HP/UX, followed by Microsoft Windows NT (Intel). In the fast changing world of Web-based applications, it is important to have access to the latest versions of software and the latest features available. If the platform you choose is not towards the top of the ship list, you may be at a competitive disadvantage.

TIP

Check the "Product Lifecycle" section under Oracle's MetaLink, http://metalink.oracle.com, to verify product availability by platform.

Service

Quality of vendor service should play a key role in selecting a hardware platform. Especially with an external Web site, you must ensure that hardware installations, upgrades, and replacements will go smoothly to avoid costly downtime. In particular, be careful when choosing a vendor that requires the use of proprietary parts or components. It is much easier to pick up a video card at your local computer store on a Saturday afternoon than it is to custom order a replacement part. You may want to review the vendors' support sites, including Web sites, FTP facilities, or bulletin board services (BBS). Determine how much information they have made available to customers, how easy it is to locate, and the amount of detail in the documentation.

A recent outage at eBay cost the company several millions of dollars in lost commissions—in addition to reduced consumer confidence and nearly 25 percent of its market value—in one day. One of the lessons to be learned is to understand in full and to receive in writing your warranty and support contracts, including their response time obligations and your right to compensation for business losses, if any.

Several publications periodically rate hardware vendors' service. While these surveys are a useful guide, no substitute exists for talking with people who are using the hardware. Speak with as many people as you can. Ask the vendors for references of former customers to understand why they have switched platforms. Ensure the issues causing unsatisfied customers have been remedied.

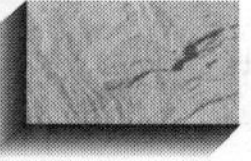

TIP
Before making a major hardware purchase, talk with as many references as possible.

Compatibility

Ensure your choice of hardware vendor is in line with the information systems strategy of your company. Make sure a solid reason exists to justify deviating from the accepted standards. If your company is running nothing but Linux servers, there are consequences to installing a database server, a Web server, or an Application Server on Windows NT.

By choosing a platform that is compatible with other servers in your company, you may have the opportunity to leverage additional hardware and administration expertise. For example, with a Sun Enterprise 10000 server, you have the capability to dynamically shift processors among several independent domains. If your workloads are staggered, this can save on hardware costs—for example, if you have a transaction processing system running on one heavily used domain during the day and a data warehousing application running on a separate domain loaded at night. You could allocate 70 percent of the processors to the transaction processing system during the day and 70 percent of the processors to the data warehouse at night.

Each vendor will offer different levels of compatibility and price. In a Windows NT environment, you can realize savings when purchasing all servers from a single vendor. A Compaq Hot Plug hard drive can be used in virtually any Compaq server with a Hot Plug drive bay, enabling you to keep a smaller part inventory and giving you the flexibility to reconfigure systems.

Having a single vendor can also minimize the variety of platform-related issues. Every platform will have issues unique to the vendor. If you only have one vendor, you can make assumptions and apply fixes across the enterprise. In addition, you have a single vendor taking responsibility for troubleshooting, which eliminates the finger-pointing when multiple vendors share the responsibility.

Upgradability

You always want to guarantee a path exists to upsize your application—you need to leave yourself room to grow. This is particularly true with external Web sites. The 800.com site is a prime example. During the 1998 Christmas season, they offered a promotion where new customers could order a combination of three CDs and DVDs for $1. Needless to say, they were swamped with requests and there were stretches of hours where their Web site was unreachable.

Make sure an easy upgrade path is available if you need to grow rapidly due to heavy system usage, and try to plan ahead for large promotions to avoid an issue. This does not necessarily mean the box you buy needs to be able to hold 64 processors and 64GB of RAM, but do not get caught in the trap of saving on an initial hardware purchase just to build in an artificial growth ceiling. Ensure that the vendor you choose can scale to your most optimistic growth estimates. Be clear on the specific configuration you will be receiving. If the system is shipping with 128MB of RAM, make sure it is one module and not four 32MB modules.

Be skeptical of scalability solutions that require more exotic hardware configurations. While technologies such as Oracle Parallel Server, clustering servers, and arrays of Web or Application Servers can be good solutions to scalability problems, they add an extra degree of administrative complexity. For fast-growing companies, the skill set to administer more complex configurations may not be available. Solutions that can scale in a single server, or a more manageable number of servers, may save you downtime because of administrator error.

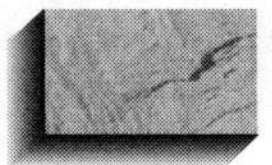

TIP

The more servers and software components supporting your applications, the more points of failure and the greater the chance of an outage. The Internet community can be extremely unforgiving of untimely outages. Imagine if you could not trade stocks online during a market crash!

Performance

Performance is more important than many people like to think. It is one of the attributes that shapes your customers' view of your company. Response times dictate a user's perception of performance. If a Web site is hosted on a site connected to the Internet through a 56KB circuit, the Web site screams "fly by night." Bandwidth is key to a successful Web site.

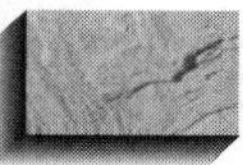

TIP

Your Web site's performance will be judged based on the performance of other Web sites. If users have become accustomed to one-second response times from Web sites they visit, your Web site will feel fast or slow by comparison.

Choosing and properly configuring the right hardware can make or break a Web site's performance. For example, RAID 1+0 can be more than 100 percent faster than RAID-5 for database servers. While performance might be improved with faster hardware, application tuning should be the first step to improving performance.

Minimizing network roundtrips through the use of JavaScript and other browser-side code can improve performance dramatically. With connection speeds that vary from 28.8 modems to greater than full T-1s and unpredictable Internet congestion, the fewer times data needs to be sent between the client and the browser, the better the performance. The ultimate test of Web site congestion immunity is to check the Web site's performance the next time a new version of Netscape Navigator or Internet Explorer is released. The day the Starr report was released on the Internet, no news site could be reliably contacted—the world's servers timed out.

TIP

Your dedicated bandwidth should exceed that of your user's connection. Do not host a Web site on a 56KB line if you expect users to be connecting from a location with a T-1 connection to the Internet.

Asynchronous operations can greatly improve perceived performance. There is no viable reason to have a user wait for a response from a browser when email notification of success or failure will suffice. A good example of asynchronous operations is when a trade is entered on E*Trade. A trade is entered, queued, and the user can continue with other work. The user does not wait idle for the trade to execute before additional tasks can be performed.

Another important and often overlooked performance factor is the speed of your internal network. Most Web applications rely on several systems, including a Web server, a database server, and a file server storing download files. The speed at which these servers communicate and the load that internal resources are putting on the systems can affect response time for your external users. A common recommendation is the use of a switched network. Building your network with switch technology offers several benefits, including increased speed by enabling servers to communicate at dedicated speeds of 100MB to 1GB. Network switches provide additional management features and fault tolerance. Recent improvements in technology and reduced cost make them an alternative that bears consideration.

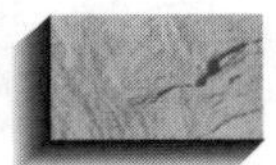

TIP
Track your Web site's bandwidth utilization. As demand increases, upgrade your bandwidth before your users can notice a slowdown.

Availability

External users will expect your Web site to be available 24×7 (see Chapter 7), and they want to access the site at their convenience. Messages such as "Under Construction," "Data Temporarily Unavailable," or "Unavailable During Backup" are not acceptable. Users quickly will become frustrated and find another site to frequent.

Several factors affect availability—choice of hardware platform, redundancy/fault tolerance, and choice of backup method are only some of the decisions that dictate Web site availability. The level of availability required should be balanced against the cost of downtime. Servers, storage, network, and Internet connection must all be available for users to access a Web site. When selecting a provider to host your Web site, confirm they have redundant Internet connections to disparate providers—otherwise you are a candidate for an unexpected outage.

Sizing the Web Server and Related Hardware

Sizing a system is more of an art than a science. Every configuration will have a bottleneck; the trick is having the system reach all of its bottlenecks at the same time. It is a waste of money and computing resources to have a 64-processor system if the I/O subsystem cannot support more than a two-processor system.

Benchmarks can be a good guideline for relative system performance. If a benchmark shows a particular configuration can process 100,000 transactions per hour, do not assume that your application will perform the same. Typically, benchmark transactions are less complex than real-world transactions. Benchmarks can be useful to determine the relative performance of two systems. If one system benchmarks 100,000 transactions per hour and another 1,000,000 transactions per hour, the second is likely to be ten times faster for your application.

Two sites to visit for benchmarks are http://www.tpc.org and http://www.spec.org. The biggest problem with benchmarks is they are rarely performed recently enough to have results for hardware you are ready to purchase. The other caveat related to benchmarks is to choose the benchmark carefully. SPECfp is not an appropriate benchmark to judge database or Web server performance, because these applications rarely perform floating-point operations.

Getting Enough Processors

Megahertz is not everything. Do not fall into the common trap of comparing processors from different vendors based on megahertz alone. The architecture of each processor is different. Some are 32-bit and some are 64-bit; some can execute two instructions at a time and some can execute four instructions at a time.

The best way to determine the number of processors of a given type you need for your system is to take your application for a test drive. Measure the CPU time required by your workload mix and scale the result to the number of users you will have. The closer you can replicate your production environment and workload, the closer your estimates will be.

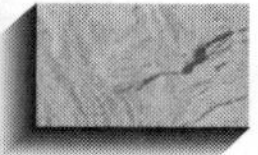

TIP

Have several people estimate the number of processors required. The closer the estimates, the better the chance the estimate is valid.

Few sites have a spare box configured identically to a proposed production box. Unfortunately, this is rarely practical. In the absence of a test box of your own, you can use information from several sources to size the number of processors. Find a standardized benchmark that best fits your application. For database servers, this is usually SPECint and SPECint rate. For Web servers, this is usually SPECWeb. Use the benchmarks as a general comparison of processors from different manufactures. Do not forget benchmarks are not perfect, but they are good in the absence of a test machine.

Processor technology rapidly improves. While the dramatic increases in processor performance cannot continue, there does not appear to be an end in sight. On average, processor logic performance has doubled every three years. In addition, the size of the trace lines used in processors has halved every seven years. These, combined with other design improvements, have kept CPU performance doubling every 18 months.

Since technology changes so rapidly, you will be able to get the most for your dollar by deferring hardware purchases as long as possible. If you plan on a project lasting six months, buy your development boxes today and defer the purchase of your production box until closer to the go-live date. In Figure 1-1, you will see the processor's logical performance increase over time.

In Figure 1-2, we look at processor trace time over time.

In general, a fewer number of fast processors perform better than a large number of slower processors. This is largely because of the inability to parallelize certain operations; if an operation cannot be parallelized, a risk of having idle CPUs is encountered. If you are compelled to run on one processor, the speed of the CPU will limit your application. The potential to have idle CPUs is mitigated by having a large number of users. Even if you are limited to a single process, you will have several users each trying to use different CPUs—keeping all of the CPUs busy.

Try to find someone else running a similar application. Ask what hardware they are using. You can always estimate what you will need, but a reasonability check is nice to have.

Another technique is to estimate the CPU seconds needed per user, then determine the number of users you need to handle during peak processing times and estimate the number of processors necessary. For example, if a user requires 10

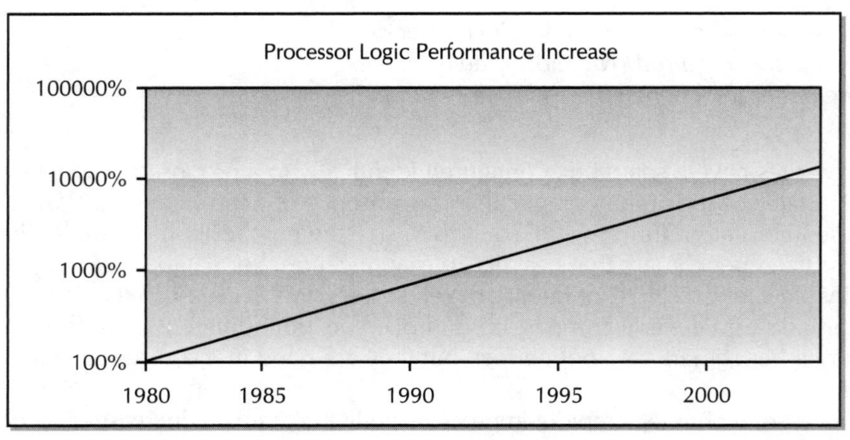

FIGURE 1-1. *Processor logical performance increase*

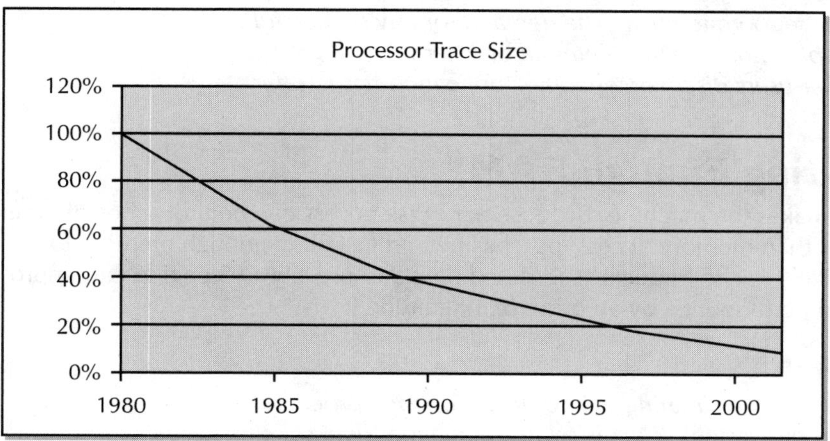

FIGURE 1-2. *Processor trace size*

seconds of CPU time to complete processing, and you need to process 2,000 users during the peak hour, you will need 20,000 CPU seconds per hour.

20,000/3,600 = 5.6

With the preceding specs, you should have at least six processors. This calculation is not always easy to do because response time does not necessarily equate to CPU time, but it is a good technique.

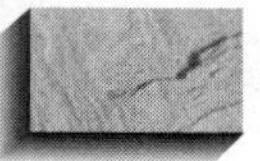

TIP
Refrain from purchasing a production box until you have run the application on a test or development box to validate sizing.

Do not be afraid to order some equipment now and some tomorrow. It is more important to have a machine that is in the right ballpark than to get the number of processors right the first try. If I buy a machine that can have 14 processors and I initially buy six, as long as I am close I will be able to fine-tune the estimate. It is far more expensive to buy a machine already at capacity and find out you need to replace it.

TIP
Leave room to grow. The demand for any successful application, whether internal or external, will grow after users discover what the application has to offer.

Getting Enough RAM

RAM makes the machine. Because hard disk access can be thousands of times slower than memory access, purchasing and installing enough memory to effectively cache frequently accessed data and prevent O/S paging can improve system performance by an order of magnitude.

TIP
Begin by estimating 1GB of RAM for each processor in your system. RAM is relatively inexpensive, so buy as much as you can.

Memory is needed by the database to cache data, by the Application Server to cache code, by the Web server to cache HTML pages, and by the O/S to cache the file system. It is rare that someone has too much memory.

As you can see from Figure 1-3, response time is directly correlated to cache hit ratios. Therefore, you should strive for 99 percent cache hit ratios. A 99-percent cache hit ratio is five times faster than a 95-percent cache hit ratio and 20 times faster than an 80-percent cache hit ratio. While not all applications can achieve a 99-percent cache hit ratio, less than a 90-percent cache hit ratio is almost certainly due to not allocating enough memory to the cache.

TIP
Know your limits. For example, on many 32-bit O/S there is a 4GB (or less) total memory limit; the hardware may allow more memory to be added, but the O/S may not be able to use it. If you cannot use it, why buy it?

Cache is not the only use for memory. Applications and user processes require memory. The amount required per user should be determined in a test environment and scaled to the number of concurrent users.

TIP
Do not neglect to take the operating system into account. Memory must be allocated for the O/S and efforts should be made to tune it.

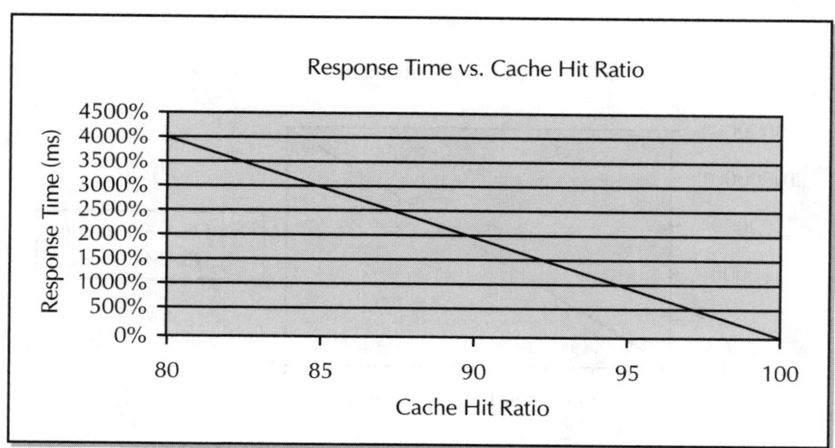

FIGURE 1-3. *Response time vs. cache hit ratio*

As a general rule, the data cache for database should be 1–5 percent of the database size. This breaks down with very large databases, where the percentage is usually less, and for small databases, where the percentage is usually more. The more important metric is the percent of the data accessed in a day rather than the total size of the database.

DRAM capacities have been quadrupled every three years. Unfortunately, DRAM speeds have not improved as rapidly. This mismatch in technology advances may lead to applications being increasingly memory bandwidth bound. In Figure 1-4, it is evident how much DRAM technology advances have improved over time.

TIP

Buy the highest-density RAM your system supports. This will avoid removing RAM if you upgrade in the future—for example, if all the RAM slots are filled and your system has 1GB RAM total, you will have to remove 1GB of RAM and purchase 2GB of RAM if you upgrade to 2GB. If you initially had higher-density RAM, you would only have to purchase 1GB of new RAM.

Getting Enough Storage

It's important to consider your storage needs from drive size to cache to host adapters.

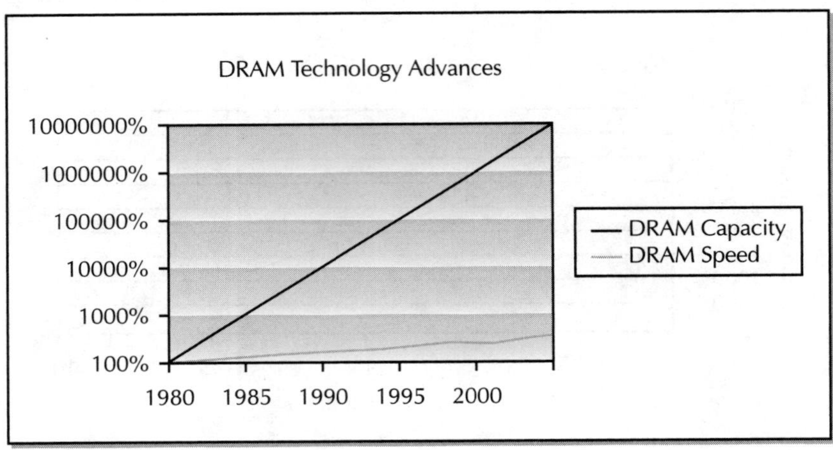

FIGURE 1-4. *DRAM technology advances*

Drive Size

With ever-increasing drive sizes, tuning application I/O becomes increasingly more challenging. The following are three typical modes of operation for an application:

- **Random I/O** Where the drive access time is the bottleneck
- **Sequential I/O** Where given enough I/O buses, drive throughput is the bottleneck
- **CPU intensive** Where the system's CPUs are the bottleneck

Of the preceding three most common performance bottlenecks listed, the first two are related to storage. Large hard drives can be particularly detrimental to the first situation.

TIP
Buy the smallest-size hard drives with the fastest RPMs practical. At the time of writing, this would be 9GB 10,000 RPM drives.

Determine if your application will be bottlenecked on random I/O. If your application might be bottlenecked on random I/O, do not be tempted by the cost savings of larger hard drives. Even with a 10,000-RPM drive, a drive typically cannot process more than a couple hundred random I/O requests per second. The way to process additional I/Os per second is to have additional hard drives. With hard drives that hold more than 36GB of information available, you have to have a good-sized application to require more than one 36GB drive.

Drive capacities have been quadrupled every three years, similar to DRAM capacities. Unfortunately, drive speeds have not improved as rapidly. This mismatch in technology advances plagues DBAs and system administrators who need to effectively tune I/O activity. When the entire application resides on one drive, very few tuning options are available. In Figure 1-5, you can see how much drive technology has improved over time.

TIP
Be sure to size drive throughput and request performance in addition to drive capacity.

Cache

A large amount of disk cache can be a double-edged sword. Disk cache can dramatically improve write performance by registering a successful write as soon as the write reaches the cache. Because memory is thousands of times faster than disk, writes can be completed 10–1,000s of times faster than writing to disk. Disk cache

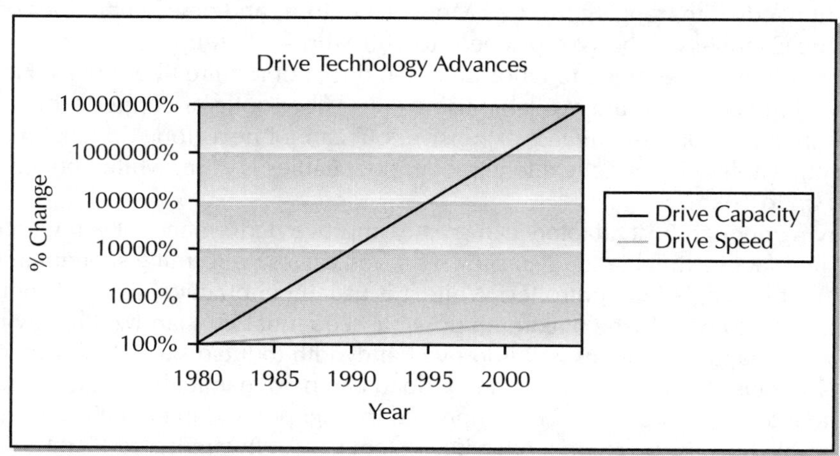

FIGURE 1-5. *Drive technology advances*

can improve read performance, if the data read can be found in the cache. The data may be in the cache from a previous read, or from read ahead intelligence in the drive or RAID unit.

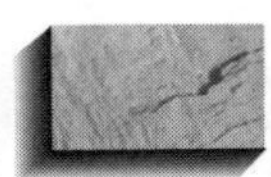

TIP
Cache is another point of failure. To avoid potential data loss, ensure your cache has battery backup.

Regardless of the amount of cache, read and write performances are ultimately limited by the underling drives. For instance, if you have one drive that can write at 10 Mbps, you may be able to achieve better throughput for short periods. Once your cache is full, you will be limited to 10 Mbps. If unexpected, it will seem as though your system has hit a brick wall.

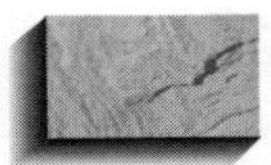

TIP
Size the throughput of the underling drives before worrying about cache. Cache helps smooth the I/O peaks but will not solve all your problems.

Host Adapters

The choice of host adapters and number of host adapters affect performance. There are many types of I/O buses in use today. The more popular interfaces for open systems are Fast-Wide SCSI, Ultra SCSI, Ultra2 SCSI, and Fibre Channel. Each has different bandwidth, ranging from 20 Mbps–100 Mbps, and new generations of SCSI and Fibre Channel will boost top speeds to 160 Mbps–400 Mbps.

Fiber Channel, renamed to Fibre Channel, does not require fiber optics. Fibre Channel interface cards are available using either fiber-optic or copper cables. The copper interfaces are usually less expensive, but cannot be as long (in length) as the fiber-optic cables. The practical length of copper cables is 25m, while fiber can extend up to 10km.

Having enough host adapters can greatly improve performance. Even with the fastest interfaces available today, as few as seven drives performing sequential reads can saturate a single I/O controller. While it is usually impractical to have enough host adapters to handle the maximum possible sequential I/O bandwidth, having as many host adapters as drives will improve bandwidth to the disks. With products, such as Veritas Volume Manager, the I/O load can be dynamically balanced across multiple interfaces, providing both improved throughput and interface failover.

Multiple host adapters are a must if a system uses software-based RAID 1. With drive mirroring, performance is degraded noticeably when both copies of a volume are on the same I/O bus.

RAID

The choice of RAID (redundant array of independent disks, formerly redundant array of inexpensive disks) level can greatly impact performance. The decision to use a particular RAID level should not be entered into lightly. The following is a brief discussion of some common RAID levels. For a further detailed discussion of RAID, refer to the "An Introduction to RAID Technology" booklet available at http://www.mti.com.

RAID 5 RAID 5 provides the most economical protection for your data. With RAID 5, any single disk can fail without interrupting access to your data. RAID 5 provides significant read performance benefits over a single disk. Because reads are spread over *n* disks, read performance can be as much as *n* times faster than a single disk. While I/O activity is spread over several disks, there is only one copy of each piece of data. The cost is a 20–50 percent performance penalty on writes over a single disk. When a RAID 5 write occurs, the original image of a block must be read, the parity information for the stripe must be read, the new data must be written, the new parity must be computed, and the new parity information must be written to disk. While there are enhancements that RAID vendors such as MTI have developed, the mechanics do not change. RAID 5 should only be used on file systems with a large read-to-write ratio or when write performance is not a consideration.

RAID 1 RAID 1 is based on mirroring. At least two copies of each data file exist. Read performance can range from 2–2*N* times the performance of a single disk. Write performance is not significantly different from a single disk. Performance is dictated by the application's capability to spread out I/O activity across several disks. If there are read hot spots, performance will be close to two times the performance of a single disk. If read activity can be spread out over several devices, read performance will be close to 2*N* times that of a single disk. RAID 1 should be used when I/O activity can be evenly spread across several file systems. Typically, RAID 1 performs well with a large number of concurrent users since the large number of users tends to randomize the I/O activity.

RAID 1+0 RAID 1+0 is based on mirroring combined with striping across several disks. As with RAID 1, at least two copies of each data file exist. Read performance is typically 2*N* times the performance of a single disk. Write performance ranges from 1–*N* times that of a single disk. The advantage that RAID 1+0 has over RAID 1 is the transparent striping of I/O activity. RAID 1+0 offers further data protection than RAID 5 since multiple disks in a RAID 1+0 can fail before there is data loss. RAID 1+0 is usually the best choice for your storage subsystem. The downside of RAID 1+0 is the additional cost. Typically, RAID 5 has 10–20 percent overhead for data protection. RAID 1+0 has 100 percent overhead for data protection.

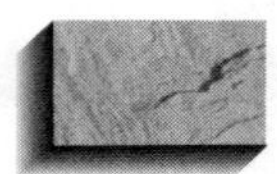

TIP
Plan for RAID 1+0 in your budget. For OLTP applications, RAID 5 has too much overhead and will be a bottleneck in active systems.

HARDWARE VS. SOFTWARE RAID Little performance difference exists between hardware and software RAID; the main difference is where the processing occurs. With software RAID, the processing occurs in the host system's CPUs. With hardware RAID, the processing occurs either in the host interface or in a RAID array. If your environment requires a storage area network (SAN), hardware RAID array is the best choice. Hardware-based RAID arrays usually offer manageability benefits, while software-based RAID solutions usually offer cost benefits. Software RAID, through such products as Veritas Volume Manager, can offer additional interface failover and interface load-balancing benefits.

Choosing an Operating System

While the choice of hardware usually dictates the operating system, several situations exist where this is not the case.

Compaq Tru64 UNIX vs. Windows NT on Alpha Processors

Traditionally, this has been an easy decision. Tru64 UNIX, formerly Digital UNIX, was usually a better choice than Windows NT. Digital UNIX had better driver support, better support from software vendors, and was considerably more stable.

With Compaq acquiring Digital, the choice may not be as clear. Even though, publicly, Compaq has stated they intend to continue to actively support Tru64 UNIX, the empirical evidence is clouded. For example, Compaq was shipping a PCI Fibre Channel host adapter for Alpha machines running Windows NT for nearly one year before Compaq made drivers available for Tru64 UNIX.

With Oracle, all evidence points to Tru64 UNIX being the preferred operating system. Oracle consistently has shipped products for Tru64 UNIX prior to shipping for Windows NT on Alpha.

While the future direction may not be clear, unless you have a compelling reason to run Windows NT on Alpha, Tru64 UNIX is more stable and is better supported by Oracle.

Windows NT vs. Linux on Intel Processors

Windows NT, soon to be Windows 2000, on Intel hardware is a very widely supported operating system. The downsides to Windows NT have traditionally been stability, scalability, and overhead. While Linux was thrust into the limelight by many factors, including a government antitrust investigation of Microsoft, it is a viable alternative to Windows NT.

Who has the performance edge? It is hard to say because it changes all the time. Several benchmarks can be performed with conflicting results—each side claiming the other did not properly tune the other system. Refer to the following result summary.

From Sm@art Reseller:

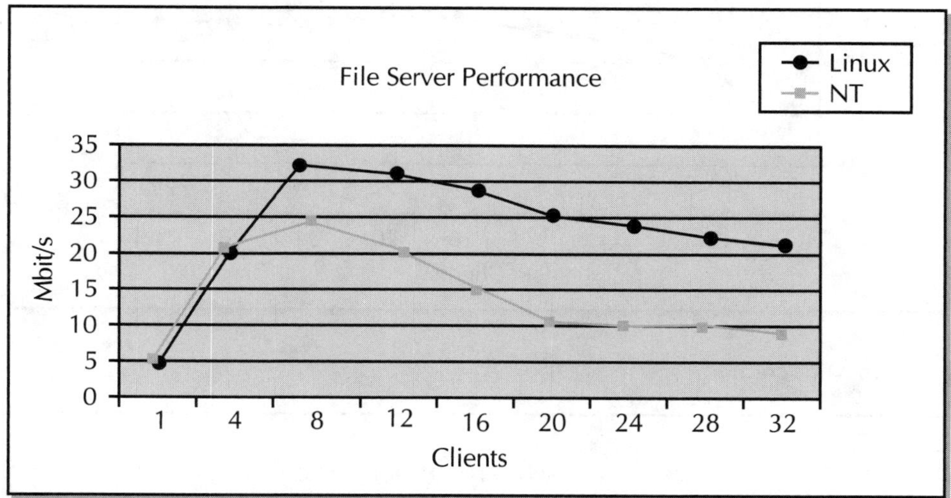

From Mindcraft:

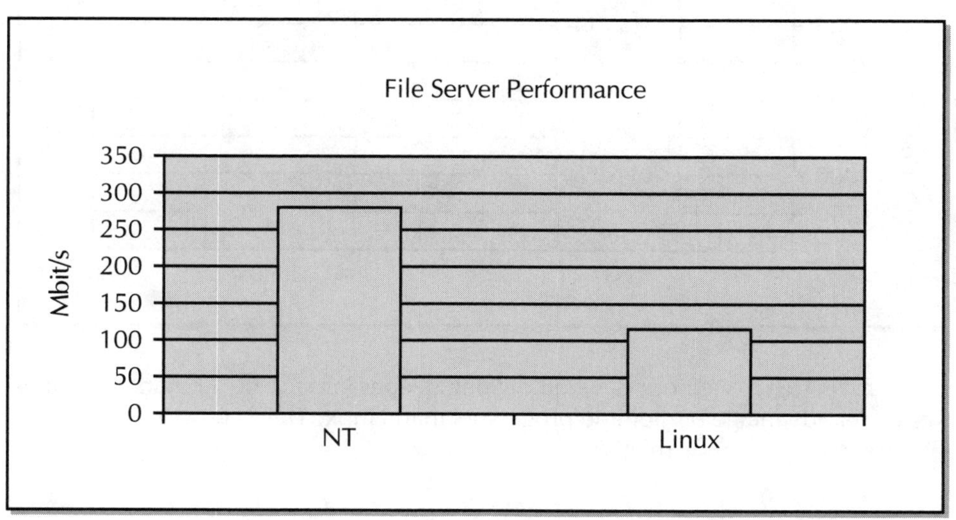

From Sm@art Reseller:

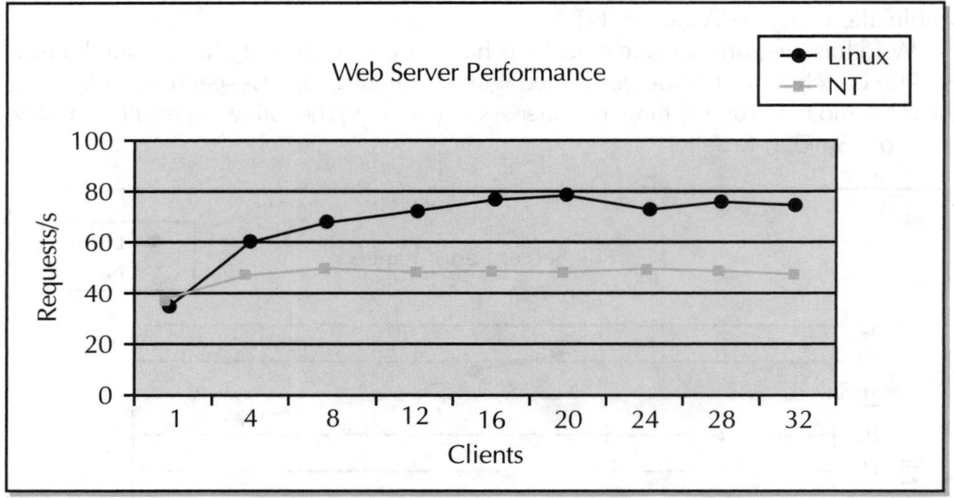

From Mindcraft:

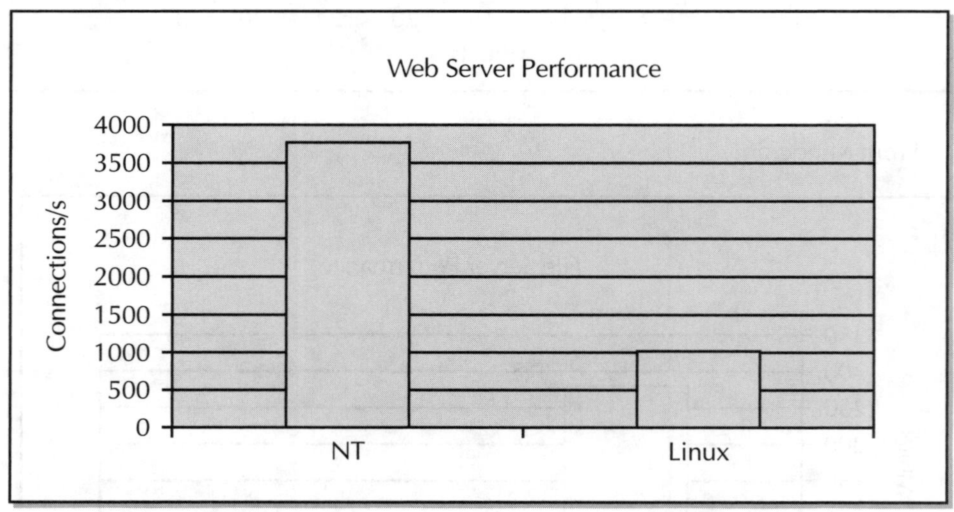

The main trend one notices when digging deeper into the benchmarks is that NT takes better advantage of multiple processors than Linux. This is probably because multiprocessor support is relatively new to Linux.

As Linux continues to mature, expect the multiprocessor performance gap to close. Linux is a less resource-intensive operating system than NT (Linux runs respectably on a 486 with 32MB of RAM); therefore, performance will likely be better on Linux. The systems we have worked with running Linux and Oracle perform very well with better stability than Windows NT.

Based on recent product release dates, Windows NT is better supported by Oracle. However, Oracle has stated that it intends to fully support Linux. At the time of writing, Oracle8i, Oracle Application Server 4, and WebDB were all available for Linux. In addition, Developer Server 6.0 was available in beta release. Oracle has plans to release Oracle Applications for Linux.

With major hardware vendors including Dell, Compaq, and IBM supporting Linux, it will be around for the long haul. Silicon Graphics has even talked about dropping Irix in favor of Linux.

For people who are cost conscious, already have UNIX expertise in-house, or do not have a compelling reason to run Windows NT, Linux is a good option. If you only have Windows NT expertise in-house, Windows NT is probably the better choice.

Linux on Non-Intel Processors

While Linux is available on many non-Intel platforms, the other platforms are not as well supported at this time. At the time of writing, running Linux on anything other than Intel-based hardware is not recommended. Currently, Oracle only supports Linux on Intel.

Researching Available Patches

Staying current with operating system and firmware patches can improve system security, stability, and performance. The best place to look for patches is usually the vendor's Web site.

Security-related patches are particularly important for machines connected to the Internet. One does not have to look far for a headline about SPAM being bounced off an unsuspecting email server, or a corporate or government Web site being hacked into and taken hostage.

Some vendors, such as Sun, provide a patch analysis tool. Sun's patchdiag uses a configuration file that is updated nightly to check the installed versions of patches on your system against what is current. The patchdiag tool can be downloaded from http://sunsolve.sun.com.

Microsoft has a security patch email list. Every time Microsoft finds and patches security vulnerabilities, an email is sent to subscribers of the list. To subscribe to the list, visit http://www.microsoft.com/security.

Another useful mailing list to be on is the CERT advisory email list. Visit http://www.cert.org. CERT advisory emails are sent out as Internet-related security vulnerabilities are found.

Available patches for Oracle can be found on Oracle's MetaLink Web site, http://metalink.oracle.com.

Summary

Hardware is one of the more important components of your Web applications. It is also the place to begin your Web journey. Take time to build a powerful infrastructure for the future. Think through your decisions, ask others for their opinions, and make choices that last.

References

"Technology Trends, Cost/Performance, and Instruction Sets," Prof. Saul Levy – Rutgers University, 1997

Sm@rt Reseller, January 28, 1999

Mindcraft, June 15, 1999

CHAPTER 2

Installation

After you have addressed all of your hardware needs, you are ready to begin. This chapter will assist in the installation of OAS. Even though the installation of OAS is typically uneventful, it's important to know what items to select, what options to change, and which items should be left alone. If you have installed a prior version of OAS, such as OWAS 3.0 or OWS 2.1, and are upgrading, you will quickly realize the installation is familiar territory. Not much has changed in the installation over the versions. A few more options have been added to each subsequent version. If this is your initial installation of OAS, do not install a prior version and then upgrade to OAS 4.0.7—on any hardware platform! As with any software product, do not install an old version with the immediate intention of upgrading. The prior versions are full of bugs, but the current version is very stable. OAS 4.0.8.1 is also available and stable. OAS 4.0.8 was originally considered internally by Oracle as OAS 5.0. This should indicate the number of enhancements between versions 4.0.7 and 4.0.8.

In this chapter, the following topics will be covered:

- Reviewing the system requirements
- Preparing for the client requirements
- Installing OAS
- Completing the installation
- Changing the Node Manager password (or port) after installation
- Correcting the internal error
- Correcting ORA-600 error
- Changing the NT service startup order
- Loading OAS and the database on the same machine
- Deciding if IIS is a problem
- Determining how buggy the beta is
- Transacting high-volume Web sites
- Finding platform-specific installation information
- Reviewing the partner CD

Reviewing the System Requirements

Before installing OAS, make sure you have the minimum system requirements on your server. If you are performing the installation on an oversized/overpowered production server, this is not likely an issue, as you have several times the amount of the minimum requirements. Oracle states the minimum requirements are as follows:

Platform	**X86 NT**	**Sun Solaris**	**Recommended**
Memory	128M	128M	512M
Disk Space	200M	300M	1GB
Swap Space	256M	256M	3x memory
Operating System Level	Windows NT 4.0 w/ Pack 5	Solaris 2.5.1 or 2.6 with a number of patches or ideally Solaris 2.7	

On NT, Oracle recommends against running OAS 4.0.8 with Service Pack 4. If you call technical support about problems with your install, the first thing they will ask you is "What Service Pack are you running?" I have installed OAS 4.0.7 on machines that have Service Pack 4 and everything has worked fine. However, I have performed the installation and experienced problems due to Service Pack 4. Service Pack 4 and 4.0.8 has never worked for me. When attempting to move back to Service Pack 3, I experienced problems if a backup wasn't selected, so "installer beware."

TIP
Read the installation and release notes for your specific OAS version, platform, and operating system. These notes change with most every unique configuration.

The beta versions of OAS will only run with Oracle8 and subsequent releases; however, the production version can work the Oracle 7.3.4, 8.0.5, 8.1.5, and subsequent releases.

Getting Ready for the Client Requirements

Because OAS uses a new Java-based management tool, the client-side requirements are a bit more restrictive than prior releases. OWS 2.1 only required an HTML browser, and OWAS 3.0 added the requirement of HTML frames. These requirements are obviously still in effect. In addition, your browser needs to be Java-enabled. OAS requires the implementation of Java 1.1.4 or subsequent releases, because it was used to develop the OAS management tool. Essentially, there are only two browsers, Internet Explorer (IE) and Netscape Navigator, meaning you must use any of the following browser versions:

- **Netscape**
  - Netscape 4.04 w/ patch
  - Netscape 4.06+
- **Internet Explorer**
  - IE 4.0 and Service Patch 1
  - IE 4.01 with Service Patch 1
  - IE 5.0+

Installing OAS

After inserting the CD and starting the installation program, the prompts will begin. The first prompt will appear identical to the one shown in Figure 2-1. Enter your company name, choose the Oracle home directory, and your site's base language.

The software Asset Manager window will be displayed, as shown in Figure 2-2. At this point, you need to choose the product(s) you wish to install—at a minimum, choose Oracle Application Server. Then, click Install.

As illustrated next, you can choose whether you wish to run the normal edition or the Enterprise edition of Oracle Application Server. This would depend upon your licensing with Oracle. The Enterprise edition features are detailed in Chapter 10.

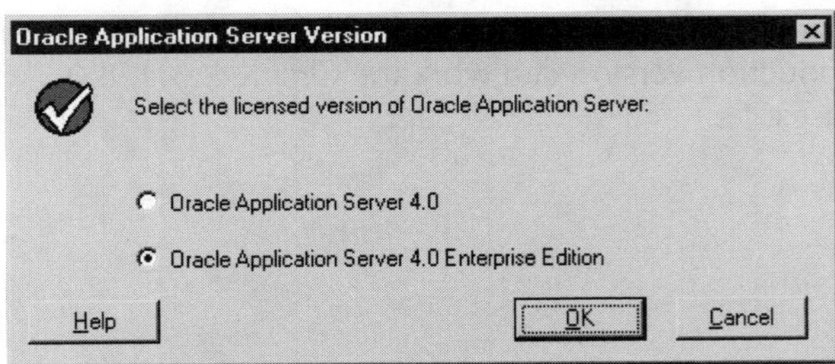

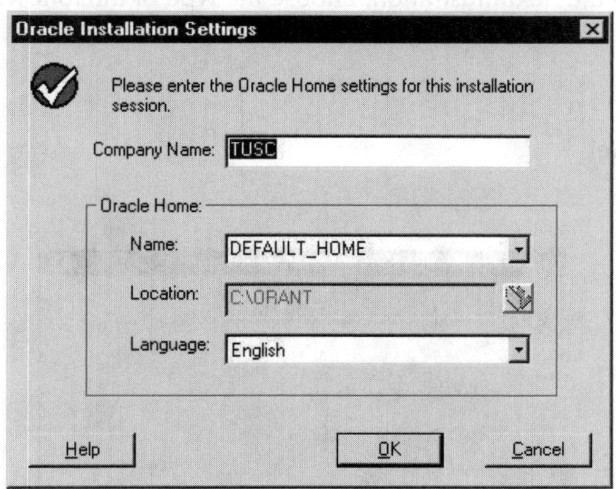

FIGURE 2-1. *Oracle installation settings*

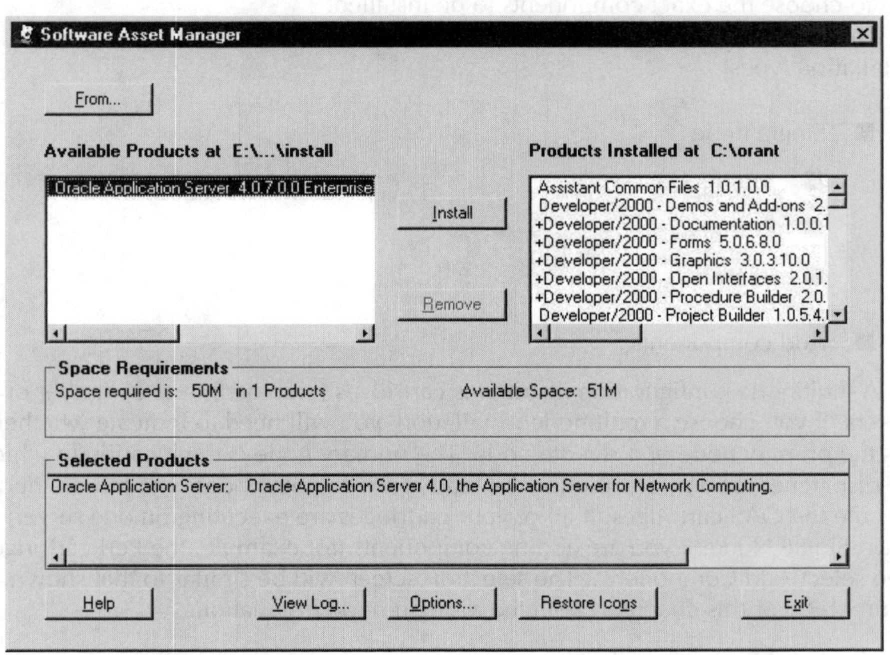

FIGURE 2-2. *Software Asset Manager window*

As evident in the next illustration, choose the type of the following installations to perform:

- Typical
- Complete
- Custom

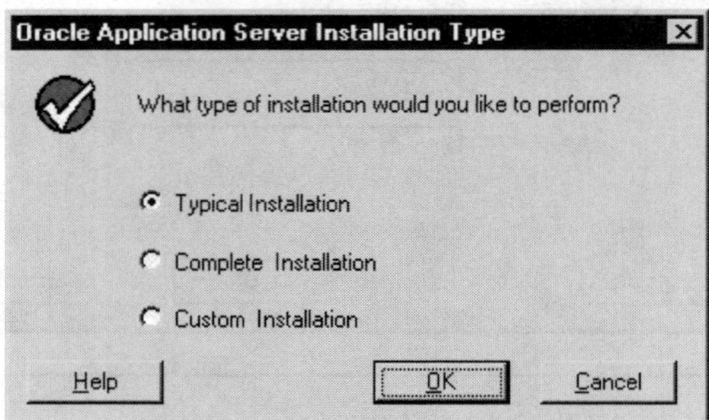

I recommend the Custom option for Oracle products you are installing, enabling you to choose the exact components to be installed.

The options shown in Figure 2-3 will display the choice of the following installation types:

- Single node
    - Multinode
    - Primary
    - Remote
- Add components

A multinode configuration distributes cartridges (and load) over a number of servers. If you choose a multinode installation, you will need to indicate whether it is the primary node or a remote node. The primary node is the location in which the dispatcher resides, distributing the load to the remote nodes. The remote nodes execute the OAS cartridges. If all of your cartridges are executing on one server, select Single Node. If you are adding components (for example, the Perl cartridge), then select Add Components. The selection screen will be similar to that shown in Figure 2-3. For this chapter, I selected a single-node installation.

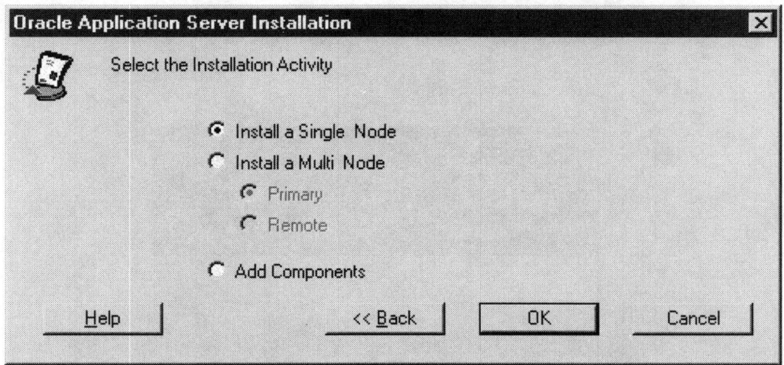

FIGURE 2-3. *Oracle Application Server Installation window*

When choosing the cartridges you wish to install, if you are still experimenting, you may want to select them all. Otherwise, choose only the cartridges your application is going to use. If you are using Java as your Application Server language, install the first three cartridges—they are all Java cartridge components. Most OAS sites currently use the PL/SQL cartridge as their primary Application Server language, in which case you would select the PL/SQL cartridge. In the screen illustrated in Figure 2-4, select the following optional cartridges you wish to install:

- Enterprise JavaBeans
- JCORBA
- JWeb
- LiveHTML
- Perl
- PL/SQL

In the screen shown in Figure 2-5, provide site installation information, and a logical name for your site. The site name is used by the OAS startup programs and for physical file locations. In addition, select the boot port. To avoid overlapping the boot port with another TCP/IP port on your server, leave the parameters set to website40 and boot port 2649.

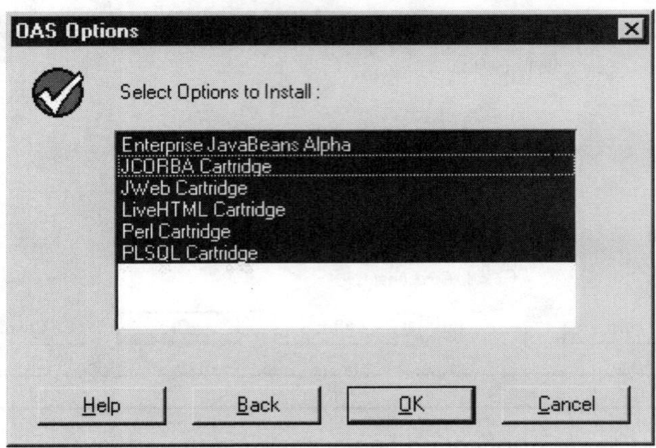

FIGURE 2-4. *Optional cartridge selection*

To this point, the installation is similar to OWAS 3.0. If you have completed prior installations, you would be anticipating the prompt for the administration port.

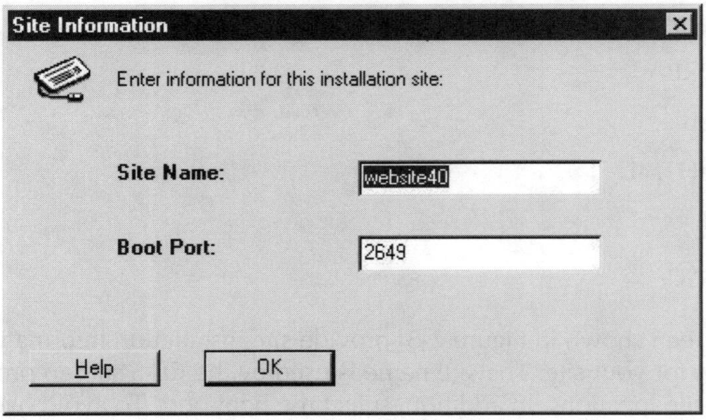

Site Information

Enter information for this installation site:

Site Name: website40

Boot Port: 2649

Help OK

FIGURE 2-5. *Site installation information*

Instead, you are prompted for the Node Manager port; this is the same as the administration port in version 3. Several reasons influenced the naming convention. The administration port administers only one Web site, and the administration port cannot manage the entire Web site. For example, you cannot restart the Web Request Broker (WRB) from the administrative port. In OWAS 3.0, you must perform the WRB "bounce" operation from the operating system's command line. The Node Manager enables you to administer an entire node—including multiple Web sites and the WRB from the browser. You no longer need to go to the command line to perform such operations.

In Figure 2-6, you are prompted for a number of the following key pieces of information about the Node Manager configuration:

- Port number
- Username
- Password
- Confirm password

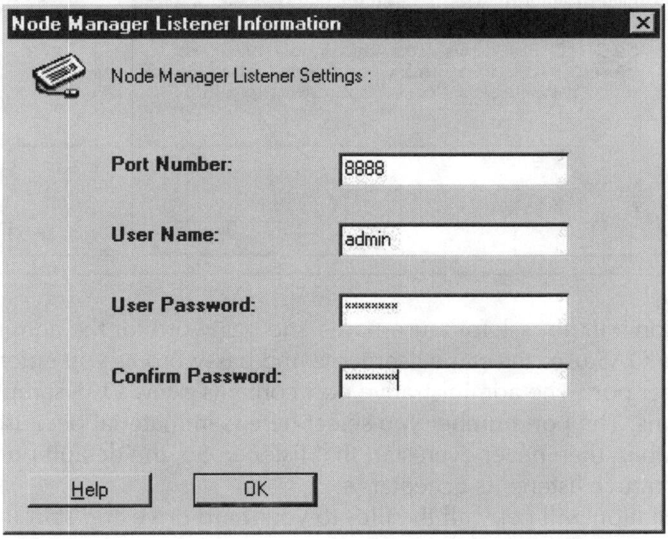

FIGURE 2-6. *Node Manager port configuration*

If the server acquiring the installation is not going to be available on the Internet, you can leave the port number as 8888, the default. However, if the server will be available on the Internet, or if the server needs to be a secure server, you should change the default to a port number only the site administrator knows. In fact, for optimum security, if you have easy access to the server's operating system command line, only bring up the Node Manager port when you need to administer sites. I would recommend setting the administrator's password to something known only to the site administrator. Use a unique password for this port—*do not* use anything that might be obvious. If someone breeches your security and gets into the Node Manager, they can destroy your entire site configuration in a short period of time. Remember that Netcraft (www.netcraft.com) keeps track of Web server usage by URL. Visit Netcraft's Web site if you are curious about what Web server a company is using. If you are curious about who's running a specific Web server or a specific version of a Web server, you can also visit Netcraft's site for a URL list by Web server. If visitors know you are running OAS and your Node Manager is running on port 8888, and the port's username and password are obvious, you are asking for security trouble.

As evident in the following illustration, OAS will prompt you for the administrative port number.

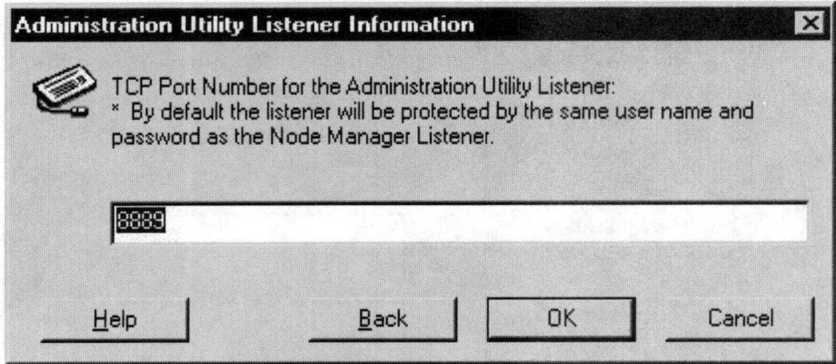

The installation will not ask for a username and password for the administrative port, because OAS uses the same username and password as you entered for the Node Manager port. The administrative port contains a few OAS samples or demonstrations. The port number you select here is immaterial because you will supply a number, then never even start that listener. So, the default port of 8889 for your administrative listener is acceptable.

The installation will copy all the files to your hard drive and start the listeners.

Completing the Installation

After you have installed OAS, beyond configuring OAS (discussed in further detail in Chapter 4), complete the installation of the internal applications and cartridge components you wish to use. All internal applications are PL/SQL packages. Therefore, you must install the PL/SQL cartridge to use the components. The following are internal applications that can be installed:

- PL/SQL Toolkit
- Logger Tables
- Log Analyzer
- Database Browser

The four optional internal applications are installed from the OAS Utilities Installation option. To use the OAS utilities, you must go to the URL of your Web server's Node Manager port and log in—using the port and username/password you defined in the preceding step.

- **PL/SQL Toolkit** In prior versions of OAS, by default, the Toolkit was installed into each PL/SQL Agent's own schema. As described in my first book, *Oracle Application Server Web Toolkit Reference* (Oracle Press, 1998), it was up to you as the administrator to do otherwise. OAS's Install PL/SQL Toolkit option automates this process by creating the PL/SQL Toolkit in a common schema (the OAS_PUBLIC schema) and then granting EXECUTE privileges to PUBLIC.

TIP

Since the OAS Toolkit has been granted EXECUTE privileges to PUBLIC, make sure you protect your PL/SQL Agent when defining your DADs (under Site | Applications | Site | Cartridge | PLSQL make sure you select Protection Enabled). If not, this OAS feature would turn out to be a security hole waiting to be exposed by wanna-be hackers!

- **Logger Tables and Log Analyzer** Because these work together, you cannot use the Log Analyzer without first installing the Logger Tables. By default, OAS writes a log file containing access information for every URL hit to your site. This file is in Oracle's proprietary XLF (extended log file) format. Using a tool, such as WebTrends, you can analyze this information—as described in further detail in Chapter 26. OAS enables you to store this XLF information in Oracle tables. The Oracle tables are called the Logger Tables. Even though I would not recommend doing this for performance reasons, the XLF logs can be written directly to the database, rather than to the file system. A better option is to batch-load the logs into the database. This option did not work in prior versions of OAS, but has been fixed for version 4. The advantage to storing this information in the database is that, once in the database, you can write your own scripts to analyze the log information or you can use the Log Analyzer, providing built-in and ad hoc reports on this information.
- **Database Browser** From tables to indexes to procedures to packages, the Database Browser enables you to view all objects in your database from your browser. If you have purchased WebDB, as detailed in Chapter 5, WebDB also provides a powerful browse database feature.

Changing the Node Manager Password (or Port) After Installation

Version 4 has finally encrypted the password in the configuration file. Prior to version 4, you could edit the administrative password by editing the listener's configuration file. To edit the password, you must go through the OAS Manager to select the site, then Oracle Application Server, Security, and finally Basic. The admin user's password is blank. Enter the new password prompt, then click on Apply.

To alter the Node Manager's port number, edit the listener configuration file. This file is in the ows/admin/website40/httpd_servername/node directory, where website40 is the name you specified at install time, and servername is the complete domain name of your server. The file containing the port information is the svnode.cfg file. The port number is the second parameter under the [Multiport] tag.

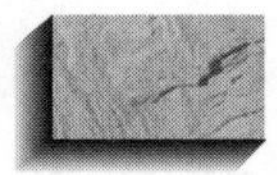

TIP
You can quickly change the Node Manager password through the command-line utility oaspasswd.

For the preceding changes to take effect, you must stop and restart the Node Manager port from the command line, by using either of the following commands:

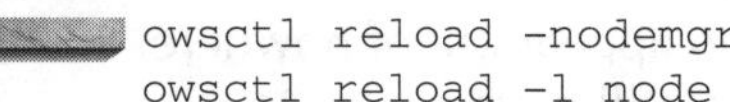

```
owsctl reload -nodemgr
owsctl reload -l node
```

Correcting the Internal Error

After installing OAS or OWAS, you may experience the infamous "internal error," also known as "the kiss of death." There appears to be no logical explanation for this error. In fact, the error may appear one time you execute a URL and not the next. Many developers have spent countless hours debugging their code and trying to capture this internal error. This message resides deep within OAS, *not* from the application code. The internal error message simply means that the cartridge you attempted to execute has failed.

If you get this error every single time, never getting a success, it is likely that the cartridge to be executed is not properly configured. If you get the internal error every time, check the WRB's log file for additional information, then fix the cartridge's configuration issues. If you are running OAS on the edge of or below the memory recommendations, there is not enough memory to load the cartridge instance, and you will experience an internal error message. Reading the error log file will clearly indicate why you are receiving this error.

If the internal error message occurs every once in a while, and particularly occurs when your server is the least busy, then most likely it is because of a bug that exists in early versions of OWAS and OAS. If you were installing OWAS v3.0, you should not consider production versions prior to version 3.0.1.0.1 for NT or 3.0.1.8 for UNIX. If you are installing OAS v4.0, do not consider production on any platform prior to version 4.0.7. In every case where the internal error was intermittent, it has been my experience that the site was running on something less than a production copy of OAS.

Another similar error occurs in OWAS version 3.0. The error is *The server had an internal error and could not process the request.* This is a completely different error than the preceding *internal error* message. Looking at the error log, you will encounter the following explanation: [OWA] Warning: Version mismatch between expected PL/SQL packages version and current packages version (0.0) or execution of PL/SQL initialization block failed.

If you upgraded from a prior version of OAS, this error probably indicates that you forgot to install the new PL/SQL Toolkit for version 4. The PL/SQL cartridge is looking for an initialization package that does not exist. OWA_INIT was new as of OWAS version 3. In version 4, this package was renamed to OWA_CUSTOM. To solve this problem, install the current version of the PL/SQL Toolkit.

If you have not recently upgraded and the error seems to appear out of nowhere, ensure all of the PL/SQL Toolkit packages are valid, and you still have access to the packages. Invalid packages or a loss of access to the packages (for example, dropped synonyms or revoked execute access) would have the same result as previously described.

Determining How Buggy the Beta Is

If you have installed any of the OAS beta versions, such as 4.0.4.3 or 4.0.5.4, you probably quickly realized it had too many bugs to make any progress with the product. There is no easy answer to determine how clean or bug infected a beta version will be. Even though Oracle may say a product is production, be wary of trusting this label. For example, Oracle said version 3.0.1.0.0 of OWAS was a production version and as previously noted (for example, the internal error), this version was far from production. However, version 3.0.1.0.1 on NT (3.0.1.8 on UNIX) was a solid production version. On the other hand, when Oracle said release 4.0.7 of OAS was a production version, by most accounts it was a stable production version of the product. If you want to be assured of a true production release, wait for the second minor revision after Oracle says it's production. This discussion seems to imply that the beta releases are not worth testing, which is not always true. Sometimes beta releases are stable—it just depends on the product.

To decipher "how buggy is the beta (or production) version x.y.z.," the best feedback can be found on list servers. The Rocky Mountain Oracle Users Group (www.rmoug.org) has an active list server (rmoug-l@fatcity.com) and Deja (www.deja.com) has a busier list server specifically for OAS. This is an excellent way to find answers. Also make a note when a major release is rolled into a minor version release—for example 4.0.8. Version 4.0.8.1 is stable, whereas 4.0.8.0 is not.

Correcting ORA-600 Error

If you are encountering an ORA-600 error message, it is likely a database issue that requires an upgrade to resolve the ORA-600. This was known to be the case for users of Oracle 7.3.3.4 who had to upgrade to version 7.3.3.6. After upgrading from 7.3.3.4 to 7.3.3.6, an error—"Authorization failed. Retry?"—occurs, requiring you to install patch #560686. Therefore, to save valuable time before upgrading to new database versions, make sure you get the required upgrades and patches first.

Changing the NT Service Startup Order

Version 3 of OWAS on NT did not establish the proper interservice dependencies. OWAS would start the database, the SQL*Net listener, the Web listener, and the OAS WRB (Web Request Broker) all at once. During automated service startup, it would encounter problems because the 3.0 listeners require the WRB to be running before they can start. You can create your own dependencies for any NT service by editing the NT registry via the Registry Editor (you must use regedt32.exe, not regedit.exe). Be sure to back up your registry before performing any operations.

In the editor, drill into HKEY_LOCAL_MACHINE, SYSTEM, CurrentControlSet, and Services. Under Services, you will find each of the NT services. Locate the NT service you wish to create a dependency for and click on it. In the right-hand frame, a list of keys (variables) and their respective values will appear. If you see variables for DependOnGroup and DependOnService, then the service already has a dependency. DependOnService is the name of the dependency. This service will not start until the DependOnService has successfully started. You may modify the DependOnService by double-clicking it and typing in another service name—note the name *is* case sensitive. If the service does not have any dependencies, in the Edit menu, select Add Value. You need to add DependOnGroup and DependOnService, and both must have a datatype of REG_MULTI_SZ. DependOnGroup is going to remain empty and DependOnService will be the *exact* name of the service this service should depend on. Be sure your dependencies are in the correct order!

To determine the startup order for the WRB processes, start the WRB from the command line and make notes.

Loading OAS and the Database on the Same Machine

"Can the database server and the Web server be loaded on the same machine?" Definitely. My laptop computer is configured this way for development, presentations, and writing this book. However, when OAS and the RDBMS are configured on the same machine, after installation the SQL*Net listener may consume all of the CPU time. When the listener.ora has not been properly configured, OAS can bring out the worst in the SQL*Net listener. The default listener.ora file contains listener configuration examples or samples. These samples are *not* valid and *must* be removed. Otherwise, when OAS hits the listener, it consumes all of your machine's CPU trying to find the bogus listener entries.

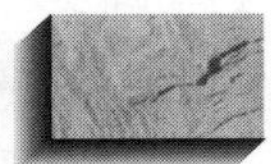

TIP

If your Oracle data is on the same machine, the net80 listener should have an entry for 'Bequeath' (local). This informs Oracle that the instance is on the local server.

"While using OAS to access PL/SQL applications on remote databases, is it required to have a local copy of an Oracle database on the same machine as OAS?"

Absolutely not. If you do not have a local database, install SQL*Net and configure access to the remote database. To avoid potential issues, be sure to install and configure SQL*Net before attempting to install OAS.

Figuring Out if IIS is a Problem

On an NT Server installation, Microsoft IIS is automatically installed for you—the default IIS listener will be running on port 80. If Microsoft Option Pack has been installed on an NT Workstation, it will start the light version of the IIS listener on port 80. This is not a problem if you do not use OAS on port 80, or if you plan to use and register IIS as an external listener to OAS. However, if you do not plan to use IIS, then shut down the IIS service and turn off the automatic startup of the service, through the Services option on the Control Panel. If you do not turn off or stop the IIS listener, then you will receive a port conflict in which the listener that starts first will remain active.

Finding Platform-Specific Installation Information

Each platform's installation procedure may be slightly different. Before performing an installation on your specific platform, look at the installation guide specific to your platform; you may also wish to find additional information on the Oracle Web pages (www.oracle.com), Metalink (http://www.oracle.com/support/), and Technet (technet.oracle.com) for installation directions and notes for each platform. Be sure to read the system requirements and the preinstallation steps. You can call Oracle Support with the operating system version and OAS version and tell them that you are requesting any information regarding specifics for a particular combination, such as patches, incompatibilities, things you *must* do (or it will not work), and so forth. For example, several changes must occur on a UNIX system ahead of time, such as kernel changes, account creations, and so forth.

Plan to throw away your first installation. In other words, try it and learn from it. Contact your system administrator to answer questions about logical volumes, mount points, and so forth. You may need to contact the system administrator to adjust SHMMAX, and perhaps other kernel parameters. Acquiring a CSI number for Oracle Support will be a big help. If you are not familiar with shell scripting, and there again, your system administrator should be your friend—particularly for postinstall tasks, such as running root.sh and setting up startup/shutdown. Definitely take the time to read the entire installation guide and do the checklists. Of particular importance to maintainability is OFA, which your DBA will understand, and which is also explained in the DBA guide.

Installing the software is the easy part, as the installer takes care of most issues. Creating the database and deciding the locations and sizes for the database files is when careful planning is important. These issues require extensive thought, and the answers may be different depending on the application. Remember to look in the logs to find the errors. You can usually ignore the "object/table to be dropped does not exist" type of errors because they will not exist on a first-time installation. Be sure to keep track of the locations of all files—if you decide to throw out the installation and reinstall, remove the entire directory tree. However, do this only on a practice installation.

Another great source of information is on Deja (www.deja.com). Even though Usenet can be frustrating, it contains gems of information.

As previously mentioned, another fine source of information is MetaLink. This is Oracle support online. If you have a valid CSI number, you can register for MetaLink. Forums and articles can assist you with operating systems specifically, and with general support questions. The more in-depth the query, the more accurate the answers that will be returned. Be specific and as unique as possible. Unlike most search engines, MetaLink's search engine assumes an operator of *and* for all words in the search. For example, a query of "owsctl status" means "owsctl" *and* "status" in the results. In most Internet search engines, this would mean "owsctl" *or* "status."

Reviewing the Partner CD

As of the release of OAS version 4.0.7, Oracle began shipping the Partner CD. This CD contains the following products, provided with a variety of the following licensing agreements:

- WebTrends Log Analyzer
- Symantec Visual Page
- OpenConnect's WebConnect
- Vital Sign's Net Medic
- Eventus' CONTROL
- Fujitsu's COBOL Cartridge

WebTrends Log Analyzer

Why reinvent the wheel? As detailed in Chapter 26, the WebTrends product is a solution for monitoring and analyzing your Web logs. WebTrends' Professional Suite is the first complete Web management solution, integrating log file analysis, proxy server analysis, Web site link analysis, and quality control in one box. The WebTrends Enterprise Suite includes all functions of the Professional Suite, as well as the capability to export WebTrends analysis to high-end database servers, such as Oracle. The award-winning WebTrends Log Analyzer is essential for anyone with a Web site, to provide critical information, such as top referring Web sites, top requested pages, top paths through the site, and much more. It offers extraordinarily fast reporting by processing log files in real time, storing the analysis in a database, and running reports on the already-analyzed data. The copy of the software on the CD is a 60-day trial license.

All WebTrends products now include FastTrends technology, enabling real-time importing, analysis, and reporting for any Web site, including an active Internet and intranet sites (10GB and larger log files supported). The LogAnalyzer offers a built-in Remote Reporting server enabling you to configure WebTrends and create, view, and email reports using only your browser. The Professional Suite is the first and only product on the market to integrate Web traffic and log analysis with proxy server analysis including link analysis and quality control—all in one box. The WebTrends Professional Suite offers a modular and scalable solution encompassing complete Web site management as one integrated solution. The Enterprise Suite is now available for e-commerce sites, high-end sites, and database developers. It includes all the features of the Professional Suite *plus* it can store the FastTrends databases in Oracle8. If you purchase the Professional Suite, upgrading to the WebTrends Enterprise Suite is available at any time.

Symantec Visual Page

Symantec's Visual Page is a powerful, easy-to-use HTML editor providing users with the fastest way to move important business documents and crucial company information to the Web. Using Visual Page's intuitive interface and drag-and-drop controls, creation and resizing of tables, frames, and images is simple. For advanced users who wish to add or modify HTML code directly, Visual Page generates clean, well-organized HTML code and includes a powerful source code editor. The copy on the partner CD is a single-user license.

Visual Page's toolbar makes it easy to change typeface sizes, align text, and set styles. Setting up document links is a snap with the Site Window. You just drag and drop files and anchor points to set up the links. No more opening other Web pages to try to link them. Symantec Visual Page provides dynamic resizing of HTML tables, frames, and images with the click of a mouse. Text wraps around images automatically, just like in your browser. Java applets and QuickTime movies run inside Visual Page. What you see is *really* what you get! The standard toolbar makes it easy to use without learning a completely new software product. The Site Window enables easy link setup—drag and drop pages and anchors to your page. The Site Window shows all your pages, anchors, and images in one convenient window. The dynamic document layout shows you how the document will look as you move and resize images. No more resizing an image and hoping the text will appear correctly.

OpenConnect's WebConnect

WebConnect Pro™ by OpenConnect Systems, Inc. enables organizations to leverage the value of their enterprise applications. With OC://WebConnect Pro, you can unleash the power of your IBM mainframe and midrange computing environments. In conjunction with OAS, you can instantly Web-enable them without changing a line of code. You will be able to revitalize your enterprise systems, not only decreasing cost but boosting sales and revenues. It enables you to provide authorized internal and external employees, customers, vendors, and business partners secure, low-cost access to your enterprise computer applications over the Internet, corporate intranet, and extranets. The partner CD includes a copy of the OC://WebConnect Pro cartridge offering a free eight-user license to access legacy systems and a copy of OpenVista.

WebConnect Pro provides easy access to legacy applications. According to OpenSystems Connect, over 70 percent of the world's information continues to be locked within an IBM SNA environment. The OC://WebConnect Pro cartridge holds the key to unleash the power of this information to corporate users through their intranets, to business partners and suppliers through extranets, and to customers of business through the Internet. No more efficient, reliable, or cost-justifiable way exists to instantly Web-enable this corporate asset than through the use of secure browser-based access to these systems. By leveraging the world's largest base of existing proven, reliable, scalable, and manageable applications without change, the barrier's between traditional platforms and today's Internet-enabled computing paradigm are immediately removed. The product's functionality is as simple as browsing and as secure as being on your own network. Access to legacy data and applications through any Java-enabled Web browser enables critical information resources to be shared among professional colleagues, customers, business partners, and suppliers. WebConnect Pro rejuvenates old-fashioned "green screens" with OpenVista. The companion to OC://WebConnect, OpenVista is a visual Java integrated development environment (IDE) enabling you to easily create simplified user screens, within traditional legacy data applications.

VitalSign's Net.Medic

VitalSign's Net.Medic software works with a user's browser to monitor, isolate, diagnose, and correct Internet or intranet performance problems. Net.Medic assists users in identifying the source of a bottleneck, whether PC, modem, or Internet service provider, and offers solution recommendations—and in some cases automatically fixes them. The copy of the product that is on the CD is a 60-day trial license. However, there is a $200 discount offer for Net.Medic Professional for OAS available from VitalSigns Software.

Net.Medic is a browser companion that monitors performance of OAS applications. It monitors browser's HTTP requests and responses, and characterizes the network delay. Net.Medic can isolate network problems by accessing OAS cartridges. By identifying these issues in seconds, Net.Medic provides system administrators and Webmasters with crucial information on end-user experience, as seen at the client desktop.

Eventus' CONTROL

On the partner CD, you receive a single-user license of Eventus' CONTROL, which is a team-oriented Web application management system designed to handle large and complex enterprise Web applications. CONTROL's collaborative framework enables teams of Webmasters, developers, and content contributors to centrally manage and deploy distributed applications through an RDBMS-based CONTROL repository. Together, CONTROL and OAS provide a scalable, enterprise-quality solution for centralized assembly, management, and delivery of network applications.

The architecture of this product is built on Oracle relational database technology, having multithreaded consoles for better performance, and is scalable to manage multiple applications with hundreds of thousands of components. CONTROL provides the tools for team collaboration that include an open framework for multiple users, applications, and servers, check-in/check-out of working files including file locking, and code reusability to minimize development efforts and ensure brand management. Real-time application analysis and correction ensures link integrity of OAS applications prior to deployment on OAS, which reduces and simplifies quality assurance tasks. Applications should be developed and released to production in less time. The monitoring and tuning capabilities provide OAS applications with usage pattern analysis for more comprehensive tuning. CONTROL also contains advanced deployment management, providing fault-tolerant deployment to multiple Web servers and transactional methods ensuring applications are deployed consistently across servers with minimal downtime. OAS and CONTROL together provide a unique, compelling solution. CONTROL stores application metadata in an Oracle repository to uniquely provide unsurpassed real-time link management capabilities, ensuring the integrity of applications before being sent to OAS. CONTROL's reliable deployment methodology ensures high-speed deployment, transformational deployment (for example, automatic link rewriting), and transactional fault-tolerant deployment (rollback, commit, pause, and so forth). CONTROL provides OAS applications with usage pattern analysis to tune Web applications. Specifically, component-level analysis (for example, hits and durations), link-level analysis, and feedback are available to development teams through the tool's active repository.

Fujitsu's COBOL Cartridge

If you have COBOL programs and would like to access Oracle from OAS using COBOL, Fujitsu has your solution. Fujitsu's COBOL cartridge provides a set of standard COBOL APIs enabling OAS functions to be invoked directly from within COBOL programs. This enables thin HTML-based clients, such as Web browsers and network computers, to access and execute COBOL programs. The partner CD includes a full user license for the Fujitsu COBOL cartridge.

This cartridge provides a number of key advantages. First, this cartridge easily enables Internet or intranet access to legacy COBOL applications. With a majority of the COBOL business applications written in the 1970s and 1980s still in use today, it is essential to leverage the vast amount of code supporting enterprise systems, and at the same time provide easy access from the browser interface. By enabling self-service to legacy applications, there is no longer a need to have specially trained personnel acting between the data and the people who want to access it. By simply creating a new Web-based user interface on top of existing business applications rather than rewriting the entire application, development time is greatly reduced. Therefore, this cartridge is the most reliable way to Web-enable COBOL applications. There is no reprogramming of the business logic. It is not only faster to deploy these applications on the Web, but it is also the safest way. With the combination of COBOL cartridge and Fujitsu COBOL, programmers can build new Web applications or adapt legacy applications to the Internet. Fujitsu COBOL is a high-performance and high-quality COBOL compiler available across hardware and software platforms—from mainframes to workstations to personal computers.

Summary

The installation process is not meant to be a painful operation. Take your time, follow the directions, and you will find that it is painless. However, if you are like most IT professionals, you are reading this chapter because the installation did not work the first time.

CHAPTER 3

Designing the Site

ven though typical client/server deployment issues are not a factor in Internet architecture projects, the graphic intensity, immaturity of the browser, and development tools create new factors for your Web projects. While management of a Web project and database design remains relatively constant with the client/server projects you have worked on, the design of a Web application involves many different factors that do not need to be considered in a typical client/server application design process. This chapter will cover issues throughout the phases of planning and development of an application on the Web. I once had a project manager who cut our design off because it was taking too long and he felt that he needed to see results sooner. We tried to explain that his decision was a mistake, but he didn't listen. He said he feared for his job if we didn't crank out some code in a hurry. Guess who was right in the end? The tips covered in this chapter include the following:

- Jump-starting your Web server knowledge
- Designing your Web team
- Making the most of the five C's
- Planning your design
- Flowing with design
- Developing coding standards
- Understanding how Internet development is different
- Organizing your directories
- Thinking thin client

Jump-Starting Your Web Server Knowledge

A number of excellent books and articles are available on the topic of Oracle Web application development. A good place to start your introduction to the Internet and OAS is my previous book titled *Oracle Application Server Web Toolkit Reference* (Oracle Press, 1998). The basic Internet topics you will need to know before starting the development and deployment of your application are covered in Chapter 1, Chapter 2, and Chapter 4. These chapters provide an excellent starting point for your Web education and provide an explanation of Internet fundamentals, such as the difference between intranets and extranets, available development tools, and how to develop practical Web applications. Chapters 1, 2, and 4 of *Oracle*

Application Server Web Toolkit Reference provide a basic understanding of the technology and provide detailed coding examples to begin your Web education.

An amazing number of resources are available over the Internet. Refer to Appendix A of this book for an extensive list of sites that can help you with your Web education. Many papers describing the technology and basic Internet design principles are available in the document download section of the TUSC site (http://www.tusc.com). On this site, you can obtain a complete picture of the Internet as a whole, including specific information on tools, technical architecture, tuning, and many other topics. Numerous sites are available for ideas regarding Internet site design. Technical references, such as http://www.htmlgoodies.com, can answer many technical questions about creating Web sites with advanced features. Many sites cover general design considerations, such as when to use animation or how information should be formatted on a page. The best examples of what *not* to do can often be found on poorly designed sites, so search the Web and find sites you do not like—then build a "Web Design Don't" list. These sites can be used as examples on how not to build a site—http://www.webpagesthatsuck.com is an example of this type of site and there are many more, such as http://www.worstoftheweb.com. These sites include many examples of how not to do things along with all of the appropriate explanations. By adhering to these recommendations, you can avoid the same pitfalls in the development of your Web site.

Other sites provide examples of how to design a good site. Again, researching and investigating numerous sites and building a "Web Design Do" list is the best way to identify what you like in a Web site and what you would like to include in your Web application.

Designing Your Web Team

A number of successful team configurations have been demonstrated across a large span of companies, from small (a one-person "team") to large. This section makes some generalizations for developing a Web team. It is not a list of rigid requirements, but should be used as an inspirational guide to building your team.

When putting together your team, the Information Technology (IT) group should manage your Internet project development. Once the application is in production, the IT group will be expected to support the technology used for the Web sites you build. Too often departments outside of IT view the idea of working with IT as a bottleneck or a negative project impact. If you view working with IT as such, I would highly recommend that you discuss that opinion with your Chief Information/Technology Officer (CIO/CTO).

Both organizations should challenge each other to ensure that the focus of all team members is to produce practical business results on (or ahead of) time and on (or under) budget.

Depending on the size of your company or project, you may not have a separate person for each of the project roles. These roles include the following:

- Internet executive steering committee
- Web master, project managers
- Web architect
- Content masters
- Content managers
- Graphics designer
- DBA
- IT operations administrators

The roles will be covered in detail in the following subsections. Refer to Figure 3-1 for a visual representation of your Web project team. If the team is too small to assign an individual to each of the positions, it is important to remember that each role should have at least one person assigned to it through your planning, development, and implementation processes. One person can wear many hats, but all hats should have an owner.

Internet Executive Steering Committee

The Internet executive steering committee represents the senior management that provides the direction and funding of Internet development projects. This group is composed primarily of senior executives from the business side. IT should have one representative, preferably the CIO or a designated direct report. This group should listen to and understand the business case for the proposed project. Once a project is approved, this group reviews and approves project plans and other deliverables. Changes in the direction and scope of projects must be justified to this group and approved before proceeding. Status reports showing performance against budget and schedule should be provided to this group.

Web Master or Commerce Manager

A number of titles exist for this position, but the mission of the person in this position is to manage your company's Internet program. This person must understand what Internet technology can accomplish for your group and its customers. This person must have both business and technology knowledge and must communicate effectively between the business users, the IT operations group, and the executive

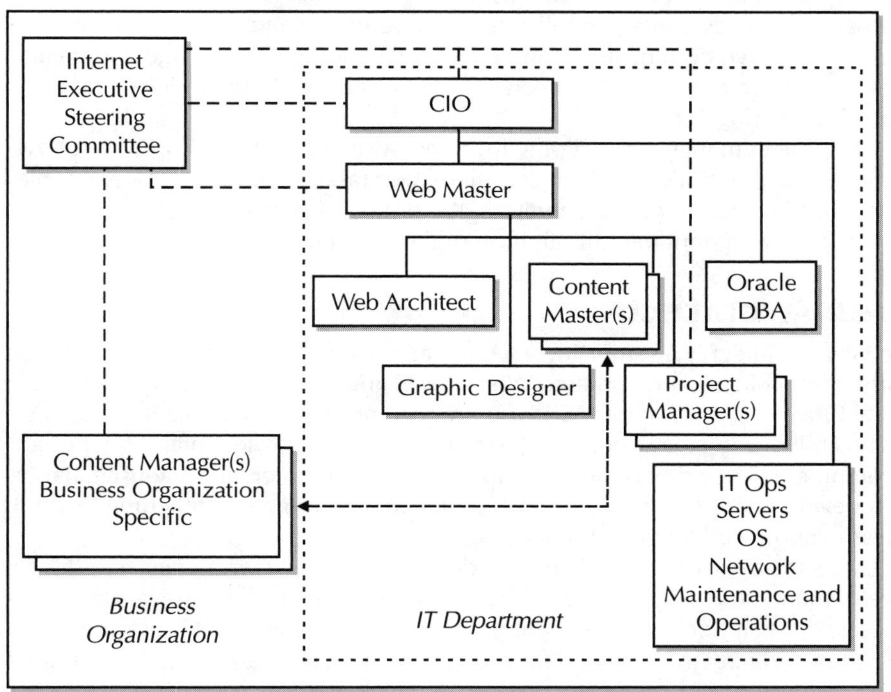

FIGURE 3-1. *Explanation of key positions*

steering committee. It is important that the Web master must have a knowledge of the industry, your business, and Internet technology. This individual should have demonstrated IT project management success within your company. The Web master should be actively involved in presenting proposed projects to the steering committee and may need to serve as project manager for the first Web project approved by the steering committee. This person's responsibility is to "know all and see all" for Web projects within your company. The Web master fills the role of corporate Web visionary.

Project Manager

A project manager must head up each project and be accountable for developing the project work plan, reporting progress towards objectives, keeping track of issues impeding progress, and driving the resolution of issues.

Similar to the Web master, the project manager needs to understand what Internet technology can accomplish for your company and your customers. This person must have both business and Internet technology knowledge and be able to communicate effectively between the business users, IT operations, and the executive steering committee.

The project manager may come from the business or from IT, but must have the talent to motivate both groups to complete their tasks. Continuity of key people is critical to IT project success. Therefore, the project manager must be committed to the project throughout the full duration of the project.

Web Architect

The Web architect is a senior-level technical person who has a proven track record implementing Internet commerce Web sites, using the technology you have chosen (likely Oracle RDBMS and OAS if you are reading this book). This individual's main responsibility is to assist your development group with project planning, design, and development. The primary qualification for this position entails extensive hands-on Web development experience, and experience mentoring and teaching technology to less experienced team members.

Large-scale, e-commerce Web site development is a component-based development effort. Many tools are available to accomplish the development process; different tools address different needs. A Web architect must understand the scope and effectiveness of different tools for different tasks. The Web architect must also understand how all the pieces fit together.

The multitude of technical options sometimes frustrates new Web developers. They often want to use a single integrated Web development product from a single vendor to simplify the development process. Some products claim to be integrated development environments, but in most cases they do a little bit of everything but do not perform any one thing exceptionally well.

Building a new corporate Web site is identical to building a new corporate headquarters. Most companies would not think of putting up a prefabricated building as a corporate headquarters. Using an off-the-shelf or canned Web development product is like putting up a prefabricated building. You get the basics, but there is nothing special about it, employees are not proud of it, and it does not impress customers or stockholders. A custom Web site looks good, performs well, and can be personalized by each visitor. The visitors who come to it are impressed and enjoy visiting the site.

The Web architect must have experience installing, programming, and teaching others how to develop with a variety of Internet development tools such as HTML editors, Web Servers, Web Listeners, JavaScript, Perl, and Oracle's PL/SQL language.

The Web architect must be able to evaluate new tools for development and testing, and help the team select from alternative development tools and approaches for particular tasks. The Web architect must not only understand how to develop using different methods, but must understand the intricate relationships between different software products. The Web architect must also understand how to add new functionality to the Web site without having to start from scratch or redo past work.

Content Master

Content masters are Web developers who understand Web development tools, your company's business processes, and the needs of particular Internet audiences. The qualifications of this role should include technical experience with Web development tools such as HTML editors, JavaScript, PL/SQL, and Perl. Experience developing user documentation or designing instructional materials is also beneficial for the role of content master. Content masters are just that—masters of the content. Ideally, they understand your business and the content of the information therein. By using this information, content masters master the content into your site.

Content Manager

Content managers are the business leaders in particular business processes. They understand current processes in detail and can provide the direction and assistance to users on proper procedures. Content managers do not have to be technical, but they need to be able to document business processes and needed improvements. Experience testing application software, developing user documentation, or training users in particular business areas is beneficial. Content managers will work with content masters to define information requirements and storyboards for Web page processing.

Graphic Designer

Graphic designers are artists who have experience developing attractive artwork for advertising campaigns, instructional materials, and/or Internet Web sites. Ideally, they have experience with a variety of graphic design tools. Their job is to make the Web site appealing and to establish graphics standards to ensure a consistent appearance and functionality throughout the Web site. It is *very* important that this person be experienced in graphic design. A "tinkerer" will not produce the same professional-looking images and layouts that a person who is trained and experienced in this field will. In the end, an experienced graphic designer will need to clean up the tinkerer's site. It is easier and more cost effective to have this input at the beginning of the process and avoid the rework. This is an effort that can be easily outsourced, too.

Graphic designers will work with content masters and content managers to implement natural, intuitive, fast, and effective Web applications for users to accomplish their intended business purposes.

Oracle Database Administrator

Oracle database administrators (DBAs) are experienced with designing, implementing, and managing Oracle databases. During the development of the Web site, the Oracle DBA designs and implements the database that the content masters will use to implement the Web application. They must understand application and database security to work with the Web architect and IT operations on application, database, system, and network security design. The DBAs will tune the application and database to accommodate the expected Web site usage. They will assist the project manager and IT operations to determine the correct server configuration required for development and production. After the system goes into production, the DBA will proactively monitor the database to ensure the performance and reliability are maintained at high levels. Again, this is not a job for a "tinkerer;" this is a serious effort that requires an experienced person. If you do not have an experienced Oracle DBA for your project, you can also outsource this effort. For example, TUSC offers a remote DBA service (rdba.tusc.com).

IT Operations Administrator

IT operations administrators manage systems and network performance to ensure users benefit from good response time. They manage the infrastructure upgrades to minimize and eliminate business disruption. The administrators establish standards for hardware and software, and establish procedures for security and disaster recovery. They also maintain contracts for hardware and software maintenance and Internet service, and maintain relations with vendors.

Making the Most of the Five C's

The following five attributes are found on all good Web sites. Jim Sterns, who has published several books on marketing on the Internet, named these attributes the Five C's: content, context, cool, contact, and control. Ignoring any of these attributes during planning or design will make your site incomplete and unprofessional. As you continue to develop sites, you may wish to add to the list of C's on your own. For example, I have my own C—"Come Back"—meaning that I want to build a site that will be addictive and that users will come back to time and time again. The following subsections provide further explanations of Jim's Five C's.

Content

Make sure you have content that will generate interest. Putting a site together just so you have a presence on the Web without adding valuable content will hurt your company more than it will help. Ensure that the information you supply on the Internet is timely, accurate, and meaningful. If the content on your site is out of date, your intended audience will not visit again. If your content is not accurate, you cost yourself and your company credibility and respect. Even though quantity should not be a measure of "good" content, a lack of content will not be good. Quality of the content is extremely important, but so is the quantity—everything must be available on your site. Lastly, if the content on your site is not meaningful to your intended audience, your development effort will be a waste of time.

Context

The information included in your site should be relevant to your users and to the specific area of your application. Related information should always be grouped together in their respective areas of the application. Multiple paths will make it easier for your users to find what they are looking for and will help your application flow more cleanly.

The user must be able to navigate forward and backward through your site easily. Links enable the user to access other areas of your application quickly and should be easily found on every page. If a user gets stuck in an area of your application or is confused as to how to navigate through the site, they will not come back.

It's important to have a site map, site search capability, and a "What's New" page within your site. For example, for one customer's What's New page, a cookie was stored with the user's date of last review of the page. Every time they visited the What's New page, we collected the value of this cookie and provided them with a custom page showing them the pages that were new since their last visit.

Cool

Your site should be appealing and use fonts, colors, and/or add-ins that make it unique from other sites. If your site contains a more attractive appearance and superior features than another site similar to yours, users will return to your site.

Contact

Your site should let a user know how they can contact a real person at your company. An email contact must be easily found. A phone number for someone who can help the user is a requirement if your business relies on your site for business contacts or e-commerce. Many times people come to your Web site to find your 800 number. Make sure these contact points (for example, email, phone, and fax) are easily found from any page within your application. You may wish to provide specific contact names on your site, but it is more common to provide contact groups—for example, sales, careers, and accounts payable.

Control

The users must feel they have control of their experience. This can be accomplished with a number of different methods. For example, for an aviation company we allowed the users to tell us about their favorite plane, what kind of pilot they were, and their favorite airline company. Using this information, we provided a custom background image (with their favorite plane) and other information specific to their interests. Yahoo figured out the concept of control long ago with my.yahoo.com, which enables the users to enter stock information, the news of interest, and much more information about who they are. Amazon keeps track of the books their customers buy and each time a customer visits Amazon's site, that person is told about books that might interest her based on her historical purchases. You want the users to feel they have control of your site to make it appearance and functionality according to the user's desire.

Planning Your Design

When it comes to designing your site, this is a serious effort. The more time you can afford to spend in this phase, the better your site will be. This is also an inexpensive part of your project overall. What costs $1 to think about during the design phase will cost you over $1,000 once the application is developed.

Audience Analysis

When a software development project begins, one of the first steps in the software life cycle is to gather requirements, hold joint application development (JAD) sessions with your IT staff and the business leaders, and obtain an understanding of the requirements. Once your project team understands the business requirements, you need to identify the audience of your site. A critical step in developing a Web application is to know your prospective audience. Who is the target group of users visiting, using, and browsing the Web application? To identify the target audience, use audience analysis.

For an audience analysis, you need to gather data that will identify the characteristics of the target audience, enabling you to break down your audience into different skill levels and groups. It's important to understand the amount of browser control your site will have. Will users be able to use *any* browser to visit your site? Will you limit the users to a specific browser and version?

When developing a Web application, you do not always have the luxury of holding interviews or JAD sessions with the individuals who will potentially be visiting your Web application or hyper-linking to your Web page. Consider the different types of users groups:

- **Frequent users** These users have been trained on your Web site or Web application, and routinely visit and use the site (intranet, and extranet users).
- **Novice users** These users possess little or no knowledge of the site and are interested in gaining an understanding of the site or performing a task with little frustration (Internet users).
- **International users** These users are from all over the world, speak many different languages, and might not understand technical terms to which we are accustomed (Internet users).

Sketching

The first sketch of your application should be kept informal. Begin by quantifying your ideas on paper and present your initial concept very loosely to your customer or user. Let the client or user imagine the power of the final design. The first sketch will get your customer excited about the project. When presenting your idea, use your instincts and always present the one idea that works. Your sketchbook will be able to show your client how you arrived at the right solution. When discussing your application with your clients, you might explain your general concept to them, but you may wish to drive the meeting by asking them their expectations of your site based on the information you provided. This often drives out expectations you may not think of. Be ready to write quickly!

Reality

Stay away from what's been done; it is better to create something no one has ever seen before than mimic an existing site. Repeating a site that someone else has already done will never get the desired response or traffic. To truly be successful, design your site with a unique approach to catapult your site to the coolest of its kind.

Oneness

Business sites need to project a professional image and enable visitors to find and obtain information on your company products quickly and easily. It is essential to give your site a uniform look throughout, making the user comfortable no matter what page they are viewing. Very few Web sites can manage to have the major sections of their Web site drastically different from one another. An exception may be game sites or companies promoting different products on the same site, with different themes or genres, that require each area to be its own "world." HTML style sheets can help provide the oneness in your appearance and functionality.

Navigation

As discussed in the "Layout and Navigation" section below, one of the primary focuses of conformity in your Web pages should be the navigation links to other areas in your site. Without conformity, visitors to your site will quickly become frustrated trying to find their way around. The visual appearance of your pages must display the same uniformity from section to section—not only in color and layout, but with the graphics and styles implemented within your main page and major subsections.

Color and Images

The main page of your site gives the visitor the baseline of what to expect from the rest of the site. Between the main page and the major subsections, your choice of graphics must be consistent. If you create a model with each major section in your site having a title bar and using four-color stock photography somewhere at the top of the page, stick with it. It would break the continuity of the site to have a different section using black and white line art icons at the top that looked nothing like the pictures in other sections.

Create a mockup of your new main page before beginning to code. Try out different layouts and colors ahead of time and find an arrangement that works for your business. When you settle on an appearance and behavior, define and document the major sections and subsections of the site and decide what kind and how many images or icons you may need for each section. Knowing all this before you code will help you keep your site pages consistent with one another and you will avoid having to go back and add links or images to completed pages.

Major Browsers

While your site is under development, make sure your site appears and functions identically under the two major Web browsers, Internet Explorer and Netscape Navigator. The subtle differences may include how both browsers render the same HTML code. The differences can be surprising and time-consuming to fix after your site has been completed. Test continuously with each new addition to the site.

Reuse

Do not start from scratch every time you begin a new project; try to leverage existing code from other successful projects. If you already have a successful design, do not reinvent the wheel. Change the layout or colors of the page, but use an existing page as a template to avoid developing the new page from scratch. If you are going to create a form on a preexisting Web site, a set of standards has already been established. The new form should match the appearance and behavior of the current Web site. Styles sheets and a code library of standard routines will help you with this effort.

Site Maintenance

When performing updates to the site, attempt to use the same employees who worked on the site originally. They will be more familiar with work completed in the past and less likely to break the chosen style of your site. They will also have access to the original images and materials of your site, creating faster turnaround times and greater consistency throughout your site.

Color

Color may be the single most important aspect of your Web page design, yet it is routinely neglected or abused. Many Web designers fail to take advantage of the potential a properly implemented color scheme can bring and others abuse it by overzealous use. A well-thought-out color scheme can tie together the graphics, ideas, and, most importantly, the information included in your Web site. Color can lead the users through your site's content, direct their attention to key items, and help associate products or information with your company or service by using an identifiable "look and feel."

Selecting a Color Scheme

Be careful when choosing the primary colors for your Web site. Color sets a mood and tells a lot about the Web site before a single word is read. Your corporate image should play a key role in the use of color. Think about the content that will go into the pages, the subject matter, and the target audience.

Your existing company logo and printed materials are the first places to look for guidance in selecting a color scheme for your Web site. If your business already has an established presence in the marketplace, it is essential to also project that image onto the Web. Your familiar business colors will tell site visitors immediately they have come to the right place. Colors can be taken from your company's logo, and when matched with other complementary shades will create a page that highlights the logo and constantly maintains an identity with your company.

The image your business has (or desires) in the marketplace also plays an important role in your color palette. A muted or subtle color scheme of light colors and pastels imparts a corporate feel on visitors and is suitable for most business sites. If your business image is designed to be up-front and exciting, a set of high-contrast or flashy colors may be more appropriate. The services of a graphic designer may be valuable in determining a color scheme for your site.

Another good place to look when choosing a color scheme is among the products or services your business offers. A landscaping company, for example, may find it a good idea to use colors that represent the spring or summer seasons, using various shades of green. Used with some select images of trees and flowers, the color scheme will set the mood for what the site has to offer. Even your business name can lend itself to your color selection. If your company name is "Red Rover," one possible primary color for your site is obvious.

Color should also be selected with your target audience in mind. IBM's Web site has a clean, sleek appearance and a definite corporate feel. That same muted color scheme would not work effectively for a site dedicated to music or computer games, which demand more flash and eye-catching colors and images.

Make sure that the colors you choose complement each other. Lime green and bright purple conflict with each other and are hard on the eyes, not to mention unattractive. Two distinct variation of the same color—for example, a light blue and dark blue—complement each other. Neutral colors like grays, and basic black and white, will work with most other colors. Make sure the information you display on your Web pages does not get lost in the color scheme. Create a quick test page and incorporate text and images to see how they will be displayed within a browser. Unless you can dictate the resolution and color depth for each user, make sure to test your color choices at 256 colors as well as millions of color. Numerous color guides are available on the Web.

Judicious Use of Color

One of the first mistakes beginning Web designers make is the overuse of color. How many Web sites have you been to where text on the page was displayed in five different colors, in five different fonts and sizes with all kinds of flashing graphics? Many beginning Web designers get caught in this trap because they desire to have their page noticed, or make it stand out. It is barely tolerable for a personal home page, but it is really unacceptable for a business site.

Color should be used to make sure sections or areas of your Web site stand out. It should definitely be used to draw attention to key areas of the page, or to direct the user's eye. If the page contains too many colors, the viewer cannot be sure what is new or important on the page, and may miss critical information. For example, look at the following text in Figure 3-2. Even though you cannot see the colors in this book, you can see by the shades of gray that all those colors do not mean too much to the user.

In Figure 3-2, the box on the left uses five different colors and your eyes alone cannot give you any hint as to where to look first. The box on the right has only one of the items highlighted with color and your eye jumps immediately to the last line. When combined with a bold and italic font, it becomes an unmistakable item for the eye, even in black and white; it is clearly different from everything else around

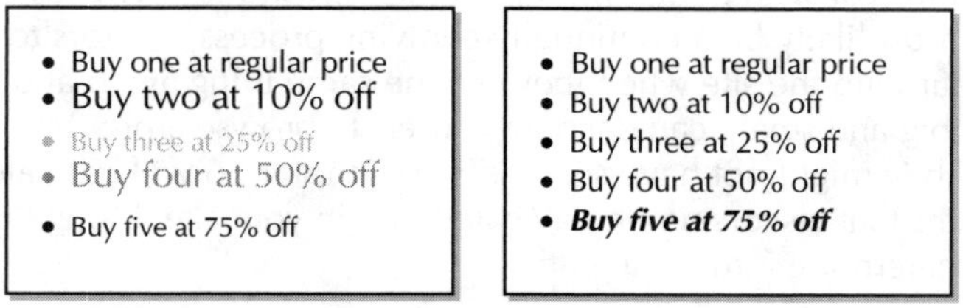

- Buy one at regular price
- Buy two at 10% off
- Buy three at 25% off
- Buy four at 50% off
- Buy five at 75% off

- Buy one at regular price
- Buy two at 10% off
- Buy three at 25% off
- Buy four at 50% off
- ***Buy five at 75% off***

FIGURE 3-2. *Too many colors proves meaningless*

it, and something to look at right away. The bullet points will help all the items stand out from other material on the Web page, and the single colored line helps the one item stand out from the other four.

The color of the font for your pages should always be black or white, depending on the background color of the page. The main body of text on your pages should be simple and readable; use color only for hyperlinks and key items. A large amount of colored text against a colored background can be difficult to read, and hyperlinks can get lost.

On the other hand, Web pages completely devoid of color should be avoided. A page that contains a press release may be fine in a single color, because it is designed to be read in its entirety. In contrast, on a page displaying quarterly profit figures, highlighting specific sections and key sums in color makes them easy to find. Used properly, color is a powerful tool to draw attention to important information on your Web pages.

Color Tips

The following are some quick tips about the use of color in your site:

- Find a selection of colors that work together and stick with them—do not overuse color.
- The main text of the body of a page is best as a simple color, such as black or white.
- Use color to draw attention to key items.

Layout and Navigation

The layout of a Web site affects how easy (or difficult) it will be for users to navigate through its contents. A well-laid-out site enables users to quickly find the information they are searching for with a minimum amount of frustration. The layout of your Web site will most likely be a continually evolving process. Visitors to Web sites become familiar with the site when they see the same thing again and again, so changes, both big and small, can encourage users to browse around for new material or in sections they might not have seen before. Chapter 26 will educate you on how to view the paths that visitors use to navigate through your site. Using this information will help you determine future site paths.

Frames or No Frames?

The use of frames in Web pages has both advantages and disadvantages, and you should decide whether you want to use them in your Web site before writing the code.

One main benefit to using frames is to display information that does not change from page to page, thus cutting down on redundant text and graphics loading as a user navigates through your site. For example, a frame can be loaded once with navigation buttons providing the user with a fixed, unchanging space to look at when navigating through your site. Frames are also good for placing related information side by side and enabling the user to scroll through the information independently.

A downside is how frames affect the appearance of your Web page. If the viewable area of the Web browser is too small to fit the contents of the frame, a scroll bar will appear in the frame and may cause an unattractive breakup of the page's graphics or layout. If you disable the scroll bar in your HTML code, users will be unable to access the hidden buttons and links without resizing their browser window. Frames take extra coding consideration, and it is possible (however remote these days) that the user's Web browser does not support the use of frames.

Make sure you consider all your business requirements, including future changes or expansion, before committing to use frames. A considerable amount of effort must be afforded to incorporate or delete frames after your site is completed.

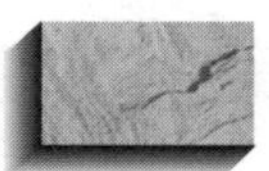

TIP
Decide whether your site needs frames before writing the code.

Location of Controls

Providing the user with the controls to navigate your Web site is essential to a positive experience when viewing your site. Navigation controls must be easy to locate and understand, as well as provide the user with the necessities to move through your site freely. Controls should be as consistent as possible from page to page and have direct links to the main points of interest on your site.

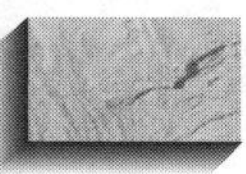

TIP
Provide links to the major areas of your site in the same, fixed location on all pages.

Most business-related Web sites have settled on placing primary navigation buttons or links across the left side of the Web page, at the top, or in some cases both. While you are not limited to these areas, they have become a de facto standard and most users will automatically look to these areas first for navigation choices.

Consistency from page to page will help keep site visitors from getting lost. Provide them with a common set of navigation features in a fixed location. Enable the user to jump to the major sections of your Web site from every page.

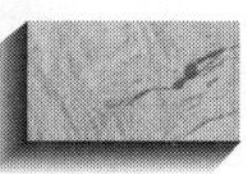

TIP
Keep navigation and header information as small as possible.

While navigation controls should be clear and easy to find, they should be unobtrusive and give as much space as possible to the main content and focus of the page. Keep the navigation controls as narrow as possible without making them unusable. A title bar of some sort is common practice on business Web sites to give the viewers an idea of their current location within your site. This header may also have other navigation controls, and should take up minimal space without making those controls unusable.

TIP
Avoid clutter that can make navigating a page difficult.

Links from the Home Page

You should provide links to all the major areas of the Web site from your main page. Users will expect to see a link to the major areas, such as Products or Services, to quickly find information on what your company has to offer. You may also wish to have links on your main page to other "hot" areas of your site, and areas that contain frequently requested information. By monitoring the user click paths, as discussed in Chapter 26, you can add items accordingly. The main page is a good place to advertise the latest news about your company's offerings and provide a direct link to new or updated information or products. Adobe's Web site (www.adobe.com) is a good example of a clean, attractive, functional home page.

Avoid a lot of clutter on your main page. Make sure the major links stand out against the other contents on the page so visitors can find them easily. Major links should be one of the most visible elements of your site.

Links from Subsections

Major subsections of your Web site should be broken down if they contain information about many different things. For example, let us assume that your business sells 12 different types of software. You could start with a Products subsection that gives a brief overview of each piece of software and provides a link to a new HTML page devoted exclusively to one particular software product. You could choose to break your 12 software products into three categories, such as Marketing and Sales, Personnel, and Accounting. Each section should then have a link back to the preceding areas.

Items No Page Should Be Without

Regardless of the pages' location within your site's hierarchy, you should provide universal features. A prominent link on each page back to the main page is absolutely essential. Your site's main page is the hub and should always be accessible from every page in your site. It is a good idea to have contact information at the bottom of each page. The business name, address, telephone number, and a way to contact the site's Web administrator are common. You may also wish to provide text links to major areas of your Web site at the bottom of each page. Several text-only Web browsers are available that have a loyal following for their speed and small size, and without text links users of these browsers will not be able to navigate your site. Remember that users may print any pages of your site and hand those pages over to someone else.

Accessibility

When designing your Web site, consider the entire audience of potential viewers. With few concessions, you can make your site accessible to the greatest number of people. When you make your Web site more accessible, you open it up to people who might not otherwise have been able to access your information or products. You are also contributing to making the World Wide Web a place where anyone can access the information they need, regardless of physical or technological challenge or handicap.

Basic Colors

Your first consideration should be choosing an appropriate background color or image. If you use a solid color for the background, make sure it is very neutral or enables text to be easily read. A good example would be a simple white or gray background with black text.

Similarly, if you use an image as your background, make sure it does not interfere with the readability of the text on the page. The image should blend into the background and use similar colors, so it will not to be distracting to the eye.

Do not forget about the "link" and "visited link" colors in your HTML code. The default colors of the browser may not work well with your background color or image. Do not leave it to chance—specify color values that look best with your page.

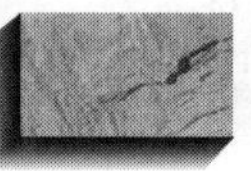

TIP
Make sure your color scheme enables text to be read easily.

Font Choices

One of the most important choices you can make from an accessibility standpoint for your HTML document is the font. The font face, size, and color are key components in making your document readable to all visitors of your Web site.

When choosing a font face, make sure it displays cleanly on the screen. Select a TrueType font for best results, and make sure the font you select is on the viewer's system. This will generally limit your choices to Arial and Times New Roman. Fortunately, when using the <FONT> tag, you can specify alternate fonts to use if your first choice is not available on the user's system, as the following syntax illustrates. In this example, the page will display using the Tahoma font, and if that font is not available, in Arial, and lastly in Helvetica:

```
<FONT FACE="Tahoma, Arial, Helvetica">
```

Style sheets also support embedding font faces within a document, so specific fonts can be used on a Web site even if the user does not have the fonts locally available within their browser. However, the support of style sheets is implemented differently in various browsers, so test this carefully.

If you use the <FONT> tag, remember to use the closing </FONT> tag. The <FONT> tag overrides the viewer's default font for browsing. When you close the tag, the browser returns to using the default font. The viewer may have difficulty reading certain faces or font sizes, so take this into account when coding the <FONT> tag.

Using the size parameter with the <FONT> tag may render the font in drastically different sizes depending on the browser and platform the viewer of your page is using. For the most consistent display, but still maintaining a degree of artistic license, you can use the <FONT> tag in conjunction with the heading (for example, <H4>) tags.

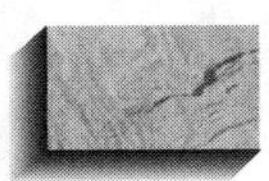

TIP
Choose larger, more readable fonts for your pages.

The main body of your document should use a font size easily read by all viewers of your site. Avoid using font sizes that are too small and difficult to read. Small fonts mixed with a lot of text or images may lose the viewer's attention, therefore, consider making key points of text in **bold** face to stand out.

Font color should be used judiciously. A Web page with many different colors is very distracting to the eye and makes it difficult to determine highlights or important points of your document. Choose a set of complementary colors and use them as part of your Web site theme. Make sure the font can be easily read on the page's background color.

TIP
Use <Hx> tags for more consistent font sizes in visitors' browsers.

Images

Images are good tools to make a point or grab the user's attention. Given a bit of thought, you can make sure everyone benefits from them.

Make sure all your images use the ALT attribute of the <IMAGE> tag. The ALT parameter enables you to specify text that appears in the area of the image. Most browsers will display this text on the screen before the images are rendered in the browser window, and also in the "ToolTip" that appears when the viewer moves the mouse pointer over the image. These are all helpful to readers of your document. If the viewer has images shut off, or is using a browser that does not display images, he or she can still get information on the image that is supposed to be there. For those who cannot see the page, the browser will "read" the ALT text to help the user understand the image.

The image itself should be designed to convey a clear message. Avoid "loud" images or distracting images with unclear meaning. Be cautious using animated GIF images with whiz-bang effects and little meaningful content to the viewer.

TIP
Use the ALT attribute with images.

Links

Links should be clear and to the point. Make sure the LINK and VLINK attributes in the <BODY> tag use colors that clearly differentiate a link from ordinary text. Avoid using underlined text in HTML documents as it can easily be confused with a link.

If you use an image as a link, be sure to provide text links on the page. Many Web designers make it a common practice to put a set of text links at the bottom of each page for simple navigation.

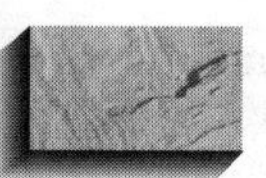

TIP
Specify appropriate colors for your <A>nchor tags.

Simplicity

Basically, design your site so a small child could use it. Provide a simple solution that will work well for everybody, because we are all big kids. Do not overanalyze your design—it will complicate and lengthen your design process and confuse your potential users. Try solving interface problems with words before applying metaphors. Give the user hints to accomplish the tasks instead of trying to create a complicated design that will walk the user through a task. Think of your site as an automated phone attendant. There should not be more than about five menu options on any page, and there should be no more than three or four levels to drill through. That is a difficult task, isn't it?

Information Rationing

Edit information into concise pieces of content, and if there is further information, use the word "more" as a link to retrieve it. Dumping all of your information onto one page is overwhelming to a user—most will not want to scroll more than a screen or two to complete a page. Ration the information to the user by giving the information in smaller, easily digestible pieces. This will also help to keep your download times shorter, and keep the user interested. Paging logic is a great solution for queries that return large amounts of data. For example, if a user's query returns 500 rows, it is easier for the user to review the information and get a faster download if you present the data to the user 20 rows at a time.

Avoiding Design Pitfalls

Designing a Web site or interface for a Web-served application can be an exciting experience. You have the opportunity to create the window that visitors or users look through and see the site. However, design pitfalls exist, and care should be taken when addressing such issues concerning clip art, animation, and unsupported code or file formats.

Clip Art

Clip art is a great tool for presentations or reports that need a little spice. However, it is rare that a piece of clip art will work well on a professional Web site.

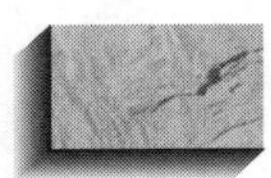

TIP
Be careful using clip art; most are not good for business Web sites.

Your Web graphics need to remain consistent with the theme of your site and a particular area should be reserved for the location of images to preserve consistency. Clip art libraries vary wildly, and generally contain a limited patchwork of stylized icons or graphics. It becomes difficult to find all the images in a particular style you will need for the various sections of your Web site, especially when making additions or modifications to the site in the future. The consistency and appearance of the site will suffer if the clip art collection does not have an image you need for a section in the same style as you have previously used.

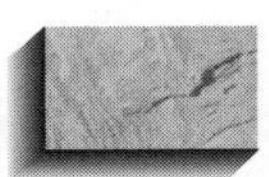

TIP
Be careful of legalities regarding using purchased clip art on your commercial Web site.

If you decide to use clip art, look for simple, more stylized, one-color images. Multicolored clip art images rarely look realistic and tend to make a site look amateurish because they cannot compete with a real photograph for flair or impact on a viewer. If you choose to include clip art on your site, try to buy a collection of clip art that contains images and icons in a single style. Plenty of clip art collections are available that contain 100,000+ images, but many are unacceptable for business and some are downright unattractive. You may pay the same price or more for a smaller set of custom style images, but you will be able to choose a collection that works for your site. The set will have more images and icons in your chosen style than you would get in a large, generic clip art collection. Also, be aware of any legalities concerning the use of clip art collections before you add images to your site. Many collections available for purchase do not provide for commercial use of the images.

An exception to clip art is stock photography. Many large clip art collections come with an assortment of stock, digital photographs on CD-ROM. With a photo-editing program, such as Adobe Photoshop, stock images can be cropped, faded, or altered in a variety of ways to work within your Web site. Most clip art cannot compete with well-chosen photographs that match the subject matter of your Web page. Few stock images will be usable directly from the CD, but with minimal effort they can be modified for your site and create far more impact and impression on the visitors.

TIP
Stock photography has good impact; use it!

Animations

Animated GIF images and newer animated formats, such as Macromedia's Flash, offer eye-catching ways to attract a viewer's attention. This razzle-dazzle effect can also ruin an otherwise good Web site when it is overused.

In real life, most of the objects surrounding you are motionless, and when something breaks that state your eyes tend to look toward what moved. The same logic applies to a Web page. Web pages are generally static information resources consisting of text and pictures. So when something is moving on the site, the first place the eye will look is at the movement.

Used in moderation, animations can be a perfect way to attract a viewer's attention toward information you would like them to know about. Using too much animation can be confusing to a user—identical to the overuse of colors and fonts. Moreover, animations can make a page appear amateurish when used without regard to page consistency and content. Lastly, they tend to be larger and more resource-intensive. Visitors with slow connections to the Internet will become frustrated with lengthy page loads that include many animations that give little substance to the page.

If you use animations on your page, try to limit them to one or two at the very most, and avoid putting them near each other. Treat them as specialty items, used to grab the viewer's attention for a specific purpose.

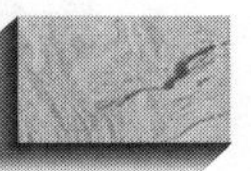

TIP
Limit your use of animated images.

Unsupported Code or File Formats

If you are creating a Web page, it is because you want someone to see the content of the page. Unless you are creating a highly customized Web application with special requirements, it is paramount that the information, pictures, and downloadable materials you use be viewable and usable by the widest audience possible.

When coding your HTML, stick to commands supported by the two major browsers, Internet Explorer and Netscape Navigator. Each browser has some custom tags the other does not support, so expect that roughly half of the viewers will not see the custom settings. New specifications like cascading style sheets (CCS) give you a newfound sense of control over your pages, but are not fully (or consistently) supported by both major browsers, and are certainly not supported in older versions of the browsers. A standard rules is to test code in both major browsers, and any others you want to fully support. This way, you will catch inconsistencies before you get too far. WebTrends.com and other sites will automatically help you validate the compatibility of your site with older browsers.

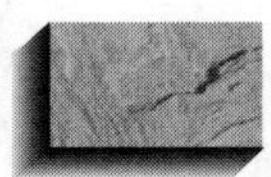

TIP
Stick with Web standard image and compression formats.

The two generally accepted image formats for viewing on the Web are GIF and JPEG. Several newer formats are available—most notably the PNG file format—but you must be careful when using a more exotic image type. While almost all Web browsers can handle GIF and JPEG images properly, only the newest can display a PNG image. While Microsoft's BMP file format is a standard on the Windows operating system, remember the large number of Macintosh and UNIX users of the Web. Unless you have a specific need, it is best to stick with GIF or JPEG.

Another consideration is files you provide for download, because your choices are somewhat limited. It is commonplace to compress downloadable files so they take the least amount of time to transfer to the user's computer, but many compression formats are not supported across platforms. Again, the best advice is to know your target audience. If you are providing UNIX programs for download, it would be reasonable to assume that Windows users will not be accessing the files; therefore, it is safe to use a UNIX file compression format. If you are providing Word documents, your audience is most likely Windows or Mac users, and you should compress using a format available to both platforms.

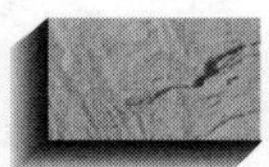

TIP
Know your target audience.

Flowing with Design

Using a standard flow of steps in designing your site can save you time in development. It can also result in a site that is more sound in terms of standards and technical architecture. If you step through your design, common functions will become apparent. Using a standard flow of steps will also give your team a common way to code your site, making later enhancements easier and cleaner. The following subsections make up a standard set of steps in a design flow.

Draw Storyboards

Storyboards should be completed without technical considerations. Your team should draw out how they envision the appearance of your Web application by drawing out how the application will flow from screen to screen, starting at your first screen. In addition, your team should consider brainstorming to determine how each page should look. This can be easily accomplished on large pieces of paper. Place these pages on a wall in the order they will appear in the application; this way, the order and grouping can be easily changed as the group brainstorms on the layout of the application. Try to put all your ideas on paper and have a general layout of your application before moving on to the next step.

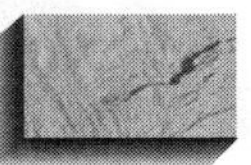

TIP
Use the Post-it large notepads when developing your storyboard.

Decide on Static, Dynamic, Semidynamic, or Semistatic

In this step, each screen or page on your storyboard should be considered to determine if the page will be a static, dynamic, semidynamic, or semistatic page. Things to consider include the fact that static pages download faster than dynamic pages and dynamic pages require processing power. Semidynamic pages are those that are partially dynamic. Semistatic pages are static pages that are dynamically generated periodically (on a frequency). Make sure you have considered each page so you get the fastest download times possible for every page. The following is a list of several options for your pages and an explanation of each:

- **Static** The static page will look the same every time it is retrieved. Text for this page is stored in an HTML file and will be exactly the same on each download. Download times for this type of page will be faster than dynamic pages because there is no processing time involved for such tools as an Oracle database or OAS to generate the content of your page. An example of this type of page could be a help page describing how to use a form within your application.
- **Dynamic** A dynamic page will not exist until it is called by the browser. Tools (a cartridge or CGI) on the server will generate all content when the page is requested. Processing times for this type of page are longer because the server must generate the content before it can be downloaded to the user's browser. However, these pages are a great asset to a Web site. With dynamic pages, you can make the user feel like the site was designed just for them by greeting them after they have registered with your site. They also enable you to supply your users with real-time, dynamic data. This type of page may look different every time your user visits, giving your users reason to return again. An example is a monitoring page for tracking who is logged in to your database at any moment. This information can change every second, driving the need for a dynamic page.
- **Semidynamic** A page that uses the semidynamic (only partially dynamic) approach may be used if small pieces of your page are dynamic, but you would like to keep most of the performance advantages of a static page.

A good example is a startup page that displays the same information for every user, but may call a CGI function to display a counter. The counter will change on every hit and would be generated dynamically.

- **Semistatic** A semistatic page is one that is generated from dynamic data but stored as a static file. Semistatic pages are static pages that are dynamically generated periodically. The advantage of a semistatic page is that when users access them, they are static and so require no processing power to generate. The disadvantage is that they are generated on a set frequency, so the information has a potential of being dated. However, if the frequency is event-based (when the data changes), this may not be an issue. If the data changes very frequently, semistatic pages do not make sense. An example where this is used is for a report to display the previous day's manufacturing production. The report would not change during that day, so it would not need to be generated for each download, but would be regenerated every night for the previous day. See the Web Publishing Assistant section in Chapter 6 for an automated solution to generating the semistatic pages.

Review Dynamic Pages in Terms of Code

During this step, decide what type of code (such as language) will be used to develop each of your dynamic pages. Assigning work to the developers in your group will be easier if you know what tools are involved with each page. Determine the level of difficulty in developing each page by rating the pages from easy to moderate to complex (E, EM, M, MC, or C). Knowing what level of developer is needed for each page will prevent you from overwhelming a junior developer or boring your senior level developers. Rating the difficulty of pages will help you estimate the time to complete each project phase. Performing this exercise will also help you to modularize your code.

Use Designer or Develop the Code by Hand?

Chapter 16 discusses using Designer to develop OAS code. In fact, it attempts to answer the question proposed here by educating you on Designer's capabilities for developing OAS code. If you're considering using Designer as a part of your tool set, be sure to read Chapter 16. A team that understands Designer inside and out wrote Chapter 16, while this section was written by a team of developers who understand and have successfully used Designer as described below.

An application development team has different options to consider when starting a project. Should a tool be used to create the application or should code be written by hand? Oracle Designer has the tools a development team needs to create an application. The other option is designing an entire application by hand. Generating code by hand is time consuming, but once done you can be sure of the substance of the code and what it accomplishes. Time, budget, and business goals must be taken into consideration before deciding which path to take. The best idea may be to consider incorporating both options.

Oracle Designer makes it easier to implement complete applications from start to finish. The Designer package includes the tools a project team needs to plan and create an application. Designer and the included Developer tool can be used to generate all your code without ever writing a line of custom code. This is a great option for the project team light on budget and time. The tools in Designer enable you to develop the business plan and approach, while the Developer tool creates the DDL statements. This is a viable tool for creating Web-based applications. Designer enables project teams to automate the task of creating an application. The Designer tools create the code needed to accomplish your desired end results by enabling the developer to tailor the application to follow the business needs from the start. It also adds code into the application to handle most any need.

Designer works well for application creation unless you consider the amount of unneeded code it creates in your application. The tool automatically adds in lines of code to handle different issues like security, whether it is a necessity or not. Designer enables users to build an entire application without ever having to manually put in lines of code to accomplish a task. Designer makes this possible by letting the developer create numerous templates to follow for different desired outcomes. However, developers who handwrite code may not be very excited to create the templates when it is easier for them to write the code. Creating your own code for simple to complex queries will drastically reduce the number of lines needed to accomplish tasks and remove the unneeded code included by Designer.

Another option is to use Designer to organize and create the basic functionality. In many cases, you can create approximately 80 percent of the code and basic structure using Designer. This leaves you with only 20 percent of the code sections to write by hand. This gives the developers the freedom to re-create sections of code to increase performance and give the option to add customized sections. The only drawback to this method is if global changes are needed late in the development stage. The risk of losing custom code and re-creating needed code that has been deleted is possible when the application is regenerated. Creating all the necessary items, such as your list of values, and using them with your custom setting will help reduce the time creating code. Creating the basic template to follow and values needed for the application using Designer, then sitting down and working through the code needed, will take less time than creating the application by hand. Using Designer to create templates and application layout, then incorporating handwritten code, can also cut the development time considerably. Be careful with custom code, as it may be changed when the application is regenerated. Using Designer will also make it easy to give a project a base plan to follow, and doing some of the back-end coding by hand will help reduce the amount of unneeded code. Designer will help get things started and cut down on the time and money needed for developers to get a project underway. Using Designer to create the basis for the application will give a team more time to concentrate on form and content without worrying about following the business plan and losing site of the objectives.

To understand the vast power and usefulness of Designer, read the documentation and related information. If you are looking to roll out a finished application quickly without having developers spend hours handwriting code, using Designer may be your answer. If you have the time and resources, and a knowledgeable staff, it is beneficial to explore the option of using Designer for part of the application and handwriting the rest of the code. This option will help reduce the unneeded code, assist in the customization of your application, and improve runtime performance.

Toolkit – Reusable Code

It is important to write generic procedures to handle certain functions or sections of a page that will be used repeatedly. An example of this is a set of links that is displayed at the bottom of each page within your site.

Calling a function from your toolkit to display the links at the bottom of the page is easier for your developers than writing the code to include all the links in every page. If you need to change one of the links at the bottom of all of your pages, this approach would enable you to change the link in only one place instead of in every page.

The toolkit approach also makes it easier to implement coding and appearance standards. If each developer only needs to call a function to set up headers, footers, navigation bars, and so forth, then it will be easier to make each page in the application appear identical to the rest of the site. It is also easier to update your site if your standards change if you have a toolkit of reusable code.

Review from Database Standpoint

After defining your toolkit, you must review what information you will need to retrieve from the database. Your design team will need to gather all information from the storyboards and identify what information will be retrieved from the database. Information that is dynamically generated to build your site pages will query information from your database. In the database review, make sure to consider the use of user profiles and security information such as user login IDs, and lookup tables.

Design and Normalize Database

The last step before building your application is designing and building your database. This step is the same as building any other database-related application.

Once the data requirements are known, the database administrators will help to develop logical and physical data models, including the appropriate level of normalization for your system. Take your time during this phase—the database you design will be the database your application is built around.

Developing Coding Standards

Developing a set of coding standards before the development of your application begins is very important. These standards should be enforced for all developers working on your application. Coding standards make it easier for other developers to help with unfinished code, debug broken code, or add new functions to the existing code. Standard indentations and case standards for SQL statements and HTML should also be developed. It is my preference to write lowercase code—it makes it easier to read the code—and to use underscores to separate words in parameter names. For example, in_last_name. More specific areas that should be considered for standardization and suggestions for these standards include those shown in Table 3-1.

Get vs. Post

Another standard to consider for Internet development is if your application will use the GET or POST method when submitting information from an HTML form.

Object	Type	Standard
Parameter Names	IN (input) OUT (output) INOUT (input and output)	IN_<name> OUT_<name> IO_<name>
Variable Names	Local Global	V_<name> G_<name>
Bind Variables	Bind	B_<name>
Package/Procedure names	Package Procedure Function	PCK_<name> SP_<name> F_<name>
Indicator Variables	Indicator	I_<name>

TABLE 3-1. *Naming Standards*

The GET method passes the form information using a URL, identical to a URL you type into the browser's address line. In fact, the URL is displayed in the browser's Address window. This is a problem if passwords or other sensitive pieces of information are being passed to the called procedure. Because this information is passed on the command line and through an operating system environmental parameter, the GET method also has a limitation on the number of characters that are passed using the method. This is most commonly an issue for the HTTP Listeners because when you send a URL that contains more than 1,000 characters using the GET method, the HTTP Listener tends to crash / die. This unpredictability is a big drawback.

The POST method, on the other hand, does not display the URL that the form information is being passed to. Instead, the POST method uses standard input to pass its information through the HTTP Listener. The POST method is a more secure method to use with forms because potential sensitive information is not being displayed to the user. There is also no maximum character limitation when using the POST method. The POST method is the most flexible and secure option of these two, and is recommended as the standard. However, if a user needs to be able to bookmark a specific page, remember that the user will not be able to bookmark the contents of a page that uses the POST method, whereas the user can bookmark a page that used the GET method.

Using the PL/SQL Toolkit or Not

Another important standards decision is whether to use htp.print ('html commands') or the PL/SQL Toolkit (htp.html_command) to build your pages. You need to decide if your application is to be written such that you use the OAS PL/SQL Toolkit or if you will use the print command for everything. The htp.print ('html commands') method removes the need for developers to learn a whole new set of commands.

Several advantages become apparent when using the PL/SQL Toolkit. First, the code generated using this method is easier to read. By using the Toolkit, your code will appear less cluttered and is easier to read, which makes the code easier to debug. Second, using the Toolkit means that your code gets initially tested when you compile your procedure. The other method will not be tested until the procedure is executed and viewed in a browser. Using the Toolkit also makes it easier to debug using this method.

Lastly, Oracle's Toolkit is continuously upgraded, which means the PL/SQL Toolkit will always generate the latest standard of HTML, XML, or new standards as they are released. This ensures you do not have to revisit all your code every time a new standard language is released for the Internet.

Using the PL/SQL Toolkit is recommended because of the reasons previously stated, but in reality this is a philosophical decision that is up to you as lead developer.

Understanding How Internet Development Is Different

In the introduction of this chapter it was mentioned that Internet design is different than client/server design. This section addresses some of those differences.

Consider State

Having to consider state is a concept new to many developers who have used Oracle Forms development tools or other standard Forms development tools in a client/server environment. Applications built for the Web do not naturally maintain the state of records as the user works through forms in an application. Using OAS, each operation normally found in a form—such as selecting, updating, and inserting records—is treated as a separate and distinct process. For example, a user can select many records from the database but none are locked at the time of the select—just like they are not locked when using Oracle Forms. The difference between client/server and Web-based becomes apparent in the next step. If a user changes a record in an Oracle Form, the record is immediately locked for update; if a user changes a record in their browser, nothing happens. In a Web application, unless you write logic to handle locking, nothing is preventing another user in a different location from updating that same record. In fact, in your Web application, both users that changed the record would be allowed to save their changes. The last person to save their changes would be the "winner" because their changes would "stick." The first user that saved his or her changes would have no idea that the second user overwrote those changes. I call this the "superoptimistic" locking scheme. If you prefer to use a locking mechanism that is more foolproof than the superoptimistic locking scheme, OAS has provided several built-in methods that provide a workaround to the locking problem. Transaction Services enables you to provide a codeless solution to locking by seamlessly defining and managing transactions for you. OAS also provides an optimistic locking package (OWA_OPT_LOCK) to help manage transactions in a different way.

Transaction Services is functionality included by Oracle in the OAS architecture. This functionality enables you to define a set of functions or procedure calls that comprise a transaction. This process can be described by comparing it to Oracle Forms. In Forms, a user can update a field for a specific record on a form. Using Transaction Services, OAS manages the entire transaction—without any code from you. The record is now protected from another user updating or deleting this record until the updating user unlocks the record by saving or rolling back his or her changes.

The transaction must be set up for each set of operations or URLs that make up a transaction. This is accomplished in the OAS Administration utility. Upon creation, the administrator must define what the entry point or procedure call is for the transaction. Once this procedure is called referencing a specific database record, the record is locked, prohibiting changes from other users. The developer also defines what other procedures are involved in a transaction. The user likely calls each of these procedures by choosing other links while changing the record. Finally, an exit (commit) and a rollback URL are defined. Once either one of these links is called, the record is saved and unlocked or just unlocked.

You may be concerned that a user can leave their browser open from anywhere in the world, lock a record, and walk away from their computer for hours, locking out all other users from this record. This is more of a problem with the Internet architecture than the client/server architecture of Oracle Forms. Tracking down a user who is locking a record unwittingly over the Internet is tougher than tracking down a user that is connected to your company's private network. This is not an issue with Transaction Services since the administrator also defines the transaction timeout period for each transaction. Once this timeout period has been exceeded, the record is automatically unlocked, eliminating orphan locked records.

Another approach is using your own optimistic locking algorithm. This approach requires that each table contain the addition of an update date-time field. Each time a user selects a record, the update date is included in the SELECT statement. The user can make changes and perform a COMMIT. If the current update date in the database does not match the one sent back by the user during their update, the user is informed that someone made changes to their record before they were saved. The record is then requeried. The user must make their changes and COMMIT again. With this method, the record is never actually locked in the database, but is only checked before the update or delete is allowed to happen.

Using the PL/SQL Toolkit's built-in optimistic locking package (OWA_OPT_LOCK), you can perform optimistic locking without adding a column to every table. This package provides a number of methods to perform optimistic locking. The easiest method to implement uses a checksum. A checksum is a unique alphanumeric value calculated based on all columns from a specific record in a table. The checksum is created at the time the record is selected from the database. Prior to updating the record, the checksum is recalculated and compared to the original checksum. If the checksum is the same, the record has not been changed. If the checksum is different, the record has been changed since it was selected.

Both of these methods will keep one user from overwriting another user's changes without being aware that he or she is doing so. Times can occur when it is advantageous to use one method over another. For example, it is better to use Transaction Services on transactions performing a set or group of operations. If you are developing transactions that consist of one DML statement (INSERT, UPDATE, or DELETE), it is probably not worth the trouble of setting up the Transaction Services. If operations perform multiple INSERT, UPDATE, and DELETE operations in the same transaction, then Transaction Services greatly simplifies your development by grouping the transaction together. Operations can be saved or rolled back together, maintaining the integrity of the records during the operation. Transaction Services are the only method of keeping a user from deleting a record while another user is updating the record. It is the only method that actually locks the record in the database to protect against such conflicts. Transaction Services are a feature of the Enterprise Edition of OAS.

Client Functions Using JavaScript

JavaScript is a scripting language that is executed on the client instead of on the server. The JavaScript code is included in the download of the HTML and is executed as inline code. Refer to Chapter 12 for further information about JavaScript. It is recommended that you place the JavaScript code before any HTML on your page. This way, the inline JavaScript will execute when the page starts up. You can also put the JavaScript in a function and call it from any point on your page, or as part of an action or event that the user executes. For example, use JavaScript to make sure a field is entered before the record is sent to the server or to fill in a product description after a product number is entered.

JavaScript vs. Database Validation

Why would you go to the trouble of learning or including another tool in your technical architecture when you can validate field information and send back messages using your PL/SQL procedures? For example, let's say that your HTML form has five required fields and your user enters only two of the fields. If you use PL/SQL to test your inputs, your PL/SQL procedure would need to verify each field and send back a meaningful error message for each empty field. This information must all be compiled on the server into one message and sent back to the browser while the user waits for the validation; then, the message can be downloaded. This can quickly become cumbersome if the user is entering a lot of data on many screens. It can also be frustrating for the user.

JavaScript makes client-side validation user friendly. You can create JavaScript functions to ensure all fields are entered after the Submit button is selected. You can also validate that product codes, customer IDs, and so forth are valid when they are entered instead of after they are sent to the server. Using client-side JavaScript code enables you to build an application that gives your users all the benefits they learned to rely on in the client/server environment.

Controlling Access

At least three methods are available for controlling access to the database: using the OAS built-in security functions, using the Oracle database user tables, and building your own user profile table.

Oracle included its own user authentication scheme for OAS. Through the OAS architecture, you can restrict access to your entire application or you can restrict access to specific packages within your application. The users, groups, and packages granted access are maintained on the OAS administration pages. Standard login dialog boxes are displayed just as they are when you log in to the Administration utility. When the user logs in using this method, a cookie is sent to the user's PC that remains persistent for the duration of time that the user's browser is open. The passing of cookies and validation that the user is logged in are maintained automatically by OAS.

Oracle database authentication uses Oracle's database user tables to perform validation. This method is best used for restricting access to specific data tables. No screens or automatic session tracking are included within this method.

Like the Oracle database authentication method, the custom-developed user profile method will not automatically maintain session information. This means a method for tracking whether the user is logged on must be developed through the use of cookies or passing login information from screen to screen. The advantage of the custom user profile method is that other information can be maintained with the user login information. This information could include custom application information such as preferred screen colors, or the number of rows to be displayed in an HTML table at once. The custom authentication method enables the user to customize the application to set personal preferences.

The built-in OAS authentication methods are the quickest way to implement security for your application. This method does not require you to develop a login form or a method for handling cookies. While it is the recommended method for implementing quick security, it comes with a caveat: past versions of OAS contain bugs causing the Listeners to freeze when the built-in security was implemented. Oracle worked on these problems for later versions, but developers should be aware of possible problems when implementing this method.

The most flexible method of implementing security is to develop your own user profile table, login form, and session tracking methods. This enables you to give the user the capability to customize the application to their preferences. It also enables you to customize login forms and methods to suit your business requirements. However, this method will take more time to develop since every restricted screen in your application will need to include code for validating user login information by using 'send and get' cookie functions.

Chapter 15 contains more information about establishing your own security routines. Chapter 10 covers the OAS built-in security methods in more detail.

Dealing with Those Who Will Not Accept Cookies

If your users will not (or cannot) accept cookies and your application relies on cookies to track user activity, such as a shopping cart model for an online store, or if the site uses cookies to validate a user login, you could have a serious problem implementing your application. Options are very limited for tracking user activity on a site or tracking user login information on a site if the user refuses to accept cookies. If your cookie is not accepted and not found, by default a PL/SQL error will occur stating the cookie could not be found. Otherwise, every time the get cookie function is called, the next screen will not be displayed because of the error interruption. In this case, a page should be developed to indicate to the user that they are unable to access your application unless they accept cookies. This will provide a detailed explanation of the problem rather than displaying the standard Oracle error, enabling the user to make a choice to accept the cookies. If you are using cookies on your site, always account for this situation. You will need to make the decision as to what to do when users will not accept cookies. Will you code around this? Will you simply tell them they must accept cookies?

Organizing Your Directories

Planning how your source code is stored on the server can make debugging easier. Place your application files in the same area on your server and keep different types of files separated in this area. All images should be grouped together, but separated from the rest of your application. The same can be said for all HTML files, PL/SQL source code, Java programs, and CGI executables. Applying organization in this area can make your maintenance activities easier in the future.

Thinking Thin Client

When developing Web applications, you need to consider thinking in thin client. You certainly do not want your application to be considered "fat" and shunned by the user community for breaking Intequette (Internet etiquette).

Minimizing Long Load Times

You have about ten seconds to capture the interest of your visitors, so testing your Web application on different browsers at different times of the day is critical. Many different companies are on the Web that will gladly check the download time of your images on your Web pages and report back any HTML problems encountered. For example, the WebTrends site (http://www.webtrends.com) is one option.

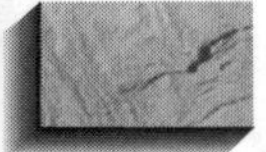

TIP

The following URLs are two Web addresses of companies that will check your Web site and provide a report on load times and HTML problems they encounter. The first is NetMechanic (http://www.netmechanic.com), and the second is Imagiware (http://www2.imagiware.com/RxHTML/).

Maximizing the Image Tag

Most browsers will display the content of your Web pages as soon as they have loaded the information. Images appear gradually and text formats from the top of the page down. To load an image on an HTML page, use the <IMG> tag. The <IMG> tag requires the browser to retrieve the image from the server and scale it before inserting it into your page.

The <IMG> tag is used to anchor a multimedia object on your HTML document. The most common images used are GIFs and JPEGs. The SRC attribute of the <IMG> tag indicates to the browser where to retrieve the image to download. The following is the URL of the image calling the TUSC logo:

```
<IMG SRC="http://www.tusc.com/images/tusc.gif" WIDTH="50"
     HEIGHT="50" ALT="TUSC Logo">
```

It is very important that you use the correct WIDTH and HEIGHT attributes for your images. If these attributes are not present, the browser must calculate the WIDTH and HEIGHT, which takes time to process. If the connection is slow or there is a delay, the image will be sized based on the browser's default image sizes. Once the image starts downloading and the image size is known, the HTML page will be rearranged. The page rearrangement will not appear professional to your user, and can add unacceptable time to the download of the page. The ALT attribute is also important because it will display text before the image is downloaded. For nongraphic browsers, it will at least give the visitor an idea of what image could have been loaded. Most HTML editors will automatically add these <IMG> attributes.

When an image is loaded by default, it will align to the left side of the page. You can change this ALIGN attribute to either right or left, or you can wrap text around your image (right or left). For example, if you want the text describing your image to show up on the left of the page and the image on the right of the page, set the ALIGN attribute equal to right. The text will display on the left side of the image.

```
<HTML>
<HEAD>
<TITLE>Aligning Text on an Image</TITLE>
</HEAD>
<BODY>
<H1> The TUSC logo.</H1>
<BR><BR>
<IMG SRC="http://www.tusc.com/images/tusc.gif" HEIGHT="105"
WIDTH="410" ALT="TUSC LOGO" ALIGN=right>
<H1> The TUSC logo.</H1>
The image on the right is the our TUSC logo.
</BODY>
</HTML>
```

Color Reducing

Reducing the number of colors from 256 to 8, 16, or 32 will also decrease the load time of an image. Experiment with the number of colors to determine what resolution works best for your image. If it is still not fast enough for your Netscape users, you can use the LOWSRC attribute of the <IMG> tag. This attribute will cause the browser to load the LOWSCR image once it encounters the <IMG> tag. The LOWSCR image will be at the lowest resolution copy of your image. Once the document has completely loaded, the browser will load the real image from the SRC attribute.

If you know what images on your Web site are causing the longest load time, use JavaScript to load these images in the background while your visitor is busy reading your main page. The following JavaScript, when placed after the <BODY> tag, will cause the browser to cache the images into the visitor's PC memory. This preloading of images occurs in the background, and when the visitor hyperlinks to the next Web page, the image will already be available for display. If you use the same set of images throughout your Web pages, once retrieved, they will be stored in the user's cache and the page will take less time to download.

```
<SCRIPT LANGUAGE="JavaScript1.1">
img1 = new Image();
img1.src = "tusc.gif";
img2 = new Image();
img2.src = "Oracle.gif";
img3 = new Image();
img3.src = " <http://www.tusc.com/images/award.gif>;
</SCRIPT>
```

By structuring your HTML, both at the Web page and Web site levels, you can offer your visitors the information they are looking for within the recommended 10-second time frame. At the same time, you want to intrigue them with your images and graphics. By structuring your HTML page, using the right resolution, setting the <IMG> attributes correctly, and (if needed) preloading images, you can safely say you have completed your part in resolving long load times.

Graphics

Another timesaver includes saving your images in the correct format. If your image contains many colors and shading (i.e., a photo), your image should be saved in the JPEG format (.jpg). Black and white or gray-scale pictures, and pictures with large areas of a few colors (i.e., line art), should be saved as GIF files. GIF compresses images by saving large areas of a single color in shorthand format. So, if your image has just a few areas of basic colors, it will be smaller in the GIF rather than the JPEG format. Image size is very important on the Web and the longer it takes a site to launch, the more people you lose.

You often cannot see a quality change between 256 and 32 colors; however, you save about 4,000 bytes if you convert to 32-color GIF, decreasing the load time for any Web page. The best way to test your site is to experiment with each image for the best quality and the maximized image size for your Web projects.

- **GIF (Graphics Interchange Format)** Used for all images under 24-bit. Most often used for line art, clip art, and images with large areas of a single color.
- **JPEG (Joint Photographic Experts Group Format)** Used for images over 24-bit.

Paging Logic

Paging logic is the process of rationing information to the user. If a query returns more than 100 rows, the download time for your page becomes unnecessarily long if you attempt to load all the rows at one time. The capability of the user to scroll through all the information and understand everything provided is greatly reduced. Presenting the data 20 rows at a time enables the user to digest the information in more manageable pieces. Several other concerns that need to be explored accompany paging logic.

First, is it reasonable to have a query in your application that returns more than 100 rows? If 10,000 rows are returned, paging through them 20 at a time to find record 5,200 will become very frustrating. A better design might be to require your users to refine their queries so fewer rows are returned. Messages asking them to refine their queries and screens capable of performing this task will have to be developed as part of your application.

Second, is it inefficient to keep executing the same cursor? The answer is probably not. The data and the query should be cached in your database, which will make retrieval time after the first retrieve faster. If you are still concerned that reexecuting your query is inefficient, there are several options.

As previously described earlier in this chapter, Transaction Services can be implemented to keep a cursor open. This way, your application can continue reading the open cursor upon subsequent executions by a user. If the user waits too long to move to the next page, the Transaction Service can timeout and the cursor will need to be reloaded anyway. This must be considered in the development of these procedures. The users would also be required to choose a "Done" link to close the transaction when they stop paging through the original query. Otherwise, transactions will be left open when they are no longer needed.

Another option is to write the query data to a temporary table. The row number for the query will be created along with an index on the row number. When retrieving the next set of records, using the temporary table retrieves this information quickly because it uses the row number index. If multiple users will access this same query functionality at once, you will need to account for this in your temporary table. For example, a login ID or randomly generated query number must be included for each query in the temporary table so each can be distinguished from the others.

Archiving Records to Be Accessed Later

If you cannot find an effective way to limit your users' queries, archive the records used for historical purposes. If your database is properly tuned, transactional systems will continue to grow and at some point you must purge and archive your transactional data. The following subsections are a few archiving options to consider.

Partition Tables

The use of partitioned tables increases performance of data retrieval. Partitioning a table enables one or more users to access multiple parts of the same table without unduly impacting other users. The key to partitioning is to ensure the partitions reside on a different disk controller. For example, create a table with two or more partitions and store the partitions to different tablespaces. Again, an assumption is made that the tablespaces reside on physically different disk controllers. This is a feature that Oracle8 brought us.

Purge Larger Tables

Purging data is always a big project. The process of deciding what to purge and what to keep can be painful. Do you have a current set of guidelines for purging old data? If possible, export your data and purge the data within each database table. This may provide the performance you need, but be careful that the data you are purging still maintains referential integrity. For example, maintaining parent-child relationships must be considered if you purge a parent table.

Design an Archival Routine

Unfortunately, an easy way to design an archival routine does not exist. Depending on the complexity of your data model, it can be beneficial to develop an archiving routine. This is not a trivial task. However, if you think about design issues for purging and archiving in the beginning of your data model design, you will not have to address such issues while your database is growing. Just as you design your model around business rules that apply to the operational data model, at the same time consider methods to archive or purge this data. The issues to consider when designing a purge and archive routine are referential integrity, setting a purge or an archive flag, and a time stamp to track the archiving process.

Use your company's data warehouse if one exists. One of the major features of a data warehouse is the storage history. One way to use a data warehouse is to create triggers on the operational tables and move data to an interface table. Initiate a process pulling the data from the interface tables and inserting the data to the data warehouse and a finial routine flagging the rows processed and remove them from the operating system. This option will still require a flag to indicate your operational data has been moved to the data warehouse.

You can purchase third-party software or services, making purging and archiving quick and easy. Most third-party products provide the following features:

- Purges data as easily as writing a query
- Adds the archiving feature to any existing purge routine *without programming*
- Requires no application or database source code
- Includes full audit trail for purged and archived operations
- Provides easy archive data backup to tape

Drop-Down List Boxes

How many rows are too many in a drop-down list? One hundred rows is a good rule of thumb. Beyond this, the download time is too extensive. The user would be required to scroll through too many rows to find the desired value. Lookup screens can be developed to address this issue. The capability to query for the desired record and bring it back to the original form will give the user more flexibility in finding the desired value than scrolling through a too-large list. When using this method, the option for the user to enter the value should be included if it is known. Forcing a user to visit a query screen every time they enter a form, when they know the desired value, will be a source of frustration and, consequently, should be avoided. Consider using the WebDB list of values routines to automate your list of values' functionality.

Summary

Designing a Web application is different than the design of a client/server application. But then, developing a client/server application was different than developing a terminal/host application. Take the time to design your application properly.

CHAPTER 4

OAS Configuration and Tuning

hen I wrote my original outline for this book, I estimated that this chapter would be about 30 pages. I never imagined that I could write an entire book on OAS configuration, management, and tuning. To obtain the short answer in tuning OAS, read the first section of this chapter.

The configuration of OAS can be the success factor for your site. Why, you might ask? If OAS is not configured correctly, you are likely to run into problems. Problems with performance are the primary potential issues, but intermittent errors and security risks could be others. Because performance of OAS is a factor in the success of most projects, this chapter will address not only the configuration of OAS but also how to configure OAS to retrieve the best overall performance. Chapter 2 provides the steps for a complete OAS installation, which should be completed prior to the steps in this chapter. The goal of this chapter is to discuss the configuration specifics once you have installed OAS and designed your application (Chapter 3). The components that require configuration are the Listeners (Chapter 8), the cartridges (discussed in a number of chapters, such as Chapters 14 and 17–21, which cover the PL/SQL, Forms, Reports, Java, Perl, and LiveHTML cartridges), applications, nodes, DADs, authentication services or security (Chapter 15), and the Logger (Chapter 26).

The following are three ways to categorize performance relating to the processing of Hypertext Transfer Protocol (HTTP) and Internet Inter-ORB Protocol (IIOP) requests. This chapter addresses the following performance categories:

- **Request latency** The time processing a request.
- **Request throughput** The number of requests processed per unit of time.
- **Scalability** The capability to handle increasing numbers of requests without adversely affecting latency and throughput.

In this chapter, the following topics will be covered:

- Jumping straight to the short tuning answer
- Analyzing and tuning performance
- Administering OAS processes
- Managing Listeners
- Configuring applications and cartridges
- Managing and configuring database access descriptors (DADs)
- Adding miscellaneous OAS objects

Jumping Straight to the Short Tuning Answer

If you prefer to read the short answer rather than reading the entire chapter, this section summarizes the major points of configuration for optimum performance and security. Because it is difficult to summarize an entire chapter into one section, it is highly recommended that you read the entire chapter. If you do not have time, the following is the "Cliff Note" version:

- Size your hardware properly.
- At a minimum distribute OAS, database, and FTP onto individual servers.
- Hardware components should operate at no more than 75 percent to 80 percent of capacity.
- Use the OAS Monitor to monitor OAS usage.
- Use top, vmstat, netstat, sar, and ps to manage memory usage, paging, swapping, and TCP/IP parameters on UNIX.
- Use Task Manager and Performance Monitor to manage memory usage, paging, and swapping on NT.
- Set the operating system swap size to three times the physical memory.
- Use directio for maximum disk performance
- Set TCP/IP parameters per the hardware vendor's specification for a Web server.
- Obtain the latest operating system patches, especially those for TCP/IP.
- Collapse process model for memory usage; do not collapse process model for stability and failure recovery.
- Distribute the load across multiple nodes.
- Require that clients use HTTP 1.1.
- Use Multithreaded Server (MTS) for SQL*Net.
- Tune Cartridge Server, instance, and thread parameters.
- Tune specific cartridge parameters.
- Tune your SQL code.
- Monitor logs for errors.

- Keep logs small (1–5MB).
- Turn off DNS resolution.
- Set up autoredirection based on system hitting 80 percent.
- Minimize directory rescans.
- Read this entire chapter when you have the time.

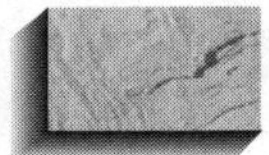

TIP
This chapter will help you to become an experienced OAS Webmaster. Because the OAS Manager is entirely Web-based, you should consider hiring an outside consultant if you do not have time to learn the intricacies of OAS configuration. An experienced OAS Webmaster can make an amazing difference in the performance and stability of your Web site.

Analyzing and Tuning Performance

You can use the OAS Manager to analyze performance, including process CPU and memory usage and connection and request statistics. A number of other ways exist to monitor the performance of your applications, servers, and sites. The following sections cover the general tuning items.

Reviewing Hardware Recommendations

In addition to the following general recommendations, make sure your hardware resources are adequate for the requirements of your specific applications. To avoid hardware-related performance bottlenecks, each hardware component should operate at no more than 75 percent to 80 percent of capacity. In the beginning of a system's life, the 80 percent of capacity rule is common sense, but is often forgotten once the application goes into production. Loading the last 20 percent of the system is what can cause the worst of performance problems.

The following is the absolute minimum hardware configuration for most OAS deployments on the Sun Solaris platform:

- Sun UltraSparc II at 168MHz or Pentium Pro at 200MHz
- 128MB of memory
- 0.5GB of disk space
- 100-Mbps network connection

Processor and memory resources should be more than adequate to handle the maximum traffic your network connections can handle. If your network becomes a bottleneck, you can upgrade to faster network interface cards, or install multiple network interface cards on each machine.

Using the OAS Monitor

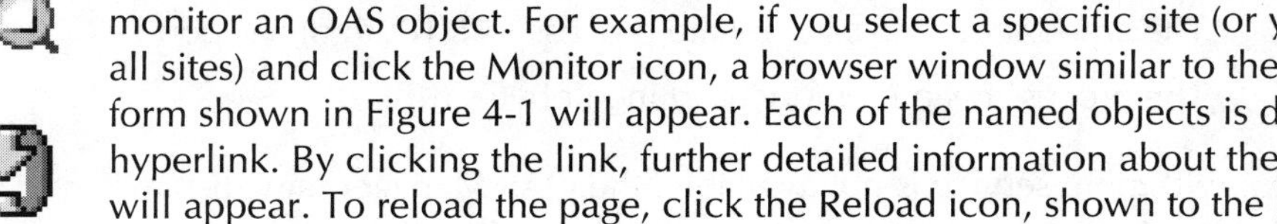

By selecting an object and clicking the Monitor icon, shown to the left, you can monitor an OAS object. For example, if you select a specific site (or you can select all sites) and click the Monitor icon, a browser window similar to the OAS Monitor form shown in Figure 4-1 will appear. Each of the named objects is displayed as a hyperlink. By clicking the link, further detailed information about the OAS object will appear. To reload the page, click the Reload icon, shown to the left.

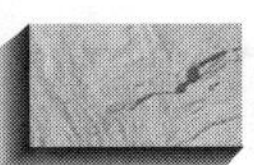

TIP
All monitoring statistics are a rough indication of the state of the server. They are not precise.

Monitor - Microsoft Internet Explorer

Site

Process Status					Connections			Requests	
Name	Node	SID	CPU	Memory	Current	Last Time	Total	Pending	Total
dispatchers/admin	tuscco_db1	510:0	696	1947	2	2 16:39:37	2	0	6663
dispatchers/emploc	tuscco_db1	652:0	2498	1963	2	2 16:39:10	2	0	6661
dispatchers/evcon	tuscco_db1	626:0	575	1963	2	2 16:39:16	2	0	6661
dispatchers/tne	tuscco_db1	553:0	801	1991	2	2 16:39:27	3	0	6665
dispatchers/trs	tuscco_db1	677:0	1840	2007	2	2 16:39:05	4	0	6664
dispatchers/wb	tuscco_db1	586:0	790	1959	2	2 16:39:21	2	0	6663
dispatchers/www	tuscco_db1	526:0	1079	2139	3	2 16:39:32	7	0	6796
orb/mncnmsrv	tuscco_db1	290:0	18150	3179	29	2 16:41:22	59	0	194880
orb/mnlogsrv	tuscco_db1	311:0	1248	901	3	2 16:41:21	3	0	6694
orb/mnorbmet	tuscco_db1	347:0	73314	1764	1	2 16:40:40	1	0	3810
orb/mnorbsrv	tuscco_db1	313:0	18376	1832	14	2 16:40:43	22	0	6690
wrb/cartxSrv/condo	tuscco_db1	454:0	2115	2086	3	2 16:40:02	3	0	3755
wrb/oassrv	tuscco_db1	351:0	0	0	0	00:00:00	0	0	0
wrb/otsfacsrv	tuscco_db1	457:0	340	1468	2	2 16:40:02	2	0	3755
wrb/wrbahsrv	tuscco_db1	351:0	35707	5951	11	2 16:40:38	25	0	53
wrb/wrbasrv	tuscco_db1	351:0	35707	5951	11	2 16:40:38	25	0	1
wrb/wrbcfg	tuscco_db1	351:0	35707	5951	11	2 16:40:38	25	0	156

FIGURE 4-1. *OAS monitoring*

The following table describes the entries that display process status information:

Column	Description
Name	The name of the process
Node	The name of the machine
SID	The process ID and (after the colon) the instance ID
CPU	The amount of time used by the process in 1/100th of a second
Memory	The process heap memory used in kilobytes (KB)

If the Monitor (wrbmon) service is not available, the OAS Manager may display incorrect or outdated status information. This occurs when either the oassrv process (in collapsed mode) or the wrbmon (in noncollapsed mode) is not running. The status information is dependent on the wrbmon process at the monitoring and dump (show state) levels.

The following table describes the entries that display connection information:

Column	Description
Current	The number of current in-bound connections to the process.
Last Time	The time of the last in-bound connection to the process in the format of [[days]hour:minutes:seconds]. This interval is measured since the process started.
Total	The total number of in-bound connections since OAS started.

The following table describes the entries that display request information:

Column	Description
Pending	The number of pending requests
Total	The total number of requests completed

Tuning OAS on Solaris

To monitor OAS performance on Sun Solaris systems, you can use the top, vmstat, sar, and ps utilities to monitor memory usage, swapping, paging, and processor usage by OAS processes.

As discussed in Chapter 1, it is best to dedicate a box to OAS for optimum performance and monitoring. Processor use will vary with each individual application. If the application is network-intensive, the Listener processes will consume the majority of processor cycles. If the application is application-intensive, the majority of the work will be consumed by cartridges; therefore, the majority of the processes are consumed by cartridges. If the application is database-intensive and the database is on the same box (not recommended for a production site) as OAS, the database processes will consume the machine with CPU and I/O.

Tuning the Operating System

Sun Microsystems updates the Solaris operating system components regularly, such as the Transmission Control Protocol/Internet Protocol (TCP/IP) subsystem. TCP/IP is heavily used by OAS, so always be sure you have installed the latest patches.

Sun also provides the Solaris Internet Server Supplement, which is a set of add-on modules specially tailored for Solaris systems that host Web sites, so be sure to obtain this supplement from Sun. The following subsections discuss items at the operating system level that you can set for optimum system performance.

FILE DESCRIPTORS Make sure the limit on file descriptors per process is set at maximum before starting OAS, which is accomplished using the unlimit command as follows:

```
$ unlimit descriptors
```

TRANSMISSION CONTROL PROTOCOL (TCP) SETTINGS The following table lists the recommended TCP parameters and values for Solaris. These values are good recommendations and have not changed in a long time, but you may wish to contact Oracle support for the most current recommendations.

Parameter	Recommended Value
tcp_conn_req_max	1024
tcp_close_wait_interval	3000
tcp_rexmit_interval_min	1500
tcp_xmit_hiwat	65536
tcp_xmit_lowat	24576
tcp_recv_hiwat	65536

To set these TCP parameters, you must first connect to the root UNIX account (su root) and then use the following command, replacing parameter with the preceding parameter name and value with the preceding suggested value:

```
# /usr/sbin/ndd -set /dev/tcp parameter value
```

USING THE NETSTAT UTILITY Solaris 2.5.1 and subsequent releases contain a new TCP/IP statistic, known as tcpListenDrop, which counts the number of times that a connection is dropped because of a full queue. You can use the Solaris netstat utility (-s option) to report networking statistics, including tcpListenDrop. Applications that have high tcpListenDrop counts should increase the size of the queue by specifying higher values for the backlog to the Listener (the listen() call). Set the maximum backlog size by adjusting the value of the tcp_conn_req_max parameter (to a higher number). In the case of an initial handshake, an incoming packet is sent with only the Synchronized Sequence Numbers (SYN) flag set. When a packet is sent, the server makes an entry in the listen queue, then sends another packet to acknowledge the first packet. It also includes a SYN flag to reciprocate the synchronization of the sequence number in the opposite direction. Then, the client sends another packet to acknowledge the second SYN, and the server process is then scheduled to return (from the accept() call), subsequently moving the connection from the listen queue to the active connection list.

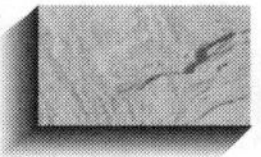

TIP
If you send an initial SYN packet without it being acknowledged with a second SYN packet, it will eventually time out, and the server will discard the client from the listen queue. The listen queue becomes full when a server has several SYN packets that do not contain valid source addresses. This causes new connections to wait for old connections to be discarded from the queue. Solaris 2.5.1 patch 103582 and IP patch 103630 correct this problem by using two separate queues, as opposed to one. These patches have been incorporated into Solaris 2.6 and Solaris 2.7.

Solaris 2.6 and subsequent releases also added two new TCP tunable parameters, tcp_conn_req_max_q and tcp_conn_req_max_q0, which specify the maximum number of completed connections waiting to return from an accept() call, and the maximum number of incomplete handshake connections, respectively.

Use the netstat utility (-s option) to monitor TCP statistics, and to determine connection drop activity, as well as the type of drops. The tcpHalfOpenDrop statistic is incremented when an in-doubt connection is dropped. The default value for tcp_conn_rq_max_q is 128, and the default value for tcp_conn_req_max_q0 is 1,024. The default values are typically sufficient and should not require tuning. However, by examining the statistics with the netstat utility, you can determine if the parameters need to be adjusted.

TCP implementations use a congestion window limiting the number of packets that can be sent before an acknowledgment. This is used to improve the startup latency and also helps avoid overloading the network. The TCP standard specifies that the initial congestion window should consist of one packet, then double up on each successive acknowledgment. This causes exponential growth and may not necessarily be ideal for HTTP servers, which typically send small batches of packets. Solaris 2.6 provides a tcp_slow_start_intital parameter that can be used to double the congestion window from its default of 1 to 2. This improves transmission throughput of small batch sizes.

Contrary to Solaris, NT version 4 does not immediately acknowledge receipt of a packet upon connection/start, which results in an increase in the connection startup latency. NT version 4 immediately acknowledges if two packets are sent. The difference between the NT and the Solaris implementation causes performance discrepancies, or higher response times, when NT clients are used to connect to Solaris servers with a high-speed or LAN-based network. Set the congestion window on Solaris to 2, using tcp_slow_start_initial equal to 2.

In Solaris 2.6, the tcp_conn_hash_size parameter can be set to help address connection backlog. During high connection rates, TCP data structure kernel lookups can be expensive and can slow down the server. Increasing the size of the hash table improves lookup efficiency. The default for tcp_conn_hash_size is 256. This parameter must be a power of 2, and can be set in the /etc/system kernel configuration file.

Use the netstat utility to monitor the overall network traffic, as well as the network traffic for a given interface, using the (-k) option. Solaris 2.6 has several new counters that report byte count statistics. Table 4-1 lists the netstat utility counter names and descriptions.

Utility Counter Name	Description
rbytes	Read byte count
obytes	Output byte count
multircv	Multicast receive
multixmt	Transmit count
brdcstrcv	Broadcast byte count
brdcstxmt	Broadcast transmit count
norcvbuf	Receive buffer allocation failure count
noxmtbuf	Transmit buffer allocation failure count

TABLE 4-1. *Monitoring Network Traffic Using the netstat Utility*

The following table lists additional Solaris 2.6 network enhancements that increase network performance:

Network Enhancement	Description
Kernel Sockets	Enables higher socket performance in addition to the TCP/IP STREAMS
TCP Large Windows	Allows TCP sessions to transmit larger packet sizes between 64KB and 1GB
Zero Copy TCP/Hardware Checksum	Avoids data copy, and uses hardware checksum logic

Monitoring Processor Use

To determine process utilization, you should gather CPU statistics. You should also monitor system scalability by adding users and increasing the system workload. Use the sar and mpstat utilities to monitor process use, as described in the following subsections.

USING THE SAR UTILITY To determine process use, use the following sar command:

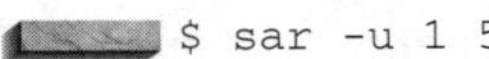

```
$ sar -u 1 5
```

When you use the sar command, you will receive a listing similar to the following:

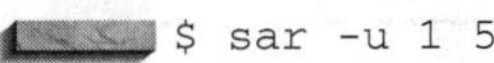

```
$ sar -u 1 5

SunOS Tuscco_oas3 5.6 Generic_sun4m

%usr     %sys     %wio    %idle
1        1        0       98
3        5        0       92
8        2        0       90
2        2        0       96
```

The sar command (-u option) provides the statistics identified in the following table.

CPU Statistics	Description
%usr	Percentage that the processor is running in user time
%sys	Percentage of processes running in system time
%wio	Percentage the processor spends waiting on I/O requests
%idle	Percentage that the processor is idle

USING THE MPSTAT UTILITY On Solaris, you can also monitor CPU processes using the following mpstat command:

```
$ mpstat 1 3
```

The mpstat utility is similar to the sar command: the first argument to mpstat is the polling interval time in seconds. The second argument to mpstat is the number of iterations. The mpstat utility reports the statistics per processor, as shown in the Table 4-2.

Monitoring the Run Queue

Monitor the run queue to determine if processes are waiting for an available processor. Use the following sar -q command to monitor the run queue:

```
$ sar -q 2 5
```

Statistic	Description
CPU	Processor ID
minf	Number of minor faults
xcal	Number of interprocessor cross calls
Intr	Number of interrupts
ithr	Number of interrupts as threads
csw	Number of context switches
icsw	Number of involuntary context switches
migr	Number of thread migrations to another processor
smtx	Number of spins for a mutex lock; therefore, the lock was not obtained on the first attempt
srw	Number of spins on reader/writer lock; therefore, the lock was not obtained on the first attempt
syscl	Number of system calls
usr	Percentage that the processor spent in user time
sys	Percentage that the processor spent in system time
wt	Percentage that the processor spent in wait time (waiting on an event)
Idle	Percentage that the processor spent in idle time

TABLE 4-2. *mpstat CPU Statistics*

When you use the sar -q command, you receive a listing similar to the following:

```
SunOS Tuscco_oas3 5.5.1 Generic_103640-14 sun4m

runq-sz %runocc swpq-sz %swpocc
1.0      1.0     17.0    1.0

Average 4.2
```

The following table describes the statistics shown when you use the sar -q utility:

Statistic	Description
runq-sz	Length of the run queue (processes waiting for CPU)
%runocc	Percentage of time occupied
swpq-sz	Number of processes that have been swapped out and are now ready to run
%swpocc	Percentage of time occupied

USING PROCESSOR SETS You can create processor sets that bind processes to a set of processors, as opposed to a single processor. Two types of processor sets exist: user-created processor sets, and system-created processor sets. User-created processor sets can be managed using the psrset command or the pset_create() system call. Processors assigned to user-created processor sets only service lightweight processes (LWPs) bound to that particular processor set. However, system-created processor sets can service other LWPs. System-created processor sets do not always exist on a particular system. System-created processor sets are useful when certain processors communicate more efficiently together than they do with other processors. System-created processor sets cannot be modified or removed, but you can bind processes to them. Processor sets are used to improve CPU use by binding a certain set of processes, such as the Oracle Listeners or cartridge processes, to processor sets. Processor sets aid in reducing the processor contention between the Listener processes and the cartridge processes.

Tuning I/O

Direct input/output (I/O) bypasses the UNIX file system cache and copies the file system-based file data directly into user space. Direct I/O on file systems is similar to raw devices. Solaris 2.6 enables direct I/O to be performed using the directio() system call. An application can use the directio() system call to perform direct I/O processing on a file. To control whether direct I/O to the file system is forced, use the mount command options: noforcedirectio and forcedirectio.

Use direct I/O to:

- Improve large sequential I/O performance
- Improve performance of large files during file transfers
- Eliminate extra buffer copies and file system cache maintenance
- Reduce CPU consumption

Tuning OAS on Windows NT

On Windows NT platforms, the available tuning options are not nearly as extensive as on UNIX platforms. You can use the Task Manager and Performance Monitor to assess hardware and operating system performance. You can also verify the application processes being used by OAS.

Tuning the Process Model

The process model enables you to choose a noncollapsed model or a collapsed model. The collapsed model has smaller memory requirements because the number of processes running is less than when using the noncollapsed model. Using a collapsed model will combine the following processes into one oassrv process:

- Config Provider (wrbcfg)
- Log Server (wrblog)
- Authentication Server (wrbasrv)
- Authentication Host Server (wrbahsrv)
- Resource Manager (wrbroker)
- Resource Manager Proxy (wrbrmpxy)
- Monitoring Daemon (wrbmon)

The Process Model form, shown in Figure 4-2, enables you to select a collapsed or noncollapsed process model for running OAS.

To change your process model, follow these steps:

1. Shut down your OAS site. The only process that should be running is your Node Manager Listener. If you do not shut down your OAS site, OAS will not allow you to change the process model; instead, OAS will display a message instructing you to shut down your site before changing the process model.

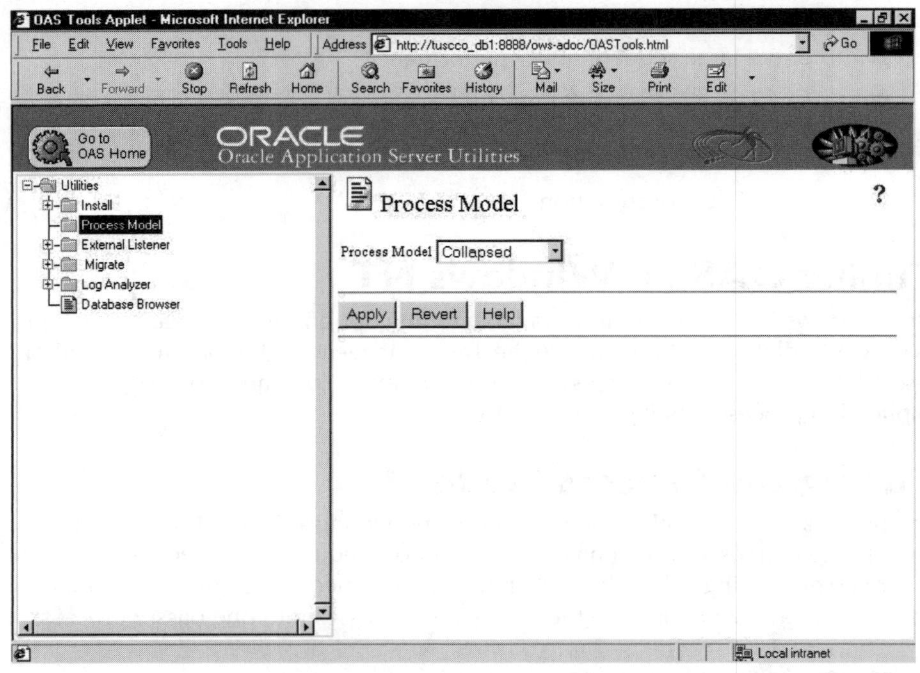

FIGURE 4-2. *Process Model form*

2. Connect to your Node Manager Listener and click the OAS Utilities icon.
3. Expand the Utilities tree and click Process Model (see Figure 4-2).
4. Select the desired process model and click Apply.

After selecting a process model, the form allows you to reload the OAS Web site.

Optimizing FTP Downloads

If your site offers a large volume of data for File Transfer Protocol (FTP) download, you will obtain better performance for these downloads, and other server accesses, by hosting the downloadable data on a separate server. This releases resources on your OAS servers for handling HTTP and application requests.

Setting Swap Space and Distributing the Load

In setting up an OAS site, you should make sure that Operating System (O/S) swap space usage does not exceed 75 percent to 80 percent. OAS will generate new processes over time. You should set up each OAS machine with three times as much swap space as physical memory. If your system begins swapping or paging excessively, you might be running too many processes on your system. In this case, add more memory or additional nodes (machines) to your site to distribute the load. Another possible cause of excessive swapping and paging is memory leakage in applications.

For smaller workloads, a single OAS node meeting the minimum hardware recommendations can run Listeners, Cartridge Servers, and databases.

Distributing Load Among Multiple Nodes

For large workloads, you can improve performance by setting up your site with multiple nodes, running Listeners and dispatchers on the primary node, and running Cartridge Servers on remote nodes. You can optimize performance by dividing responsibilities among nodes according to the workloads you anticipate.

An infinite number of server-distributed load configurations exist. The configuration for your site will depend on the load of your application. A site that is heavily based on static HTML will have a completely different configuration from a dynamically generated site. Take the time to configure your site's servers according to your site's load.

For example, for a site that is primarily dedicated to using the PL/SQL cartridge to serve database content, as illustrated in Figure 4-3, configure one node to run Listeners, several nodes to run PL/SQL Cartridge Servers, and one machine to host the database. This minimizes processor contention between OAS components and the database, especially on single-processor machines.

A failover architecture could include two or more systems with identical configurations, each hosting Listeners, Cartridge Servers, and other OAS components. Such redundant configurations provide a transparent failover mechanism in case one machine goes down.

As you gain detailed knowledge over time of the workloads your site is handling, you can fine-tune your configuration by adding or consolidating nodes to use resources more efficiently and eliminate bottlenecks. The real power of using OAS is that it can support any of these distributed architectures. Not only can OAS support these architectures, it supports them seamlessly to your application. You do not need to write your application to take advantage of a particular architecture; rather, OAS will manage this for you.

Minimizing the Number of Connections per Client

Clients using HTTP version 1.0 must use a separate HTTP connection to download each graphic used in an HTML page. Minimizing the number of graphics in static HTML pages reduces the number of separate connections from HTTP 1.0 clients.

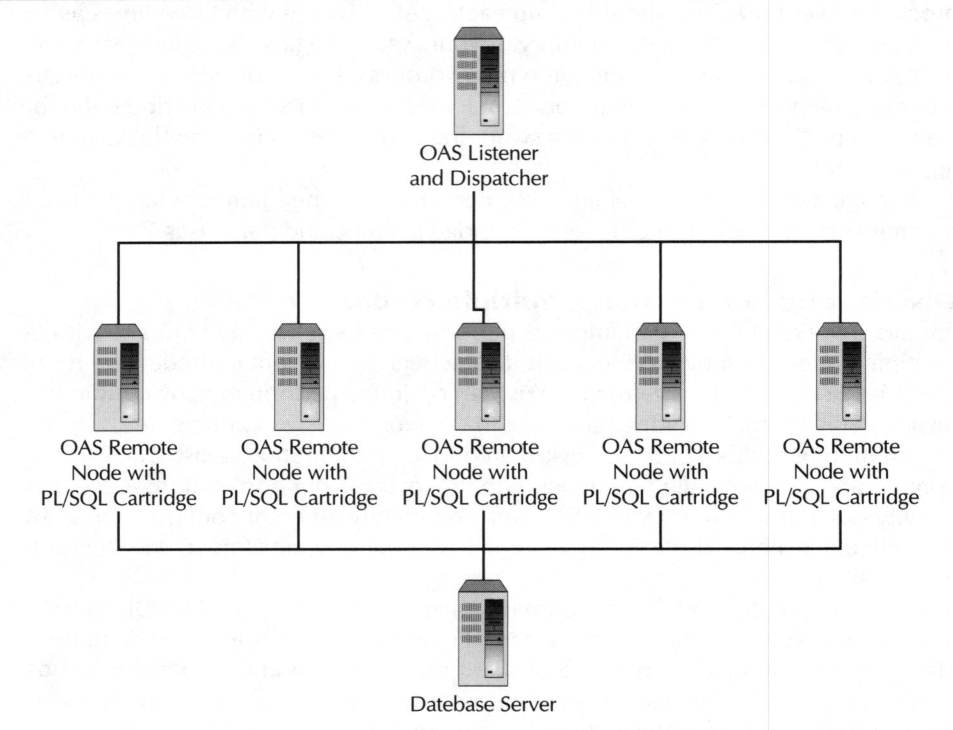

FIGURE 4-3. *Primary node, multiple remote nodes, and a database server*

Clients using HTTP version 1.1 do not have this problem. To determine the percentage of clients using each HTTP version, use Log Analyzer forms to monitor your connection statistics, and adjust the use of graphics accordingly. OAS uses HTTP 1.1, so it will help if your users (clients) are also using HTTP 1.1.

Tuning Database Access

Ideally, you should allocate a dedicated Oracle server process for each PL/SQL Cartridge Server. If you cannot do this because of memory or swap space constraints, Oracle recommends using the Oracle Multi-Threaded Server (MTS), enabling you to multiplex your database connections and ensuring that server processes are optimally used.

Database Access Descriptors (DADs)

Each PL/SQL Cartridge Server, on startup, attempts to connect to the database specified by each Database Access Descriptor (DAD) listed in the OAS configuration. To save time, you should restrict the number of DADs on each OAS node, listing only those needed by the applications on that node.

Memory Usage

OAS supports a cartridge process model. Table 4-3 contains the processes started during OAS initialization and the respective memory costs.

As Table 4-3 indicates, the memory consumed by the Fixed Cost group of processes represents a fixed cost totaling approximately 20MB. The processes in the Variable Cost group have a cost associated depending on the number of Oracle Listeners and Cartridge Servers running on the site. For each concurrent user, a

Description	Process	Average Memory Usage (MB)
Fixed cost	wrbroker	3.20
	wrbasrv	2.60
	wrbvpm	2.00
	wrbahsrv	2.20
	wrblog	2.00
	wrbcfg	1.80
	mnorbsrv	1.60
	mnaddrsrv	1.30
	mnrpcnmsrv	1.80
	wrksf	2.70
Fixed cost total		21.20
Variable cost	wwwlsnr	7.00
	wrbc	2.10
Variable cost total		9.10
Total (1 user)		30.30
Total (5 users)		38.70
Total (20 users)		70.10
Total (100 users)		238.20

TABLE 4-3. *Expected Memory Cost*

Cartridge Server is prespawned by setting the GlobalMinServers parameter in the [APPLICATION] section of the configuration file (for example, wrb.app).

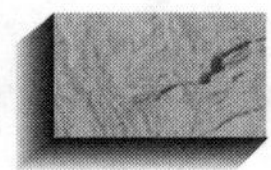

TIP
For load balancing, these processes are started five minutes after the WRB is initiated, so you will not see these processes immediately after starting OAS.

Each Cartridge Server process consumes 2–5MB of memory, depending on the type of cartridge. This represents a variable memory cost, as illustrated in Figure 4-4.

Performance Characteristics

Figure 4-5 compares the throughput (connections/second) and data throughput (Kbps) of OAS while handling requests for different-size files. This benchmark was performed on the following hardware: 4CPU X 248MHz, UltraSparc II, and 512MB memory.

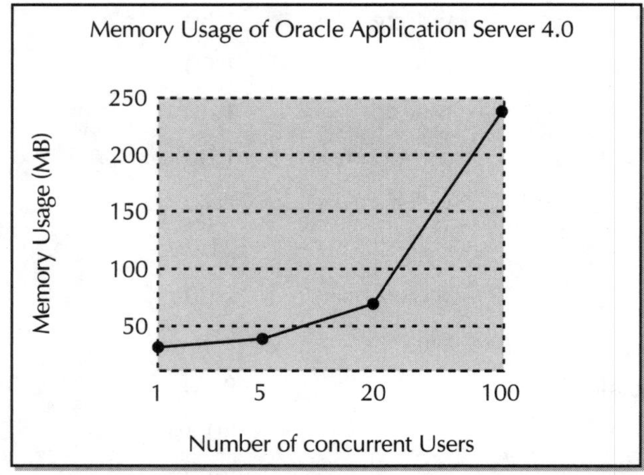

FIGURE 4-4. *Graphed OAS memory use*

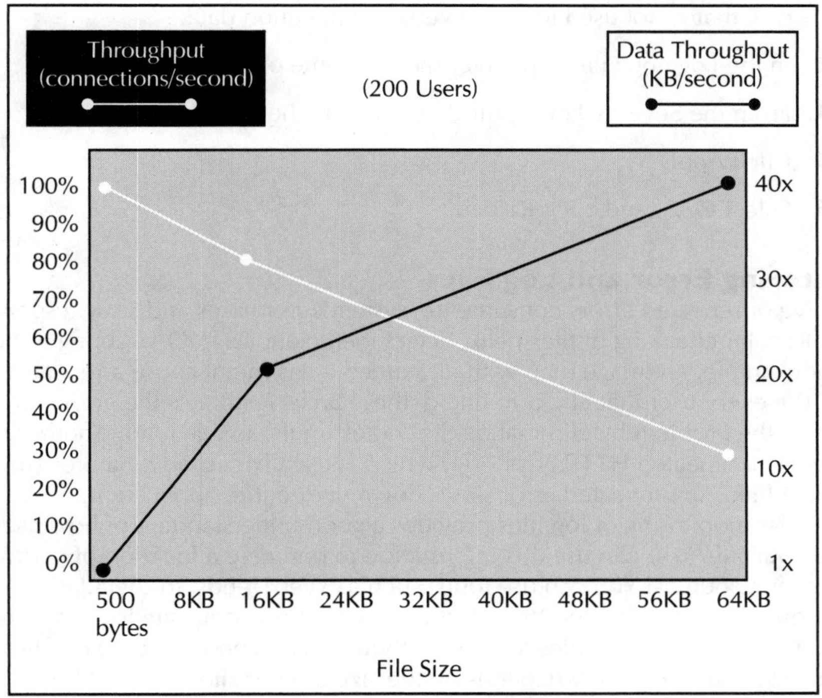

FIGURE 4-5. *Throughput for C cartridge*

As demonstrated in the example case shown in Figure 4-5, while the size of the individual files being transported increases, the throughput (connections/second) drops and the amount of Kbps (data throughput) increases.

Tuning the Logging Service

To minimize request latency on a stable system, you can specify that the Logging Service log messages for only the most severe errors. To minimize disk access contention, you can also specify that system messages be logged to a file on a separate disk that is not used to store Web or application data as follows:

1. Using the OAS Manager, navigate to the form *site-name*/OAS/Logging/System, where *site-name* is the name of your site.

2. In the Logging Directory text field, enter the full path of a directory on a disk that is not used to store Web or application data.
3. In the Logging File field, enter the full name of the logging file.
4. From the Severity Level pull-down menu, choose 1.
5. Click Apply.
6. Select OAS, and click Reload.

Monitoring Error and Log Files

Excessive or repeated errors consume the system's resources and slow response times. Regular checking of files helps detect inefficiencies in OAS configuration.

For example, an image map with undefined areas might cause a repeated HTTP Error 500; every user that clicks in one of these areas generates the error. You can eliminate the problem by eliminating the "holes" in the image map. Another example is a repeated HTTP Error 404, which is usually caused by a broken hypertext link. Any repeated error slows down your entire application.

Regular monitoring of log files provides a good understanding of how users access your site. You can use this information to optimize allocation of hardware and server resources. You can use tools, such as WebTrends, for detailed site usage monitoring. Refer to Chapter 26 for further information about site log management.

Do not allow your log files to grow without limit. When a log file reaches a certain size (the size greatly depends on the size of your site, but 1–5MB is a good standard rule), archive the file and start a new log file. This avoids the overhead of writing to a large file.

Administering OAS Processes

The Oracle Application Server form of the OAS Manager, illustrated in Figure 4-6, enables you to use several management operations to manage your Web Request Broker (WRB) processes. In the example shown in Figure 4-6, the process model is collapsed into one oassrv process. You can create (if using a noncollapsed process model), delete, stop, reload, start, or monitor a WRB process.

Table 4-4 describes all the operations you can apply.

The Oracle Application Server form contains a table of information. Table 4-5 describes all the WRB processes belonging to a site.

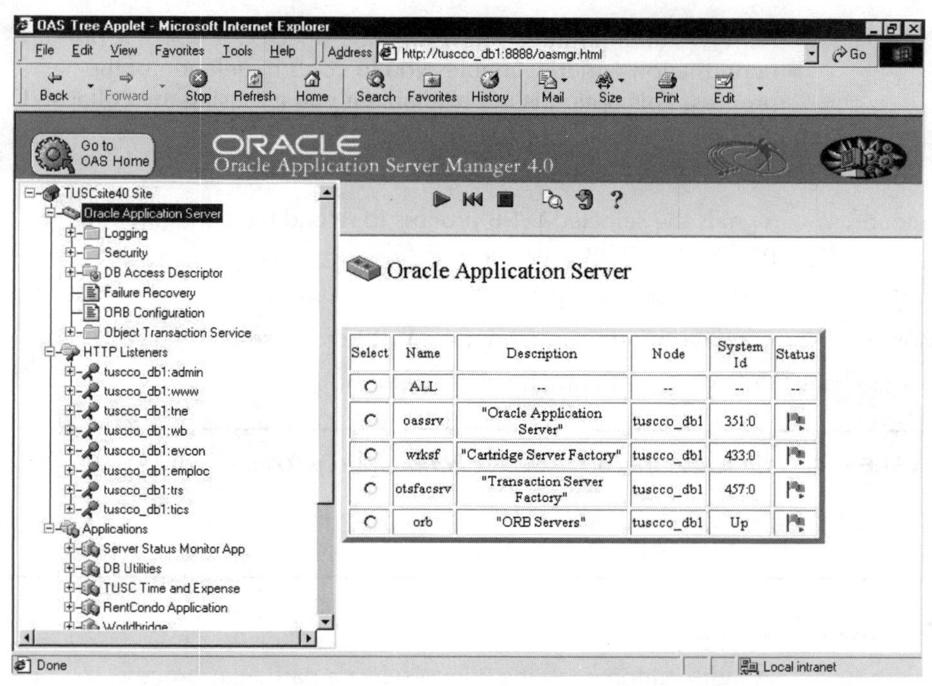

FIGURE 4-6. *Oracle Application Server form*

Operation	**Comments**
Add	Enables you to add a new process to your node for your site. You will need to input the required information on the Add WRB Process form. This option is not available if you are using the collapsed process model. Under the collapsed model, several processes, such as the Authentication Server (wrbsarv) and Monitoring Daemon (wrbmon), and others are combined into one oassrv process.

TABLE 4-4. *Oracle Application Server Form Options*

Delete	Removes all information regarding the selected process. A pop-up confirmation window enables you to confirm deletion of the process. This option is not available if you are using the collapsed process model.
Stop	Stops the selected process.
Reload	Signals the selected WRB process to reload the configuration parameters in the wrb.app.
Start	Starts the selected process.
Monitor	Displays information about the WRB processes.
Update Page	Refreshes the information in this form.

TABLE 4-4. *Oracle Application Server Form Options* (continued)

Operation	**Comments**
Select	A radio button enabling you to select a particular process, so you can use the operations described in Table 4-4.
Name	Contains the executable name of all the processes running on this site—for example, wrksf.
Description	Provides descriptive information about the process.
Node	Specifies the different machine names—for example, tuscco_db1.
System ID	Indicates the process id and instance—for example, 351:0 where 351 is the process ID and 0 is the instance of the process. If a process is down, this column does not display a system ID.
Status	Indicates whether the process is up or down. A red flag means the process is down; a green flag means the process is up. If wrbmon is down, the status of all other processes is unknown and they are shown as down. If you think your processes are up, try to start wrbmon. This is a technical limitation in OAS. Therefore, in collapsed mode, oassrv has to be running since wrbmon is part of oassrv. In noncollapsed mode, wrbmon is a separate process and it has to be running for the front end to get all the status information.

TABLE 4-5. *Description of Oracle Application Server Form Fields*

Managing Listeners

This section describes the basic operations to manage and monitor your HTTP Listeners. HTTP Listeners are capable of accepting requests for hypermedia documents, such as HTML, from multiple TCP/IP ports. You can run several HTTP Listener processes at once, with each accepting connections on a different set of ports.

TIP
Only one Listener can be assigned to a specific TCP/IP port. Two Listeners cannot be assigned to the same TCP/IP port.

Stopping and Starting Listeners

When you make changes affecting an application's virtual paths, you must stop and restart the Listeners for the change to take effect. This is in addition to reloading the Cartridge Server for the application.

Whenever you stop and restart the OAS components, you also have to stop and restart the Listeners.

To stop and restart the Listeners, follow these steps:

1. Click Http Listeners in the navigational tree to display the list of Listeners.
2. Select the Listeners that you want to stop. You must select all the Listeners that will be handling the request for the application.
3. Click the Stop icon to stop the Listeners.

4. Click the Start icon to restart the Listeners.

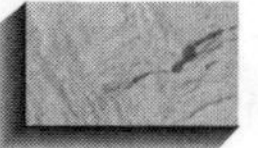

TIP
You can click the Reload icon to stop and start the Listener.

Understanding Ports

Ports are virtual divisions within an IP address on a machine. Even though a Listener can operate on any port (providing you have the privilege and the port does not conflict with another service), in general, ports with a number less than 1025 are used as system-level ports—typically assigned by the TCP/IP commission that sets standards for these port numbers. Port 80 is the industry standard TCP/IP port for HTTP.

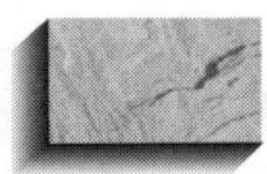

TIP
So as to not conflict with industry standard port numbers, if you plan to put a Listener on a port other than 80 or 443, you should use a number greater than 1024.

TIP
Most proxy servers limit users to ports 80 and 443 for HTTP and HTTPS. If you plan to deploy an application on the Internet, be aware that choosing a port outside these numbers could cause your users proxy issues.

The following table addresses the standard port assignments and uses:

Port Numbers	Standard Assignments
Port 80	The default HTTP Listener port
Port 443	The default HTTPS Listener (SSL - Secure Sockets Layer) port
Port 21	The FTP (File Transfer Protocol) port
Port 23	The telnet port
Ports 1–1024	Reserved for system level duties

Web Listener Configuration Tips

On NT, the stopping and starting of a Listener does not always work when performed through the OAS Manager interface. For this reason, you are usually better off using the command line to perform this operation by typing the **owsctl stop listener_name** command.

For Listener changes to take effect, you must "reload" (stop and start) the Listener.

If you have a problem starting a Listener and no error message appears, be assured that errors are logged in the listener.err file for debugging purposes.

Under the Listener configuration you will find virtual hosts. Virtual hosts enable the same machine to act as if it is several machines. Based on the domain name provided by the user (in the browser), the Web server will react accordingly.

Table 4-6 covers a few other Listener parameters you should know.

Three types of directories are shown in Table 4-7.

Parameter	Description
Redirection server	If you set the maximum number of connections for this Listener, when that number is reached, all connections beyond that point are routed to the redirection server (or URL).
Initial file	If a file is not entered for the virtual path, OAS uses index.html as the default file. If you change the initial file, you must change the base directories.
Directory indexing	Set this to False for production systems and True for test systems. By default, if you specify a virtual directory but no filename is specified, it will look to the initial file (as mentioned above). However, if the initial file does not exist and if directory indexing is set to True, the Listener will display a list of files in the virtual directory. If this parameter is set to False, the Listener will report an error indicating that the URL is not found.
MIME types	If a nonstandard file type exists for the user to view, you must define MIME types for the nonstandard file types so the Listener can inform the browser what type of data is in the file. For example, SQR outputs a file with an extension of .htm and a file with an extension of .h0. Htm files are defined as a MIME type of text/html, meaning that the Web server should send an HTTP header to the browser indicating the proper MIME type. However, a file with an extension of .h0 is not defined by default. Therefore, if you put an h0 file in a normal directory and reference it with your browser's URL, the browser will prompt you with a Save As dialog box. By adding a MIME type of h0 to the Listener and defining it as a text/html file type, your browser will know what kind of file an h0 file is because the Listener will identify the file accordingly.
Directory mappings	See Table 4-7.

TABLE 4-6. *Listener Parameters*

Mapping Type	Reason for the Mapping
N	Normal files downloaded to the Listener—for example, HTML files
C	CGI files or programs executed—for example, a C program or a Perl script
W	CGI programs that require Windows (vs. the command line) to function

TABLE 4-7. *Directory Mappings*

In addition to the mapping type, each directory type can be classified as R (recursive) or N (nonrecursive). Recursive means that the virtual path should be interpreted throughout or recursively through the actual physical path thereafter. Nonrecursive means that the mapping should only apply to the single directory, not its subdirectories.

Listener Performance

The OAS architecture enables you to scale Listener performance by configuring multiple Listeners on a single node, or multiple Listeners on several nodes. The Web Listener offers further performance enhancements by redirecting requests to other Listeners when its maximum number of concurrent connections is reached. This automatic redirection feature provides a transparent load balancing among Listeners.

Administering Your HTTP Listeners

The HTTP Listeners form, shown in Figure 4-7, enables you to use several management operations to manage your HTTP Listeners. You can create, start, stop, or delete a Web Listener process.

Table 4-8 describes all operations applicable to the HTTP Listeners.

The HTTP Listeners form you saw in Figure 4-7 contains a table of information describing all the Listeners belonging to a site. Table 4-9 explains the fields in this table.

Monitoring Your HTTP Listeners

The HTTP Listeners Monitoring form, illustrated in Figure 4-8, displays the results for the Listeners you selected to monitor.

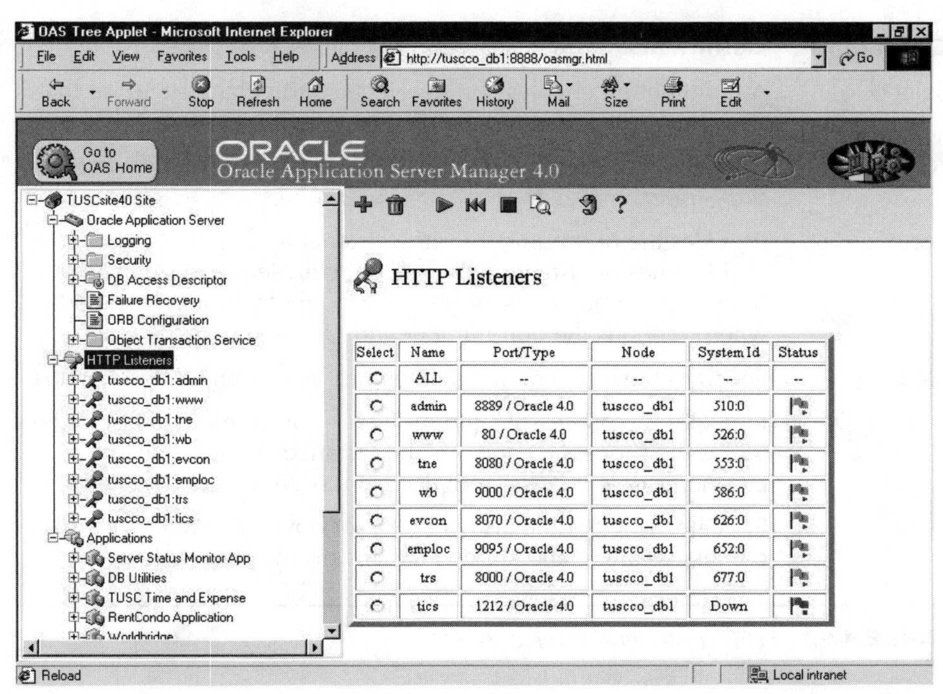

FIGURE 4-7. *HTTP Listeners form*

Operation	**Comments**
Add	Enables you to add a new Listener to your node. You will need to input the required information on the Add Listener form.
Delete	Removes all information regarding the selected Listener. A pop-up confirmation window enables you to confirm deletion of the Listener.
Stop	Stops the selected Listener.
Reload	Reloads configuration values from the wrb.app file.
Start	Starts the selected Listener.
Monitor	Displays statistics about the dispatcher on the selected Listeners.
Update Page	Refreshes the information in this form.

TABLE 4-8. *HTTP Listener Operations*

Operation	**Comments**
Select	A radio button enables you to select a particular Listener so that you can use the operations mentioned in Table 4-8.
Name	Contains the Listener name of all the registered Listeners in this site—for example, tne.
Port/type	Provides the port number for the Listener and the Listener type. Valid values of Listener types are Oracle, Netscape, Apache, and Microsoft (if you are using NT)—for example, 8080/Oracle 4.0 where 8080 is the port number and Oracle 4.0 is the type.
Node	Specifies the different machine names. For example, tuscco_db1.
System ID	Indicates the process ID and instance—for example, 553:0 where 553 is the process ID and 0 is the instance of the process. If a Listener is down, it does not display a system ID.
Status	Indicates whether the Listener is up or down. A red flag means the process is down, and a green flag means the process is up.

TABLE 4-9. *HTTP Listener Form Fields*

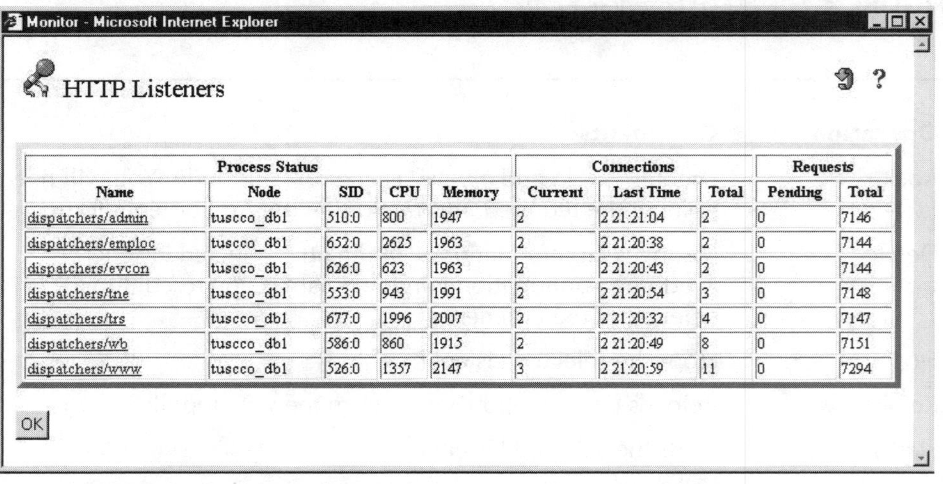

Process Status					Connections			Requests	
Name	Node	SID	CPU	Memory	Current	Last Time	Total	Pending	Total
dispatchers/admin	tuscco_db1	510:0	800	1947	2	2 21:21:04	2	0	7146
dispatchers/emploc	tuscco_db1	652:0	2625	1963	2	2 21:20:38	2	0	7144
dispatchers/evcon	tuscco_db1	626:0	623	1963	2	2 21:20:43	2	0	7144
dispatchers/tne	tuscco_db1	553:0	943	1991	2	2 21:20:54	3	0	7148
dispatchers/trs	tuscco_db1	677:0	1996	2007	2	2 21:20:32	4	0	7147
dispatchers/wb	tuscco_db1	586:0	860	1915	2	2 21:20:49	8	0	7151
dispatchers/www	tuscco_db1	526:0	1357	2147	3	2 21:20:59	11	0	7294

FIGURE 4-8. *HTTP Listeners Monitoring form*

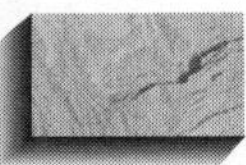

TIP
All monitoring statistics are a rough indication of the state of the server. They are not precise. For example, the "total number of requests completed" includes other internal calls of the OAS.

The following table describes the entries that display process status information:

Column	Description
Name	The name of the process
Node	The name of the machine
SID	The process ID and (after the colon) the instance ID
CPU	The amount of time used by the process in 1/100th of a second
Memory	The process heap memory used in kilobytes (KB)

The following table describes the entries that display connection information:

Column	Description
Current	The number of current in-bound connections to the process.
Last Time	The time of the last in-bound connection to the process in the format [[days]hour:minutes:seconds]. This interval is measured since the process started.
Total	The total number of in-bound connections so far.

The following table describes the entries that display request information:

Column	Description
Pending	The number of pending requests
Total	The total number of requests completed

Adding a New Listener

By clicking on the Add icon, shown to the left, the Add Listener Node Selection form, shown in Figure 4-9, will enable you to select a node in which you want to create a new Web Listener.

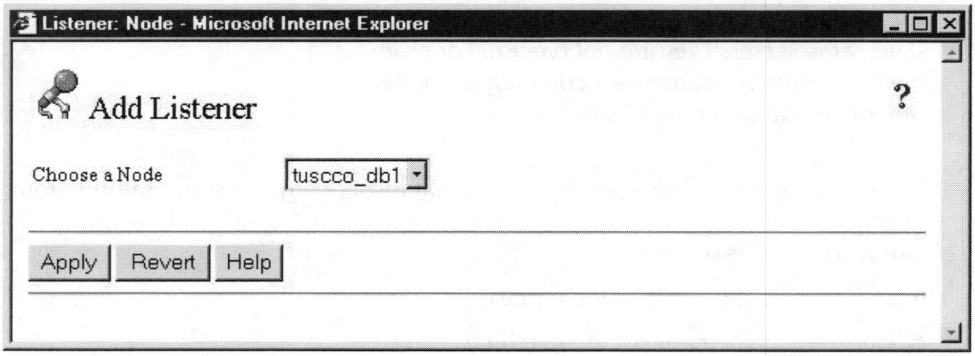

Listener: Node - Microsoft Internet Explorer

Add Listener

Choose a Node: tuscco_db1

Apply | Revert | Help

FIGURE 4-9. *Add Listener Node Selection form*

After selecting the node and pressing the Apply button, the Add Listener form, shown in Figure 4-10, appears, enabling you to create the new Listener.

You can reload OAS from the command line or through the browser. To reload OAS at the command line, type the following syntax:

```
owsctl reload
```

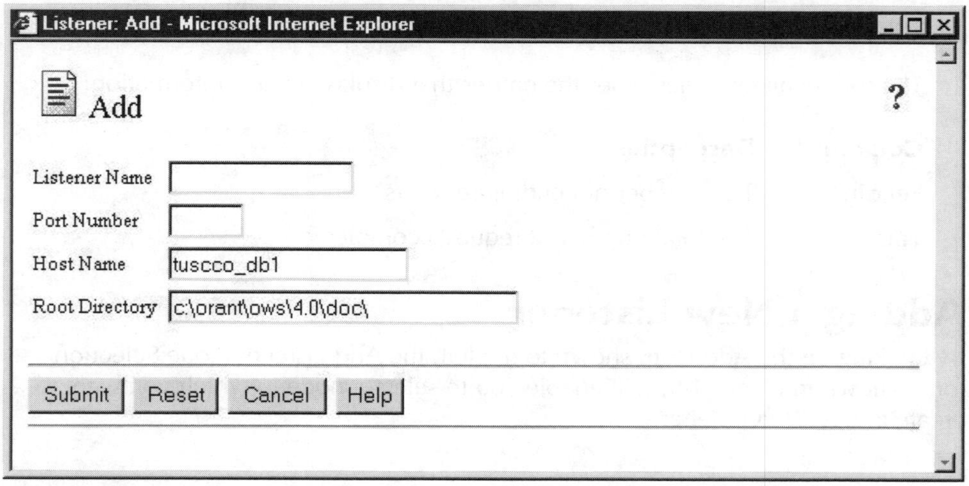

Listener: Add - Microsoft Internet Explorer

Add

Listener Name

Port Number

Host Name: tuscco_db1

Root Directory: c:\orant\ows\4.0\doc\

Submit | Reset | Cancel | Help

FIGURE 4-10. *Add Listener form*

To reload OAS from your browser, in the OAS Manager, select the node and click on the Reload icon.

After adding or deleting a Listener, you must refresh the navigational tree by holding the SHIFT key and clicking Reload in your browser's toolbar to view your changes.

For configuration changes to take effect, reload the Listeners:

1. At the OAS level, select All and click the Reload button.
2. At the HTTP Listeners level, select each listener and click the Reload button.

Table 4-10 explains the Listener fields.

Field	Description
Listener Name	An alphanumeric string of your choice, no longer than six characters, that uniquely identifies the Web Listener.
Port Number	A TCP/IP port on which the Web Listener can accept connections. You can choose any number from 1 to 65535 except for those port numbers already assigned to other programs. To access ports 1 through 1023, the Web Listener process must execute with root privileges.
Host Name	The name the Web Listener will use to identify itself. You should use your OAS machine's primary host name, such as tuscco_db1.tusc.com, or an alias, such as www.rentcondo.com, by which you can identify your Web Listener on the Internet. Refer to your operating system documentation to learn how to create a host name alias. When you connect to this Listener, you must specify the host name exactly as you enter it here. For example, if you specify your host name as tuscco_db1.tusc.com listening on port 8080, you must type **http://tuscco_db1.tusc.com:8080** to access it. Unless you specifically define aliases in the Network Parameters form, you will not be able to access it using a variation of this URL. For example, http://tuscco_fs1:8080 will return an error. If you wish to specify aliases for a host name, go to the Network Parameters form for the desired Listener. You must add all aliases to this form to use aliases to access this Listener.

TABLE 4-10. *Listener Fields*

Root Directory	The file-system directory that serves as the physical root of the Web Listener's virtual file system. Make sure to use a / at the end of the directory. This is the directory in the local file system to which the URL http://hostname/ will refer. Make sure to use a / at the end—for example, /private/tusc/oas/condo/.
User ID	The user identity that the Web Listener assumes after it completes its configuration. You can specify either a username or numeric user ID in this field. To denote the root ID, you must specify "root" rather than "0". The User and Group ID fields specify the privileges the Web Listener assumes while running. When the Web Listener process starts up, it runs with root privileges until it completes its configuration. Then, the Web Listener assumes the user and group identities specified in the User ID and Group ID parameters. The User ID and Group ID fields must give the Web Listener the following access permissions to certain files and the directories in which they reside: Read access to the configuration file Read access to all files that provide content for servicing requests Read access to all image map files Execute access to all OAS binaries and program files that the Web Listener must execute Write access to the log and error files Read access to user directories. However, for security reasons, you should beware of enabling a Web Listener with privileged user ID, such as root or oracle, or group ID, such as DBA to launch programs, because these programs inherit the Web Listener's privileges. You can also assign your Web Listeners an unprivileged user identity, such as nobody.
Group ID	The group identity that the Web Listener assumes after it completes its configuration. You can specify either a group name or a numeric group ID in this field.

TABLE 4-10. *Listener Fields* (continued)

Configuring a Listener

After adding a Listener, you can configure several parameters. These parameters enable you to control how the Listener uses the network, define a virtual file system by mapping specific virtual pathnames used in URLs to the file system pathnames of local directories, and configure various defaults for the Listener.

Configuring Network Parameters

The Listener Network form, shown in Figure 4-11, enables you to specify the network identity of the host on which the Web Listener runs, and controls how the Web Listener uses the network.

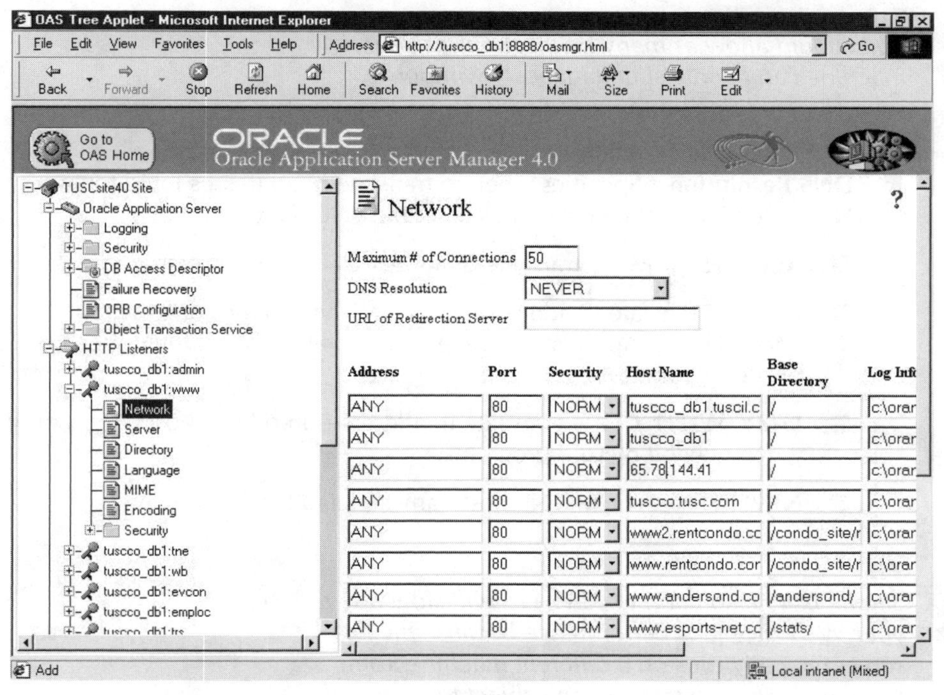

FIGURE 4-11. *Listener Network form*

For configuration changes to take effect, after clicking Apply in the form, click the Reload button at both the OAS level and the HTTP Listener level. Refreshing the navigational tree will not reload the server processes.

In addition, HTTP Listeners must be restarted from the HTTP Listener level by selecting each listener and clicking the Reload button.

The Listener Network form's fields are discussed next:

- **Maximum # of Connections** The maximum number of Web Listener connections that may be active at one time. The default is 600 on Windows NT and 500 on Solaris. The maximum value for this parameter is 700 for both Windows NT and Solaris.

TIP
You should allow as many connections as your machine can handle simultaneously without severely impairing performance.

- **DNS Resolution** Specifies when to translate IP addresses into Domain Name Service (DNS) host names. Possible values are as follows:
  - **ALWAYS** Always translate IP addresses into DNS hostnames.
  - **LAZY** Translate IP addresses into DNS host names only when needed by an Application Development Interface (ADI) application or security module.
  - **LAZY_WITH_CGI** Translate IP addresses into DNS host names only when needed by CGI programs.
  - **NEVER** Never use DNS host names (default).

TIP
Setting DNS resolution to ALWAYS will slow down your Web Listener's performance because the DNS server typically runs on a different machine from OAS, making each transaction subject to a time-consuming DNS query. On the other hand, if you use domain-based restriction for access control, do not set DNS resolution to NEVER. Rather, setting DNS Resolution to LAZY_WITH_CGI is often a good compromise.

- **URL of Redirection Server** The URL of a Web Listener process to which requests can be redirected when the selected Listener's maximum number of connections has been reached. The URL must be of the form: http://*HostName*:*PortNumber*. The redirection server must have all the capabilities of the selected Web Listener to fulfill the same requests.

TIP
If you are consistently receiving the maximum number of connections on a certain Web Listener process, create another Listener by copying the original Listener configuration and use the new Listener as a redirection server for the original.

- **Listener PID file** This parameter is valid only for UNIX. Specifies a file that contains the Process ID PID of the Web Listener process.

TIP
You must use the HTTP Listeners form to stop a Web Listener before changing its Listener PID file. If you do not stop the Listener, the HTTP Listeners form loses track of the Web Listener process. Each Web Listener process is capable of accepting connections on multiple TCP/IP ports. Each entry in this section specifies the network identity the Web Listener assumes for connections on a particular port.

- **Address** The IP address associated with the specified port. On machines with more than one IP address, you may assign a different IP address to each port. A value of zero or ANY indicates the Web Listener accepts the connections from the specified port on any of the machine's available addresses.
- **Port** A TCP/IP port on which the Web Listener can accept connections. You can choose any number from 1 to 65535.

TIP
To use ports 1 through 1023, you must give the Web Listener process root privileges. (Refer to the user and group parameters sections below.)

- **Security** Specifies the security module to handle incoming requests through the address and port combination. Possible values are as follows:
  - **NORM** Does not support Secure Sockets Layer (SSL) on a port.
  - **SSL** Adds support for SSL.
- **Host Name** The name by which the server identifies itself on this address/port combination. You can use your machine's primary host name or an alias, such as www.rentcondo.com, by which you want to identify your Web Listener on the Internet. Refer to your operating system documentation to learn how to define a host name alias. This must be a valid name recognized by DNS. You can specify more than one host name (domain) per port. You can enter more than one host name for a Listener instance, thus enabling the Listener to respond to requests using more than one host name. Add an additional entry to the Network section for the Listener instance to indicate that the Listener should also respond to requests for, say, www.rentcondo.com and rentcondo.com.
- **Base Directory** The directory name to which URL-encoded pathnames addressed to this port are to be appended. For example, if the base directory is /condo_site, the URL http://www.rentcondo.com/file is converted to http://www.rentcondo.com/condo_site/file.
- **Log Info Directory** The log information directory containing log information files that the Listener uses to write informative messages for this port.
- **Authentication** Determines if OAS authenticates a client over an SSL port. Possible values are as follows:
  - **NONE** Does not authenticate the client.
  - **OPT** Authenticates the client, but does not require a certificate.
  - **REQ** Authenticates the client and aborts the SSL handshake if the client does not send a certificate. This parameter is used for clients implementing SSL 3.0 only. OAS never authenticates clients implementing SSL 2.0.
- **Certificate Label** The label pointing to certificate files in the Security field. You can only have one certificate label per port. If you selected NORM under Security, leave this field blank.

MULTIPLE ADDRESSES AND PORTS OAS supports communication through multiple address/port combinations, such as multiports. It simultaneously

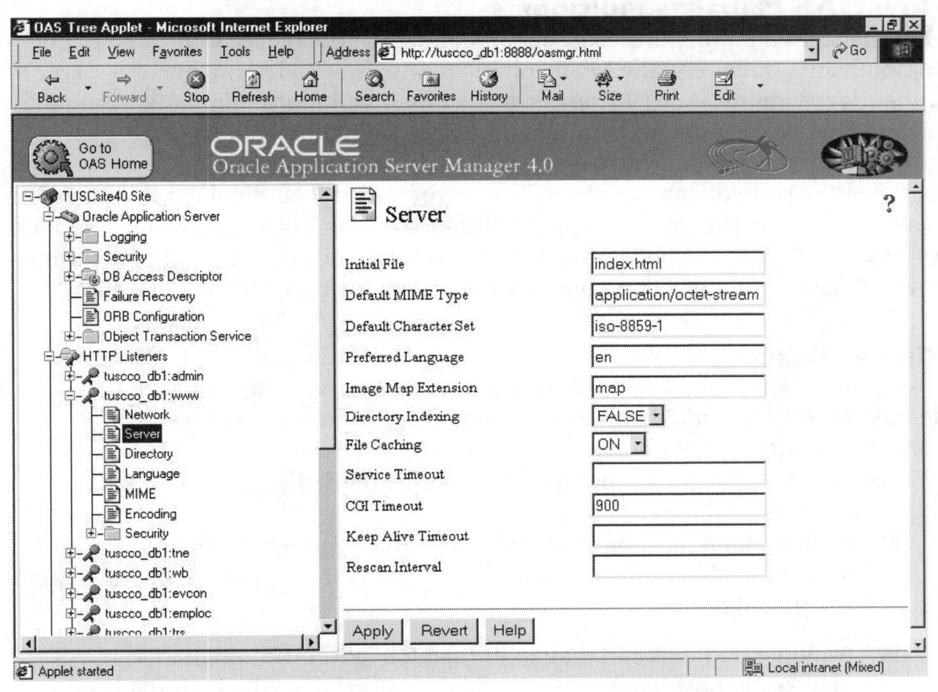

FIGURE 4-12. *Listener Server form*

listens on each address/port combination and tracks every request according to the combination through which it arrived.

The advantage of multiports is that OAS can present itself as multiple servers, each providing different services or configurations. The server can treat requests differently depending upon which address/port combination the request arrives in terms of the following:

- Security applied to the request
- The file system that provides information for the request
- The log information collected about the request

DUPLICATE PORT NUMBERS AND IP ADDRESSES You can specify more than one IP address per port and more than one port per IP address. You cannot specify the same IP address and port number combination more than once.

How OAS Manages Multiports

OAS manages all multiports as a suite; therefore, an operation applicable to one combination applies equally to all combinations. For example, when the server suspends communication, it stops listening on all multiports. Similarly, when the server commences listening, it starts listening on all combinations.

In addition, OAS considers an error that occurs with any multiport as an error for the entire suite of combinations. The server reacts accordingly in this case. For example, the server considers failing to listen on a particular combination a failure to listen on all combinations. In this case, the server does not start until it reads a new configuration file with a correct set of multiports on which it can listen.

Virtual Hosts

OAS can present itself as multiple domains or virtual hosts on one port. Each domain must be specified in the Host Name field. When a client requests a nonspecified domain, the server returns an error message.

Consider the following when you are configuring virtual hosts:

- Each domain must be specified in the Host Name field; therefore, if you want to enable users to enter a partial domain, you must explicitly define the partial domain.
- Multiple domains can map to the same IP address through DNS. OAS checks the host request-header field to determine which virtual host or domain name is requested.
- Each domain can supply content from its own base directory.

Configuring Server Parameters

The Listener Server form, illustrated in Figure 4-12, enables you to configure various defaults for the Web Listener, such as default character set and time-outs.

The fields in the Listener Server form are as follows:

- **Configuration Directory** The directory where you want the Web Listener configuration file to reside. The name of the file is **sv***ListenerName*.cfg. If you choose a different directory than the default value provided, make sure the permissions on the directory enable the Web Listener to read the file.
- **Initial File** The default file to retrieve from a directory when a URL specifies only the directory. The default filename is index.html. For example, if you set this field to index.html, the requested URL http://www.rentcondo.com/ will translate to http://www.rentcondo.com/index.html.

- **User Directory** This parameter is valid only for UNIX and is the default subdirectory to search in a user's home directory if a URL specifies only the user's home directory. For example, if the user directory is condo_site and a browser requests http://www.rentcondo.com/~8125, the URL is converted to http://www.rentcondo.com/~8125/condo_site/. There is no default. There are several restrictions imposed on user directories:
    - For security, no CGI scripts may be executed from a user directory.
    - The Web Listener performs no filename negotiation within user directories; the URL must specify the requested filename exactly.
    - If several browsers access the same file within a user directory at the same time, they do not share a common memory-mapped copy of the file, which makes accessing user directories less efficient than access to other directories.
- **Default MIME Type** Specifies a Multipurpose Internet Mail Extension (MIME) type to use in interpreting requested files of an unsupported MIME type. The default is application/octet-stream, which means that by default the Web Listener treats any requested file of unidentified MIME type as a binary file. You can review the RFCs that define MIME at http://www.oac.uci.edu/indiv/ehood/MIME/MIME.html.
- **Default Character Set** The character set to use in interpreting a file that uses an unrecognized character set. You must use a character set name defined by RFC 1521. The default is ISO-8859-1: the character set used for English.
- **Preferred Language** The language to choose when handling a request for a file available in more than one language, if the request does not specify a language. You must use a language identifier defined by RFC 1766. The default is "en" (English).
- **Image Map Extension** Filename extensions that the Web Listener should use to identify image map files. There is no default; therefore, if you want this Web Listener to support image maps, you must set this field to the filename extension, such as map. This extension indicates the files that will be used for your image maps.
- **Directory Indexing** Specifies whether the Web Listener should provide a directory listing when a URL resolves to a directory that does not contain a file named by InitialFile. If you enter False, such a URL will produce an error. Directory listings can sometimes help requestors correct spelling

errors in their request URLs. The default is True. If Directory Indexing is set to True, the listing will always be set to local time.

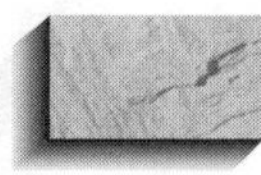

TIP
For security or privacy, and without exposing the directory contents to clients, in this case, set this field to False.

- **File Caching** This parameter is valid only for Windows NT. It determines whether the Web Listener is going to cache a file. Possible values are as follows:
  - **ON** Use file caching. The cached files may not be editable from all editors. This is the default.
  - **OFF** Do not use caching.

TIP
If you want to edit files while they are being serviced by OAS, you need to set this value to OFF.

- **Service Time-out** This parameter is valid only for Windows NT. It specifies the number of seconds the control panel service waits for a start, stop, or continue operation to finish before reporting a failure.
- **CGI Time-out** Specifies the number of seconds to wait before a CGI program times out.
- **Keep Alive Time-out** Specifies the number of seconds the Oracle Web Listener keeps a connection open without any activity on that connection. If you leave this field empty, the default value is 10 seconds.
- **Rescan Interval** Specifies the minimum amount of time (measured in seconds) between directory rescans. When a directory is accessed, the server determines when the directory was last scanned. If the directory has not been scanned within a number of seconds specified in this field, the server determines if the directory has been modified since the last scan. If it has been updated, the server rescans the directory. By default, the rescan interval is set to 0, which means that a directory is checked for changes each time it is accessed. By increasing the value of this parameter, you can reduce the frequency at which directories are checked for changes. Changing this value can slightly improve the performance of OAS.

Configuring User/Group Parameters

The User/Group form enables you to specify the user and group identities the Web Listener assumes when it runs. This form is applicable only for the UNIX version of OAS.

When the Web Listener process starts up, it runs with root privileges until it completes its configuration. Then, the Web Listener assumes the user and group identities specified in the User ID and Group ID parameters.

The User ID and Group ID parameters you use must give the Web Listener the following access permissions to certain files and the directories in which they reside:

- Read access to the configuration file
- Read access to all files that provide content for servicing requests
- Read access to all image map files
- Execute access to all OAS binaries and program files that the Web Listener must execute
- Write access to the log and error files
- Read access to user directories

For security, care should be taken when enabling a Web Listener with a privileged user ID, such as root or oracle, or a group ID, such as dba, to launch programs, because these programs inherit the Web Listener's privileges. You might consider assigning your Web Listeners an unprivileged user identity, such as nobody.

The following table describes the fields in the User/Group form:

Field	Description
User ID	Specifies the user identity that the Web Listener assumes after it completes its configuration. You can specify either a username or numeric user ID in this field. To denote the root ID you must specify root rather than 0.
Group ID	Specifies the group identity that the Web Listener assumes after it completes its configuration. You can specify either a group name or a numeric group ID in this field.

Configuring Directory Mappings

The Listener Directory form, illustrated in Figure 4-13, enables you to define a virtual file system by mapping specific virtual pathnames used in URLs to the file system pathnames of local directories.

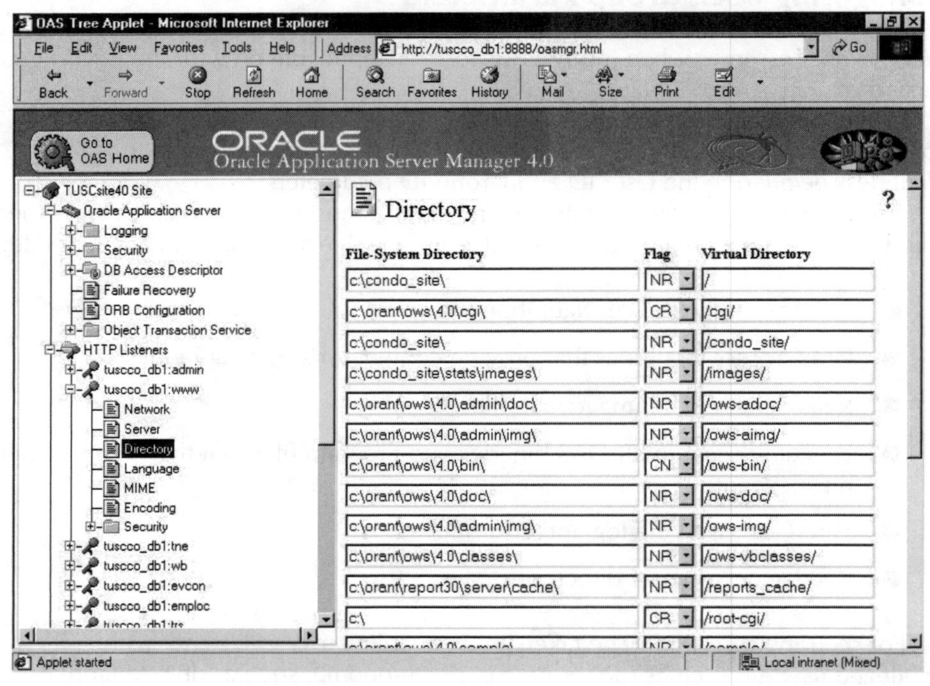

FIGURE 4-13. *Listener Directory form*

When the Web Listener starts up, it checks to make sure it has access to the file system directories specified in this section, but it does not verify that individual files in the directories exist or can be accessed. If a subsequent request refers to a file that the Web Listener cannot access, the Listener returns a "404: Not found" error.

Descriptions of the fields for each directory entry are as follows:

- **File System Directory** Specifies the pathname of a directory in the local file system. Make sure to include a trailing slash (UNIX) or a backslash (NT)—for example, /condo_site/html/.
- **Flag** The first code in this field specifies whether CGI programs may run from the specified virtual directory. Possible values are as follows:
  - **N (Normal)** Does not allow CGI programs to run from this directory
  - **C (CGI)** Enables CGI programs to run from this directory

- **W (WinCGI)** (Windows NT only) Enables WinCGI programs to run from this directory

The second code specifies whether subdirectories of the specified file system directory should be mapped recursively—that is, whether the directory tree rooted at the specified file system directory should be accessible through the specified virtual directory. Possible values are as follows:

- **N (Nonrecursive)** Do not map subdirectories recursively.
- **R (Recursive)** Map subdirectories recursively. If you do not want to make the subdirectories of the mapped file-system directory accessible to clients, set the directory mapping to nonrecursive.

- **Virtual Directory** Specifies the virtual directory through which the file system directory will be accessed. The first entry in the Directory Mappings section must specify the virtual root directory (/). Make sure to include a trailing slash (for all operating systems)—for example, /condo_site/.

Accessing Network Mapped Directories

On Windows NT, to access a file on a network system, you must map your Listener to the network path, as follows:

1. Select Services from the Control Panel and choose the Listener that you want to access the network paths.
2. Click Startup.
3. In the Service dialog box, enter the user account and password in the Log On As section. The password will not be validated until the service has been started.

   By default, the HTTP Listener uses the System Account. This account does not have access to files in network mapped directories.
4. Click OK.
5. Close the Services window.

To grant the new user the right to log on as a service, follow these steps:

1. Go to Start | Programs | Administrative Tool (Common) | User Manager. The User Manager window appears.
2. Select User Rights from the Policies pull-down menu.

3. Check the Show Advanced User Rights box.
4. From the pull-down menu, select Log On As a service. If the user is not listed in the Grant To box, click Add to add the user.
5. Select the user from the Grant To box and click OK.

Configuring Language Extensions

The Listener Language form, illustrated in Figure 4-14, maps various abbreviations identifying human languages to appropriate character sets and filename extensions.

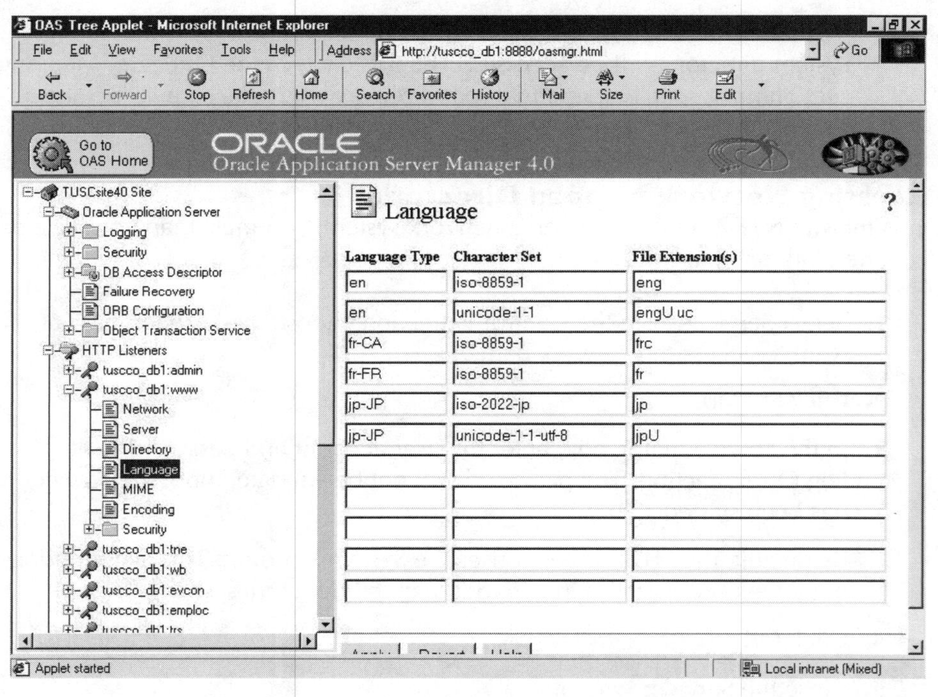

FIGURE 4-14. *Listener Language form*

Because character set specifications apply only to text files, language extensions for nontext files are ignored. For example, the files image.en.jpg and image.uc.jpg would be considered equivalent.

The following table describes each entry in this form, which has the following fields:

Field	Description
Language Type	A language identifier, such as en, as defined by RFC 1766.
Character Set	The name of the character set used for the specified language, such as ISO-8859-1, as defined by RFC 1521.
File Extension(s)	Extensions used to identify files encoded for the specified language, such as en. Filename extensions are case sensitive; if you specify more than one extension, you must separate them with spaces or commas.

Configuring MIME Types

The Listener MIME form, illustrated in Figure 4-15, enables you to map Multipurpose Internet Mail Extension (MIME) types to filename extensions representing each type that the Web Listener recognizes.

The following table describes each entry in this form, which has the following fields:

Field	Description
MIME Type	A MIME type, such as text/html, as defined by RFCs 1521 and 1522.
File Extension(s)	Extensions, such as htm or html, used to identify files of the specified MIME type. File extensions are case sensitive; if you specify more than one extension, you must separate them by spaces or commas.

Configuring Encoding Extensions

The Listener Encoding form, illustrated in Figure 4-16, enables you to specify the processing performed on a file, such as compression.

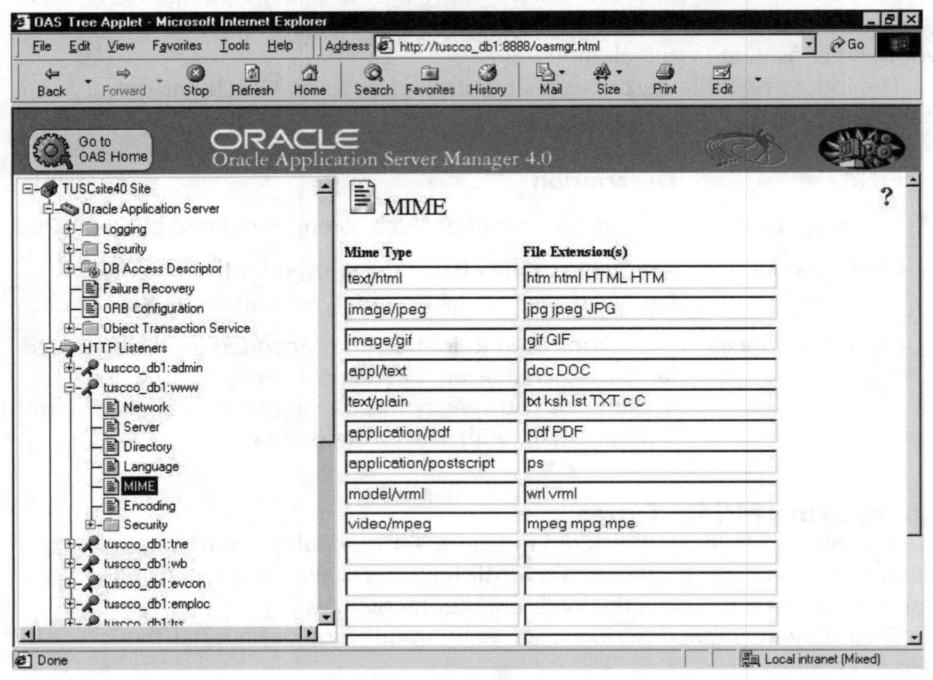

FIGURE 4-15. *Listener MIME form*

The following table describes each entry in this form, which has the following fields:

Field	Description
Encoding	The name of a helper application, such as compress or gzip, used to encode files
File Extension(s)	Extensions, such as Z or gz, used to identify files encoded by the specified helper application

Tuning Listeners

Because Listeners can consume a considerable amount of your system's CPU, it is important to tune all of your Listeners. To distribute the request load on a site, if possible, create multiple Listeners on the site, each listening on a different TCP

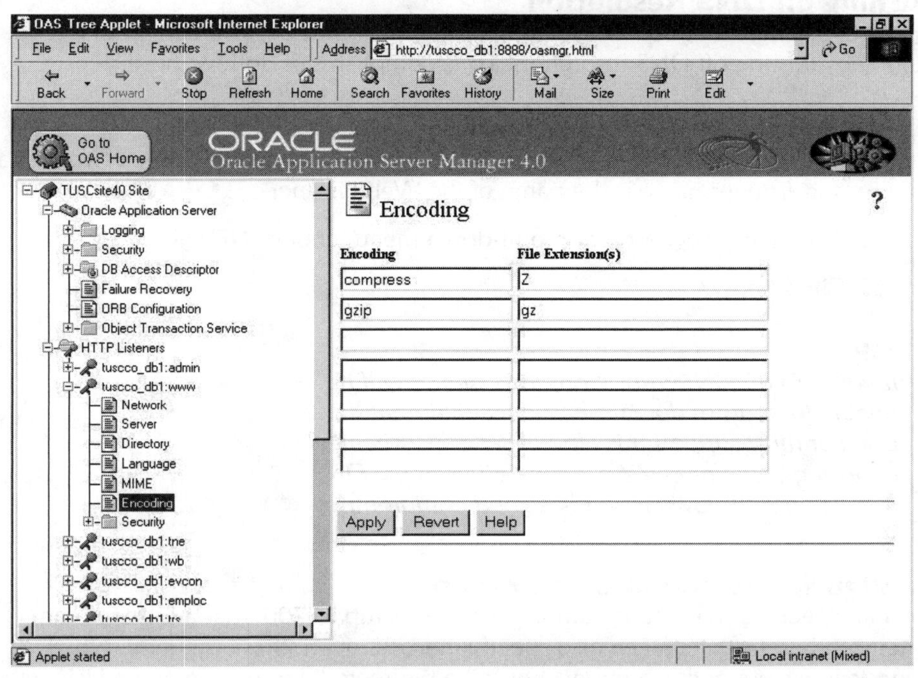

FIGURE 4-16. *Listener Encoding form*

port. On multiprocessor machines, this increases throughput by enabling more concurrent connections.

TIP
Ports 80 and 8080 are the only standard ports available. Using a port other than a standard port for an Internet application could create proxy server issues for your remote application users.

Avoid storing a large number of files in a directory served by a Listener. The more files stored in a directory, the longer it takes to search the directory for a requested file. Because your virtual root directory is usually hit the most, keep it clean. To store a large number of files, distribute the files among several directories, minimizing the number of files in the directory.

Turning off DNS Resolution

For Web Listeners that do not use domain-based restriction, you can reduce request latency by turning off DNS resolution. To accomplish this, follow these steps:

1. Using the OAS Manager, navigate to the form *site-name*/Http Listeners/*listener-name*/Network, where *site-name* is the name of your site and *listener-name* is the name of the Web Listener.
2. From the DNS Resolution pull-down menu, choose NEVER.
3. Click Apply.

TIP
If you turn off DNS resolution, the Listener will be unable to perform domain-based restriction. If the Listener must support this kind of security scheme, choosing LAZY or LAZY_WITH_CGI from the DNS resolution pull-down menu is a good compromise.

Configuring Automatic Redirection

You can specify a maximum number of requests (up to 700) that a Listener can concurrently satisfy. You can also specify the URL of another Listener to which any requests in excess of this number should be redirected. For example, if a Listener's maximum number of requests is set to 100, the 101st request is sent back to the browser with a redirection status and the URL of the second Listener. The browser interprets this status and sends a request to the second Listener. This operation is transparent to the user of the browser.

To calculate an optimum maximum number of concurrent requests for a Listener, first estimate the peak number of concurrent requests you expect to receive on the Listener. Then try setting the maximum number of concurrent requests between 50 percent and 85 percent of this peak estimate. You can set this parameter as follows:

1. Using the OAS Manager, navigate to the form *site-name*/Http Listeners/*listener-name*/Network, where *site-name* is the name of your site, and *listener-name* is the name of the Listener.
2. In the Maximum # of Connections text field, enter the number you calculated based on your peak estimate.
3. In the URL of Redirection Server text field, enter the URL of the Listener you want to handle redirected requests from this Listener.
4. Click Apply.

Minimizing Directory Rescans

By default, an OAS Listener rescans a directory looking for new, changed, and deleted files every time the directory is accessed. Because most directories do not change frequently, it is usually acceptable to rescan directories only once per hour, eliminating the per-access rescan overhead. Setting the directory rescan parameter can be accomplished as follows:

1. Using the OAS Manager, navigate to the form *site-name*/Http Listeners/*listener-name*/Server, where *site-name* is the name of your site, and *listener-name* is the name of an Oracle Web Listener.
2. In the Rescan Interval text field, enter 3600 for the number of seconds (one hour).
3. Click Apply.

Configuring Applications and Cartridges

Configuration values for cartridges depend on the cartridge and the language your application uses. Some values are always required, such as the virtual path and name for the cartridge. Users of your site will enter a cartridge's virtual path to access the cartridge. Most likely, the users will not actually type the virtual path, but will click their way through hyperlinks to get to the virtual path.

An application also contains configuration values that apply to all its cartridges. This enables you to manage cartridges in an application by adjusting values for the application that contains the cartridges. Examples of values that can be applied to all cartridges within an application include the names of machines running the applications, logging information, transaction information, and session information.

You can write Common Gateway Interface (CGI) applications handled by the Listener component of OAS. However, when you are creating new applications, CGI applications are not recommended because they do not take advantage of the load-balancing and scalability features of OAS. In addition, cartridge-based applications tend to run faster than CGI applications because they are persistent (remain in memory and cycling to answer your user's requests immediately). CGI applications run through the Listener, and do not use the OAS Web Request Broker. Any Listener can execute CGI programs. Because it is actually the Listener that runs CGI applications, OAS does not actually execute CGI requests at all.

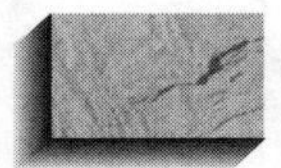

TIP
Because an Application Server, such as OAS, is not required to service CGI requests, put your CGI applications on another Web server to distribute processing loads.

Applications and Cartridge Servers

Each application (and the cartridges contained within the application) runs within a Cartridge Server process, and each Cartridge Server process can run only one application. You can equate applications with Cartridge Servers.

When an application runs, the Cartridge Server process creates instances of its cartridges. The cartridge instances handle client requests. Within a Cartridge Server process, the cartridge factory object instantiates cartridges in the process.

When configuring and tuning OAS, you can specify the minimum and maximum number of cartridge instances running within a Cartridge Server. You can also specify how many Cartridge Servers each application can run. You can adjust these numbers to improve performance. If you run OAS over multiple nodes, the number of Cartridge Servers applies to the entire site. Each node will run the same number of Cartridge Servers for the application, but you can distribute the load among your servers.

Figure 4-17 illustrates an application, the RentCondo application based on the PL/SQL cartridge. One instance of the Condo cartridge is running, and the cartridge's configuration values enable the cartridge to execute the appropriate procedures for the Condo application. Further information about Cartridge Servers will be provided shortly.

Application and Cartridge Life Cycle

When the Resource Manager (RM) component of the Application Server starts up, it starts up the minimum number of Cartridge Servers automatically for each application. Each Cartridge Server process then starts up the minimum number of cartridge instances for each cartridge.

If you set the minimum number of servers to 0, no Cartridge Servers are started until the Application Server receives a request from a client. When it receives the request, it starts up a Cartridge Server and the minimum number of cartridge instances.

If you set the minimum number of cartridge instances to 0, the Cartridge Server does not start up any cartridge instances until it receives a request.

After starting up the minimum number of cartridge instances, the Cartridge Server starts up additional cartridge instances when more requests than cartridge

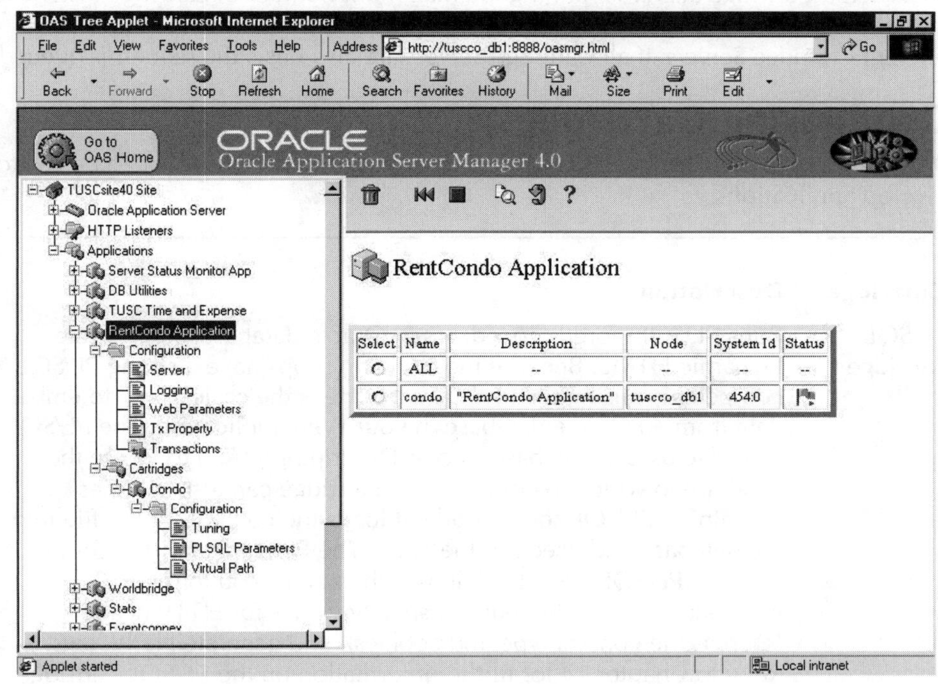

FIGURE 4-17. *Configuration values for RentCondo application*

instances are available. A Cartridge Server process can start up additional cartridge instances until it reaches the specified maximum number.

The RM terminates cartridge instances not in use. It terminates cartridge instances in Cartridge Servers until only the specified minimum number remains. For example, if you set a cartridge to have a minimum of three and a maximum of ten instances, the Cartridge Server starts up three cartridge instances. As requests come in, it starts up more cartridges—up to ten cartridge instances. When the number of requests decreases, the RM terminates the idle cartridge instances. It does not terminate all the cartridge instances, however; it stops terminating cartridge instances when the minimum number of cartridge instances are left.

The Cartridge Server process itself is terminated by the Application Server when it does not contain any cartridge instances. Similar to how the Cartridge Server terminates cartridge instances, the Application Server stops terminating Cartridge Servers when the minimum number of Cartridge Servers is left.

When a Cartridge Server is running the maximum number of cartridge instances, and all the instances are servicing requests, the RM routes additional requests to different Cartridge Servers. If all Cartridge Servers are also busy, the request is queued.

Configuring Cartridges

OAS comes with the cartridges shown in Table 4-11. These cartridges can be use to develop applications.

Cartridge	Description
PL/SQL cartridge	Runs PL/SQL stored procedures in Oracle databases to generate Dynamic HTML. Because most Oracle shops have a strong PL/SQL competency, using the PL/SQL cartridge is the easiest way to embed data from an Oracle database in your Web application. The PL/SQL cartridge uses a Database Access Descriptor (DAD) to locate the database to which to connect. The cartridge can also run files containing PL/SQL source code; it loads the contents of the file into the database and executes the code. The PL/SQL cartridge comes with the PL/SQL Web Toolkit, which enables you to retrieve information about the request, specify values for HTTP headers (such as the content type and cookies), and generate HTML tags. Refer to Chapter 14 for further information on the PL/SQL cartridge.
JWeb cartridge	Runs Java applications. The JWeb cartridge contains a Java Virtual Machine (VM) that interprets the bytecodes for the Java application. When you configure the cartridge, specify where the class files for the applications are located. You can also use the JWeb cartridge to connect to and access data from databases in two different ways: 1. You can use the pl2java utility, which generates Java methods for procedures and functions in the database. Then, invoke the methods from your Java application similar to typical Java methods. 2. You can use the JDBC interface, enabling you to execute SQL statements. The JWeb cartridge comes with the JWeb Toolkit, which enables you to get information about the request, connect to the database, specify values for HTTP headers (such as the content type and cookies), and generate HTML tags. Refer to Chapter 19 for further information regarding the JWeb cartridge.

TABLE 4-11. *OAS Cartridges*

LiveHTML cartridge	Interprets server-side includes (SSI) documents. SSI is a standard that enables you to embed dynamic data in an otherwise static HTML document. You use special tags in your document to mark the places where the cartridge will substitute dynamic data. You can also embed Perl scripts in documents for the LiveHTML cartridge to generate dynamic data. This feature enables you to generate more complex dynamic data than what is supported by SSI. The LiveHTML cartridge supports Web Application Objects. This feature enables you to group pages into an application object and share data across requests or even between users. Refer to Chapter 21 for further information about the LiveHTML cartridge.
Perl cartridge	Runs Perl scripts. The Perl cartridge comes with modules, such as DBI, DBD::Oracle (which you can use to access Oracle databases), CGI, and Net. Refer to Chapter 20 for further information on the Perl cartridge.
C cartridge	Runs C applications. To use this cartridge, implement callback functions invoked by the Application Server. The C cartridge comes with the WRB API, which contains functions and data structures that you can use to retrieve information about the request, specify values for HTTP headers (such as the content type and cookies), and send requests to other cartridges.
JCORBA	Runs JCORBA objects, which are CORBA objects written in Java. Clients of JCORBA objects can be applets, stand-alone applications, or applications based on cartridges. Refer to Chapter 19 for further information about the JCorba cartridge.
Enterprise JavaBeans (EJB)	Runs EJB objects, which are Enterprise beans that meet the guidelines specified in the Enterprise JavaBeans 1.0 specification, as CORBA objects. Clients of EJB objects are the same as those for JCORBA objects. Refer to Chapter 19 for further information about the EJB cartridge.
ODBC cartridge	Accesses ODBC databases, such as Sybase or Informix.

TABLE 4-11. *OAS Cartridges* (continued)

Multiple Instances and Threads in Cartridges

Because the Cartridge Server is multithread (MT)-safe, it can run multiple threads for one or more cartridge instances, but only if these cartridge instances are MT-safe. When you configure your cartridges, specify the number of cartridge instances and the number of threads that a cartridge Server can execute.

Figure 4-18 illustrates the possible instance and thread configurations. Each quadrant shows a Cartridge Server. Only four configurations are possible:

- You will create configuration A when you have one thread and one cartridge instance in a Cartridge Server.
- You will create configuration B when you have one cartridge instance, but multiple threads in a Cartridge Server.
- You will create configuration C when you specify multiple cartridges and multiple threads in a Cartridge Server. In this case, the number of threads and the number of cartridge instances should be the same (for example, the minimum number of threads = minimum number of instances, and maximum number of threads = maximum number of instances).

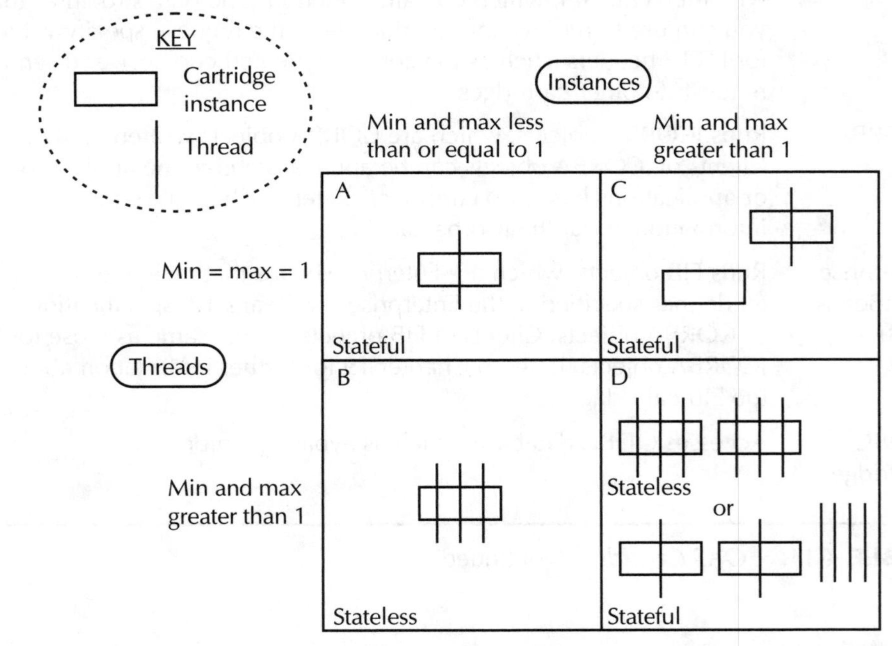

FIGURE 4-18. *Threads and instances in a Cartridge Server*

- You will create configuration D when you specify the maximum number of clients a Cartridge Server can service simultaneously.

STATEFUL AND STATELESS CARTRIDGES A stateful cartridge can run only one thread per cartridge instance. Stateful cartridges are not designed to work in a multithreaded environment because they contain unprotected structures or variables. Using stateful cartridges in an MT environment can lead to deadlock situations where two (or more) clients wait for resources locked by the other client. In Figure 4-18, configuration A, C, and the bottom half of configuration D show stateful cartridges. You can run any cartridge types in stateful mode.

A stateless cartridge can run multiple threads safely per cartridge instance. Consider this task: say you want one cartridge instance to handle more than one request simultaneously. Each thread handles one request. In Figure 4-18, configuration B and the top half of configuration D show stateless cartridges. Only the C cartridge, JCORBA, and EJB can be stateless. You have to run other cartridges in stateful mode because they are not stateless cartridges.

To configure a cartridge to be stateless, set the cartridge's min and max threads to be greater than 1. The cartridge's min and max instances can be equal to or greater than 1. If you set the min/max instances and threads to other combinations, the cartridge is stateful.

For C cartridges only, you can also designate a C cartridge as stateless in the CWeb Parameters form, illustrated in Figure 4-19. On this form, set the Stateless field to True to mark a C cartridge as stateless.

The field enables you to have stateless C cartridges with multiple instances and multiple threads. Each Cartridge Server runs multiple cartridge instances, and each instance runs one or more threads. Figure 4-20 shows a Cartridge Server with three instances and seven threads.

If you do not designate the cartridge as stateless, the cartridge cannot run multiple threads per instance. A stateful cartridge with the same configuration (three instances and seven threads) is not optimal because each cartridge instance can run only one thread at the same time. Because only three instances exist, you should have at most only three threads. As illustrated in Figure 4-21, stateful cartridges cannot use threads.

OAS uses the following algorithm to determine whether a cartridge is stateless or stateful:

- If the stateless flag is set to True, the cartridge is stateless; this flag should be used for C cartridges only.
- If no stateless flags exist, the Application Server looks at the number of cartridges and threads. If max thread is greater than 1 and max instance is equal to 1, then the cartridge is stateless.
- Otherwise, the cartridge is stateful.

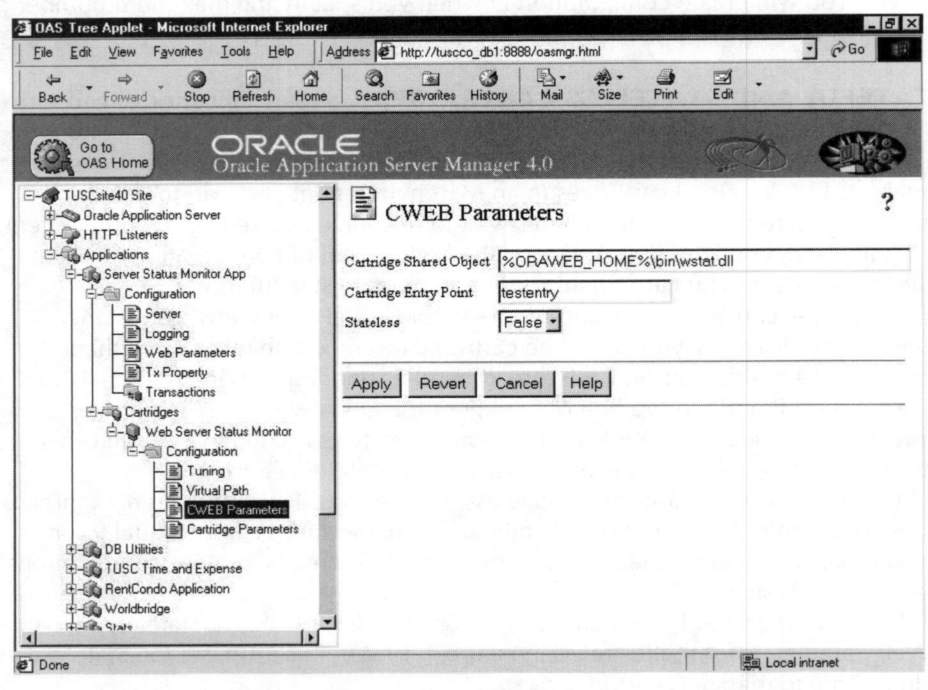

FIGURE 4-19. *CWeb Parameters form*

Stateless cartridges have a "MaxClients" parameter that specifies the maximum number of clients that a Cartridge Server can serve at any time. The max clients parameter does not apply to stateful cartridges.

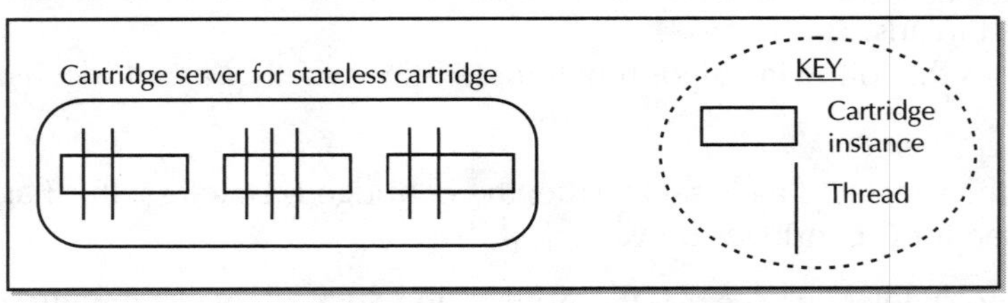

FIGURE 4-20. *Threads and instances in the stateless C cartridge*

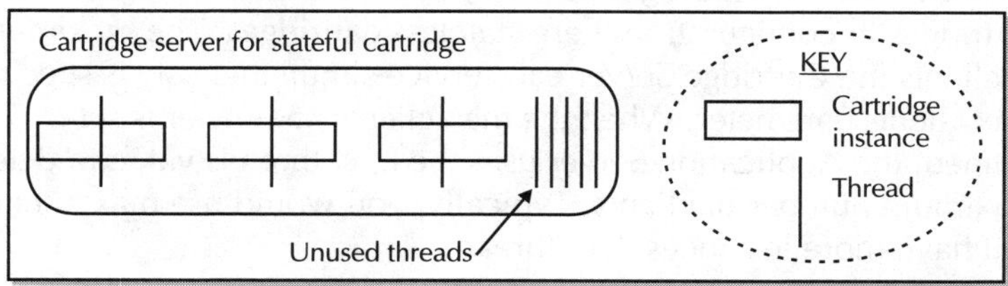

FIGURE 4-21. *Threads and instances in a stateful cartridge*

Table 4-12 shows which configurations are suitable for which cartridges.

NUMBER OF CLIENTS The maximum number of clients that a Cartridge Server can handle at any one time depends on how the cartridge is configured.

- For a cartridge defined like configuration A (refer to Figure 4-18 for the configurations), the corresponding Cartridge Server has only one instance and one thread. Thus, at any point in time it can service only one client.
- For a cartridge defined like configuration B, the corresponding Cartridge Server has one instance but multiple threads. This configuration can be

Cartridge type	Configuration
PL/SQL cartridge	Stateful
JWeb cartridge	Stateful
LiveHTML cartridge	Stateful
Perl cartridge	Stateful
C	Stateful or stateless (depends on whether the C cartridge is MT-safe)
JCORBA	Stateful or stateless (depends on whether the JCORBA object is MT-safe)
EJB	Stateful or stateless (depends on whether the EJB object is MT-safe)

TABLE 4-12. *Stateful or Stateless Cartridges*

used only with C cartridges or with JCORBA and EJB applications. All cartridges in configuration B are stateless cartridges. The maximum number of clients the Cartridge Server can service simultaneously is specified by the max clients parameter. When the max clients parameter is set to 0 or not defined, the Application Server uses the max threads value to determine the maximum number of clients. Typically, you would use max clients when you have more instances than threads.

- For a cartridge defined like configuration C, the corresponding Cartridge Server can have different numbers of instances but only one thread. Thus, at any point in time it can service only one client.
- For stateless cartridges in configuration D, the maximum number of clients a Cartridge Server can service simultaneously is specified by the max clients parameter. If the max clients parameter is set to 0 or not defined, the Application Server uses the max threads value to determine the maximum number of clients. Typically, you would use max clients (in a stateless cartridge) when you have more instances than threads. For example, if you have five instances but only three threads, you can set max clients to 5 so that the Cartridge Server can handle two more clients. (Otherwise, the Application Server would direct the clients' requests to other Cartridge Servers.) In the Cartridge Server, if all three threads are busy, the Cartridge Server places the two clients' requests in a queue until a thread is available.
- For stateful cartridges in configuration D, the maximum number of clients a Cartridge Server can service simultaneously is specified by the max threads value. For stateful cartridges, the recommended configuration is to have the number of threads equal to or less than the number of instances. You should not have more threads than instances because the extra threads are not used and consume the machine's CPU cycles. You should choose to have fewer threads than instances if you are running OAS on a machine with limited resources.
- For stateful cartridges in configuration D, the maximum number of clients a cartridge server can service simultaneously is directly related to the number of active cartridge instances. For stateful cartridges, the recommended configuration is to set the min and max number of threads to 1. OAS assigns, by default, at least 1 thread for each cartridge instance. If you have more threads than instances, OAS will consume unnecessary CPU cycles maintaining threads that do not belong to a cartridge instance.

Cartridge Performance – Load Balancing

OAS balances incoming requests among the following:

- **Nodes** For maximum scalability, OAS automatically distributes requests evenly among all nodes that comprise a site.
- **Cartridge Servers** For each cartridge type, OAS distributes requests among Cartridge Servers according to configurable site-wide minimum and maximum numbers of Cartridge Servers.
- **Cartridge instances** For each cartridge type, OAS assigns requests to cartridge instances according to configurable minimum and maximum numbers of instances per Cartridge Server.

In addition to the load-balancing features provided by the Standard edition, OAS Enterprise edition enables you to configure the load balancing among the following nodes using the OAS Manager:

- **Weighted node** Use the HostServerWeight parameter to specify the percentage of Cartridge Servers that should run on each node. For example, if node A is a large, fast machine, you might specify that it run 50 percent of Cartridge Servers. If nodes B and C are smaller, less powerful machines, you might assign each 25 percent of the Cartridge Server load.
- **Host maximum** Use the HostMaxServers parameter to limit the number of cartridge instances that you execute on a per-host basis. The limits on each host can be different.
- **Adding hosts at runtime** Use the HostMinServers parameter to monitor and adapt to changes in the Cartridge Server load, and to distribute the Cartridge Server load evenly across the nodes. This feature also enables you to add new nodes to a running system to handle additional load.
- **Adapting to system resource usage** OAS monitors system resources on each node, such as CPU, memory, and swap space usage, and adjusts the Cartridge Server load on each node accordingly.

Multi-Threaded Cartridge Servers

Unlike Oracle Web Application Server 3.x, in which a single Cartridge Server handles only one user request at a time, OAS 4.0 is multithreaded. In this architecture, multiple instances of the same cartridge can run simultaneously in the same process, which is called a Cartridge Server. To take advantage of multithreading, the cartridge code must be thread-safe; cartridges can be thread-safe in two ways:

- **Globally thread-safe** Global resources shared by cartridge instances are protected from corruption by out-of-sequence accesses using a programmatic locking mechanism.
- **Instance-context thread-safe** Cartridges are coded using multiple threads. Data shared by threads within an instance is protected from corruption by out-of-sequence accesses using a programmatic locking mechanism.

For more information on writing globally thread-safe and instance-context thread-safe applications, refer to Chapter 19. Figure 4-22 illustrates the threading policy for cartridges.

Depending on the thread safety of a cartridge, performance can be tuned by adjusting the minimum and maximum number of concurrent instances of the cartridge, as well as the minimum and maximum number of threads per server.

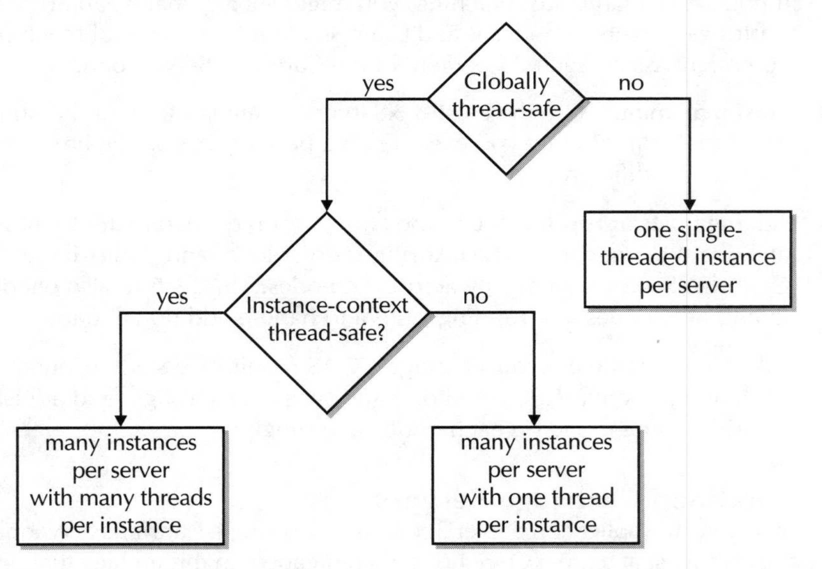

FIGURE 4-22. *Threading policy for cartridges*

Tuning and Managing Cartridges

The instructions in this section apply only to globally thread-safe cartridges and instance-context thread-safe cartridges.

Tuning Cartridge Servers

Increasing the minimum and maximum number of cartridge instances per Cartridge Server and the minimum and maximum number of threads per instance from one to ten (for all values) results in about a 10 percent performance improvement.

To avoid consuming unnecessary memory, Oracle recommends setting the minimum parameter to 1 and the maximum parameter to 10, as follows:

1. Using the OAS Manager, navigate to the form *site-name*/Applications/ *app-name*/Cartridges/*cart-name*/Configuration/Tuning, where *site-name* is the name of your site, *app-name* is the Cartridge Server you want to tune, and *cart-name* is the name of a cartridge in the application.
2. In the Minimum # of Instances text field, enter 1.
3. In the Maximum # of Instances text field, enter 10.
4. In the Minimum # of Threads text field, enter 1.
5. In the Maximum # of Threads text field, enter 10.
6. Click Apply.
7. Select the application in the navigational tree and click Reload.

Scaling Cartridge Server Load

Use the following formulas to calculate optimum values for the global minimum and maximum numbers of Cartridge Servers of a particular type:

- *min-servers = avg-connections/min-instances*
- *max-servers = peak-connections/max-instances*

where *avg-connections* is the estimated average number of concurrent connections that your site must support, *peak-connections* is the estimated peak number of concurrent connections, *min-instances* is the value you entered in the Minimum # of Instances text field, and *max-instances* is the value you entered in the Maximum # of Instances text field, as described in the previous section.

You can use these values to configure the minimum and maximum numbers of Cartridge Servers for a particular cartridge type:

1. Using the OAS Manager, navigate to the form *site-name*/Applications/*app-name*/Configuration/Server, where *site-name* is the name of your site, and *app-name* is the type of Cartridge Server you want to tune.
2. Click Hosts.
3. In the Minimum # of Servers text field, enter the minimum number of servers.
4. In the Maximum # of Servers text field, enter maximum number of servers.
5. In the Weight text field, enter the percentage of weight distribution to be allocated to a host—for example, 50 percent.
6. Click Apply.

Tuning the LiveHTML Cartridge

These guidelines can assist in the design and deployment of your server-side includes (SSI) files for efficient access, reducing request latency:

- Avoid including SSI files within other SSI files (nested includes). Nested includes slow response time and add load on the system.
- Do not mix SSI files and static files in the same directory. Because directories containing SSI files are always accessed using the LiveHTML cartridge, even static files in these directories are served by the LiveHTML cartridge. By separating static and SSI files, you can avoid the cartridge call overhead for static files.

Tuning the OCI Cartridge

The Oracle Call Interface (OCI) cartridge is used to develop applications requiring access to database information. Oracle8 provides an interface for applications using the OCI. OCI8 provides many performance enhancements that can be used to improve the performance of an OCI application.

An interface for the development of multithreaded applications is provided with OCI8. By allocating separate session handles and service contexts, each thread can establish a separate database session and submit SQL statements. OCI8 also provides an asynchronous callback service, where long-running SQL statements can be submitted to the server while control is returned to the application. The application can check the status of outstanding tasks. Application performance is improved by submitting multiple requests in parallel without having to block individual requests.

An array-processing interface that can be used to process transactions is also provided with OCI8. The array interface enables you to declare a local C array populated with values. The array can then be used to perform insert, update, or delete operations. Arrays can also be used to retrieve database information. The array interface increases performance by reducing SQL calls from the number of records to be processed to a single call. For example, if you want to read 10,000 rows from the database, the traditional method is to open a cursor and loop through each fetch until all 10,000 rows are retrieved, which results in 10,000 fetch calls. If you are running in a network environment where OAS runs on a server other than the database server, this can increase the network traffic and reduce overall performance. Using an array of 10,000 elements results in only one SQL fetch call.

Using arrays to perform SQL operations considerably reduces SQL call overhead, as well as network overhead running in a distributed environment. OCI8 enables you to use an array of structures to perform batch SQL and other object-type operations. An array of structures allows more elegant programming and offers more flexibility in organizing data structures.

When using arrays in OCI, use bind variables to specify predicate values in the where clause. Using bind variables avoids queries hardcoded with scalar values. Bind variables also enable SQL statements to be reused. The SQL statement is exactly the same, but the value of the runtime bind variable changes, increasing application performance by reducing hard parses and improving library cache use.

A feature known as *prefetching,* which helps increase application throughput when dealing with batches of rows, is provided with OCI8. Use OCI_ATTR_PREFETCH_ROWS to specify the number of rows that should be prefetched from the server into the client cache. Use OCI_ATTR_PREFETCH_MEMORY to specify the amount of memory that should be used for memory. You can specify either the number of rows that should be prefetched, or the amount of memory that should be used to hold the prefetched rows. The more rows that you prefetch into the client cache, the more Application Server to database server roundtrips can be reduced. Fetching latency can also be reduced because the data is located in the local client cache. Use OCIAttrSet()to set the values of the prefetching attributes. The optimal setting for the prefetch attributes depends on the amount of data, as well as the size of a row piece.

Increased client-side processing and client-side object caching are provided with OCI8. The object cache maintains object instances and objects currently in memory, which reduces the number of network trips.

Tuning the PL/SQL Cartridge

PL/SQL provides the capability to create PL/SQL tables (i.e., arrays). The index of the table is the binary integer ranging from -2147483647 to +2147483647. This table index option is known as *sparsity,* and enables meaningful index numbers such as customer numbers, employee number, or other useful index keys. Use PL/SQL tables to process large amounts of data.

PL/SQL tables can also be used in OCI applications, enabling you to pass arrays from OCI into PL/SQL stored procedures to process large batches of data. PL/SQL tables increase performance by operating on tables rather than single rows.

PL/SQL provides TABLE and VARRAY (variable size array) collection types. The TABLE collection type is called a nested table. Nested tables are unlimited in size and can be sparse; therefore, elements within the nested table can be deleted using the DELETE procedure. Variable-size arrays have a maximum size and maintain their order and subscript when stored in the database. Nested table data is stored in a system table that is associated with the nested table. Variable-size arrays are suited for batch operations in which the application processes the data in batch array style.

TUNING SQL To maximize performance and minimize execution time, optimize application SQL statements. Tuning SQL is often the effort of rewriting SQL statements either to do less work or to improve the parallelization factor of the query.

Explain plans are crucial to tuning SQL and examining the execution path. The Explain Plan lists the execution path Oracle's Optimizer chooses for a given query, enabling you to review the Execution Path before it is submitted. Use the Explain Plan to analyze queries, and to tune the query before it is executed. If the Explain Plan reveals a poor execution path, you can tune the SQL statement using hints to obtain a better Execution Path.

To use the Explain Plan utility, select permissions must be granted on the tables that you are attempting to explain. You must also have select and insert permissions on the PLAN_TABLE table. To create the Explain Plan table, run the $ORACLE_HOME/rdbms/admin/utlxplan.sql script.

You can also generate a SQL trace file and use it with the tkprof utility, which shows the different phases including parsing, fetching, and execution.

Reloading Cartridge Servers

With the OAS Manager, you can reload Cartridge Servers for all applications or Cartridge Servers for a specific application.

RELOADING ALL CARTRIDGE SERVERS FOR ALL APPLICATIONS

To reload all Cartridge Servers for all applications, follow these steps:

1. In the navigational tree, select Applications. Selecting Applications displays a list of all Cartridge Server processes, as shown in Figure 4-23.
2. Select the radio button next to All.
3. Click the Reload icon to reload the Cartridge Servers.

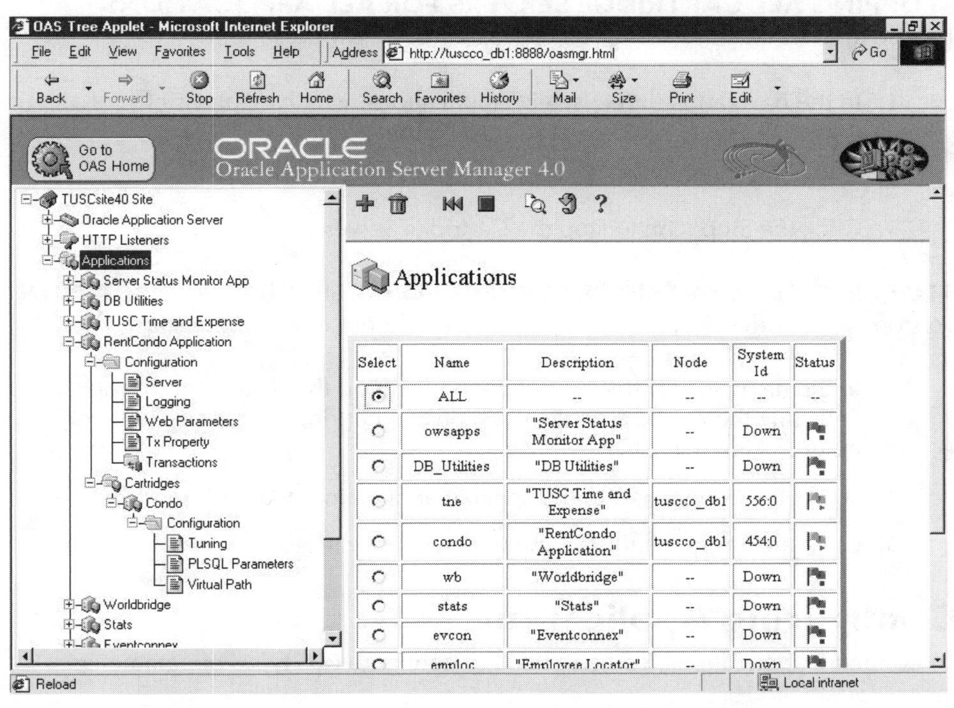

FIGURE 4-23. *OAS Manager Application form*

RELOADING ALL CARTRIDGE SERVERS FOR A SPECIFIC APPLICATION

To reload all Cartridge Servers for a specific application, follow these steps:

1. In the navigational tree, select the application that you want to stop. Selecting the application displays a list of cartridges in the application, as illustrated in Figure 4-23.
2. Select the radio button located adjacent to the specific application you wish to reload.
3. Click the Reload icon to reload the Cartridge Servers.

Stopping Cartridge Servers

Using the OAS Manager, you can stop Cartridge Servers for all applications, or Cartridge Servers for a specific application, or stop just a single Cartridge Server process.

STOPPING ALL CARTRIDGE SERVERS FOR ALL APPLICATIONS

To stop all Cartridge Servers for all applications, follow these steps:

1. In the navigational tree, select Applications, which displays a list of all Cartridge Server processes (refer to Figure 4-23).
2. Select the radio button next to All.
3. Click the Stop icon to stop the Cartridge Servers.

STOPPING ALL CARTRIDGE SERVERS FOR A SPECIFIC APPLICATION

To stop all Cartridge Servers for a specific application, follow these steps:

1. In the navigational tree, select the application that you want to stop. Selecting the application displays a list of cartridges in the application (refer to Figure 4-23).
2. Select the button next to the specific application you wish to stop.
3. Click the Stop icon to stop the Cartridge Servers.

Configuring Applications

To configure applications, you will need to configure two types of parameters:

- Application-level parameters
- Cartridge-level parameters

Application parameters affect the Cartridge Server processes running the application, while cartridge parameters affect only individual cartridges.

Understanding Application-Level Parameters

OAS allows you to set the following application-level parameters:

- Number of seconds a cartridge instance can be idle before it is terminated
- Routing of requests
- Logging parameters
- MIME types that the application handles
- Whether clients need certificates to access the application

- Whether each cartridge instance is bound to a client
- Number of seconds before a session times out
- The HTML page that is returned to the client if an error occurs
- Transaction service for the application

Application-level parameters are located in the Configuration section under the application name. The four forms include Server, Logging, Web Parameters, and Transaction Property. Table 4-13 describes the application-level parameters you can set using these forms.

The following subsections describe the parameters set at the application level and are applicable to all cartridges within the application.

CARTRIDGE TIME-OUT When a cartridge instance has been idle for this specified amount of time, the Cartridge Server can terminate the instance. This is independent of whether the instance is session-enabled. The time-out is specified in seconds.

SCHEDULING This load-balancing option enables you to specify how requests to the cartridges in the application are routed.

LOGGING PARAMETERS You can enable or disable logging. If enabled, you specify the directory and file to which the logged messages are written. You also need to specify the severity levels (between 0 and 15), where low values indicate serious problems. Specifying a high value will cause the Logger to log more messages because it writes all messages up to and including that severity level. For example, if you set the severity level at 3, the Logger logs messages of severity levels 0, 1, 2, and 3.

APPLICATION MIME TYPES The Application MIME Types provides a list of file extensions that the application does or does not process.

To list the file extensions that the application will process, prefix the list with a + character (for example, "+html, txt").

To list the file extensions that the application will not process, prefix the list with a - character (for example, "-jpeg, gif").

CLIENT CERTIFICATE You can require clients to have an appropriate SSL certificate to access your application.

CLIENT SESSIONS You can bind clients to a specific cartridge instance. The session between a client and a cartridge instance is valid until the session times out.

To Set this Item	Use this Parameter	Set In this Form	Default Value
How long (in seconds) a cartridge instance can be idle before it is terminated	Cartridge time-out	Server	86400
How requests are routed	Scheduling	Server	
Logging parameters		Logging	On
MIME types that the application handles	Application MIME Types	Web Parameters	jpeg, gif
Whether clients need certificates to access the application	Client certificate	Web Parameters	Disabled
Whether each cartridge instance is bound to a client	Client sessions	Web Parameters	Disabled
The number of seconds before a session times out	Max session idle time	Web Parameters	15
The page that is returned to the client if an error occurs	Error page	Web Parameters	No default
Enable transaction service for the application	Transactions	Tx Property	
The transactional DADs used by the application	Transactional DADs	Tx Property	

TABLE 4-13. *Application-Level Parameters*

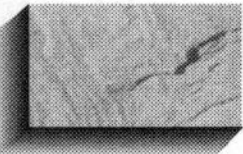

TIP
If you are developing applications that use HTML frames with session-enabled cartridges and more than one frame is sending requests to the cartridge at the same time (for example, you have an HTML frameset and the frames in the frameset send requests to the same session-enabled cartridge), make sure that the first request to the cartridge, which establishes the session, returns before you send subsequent requests. Make sure that you do not have more than one frame in the HTML frameset sending requests to the cartridge at the same time to establish a session. The reason for this is that the Application Server uses cookies to store session information. The browser does not store the cookie information until it gets a response to the request.

MAX SESSION IDLE TIME This parameter sets how long (measured in seconds) before a session between a client and a cartridge instance times out.

ERROR PAGE You can create an HTML page to appear if the client encounters an error. If you do not create one, a default page ($ORAWEB_HOME/admin/doc/wrberr.html) appears.

MINIMUM AND MAXIMUM NUMBER OF SERVERS These values specify the global minimum and maximum number of Cartridge Servers—for example, the number of Cartridge Servers running on all the nodes.

Each Cartridge Server runs one application, and each Cartridge Server can service one or more clients, depending on the number of cartridge instances and threads.

In environments where OAS is running on multiple nodes, the minimum number of Cartridge Servers is not spawned immediately when the Application Server is started. If you are running the Application Server on multiple nodes, the Application Server enforces the specified minimum number of Cartridge Servers only after allowing time for the Cartridge Server factories on all the remote nodes to start. (The Cartridge Server factories start up Cartridge Servers.) The time that is allowed is approximately five minutes.

As it receives requests beyond what the minimum number of Cartridge Servers can handle, it starts up more Cartridge Servers to the maximum number that is specified.

WEIGHTS You can specify the number of requests to be routed to specific machines. The higher a machine's weight, the more requests it will receive.

Understanding Cartridge-Level Parameters

Cartridge-level parameters vary depending on the cartridge type. For example, if you are developing a PL/SQL application, the cartridge will have different parameters from the cartridges in a Perl application.

OAS enables you to set the following cartridge-level parameters:

- Virtual path for the cartridge
- Security scheme associated with the virtual path
- Minimum and maximum number of instances for each cartridge
- Minimum and maximum number of threads per Cartridge Server
- Maximum number of clients that a stateless cartridge can handle

Cartridge-level parameters are located in the Configuration section under each cartridge. The Configuration sections under cartridges vary depending on the cartridge type. For example, if you are creating a PL/SQL cartridge, then your cartridges will have different configuration information from cartridges in a Perl application.

Two forms common to all cartridges are the Virtual Paths form, shown in Figure 4-24, and the Tuning form, shown in Figure 4-25. The Virtual Paths form enables you to specify the virtual path for the cartridge and authentication schemes for the virtual path. The Tuning form enables you to specify the number of instances for the cartridge and the number of threads. Table 4-14 describes the cartridge-level parameters you can set using these forms.

TIP
The Windows NT environment has a 512-byte limit on the expanded length of some environment variables (for example, CLASSPATH, JAVA_HOME). Make sure that your environment variables are not longer than 250–300 characters because some cartridges and JCORBA objects try to expand environment variables.

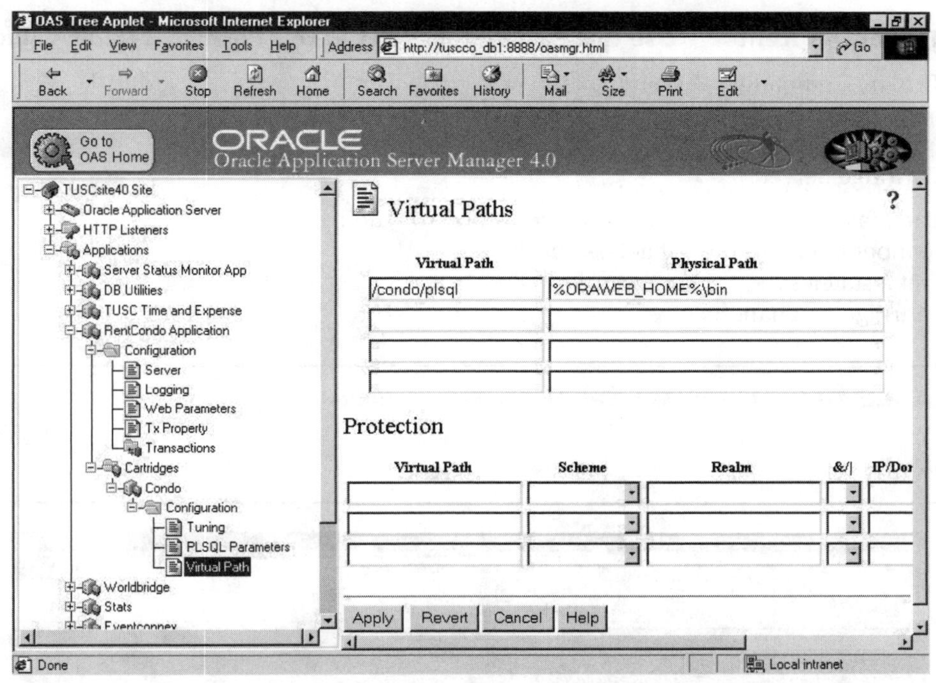

FIGURE 4-24. *Virtual Paths form*

To Set this Item	Use this Parameter	Set In this Form	Default Value
The virtual path for the cartridge	Virtual path/physical path	Virtual Paths	None
Security scheme associated with the virtual path		Virtual Paths	None
The minimum and maximum number of instances for each cartridge	Min/max instances	Tuning	Min: 1 Max: 10

TABLE 4-14. *Cartridge-Level Parameters*

To Set this Item	Use this Parameter	Set In this Form	Default Value
The minimum and maximum number of threads per Cartridge Server	Min/max threads	Tuning	Min: 1 Max: 1
The maximum number of clients that a stateless cartridge can handle	Max # of clients (for stateless cartridges)	Tuning	0

TABLE 4-14. *Cartridge-Level Parameters* (continued)

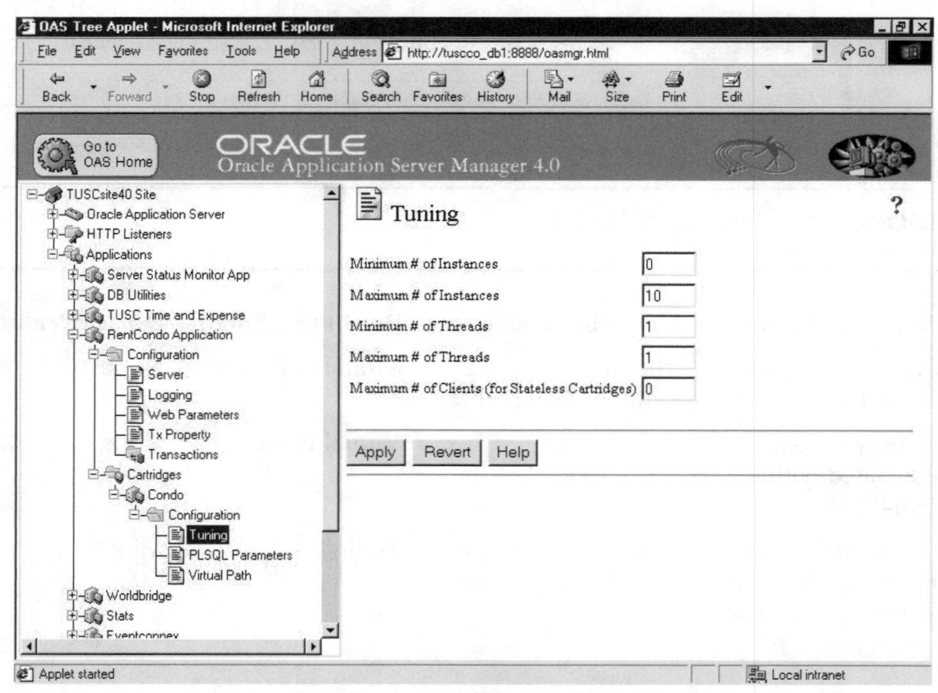

FIGURE 4-25. *Tuning form*

The following subsections describe the parameters common to all cartridge types (for example, the PL/SQL cartridge, the JWeb cartridge, and the LiveHTML cartridge).

VIRTUAL PATH AND PHYSICAL PATH Each cartridge is associated with one or more virtual paths. To invoke a cartridge, a browser invokes one of the virtual paths associated with the cartridge.

A virtual path can be associated with a physical path. This is cartridge-dependent.

PROTECTION You can associate virtual paths with security schemes.

MINIMUM AND MAXIMUM NUMBER OF INSTANCES These values specify the number of cartridge instances that can execute within each Cartridge Server process for the application.

When a Cartridge Server process starts up, it starts up the minimum number of cartridge instances for each cartridge. As it receives requests beyond what the minimum number of instances can handle, it starts up more instances, up to the maximum number.

MINIMUM AND MAXIMUM NUMBER OF THREADS The minimum and maximum values specify the number of threads per Cartridge Server.

MAXIMUM NUMBER OF CLIENTS FOR STATELESS CARTRIDGES This value specifies the maximum number of clients that stateless cartridges in a Cartridge Server can handle. Use this parameter to increase the number of clients handled by a cartridge.

Displaying Configuration Information

The Configuration form, shown in Figure 4-26, enables you to view configuration information for your application.

Table 4-15 explains the values of the fields in the Configuration form.

Configuring Server Parameters

The Cartridge Server form, shown in Figure 4-27, enables you to configure several parameters for your Cartridge Server. A Cartridge Server runs one application, consisting of one or more cartridges. The Cartridge Server process can run multiple instances of the cartridges; the number of instances is configurable.

The fields on the Cartridge Server form are described next:

- **Cartridge Time-out** Specifies the time-out (measured in seconds) for a cartridge that has not been invoked. After the specified time, the ORB closes the connection with the client.

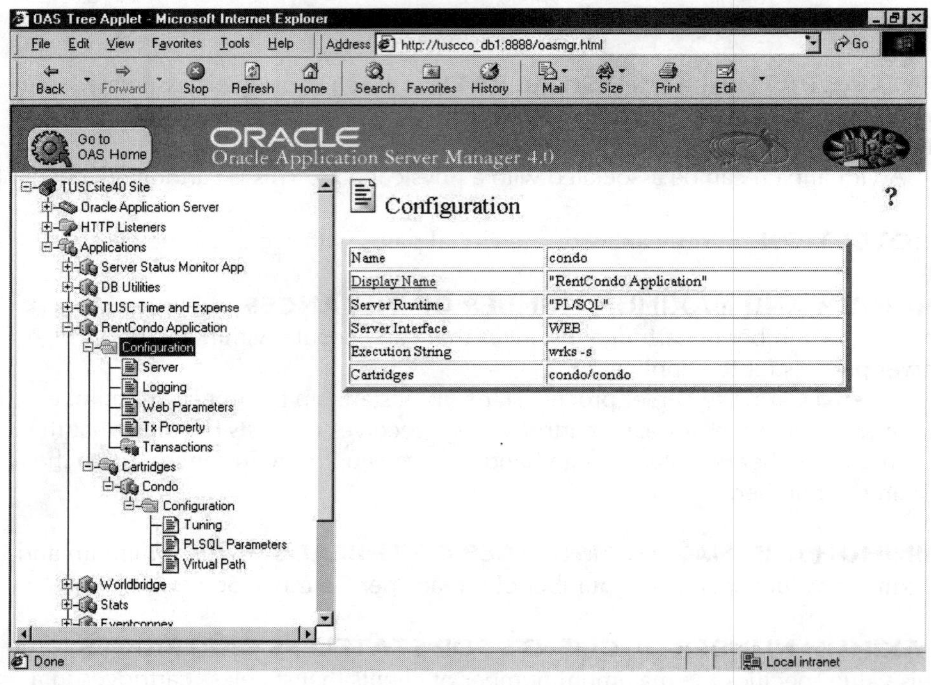

FIGURE 4-26. *Configuration form*

Field	Description
Name	Displays the short name for the application.
Display Name	Displays the complete name for the application. This is the name that is used in the navigational tree.
Server Runtime	Displays the server runtime. The possible values are CWeb, JWeb, Perl, LiveHTML, PL/SQL, and JCORBA.
Server Interface	Displays the server interface. The possible values are WEB or CORBA.
Application Version	Displays the application version for the application—for example, 1.0.

TABLE 4-15. *View Configuration Fields*

Field	Description
Execution String	Displays the execution string for the application—for example, wrks -s.
Client Jar File	Displays the complete path to the client jar file—for example, %ORACLE_HOME%/ows/cartx/Beans/order/install/client.jar.
Server Jar File	Displays the complete path to the server jar file—for example, %ORACLE_HOME%/ows/cartx/Beans/order/install/server.jar.
Application File	Displays the complete path to the application .app file—for example, %ORACLE_HOME%/ows/cartx/Beans/order/install/order.app.
Cartridges	Displays the complete cartridge name running in the application—for example, Order_Enter.

TABLE 4-15. *View Configuration Fields* (continued)

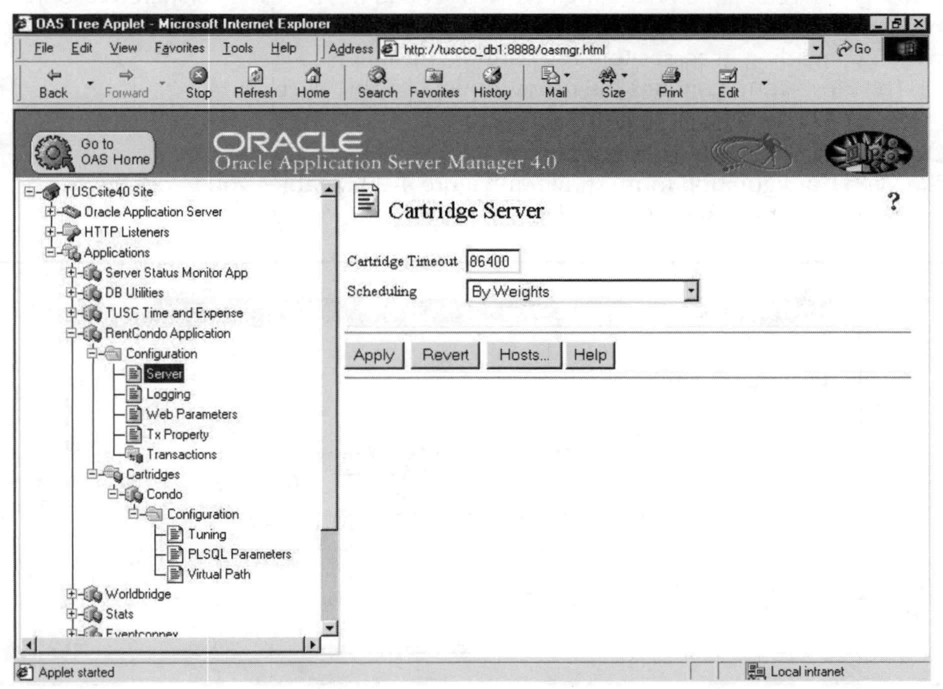

FIGURE 4-27. *Cartridge Server form*

- **Scheduling** Enables you to determine the distribution of your applications. The load-balancing valid options are as follows:
  - **By Weights** Use only the weight proportional to each host. This is the default.
  - **By Machine Load** Use only the load of the machine CPU and memory to dynamically calculate host weights, depending on each node's load. You do not need to enter a weight in the Hosts form.
  - **By Weights and Machine Load** Use both the weight and load of the machine.

After entering the appropriate information in the Configuration form, click the Apply button to process the form. If you have a distributed site (multiple servers that make up your site) and you wish to configure load-balancing parameters, click the Hosts button to go to the Hosts form.

CONFIGURING HOSTS FOR LOAD BALANCING The Hosts form, shown in Figure 4-28, enables you to use several hosts to balance the load for your Cartridge Servers. Load balancing involves scheduling accesses to shared resources. In OAS, the resources are the cartridge instances in the system. Load balancing involves shielding accesses to these cartridge instances.

The Hosts form contains the fields shown in Table 4-16.

Configuring Web Parameters

The Web Configuration form, shown in Figure 4-29, enables you to configure several parameters for your cartridge.

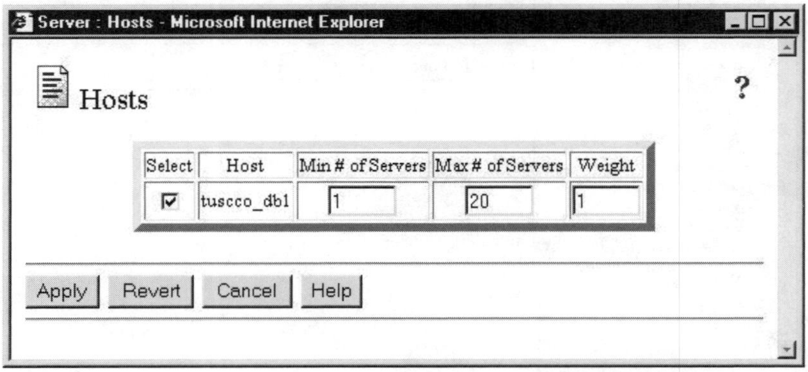

FIGURE 4-28. *Hosts form*

Field	Comments
Select	A checkbox option to select a particular host.
Host	Displays the host name—for example, isp-sun31.
Min # of Servers	Specifies the minimum number of Cartridge Servers running on the node. When the Application Server starts up, it starts up the minimum number of Cartridge Servers. As it receives requests beyond the minimum number that the Cartridge Servers can handle, OAS starts up more Cartridge Servers, up to the maximum number.
Max # of Servers	Specifies the maximum number of Cartridge Servers running on the node. When the Application Server starts up, it starts up the minimum number of Cartridge Servers. As it receives requests beyond what the minimum number of Cartridge Servers can handle, it starts up more Cartridge Servers, up to the maximum number.
Weight	Displays the percentage of Cartridge Server processes of this Cartridge Server type that should run on each host. This is useful in situations where a particular host can handle higher loads than other hosts. Valid values are 0.04 to 1. If you enter 0, OAS uses 0.5 as the weight value. For example, if host A is a large, fast machine, specify that it run 0.5, or 50 percent of your cartridge servers. If hosts B and C are smaller, less powerful machines, assign each host machine 0.25, or 25 percent, of the Cartridge Server load.

TABLE 4-16. *Host Form Fields*

Table 4-17 describes the fields in the Web Configuration form.

Modifying Applications

When you modify applications, you must either reload or stop/restart certain components for the changes to take effect. Changes you make can be grouped into two categories:

- **Changes to the application logic** For example, while you are developing a PL/SQL application, you could be changing the stored procedure that a request invokes, or if you are developing a JWeb application, you could be changing Java classes.
- **Changes to the application and cartridge configuration** For example, you add or remove cartridges from an application, change the logging levels, or

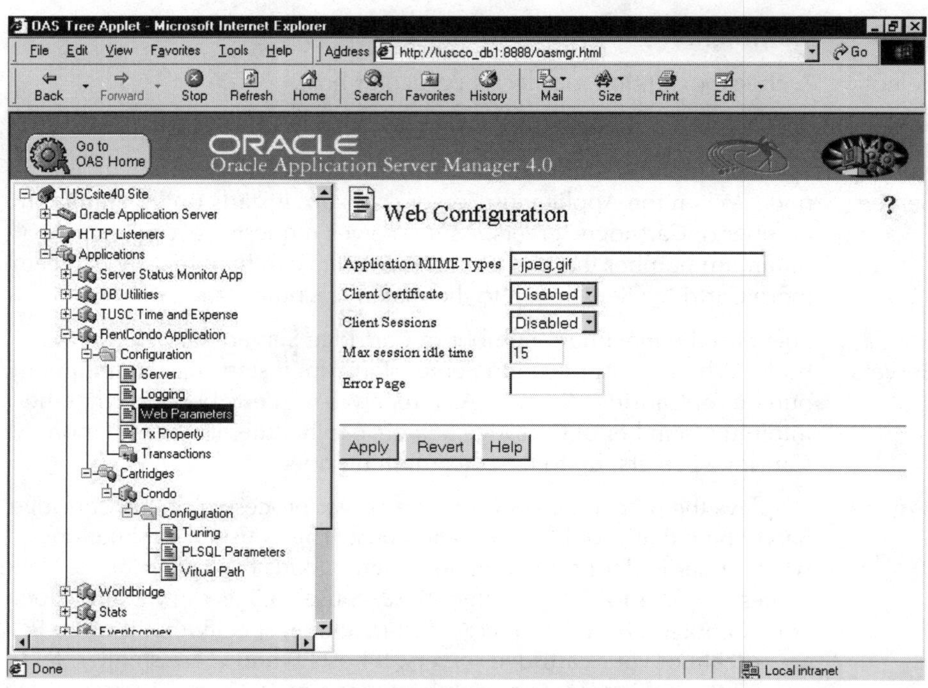

FIGURE 4-29. *Web Configuration form*

Field	Description
Application MIME Types	Specifies the file extensions (a further level of selection) the cartridge can handle. For example, to specify that a cartridge accept all extensions except certain file extensions, you can enter the following: jpg, or gif, which makes the WRB send all files with extensions other than jpg and gif to the cartridge. Files with extensions of jpg and gif are not sent to the cartridge. If you do not enter a value, then the cartridge accepts all file extensions and all URLs are sent to the cartridge.

TABLE 4-17. *Web Configuration Form Fields*

Field	Description
Client Certificate	A pull-down menu to specify if the dispatcher needs to retrieve the client-side SSL certificate for the cartridge. This certificate is then made available to that cartridge in the form of an API. The possible values are as followed: **Disabled** Do not retrieve the client-side SSL certificate for the cartridge. This is the default. **Enabled** Retrieve the client-side SSL certificate for the cartridge.
Client Sessions	A pull-down menu to inform the dispatcher the cartridge is session-enabled; requests originated from the same client receive the same cartridge instance. This is true as long as the idle time is less than the specified seconds in the "Max session idle time" field. The possible values are as follows: **Disabled** The cartridge is not session-enabled. This is the default. **Enabled** The cartridge is session-enabled. If you select this option, you also need to enter a value for the "Max session idle time" field.
Max session idle time	Specifies the idle time (measured in seconds) for a session-enabled cartridge. Once the idle time exceeds the time specified in this field, the cartridge instance is no longer associated with the request and can be bound to any other incoming request. After the instance expires, the client asking for the expired cartridge receives a page back indicating that the session expired. The subsequent request starts a whole new session. Use the "Max session idle time" field with caution. If you set this field to a large number, during the idle time the cartridge is unavailable to any other request. The optimal value is dependent on the functionality of the cartridge. Set it to a value that is large enough to allow multiple requests within the session to complete, but small enough that it does not stop the cartridge from being used by other requests. The default for this field is 0.
Error Page	Specifies the page to display if an error occurs in executing a request.

TABLE 4-17. *Web Configuration Form Fields* (continued)

change the number of threads or instances. These changes affect the wrb.app configuration file. Whether you reload the Cartridge Server or need to stop and restart it depends on the configuration parameter.

Changes to the Application Logic

Table 4-18 shows which components you have to stop and restart when you make a change to the application logic.

TIP
When you stop Cartridge Servers and cartridge instances, you do not restart them. The Application Server restarts them automatically for you when it receives a request for the cartridge.

Changes to Application and Cartridge Configuration

Table 4-19 lists the configuration parameters that can be reloaded. If you change a parameter that is not listed, you have to stop and restart the Cartridge Server. Changes affecting the virtual path require you to stop and restart the Listener; this is in addition to reloading the Cartridge Server.

Type	If You Change:	You Have to Stop and Restart:
PL/SQL	Procedure in the database	Cartridge instances that invoked the procedure
JWeb	Java classes	Cartridge Servers that invoked the class
LiveHTML	Files called by the LiveHTML cartridge	Nothing
LiveHTML	Perl scripts called by LiveHTML cartridge	Cartridge Servers that invoked the script
Perl	Perl scripts called by the Perl cartridge	Nothing
Perl	Packages called by the Perl scripts	Cartridge Servers that invoked the Perl script
C	The library file (.so or .dll)	Cartridge Server
JCORBA or EJB	Java classes for the JCORBA or EJB objects.	JCORBA or EJB server (you also have to reinstall the application)

TABLE 4-18. *Modifying Applications and Affected Components*

Action	**Effects**
Adding an application	The Resource Manager (RM) creates the minimum number of Cartridge Servers for new applications. You have to stop/restart the Listener.
Removing an application	The RM shuts down all existing Cartridge Servers for the removed application. You have to stop/restart the Listener.
Adding a cartridge to an existing application	The RM creates the minimum number of instances of the added cartridge. You have to stop/restart the Listener.
Removing a cartridge from an application	The RM removes all instances of the removed cartridge from all Cartridge Servers. You have to stop/restart the Listener.
Modifying the minimum/maximum number of Cartridge Servers and cartridges	The RM enforces the maximum value for Cartridge Servers immediately if the new maximum value is greater than the previous maximum value. If the new maximum value for Cartridge Servers is less than the previous value and the current server count is greater than the new maximum value, the RM enforces the new maximum value after all cartridge instances in a Cartridge Server are terminated. The RM enforces the new minimum value for cartridge servers in its next RM heartbeat check.
Adding/removing hosts for an application	The RM stops Cartridge Servers from the removed hosts. The RM uses the new host list when it counts the number of Cartridge Servers for the application.
Modifying load-balancing information (weights and load-balancing method)	The RM uses the new configuration when it checks the number of Cartridge Servers for the application.
Modifying Logger parameters	The new configuration goes into effect with the next logged message.

TABLE 4-19. *Reloadable Parameters*

Managing and Configuring Database Access Descriptors (DADs)

You can configure Database Access Descriptors (DADs) containing the information needed by OAS components to connect to Oracle databases. These DADs can be used by any component that supports configurable database access.

Administering Your DADs

The Database Access Descriptor form, illustrated in Figure 4-30, enables you to add and delete DADs.

The following table describes all the operations you can apply to the DADs:

Operation	Comments
Add	Enables you to add a new DAD. You will need to input some required information on the DAD: Add form.
Delete	Removes all information regarding the selected DAD. A pop-up confirmation window appears to confirm deletion of the DAD.
Update Page	Updates this form.

The Database Access Descriptor form contains a table, shown below, which describes all the DADs belonging to a site:

Operation	Comments
Select	Enables you to select a particular DAD so that you can use the operations mentioned above
DAD	Contains the names of all the DADs

To add a new DAD, select the Add icon on the Database Access Descriptor form. This takes you to the DAD: Add form, described in Table 4-20 and illustrated in Figure 4-31 in the next section.

To delete an existing DAD, select it from the list on the Database Access Descriptor form and click the Delete icon, shown to the left. You will then be asked to confirm the deletion.

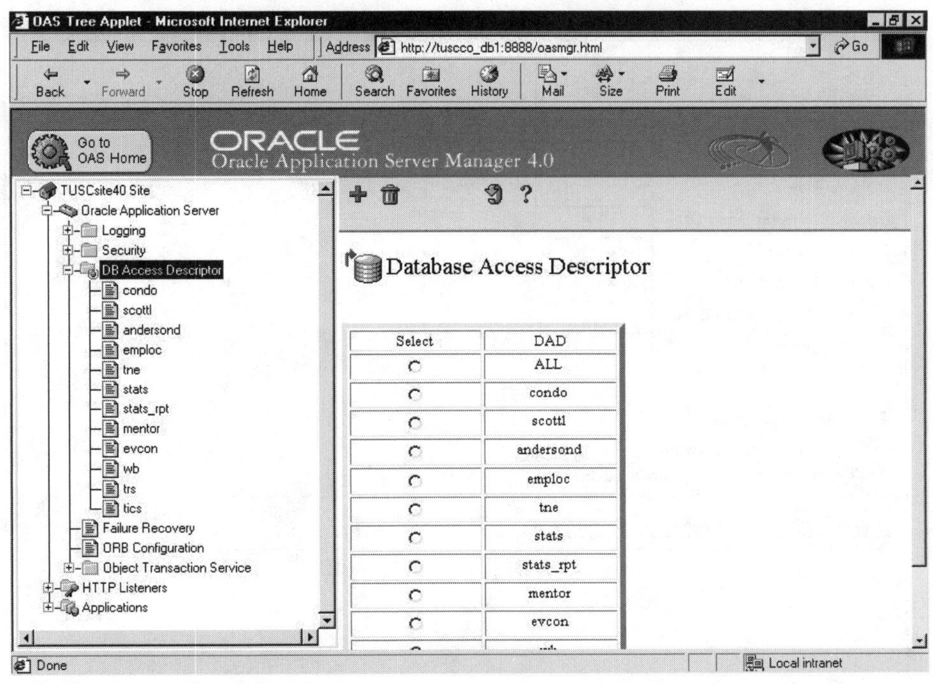

FIGURE 4-30. *Database Access Descriptor (DAD) form*

Adding a DAD

The Add DAD form, illustrated in Figure 4-31, enables you to add a DAD. A DAD contains a set of values that specify how a cartridge is to connect to an Oracle database server to fulfill an HTTP request. Each cartridge is associated with a DAD. The information in the DAD includes the username, password, connect string, error log file, standard error message, and the language to use.

After entering the required information, click the Apply button. If you checked the Create Database User checkbox, you are prompted to enter a DBA username and password in the DBA Account Info form.

Table 4-20 describes the Add DAD form's fields.

Adding Transactions

After creating a DAD, you can click the Transactions button to enable the Database Access Descriptors as transactional. Figure 4-32 illustrates the DAD Transactions form.

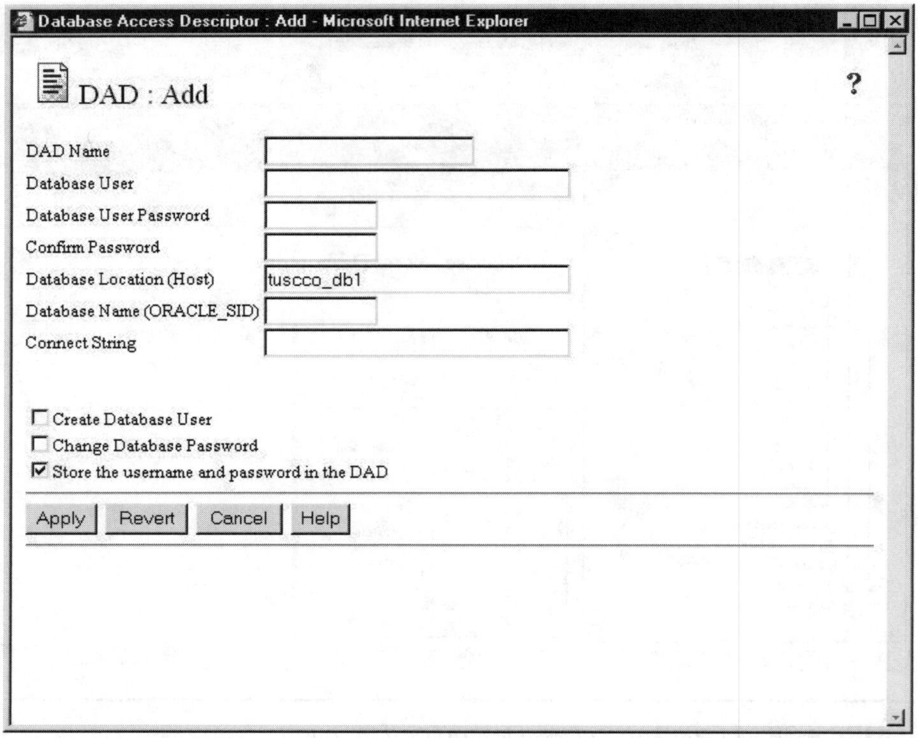

FIGURE 4-31. *Add DAD form*

Field	Description
DAD Name	The name of the DAD you are creating. DAD names are case sensitive.
Database User	The user ID the new DAD is to assume. If the username you choose has not been created in the database, click the Create/Change Database User checkbox near the bottom of the form. If the database is a remote database, you must also provide a DBA username and password in the DBA Username and Password fields at the bottom of the form.

TABLE 4-20. *Add DAD Form Fields*

Field	Description
Database User Password	Enter the login password for this user ID.
Confirm Password	Reenter the login password to make sure you have typed it correctly.
Database Location (Host)	Specifies the host name. For example, john-sun.
Database Name (ORACLE_SID)	For a DAD accessing a database in the same ORACLE_HOME as OAS, you must specify the ORACLE_SID of the database with which to connect.
Connect String	For a DAD that accesses a database on a remote host, you must specify a SQL*Net V2 service name to be used in connecting this DAD with the database on the remote host. If your database is installed on the same host as OAS but is in a separate ORACLE_HOME, it is regarded as a remote database and you must enter a SQL*Net V2 service name. The connect string specified in a DAD should be valid from all the nodes the cartridge can potentially run. Tip: For transactional DADs, it is mandatory that the connect string be specified for the DAD, regardless of whether your database is local or remote.
Create Database User	Click this checkbox if the username specified in the Database User field has not been created in the database. If you have installed the PL/SQL Toolkit from the current OAS release, the new user will also be granted proper privileges to content service database objects.
Change Database User Password	Click this checkbox to change the password specified in the Database User Password field.
Store The Username And Password In The DAD	Click this checkbox to store the username and password in the Database Access Descriptor.

TABLE 4-20. *Add DAD Form Fields* (continued)

Database Access Descriptor : Transactions - Microsoft Internet Explorer

DAD : Transactions

Distributed Transactions	Enabled
DatabaseType	Oracle 8
Lock Timeout	600
Global DB Name	
Heterogeneous OTS Agent Connect String	

Apply Revert Cancel Help

FIGURE 4-32. *DAD Transactions form*

TIP
The Transactional DAD feature is available only in the Enterprise edition of OAS.

Declared transactional DADs enable applications to participate in distributed transactions. A transaction links together multiple operations and resource changes (database updates, file changes) into a single unit, whether they occur within single or multiple applications.

The DAD Transaction form's fields are described next:

- **Distributed Transactions** Specifies whether to enable transactions for the DAD. Possible values are as follows:
  - **Enabled** Make the DAD transactional. This is the default.
  - **Disabled** Make the DAD nontransactional.

- **Database Type** Specifies the database to which the DAD connects. Possible values are as follows:
  - **Oracle8** The DAD connects to an Oracle8.x database
  - **Oracle7** The DAD connects to an Oracle7.x database
- **Lock Time-out** If two requests are in contention for the Resource Manager's resources, the second request waits for the first to finish before its request is handled. This may produce a performance or deadlock situation. This value is the total time (measured in seconds) the second request is to wait before it is rejected. The default is 600 seconds.
- **Global DB Name** The global database name is the combination of the database name and domain specified in the Oracle database initialization file (INITxxx.ORA). For example, if the file contains the lines "db_name = ORCL db_domain = tusc.com", the global database name is ORCL.tusc.com. This field requires the global database name of the database acting as the Resource Manager. Components of the transaction service include the Transaction Manager and the Resource Manager (RM). The Resource Manager component is usually an Oracle7 or Oracle8 database managing data integrity for transaction resource changes. Multiple RMs can exist in an environment to serve requests.
- **Heterogeneous OTS Agent Connect String** This field is required if your RM is an Oracle7 database. A heterogeneous Object Transaction Service (OTS) Agent is necessary to interact between an Oracle8 Distributed Transaction Coordinator (DTC) and an Oracle7 RM. If your RM is an Oracle7 database, you must configure an HO Agent to interact between them. This configuration field requires the heterogeneous OTS Agent's service name to be configured in the DTC Oracle8 TNSNAMES.ORA file.

Adding a New Database Access Descriptor (DAD): Advanced

After creating a DAD, use the Database Access Descriptor: Advanced form, illustrated in Figure 4-33, to add advanced features to a new DAD. After entering the required information, click the Apply button to create the DAD.

Table 4-21 describes the Advanced DAD form's fields.

Adding Nodes and Processes

The following subsections provide the instructions on how to add nodes and processes in OAS.

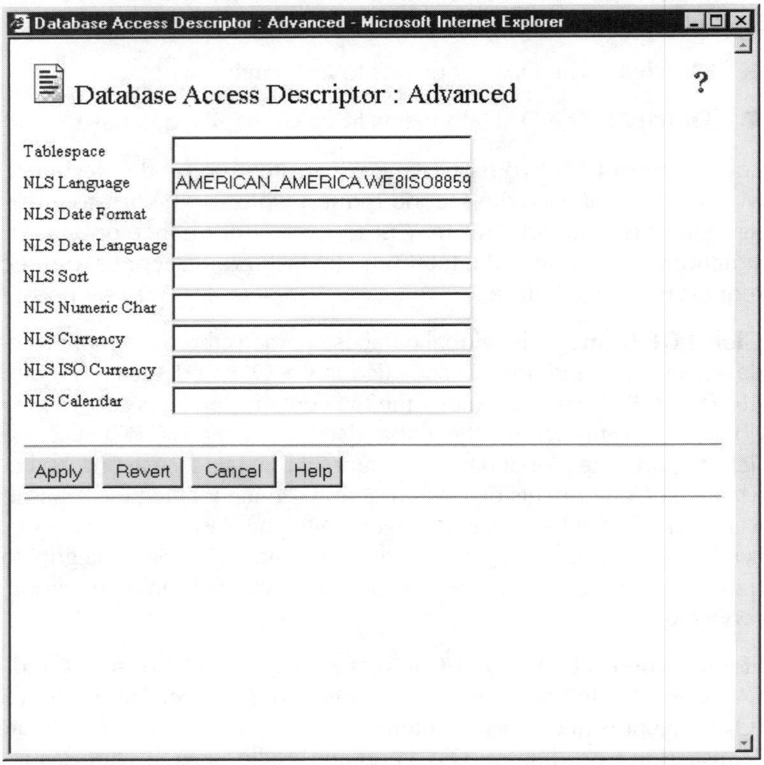

FIGURE 4-33. *Database Access Descriptor: Advanced form*

Field	Description
Tablespace	The tablespace the DAD will use instead of the SYSTEM tablespace. Every Oracle database contains a tablespace named SYSTEM, which Oracle creates automatically when the database is created. Make sure the parameter is valid; otherwise, you will receive a submission error or missing/invalid option. Tip: When modifying the DAD configurations, make sure all NLS-related information is valid. The OAS Manager does not validate these fields.

TABLE 4-21. *Advanced DAD Form Fields*

Field	Description
NLS Language	Language and character set for this DAD to use—for example AMERICAN_AMERICA.US7ASCII.
NLS Date Format	The date format to use with the TO_CHAR and TO_DATE functions—for example, MM/DD/YYYY. You may leave this field blank, as it is optional.
NLS Date Language	The language to use for day and month names and date abbreviations (AM, PM, AD, BC). You may leave this field blank, as it is optional.
NLS Sort	The sorting sequence to use: BINARY or valid linguistic definition name. If the value is BINARY, then the collating sequence for order by queries is based on the numeric value of characters (a binary sort requires less system overhead). If the value is a named linguistic sort, sorting is based on the defined linguistic sort. You may leave this field blank, as it is optional.
NLS Numeric Char	The characters to use as the group separator and decimal. You may leave this field blank, as it is optional.
NLS Currency	The string to use as the local currency symbol for the L number format element. For example, L099 represents the L format element to return the default local currency symbol for the territory France. You may leave this field blank, as it is optional.
NLS ISO Currency	The string to use as the international currency symbol for the C number format element. For example, C099 represents the C format element to return the default local currency symbol for the territory France. You may leave this field blank, as it is optional.
NLS Calendar	The calendar format to use, because many calendar systems are in use throughout the world. For example, if NLS_CALENDAR is set to Japanese Imperial, the date format is YY-MM-DD. You may leave this field blank, as it is optional.

TABLE 4-21. *Advanced DAD Form Fields* (continued)

Adding a New Node

To add a node to your Web site, from the OAS Manager, click on the top-level site description and then click on the Add icon. This will display the Add Node form, shown in Figure 4-34, enabling you to add a new node to your Web site.

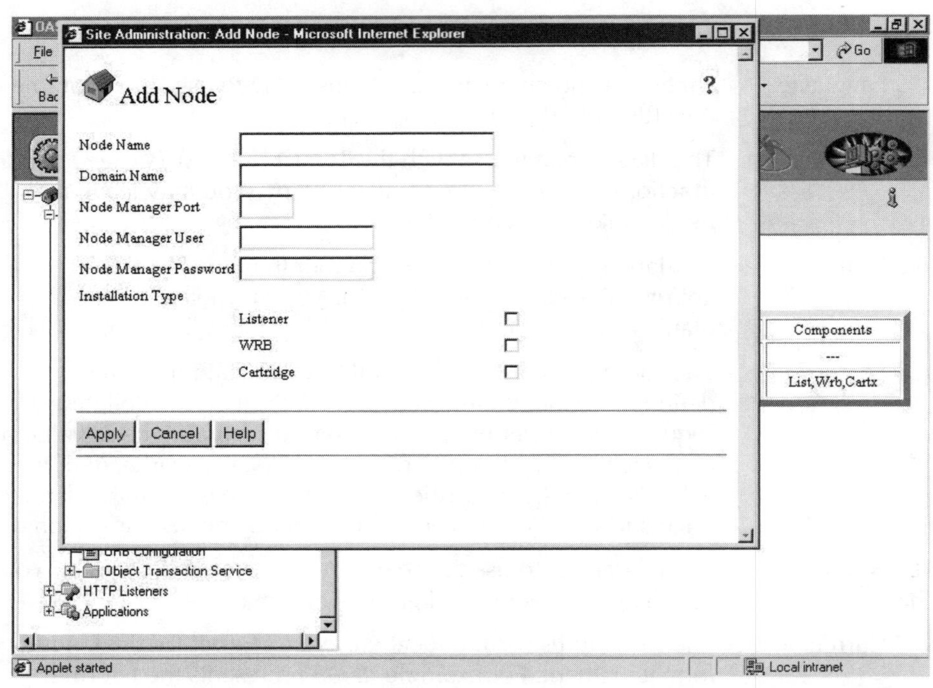

FIGURE 4-34. *Add Node form*

Table 4-22 explains the fields shown on the Add Node form.

Adding a New Process

To add new WRB processes to your Web site, you will use the Add WRB Process form, illustrated in Figure 4-35.

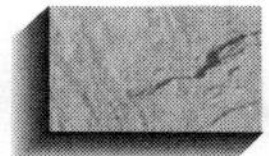

TIP
If you are using the collapsed process model, you cannot add a new process. Under the collapsed model, several processes, such as the authentications server (wrbsarv), the monitoring daemon (wrbmon), and others are combined into one oassrv process.

Field	**Description**
Node Name	An alphanumeric string of your choice no longer than 30 characters that uniquely identifies the machine name.
Domain Name	Enter the domain name by which the machine identifies itself when serving requests. This must be a valid name recognized by DNS.
Node Manager Port	A TCP/IP port identifying the port number of the Node Manager Listener. You can choose any number from 1 to 65535, except for those port numbers already assigned to other programs.
Node Manager User	Enter the user identity. You can specify either a username or numeric ID in this field. To denote the root ID, you must specify root rather than 0.
Node Manager Password	Enter the password for the Node Manager user.
Installation Type	A checkbox option to select a combination of Listener, WRB, and cartridge installation types for the new node. If you check Listener, you can install HTTP Listeners on the node. By checking WRB, you can run any WRB process or component on the node. Selecting Cartridge allows you to run cartridges on the node.

TABLE 4-22. *Add Node Fields*

The fields shown on the Add WRB Process form are explained next:

- **Node Name** A pull-down menu to select the machine name where you want to add the new process.
- **WRB Process** A pull-down menu to select the WRB process to add. Valid WRB processes are as follows:
  - **wrbcfg** Configuration Provider
  - **wrblog** Log Server
  - **wrbmon** Monitoring Daemon

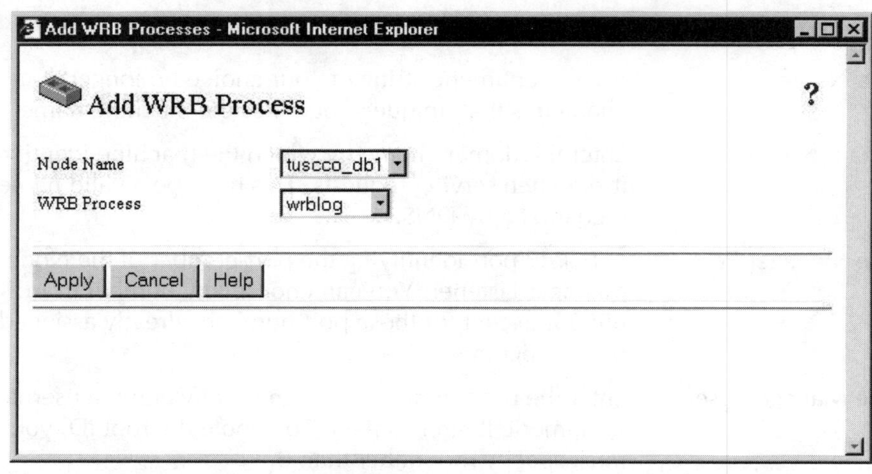

FIGURE 4-35. *Add WRB Processes form*

- **wrbasrv** Authentication Server
- **wrbahsrv** Authorization Host Server
- **wrbroker** Resource Manager
- **wrbrmpxy** Resource Manager Proxy
- **wrksf** Cartridge Server
- **wrbvpm** Virtual Path Manager
- **wrbfac** Cartridge Factory

Summary

OAS is a complex and powerful product. With a multitude of tuning options available, OAS is the perfect Application Server for any business, from a small company to the largest dotcom in the world. Invest the time to fully understand this chapter inside and out—it will pay off 10 times over.

CHAPTER 5

WebDB

ebDB is a self-service Web publishing solution for end users and developers to build dynamic Web sites from just a Web browser. One of the primary benefits of WebDB to an organization is to provide a rapid way for employees to share documents and relevant business information from a common location without having to involve IT staff with every update. WebDB is meant to free Webmasters from being a bottleneck, and to return the task of Web site content management back to the users—the content providers within an organization.

In future releases, WebDB sites will evolve from its self-service Web publishing beginnings into a full-fledged business portal. A business portal is an intranet site that delivers personalized access to business applications and information to all employees.

WebDB has steadily evolved in its subsequent releases to provide the customer ever-increasing levels of integration with the rest of the Oracle product family, including Oracle InterMedia Text, and with WebDB 2.1 provides extensive integration with Oracle Reports 6i, where customers can access and schedule reports with the Oracle Reports Server via the WebDB browser interface. To provide a bit of background, Oracle WebDB is developed from the Enterprise Internet Tools Division—the same group that brought you longstanding Oracle products such as Oracle Developer and Oracle Reports. It should also be noted that Oracle Forms is not going to replace WebDB (nor is JDeveloper), but rather it will augment WebDB.

To expand upon future plans for WebDB, if you are familiar with Websites such as my.yahoo.com or my.excite.com, WebDB 3.0 will provide an infrastructure that will allow users to "plug-in" different application components to form their own personalized, customizable Web pages. Plug-ins within the WebDB 3.0 infrastructure are known as "portlets," and applications that provide portlets to WebDB are called portlet providers. In the future, Developer Forms will become a portlet provider to WebDB, allowing sites built with WebDB to display an Oracle Developer Form or sections of Oracle Form(s) on a page within a WebDB Web site.

In addition to the above-noted capabilities of WebDB (building sites), I also feel that WebDB can help augment your OAS development without nearly as much code. WebDB is especially useful for developing the simple table maintenance routines for your OAS applications. WebDB originated out of the Government Oracle Consulting group. Previously, you could download the original (free) version of WebDB from the government consulting Web site—it was called WebView. As a matter of fact, in early WebDB versions (e.g., version 2.0) there were even areas within the tool that still said "WebView," such as in the title of the General Help window. However, since WebDB is now a viable development tool, Oracle has since removed the free version and sells its predecessor.

Early on in WebDB's life, WebDB may have been identified as an interim product, as OraCard once was, causing the more experienced Oracle crowd to be a little nervous. It might appear that WebDB is an interim solution. A quick history lesson: Oracle Developer, particularly Oracle Forms, has not been a primetime Internet solution. The browsers were not sufficient to support the robust and powerful user interactivity provided by Oracle Forms. Historically, when an Oracle product has been in the catching up to the competition mode, Oracle purchased or invented an interim technology such as OraCard. The last time Forms fell behind the competition was when the true graphical user interface (GUI) became popular quickly—this is when OraCard suddenly appeared. However, once Forms got its GUI, Oracle disbanded OraCard. Another disbanded product was PowerObjects. When the scripting language in Forms was not as powerful as Visual Basic, Oracle introduced PowerObjects. Once the PL/SQL packages and capabilities in Forms matched Visual Basic's stamina, PowerObjects encountered a quick death. When Forms did not provide the thin-client Internet capabilities one might hope, WebDB was introduced. So, will Forms replace WebDB? No. WebDB is not a Forms or Reports or any other development tool's replacement; it is a content generation tool—it augments other Oracle products but does not replace them. Will Forms and Reports someday provide as thin a footprint as WebDB? Hopefully, yes! WebDB is a wizard-driven tool, useful for browsing, building, managing, and self-servicing applications. Although end users may publish the content and generate code using the WebDB interface, WebDB works best as a developer's Toolkit. You can develop an entire application with zero coding or you can extend the product with your own code and libraries of code, demonstrated in this chapter. If you look through the WebDB marketing literature, you'll find it's primarily discussed as if it's a content management tool. However, the product is much more than a content management tool—it is a wizard-based development suite.

In this chapter we will discuss the following topics:

- Considering why you should use WebDB
- Looking at primary functionality
- Installing WebDB
- Using the navigation toolbar
- Helping yourself
- Reviewing some frequently asked questions
- Browsing the database
- Building objects and components
- Administering WebDB
- Monitoring your objects
- Building sites

Considering Why You Should Use WebDB

WebDB serves multiple needs—from code generation or Web development to content management. WebDB will help develop code and Web applications quickly. WebDB will browse or view the structures held within the database—from tables, to indexes, to procedures. DBAs feel comfortable using WebDB because it provides a number of scripts for database monitoring. One of the primary benefits of WebDB is that you can build and manage your entire site through a browser. Client-side tools (beyond a browser and network connectivity) are unnecessary.

Looking at Primary Functionality

The main functions of WebDB are evident by looking at the Main menu (see Figure 5-1). The major functions available from the Main menu are Browse, Build, Administer, Monitor, and Sites. The Browse functionality enables you to scan the database components by schema, object type, or name. Under Build, you can construct user interface components and database objects. Administer enables you to manage privileges and establish Listener settings. Monitor provides the capability to view end-user and database activity, and Sites is the location to construct and monitor a Web site wholly contained within the database. The Sites functionality contains the content management portion of WebDB.

Installing WebDB

WebDB is a stand-alone product, containing its own Web Listener and the components needed to operate independently of OAS. WebDB is fully functional, with no need for other Web servers; therefore, it is irrelevant whether OAS was installed. The code generated from WebDB is executed via the WebDB Listener or through OAS 4.0 when used with WebDB's PL/SQL Cartridge.

The WebDB product installation is quite similar to other Oracle product installations. On NT, you can run orainst.exe or setup.exe from the CD. As shown in Figure 5-2, the installation will prompt you for your company name, the Oracle home directory, and your language. Enter the answers to the questions, then perform a typical install or a custom install, as illustrated in Figure 5-3. Unlike most Oracle installations, for WebDB I recommend using the typical installation. I usually recommend performing a custom installation because I don't want to install the entire product. However, with WebDB I prefer to install the entire product, which is the functionality behind a typical installation.

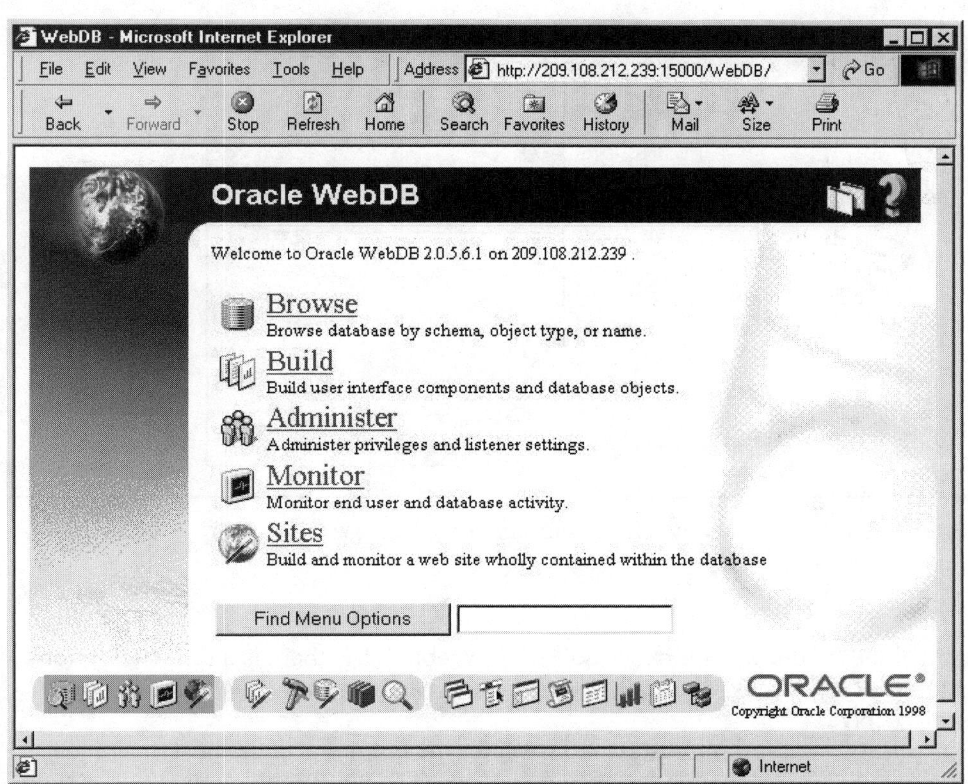

FIGURE 5-1. *WebDB Main menu*

The following pieces (see Figure 5-4) of information are critical to the success of your WebDB installation. The password prompt is asking for the password for your SYS account. The information will be provided by your DBA. In WebDB 2.0, the only trick to installing WebDB existed when the WebDB install involved a remote database (where the database is actually on another physical machine). In this case, you will need to provide a SQL*Net connect string to connect to the Oracle database. However, there is not a prompt for the connect string of the SYS account. Therefore, if your database is local, specify just the password—for example, change_on_install. Odd as it may seem, if your database is remote, you want to be sure to specify the password, an @ symbol, and the SQL*Net connect string in the Password field—for example, change_on_install@sales. This tells WebDB to install to a remote machine. I was confident that this would be resolved in a future version

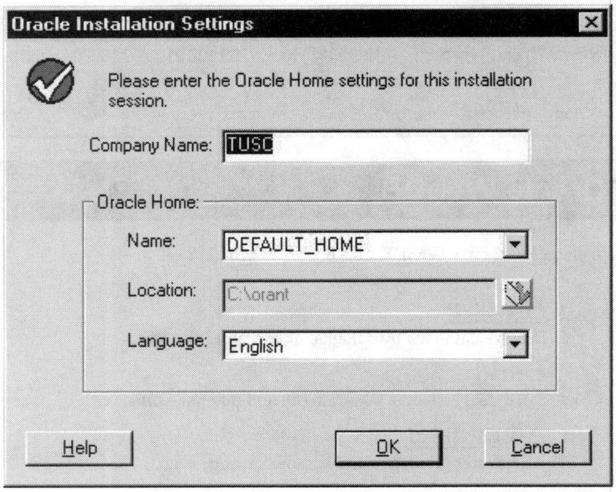

FIGURE 5-2. *Company, Oracle home, and language*

of WebDB, and it was quickly resolved. In WebDB 2.1, there is a separate option that explicitly allows for installation to remote database instances. Ask and you shall receive.

The second prompt, host name, specifies the full name of the host machine. The default host name may be acceptable, and if so you should maintain it as such. The host name specified is the virtual host name that you will be specifying in the browser to connect to the WebDB Listener. If you plan to access WebDB using an IP address, specify the appropriate address here rather than a virtual host name.

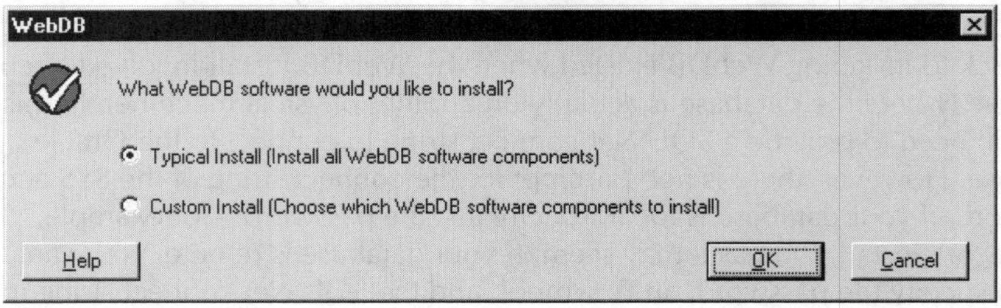

FIGURE 5-3. *Typical or custom installation*

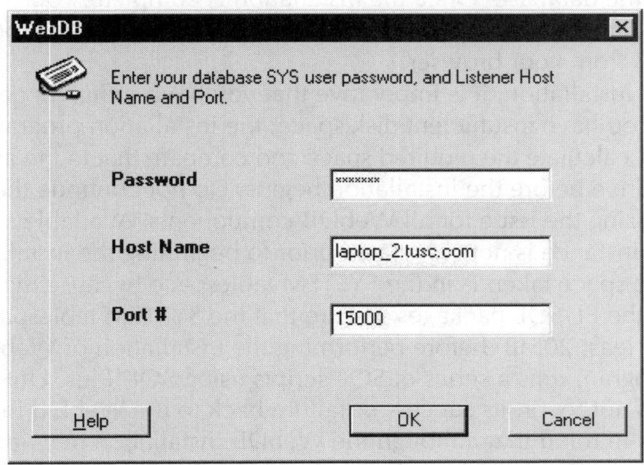

FIGURE 5-4. *SYS password, host name, and port number*

Either way, the value you specify will need to be an IP address or a valid domain name entry. The final parameter defaults to a port of 80, which is dangerous because it is not likely to be appropriate. However, if WebDB is the only Web Listener on the machine (though unlikely), port 80 would be ideal. I like to establish company-wide port numbers for different functions. For example, port 80 is the logical choice for standard Web site Listeners, port 443 is for SSL Listeners, and port 15000 (or you could try a number a bit lower such as 120, but see Chapter 8 for issues surrounding ports numbered less than 1024) is for WebDB. Then, I use this standard for every server in the entire company. Therefore, typically I'd recommend changing the port value to 15000 (or the port of your choice). If you leave the default parameter set to port 80, you can change the port number later from the WebDB Listener icon on the Windows NT Control Panel.

The installation procedure will verify the SYS password, then analyze the Toolkit dependencies. If the Toolkit already exists, you will be prompted with the choice to drop and re-create it or rename it (manually) and try again later. The next prompt is curious to me, as it asks which database version is installed—can't Oracle read this from the v$version virtual table? (It already logged in to the SYS account, didn't it?) Once the questions have been answered (e.g., you may need to answer more if you're out of disk space), WebDB will be installed. The installation takes a while (30 minutes to 8 hours—most typically about 1–2 hours) because a number of packages are created in the database. Once the installation is complete, your WebDB Listener will be running on the port you have specified in the step above. From here on, you access WebDB from your browser.

During the installation, it is imperative that you have sufficient database and disk space. If you have insufficient disk space, the installation program will display a warning. It will calculate the required space and compare that to the available space on your hard drive before the installation begins. Do not continue the installation without addressing the issue for all WebDB components. Available space within your database instance is not calculated prior to beginning the installation. Most of the database space taken is in the SYSTEM tablespace because most of WebDB Is made up of the PL/SQL packages. Ensure that the SYSTEM tablespace available is sufficient (at least 20MB) before performing the installation of WebDB. The installation program runs a series of SQL scripts using SQL*Plus. Unfortunately, SQL*Plus does not report its success or failure back to the WebDB installation program. Keep in mind that although the WebDB installation may indicate success upon completion, it may not have been completely successful. I couldn't find an error log for the installation scripts, so the only way I noticed that I ran out of database space was that I watched the scripts run in SQL*Plus during the installation—painful as it is. My assumption is that this will be fixed in a future installation release.

After the installation, change the passwords for the accounts WebDB creates. The installation does not prompt for any password information, and therefore WebDB creates two accounts with the same password as the username, the most dangerous of which is the *webdb* account (a DBA account). This could be an obvious security risk. The other account created is the oas_public schema, which has CONNECT and RESOURCE privileges. It is highly recommended that you change the password of both of these Oracle accounts immediately after your installation.

Using the Navigation Toolbar

In Figure 5-1, the navigation toolbar is located at the bottom of the page. The navigation toolbar is useful for accessing WebDB features quickly. The images are not necessarily intuitive at first glance. Fortunately, each image contains a corresponding ALT tag, which provides you with a tooltip explaining each image. If you put your cursor over an image, it will display the name of the function represented by the image. The images are grouped into three distinct sections. The first grouping contains items from the Main menu (Browse Database Objects, Build UI Components, Administer Privileges, Monitor Activity, and Build Sites). The second grouping is the items contained in the Build UI Components section (User Interface Components, Utilities, Build Database Objects, Shared Component Library, and Component Finder). The final grouping contains all of the items found in the User Interface Components section of the WebDB application (Forms, Menus, Frame Drivers, Dynamic Page, Reports, Charts, Calendars, and Hierarchies). The navigation toolbar is consistent throughout WebDB's entire application building interface.

Helping Yourself

Within WebDB there are typically two levels of help available to you as the developer: Generic help (big Help icon or the big Question Mark icon) and context-specific help (little Help icon or the little Question Mark icon). Both of the icons are located on most WebDB pages (see Figure 5-7 in the next section). If you click on the generic Help icon, a page is displayed identical to the one shown in Figure 5-5. If you click on the context-sensitive Help icon, a context-sensitive Help page will be displayed such as the one illustrated in Figure 5-6.

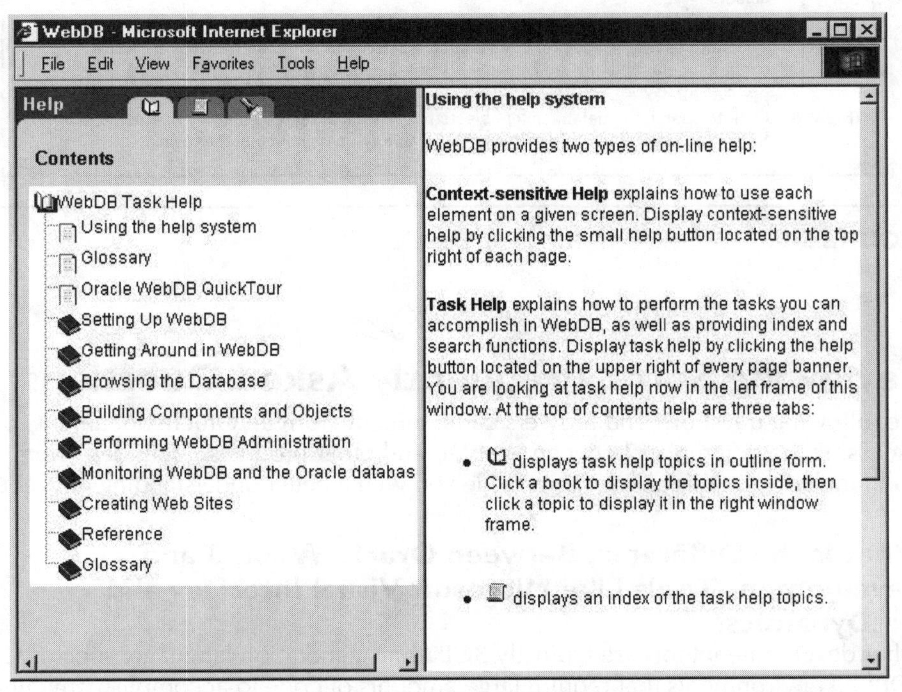

FIGURE 5-5. *Generic Help page*

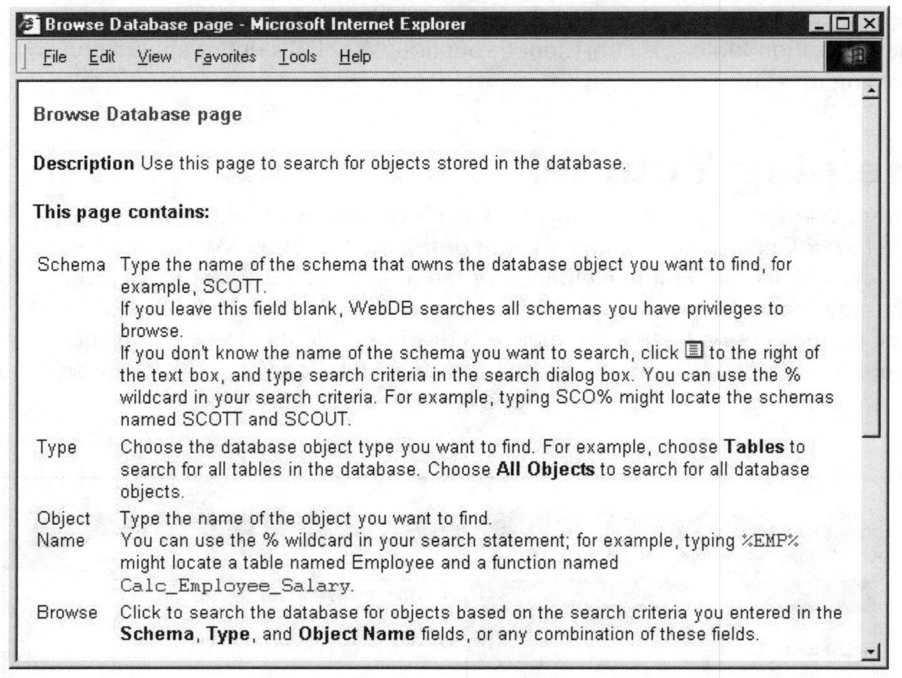

FIGURE 5-6. *Context-sensitive Help page*

Reviewing Some Frequently Asked Questions

The following questions and answers came directly from an Oracle document discussing the differences between WebDB and other products. I felt these were worth including in this chapter to provide you with a better understanding of WebDB.

What Is the Difference Between Oracle WebDB and Development Tools Like Microsoft Visual InterDev and NetDynamics?

Other development tools are typically 3GL (third-generation language, such as C or COBOL) environments that require large amounts of code to accomplish anything useful. Additionally, 3GL environments treat the database as an afterthought, requiring callouts or external server components to access the database. Oracle WebDB, on the other hand, is a Web environment that allows fast, native access to information in the database without any programming. Using only a browser, application authors can create everything from simple database queries to complicated, dynamic database applications that would require an extraordinary amount of time if done with other tools.

What Is the Difference Between Oracle WebDB and Web Page Authoring Tools Like Microsoft FrontPage and NetObjects Fusion?

Web authoring tools excel at creating static Web pages requiring little or no modification. For these types of Web pages, Oracle WebDB includes Symantec Visual Page (30-day trial on the partner CD). Oracle WebDB excels at creating dynamic Web pages using information from the database. When information in the database changes, the Oracle WebDB Web pages automatically change to reflect the new data.

What Is the Difference Between Oracle WebDB and Oracle Developer?

Oracle Developer is an extremely powerful application development environment for developing enterprise class applications for both the client/server and the Web. Typically, Oracle Developer is used for high-throughput OLTP SYStems. Both products share the ability to create multilingual database forms, reports, and charts using powerful declarative capabilities to build applications without writing code. Oracle WebDB provides a lightweight yet complete set of tools for application development, database management, and performance tracking, emphasizing simplicity, database integration, and ubiquitous access through a completely browser-based user interface. Oracle WebDB sacrifices some of the fine-grain control of Oracle Developer for a very short learning curve and an even shorter development cycle. Oracle WebDB is typically used for self-service applications.

What Is the Difference Between Oracle WebDB and Oracle Designer Web Server Generator?

Oracle Designer is a model-based application development environment used to generate server DDL, client/server, and Web-based applications with Java and HTML user interfaces. Oracle WebDB is a lightweight, purely HTML tool for rapid development of both Web database applications and Web sites. It is focused more on getting the task at hand done quickly and effectively, rather than on the process modeling that makes Oracle Designer such a powerful tool.

Will Oracle Designer Generate Oracle WebDB Components?

The future versions of Oracle Designer will be able to read the Oracle WebDB repository and provide roundtrip engineering for Oracle WebDB components.

What Is the Difference Between Oracle WebDB and Oracle Discoverer?

Oracle Discoverer is an ad hoc query, reporting, exploration, and analysis tool for accessing the information in data warehouses, typically used in decision support. It enables users to pivot and drill down through their data. The final results from Discoverer notebooks can be published to the Web in HTML format. Both products are designed to be easy to use and administer. Oracle WebDB is a HTML-based, thin-client tool that provides nonprogrammers with a quick and easy way to author content-driven Web sites and Web database applications without scripting. Oracle WebDB is generally an HTML-based software development tool, whereas Oracle Discoverer is desktop software with a slant towards data mining and decision support.

What Is the Difference Between Oracle WebDB and Oracle JDeveloper?

Oracle JDeveloper is a Java development tool containing significant productivity enhancements for database programmers and multitier application developers. Developers can use JDeveloper to create middle-tier Java servlets for dynamically generating HTML. Oracle WebDB is an easy to use browser-based, wizard-driven environment used to build data-driven HTML pages for your Web sites, as well as an environment in which you can code simple HTML-based applications. Oracle WebDB support for Java servlets is currently under consideration.

Browsing the Database

OAS comes with a Browse database functionality. Although the Browse database functionality of WebDB is similar to that of the OAS, the WebDB Browse database functionality is more powerful. In WebDB, you are able to view all database objects, whether in a specific schema or any database schema. You can search for objects by the schema, type (clusters, functions, indexes, libraries, packages, procedures, sequences, snapshots, synonyms, tables, triggers, and views), or name. From the Main menu of WebDB, you simply select Browse. Figure 5-7 illustrates the first screen viewed when conducting a search.

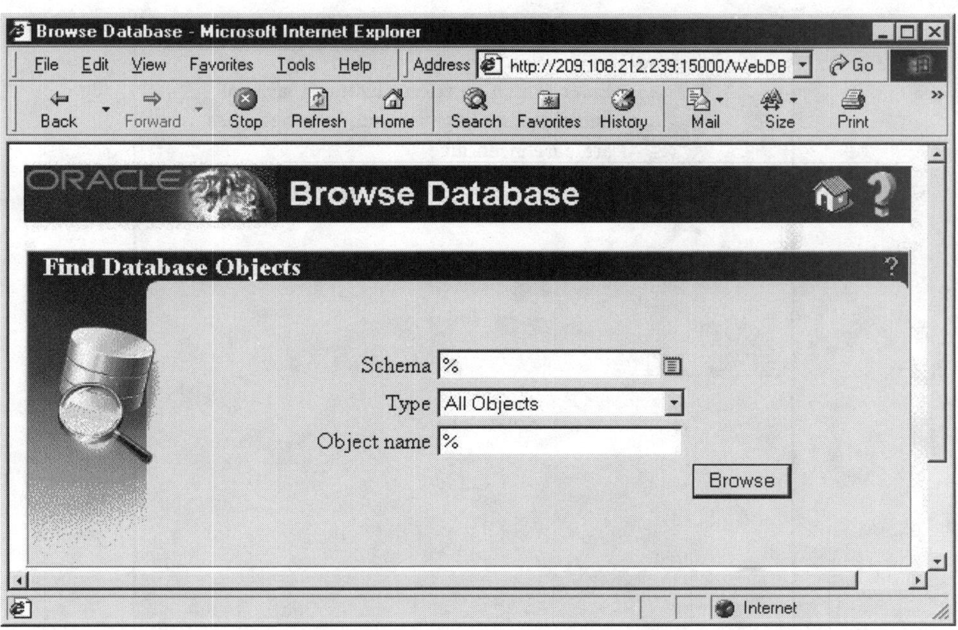

FIGURE 5-7. *WebDB search screen*

WebDB's Browse is a great feature for viewing database objects. If I plan to edit database objects, I typically use a tool identical to TOAD or SQL*Programmer, but if I am viewing the database objects, I like WebDB's Browse function because it's Web-enabled. A feature common throughout WebDB is the pop-up list. As illustrated in Figure 5-7, the Schema field contains the List icon off to the right. If you click on the List icon, a schema search window identical to the one shown in Figure 5-8 will pop up. In Figure 5-9, the search criteria uses a standard Oracle LIKE clause, therefore using standard LIKE syntax. In Figure 5-8, the search specifies all schemas beginning with an S having anything after the S (1–*n* letters is represented by the % sign) and ending with a T. Once you click on BROWSE, WebDB's query will

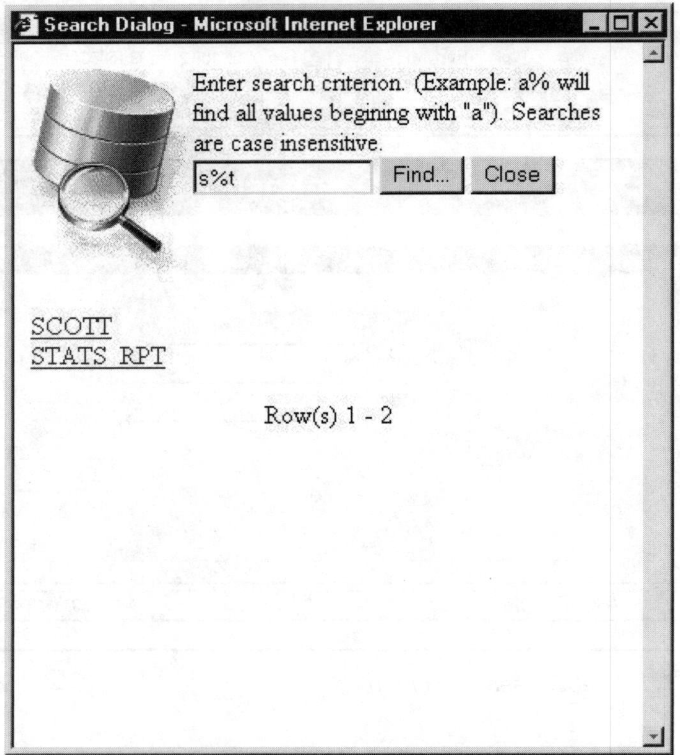

FIGURE 5-8. *WebDB pop-up list for schema selection*

retrieve the objects matching the criteria you specified. Depending on how detailed a query you make it, the WebDB results will vary. If you did not specify a schema or an object name, or you performed a totally blank query, as in Figure 5-9, WebDB will show you the list of schemas, then ask you to choose a schema whose objects you'd like to view. After picking a schema, WebDB will show you all of the object

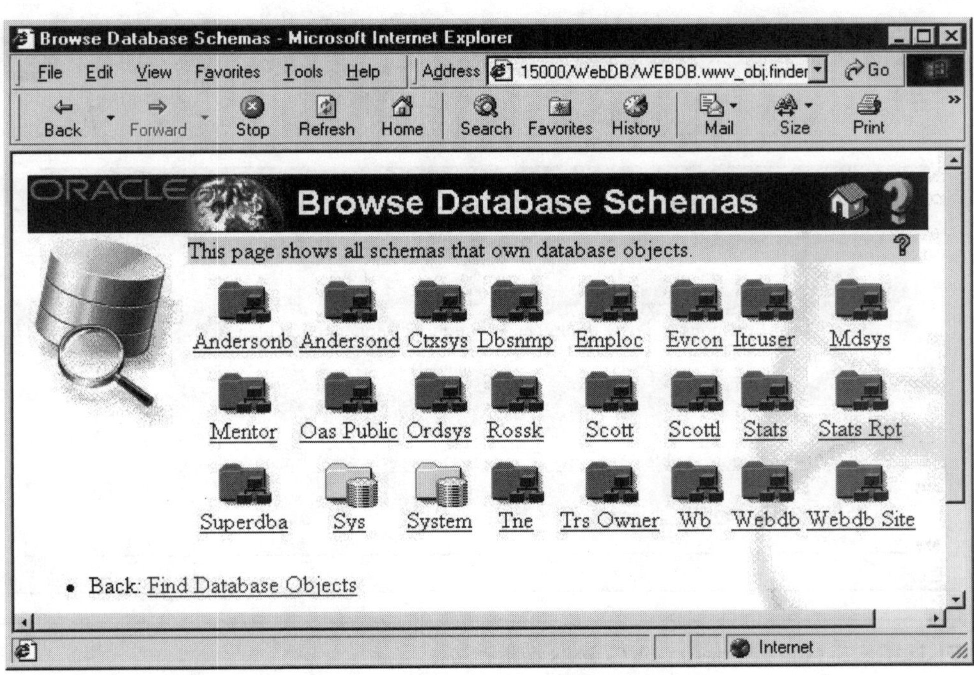

FIGURE 5-9. *No search criteria specified, choose a schema*

categories that exist for that schema, as illustrated in Figure 5-10. From this view, you can drill into specific object types, then into a specific object.

If you specify a specific or wildcard schema and/or object name, such as a schema name like "S%T" and an object name like "%EP%," as illustrated in Figure 5-11, then the results page will show all of the objects matching the criteria within each respective schema. Each specific object type has its own graphical representation. Drilling into specific objects, the pages will appear different for each object type. For example, a package drills into the procedures and functions within,

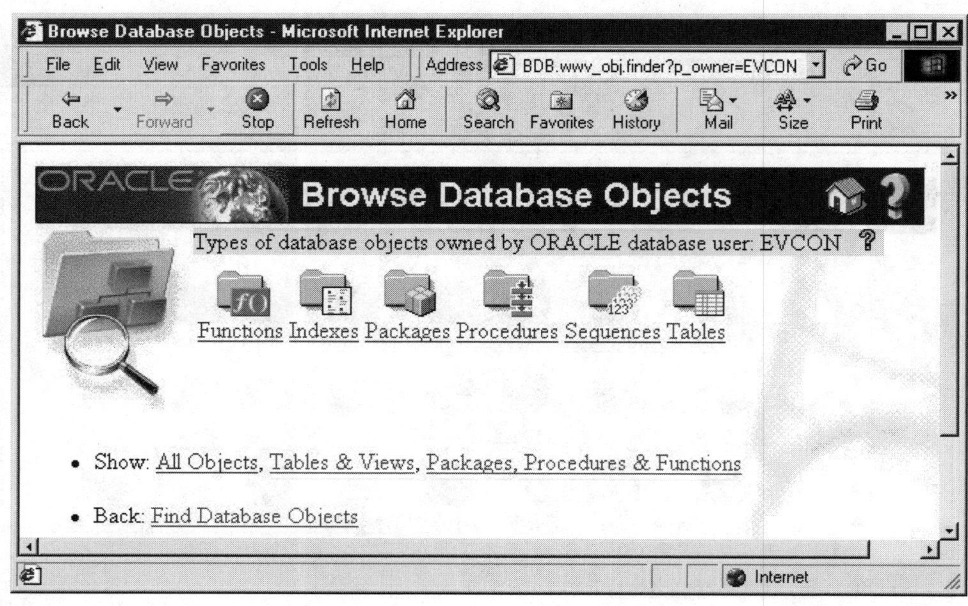

FIGURE 5-10. *Schema EVCON's object list*

whereas drilling into a table enables you to query from the table or view the table attribute details.

NEW If an object was created within the last seven days, you will see the New icon shown next to the object name. For objects that have a state or status, such as packages, procedures, functions, and triggers, you will also see their respective state next to the object name if the object is invalid.

For each specific object type, different operations may be performed. For example, tables and views may not only be queried, but data can be changed (INSERT, UPDATE, DELETE). You can also execute database procedures and functions (WebDB will prompt for the required parameters) or view the contents of packages, view information about triggers, synonyms, or indexes, and much more.

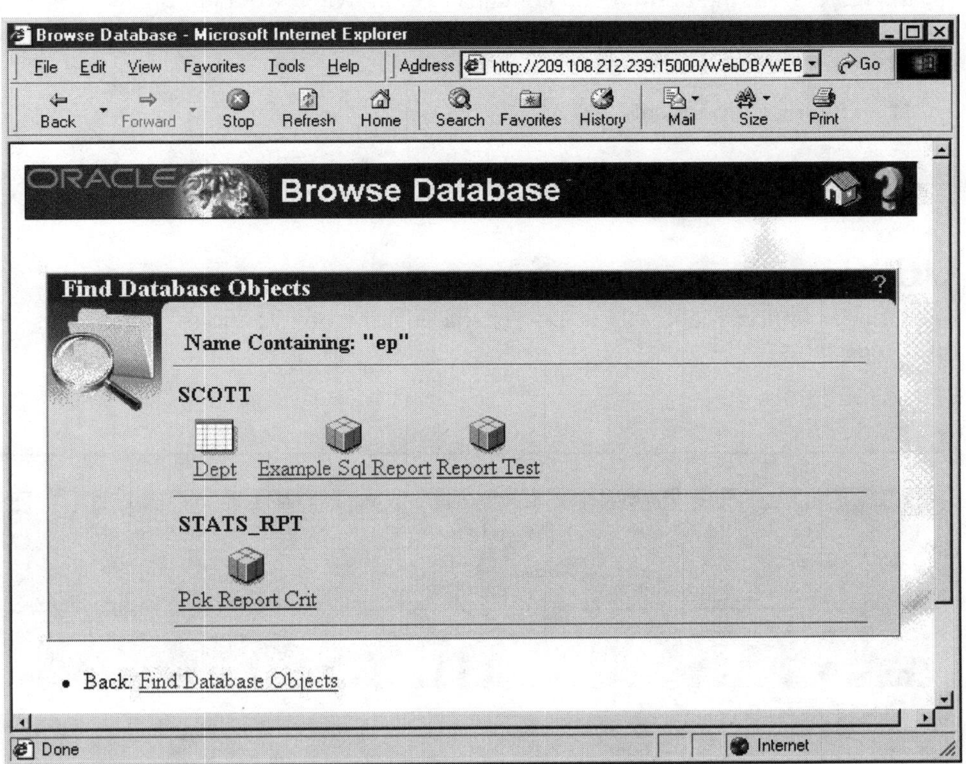

FIGURE 5-11. *All schemas like "S%T" and objects like "%EP%"*

Building Objects and Components

Building objects and components with WebDB can be broken into the following three sections:

- Building WebDB components
- Building shared components
- Building Oracle database objects

In Figure 5-12, the Build menu contains the following two additional options:

- Utilities
- Finding Components

Because the last two options are the easiest to describe, let's start with these—utilities and finding components.

Utilities

The Utilities option enables the export of shared components and manages locks on components.

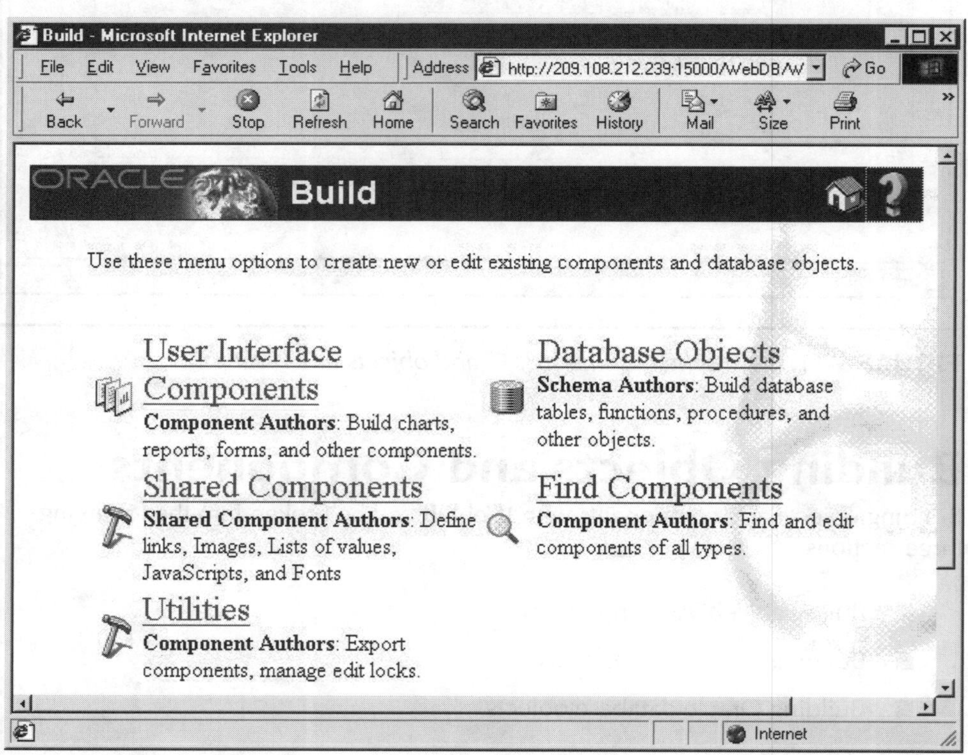

FIGURE 5-12. *WebDB's Build menu*

Exporting Shared Objects

The term "export" is a bit misleading. This isn't the Export utility that DBAs will think of when they see the word export; rather, this export creates a SQL script deleting all records from the specific shared component's table(s) and then inserting each of the records needed to support the shared components on another machine. For example, if you exported the colors shared component, WebDB will create a script (and display it in the browser window for you to cut and paste into SQL*Plus) identical to the following:

```
delete from WWV_COLORS
/
insert into WWV_COLORS values (1002, 'Black', 'black')
/
insert into WWV_COLORS values (1003, 'Red', 'red')
/
insert into WWV_COLORS values (1004, 'Green', 'green')
/
...
```

Managing Component Locks

When developers go into the Edit option for an object, WebDB puts a lock on that object so developers don't have a version conflict. This is a pessimistic locking method; it works most of the time. It does not work if the developer gets distracted in the middle of making changes and closes his or her browser or types in a new URL. When a developer is working with the object, he or she will see the status of each version of the object. In Figure 5-13, user WebDB has locked version 3 in edit mode. If the developer did not notice the status upon clicking on the Edit option, the developer would see a page similar to the page illustrated in Figure 5-14.

When locked components cannot be checked out, your WebDB SYStem administrator will need to navigate from the main WebDB menu into the Build menu, then into the Utilities menu, and finally into the "manage locks on components" option. Upon selecting this option, your administrator will see a list of all locked components and the length of time these objects have been checked out (in minutes). There are only 1,440 minutes in a day. As illustrated in Figure 5-15, many of these components have been locked for a long time. If the same developer comes back to edit the object, WebDB will recognize the user as the same person and enable the user to continue where they left off. If you click the Unlock link (to override the locked objects), WebDB simply displays a message stating that the

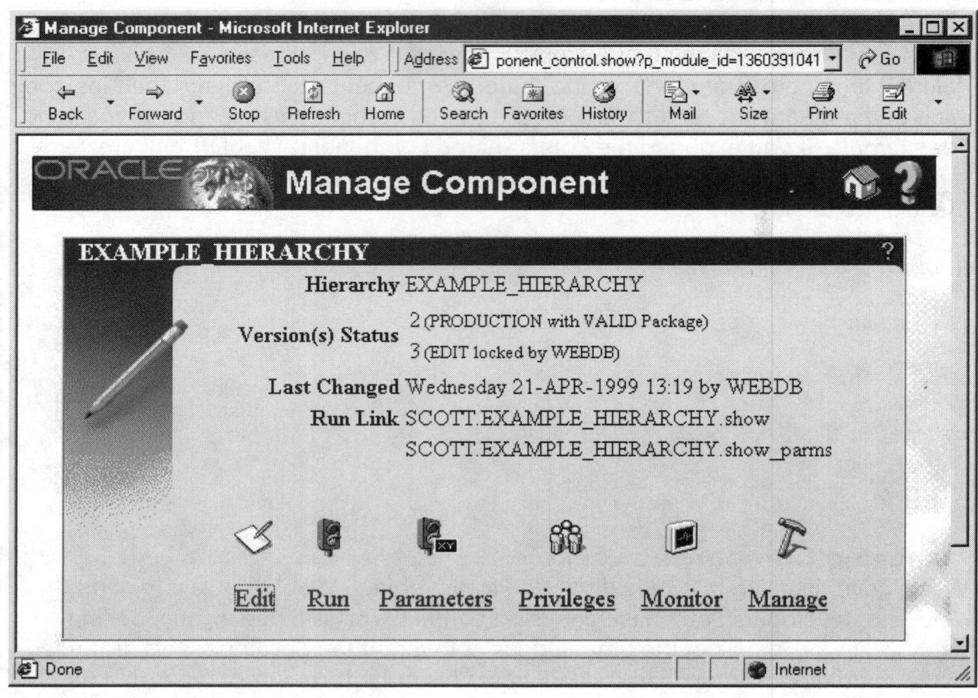

FIGURE 5-13. *Component is locked by another user*

component is now unlocked. If locked objects do not exist, a message will be displayed stating "No components are locked."

Finding Components

Finding components can be confusing because at first you may think this feature is identical to the Browse functionality on the Main menu. The Browse functionality accessible from the WebDB Main menu enables you to find database objects,

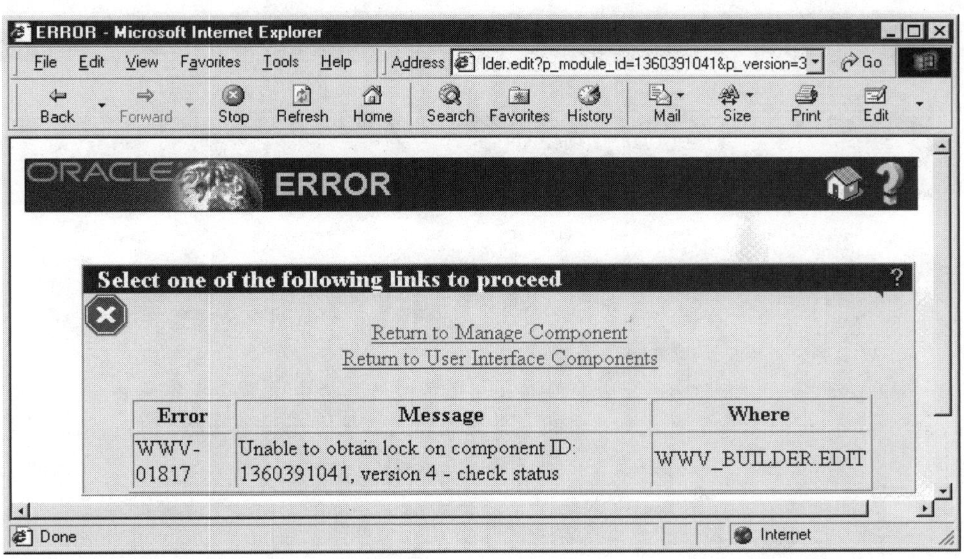

FIGURE 5-14. *Locked components cannot be checked out*

whereas the Find Component feature within the Build component enables you to find user interface and shared components you have built previously using WebDB. Remember that components built in WebDB may or may not be database objects. For example, if you create a list-of-values shared component, it is simply an entry in a WebDB table, and there will not be an associated database object. However, if you build a report with WebDB, WebDB will create a database package to support this report. Since you may have a large number of database packages, you may find it much easier (and more practical since you can edit the component through WebDB using this search engine) to search for the component within the Find Component feature. As illustrated in Figure 5-16, you have the capability to search (by schema, name, type, or status) and find components built with WebDB. The results of your query will appear similar to the output in Figure 5-17. A powerful

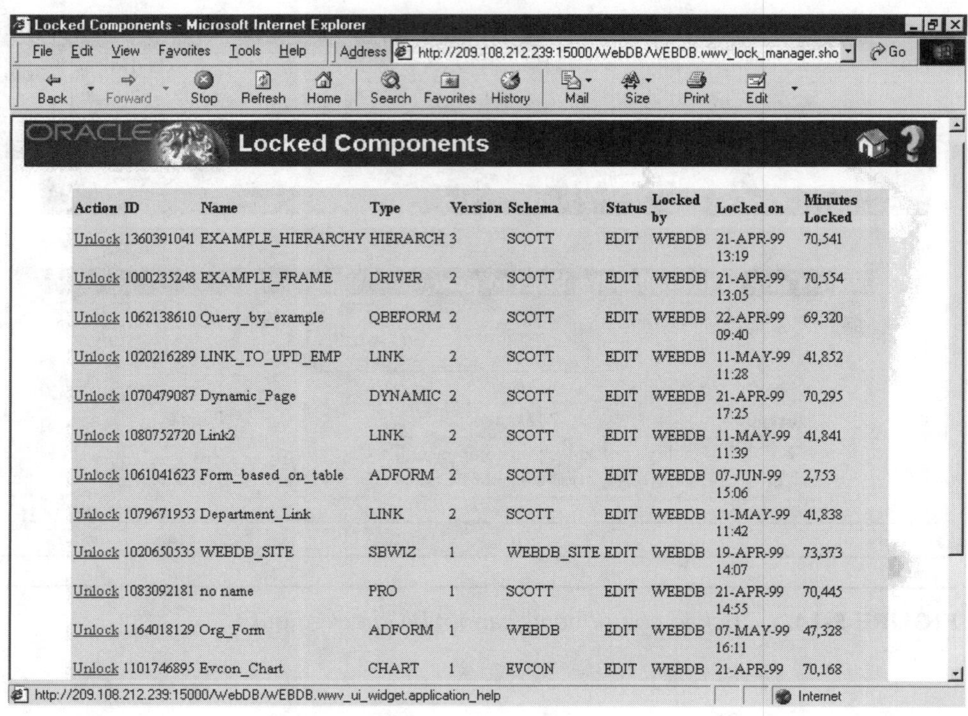

FIGURE 5-15. *Locked components*

feature of this search function is the capability to manage the component by simply clicking on the link provided for each component.

Building WebDB Components

By clicking on the User Interface Components link, shown in Figure 5-12, you will navigate to Main menu, shown in Figure 5-18, to build WebDB components. WebDB enables you to create forms, reports, charts, menus, frame drivers, dynamic pages, calendars, and hierarchies. All of the build components use a friendly wizard interface to create (and edit) the objects that you build.

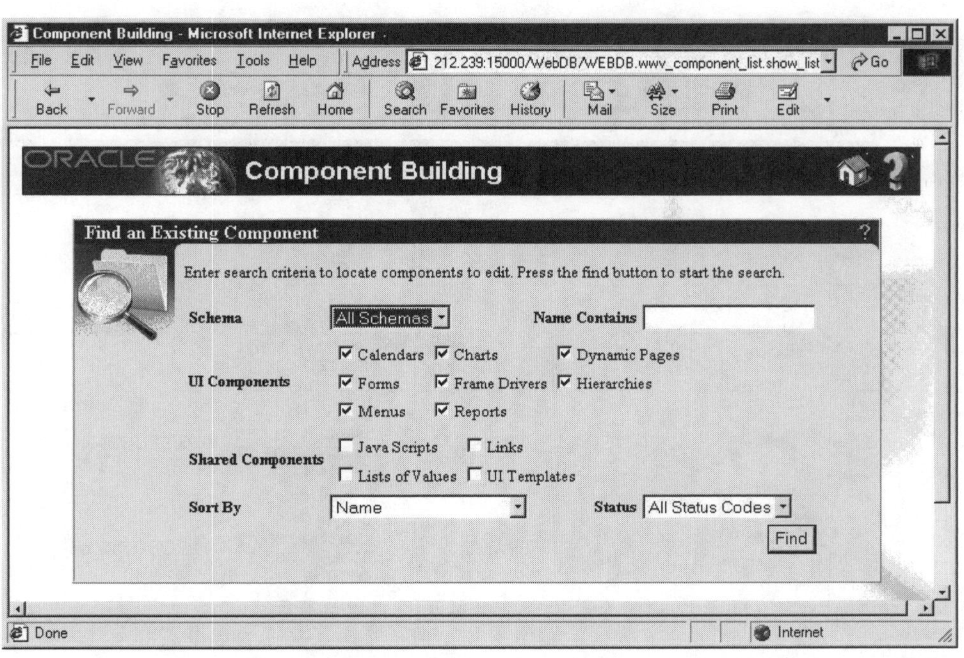

FIGURE 5-16. *Find Components Search page*

Building Forms

When it comes to building forms with WebDB, four types of forms are available: forms on stored procedures, forms on tables/views, master-detail forms, and query by example (QBE) forms. In Figure 5-19, each of the options available is displayed.

Creating Forms for Stored Procedures

In existing applications, you may have a number of procedures that accept a set of parameters and then process that information. For example, you may have a

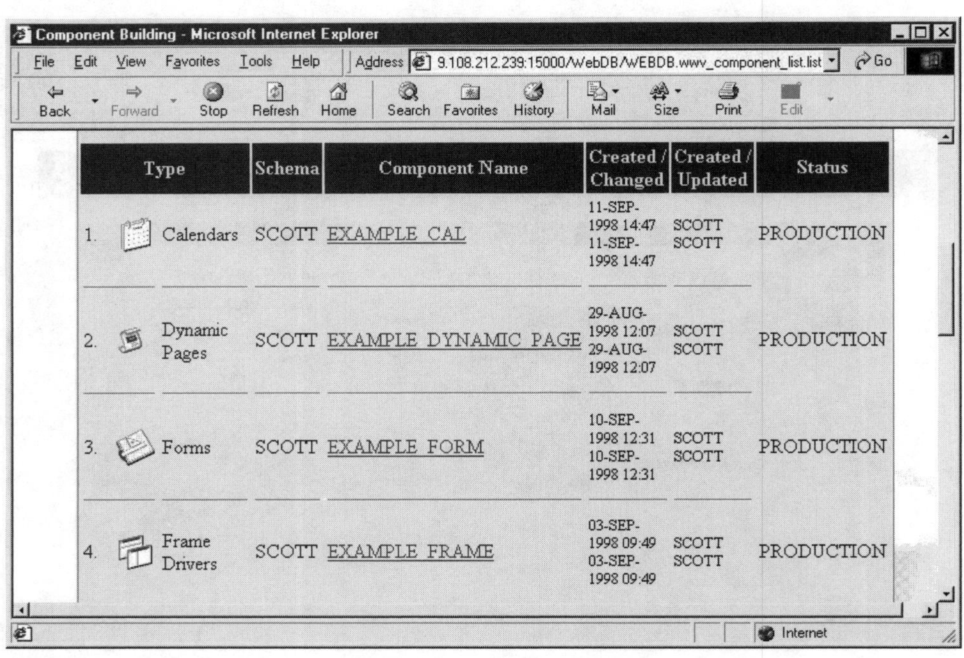

FIGURE 5-17. *Results of Find Components feature*

procedure that accepts a department number and a percentage to increase salaries for the department. Or, you may have a procedure that accepts a name, address, city, state, ZIP, and other information, determines if a current record in the table matches the requested information, and inserts or updates records accordingly. If you have such procedures, the WebDB Forms for Stored Procedures Wizard will prompt to assist in determining the schema and procedure or packaged procedure to call, and based on the information provided will pull the necessary fields needed by the procedure. Then, as illustrated in Figure 5-20, you can set a default value for each parameter, prompt for a specific type of list of values, provide a URL link, and

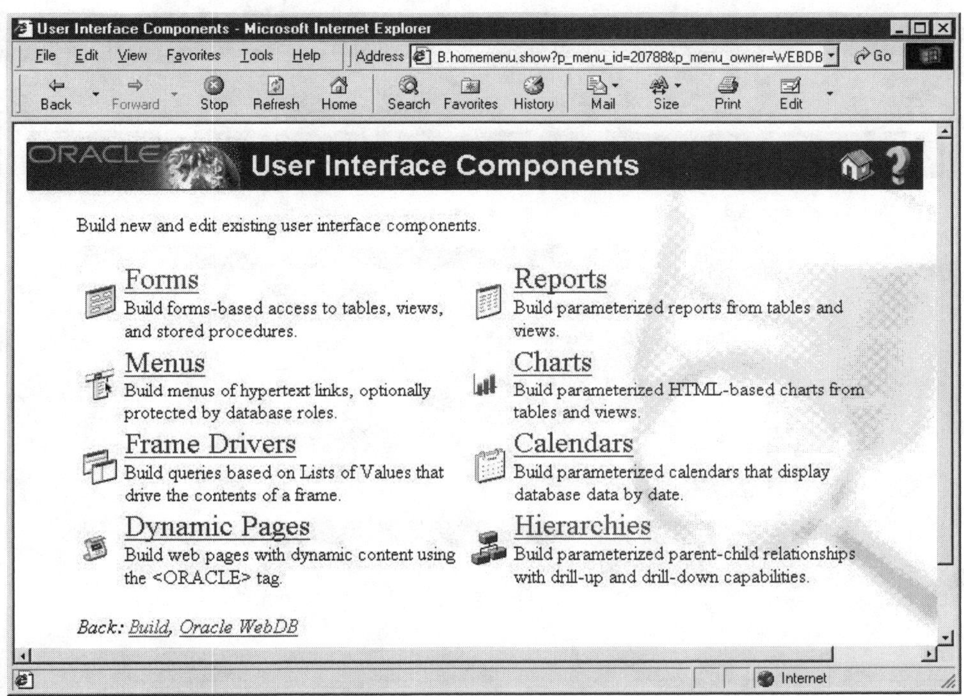

FIGURE 5-18. *User Interface Components Main menu*

much more. In other words, by using all of the information provided, WebDB will build a front end to call your procedure.

The results of the front-end form will be passed on to the procedure upon submission by the end user. Figure 5-21 shows an example of a procedure-based form that a user might use to increase salaries across an entire department. After creating a form using the wizard, you can go back and add blocks of PL/SQL code to several sections of the final generated procedure (this is true for most objects—forms, reports, charts, etc.).

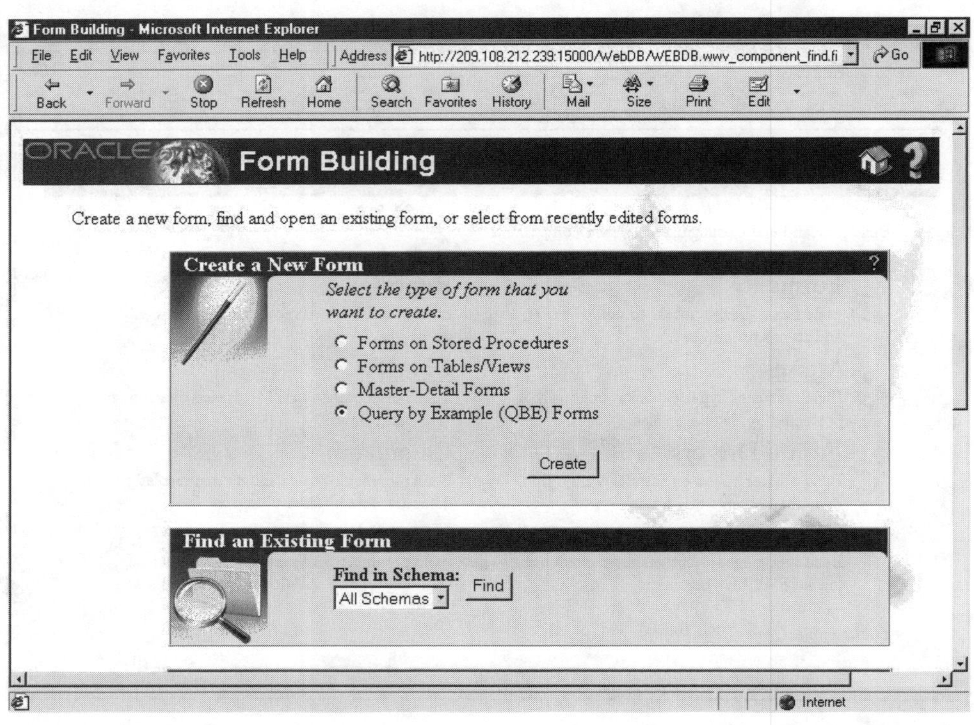

FIGURE 5-19. *Form Building Main menu*

TIP

Although you could edit the procedure created by WebDB with a PL/SQL editor, the WebDB application editing interface is the ideal location to append any custom PL/SQL code. WebDB does not recognize direct code changes to the underlying generated code. If you decide to hand-edit the code that WebDB generates directly, be aware that your changes may be lost if you ever try to regenerate your package using the traditional wizards provided by WebDB. Use the reentrant wizards supplied by WebDB to invoke your custom PL/SQL code.

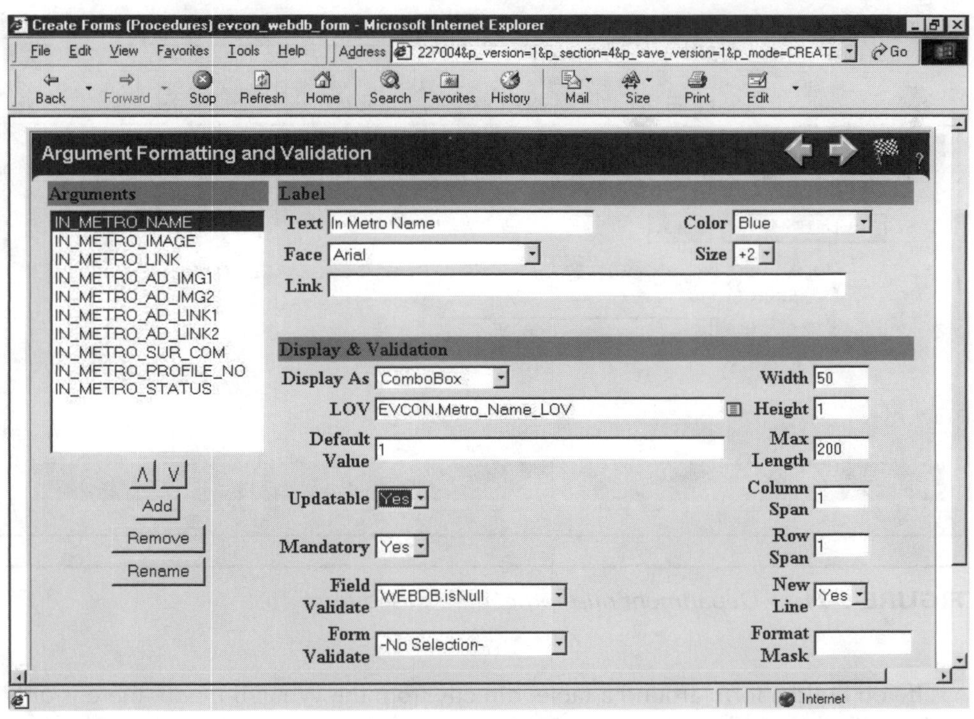

FIGURE 5-20. *Building a form based on a procedure*

Creating Forms to Edit a Table or View

Often the database structure has been built, but the procedures to maintain data in those structures has not. The Forms to Edit a Table or View feature will build a data entry form for a table or view; this is a simple method of creating table maintenance screens for applications. I've found that typically 80 percent of my work goes into 20 percent of my forms—Web forms or otherwise. It's my feeling that WebDB will be able to create 80 percent of your forms, which unfortunately is only about 20 percent of your work. However, I'll take the 20 percent of the work (or time). In other words, this feature alone will help you build 80 percent of your forms (in terms of count—or numbers) in nearly no time at all. A great feature of this WebDB interface is its ability to modify a form even after it has been initially created by the wizard. The wizard enables you to dynamically create and modify your forms.

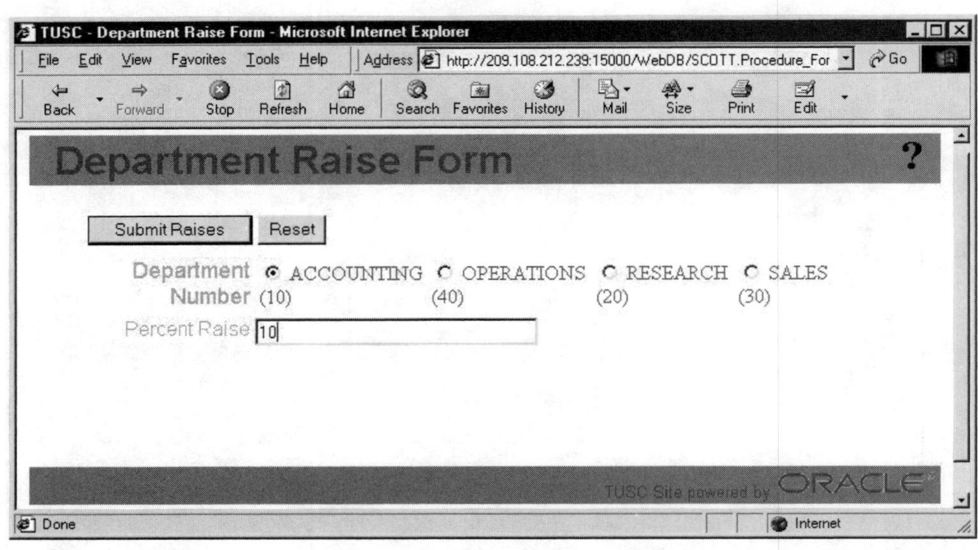

FIGURE 5-21. *Department raise procedure-based form*

If you build a form around a table, directly from the WebDB menu, there is only an Insert option, which allows you to enter records that are inserted into your table. You can, however, call the form to update and delete rows, but this is typically done with a query by example (QBE) form that uses a shared object called a link. To call the form in update mode, the URL looks like this:

```
http://www.webdb.com:15000/WebDB/SCOTT.EXAMPLE_FORM.show?p_arg_names
=_show_
header&p_arg_values=YES&p_arg_names=_rowid&p_arg_values=KING&p_arg_
names=_alt_rowid&p_arg_values=ENAME
```

Notice the name of my form is example_form, which is in the scott schema. The called procedure within the package is show. Each of the columns is passed into arrays—specifically, the p_arg_names array, which is the name of each array value, and the p_arg_value array, which contains the value of the respective named object. In the preceding example, the _show_header argument is set to Yes, rowid is set to 'KING', and _alt_rowid is set to ename. The show procedure parses out _rowid and _alt_rowid as the field names. In other words, the above URL is pulling a record where ename='KING'. The link shared object builds the URL to retrieve the correct record based on a unique field (i.e., empno would be a better unique number than ename). I realize this may be confusing as you read this, but give it a try. You'll find that it's not really that confusing at all.

Creating Master-Detail Forms

A master-detail form displays a master row and multiple detail rows—for example, a department and the employees in the department. To create a master-detail form using the WebDB Wizard, you will need to provide the master and detail tables and respective columns for each table. Unlike calling (and passing parameters to) the underlying packaged procedure for table/view forms, the values are not passed into the packaged procedure using an array, but using specific field names. To call the packaged procedure example_md_form.show to retrieve a record where deptno=10, you would use the following URL:

```
http://webdb.tusc.com:15000/WebDB/SCOTT.EXAMPLE_MD_FORM.show?p_rowid=
10&p_alt_rowid=DEPTNO
```

Calling the show_parms procedure will pull up a query by example form to retrieve specific master records and allow editing of those records matching the query:

```
http://webdb.tusc.com:15000/WebDB/SCOTT.EXAMPLE_MD_FORM.show_parms
```

Creating a Query by Example (QBE) Form

The QBE form will typically be used as the front end for your table/view forms, as previously described. The QBE form enables you to prompt for column values to be used in the where clause, specify how to order the retrieved records, and specify in which columns you would like to display a sum. The output can be displayed as HTML, in an Excel spreadsheet, or as ASCII. If you execute the show_parms procedure within your QBE form's package, the QBE form will prompt the user for the preceding information, whereas if you call the show procedure and don't pass any parameters, the QBE form will execute the query without a where clause.

Building Reports

When building reports, you have two choices: build the query statement using the Query Wizard (WebDB prompts for the table, columns, and where clause) or type the SQL statement. If you have written the SQL statements previously, they probably exist in a file somewhere on your system. If that is the case, you can cut and paste the query into WebDB. If you are an experienced developer, you may find it easier and less painful to type the SQL statement rather than stepping through the Query Wizard. The Query Wizard will only enable you to pick any one table or view to base your report on. Therefore, if you would like to build a report based on a complex query, type the SQL statement. One might think the end result (internal to WebDB) of both methods is a SQL statement; however, it is not. Each method is maintained by a completely separate editor. Therefore, you need to choose the proper report type before you create the report. My general recommendation would be to type the SQL statement. Identical to the QBE forms, the results can be output to HTML, Excel, or ASCII.

Building Charts

In the same manner as used to create reports, charts can be built from the chart's SQL Wizard or by typing a SQL statement. After creating your chart package, the user can be prompted to build a where clause for the chart through the point-and-click interface. The charts are flexible during development and even at runtime (if you so choose). You can only generate bar charts (displayed horizontally or vertically). You can also enable users to set the axis (zero, average value, first value, last value, maximum value, minimum value) and include a number of statistics at the bottom of the chart (average value, axis name, count of values, first value, last value, maximum value, sum of values). WebDB's charting mechanism uses a package called OWA_CHART, which is discussed in detail in Chapter 6.

Building Menus

Menus enable you to build Web-based menus for your Web applications. Menus can have submenus. Each menu item is assigned to a database role, granting users view privileges to menu items. Each menu item is assigned a bullet icon (from the images shared library), a name to be displayed, help text, and more. Menu items can be assigned to a specific URL (e.g., www.tusc.com) or they can reference components of WebDB.

Building Frame Drivers

A frame driver enables you to divide the HTML page up into two logical pages (driving frame and target frame) with different URLs (a specific URL, a PL/SQL routine, or a static HTML page) for each subpage (or frame) assigned to each logical frame. The first frame enables you to write a query and retrieve records in a list (combo box, radio button, etc.). Upon the completion of the user's selection, the results will be returned to the target frame. The page can be broken up into a frame size(s) you desire.

Building Dynamic Pages

Dynamic pages are similar to the Cold Fusion or Microsoft's ASP approach to building Web pages. This approach is also very similar to the industry standard server-side includes (SSI) or Oracle's LiveHTML approach. All of these approaches use HTML files with embedded server-side tags. A WebDB dynamic page is a page containing HTML with embedded <ORACLE> tags. The Oracle tag contains your PL/SQL code. For example, the PL/SQL code in the following script checks to see if the current time is before or after 12 P.M., then displays a message accordingly:

```
<HTML>
<HEAD>
<TITLE>This uses Oracle Tag</TITLE>
</HEAD>

<BODY>
<ORACLE>
if to_number(to_char(sysdate,'hh24'))>12 then
   htp.header(1,'Good Afternoon');
else
   htp.header(1,'Good Morning');
end if;
</ORACLE>
<H2>Example of A Dynamic Page</H1>
<ORACLE>select * from scott.emp where sal>1000</ORACLE>
</BODY>
</HTML>
```

TIP
Dynamic pages provide an extremely powerful way to build highly customized data-driven HTML pages for your Web sites and applications.

Building Calendars

OAS provides a packaged Toolkit utility called owa_util.calendarprint to display a calendar based on data in a table. The calendar-building capabilities of WebDB use the calendarprint routine. To build a calendar, supply a SQL statement containing the date (to display on the calendar), the value to display on that date, and, optionally, a target URL to branch to if the displayed value is selected. Be sure to order your query by date.

Building Hierarchies

SQL provides a component of the SELECT statement called a "connect by" providing a hierarchy of data. A good example of such a query would be a company's organizational chart where the organization chart starts with the president of the company, showing each direct report, subordinates, and so on. The hierarchy functionality within WebDB enables you to build a connect by showing the information graphically, to be drilled into one level at a time as shown in Figure 5-22.

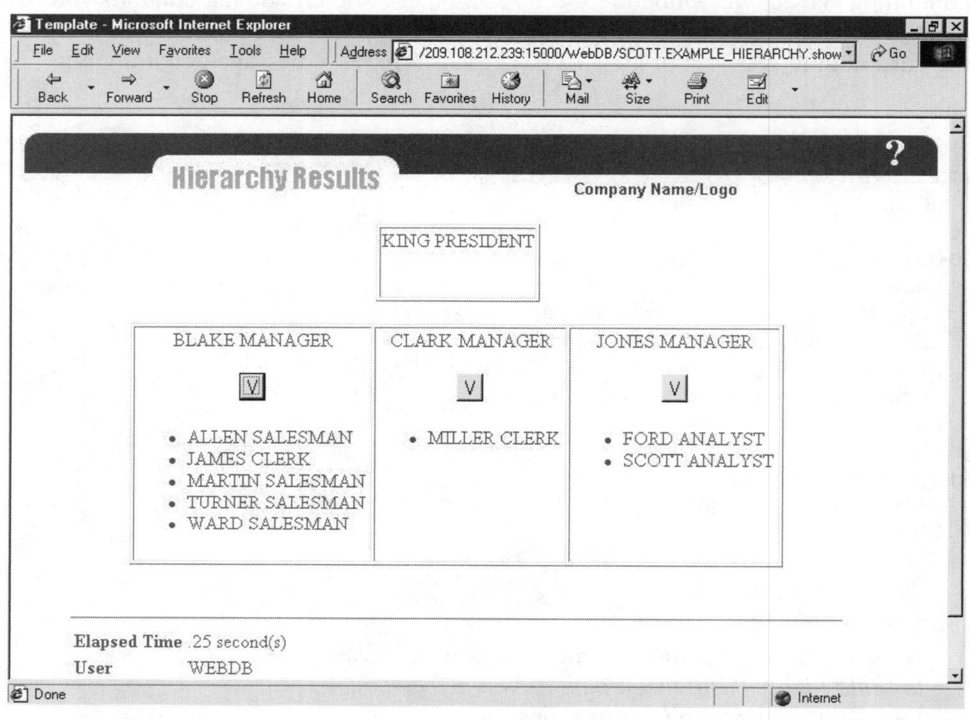

FIGURE 5-22. *Hierarchy of the famous EMP table*

Building Shared Components

Shared components within WebDB include colors, fonts, images, a JavaScript library, links, lists of values, and user interface templates. These features are powerful because they provide inheritable objects for your WebDB application components. WebDB comes with examples and usable components for each shared component type. Prior to writing your complete WebDB application, you will want to define your shared components as much as possible.

Assigning Shared Colors

WebDB comes with a predefined list of about 35 colors. You can define many colors (or just a few) for use throughout your Web application. To define colors, you can provide a logical name for the color or a hex value (using #rrggbb where rr is the hex code 00-FF for red, gg is green, and bb is blue). In forms, reports, and other components, you can specify colors for fonts and other attributes.

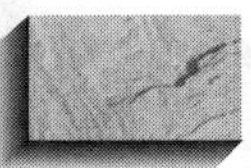

TIP

If you define color names such as <application>_background and <application>_text_color (i.e., iw_background and iw_text_color) it will be easier to change the color scheme of an entire application by simply changing the underlying hex values!

Defining Shared Fonts

Font support depends on the user's browser, platform, loaded fonts, and more. However, WebDB enables you to define the fonts that your application will support. There are about 20 predefined fonts. To define a font, provide the name of the font as it would be recognized by the <FONT> tag in HTML. When you select the Fonts option within the shared components, the same text is displayed in each of the defined fonts. You will likely notice that many of the test fonts look the same. This is because unrecognized fonts will be displayed using the browser's default font.

Pointing to Your Images

Organizing your images within WebDB is actually quite simple. WebDB supports a number of image types, including arrows, backgrounds, database browsing, database objects, icons, logos, template art, and wizard images. These images are typically provided as drop-down lists throughout WebDB.

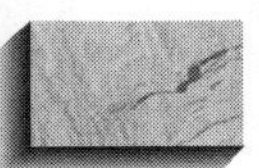

TIP

When specifying the name of the image file, be sure to prepend the logical directory. The logical directory is relative to the root directory for the site that will be using the image (i.e., /images/myLogo.gif).

Creating a JavaScript Library

The JavaScript library is absolutely one of the finest features of WebDB, enabling you to build your own library with components to be included in any form. Not only can the routines be included for field-level validation, but WebDB also supports form-level validation. WebDB comes with three predefined JavaScript scripts that cannot be modified; however, you may copy and modify any of the predefined scripts. The predefined JavaScript routines are as follows:

- **isNumber** Ensuring the field value is a number
- **inRange0_100** Ensuring the specified value is between 0 and 100
- **isNull** Ensuring the user did not leave the field blank

It's unlikely that you would copy and edit the isNumber or isNull routines, but it is likely that you'll copy the inRange routine. Each script you create can be tested using both field- and form-level validation. The scripts you create can be any valid JavaScript function. The following script is not a complex JavaScript function, but it shows the required parameters (both of them) and how to display the name and value of the passed parameters:

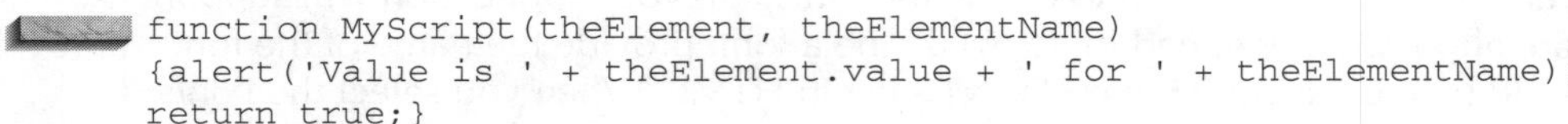

```
function MyScript(theElement, theElementName)
{alert('Value is ' + theElement.value + ' for ' + theElementName);
return true;}
```

An important feature of WebDB is that JavaScript routines (and actually all shared components) are dynamically pulled from your shared component library. If you change a JavaScript routine, the changes will be inherited by *all* of the forms that reference the shared component.

TIP
If you wish to use a JavaScript function from WebDB in your custom OAS applications, you can use the following code to extract the JavaScript from WebDB:

```
WEBDB.wwv_javascript.open_script;
WEBDB.wwv_javascript.print_script(routine_name);
WEBDB.wwv_javascript.close_script;
```

For example, if you wanted to use the built-in isNumber JavaScript library routine, your OAS code would look like this:

```
WEBDB.wwv_javascript.open_script;
WEBDB.wwv_javascript.print_script('WEBDB.isNumber');
WEBDB.wwv_javascript.close_script;
```

Defining Links

Defining links is a powerful feature that allows you to build and manage a list of associations between column names and stored procedure calls. For any field shown in a report or on a form, you can provide a stored procedure call enabling the user to drill further into the information. In effect, the links you define provide context-sensitive links in your reports, graphs, and forms. Links can be defined to point to a specific WebDB component or run a specific graph, report, form, or a specific hardcoded URL.

Defining List of Values

Another powerful shared component is the list of values. Your list of values can be defined from a dynamic (based on a SQL query) or a static source (based on hardcoded values). A list of values can be displayed a number of ways, including a combo (drop-down list box), multicombo (multiple selection box), radio (radio buttons), check (checkboxes), or pop (pop-up list—separate window). To make it easier during your development, choose one display method as your default method. Once you specify the criteria for your list of values, test it using WebDB.

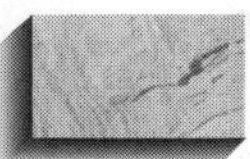

TIP

Defining a list of values is a great way to implement cross-table validation!

Creating User Interface Templates

The final shared component left to discuss is the user interface (UI) template. This is the HTML used as the shell to display the HTML page. The UI template is the definition that you will use to set a standard look and feel for your Web pages throughout your application. Like all other shared components, the templates are dynamically read from the database, providing you with the capability to change your templates at any point in time. This inheritance-based feature allows you to change the entire look of your site all at once. The templates are basic HTML, so you can use any HTML design tool (even Notepad or vi) to create your templates. Pieces of information are dropped into the template using substitution tags, which include the following:

- #TITLE# Component title
- #HEADING# Component heading
- #HELPLINK# Help link
- #HOMELINK# Home link
- #FRAMELINK# Frame link, for use with menus
- #BODY# Body
- #IMAGE_PREFIX# /images/

TIP
Defining your standard navigation bar (copyright or legal disclaimers) inside the template allows for a consistent look and feel as well as eliminating the need for repeating code.

Building Oracle Database Objects

Using the Build Oracle Database Objects feature of WebDB, you can build (not maintain) tables, views, indexes, sequences, synonyms, triggers, packages, procedures, and functions. WebDB is consistent with its wizard-like interface because all of the components are built through the standard interface here. Figure 5-23 illustrates the initial page that enables you to define the type of object you wish to create. Keep in mind that your DBA may not like it if new objects are created through WebDB and not in their build DDL scripts or their CASE tool, so be sure to verify with your DBA that it is acceptable to use WebDB to create objects in your database.

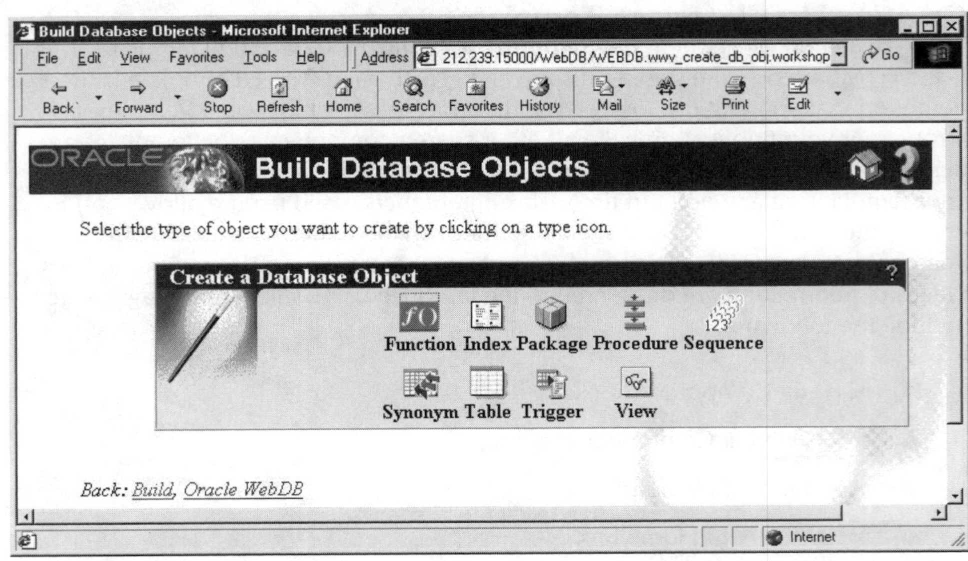

FIGURE 5-23. *Build Database Objects feature*

Administering WebDB

The administration portion of WebDB assists in overseeing components and database objects from user privileges to Listener settings. Figure 5-24 shows the complete WebDB Administration menu.

Making the Most of the User Manager

The User Manager enables you to create or edit database accounts. When editing accounts, you can change everything from a specific user's password or the default tablespace or temp tablespace, to their profile, to granting access, assigning roles, and issuing WebDB browse and build privileges.

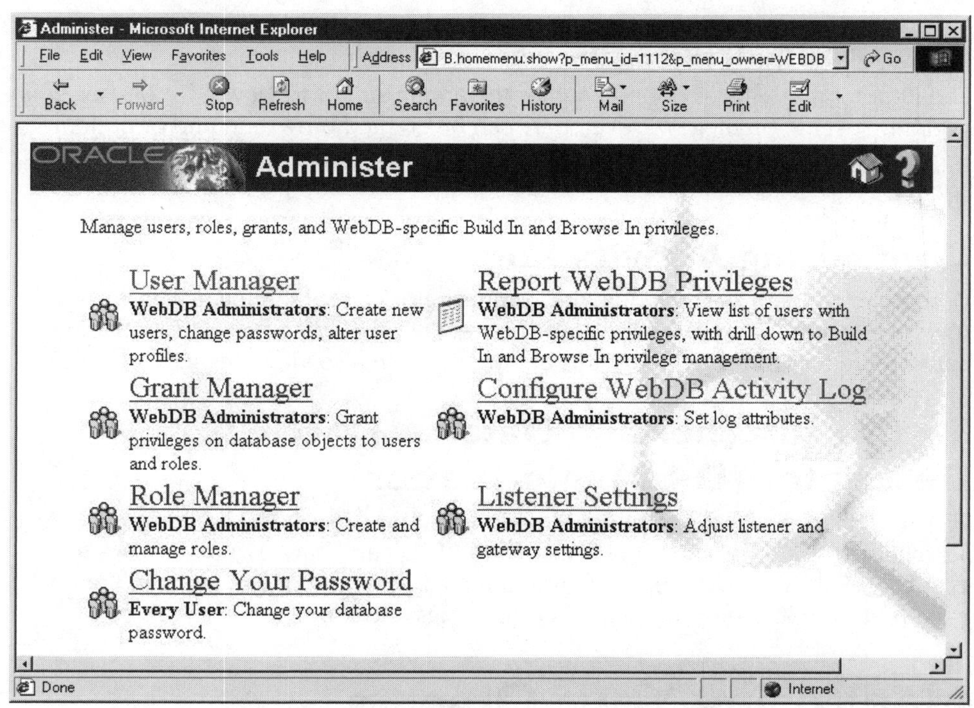

FIGURE 5-24. *WebDB's Administration Main menu*

Using the Grant Manager

The Grant Manager enables you to grant specific users or roles the privilege to access specific database objects.

Using the Role Manager

The Role Manager assists in creating and managing roles. Prior to Oracle8i, procedures could not use roles or the privileges of the executing user. However, WebDB has implemented their own powerful Role Manager, checking the identity of the originating user and the grants and roles assigned to that specific user.

Changing Your Password

The "Changing your password" menu option is available to every user of WebDB, enabling the user to change his or her personal Oracle schema password.

Reporting Privileges

The Reporting Privileges option enables the administrator to view a list of users with WebDB-specific privileges. Developers can be granted browse in and/or build in access to specific schemas. From this page, the administrator can drill into the administration of specific users privileges, grants, and settings.

Configuring Activity Log

Within the configure activity log, the administrator can set the log attributes—specifically, the log switch interval (default every 14 days) to the number of days appropriate for your site. Under this option, you can also view the activity logs.

Setting Listener and Database Access Descriptor (DAD) Information

Within the Listener Setting option, the administrator can adjust Listener and gateway settings. The administrator can set the default DAD and each DAD's settings for WebDB. Within the Listener configuration, the administrator can manage the thread maximums and establish the directory mappings and MIME types.

Monitoring Your Objects

WebDB provides an administrator with a number of monitoring options. Each user interface component created by your developers contains the option of logging performance information. If you plan to analyze the performance of your site, it would be wise to take advantage of this feature. There are four types of objects that can be monitored within WebDB, as is evident from Figure 5-25:

- User interface components
- Activity log
- Database objects
- Batch jobs

Monitoring User Interface Component Performance

As is apparent in Figure 5-26, analyzing the performance of your WebDB application can be conducted in a number of ways. The Monitoring User Interface Component Performance option enables you to monitor all end-user requests for components. The information can be reviewed by response times, component name, day and hour, database user, browser type, IP address, page type, and rows returned.

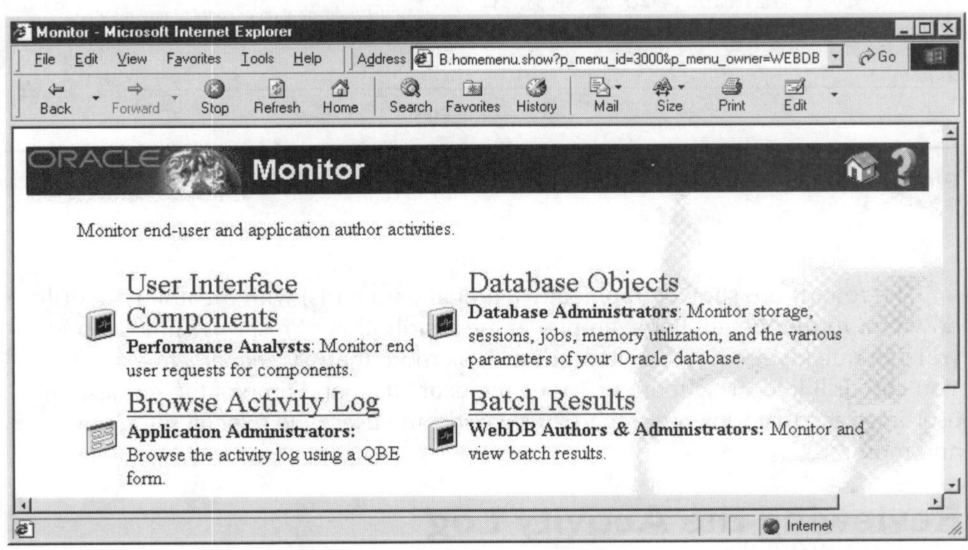

FIGURE 5-25. *WebDB's Monitor Main menu*

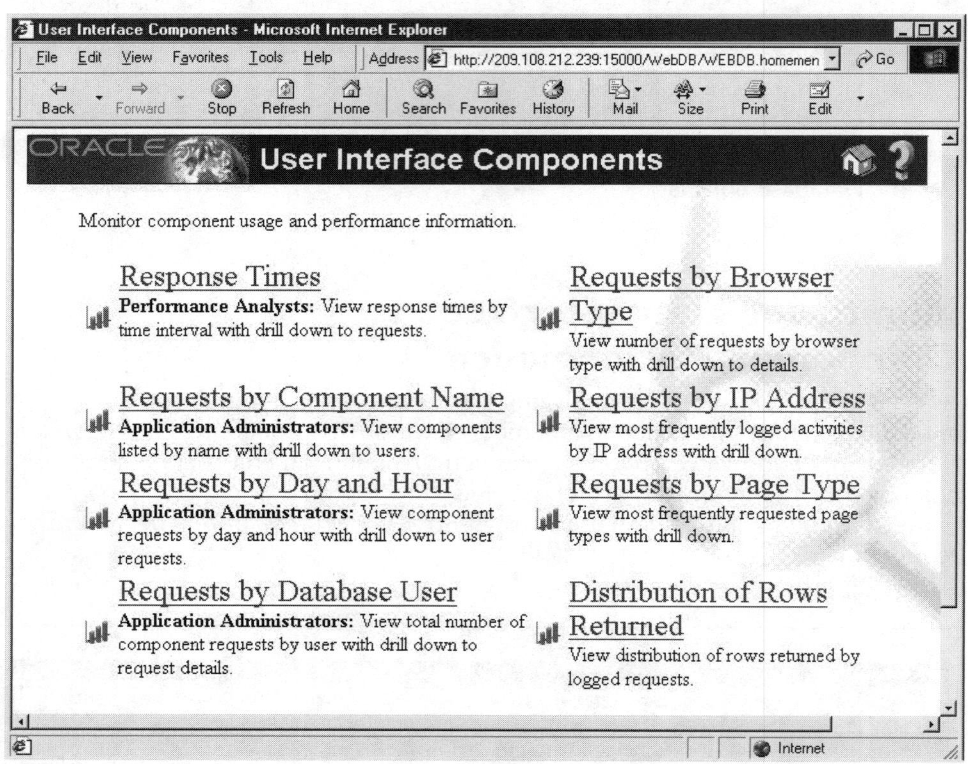

FIGURE 5-26. *Monitoring User Interface Components feature*

The reports are shown graphically (vertical bar charts) with the ability to drill down for further detail. For example, in the distribution of response times report, you can quickly see how many requests took more than 20 seconds to execute. You can drill into these requests to see the exact date and time of the request, the user interface that took more than 20 seconds, the user who executed the query, and more.

Reviewing the Activity Log

The Reviewing the Activity Log feature is a good example of WebDB recursively using itself. Within Reviewing the Activity Log, you can browse the activity log using a QBE form as we reviewed above. You have the capability of displaying specific fields as well as building your where clause, order by, output format, and more.

Monitoring Database Objects

The Monitoring Database Objects feature within WebDB is great for monitoring locks, redo logs, rollback segments, storage, sessions, jobs, memory utilization, and various init.ora parameters of your Oracle database. Monitoring database objects provides you with some of the top DBA scripts. The advantage is that the scripts can be run and displayed from any browser, and many of them provide graphs of the information. The features in the Monitoring Database Objects option make for the beginning of a great DBA Toolkit.

Reviewing Batch Job Results and Performance

The Review Batch Job Results and Performance option enables the administrator to monitor and view batch results. Because the Batch Manager requires the job_queue_processes init.ora parameter be set to a value greater than one and there are two other init.ora parameters affecting the timing frequency of duration/execution of batch jobs, this menu option enables you to check these init.ora parameters and make sure that they are properly set. If they are not properly set, you will want to let your DBA know so the values can be corrected.

Building Sites

If you would like to pull together your application into a site (more than just a front-end menu), the Sites section of WebDB will help you do this. The Sites feature will not only enable you to store this information, but will allow you to build and monitor a Web site wholly contained within the database.

TIP

"Wholly contained within the database" means that all components used to build the site were defined by and are stored within WebDB. For example, you cannot use server-side JavaScript functionality because the .js file is not within WebDB.

If you wish to use the Sites section of WebDB, you must first create a site using the Site Creation Wizard. Creating a WebDB site creates a number of tables, packages, data, and more, taking a "little while" to run, as mentioned above. As the creation is progressing, WebDB will provide you with an installation status progression bar, and the current step. WebDB creates an entire site in a schema of its own. There are a total of 13 steps, defined in the following section.

From the WebDB Site Install Menu page, you have two initial links to your newly-created Website:

- Site administration
- Site home page

Clicking on the Site Home Page enables you to view the site as a public user would. The URL that it branches to is the URL you would distribute to your site users. Clicking on Site Administration will present you with a number of options available as discussed in the following section.

Administering Your Site

Upon clicking on the Site Administration link, WebDB will prompt you for a username and password for the name of your site administrator schema. The site administrator is the account that created the site. Typically, the account will be named webdb, but it might be another account as well. When you created the site (using whatever account has these privileges), you also created a new schema that contains the tables, procedures, etc. The username and password for that schema will be the same initially—change this immediately! When you created the site, WebDB prompted you for the username. Although this account owns the database objects, it does not technically own the site—WebDB does. Figure 5-27 is an example of the main Administration menu that you'll see for a site if you log in as the database object owner—note that only four options are available. If you log in as the true site administrator, you should see that there are 13 primary options available to the administrator as shown in Figure 5-28 and Figure 5-29:

- Site Map
- Site
- Style
- Folder
- Category
- Perspective

- Custom Item Type
- Group
- User
- Privilege
- Personal Information
- Site Statistics
- Search

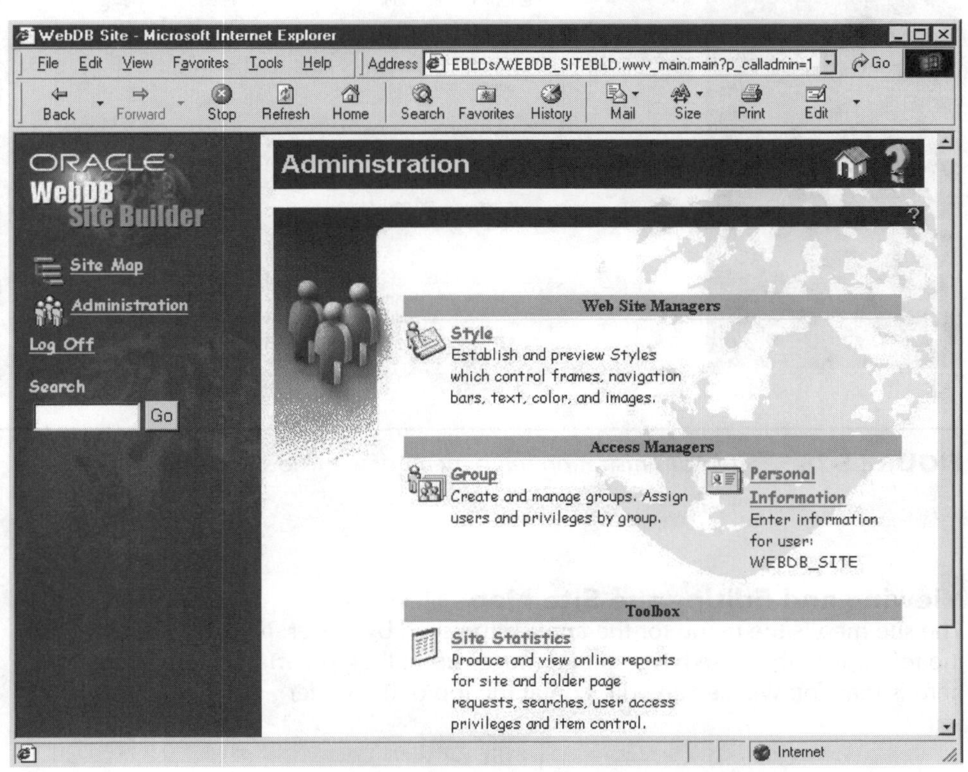

FIGURE 5-27. *Site Administration main menu of the database object owner*

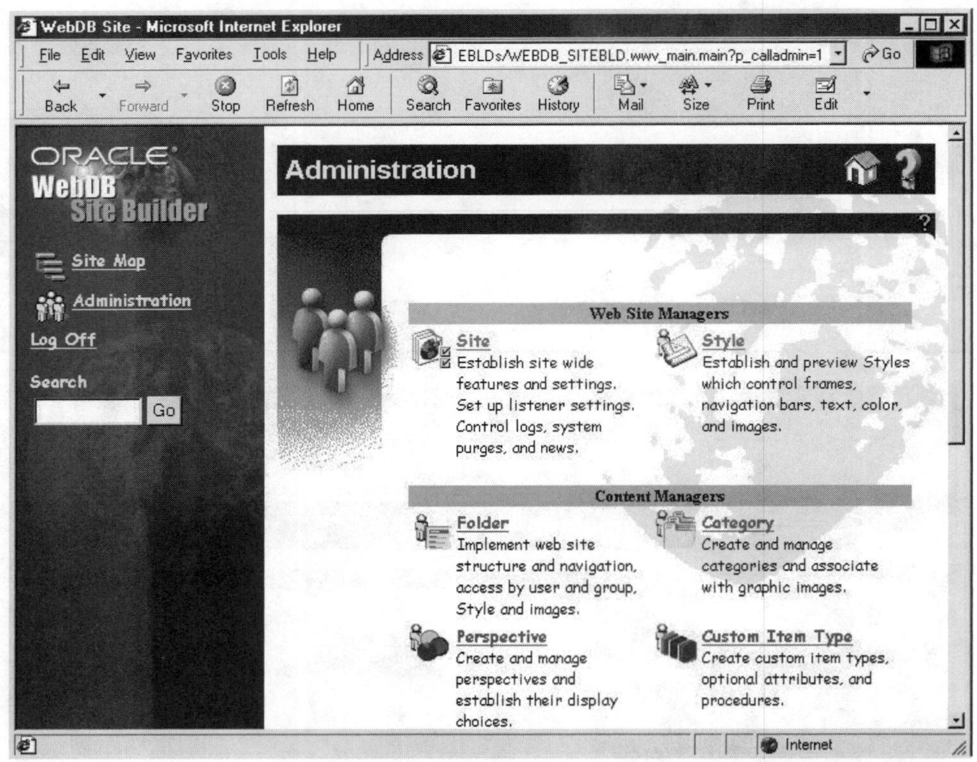

FIGURE 5-28. *Site Administration main menu of the true site owner – part 1*

Viewing and Editing the Site Map

The site map is the menu for the application seen by a user. If you're the owner of the folder (or otherwise have edit privileges upon that folder), then the exception here is that you will see an edit icon at the top of the folder.

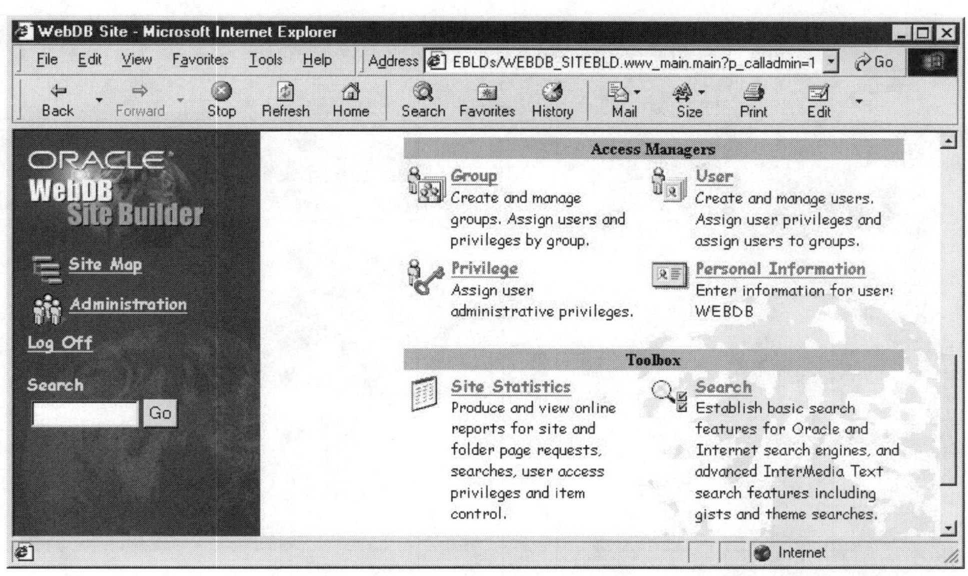

FIGURE 5-29. *Site Administration main menu of the true site owner – part 2*

By clicking on this icon, the folder will be displayed in edit mode enabling you to add items, add folders, set folder properties, set navigation bar properties, edit styles, edit objects, delete specific objects, or move objects to other folders as is seen in Figure 5-30.

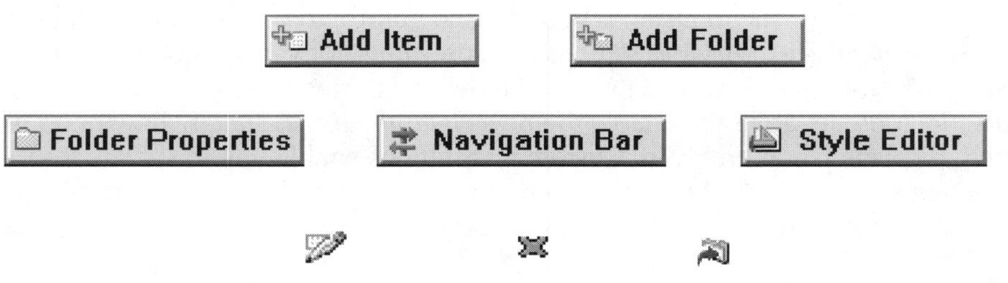

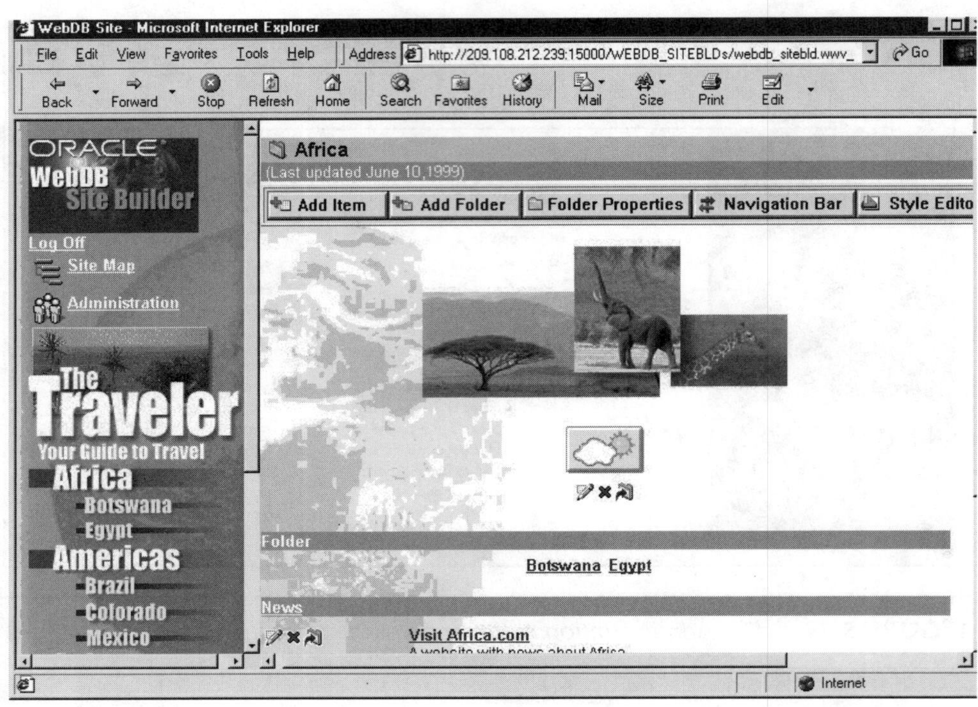

FIGURE 5-30. *Administration of the Africa folder*

Establishing Site-Wide Features and Settings

Through the Site link on the Administrative page, you can establish site-wide features and settings, set up Listener settings, and control logs, system purges, and news. System-wide features and settings include values for version control, item deletion, keyword searches, and items to be deleted during a system purge. News features include the ability to enable the news feature, and to specify how news is created, displayed, and archived. Custom text settings enable you to specify the display text for each of the links displayed in the navigation bar and the content area. These links include the text displayed for:

- Category link
- Log on link
- Log off link

- News link
- Perspective link
- Folder banner
- Site map link

Establishing and Previewing Styles

You can establish and preview styles through the Style link on the administrative page. Styles enable you to control the frames, text/font, color, and images for your site's navigation bars, banners, and content area.

Implementing Folder Characteristics

Implementing folder characteristics is accomplished from the Folder link on the Administrative page. Web site structure and navigation are definable within this area. New folders can be added, and existing folders can be edited or deleted. Upon editing a folder, access levels can be established by user and group. The folder's style and images (banner and title) can be set. You can also establish the size of the folder images. The default is blank, in which case the browser will display the actual size of the image. If all of your images are roughly the same size (and small), this should work just fine. However, if your images are large or of a great variety of sizes, the images may vary greatly in size, which will create a disproportional-looking page. Therefore, I'd recommend that all of your images be about the same size (or at least of proportional dimensions) and that you set the size parameters accordingly.

Creating and Managing Categories

From the Categories option on the Administrative menu, you can create and manage categories and associate the categories with graphic images. Categories are captions or subheadings within a folder. When regular items are added to a folder, they are put into a category.

Creating and Managing Perspectives

The Perspectives link on the Administrative menu enables you to create and manage perspectives and establish each perspective's display choices. Regular items can be placed into 0, 1, or many perspectives.

A perspective is a cross-category grouping of an item. By assigning a perspective, you answer the question, "Who will be interested in this item?" For example, you can add links to diverse vacation spots around the world and assign perspectives such as "Vacations for Nordic Enthusiasts," "Archaeology Expeditions," "Extreme Vacations for Adventurers," and so on.

The Perspective Manager lets you create perspectives for items that your audience might be interested in, and optionally display the perspective pop-up or specific perspective links directly from the navigation bar. However, the folder owner or site administrator must have configured perspective links to display. This task is performed from the Folder Manager (Navigation Bar tab).

When you add or edit items, you have the option of assigning one or more perspectives to that item. You can assign perspectives only to "Regular Items," not to Quickpicks, Announcements, and News.

Unlike categories, you are not required to assign perspectives to an item. However, when perspectives are assigned, they can be used by your end users to filter information. For example, let's say you have a Human Resources Web site built with WebDB's Sitebuilder. If you have a perspective for new employees, new employees can then use the new employees perspective to instantly retrieve all the documents across the Web site that belong to that perspective. Users can view items by perspective and also specify perspectives when they perform an advanced search.

TIP
If you want to add more than one perspective to an item, hold down the CTRL *key and click on each perspective you want to add from the list. This can be done while adding a new item or editing an existing item.*

TIP
To remove a perspective from an item, hold down the CTRL *key and click the selected perspective on the list.*

Creating and Managing Custom Item Types

You can create custom item types, optional attributes, and procedures from the Custom Item Types link on the Administrative menu. Upon adding a customer item type, you can set the attributes and default values, and whether the attribute is displayed, passed to the procedure, and/or required. A predefined item type is a URL—when the link is selected, the user will be branched to a URL. Custom items enable you to call a procedure and pass a specific set of parameters to the procedure.

Creating and Managing Groups

Under the Group option on the Administrative menu, you can create and manage groups. Users and privileges are then assigned to the group. Members can be assigned as administrators or as typical users in the group.

Creating and Managing Users

Within the Users option on the Administrative menu, you can create and manage users. This function also provides the capability to assign user privileges and assign users to groups. For any user, you can grant administrator privileges (site, style and news administrator, style administrator, news administrator), set passwords, create a personal folder for the user, and view and maintain personal information (first name, last name, nickname, email, telephone, etc.).

Assigning Privileges

Under the Privileges link on the Administrative menu, you can quickly assign administrative privileges to users. Users are added to the list of administrators and then can be assigned as an administrator of site, news, and style information by simply selecting checkboxes.

Editing Personal Information

The Personal Information link on the Administrative menu enables you to set your own password, create a personal folder, and view and maintain personal information (first name, last name, nickname, email, telephone, etc.).

Viewing Site Statistics

The Site Statistics option on the Administrative menu enables you (the site's administrator) to produce and view online reports for site and folder page requests, searches, user access privileges, and items (on the menus) control. The statistics can be reported by folder, IP address, date, time, or browser for all dates or for a specific date range. The graphs are more appealing to the eye and fancier than those from the OWA_CHART routine. Unfortunately, the developers hardcoded the charting capabilities into the sitestats1 and sitestats2 packages, so you can't call the routine yourself, but you could use the code to develop your own charting routine. The charts are horizontal bar charts with colorful bars, as illustrated in Figure 5-31.

Establishing Search Features

From the Search link on the Administrative menu, you can establish basic search features for Oracle and Internet search engines. You can also set advanced InterMedia Text search features, including gists and theme searches. You can specify a search box size and an Internet search engine for use with the basic Search feature. Under the advanced (InterMedia Text) configuration, you can set the number of text entry fields, text entry field display width, maximum allowable characters, and date field length. To use the InterMedia Text option (context server with gists and themes), Content Server must be installed within your database server.

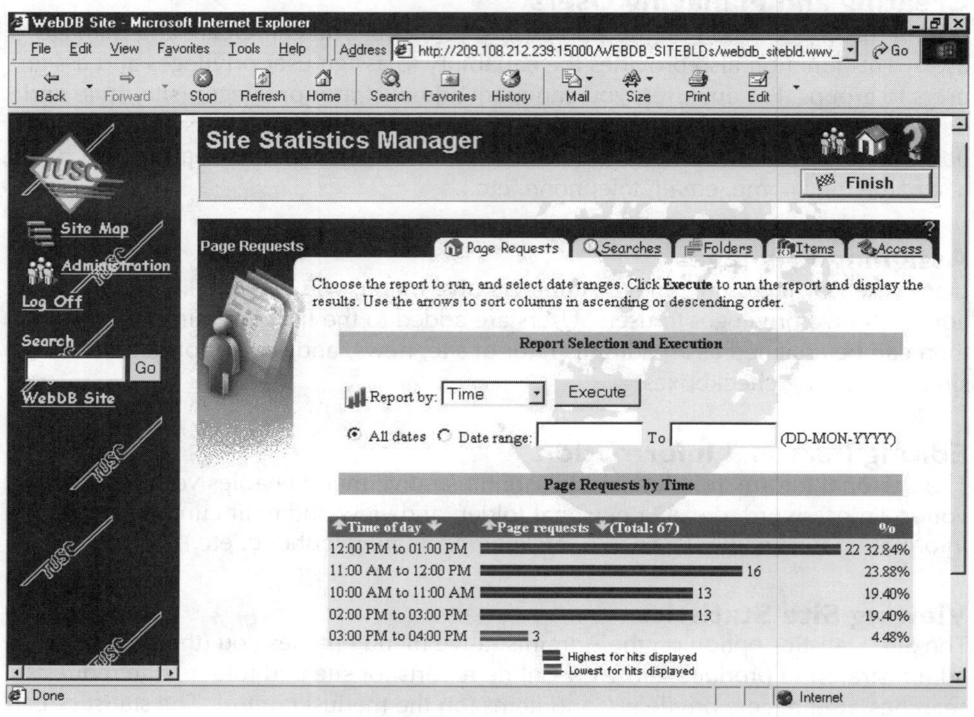

FIGURE 5-31. *Site statistics, page requests by time of day*

Summary

WebDB is a great product to conserve time and energy during development and for ongoing support. I'm confident future versions will provide advanced functionality. Become acquainted with the navigation toolbar located at the bottom of WebDB's Application Builder—it will save you time. WebDB itself will save you hours of time and frustration in otherwise tedious application development. Oracle WebDB is the self-service Web publishing solution for end users and developers to build, manage, and deploy dynamic Web sites using just a Web browser. It combines an intuitive HTML interface with a complete set of robust, browser-based HTML tools. Oracle WebDB allows people to share and access important business information and documents right from their Web browsers while still having time to concentrate on their real jobs.

CHAPTER 6

Oracle Extras

As developers, we are on a constant search for tools and utilities to make our lives easier in the Web development world. A number of tools, toolkits, other miscellaneous Oracle products, applications, and freebies will be covered. Today, Oracle offers most of their freebies on their TechNet site (technet.oracle.com).

This chapter will cover these offerings as they relate to OAS. Plus, we will take a look at creating your own development toolkit. Additional products you may find useful to develop your applications with OAS are covered in further detail in Chapter 23, which covers non-Oracle utilities to improve your Web development life.

In this chapter, the following topics will be covered:

- Establishing a Web development toolkit
- Using WebAlchemy
- Generating graphs using OWA_CHART
- Using Oracle's Java plug-in—JInitiator
- Using the Web Publishing Assistant
- Configuring SQL*Net
- Configuring and using SQL*Plus
- Using SQL*Loader
- Making the most of Oracle File Packager
- Using Oracle's Enterprise Manager
- Using Oracle's GUI PL/SQL editor—Procedure Builder

Establishing a Web Development Toolkit

Do you always have access to necessary programs or code to complete the task at hand? Maybe they are on your laptop, your machine at home, or at the office. Wherever you are working, you are bound to run into the situation where you need your tools and do not have them, unless you have a library of specific code and/or programs right at your fingertips. Having the necessary tools, and being prepared and knowledgeable, is the basis of Rapid Application Development (RAD). This can be accomplished with little effort.

Throughout this chapter, tips and techniques are presented relating to Web design. Couple this with your own toolkit of code and programs, and you will attain your customers' (whether they are internal or external to your company) and your own objectives. These tools will enable you to create your applications rapidly, efficiently, and effectively.

Jump-Starting Your Applications

I am never without my trusty CD of programs and code examples. Everyone has code examples and programs, but they are often located in one location or strewn about on a multitude of floppies and Zip disks. The solution is to create your own CD of cool tools and code that you need constantly. The price to produce your own CDs has come down significantly over the past couple of years. In fact, you can buy the media for about one dollar. If you do not have a writeable CD drive, I am sure you know somebody who has a CD burner; they might even have one in your local library. We build and mass-produce CDs for our consultants. What you put on your CD is up to you, but I would recommend filling your CD with shareware, freeware, and programs that you have licensed. Another important component on the CD should be your code library, which should contain code from every project that you have worked on, code received from coworkers, and so forth. Nothing is spared; treat everything like it is gold. You never know where or when you will need a certain snippet of code or a specific program.

If you are certain you will always have access to the Web, store this information on a Web server for quick access at anytime. Web-deploying your toolkit can make it easier to publish it to your group. However, the CD has proven to be the best all-round media, primarily because it is available anywhere, anytime, and you do not need to dial up to the network or to the Internet to access the information. Web-deploying your toolkit might be your best answer to get to your real-time, easiest to publish, most current toolkit, but your CD is probably your trusty (and fastest) toolkit. So, as we used to say in the Boy Scouts, "Always be prepared."

Using your CD-based toolkit, your development will be faster—it will truly be RAD. The following are the benefits to using a CD-based toolkit:

- You will not need to download tools from the Web.
- You will not need to call or ask other developers for assistance, because you will have all the reference material and tools you will need.
- You will have code examples that you can reuse.
- Most important, you do not have to (nor will you) reinvent the wheel.

Finding Cool Tools

Where do you find these cool tools? Finding the tools is easier than you might think. First, you can download many of the tools from the TUSC Web site (www.tusc.com). You can also find useful tools at www.jumbo.com, www.download.com, and www.shareware.com. Tremendous resources are available at your fingertips, and you can find a large list of Web sites containing cool tools in Appendix A.

Creating Your Toolkit

You need to determine what should be included in your toolkit. While each person's toolkit is different, they will have some similarities. The following is a list of what I believe should be included in every toolkit:

- Code examples for every language that you have encountered. For example, JavaScript, PL/SQL, HTML, Java, and Perl
- Reference material and documentation for every language and tool that you have encountered. For example, HTML, DHTML, JavaScript, SQL*Plus, PL/SQL, OAS, Java, Perl/CGI, VBScript, and JScript
- Graphics software, such as Paintshop Pro or Adobe Photoshop
- An image map editor, such as MapEdit
- Text and language editors, such as PFE, TOAD, and SynEdit
- FTP software, such as WS_FTP
- GIF animation software, such as Animation Shop and GIF Construction Set
- Design tools, such as Dreamweaver (HTML), NetObjects ScriptBuilder (JavaScript), and WebAlchemy (HTML to PL/SQL)
- Browser plug-ins, such as the Adobe Acrobat Reader, Shockwave, and JInitiator
- Miscellaneous software, such as WinZip

Finding and Using Oracle Freebies

You will find that Oracle offers utilities and scripts available at no charge. Usually, these are unsupported, or offered as beta versions. Some utilities, such as WebAlchemy, are available for download and widely used, but are unsupported and seemingly lost in the OAS shuffle. You will usually find the Oracle freebies on the Oracle TechNet site (technet.oracle.com).

Using WebAlchemy

WebAlchemy is a GUI tool written in MS Visual C++ for translating HTML pages into PL/SQL procedures to be used with the OAS PL/SQL cartridge. You can obtain WebAlchemy from your local Oracle representative. At the time this book was written, WebAlchemy was not available on the TechNet site, however, watch the TUSC site for further information on this tool.

Converting from HTML to PL/SQL

Start the WebAlchemy application and then click the Open File icon, shown on the left, choose Open on the File menu, or hit CTRL-O, to open the desired HTML file to convert into PL/SQL Toolkit code. Once you have the HTML file open, convert the file to PL/SQL by clicking the Generate icon, shown on the left, by choosing Generate PL/SQL on the Generate menu, or by pressing CTRL-G. My previous book, *Oracle Application Server Web Toolkit Reference* (Oracle Press, 1998), contains a detailed explanation of how to use WebAlchemy to convert not only HTML to PL/SQL, but also Cold Fusion or Microsoft Active Server pages to PL/SQL.

Using Positional Versus Named Notation

You can configure WebAlchemy to convert the HTML into PL/SQL with positional notation, as opposed to named notation for input parameters. This is a matter of personal preference and standards within your organization, but WebAlchemy can support the generation of either notation.

The following is an example of positional notation:

```
htp.tableRowOpen(  NULL, NULL, NULL, NULL, ' BGCOLOR="#303080"' );
```

The following is the same example using named notation:

```
htp.tableRowOpen(  cattributes => ' BGCOLOR="#303080"' );
```

To switch WebAlchemy from generating named notation to positional notation, select Preferences from the Generate menu. For the option entitled Procedure Call Notation, click the Positional radio button. When you have finished setting any other preferences, press the OK button.

TIP
The Undo command only works for one command; make sure the command you are executing is the one that you want to undo! In other words, you cannot undo the undo.

Generating Graphs Using OWA_CHART

OWA_CHART is also available from your Oracle representative, but also keep an eye on the TUSC site for further information about OWA_CHART. This package enables you to draw horizontal and vertical bar charts from data extracted using a select statement. In the words of OWA_CHART developer, it is a "package to display the results of a query in a bar chart."

For example, the following is a PL/SQL call to the OWA_CHART package to graph the count of the distinct IP addresses that visited our site by day:

```
owa_chart.show_chart(
    q => 'select   ''get_ip_details?in_date=''||trunc(entry_date) the_link, ' ||
         '         trunc(entry_date)                           the_text, ' ||
         '         count(distinct c_ip)                        the_value ' ||
         'from     inet.logxlf '||
         'group    by trunc(entry_date) '||
         'order    by trunc(entry_date) desc',
    chart_type   => 'VBAR',
    bar_image    => 'MULTI',
    image_locat  => '/condo/images/',
    chart_title  => 'Distinct URL Hits by Day',
    font_size    => '-2',
    show_summary => 'CAMXVS');
```

As evident in the preceding example, the package supports a number of parameters. This package will take in either a query or a cursor of a query. The following is the format for the query itself:

```
select the_link,
       the_text,
       the_value
from   my_table
where  my_constraints
```

In the preceding query, the_link is the link that will be associated to the_text (the label describing the charted number) of the chart. The_value is the numeric value of the bar.

Parameters that can be passed to OWA_CHART for graphing can be passed in one of three ways: a query, a list of parameters in a PL/SQL table (i.e., array), or through a cursor. The following are the respective parameter names:

- **q** The query itself as previously described
- **parm_name** An array containing parameters to be passed into the query. For example, my_parm_name(1) := 'job_type'; my_parm_name(2) := 'h_date';

- **parm_value** An array containing the respective parameter values. They correspond to the parm_name. For example, may_parm_value(1) := 'MANAGER'; may_parm_value(2) := '01-JAN-90';
- **c** A cursor of a parsed query

The following are other parameters that can be passed to the OWA_CHART package:

- **chart_type** Determines whether the chart will be a horizontal bar chart (HBAR) or a vertical bar chart (VBAR).
- **bar_image** The name of the image file that will fill the bars of the chart. You can either use your own image (for example, telephone.gif) or use the value of MULTI, which indicates the chart should be color-coded by value. In other words, all values in the top 12 1/2 percent of the values will be red, the next 12 1/2 percent will be orange, then yellow, green, blue, purple, brown, and black.
- **chart_title** An optional title that can be displayed on the chart.
- **axis** The axis of the chart. Valid values are as follows:
  - **ZERO** Chart is relative to zero
  - **FIRST** Chart is relative to the first value
  - **LAST** Chart is relative to the last value
  - **MAX** Chart is relative to the maximum or highest value
  - **MIN** Chart is relative to the minimum or lowest value
  - **AVG** Chart is relative to the average value
- **scale** A proportion of how big to make the bars. Any positive integer is valid.
- **bar_width** How many pixels wide the bar will be. Valid for vertical charts only.
- **bar_height** How many pixels tall the bar will be. Valid for horizontal charts only.
- **num_mask** The number mask for the displaying of the value of the bar.
- **font_size** The relative size of the font for the text and title of the chart. For example, –2 or +1.
- **max_rows** The maximum number of bars to display.

- **image_locat** The virtual directory where the images are located.
- **show_summary** Determines whether OWA_CHART will display a chart summary and what summary information will be shown. This parameter should contain a string of letters corresponding to the different summary information, and the order of the letters corresponds to the order of displaying of the information. For example, if a value of CAS is supplied for show_summary, the summary information will contain the count, the average value, and then the sum of all values. Possible values are as follows:
  - **C** Count of records/bars returned
  - **A** Axis
  - **M** Minimum value
  - **X** Maximum value
  - **V** Average value
  - **S** Sum of all values
  - **F** First value
  - **L** Last value

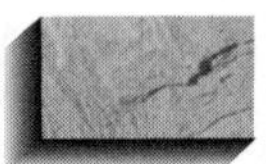

TIP
Be sure to sort the information using an order by *in your SQL statement.*

Using Oracle's Java Plug-In - JInitiator

Oracle JInitiator is Oracle's version of JavaSoft's Java Plug-In. Oracle JInitiator is implemented as a plug-in for Netscape Navigator or an ActiveX component for Microsoft Internet Explorer. JInitiator provides the capability to specify the use of a specific Java Virtual Machine (JVM) on Web clients instead of relying on a browser's default JVM. Oracle JInitiator enables customers to execute Oracle Developer Server applications in any Netscape Navigator 4.0 browser or subsequent releases and in Microsoft Internet Explorer 4.0 browser or subsequent releases. Oracle JInitiator is currently available for Windows 95 and Windows NT 4.0. Certification for Windows 98 will follow shortly. You can download JInitiator from technet.oracle.com.

TIP
The version number for JInitiator is currently 1.1.7.18. The first three digits reflect the JDK version (1.1.7), and the fourth digit represents the JInitiator version.

Using the Web Publishing Assistant

The Web Publishing Assistant (WPA) aids in the publishing of data from queries against your Oracle database in an HTML format. Queries can be executed and published once or scheduled to execute on a regular basis. The Web Publishing Assistant uses a Create Web Page Wizard to help you publish your data quickly and easily. Web Publishing Assistant is a great way to publish data on a daily, weekly, or monthly basis—such as a weekly management report. Even though the Web Publishing Assistant cannot generate dynamic reports, the advantage of the tool is that queries are executed and published as static HTML data. This way, if 100 managers need the weekly management report, all 100 of them are viewing a single static HTML file rather than taking valuable processing power to dynamically execute the same report 100 times.

Creating a New Web Page

Figure 6-1 illustrates the initial Web Publishing Assistant page. After clicking on the Create Web Page button, the wizard will prompt you through four steps to publish the data.

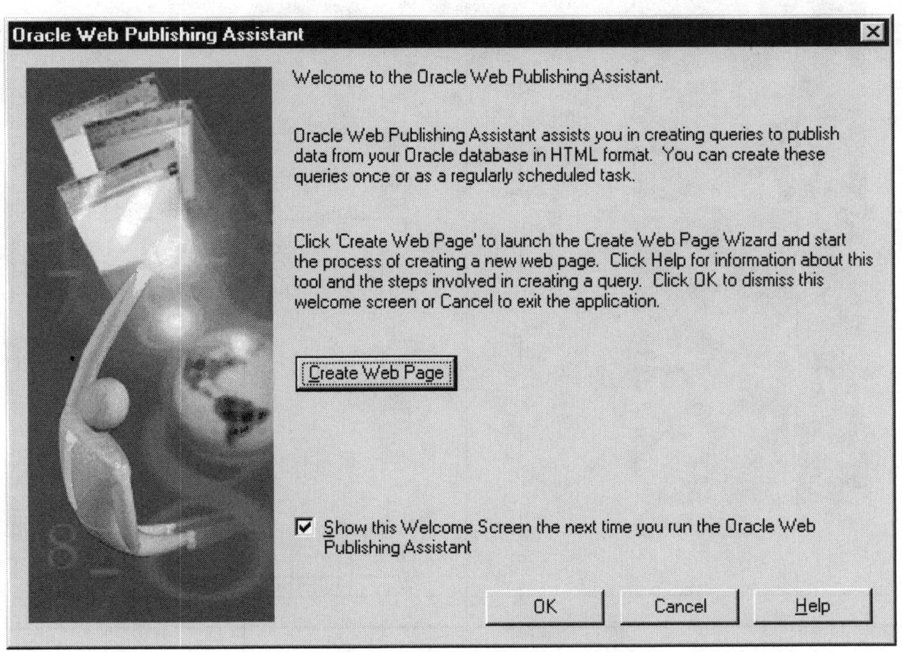

FIGURE 6-1. *Web Publishing Assistant initial page*

Logging into a Database

Step 1 of 4 is illustrated in Figure 6-2. In the first step, you are logging in to the Oracle database (local or remote).

Building Your Query

Step 2 of 4, as illustrated in Figure 6-3, enables you to either build a query with the wizard (labeled "Build a query from a database hierarchy") or type the SQL statement (labeled "Enter a query as a SQL statement"). The Database Hierarchy Wizard enables you drill down into tables, synonyms, or views. After selecting an object type (for example, table), select a schema that contains objects of that type (for example, SCOTT). Once you select a schema, you will see detailed objects (for example, a specific table in the SCOTT schema, emp), which you can select. Within

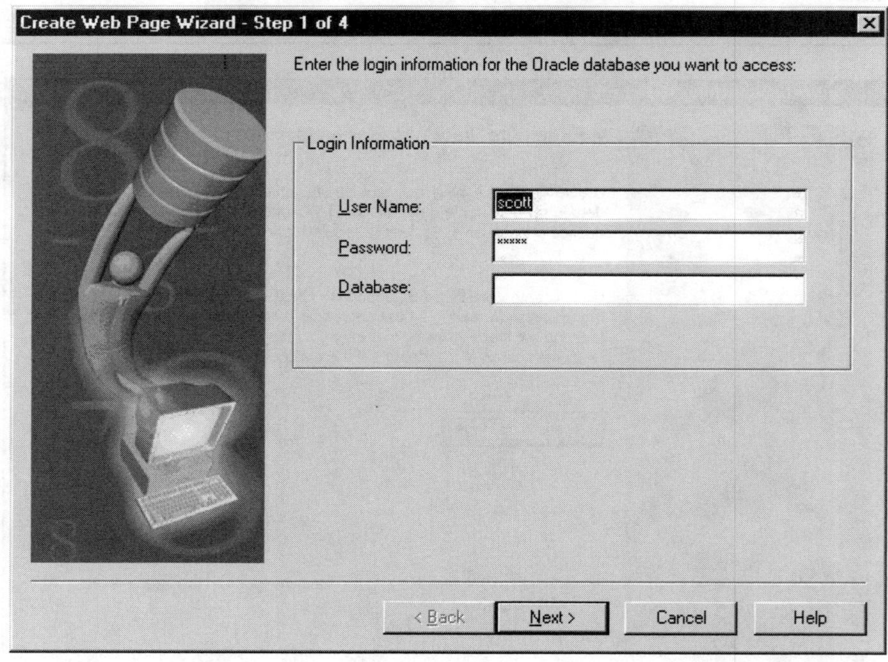

FIGURE 6-2. *Web Publishing Assistant Step 1 – Login*

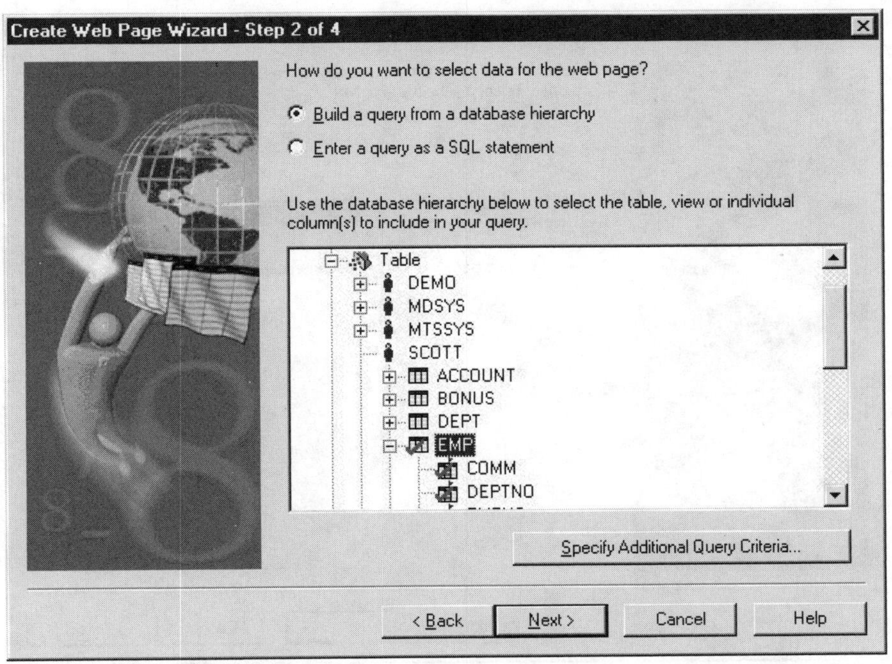

FIGURE 6-3. *Web Publishing Assistant Step 2 – Developing the Query*

an object, you can select object attributes (for example, columns in a table). By clicking on Specify Additional Query Criteria, you can enter a where clause for your SQL statement. If you enter your own query, you have the option of either typing your SQL statement directly into the wizard or importing a SQL script from another file.

Scheduling Your Query

In step 3 of 4, illustrated in Figure 6-4, you schedule the frequency at which the query should be executed to generate a new static HTML file. Your frequency options include immediately, once, on specific day(s) of the week, on specific day(s) of the month, at regular intervals (for example, daily), when data changes, or manually. The capability to schedule reports to execute when data changes is powerful.

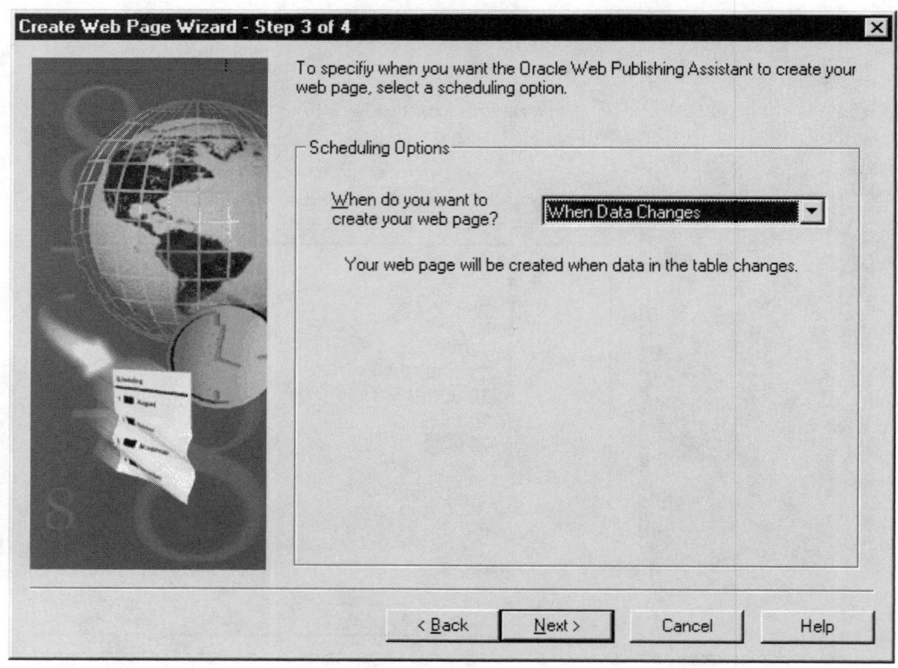

FIGURE 6-4. *Web Publishing Assistant Step 3 – Scheduling*

TIP

If you schedule a query frequency of When Data Changes, an important Windows registry parameter, OWASTDBC, will indicate the number of seconds between database polls to determine if database information has changed since the last poll. A lower number means a shorter amount of time between database data change and Web page generation, but a lower number also increases CPU usage. The default value for this parameter is 1,000, which is roughly every 17 minutes. The available range is 1 to infinity. If this value is not present in the registry, then Oracle Web Publishing Assistant is using the default value of 1,000.

Defining File Options and Picking a Template

In step 4, illustrated in Figure 6-5, you specify the location where the static HTML file should be written. This should be a directory on your system virtually mapped with OAS. Users will be able to view the reports through their Web browser from this virtual directory. Templates can be used to format the data that is published. The default template uses a Java applet to display the data in a table format. The following examples are explained in further detail. Once you create a query, you can double-click on it or click on Preview to view the results. By clicking on the Generate icon, your query will be executed and a new HTML file will be written. For any query you create, you can edit all of the parameters specified in steps 1 through 4. You can also edit the template used by the Web Publishing Assistant.

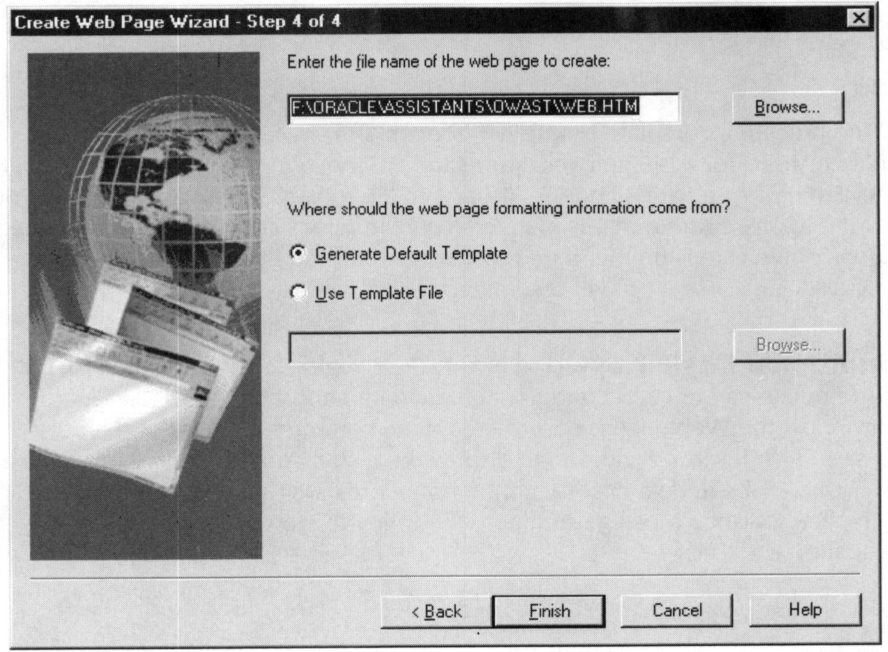

FIGURE 6-5. *Web Publishing Assistant Step 4 – File Placement*

Understanding the Web Publishing Assistant Template Language

Three sample templates are included with the Web Publishing Assistant. By opening the sample templates and reading them, you will quickly discover the intricacies of templates. However, these are simple examples compared to the power and capability of the complete template language.

Keyword <%begindetail%>, <%enddetail%>

These keywords, begindetail and enddetail, surround a section of the HTML template that the data output from the Oracle database will be merged with. Within this section, the column names are denoted with <% and %>, used to mark the position of the data returned from the query, as illustrated in the following example:

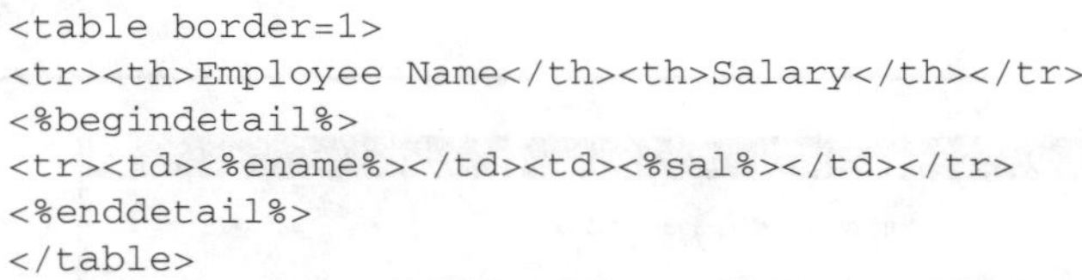

```
<table border=1>
<tr><th>Employee Name</th><th>Salary</th></tr>
<%begindetail%>
<tr><td><%ename%></td><td><%sal%></td></tr>
<%enddetail%>
</table>
```

The preceding template example will open an HTML table with a border, display headers for the Employee Name and Salary columns, and list the columns ENAME (employee name) and SAL (salary) in table data values for each row. You can refer to any column in this manner. You can refer to column names in other sections of the extension file. If no records are returned from the query, the <%begindetail%> section will be omitted.

Conditional Logic Keyword <%if%>, <%else%>, and <%endif%>

Your template can contain conditional logic with an if-then-else statement to control how the Web page is constructed. One common use of an if-then-else statement is to insert a condition to display the results from the query on the first row with a <%begindetail%> section. If no records are returned by the query, you typically want a message similar to the following to appear in the resulting HTML file:

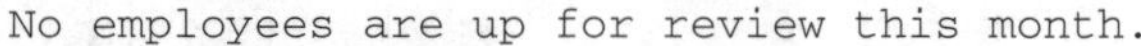

```
No employees are up for review this month.
```

By using the <%if%> statement and a built-in variable named CurrentRecord, you can tailor the output, so a message is displayed when no records are returned by the query. Conditional logic statements must exist entirely before, inside, or after the <%begindetail%> and <%enddetail%> block; they cannot span the begin and end detail commands. Nested <%if%> statements are not allowed; you cannot place an <%if%> statement within a <%if%> statement.

The following code segment is the syntax for the <%if%> statement:

```
<%if condition%>
  HTML text
[<%else%>
  HTML text ]
<%endif%>
```

Condition uses the following syntax:

```
value1 operator value2
```

Operator is defined as:

- **eq** Verify if value1 equals value2
- **lt** Verify if value1 is less than value2
- **gt** Verify if value1 is greater than value2
- **contains** Verify if any part of value1 contains the string in value2

The operands *value1* and *value2* can be column names, a built-in variable, or a constant. CurrentRecord is a pseudocolumn that is also available.

The following is an example that incorporates an <%if%> statement and CurrentRecord variable:

```
<HTML>
<BODY>
<table border=1>
<tr><th>Employee Name</th><th>Salary</th></tr>
<%begindetail%>
<tr><td><%ename%></td><td><%sal%></td></tr>
<%enddetail%>
</table>
<%if CurrentRecord EQ 0 %>
<B>No Employees Match the Criteria Specified<BR></B>
<%endif%>
</BODY>
</HTML>
```

When used in an <%if%> statement, column names are not denoted between **<%** and **%>**. For example, the following code processes salaries greater than $5,000 per month with a special note.

```
<%begindetail%>
<%if sal GT 5000%>
Our records show that <%ename%> makes <b>a lot</b> of coin!<br>
<%endif%>
<%enddetail%>
```

Special Psuedovariables

Special pseudovariables are available to help you perform special processing in your template, including the following:

- CurrentRecord
- CurrentDate
- MaxColumn
- QueryID

CURRENTRECORD The CurrentRecord variable contains the number of times the <%begindetail%> section has been processed. The first time through the <%begindetail%> section, the value is zero. The value of CurrentRecord changes every time another record is retrieved from the database.

CURRENTDATE The CurrentDate variable shows the date and time of the Web page generation. This variable cannot be used inside <%if%> statements. If you do not specify a date format, the default format used is DD/MMM/YYYY (for example, 05/OCT/2002). The default time format is HH:MM:SS A.M./P.M. (for example, 10:01:15 A.M.). You can change the date and time format using the codes shown in Table 6-1.

Format Code	Description
%a	Abbreviated weekday name
%A	Full weekday name
%b	Abbreviated month name
%B	Full month name

TABLE 6-1. *Date and Time Format Codes*

Format Code	Description
%c	Date and time representation appropriate for locale
%#c	Long date and time representation, appropriate for current locale; for example, Tuesday, March 14, 1995, 12:41:29
%d	Day of month as decimal number (01–31)
%#d	Day of month as decimal number without leading zero (1–31)
%H	Hour in 24-hour format (00–23)
%#H	Hour in 24-hour format without leading zero (0–23)
%I	Hour in 12-hour format (01–12)
%#I	Hour in 12-hour format without leading zero (1–12)
%j	Day of year as decimal number (001–366)
%#j	Day of year as decimal number without leading zero (1–366)
%m	Month as decimal number (01–12)
%#m	Month as decimal number without leading zero (1–12)
%M	Minute as decimal number (00–59)
%#M	Minute as decimal number without leading zero (0–59)
%p	A.M./P.M. indicator for 12-hour clock in current locale
%S	Second as decimal number (00–59)
%#S	Second as decimal number without the leading zero (0–59)
%U	Week of year as decimal number, with Sunday as first day of week (00–51)
%#U	Week of year as decimal number, with Sunday as first day of week without the leading zero (0–51)
%w	Weekday as decimal number (0–6; Sunday is 0)
%W	Week of year as decimal number, with Monday as first day of week (00–51)

TABLE 6-1. *Date and Time Format Codes* (continued)

Format Code	Description
%#W	Week of year as decimal number, with Monday as first day of week without the leading zero (0–51)
%x	Date representation for current locale
%#x	Long date representation, appropriate to current locale; for example, Tuesday, March 14, 1995
%X	Time representation for current locale
%y	Year without century, as decimal number (00–99)
%#y	Year without century, as decimal number without the leading zero (0–99)
%Y	Year with century, as decimal number (for example, 1998)
%#Y	Year with century, as decimal number without the leading zeros (for example, 1998)
%z	Time zone abbreviation; no characters if time zone is unknown
%Z	Time zone name; no characters if time zone is unknown

TABLE 6-1. *Date and Time Format Codes* (continued)

The following is an example using the CurrentDate variable:

```
<%CurrentDate:Today is %A, day %d of %B in the year %Y %>
```

The preceding code translates into output similar to the following:

```
Today is Friday, day 31 of May in the year 2002
```

MAXCOLUMN The MaxColumn variable, <%MaxColumn%>, specifies the number of columns returned by the query executed.

QUERYID The QueryId variable, <%QueryId%>, provides a unique identifying number for the generated Web page. You can use this number when troubleshooting Oracle Web Publishing Assistant.

TIP

The limit to the number of queries stored in the Oracle Web Publishing Assistant repository is 65,535 queries, and the limit is not changeable. Another limit of the software is that the maximum number of characters per column returned from the database is 4,000 characters.

Configuring SQL*Net

SQL*Net is a fundamental component of the Oracle product line. In this section, SQL*Net as it relates to OAS will be covered. If you install the Oracle database on one machine and OAS on another, you will need SQL*Net to connect OAS to the database. If OAS and the database reside on the same machine (refer to Chapter 1 for further recommendations), you will not need SQL*Net.

Understanding SQL*Net Parameters

To connect to a database, you will need to edit the following two files that will be created during the SQL*Net installation:.

- sqlnet.ora
- tnsnames.ora

Reviewing the sqlnet.ora File

The sqlnet.ora file is used on the database server to establish parameters every time you connect to the database, from any client tool (i.e., OAS, TOAD, Procedure Builder, or SQL*Plus). The sqlnet.ora file is a server-side SQL*Net file. The sqlnet.ora file is made up of profile parameters and contains several types of information, including the following:

- The amount of time between probes sent to determine whether a client/server connection is still alive (dead connection detection)
- Optional tracing and logging parameters
- Default domains
- Names resolution services
- Client parameters for use with Oracle Names
- Other optional parameters

A partial list of valid parameters includes the following (the recommended values are shown for each parameter):

- **SQLNET.EXPIRE_TIME = 60** Determines how often SQL*Net sends a probe to verify a client/server connection is still active. If a client is abnormally terminated (dies or is disconnected), a database connection may be left open indefinitely unless identified and closed by the machine the database resides on. If this parameter is specified, SQL*Net sends a probe periodically to determine whether an invalid connection should be terminated. If SQL*Net finds a dead connection—or a connection no longer in use—it returns an error, causing the server process to exit.
- **AUTOMATIC_IPC = ON** Indicates whether Oracle will try to convert a client/server connection to a bequeath connection if the client is detected on the same server as the database. This parameter is obsolete in Oracle8.1.5.
- **TRACE_LEVEL_CLIENT = OFF** Controls server-side SQL*Net tracing. This is different than a session trace that you would run through TKPROF; this is a trace file to help debug networking issues.
- **NAMES.DIRECTORY_PATH = (TNSNAMES)** Specifies how TNS resolves service names. TNSNAMES indicates using the local tnsnames.ora file, ONAMES is Oracle Names, and HOST is the OS host name resolver (/etc/hosts file or DNS); others are less common.
- **NAMES.DEFAULT_DOMAIN = world** The default TNS domain. This enables you to type DB8 to reference a database called DB8.WORLD in your tnsnames.ora or any other default names extension. For example, if the domain was TUSC.COM you could reference WORK.TUSC.COM by specifying just WORK.

The following illustrates an example of a sqlnet.ora file:

```
AUTOMATIC_IPC = OFF
TRACE_LEVEL_CLIENT = OFF
NAMES.DIRECTORY_PATH = (TNSNAMES)
NAMES.DEFAULT_DOMAIN = world
```

Reviewing the tnsnames.ora File

The tnsnames.ora file is used by the client to connect to a database. The tnsnames.ora file is used by clients and distributed database servers to identify potential destinations and contains local naming parameters. The tnsnames.ora file will contain an entry for each database to which you have access.

Valid file input includes the following:

- **TRAIN.world** Service name
- **DESCRIPTION** Descriptor list
- **ADDRESS_LIST** List of addresses for the service name
- **ADDRESS** An individual address for the service name
- **COMMUNITY = tcp.world** Required only if you use InterProtocol Exchange; that is, if you have a PC on Novell only configured for IPX and you need to go through an Oracle InterProtocol Exchange server to convert the connection request to TCP
- **PROTOCOL = TCP** Protocol to communicate over (TCP, IPX, IPC, etc.), usually TCP or IPC
- **Host = TRAINING** Host name of the server (could also be the IP address)
- **Port = 1521** TCP/IP port to use for communications on the server (must match the listener.ora—1521 is the Oracle default)
- **CONNECT_DATA = (SID = TRN8)** SID of the database you are connecting to (SID= is obsolete in 8.1.5; it becomes SERVICE_NAME)

The following code segment is an example of the tnsnames.ora file:

```
TRAIN.world =
  (DESCRIPTION =
    (ADDRESS_LIST =
        (ADDRESS =
          (COMMUNITY = tcp.world)
          (PROTOCOL = TCP)
          (Host = TRAINING)
          (Port = 1521)
        )
        (ADDRESS =
          (COMMUNITY = tcp.world)
          (PROTOCOL = TCP)
          (Host = TRAINING)
          (Port = 1526)
        )
    )
    (CONNECT_DATA = (SID = TRN8)
    )
)
```

Establishing Your SQL*Net Parameters

You can edit the tnsnames.ora file manually with any text editor. The file is located in the following directory:

- **On Windows95** Orawin95/Network/Admin
- **On Windows NT** Orant/Network/Admin
- **On UNIX** \$ORACLE_HOME\network\admin

To edit the tnsnames.ora file through a GUI tool, you can use the SQL*Net Easy Configuration. To use the Easy Configuration program, complete the following steps:

1. Start the SQL*Net Easy Configuration tool.
2. When the dialog box appears, choose the Add Database Alias radio button.
3. In the next window, choose a name you want to use to connect to your remote database, usually four to six characters, such as TRAIN. Your SQL*Plus connect string would be dev/dev@TRAIN.
4. Choose your network protocol for connecting to the database—most connections are TCP/IP.
5. In the last window, enter the IP address or the machine name where the database resides, and enter the database instance name.

In most cases, you will need to get both of these parameters from your network/database administrator.

Configuring and Using SQL*Plus

Another fundamental component of the Oracle RDBMS is SQL*Plus. SQL*Plus enables you to access the database to perform queries, database modifications, and other maintenance operations. At one point, SQL*Plus was used by end users to perform ad hoc queries, by database administrators, and as the primary reporting tool. A variety of tools are used for reporting and maintenance today, even though SQL*Plus remains a useful tool.

Modifying SQL*Plus Configure Files

The glogin.sql and login.sql files can be configured to make your life easier when using SQL*Plus. These files enable you to set SQL*Plus parameters at the time of login, instead of manually setting them each time. The glogin.sql file is used globally on the machine where SQL*Plus is installed. When someone starts SQL*Plus, these parameters will be used. The login.sql can be customized for each individual user. Each person could create his or her own login.sql file.

Setting Your Working Directory in SQL*Plus

To create a shortcut of the Sql*Plus executable in Windows, right-click the executable and choose Create Shortcut from the menu. Once you have a shortcut created, right-click on it and select Properties from the menu. When the dialog box appears, click the Shortcut tab. Change the "Start in" directory to the directory where you will be working.

Creating Your glogin.sql and login.sql Files

The glogin.sql is located in the following directory: d:\orawin95\plus33 for Oracle 7.x and d:\orawin95\plus80 for Oracle 8.x. The login.sql file is located in the directory you set as your working directory. The following is an example of what you may include in the login.sql file:

```
set numwidth 9
set linesize 100
set pagesize 24
-- below sets your sql prompt
set termout off
column dbname new_value prompt_dbname
select substr(global_name,1,instr(global_name,'.')-1) dbname
from global_name;
set sqlprompt "&&prompt_dbname> "
set termout on
```

SQL*Loader

SQL*Loader is a fast and easy way to load data into the database. It is comprised of three simple steps:

1. Create a comma-delimited text file, a .csv file.
2. Create a control file.
3. Run the program.

To load data into the database, perform the following steps:

1. If you intend to run SQL*Loader locally, make sure that you have installed the Oracle7 or Oracle8 utility. The executable is entitled Sqlldr73.exe or Sqlldr80.exe.

2. Create a comma-delimited text file. This can be accomplished by using Excel to create a (*.csv) file, or you can create your own data input file with another program.
3. Create a control file with the extension .CTL.
4. Before running the SQL*Loader executable, make sure the *.ctl and *.csv files reside in the same directory as SQL*Loader.
5. Make sure that the columns in the .ctl file match the columns, number of columns, and the order from the .csv file.
6. Run the SQL*Loader executable.

Even though the following example does not cover all the possibilities, it will get you started. If you have further questions, consult the SQLLOAD section in *Oracle: The Complete Reference*. The following is an example of a comma-delimited text file and a control file:

Sample .csv file

```
1999,4,004,1,2/2/99,2/5/99,2/9/99,2/13/99,
1999,4,000,2,3/2/99,3/5/99,3/9/99,3/13/99,
1999,4,002,3,4/2/99,4/7/99,4/9/99,4/15/99,
1999,4,010,4,5/4/99,5/7/99,5/11/99,5/15/99,
1999,4,000,5,6/2/99,6/7/99,6/9/99,6/15/99,
1999,4,005,6,7/2/99,7/8/99,7/12/99,7/16/99,
1999,4,007,7,8/3/99,8/6/99,8/11/99,8/14/99,
1999,4,000,8,9/2/99,9/8/99,9/10/99,9/16/99,
1999,4,000,9,10/4/99,10/7/99,10/11/99,10/15/99,
1999,4,000,10,11/2/99,11/5/99,11/9/99,11/13/99,
1999,4,011,11,12/2/99,12/7/99,12/9/99,12/15/99,
1999,4,200,12,1/4/00,1/7/00,1/11/00,1/17/00,
...
```

Sample .ctl file

```
load data
infile 'fstdates.csv'
insert into table month_calendar
FIELDS TERMINATED BY ","
(b_yr position (*) integer external,
weeks position (*) integer external,
service position (*) char,
mon_id position (*) char,
first_close position (*) date "MM/DD/YY",
second_close position (*) date "MM/DD/YY",
third_close position (*) date "MM/DD/YY",
open_date position (*) date "MM/DD/YY")
```

Making the Most of Oracle File Packager

The Oracle File Packager enables you to create an installation script to be executed using the standard Oracle Installer utility. Oracle File Packager creates the files and the necessary install script all in the directory you specify. Once the files are in the directory, you can copy them to a CD or the media of your choice.

Using the Oracle File Packager

To use the Oracle File Packager, follow these steps:

1. Start the Oracle File Packager application, then press the Next button.
2. When the dialog box appears, choose the type of installable product you will create. If you choose Standalone Product, the product you are creating the installation script for can be installed only on singular machines. If you choose Sharable Product, it can be installed on a server and then accessed by many machines. Click the radio button of your choice, then hit the Next button.
3. In the following dialog box, you will input the Product Name, Internal Name, and the Product Description. The Product Name is the label that is shown when the user runs the Oracle Installer for your product. The Internal Name is a unique, eight character name. This name will remain with your product when you are creating the installer for any language. The name length is limited to eight characters, and the field accepts only characters A–Z, 0–9, and underscores. Press the Next button.
4. The following screen contains the Version information and the Operating System choice. The first text box is used for a Version number, in the format AA.BB.CC.DD.EEA where the letters correspond to numbers; the letter at the end would be for patch releases. An example would be 3.0, 14.45.55, or 12.12.12a. After you have chosen your version identification, pick the operating system (O/S) you will use to install. After picking the O/S, press the Next button.
5. In the next window, the default directory is chosen for you. To change the default directory, hit the Browse button and navigate to the desired directory; otherwise, press the Next button.
6. In the next dialog box, pick the files to include in your install. Press the Add button. When the Add Files To Product browse window comes up, choose the files you wish to add and click the Open button. After you have picked

the files that you want to include, click Select All. Once you have the files selected that you want to install, press the Next button.

7. In the next dialog box, choose the destination directories for the files. If you do not want the files installed into the Oracle home directory, select the file that you want to change and click the Assign Destination button. If you click the Assign Destination button, you are not able to browse your file system. If you want the change the directory and you do not see it in the choices of the drop-down box, you will have to type in the full directory location. After you have completed this, press the Next button.
8. In the next dialog box, if everything looks good, press the Finish button.
9. To run your newly created install script, start the Oracle Installer and select your install file. It is entitled, win{*os*}.prd, such as win95.prd.

Using Oracle's Enterprise Manager

This section will address Enterprise Manager only from a Web development perspective. Oracle Enterprise Manager is primarily meant to be used by DBAs; therefore, many of the functions will not be discussed, including Backup Manager, Data Manager, and Storage Manager.

Instance Manager

The Instance Manager is useful when developing Web applications because from time to time you may need to abort or kill sessions that are taking an unusually long time to execute, or perhaps if an infinite loop has occurred. The Instance Manager enables you to click on the Sessions menu and click Disconnect to kill the specific session.

Schema Manager

The Schema Manager is useful to view, create, and edit database objects, including clusters, database links, functions, indexes, package bodies, package specifications, procedures, refresh groups, sequences, snapshot logs, snapshots, synonyms, tables, triggers, and views. Privileges can also be granted on objects through the Schema Manager. The Schema Manager uses an Explorer-like interface to enable you to drill into an object type (for example, functions), then shows the schemas containing the object type that can be drilled into to view the specific object. The object can be edited directly in the window. For Web development, the Schema Manager is probably the most useful Enterprise Manager utility because it enables you to create and edit objects through a GUI interface.

Security Manager

If your application uses database authentication, the Security Manager is useful for granting and revoking privileges to your packages and procedures. The Security Manager enables you to grant and revoke (system and object) privileges and roles to users. Profiles can also be managed through the Security Manager. Profiles enable you to control a session's resources, including CPU time per session, CPU time per call, overall connect time, and session maximum idle time. Database services can also be limited through the use of profiles. Database services include the maximum number of concurrent sessions per user, maximum reads per session/call, and maximum private SGA Kbytes. If your Web application does not use database authentication, all users use the same username in Oracle. You can limit the maximum amount of time a query can run before killing the session, but this could be dangerous because the users will see a blank page when they have exceeded the time limit.

SQL Worksheet

The SQL Worksheet is more effective than using SQL*Plus for your ad hoc queries during Web development. The SQL Worksheet is a GUI and contains a command history, so you can retrieve, edit, and execute your previously typed SQL queries.

Software Manager

Oracle Software Manager (OSM) enables you to automate many of the administrative tasks common in a distributed environment. Fortunately, in a Web environment, the browser is often the only piece of software that resides on the client. However, if you are using Oracle JInitiator, that is another client component—and there may be more depending on your implementation. OSM could be used to manage the distribution of your client software. In a large development environment, OSM could be used to manage the distribution of all development software. In conjunction with Oracle Enterprise Manager, OSM registers, distributes, installs, and tracks all software on network machines with Oracle Intelligent Agents.

Using Oracle's GUI PL/SQL Editor – Procedure Builder

Procedure Builder is a great product when it comes to Web development because it enables you to create, edit, and debug your Web packages, procedures, and functions through a GUI tool. For Web development, use only the server-side editing capabilities of Procedure Builder.

Procedure Builder enables you to drill into database objects by schema. The Object Navigator is Procedure Builder's browser for locating and working with both client and server program units, libraries, and triggers. You can expand and collapse nodes in the Object Navigator to view or hide object information, such as cross-reference and dependency information. Different icons are used in the Navigator to represent different classes of objects.

Building Program Units

By selecting the Program Units node in the Object Navigator and clicking the Create button, you can create a new program unit. Upon clicking the Create button, Procedure Builder will open the Program Unit editor. To opens the Program Unit editor for an existing program unit, you can double-click on the icon next to the unit. When you select a program unit in the Object Navigator, it also becomes the active program unit in Procedure Builder's debugging window, called the PL/SQL Interpreter.

The Object Navigator enables you to drag and drop objects to change the relationships between objects. For example, if you drag a program unit into an open library, the program unit will be added to the library. For Web development, it is important to execute your code on the server. Program units in the Stored Program Units node are executed directly from the server.

The development of a program unit involves the processes of editing, compiling, testing, and debugging. When creating a new program unit, you are prompted for a name and the type of program unit you want to create. This information is used to provide you with a program unit template when the editor is displayed. The Program Unit editor provides you with full text editing capabilities for entering and editing your program unit source code. You can import source from or export source to text files in the file system. The drop-down list in the Name box of the Program Unit editor enables you to quickly navigate to other program units. The taskbar provides common operations you can perform on program units.

Debugging Program Units

The PL/SQL Interpreter is the central debugging workspace where you can set debug actions and test the program unit in runtime simulation. Click a program unit icon in the Object Navigator to display its source in the Source pane of the Interpreter window, including line numbers. Breakpoints suspend execution of a compiled program unit, enabling you to step through code and troubleshoot runtime errors. You can also set conditional breakpoints, called debug triggers. When the procedure is running, execution will halt at these breakpoints so you can debug your PL/SQL code. You can execute the program unit by typing its name and any required arguments at the command-line prompt. Execution of the program unit is suspended at the line just prior to the breakpoint. Double-click on an executable line in the source pane to set a breakpoint. The following command buttons in the Interpreter enable you to step through the code of a suspended program unit to pinpoint the location of runtime errors:

- **Step Into** Advances execution to the next line of code.
- **Step Over** Advances execution to the next line of code in the current program unit only.
- **Step Out** Advances through the rest of the current program unit and returns to the outer program unit.
- **Go** Resumes execution to the end of the program unit, or until another breakpoint is encountered.
- **Reset** Aborts suspended execution.

During the debugging process, you can examine any of the program unit's local variables or parameter values to identify where problems may be occurring. You can also edit local variables or parameter values to force branching conditions and test alternate code paths. The Stack node in the Object Navigator displays a call stack history ending with the suspended program unit. Expand any node in the stack to view variable and parameter values at the time of suspension.

Building a Library

Libraries (packages) are collections of program units stored on the client side or server side for easy reuse by multiple applications. For Web development, remember that you only want server-side development. Libraries also offer performance benefits because library program units are not loaded into memory until they are called.

To build a library, perform the following steps:

1. Create or open an existing library in the Object Navigator.
2. Add program units by dragging and dropping them into the open library.
3. Save the library.

Summary

When you review the extensive list of Oracle products and tools, it is amazing. At one point in time, if you knew SQL*Plus, SQL*Forms, and RPT, you were king of the Oracle development world—no more. From WebAlchemy to OWA_CHART to

JInitiator to the Web Publishing Assistant, Oracle's depth of Web tools is extensive. SQL*Net has provided Oracle with a competitive scalability and distributability advantage for years. SQL*Loader provides powerful capabilities for mass loading and converting data from other systems. Oracle's Enterprise Manager and Procedure Builder get you into the GUI world of database management and development. No matter what, when it comes to developing a Web solution, Oracle certainly will exceed your expectations with their breadth of tools to help you to do the job.

CHAPTER 7

24x7 Uptime

The notion that an e-business site should never sleep is universally acknowledged. Customers can potentially access your Web site at any time of day or night. When your site is down or unavailable, it will directly result in lost revenue and bad publicity, and worst of all, the customer may retain a bad impression about the site and never return. There are also other indirect site costs, such as resource idleness during downtime, additional expert manpower required to urgently restore services, and so on. In spite of realizing the criticality behind keeping systems online and running 24 hours a day, 7 days a week, it is also commonly acknowledged that the task is highly challenging, if not downright impossible. The fundamental reason for 24x7 uptime being a Herculean act is the overall complexity. When a Web site functions properly, it is seamless to the eyes of the end user. However, behind the scenes, a large number of hardware and software components are associated with most commercial Web sites. Each of these components is prone to failure, and therefore prone to failure resulting in downtime. The challenge is to identify every component, categorize them appropriately, list potential failures, and take concrete steps to avoid and/or minimize such failures. In other words, each component has to be explicitly fault tolerant.

The following are common, broadly classified components that you may encounter:

- **Hardware** Including physical components such as memory boards, CPUs, disks, controllers, etc. on all tiers, including the back-end database server, the Web servers, and others, including the servers housing transaction processing (TP) monitors and application servers (i.e., OAS) in an *n*-tier environment.
- **Operating system (OS)** Refers to the OS layer on top of all hardware. The OS may be diverse, depending on the hardware in place. For instance, the back-end database servers could be using a UNIX flavor, whereas the Web servers may be using Windows NT. Even in case of the Oracle8*i* Database Appliance, there is an OS component—the microkernel—used within the appliance.
- **Network** The network backbone has to be sufficiently powerful for any commercial Web site to function decently. This category includes the various components that make up the network, such as interface cards, cables, routers, multiplexers, and other media.
- **Server software** Pertains to server software, used within all the tiers, including the RDBMS itself (i.e., Oracle), Web servers (for example, Apache Server, Microsoft IIS, Oracle) and Application Servers (for example, Oracle Application Server).

- **End-user applications** Consist of various critical off-the-shelf and custom applications in use within the company, such as inventory management and sales management systems. These applications are often necessary to process orders in an e-business environment. This category also includes the applications that create the actual Website interfaces and enable end users to navigate the site using a browser.
- **Data within the database** Finally, the actual data (rows in the tables, objects pertaining to specific classes) that is present within the database—such as item catalogs, prices, order details, tax information, and so on—should not be forgotten. This is the real hidden "wealth" of any site, and all the other components merely allow ways to use the data in meaningful ways and accumulate additional data in the process.

The failure of any component listed above could potentially result in downtime. Each distinct category has to be treated uniquely. Single points of failure pertaining to each component have to be identified so that failure can be avoided, and if failure is inevitable, so that it can be masked adequately. Ideally, failure resistance needs to be built into all components from the time of installation/configuration. The cost of not doing so can be immense and manifest itself through frequent failures down the line. Once the site is live, very few opportunities are available to address these failures and repair them on an ongoing basis, since downtime is very expensive. As such, the importance of doing things right the "first time" and not on an incremental basis needs to be emphasized. Such a detailed initial architectural design and deployment process generally may take weeks or even months. However, time to market is also a very stringent requirement for most (if not all) e-business sites, which tend to be in an extreme hurry to deploy solutions and go live. This rapid-fire solution may not be robust enough or insulate all components; however, the fear of competitors catching up or even racing past is a genuine fear and is enough to warrant deploying a lukewarm solution. The danger is not in deploying anything suboptimal, but living with it as it breaks.

The trick is to be familiar enough with your most readily available options to rapidly design and deploy an appropriately robust solution that is well thought out, accounts for all components within all categories, and can be deployed sensibly using the right hardware, software, and middleware. Towards this end, Figure 7-1 illustrates an architecture that provides redundancy at multiple tiers, thus eliminating single points of failure. In addition to failover capabilities, redundant components help performance by allowing load-balancing features. However, such load balancing may not be automatic, and you need to ensure that all applications and data are designed for explicit load balancing. For instance, when using Oracle across multiple nodes in a Parallel Server configuration, data and user access needs to be partitioned either horizontally or vertically (or as a combination of both) across all participating nodes/instances. (Refer to the Oracle Parallel Server documentation for further information.)

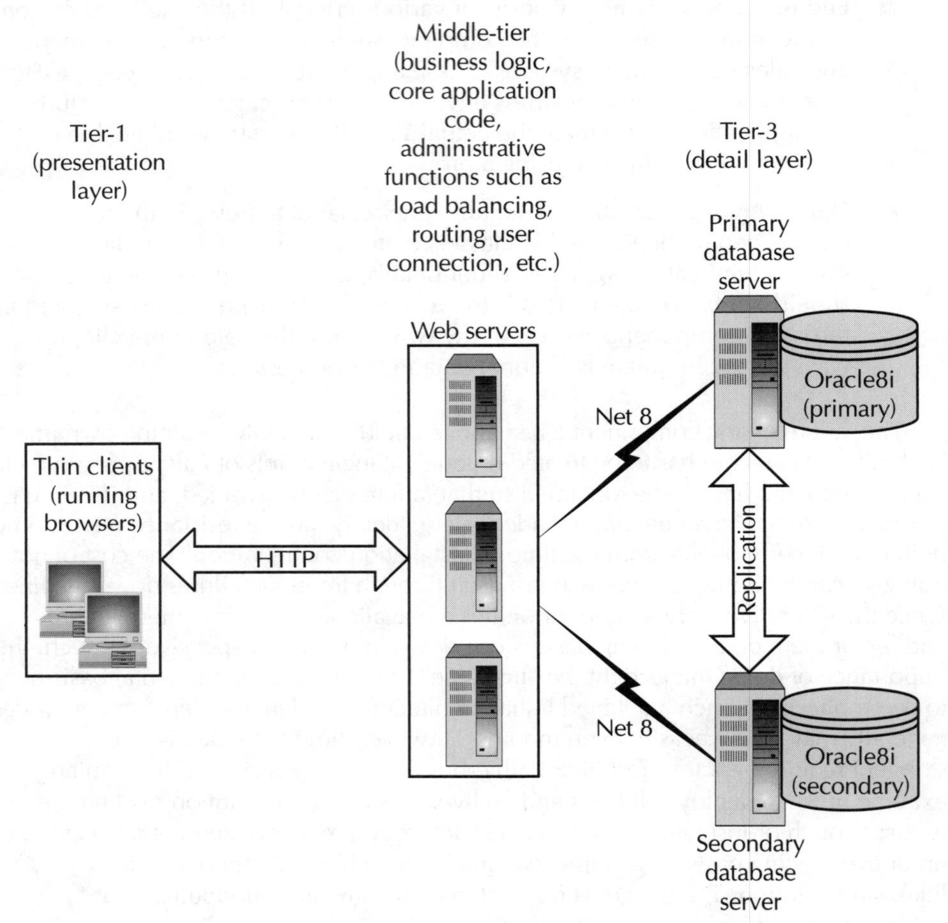

FIGURE 7-1. *Redundancy at different tiers prevents single points of system failure*

Since the previously mentioned components and categories are far too many and diverse to discuss meaningfully in any depth, this chapter only discusses some of the high-availability solutions available within Oracle to insulate the actual database from failure. Entire books are written on the topics of configuring and managing the hardware, OS, network, and so forth, to prevent failures. The following are some of the high-availability solutions:

- Oracle Parallel Server
    - Advantages of OPS
    - Disadvantages of OPS
    - Automatic failure recovery under OPS
- Advanced Replication
    - Advantages of Advanced Replication
    - Disadvantages of Advanced Replication
    - Automatic failure recovery with Advanced Replication
- Standby instances
    - Advantages of standby instances
    - Disadvantages of standby instances
    - Automatic failure recovery with standby instances
- Standby databases
    - Advantages of standby databases
    - Disadvantages of standby databases
    - Automatic failure recovery with standby databases
- Third-party solutions
- Combining multiple solutions together
- Custom standby database strategies
- End-user session disruption and application failover

Oracle Parallel Server

Simply described, Oracle Parallel Server (OPS) is a database configuration in which multiple instances can be up and running simultaneously, with each instance referring to the same physical set of data files (refer to Figure 7-2). OPS is configured on specific environments that support such a configuration of multiples systems (nodes), all sharing the disks on which the files reside—namely, clusters and massively parallel processing (MPP) systems. The OPS implementation on each architecture differs slightly. For example, on MPP, different nodes can be simultaneously used to distribute query processing and increase throughput due to fast data movement through the high-speed interconnect. This may not be the case on certain cluster platforms. Refer to your platform-specific documentation for further details. Each node that supports an instance accesses the shared disks and is referred to as a "participating" node. Each instance shares a sibling relationship with the other, rather than the parent/child association that is common with other similar configurations. As such, failure of one or more ("parent" instances) does not cause the entire database to be inaccessible. Theoretically, as long as there is at least one surviving instance, database availability should not be impacted. From a unilateral perspective, each participating node's instance can be viewed as a regular (non-OPS) instance. Thus, two or more of these instances make up an OPS configuration. Each instance's access to the shared disks is synchronized and controlled through a specialized piece of software called the DLM (Distributed Lock Manager). In versions prior to Oracle8, the DLM was a vendor-specific component (external to Oracle). Starting with Oracle8, it has been integrated within Oracle OPS and is referred to as the Integrated Distributed Lock Manager (IDLM).

Under OPS, if one node crashes (due to component malfunctions or network failures), the database is still accessible through the other nodes. This prevents the entire node from being a single point of failure. When single-node failure occurs and the instance on that node crashes, a surviving node (the one that detected the instance failure) performs the necessary instance recovery. If the failure is not automatically detected, the instance recovery occurs when the crashed instance is manually restarted.

Advantages of OPS

OPS provides the following primary advantages:

- Availability during node failure. It automates instance recovery after intermittent node failures, thus enhancing MTTR.
- Enhanced performance through load balancing (access being distributed across instances, allowing memory and CPUs from different nodes to be used concurrently).

- Higher capacity and scalability, especially in MPP configurations, by allowing a large number of nodes to be used. Also, a new node can be incrementally "plugged in" as necessary.

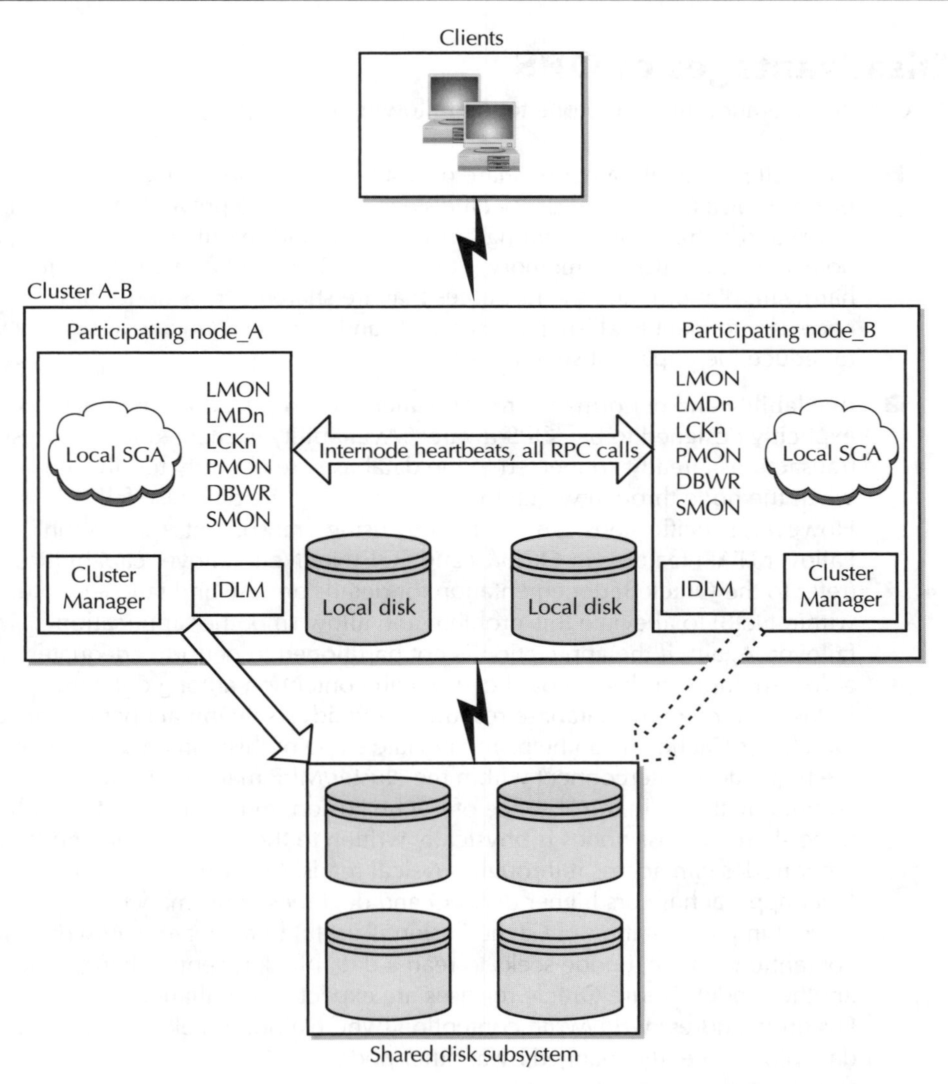

FIGURE 7-2. *OPS architecture*

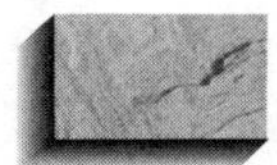

TIP
OPS requires an appropriate design and explicit manual configuration for these features to be used. That is, concurrent multinode access is not automatic in an OPS environment.

Disadvantages of OPS

An OPS configuration may be prone to the following issues:

- Since all participating nodes share disk subsystems, the configuration is still prone to disk failures unless specific steps are taken to prevent them, such as OS and/or hardware mirroring (RAID 1, 0+1, and so on). Also, other single points of failure (CPUs, memory, I/O channels) depend on your specific hardware platform and the resources that are shared across nodes. It is necessary to identify all such components and provide adequate redundancy to reduce the impact of such failures.
- Availability and performance may be affected if applications are not explicitly designed to be "OPS-aware." Availability is affected if in-process transactions already connected to the database are abruptly terminated when the node through which they are accessing the database fails. However, specific steps can be taken by using Transparent Application Failover (TAF) features in OCI8/8*i* and SQL*Net/Net8 failover capabilities (refer to the Oracle8*i* documentation for details on TAF and failover features within Net8) to alleviate this problem and allow smoother application failover. Again, if the application is not partitioned to perform adequately across multiple nodes, it could cause high contention among different instances for various database resources and adversely impact performance. Oracle8*i*'s Cache Fusion helps to alleviate some of this contention by using the high-speed interconnect within the cluster/MPP machine for internode communications. In the absence of Cache Fusion, much of the data that has to be shared across nodes is physically written to the disk from one node so other nodes can access it through physical reads. Obviously, the older, latter approach incurs higher disk I/O and degrades performance. The current implementation of Cache Fusion is useful to alleviate read/write contention (where a node seeks to read a data block recently changed by another node). Future Oracle releases are expected to enhance Cache Fusion to address write/write contention (where a node seeks to change a data block recently changed by another node).

- Maintenance requirements and system complexity generally increases. The greater the number of components and the additional tuning increases the amount of servicing and monitoring that is required to ensure smooth running.
- OPS is not designed for failover through a WAN, and as such, cannot be used for disaster recovery (since the physical distance between the participating nodes is not great—generally, only a few meters).
- System cost goes up. However, if the cost of downtime is higher than the system cost, the investment toward OPS-capable architecture ought to be easily justifiable.

Automatic Failure Recovery Under OPS

Failure could be due to a variety of reasons—such as node component failure, network failure, or instance failure. After a node fails, recovery must occur at the hardware/OS level, as well as within Oracle at the instance level. If only the instance has crashed, no hardware/OS-level recovery is necessary.

The vendor-specific CM (Connection Manager) ensures that each node in the cluster is alive by periodically exchanging heartbeat messages. Node failure is indicated by persistent time-outs of consecutive heartbeat messages. Occasional time-outs may indicate that the node is too busy with other processes to respond to heartbeat messages. **Consecutive** time-outs are a clear indication that the node is indeed down. Once node failure is determined, the connection is marked as broken and cluster reorganization occurs to exclude the broken node.

After the cluster reorganization, the DLM immediately rebuilds its lock database. The DLM database is primarily in the cache of each instance. One or more instance failures cause a portion of the database to be lost. The surviving instances help in reconstructing the lost information.

Finally, instance recovery is initiated. Instance recovery is very similar to crash recovery that is performed on startup in non-OPS configurations. The only difference is that instance recovery is performed by another (surviving) instance. Instance recovery involves two primary operations—restoration of the cache integrity (cache recovery) and restoration of the transaction state (transaction recovery). This involves writing dirty buffers to disk such that all committed transactions are reflected in the data files. Conversely, uncommitted transactions are removed from the buffer and not written to disk. Whereas transaction recovery can be performed in parallel by multiple instances (in configurations with more than two nodes) to speed up the process, cache recovery can only be done by a single instance. User activity in the failed instance freezes during the failure and cache recovery. Activity can resume during transaction recovery, but it will likely experience a loss of performance. However, the surviving instances can pick up the load. Any user/application process connected to the failed instance needs to be switched over to a surviving instance either automatically or through the explicit reconnection. The end users and associated applications may see an Oracle error message (for example, ORA-3113, ORA-3114, or a similar error number) regarding the instance failure. The SMON process belonging to the node that detects the failure performs instance recovery on the failed node to clean up all resources pertaining to the failed instance and to bring the database to a consistent state. Evidence of cache recovery can be observed through instance recovery messages in the database *alert log.*

Advanced Replication

Advanced Replication (AR) is a sophisticated replication mechanism available in Oracle. AR enables one or more source databases, certain predetermined schemas, and even specific segments within each database to be replicated to one or more target database in a one-way or multiway replication scheme. Thus, both the source and the target databases can concurrently handle reads and writes. From a logical perspective, AR provides a "hot" standby database. Unlike in a conventional standby database scenario, the target database is open and available for immediate failover if the source database crashes (refer to Figure 7-3). Ideally, the target should be maintained on a separate machine at a remote location for disaster recovery purposes. Due to the target being continuously open, it can be utilized as a reporting instance, enabling end users or DSS-type applications to use it for issuing complex queries that cannot normally be issued in the production OLTP database (for fear of hurting production performance).

Under AR, multiple copies of the entire database or specific subsets can be concurrently written to and they can be kept synchronized in nearly real-time fashion. Such a configuration is called a multimaster configuration (because there are multiple master copies). If immediate synchronization is not desired, then an event-based approach may be taken to propagate the transactions from each master to the others. For instance, the propagation can be time-based, where the propagation occurs during specific low-usage hours. However, if replication is being done for failover purposes, synchronization would typically be immediate. Thus, each database copy should be maintained in a "peer-to-peer" manner. All writes are initially stored locally and then forwarded to each target database through the "push" mechanism as opposed to simple replication snapshots, which "pull" the data from the source database.

Each transaction is propagated in a consistent fashion to prevent data integrity violations. If there are integrity violations or conflicts, specific conflict resolution

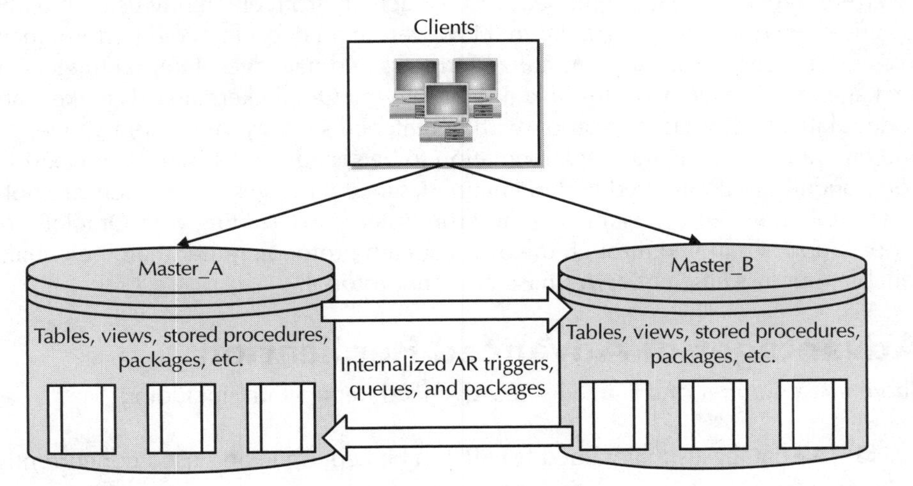

FIGURE 7-3. *Advanced replication configuration*

schemes can be set. Conflicts could occur for a variety of reasons. For instance, if the same copy of the row has been changed differently in each database by different users, a conflict would be recognized. A unique-key violation is another example of such conflicts. Conflicts need to be detected and resolved amicably. AR provides powerful algorithms for conflict detection and resolution. Conflict resolution can be consistent across the database or vary at the segment or even column level. Multiple conflict resolution techniques are available, such as using the latest change, using the earliest change, using changes specific to a certain site/database, using the maximum value, and so on.

As transactions are being forwarded, if a specific target database is unavailable, the transactions are retained at the source in the local deferred queue. When the target database is available again, the transactions are applied to it. The absence of one or more target databases will not prevent the transactions from being propagated to the remaining database copies. Both DML and DDL statements are propagated across all the masters. AR has traditionally used triggers, asynchronous queues, and various journal tables to implement different replication schemes. Trigger-based replication is effective under certain scenarios. However, in environments with large-scale concurrent DML, overall response time and throughput are adversely affected due to high trigger activity and the resultant recursive SQL. Traditionally, the trigger-based approach in AR has been a major deterrent, preventing sites with heavy OLTP activity from efficiently using it without significant performance degradation. However, in an effort to avoid performance loss, AR in Oracle8/8*i* uses internalized triggers and packages. Internal triggers and packages are C code modules linked right into the Oracle kernel. This makes the code relatively more tamperproof (with heightened security) and very lightweight and efficient, allowing the implementation to be speedy and scalable. No external components are configured and maintained. Since packages and triggers are not generated, they can be instantiated and run faster. Also, starting with Oracle8*i*, data propagation is handled through the direct stream protocol, rather than the equally reliable, but less efficient, two-phase commit protocol.

Advantages of Advanced Replication

There are a number of advantages to Advanced Replication, including

- All databases maintained by AR can be kept open and used concurrently.
- AR can be used for disaster recovery by having a database copy maintained at a remote site.
- Hardware independence exists, because the machines on which these databases are created can be of varying manufacturers, platforms, and OS versions.
- Load balancing across all replicated databases is possible.

Disadvantages of Advanced Replication

There are also a few disadvantages to Advanced Replication, including

- Propagation may not always be immediate. Therefore, changes to data in one database may not be immediately visible in all the other databases.
- During disasters, there is a distinct possibility of some data loss, since a site's database may be destroyed prior to the latest changes being propagated. In case the database at a site only fails and is not destroyed, the data loss will be temporary and all database copies can be synchronized once the failed database comes back up.
- Conflict resolution mechanisms must be well thought out and address scenarios in which all database copies can be directly written to (in master/master and master with updatable snapshot configurations) to prevent logical data corruption.

Automatic Failure Recovery with Advanced Replication

In the case of AR, during failure of a specific database copy, the cause of failure needs to be determined and the database recovered/rebuilt from the latest copy or from the backups. As previously mentioned, there is a chance of some data loss (most recent writes) during such failure. Whenever a specific database copy fails, the other copies will continue to function unless a major disaster occurs in which all existing copies are wiped out. The chances of this are very rare. During such situations, the downtime interval would be significant, because the database would have to be rebuilt using the last available backup. All client/user traffic can be redirected through the TAF (if the applications are written in OCI8/8*i*) or Net8 (automatic or explicit reconnection) to surviving copies of the database.

Standby Instances

A standby instance is basically a second instance that enables failover during specific database/system failures (refer to Figure 7-4). A standby instance is an HA (high-availability) option available on cluster-based architectures, such as IBM's HACMP/6000, NCR's LifeKeeper, HP's HP ServiceGuard, and Sun's Sun Clusters. Many vendors providing cluster solutions have an "Oracle configuration pack" that preconfigures a standby instance on a nonprimary node to take over during disasters. For Windows NT, Oracle provides Fail Safe, which can be implemented on Microsoft Cluster Server. Additionally, third-party software, such as VERITAS FirstWatch and VERITAS Cluster Server, is available for monitoring and managing failover.

A standby instance is not to be confused with OPS. With OPS, multiple (parallel) instances concurrently mount a single database resident on the cluster's shared disks. Thus, with OPS, concurrent access to the database is possible through any node that houses an instance. In the case of a standby instance, there is only one instance mounting a database at any time. This instance is referred to as the *primary instance.* The database remains resident on the cluster's shared disks so that any node can access it. When the node on which the primary instance resides fails, another predesignated node takes over control of the shared disks and immediately starts up another instance to mount the database, performs crash recovery, and reopens the database. All client processes that were connected to the database through the earlier instance experience a service disruption. Any new, incoming client connections that come in during the failover will get an error message that the connection request has failed (unless a middle-tier TP Monitor or an Application Server is configured to insulate the client from the error and, if necessary, connect instead to a remote geo-mirrored database; also as previously mentioned, OCI applications can use TAF

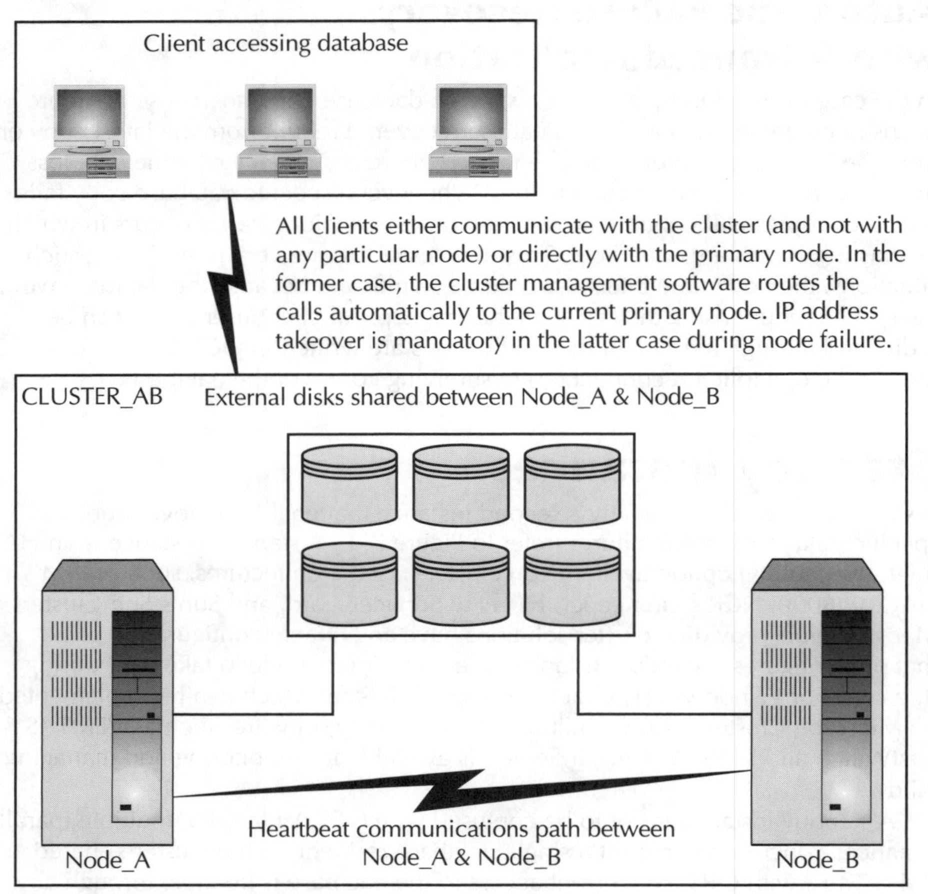
Client accessing database
All clients either communicate with the cluster (and not with any particular node) or directly with the primary node. In the former case, the cluster management software routes the calls automatically to the current primary node. IP address takeover is mandatory in the latter case during node failure.
CLUSTER_AB
External disks shared between Node_A & Node_B
Heartbeat communications path between Node_A & Node_B
Node_A
Node_B

FIGURE 7-4. *Standby instance configuration*

features in Oracle8/8*i*). However, as soon as the failover completes and the new instance is up and running, they can all reconnect and continue processing. The reconnection is seamless; they do not need to have any major application code changes implemented (other than putting in messages asking users to reconnect after three or so minutes if the database connection is broken or cannot be established) or SQL*Net/Net8 failover features enabled. They attempt to reconnect as they normally would, and their connection requests are routed to the new node. As expected, uncommitted transactions will be lost during the brief service disruption. The duration of the disruption is generally a few minutes during failover, and is particularly dependent on the time required to perform crash recovery.

Standby instances are sometimes viewed as "poor man's OPS." However, this is may be discounting the approach. It is true that, in the case of OPS due to another parallel instance already being up and available, failover is instantaneous—the connected client sessions will still experience a disruption. However, users can immediately reconnect and continue without having to wait for the standby instance to come up. Additionally, OPS offers higher scalability than standby instances. In the case of the latter, the scalability is limited to a single node's maximum capacity. However, standby instances have other advantages.

Advantages of Standby Instances

The advantages of standby instances are as follows:

- The most important advantage is the lowered cost and maintenance/administrative overhead. With standby instances, your site does not need to purchase an OPS license. Additionally, no raw devices are required as they are mandatory in an OPS configuration. To compound the situation, raw devices are relatively more difficult to manage than are cooked file systems. There is only a single instance to be monitored and tuned. The very same tuning changes will apply to the standby instance.
- There's no need to worry about explicit application partitioning.
- Generally, no data loss is experienced during failures since the standby instance takes over immediately after the primary instance fails.

Disadvantages of Standby Instances

The following are some disadvantages to standby instances:

- An important point to keep in mind is that, generally, cluster-based solutions such as standby instances (and even OPS, for that matter) are not capable of providing disaster recovery due to the close proximity of the nodes in the cluster. A remote solution will still need to be configured if your availability requirements are stringent enough to warrant one.
- A brief service disruption occurs, as the standby node detects that the primary node has failed and takes over. The standby instance has to, at the very least, perform crash recovery prior to reopening the database. This may take some time (generally, a few minutes) and, as such, may not be suitable for sites seeking true 24x7 uptime.
- Standby instance configurations are not capable of load balancing (at least, not as much as OPS), since only one instance is up and running at any given point in time.

TIP
Considering the very few occasions that failures do occur, and depending on the overall availability requirements of your organization (as determined by your service level agreement), standby instances may very well be the answer to your availability needs.

Automatic Failure Recovery with Standby Instances

In a standby database configuration, the IP address of the failed node is usually taken over by the standby node. So, once the failed instance is restarted by the standby, database access is seamless. Existing client/user processes would experience a service disruption during failure. However, after a few minutes, they may reconnect and continue their work (all uncommitted transactions would have been rolled back and would need to be reissued). If the IP address takeover is not supported in a specific cluster, the client/user processes will need to explicitly reconnect to the standby instance. Alternatively, TAF and Net8 automatic failover capabilities can be utilized to make the connection to the standby instance seamless.

Standby Databases

A standby database, as the name implies, is a copy of a functioning database, kept ready to be used in lieu of the latter for availability during disasters and system/database failures (when the functioning primary database has crashed and is unavailable). Figure 7-5 illustrates a standby database. The functioning database is referred to as the "primary" database. The mechanics for implementing a standby database have been officially available within Oracle since v7.3. However, with every new release, the standby database feature becomes more robust and automatic. Additionally, in Oracle8*i*, a standby database may be periodically kept open for reporting (query only) purposes. Also, an application support benefit may be realized as the standby database can be used to recreate failed operations for debugging.

The transactions occurring in the primary database are applied to the standby database through the former's archived redo logs. As transactions get written to the online redo logs, the logs get full, switch, and are archived by ARCH prior to being overwritten. Thus, both the primary and standby databases need to be in ARCHIVELOG mode. The archived logs are copied across the network to the remote standby server. (Note that in Oracle8*i*, the archived logs can be directly written to a remote standby location). The standby database is continuously in a state of recovery (mounted, but not open). All archived logs copied over are applied to the

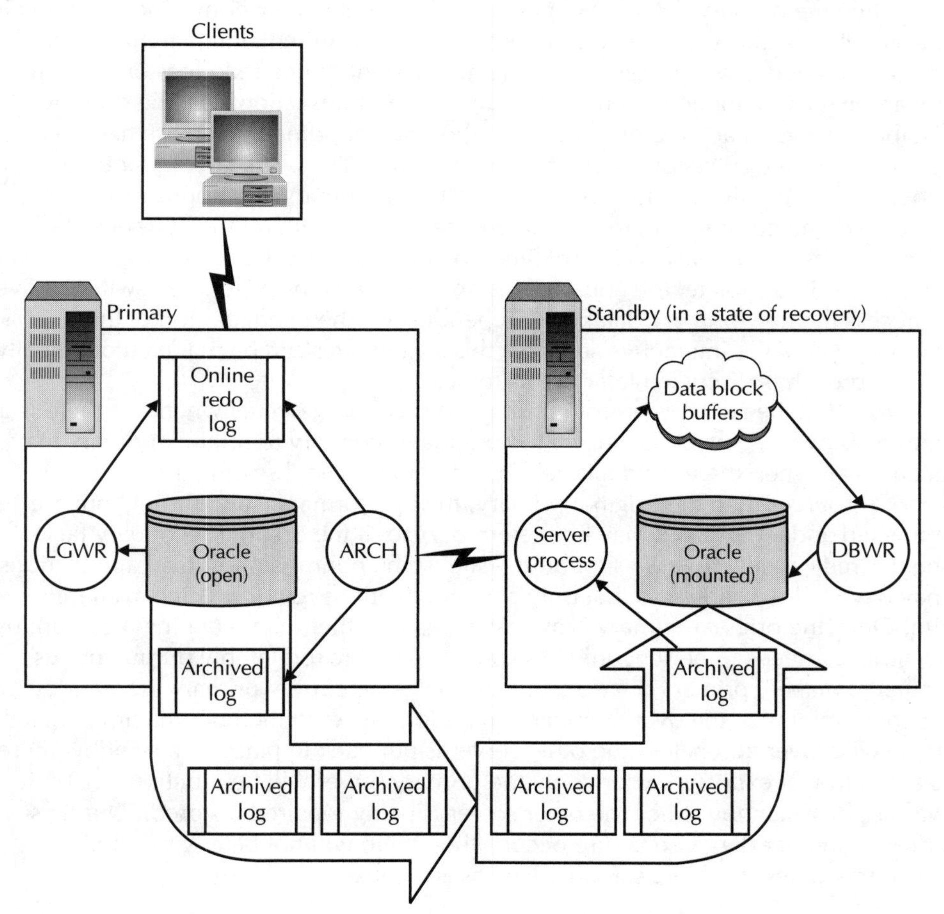

FIGURE 7-5. *Standby database configuration*

standby database to allow it to catch up to the primary database. The standby database is always behind the primary database. Even if all the archived logs generated thus far have been already applied, it still lags behind if transactions are currently being written to the primary's online redo logs. These redo-logs can be applied only after they are archived and copied over. Backups of both the primary and standby databases need to occur. In other words, the standby implementation is not a substitute for taking backups.

When the primary database experiences failure, switchover may occur, wherein the standby database is taken out of recovery mode. All remaining archived redo logs are applied and, whenever possible, the current online redo logs of the primary are archived and applied to ensure that there is no transaction loss.The standby database is then made the primary. After the original primary database has been repaired/restored, it becomes the standby database. Thus, it is kept in mounted mode and all archived redo logs (from the current primary) are applied to it. Whenever the current primary database experiences a failure, the current standby takes over as the primary with very little downtime during the switchover. Once the switchover is complete, the applications and user sessions need to be switched over to access the new primary database. Depending on the configuration of the connectivity of the interactive sessions, this switch over can be made automatically. This approach is discussed later in this topic.

Note that the switchover from primary to secondary occurs whenever there is a failure. However, switchback from the original secondary to original primary may occur even when there is no failure. That is, if the original secondary server has lower resources than the original primary, then performance and throughput are impacted and switchback may be preferred. Also, if the original secondary lacks the desired capacity to fully support the site, some nonmission-critical applications may have to be disabled so that only core applications requiring high availability run. Once the original primary is available again, rather than retaining it as standby, switchback needs to be scheduled as soon as possible (preferably during low-use hours) to make it primary once again (and make the current primary the standby again) to minimize the overall impact on performance. Remember that immediately after switchover and before the other server is put back in place as a standby, there is a window of exposure where only the primary server will be functioning. There will not be a standby (since the other server is being repaired/restored). During such times, if another database failure occurs, then there will not be any way to limit downtime unless multiple standby databases are used.

TIP

Multiple standby databases need to be considered as a serious alternative for limiting the window of exposure caused by a single standby database. The first standby can be kept behind the primary database for 15 minutes to a half hour (one or two archived redo logs behind) and a second standby database can be kept behind the primary by two hours or more (six or more archived redo logs behind). This will allow fast switchover, using the first standby database during primary database failures, and also allowing adequate time for preventing user errors (such as a table deletion or truncation) from being propagated to the second standby, since it is behind by two or more hours. Generally, with user errors, the first standby may already have the errors propagated to it. Since it is only one or two archived redo logs behind, there is a higher chance that the error was propagated prior to being detected and the propagation stream stopped). Also, in Oracle8i, having multiple standby databases allows the second standby to be kept open for higher periods of time for query access. Also, the second standby can be maintained remotely, allowing disaster recovery. However, as may be obvious, a higher cost is involved with keeping multiple standby servers, since an organization has to invest in multiple database servers. Also, maintenance and monitoring requirements increase. Whether one or more standby databases are used, it is recommended that any scheduled or discretionary processes, such as nightly reporting, be suspended while the primary database is out of operation. This will help to reduce the possibility of introducing further failures.

As you have seen, the standby database is in a state of constant recovery. This means the database cannot be used (for reporting, ad hoc queries, and so on) by end users. This may be perceived to be a waste of resources by management. As previously mentioned, in Oracle8*i*, the standby database can be kept open for certain periods in read-only mode. However, when the database is open, archived redo logs from the primary database cannot be applied to it, because recovery and open access are mutually exclusive (at least, in current releases). But once access is complete, the database can be put back in recovery mode and the process of applying archived logs can continue. The standby database is a very useful feature for certain environments where maintaining dual environments is necessary. Thus, during the daytime, when users need to issue ad hoc queries, the standby database can be kept open in read-only mode. The archived logs from the primary database that need to be applied can be accumulated on the standby server. Once the day ends, the standby database can be closed and placed in recovery mode again. Then the accumulated archived logs can be applied. For example, in the eight hours of regular business hours, there may be 20 to 25 archived logs that get accumulated, that can be applied in the evening. In case the primary database fails during business hours, the MTTR will be higher because the remaining archived logs are applied to make the standby relatively current and switchover occurs. However, the higher MTTR needs to be reconciled with organizational availability requirements to see whether it is acceptable. Obviously, in true 24x7 environments, trading potential downtime for better usage of dormant resources won't be an acceptable alternative.

Advantages of Standby Databases

The advantages of standby databases are:

- They allow disaster recovery if the standby database is maintained at a remote location.
- They are very flexible because a standby database can be maintained automatically (Oracle8*i*) or through the manual means with user input and/or scripts.
- Network bandwidth requirements are less intensive compared to other high-availability solutions, since only the archived redo logs need to be copied on a regular basis from the primary to the standby.
- With Oracle8*i*, the standby database can be kept open for read-only access.

Disadvantages of Standby Databases

Standby databases have the following disadvantages:

- There may be some data loss during failover to the standby database. If the online redo logs on the primary are lost, they cannot be archived and applied to the standby prior to failover. As such, the lost transactions would need to be identified and reentered. The LogMiner utility in Oracle8*i* would be very useful during such circumstances. Also, any archived redo logs that have not been applied prior to activating the standby cannot be applied later (after the standby has been activated).
- There is no easy fallback mechanism to return to the original primary machine after the standby database has been activated. The standby database must be reconstructed as the original primary and a failover to the original primary (now the standby) has to be initiated.
- While the standby database is open in read-only mode, it cannot be kept synchronized with the primary database (that is, the archived redo logs cannot be applied while it is open).

- Once the standby database is open in read/write mode, it becomes an independent database and cannot be made the standby again. At that point, a new standby has to be rebuilt from scratch (from the latest backup).
- Data not present in the archived redo logs (such as tables and indexes created through the NOLOGGING/UNRECOVERABLE option) will not be propagated to the standby. As such, the commands that disable redo need to be avoided or explicit measures need to be implemented to record and manually propagate such commands. Implementation of a robust database patch procedure can help to propagate such changes to all standby databases.
- User errors (accidental table deletions and so on) and logical corruption (index keys not matching the table column values) within the primary database may get propagated to the standby database via the archived redo logs if not detected and rectified on time.
- Failover is not immediate. It generally takes a few minutes to detect the failure of the primary database, apply the remaining archived redo logs, as appropriate, to the standby, and activate and open the standby for user access. In other words, users would experience a service disruption. As such, standby databases may not be acceptable to sites seeking true 24x7 uptime.
- The standby database must be the same Oracle version as the primary database. This does not allow the use of standby databases to provide uptime during version upgrades/downgrades (since the primary database cannot be synchronized with the standby database once the major version number changes).

Automatic Failure Recovery with Standby Databases

As mentioned previously, client/user processes will experience a brief service disruption during failure detection and failover to the standby database. Automatic failure recovery can be attained through the TAF and/or Net8 failover capabilities by automatically rerouting all client/user processes to the standby database after it is up and running. Alternatively, all client/user processes can explicitly connect to the standby database by directly using the appropriate service name. All applications can be coded to reconnect to the standby database if they are disconnected from the primary database.

Third-Party Solutions

In addition to the Oracle-based solutions discussed in the preceding sections, there are various third-party hardware and software high-availability solutions on the market. These ought to be considered during the initial design stage. For instance, standby databases can also be maintained through hardware-based geo-mirroring solutions. Rather than relying on the archived redo logs, you can set up all writes to the primary system to be synchronously copied to a remote standby system across a high-speed network link. I have seen the industrial strength of many of these third-party solutions proven in a variety of failure recovery scenarios. Of course, these solutions come with their own, sometimes similar, weaknesses, too. *Oracle 24x7 Tips and Techniques* from Oracle Press/Osborne discusses certain third-party hardware and software solutions in further detail.

Combining Multiple Solutions

You often may find that any single high-availability solution proves inadequate for allowing database access during all failures and disasters. Two or more such solutions may be combined to form a comprehensive solution and prevent a wide variety of outage-causing situations. For instance, you can supplement an OPS configuration with a remotely placed standby database. The OPS configuration would enable immediate seamless failover during local node failure. If all nodes fail due to a disaster or the shared disk system fails (in spite of RAID 1, 5, etc.), then OPS would not continue to provide database availability. In such situations, resort to using the remote standby database. A brief service interruption will occur as the standby database is made relatively up-to-date and activated. However, such a combined solution will prevent any outage lasting more than a few minutes.

In a similar fashion, you can also combine an Oracle solution with a third-party solution. An example is using the Oracle standby database in conjunction with third-party geo mirroring. You can use the geo-mirroring features to synchronously replicate the smaller online redo logs and control files (to prevent any performance degradation due to synchronous replication), whereas the data files and the archived redo logs can be replicated using regular and/or manual standby database features in an asynchronous fashion. Since the data files and archived redo logs form the bulk of the data that is replicated in a standby database environment, there is no significant strain on the geo-mirroring mechanism. Most geo-mirroring solutions can operate in both synchronous and asynchronous modes. However, Oracle recommends operating them only in synchronous mode (at least in Oracle environments). Such synchronous operation may delay writes on the primary database if the network latency is high. However, this ensures that only small, important, files are written synchronously. On the other hand, large files get written asynchronously, enabling you to acquire the best of both worlds—operating in a robust standby mode without impacting the performance of the primary database.

Custom Standby Database Strategies

Most of the solutions discussed earlier do not provide database availability during OS/Oracle patch application or upgrades. For instance, you cannot maintain a standby database across different Oracle versions. If you are on Oracle7, you cannot upgrade the primary database to Oracle8 while clients/user processes continue to use the v7 standby database. The new transactions generated in the v7 database cannot be applied to the new v8 database via the archived redo logs (the v7 and v8 archived log formats are incompatible). OPS permits a limited extent of rolling upgrades (where one node is upgraded at a time, while the other nodes continue to provide database access) on certain platforms. However, in order to attain true 24x7 uptime, you obviously need to have seamless access to the database during any major upgrade process. When uptime during upgrades/patch applications is a serious consideration, you may have to resort to custom standby strategies. *Oracle 24x7 Tips and Techniques* from Oracle Press/Osborne outlines a few custom standby strategies that may be utilized during such situations (only after due analysis of your specific environment to gauge whether any custom solution is appropriate).

End-User Session Disruption and Application Failover

I've been constantly making reference to Net8 and TAF features in Oracle8/8*i* to enable smooth application failover, where the end user does not notice database failure (as much as possible). Application failover is just as important as preventing and managing database failure in a 24x7 environment. An application is an end user's "window" into the database. Frequent service disruptions, no matter how brief, will frustrate any end user. As such, applications must be designed and built to be fault tolerant and enable seamless reconnection, wherever appropriate to the same primary database service name or explicitly to a standby database service name. Only in rare or extreme cases should the end user be forced to reconnect explicitly, especially in the disconnected/stateless Internet architecture. In order to achieve this, one needs to be highly familiar with TAF and Net8 failover capabilities. As such, a detailed study of the Oracle8*i* documentation set regarding these features is recommended prior to designing any application failover strategies.

Finally, there are also some application-specific ways to achieve data redundancy for failover. For instance, you can use "transaction splitting" for this purpose. Transaction splitting is a technique where all writes (or specific predetermined ones) are directed simultaneously through threads or sequentially to multiple databases (for instance, the primary database and an open standby database copy). Thus, all copies of the database would have up-to-date writes directly from the application. This eliminates the need for any backend synchronization, such as Advanced Replication. Furthermore, the application can be built to ignore write failure (in case a database copy has experienced failure). As long as the master database copy has recorded the write accurately, the application can continue to function after sending an alert to administrative personnel regarding the failure of the write (so appropriate corrective action can be taken). In case the master copy itself experiences write failure or a related error, such as disconnection from the database, the application can again send a similar alert to administrative personnel and continue accessing a predesignated copy of the database.

Summary

This chapter outlined possible ways of attaining 24x7 uptime for database-driven Web sites. It emphasized the importance of identifying all single points of failure and taking steps to prevent such failure as much as possible by designing and deploying appropriately robust architecture. In the event that failure does occur, certain failover configurations within Oracle can minimize, and at times avoid, any downtime. Finally, the utility of masking failure, from an end-user application perspective, and devising custom high-availability solutions for enabling database uptime during routine patch application/upgrades was highlighted.

References

- Oracle7 v7.3.4 documentation set
- Oracle8 v8.0.5 documentation set
- Oracle8i v8.1.5 documentation set
- Devraj, Venkat S., *Oracle 24x7 Tips and Techniques.* Oracle Press/Osborne McGraw-Hill; 1999.
- Several Oracle Corporation and Oracle Support white papers and bulletins. (Authors include Erik Peterson, Paul Manning, Nitin Vengurlekar, Hasan Rizvi, Anjo Kolk, Sameer Patkar, Lawrence To, Basab Maulik, Carol Colrain, Prabhakar Gongloor, Roderick Manalac, J. Diet, Stefan Pommerenk, Shari Yamaguchi, Brian Quigley, Deepak Gupta, Erik Peterson, B. Klots, Rama Velpuri, Satish Mahajan, Cristina Añonuevo, Betty Wu, and others.)

CHAPTER 8

HTTP Listeners

The Hypertext Transfer Protocol (HTTP) Listener is a process that communicates using HTTP and cycles as it waits for requests coming across TCP/IP on a specific port (or on multiple ports). The HTTP Listener, generically called the Web Listener, translates virtual directories into physical directory locations. HTTP Listeners traditionally support two types of virtual directories, defined as "normal" and "cgi" directories. The main difference between the two is how the files are handled. When users request a file from a normal directory, the file is sent directly to the browser (e.g., an HTML file). A file requested from a cgi directory is assumed to be a program that needs to be executed, which will, in turn, dynamically generate HTML or HTTP data. A Web server is a server that contains 1 or more Web Listeners. If you are looking for a *standard* Web server, I have found more than 150 on the market. You can find a good list of Web servers (and other information, such as marketshare statistics, who is using each Web server, and so forth) at www.netcraft.com. The most popular Web servers are free. Oracle's Application Server, however, is much more than a standard Web server. Because most Web servers are free, I can only assume that Oracle never intended on being in the Web server business. The Spyglass listener is packaged with the Web Listener. OAS is licensed by Oracle. Oracle's Web solution, OAS, provides the base functionality of a standard Web server and much more, which will be discussed in this chapter.

In this chapter, the following topics will be covered:

- Using the Oracle Listener
- Configuring IIS, Netscape FastTrack, Netscape Enterprise, or the Apache Listener with OAS
- Unregistering IIS, Netscape FastTrack, Netscape Enterprise, or the Apache Listener from OAS
- Comparing IIS speed with Oracle (Spyglass)
- Turning file caching off
- Tuning your TCP/IP parameters
- Guarding your base domain name
- Monitoring your site for crashes
- Starting and stopping OAS
- Setting the rescan interval
- Analyzing why the listener does not notice that file permissions have changed

- Troubleshooting why you cannot access the Node Manager
- Copying a listener from another server
- Configuring the listener to run on port 80 on a UNIX machine

Using the Oracle Listener

As previously mentioned, Oracle's listener is actually the Spyglass listener. If you install OAS and set up listeners through the Node Manager port, you will actually be configuring the underlying Spyglass listeners. From an integration and support standpoint, I feel it's easiest to use one vendor's product—keep it simple silly (KISS). In other words, use the Oracle listener. If you are already running one of the following listeners: Microsoft IIS, Netscape FastTrack, Netscape Enterprise, or Apache—you can register the listener with OAS, or you can elect to use the Oracle/Spyglass listener. If you are using a listener not previously mentioned, you would need to decide whether you want to run the Oracle listener on a different port. The decision is up to you, the lead architect.

TIP
Keep OAS configuration simple by using the Spyglass (Oracle) listener.

A number of tests were conducted to determine if one listener outperformed another in terms of reliability. The findings basically indicated that a listener is a listener. If you wish to run performance tests yourself, the following script will get you started. Most listeners will crash when you reach about 1,000 characters in a GET operation.

TIP
Try to limit the length of your URLs to less than 1,000 characters to avoid crashing your listener. HTML forms should use the POST operation to avoid excessively long URLs.

```
CREATE OR REPLACE PROCEDURE test_listener
  (in_base_url  varchar2 default
  'http://myserver/plsql/routine?in_name=Testing',
   in_how_many  varchar2 default 100,
   in_grow_flag varchar2 default 'N')
 is
  url                  long := in_base_url;
```

```
  html                 utl_http.html_pieces;
  start_time          number;
  very_start          number;
begin
  -- Open the html page
  htp.htmlOpen;
  htp.bodyOpen;

  -- Set the starting time of the entire routine
  very_start := dbms_utility.get_time;

  -- Call the site the number of times requested
  for x in 1 .. to_number(in_how_many) loop
     -- If the grow_flag is set, then add a character onto
     -- the URL, most listeners will die at about 1000 characters
     -- on a GET operation.
     if in_grow_flag = 'Y' then
           url := url || 'x';
     end if;

     -- Set the starting time, just before calling the page
        start_time := dbms_utility.get_time;

     -- Call the page returning each 4000 character's worth
     -- into the html array
     html        := UTL_HTTP.request_pieces(url);

    -- Print some stats - the URL that was called, length of the
    -- URL, how many 4000 character pieces were returned, and the
    -- amount of time it took to fetch the data.
    htp.print('URL.............: ' || url                  || htf.br);
    htp.print('URL Length.......: ' || length(url)          || htf.br);
    htp.print('Segments Returned: ' || to_char(html.count) || htf.br);
    htp.print('Time to Retrieve.: ' ||
               to_char(dbms_utility.get_time - start_time)||
               ' (1/100 seconds) ' || htf.hr);
 end loop;

 -- Draw another line and print the total amount of
 -- time it took to call this routine x times
 htp.hr;
 htp.print(  'Total Retrieve Time.: ' ||
              to_char(dbms_utility.get_time - very_start) ||
             ' (1/100 seconds) ');

  -- close html page
  htp.bodyClose;
  htp.htmlClose;
end test_listener;
```

The preceding script may crash your listener when the URL grows to more than 1,000 characters in length. The preceding script will report the results of your listener's performance.

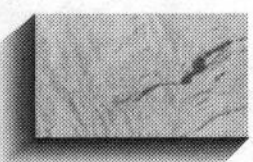

TIP
If your in-house proxy server is caching the requested page, you may get skewed results because the request is not actually hitting the Web server. In this case, you would want to be sure to use the PRAGMA NO-CACHE Meta tag.

Configuring IIS, Netscape FastTrack, Netscape Enterprise, or the Apache Listener with OAS

To register Microsoft's IIS listener with OAS, perform the following steps:

1. Install Microsoft's Option Pack 4 (note this is not Service Pack 4, but Option Pack 4) for NT (if you are running Microsoft NT Server, rather than NT Workstation, IIS will already be installed). This installation provides an IIS listener running on port 80.
2. Reboot server PC and wait for all of the services to come up.
3. Navigate to the OAS Node Manager (i.e., port 8888) through the browser.
4. From the Node Manager, run OAS Utilities. Drill into Register External Listeners and select Microsoft. When you do this, OAS then scans the standard ports (80, 443, and 8080) to determine if there is an IIS listener on one of those ports. If not, it will prompt you for the port to scan. Otherwise, OAS will show you a list of server names and ports that are running IIS.
5. Select the server (click the checkbox) and port to register. The final step is pretty simple, too. Simply select Register Checked Listeners. At that point, you should get a "success" message.
6. Even though I did not find this anywhere in the documentation, I rebooted the server once again.
7. After the reboot, go back to the Node Manager and start OAS.
8. To verify everything works properly, just execute a cartridge URL like a PL/SQL procedure from the IIS port. For example: http://hp1.tusc.com/plsql/test_procedure
9. The external listener should now work just fine.

TIP

If the version and vendor of the other Web server isn't specifically listed, then it is not supported and probably won't work. OAS prompts for the physical directory of the executable and configuration files and replaces shared libraries of the other Web server. What this also means is that you can't make changes to the port (i.e., adding more virtual directories) unless you first deregister the OAS port. The process of deregistering the external listener will swap back the original shared libraries. See Oracle bulletin 70061.1.

NOTE

Administration of IIS is under Windows NT 4.0 Option Pack in the Microsoft Personal Web Server option and the Personal Web Manager.

Undoing the Registration of IIS, Netscape FastTrack, Netscape Enterprise, or the Apache Listener from OAS

If you change your mind and decide you would rather not use one of these listeners as your externally registered listener, it's simple to undo the registration. Perform the following steps:

1. Start up the Node Manager (i.e., port 8888) through the browser.
2. Run OAS Utilities and drill into Unregister External Listeners.
3. Similar to the registration process, you will then see the name(s) of the server(s) and ports that are external and registered. Select the server (click the checkbox) and port that you wish to unregister. Select Unregister Checked Listeners.
4. You should then receive a success message.
5. Once again, even though I did not see this step in any documentation, I rebooted the server.
6. After the server started back up, I went back to the Node Manager, started OAS, and away we went.

Comparing IIS Speed with Oracle (Spyglass)

Previously, I stated that a listener is a listener in terms of reliability. Well, what about performance? To test a listener's performance in terms of URL execution speed, I ran a PL/SQL routine that takes about 1/100th of a second to execute if executed by itself. The PL/SQL routine is called get_emps. Then, I wrote a second routine (named get_emps_100_times) using UTL_HTTP to call the get_emps URL 100 times. I figured that this method served as a good benchmark to test each of the listeners. From the browser, I executed the get_emps_100_times routine 11 times in a row using each of the listeners (Oracle and IIS).

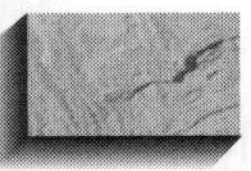

TIP
Execute performance tests in your own OAS environment.

When using the Oracle listener, the first time OAS ran get_emps_100_times, it took 8.52 seconds. The first time you execute a PL/SQL procedure, it will take a little longer because the Oracle DB has to physically read the data from the disk. Thereafter, the data is cached in the SGA. The average time for subsequent executions was 4.57 seconds.

Then, I removed the Oracle listener and installed Microsoft's IIS listener. The first time I executed get_emps_100_times, the routine took 12.96 seconds. Thereafter, on average, the routine took 5.83 seconds for the next 10 executions.

Using this performance benchmark, you can see that it takes longer to run OAS components (in this case, the PL/SQL cartridge) using the IIS than it does through the Oracle listener.

Turning File Caching Off

If you have used OWAS version 3 on NT, especially while in the development phase of your project, you were probably extremely frustrated by locked static HTML files. If you are not familiar with this problem, you are fortunate. In version 3, all static HTML files were cached and locked once the server called the HTML page. If you had any hopes of editing the file, you needed to stop the listener, edit the file, and restart the listener. In a development environment, this got old quickly.

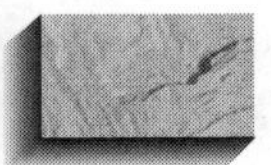

TIP
Turn file caching off during development, but on for a production environment.

If you liked this feature, you can still enable it in OAS version 4. However, in version 4, fortunately, you have the option to turn the file caching off. This is a great enhancement. To enable or disable this feature, go to the OAS Manager in the Node Manager (i.e., port 8888); then, drill into your Web site and then to HTTP Listeners. Now, drill into the specific listener and click on Server. You will see File Caching in the right-hand frame. Turning this On will lock the files once they are accessed. The advantage to this feature is that the file is cached, which makes access to files considerably faster. Therefore, on a production system, this parameter should be set to On. Turning this feature Off will cause the file to be read from the disk every time—in other words, it is not cached (or locked); therefore, you can edit the file any time you wish.

Tuning Your TCP/IP Parameters

Sun regularly updates the Solaris operating system components, such as the Transmission Control Protocol/Internet Protocol (TCP/IP) subsystem, that are heavily used by OAS. Whatever your operating system, make sure you have installed the latest patches. Also available from Sun is the Solaris Internet Server Supplement, which is a set of add-on modules specially tailored for Solaris systems that host Web sites. See Chapter 4 for additional information on parameters. The following table contains Oracle's recommended TCP/IP parameter settings for a Web server:

Parameter	Recommended Value
tcp_conn_req_max_q	1,024
tcp_close_wait_interval	3,000
tcp_rexmit_interval_min	1,500
tcp_xmit_hiwat	65,536
tcp_xmit_lowat	24,576
tcp_recv_hiwat	65,536

TIP
On at least a monthly basis check to see if your hardware vendor has any operating system patches, updates, series or recommendations that could affect your performance.

After you su to the root account, execute the following command to set these TCP/IP parameters:

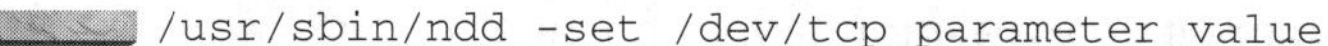

```
/usr/sbin/ndd -set /dev/tcp parameter value
```

where *parameter* is a parameter listed in the first column of the preceding table, and *value* is the respective value listed in the second column. For example:

```
/usr/sbin/ndd -set /dev/tcp tcp_conn_req_max_q 1024
```

Guarding Your Base Domain Name

By now, most companies have registered their company domain name. For example, our base domain is tusc.com. Typically, your email address is the same name as this base domain name (e.g., Bradley_Brown@tusc.com). If you are using Microsoft Exchange Server on an NT box, be careful. Your base domain name, in this example tusc.com, is registered to a specific IP, and if a user types **tusc.com** in their browser, the browser will attempt to perform an HTTP operation on port 80 to that specific box (i.e., your mail server). When you install Microsoft NT Server, it automatically installs IIS on that server. Therefore, if a user simply types **tusc.com**, which resolves to the IP address of the Exchange Server, the user may see the default IIS home page. This would certainly confuse users. I have seen smaller ISPs who are not aware of this problem. Because ISPs typically virtually host a number of sites, the page that displays may be a totally different company's Web site. Oops! To disable IIS on this server, simply go to the Services option of the Control Panel, stop the service, and set the default startup method to Manual. This will protect your base domain name, so users will not see the default Web server page. Another option would be to include a redirect option in the IIS server that points to www.tusc.com. Either of these methods is acceptable, even though I certainly prefer the latter. For security reasons, you may want to turn off other services, such as ping and FTP on that server. A firewall will also fix this problem, because you can easily limit the protocols permitted to communicate to each of your servers on specific TCP/IP ports.

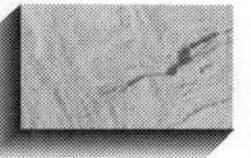

TIP
Test out your base domain name through the Internet to see if you see any surprises.

Monitoring Open Connections

If you are curious about the number of open sessions (at the listener-level), then you can issue the following netstat command (from UNIX):

```
netstat -an | grep \.80 | grep EST
```

In the preceding example, 80 is the Web Listener port and EST is short for ESTABLISH. This simply shows in detail how many concurrent connections you have. The following script shows more extensive information, but at a higher level—specifically, it counts how many occurrences you have of each. This script looks at port 80 and then port 443 for all connections, whether active or not. ESTablished connections are those that are currently active. If you have a lot of connections and not a lot of ESTablished connections, you should probably reduce the amount of time that connections are kept open—as described in the previous section.

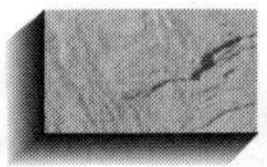

TIP
Write a script to automate the monitoring of open connections. Based on your own thresholds, you may wish to send yourself email warnings.

The following script displays various TCP/IP information:

```
echo 'hostname'

echo netstat to 80:
netstat -an | grep \.80 | grep -v grep | wc -l

echo netstat to 443:
netstat -an | grep \.443 | grep -v grep | wc -l

echo netstat established
netstat -an | grep ESTABLISHED | grep -v grep | wc -l

echo netstat listen
netstat -an | grep LISTEN | grep -v grep | wc -l

echo netstat close_wait
netstat -an | grep CLOSE_WAIT | grep -v grep | wc -l

echo netstat fin_wait_1
netstat -an | grep FIN_WAIT_1 | grep -v grep | wc -l

echo netstat fin_wait_2
netstat -an | grep FIN_WAIT_2 | grep -v grep | wc -l

echo netstat total
netstat -an | grep -v grep | wc -l
```

The following script looks at the OAS processes:

```
echo Number of wrks [Cartridge Server] processes:
ps -ef | grep "wrks" | grep -v grep | wc -l

echo Number of mnmon [Monitor] processes:
ps -ef | grep "mnmon" | grep -v grep | wc -l

echo Number of oraweb [Listener] processes:
ps -ef | grep "oraweb" | grep -v grep | wc -l

echo Number of otsfacsrv [Cartridge Server] processes:
ps -ef | grep "otsfacsrv" | grep -v grep | wc -l

echo Number of mnorbsrv [ORB] processes:
ps -ef | grep "mnorbsrv" | grep -v grep | wc -l

echo Number of oassrv [Collapsed Config, Log, Auth, Broker,
echo Monitor, Proxy] processes:
ps -ef | grep "oassrv" | grep -v grep | wc -l

echo Number of mncnmsrv [ORB Config Mgr] processes:
ps -ef | grep "mncnmsrv" | grep -v grep | wc -l

echo Number of mnlogsrv [ORB Log] processes:
ps -ef | grep "mnlogsrv" | grep -v grep | wc -l

echo Number of mnorbmet [ORB Metric Server] processes:
ps -ef | grep "mnorbmet" | grep -v grep | wc -l
```

The netstat command is a powerful UNIX utility. The following syntax is the entire command:

```
Usage:  netstat [-an] [-f address-family] [system [core]]
        netstat [-Mnrsv] [-f address-family] [-p protocol]
                [system [core]]
        netstat [-gin] [-I interface] [interval] [system [core]]
        -a      show state of all sockets, including passive sockets
        -f      show statistics only for specified address family
        -g      show multicast information for network interfaces
        -i      show statistics for network interfaces
        -I      show statistics only for specified network interface
        -M      show multicast routing tables
```

```
-Ms      show multicast routing statistics
-n       display network addresses numerically
-p       show statistics only for specified protocol
-r       show routing tables
-rv      show additional information for the routing table
-s       show statistics for all protocols

interval        display interface statistics continuously
system          replaces the default kernel /stand/vmunix
core            replaces the default core file /dev/kmem
```

Monitoring Your Site for Crashes

Proactively monitoring your Web site to ensure it's up and running 24 hours a day, 7 days a week is important. If your site is down, there is a script you can run that will automatically send you an email or have a message sent to your pager notifying you of your site's status. You can also pay a service company to monitor for you.

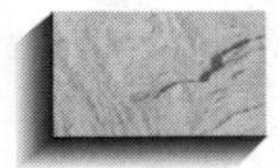

TIP
Oracle has established a goal for OAS 4.1 such that OAS will not have a single point of failure. Until this is true, you will need to proactively monitor your production Web sites.

The following script was published by Jeff Francis (jfrancis@frii.com). If you take the following shell script, put it on your UNIX box, and then add the script execution to crontab, it should do the trick. The script will cause an email to be sent to your alphanumeric pager whenever your Web page is down. It requires bash (or ksh) and lynx (or wget) to work. To avoid repetitious email messages to your alphanumeric pager, modify this script so it only sends you a message for each state change. The following script will send a message every single time the script checks your site and it's down.

OAS version 4.0 will monitor each of the site processes and automatically restart failed components for you. The monitoring and auto restart functionality is available under the Node Manager (i.e., port 8888) in the OAS Manager, under Oracle Application Server; click on Failure Recovery. By using the built-in failure recovery, you can configure the state save interval and the state detection interval, and enable or disable failure recovery for any (or all) of the following processes:

- Configuration provider
- Authentication server
- Broker

- Logger
- Cartridge Server Factory
- Dispatcher
- Monitoring Daemon
- RM Proxy

However, the following script would provide more flexibility for OAS failures:

```
#!/usr/local/bin/bash
# web_monitor.ksh
#
# Simple web server monitoring script.  Designed to be placed in cron
# and run periodically.  There are several known limitations with this
# script, the most important of which is that it will send email
# *every* time it checks, and the site is down.  If you run the script
# too often (say, every five minutes), and your site is down for an
# extended period of time, you will quickly go insane with the number
# of pages you'll receive (and probably rack up a substantial bill
# from your paging service).

# This script should run under either 'bash' or 'ksh'.  Probably even
# 'sh', though I haven't tried it.

# This script could probably be made to run under Windows NT without a
# great deal of trouble if you install the UNIX utils (bash in
# particular) from Cygnus (www.cygnus.com).  The limiting factors are
# finding a command-line-driven (non-GUI) mail program (sendmail) and web
# browser.

# Jeff Francis (jfrancis@frii.com)

# This is the URL of the page you wish to monitor.
URL="http://www.tusc.com/index.html"

# This is the string you want to search for to make sure you got a
# valid page.
STRING="TUSC (The Ultimate Software Consultants)"

# Here's the message to send to the user when things get wonky.  You
# can get as specific as you like here; just remember that most
# alphanumeric pagers have a message length limitation.
MESSAGE="Danger, Danger. The TUSC Web site is down."

 # Here's the subject line of the email.  Keep it short for sanity.
```

```
SUBJECT="TUSC Site Down"

# This is the email address to send a message to if the web page is
# down.
MAILTO=administrator@your_domain.com

# Here's the full path to your text-only web browser
# (could be 'lynx' # or 'wget' to name a couple).
BROWSER="/usr/local/bin/lynx"

# Here's the full path to your mail program (could be 'mutt', 'elm',
# 'mail', or 'mailx', or darned near anything, depending on
# what flavor of UNIX you're running).
MAIL="/usr/local/bin/mutt"

# Dump the web page and make sure the specified string
# matches somewhere within the returned text.
if [ `${BROWSER} -dump ${URL} | grep -c -i "${STRING}" 2>&1` -eq 0 ]
then
  echo "${MESSAGE}" | ${MAIL} -s \"${SUBJECT}\" ${MAILTO}
fi
```

Starting and Stopping OAS

Each version of OAS not only had a unique name, but also had a unique way of starting the services. To start Oracle Web Server (OWS) version 1, the following was the syntax:

```
V1:    wlctl   start <port_number>       eg. wlctl   start 8888
       wlctl   stop  <port_number>
```

Even though the product names stayed the same in OWS version 2, the syntax changed. Starting and stopping used a logical port name rather than a port number. The reason behind this is that Oracle was positioning OWS to be able to control multiple ports with one listener. Start and stop Oracle Web Server versions 2.0 and 2.1, as illustrated in the following syntax:

```
V2.0: wlctl2  start <listener_name>     eg. wlctl2  start admin
      wlctl2  stop  <listener_name>

V2.1: wlctl21 start <listener_name>     eg. wlctl21 start admin
      wlctl21 stop  <listener_name>
```

As of Oracle Web Application Server (OWAS) version 3, the WRB came into play. So, to start version 3, you had to start the WRB and then each of the listeners.

To stop version 3, the commands are entered in reverse order and appear identical to the following:

```
V3.0: Starting the webserver (note the sequence):
      owsctl start wrb    ... starts webrequest broker
      owsctl start admin ... start admin listener
      owsctl start yourweb ... start your weblistener

      Stopping the webserver (note the sequence):
      owsctl stop yourweb
      owsctl stop admin
      owsctl stop wrb
```

In Oracle Application Server (OAS) version 4, the WRB is still around, but Oracle simplified the command to start and stop the entire site. You can still start and stop individual processes if you wish. One of my favorite features of the OAS owsctl process is the reload feature. This command stops and starts the entire site, all in one command. Prior to version 4, you could not stop the WRB through a browser; you always had to perform this function through the command line. However, version 4 enables you to start and stop the WRB and all of the listeners (with the exception of the Node Manager) through the Node Manager. The reload feature is also available from the GUI features of the OAS Manager. In prior versions, I usually wrote a script to stop and start the entire Web server. I usually called this script something like bounce. The syntax for version 4 appears identical to the following:

```
V4.0: Starting everything:
      owsctl start

      Stopping everything:
      owsctl stop

      "Bounce" everything:
      owsctl reload
```

Setting the Rescan Interval

The default value for the rescan interval parameter is 0, meaning that directories are checked for file changes each time a file is accessed. Ideally, you would set this value to a high number on a production site, since changes to static files would rarely be made—or at least scheduled. However, if you then change a file, the changes will not be picked up until the rescan interval is reached. Therefore, an ideal setting for this parameter is between one minute (60 seconds) and five minutes (300 seconds). This parameter does not affect performance too greatly, so setting it super high will not provide much value. Leaving the parameter set to 0 does not make much sense either.

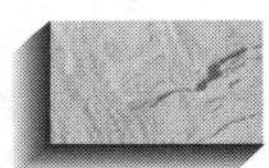

TIP
Set the rescan interval to 300 seconds for a production environment.

Analyzing Why the Listener Does Not Notice that File Permissions Have Changed

The listener caches the modification date and time of the directory and all the files within. If a URL is unavailable because of permission problems, and you fix that problem, the listener will continue to say that the URL is unavailable because the directory modification date and time have not changed; it does not check the file itself. Renaming the file and then changing it back again will force the listener to see the change—the modification date and time will be set accordingly. As previously mentioned, setting the *rescan interval* determines how long the listener will go without rescanning a directory that appears not to have changed, including the ability to never rescan unless the modification date changes.

Troubleshooting Why You Cannot Access the Node Manager

After installing OAS, you might find that you could not access the Node Manager port. During the installation, OAS prompts you for the name of the server. I typically do not recommend that you change this parameter, but it's important to note the value that it retrieves. The value displayed is typically the name of the machine, including the full domain name. You may have many aliases by which you can refer to the machine. However, OAS likes to refer to the machine with the full domain name. Try accessing the Node Manager by specifying the entire name of the machine, including the domain name. If that does not work, look in the file %oraweb_admin/site_name/http…/node/svnode.cfg—you will typically see two entries in the file that indicate how to specify the name of the machine from the browser. In version 3.x, only one entry was added, which was the full domain name of the machine. You can edit this CFG file (be careful if you do) to add additional entries if you wish.

Copying a Listener from Another Server

The easiest way to copy the configuration information from one server to another is to copy the listener.cfg file. Before copying the file, create a listener with the virtual name you wish to use and shut the listener down. Then, back up the listener.cfg file that OAS creates, and copy the listener.cfg file from the other server to the newserver. You may need to edit the configuration for the new server's directory structure and the like. You can edit the listener.cfg file, or you can use the OAS listener configuration tool in the OAS Manager. Once you've edited the configuration, you can start the listener. You have just copied a listener from another server.

TIP
Copying a listener from another server is as simple as copying the CFG file. Be sure to modify the directories and other server specific information before attempting to start the listener.

Configuring the Listener to Run on Port 80 on a UNIX Machine

On UNIX, all ports less than 1,024 are restricted ports. Therefore, port 80 is a restricted port. There is a script located at $ORACLE_HOME/orainst/oasroot.sh that will modify permissions on the oraweb process such that it can run on the protected port of 80. If you don't run this script, you will have to start and stop port 80 as a superuser. Note that the oasroot.sh script must be run by the root user.

Summary

So, is a listener a listener? That all depends on what you're looking for. Almost any listener can provide base functionality, and tests indicate that most listeners are fairly reliable. However, if speed, flexibility, and additional features are important to you, the list of options narrows considerably. Oracle's Spyglass listener is one of the best I have found, but you will need to make that call yourself, based on your business requirements.

CHAPTER 9

Oracle8*i* Built-In Packages

hen it comes to developing applications using Oracle as your database engine, the built-in database packages continue to multiply and become more powerful with each new database version. This chapter will cover the built-in packages as important components of any Web development project using Oracle. These packages can be used regardless of which Web server you are using. This chapter has grouped the built-in packages into the following categories:

- Messaging with dbms_alert
- Setting SGA variables with dbms_application_info
- Executing DDL with dbms_ddl
- Queuing with dbms_job
- Accessing objects with dbms_lob
- Writing output with dbms_output
- Messaging with dbms_pipe
- Setting session properties with dbms_session
- Executing Dynamic SQL using dbms_sql
- Setting the trace level with dbms_trace
- Making the most of dbms_utility
- Accessing operating system files with utl_file
- Maximizing utl_http

Messaging with dbms_alert

The dbms_alert package provides support for the asynchronous (as opposed to polling) notification of database events. This package is used in combination with database triggers to cause the application to notify itself when the values of interest in the database have been changed. The dbms_alert package registers that you are waiting for a specific alert by setting a flag in the SGA and then watches for the specified alert. Because the Web does not maintain state, your procedures typically execute in less than a second. Use the dbms_alert to monitor a database change occurring from the time your procedure starts until it ends. It is possible to use a hidden frame on your Web page that cycles using dbms_alert, waiting for a condition to occur to force the page refresh.

For example, suppose you are displaying or graphing key company information stored in the database (such as time and expense reporting, employee vacation information, stock prices, earnings estimates, and so forth) for your corporate executives. After reading, displaying, and graphing the data, this procedure can check for or wait for a database alert (using dbms_alert.waitone) covering the data just read. The routine could verify if an alert was generated since the procedure started, or it could wait until an alert is generated and automatically wake when the data is changed by any other user. To perform this task, a trigger must be placed on the database table that signals an alert (using dbms_alert.signal) when changed. Alerts are transaction-based, which means the waiting session does not receive the alert until the transaction signaling the alert performs a COMMIT.

A number of concurrent signalers of an alert exist, and a number of concurrent waiters on a given alert can also exist. Because a waiting application will be locked in the database and cannot perform other tasks, you must be careful about waiting too long in the Web world or the user's browser could time out.

Suppose your Web page calls a PL/SQL procedure that graphs earnings information, and the procedure needs to know if income or expense data has changed since the procedure started. At the beginning of the procedure we need to register the alert, as the following snippet of code illustrates:

```
dbms_alert.register('earnings_alert');
<<beginning>>
```

The rest of the procedure would not change; however, it would collect and graph the earnings information. At the end of the procedure, if you want to verify if an alert was signaled since this procedure started, apply the following syntax:

```
dbms_alert.waitone('earnings_alert', message, status, 0);
```

Message and status are output variables from the waitone procedure. Message will be NULL and status will be 0 if an alert has not been raised. If the status is greater than 0, an alert was sent. At this point, our routine will clear the HTML buffer and go back to the top of our procedure to start over. The following code illustrates how to check the status and how the earnings_alert is removed when finished:

```
-- 0 means an alert occurred, 1 means a timeout occurred
if status = 0 then
   owa_util.showpage;
   -- Could display message and status here, if appropriate
   goto beginning;
end if;

--  When the application is no longer interested in the alert,
--  it needs to remove the alert. This is important since it reduces
--  the amount of work required by the alert signaler.


dbms_alert.remove('earnings_alert');
```

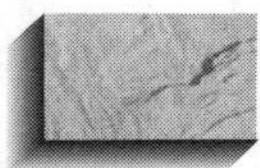

TIP
In the preceding example, the owa_util.showpage was used to clear the HTML buffer. This routine moves the HTML buffer (stored in a PL/SQL table) to the dbms_output PL/SQL table and clears the HTML buffer.

Each of the tables that could affect our earnings numbers would need to have a trigger similar to the following example:

```
create trigger income_trig after insert or update or delete on income
begin
  dbms_alert.signal('earnings_alert', 'Data changed in income table');
end;
```

Your procedure can be registered for multiple events and wait for any of them to occur using the waitany call. Your procedure can also supply an optional time-out parameter to the waitone or waitany procedure calls. A time-out of 0 will be returned immediately if there is no pending alert.

Alerts are processed in real time and may be signaled more often than the corresponding application wait calls. In such cases, the older alerts are discarded. Your procedure will always get the latest alert based on transaction COMMIT times. If your application requirements do not need transaction-based alerts, the dbms_pipe package may provide a useful alternative.

If the transaction is rolled back after the call to dbms_alert.signal, no alert will occur. This package uses the dbms_lock package for synchronization between signalers and waiters and the dbms_pipe package for asynchronous event dispatching. Dbms_alert uses one database pipe and two locks for each alert registered by a session.

Even though you cannot pass a specific status number using the dbms_alert package, you can pass a specific message. The message can contain a text message, or it can contain table information such as a unique key or other specific data. The waiting session may be able to avoid reading the database after the alert occurs by strategically using the information in this message.

register

The register procedure registers interest in an alert. A session may register interest in an unlimited number of alerts. Alerts should be deregistered when the session no longer has any interest—"interest" meaning that we wish to monitor the alert. If no users have registered an interest in an alert, valuable processing time is not spent monitoring the alert or saving the information in the SGA. The only input parameter is the name of the alert this session is interested in. The following code illustrates the syntax of the register procedure:

```
procedure register(name in varchar2);
```

remove

The remove procedure removes an alert from a session's registration list. This should be completed when the session is no longer interested in the alert. Removing an alert is important because it will reduce the amount of work performed by signalers of the alert. The only input parameter is the name of the alert to remove from this session's interest. The following code illustrates the remove procedure's syntax:

```
procedure remove(name in varchar2);
```

removeall

The removeall procedure removes all alerts for this session from the registration list. Execute this procedure when the current session is no longer interested in *any* alerts. The removeall procedure is automatically called on the first reference to the dbms_alert package from a session. Therefore, no alerts from prior sessions, which may have terminated abnormally, can affect this session. The following code illustrates the removeall procedure's syntax:

```
procedure removeall;
```

waitany

The waitany procedure will wait for an alert to occur for any of the alerts for which this session is registered. The only input parameter for this procedure is time-out, which is the maximum time to wait for an alert. If no alert occurs before time-out seconds has expired, this call will return with status of 1. The other variables are all output parameters, including:

- **Name** The name of the alert that occurred, in uppercase
- **Message** Containing the message associated with the alert (this is the message provided by the signal call)
- **Status** Set to 0 (alert occurred) or 1(time-out occurred)

If multiple signals for this alert occurred before the waitany call, the message will correspond to the most recent signal call. The message is a maximum of 1,800 characters. Messages from prior signal calls will be discarded. If you do not register any alerts before waiting for an alert, you will receive an ORU-10024 error, indicating that no alerts have been registered. The default maxwait for time-out is defined as 1,000 days by default; that's a long time! The following code illustrates the syntax of the waitany procedure:

```
procedure waitany (name  out varchar2,
         message out varchar2,
         status out integer,
         timeout in number  default maxwait);
```

waitone

The waitone procedure will wait for a specific alert to occur. If the alert was signaled since the register or last waitone/waitany procedure was executed, a call to waitone will return immediately. The waitone procedure contains the same parameters as the waitany procedure. The difference between waitone and waitany is the input parameter in the waitone parameter; it contains the name of the alert for which it waits. The following code illustrates the syntax of the waitone procedure:

```
procedure waitone(name  in varchar2,
         message out varchar2,
         status out integer,
         timeout in number default maxwait);
```

signal

The signal procedure will signal a specific alert. The only input parameters to this procedure are the name of the alert and the message. As noted before, the signal call only occurs when the transaction in which it is made performs a database COMMIT. If the transaction rolls back, then the signal call is also retracted. When this alert is sent, all sessions that have registered interest in this alert will be notified. If the interested sessions are currently waiting, they will be awakened. If the interested sessions are not currently waiting, they will be notified the next time a wait call is performed. The message indicates the message that is to be associated with this alert and will be passed to the waiting session. The following code illustrates the syntax of the signal procedure:

```
procedure signal(name  in varchar2,
         message in varchar2);
```

Setting SGA Variables with dbms_application_info

The dbms_application_info package provides a mechanism for registering the name of the application module currently running and its current action within the database. Registering this information enables DBAs to monitor how the system is being used, conduct a performance analysis, and track resource accounting by module. Client information is stored in the client_info column. The name registered through this package will appear in the module column, and the current action is represented in the action column of the V$SESSION and V$SQLAREA virtual tables.

The dbms_application_info package is extremely useful in Web development. The module name is normally set to a user-recognizable name for the program currently executing. For example, this could be the name of the Web procedure executing, which identifies the high-level function being performed. The action name is normally set to a specific action a user is performing within a module. For example, the procedure the user is executing could be checking_credit or registering_profile—in other words, identifying logical breakpoints in the procedure. Using the dbms_application_info procedure is meant to specifically identify what a user's procedure is currently doing. As the developer, you can set these two fields to values you feel will provide valuable information to your DBAs. It is recommended you establish a standard throughout your company for setting these fields.

Additionally, the client_info field can provide valuable information to your DBA. This field is available for client-specific information. For example, if your application does not use database authentication but uses a cookie to store user information, by storing user information in this column your DBA will not know the "real" user running the procedure. You can store the "real" user ID (retrieved from the cookie) in the client_info column. This will help the DBA determine usage and performance by "true" users.

If your DBA would like to gather his or her own statistics based on module, the DBA can implement a wrapper around this package by writing a version of this package in another schema that first gathers statistics, then calls the sys version of the package. The public synonym for dbms_application_info can be changed to point to the DBA's version of the package to implement this type of tracking.

set_module

The set_module procedure sets the name of the module currently running and sets the *action* of the module. For non-Web applications, when the current module terminates, set_module should be called with the name of the new module if one exists, or set to NULL if a new module does not exist. In the Web world, unless you are using Transaction Services, do not be concerned with setting the module to NULL, because after the request is finished, OAS logs the user off.

The only input parameters for this procedure are module_name and action_name. The module_name should contain the name of the module or procedure name executing in this session. The action_name can contain the name of the action that will then be running. The maximum length of the module_name is 48 bytes and the maximum length of the action_name is 32 bytes. Longer names will be truncated. If the action_name is not being specified, then NULL should be passed for this value. The following code illustrates the syntax of the set_module procedure:

```
procedure set_module(module_name varchar2, action_name varchar2);
```

set_action

The set_action procedure sets the name of the current action within the current module. The only parameter, action_name, which follows the preceding rules, is illustrated in the following syntax:

```
procedure set_action(action_name varchar2);
```

read_module

If you can set the module and action names, it is only logical that you should be able to read them. The read_module procedure has two output parameters, module_name and action_name, illustrated in the following syntax:

```
procedure read_module(module_name out varchar2,
                      action_name out varchar2);
```

set_client_info

The set_client_info procedure sets the client_info field of the current session as previously described. The client_info field is provided for the use of individual applications; the Oracle system does not use this field for any purpose. After being set, the client_info field can be queried from V$SESSION. The only parameter for this routine is the client_info field, which may contain any character data regarding the procedure, storing up to a maximum of 64 bytes; longer values will be truncated. As suggested previously, you may elect to set this to the "true" user information for a Web application. The following code illustrates the syntax of the set_client_info procedure:

```
procedure set_client_info(client_info varchar2);
```

read_client_info

The read_client_info procedure performs the opposite operation of the set_client_info procedure; it reads the value of the client_info field of the current session. The only output argument will be provided by the client_info column. Use this procedure to retrieve the last value the client_info field was set to using the set_client_info procedure. The following code illustrates the syntax of the read_client_info procedure:

```
procedure read_client_info(client_info out varchar2);
```

set_session_longops

Application performance in the Web world is important. Calling the set_session_longops procedure sets a row in the v$session_longop table that can be used to indicate the ongoing progress of a long-running operation. Some Oracle functions, such as Parallel Query and Server Managed Recovery, use rows in this table to indicate the status of a database backup. The parameters for this procedure include rindex (actually an input and output parameter), and should contain a token that represents the v$session_longops row to update. Set rindex to set_session_ longops_nohint (reserved variable) to start a new row. Use the returned value from the prior call to reuse a row.

The slno parameter, also an input and output parameter, is used to save information across calls to set_session_longops. It is for internal use and should not be modified by the caller. The op_name parameter specifies the name of the long- running task, and will appear as the opname column of v$session_longops. The maximum length of op_name is 64 bytes. Target specifies the object that is being worked on during the long-running operation—for example, it could be a table ID that is being sorted. It will appear as the target column of v$session_longops. Context contains any number the client wishes to store. It will appear in the context column of v$session_longops.

The sofar parameter can contain any number the client wishes to store. It will appear in the sofar column of v$session_longops. Sofar typically contains the amount or percentage of work that has been completed so far. Totalwork should be set to any number the client wishes to store. It will appear in the totalwork column of v$session_longops. This is typically the total amount of work needing to be completed during this long-running operation. If the sofar parameter is a percentage, totalwork would be set to 100. Target_desc specifies the description of the object being manipulated in this long operation. This provides a caption for the preceding target parameter. The value will appear in the target_desc field of v$session_longops. The maximum length of target_desc is 32 bytes. Finally, units specifies the units in which sofar and totalwork are being represented. An example of units might be percentage. This information will appear as the units field of v$session_longops. The maximum length of units is 32 bytes. The following code illustrates the syntax of the set_session_longops procedure:

```
procedure set_session_longops(
          rindex      in out pls_integer,
          slno        in out pls_integer,
          op_name     in     varchar2 default null,
          target      in     pls_integer default 0,
          context     in     pls_integer default 0,
          sofar       in     number default 0,
          totalwork   in     number default 0,
          target_desc in     varchar2 default 'unknown target',
          units       in     varchar2 default null);
```

Executing DDL with dbms_ddl

Occasionally you may need access to data definition language (DDL) statements from within stored procedures. DDLs include the CREATE and ALTER statements.

alter_compile

The alter_compile procedure is equivalent to the SQL statement of the following syntax:

```
alter procedure|function|package [<schema>.]<name> compile [body]
```

The parameters for this procedure include type, schema, and name.

- **Type** The object type to be compiled, which must be procedure, function, package, package body, or trigger.
- **Schema** The schema name the object exists within. If this is NULL, then the procedure will use the current schema.
- **Name** Contains the name of the object to be compiled.

The following code illustrates the syntax of the alter_compile procedure:

```
procedure alter_compile(type varchar2,
                        schema varchar2,
                        name varchar2);
```

analyze_object

The analyze_object procedure is equivalent to the SQL statement of the following syntax:

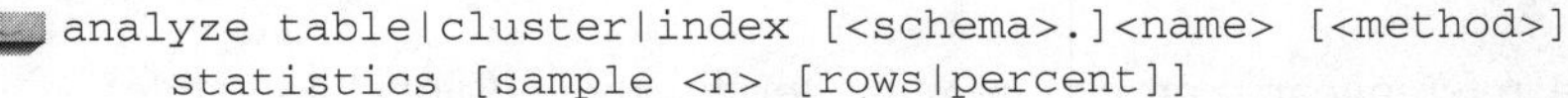

```
analyze table|cluster|index [<schema>.]<name> [<method>]
  statistics [sample <n> [rows|percent]]
```

The input arguments include:

- **type** Table, cluster, or index
- **schema** Object to analyze If NULL, indicates the current schema
- **name** Object to analyze,
- **method** Estimate, compute, or delete
- **estimate_rows** Number of rows to estimate
- **estimate_percent** Percentage of rows to estimate
- **method_opt** [for table], [for all [indexed] columns] [size n], [for all indexes]
- **partname** Specific partition to be analyzed

The following code illustrates the syntax of the analyze_object procedure:

```
procedure analyze_object
   (type             varchar2,
    schema           varchar2,
    name             varchar2,
    method           varchar2,
    estimate_rows    number   default null,
    estimate_percent number   default null,
    method_opt       varchar2 default null,
    partname         varchar2 default null);
```

alter_table_referenceable

The alter_table_referenceable procedure is equivalent to the SQL statement of the following syntax:

```
alter table [<table_schema>.]<table_name>
     referenceable for <affected_schema>
```

The alter_table_not_referenceable procedure is equivalent to the SQL statement of the following syntax:

```
alter table [<table_schema>.]<table_name>
      not referenceable for <affected_schema>"
```

The alter_table_referenceable procedure will alter the given object table table_schema.table_name; it becomes the referenceable table for the given schema affected_schema, which is currently not supported or available as a DDL statement.

The alter_table_not_referenceable procedure will alter the given object table table_schema.table_name; it will no longer be the default referenceable table for the schema affected_schema.

Both procedures include the arguments table_name (name of the table to be altered), table_schema (name of the schema owning the table to be altered), and affected_schema (name of the schema affected by this alteration). The following code illustrates the syntax of the alter_table_referenceable and alter_table_not_referenceable procedures:

```
procedure alter_table_referenceable
         (table_name      varchar2,
          table_schema    varchar2 default null,
          affected_schema varchar2 default null);

procedure alter_table_not_referenceable
         (table_name      varchar2,
          table_schema    varchar2 default null,
          affected_schema varchar2 default null);
```

Queuing with dbms_ job

Have you ever wanted to execute an Oracle procedure every hour? You can execute scripts from the operating system using the UNIX cron utility, but what if you want to use Oracle to schedule the execution of your package? The dbms_job package is Oracle's version of the cron utility. Dbms_job can be used to schedule the execution of specific Oracle packaged procedures at a specific time and on a recurring basis. The dbms_job utility makes use of a number of parameters, including:

- **job** The number of the job being executed
- **what** The PL/SQL procedure to execute, including the final semicolon
- **next_date** The date at which the job will be executed
- **interval** A date function, evaluated immediately before the job starts executing

If the job completes successfully, this new date is placed in next_date and no_parse, indicating not to parse this statement before execution. Examples of legal intervals include the following:

- **'sysdate + 7'** Execute once a week
- **'next_day(sysdate, "tuesday")'** Execute once every Tuesday
- **'null'** Execute once, then the job will be deleted from the queue

Other parameters include force and instance. If force is True, a positive integer is acceptable as the job instance. If force is False, the specified instance must be running; otherwise, the routine raises an exception.

For Web development, you could use dbms_job to execute a package that uses utl_file to output an HTML file. This can be used to dynamically write a static HTML file, often referred to as "semistatic" Web pages. Creating semistatic pages is more efficient than creating dynamic pages, since dynamically creating content (HTML pages) takes more processing power than it does to read a static HTML file. Therefore, creating static HTML files could save you valuable processing power and make your application more scalable. As described in Chapter 6, you can also use the Web Publishing Assistant to periodically write static files from dynamic Oracle data. What if you wanted to use utl_http to periodically pull data from another Web site? You can use dbms_job to schedule the periodic querying of another Web site. When it comes to developing Web applications, requests will arise to periodically run a PL/SQL procedure; dbms_job will perform this task for you.

You can specify the job number or allow Oracle to assign a job number. The following code submits a new job with a specific job number using isubmit:

```
procedure isubmit (job       in  binary_integer,
                   what      in  varchar2,
                   next_date in  date,
                   interval  in  varchar2       default 'null',
                   no_parse  in  boolean        default false);
```

The following code submits a new job and Oracle chooses the job number from the sequence sys.jobseq:

```
procedure submit ( job       out binary_integer,
                   what      in  varchar2,
                   next_date in  date           default sysdate,
                   interval  in  varchar2       default 'null',
                   no_parse  in  boolean        default false,
                   instance  in  binary_integer default any_instance,
                   force     in  boolean        default false );
```

The following code removes an existing job from the job queue by executing the remove procedure. Removing the job from the dbms_job queue does not stop the execution of a job once it has started.

```
procedure remove   (job       in  binary_integer );
```

The following code changes the job parameters by using the change procedure. Parameters defined as NULL will remain as-is. This can be used to alter the execution or frequency of the job execution.

```
procedure change   (job       in  binary_integer,
                    what      in  varchar2,
                    next_date in  date,
                    interval  in  varchar2,
                    instance  in  binary_integer default null,
                    force     in  boolean        default false);
```

The following code changes only the command being executed (not the schedule or any other parameters) by using the what procedure:

```
procedure what      ( job       in  binary_integer,
                      what      in  varchar2 );
```

The following code changes when an existing job will next execute by using the next_date procedure:

```
procedure next_date ( job       in  binary_integer,
                      next_date in  date     );
```

The following code changes the instance or force parameters by using the instance procedure:

```
procedure instance ( job          in binary_integer,
                     instance     in binary_integer,
                     force        in boolean default false);
```

The following code changes the interval (how often the job executes) of an existing job by using the interval procedure:

```
procedure interval  ( job       in  binary_integer,
                      interval  in  varchar2 );
```

Jobs can be broken if they have failed to execute after 16 tries, or they can be manually set to broken to prevent them from running. Because broken jobs are never executed, to set the broken flag back to False (not broken), use the broken procedure, as illustrated in the following example:

```
procedure broken     ( job        in  binary_integer,
                       broken     in  boolean,
                       next_date in  date          default sysdate );
```

The following code forces a job to execute immediately (even if broken) by using the run procedure. Executing the job will recompute the next_date parameter.

```
  procedure run  ( job        in  binary_integer,
                   force      in  boolean default false);
```

The status of jobs in the queue can be viewed by querying the dba_jobs or user_jobs table, and currently running jobs can be seen in dba_jobs_running.

Accessing Objects with dbms_lob

The dbms_lob package provides general-purpose routines for operations on Oracle Large Object (LOB) datatypes: Binary Large Objects (BLOB), Character Large Objects (CLOB, which are read-write), and Binary Files (BFILE, which are read-only). The dbms_lob package contains many procedures and functions. Rather than going through each function in detail, I have opted to demonstrate how to save an operating system file (image) into the database, how to retrieve it from the database, and how to display the image on a Web page.

The following code segment illustrates the syntax to read a file from the operating system and load it into the database:

```
Declare

lob_temp   blob;
os_file    bfile := bfilename('/website40/images/', 'image.jpg');
ignore integer;
begin
  dbms_lob.fileopen(os_file, dbms_lob.file_readonly);
  dbms_lob.loadfromfile(lob_temp, os_file,
                        dbms_lob.getlength(os_file));
  dbms_lob.fileclose(os_file);
end;
```

The following code segment demonstrates how to pull the image from the database, save it to an operating system file using utl_file, and display it on an HTML page using htp.image:

```
declare

lob_temp     blob;
data_buffer raw(1);
amount       binary_integer := 1;
```

```
pos          integer         := 1;
filehandle   utl_file.file_type;
count_down   integer;
begin
  select image_col
  into   lob_temp
  from   images_table
  where  image_index = in_img_no;
  count_down := dbms_lob.getlength(lob_temp);
  image_fn   := '/website40/images/i'||to_char(in_img_no)||'.jpg'
  filehandle := utl_file.fopen(image_fn, 'get_lob.out','w');
while count_down <> 0 loop
       dbms_lob.read (lob_temp, amount,
                      pos, data_buffer);
       utl_file.put (filehandle, data_buffer);
       pos := pos + 1;
       count_down := count_down - 1;
       data_buffer := null;
  end loop;
  utl_file.fclose(filehandle);
  htp.image(image_fn);
  ...
end;
```

Writing Output with dbms_output

The procedures within dbms_output accumulate information in a buffer using put and put_line so the information can be retrieved later (through get_line or get_lines). If this package is disabled, all calls to this package are ignored. By disabling the dbms_output package, these routines are only active when the client deals with the information. Dbms_output is useful for debugging or for reports to SQL*DBA or SQL*Plus. The default buffer size is 20,000 bytes. The minimum is 2,000 bytes and the maximum is 1,000,000 bytes.

For Web development, dbms_output provides valuable information when debugging from SQL*Plus or a GUI PL/SQL editor, but if you are testing through the browser the htp.comment is equally useful.

For example, dbms_output can be used in your Web procedure to keep track of each step through your procedure, or possibly to review variables and their current settings. Use the following code to output information about the current procedure processing:

```
dbms_output.put_line('Procedure x is at reference point xyz.abc');
```

If your Web procedure was executed from SQL*Plus, this put_line command would be buffered, and will not be displayed unless the client has enabled the dbms_output package. Within SQL*Plus, to see the dbms_output messages you must type the following command:

```
set serveroutput on
```

The following code is another option the procedure could execute to receive a line from the dbms_output buffer:

```
dbms_output.get_line(received_buffer, received_status);
```

The preceding syntax would retrieve the line of information into the received_buffer variable. Your procedure could then display the buffer on the screen (or in the HTML code using htp.comment). Your procedure would need to repeat calls to get_line until received_status came back as nonzero. To increase performance, use the get_lines procedure instead to return an array of lines.

enable

The enable procedure enables calls to put, put_line, new_line, get_line, and get_lines. Calls to these procedures are ignored if the package has not been enabled. The enable procedure also can set the default amount of information to buffer and will clean up data buffered from any dead sessions. Multiple calls to enable are allowed.

When enabling the dbms_output package, set the buffer_size to indicate the amount of information to be sent to the buffer. Buffer size is indicated in bytes. Varchar2, number, and date items are stored in their internal representation. The information is stored in the System Global Area (SGA) or the system memory; therefore, access to this information is fast. An error is raised if the buffer size is exceeded. If multiple calls are to be enabled, the buffer_size is generally the largest of the values specified, and will always be greater than or equal to the smallest value specified. The following code illustrates the syntax of the enable procedure:

```
procedure enable (buffer_size in integer default 20000);
```

disable

The disable procedure disables or ignores calls to put, put_line, new_line, get_line, and get_lines and purges the buffer of any remaining information. For example, it can be used to turn off messaging from the procedures when testing or debugging is done. The following code illustrates the syntax of the disable procedure:

```
procedure disable;
```

put

The put procedure places a piece of information into the dbms_output buffer. When retrieved by get_line(s), the number and date items will be formatted with to_char using the default formats. If you want to use another format, then format it explicitly. This routine is overloaded: it accepts varchar2, number, or date datatypes. The following code illustrates the overloaded syntax of the put procedure:

```
procedure put(a varchar2);
procedure put(a number);
procedure put(a date);
```

put_line

The put_line procedure places a piece of information into the buffer followed by an end-of-line marker. When this information is retrieved by the get_line(s) procedure, the number and date items will be formatted with to_char using the default formats. Everything is stored internally in the buffer as a character (varchar2) value. The put_line routine is also overloaded. The following code illustrates the syntax of the overloaded put_line procedure:

```
procedure put_line(a varchar2);
procedure put_line(a number);
procedure put_line(a date);
```

new_line

The following new_line procedure will add an end-of-line marker to your dbms_output buffer. Get_line(s) returns "lines" delimited by new_lines. The following code illustrates the syntax of the new_line procedure:

```
procedure new_line;
```

get_line

The get_line procedure will retrieve a single buffered line. The lines are delimited by calls to put_line or new_line. The line is constructed taking all the items up to a newline, converting the items to varchar2, and concatenating them into a single line.

If the client application fails to retrieve all lines before the next put, put_line or new_line, the nonretrieved lines will be discarded.

The output parameters of this procedure include line and status. Line will contain the varchar2 line of information previously stored and allows the maximum length of 255 bytes. Status will be set to 0 (upon successful completion of the call) or 1 (no more lines exist). The following code illustrates the syntax of the get_line procedure:

```
procedure get_line(line out varchar2, status out integer);
```

get_lines

The final dbms_output procedure is the get_lines procedure. Get_lines retrieves multiple lines that have been buffered. The lines are delimited by calls to put_line or new_line. The line is constructed taking all the items up to a new_line character, converting all the items to varchar2, and concatenating them into a single line.

Once get_lines is executed, the client should continue to retrieve all lines because the next put, put_line, or new_line will purge the buffer of leftover data. Numlines is actually an input and output parameter. On calling the routine, numlines should be set to the maximum number of lines the caller is prepared to accept. After the procedure is called, numlines will be set to the actual number of lines returned. This procedure will not return more than the specified number of lines. Another output parameter of get_lines procedure is the lines parameter. Lines is a PL/SQL table or array containing each of the dbms_output lines. The following code illustrates the syntax of the get_lines procedure:

```
procedure get_lines(lines out chararr, numlines in out integer);
```

Messaging with dbms_pipe

The dbms_pipe package provides a mechanism enabling messages to be sent between sessions. Messages are not stored in a table; they are stored in the SGA. You can think of a pipe as a message queue; the first message in will be the first message pulled out. Each pipe can be uniquely named—similar to calling a unique phone number. Unlike a phone call, however, when the sender sends a message, the recipient will not receive the message unless they check the pipe to see if any messages exist in the queue.

You can imagine how useful this package could be in a Transactive Content site (a concept discussed in further detail in *Oracle Application Server Web Toolkit Reference* by Brad Brown (Oracle Press, 1998)). If you enable users to converse directly with a live operator for site direction, this interaction can be accomplished with the dbms_pipe package. The dbms_pipe package is commonly used to send a command to a job execution process. If you want to execute a report on the server, send the message through dbms_pipe of the job to be executed. When the job is complete, you will receive a URL pointing to the report's output. The recipient end of the request is typically handled by a process running on the database server. This process cycles (loops indefinitely), waiting for requests to come in through a specific dbms_pipe message, and then acts accordingly. Messages are sent to a specific pipename using dbms_pipe.send_message, and messages are received from a specific pipename using dbms_pipe.receive_message. Before sending a message, it must be "packed," or placed into the static buffer. To read the message, you must "unpack" it, extracting the message from the static buffer.

The pipename used can be any name you choose. For example, the pipename could be a username, enabling private user to user communications, or it could be a generic name, such as "messages," enabling all database users with execute privilege on dbms_pipe and knowledge of the pipe to read or write to the pipe.

Pipes operate independently of transactions. They also operate asynchronously. Multiple readers and writers can reside within the same pipe. However, pipes only operate between sessions in the same instance and cannot be used for cross-instance messages. Pipes can be explicitly created using dbms_pipe.create_pipe and removed using dbms_pipe.remove_pipe. A pipe created using the explicit create command should be removed explicitly using the remove function. A pipe can also be created implicitly. Pipes automatically come into existence the first time they are referenced. Pipes disappear when they contain no more data, although some overhead remains in the SGA until it is aged out. As previously mentioned, pipes are stored in the SGA; therefore, pipes take up space in the SGA.

As Oracle suggests, other potential applications are available for the dbms_pipe function, including:

- **External service interface** You can provide the capability to communicate with (user-written) services external to the RDBMS. This can be accomplished in a multithreaded manner so several instances of the service can be executing simultaneously. Additionally, the services are available asynchronously; the requestor of the service does not need to wait for a reply. The requestor can check (with or without time-out) for a reply at a later time. The service can be written in the 3GL languages supported by Oracle, not just in C.
- **Independent transactions** The pipe can be used to communicate to a separate session performing an operation in an independent transaction, such as logging an attempted security violation detected by a trigger.
- **Alerters (nontransactional)** You can post another process without requiring the waiting process to poll. If an after-row or after-statement

trigger should alert an application, then the application would treat this alert as an indication the data has changed. The application would then go read the data to retrieve the current value. Because this is an after trigger, the application would want to perform a SELECT for update to ensure it read the correct data.

- **Debugging** Triggers and/or stored procedures can send debugging information to a pipe. Another session can read out of the pipe, display it on the screen, or write it out to a file.
- **Concentrator** Useful for multiplexing large numbers of users over a fewer number of network connections, or improving performance by concentrating several user transactions into one RDBMS transaction.

For example, you have written a C program performing a number of calculations based on a pricing algorithm used to price products for your customers. You must provide this routine with the customer number, the product number being purchased, the cost for the product, and the pricing algorithm for this customer. This would typically all be information you gathered from the database. Because of the complexity of the pricing algorithm, this operation is performed using a C program. The following code calls the pricing algorithm:

```
customer_price := pricing_routine.get_price(cust_no,
                      item_no, unit_cost, cust_price_algorithm);
```

The following is an example of the pricing_routine:

```
create or replace function pricing_routine
                              (cust_no              number,
                               item_no              number,
                               unit_cost            number,
                               cust_price_algorithm varchar2)
return number is
sts         integer;
price       number;
errormsg    varchar2(512);
begin
     dbms_pipe.pack_message('1');  -- protocol version
     -- return pipe
     dbms_pipe.pack_message(dbms_pipe.unique_session_name);
     dbms_pipe.pack_message('getprice');
     dbms_pipe.pack_message(cust_no);
     dbms_pipe.pack_message(item_no);
     dbms_pipe.pack_message(unit_cost);
```

```
      dbms_pipe.pack_message(cust_price_algorithm);
      sts := dbms_pipe.send_message('get_customer_price');
      if sts <> 0 then
         raise_application_error(-20000, 'Error:'||to_char(sts)||
                                         ' sending on pipe');
      end if;
      sts := dbms_pipe.receive_message(dbms_pipe.unique_session_name);
      if sts <> 0 then
         raise_application_error(-20000, 'Error:'||to_char(sts)||
                                         ' receiving on pipe');
      end if;
      dbms_pipe.unpack_message(errormsg);
      if errormsg <> 'SUCCESS' then
         raise_application_error(-20000, errormsg);
      end if;
      dbms_pipe.unpack_message(price);
      return price;
end;
```

pack_message

The pack_message procedure will pack an item into the message buffer. The procedure is overloaded to handle all data types. The only input parameter is item, containing the item to be packed into the local message buffer. The following code illustrates the syntax of the overloaded pack_message procedure:

```
procedure pack_message(item in varchar2 character set any_cs);
procedure pack_message(item in number);
procedure pack_message(item in date);
procedure pack_message_raw(item in raw);
procedure pack_message_rowid(item in rowid);
```

unpack_message

The unpack_message procedure unpacks an item from the local message buffer. This procedure is also overloaded to retrieve all datatypes. The only output parameter is the item, containing the argument to receive the next unpacked item from the local message buffer. The following code illustrates the syntax of the overloaded unpack_message procedure:

```
procedure unpack_message(item out varchar2 character set any_cs);
procedure unpack_message(item out number);
procedure unpack_message(item out date);
procedure unpack_message_raw(item out raw);
procedure unpack_message_rowid(item out rowid);
```

next_item_type

The next_item_type function will retrieve the type of the next item in the local message buffer. It will return one of the following values:

- **0** no more items
- **9** varchar2
- **6** number
- **11** rowid
- **12** date
- **23** raw

The following code illustrates the syntax of the next_item_type procedure:

```
function next_item_type return integer;
```

create_pipe

The create_pipe function creates an empty pipe with the name provided and returns the status of the new pipe. The first input parameter for this routine is the pipename, which is the name of pipe to be created. The next parameter is maxpipesize, which is the maximum allowed size for the pipe. The total size of all the messages in the pipe cannot exceed this amount. The maxpipesize for a pipe becomes part of the pipe and persists for the lifetime of the pipe. Callers of send_message with larger values will cause the maxpipesize to be increased. Callers with a smaller value will use the larger value. The specification of maxpipesize enables you to avoid its use in future send_message calls. The private parameter contains a Boolean value indicating whether the pipe will be True for private (and for the use of the creating user ID only), or False if the pipe is public. A private pipe can be used directly through calls to this package by sessions connected to the database as the same user as the one that created the pipe. It can also be used through stored procedures owned by the user who created the pipe. The procedure may be executed by anyone with execute privilege on the pipe. A public pipe can be accessed by anyone who has knowledge of its existence and has execute privilege on dbms_pipe. The only return value is a 0, which means the pipe creation was successful. This is returned even if the pipe was created in a mode that permits its use by the user executing the create call. If a pipe already exists, it is not emptied. If the pipe fails to create, your procedure will receive an exception.

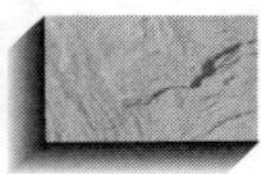

TIP
Do not use pipenames beginning with ORA$. These are reserved for use by procedures provided by Oracle Corporation. Pipename should not be longer than 128 bytes, and is case insensitive. The pipename cannot contain NLS characters.

The following code illustrates the syntax of the create_pipe function:

```
function create_pipe
         (pipename    in varchar2,
          maxpipesize in integer  default 8192,
          private     in boolean  default TRUE)
return integer;
```

remove_pipe

The remove_pipe function will remove the named pipe. The input parameter is the pipename, and should contain the name of pipe to remove. The only return value is 0, meaning success. Calling remove on a pipe that does not exist returns 0. If the remove_pipe function fails, your procedure will receive an exception. The following code illustrates the syntax of the remove_pipe function:

```
function remove_pipe(pipename in varchar2)
return integer;
```

send_message

The send_message function sends a message on the named pipe and returns a status code. The message is contained in the local message buffer that is filled with calls to pack_message. As previously discussed, a pipe will be created explicitly using create_pipe, or it will be created implicitly the first time it is called. The input parameters used in this procedure include:

- **pipename** Name of pipe to place the message on
- **timeout** Time to wait while attempting to place a message on a pipe, in seconds
- **maxpipesize** Maximum allowed size for the pipe

The return values include 0 (meaning success), 1 (meaning the send_message timed out, either because a lock on pipe cannot be established or the pipe stays too full), and 3 (meaning an interruption has occurred). The following code illustrates the syntax of the send_message function:

```
function send_message
          (pipename    in varchar2,
           timeout     in integer  default maxwait,
           maxpipesize in integer  default 8192)
return integer;
```

receive_message

The receive_message function receives a message from a specified pipe, copies the message into the local message buffer, and returns a status. You need to use the unpack_message function to access the individual items in the message. The pipe can be created explicitly using the create_pipe function, or it will be created implicitly. The input parameters include pipename (name of pipe from which to retrieve a message), and time-out (time to wait for a message—a time-out of 0 allows you to read without blocking). The return status values can be 0 (meaning success), 1 (meaning timed out), 2 (meaning the record in the pipe is too big for the buffer), and 3 (meaning an interruption has occurred). The following code illustrates the syntax of the receive_message function:

```
function receive_message
          (pipename in varchar2,
           timeout  in integer  default maxwait)
return integer;
```

reset_buffer

The reset_buffer procedure resets pack and unpack positioning indicators to 0. Generally, this routine is not needed, but it can be used in the event of an error or special processing to clear the buffer. The following code illustrates the syntax of the reset_buffer procedure:

```
procedure reset_buffer;
```

purge

The purge procedure will empty out the named pipe. An empty pipe is a candidate for least recently used (LRU) removal from the SGA; therefore, purge can be used to free all memory associated with a pipe. The only input parameter is pipename, which is the name of the pipe from which to remove all messages. The following code illustrates the syntax of the purge procedure:

```
procedure purge(pipename in varchar2);
```

unique_session_name

The unique_session_name function will retrieve a name unique among all sessions currently connected to this database. Multiple calls to this routine from the same session will always return the same value. There are no input parameters—just call the procedure and it will return a unique name. The returned name can be up to 30 bytes long. The following code illustrates the syntax of the unique_session_name function:

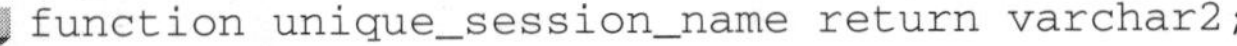

```
function unique_session_name return varchar2;
```

Setting Session Properties with dbms_session

In any client/server application, there will be times when you want to set a user's role on the fly. This type of operation is often used when users have minimal privileges under their default role, but a particular procedure or function may require additional privileges to execute the procedure/function.

The dbms_session package provides access to the sql alter session statements and other session information from stored procedures.

set_role

The set_role procedure is equivalent to the sql set role statement. The only input parameter is role_cmd, which contains the text to be appended to set role and executed as SQL. This is useful to assign a user a role only when they require it, and remove the privileges of that role when it is no longer necessary. The following code illustrates the syntax of the set_role procedure:

```
procedure set_role(role_cmd varchar2);
```

set_sql_trace

The set_sql_trace procedure is equivalent to the sql alter session set sql_trace statement. The only input argument to this procedure is sql_trace, which is a Boolean variable (True or False) indicating whether to turn tracing on or off. The following code illustrates the syntax of the set_sql_trace procedure:

```
procedure set_sql_trace(sql_trace boolean);
```

set_nls

The set_nls procedure is equivalent to the sql alter session set <nls_parameter> = <value>statement. The input parameters to this procedure are param and value.

Param is the NLS parameter. The parameter name must begin with NLS. Value is the value to set the NLS parameter to. If the parameter is a text literal, it will need embedded single quotes, as illustrated in the following syntax:

```
set_nls('nls_date_format','''DD-MON-YY''')
```

The following code illustrates the syntax for the set_nls procedure:

```
procedure set_nls(param varchar2, value varchar2);
```

close_database_link

The close_database_link procedure is equivalent to the SQL statement alter session close database link <name>. The only input parameter to this procedure is dblink, which is the name of the database link to close. The following code illustrates the syntax of the close_database_link procedure:

```
procedure close_database_link(dblink varchar2);
```

reset_package

The reset_package procedure deinstantiates all packages in this session. In other words, it frees all package states and releases memory used by those packages. All package states are free at the beginning of a session. The following code illustrates the syntax of the reset_package procedure:

```
procedure reset_package;
```

unique_session_id

The unique_session_id function will return an identifier unique for all sessions currently connected to this database. Multiple calls to this function during the same session will always return the same result. The return value from this function, unique_session_id, can return up to 24 bytes. The following code illustrates the syntax of the unique_session_id function:

```
function unique_session_id return varchar2;
```

is_role_enabled

The is_role_enabled function returns a Boolean value (True or False) indicating whether the named role is enabled for this session. The only input argument for this function is the rolename, which indicates the name of the role. The following code illustrates the syntax of the is_role_enabled function:

```
function is_role_enabled(rolename varchar2) return boolean;
```

is_session_alive

The is_session_alive function determines if the specified session is alive. The return value is a Boolean value (True or False). The only input argument to this procedure is uniqueid, which is the unique ID of the session to check to see is it's alive. The following code illustrates the syntax of the is_session_alive function:

```
function is_session_alive(uniqueid varchar2) return boolean;
```

set_close_cached_open_cursors

The set_close_cached_open_cursors procedure is equivalent to the sql alter session set close_cached_open_cursors statement. The only input argument is close_cursors, which is a Boolean value (True or False) indicating whether to turn close_cached_open_cursors on or off. The following code illustrates the syntax of the set_close_cached_open_cursors procedure:

```
procedure set_close_cached_open_cursors(close_cursors boolean);
```

free_unused_user_memory

The free_unused_user_memory procedure will reclaim unused memory after performing operations requiring large amounts of memory (where large is >100KB). This procedure should only be used in cases where memory is at a premium, such as any high-volume or high-transaction Web site. The following are example operations using a considerable amount of memory:

- Large sorts where entire sort_area_size is used and sort_area_size is hundreds of kilobytes
- Compiling large PL/SQL packages/procedures/functions
- Storing hundreds of kilobytes of data within PL/SQL indexed tables

You can monitor user memory by tracking the session uga memory and session pga memory statistics in the V$SESSTAT/V$STATNAME fixed views. Monitoring these statistics will also show how much memory this procedure has freed. This routine should be used infrequently and judiciously. The following code illustrates the syntax of the free_unused_user_memory procedure:

```
procedure free_unused_user_memory;
```

Executing Dynamic SQL Using dbms_sql

The dbms_sql package provides a means to use Dynamic SQL to access the database. Because Dynamic SQL, or more specifically ad hoc SQL, can kill system performance unless your entire development staff has excellent dynamic SQL tuning skills, the use of dbms_sql should be restricted, if not prohibited, in most environments. Because the dbms_sql package is described in a number of books and other reference materials, I will not go into great detail regarding this package.

In dbms_sql, bind variables of a SQL statement are identified by their names. When binding a value to a bind variable, the string identifying the bind variable in the statement may optionally contain the leading colon. For example, if the following SQL statement is parsed binding the variable to a value, it can be identified using either of the strings :X and X.

```
select ename from emp where sal > :x
```

Columns of the row selected in a SELECT statement are identified by their relative positions (1, 2, 3, and so forth) as they appear on the select list from left to right.

The flow of procedure calls is typically as follows:

- open_cursor
- parse
- bind_variable
- query?
  - Yes
  - define_column
  - execute
- No
  - execute
- variable_value
- fetch_rows
- column_value
- close_cursor

open_cursor

The open_cursor function opens a new cursor. When the cursor is no longer needed, the cursor *must be closed* explicitly by calling the close_cursor function. The return value is the cursor ID number of the newly opened cursor. This number is used to reference this cursor in other statements. The following code illustrates the syntax of the open_cursor function:

```
function open_cursor return integer;
```

is_open

The is_open function will return True if the given cursor is currently open. The only input parameter is c, which is the ID number of the cursor you wish to check to see if it's open. The return value will be True if the given cursor is open or False if it is not currently open. The following code illustrates the syntax of the is_open function:

```
function is_open(c in integer) return boolean;
```

close_cursor

The close_cursor procedure will close the given cursor. The only input parameter to this procedure is c, which indicates the cursor ID number of the cursor to close. The following code illustrates the syntax of the close_cursor procedure:

```
procedure close_cursor(c in out integer);
```

parse

The parse procedure will parse the given statement for the cursor. Be careful, because parsing and executing DDL statements can cause your application to hang. The input parameters are c, statement, and language_flag. The input parameter c is the cursor ID number of the cursor in which to parse the statement, retrieved from a call to open_cursor. Statement is the SQL statement to parse. Language_flag specifies behavior for statement for which the valid values are v6, v7, and native. Using a value of v6 or v7 specifies behavior according to version 6 and version 7 of Oracle, respectively. Native specifies behavior according to the version of the database to which the program is connected, which is the default behavior. All DDL statements are executed immediately when parsed; you do not need to explicitly execute them. The following code illustrates the syntax of the parse procedure:

```
procedure parse(c             in integer,
                statement     in varchar2,
                language_flag in integer);
```

bind_variable, bind_variable_char, bind_variable_raw, bind_variable_rowid, bind_array

The bind_variable, bind_variable_char, bind_variable_raw, bind_variable_rowid, and bind_array procedures bind the specified value to the variable identified by its name in the parsed statement in the cursor. If the variable is an in or in/out variable, the given bind value should be valid. If the variable is an out variable, the bind value is ignored. A number of input parameters can be used if each of the bind procedures is heavily overloaded. The input parameter c indicates the cursor ID number of the cursor to bind. Name specifies the name of the variable in the statement. Value is the value to bind to the variable in the cursor. If the variable is an out or in/out variable, its type is the same as the type of the value being passed in for this parameter. Out_value_size indicates the maximum expected out value size in bytes for the varchar2 out or in/out variable. If out_value_size is not specified for the varchar2 out or in/out variable, the size is the length of the current value. The parameters n_tab, c_tab, d_tab, bl_tab, cl_tab, and bf_tab are specified for array execute operations when the user wishes to execute the SQL statement multiple times without returning control to the caller. A list of values can be bound to this variable. This functionality is identical to the array execute feature of OCI, where a list of values in a PL/SQL index table can be inserted into a SQL table with a single (parameterized) call to execute. Parameters index1 and index2 are also used for array execute operations. Instead of using the entire index table, the user may chose to limit the array to a range of values. The following code illustrates the syntax of the overloaded bind_variable procedure:

```
procedure bind_variable(c               in integer,
                        name            in varchar2,
                        value           in number);
procedure bind_variable(c               in integer,
                        name            in varchar2,
                        value           in varchar2
                                        character set any_cs);
procedure bind_variable(c               in integer,
                        name            in varchar2,
                        value           in varchar2
                                        character set any_cs,
                        out_value_size  in integer);
procedure bind_variable(c               in integer,
                        name            in varchar2,
                        value           in date);
procedure bind_variable(c               in integer,
                        name            in varchar2,
```

```
                                value           in blob);
procedure bind_variable(c                       in integer,
                        name                    in varchar2,
                        value                   in clob character
                                                        set any_cs);
procedure bind_variable(c                       in integer,
                        name                    in varchar2,
                        value                   in bfile);
```

The following code illustrates the syntax of the overloaded bind_variable_char procedure:

```
procedure bind_variable_char(c                  in integer,
                             name               in varchar2,
                             value              in char
                                                character set any_cs);
procedure bind_variable_char(c                  in integer,
                             name               in varchar2,
                             value              in char
                                                character set any_cs,
                                              out_value_size in integer);
```

The following code illustrates the syntax of the overloaded bind_variable_raw procedure:

```
procedure bind_variable_raw(c                   in integer,
                            name                in varchar2,
                            value               in raw);
procedure bind_variable_raw(c                   in integer,
                            name                in varchar2,
                            value               in raw,
                            out_value_size      in integer);
```

The following code illustrates the syntax of the bind_variable_rowid procedure:

```
procedure bind_variable_rowid(c      in integer,
                              name   in varchar2,
                              value in rowid);
```

The following code illustrates the syntax of the overloaded bind_array procedure:

```
procedure bind_array(c       in integer,
                     name    in varchar2,
                     n_tab   in Number_Table);
```

```
procedure bind_array(c      in integer,
                     name   in varchar2,
                     c_tab  in Varchar2_Table);
procedure bind_array(c      in integer,
                     name   in varchar2,
                     d_tab  in Date_Table);
procedure bind_array(c      in integer,
                     name   in varchar2,
                     bl_tab in Blob_Table);
procedure bind_array(c      in integer,
                     name   in varchar2,
                     cl_tab in Clob_Table);
procedure bind_array(c      in integer,
                     name   in varchar2,
                     bf_tab in Bfile_Table);
procedure bind_array(c      in integer,
                     name   in varchar2,
                     n_tab  in Number_Table,
                     index1 in integer,
                     index2 in integer);
procedure bind_array(c      in integer,
                     name   in varchar2,
                     c_tab  in Varchar2_Table,
                     index1 in integer,
                     index2 in integer);
procedure bind_array(c      in integer,
                     name   in varchar2,
                     d_tab  in Date_Table,
                     index1 in integer,
                     index2 in integer);
procedure bind_array(c      in integer,
                     name   in varchar2,
                     bl_tab in Blob_Table,
                     index1 in integer,
                     index2 in integer);
procedure bind_array(c      in integer,
                     name   in varchar2,
                     cl_tab in Clob_Table,
                     index1 in integer,
                     index2 in integer);
procedure bind_array(c      in integer,
                     name   in varchar2,
                     bf_tab in Bfile_Table,
                     index1 in integer,
                     index2 in integer);
```

define_column, define_column_char, define_column_raw, define_column_rowid, and define_array

The define_column, define_column_char, define_column_raw, define_column_rowid, and define_array procedures define a column to be selected from the specified cursor; this procedure is applicable only to SELECT cursors. The column being defined is identified by its relative position in the SELECT statement in the specified cursor. The type of the column to be defined is the type of the value being passed in for parameter column.

A number of input parameters and procedures are heavily overloaded, as is apparent in the following syntax. The input parameter c is the cursor ID number of the cursor to define the row to be selected. Position is the position of the column in the row being defined. Column is the type of the value being passed for this parameter, and is the type of the column to be defined. Column_size indicates the maximum expected size of the value in bytes for the varchar2 column. The other parameters have the same definition as in the preceding define procedures. The following code illustrates the syntax of the overloaded define_column procedure:

```
procedure define_column(c           in integer,
                        position    in integer,
                        column      in number);

procedure define_column(c           in integer,
                        position    in integer,
                        column      in varchar2 character set any_cs,
                        column_size in integer);
procedure define_column(c           in integer,
                        position    in integer,
                        column      in date);
procedure define_column(c           in integer,
                        position    in integer,
                        column      in blob);
procedure define_column(c           in integer,
                        position    in integer,
                        column      in bfile);
```

The following code illustrates the syntax of the overloaded define_column_char procedure:

```
procedure define_column_char(c           in integer,
                             position    in integer,
                             column      in char character set any_cs,
                             column_size in integer);
```

The following code illustrates the syntax of the overloaded define_column_raw procedure:

```
procedure define_column_raw(c            in integer,
                           position    in integer,
                           column      in raw,
                           column_size in integer);

procedure define_column_rowid(c        in integer,
                             position in integer,
                             column   in rowid);
```

The following code illustrates the syntax of the overloaded define_array procedure:

```
procedure define_array(c              in integer,
                       position       in integer,
                       n_tab          in Number_Table,
                       cnt            in integer,
                       lower_bound    in integer);
procedure define_array(c              in integer,
                       position       in integer,
                       c_tab          in Varchar2_Table,
                       cnt            in integer,
                       lower_bound    in integer);
procedure define_array(c in integer,
                       position       in integer,
                       d_tab          in Date_Table,
                       cnt            in integer,
                       lower_bound    in integer);
procedure define_array(c in integer,
                       position       in integer,
                       bl_tab         in Blob_Table,
                       cnt            in integer,
                       lower_bound    in integer);
procedure define_array(c in integer,
                       position       in integer,
                       cl_tab         in Clob_Table,
                       cnt            in integer,
                       lower_bound    in integer);
procedure define_array(c in integer,
                       position       in integer,
                       bf_tab         in Bfile_Table,
                       cnt            in integer,
                       lower_bound    in integer);
```

execute

The execute function executes the given cursor and returns the number of rows processed (valid and meaningful only for INSERT, DELETE, or UPDATE statements; for other types of statements, the return value is undefined and should be ignored). The only input parameter is c, which is the cursor ID number of the cursor to execute. The return value indicates the number of rows processed if the statement in the cursor is an INSERT, DELETE, or UPDATE statement; otherwise, it is undefined. As noted above, DDL statements execute automatically when parsed and do not need to be executed explicitly. The following code illustrates the syntax of the execute procedure:

```
function execute(c in integer) return integer;
```

fetch_rows

The fetch_rows function fetches rows from the given cursor. As long as fetch_rows is able to fetch a row, it can be called repeatedly to fetch additional rows. The fetch_rows function will return a 0 when no rows are available to return. The only input parameter is c, which is the cursor ID number of the cursor to fetch. The function's return value indicates the number of rows actually fetched. The following code illustrates the syntax of the fetch_rows procedure:

```
function fetch_rows(c in integer) return integer;
```

execute_and_fetch

The execute_and_fetch function executes the specified cursor and fetches rows from it. This function provides the same functionality as a call to the execute function followed by a call to the fetch_rows function. However, this function can potentially cut down on the number of message roundtrips to the database from the application server compared to calling execute and fetch_rows separately. The input parameters are c and exact. The parameter c specifies the cursor ID number of the cursor to execute and fetch. The exact parameter is a Boolean variable indicating that an exception should be raised if the number of rows matching the query is not exactly 1. The return value for this procedure indicates the number of rows actually fetched. The following code illustrates the syntax of the execute_and_fetch function:

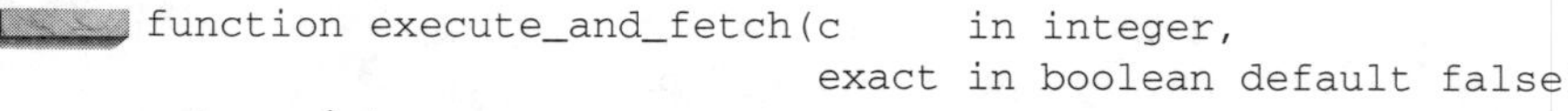

```
function execute_and_fetch(c     in integer,
                           exact in boolean default false)
return integer;
```

column_value

The column_value procedure will retrieve a value of the column identified by the given position and the specified cursor. This procedure is used to access the data retrieved by fetch_rows. The input parameters are c and position. The parameter c indicates the cursor ID number of the cursor from which to get the value. Position indicates the position of the column in which to get the value. The output parameters are value, column_error, and actual_length. Value is the value of the column. Column_error is any column error code associated with value returned. Actual_length is the actual length of value in the table before any truncation during the fetch. The following code illustrates the syntax of the overloaded column_value procedure:

```
procedure column_value(c        in  integer,
                       position in  integer,
                       value    out number);
procedure column_value(c        in  integer,
                       position in  integer,
                       value    out varchar2 character set
                                      any_cs);
procedure column_value(c        in  integer,
                       position in  integer,
                       value    out date);
procedure column_value(c        in  integer,
                       position in  integer,
                       value    out blob);
procedure column_value(c        in  integer,
                       position in  integer,
                       value    out clob character set any_cs);
procedure column_value(c        in  integer,
                       position in  integer,
                       value    out bfile);
```

The following code illustrates the syntax of the column_value_char procedure:

```
procedure column_value_char(c        in  integer,
                            position in  integer,
                            value    out char character set
                                           any_cs);
```

The following code illustrates the syntax of the column_value_raw procedure:

```
procedure column_value_raw(c        in  integer,
                          position  in  integer,
                          value     out raw);
```

The following code illustrates the syntax of the column_value_rowid procedure:

```
procedure column_value_rowid(c        in  integer,
                             position in  integer,
                             value    out rowid);
```

variable_value, variable_value_char, variable_value_raw, variable_value_rowid

The variable_value, variable_value_char, variable_value_raw, and variable_value_rowid procedures will retrieve a value(s) of the variable identified by the name and the specified cursor. The input parameters are c and name. C indicates the cursor ID number of the cursor from which to get the value. Name is the name of the variable of which to get the value. The value output parameter is the value of the variable. This function provides the same function as the column_value procedure, but rather than specifying a relative column number, you specify the column name. The following code illustrates the syntax of the overloaded variable_value procedure:

```
procedure variable_value(c     in  integer,
                         name  in  varchar2,
                         value out number);
procedure variable_value(c     in  integer,
                         name  in  varchar2,
                         value out varchar2 character
                                           set any_cs);
procedure variable_value(c     in  integer,
                         name  in  varchar2,
                         value out date);
procedure variable_value(c     in  integer,
                         name  in  varchar2,
                         value out blob);
procedure variable_value(c     in  integer,
                         name  in  varchar2,
                         value out clob character set any_cs);
procedure variable_value(c     in  integer,
                         name  in  varchar2,
                         value out bfile);
procedure variable_value(c     in  integer,
                         name  in  varchar2,
                         value in  Number_table);
procedure variable_value(c     in  integer,
                         name  in  varchar2,
                         value in  Varchar2_table);
procedure variable_value(c     in  integer,
                         name  in  varchar2,
```

```
                          value in  Date_table);
procedure variable_value(c     in  integer,
                          name  in  varchar2,
                          value in  Blob_table);
procedure variable_value(c     in  integer,
                          name  in  varchar2,
                          value in  Clob_table);
procedure variable_value(c     in  integer,
                          name  in  varchar2,
                          value in  Bfile_table);
```

The following code illustrates the syntax of the variable_value_char procedure:

```
procedure variable_value_char(c        in  integer,
                              name     in  varchar2,
                              value    out char character
                                           set any_cs);
```

The following code illustrates the syntax of the variable_value_raw procedure:

```
procedure variable_value_raw(c         in  integer,
                             name      in  varchar2,
                             value     out raw);
```

The following code illustrates the syntax of the variable_value_rowid procedure:

```
procedure variable_value_rowid(c       in  integer,
                               name    in  varchar2,
                               value   out rowid);
```

last_error_position, last_sql_function_code, last_row_count, and last_row_id

The last_error_position, last_sql_function_code, last_row_count, and last_row_id functions retrieve various types of information for the last-operated cursor in the session. To ensure the information relates to a particular cursor, the functions should be called after an operation on that cursor and before any operation on another cursor. The respective return values for these functions include the following:

- **last_error_position** The relative position in the statement when the error occurs
- **last_sql_function_code** The SQL function code of the statement
- **last_row_count** The cumulative count of rows fetched
- **last_row_id** The ROWID of the last processed row

The following code illustrates the syntax of the last_error_position, last_sql_function_code, last_row_count, and last_row_id functions:

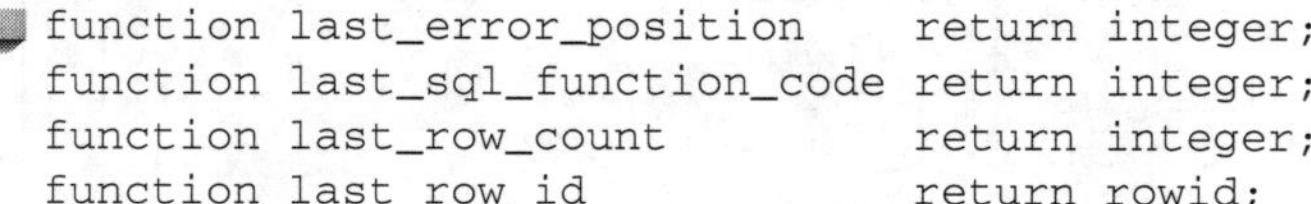

```
function last_error_position     return integer;
function last_sql_function_code return integer;
function last_row_count          return integer;
function last_row_id             return rowid;
```

Setting the Trace Level with dbms_trace

When developing Web applications, tuning is the key to the performance of your entire application. One poorly designed query can pull down the entire system. To track (or trace) performance and execution plans, you can use the dbms_trace package to turn tracing on and off. The trace levels are defined as constant variables, and are named trace_all_calls, trace_enabled_calls, trace_all_exceptions, and trace_enabled_exceptions.

set_plsql_trace

The set_plsql_trace procedure is used to start trace data dumping in the current session. The following code illustrates the syntax of the set_plsql_trace procedure:

```
procedure set_plsql_trace(trace_level integer);
```

clear_plsql_trace

The clear_plsql_trace procedure will stop trace data dumping in the current session. The following code illustrates the syntax of the clear_plsql_trace procedure:

```
procedure clear_plsql_trace;
```

plsql_trace_version

The plsql_trace_version procedure will retrieve the version number of the trace package. The following code illustrates the syntax of the plsql_trace_version procedure:

```
procedure plsql_trace_version(major out binary_integer,
                              minor out binary_integer);
```

Making the Most of dbms_utility

The dbms_utility package contains a number of utility routines to assist in your Web development. For space considerations, a number of procedures and functions that are a part of dbms_utility will not covered in this section.

compile_schema

The compile_schema procedure will compile *all* procedures, functions, packages, and triggers in the specified schema, regardless of their status. After calling this procedure you should select from view all_objects for items with status of INVALID to verify if all objects were successfully compiled. You may use the SQLDBA command "SHOW ERRORS *<type>* *<schema>*.*<name>*" to view the errors associated with INVALID objects. The only input argument to this procedure is schema, which should contain the name of the schema to compile.

TIP

Oracle PL/SQL Tips and Techniques *by Joe Trezzo (Oracle Press, 1999) provides a script that will compile only the routines that need to be compiled (for example, those that are invalid), and will compile recursively until all possible program units are validated.*

The following code illustrates the syntax of the compile_schema procedure:

```
procedure compile_schema(schema varchar2);
```

analyze_schema

The analyze_schema procedure will analyze all the tables, clusters, and indexes in a schema. The input parameters include the schema and all the estimation parameters (method, estimate_rows, and so forth). Schema is the name of the schema. The following code illustrates the syntax of the analyze_schema procedure:

```
procedure analyze_schema(schema           varchar2,
                          method           varchar2,
                         estimate_rows    number default null,
                         estimate_percent number default null,
                         method_opt       varchar2 default null);
```

analyze_database

The analyze_database procedure will analyze all the tables, clusters, and indexes in the entire database. The input arguments are the same as the preceding analyze_schema procedure, with the exception that there is no schema specified. The following code illustrates the syntax of the analyze_database procedure:

```
procedure analyze_database(method            varchar2,
                           estimate_rows     number default null,
                           estimate_percent  number default null,
                           method_opt        varchar2 default null);
```

format_error_stack

The format_error_stack function formats the current error stack. This can be used in exception handlers to view the full error stack. Refer to Chapter 25 for further information and examples of this procedure. The output argument format_error_stack returns the error stack, which may be up to 2,000 bytes. The following code illustrates the syntax of the format_error_stack function:

```
function format_error_stack return varchar2;
```

format_call_stack

The format_call_stack function will format the current call stack. This can be used on any stored procedure or trigger to access the call stack. It can also be useful for debugging. The output argument, format_call_stack, returns the call stack, which may be up to 2,000 bytes. The following code illustrates the syntax of the format_call_stack function:

```
function format_call_stack return varchar2;
```

is_parallel_server

The is_parallel_server function will figure out if the current database is running in parallel server mode. The return argument is_parallel_server will return True if this instance was started in parallel server mode; otherwise, it will return False. The following code illustrates the syntax of the is_parallel_server function:

```
function is_parallel_server return boolean;
```

get_time

The get_time function will return the current time in hundredths of a second. This function is extremely useful for performance measurements down to the hundredth of a second. The return variable, get_time, is the time in the number of hundredths of a second from some arbitrary epoch. To actually measure time to the hundredth of a second, you must use get_time at the beginning and end of the procedure, and then subtract the two numbers. The following code illustrates the syntax of the get_time function:

```
function get_time return number;
```

The following code is an example using the get_time function. The call_url_100_times procedure starts by retrieving the current time. It then calls another routine, which could be any URL. Perhaps you want to verify how quickly your competitors handle 100 requests. At the end of the 100 calls, it will print the total amount of time it took to retrieve the page 100 times. In the following example, call_url_100_times calls the get_employees procedure to calculate the amount of time the routine takes to execute, along with the concurrent user count:

```
procedure call_url_100_times
is
timer_start  number := dbms_utility.get_time;
timer_end    number;
html utl_http.html_pieces;
begin
for x in 1 .. 100 loop
    html := utl_http.request_pieces(
             'http://hp1.tusc.com/plsql/get_employees');
    htp.print(html(1));
end loop;
htp.hr;
timer_end := dbms_utility.get_time;
htp.header(5,to_char((timer_end - timer_start)*
           .01, '999,990.99')||' seconds');
end;

procedure get_employees
is
cursor emp_cur is
       select *
       from   emp;
cursor cnt_cur is
       select count(*) user_count
       from   v$session
       where  program like '%wrks%'
       and    status  =    'ACTIVE';
today varchar2(50) := to_char(sysdate,'mm/dd/yy hh:mi:ss pm');
timer_start  number := dbms_utility.get_time;
timer_end    number;
```

```
user_counter number;
begin
htp.header(1,today);
for cnt_rec in cnt_cur loop
    htp.header(6,to_char(cnt_rec.user_count,'999')||
                ' concurrent users at start');
end loop;
select counter.nextval into user_counter from dual;
htp.header(2,user_counter);
htp.tableOpen;
for emp_rec in emp_cur loop
htp.tableRowOpen;
htp.tableData(emp_rec.emp_name);
htp.tableRowClose;
end loop;
htp.tableClose;
timer_end := dbms_utility.get_time;
htp.header(5,to_char((timer_end - timer_start)*
               .01, '999,990.99')||' seconds');
for cnt_rec in cnt_cur loop
    htp.header(6,to_char(cnt_rec.user_count,'999')||
                   ' concurrent users at end');
end loop;
htp.hr;
end;
```

get_parameter_value

The get_parameter_value function retrieves the value of a specified init.ora parameter. The input argument parnam indicates the init.ora parameter name. The two input/output parameters are intval and strval. Intval is the value of an integer parameter or value length of a string parameter. Strval is the value of a string parameter. This function returns partyp, which is the parameter type (0 if parameter is an integer/Boolean parameter, and 1 if parameter is a string/file parameter). The following code illustrates the syntax of the get_parameter_value function:

```
function get_parameter_value(parnam in     varchar2,
                             intval in out binary_integer,
                             strval in out varchar2)
return binary_integer;
```

name_resolve

The name_resolve procedure will resolve the given name, performing synonym translation if necessary. The input arguments include name and context.

Name is the name of the object. The name can be of the form [[schema.]object.]subobject[@dblink]—for example, scott.myPackage.myProcedure@sales. Context must be an integer between 0 and 8. The output parameters for this function include schema, part1, part2, dblink, part1_type, and object_number. Schema is the schema that the object truly exists within. If no schema is specified in name, the schema is determined by resolving the name. Part1 is the first part of the name. The type of this name is specified in part1_type (for example, synonym, procedure, or package). Part2 contains a procedure name within the package indicated by part1 (if it is not NULL). Dblink is a database link that was either specified as part of name, or name was a synonym that resolved to an object with a database link. In this latter case, part1_type will indicate a synonym. The part1_type parameter indicates the type of part1, which can be 5 (synonym), 7 (procedure, top level), 8 (function, top level), or 9 (package). If part1_type is a synonym, it means name is a synonym that translates to something with a database link. In this case, if further name translation is desired, you must call the dbms_utility.name_resolve procedure on this remote node. The final output parameter is object_number, which contains the object number to which name was resolved. The following code illustrates the syntax of the name_resolve procedure:

```
procedure name_resolve(name          in  varchar2,
                       context       in  number,
                       schema        out varchar2,
                       part1         out varchar2,
                       part2         out varchar2,
                       dblink        out varchar2,
                       part1_type    out number,
                       object_number out number);
```

name_tokenize

The name_tokenize procedure will call the parser to parse the given name as schema [.object [.subobject]][@ dblink], where schema is parameter a, object is parameter b, and subobject is parameter c. This procedure will strip double quotes, or convert to uppercase if there are no quotes—identical to SQL. It will also ignore comments of all sorts. Any missing values are treated as NULL. The following code illustrates the syntax of the name_tokenize procedure:

```
procedure name_tokenize( name    in  varchar2,
                         a       out varchar2,
                         b       out varchar2,
                         c       out varchar2,
                         dblink  out varchar2,
                         nextpos out binary_integer);
```

comma_to_table

The comma_to_table procedure will convert a comma-separated list of names into a PL/SQL table of names. This uses name_tokenize to figure out what are names and what are commas. The following code illustrates the syntax of the comma_to_table procedure:

```
procedure comma_to_table( list   in  varchar2,
                          tablen out binary_integer,
                          tab    out uncl_array);
```

table_to_comma

The table_to_comma procedure performs the opposite operation of the preceding comma_to_table procedure. This procedure will convert a PL/SQL table of names into a comma-separated list of names. The following code illustrates the syntax of the table_to_comma procedure:

```
procedure table_to_comma( tab    in  uncl_array,
                          tablen out binary_integer,
                          list   out varchar2);
```

port_string

The port_string function will return a string that uniquely identifies the port (operating system) and the two-task protocol version of Oracle—for example, IBMPC/WIN_NT-7.0.0. The maximum length is port specific. The following code illustrates the syntax of the port_string function:

```
function port_string return varchar2;
```

db_version

The db_version procedure will return the version information for the database, including version (for example, 7.1.0.0.0) and the compatibility setting of the database determined by the "compatible" init.ora parameter. If the parameter is not specified in the init.ora file, NULL is returned. The following code illustrates the syntax of the db_version procedure:

```
procedure db_version(version       out varchar2,
                     compatibility out varchar2);
```

analyze_part_object

The analyze_part_object procedure is equivalent to the following SQL statement:

```
analyze table|index [<schema>.]<object_name>  partition <pname>
       [<command_type>] [<command_opt>] [<sample_clause>]
```

For each partition of the object, the table or index will be analyzed in parallel using job queues. The package will submit a job for each partition. It is the user's responsibility to control the number of concurrent jobs by setting the init.ora parameter job_queue_processes correctly. There is minimal error checking for correct syntax. Errors will be reported in SNP trace files. The input arguments include:

- **schema** Schema of the object_name
- **object_name** Name of object to be analyzed, and it must be partitioned
- **object_type** Type of object, and it must be a T(able) or an I(ndex)
- **command_type** Must be one of the following: C(ompute statistics), E(stimate statistics), D(elete statistics), or V(alidate structure)
- **command_opt** Other options for the command type

Other command options (command_opt) for compute or estimate statistics can be for table, for all local indexes, for all columns, or a combination of some of the options of analyze statistics (table). For validating a structure, the only option is that it can be cascade when object_type is a table. The sample_clause parameter specifies the sample clause to use when command_type is estimate statistics. The following code illustrates the syntax of the analyze_part_object procedure:

```
procedure analyze_part_object
   (schema        in varchar2 default null,
    object_name   in varchar2 default null,
    object_type   in char     default 'T',
    command_type  in char     default 'E',
    command_opt   in varchar2 default null,
    sample_clause in varchar2 default 'sample 5 percent');
```

exec_ddl_statement

The exec_ddl_statement procedure will execute the DDL statement in the parse_string parameter. The following code illustrates the syntax of the exec_ddl_statement procedure:

```
procedure exec_ddl_statement(parse_string in varchar2);
```

current_instance

The current_instance function will return the current connected instance number and will return NULL when the connected instance is down. The following code illustrates the syntax of the current_instance function:

```
function current_instance return number;
```

active_instances

The active_instances procedure will return a PL/SQL table (instance_table) containing a list of the active instance numbers and names. When no instance is up and running, the list is empty. The instance_count parameter will contain the number of active instances. The following code illustrates the syntax of the active_instances procedure:

```
procedure active_instances(instance_table   out instance_table,
                           instance_count   out number);
```

Accessing Operating System Files with utl_file

The utl_file package enables you to perform operating system file operations from PL/SQL. Remember, utl_file executes on the database server; therefore, you can perform operations on files on the database server using utl_file.

The following code uses dbms_lob to read a file from the operating system and insert the file into a database record:

```
create or replace procedure load_lob is
  lob_temp    blob;
  os_file     bfile := bfilename('dir_store', 'in_file.gif');
  ignore integer;
begin
  dbms_lob.fileopen(os_file, dbms_lob.file_readonly);
  select blob_col
  into lob_temp
  from db_table_1
  where col1 = 1
  for update;
  dbms_output.put_line('Size of the external file is: '||
                       dbms_lob.getlength(os_file));
  dbms_lob.loadfromfile(lob_temp,
```

```
    os_file, dbms_lob.getlength(os_file));
  dbms_lob.fileclose(os_file);
  dbms_output.put_line('Size of the internal blob is: '||
                       dbms_lob.getlength(lob_temp));
  commit;
end;
```

Once in the database, use utl_file to extract the file. The following is the procedure that retrieves the blob_col (1 character at a time) from db_table_1 and stores the BLOB into the get_lob.gif file:

```
create or replace procedure get_lob is
    lob_temp    blob;
    data_buffer raw (1);
    amount      binary_integer := 1;
    pos         integer        := 1;
    filehandle  utl_file.file_type;
    err_num     number;
    err_msg     varchar2(100);
    count_down  integer;
begin
    select blob_col into lob_temp from db_table_1 where col1 = 1;
    count_down := dbms_lob.getlength(lob_temp);
    dbms_output.put_line('The size of the internal lob is:  ' ||
                         count_down);
    filehandle := utl_file.fopen('/bdb/images/','get_lob.gif','w');
    while count_down <> 0 loop
       dbms_lob.read (lob_temp, amount, pos, data_buffer);
       utl_file.put (filehandle, data_buffer);
       pos := pos + 1;
       count_down := count_down - 1;
       data_buffer := null;
    end loop;
    dbms_output.put_line('We just exited the loop');
    utl_file.fclose(filehandle);
    dbms_output.put_line('We just closed the file');
    exception when others then
       begin
          err_num := sqlcode;
          err_msg := substr(sqlerrm ,1 ,100);
          dbms_output.put_line('Error #: ' || err_num);
          dbms_output.put_line('Error message: ' || err_msg);
          dbms_output.put_line('Count down:  ' || count_down);
          utl_file.fclose_all;
       end;
end;
```

fopen, Version 1

The fopen function will open a file (no maximum line size). This version of fopen does not take a parameter for the maximum line size. Thus, the default (which is 1,023 on most systems) will be used. To specify a different maximum linesize, use the following version of fopen found below. As of Oracle 8.0.6, you can have a maximum of 50 files open simultaneously. There are the following three input parameters:

- **location** Directory location of file
- **filename** Filename (including extension)
- **open_mode** Open mode (r, w, or a). r stands for read, w for write, and a for append

The fopen function returns file_type, which is the handle (pointer number) to the open file. The following code illustrates the syntax for the fopen function:

```
function fopen(location  in varchar2,
               filename  in varchar2,
               open_mode in varchar2)
return   file_type;
```

fopen, Version 2

The second version of the fopen function opens a file and enables you to provide a user-specified maximum line size. The three preceding input parameters also apply for this version. The only additional parameter for this version of the fopen function is max_linesize, containing the maximum number of characters per line, including the newline character for this file. For this function, the minimum value is 1 and the maximum value is 32767. This version also returns file_type, containing the handle to the open file. The following code illustrates the syntax for the fopen function:

```
function fopen(location     in varchar2,
               filename     in varchar2,
               open_mode    in varchar2,
               max_linesize in binary_integer)
return   file_type;
```

is_open

The is_open function will verify whether a specific file handle is open. The only input parameter is file, which will contain a file handle to check. This function will return a Boolean value indicating if the file handle specified is open. The following code illustrates the syntax for the is_open function:

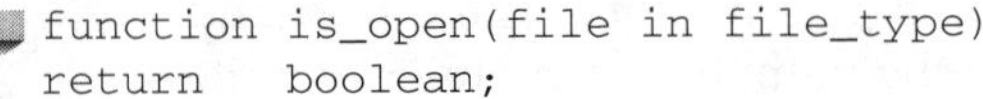

```
function is_open(file in file_type)
return   boolean;
```

fclose

The fclose procedure will close an open file. The input parameter is file, containing the file handle of the file to close. The following code illustrates the syntax for the fclose procedure:

```
procedure fclose(file in out file_type);
```

fclose_all

The fclose_all procedure will close all open files for this session. This should be used for emergency cleanup use only. The file_type handles will not be cleared. In other words, is_open will still indicate the files are open. The following code illustrates the syntax of the fclose_all procedure:

```
procedure fclose_all;
```

get_line

The get_line procedure will get (read) a line of text from the file. The only input parameter is file, which should contain the file handle. The file must be opened in read mode. The output parameter buffer will contain the next line of text in file. The following code illustrates the syntax of the get_line procedure:

```
procedure get_line(file   in  file_type,
                   buffer out varchar2);
```

put

The put procedure will put (write) text to a specific file. The file must be opened in write or append mode. The input parameters are file and buffer. The parameter file must contain the file handle and buffer is text to write to the file. The following code illustrates the syntax of the put procedure:

```
procedure put(file   in file_type,
              buffer in varchar2);
```

new_line

The new_line procedure will write a line terminator(s) to a specific file, if that file is opened in write or append mode. The input parameter file is the file handle, and the second parameter line will contain the number of new lines to write. The default number of lines is 1. The following code illustrates the syntax of the new_line procedure:

```
procedure new_line(file  in file_type,
                   lines in natural := 1);
```

put_line

The put_line procedure will write text to a specific file and place a new_line character after the text. The file must be opened in write or append mode. The input parameters are file and buffer. The parameter file must contain the file handle and buffer is text to write to the file. The following code illustrates the syntax of the put_line procedure:

```
procedure put_line(file   in file_type,
                   buffer in varchar2);
```

putf

The putf procedure will write formatted text to a specific file that is opened in write or append mode. The input parameters are file and buffer. The parameter file should contain the file handle. The second parameter is format, which uses its own special formatting rules. The following code illustrates the syntax of the putf procedure:

```
procedure putf(file   in file_type,
               format in varchar2,
               arg1   in varchar2 default null,
               arg2   in varchar2 default null,
               arg3   in varchar2 default null,
               arg4   in varchar2 default null,
               arg5   in varchar2 default null);
```

fflush

The fflush procedure will force a physical write of buffered output to a specified file. The only input parameter is file, which contains the file handle to flush. This file must be opened in write or append mode. The following code illustrates the syntax of the fflush procedure:

```
procedure fflush(file in file_type);
```

Maximizing utl_http

The utl_http package contains functions request and request_pieces for making HTTP callouts from PL/SQL programs. This is an extremely powerful function. This function is a built-in PL/SQL package deployed as part of the database, not OAS! It was released in the database Oracle 7.3.3. The procedure utl_http makes HTTP calls from the database engine. If you build a procedure using utl_http, you could schedule the procedure to execute in conjunction with dbms_jobs. You can extract this information and store it in the database or in a file using utl_file, as previously described.

Two exceptions should be declared when using the utl_file function. Otherwise, for any error you'll receive the infamous ora-6510 error, indicating there was a PL/SQL: unhandled user-defined exception. The following are the two exceptions that must be declared:

```
declare init_failed    exception;
declare request_failed exception;
```

The init_failed exception will occur when initialization of the http callout subsystem fails. This could occur if an environmental failure has occurred, such as lack of available memory. The request_failed exception will occur when the HTTP call fails. This could occur if a failure of the HTTP daemon has occurred or if the url argument cannot be interpreted as a URL because it is NULL or has non-HTTP syntax. If the site is down or does not respond, you would receive the request_failed error.

To follow good programming practice, you should use the request_lines function to read the entire Web page rather than truncating at 4,000 characters. However, if you know the information you need is within the first 4,000 characters, then feel free to use the request function.

From your database, you can read a Web site and process it as you deem necessary. There are a number of possible uses of this function for your company. For example, you can use utl_http for stock price tracking, to gather your competitors' price lists, to collect vendor comparison price lists as a cyber robot (gathering keyword and URL information), to create semistatic pages (such as a static home page from data like weekly news), to read templates, to call other CGI programs, for load testing, and more.

Remember that cookies will not be sent in the HTTP header from utl_http. Because it is not a browser, it does not store cookies. Therefore, when calling a page, if the application functions without cookies, the results will be as expected. However, if a cookie is required, the application may fail without it.

If you want to collect Oracle's stock price each day to track your portfolio, track your companies stock price, or provide real-time and historical stock information on your company's Web site, utl_http can be used. Where can you gather stock information? From about a thousand different sites, so pick your favorite. To view a stock quote from Yahoo (as HTML), use the browser to traverse down to the stock price for Oracle. The following code is the final result that will retrieve the requested information:

```
http://quote.yahoo.com/q?s=orcl&o=t
```

View the source code for that page, which appears similar to the following subset of code:

```
...
<a href="/q?s=ORCL&d=t">ORCL</a>     Nov 25       <b>34 5/8</b>
<font color="#ff0020">-3/8</font>
<font color="#ff0020">-1.07%</font> 4,019,400 <small>
...
```

Using utl_http, you could retrieve the HTML for this page using a statement similar to the following:

```
html := utl_http.request_lines('http://quote.yahoo.com/q?s=orcl&o=t');
```

Once executed, the results of the query from Yahoo are placed into a PL/SQL table called html, which can be parsed to extract key information like the following:

```
start_pos       := instr (html(x), '>orcl</a>');
end_pos         := instr (html(x), '<small>', start_pos+1);
key_information := substr (html(x), start_pos,
                           end_pos - start_pos);
```

At this point, you can further break down key_information, store the information in the database, write a file (using utl_file), or perform other tasks. You can schedule this procedure to execute on a regular frequency using dbms_jobs.

Similar to the preceding stock price logic, you can gather your competitors' price lists or collect price lists from all of your vendors to enable vendor price comparisons directly from your data. In other words, anything containing key information on a specific URL will use logic similar to the preceding procedure logic. You can even develop a generic routine to extract this key information from any page. Another example use mentioned was the cyber robot. Use utl_http to read through an entire site or component thereof and to build data for searches, site maps, "what's new" pages, and more. Collect tables containing keywords and URLs with an intersection entity containing the keywords in each URL. The pseudo logic might appear similar to the following:

- Loop
  - Read page
  - Ignore tags (from < to >)

- For each keyword
  - Does keyword exist in table?
    - **Yes** insert keyword_url record
    - **No** insert keyword and keyword_url
- Find all anchors, insert url, site_tree records
- Read next unprocessed url record

Yet another use of utl_http might be to create what is referred to as a semistatic home page. This type of page is useful if you want a page to contain dynamic content, but you do not want to dynamically generate that content every time someone requests the page. This is especially true for your home page. If you are going to experience thousands of hits every hour or minute, you certainly do not want to generate the home page dynamically for each user, do you? Even if the content on the page only changes every minute, every five minutes, or hourly, this technique will save valuable processing power. You might also have daily updates, a weekly news page, or even a monthly manager's report that can be created in a similar manner. The less frequent the data changes, the more powerful this use. You can drive the re-creation of the page by a database event, such as an update. Using utl_http, dynamically generate the page's contents and retrieve the HTML for the page. The next step is to write the HTML to a static file, which can be accomplished using utl_file. Your final determination is the method of regeneration. If it is manual, simply execute the procedure whenever necessary. If it is a frequency-based regeneration, you can use dbms_job to execute your procedure on whatever frequency you choose. If it is based on a table event, you can use a table-based trigger to execute your procedure or use dbms_pipe to queue the execution.

Another use for utl_http is to dynamically change content on a static page, such as a template. Maybe you prefer maintaining your HTML with an HTML editor, such as DreamWeaver. Using utl_http, you can read a static HTML file from the Web server, then change the contents, such as the background image, on the fly. The following procedure employs this functionality by looking up this user's preferred background image and replacing it accordingly:

```
procedure use_template
(in_url varchar2)
as
profile_rec         tusc_util.profile_cur%rowtype :=
                       tusc_util.get_profile_info;
html_pieces         utl_http.html_pieces;
html                varchar2(4000);
html2               varchar2(4000);
upper_html          varchar2(4000);
head_pos            number(4);
```

```
ss_pos              number(4);
ls_pos              number(4);
ls2_pos             number(4);
body_html           varchar2(4000);
protocol            varchar2(100);
begin
  /*
  This procedure uses any url (html
  file) and replaces the body command w/
 our own body command with the background
 image of this user.
  */
  html_pieces    := utl_http.request_pieces(in_url);
  html           := substr(html_pieces(1),1,2000);
  upper_html     := upper(html);
  html2          := substr(html_pieces(1),2001);
  head_pos       := instr(upper_html, '<head>');
  ss_pos         := instr(in_url, '//');
  ls_pos         := ss_pos + 2;
  <<search_last_slash>>
  ls2_pos        := instr(in_url, '/', ls_pos+1);

  if ls2_pos > 0 then
     ls_pos   := ls2_pos;
     goto search_last_slash;
  end if;

  html           := substr(html, 1, head_pos-1) ||
                    '<head><base href=' || substr(in_url, 1, ls_pos) ||
                 '>' || substr(html, head_pos+6);
  upper_html     := upper(html);
  ss_pos         := instr(upper_html, '<body');
  ls_pos         := instr(upper_html, '>', ss_pos);
  body_html      := htf.bodyopen(profile_rec.custom_background_image,
                      cattributes => 'bgcolor="#ffffff"');
  html           := substr(html, 1, ss_pos-1) || body_html ||
                      substr(html, ls_pos+1);
htp.prn(html || html2);
for x in 2 .. html_pieces.count loop
    htp.prn(html_pieces(x));
end loop;
```

Another use (and one of my favorites) for utl_http is to execute any CGI program directly from PL/SQL. Remember, you can call any valid URL using this procedure. This can obviously include a URL executing a CGI program that executes and returns HTML. By using utl_http to execute the CGI program, the information (HTML) is then returned to PL/SQL. For example, you can have a CGI program performing credit card processing, Notice to Airman (NOTAM) information for airlines, access to TCP/IP ports, and more. This enables you to write the complex code in another language (for example, C, Java, or Perl) and to save PL/SQL for the graphic user display of information.

In the preceding dbms_utility.get_time example, we also used utl_http to repeatedly call a specific URL. You can use this functionality for performance benchmarks of your applications (or your competitor's) or for testing. You can also execute this procedure on a scheduled basis (using dbms_job) and collect statistics. For testing purposes, you can put the call into a for loop, as illustrated in the following syntax:

```
for i in 1 .. 10000 loop
    html_pieces := utl_http.request_pieces(url_to_call);
end loop;
```

Or, you could store a set of URLs in a table and loop through the table using the following:

```
for i in 1 .. 10000 loop
    for test_urls_cur in test_urls_rec loop
        html_pieces := utl_http.request_pieces(test_urls_rec.url);
    end loop;
end loop;
```

The utl_http is a powerful package, especially when used with other built-ins packages such as dbms_job or utl_file. Take a moment to examine the possibilities for your environment!

request

The request function accepts a URL as its argument. Its return type is a string of 4,000 bytes or less in length. It will display the first 4,000 bytes of the html result returned from the HTTP request to the argument URL.

The following is an example of the utl_http.request:

```
declare html_results varchar2(4000);
begin
   html_results :=
        utl_http.request('http://www.tusc.com');
   .... -- process html_results
end;
```

The preceding example requests the HTML for the www.tusc.com Web site and places the HTML into a PL/SQL varchar2 variable named html_results. The HTML can be processed as deemed necessary, but remember, html_results will only contain the first 4,000 characters from the site's requested page.

The input parameter url is the URL you wish to call from the database. It is worth noting that http:// must be specified at the beginning of the URL, as you can see in the preceding examples. The proxy parameter includes the IP address or domain name of the proxy server. The following code illustrates the syntax for the request function:

```
function request (url   in varchar2,
                  proxy in varchar2 default NULL)
return   varchar2;
```

request_pieces

The request_pieces function also takes a URL as its argument. The return type for the request_pieces function is a PL/SQL table of type utl_http.html_pieces. Each element of the PL/SQL tables is a string of 4,000 bytes. The final element may be shorter than 4,000 characters.

The following is a quick example of the utl_http.request_lines:

```
declare pieces utl_http.html_pieces;
 begin
   pieces :=
       utl_http.request_lines('http://www.tusc.com');
   for i in 1 .. pieces.count loop
     .... -- process each piece
     .... -- refer to each piece as pieces(i)
   end loop;
 end;
```

The preceding example requests the HTML for the www.tusc.com Web site and places the HTML into a PL/SQL table named pieces. The HTML can be processed as you deem necessary.

The input parameters url and proxy are the same within the request function. The variable max_pieces is optional; it must be a positive integer, and must specify the maximum number of PL/SQL table array elements to retrieve. The following code illustrates the syntax for the request_pieces function:

```
function request_pieces (url    in varchar2,
                         max_pieces natural default 32767,
                         proxy   in varchar2 default NULL)
return html_pieces;
```

Summary

A number of powerful built-in database packages are available. In this chapter, we covered these packages from a Web development perspective. With each new database version, I always scan through the packages in the SYS schema to see what has been added. Often, the new packages are not documented, but you can usually find some documentation within the package specification.

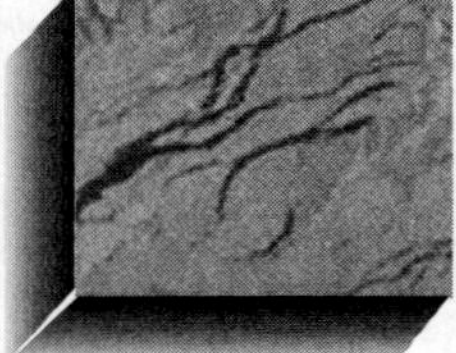

PART II

Core Concepts

CHAPTER 10

Differences Among the Various Oracle Web Server Versions

The Oracle Web Server has come a long way since the first release. Most people considered the first release to be a rushed release, enabling Oracle to enter the Web world. Version 2 brought considerable promise to the product's future. Version 3 was a disappointment at first, because of bugs, but quickly became a powerful, scalable solution. By version 3, the name of the product was beginning to evolve. In version 1 and version 2, it was just Oracle Web Server. Version 3 added "application" into the name—becoming Oracle Web Application Server, or OWAS, to stress it was not just a Web server. The name changed in version 4. Aside from its new name—Oracle Application Server (OAS)—with many new features it became a robust Application Server for a Web environment. Table 10-1 highlights the advancement of features and functionality for the succession of releases in the development of the Oracle Web Server through OAS. As of OWAS 3.0, the DCD (Database Connect Descriptor) became the DAD (Database Access Descriptor).

Feature	V1	V2.1	V3	V4
Web browser administration interface		X	X	X
Java administration interface				X
Multithreading				X
Load-balancing			X	X
Advanced load-balancing				X
Failure recovery				X
PL/SQL cartridge		X	X	X
Java cartridge		X	X	X
JWeb cartridge				X
Perl cartridge			X	X
ODBC cartridge			X	X
LiveHTML cartridge			X	X
C cartridge			X	X
VRML cartridge				X

TABLE 10-1. *Oracle Web Server Version Differences*

Feature	V1	V2.1	V3	V4
CORBA 2.0 infrastructure				X
WebConnect				X
COBOL cartridge			X	X
XA transaction management			X	X
OTS/JTS				X
ICX (Intercartridge Exchange)				X
Cartridge Server				X
Netscape FastTrack Server usable				X
Netscape Enterprise Server usable		X	X	X
Microsoft Internet Information Server usable			X	X
Apache Server usable				X
Third-party tools bundled			X	X

TABLE 10-1. *Oracle Web Server Version Differences* (continued)

The following topics will be covered in this chapter:

- Taking a look at what's new in OAS 4.0
- New features in administration
- Enhancements in OAS architecture
- Advancements in cartridges
- Working with OAS 4.0 and other Oracle products
- Comparing OAS 4.0 to OAS 4.0 Enterprise edition
- Checking out third-party tools bundled with OAS
- Reviewing OAS 4.0 requirements

Taking a Look At What's New in OAS 4.0

The new features of OAS 4.0 can be broken down into four primary areas:

- **Administration** The administration front end has been reconstructed to ease the administration of a Web site through a Web browser. OAS 4.0 includes additional example applications and extensive documentation compared to previous releases.
- **Architecture** The Object Request Broker technology (ORB) has been implemented to address the resource and communication requirements among different server processes. Many new features have been added in the load-balancing, tuning, and failure recovery areas.
- **Cartridges** Java technology has been the driving force in the new OAS 4.0 features. Four Java-related cartridges are now available—JWeb, JSQL, JCorba, and EJB. An enhanced version of the LiveHTML cartridge has been released, using Perl as its server-side scripting language—refer to Chapter 20 and Chapter 21 for further information on Perl and LiveHTML, respectively. The PL/SQL cartridge implemented new ways of tackling parameters and authentication.
- **Third-Party CD** OAS comes with a CD of Oracle's choice for best-of-breed products compatible with OAS.

New Features in Administration

The OWAS 3.0 administration front end has been replaced with a new, cleaner, easier to follow Web interface, as illustrated in Figure 10-1.

The Welcome page contains the following components:

- **OAS Manager** A Java/HTML-based Node Manager replaced the OWAS 3.0 Web administration front end, as illustrated later in Figure 10-2. OAS Manager is the location to configure the WRB, HTTP listeners, and Web applications.
- **OAS Utilities** An extension of the Node Manager, and the location to install the Logger Tables and PL/SQL Toolkit, configure Apache, Microsoft IIS, or Netscape Web listeners, migrate previous versions of the Oracle Web Server, and more.

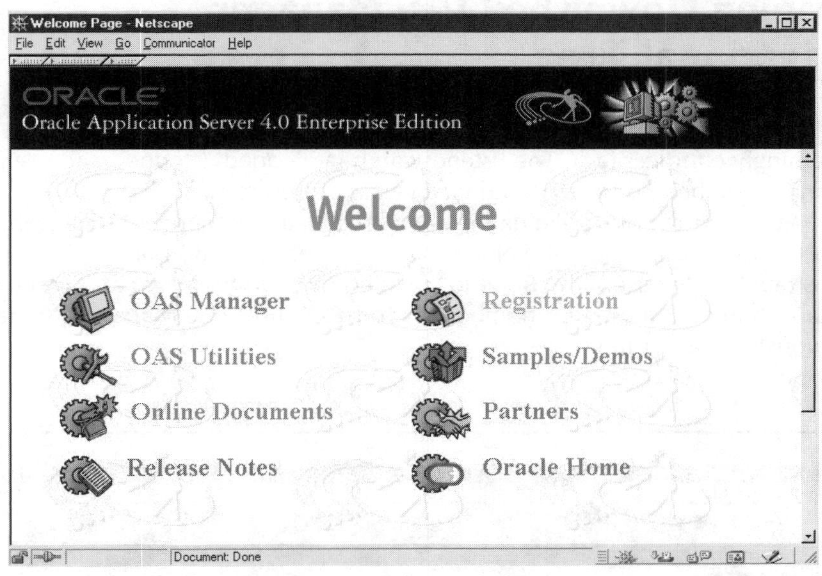

FIGURE 10-1. *OAS administration Welcome page*

- **Online Documents** OAS 4.0 complete product documentation is available in Adobe Acrobat PDF format. The documentation includes a powerful Java applet for ease of navigation and searching.
- **Release Notes** A link to documents containing OAS 4.0 notes pertaining to outstanding issues or problems not addressed in the initial product documentation.
- **Registration** A link to the Oracle Application Server registration page, www.olab.com.
- **Samples/Demos** A link to the OAS 4.0 Samples component of your Application Server, automatically installed on the administrative port of your Web server.
- **Partners** A link to the partners Web site, www.olab.com.
- **Oracle Home** A link to the Oracle's main Web site, www.oracle.com.

Climbing Down the OAS Manager Navigational Tree

An administrator-friendly approach to OAS site manageability is a distinguishing feature of the OAS Manager. Starting and stopping the listeners and the applications is a seemingly effortless task. The listener can be 'reloaded' (stopped and restarted) independent of the applications and vice versa, as illustrated in Figure 10-2.

The Microsoft Explorer–like navigational tree feature enhances manageability of your OAS site. By default, the Node Manager uses the 8888 port, and the demonstrations use port 8889. Refer to Chapter 2 for further information regarding the establishment of these port numbers. By default, the Node Manager listener is continuously up and running.

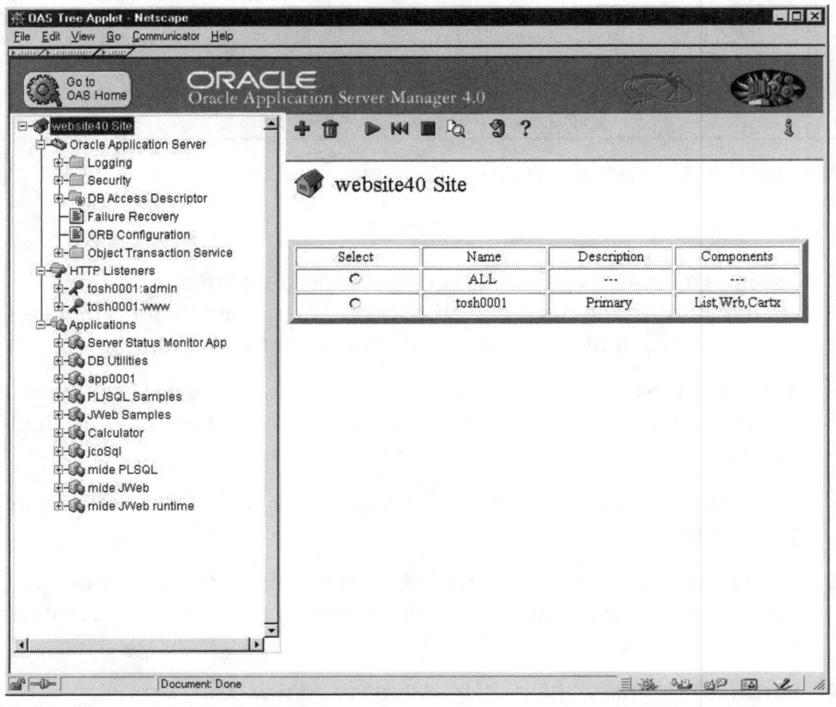

FIGURE 10-2. *OAS Manager*

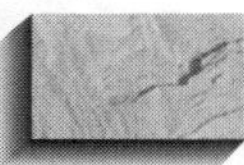

TIP
The Tree prior to OAS 4.0.8 does not always automatically refresh itself when components are reconfigured. To force the applet to reload, press the SHIFT *key and click the Reload button on your browser. Follow the same procedures if the "Tree Applet can't start" message occurs when attempting to display the navigational tree.*

Oracle Web Server administration is composed of three components, namely:

- Oracle Application Server
- HTTP Listeners
- Applications

The Oracle Application Server subcomponents include logging, security, Database Access Descriptor (DAD), failure recovery, Object Request Broker (ORB), and Oracle Transaction Service (OTS) configurations. You can leave all the subcomponents as originally defaulted, except for the DAD, which should be configured if you want your Web applications to connect to a particular Oracle database.

The HTTP Listener component defaults to a standard HTTP listener configuration. OAS enables you to configure these HTTP listeners. If you want to use a non-Oracle listener with your OAS, register it through the OAS Utilities as an external listener component. When OAS 4.0 has been installed, it will enable two preinstalled listeners—admin and www. The admin port is used by the demonstration applications. The www port is used by your new applications accessing port 80; you can also create new Oracle-based HTTP listeners.

The Application component, also known as the Cartridge Server, is the location to define your Web applications. When you define a Web application, you can use any of following cartridges: C (C Web), Enterprise Java Beans (EJB), Java/Corba (JCorba), Java (JWeb), Perl, or PL/SQL cartridges.

In OAS 4.0, the PL/SQL Agent concept is no longer used. The configuration information in PL/SQL Agents has become a part of the cartridge configuration. The PL/SQL application can be called from multiple HTTP listeners; each may be listening on different ports, unlike in OWAS 3.0 when a PL/SQL Agent was tied to a specific HTTP listener port. You are no longer required to list the ports tied to an agent.

TIP

When configuring the OAS Node Manager, if you destroyed or corrupted the configuration file, the navigational tree applet will no longer appear; the applet may indicate an error has occurred or prompt you to install the latest version of the JDK. To address this issue, find the latest backup copy of the wrb.app and site.app files, by looking at the files' date stamps. These files contain correlating numbers as their file extensions. Back up the current wrb.app and site.app files, replace them with the backup copies, then reload your OAS Node Manager listener (for example, owsctl reload –nodemgr).

TIP

Never hand modify the wrb.app and site.app files without first making a backup copy. Even though not obvious, there exist interfield relationships within those files such that, if certain values are changed, other values must also be changed. The OAS architecture will not start if these files are corrupted.

Understanding the OAS Manager Operational Buttons

The OAS Utilities Manager navigational tree is primarily used for site configuration. Figure 10-3 illustrates operational buttons shown on the upper part of the right frame, including the following:

- Add a new record, such as a node, listener, application, or DAD.
- Delete an existing record, such as a node, listener, application, or DAD.
- Start a listener, the WRB, or individual WRB components.
- Reload (or bounce) the node, HTTP listeners, or WRB components. A reload is necessary when configuration of a component has changed.
- Stop a node, listener, the WRB, or individual WRB components.
- Monitor node status, including the Oracle HTTP listeners and WRB components.

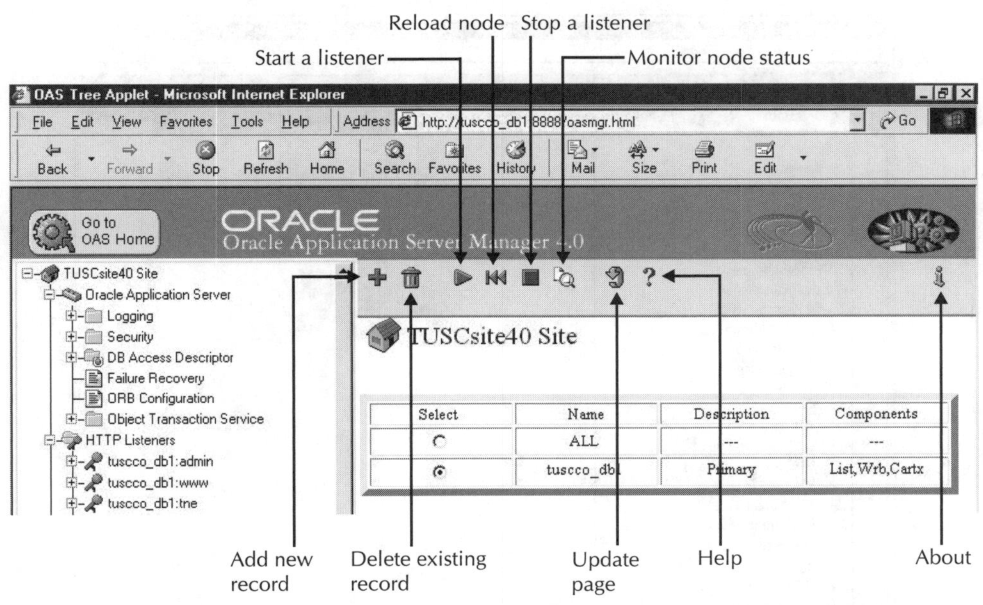

FIGURE 10-3. *OAS Utilities Manager page*

- Update Page is used to reload the current page.
- Help loads a help page to the Web browser.
- About indicates the current OAS version.

Climbing the OAS Utilities Navigational Tree

The Explorer-like navigational feature of the OAS utilities is similar to the OAS Node Manager, as illustrated in Figure 10-4. When you click on the folder, subfolders will appear—namely, Install, Process Model, External Listener, Migrate, Log Analyzer, and Database Browser—each of which will be covered in the following sections.

Installing OAS Components – Install

From the Install subfolder, you can install the Database Browser packages, enabling you to browse database objects. You can also install the Logger Tables to store log information to the database; refer to Chapter 26 for further information. After installing the Logger Tables, you can install the Log Analyzer. The Log Analyzer enables you to report on the raw data stored by the Logger and display site statistics. The Log Analyzer uses the PL/SQL cartridge and, therefore, relies on the PL/SQL Web Toolkit.

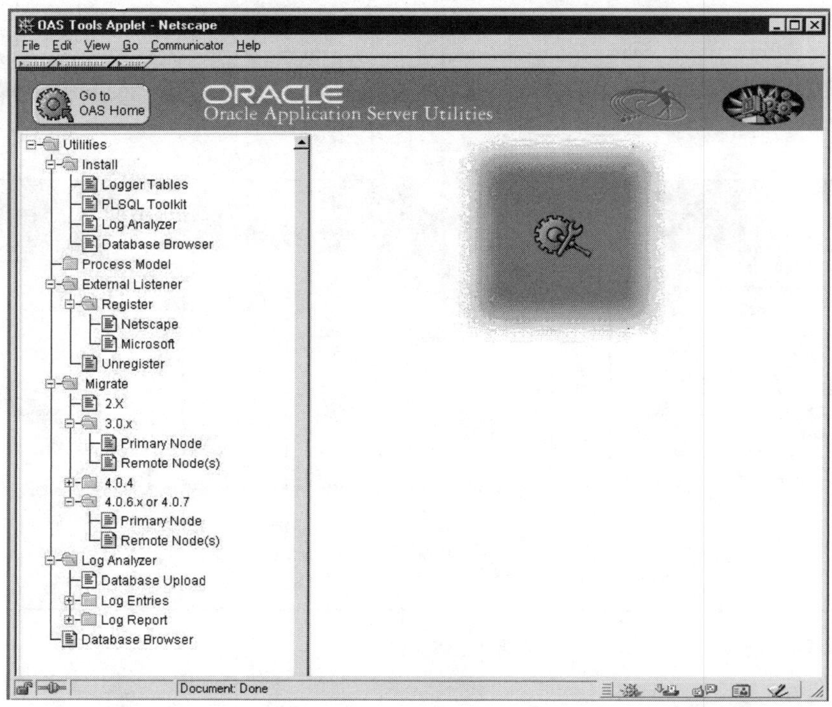

FIGURE 10-4. *OAS Node Manager page*

Installing the PL/SQL Web Toolkit is a breeze to install and manage with OAS 4.0. You only need to install the PL/SQL Web Toolkit once per database instance. The installation of the PL/SQL Web Toolkit option places the OAS Content Services API components into the WEBSYS schema and the standard PL/SQL Web Toolkit components are placed into the OAS_PUBLIC schema. The installation creates public synonyms for the packages in OAS_PUBLIC and grants execute privilege to PUBLIC. OAS 4.0 makes it easy because the installation provides for any user in the database to access the PL/SQL Web Toolkit.

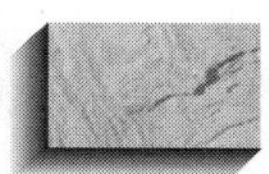

TIP
The OAS Content Service API is usable only if you are running the Enterprise edition of OAS 4.0.

Collapsing the Process Model – Process Model

You can switch from collapsed (default) model to noncollapsed, and vice versa. The collapsed model combines various WRB processes into one OAS server process. The collapsed model requires fewer resources because the number of processes running is fewer than with the noncollapsed model. The collapsed model, however, was less reliable than the noncollapsed model and was renamed as of OAS 4.0.8.

Registering or Unregistering an External Listener – External Listener

You can register and deregister external HTTP listeners, such as Netscape Enterprise Server, Microsoft Internet Information Server, or the Apache Server through this option.

TIP
You can currently register an Apache listener only if you are using the Solaris platform.

Migrating from Prior OAS Versions – Migrate

You can migrate your configuration files from previous versions of your Oracle Web Servers—including versions 2, 3, and 4—using the Migrate option. To convert the configuration (*.cfg and *.app) files from a prior OAS version into the new OAS 4.0 formats, supply the (primary or remote) node's ORACLE_HOME directory to the Migrate utility. The *.cfg files contain your HTTP listener and DAD configurations. The *.app files contain your WRB and cartridge information.

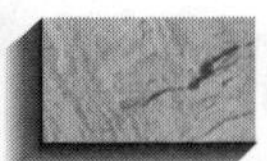

TIP
Because of disk space issues, I often save my cfg and app files to a special directory, but manually remove the prior OAS installation—in which case, by removing the prior version of OAS, I am not able to use the Migrate utility. However, manual configuration isn't usually all that time-consuming. If you have enough disk space to install both versions, you will be able to use the Migrate utility.

Using Log Analyzer – Log Analyzer

You must first install the Log Analyzer to be able to use the Log Analyzer options. The Log Analyzer component of the OAS Utilities enables you to upload log data from existing files. I would not recommend using the Log Analyzer as the method to load log data into the database, unless you require real-time log information in your database. The other components available under the Log Analyzer menu item relate to log entries and log reports. The Log Entries option enables you to view current XLF and system message log entries contained in the Logger Tables. The

Log Reports option enables you to run the XLF Log Report, System Message Log Report, Concurrent User Report, and modify the Concurrent User Report. The entire Log Analyzer component requires the Logger Tables, PL/SQL Web Toolkit, and Log Analyzer to be installed. This component is executed through the admin port's listener. See Chapter 26 for more information.

Using the Database Browser – Database Browser

The Database Browser enables you to view schema objects (tables, views, and stored PL/SQL), users, sessions, rollback segments, database files, tablespace usage, and tablespace free space summaries.

Reviewing the OAS Command-Line Utilities

Table 10-2 contains the OAS documentation's appendix describing OAS command-line utilities.

Administrators familiar with OWAS 3.0 should discover the syntax of the owsctl command has changed significantly for OAS 4.0.

Oracle strongly recommends using the OAS Node Manager to administer your site. If you choose to use the command-line utility to start OAS, you should also use the command-line utility to stop OAS. Likewise, if you use the OAS Node Manager to start OAS, you should also use it to stop OAS.

Accessing the Online Documentation

The OAS 4.0 online documentation uses a Java interface for searching and browsing different chapters and sections. The main OAS documentation can be accessed from the OAS 4.0 Welcome page through the Online Documents menu item. The documents contain links to the Adobe Acrobat PDF files. Oracle did a considerable amount of research into the documentation and its use for administrators and developers. Most

Name	Description
owsctl	Start, stop, reload, and display the status of the Oracle Web Listener, Oracle Web Status Monitor, Web Request Broker, Object Request Broker, and cartridge processes
owsstat	Monitor the status of the Oracle Web Listener
oasnetconf	Modifying certain node properties on different machines
oaspasswd	Change the Node Manager, ORB, and Wallet Manager passwords

TABLE 10-2. *Command-Line Utilities*

of the suggestions were taken from the documentation team and implemented in each version. Your feedback is important, and can be provided at the TUSC Web site (www.tusc.com), or directly to Oracle.

Enhancements in OAS Architecture

Many different layers exist within the OAS architecture, as illustrated in Figure 10-5—for example, the HTTP listener layer, the WRB (or OAS) layer, and the new applications layer.

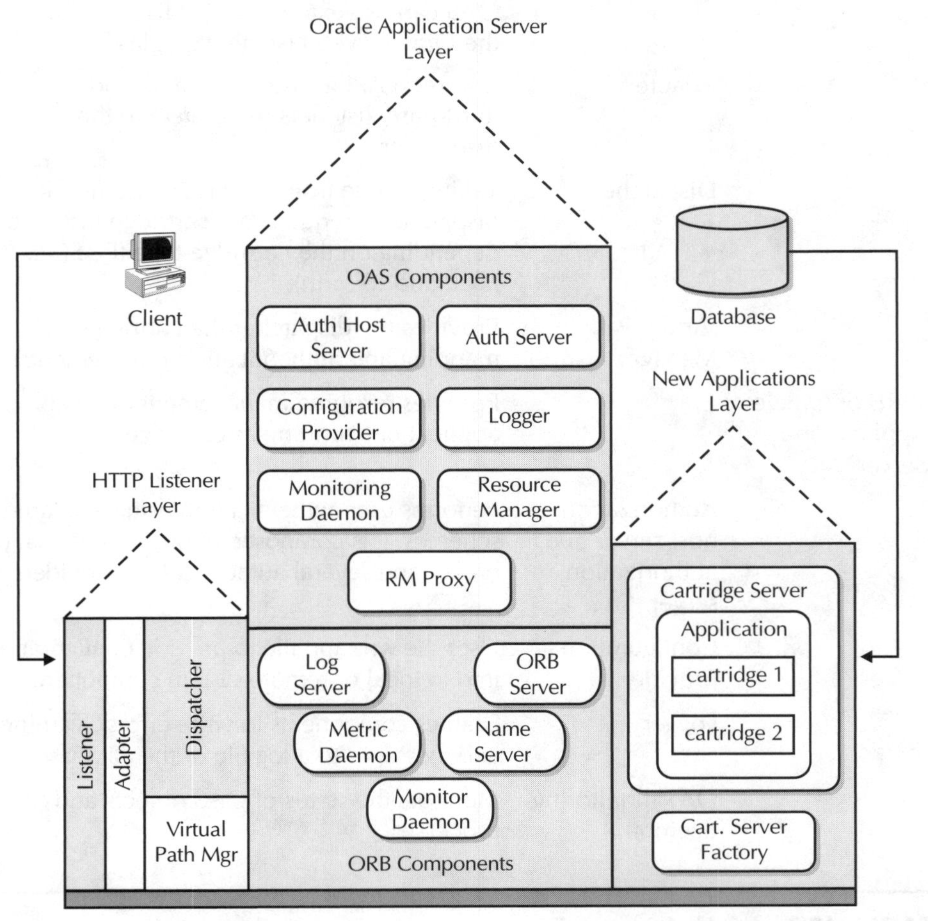

FIGURE 10-5. *OAS 4.0 architecture overview*

Table 10-3 lists OAS layer components and briefly describes each component.

Layer	Components	Description
HTTP Listener		Front end for all Web requests from clients across the network (Internet, intranet, and extranet).
	Listener	HTTP servers or listeners handle incoming requests and route them to the dispatcher. OAS can use external HTTP listeners besides the Oracle Web Listener (Spyglass).
	Adapter	Common API for use by Oracle and third-party listeners to connect to the dispatcher.
	Dispatcher	Taking its cue from the HTTP Listener, it dispatches a request to a cartridge instance depending on the cartridge type (PL/SQL, Java, and so forth).
	Virtual Path Manager	Provides the dispatcher the cartridge mapping and authentication requirements.
WRB or Oracle Application Server		Provides resource management for Web applications running as cartridges.
	Authorization host server and authorization server	Performs user authentication using available schemes. It is composed of one authentication broker and several authentication providers.
	Configuration provider	Uses the wrb.app file to provide configuration info to local or remote system components.
	Logger	Enables components to write errors, warnings, and messages to a log file or the database.
	OAS monitoring daemon	Monitors the status of OAS objects and processes.

TABLE 10-3. *OAS 4.0 Layer Components*

Layer	Components	Description
	Resource Manager	Watches the Cartridge Server processes and instances, manages OAS processes, and evaluates and responds to requests.
	RM proxy	Obtains object references from JCORBA and EJB objects and returns them to clients.
	ORB log server	Used by ORB processes to log error and status messages.
	ORB server	Main ORB process facilitating the distribution of object requests.
	ORB metrics daemon	Collects statistics for the OAS monitoring daemon for enhanced load-balancing.
	ORB name server	Registry for OAS processes including ORB, OAS components, cartridges, and listeners, except the Node Manager.
	ORB monitor daemon	Brings up and monitors ORB components.
Applications		Consisting of applications, cartridges, and Cartridge Servers.
	Application	Controls cartridges executing application code.
	Cartridge	Uses configuration data and passed parameters to execute code in the server. Cartridges are contained within applications. If under an application, they must be components of the same cartridge type.
	Cartridge Server	Process that runs an application using one or more cartridges.
	Cartridge Server factory	Component of the Cartridge Server that instantiates a cartridge. It does this when the Cartridge Server first starts up and when requests for cartridges come in.

TABLE 10-3. *OAS 4.0 Layer Components* (continued)

Understanding that Applications Now Contain Cartridges

The OAS 4.0 architecture involves a new important component called *application*. Application is a method of grouping a set of similar cartridges. Requests from the Web that require processing and database access code to be executed in the server are executed through an application. An application is configured to use cartridges of the same type. For example, a PL/SQL cartridge provides access to the database and a way to execute PL/SQL code. A JWeb cartridge contains a Java Virtual Machine, or JVM, to execute Java class files. The Perl cartridge includes a Perl interpreter that executes Perl scripts. Multiple cartridges, which must be of the same type, can be configured and reside within an application.

Tuning the Cartridge Server, Which Can Run Multithreaded Cartridges

Unlike OWAS 3.0, in which a single Cartridge Server handles only one user request at a time, OAS 4.0 is multithreaded. In this architecture, multiple instances of the same cartridge can run simultaneously in the same process, which is called a Cartridge Server. In OWAS 3.0, each cartridge instance was a separate process, but the new architecture enables multiple cartridge instances to share memory and processing space. Each Cartridge Server has a queue of threads servicing requests as they are received. To take advantage of multithreading, the cartridge code must be thread-safe; cartridges can be thread-safe in two ways:

- **Globally thread-safe** Global resources shared by cartridge instances are protected from corruption by out-of-sequence accesses using a programmatic locking mechanism.
- **Instance-context thread-safe** Cartridges are coded using multiple threads. Data shared by threads within an instance is protected from corruption by out-of-sequence accesses using a programmatic locking mechanism.

Depending on the thread safety of a cartridge, performance can be tuned by adjusting the minimum and maximum number of concurrent instances of the cartridge, and the minimum and maximum number of threads per server.

The number of threads and instances is configurable depending on whether the cartridge you are using is "multithread safe", meaning your application can run without the possibility of locking out some of the process resources. Multithread safe cartridges are synonymous with stateless cartridges (that can run multiple threads safely per cartridge instance). Stateful cartridges, on the other hand, can only run one thread per cartridge instance. They are not designed to work in a multithreaded environment because they contain structures or variables that are not protected. Table 10-4 indicates which cartridges are stateless and which ones are stateful.

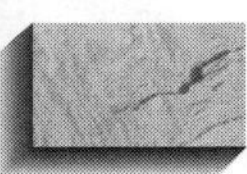

TIP
When you stop Cartridge Servers and cartridge instances, they do not need to be restarted. The Application Server will be automatically restarted when it receives a request for the cartridge.

TIP
As evident in Table 10-4, many of the cartridges, including the PL/SQL cartridge, are not multithreaded. If you set the number of threads to a number greater than 1, the Cartridge Server still reserves spaces for the additional threads, which will never be used. Be sure not to set the maximum number of threads for stateful cartridges to a number higher or lower than the number of cartridge instances. Identical to OWAS, you still need to configure your cartridge instance minimums and maximums as in previous releases.

Cartridge Type	Configuration
PL/SQL	Stateful
JWeb	Stateful
LiveHTML	Stateful
C	Stateful or stateless depending on the C cartridge being multithread safe
JCORBA	Stateful or stateless depending on the JCORBA object being multithread safe
EJB	Stateful or stateless depending on the EJB object being multithread safe

TABLE 10-4. *Stateful or Stateless Cartridges*

Understanding OAS Transactions

The Transaction Service in OAS enables applications to perform distributed transactions, which are transactions spanning HTTP requests and/or cartridges and/or databases. Transaction Services gives state (meaning that the application knows who the user is from request to request) to your Web applications. This is a zero-code implementation creating transactions in OAS. In OWAS 3.0, the zero-code method was available for PL/SQL only. In OAS 4.0, this zero-code method is also available for Java, C, and Live HTML.

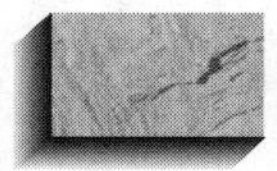

TIP
The Transaction Service feature is available only in the Enterprise edition of OAS.

The Transaction Service enables you to perform distributed transactions. It demarcates transactions (it begins, commits, and rolls back transactions) and tracks operations within the transaction scope.

You use the Transaction Service in conjunction with a database access API, such as OCI or JDBC. The database access API performs database operations, such as parsing SQL statements, executing statements, and fetching the execution results. However, instead of using the database access API mechanism for beginning, committing, or rolling back transactions, or establishing connections to the database, let the transaction service perform these operations for you.

The Transaction Service includes the Transaction Manager and the Resource Manager. When a cartridge demarcates a transaction using the Transaction Service or performs an operation within the scope of a transaction, the call goes to the Transaction Manager. The Transaction Manager coordinates transaction requests from cartridges: it analyzes requests and forwards them to the Resource Manager with the proper transaction identification. The Resource Manager component is usually a database, such as Oracle7 or Oracle8.

Transactions can span HTTP requests; these transactions are known as *conversational transactions.*

Determining When to Use the Transaction Service

You should use the Transaction Service when you need to group database operations into transactions, and when those operations span multiple requests or databases. The cartridges that support the Transaction Service are as follows:

- PL/SQL
- JWeb
- C
- LiveHTML
- JCORBA and EJB objects

Balancing the Load

OAS has considerable load-balancing capabilities. OAS balances incoming requests among the following:

- **Nodes** For maximum scalability, OAS automatically distributes requests evenly among all nodes that comprise a site.
- **Cartridge Servers** For each cartridge type, OAS distributes requests among Cartridge Servers according to configurable site-wide minimum and maximum numbers of Cartridge Servers.
- **Cartridge Instances** For each cartridge type, OAS assigns requests to cartridge instances according to configurable minimum and maximum numbers of instances per Cartridge Server.

In addition to the load-balancing features provided by the standard edition, OAS 4.0 Enterprise edition enables the configuration of load-balancing among nodes using the OAS Manager. OAS 4.0 Enterprise edition enables you to configure the following types of load-balancing using OAS Manager:

- **Weighted Node** Use the HostServerWeight parameter to specify the percentage of Cartridge Servers running on each node. For example, if node A is a large, fast machine, you might specify that it run 50 percent of the Cartridge Servers.
  If nodes B and C are smaller, less powerful machines, you might assign each 25 percent of the Cartridge Server load.
- **Host Maximum** Use the HostMaxServers parameter to limit the number of cartridge instances running on a per-host basis. The limits on each host can be different.
- **Host Minimum** Use the HostMinServers parameter to monitor and adapt to changes in the Cartridge Server load, and to distribute the Cartridge Server load evenly across the nodes.

- **Adding Hosts at Runtime** This features enables you to add new nodes to a running system to handle additional loads.
- **Adapting to System Resource Usage** OAS monitors system resources on each node, such as CPU, memory, and swap space usage, and adjusts the Cartridge Server load on each node accordingly.

Balancing Cartridge Server Load

The Hosts form enables the use of several hosts to balance the load for your Cartridge Servers. Load-balancing involves scheduling accesses to shared resources. In OAS, the resources are the cartridge instances in the system. Load-balancing involves shielding accesses to these cartridge instances.

The Hosts form contains the following fields, as illustrated in Table 10-5.

OAS enables you to determine the distribution of your applications. The load-balancing options are as follows:

- **By weights** Use only the weight proportional to each host, which is a percentage you establish. This is the default load-balancing method.
- **By machine load** Use only the load of the machine CPU and memory to dynamically calculate host weights, depending on each node's load. You do not need to enter a weight in the Hosts form.
- **By weights and machine load** Use both the weight and load of the machine.

Balancing Listener Load

The OAS architecture enables you to scale listener performance by configuring multiple listeners on a single node, or multiple listeners on several nodes. The Web Listener offers further performance enhancements by redirecting requests to other listeners when its maximum number of concurrent connections is reached. This automatic redirection feature provides a transparent load-balancing among listeners.

Being Ready with Failure Recovery

OAS 4.0 provides enhanced mechanisms for failure detection and recovery of listeners and Cartridge Servers. It is also distributed and self-monitoring. Upon detection of a failure, OAS restarts the failed component and attempts to restore it to the state just before the failure.

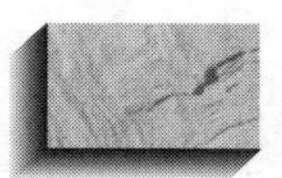

TIP
By default, many of the failure recovery components are not enabled.

Field	Comments
Select	A checkbox option to select a particular host.
Host	Displays the host name—for example, isp-sun31.
Min # of servers	Specifies the minimum number of Cartridge Servers running on the node. When the Application Server starts up, it starts up the minimum number of Cartridge Servers. As it receives requests beyond the minimum number of Cartridge Servers it can handle, it starts up more Cartridge Servers, up to the maximum number.
Max # of servers	Specifies the maximum number of Cartridge Servers running on the node. When the Application Server starts up, it starts up the minimum number of Cartridge Servers. As it receives requests beyond the minimum number of Cartridge Servers it can handle, it starts up more Cartridge Servers, up to the maximum number.
Weight	Displays the percentage of Cartridge Server processes of this Cartridge Server type running on each host. This is useful in situations where a particular host can handle higher loads than other hosts. Valid values are 0.04 to 1. If you enter 0, Oracle Application Server uses 0.5 as the weight value. For example, if host A is a large, fast machine, you might specify it to run 0.5, or 50 percent of your Cartridge Servers. If hosts B and C are smaller, less powerful machines, you might assign each 0.25, or 25 percent of the Cartridge Server load.

TABLE 10-5. *Host Form Fields*

Clamping Down on Security

OAS 4.0 supports the following authentication mechanisms:

- Basic
- IP address–based
- Domain name–based

- Basic Oracle
- LDAP-based

LDAP-based security is new as of OAS 4.0 and is available only in OAS 4.0 Enterprise edition. You can configure virtual paths so users requesting access to the paths are verified against a directory server using X.509 digital certificates. OAS can access the contents of directory servers that support Lightweight Directory Access Protocol (LDAP) v3.

LDAP is a protocol enabling clients to access information from a directory server. This protocol enables corporate directory entries to be arranged in a hierarchical structure reflecting geographic and organizational boundaries. In the context of OAS, you can protect URLs by associating them with certificates. The certificate provider accesses a directory server, possibly over Secure Sockets Layer (SSL, which is described in further detail in Chapter 15), to verify the user has a certificate enabling the execution of a specific URL.

OAS has been tested with LDAP-compliant servers. Directory servers are used by organizations to define a hierarchical view of the organization's employees, units, and other resources.

Directory servers use standard attribute names to define entries in the server. For example, "o" stands for organization, "ou" stands for organizational unit, and "uid" stands for user ID.

When you protect virtual paths using directory servers, you can limit access to the virtual paths to particular branches in a directory server. For example, given the preceding structure, you can specify that only users in the finance branch can access a virtual path.

Users identify themselves using X.509 v3 certificates. OAS reads the certificate and verifies the user specified by the certificate is in the allowed portion of the directory server.

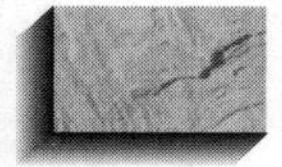

TIP

You can use certificates and directory servers to protect only virtual paths associated with cartridges. You cannot use them to protect virtual paths associated with static files or CGI scripts.

Advancements in Cartridges

The PL/SQL cartridge has enhanced parameter passing and improved custom authentication mechanisms. LiveHTML uses Perl as its server-side scripting language. Java support has been enhanced with the introduction of JWeb, JSQL, JCorba, and EJB. The following sections discuss each of these advancements.

Installing the PL/SQL Cartridge Web Toolkit

The PL/SQL Web Toolkit is installed in a common, system-specified schema, installing the Web Toolkit once per database. The PL/SQL Web Toolkit is now installed using the schemas located in Table 10-6.

When the OAS_PUBLIC packages are installed, they are granted EXECUTE privilege to PUBLIC; then, PUBLIC synonyms are created. Virtually any user in the database will be able to access the Web Toolkit.

The WEBSYS packages are granted EXECUTE privileges to a role named OWS_STANDARD_ROLE. These packages are used for Content Services, which are discussed shortly.

Schema	Tables	Packages
OAS_PUBLIC	None	htf
		htp
		owa
		owa_cookie
		owa_custom
		owa_image
		owa_opt_lock
		owa_pattern
		owa_sec
		owa_text
		owa_util
WEBSYS	ows_attributes	owa_content
	owa_content	ows_cs
	ows_fixed_attrib	
	ows_object	

TABLE 10-6. *PL/SQL Web Toolkit Installation Map*

Comparing Applications to PL/SQL Agents

In OAS 4.0, the PL/SQL Agent concept is obsolete. PL/SQL cartridges, separately configured, can be grouped into applications. An application enables you to manage a set of cartridges as one entity, because it runs in the same Cartridge Server process. This includes stopping all cartridges within an application, or changing logging parameters for all cartridges in a specified application.

A PL/SQL cartridge can be associated with a specific virtual path. By default, it adds a virtual path record to the cartridge configuration containing the application and cartridge name. The following is an example of the URL:

http://www.tusc.com/appname/cartname/pkgname.procname?param=value

In OWAS 3.0, you were required to specify port numbers in the PL/SQL Agent configuration. These port numbers identified the HTTP listeners using the PL/SQL Agent. In OAS 4.0, these port numbers are no longer required.

The following indicates how OAS uses the PL/SQL cartridge to handle requests:

1. The HTTP listener receives a request from a client browser, and determines if the request can be handled by the listener (for example, static pages), or if the WRB should handle the request. This request's virtual path is a cartridge; therefore, the dispatcher forwards the request to the Web Request Broker (WRB).

2. From the virtual path, the WRB determines which PL/SQL cartridge should handle the request, and sends the request to a Cartridge Server running within the application.

3. In the Cartridge Server, the PL/SQL cartridge uses the DAD's configuration values to determine which database to connect and how to set up the PL/SQL database client configuration.

4. The PL/SQL cartridge connects to the database, prepares the call parameters, and then invokes the stored procedure.

5. The stored procedure generates an HTML page, which can include data accessed from database tables.

6. The output from the stored procedure is then sent back to the PL/SQL cartridge, then on to the client browser.

TIP

Currently, the NT environment has a 512-byte limitation on the expanded length of some environment variables (CLASSPATH, JAVA_HOME, and so forth). Some OAS cartridges and JCO objects will try to expand environment variables. Therefore, make sure your environment variables are not longer than 250–300 characters long.

Using Flexible Parameter Passing

With the new Flexible Parameter Passing feature you do not have to match HTML form parameter names with your PL/SQL stored procedure parameter names. The parameter name obtained from the Web environment QUERY_STRING is now regarded as data. The follow procedure shows an example of the parameter types required to use Flexible Parameter Passing:

```
proc_name(
    num_entries  in number,
    name_array   in owa.vc_arr,
    value_array  in owa.vc_arr,
    reserved     in owa.vc_arr)
```

The following list explains the components of the preceding procedure:

- proc_name is the name of the PL/SQL procedure to be invoked.
- num_entries specifies the number of name-value pairs in the Web environment QUERY_STRING. This could also be determined from the PL/SQL variable name_array.count or value_array.count.
- name_array specifies the parameter names passed in the query string.
- value_array specifies the values passed in the query string.
- reserved is not used currently. It is reserved for future use.

The following is an example of an actual procedure that prints out the name-value pairs in the query string:

```
create or replace procedure list_query_string(
    num_entries  in number,
    name_array   in owa.vc_arr,
    value_array  in owa.vc_arr,
    reserved     in owa.vc_arr)
is
begin
    htp.htmlopen;
    htp.headopen;
    htp.title('Flexible Parameter Passing Example');
    htp.headclose;
    htp.bodyopen;
    htp.header(1, 'Flexible Parameter Passing Example');
    htp.print('QUERY_STRING contains ' || to_char(num_entries) ||
              ' name-value pairs.');
    htp.dlistopen;
    for counter in 1 .. num_entries
```

```
    loop
        htp.dlistterm(name_array(counter));
        htp.dlistdef(value_array(counter));
    end loop;
    htp.dlistclose;
    htp.bodyclose;
    htp.htmlclose;
end;
```

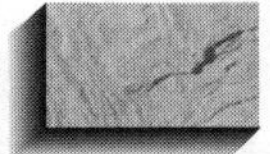

TIP
Using prerelease versions of Oracle 8i (8.1.4) and OAS with stored procedures having more than 20 parameters will result in ORA-65513 error (OAS 4.0 release notes). Using the Flexible Parameter Passing feature is a method to avoid this problem.

Using Positional Parameter Passing

The PL/SQL cartridge makes two database hits each time it handles a request for a stored procedure. The first database hit verifies the procedure exists within the database. The second database hit executes the stored procedure.

You can force the PL/SQL cartridge to execute the procedure on the first hit by using a ^ (caret) character in the URL. When using this feature, it causes parameters for the procedure to be matched by position instead of by name. The parameter names do not have to match—they just have to be complete and in the same order.

TIP
You must check your procedure and parameter lists carefully, because error messages will occur if mismatched parameters exist, and this will be difficult to debug.

The following examples demonstrate both the traditional (call by name) method and the new Positional Parameter Passing method. The first example is the traditional call to a procedure chk_emp with the parameters emp_name and dept_id:

```
http://www.tusc.com/hr/plsql/chk_emp?emp_name=BILL&dept_id=20
```

If you use the traditional (call by name) method, your procedure declaration should appear identical to one of the two following examples:

```
procedure ckh_emp (emp_name in varchar2, dept_id in varchar2) is
```

or

```
procedure ckh_emp (dept_id in varchar2, emp_name in varchar2) is
...
```

When you use the Positional Parameter Passing feature, the parameters must be defined in the correct order. Therefore, your procedure must be declared, as follows:

```
procedure ckh_emp (emp_name in varchar2, dept_id in varchar2) is
```

and is called with this syntax:

```
http://www.tusc.com/hr/plsql/^chk_emp?emp_name=BILL&dept_id=20
```

In the preceding example, the caret (^) appears before the procedure name chk_emp and different parameter names are used. We used Positional Parameter Passing; therefore, the parameter names are ignored.

TIP
The Positional Parameter Passing feature does not work with the Flexible Parameter Passing feature.

Executing PL/SQL Source Files from Script

PL/SQL source files can be directly executed from the file system without storing the procedure code in the database. This new feature is convenient for developers who do not want to store development code in the database because of time constraints in reloading the procedures into the database during application development.

Anonymous PL/SQL blocks must be used on the file when executed from the Web; in other words, the PL/SQL block should not be defining a procedure or function. The file must start with a DECLARE or BEGIN statement. Name your PL/SQL source files with the .sql extension. You will need to indicate the extension in the URL, as well.

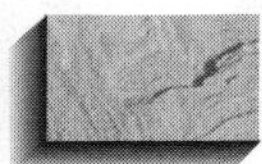

TIP
If you are using the PL/SQL cartridge to run SQL files from the file system, the SQL file cannot have a forward slash (/) at the end of the file. If a forward slash is present at the end of the file, the PL/SQL cartridge will be unable to execute the specified file.

The location of your SQL files is configured through the virtual mapping scheme of a specified PL/SQL cartridge. The DAD named in the PL/SQL cartridge will be used to connect to the database when the SQL file is executed. The following is an example of the URL to execute a PL/SQL script existing in a file (hello.sql):

```
http://www.tusc.com:9001/test/sql/hello.sql
```

In the preceding syntax, /test/sql is a virtual map configured in a PL/SQL cartridge mapping to a physical directory, such as the c:\mywebsql\ directory. The hello.sql script must be placed in the c:\mywebsql\ physical directory.

Parameters can be passed to the PL/SQL source file in the URL's QUERY_STRING environment in the same way they can be passed to the Common Gateway Interface (CGI), as name-value pairs. In the PL/SQL code, you can access the name-value pairs using bind variables syntax, which uses a colon (**:**) to indicate a passed variable.

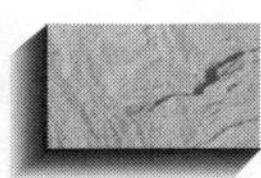

TIP
You cannot bind arrays in PL/SQL files because arrays are not supported as bind variables.

TIP
You cannot use the source file execution feature with the Positional Parameter Passing feature because the parameter passing feature only applies to stored procedures.

The following source code demonstrates how easy it is to create a Web application using PL/SQL source from files. The SQL script named qry_pkg.sql displays all packages created in the DAD schema. The SQL script named qry_pkg_dtl.sql displays the package specification or body, depending on the parameter passed from the URL.

The results of the source code for qry_pkg.sql are shown in Figure 10-6, and the source code itself in the following code listing.

```
--
--qry_pkg.sql - Displays packages owned by current schema
-- in the executing DAD
-
 declare
  cursor c_pkg is
  select distinct name
  from   user_source
  where  type = 'PACKAGE'
  order  by name;
begin
  htp.htmlopen;
```

```
  htp.headopen;
  htp.title('Packages');
  htp.headclose;
  htp.bodyopen;
  htp.header(3, 'Packages for user '||user);
  for r_pkg in c_pkg loop
     htp.anchor('qry_pkg_dtl.sql?pkg_name='||r_pkg.name||'&'||
                'pkg_type=spec',r_pkg.name);
     htp.br;
  end loop;
  htp.bodyclose;
  htp.htmlclose;
end;
 -- NOTE, do not put a / here
```

Figure 10-7 is an example of a Web page generated by PL/SQL source file qry_pkg_dtl.sql with parameters pkg_name and pkg_type passed with values of *EMPLOYEE* and Spec, respectively. The source code itself is shown next.

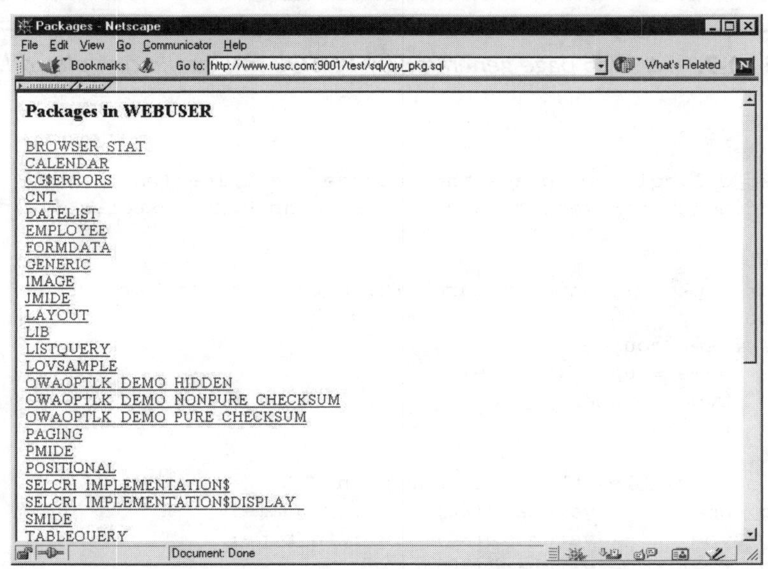

FIGURE 10-6. *A Web page generated by PL/SQL source file qry_pkg.sql*

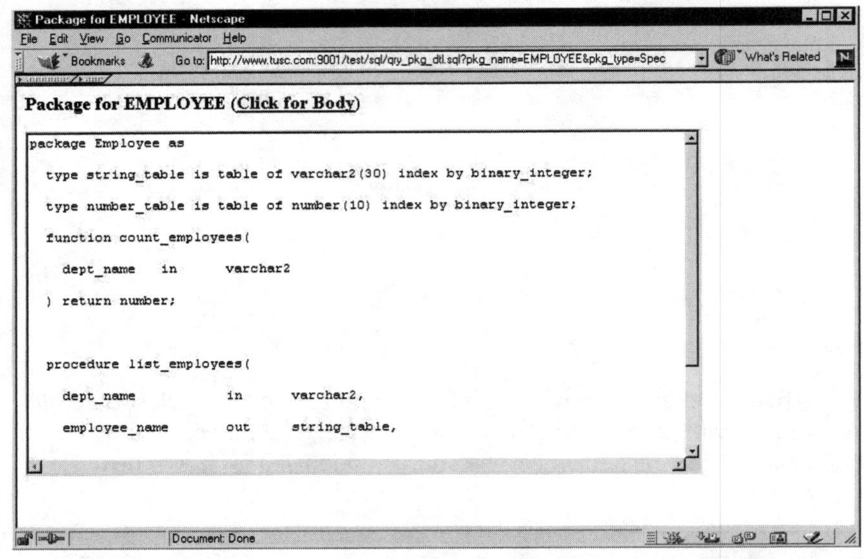

FIGURE 10-7. *A Web page generated by PL/SQL source file qry_pkg_dtl.sql*

```
--
--qry_pkg_dtl.sql - Displays the package specification or body
--(depending on parameters passed) inside an HTML textarea field.
-
 declare
   cursor c_pkg_s(p_name in varchar2, p_type in varchar2) is
   select *
   from   user_source
   where  name = upper(p_name)
   and    type = upper(p_type)
   order  by line;

   -- Bind variables that are passed in URL
   l_pkg_name       varchar2(60)  := :pkg_name;
   l_pkg_type       varchar2(30)  := :pkg_type;
   l_pkg_other_type varchar2(30);
begin
  if l_pkg_type = 'SPEC' then
     l_pkg_type       := 'PACKAGE';
     l_pkg_other_type := 'BODY';
  else
     l_pkg_type       := 'PACKAGE BODY';
     l_pkg_other_type := 'SPEC';
```

```
  end if;
  htp.htmlopen;
  htp.headopen;
  htp.title(initcap(l_pkg_type) ||' for '||l_pkg_name);
  htp.headclose;
  htp.bodyopen;
  htp.header(3, initcap(l_pkg_type) ||' for '||l_pkg_name||' ('||
          htf.anchor('qry_pkg_dtl.sql?pkg_name='||l_pkg_name||'&'||
                     'pkg_type='||htf.escape_url(l_pkg_other_type),
                     'click for '||l_pkg_other_type)||')');
  htp.formopen('pkgspecform');
  htp.formtextareaopen('pkgspec',20,80);
  for r_pkg_s in c_pkg_s(l_pkg_name,l_pkg_type) loop
     htp.print(r_pkg_s.text);
  end loop;
  htp.formtextareaclose;
  htp.formclose;
  htp.bodyclose;
  htp.htmlclose;
end;
 -- NOTE, do not put a / here
```

Implementing Your Own Custom Authentication

Custom Authentication was implemented in OWAS 3.0 using the privinit.sql file. OAS 4.0 uses the privcust.sql file. The privcust.sql file contains a copy of the OWA_CUSTOM package body, enabling developers to easily provide custom authentication. The privcust.sql file can be found in the $ORACLE_HOME/ows/cartx/plsql/admin subdirectory.

The Custom Authentication feature is useful when controlling the access to your applications—for example, access of stored procedures for an application by different types of users.

TIP
Custom authentication cannot be mixed with the BASIC_ORACLE or dynamic database authentication features. The username and password for the DAD must be stored in the configuration file.

TIP
If you implemented owa_init.authorize in each user's schema in version 3.0, you will need to migrate the function for each schema to the OWA_CUSTOM package in OAS 4.0.

The following describes the available OWA_SEC.SET_AUTHORIZATION options for using the OWA_CUSTOM package:

- **NO_CHECK** Any user will be able to access any package in a DAD schema and will *not* be prompted by a custom authentication login. If NO_CHECK is used, you may use types of authentication other than the custom authentication; therefore, this is referred to as the "no check" custom authentication scheme.
- **GLOBAL** Before any user can access any package in any DAD schema, the user will be subject to pass the criteria in the authorize function of the OWA_CUSTOM package.
- **PER_PACKAGE** Before any user can access procedures in a package, the user will be subject to pass the criteria in the authorize function of the package executed. If the procedure executed is not in a package, or if the package does not contain an authorize function, the user will be subject to pass the criteria in the OWA_CUSTOM package's authorize function.
- **CUSTOM** Only selected users can access any package in certain DAD schemas, requiring a login—referred to as the CUSTOM authentication scheme.

Understanding the NO_CHECK Option

If you want the no check authentication scheme to be enabled, modifications are not required as long as the default Web Toolkit installation has not been altered. To reset the no check authentication scheme, perform the following steps:

1. Modify the privcust.sql file and edit the OWA_CUSTOM package body to pass the *OWA_SEC.NO_CHECK* as the parameter to the *owa_sec.set_authorization* function in the anonymous PL/SQL block. For example:

   ```
   owa_sec.set_authorization(OWA_SEC.NO_CHECK)
   ```

2. Execute the privcust.sql file in SQL*Plus in the OAS_PUBLIC schema, which will recompile the OWA_CUSTOM package body for the entire site.

TIP
For authorization scheme changes to take effect in the client browser, exit and reopen the browser. When switching authorization schemes, you will need to bounce the OAS site on the server.

The following script is a copy of the original version of the OWA_CUSTOM package body as distributed in privcust.sql file:

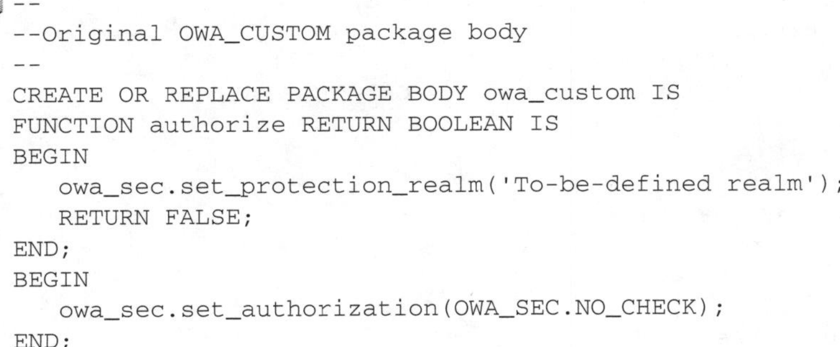

```
--
--Original OWA_CUSTOM package body
--
CREATE OR REPLACE PACKAGE BODY owa_custom IS
FUNCTION authorize RETURN BOOLEAN IS
BEGIN
   owa_sec.set_protection_realm('To-be-defined realm');
   RETURN FALSE;
END;
BEGIN
   owa_sec.set_authorization(OWA_SEC.NO_CHECK);
END;
```

Understanding the GLOBAL Option

To implement the GLOBAL custom authentication scheme, perform the following steps:

1. Modify the privcust.sql file and edit the OWA_CUSTOM package body, to pass OWA_SEC.GLOBAL as the parameter to the owa_sec.set_authorization function in the OWA_CUSTOM anonymous PL/SQL block, as illustrated in the following line of code:

   ```
   owa_sec.set_authorization(OWA_SEC.GLOBAL)
   ```

2. Modify the authorize function in OWA_CUSTOM package body to authenticate the user as you wish users to be authenticated—for example, accessing a custom-made acme_web_users table or other criteria, then returning True or False depending on the results of the authentication. Returning a value of True will grant the user access (authentication succeeded), and returning a value of False will deny access to the user.
3. Modify the line in the authorize function, *set_protection_realm*, to a desired login prompt label, as illustrated in the following line of code:

   ```
   owa_sec.set_protection_realm('For Authorized Members Only');
   ```

4. Execute the privcust.sql file in SQL*Plus in the OAS_PUBLIC schema, which will recompile the OWA_CUSTOM package body for the entire site.

The following is an example of an OWA_CUSTOM package compiled in OAS_PUBLIC, modified for the GLOBAL custom authentication scheme:

```
--
-- Modified OWA_CUSTOM package body for the GLOBAL
-- authentication scheme
--
create or replace package body owa_custom is
function authorize return boolean is
   username varchar2(30) := owa_sec.get_user_id;
```

```
   userpwd  varchar2(30) := owa_sec.get_password;
   dummy    varchar2(1);
begin
   owa_sec.set_protection_realm('For Members Only (GLOBAL)');
   select 'x'
   into   dummy
   from   acme_web_users
   where  uname = username
   and    upass = userpwd;
   return true;
exception
   when no_data_found then
        return false;
end;
begin
   owa_sec.set_authorization(owa_sec.global);
end;
```

The following dialog box is displayed upon success when invoking the GLOBAL custom authentication scheme.

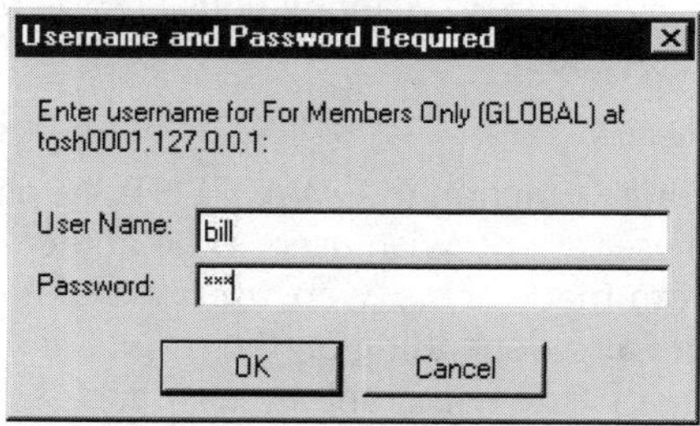

The following dialog box demonstrates the Alert box viewed if authorization has failed.

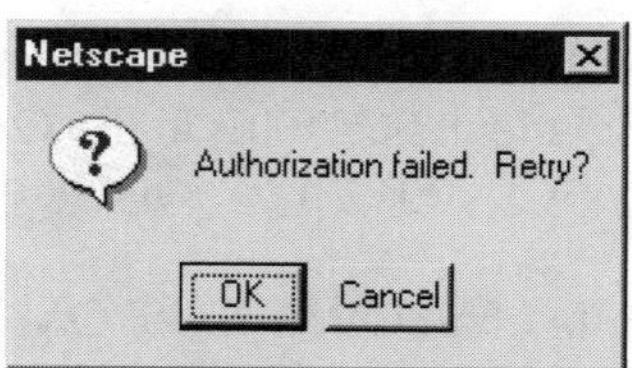

Understanding the PER_PACKAGE Option

To implement the PER_PACKAGE authentication scheme, you need to do the following:

1. Modify the privcust.sql file and edit the OWA_CUSTOM package body, to pass *OWA_SEC.PER_PACKAGE* as the parameter to the *owa_sec.set_authorization* function in the OWA_CUSTOM anonymous PL/SQL block, as illustrated in the following line of code:

   ```
   owa_sec.set_authorization(OWA_SEC.PER_PACKAGE)
   ```

2. If desired, you can modify the authorize function in the OWA_CUSTOM package body to authenticate the user as you wish users to be authenticated, as in the preceding GLOBAL example. This package will be used as the catchall for packageless procedures and packages without an authorize function.
3. Execute the privcust.sql file in SQL*Plus in the *OAS_PUBLIC* schema to recompile the OWA_CUSTOM package body as the site default.
4. Create an authorize function in each of the packages accessed from the Web. Declare the authorize function in these packages. This function can be copied from the originally installed authorize function in OWA_CUSTOM. Code the authorize function in each package to authenticate the user using a custom-made user table and/or some other criteria and then return True or False, depending on the results of the authentication. Returning True will enable the user to execute the procedure requested in the URL, while returning False will deny access to the user. For example, you could modify the line in the authorize function to set the protection realm to a desired login prompt label, as the following syntax illustrates:

   ```
   owa_sec.set_protection_realm('For Special Authorized Members Only');
   ```

5. Execute the source SQL file for your package in SQL*Plus (in your DAD's schema), which will recompile the package body.

TIP
If you do not create an authorize function for a package or a schema whose anonymous procedure is being accessed from the Web, a request failed error will occur.

The following code illustrates both the modified OWA_CUSTOM package body and a sample package protected by using the PER_PACKAGE custom authentication scheme:

```
--
--Modified OWA_CUSTOM package body for the PER_PACKAGE authentication
```

```
--scheme
--
create or replace package body owa_custom is
-- This function will be used under the PER_PACKAGE scheme only
-- when an unpackaged procedure is executed or when a package does
-- not contain an authorize function.
function authorize return boolean is
begin
   return true;
end;
begin
   owa_sec.set_authorization(owa_sec.per_package);
end;
--
-- Sample package protected using the PER_PACKAGE scheme
--
create or replace package sample is
function  authorize return boolean;
procedure startpage;
end;

create or replace package body sample is
function authorize return boolean is
   username varchar2(30) := owa_sec.get_user_id;
   userpwd  varchar2(30) := owa_sec.get_password;
   dummy    varchar2(1);
begin
   owa_sec.set_protection_realm('For Special Authorized Members Only');
   select 'x'
   into  dummy
   from  acme_web_users
   where upass          = username
   and   upass          = userpwd
   and special_user     = 'Y';
   return true;
exception
   when no_data_found then
        return false;
end;
procedure startpage is
--
-- Displays packages owned by schema in DAD
--
cursor c_pkg is
   select distinct name
   from  user_source
   where type = 'PACKAGE'
   order by name;
begin
```

```
  http.htmlopen;
  http.headopen;
  http.title('Packages');
  http.headclose;
  http.bodyopen;
  http.header(3, 'Packages in '||user);
  for r_pkg in c_pkg loop
     http.anchor('qry_pkg_dtl.sql?pkg_name='||r_pkg.name||'&'||
                'pkg_type=spec',r_pkg.name);
     htp.br;
  end loop;
  http.bodyclose;
  http.htmlclose;
end startpage;
end sample;
```

Understanding the CUSTOM Option

To implement the CUSTOM authentication scheme, perform the following steps:

1. Modify the privcust.sql file containing the OWA_CUSTOM package body to pass *OWA_SEC.CUSTOM* as the parameter to the *owa_sec.set_authorization* function in the OWA_CUSTOM anonymous PL/SQL block, as illustrated in the following line of code:

   ```
   owa_sec.set_authorization(OWA_SEC.CUSTOM)
   ```

2. Modify the authorize function in the OWA_CUSTOM package body to handle "catchall" situations. If the authentication server does not find an OWA_CUSTOM package in the user schema, it will call the authorize function in the OWA_CUSTOM package in the *OAS_PUBLIC* schema.
3. Execute the privcust.sql file in SQL*Plus, which will recompile the OWA_CUSTOM package body in *OAS_PUBLIC* schema.
4. Create an OWA_CUSTOM package (you could copy the OWA_CUSTOM package in the *OAS_PUBLIC* schema for a foundation) containing an authorize function in each DAD's schema that you want secured individually. Code the authorize function in each DAD schema to authenticate the user accessing a custom-made user table and/or some other criteria, and then return True or False depending on the results of the authentication. Returning True will let the user through, and returning False will deny access to the user.
5. Modify the line in the authorize function, *set_protection_realm*, to a desired login prompt label, as illustrated in the following line of code:

   ```
   owa_sec.set_protection_realm('For Custom Members Only (Global)');
   ```

6. Compile the modified OWA_CUSTOM package in the DAD schema to be protected.

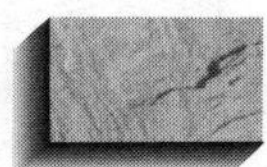

TIP
If you do not have an OWA_CUSTOM.AUTHORIZE function for a schema package procedure accessed from the Web, the PL/SQL cartridge will use the OWA_CUSTOM.AUTHORIZE function in the OAS_PUBLIC schema as the default.

The following code illustrates the modified OWA_CUSTOM package body in *OAS_PUBLIC*, and the OWA_CUSTOM package for a protected DAD schema using the CUSTOM authentication scheme:

```
--
--Modified OWA_CUSTOM package body in OAS_PUBLIC for CUSTOM scheme.
--
create or replace package body owa_custom is
-- This function will be called by default
function authorize return boolean is
begin
   -- Always returns true, which makes owa_custom
   -- defaults to no authentication required
   return true;
end;
begin
   owa_sec.set_authorization(owa_sec.custom);
end;

--
-- Modified owa_custom package body in DAD schema for custom scheme.
--
create or replace package body owa_custom is
function authorize return boolean is
   username varchar2(30) := owa_sec.get_user_id;
   userpwd  varchar2(30) := owa_sec.get_password;
   dummy    varchar2(1);
   --
begin
   owa_sec.set_protection_realm('For Custom Members Only (Global)');
   select 'x'
   into   dummy
   from   acme_web_users
   where uname= username
   and    upass       = userpwd
   and    custom_user = 'Y';
   return true;
exception
   when no_data_found then
```

```
        return false;
end;
begin
   owa_sec.set_authorization(owa_sec.custom);
end;
```

Regardless of the custom authentication scheme you choose, the main advantage of using custom authentication over the dynamic database authentication or BASIC_ORACLE authentication scheme is you have total control in securing the applications by prompting and checking for usernames and passwords tailored to your security policies. You can also add authentication criteria, including an IP address identification and cross-checks. Refer to other functions in the OWA_SEC package for further information on IP address retrieval.

Uploading and Downloading Files to and from the Database

The OAS Enterprise edition's OWA_CONTENT package enables you to upload and download files between the client (browser) and database. This new feature proves extremely useful for automating an Internet-based file management system. This package is powerful and enables considerable extensibility so you can add attributes as deemed necessary.

Look at this package in logical steps. First, if you want to upload files into the database, you might want to create an HTML script similar to the following upload.html script. The HTML files require the enctype attribute, which is unique to file uploads and automatically indicates to the PL/SQL cartridge to use the OWA_CONTENT package. The field named file, which is a type = "file," enables the user to pick a filename in the browser:

```
<html>
<head>
<title>Upload a File</title>
</head>
<body>
<h1>Upload a file</h1>
<h2>Please fill in the information below</h2>
<table>
<form enctype="multipart/form-data" action="/plsql/write_info"
      method="POST">
<tr><th>Your Name</th>
<td><input type="text" name="who"></td></tr>
<tr><th>File Description</th>
<td><input type="text" name="description"></td></tr>
<tr><th>File to upload</th>
<td><input type="file" name="file"></th></tr>
```

```
<tr><td></td>
<td><input type="submit" value="Upload File"></td></tr>
</form>
</table>
</body>
</html>
```

The preceding HTML file generates a page identical to the browser page illustrated in Figure 10-8.

The action from the preceding upload.html page calls a PL/SQL routine called write_info, which is shown below. The following script does not explicitly call the OWA_CONTENT package to insert the data into the database. As previously mentioned, this is automatically done. However, if you wish to set the parameters, use the OWA_CONTENT procedures and functions.

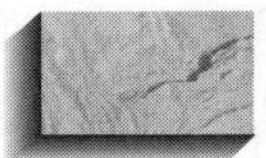

TIP

To update the database, you must add a forward slash (/) in front of the filename.

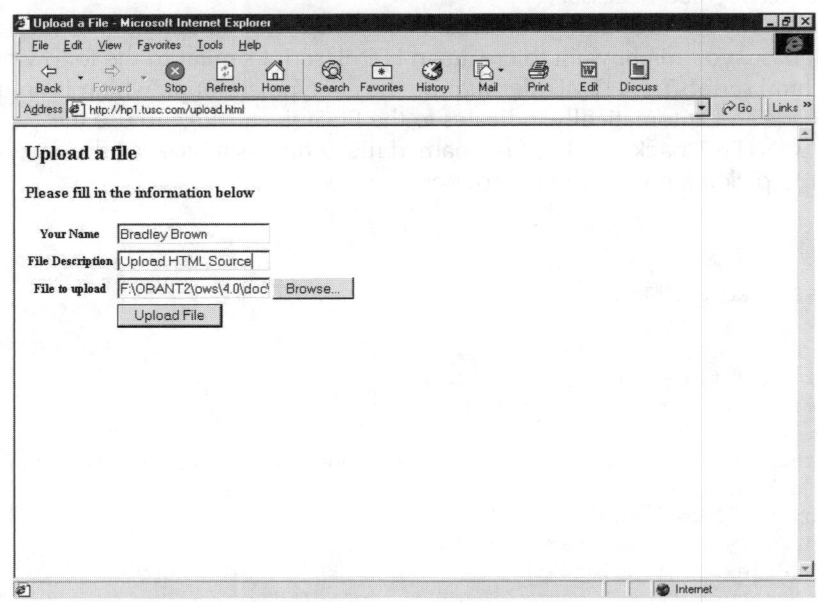

FIGURE 10-8. *Upload.html in the browser*

```
CREATE OR REPLACE procedure write_info (
    who         in varchar2,
    description in varchar2,
    file        in varchar2) as
begin
    owa_content.set_author('/'||file,who);
    owa_content.set_description('/'||file,description);
    htp.htmlopen;
    htp.headopen;
    htp.title('File Uploaded');
    htp.headclose;
    htp.bodyopen;
    htp.header(1, 'Upload Status');
    htp.print('Uploaded ' || file || ' from ' ||
              who || ' successfully.');
    htp.bodyclose;
    htp.htmlclose;
end;
```

After uploading the file, a page identical to Figure 10-9 will be displayed.

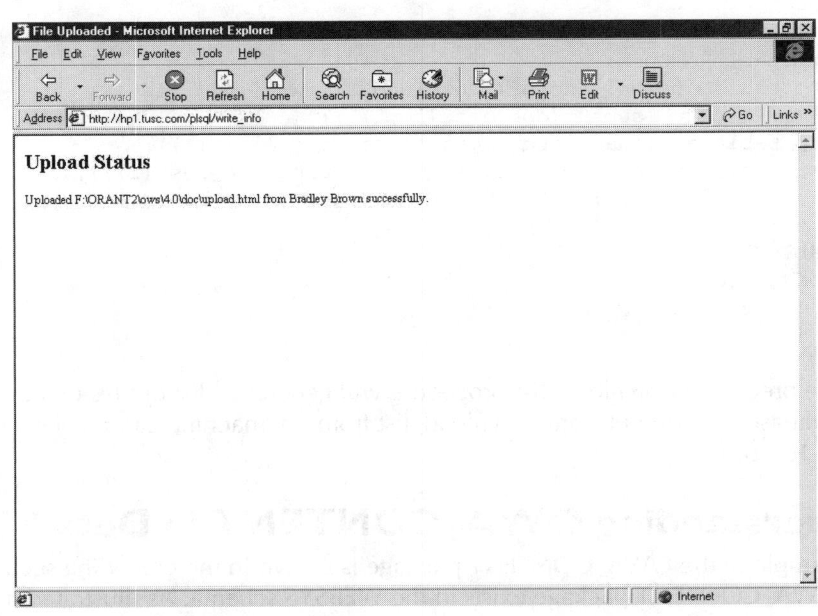

FIGURE 10-9. *Upload complete status page*

When you are ready to retrieve the files out of the database, you can use a procedure similar to the following code, called download_list:

```
create or replace procedure download_list
as
sts number;
doc_list owa_content.string_arr;
begin
sts := owa_content.list_documents(doc_list);
htp.htmlOpen;
htp.headOpen;
htp.title('Download a file');
htp.headClose;
htp.bodyOpen;
htp.header(1,'Choose a file to download');
htp.tableOpen('BORDER=1');

htp.tableRowOpen;
htp.tableHeader('Filename');
htp.tableHeader('Author');
htp.tableHeader('Description');
htp.tableRowClose;

for i in 1 .. doc_list.count loop
    htp.tableRowOpen;
    htp.tableData(htf.anchor('download?filex='||doc_list(i),
                  substr(doc_list(i),2)));
    htp.tableData(owa_content.get_author(doc_list(i)));
    htp.tableData(owa_content.get_description(doc_list(i)));
    htp.tableRowClose;
end loop;
htp.tableClose;
htp.bodyClose;
htp.htmlClose;
end;
```

The preceding download_list procedure will generate a list of files uploaded to the database. The output from download_list from my machine can be viewed in Figure 10-10.

Understanding OWA_CONTENT in Detail

An example of the OWA_CONTENT package is shown in the preceding section. The OWA_CONTENT package exists in the WEBSYS schema. As illustrated in the preceding example, the OWA_CONTENT package is automatically called and the file contents are inserted into the database, but that is all that is automatic. In other words, most of the file attributes (for example, title and description) are not set

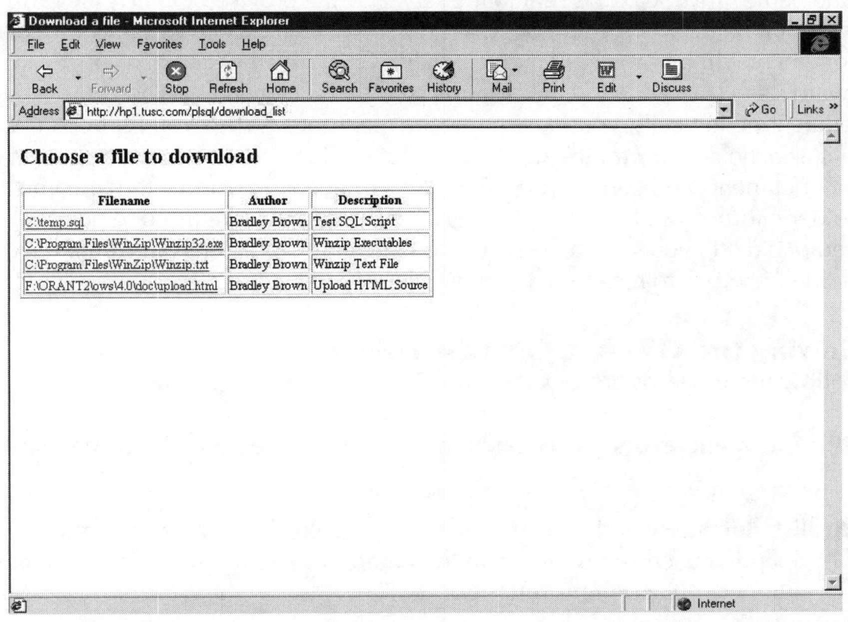

FIGURE 10-10. *Download_list output*

automatically—you must set them all manually. However, the document length attribute is automatically set.

Reviewing the OWA_CONTENT Datatypes

The OWA_CONTENT package contains three PL/SQL tables (i.e., arrays). Two are string arrays and the other is a number array. The PL/SQL tables are defined as follows:

- string_arr varchar2 (256)
- bigstring_arr varchar2 (2000)
- number_arr number

Understanding the Document's Fullname Parameter

The variable, doc_fullname, used throughout the procedures and functions, is the full path-qualified name of the document. For example, '/folder1/myfile' or '/myfile2.txt'. If you have uploaded a document ('mydoc.txt') through the PL/SQL cartridge, on Solaris, only the name ('mydoc.txt') is sent to the server by the browser. On NT, the browser sends the full path, which could be 'C:\Temp\mydoc.txt'. Once reaching the server, the document will be saved as /mydoc.txt and /C:\Temp\mydoc.txt, respectively. A forward slash (/) is added to the beginning of all the filenames. When you make procedure/function calls, you *may* supply the forefront **/**. When you list documents, you will see the added **/** for the documents that originally did not have a **/** supplied. After a document is uploaded, you can call rename_document to either rename it or add folder information. For example, on NT, if the doc uploaded is originally named 'C:\Temp\old.txt', you can call owa_content.rename_document ('C:\Temp\old.txt', 'newfolder/new.txt') to rename it to 'newfolder/new.txt'.

Reviewing the OWA_CONTENT Functions

The following functions are a part of the OWA_CONTENT package:

- **document_exists** This function will return True if the document exists.

```
function document_exists(doc_fullname in varchar2) return boolean
```

- **list_documents** This procedure retrieves the full names of all the documents currently stored in the database. The returned value contains the number of documents returned.

```
function list_documents(doc_list out string_arr) return binary_integer
```

- **get_attributes** This function will retrieve all of the attributes, including reserved and user-defined attributes, for a specific document. The predefined attributes will precede the user-defined attributes. The return value contains the number of attributes returned.

```
function get_attributes(doc_fullname in varchar2,
                        attrib_name  out string_arr,
                        attrib_type  out number_arr,
                        attrib_val   out bigstring_arr) return number
```

- **get_content_type** This function retrieves the contents stored in the predefined attribute content type.

```
function get_content_type(doc_fullname in varchar2) return varchar2;
```

- **get_author** This function retrieves the contents stored in the predefined attribute author.

```
function get_author(doc_fullname in varchar2) return varchar2;
```

- **get_expiration** This function retrieves the contents stored in the predefined attribute expiration.

```
function get_expiration(doc_fullname in varchar2) return date;
```

- **get_language** This function retrieves the contents stored in the predefined attribute language.

```
function get_language(doc_fullname in varchar2) return varchar2;
```

- **get_char_set** This function retrieves the contents stored in the predefined attribute char_set.

```
function get_char_set(doc_fullname in varchar2) return varchar2;
```

- **get_description** This function retrieves the contents stored in the predefined attribute description.

```
function get_description(doc_fullname in varchar2) return varchar2;
```

- **get_title** This function retrieves the contents stored in the predefined attribute title.

```
function get_title(doc_fullname in varchar2) return varchar2;
```

- **get_encoding** This function retrieves the contents stored in the predefined attribute encoding.

```
function get_encoding(doc_fullname in varchar2) return varchar2;
```

- **get_length** This function retrieves the contents stored in the predefined attribute length. The length attribute is automatically set by the OWA_CONTENT package.

```
function get_length(doc_fullname in varchar2) return number;
```

Reviewing the OWA_CONTENT Procedures

The following are the procedures that are a part of the OWA_CONTENT package:

- **delete_document** This procedure will delete a specific document.

```
procedure delete_document(doc_fullname in varchar2)
```

- **delete_documents** This procedure will delete a set of documents as defined in the string array that is passed to the procedure.

```
procedure delete_documents(doc_fullname_list in string_arr)
```

- **rename_document** This procedure will rename a specific document from old_fullname to new_fullname. The procedure will create a NO_DATA_FOUND exception when the document old_fullname does not exist.

```
procedure rename_document(old_fullname in varchar2,
                          new_fullname in varchar2)
```

- **get_attribute** This procedure returns information for one attribute. This could be a predefined or user-defined attribute. The procedure will create a NO_DATA_FOUND exception when the attribute (for example, attrib_name) does not exist.

```
procedure get_attribute(doc_fullname in varchar2,
                        attrib_name  in varchar2,
                        attrib_type  out number,
                        attrib_val   out varchar2)
```

- **set_attribute** This procedure only applies to user-defined attributes. Use each specific procedure (for example, set_author and set_description) for setting the predefined attributes for a document.

TIP
Not all of the predefined attributes are updatable. If the attribute name (i.e., attrib_name) specified is not found, the set_attribute procedure will create a new one. If the attribute name already exists, this procedure will update its value.

```
procedure set_attribute(doc_fullname in varchar2,
                        attrib_name  in varchar2,
                        attrib_type  in number,
                        attrib_val   in varchar2)
```

- **set_content_type** This procedure sets the predefined attribute content type.

```
procedure set_content_type(doc_fullname     in varchar2,
                           content_type_val in varchar2)
```

- **set_author** This procedure sets the predefined attribute author.

```
procedure set_author(doc_fullname in varchar2,
                     author_val   in varchar2);
```

- **set_expiration** This procedure sets the predefined attribute expiration date.

```
procedure set_expiration(doc_fullname in varchar2,
                         expire_val   in date);
```

- **set_language** This procedure sets the predefined attribute language.

```
procedure set_language(doc_fullname in varchar2,
                       language_val in varchar2);
```

- **set_char_set** This procedure sets the predefined attribute character set.

```
procedure set_char_set(doc_fullname in varchar2,
                       char_set_val in varchar2);
```

- **set_description** This procedure sets the predefined attribute description.

  ```
  procedure set_description(doc_fullname in varchar2,
                            desc_val     in varchar2);
  ```

- **set_title** This procedure sets the predefined attribute title.

  ```
  procedure set_title(doc_fullname in varchar2,
                      title_val    in varchar2);
  ```

- **set_encoding** This procedure sets the predefined attribute encoding.

  ```
  procedure set_encoding(doc_fullname in varchar2,
                         encode_val   in varchar2);
  ```

- **list_attributes** This procedure retrieves a list of all of the attribute names for a specific document.

  ```
  procedure list_attributes(doc_fullname in  varchar2,
                            attrib_name  out string_arr);
  ```

- **list_system_attributes** This procedure retrieves a list of all of the predefined (i.e., system) attribute names for a specific document.

  ```
  procedure list_system_attributes(doc_fullname in  varchar2,
                                   attrib_name  out string_arr);
  ```

- **list_user_attributes** This procedure retrieves a list of all of the user-defined (i.e., system) attribute names for a specific document.

  ```
  procedure list_user_attributes(doc_fullname in  varchar2,
                                 attrib_name  out string_arr);
  ```

- **delete_attribute** This procedure deletes an attribute for a specific document.

  ```
  procedure delete_attribute(doc_fullname in varchar2,
                             attrib_name  in varchar2);
  ```

Understanding the Content Helper (OWS_CS)

The package OWS_CS contains various helper routines used by the content services to insert/delete objects from the content schema. The OWA_CS package exists in the WEBSYS schema. For application development, use the OWA_CONTENT package to retrieve content data; the OWA_CS package is primarily for internal use only.

Using the New OWA_UTIL.MIME_HEADER Parameter

The owa_util.mime_header procedure takes a CHARSET parameter, in addition to the CCONTENT_TYPE and BCLOSE_HEADER parameters.

The CHARSET parameter is a VARCHAR2 variable and is optional. It represents the character set being used for this HTTP header and defaults to NULL.

Using the New OWA_UTIL.CELLSPRINT Parameter

The OWA_UTIL.CELLSPRINT procedure is overloaded. There is a new overloaded definition that contains an additional output parameter (P_RECCNT) specifying the number of rows that have been returned by the query.

Decommissioning of the OWA_INIT Package

The OWA_INIT package is obsolete in OAS version 4.0. It has been replaced by the OWA_CUSTOM package. Refer to the preceding section on OWA_CUSTOM for further information.

Thinking About the Perl Cartridge Enhancements

As of OAS 4.0, the Perl cartridge is considered a production cartridge. For further information regarding the Perl cartridge, refer to Chapter 20.

Considering LiveHTML Cartridge Is Now Real

OAS 4.0 uses Perl scripting for its LiveHTML cartridge. Perl scripts can be embedded inside HTML pages to include dynamic content when the HTML page is accessed. Perl accesses the Oracle database using the DBI/DBD interface. Refer to Chapter 21 for further information regarding the LiveHTML cartridge.

From LiveHTML scripts, you can access Web application objects (WAO). These objects provide a set of objects to interact with the runtime environment of Web applications. Use WAO to retrieve HTTP header values, set cookies, control the transactional attributes of a page, and access objects and methods in other cartridges.

Use WAO to set transaction features for each LiveHTML page with the transaction property enabled in the LiveHTML cartridge. Transactions span more than one cartridge if the cartridges have the transaction property enabled.

Looking at the Java Cartridges

Oracle8i is primarily focused around the Internet and Java; therefore, considerable enhancements have occurred in the Java components. For further information regarding Oracle and the Java cartridges, refer to Chapter 19.

Reviewing JWeb enhancements

The JWeb cartridge contains a Java Virtual Machine and Java class libraries. It provides a runtime environment for server-side Java applications. A Java application is a Java class that starts executing from its main() method. Java applications are platform-independent and they can access all the functionality of Java, including database access and running legacy libraries (in C) through native method interface.

The advantages of using the JWeb cartridge are as follows:

- The JWeb cartridge provides better performance than CGI, because there is no startup and shutdown of the Java Virtual Machine required for each request.
- The JWeb cartridge takes advantage of load-balancing, scalability, monitoring, logging, sessions, and other features of the Web Request Broker (WRB).
- The JWeb cartridge minimizes use of resources by running multiple Java applications on the same virtual machine and/or handling multiple requests for the same application using the same instance of the application.
- The JWeb cartridge comes with the JWeb Toolkit; the Toolkit is a set of classes that you can use to generate HTML, access databases, retrieve and set HTTP headers, and access WRB services.
- The JWeb cartridge runs Java applications on the server. It is not involved with running applets, which are downloaded and run on the client.

To invoke a Java application through the JWeb cartridge, provide the cartridge with configuration information such as virtual path and authentication information. You configure the cartridge using the OAS Manager.

The following features are new for the JWeb cartridge in OAS 4.0:

- The JWeb cartridge supports JDK 1.1.6.
- OAS 4.0 introduces the concept of applications, containing values for environment variables, such as JAVA_HOME, CLASSPATH, and LD_LIBRARY_PATH. This enables you to configure each application independently. In OWAS 3.0, these values were set for the JWeb cartridge and were used for all Java applications.
- Applications contain cartridges, and you can specify the number of instances and threads for each cartridge.
- The JWeb cartridge is multithreaded. This improves performance because multiple requests can be handled simultaneously.
- The classes in the ORACLE.OWAS.WRB.SERVICES.LOGGER package are deprecated. To log messages, use the classes in ORACLE.OAS.SERVICES.LOGGER.

Looking in to the New JCorba

OAS 4.0 supports a component-based application model in the form of JCORBA. In a component-based application model, you build an application's integrating components using development tools, often referred to as an integrated development environment (IDE). Additional examples of component-based application technologies include COM/DCOM and OpenDoc.

The JCORBA model deploys components written in Java as CORBA components. Components in the JCORBA model are JCORBA objects (JCOs). JCOs are Java classes packaged together to form an application running on OAS. Objects of these classes can be instantiated and accessed from different types of clients, such as Java applets, Java applications, CORBA, and DCOM.

JCORBA objects typically provide the business logic in JCORBA applications. The objects define methods that clients can invoke to perform a specific operation. A JCORBA application consists of one or more JCORBA objects.

When you write JCORBA applications, you receive the benefits of the Java language and the CORBA/IIOP scalability features, plus additional features provided by OAS such as load-balancing, management, monitoring, and logging capabilities. The following list details the scalability features of OAS:

- The management of JCORBA applications is integrated into the Application Server's management functions. Using the Oracle Application Server Manager, you can manage your JCORBA application and the objects within the application identical to other OAS applications.
- You can distribute your application and run it on multiple nodes on the network.
- You can perform load-balancing to achieve maximum performance.
- You do not have to become familiar with CORBA's infrastructure to create JCORBA objects because it is generated automatically for you.
- You can incorporate JCORBA objects developed by third parties in your application.

TIP

JCORBA objects run on the server and therefore do not have a GUI or any other visual representation. They contain methods that perform operations and return values to the clients. The client can display them to the user, if appropriate.

There are significant differences between JCORBA applications and other applications in the application server environment.

To develop the objects for JCORBA applications, you can use any Java development environment, Oracle JDeveloper, or the JDK from Sun Microsystems that supports Java 1.1.6 or later. Oracle JDeveloper provides tighter integration than other IDEs. It provides wizards to assist in the development and deployment processes, while providing local debugging capabilities.

You need the jar utility to package the application. This utility accompanies the distribution of JDK 1.1.6 from Sun.

Working with OAS 4.0 and Other Oracle Products

Aside from OAS 4.0 distributed as a standalone product, it is also included and used by the Oracle products outlined in the following sections. Please check with your Oracle representative for updated information regarding these products.

Looking at the Oracle Enterprise Developer Suite

Enterprise Developer Suite is a set of tools for building scalable, reliable, secure enterprise class database applications for client/server and Web deployment. Aside from OAS, it also includes Oracle Designer and the Object Extensions, Oracle Developer and Oracle Developer Server, Oracle Database Server version 7 and 8 Enterprise edition, Oracle JDeveloper, and informative documentation with code examples. Oracle Designer enables you to generate PL/SQL code to be deployed on the Web using OAS.

Thinking About the Oracle JDeveloper Suite

JDeveloper Suite provides a complete set of products for building component-based server-centric applications in Java for Web deployment. It also includes the Oracle JDBC drivers, and built-in support for SQLJ to access the Oracle database with Java code. The JDeveloper Suite includes utilities for generating Java wrappers to existing PL/SQL procedures.

Using Oracle Developer Server

Developer Server is a deployment platform enabling you to deploy your existing Oracle Developer Forms or Reports in the Web without modifying your form or report code. The Developer Server process runs as a cartridge from within Oracle Application Server. Refer to Chapter 17 and Chapter 18 for further information regarding Oracle Developer Web deployment.

Combining Oracle Applications with OAS

Web-enabled versions of the Oracle Applications product (release 11 and subsequent releases) use OAS for thin-client and wide area network deployment of back-office applications. Oracle Applications use OAS's configuration, load-balancing, failover, and management capabilities.

Using Oracle Enterprise Manager

Newer versions of the Enterprise Manager (version 2 and subsequent releases) are written in Java to achieve consistency in the user interface. The Enterprise Manager is used by DBAs and system administrators to manage distributed Oracle databases and OASs from a single browser. Enterprise Manager actually uses the OAS core ORB server to run in distributed mode and provide browser access.

Implementing Oracle Internet Commerce Server

Oracle Internet Commerce Server is Oracle's e-commerce platform for the Internet using a thin-client access to the Oracle database. ICS uses OAS's features, such as Java and PL/SQL cartridges, session management, scalability, and manageability. Refer to Chapter 22 for further information regarding the Oracle Internet Commerce Server.

Using Oracle Payment Server

Oracle Payment Server facilitates business-to-business commerce by providing thin-client access and platform for running business logic. It also uses OAS's features, such as Java and PL/SQL cartridges, session management, scalability, and manageability.

Purchasing Oracle Data Mart Suite

The Data Mart Suite warehousing product enables Web access for analysis tools. It uses OAS PL/SQL cartridges.

Using Oracle Express OLAP Server

Express OLAP Server (version 3 and subsequent releases) is an OLAP product enabling Web access for analysis plus a distributed platform for running Express agents. OAS features used include thin-client access, C++ cartridge, load-balancing, and IIOP for communication.

Reviewing Oracle Discoverer

Discoverer (version 3 and subsequent releases) is a data analysis tool using OAS features such as thin-client access, C cartridge, CORBA, scalability, and manageability.

Implementing Oracle Video Server

Video Server (version 3.0 and subsequent releases) uses OAS for Web access, scalability, manageability, and ORB for communication. This product is used for storing and playing multimedia data and capturing end-user interactions.

Comparing OAS 4.0 to OAS 4.0 Enterprise Edition

Oracle Application Server comes in two different editions—4.0 and 4.0 Enterprise editions are shipped within the same CD. You will need to indicate which version you are entitled to use when installing the product.

Table 10-7 illustrates the features found in Application Server 4.0, and the additional features found in the 4.0 Enterprise edition.

Feature	Application Server 4.0	Application Server 4.0 Enterprise Edition
Load–balancing and request scheduling	Round-robin scheduling algorithm	Node weight scheduling Adaptive request scheduler based on system load metrics Hybrid combination of node weight and system load monitoring
Server failover and component recovery support	HTTP listener process death detection and restart, dead cartridge cleanup, manual restart, process restart for Listener/dispatchers, Cartridge Server Factory, RM Proxy, Config Provider, Auth Server, Log Server	All the features of Application Server 4.0 plus automatic failover support for the following software component failures: Broker/Resource Manager state is persistent and enables greater system robustness and reduced downtimes

TABLE 10-7. *OAS 4.0 and 4.0 Enterprise Edition*

Feature	Application Server 4.0	Application Server 4.0 Enterprise Edition
Security	Basic IP Domain Oracle Basic SSL/IIOP	All of the security mechanisms from the Application Server 4.0 plus the following additional providers: LDAP provider to authenticate/authorize based on X509V3 digital certificate
Application Server services	Logger Sessions ICX	All of the Application Server 4.0 services plus the following additional services: X/Open TX API Declarative transactions OTS/JTS Content services
Cartridges	PL/SQL JWeb JServlet LiveHTML Perl CWeb VRML JCORBA Objects C++ Enterprise JavaBeans (EJB)	All of the cartridges from the Application Server 4.0 plus the following additional cartridges: WebConnect from OpenConnect Fujitsu Cobol cartridge ODBC

TABLE 10-7. *OAS 4.0 and 4.0 Enterprise Edition* (continued)

Third-Party Tools Bundled with OAS

The tools listed in Table 10-8 are bundled with OAS 4.0. For further information about these tools, refer to Chapter 2.

Reviewing OAS 4.0 Requirements

Tables 10-9 and 10-10 display the system requirements referenced in the Oracle Application 4.0.8 Release Notes.

Product	Vendor	Description	Platform
Control 1.5.220	Eventus	Web application assembly tool	Windows NT
Cobol Cartridge 1.0.0	Fujitsu	COBOL cartridge	Windows NT, Solaris
OC://WebConnect Pro	OpenConnect	Legacy-to-Web connectivity solution	Windows NT, Solaris
OpenVista OV1_8_2 (bundled with WebConnect)	OpenConnect	Legacy-to-Web connectivity solution	Windows NT
Visual Page 2.0	Symantec	HTML editor	Windows NT
Net.Medic 1.2	VitalSigns	Performance monitoring client	Windows NT
LogAnalyzer 4.0	WebTrends	Web site usage tracking and reporting software	Windows NT
Pro Suite 1.0	WebTrends	Web site usage tracking and reporting software	Windows NT
Enterprise Suite 1.5	WebTrends	Web site usage tracking and reporting software	Windows NT

TABLE 10-8. *Third-Party Tools Bundled with OAS*

Hardware	Minimum Requirement	Recommended
CPU	A SPARC processor	
Memory	128MB	512MB
Disk space	400MB	1GB
Swap space	256MB	3xmemory

TABLE 10-9. *Sun Solaris System Requirements*

Software	Requirement
Operating System	Solaris 2.5.1 O/S patches required
	Solaris 2.6 O/S patches required
	Solaris 2.7
Netscape Communicator	4.51 or 4.6
Microsoft Internet Explorer	5.0
Certified Software	**Requirement**
HTTP Listeners	Oracle 40-bit (v2.14) Oracle 128-bit (v2.14) Netscape Enterprise Server 3.6.2 Apache 1.3.6
Oracle RDBMS	7.3.4 8.0.5 8.1.5

TABLE 10-9. *Sun Solaris System Requirements* (continued)

Hardware	Minimum Requirement	Recommended
CPU	A Pentium-level processor	PIII
Memory	128MB	512MB
Disk space	240MB	1GB
Swap space	256MB	3x memory

TABLE 10-10. *Microsoft Windows NT System Requirements*

Software	Requirement
Operating system	Windows NT 4.0 with Service Pack 5 version 1280 dated June 10, 1999, or later
Microsoft Internet Explorer	5.0
Netscape Communicator	4.5.1 or 4.6
Certified Software	**Version**
HTTP Listeners	Oracle 40-bit (v2.14) Oracle 128-bit (v2.14) Netscape Enterprise Server 3.6.2 Microsoft Internet Information Server 4.0
Oracle RDBMS	7.3.4 8.0.5.1 8.1.5

TABLE 10-10. *Microsoft Windows NT System Requirements* (continued)

Summary

Before you read this chapter, you may have wondered if OAS 4.0 was marketing hype or real enhancements. With the obvious advancements in OAS 4.0, it is evident that OAS 4.0 excels beyond the capabilities of OWAS 3.0's architecture. It's exciting to contemplate the potential enhancements of OAS 5.0.

CHAPTER 11

HTML Development

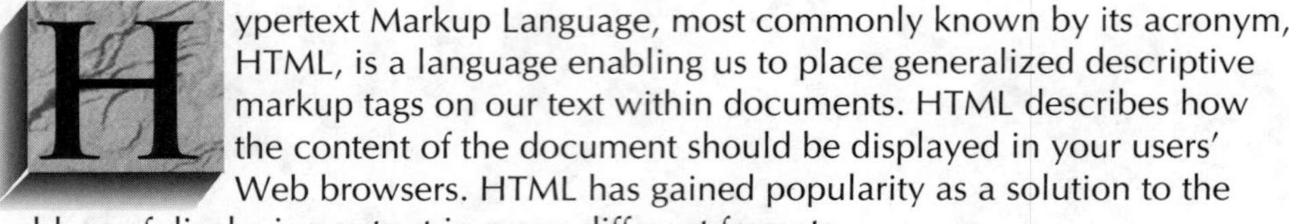

Hypertext Markup Language, most commonly known by its acronym, HTML, is a language enabling us to place generalized descriptive markup tags on our text within documents. HTML describes how the content of the document should be displayed in your users' Web browsers. HTML has gained popularity as a solution to the problem of displaying output in many different formats.

HTML documents can be created using any text editor (for example, NotePad, vi, PFE, or Microsoft Word). HTML documents are typically viewed in a Web browser (for example, Internet Explorer or Netscape Navigator). HTML is designed to lay out and structure the contents of a text document. HTML is not a programming language like C, Java, or Perl; rather, HTML is a markup language providing a standard specification to describe how text and images should be displayed.

This chapter is not meant to be an extensive HTML reference chapter. It is meant to provide you with valuable tips and techniques for developing applications with OAS and using HTML in the browser.

TIP
You can read detailed information on the HTML specifications from the organization responsible for standardizing any software standards related to the World Wide Web—the World Wide Web Consortium (W3C)—which can be located at http://www.w3.org.

This chapter will cover HTML as it relates to development of Web applications using Oracle technology. It is not intended to teach you HTML. If you are seeking more detailed information on HTML, there are numerous books on the subject—for example, *HTML: The Complete Reference* by Thomas A. Powell, published by Osborne/McGraw-Hill.

In this chapter, the following topics are covered:

- Writing HTML
- Viewing the HTML source without the results
- Refreshing a Web page after a given interval
- Using HTML tables
- Adding images
- Creating an HTML form

- Forcing side-by-side forms
- Implementing cascading style sheets—advantages and disadvantages
- Creating subject and/or text for email
- Sending email from an HTML form
- Indenting your text
- Placing two headings on the same line
- Creating the TV look
- Clearing all frames
- Referencing CGI scripts
- Inserting a page counter

Writing HTML

As previously mentioned, HTML can be written by hand in any text editor. Numerous "what you see is what you get" (WYSIWYG, pronounced wizzy wig) GUI tools enable you to paint your pages and then generate the HTML code. These tools also enable you to open an existing HTML file for editing directly from the GUI editor. HTML editors often extend beyond writing HTML code. Some tools aid you in developing JavaScript, DHTML, layers, animation, and more. HTML editors include MacroMedia's Dreamweaver, Symantics' Visual Page, HotMetal, and Microsoft FrontPage. Many of the current versions of the Microsoft products (for example, Word, PowerPoint, and Excel) have the capability to save documents as an HTML document.

Even though you can generate HTML using a GUI editor, I would highly recommend that you learn how to write HTML "the long way" first. It is important to understand the fundamentals of HTML before writing HTML in a GUI tool. When you develop dynamic code with an Oracle cartridge or a CGI program (for example, PL/SQL, Java, Perl, or C), you will not be able to edit the code in a GUI editor. You will need to understand the HTML tags. Take the time to understand HTML, become familiar with all versions of HTML, then use a tool.

It is also important to understand the standards for writing HTML, many of which are not followed by the GUI HTML editors. For example, early versions of Microsoft FrontPage were particular infamous for generating code that would embarrass any HTML programmer. Within Chapter 20, references are made to a program called the Demoroniser, which cleans up the HTML code generated by Microsoft products. As a part of your selection process, be sure to pick a tool that does not "moronize" you.

Working with the Browsers

Even though the world has essentially standardized on two browsers (Microsoft Internet Explorer and Netscape Navigator), multiple versions of each of these browsers are available. Other Web browsers are available, including the subset shown in Table 11-1.

Browser	Manufacturer	Description
Opera	Opera Software	User friendly, versatile, and fast browser that is keyboard-based. Opera has a small footprint and provides features for users with disabilities. http://www.operasoftware.com/download.html
Amaya	W3C/Amaya	Web browser and authorizing tool designed to be a test bed for experimentation of new specifications and extensions of Web protocols and standards. http://www.w3.org/Amaya/
NetCaptor	Stilesoft Inc.	Enables you to display multiple Web sites at one time on separate tabs. Also has the capability to open up groups of sites at the click of a mouse button
NeoPlanet	NeoPlanet Inc	Customizable Web browser with a built-in Web directory. http://www.neoplanet.com
ChiBrow	KCS & Associates	A browser designed for children browsing the Web. It comes with a preselected list of safe sites and enables parents to administer a list of approved sites. http://www.chibrow.com
Cyberworld Viewer	Cyberworld Int'l Corp	Enables you to view the World Wide Web through photorealistic 3D environments optimized for the Web
1st Choice Browser2000	Sabine Consulting	Displays multiple Web sites and can connect up to 200 URL's at a time
Lynx	The University of Kansas	Full-featured text-based browser intended primarily for local access. http://lynx.browser.org/

TABLE 11-1. *HTML Browsers*

TIP
You can read detailed information on Web browsers by visiting www.browsers.com.

When it comes to developing Web applications, you will have a number of decisions to make. Is your application going to support every possible Web browser? Or, are you going to support the least common denominator approach? Is your application going to support a specific subset of browsers—for example, version 5.0 browsers or subsequent versions? Or, will your application support only a specific browser, such as Internet Explorer 5.0? The decisions you make regarding browser support will greatly affect the time it takes to develop your application. For example, if you plan to support every possible browser and you plan on using JavaScript, you will need to be extremely careful about how you code your application in order to allow earlier versions of browsers to display your pages. To support a specific subset of browsers, you must test your application on each of the browsers within your subset, which includes each unique platform (operating system). For intranet application development, you can often choose only one browser version and platform to support.

If a browser does not understand (or support) a tag, most browsers will ignore the tag but display the contents of the information between the tags. For example, if your HTML file contained <BIG>This is big.</BIG> and your browser did not support the <BIG> tag, then the browser would display "This is big." in a normal font. If you plan to notify users who are using an older browser version that they need to upgrade, tags can be used to accomplish this task. For example, the <NOSCRIPT>, <NOFRAMES>, <NOEMBED>, and <NOLAYER> tags can be included in your HTML document and enable you to display alternate content on older browsers. For example, the <NOSCRIPT> tag enables any message (or HTML code) between these tags to be displayed on browsers that cannot understand the <SCRIPT> tag, which is used to support languages, such as JavaScript.

<NOSCRIPT>

The <NOSCRIPT> tag can be used to inform a user that their Web browser does not support the <SCRIPT> tag. As previously noted, older browsers actually do not understand the <NOSCRIPT> tag, so the information between the tags will be displayed in the user's browser. A browser that is JavaScript-compatible will correctly ignore the <NOSCRIPT> tag and the contents between the tags will not display.

If your browser does not support the <SCRIPT> tag, this tag will also be ignored and the contents therein will be treated as text. Therefore, as is noted in Chapter 12, JavaScript developers typically place their JavaScript code between HTML comment tags, so users with older browsers will not see the JavaScript code. The following code segment demonstrates how the <NOSCRIPT> command is used to inform the user that their browser does not support JavaScript:

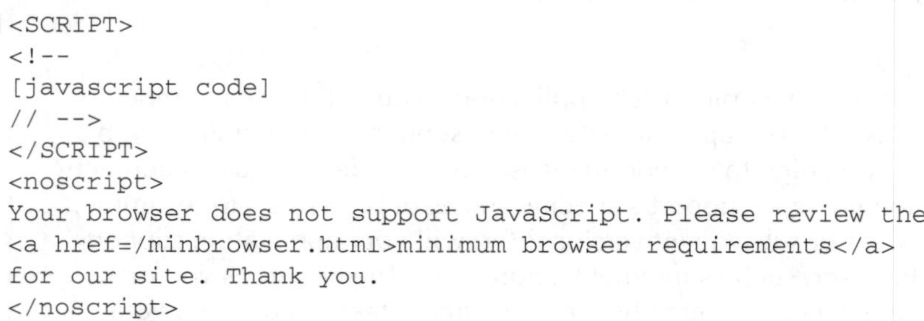

```
<SCRIPT>
<!--
[javascript code]
// -->
</SCRIPT>
<noscript>
Your browser does not support JavaScript. Please review the
<a href=/minbrowser.html>minimum browser requirements</a>
for our site. Thank you.
</noscript>
```

Please do not make a Web site for general public consumption without providing an out. Remember that some people surf without JavaScript. You would not want your site to be totally dysfunctional without JavaScript. You should provide contact information or a link to a static Web page as an alternate site. At a minimum, display a message stating, "You need JavaScript for our site, please turn it on!"

TIP
From a user perspective, informing the user they must use JavaScript to view your site is a hostile message…people do not like to be told that they have to have a specific browser or resolution. Unless you are supporting a small subset of browsers, you should—if you want to keep customers—provide an alternate procedure to access a static page or an information/contact page of some sort.

<NOFRAMES>

The <NOFRAMES> tag is typically used to inform the user that their browser does not support frames. The <NOFRAMES> tag could also be used to display your Web site in a nonframes-based browser. A browser that supports frames ignores the <NOFRAMES> tag. If you do not use this tag and a browser does not support frames, the user will only see a blank page. By using this tag, you can alert your user that their browser does not support frames. The following is an example of how the <NOFRAMES> tag could be used:

```
<noframes>
<head>
<title>Please download a new browser</title>
</head>
```

```
<body>
<font size="2" face="Arial, Geneva, Helvetica, Verdana">
Your browser does not support frames. Please review the
<a href=/minbrowser.html>minimum browser requirements</a>
for our site. Thank you.
</font>
</body>
</noframes>
```

<NOEMBED>

The <NOEMBED> tag is used to inform the user that their browser does not support the <EMBED> tag. Browsers that do not support the <EMBED> tag will display the contents between the <NOEMBED> tags. For example:

```
<noembed>
<font size="2" face="Arial, Geneva, Helvetica, Verdana">
Your browser does not support plug-in objects. Our site uses
the MacroMedia Shockwave plug-in. Please review the
<a href=/minbrowser.html>minimum browser requirements</a>
for our site. Thank you.
</font>
</noembed>
```

<NOLAYER>

The <NOLAYER> tag is used to advise the user that their browser does not support the <LAYER> tag. In 1997, Netscape developed the nonstandard proprietary tags <LAYER> and <ILAYER>, enabling you to define a self-contained unit of HTML within your document. The <LAYER> tag enables you to stack transparent sheets on your HTML document that can be moved around and stacked as the developer pleases. The <NOLAYER> tag can be used to direct the user to a nonlayered version of your HTML document.

```
<nolayer>
<head>
<title>This site is best viewed by a new browser</title>
<meta http-equiv=refresh content=10;url=nolayer_index.html>

</head>
<body>
<font size="2" face="Arial, Geneva, Helvetica, Verdana">
Your browser does not support layers. For the best viewing
of our site, please upgrade your browser to our minimum site
requirements. If your browser does not automatically display
our non layer-based version of our site, please click
<a href=nolayer_index.html>here</a> now or review the
<a href=/minbrowser.html>minimum browser requirements</a>
```

```
for our site. Thank you.
</body>
</nolayer>
```

Viewing the HTML Source Without the Results

While developing your Web application, you can view the source code without viewing the results in the browser. This can be accomplished from the browser by putting "view-source:" in front of the URL for the site or page. This can be particularly useful when a site is under development or when you are debugging the site. For example, in the browser, type the following address:

```
view-source:http://www.tusc.com
```

Refreshing a Web Page After a Given Interval

Occasionally you might wish to refresh or reload a Web page after a given interval. For example, you would like to refresh the contents of the page every 10 seconds. Of course, this only makes sense if the page's contents are dynamically generated. The following HTML example refreshes the page every 10 seconds:

```
<HTML>
<HEAD>
<META HTTP-EQUIV="REFRESH" CONTENT="10">
<TITLE>Stay tuned! I refresh every 10 seconds.</TITLE>
</HEAD>
<BODY>
...Page contents here...
</BODY>
</HTML>
```

You can also branch to another page after a specified period of time. The following example branches to another page after 300 seconds (5 minutes). This type of logic could be useful if you wanted to log the user off if they do not perform an activity in a specified period of time.

```
<HTML>
<HEAD>
<META HTTP-EQUIV="REFRESH" CONTENT="300; URL=auto_logoff">
<TITLE>Keep active, otherwise I log off in 5 minutes!</TITLE>
</HEAD>
<BODY>
```

```
…Page contents here…
</BODY>
</HTML>
```

Another method of forcing the refresh of a specific page is to age or expire the page. At the desired expiration date, the browser will refresh the page and will no longer display the expired page. This method can also be used when you don't want the user to be able to navigate "back" to a particular page. The following is an example of the expires Meta tag:

```
<META HTTP-EQUIV="Expires" CONTENT="{timestamp for expiration}">
```

Multiple HTTP-EQUIV tags can be used in a single page. Perhaps you want to refresh the page every 10 seconds until it expires. HTTP-EQUIV tags can also pass keywords and content type to the browser.

Using HTML Tables

HTML tables are widely used to display tabular data and control your document's layout. Tables are one of the most valuable formatting features of HTML. If you set up an HTML document with images, text, and data without using tables to control the format, you are in for a surprise. A nontable HTML document may look great on your browser, but may be rearranged and distorted in another user's browser. Sometimes changing your browser's window size can greatly affect the look of your site.

HTML tables are made up of rows, columns, and cells. HTML table cells can contain images, form fields, text, rules, headings, and even another table.

In HTML, a table starts with the <TABLE> tag and *must* end with the </TABLE> tag. These two tags encapsulate a table and its elements within the HTML document. Within the <TABLE> tags, use the following tags to format information in the table:

Table Tag	Definition
<TR></TR>	Defines a table row
<TH></TH>	Defines the table header cell (and will be in a bold font)
<TD></TD>	Defines the table's data in a cell
<CAPTION></CAPTION>	Defines the title of the table, which can appear at the top, bottom, left, or right of the table

The following example displays the preceding table using HTML:

```
<HTML>
<HEAD>
<TITLE>Sample HTML Table</TITLE>
</HEAD>
<BODY>
```

```
<TABLE BORDER=1>
<CAPTION ALIGN=TOP>HTML Table Tags</CAPTION>
<TR>
      <TH>Table Tag</TH>
      <TH>Definition</TH>
</TR>
<TR>
      <TD>TR</TD>
      <TD>Defines a table row</TD>
</TR>
<TR>
      <TD>TH</TD>
      <TD>Defines the table header cell (and will be in a bold font)</TD>
</TR>
<TR>
      <TD>TD</TD>
      <TD>Defines the tables data cell</TD>
</TR>
<TR>
      <TD>CAPTION</TD>
      <TD> Defines the title of the table which can appear
           at the top, bottom, left or right of the table</TD>
</TR>
</TABLE>
</BODY>
</HTML>
```

Tables can be fixed size, <table width=300>, or they can be variably sized, <table width=50%>. If you omit the width attribute, the table will be only as wide as necessary to accommodate the widest cells. HTML treats tables as objects, which can be centered or aligned to the margin with other text flowing around them.

Adding Images in a Table

A number of attributes are available for each of the HTML table commands. For example, the BORDER attribute on the <TABLE> tag defines the border thickness in pixels. If you would like to turn off the border, you can leave off the BORDER attribute or you can set the BORDER attribute equal to 0 (for example, BORDER=0).

In the following example, a background image has been added to the table definition. Just as you use the BACKGROUND attribute in the BODY tag, you can use the BACKGROUND attribute in the <TABLE> tag, as the following syntax illustrates:

```
<TABLE BORDER=1 BACKGROUND="background.jpg">
```

Netscape and IE treat the background attribute differently for tables. Netscape uses the upper-left corner of the background image in each cell and separates the cells with a blank border, even with the BORDER attribute set to 0; Explorer centers the image behind the entire table. Both browsers will tile small images to fill the entire cell. Test background images for your tables carefully if they are large or complex, as this can make your carefully drawn tables unreadable.

Within the following example, the text was included into the table cells. Inserting an image into a table cell is accomplished by embedding the <IMG> tag in the <TD> tag. When the browser constructs the table, the image will be downloaded and inserted into that particular cell, as the following example illustrates:

```
<TABLE BORDER=1 BACKGROUND="background.jpg">
<TR>
<TD>
This image represents our customer demographics
</TD>
<TD>
<IMG BORDER=0 HEIGHT=20 WIDTH=30 SRC="/images/world.gif">
</TD>
</TR>
</TABLE>
```

Creating an HTML Form

HTML forms enable you to prompt a user for input, then pass that information to an Oracle cartridge or a CGI script. The information is passed to the script either using a URL (the GET method) or through standard input (the POST method). The contents of the form (for example, fields and buttons) must be enclosed within the <FORM> tag.

The <FORM> tag itself contains attributes. One of the attributes is ACTION, which contains the URL of the script to execute. Another attribute is METHOD, which instructs the browser to use the GET or POST method of sending the information to the server. In addition to form elements, such as the input fields and text, you must include a Submit button, which sends the information to the server. Optionally, you can include a Reset button in your form, which will enable the user to quickly reset the form input fields to their default values.

The JavaScript-aware browsers have event handlers that can be used to execute a script defined in the document. Table 11-2 contains the most commonly used JavaScript event-handler tag attributes that can be used with the <FORM> tag.

The following example demonstrates the use of the onSubmit event, which will execute a JavaScript function called checkInsertForm(). When the user presses the

Event Handler	Description
onSubmit	Event is triggered when a user activates the Submit button
onReset	Event is triggered when the Reset button is clicked
onSelect	Event is triggered when the current selection on a form field changes
onChange	Event is triggered when the contents of an object, text, or text area field are changed

TABLE 11-2. *JavaScript Form Events*

Submit button, the onSubmit event will occur and the checkInsertForm() JavaScript function will execute.

```
<form name="InsertMemberForm" onSubmit="return(checkInsertForm())"
      action="http://myserver.com/ougTool/cart1/insertMember" >
```

The following code is the checkInsertForm() JavaScript code. This function checks the value of each field in the form. If the value of a field is empty, an alert() message box is displayed and the cursor is placed into the empty field.

```
<SCRIPT LANGUAGE="JavaScript">
<!--
       //check valid field entries
        function checkInsertForm()
       {
           if (document.InsertMemberForm.in_FirstName.value == "")
           {
              alert("Missing First Name");
              document.InsertMemberForm.in_FirstName.focus();
              return(false);
           }
...
// -->
</SCRIPT>
```

The following example is an HTML form requesting the first and last name from the user, which is then submitted to the information to the server using a CGI script called insertMember.cgi. This example also includes a Submit and a Reset button.

```
<HTML>
<HEAD>
<TITLE>Example HTML Form</TITLE>
</HEAD>
<BODY>
<H1> Name Verification<H1>
<FORM METHOD=POST ACTION="http://myserver.com/cgi_bin/process_name.cgi" >
First Name <INPUT TYPE=TEXT NAME="first_name" size=10 MAXLENGTH=10 ><BR>
Last Name <INPUT TYPE=TEXT NAME="last_name" size=20 MAXLENGTH=20 ><BR>
<INPUT TYPE="submit" VALUE="Send Name" >
<INPUT TYPE="reset" >
</FORM>
</BODY>
</HTML>
```

Limiting Data That Can Be Entered

In the preceding example, the <INPUT> tags are used to set up the input fields in the form. The following example form uses input fields for City, State, ZIP Code, and Country. The SIZE attribute of the <INPUT> tag limits the display size of the input fields being entered to a maximum number of characters displayed at a time. The MAXSIZE parameter limits the maximum number of characters to be entered into a field. In the following example, the user will only be able to see 20 characters in the City field. The other attribute is the TYPE attribute, which indicates the datatype. In the following example, all of the fields are text fields.

```
<td><input type=text name = "city"    size=20></td><td><input type=text
name = "state"   size=2></td><td><input type=text name = "zipCode"
size=5></td>
<td><input type=text name = "country" size=15></td>
```

The NAME attribute in the preceding example indicates the name of each variable or field. The TYPE attribute specifies the type of GUI control that is going to be used for the field; many different types of controls can be used including those shown in Table 11-3.

The NAME attribute is used as a unique name assigned to each field. The name given to a field should be treated the same way a variable field is within a coded script. The name you select should not use embedded spaces or punctuation that can cause problems when passing information to and from a server-side script. When naming your input fields, use characters, numbers, or underscores and use a name that describes the data the user is to input. The name used in the HTML document for an input form field should also be the name used on the server-side script. For example, if you name an input field password1 in your HTML form, then the server-side script must accept a field called password1.

<INPUT> Type	**<INPUT> Tag**
Buttons	<INPUT TYPE="BUTTON">
Checkbox	<INPUT TYPE="CHECKBOX">
Files	<INPUT TYPE="FILE">
Hidden fields	<INPUT TYPE="HIDDEN">
Images	<INPUT TYPE="BUTTON">
Text box	<INPUT TYPE="TEXT">
Password	<INPUT TYPE="PASSWORD">
Reset	<INPUT TYPE="RESET">
Submit	<INPUT TYPE="SUBMIT">
Text window	<TEXTAREA> ... </TEXTAREA>
Menus	<SELECT>...<OPTION>...</SELECT>

TABLE 11-3. *HTML Input Tags*

The following HTML script example creates two input fields, in_password1 and in_password2. They are input type=password fields and contain text titles of "*Password" and "*Re-enter Password" preceding the input field.

```
<table><tr>
        <td><Font color="RED">*Password</FONT></td>
        <td><table  border=0 cellpadding=0>
           <tr>
           <td><input type=password name = "in_Password1" size =10 maxlength=10>
               </td>
           <td></td>
           <td><Font color="RED">*Re-enter Password</FONT> </td>
           <td><input type=password name = "in_Password2" size=10 maxlength=10>
               </td>
           </tr>
      </table></td>
</tr></table>
```

The SIZE and MAXLENGTH attributes give the developer control to limit the size of the field and the maximum amount of characters a user can enter. In the preceding code, the password field's SIZE field is set to 10. Therefore, an input field the size of 10 characters will display on the document. The MAXLENGTH field is also set to 10, which restricts the user from entering more than 10 characters. If the MAXLENGTH attribute is set to greater than the SIZE of a field, the user would be able to scroll in the input field and enter characters up to MAXLENGTH.

If you still need to validate your input data, you might write a JavaScript called from the <FORM> tag. Two event handlers can be used at the form level, onSubmit and onReset. The name of the script specified on the onSubmit="script()" and onReset="script()" event handlers instructs the browser to invoke the script after the user presses the Submit or Reset button. The onSubmit attribute will enable you to evaluate the input data on the client-side before it is sent across the Internet to the server-side script for processing. The script assigned to the onReset attribute is executed once the user presses the Reset button.

```
<!-- OnSubmit example. -->
<FORM ACTION="insertMember.cgi" onSubmit="verify_input()" >

<!-- OnReset example. -->
<FORM ACTION="insertMember.cgi" onReset="clear_input()" >
```

Creating Images That Act Like Buttons

Besides the Submit and Reset buttons created in an HTML form with the <INPUT> tag, you can also add images that will act as buttons. This is supported in Explorer 5.0, but not in Navigator 4.6.

HTML 4.0 provides the <BUTTON> tag. The <BUTTON> tag is similar to the button created by <INPUT TYPE=IMAGE> with improved presentation features. This tag enables you to add an image. For example, the button could be of a type Submit or Reset that will appear and behave identical to a three-dimensional button. The button can move up and down as it is pressed, giving the user a bit of animation. Text placed between the <BUTTON> and </BUTTON> tags will display on the button face. An <IMG> placed between the <BUTTON> and </BUTTON> tags will cause the browser to display the image as the button.

TIP
If you want your image to appear as a button, many of the graphic editors enable you to turn your image into a button.

The following is an HTML example of the <BUTTON> tag used for Submit and Reset:

```
</HEAD>
<BODY>
<H1>Example Special Buttons</H1>
<FORM METHOD=POST ACTION=http://www.tusc.com/cgi_bin/process_name.cgi >
First Name <INPUT TYPE=TEXT NAME=first_name size=10  MAXLENGTH=10><BR>
Last Name <INPUT TYPE=TEXT NAME=last_name size=20 MAXLENGTH=20><BR>
<BR><BR>
```

```
<!-- Submit Button -->
<BUTTON TYPE=SUBMIT NAME="submit" VALUE="Submit" STYLE="font: 12pt
Arial Blue; background:red" >
<IMG SRC="check.gif" WIDTH=30 HEIGHT=20 ALT="">
Check Me Out
</BUTTON>
<!-- Reset Button -->
<BUTTON TYPE=reset NAME="reset" VALUE="reset" " STYLE="font: 12pt Arial
Blue; background:red" >
<IMG SRC="check.gif" WIDTH=30 HEIGHT=20 ALT="">
Clear Form
</BUTTON>
</FORM>
</BODY>
</HTML>
```

The Web page generated by this code is demonstrated in Figure 11-1.

The JavaScript-aware browsers have event handlers that can be used to create a button executing a script defined in your HTML document. Refer to Chapter 12 for

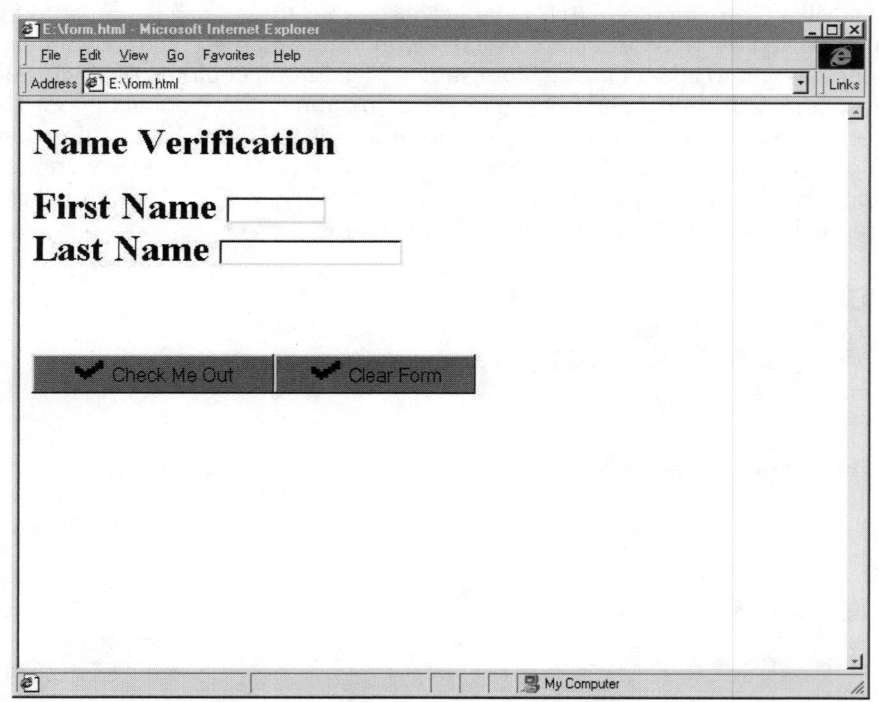

FIGURE 11-1. *Sample HTML output using the <BUTTON> tag*

Event Handler	Event Is Triggered when the User:
OnBlur	Moves out of a form field that has focus
OnClick	Presses down and then releases the mouse button
onDblClick	Presses down and releases the mouse button twice
onFocus	Enters a field to makes it active
onKeyDown	Depresses a key on the keyboard
onKeyPress	Depresses and releases a key on the keyboard
onKeyUp	Releases a key on the keyboard
onMouseDown	Presses the mouse button down and before it is released
onMouseMove	Moves the mouse pointer around the display region of an HTML element
onMouseOut	Moves the mouse pointer away from the display region of an HTML element
onMouseOver	Moves the mouse pointer into the display region of an HTML element
OnMouseUp	Releases the mouse button

TABLE 11-4. *Button Event Tags*

further information on JavaScript and OAS. Table 11-4 contains a list of "on" event tag attributes that can be used with the <BUTTON> tag.

The following script is an example of a button executing a script when the browser detects the onClick event. The script will execute after the user has selected the display region of your image (the button) and presses and releases the mouse button.

```
<HTML>
<HEAD>
<TITLE>Example JavaScript for Button</TITLE>
</HEAD>
<BODY>
<H1>Example JavaScript for Button</H1>
<FORM METHOD=POST ACTION=http://www.tusc.com/cgi_bin/process_name.cgi>
First Name<INPUT TYPE=TEXT NAME=first_name size=10  MAXLENGTH=10 ><BR>
Last Name<INPUT TYPE=TEXT NAME=last_name size=20 MAXLENGTH=20 ><BR>
<BR><BR>
<!-- Submit Button -->
<BUTTON NAME="submit_button"
        onClick="alert('Submit button was pressed')"
        STYLE="font: 12pt Arial Blue; background:red" >
```

```
<IMG SRC="check.gif" WIDTH=30 HEIGHT=20 ALT="Check Me Out">
Check Me Out
</BUTTON>
<!-- Reset Button -->
<BUTTON NAME="reset_button"
        onClick="alert('Reset button was pressed')"
        STYLE="font: 12pt Arial Blue; background:red" >
<IMG SRC="check.gif" WIDTH=30 HEIGHT=20 ALT="Clear Form">
Clear Form
</BUTTON>
</FORM>
</BODY>
</HTML>
```

Working with URLs and Hyperlinks

The Uniform Resource Locator (URL) is the address schema of the World Wide Web. URLs are defined by RFC 1738. When you start up your browser and attempt to enter the Internet, you will be using an HTTP URL to locate the home Web page of your Internet provider. Many different protocols and types of URLs exist, including but not limited to the following:

- **File URL** A URL that retrieves a specific file on a site.
- **File Transfer** A URL that will transfer a file from one machine to another.
- **Gopher URL** A URL that pulls information from a Gopher server.
- **News URL** A URL that pulls information from a Usenet newsgroup site.
- **HTTP URL** Hypertext Transport Protocol (HTTP) URL that pulls information from an HTTP server that serves HTML documents.
- **Partial or relative URL** Once you reach a hypertext document with a URL, you can access other documents on the server by entering the document name or a partial URL (for example, myOtherDoc.HTML).

Table 11-5 shows examples of valid URLs.

Hyperlinks or hypertext links can be created in HTML with the <A> tag ("A" meaning anchor) and the HREF attribute. Hyperlinks give your visitors a road map to information on the World Wide Web that you feel pertains to your topic. As previously mentioned, you can hyperlink to different resources on the WWW with a partial or relative URL.

When you visit a Web site with a browser, the hyperlinks are usually underlined and the hyperlink text has a different color than the text on the rest of the document.

URL	Description
ftp://www.myftpserver.com/ myftpfile.doc	Use the File Transfer Protocol (FTP) to download a specific file (myftpfile.doc) from a specific server (www.myftpserver.com).
http://www.myhttpserver.com/ myhtml.html	Using Hypertext Transfer Protocol (HTTP), a specific document (myhtml.html) will be transferred from the virtual root directory (because no directory was specified) from a specific server (www.myhttpserver.com).
http://www.myhttpserver.com/ myhttpdirectory/	Refers to a specific server (www.myhttpserver.com) and refers to a specific directory (myhttpdirectory), but does not refer to a specific file. In this case, the HTTP server will use its default initial file (usually, index.html).
myfile.html	This URL does not specify a protocol or directory. Because URLs are relative to the last URL, the prior URL's protocol, server, and directory will be used by the browser.

TABLE 11-5. *Sample URLs*

Images can also be "hot," or active, providing links used to direct your visitors to other resources on the Web.

The HTML <A> tag with an HREF attribute is used to direct your visitors to an anchor within your document or to another document. The HREF can contain an absolute URL reference (including protocol, server, directory, and file) or it can include a fragment identifier or a JavaScript code fragment. Place text, an image, line breaks, and headings to mark a visible area that users can select to hyperlink between the tags <A> and </A>.

Attributes can be set in the <BODY> tag to change and set the color of visited, unvisited, and active (currently being viewed in another browser window) hyperlinks, including the following examples:

<BODY> Attribute	Description
ALINK=	Set the color of active links
LINK=	Set the color of unvisited links
VLINK=	Set the color of visited links

For example, the following HTML code segment would set the preceding links accordingly:

```
<BODY BGCOLOR="white" TEXT="black" LINK="blue"
      VLINK="red" ALINK="yellow" >
```

Colors can be referenced by name or by RGB value. The ALINK, LINK, and VLINK attributes are noted as being deprecated in the specification for HTML 4.0. They are being replaced by font items in the specification for CSS (cascading style sheets), even though they will still be supported in current versions.

Keyboard shortcuts (hot keys) and tab orders (TAB key) can also be added to your hyperlinks, giving the user keyboard control. The hot keys can be set with the ACCESSKEY attribute of the <A> tag. The tab order enables the user to tab to hyperlinks and is set with the TABINDEX attribute. The following hyperlink examples use hot keys and tab orders. Notice the LINK, VLINK, and ALINK attributes set in the <BODY> tag. The example shows HTML output containing hyperlinks.

```
<HTML>
<HEAD>
<TITLE>Hyperlinks to Web sites</TITLE>
<BODY BGCOLOR="white" TEXT="black" LINK="blue"
      VLINK="red" ALINK="yellow" >
<H1>Cool Web Sites to Browse</H1>
<BR><A HREF="http://www.internet.com"
       ACCESSKEY=w
       TABINDEX=1> Web Developers Channel (ALT-W)
   </A>
<BR><A HREF="http://www.webplaces.com"
       ACCESSKEY=g
       TABINDEX=2> Web Graphics (ALT-G)
   </A>
<BR><A HREF="http://www.inquiry.com"
       ACCESSKEY=a
       TABINDEX=3> Ask the professionals web related questions (ALT-A)
   </A>
<BR><A HREF="http://www.webdeveloper.com"
       ACCESSKEY=d
       TABINDEX=4> Resources and technical information
                   on Web Development (ALT-D)
   </A>
<BR><A HREF="http://www.webreference.com"
       ACCESSKEY=i
```

```
        TABINDEX=5> Information on web development. (ALT-I)
    </A>
<BR><A HREF="http://www.wdvl.com"
        ACCESSKEY=v
        TABINDEX=6> Web Developers Virtual Library. (ALT-V)
    </A>
<BR><A HREF="http://www.browserwatch.com"
        ACCESSKEY=b
        TABINDEX=7> Information on browsers and plugins. (ALT-B)
    </A>
<BR><A HREF="http://web1.w3.org/markup/html-spec/html-spec_13.html"
        ACCESSKEY=h
        TABINDEX=8> Document on the HTML Coded Character Set (ALT-H)
    </A>
</BODY>
</HTML>
```

The Web page generated by this code is demonstrated in Figure 11-2.

Removing Hypertext Underline Links

For users that do not like the underlined hypertext links, the feature can be turned off through their browser settings.

- For IE users, go to View on the top task bar, then Internet Options, then select the Advanced tab. Under Browsing, go down to "Underline links," then select the Never radio button. Then, click the OK button.
- For Netscape users, go to Options at the top of the task bar. Click on General Preferences, then Appearance. Under Link Styles, uncheck the Links are Underlined box. Then, click the OK button.

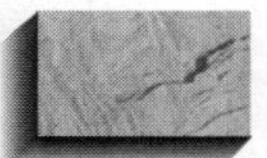

TIP
If you as a developer prefer not to underline the links, you can use HTML 4.0 cascading style sheets to accomplish this task.

When the user passes over a hyperlink, the mouse pointer turns into a hand notifying the user that a hyperlink is present. Some feel that different-colored text, an underline, or changing the mouse pointer is overkill for hyperlinks. If you are using cascading style sheets (CSS), the following technique enables you to remove

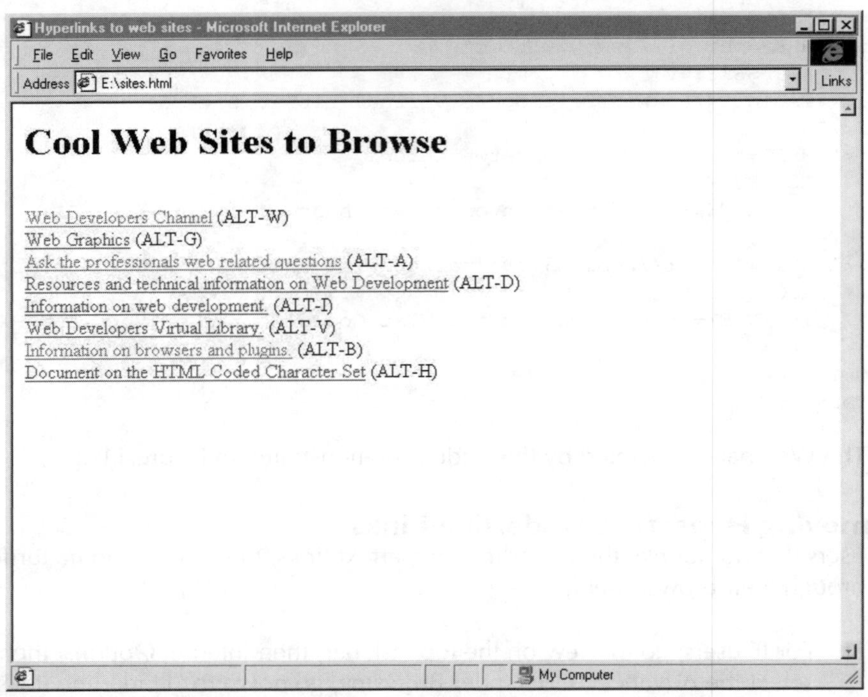

FIGURE 11-2. *Sample HTML output of Hyperlinks to Web sites*

the hyperlink underline. Place the following code at the head of your document to eliminate the hyperlink underlines. When the user passes over the hyperlink, the mouse pointer will still change to a hand and the text will be colored blue.

```
<style type="text/css">
a { text-decoration: none;
color: blue ;}
</style>
```

If the preceding HTML example "Cool Web Sites to Browse" is changed to include the preceding style tags, the page would appear identical to the one shown in Figure 11-3.

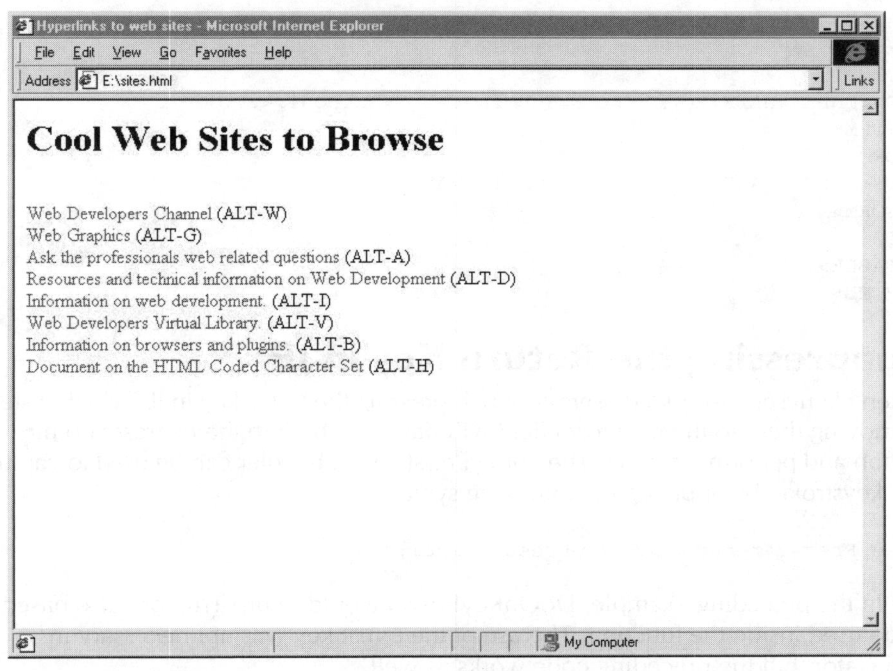

FIGURE 11-3. *Sample HTML output of Cool Web Sites with no URL underlines*

Forcing Side-by-Side Forms

HTML tables can be used to force Submit buttons to be side by side for different forms. The </FORM> tag implies a new line, so if another <FORM> is opened, the Submit button for that form will appear below the first form. To force the buttons to appear on the same line, use an HTML table. The following code would enhance the preceding description:

```
<HTML>
<FONT COLOR=#FF0000 SIZE=4>Without a table</FONT>
<FORM 1>
<INPUT NAME=Form1 TYPE=Submit VALUE=Button1>
</FORM>
<FORM 2>
<INPUT NAME=Form2 TYPE=Submit VALUE=Button2>
</FORM>
```

```
<FONT COLOR=#006010 SIZE=4>With a table</FONT>
<TABLE>
<TR>
<FORM 1>
<TD><INPUT NAME=Form1 TYPE=Submit VALUE=Button1></TD>
</FORM>
<FORM 2>
<TD><INPUT NAME=Form2 TYPE=Submit VALUE=Button2></TD>
</FORM>
</TR>
</TABLE>
</HTML>
```

Suppressing the Return Key in IE

Often client/server-minded users continue pressing the ENTER key in IE, which instead of moving them to the next form field will navigate them to the nearest Submit button and perform a submit. The onKeyPress() event handler can be used to capture the keystroke, by applying the following syntax:

```
onKeyPress="return DoOnKeyPress(event);"
```

In the preceding example, DoOnKeyPress() would return True or False based on code used inside the function. The use of the ENTER key was not necessary in Navigator, but the preceding code works as well.

Implementing Cascading Style Sheets—Advantages and Disadvantages

Cascading style sheets (CSS) enable you to change the browser defaults for page display. They can be created for individual elements, whole pages, or entire sites. You can turn off underlining on links; change the default font, size, and line spacing; control the placement of objects; and set special attributes to anything that falls within an <H1> tag or any other tag. CSS makes it easy to bring consistency to your entire Web site. The idea is to save time and simplify things, but the erratic implementations of style sheets between browsers and versions will probably increase the time to complete the same tasks with the current releases.

CSS was released with the version 4.0 HTML specification. Unfortunately the 4.0 versions of IE and Navigator were released prior to the final specification of CSS. The two browsers implement style sheets differently. This leads to the confusing mix of CSS1, CSS2, and Layers. You must be careful regarding the browsers your site supports, or limit your implementation of style sheets to the features supported by both IE 4.x and Netscape 4.x. When implementing CSS features, test the appearance and effects on both IE and Netscape 4.x and 3.x. This implementation results in enhanced effect for those with browsers that support the CSS and no diminished effect for those that do not.

Do not implement unsupported features, as this may make any information on your site inaccessible to users with 3.x or subsequent browsers. For example, DHTML is IE-centric and is lost on the Netscape browser. Conversely, be careful about implementing the functionality of Netscape-specific tags that are not supported by Microsoft. Some rework may be necessary to make all of your pages appear appropriately in all browsers. For example, make sure there are <P> (paragraph) tags before text that follows other tags when defining the size and font of the tags.

As a redesign of a Web site is inevitable, you will want to position yourself for less pain when you change the colors, fonts, sizes, and backgrounds of the entire site. When implementing CSS, take the opportunity to change your links to conform to one of the standards common on the Web—unvisited links a "hot" color and visited links subdued. For example, have links on pages in maroon (or another color that works well with your color scheme) and visited links grayed out.

The Safe List contains a list of what you may use to decide which features to use and which to forego. You can find this list at http://style.webreview.com/. When you decide to enhance the CSS structure of your site, revisit the Safe List to make sure the popular browsers support the new features you add. WebReview also contains a Danger List, containing the features that will cause different browsers to display erratic results. The primary features that work on all major browsers are simple formatting features.

The full benefit of CSS will be more fully realized when browsers support it better. However, design, redesign, and consistency of your Web pages will become easier by implementing the "linked" style sheet in all of your pages. You should still rely on body tags for those who are using Netscape 3.x and IE 3.x browsers, but your pages can appear more readable and consistent under the version 4.x of each browser. This is not particularly painful to implement. As the site grows, it becomes more difficult to make mass changes every day. Making modifications now and knowing that they are implemented consistently throughout your site is incredibly easy when you only have to edit a single page.

Perhaps the most daunting aspect of implementing CSS is the consideration of what is supported by the various browsers. The resources at the WebReview site, http://www.webreview.com, are useful. They present a good tutorial about CSS and include a terrific Browser Compatibility Chart of the features supported by specific versions of particular browsers and several other tools (specs, master list, Safe List, and a Danger List), depending on in your implementation.

Another good site for how-to information is found at http://www.stars.com/Authoring/Style/Sheets/WDVL.html, a part of the Web Developers Virtual Library at http://www.stars.com that includes a tutorial and a wealth of resources.

Tools for implementing CSS are also improving. HomeSite, a popular site creation package, provides capability for CSS. A tool dedicated to style sheets is available at the Sheet Stylist page at http://homepages.tcp.co.uk/~drarh/Stylist/. Many tools are affordable and provide a demonstration to download and try before you purchase.

By understanding the benefits and limitations of CSS, you are more likely to produce a new site without erratic display behavior.

Creating Subject and/or Text for Email

Did you know that you can automatically enter the subject line for visitors that click a link on your site to send you email? The following syntax is a standard email link in HTML:

```
<A HREF="mailto:bradley_brown@tusc.com">Click here to send me email</A>
```

With just a slight modification, you can automatically enter the subject line for Web surfers that click the link, making it easier to track email from your Web site:

```
<A HREF="mailto:bradley_brown@tusc.com?subject=About
      your book">Click here to send me email about my book</A>
```

In the preceding example, if the user clicked the line "Click here to send me email", the user's default email program would start, which will create a new email message and automatically enter the subject line with the text, "About your book." Taking this one step further, if you would like to populate the message for the user, this is done with the BODY attribute.

```
<A HREF="mailto:bradley_brown@tusc.com?subject=About
       your book"&body="I would like to ask you a question,
       which is:">Click here to send me email about my book</A>
```

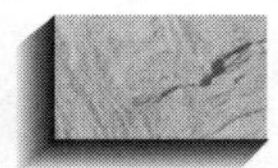

TIP
The mailto: address was not supported in early versions of Internet Explorer and it is not supported by many of the online HTML email functions available. Unless you are sure that all your users are using an IE or Netscape browser and a POP3 email package, choose another approach.

Sending Email from an HTML Form

If you want the user to enter the information into an HTML form and submit that message through email, the following code will automatically send email—email that contains not only the to, from, and subject, but also the message body.

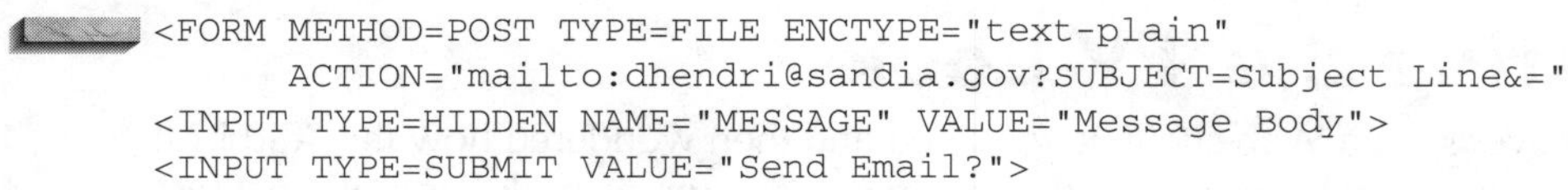

```
<FORM METHOD=POST TYPE=FILE ENCTYPE="text-plain"
      ACTION="mailto:dhendri@sandia.gov?SUBJECT=Subject Line&=">
<INPUT TYPE=HIDDEN NAME="MESSAGE" VALUE="Message Body">
<INPUT TYPE=SUBMIT VALUE="Send Email?">
</FORM>
```

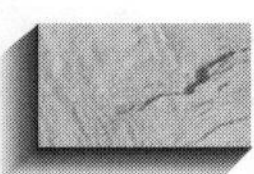

TIP

Note the "&=" after "Subject Line." This is needed to force the text to display the data in the message body.

Indenting Your Text

Because tabs are not directly supported in HTML, you can create a placeholder by using a single-pixel GIF image. When displaying the GIF image, you can set the height and width using the respective <IMG> attributes, as the following line of code illustrates:

```
<img src="one_pixel.gif" height=1 width=20>
```

The preceding syntax enables you to create an exact-size placeholder. The download time is not an issue because the GIF is small.

If you are deploying your site to Netscape browsers only, you can use the Netscape tag <SPACER> to indent paragraphs. IE does not understand this tag, and will simply ignore it.

```
<SPACER TYPE=horizontal SIZE=20>
```

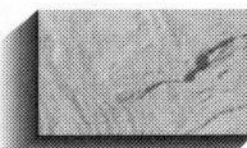

TIP

Another way to accomplish formatting in which you do not need to "placehold" more than the vertical height of the character is to use several consecutive nonbreaking spaces ( ). Remember that HTML ignores multiple "normal" spaces within a document—you must use .

Placing Two Headings on the Same Line

To get two different-size headings on the same line, you cannot use the <H> (heading) tag, because an implicit break (<BR>) will occur when headings are used. However, you can mimic two headings on the same line by using the <FONT> tag, as the following example illustrates:

```
<font size=+1 font=arial>Welcome to </font>
<font size=+3 font=arial>TUSC</font><br>
```

Creating the TV Look

Have you ever seen a Web site that you liked and then wondered how they did it? If so, you probably quickly looked at their source code. For example, one site that we created contained a frame on all four sides, giving it a TV-screen look. The reason for the appearance was to support multiple browser window sizes without recoding the application. By putting the black frames around the page, we kept the same look and feel no matter what window size was used.

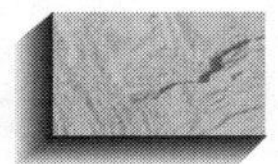

TIP

If you want to butt graphics up against the edge of the window, put your HTML page in a frame and add the tag MARGINWIDTH=0 MARGINHEIGHT=0.

Clearing All Frames

You have a vision of how your page will look and you typically spend a considerable amount of effort sizing objects, so your site is a work of art. You do not want to see your page displayed in a frame. At least three ways exist of eliminating all frames before your page is displayed. First, there is a Meta tag specifically to set the target frame to _top, meaning wipe out all frames. The syntax would appear identical to the following:

```
<META HTTP-EQUIV="Window-target" CONTENT="_top">
```

If you have control of the link itself, you can use a target frame of _top, as illustrated in the following example:

```
<A HREF="main.html" TARGET="_top">
<IMG SRC="home1.gif" alt="TUSC Main Page"
    WIDTH=90 HEIGHT=42 BORDER=0 ALIGN=bottom>
</A>
```

Another method is to use JavaScript to accomplish the preceding task, as illustrated in the following example:

```
<script language=javascript>
if (parent.frames[1])
   parent.location.href = self.location.href;
</script>
```

Make sure you return the favor to any links you include on your site to outside Web sites. It is poor form to open another site within your own frames, so include the TARGET="_top" attribute for all external links you create.

Referencing CGI Scripts

Web pages on the Internet can request user input, such as search pages, surveys, credit card information, and online registrations. The data can be accepted from an HTML Web page and sent to a program through a Common Gateway Interface (CGI) script.

A CGI script is a simple protocol used to communicate between a form on the Web and a program on a server. CGI scripts use UNIX/C concepts, such as STDIN (standard in), STDOUT (standard out), and environment variables. No specific programming language exists for CGI scripts, so use C, PRO*C, Perl, and/or UNIX shell scripting. The only requirement of the programming language used is it must be able to handle STDIN and STDOUT.

A CGI script has the capability to send and receive information to and from the browser. This feature gives the Web its interactive nature. A CGI program receives two types of information from the browser.

The CGI script can gather pieces of information about the browser, server, and the CGI script itself. The server provides this information to the CGI script through environment variables. The CGI script can be passed information entered by the user. This information is encoded by the browser and sent through an environmental variable (specifically, QUERY using the GET method) or through the standard input (STDIN using the POST method).

The workings of a CGI script are simple:

1. The user submits input, usually by entering data and pressing a Submit button. The CGI script receives the data from the input form as a set of name-value pairs. The names are defined by the URL or by the HTML form elements in the HTML script. The input is read from STDIN.
2. The CGI script takes the data and parses the information by name. The script can also send the information off to be processed by other programs.
3. The CGI script prepares the data to be written in HTML format and sends out through STDOUT.

For example, you as the developer are debugging a Web application and would like to see what some of the environment variables contain. You would also like the browser to display the environment variables and their values. The following example is a CGI script, written in C, to determine the environment variables and their values to print the results to the browser:

```
#include <stdio.h>
extern char **environ;
int main()
 {
   char **p = environ;
```

```
    printf("Content-Type: text/html\r\n\r\n");
    printf("<html> <head>\n");
    printf("<title>CGI Environment</title>\n");
    printf("</head>\n");
    printf("<body>\n");
    printf("<h1>CGI Environment</h1>\n");
    while(*p != NULL)
      printf("%s<br>\n",*p++);
    printf("</body> </html>\n");
}
```

By using HTML you can build URLs that call other URLs. CGI programs can be used to accomplish the processing of this information. The OAS cartridges implemented by Oracle are smart CGI programs. You can obtain further information about the OAS cartridges in Chapter 14 and Chapters 17–20.

Adding a Page Counter

In any application, you would like to know what kind of activity your Web page is receiving, such as the following:

- How many visitors has your Web page received?
- How many guests have registered a profile?
- Where are your visitors coming from?
- What time of the day did your visitors arrive?
- Where did they travel to from your site?
- Where are they coming from?

If all you want to know is how many guests have registered a profile, write a PL/SQL procedure to select the count of the profiles registered in your database and return the results to your Web page. If you want to count the number of hits to a page, use a sequence number or a counter table. If you are using OAS, a number of methods are available to gather this information.

If your Internet service provider (ISP) hosts your site, you may not be able to use OAS or a CGI program to generate this information. Therefore, contact your ISP and inquire if they allow page counters. If they do, they will probably provide you with a Frequently Asked Questions (FAQ) list on how to add their page counter. Or, if they allow CGI scripts, you can write a CGI script that keeps a tally of your visitors and displays the counter on your Web page. A number of free page counters are available on the Web.

If you cannot use a CGI program for your counter, you can use a public counter. Many Web sites can provide statistics on your Web site. Usually, the "fee" for this type of page counter requires that you include their advertising on your site.

One of the public counters you can use is XOOMCounter, located at www.pagecount.com. They offer a free graphical page counter that provides you with an easy but powerful site management tool that gives you access to stats about your site. When you attempt to incorporate their services into your site, they will send you a set of instructions that include an anchor tag containing an image referencing their site.

If you are using Active Server Pages (ASP), an ASP Component can be used to keep track of your visitors. The ASP component is called Page Counter Component. With this component, you can determine the number of times a page from your Web site has been requested. To perform this task, you would use the server's CreateObject method to create an instance of the Page Counter Component. The following line of code illustrates an example of creating an instance of the Page Counter Component:

```
Set pc = Server.CreateObject( "MSWC.PageCounter")
```

Then, use the Page Counter Component's methods (PageCnt.dll) to retrieve and save the number of accesses to your Web site.

Summary

Web developers have encountered many limitations with HTML. HTML is only a small part of the Standard Generalized Markup Language (SGML) specifications created for the Web. HTML only determines how the information is displayed on a browser instead of describing the content. Web developers are looking towards smarter documents that identify what information is in the document. Now the World Wide Web (WC3) is looking for the HTML++. They have found it. It is called Extensible Markup Language (XML) and is described in detail in Chapter 13.

Both HTML and XML are based on the SGML specifications. HTML is an implementation of SGML for visual presentation, while XML is a subset of SGML for writing markup languages specifying the format for expressing data content. Businesses will be able to create their own self-describing markup language.

So, if you want to stay up on the cutting edge of technology, XML is the next wave for the World Wide Web, but HTML is certainly the foundation for it all.

CHAPTER 12

JavaScript Development

The JavaScript language was created to add procedural power to HTML documents. Alone, HTML documents have limited capabilities. They can display data, accept data entered by the user, and send entered data to a server to be processed; however, HTML does not consist of events associated with actions. JavaScript, with the capability to relate to HTML objects, exists to manipulate data within the HTML document with respect to form and content. JavaScript is an event-based addition to HTML.

JavaScript is a simple to learn, dynamic, and powerful object-based language. HTML is a markup language (not a programming language), whereas JavaScript is an interpretive programming language. If you are familiar with other programming languages, you will find JavaScript easy to learn. The initial specification for JavaScript was developed by Netscape, then published as an open specification. Today, we only have two browsers; therefore, there are merely two versions of JavaScript we must accommodate. Browser implementation differences are the thorns in the JavaScript rose.

JavaScript is not Java. In presentations, I often ask if people know the four similarities that Java and JavaScript share. As time passes, more people know the answer to this question—it's J.A.V.A. Maybe, it's not quite that simple. Similarities exist between Java and JavaScript, but not more than other programming languages. When Netscape invented JavaScript, originally called LiveScript, Java was also beginning to gain popularity. Netscape asked Sun if they could use the name JavaScript—the name was changed, purely for marketing reasons. In hindsight, I am not sure if Sun or Netscape would make this choice again. It's caused more confusion than it's been worth (for both companies); but then again, they fed off each other. The confusion may have been a good thing for both. A server-side version of JavaScript is available, called LiveWire. To date, I have found *one* person whose predecessors used LiveWire. His team was converting their LiveWire application to use the PL/SQL cartridge for performance and scalability reasons.

JavaScript runs on the client, in the browser; therefore, your browser must support JavaScript. Netscape and Microsoft browsers support JavaScript on a number of platforms. This enables JavaScript to be a portable language. JavaScript is more of a scripting language than a full-fledged programming language (for example, Java or C++), and JavaScript requires less code to accomplish more. The downside of less code is that it is not as powerful or flexible as a full-blown programming language. Another disadvantage is JavaScript is inline with your HTML; therefore, users can view your source code, making it more difficult to protect your code. JavaScript can be used inside an HTML document in many ways. Before you learn JavaScript, you should learn HTML. JavaScript is embedded into your HTML document and supports events based on your HTML-based objects. Therefore, you need to obtain an understanding of HTML, its objects, and the browser's object hierarchy. In JavaScript, objects have both properties (data or information about the object) and methods (behaviors of the object). Objects can also have associated events. JavaScript uses dot notation similar to the Oracle dot notation (for example, Oracle uses schema.table.column to reference a column in a specific table in a specific schema) to reference objects.

JavaScript can perform data validation, event handling, navigation, document content creation, and calculations to enhance HTML forms and frames, provide cookie management, interface with other objects (for example, Java programs), provide for complete client-side applications, generate other HTML documents in pop-up windows, and more. Using JavaScript's client-side processing can make server-side calls unnecessary, enabling HTML and JavaScript to become a useful platform for reporting and collecting data. Through JavaScript, needed functionality can be performed through the client's browser.

In this chapter the following topics will be covered:

- Comparing JavaScript to PL/SQL
- Intricacies of OAS
- Handling browser incompatibilities
- Writing browser-specific code from PL/SQL
- Reusing your JavaScript code
- Programming user-defined alert processing
- Displaying properties on the screen
- Opening a new window and passing parameters to the window
- Assigning JavaScript variables
- Using the Submit button
- Validating form fields
- Handling exceptions with the onError event handler
- Working with PL/SQL code and various browsers
- Making a two-dimensional array in JavaScript
- Assigning JavaScript variables
- Invoking a PL/SQL procedure from a pick list
- Changing frames simultaneously
- Resolving the access denied error

- Building JavaScript menus
- Passing spaces as a part of the URL
- Debugging onFocus with alert
- Subscribing to the JavaScript OnFocus newsletter
- Reviewing visual JavaScript tools

Comparing JavaScript to PL/SQL

In versions 1–6 of Oracle, SQL was the foundation to Oracle and Oracle solutions. As of the release of version 7, PL/SQL became the basis of Oracle solutions. Oracle8i promises to make Java the next foundation of Oracle's solution. Based on surveys I have performed at Oracle users groups, most developers have a solid knowledge of PL/SQL. In this section, I am going to assume you know PL/SQL. If you are not familiar with PL/SQL, I would highly recommend *Oracle PL/SQL Tips and Techniques* by Joseph Trezzo (Oracle Press, 1999). In this section, a quick JavaScript introduction comparing JavaScript to PL/SQL is provided.

TIP
JavaScript is case-sensitive. If you have not worked with case-sensitive languages, I can assure you this fact will haunt you numerous times...so, say it with me. "JavaScript is case-sensitive." When you are debugging code and you just cannot figure it out, stop and think—is case-sensitivity getting the best of you?

Using Semicolons or Not

A second difference between PL/SQL and JavaScript: in JavaScript the semicolon at the end of the line is optional. It is only required if two commands are placed on the same line. Otherwise, the newline character indicates the end of the command. Remember, if you use separate htp.print commands to print your JavaScript code from within OAS, OAS will send a newline character after each htp.print command. If you use a tool, such as WebAlchemy, to convert your static HTML and JavaScript file into PL/SQL code, you will discover many tools will convert the entire script into one htp.script or htp.print command. Use semicolons to separate every command eliminating potential problems. If you do not use semicolons, your JavaScript is likely to fail after the conversion.

Defining Variables

In JavaScript you can define variables, used to store information within your program. Variables in JavaScript must begin with a letter or an underscore. Subsequent characters can be letters, numbers, or underscores, but cannot be spaces or hyphens. In addition, variables cannot be reserved words.

Reviewing the JavaScript Keywords and Reserved Words

As with every programming language, JavaScript contains keywords. Keywords of the JavaScript language include break, continue, do, else, false, for, function, if, in, int, labeled, new, null, return, switch, this, true, typeof, var, while, and with. Additionally, all languages contain reserved words; in JavaScript, they include abstract, Boolean, break, byte, case, catch, char, class, const, continue, default, delete, do, double, else, extends, false, final, finally, float, for, function, goto, if, implements, import, in, instanceof, int, interface, labeled, long, native, new, null, package, private, protected, public, return, short, static, super, switch, synchronized, this, throw, throws, transient, true, try, typeof, var, void, while, and with. Remember, JavaScript is case-sensitive.

Looking at JavaScript Literals

Literals in PL/SQL include text, numbers, and Boolean literals. JavaScript has more extensive literal declarations than PL/SQL. JavaScript's literal declarations include integer literals (decimal, hexadecimal, and octal), floating-point literals (decimal numbers with fractional parts), Boolean literals (1-True or 0-False), string literals (0 or more characters enclosed in single or double quotation marks), and special characters (for example, \b for backspace, \f for formfeed, \n for newline, and \r for carriage return).

Separating and Beautifying Your Code

Identical to PL/SQL, JavaScript uses separators between characters. The interpreter removes separators, and the use of separators is a matter of aesthetics. JavaScript's separators are spaces, tabs, and newlines.

Commenting JavaScript

Many programmers do not like to include comments within their source code; however, comments are an important component to a programming language. Comments are used to make the code easier to read, understand, and debug. In JavaScript, there are single-line comments (denoted by two forward slashes (i.e., //))

and multiline comments (denoted by a forward slash and an asterisk (i.e., /*) and ending with an asterisk and forward slash—i.e., */.

Understanding JavaScript Operators

Similar to PL/SQL, JavaScript operators enable the programmer to act or react upon variables. Operators are used to assign values, make changes, and perform calculations to variables. Unlike PL/SQL, most JavaScript operators are direct descendants from C++. For assignment, PL/SQL uses colon-equals (i.e., :=), whereas JavaScript uses equals (i.e., =). Many of the arithmetic and comparison operators are the same for PL/SQL and JavaScript, such as addition or plus (i.e., +), subtraction or minus (i.e., -), multiplication (i.e., *), division (i.e., /), not equal to (i.e., !=), greater than (i.e., >), greater than or equal to (i.e., >=), less than (i.e., <), and less than or equal to (i.e., <=). Some of JavaScript's nice C++ descendents include increment a variable (i.e., ++), decrement a variable (i.e., --), and add a variable to another (i.e., +=). For comparison, PL/SQL uses equals (i.e., =), whereas JavaScript uses double equals (i.e., ==). Another important operator is the concatenation operator, which in PL/SQL is the double pipe (i.e., ||) while JavaScript uses a plus sign (i.e. +).

Controlling Your Structures

JavaScript contains full control structures including if-then-else, for, while, do, and more. The syntax for the if-then-else is a little different than PL/SQL. The condition statement must be placed between parentheses (i.e., ()) in JavaScript. The statements are placed between curly braces (i.e., {}). For example, the if-then-else syntax in JavaScript is as follows:

```
if (condition)  {
   [statements]
}  else  {
   [statements]
}
```

An example of actual JavaScript code might appear identical to the following:

```
if (a==b)  {
   c=200
}  else  {
   c=300
}
```

The PL/SQL for statement is considerably more extensive in JavaScript than it is in PL/SQL:

```
for   ([initializing_expression]; [conditional_expression]; [loop_expression])  {
     [statements]
}
```

The following is an example of actual JavaScript code using the for statement:

```
for  (x = 0;  x<100; x++)  {
     document.write(x + " ")
}
```

JavaScript includes a while statement that is similar to the JavaScript for statement without the initializing and loop expressions. The following syntax illustrates the while statement:

```
while (conditional_expression)  {
      [statements]
}
```

Identical to PL/SQL *labels*, JavaScript labels can be used within a loop. JavaScript labels are supported in JavaScript version 1.2 and subsequent releases. JavaScript labels are indicated with a colon after the label. Labels are typically used with the break and continue statements, referencing a specific label. The following example includes while, if, label, and a break statement. The break statement enables you to reference a label outside of another loop structure (the while loop used in the following example):

```
y=0
start_loop:
y++
x=0
while (y<5) {
  x++
  document.write(x + " " + y)
  if (x==20) {
      break start_loop
  }
}
```

Modeling the Objects or Object Modeling?

JavaScript's object model enables the programmer to implement powerful and versatile models for application development. The object model eases the design and implementation details of complex programs and enables the use of previously created objects in current projects. Remember that JavaScript is object-based, not object-oriented. You cannot create your own complex objects in JavaScript; however, you can refer to JavaScript objects. If that is not confusing enough, object-based versus object-oriented means that JavaScript does *not* provide several basic functions of object-oriented languages. These basic functions would include abstraction, inheritance, and encapsulation. Java is an object-oriented language.

JavaScript can use or refer to objects created in Java. The JavaScript object model is simple to understand. The following is an example of a simple HTML script:

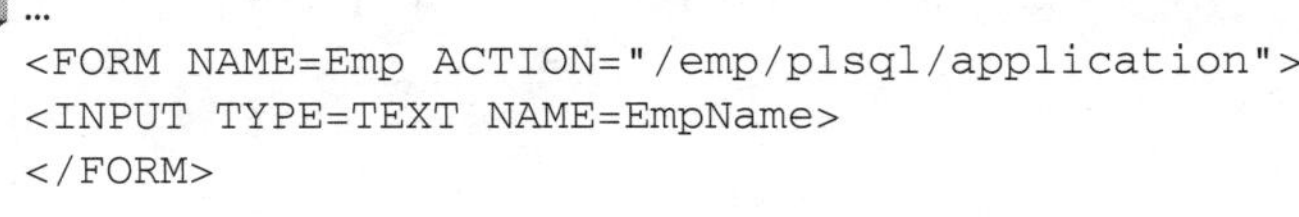

```
...
<FORM NAME=Emp ACTION="/emp/plsql/application">
<INPUT TYPE=TEXT NAME=EmpName>
</FORM>
...
```

In JavaScript, the object model to reference the value in the *empName* field in the *emp* form would be referred to as the following line of code:

```
window.document.Emp.EmpName.value
```

Everything is case-sensitive! In the preceding example, we retrieved the value of the field. The value is a property of the field. Form text fields have other properties, including defaultValue and name.

While noting the preceding properties, you might wonder about the name property. Why would you need the name of the field when you had to specify the name in the object model specification (window.document.Emp.EmpName.name)? Because there are a number of ways to reference objects in JavaScript. For example, "this" refers to the current object. Therefore, if you wanted to access the name of the current object, it would be referenced as the following syntax illustrates:

```
this.name
```

You can also reference objects based on array values. For example, forms on a page or fields within a form. For example, you could refer to the first form and the first field on the form, as the following line of code illustrates:

```
window.document.forms[0].fields[0].name
```

As evident in the preceding syntax, JavaScript's object model can quickly become complex. I would highly recommend you picking up at least one JavaScript book for your library. A good JavaScript book will explain the object model, and describe all properties, methods, and event handlers available for each object type. I own a JavaScript Quick Reference Guide that I carry every place I go.

Each object type has properties and methods associated with it. For example, the methods associated with form text fields include blur(), eval(), focus(), select(), toString(), and valueOf(). It is also programmatically possible to force these methods to occur.

Text fields also have event handlers associated with them. The events that could occur include onBlur, onChange, onFocus, and onSelect.

Table 12-1 illustrates a quick reference of the events available for each object type.

Object	onClick	onSubmit	onChange	onFocus	onBlur	onLoad	onUnload	onMouseOver	onSelect	onAbort	onError	onMouseOut	onReset
Button	x												
Reset	x												
Submit	x												
Radio	x												
Checkbox	x												
Link	x							x				x	
Form		x							x				x
Text			x	x	x				x				
Textarea			x	x	x								
Select			x	x	x					x	x		
Image													
Area	x							x				x	
Window						x	x				x		

TABLE 12-1. *Events per Object Type*

The Intricacies of OAS

JavaScript is embedded into your HTML code. Therefore, if you are using a cartridge or CGI, no setup is required—JavaScript is included into your HTML document. JavaScript code is typically placed in the <HEAD> section of your HTML. As noted in the preceding section, if you use WebAlchemy to convert your HTML code to PL/SQL, be sure to use semicolons between each line of JavaScript code. You can write your HTML (and JavaScript) code in your favorite editor (visual or text) and convert it to PL/SQL, or write straight PL/SQL using the htp.script procedure for your JavaScript or a series of htp.prints. No special procedures are required to write JavaScript with OAS.

Handling Browser Incompatibilities

Browser compatibility is the bane of Web developers. It is painfully common to develop a routine or function in JavaScript for one vendor's (Netscape or Microsoft) browser and test it in another, only to discover that the same code does not work. Unfortunately, the bad news is that dealing with browser incompatibility is something of an art and not a science. No particular "magic" exists to solve all compatibility problems. Most of the current JavaScript books indicate command compatibility and incompatibility of the "Big Two" browsers.

The good news is that the various browsers supporting client-side JavaScript *are* compatible, at least regarding the more common and basic features of the language. As you extend JavaScript into Dynamic HTML (DHTML), style sheets, and the HTML 4.0 specifications, more incompatibilities will be evident. Documentation regarding these general features is also widely available online, at the vendors' Web sites, and in reference books—and therefore will not be addressed in this chapter.

The simplest remedy for browser incompatibility is to avoid the issue entirely by only supporting one browser. If you have a choice in the matter, choose one browser to support—and a specific version of that browser. Otherwise, you are destined to fight JavaScript differences. By choosing one browser to support, you will completely eliminate the whole issue of keeping code running on different platforms, an advantage not to be underestimated. It can be difficult enough keeping a single application running properly for one browser and version, let alone adding another browser and more versions to the situation. Potential problems are not always under the developer's influence. An infinite number of factors, well beyond the developer's control, can affect browser performance, including but not limited to firewalls, ISPs, the user's connection to the network, the Internet (i.e., direct or by modem, with baud rate considered), the user's operating system, the server's operating system, and even operating system settings (for example, environmental parameters). Intranets (for example, local applications where the user base can be strictly controlled) are easier to support than the Internet. A certain amount of control can be enforced, such as user access, versions, and which browsers are supported. By eliminating the complication of having to support multiple browsers, support issues become simpler—and the simplest approach seems to work best.

It is not always possible to limit users to one specific browser and version, particularly on Internet applications. This opens a whole Pandora's box of compatibility problems that *must* be dealt with carefully. As previously mentioned, specific instances of compatibility will not be addressed. When supporting multiple browsers, careful testing on every supported browser, platform, *and* version is essential. Some testing software can help to automate testing; however, testing is complicated because multiple versions of a browser often cannot exist on the same machine. At a minimum, perform testing on the least common denominator. If multiple browsers must be supported, to avoid problems, do not implement browser-specific features. The identity of these features can be obscure, and thorough testing of multiple-browser applications is essential. Some information on this topic can be gained from research on the Web and from reference books, but you as a developer will want to compile your own list of incompatibilities *with* workarounds. Generally speaking, the oldest and most basic features of JavaScript are supported by the various browsers in the same way and offer little resistance to compatibility. It is primarily the newer features in which the browsers will differ. It is always possible to write generic code for one browser and have it not work in another. This is where testing and debugging must be enforced.

TIP
At a minimum, perform testing on the least common denominator of a browser and version.

For those instances where incompatibilities cannot merely be avoided, careful coding techniques can address such problems. JavaScript is an interpretive language (interpreted on the fly). It provides the capability to create objects and properties on the fly, and with the careful use of the JavaScript tag—and browser-specific code in JavaScript itself—you will be able to work around all incompatibilities.

Creating objects and properties is a fairly elegant way to work around some browser incompatibilities, at least, to avoid JavaScript errors. You can implement the code in your application to check if a given object exists. If the object does not exist, you can create the object to avoid errors when referencing the object or property later. For example, the disabled form object property in Internet Explorer is not supported by Netscape Navigator. However, for the affected form fields, you can create a form property called disabled. This can be accomplished within an onLoad() event handler for designated form objects. The result is that the future references to that property in your mainline code *will* locate the disabled property. This is because the new programmer-defined property is now there—you created it.

The end result is that a JavaScript error can be avoided neatly. Creating the form property only avoids a JavaScript error—merely creating a property called disabled for the appropriate objects will not cause Navigator to do anything with the new property; in other words, the object will not actually be disabled. However, creating the object property will enable the same code to work in both browsers.

Another way to handle incompatibilities in browser versions is to use the JavaScript tag with specific version numbers. If the browser does not support the appropriate version, the browser will ignore the block of code. Again, this must be a satisfactory solution for your application. For example, to use this "feature," browsers not supporting JavaScript version 1.2 would ignore the following script. Therefore, this code would not cause problems during execution in older browsers—of course, with the exception of the loss of processing this code, which cannot be avoided, because that browser is entirely ignoring the code.

```
<SCRIPT LANGUAGE="JAVASCRIPT1.2">
// JavaScript 1.2 code goes here
// Will be ignored by older browsers that
// don't support JavaScript version 1.2 or above.
</SCRIPT>
```

The most difficult and time-consuming workaround is the most powerful of the techniques—writing browser-specific code. To identify the actual browser being used by the user, you use the appVersion property of the navigator object. The following line of code continues the JavaScript appVersion variable:

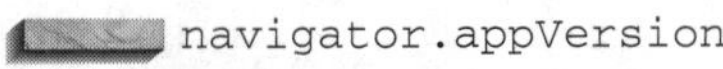

```
navigator.appVersion
```

The preceding variable will identify the actual browser and version being used. The power behind this information is undeniable and should not be underestimated; it enables you to write browser-, version-, and platform-specific code.

TIP
Using the browser version information, you could maintain browser-specific code with simple if-then-else logic, but your code may quickly become difficult to maintain.

Writing Browser-Specific Code from PL/SQL

The ways of addressing browser incompatibilities can be accomplished *outside* of JavaScript and outside of the HTML document. This can be accomplished when dynamic Web pages are being dynamically generated, identical to the procedures within OAS. Even though this technique references generating Web pages in PL/SQL, the principles follow through to other dynamic means of generating server-side Web pages (for example, using Perl or another cartridge or CGI).

The theory behind this process is quite simple. Using the PL/SQL package OWA_UTIL's get_cgi_env function for the http_user_agent, OAS will identify the user's browser and operating system. Using this information, you can dynamically send JavaScript (and HTML for that matter) browser-, version-, and platform-specific information. This is useful, for example, if you want to reference the disabled property in Internet Explorer, but not within Netscape Navigator (where it does not exist). By querying the user_http_agent, you can write the correct PL/SQL if-then-else logic to accomplish this task. This function might return a value identical to 'Mozilla/3.0.1 (WinNT;1)', meaning, the user is using Netscape Navigator version 3.0.1 on Windows NT. The following is an example of the PL/SQL code:

```
field_attributes := null;
-- User is using Netscape Navigator 3.0.1
if (owa_util.get_cgi_env('HTTP_USER_AGENT') =
     'Mozilla/3.0.1 (WinNT;1)') then
     field_attributes := ' onChange="this.disabled=true";';
end if;
htp.formText(cname => 'Name', cattributes => field_attributes);
```

The field_attributes parameter is used in the preceding htp.formText command. If the user is using any browser other than the specific version and operating system (Netscape Navigator on Windows NT), the field_attributes will be NULL. If the user's browser is the specified browser, then the field_attributes variable will be assigned accordingly. For purists, the same thing could have been accomplished by doing the comparison, and using an else clause to do the initial assignment. In turn, correct JavaScript code will be included based on the browser.

As with any powerful programming technique, the advantages and the disadvantages must be considered. The advantages include processing power and versatility in code. The main disadvantage is not immediately obvious. The comparison in the if statement must be absolute (if the = operator is used) and there are countless variations existing even for the same version of the same browser, all of which will be identified by a specific string (usually with only minor variations). Maintaining lists of such browsers can be tedious, and it may be necessary to store lists of the browsers in a database table to be checked instead of the simple preceding hardcoded example. For instance, you could check the table to verify if the current browser is in the supported browsers list, then use the if-then-else logic to check status instead of the browser identity directly.

With a similar technique using PL/SQL, it is possible to produce completely different dynamic documents, depending on variable values. For instance, displaying certain columns on the screen depending on a user's security level, or perhaps even using similar if-then-else logic to govern the display and use of entire HTML forms. Within Chapter 14, the power of using PL/SQL logic to control what is generated into the HTML document is detailed.

Reusing Your JavaScript Code

When it comes to JavaScript code in your HTML documents, and in turn in your PL/SQL packages, a number of ways exist to include JavaScript. Obviously, you could hardcode your JavaScript code into your HTML document, or in PL/SQL you might use htp.script or htp.print commands. However, if we analyze this from a coding practice standpoint, does this make sense? Wouldn't you like to share your JavaScript code and reuse it? Of course you would. Many ways exist for you to share your JavaScript code. I have provided more resuable and modular approaches that will enable you to share your code, in the following subsections.

TIP

You can use WebDB for your JavaScript repository. In Chapter 5, the "Creating a JavaScript Library" section detailed the procedures when using WebDB to create and maintain a JavaScript library. The following subsections will outline the PL/SQL code required to extract specific JavaScript functions from WebDB using WebDB's wwv_javascript package.

Mocking WebDB's JavaScript Library Functionality

If you do not have WebDB, you could develop similar functionality. You would need to create a table containing the JavaScript routines. Each routine will be located in a record of this table. You could also write a package similar to the functionality behind the WWV_JAVASCRIPT package.

Writing a PL/SQL JavaScript Library Package

You can also write a PL/SQL package full of JavaScript routines. For example, you might call the routine js_lib. In this package, you would define each of your JavaScript functions in a separate procedure. Your PL/SQL code would call each of the js_lib procedures needed for each application component.

Yet another advantage of using PL/SQL to generate the JavaScript code is that the contents of the JavaScript code can be dynamically generated. For example, not only could the JavaScript be stored in a table, but the JavaScript routine could dynamically pull information from another table, offering a considerable amount of power in your development.

Using a JavaScript Library Instead of Inline JavaScript

Rather than including your JavaScript code directly into the HTML, you can also reference a source document containing the JavaScript code. This is accomplished using the SRC attribute of the SCRIPT command, as illustrated in the following line of code:

```
<SCRIPT SRC="jslib.js">  </SCRIPT>
```

The preceding reference will retrieve the jslib.js file and include it as a JavaScript routine into the current HTML source. Remember that URLs are always relative. In other words, the directory that the browser requests the JavaScript code be pulled from is relative to the HTML source itself. Therefore, if the source were a static HTML file (the relative path for the JavaScript routine in this example), it would be the same directory as the static HTML file. If the HTML was dynamically generated by a programming language, like PL/SQL, the relative path would be the relative path to the PL/SQL cartridge.

Why not develop a PL/SQL package that contains a procedure called js? Then, for all of your PL/SQL-generated HTML, you can refer to your library of routines with the SRC (source) command. The only downside to this method is that then every routine would contain all of the functions, which may be overkill for your HTML documents.

To accomplish this task, make sure you have established a listener MIME type for .js, which should be set to application/x-javascript. Next, create a package with a procedure name of js (e.g., a package named jslib that contains a procedure called js). Your package specification and body might appear identical to the following example:

```
create or replace package jslib as
   procedure js;
end;

create or replace package body jslib as
   procedure js is begin
     htp.print('function lib1(var1){
                          alert("You passed " + var1 + " to me !")  }');
```

```
    http.print('function lib2(message){
                    if (confirm(message)){
                          alert("You pressed ok. ")
                   }else{
                         alert("you pressed cancel") }}');
  end;
end;
```

The following procedure illustrates the procedures to include referencing to your jslib.js library:

```
create or replace procedure javalibtest as
begin
      htp.htmlopen;
      htp.headopen;
      htp.title('Javascript Library Example');
      htp.headclose;
      htp.bodyOpen;
      htp.print('<script src="jslib.js"> </script>');
      htp.script('lib1("Hello World")');
      htp.script('lib2("This is really cool! ")');
      htp.big('Press reload or refresh to run the example again.');
      htp.bodyClose;
      htp.htmlclose;
end;
```

Referencing a Static JavaScript Library

Another method similar to the preceding section would be to develop a set of JavaScript routines that are static .js files. Your HTML and PL/SQL code can refer to any libraries easily by referencing the specific .js file. The advantage to this approach is that the static files are typically faster than dynamically generated files.

Programming User-Defined Alert Processing

JavaScript is an interpretive language; therefore, you may encounter runtime errors as a result of syntax errors, errors in the code, or as a result of datatypes created on the fly. Syntax errors can be addressed by editing the source code, thereby eliminating the error. Runtime errors are caused by a statement that is syntactically correct, but it attempts to perform an impossible task. The most puzzling of errors are logic errors, occurring when the program does not perform the way it was expected to.

One of the less obvious features of JavaScript revolves around JavaScript being an interpretive language. This is identical to the interpretive BASIC language of old, meaning every line of code must be interpreted byte by byte as it is executed. This can be slow, and noticeable pauses can occur during intense periods of processing. Therefore, it can be helpful to raise programmer-defined alert windows when this happens to keep users from thinking the computer has frozen.

The trick is to open a new window and use the new window's document.write() method to fill the window with a short message, do the processing, then close the window. The JavaScript code to open, write to, and close the window is as follows:

```
var w = window.open();                //open new window. "w" is the name
w.document.open();                    //open w's document
w.document.write("<HTML>");           //HTML tag for new window's contents
w.document.write("<BODY>");           //BODY tag to define document properties
w.document.write("Working…");         //message to put in new window
w.document.write("</BODY>");          //closing BODY tag
w.document.write("</HTML>");          //closing HTML tag
w.document.close();                   //close document
//processing logic goes here
w.close();                            //close window when done
```

To explain the preceding code, "w" is the object assigned to the window opened by the window.open() method; putting the return value from window.open into a JavaScript variable will enable you to reference that window object at a later time. To write to the new window, we must open the new window's document object. The window document can then be written to using the document.write() method. Upon completion, the document (not the window) must be closed. The actual processing will occur before the window is closed. Finally the new window itself must be closed.

Displaying Properties on the Screen

One of the more difficult aspects of JavaScript programming is the relationship of one object to another. JavaScript is an *object-based* language, which means parts of the language are referred to as *objects*. Anything belonging to an object is called a *property*, even though properties can be objects in their own right and have properties of their own. Working through the *object* hierarchy in JavaScript can be difficult and confusing, because different vendors' browsers have differences in the built-in objects and properties. An alternative is to use a short utility to display object properties in the document or a simple alert window using a long character string of captured object properties. The short utility is defined as a *function*. This function can be called for any object specified.

It is possible to collect object properties in JavaScript because of JavaScript's support of *associative arrays. Normal arrays* use a number or record identifier as an array index—for example, states[1] where the number 1 is the array index number for the state's array. Associative arrays use a string as a unique identifier instead of a simple number. For an associative array, the reference could be similar to states['Illinois'] as a valid identifier. Object properties in JavaScript can be referenced using either normal or associative arrays. To display properties on the screen, a method of reading the object properties from the object is needed. JavaScript also provides this capability with the object-based for loop, as the following syntax illustrates:

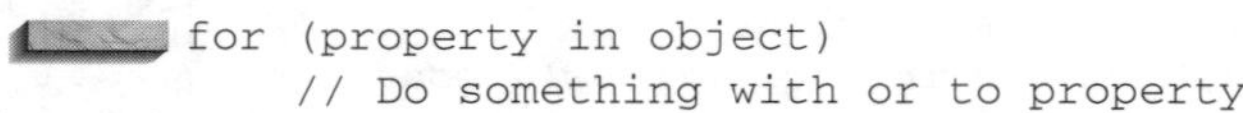

```
for (property in object)
    // Do something with or to property
```

The preceding functionality is similar to the UNIX Bourne Shell's for loop. The properties are read from the object, put into the index variable, and then manipulated by the line of code following the for loop.

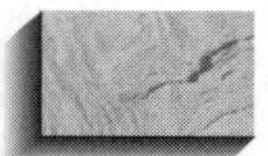

TIP
Remember, in JavaScript only the first line after the for loop command will be executed repeatedly. To execute multiple lines, enclose them within curly braces ({}).

Thus, it is easy to produce a list of supported properties for a specified object within JavaScript in an alert window. In the following example, we will collect the properties and put them into a long string variable. After every 20 items, the alert window is displayed in the browser, the list is reset to NULL, and the next set of items is displayed. This continues until all properties of the specified object have been displayed, as shown in the following illustration:

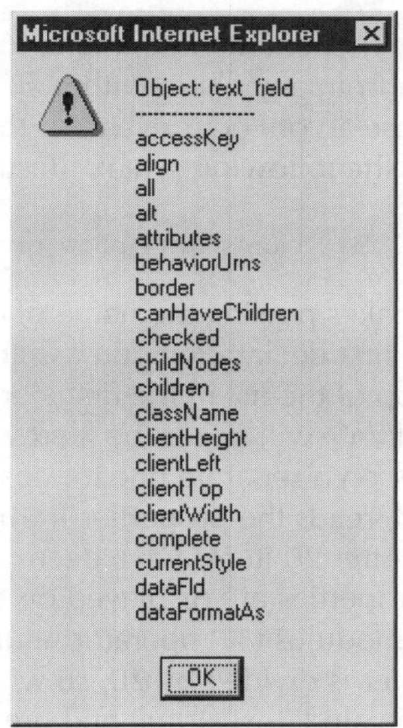


```
function show_properties (input_object) {
  // \n is a newline; Simply puts entries on different lines
  var alert_text = "Object: " + input_object.name +
                   "\n" + "--------------------" + "\n";
  var counter    = 0;
  for (i in input_object) {
     // Build alert text string.  Special handling for strings, show value
     alert_text = alert_text + i + '\n';
     // Increment property counter
     ++counter;
     // Modulus operator returns remainder of division, if 0, every 20 items
        if (counter % 20 == 0) {
        alert(alert_text);
        alert_text = null;
     }
  }
  // Print the last set
  alert(alert_text);
  input_object.blur();    // required when debugging Alert with OnFocus
}
```

By putting the preceding functionality into a function, you will be able to call the show_properties function from anywhere within an HTML document. A simple way to call the routine is to use an onFocus event for the object and call the show_properties function, as the following syntax illustrates:

```
<input type=text name=text_field onFocus="show_properties(this)">
```

Using the keyword this makes passing the name of object simple. To explain the preceding code in detail, the first declaration and assignment of alert_text is merely placing a short heading on top of the list in the first alert window with a dashed line underneath it. The newlines ("/n") will cause the alert window to put everything that follows the newline character on a separate line for cosmetic purposes. The for loop, as previously described, reads the properties from the object and concatenates them to the string alert_text. After 20 items have been collected (or when the routine runs out of properties), the properties are displayed on the screen—each separated by a newline character. The modulus (**%**) operator returns the *remainder* of a division operation. The counter is divided by 20, so when the remainder is 0, it will display the alert box, clear the alert_text string, and prepare to process another group of properties. The last group of records is displayed in an alert window and the function ends.

This particular routine has its limitations, despite its advantages. The alert window is a piece of prepackaged software; therefore, it is easiest to keep its arguments simple. Still more useful would be a method to display other attributes of the properties listed (besides just the name), such as datatype (string, object, number, and so forth) and value. This would be a bit difficult to arrange in an alert window as used in the preceding example. How would different values and columns be aligned for a readable display? Though the procedures are not immediately obvious, they do exist. Instead of using an alert window to display the properties list, a pop-up window could be opened and, combining the techniques of this discussion and the previous alert window, an HTML display (with HTML tables to control spacing) could be used to dynamically populate the new window.

The advantages of the pop-up window approach are many, and in many ways overcome the disadvantages of having to use pop-up alert messages and Dynamic HTML through JavaScript. The power and flexibility of being able to use HTML to control the display is a substantial advantage.

The disadvantages to using the pop-up alert message approach should be considered. Extra effort may be expended toward achieving the appearance of the output right, and the more complex the approach, the more effort required.

The following example, illustrated in Figure 12-1, uses a pop-up HTML window to display properties. Instead of displaying generic properties, a specialized example

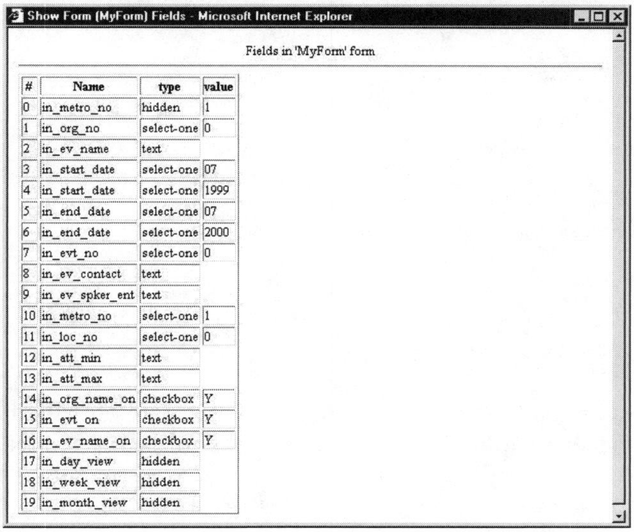

Show Form (MyForm) Fields - Microsoft Internet Explorer

Fields in 'MyForm' form

#	Name	type	value
0	in_metro_no	hidden	1
1	in_org_no	select-one	0
2	in_ev_name	text	
3	in_start_date	select-one	07
4	in_start_date	select-one	1999
5	in_end_date	select-one	07
6	in_end_date	select-one	2000
7	in_evt_no	select-one	0
8	in_ev_contact	text	
9	in_ev_spker_ent	text	
10	in_metro_no	select-one	1
11	in_loc_no	select-one	0
12	in_att_min	text	
13	in_att_max	text	
14	in_org_name_on	checkbox	Y
15	in_evt_on	checkbox	Y
16	in_ev_name_on	checkbox	Y
17	in_day_view	hidden	
18	in_week_view	hidden	
19	in_month_view	hidden	

FIGURE 12-1. *Show Form Fields in HTML pop-up*

is used to list attributes of an HTML form and lists the fields defined for the specified HTML form.

```
function show_form_fields(oForm) {
  // Text to be displayed
  var t = "";
  // Open a window to display this information
  var w = window.open("","properties","scrollbars=yes,width=600,height=200");
  w.document.write("<HTML><TITLE>Show Form [" + oForm.name + "] Fields</TITLE>");
  w.document.write("<BODY><CENTER>");
  // Makes sure the form has a name before displaying it
  if (oForm.name.length > 0) {
     t = "'" + oForm.name + "'";
     // Display name of HTML form
     w.document.write("Fields in " + t + " form");
     w.document.write("<HR>");
     // Table definition
     w.document.write("<TABLE BORDER=1>");
     // Table headings
     w.document.write("<TH>#</TH>");
     w.document.write("<TH>Name</TH>");
     w.document.write("<TH>type</TH>");
     w.document.write("<TH>value</TH>");
```

```
      // Cycle through form fields
      for (i=0;i<oForm.length;i++) {
        // Put new entry on new line
        w.document.write("<TR><TD>" + i + "</TD>");
        // Name of field
        w.document.write("<TD>" + oForm[i].name + "</TD>");
        // Type of field
        w.document.write("<TD>" + oForm[i].type + "</TD>");
        // Value of field
        w.document.write("<TD>" + oForm[i].value + "</TD>");
      }
      w.document.write("</TABLE>");
    }
  w.document.write("</CENTER></BODY></HTML>");
  w.document.close();
  // Return window object to caller
  return w;
}
```

A simple way to call the preceding routine is to use an onSubmit event for the form and call the show_form_fields function, as the following syntax illustrates:

```
<form name=DansForm onSubmit="show_form_fields(this)">
```

Comparing the preceding code to the prior section, the prior section used a for loop to traverse through the objects, taking the advantage that JavaScript represents HTML form objects as normal array objects as well as associative array objects belonging to the specified form. JavaScript represents HTML form fields as regular (number index) array objects and associative array (named index) structures. This dual representation can be confusing. It is often less complicated to represent the data in the easiest way for the manipulation to be performed. To avoid errors for dual representation specification, walk through the form fields individually by numeric index. The length attribute of the form is used to control the loop, and form.length is the number of elements in the form array. When multiple objects have the same name, JavaScript defines them as array elements, so two fields in a form called 'RecordStatus' would *have* to be referred to as numbered array elements to tell them apart. In other words, to retrieve the value of a specific occurrence of RecordStatus in ValuesForm, the correct syntax to retrieve the first value is ValuesForm.RecordStatus[0].value. It is for these situations that the show_properties routines previously discussed are most useful.

On Internet Explorer 4.0.1, window.screen properties will not return values for the associative for loop, even though its properties can be referenced directly. Writing the properties to a pop-up window rather than an alert window can generally be more useful—it may be a good idea to have both routines in case of problems. Occasionally, certain kinds of object references may be problematic for a specific browser, so an easier alternative to a complex routine may be desired. Finally, certain object property values when rendered on the screen appear not as their actual values, but as HTML objects because of how HTML evaluates them when drawn on the page. The HTML objects can take up a lot of space in the document window.

Opening a New Window Passing Parameters

Times may occur when you want to pass parameters to a PL/SQL routine (or any CGI routine) either in the current window or in a new window. The following script will either open a new page or replace the existing page:

```
<HTML>
<HEAD>
<TITLE>Passing a Variable to a Link</TITLE>
<SCRIPT LANGUAGE="JavaScript">
function CallNewWindow () {
  myWindow = window.open(
           'RoutineToCall?in_text_value=' +
            MyForm.in_text_variable.value,
           'myWin',
           'toolbar=yes,location=yes,width=500, height=300')
}
function CallSameWindow () {
  window.location =
           'RoutineToCall?in_text_value=' +
            MyForm.in_text_variable.value
}
</SCRIPT>
</HEAD>
<BODY>
<A href="javascript:CallNewWindow ()">Call New Window w/ Text Value</A><BR>
<A href="javascript:CallSameWindow ()">Call Same Window w/ Text Value</A>
<FORM NAME="MyForm" ACTION="FormAction" METHOD="GET">
<INPUT TYPE="text" NAME="in_text_variable" VALUE="12/31/1999"></TD>
</FORM>
</BODY>
</HTML>
```

Assigning JavaScript Variables

JavaScript variables are created and handled similar to other languages, and can be declared before they are used. For reasons of scope (which part of the application knows about a particular value), it is advisable to declare variables before using them.

JavaScript variables can have a *local* or *global* scope. Global variables are referenced throughout the whole document, but local variables are known only in the current block of code—usually an object definition, event handler, function, or merely lines enclosed within curly braces ({}). Generally speaking, local variables are easier to address, by their nature, because global values can be assigned anywhere in a document and it can be difficult to trace the source of their values.

Operationally, no difference exists between local and global variables in JavaScript. The difference is where they are defined, how they are used, and where they retrieve their values. Global variables are defined outside functions and blocks, while local variables are defined inside.

In the following example, the variable myGlobal would be global, but myLocal, being defined within the current block of JavaScript code (the curly braces), would be local and recognized only within that block. A reference to myLocal outside the curly braces would produce an error. The myGlobal variable could be referenced anywhere in the document, as well as within another pair of script tags.

```
<SCRIPT>
var myGlobal;
if (typeof myGlobal == "undefined") {
   var myLocal;
}
```

Use of global variables can have unexpected consequences and should be minimized for two reasons. It can be difficult to trace them back to their source. More importantly, under the right conditions, global variables can interfere with one another to produce incorrect results. Consider the following example:

```
function Function1 {
  for (j=0; j<25;j++)
}

function Function2 () {
  for (j=0;j<10;j++)
      function1();
}
```

In the preceding example, Function2 will call function1, but *not* 10 times as the for loop suggests. Instead, because variable j was defined in neither procedure, it will be defined on the fly in procedure 2 and the same instance of j will be used by procedure 1, returning 25 and immediately exiting the function 2 loop. Defining variable j in both functions would have kept the actual variable local and the problem would have been avoided.

Using the Submit Button

One of the primary uses of HTML forms is to collect data from users and send it to a server to be processed. This process of sending data to a server is called the *submission.* The primary way of performing submit operations is through the use of a *Submit button* from which HTML performs all submit processing for the user, as the following line of code illustrates:

```
<INPUT TYPE="SUBMIT" VALUE="Submit Button">
```

The preceding HTML code would place a Submit button on the screen and when pressed, would send the fields in the HTML form to the server. Only *named* form fields will be sent. As in the preceding example, the Submit button typically lacks the name attribute; therefore, the Submit button itself would not be included as a value. If you supply the name attribute for the Submit button, it will send its value to the server.

Using the built-in Submit button has disadvantages. The primary disadvantage is that pressing it is absolute, meaning that once initiated, such a submission cannot be easily stopped or canceled. A somewhat more versatile approach is to define and use a submit procedure, performing the submission with an ordinary HTML button and using the form fields submit method, as illustrated in the following syntax:

```
<INPUT TYPE="BUTTON" VALUE="Submit" onClick="doSubmit(this.form) ">
```

Consider the previous code defining an ordinary button invoking a JavaScript function which, when pressed, will enable presubmit processing before invoking the form's submit method. The following example illustrates this function:

```
function doSubmit(oForm) {
  // Check to be sure that the district value is set to D.C.
  // If it is not, display a message and do not submit the form
  if (oForm.District.value != "D.C.") {
      alert('"' + oField.value + ' "' + " is not a valid district");
      oForm.District.focus();
      return;
  }
  // Continued pre-submit processing could occur here
  // Submit the form using the form's submit method.
  oForm.submit();
}
```

The preceding function validates a form field and cancels the submission if the validation fails. The return statement ensures that the oForm.submit() method is never invoked if the validation fails.

Validating Form Fields

One of the more useful functionality features of JavaScript is to validate form fields before sending data to a server to be processed. Validating form fields before they are sent eliminates the need for sending data to a server, validating it, and sending it back to a form for correction. All of this can be handled in the form without having to send it to a server for processing.

JavaScript provides several event handlers to be used for form validation, including the onFocus() handler (invoked when a form field becomes the current field or gains focus), onBlur() (invoked when a form field stops being the current field or loses focus), and onChange() (invoked when the value of a form field changes and loses focus). The first two event handlers can be used to store and restore form field values programmatically. The onChange() event handler is used most often for validation purposes, invoked when a form field changes value (from the field itself; not when assigned programmatically). When an event handler is invoked (or triggered), the JavaScript code following the event handler as defined in the field tag is immediately executed, as the following line of code illustrates:

```
<INPUT TYPE="TEXT" NAME="District" onChange="alert('District changed');">
```

The preceding code will raise an alert window each time the district field is changed by entering a new value in the text field. Alternatively, it is preferred to define a function at the top of your HTML script and execute a JavaScript function, thus eliminating the problem of limited space in the form field tag. For example, the following syntax makes use of the this object:

```
<INPUT TYPE="TEXT" NAME="District" onChange="onChangeDistrict(this);">
```

In the preceding example, onChangeDistrict() is a JavaScript function defined elsewhere in the form and "this" is a reference to the current object, in this case the "District" form field.

Structurally, the best way to perform field validation is to create special-purpose functions to validate each form field independently of the others. Your code is kept simple, and the processing occurring in one function should not affect the processing happening in other functions. Any kind of processing permissible through JavaScript can happen in these validation functions, including validation and navigation back to the offending field when data fails validation. The onChangeDistrict() function could appear identical to the following snippet of code:

```
function ChangeDistrict(oField) {
      if (oField.value != "D.C.") {
          alert('"' + oField.value + '"' + " is not a valid district");
          oField.focus();
          return;
      }
}
```

The field is called oField in the preceding validation function. oField is passed in as the "this" keyword in the preceding text tag, but will be referenced as oField in the function. References to oField point to the field object passed to the function, in this case the District form field. The value is compared to the valid value (D.C.) and, if not equal, then the alert (which displays the incorrect value in the message) is raised. The form field's focus method is used to return focus to the field and the return command ensures that the function will exit at that point.

The process of validating form fields is not *quite* this simple. It is ridiculously easy to circumvent the preceding validation by exiting the field a second time. The field has not technically changed, so the onChange() event will not occur the second time. Prior to submission, another round of validation, this time in a submit procedure as previously described, is required to maintain data integrity. The same checks performed at the field level must again be applied to each field before submission to prevent clever users from slipping past field validation.

Handling Exceptions with the onError Event Handler

JavaScript provides a powerful way to perform exception handling with the onError event handler. When an object is assigned a user-defined onError function, it will be executed when a JavaScript error occurs. Two things must take place for the validation to occur. First, the exception handler (function) must be defined. Second, the onError event handler must be initialized to the error handler.

The function defined to handle errors must accept three arguments to process JavaScript errors. These required arguments are the error message, line number, and URL of the offending document. These can be easily collected and passed to a server for handling (perhaps stored in a log table). The following is an example of an error handler; the results can be viewed in the following illustration:

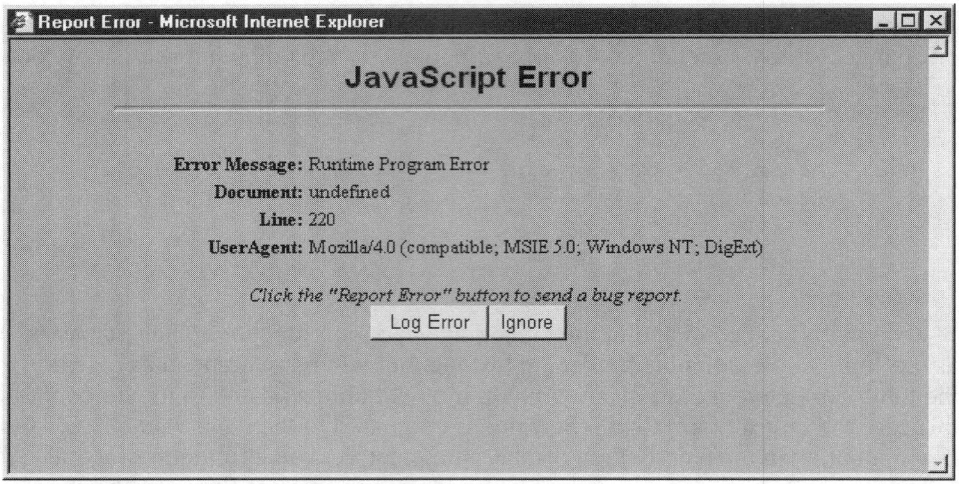

```
<SCRIPT>
function report_error (msg,url,line) {
   // Parameters to open a window are
   //           URL (none specified here),
   //           Window name (it should be unique)
   //           Window attributes
   var w = window.open("", "error_window",
                        "scrollbars=yes,width=625,height=300");
   // Open the window now
   w.document.open();
   w.document.write('<HTML><BODY BGCOLOR="AABBCC">');
   w.document.write('<CENTER><FONT SIZE=5 FACE="helvetica"><B>');
   w.document.write('JavaScript Error');
   w.document.write('</B></FONT></CENTER>');
   w.document.write('<HR SIZE=4 WIDTH="80%">');
   w.document.write('<FORM ACTION="" METHOD=POST ENCTYPE="text/plain">');
   w.document.write('<INPUT TYPE=HIDDEN NAME="msg" VALUE="' + msg + '">');
   w.document.write('<INPUT TYPE=HIDDEN NAME="url" VALUE="' + url + '">');
   w.document.write('<INPUT TYPE=HIDDEN NAME="userAgent"' +
                '        VALUE="' + navigator.userAgent + '">');
   w.document.write('<FONT SIZE=3>');
   w.document.write('<DIV align=CENTER>');
   w.document.write('<TABLE BORDER=0>');
   w.document.write('<TR><TD ALIGN=RIGHT><B>Error Message:</B></TD>');
   w.document.write('    <TD>' + msg + '</TD></TR>');
   w.document.write('<TR><TD ALIGN=RIGHT><B>Document:</B></TD>');
   w.document.write('    <TD>' + url + '</TD></TR>');
   w.document.write('<TR><TD ALIGN=RIGHT><B>Line:</B></TD>');
   w.document.write('    <TD>' + line + '</TD></TR>');
   w.document.write('<TR><TD ALIGN=RIGHT><B>UserAgent:</B></TD>');
   w.document.write('    <TD>'+navigator.userAgent+'</TD></TR>');
   w.document.write('</TABLE>');
   w.document.write('<BR><I>Click the "Report Error" button to send a bug report.</I>');
   w.document.write('<BR>');
   w.document.write('<INPUT TYPE="SUBMIT" VALUE="Log Error">');
   w.document.write('<INPUT TYPE="BUTTON" VALUE="Ignore" ' +
                '        onClick="self.close()">');
```

```
   w.document.write('</DIV></FORM></BODY></HTML>');
   w.document.close();
   return true;
}
// Inline script is called immediately, which
// calls the report_error function on an error
window.onerror = report_error();
</SCRIPT>
```

Working with PL/SQL Code and Various Browsers

A developer reported that he had included the following JavaScript in his PL/SQL procedure, which worked fine in IE, but it does not show up in Netscape. Therefore, it must be a JavaScript difference, right?

```
htp.print('<input type="button" value="Return"
                  onClick="history.back()"');
```

The problem had nothing to do with JavaScript. The problem is that Netscape Navigator requires form objects to be placed between the HTML form tags or it ignores the form. Remember, HTML differences may also exist. By changing the following script, it work in both browsers:

```
htp.formOpen('package.procedure');
htp.print('<input type="button" value="Return"
                  onClick="history.back()"');
htp.formClose;
```

Making a Two-Dimensional Array in JavaScript

How to create a two-dimensional (or more) array in JavaScript may not be obvious, but what you need to do to accomplish this is create an array of arrays. First, declare the initial list of values array, which will be your two-dimensional array as a result. The following example uses states and cities within the state. The following example demonstrates the JavaScript code to accomplish this task; however, you could develop a generic procedure pulling the data from a table to load these arrays.

```
// Declare our initial array
list_of_value     = new Array()
// Now within each array element we create another array as our
// second dimension.
list_of_value ["AL"] = new Array("Huntsville","Mobile","Montgomery")
list_of_value ["AR"] = new Array("Little Rock","Conway","Springdale")
list_of_value ["CO"] = new Array("Evergreen","Denver","Aurora","Keystone")
list_of_value ["IL"] = new Array("Naperville","Lombard","Princeton")
```

For the cities in Illinois ("IL"), loop through y for the variable list_of_value ["IL"][y].

Assigning JavaScript Variables

Did you ever wonder how to pass a JavaScript variable's value to a variable in a PL/SQL procedure in OAS? The following script prompts for the username and writes that name in another HTML page.

```
<html>
<head>
<SCRIPT>
  function dispname() { return prompt("Enter your name:","");
</SCRIPT>
</head>
<body>
<SCRIPT>
  document.write(dispname());
</SCRIPT>
</body>
</html>
```

How do you pass this name to a PL/SQL procedure? The following script illustrates the initial steps in this process. After refining the preceding script, the following script will pass the above prompted for value onto a PL/SQL procedure (or any cartridge or CGI):

```
<html>
<head>
<SCRIPT>
   function get_name(form) {
      var name=prompt("Enter your first and last name:","");
           document.welcome.u_name.value=name;
           return document.welcome.u_name.value;
        }
</SCRIPT>
</head>
<body>
<form name="welcome" action="/plsql/my_proc"
onSubmit="get_name(this);">
<input type=hidden name=u_name value="">
<input type=submit value=Submit>
</form>
</body>
</html>
```

Invoking a PL/SQL Procedure from a Pick List

Normally, a form Submit button will call another PL/SQL procedure (or any other URL). The user must click on the Submit button for this to occur. What if you wanted to call the next PL/SQL procedure as a result of the user selecting an item from a pick list or when the user clicked on a radio button, but without requiring the user to click the Submit button?

For example, you want to call the get_employee routine with the specific employee number when the user selects an employee from a drop-down list. The following HTML code is dynamically generated to pull employees from the table and illustrates the procedures described previously:

```
<html>
<head>
<title>Pick an Employee</title>
<script language="javascript">
function jump (page) {
      if ( page != "" ) self.location = page;
}
</script>
</head>
<body>
    <h1>Pick an Employee</h1>
    <form method="POST" name="vform" action="#">
    <b>Employees</b>
      <select onchange="jump (this.options[ this.selectedIndex ].value)">
        <option value="">
        <option value="/plsql/get_employee?in_id=1204">Austin Brown
        <option value="/plsql/get_employee?in_id=4023">Fred Flintstone
        </select>
    </form>
</body>
</html>
```

Once the employee name is selected from the list, the jump function is executed and control is passed to the stored procedure.

Changing Frames Simultaneously

What if you want to change the contents of two (or more) frames simultaneously upon clicking a link? This task requires a snippet of JavaScript similar to the following example:

```
<html>
<head>

<title>Changing multiple frames<title>
<SCRIPT LANGUAGE=JavaScript>
function change_all_frames(in_emp) {
  top.frame2.location.href = "get_emp_info?in_emp="+in_emp;
  top.frame3.location.href = "get_hours?in_emp="+in_emp;
  top.frame4.location.href = "get_expenses?in_emp="+in_emp;
}
</script>
</head>
<body>
...
</body>
</html>
```

Resolving the Access Denied Error

At some point, you may receive the infamous "Access Denied" message from a JavaScript routine. The "Access Denied" message occurs when you have multiple frames and from one frame you attempt to refer to a URL from another machine. This can occur when the host name is hardcoded on one frame and is not hardcoded in another frame in which the relative path is used. In other words, one frame contains an absolute path (hardcoded) and the other is relative. If this error occurs, check the URLs specified.

For example, your home page contains a number of frames, which are sourced from a frameset tag displaying the initial home page. In one of the frames, you placed a navigation bar, which had a source equal to the IP address of the machine—for example, src=209.108... And the other frames come from the database. If I came to your site through the site's domain name—for example, www.esports-net.com—the other frames have a source pointing to the domain name. To JavaScript, this is considered two different machines; therefore, it will not allow one page to reference another frame's source (for security reasons).

Building JavaScript Menus

If you wish to build menus with JavaScript, search the Web and you will find plenty of menu examples.

Passing Spaces as a Part of the URL

If you wish to pass spaces in a URL, you need to convert the spaces to pluses (+), or you can convert the spaces to %20 (hex for char 32 or a space). If the conversion is accomplished with PL/SQL, using the replace function will perform the conversion automatically. If you are prompting for a parameter in an HTML form and the JavaScript is passing the parameter, you need to use your own function, identical to the following stringReplace function, to convert spaces to pluses. However, if the parameter is part of a form, not the standard form submit functionality, the browser will automatically convert spaces to pluses. If you use a specialized onSubmit event handler, you will need to replace spaces in JavaScript. The following stringReplace function will convert any character in a string to another character:

```
function stringReplace(orig, find, replace) {
  var pos = 0
  pos     = orig.indexOf(find)
  while (pos != -1) {
    orig = orig.substring(0,pos) + replace +
           orig.substring(pos+find.length,orig.length)
    pos  = orig.indexOf(find)
  }
  return orig
}
```

To replace spaces with pluses, you would call stringReplace identical to the following line of code:

```
stringwithoutspaces = stringReplace(stringwithspaces," ","+")
```

Debugging onFocus with Alert Will Not Work

An onFocus event will be called after an alert box is displayed. Do not use alert boxes for debugging when onFocus and onBlur events are present. The following is an example of a snippet of JavaScript code that could cause trouble if you add an alert (for example, for debugging):

```
/*-------------------------------------------------------------
- Function: jf_field_entry
- Purpose:  Save value of field when OnFocus event occurs
-
- WARNING!!!  WARNING!!!  WARNING!!!  WARNING!!!  WARNING!!!
- When any ALERT message box is displayed while focus is set to
- an object having this onFocus event defined, this function
- will execute!!!  If you put an ALERT anywhere, then you
- could easily get weird results.
- WARNING!!!  WARNING!!!  WARNING!!!  WARNING!!!  WARNING!!!
-------------------------------------------------------------*/
function jf_field_entry(p1) {
  if((p1.name == "in_task_id")      ||
     (p1.name == "in_subproj_id"))  {

    // save values into global javascript variables for future processing
    jv_entry_value = p1.options[p1.selectedIndex].value;
    jv_entry_index = p1.selectedIndex;

    // this alert (whether in this function or another javascript
    // function) will re-save the erroneous value - wrong!
    alert("Initial value = " + jv_entry_index);
  }
  return;
}
```

Subscribing to the JavaScript OnFocus Newsletter

The weekly newsletter of JavaScripts.com contains great tips and techniques along with a library of scripts. You can subscribe to their weekly newsletter from their site, located at http://www.javascripts.com/. If you are an advertiser, you can reach more than 90,000 developers with your message through sponsorship of javascripts.com's weekly newsletter. Their advertising department can be contacted at advertising@earthweb.com.

Reviewing Visual JavaScript Tools

If you are more comfortable developing code using graphical development environments, tools exist enabling you to graphically build JavaScript code. Two tools worth mentioning are NetObjects ScriptBuilder and Netscape's Visual JavaScript.

Talking About NetObjects ScriptBuilder

Infuse supplied the first visual editor for JavaScript available on the market. In February of 1998, NetObjects acquired Infuse. Further information about the product can be found at http://www.netobjects.com. The current product version is 3.0.

Taking a Quick Look at Netscape's Visual JavaScript

Netscape's Visual JavaScript also enables you to visually develop JavaScript code. The product is written in Java, which because of the speed issues was a disadvantage originally, but today, because of faster *just in time* compilers, Visual JavaScript's speed is not as much of an issue. The advantage is that the product is platform-independent. This product shows the page as it is being created.

Summary

JavaScript is a large portion of any Web project. It is a powerful scripting language putting the 'life' into your site. A number of topics from data validation to pop-up windows have been covered. Great books on JavaScript are available. One of my favorite references is a *JavaScript Pocket Reference* by David Flanagan (O'Reilly & Associates, 1998)—I carry it with me everywhere I go.

CHAPTER 13

XML

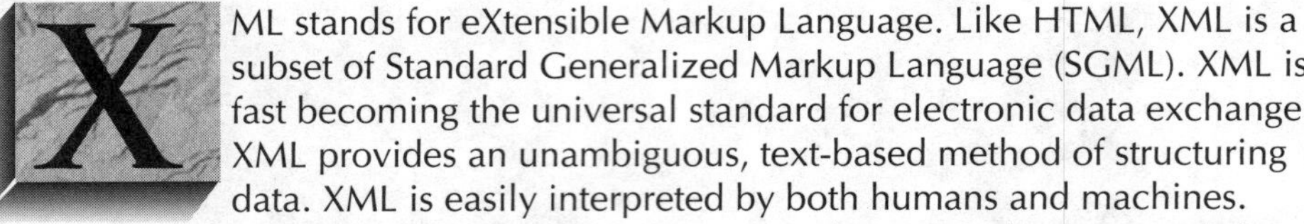

XML stands for eXtensible Markup Language. Like HTML, XML is a subset of Standard Generalized Markup Language (SGML). XML is fast becoming the universal standard for electronic data exchange. XML provides an unambiguous, text-based method of structuring data. XML is easily interpreted by both humans and machines.

Data in XML documents is represented using markup tags. The tags are defined by the user to describe the content of the data, but do not address the presentation of the content (as in HTML). XML identifies what the data means versus how the data looks, as the following example illustrates:

```
<BOOK>
      <TITLE>Oracle8i Web Development Tips and Techniques</TITLE>
       <AUTHOR>Bradley D. Brown</AUTHOR>
       <PUBLISHER>Oracle Press</PUBLISHER>
</BOOK>
```

Why is XML important to e-business? XML presents a simple, nonproprietary means of sharing data. Manufacturers, wholesalers, retailers, consumers, and financial institutions can share the same data. XML is a nonproprietary language; the same data can be accessed through multiple devices, such as Web browsers, pagers, cellular phones, and personal data assistants. XML essentially streamlines the process of communication between business and the consumer.

Oracle's strategy for implementing XML is to *"deliver the best platform for developers to productively and cost effectively deploy reliable and scalable Internet applications exploiting XML."*

Oracle8i will provide developers with core XML support implemented in Java and running on the Oracle8i built-in Java Virtual Machine (VM). XML support will be included in other products, such as OAS, and in tools such as JDeveloper.

The following topics will be covered in this chapter:

- Understanding the basic rules of XML
- Examining XML document syntax and structure
- Examining common XML document APIs
- Comparing XML and HTML
- Creating a sample XML document
- Using XSL to format and display XML documents
- XML support in Oracle8i
- Examining XML and Oracle Context
- Examining the Oracle XML Parser

- Examining the Oracle XML Class Generator
- Examining the Oracle XML SQL utility
- Examining the Oracle XSQL Servlet

Understanding the Basic Rules of XML

XML contains specific rules, which must be strictly followed when creating a document. A document must be well-formed, and meet the validity requirements set forth in the Document Type Declaration (DTD). XML is not flexible with respect to these rules.

Defining Document Type Declarations (DTD)

The structure of an XML document consists of a strict hierarchy of elements with a single root. Each element can consist of character data, child elements, and element attributes. The DTD formally defines the structure of an XML document based on these elements. The DTD is the blueprint for the document.

In the following example, a DTD is created for an XML document describing a car. The root element is CAR, which has one attribute—manufacturer—which may contain the values Chrysler, Chevrolet, Ford, or Unknown. The elements MAKE, MODEL, and COLOR are children of CAR. COLOR contains two optional children, UPPER and LOWER. DTD syntax will be covered in a later section within this chapter.

```
<!DOCTYPE CAR [
    <!ELEMENT CAR (MAKE,MODEL,COLOR)>
    <!ATTLIST CAR manufacturer (Chrysler|Chevrolet|Ford|Unknown)
       #IMPLIED>
    <!ELEMENT COLOR(UPPER*,LOWER*)>
    <!ELEMENT MAKE   (#PCDATA)>
    <!ELEMENT MODEL (#PCDATA)>
    <!ELEMENT UPPER (#PCDATA)>
    <!ELEMENT LOWER (#PCDATA)>
]>
```

Defining Well-Formed

The requirement that an XML document be well-formed refers specifically to the document syntax. A document is said to be *well-formed* if the document contains intelligible markup. Every tag must have a beginning and ending tag, when required, in a well-formed document. While most browsers will correctly process HTML tags that are not closed or nested properly, XML documents have a strict tag structure, which is defined by the DTD. A tag starting within the scope of another tag must also end within the same scope.

The following is an example of a well-formed XML document, which conforms to the DTD defined in the preceding section:

```
<?xml version="1.0" ?>
<CAR manufacturer="Chrysler">
    <MAKE>Jeep</MAKE>
     <MODEL>Cherokee</MODEL>
     <COLOR>
            <UPPER>Green</UPPER>
            <LOWER>Grey</LOWER>
     </COLOR>
 </CAR>
```

In the preceding example, every start tag has an end tag, and each tag is nested correctly and conforms to the document hierarchy defined in the DTD.

Defining Validity

An XML document is said to be *valid* if the document actually conforms to a DTD. Every element must be in its place within the hierarchy defined by the DTD for a document to be considered valid.

The following document is well-formed because all of the tags are matching, but it is not valid because it violates the defined hierarchy of the DTD (the lower color is outside the color specification. To be valid, the <LOWER> tag must be enclosed within the <COLOR> tags, because <LOWER> is a child element of <COLOR>.

```
<?xml version="1.0" ?>
<CAR manufacturer="Chrysler">
     <MAKE>Jeep</MAKE>
     <MODEL>Cherokee</MODEL>
     <COLOR>
            <UPPER>Green</UPPER>
     </COLOR>
 <LOWER>Grey</LOWER>
</CAR>
```

Examining XML Document Syntax and Structure

XML, like most other languages, has strict rules for syntax. We took a brief look at syntax in the preceding section on *Understanding the Basic Rules of XML*. The following section will take a further look at XML document syntax rules.

Looking at Case

XML is case-sensitive. The tags <CAR>, <Car>, and <car> are treated as separate elements. If the DTD specifies an element in a particular case, all XML documents referencing the DTD must follow the case rules specified for each element. As with any case-sensitive language, defining corporate standards becomes increasingly important.

Examining Element Type Declarations in the DTD

Element type declarations define the name and content model for that element. The content model specifies what other element types are allowed inside an element of the declared type, and which child elements can be present. An element can be defined as one or more of the following content models.

EMPTY

The element can only be present as an empty element tag.

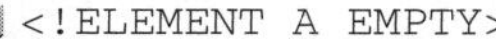

```
<!ELEMENT A EMPTY>
```

ANY

The element can contain any mixture of character data and elements.

```
<!ELEMENT B ANY>
```

Element-Only Content Models

The following elements contain only other elements as children. They cannot contain text. Special characters are used to represent element grouping.

FIXED ORDER IS INDICATED BY A COMMA <!ELEMENT A (B,C)> indicates that element A consists of element B followed by element C.

CHOICE IS INDICATED BY A VERTICAL BAR (OR PIPE) <!ELEMENT A (B|C)> indicates that element A consists of either element B or element C.

A REPEAT RULE IS INDICATED BY THE CHARACTERS *, ?, +, OR BY NO CHARACTER <!ELEMENT A (B,C)*> indicates that element A consists of zero or more instances of B followed by C.

<!ELEMENT A (B,C)?> indicates that element A consists of zero or one instances of B followed by C.

<!ELEMENT A (B,C)+> indicates that element A consists of one or more instances of B followed by C.

<!ELEMENT A (B,C)> indicates that element A consists of one and only one instance of B followed by C.

ROUND BRACKETS GROUP EXPRESSIONS FOR TREATMENT AS A UNIT (B,C) indicates that element B is grouped with element C.

Mixed Content Models

These elements enable the mixture of both elements and text as content. Two forms of the mixed content model exist.

<! ELEMENT A (#PCDATA)> indicates that element A may only contain character data consisting of zero or more characters.

<! ELEMENT A (#PCDATA|B|C)> indicates that element A may contain character data or element B or element C.

#PCDATA stands for parsed character data; the text following the element tag is parsed as a markup tag.

#CDATA is unparsed character data and can also be used on the page.

Other Rules

Only one element type declaration is allowed per element type. XML does not support overloading of elements.

Examining Attribute-List Declarations in the DTD

An element can have zero or more attributes. The set of attributes associated with a given element is defined by an attribute-list declaration. An attribute list declaration has the following basic form:

```
<!ATTLIST element-name attribute-definitions>
```

The element-name refers to the element type for the attribute list defined. The attribute-definitions are a sequence of properties defining name, type, and default value for each attribute associated with the element type.

Attribute Definition

The general form of an attribute definition is *attribute-name type default-declaration*. The attribute-name is the name of the attribute. The type is an expression or keyword, which defines the type of the attribute. The default-declaration defines the default value. The default-declaration can take on four possible values:

- **#IMPLIED** The attribute can be specified optionally in elements of the declared type. There is no default value.

- **#REQUIRED** The attribute must be specified in all elements of the declared type. There is no default value.
- **attr-value** The attribute can be specified optionally in elements of the declared type. A default value is given by the value inside the quotes.
- **#FIXED attr-value** The attribute value cannot be assigned a different value in an element instance. Every element of #FIXED type has a fixed value given within quotes.

Every attribute has a type. The following examples illustrate the various possible types:

- **String-Type** Attributes are indicated by the keyword CDATA.

```
<!ATTLIST X x CDATA #IMPLIED>
```

- **Enumerated-List Type** Attributes are lists of predefined values. An attribute value can take only one of the listed values.

```
<!ATTLIST X  x (male|female|unknown) #IMPLIED>
```

- **ID Type** Attributes define an attribute as element identifier. The following example illustrates two methods of expressing the ID type:

```
<!ATTLIST X id ID #IMPLIED>
<!ATTLIST X id ID #REQUIRED>
```

The only default value declarations allowed in the ID type are #IMPLIED and #REQUIRED.

- **IDREF Type** Attributes reference elements labeled by ID attributes.

```
<!ATTLIST X ref IDREF #IMPLIED>
```

- **ENTITY Type** Attributes accept a single unparsed entity reference. They are used to point to external data.

```
<!ENTITY my-car SYSTEM "images/car.jpg" NDATA JPG>
<!ATTLIST CAR-PIC car ENTITY #FIXED "my-car">
```

The attribute car refers the entity my-car.

- **ENTITIES Type** Attributes accept multiple unparsed entity references.

```
<!ATTLIST CAR-PIC car ENTITIES #IMPLIED>
```

- **NMTOKEN Type** Attributes can accept only tokens.

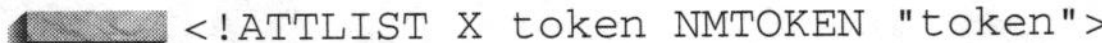

```
<!ATTLIST X token NMTOKEN "token">
```

- **NMTOKENS Type** Attributes may accept multiple tokens as values.

```
<!ATTLIST X tokens NMTOKENS "token1 token2 token3">
```

For further information regarding the syntax and structure introduced in the preceding section, refer to the XML specification found at www.w3.org.

Examining Common XML Document APIs

Two popular XML document APIs currently exist. One is the Document Object Model, or DOM, and the other is the simple API for XML, or SAX. The DOM is a tree-based API and SAX is event-based.

Looking at the Document Object Model (DOM)

The Document Object Model (DOM) is a programming API for both XML and HTML. The DOM defines the logical structure of a document and the way a document is accessed and manipulated. Programmers can create documents, manipulate their structure, and add or delete elements and constructs with the DOM. DOM documents have a structure that closely represents a tree, as illustrated in the following example:

```
<ANIMAL>
     <MAMMAL>
            <FOURLEGS>DOG</FOURLEGS>
            <TWOLEGS>MAN</TWOLEGS>
     </MAMMAL>
     <REPTILE>
            <AMPHIBIOUS>CROCODILE</AMPHIBIOUS>
            <DESERT>MONITOR LIZARD</DESERT>
     </REPTILE>
</ANIMAL>
```

The DOM in Figure 13-1 represents the preceding example.

Each of the boxes in Figure 13-1 represents a tag or node. The rounded boxes represent the node value, or data between the tags. The XML document is broken down based on the hierarchical or tree structure. The document's hierarchical

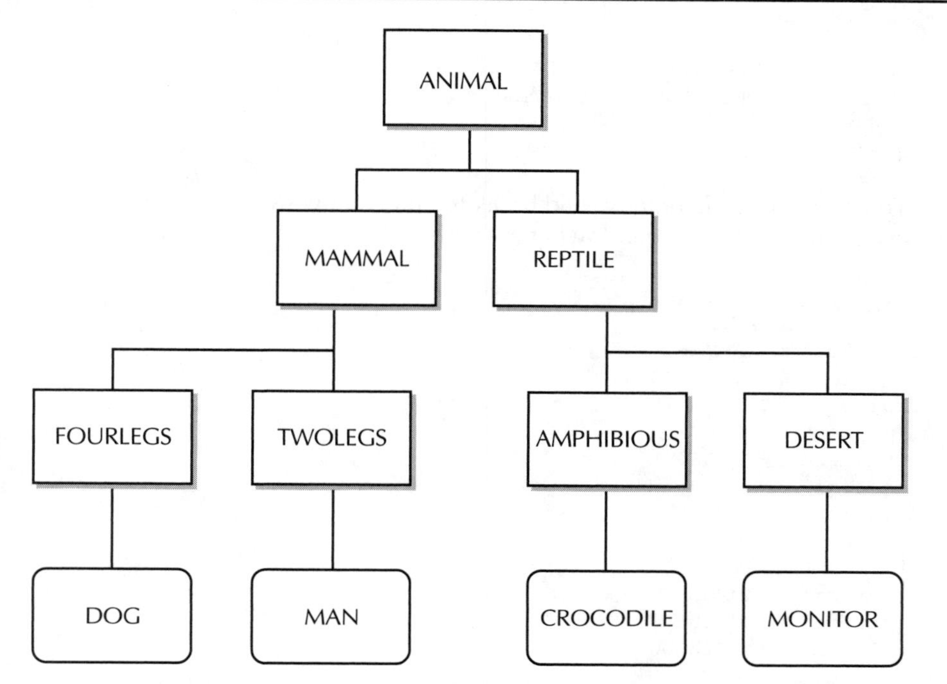

FIGURE 13-1. *DOM hierarchy of XML document*

structure is referred to as the structure model. The World Wide Web Consortium defined the DOM API specification. The complete API specification is available at http://www.w3.org.

Looking at SAX (Simple API for XML)

The SAX API is event-based as opposed to tree-based. Event-based means that SAX API reports parsing events, such as start and end tags, directly to the parsing application through callbacks and does not build an internal tree. The application implements event handlers, identical to the way a GUI application handles events. The following example illustrates how an event-based API would parse an XML document:

```
<ANIMAL>
     <MAMMAL>
            <FOURLEGS>DOG</FOURLEGS>
            <TWOLEGS>MAN</TWOLEGS>
```

```
        </MAMMAL>
      <REPTILE>
              <AMPHIBIOUS>CROCODILE</AMPHIBIOUS>
               <DESERT>MONITOR</DESERT>
      </REPTILE>
</ANIMAL>
```

The event-based handler would break the preceding XML into a series of linear events, as illustrated in the following example:

```
start document
start element ANIMAL
start element MAMMAL
start element FOURLEGS
characters DOG
end element FOURLEGS
start element TWOLEGS
characters MAN
end element TWOLEGS
end element MAMMAL
start element REPTILE
start element AMPHIBIOUS
characters CROCODILE
end element  AMPHIBIOUS
start element DESERT
characters MONITOR LIZARD
end element DESERT
end element REPTILE
end element ANIMAL
end document
```

The SAX approach to XML parsing is more straightforward than the DOM, but it is not as flexible or visual. Further information concerning SAX, including the JAVA implementation of the API, is available at http://www.microstar.com.

Comparing XML and HTML

XML and HTML are markup languages. They are based on sets of tags. They are used as a medium of data exchange on the World Wide Web. As mentioned in the introduction, HTML and XML are both subsets of SGML. Despite all of these commonalties, XML and HTML are quite different. XML represents data content, while HTML represents the presentation of data. They also differ in syntax and structure.

Looking at Common Ancestry

XML and HTML are siblings. They are subsets of Standard Generalized Markup Language (SMGL). SGML was created in 1974 by a development team at IBM led by Charles Goldfarb, and was standardized in 1986. SGML became the world standard for the interchange of computer documents. SGML uses tags to mark up the text of a document in the same manner as HTML or XML.

Looking at Differences in Syntax and Structure

As previously mentioned, XML and HTML are similar; they both use tags as markup. However, the similarities are only superficial; XML and HTML have more differences than similarities. The following is a list of these differences:

- XML elements and attributes are case sensitive, while HTML is not case sensitive.
- XML attributes must have an assigned value and be quoted. In HTML, quotes are optional in some cases and attribute values can be omitted.
- End tags are always required in XML. For some tags, such as <P>, end tags are optional in HTML.
- XML uses the special character **/** to represent empty elements <emptyelement/>. HTML contains no special character for empty elements.
- XML contains only five predefined entities (quot, amp, apos, lt, and gt). HTML has a large set of entities, which represent common mathematical or symbol characters.
- XML enables arbitrary attribute and element names. HTML is defined by a fixed set of elements and attributes.
- XML supports multiple, user-defined DTDs. HTML is defined by a single DTD, and contains a fixed grammar.

Creating a Sample XML Document

The following sections cover the creation of an XML DTD and an XML document based on that DTD. A DTD will be defined representing suspect demographic data to be shared among the law enforcement agencies.

Creating the Suspect DTD

What kind of information would we need about a suspect? How about basic demographic information such as descriptions, addresses, and phone numbers? The following DTD addresses these items:

```
<?xml version="1.0"?>
<!DOCTYPE suspect[
   <!ELEMENT suspect (name*,demographics*,address*,comms*)+>
   <!ATTLIST suspect id CDATA #IMPLIED>
   <!ELEMENT name (first, middle*, last)+>
   <!ELEMENT demographics (age*,height*,weight*)>
   <!ATTLIST demographics gender (male|female|unknown) #IMPLIED>
   <!ATTLIST demographics race
     (black|white|hispanic|asian|unknown) #REQUIRED>
   <!ATTLIST demographics hair (black|blond|brown|white|unknown)
     #IMPLIED>
   <!ATTLIST demographics eyes (blue|brown|green|hazel|gray)
     #IMPLIED>
   <!ELEMENT address (street*,city*,state*,zip*)+>
   <!ATTLIST address type (home|work|other) #IMPLIED>
   <!ELEMENT comms (phone*)+>
   <!ELEMENT phone (areacode*,prefix*,suffix*)+>
   <!ATTLIST phone type (cellphone|pager|residential|work)
     #IMPLIED>
   <!ELEMENT first    (#PCDATA)>
   <!ELEMENT middle   (#PCDATA)>
   <!ELEMENT last     (#PCDATA)>
   <!ELEMENT age      (#PCDATA)>
   <!ELEMENT height   (#PCDATA)>
   <!ELEMENT weight   (#PCDATA)>
   <!ELEMENT street   (#PCDATA)>
   <!ELEMENT city     (#PCDATA)>
   <!ELEMENT state    (#PCDATA)>
   <!ELEMENT zip      (#PCDATA)>
   <!ELEMENT areacode (#PCDATA)>
   <!ELEMENT prefix   (#PCDATA)>
   <!ELEMENT suffix   (#PCDATA)>
 ]>
```

An XML document based on the preceding DTD must comply with the following rules:

- It must contain one or more suspect elements.
- Each suspect element can have an optional ID attribute.

- Each suspect element will consist of one or more sets of zero or more name elements, zero or more demographic elements, zero or more address elements, and zero or more comms elements.
- Each name element will consist of one or more sets of first elements, zero or more middle elements, and last elements.
- Each demographic element can consist of zero or more age elements, zero or more height elements, and zero or more weight elements.
- Each demographic element can have an optional gender attribute, which must be male, female, or unknown.
- Each demographic element must have a race attribute, which must be black, white, hispanic, asian, or unknown.
- Each demographic element can have an optional hair attribute, which must be black, blond, brown, white, or unknown.
- Each demographic element can have an optional eyes attribute, which must be blue, brown, green, hazel, or unknown.
- Each address element will consist of one or more sets of zero or more street elements, zero or more city elements, zero or more state elements, and zero or more zip elements.
- Each address element will have an optional type attribute, which must be home, work, or other.
- Each comms element will consist of one or more sets of zero or more phone elements.
- Each phone element will consist of one or sets of zero or more area code elements, zero or more prefix elements, and zero or more suffix elements.
- Each phone element can have an optional type attribute, which must be either cellular phone, pager, residential, or work.
- Elements first, middle, last, age, height, weight, street, city, state, zip, area code, prefix, and suffix will be composed of character data.

Creating the Document

The following XML document is based on and complies with the DTD defined in the preceding section:

```
<?xml version="1.0"?>
<!DOCTYPE suspect SYSTEM "suspect.dtd">
```

```
<suspect id="S1">
   <name>
         <first>Joe</first>
         <last>Jackson</last>
   </name>
   <demographics gender="male" race="white" hair="blond"
     eyes="blue">
         <age>32</age>
         <height>6ft</height>
         <weight>175</weight>
   </demographics>
   <address type="home">
         <street>821 ELM</street>
   </address>
   <comms>
      <phone type="residential">
        <areacode>704</areacode>
        <prefix>333</prefix>
        <suffix>1234</suffix>
      </phone>
    </comms>
</suspect>
```

Using XSL to Format and Display XML Documents

If XML is to become the standard for electronic data interchange, there must also be a standard for presenting the data. HTML uses cascading style sheets to format and control the presentation of HTML documents. The same control is possible for XML documents with eXtensible Style Language (XSL).

Defining XSL

XSL is the proposed standard for expressing style sheets for XML. XSL is a scripting language used to describe rules for presenting XML source documents. XSL can present XML data in a variety of formats, such as HTML, speech, paper, or other media. XSL scripts are also referred to as XSL style sheets. Figure 13-2 demonstrates the relationship between an XML document, an XML processor, an XSL style sheet, and the possible representations of the data in the XML document.

The complete specification for XSL can be found at http://www.w3.org/TR/WD-xsl.

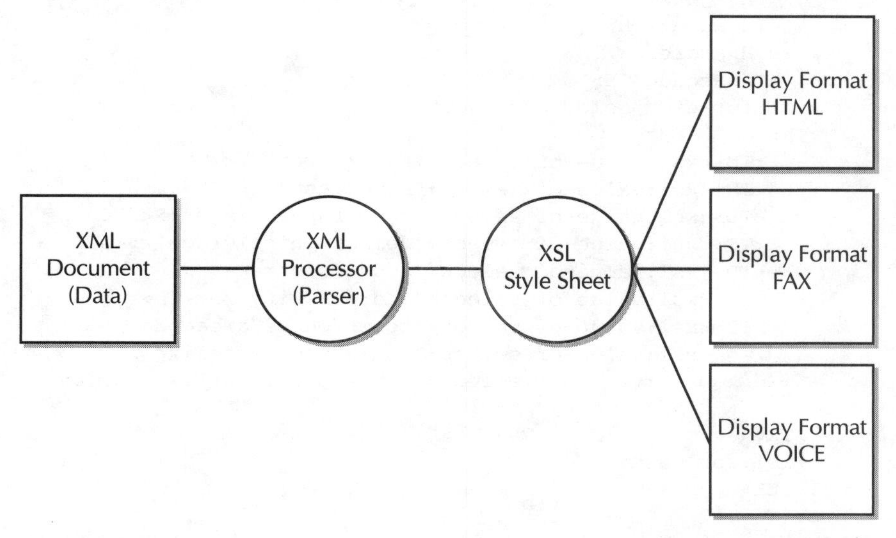

FIGURE 13-2. *Relationship between XML document, XML processor, and an XSL style sheet*

Using XSL to Display XML Data as HTML

The following XSL script will take an XML document and display the data in an HTML table. The following example uses the suspect XML document defined in a previous section:

```
<?xml version='1.0' ?>
 <xsl:stylesheet xmlns:xsl="http://www.w3.org/TR/WD-xsl">
   <xsl:template match="/">
     <HTML>
     <TITLE> XML Displayed with XSL Example </TITLE>
     <BODY bgcolor="#C0C0C0">
     <H1>XML Displayed with XSL Example</H1>
     <BR></BR>
     <H2>Suspect List</H2>
     <TABLE border="10">
           <TH>First</TH>
           <TH>Last</TH>
```

```
            <TH>Age</TH>
            <TH>Race</TH>
            <TH>Address</TH>
            <TH>Phone</TH>
        <xsl:for-each select="suspect">
        <TR>
            <TD><xsl:value-of select="name/first"/></TD>
            <TD><xsl:value-of select="name/last"/></TD>
            <TD><xsl:value-of select="demographics/age"/></TD>
            <TD><xsl:value-of select="demographics/@race"/></TD>
            <TD><xsl:value-of select="address/street"/>
                <xsl:value-of select="address/city"/></TD>
            <TD><xsl:value-of select="comms/phone/areacode"/>
                <xsl:value-of select="comms/phone/prefix"/>
                <xsl:value-of select="comms/phone/suffix"/></TD>

        </TR>
        </xsl:for-each>
      </TABLE>
    </BODY>
    </HTML>
  </xsl:template>
  </xsl:stylesheet>
```

The following XML document references the XSL script previously defined:

```
<?xml version="1.0"?>
<?xml-stylesheet type="text/xsl" href="suspect.xsl"?>
<!DOCTYPE suspect[
   <!ELEMENT suspect (name*,demographics*,address*,comms*)+>
   <!ATTLIST suspect id CDATA #IMPLIED>
   <!ELEMENT name (first, middle*, last)+>
   <!ELEMENT demographics (age*,height*,weight*)>
   <!ATTLIST demographics gender (male|female|unknown) #IMPLIED>
   <!ATTLIST demographics race
     (black|white|hispanic|asian|unknown) #REQUIRED>
   <!ATTLIST demographics hair (black|blond|brown|white|unknown)
     #IMPLIED>
   <!ATTLIST demographics eyes (blue|brown|green|hazel|gray)
     #IMPLIED>
   <!ELEMENT address (street*,city*,state*,zip*)+>
   <!ATTLIST address type (home|work|other) #IMPLIED>
   <!ELEMENT comms (phone*)+>
```

```
   <!ELEMENT phone (areacode*,prefix*,suffix*)+>
   <!ATTLIST phone type (cellphone|pager|residential|work)
    #IMPLIED>
   <!ELEMENT first    (#PCDATA)>
   <!ELEMENT middle   (#PCDATA)>
   <!ELEMENT last     (#PCDATA)>
   <!ELEMENT age      (#PCDATA)>
   <!ELEMENT height   (#PCDATA)>
   <!ELEMENT weight   (#PCDATA)>
   <!ELEMENT street   (#PCDATA)>
   <!ELEMENT city     (#PCDATA)>
   <!ELEMENT state    (#PCDATA)>
   <!ELEMENT zip      (#PCDATA)>
   <!ELEMENT areacode (#PCDATA)>
   <!ELEMENT prefix   (#PCDATA)>
   <!ELEMENT suffix   (#PCDATA)>
 ]>
 <suspect id="S1">
   <name>
         <first>Joe</first>
         <last>Jackson</last>
   </name>
   <demographics gender="male" race="white" hair="blond"
     eyes="blue">
         <age>32</age>
         <height>6ft</height>
         <weight>175</weight>
   </demographics>
   <address type="home">
         <street>821 ELM</street>
   </address>
   <comms>
      <phone type="residential">
        <areacode>704</areacode>
        <prefix>333</prefix>
        <suffix>1234</suffix>
      </phone>
    </comms>
</suspect>
```

An XML/XSL-capable Web browser, such as Internet Explorer 5.0, will display the preceding document as HTML. Figure 13-3 demonstrates the result of executing the preceding XML document through IE5.

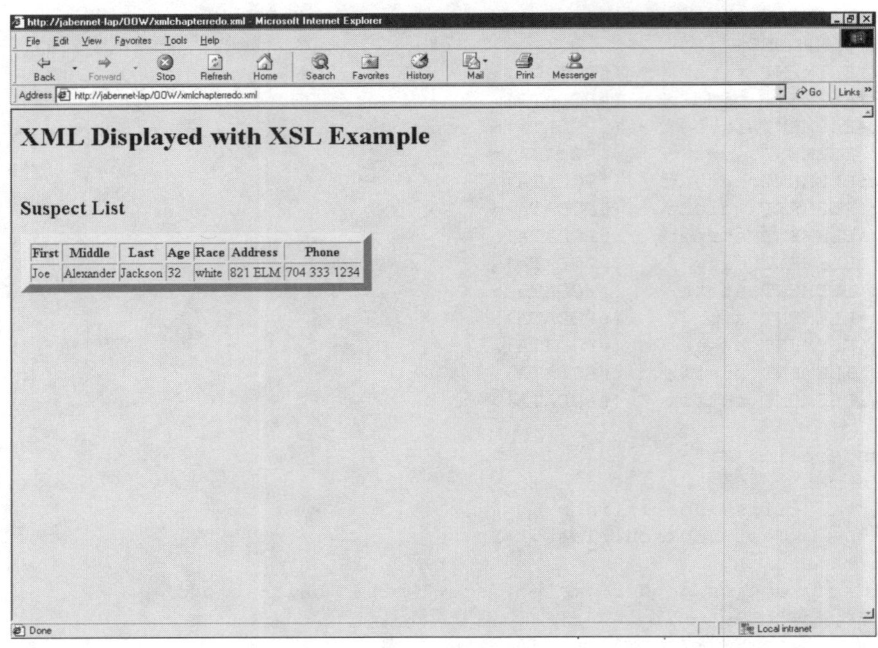

FIGURE 13-3. *XML document formatted as HTML with an XSL style sheet*

XML Support in Oracle8i

Oracle8i release 8.1.6 and subsequent releases will include a set of core XML support features. These features are comprised of the Oracle XML Parser, XML support in iFS, and XML-enabled searching in context for precise search capabilities. Oracle8i with the Oracle XML Parser will also support such features as XML SQL, an XML Class Generator, and an XSQL Servlet. The Oracle XML Parser, Oracle XML Class Generator, Oracle XML SQL Utility for Java, and the Oracle XSQL Servlet are available for download from Oracle Technet at http://technet.oracle.com/tech/xml/. The following sections will identify each of the XML features.

Examining XML and Oracle ConText

The Oracle ConText cartridge for Oracle8 is a powerful tool enabling users to quickly access and pinpoint textual information from large volumes of text data.

With the release of Oracle8i, ConText has been improved to enable developers to limit their searches to specific sections of a document. These sections of text are defined by XML tags in the document and stored as text "blobs" in the database.

The following XML document could be stored in the database in a table called empReviews:

```
<?xml version="1.0"?>
<EmployeeReviews>
    <EmpId>123456</EmpId>
    <EmpName>
       <First>John</First>
       <Last>Jones</Last>
    </EmpName>
    <Reviewer>Bob Smith</Reviewer>
    <ReviewPeriod>
        <Start>01/01/1999</Start>
        <End>06/30/1999</End>
    </ReviewPeriod>
    <ReviewText>John Jones is an outstanding employee.  He is rated a
    <Rating>10</Rating></ReviewText>
</EmployeeReviews>
```

A developer could count how many employees Bob Smith has rated a 10 in a specific review period using the following SQL statement:

```
SELECT COUNT(*)
  FROM empReviews
WHERE
       reviewer = 'Bob Smith'
AND    CONTAINS (ReviewText, '10 WITHIN Rating');
```

The preceding example was simple, but imagine how powerful the XML in ConText feature can be if used to search legal documents, criminal arrest reports, or news articles. The XML in context feature also lends itself towards analyzing marketing data.

Examining the Oracle XML Parser

The Oracle XML Parser is implemented in Java and conforms to the XML 1.0 specification. The Oracle XML Parser can be used as both a validating and a nonvalidating parser. The Oracle XML Parser also supports both the DOM and SAX APIs. Because the Oracle XML Parser is implemented as Java, it can be executed within Java applications running outside the database. The Oracle XML Parser can also execute in Java applications inside the database using the Oracle8i Java VM.

Installing the Oracle XML Parser

The Oracle XML Parser is a collection of Java classes contained in a .jar file called xmlparser.jar. The Oracle XML Parser can be installed in two ways. The first method is to include the .jar file in the CLASSPATH of the machine, which will be executing Java applications that include the Oracle XML Parser Java classes. The second method is to load the .jar file into Oracle8i using the new loadjava utility. This method leverages the power of the new Oracle8i Java VM.

Running the Oracle XML Parser Outside of the Database

The Oracle XML Parser is implemented in Java. Therefore, we can use the features outside of the database. The developer has the choice of using the DOM or SAX API for parsing an XML document.

DOM

The following Java program will read an external XML document and display its elements, attributes, and the values for both using the DOM API.

```
import java.io.*;
import java.net.*;
import org.w3c.dom.*;
import org.w3c.dom.Node;
import oracle.xml.parser.v2.DOMParser;
public class domXMLParser {

  //Document Object Model Parser
   public static void main(String[] args) {
      try
      {
         if (args.length != 1)
         {
            // Verify that an XML file was passed
            System.err.println("XML source file expected.") ;
            System.exit(1);
         }
         // Get an instance of the parser
         DOMParser XMLparser = new DOMParser();

         // Build a URL from the filename.
           URL url = buildFileURL(args[0]);
```

```
        // Set parser options: validation on,
        // warnings shown, error stream set to stderr.
        XMLparser.setErrorStream(System.err);
        XMLparser.setValidationMode(true);
        XMLparser.showWarnings(true);

        // Parse the document.
        XMLparser.parse(url);

        // Get the document.
        Document XMLdoc = XMLparser.getDocument();

        // Display document elements
        System.out.print("Document Element, Attributes, and
        values are: ");
        //printElements(doc);
          displayElements(XMLdoc);
        // Display document element attributes
        System.out.println("Parsing Complete. ");

     }
     catch (Exception e)
     {
        System.out.println(e.toString());
     }
  }

  //Build a URL which points to the file
  static URL buildFileURL(String fileName)
  {
     URL url = null;
     try
     {
        url = new URL(fileName);
     }
     catch (MalformedURLException ex)
     {
        File file = new File(fileName);
        try
        {
           String UrlPath        = file.getAbsolutePath();
           String fileSeparator  =
System.getProperty("file.separator");

           if (fileSeparator.length() == 1)
           {
```

```
              char separator = fileSeparator.charAt(0);
              if (separator != '/')
                 UrlPath = UrlPath.replace(separator, '/');
              if (UrlPath.charAt(0) != '/')
                 UrlPath = '/' + UrlPath;
           }
           UrlPath = "file://" + UrlPath;
           url = new URL(UrlPath);
        }
        catch (MalformedURLException e)
        {
          System.out.println("Failed to create url for: " +
            fileName);
          System.exit(0);
        }
     }
     return url;
  }

  //Not finished.  Use modified PL/SQL DOMSample as ref
  static void displayElements(Document doc)
  {
     NodeList      nodeList       = doc.getElementsByTagName("*");
     NodeList      nodeChildren;
     Node          node;
     Node          childNode;
     Node          attributeNode;
     Element       nodeElement;
     NamedNodeMap  namedNodeMap;
     String        attribute      = new String();
     String        attributeValue = new String();

     for (int i=0; i<nodeList.getLength(); i++)
     {
        node         = nodeList.item(i);
        nodeElement  = (Element)nodeList.item(i);
        namedNodeMap = nodeElement.getAttributes();

        System.out.print(node.getNodeName());

        if (namedNodeMap != null)
        {
           for (int x=0; x<namedNodeMap.getLength(); x++)
           {
              attributeNode  = namedNodeMap.item(x);
              attribute      = attributeNode.getNodeName();
              attributeValue = attributeNode.getNodeValue();
```

```
                System.out.print(" " + attribute + " = " +
                                attributeValue);
            }
        }

        nodeChildren = node.getChildNodes();

        if (nodeChildren.getLength() > 0){

            for (int x=0; x <nodeChildren.getLength(); x++){
                childNode = nodeChildren.item(x);
                if (childNode.getNodeValue() != null){
                  System.out.print(":"+childNode.getNodeValue()+"
                    ");
                }
            }
        }

        System.out.println("");
    }
  }
}
```

Run the preceding program against the following XML document, which contains data tagged within in the XML tags:

```
<suspect id="S1">
   <name>
         <first>Joe</first>
         <last>Jackson</last>
   </name>
   <demographics gender="male" race="white" hair="blond"
     eyes="blue">
         <age>32</age>
         <height>6ft</height>
         <weight>175</weight>
   </demographics>
   <address type="home">
         <street>821 ELM</street>
   </address>
   <comms>
      <phone type="residential">
        <areacode>704</areacode>
        <prefix>333</prefix>
        <suffix>1234</suffix>
      </phone>
    </comms>
</suspect>
```

After executing the preceding syntax, the following document element, attributes, and values are displayed:

```
suspect
 id = S1
name
first: Joe
last: Jackson
demographics gender = male race = white hair = blond eyes = blue
age: 32
height: 6ft
weight: 175
address type = home
street: 821 ELM
comms
phone type = residential
areacode: 704
prefix: 333
suffix: 1234
Parsing Complete.
```

SAX

The following Java program will read an external XML document and display the elements and attributes, and the values for both, using the SAX API:

```
import org.xml.sax.*;
import java.io.*;
import java.net.*;
import oracle.xml.parser.v2.*;

public class saxXMLParser extends HandlerBase {

   // Store the locator
   Locator locator;

  public static void main(String[] args) {

      try
      {
         if (args.length != 1)
         {
            // Make sure name of XML file was entered.
            System.err.println("Usage: saxXMLParser filename");
            System.exit(1);
         }
         // Create a new handler for the parser
         saxXMLParser saxHandler = new saxXMLParser();
```

```
        // Get an instance of the parser
        Parser saxparser = new SAXParser();

        // Set Handlers in the parser
        saxparser.setDocumentHandler(saxHandler);
        saxparser.setEntityResolver(saxHandler);
        saxparser.setDTDHandler(saxHandler);
        saxparser.setErrorHandler(saxHandler);

        // Convert file to URL and parse
        try
        {
           saxparser.parse(buildFileURL(new
            File(args[0])).toString());
        }
        catch (SAXParseException e)
        {
           System.out.println(e.getMessage());
        }
        catch (SAXException e)
        {
           System.out.println(e.getMessage());
        }
     }
     catch (Exception e)
     {
        System.out.println(e.toString());

     }
  }

  //Build a URL which points to the file
  static URL buildFileURL(File filename)
  {
     String path          = filename.getAbsolutePath();
     String fileSeparator = System.getProperty("file.separator");
     if (fileSeparator != null && fileSeparator.length() == 1)
        path = path.replace(fileSeparator.charAt(0), '/');
     if (path.length() > 0 && path.charAt(0) != '/')
        path = '/' + path;
     try
     {
        return new URL("file", null, path);
     }
     catch (java.net.MalformedURLException e)
     {
        throw new Error("unexpected MalformedURLException");
     }
```

```
}

// Implementation of DocumentHandler interface.

public void setDocumentLocator (Locator locator)
{
   System.out.println("Set Document Locator:");
   this.locator = locator;
}

public void startDocument()
{

   System.out.println("Start Document");
}

public void endDocument() throws SAXException
{
   System.out.println("End Document");
}

public void startElement(String name, AttributeList
     attributes) throws SAXException
{
   System.out.println("Start Element:"+name);
   for (int i=0;i<attributes.getLength();i++)
   {
      String attrname = attributes.getName(i);
      String type     = attributes.getType(i);
      String value    = attributes.getValue(i);

      System.out.println("
        "+attrname+"("+type+")"+"="+value);
   }

}

public void endElement(String name) throws SAXException
{
   System.out.println("End Element:"+name);
}

public void characters(char[] cbuf, int start, int len)
{
   System.out.print("Characters:");
   System.out.println(new String(cbuf,start,len));
}
```

```
public void ignorableWhitespace(char[] cbuf, int start, int
 len)
{
   System.out.println("IgnorableWhiteSpace");
}

public void processingInstruction(String target, String data)
          throws SAXException
{
   System.out.println("ProcessingInstruction:"+target+"
    "+data);
}

// Implementation of the EntityResolver interface.

public InputSource resolveEntity (String publicId, String
    systemId)throws SAXException
{
   System.out.println("ResolveEntity:"+publicId+" "+systemId);
   System.out.println("Locator:"+locator.getPublicId()+" "+
               locator.getSystemId()+
               " "+locator.getLineNumber()+"
                "+locator.getColumnNumber());
   return null;
}


// Implementation of the DTDHandler interface.

public void notationDecl (String name, String publicId, String
  systemId)
{
   System.out.println("NotationDecl:"+name+" "+publicId+"
    "+systemId);
}

public void unparsedEntityDecl (String name, String publicId,
                      String systemId, String notationName)
{
   System.out.println("UnparsedEntityDecl:"+name + "
    "+publicId+" "+systemId+" "+notationName);
}


// Implementation of the ErrorHandler interface.

public void warning (SAXParseException e)
          throws SAXException
{
```

```
      System.out.println("Warning:"+e.getMessage());
   }

   public void error (SAXParseException e)
            throws SAXException
   {

      throw new SAXException(e.getMessage());
   }


   public void fatalError (SAXParseException e)
            throws SAXException
   {
      System.out.println("Fatal error");
      throw new SAXException(e.getMessage());
   }
}
```

If we run the preceding program against the previous XML document, we get the following output:

```
Set Document Locator:
Start Document
Start Element:suspect
   id(CDATA)=S1
IgnorableWhiteSpace
Start Element:name
IgnorableWhiteSpace
Start Element:first
Characters:Joe
End Element:first
IgnorableWhiteSpace
Start Element:last
Characters:Jackson
End Element:last
IgnorableWhiteSpace
End Element:name
IgnorableWhiteSpace
Start Element:demographics
   gender(CDATA)=male
   race(CDATA)=white
   hair(CDATA)=blond
   eyes(CDATA)=blue
IgnorableWhiteSpace
```

```
Start Element:age
Characters:32
End Element:age
IgnorableWhiteSpace
Start Element:height
Characters:6ft
End Element:height
IgnorableWhiteSpace
Start Element:weight
Characters:175
End Element:weight
IgnorableWhiteSpace
End Element:demographics
IgnorableWhiteSpace
Start Element:address
   type(CDATA)=home
IgnorableWhiteSpace
Start Element:street
Characters:821 ELM
End Element:street
IgnorableWhiteSpace
End Element:address
IgnorableWhiteSpace
Start Element:comms
IgnorableWhiteSpace
Start Element:phone
   type(CDATA)=residential
IgnorableWhiteSpace
Start Element:areacode
Characters:704
End Element:areacode
IgnorableWhiteSpace
Start Element:prefix
Characters:333
End Element:prefix
IgnorableWhiteSpace
Start Element:suffix
Characters:1234
End Element:suffix
IgnorableWhiteSpace
End Element:phone
IgnorableWhiteSpace
End Element:comms
IgnorableWhiteSpace
End Element:suspect
End Document
```

Running the Oracle XML Parser Inside of the Database

As mentioned previously, the Oracle XML Parser can be executed from within the database using the Oracle8i Java VM. To access the Java methods of the XML Parser, they must be "wrapped" in PL/SQL. Oracle provides a set of 16 PL/SQL packages whose procedures and functions map to the Java methods in the Oracle XML Parser. The group of packages is called the Oracle XML Parser for PL/SQL. The parser will verify the XML document is well-formed and, optionally, if the document is valid. The parser will construct an object tree that can be accessed through the PL/SQL packages.

Parsing an XML Document with PL/SQL

The following example illustrates the use of Oracle XML Parser for PL/SQL by parsing an XML document and displaying the elements and attributes.

The following PL/SQL procedure reads an XML document from the operating system, parses the document, and either displays the document's elements and attributes or displays an error message:

```
CREATE OR REPLACE PROCEDURE PLSQLXML(directory VARCHAR2,
                                     inputFile VARCHAR2,
                                     errorFile VARCHAR2) is

   parser    xmlparser.Parser;
   document  xmlparser.DOMDocument;

-- prints elements in a document
   PROCEDURE printElements(document xmlparser.DOMDocument) is


   nodeList   xmlparser.DOMNodeList;
   listLength NUMBER;
   node       xmlparser.DOMNode;

   BEGIN
   -- get all elements
      nodeList   := xmlparser.getElementsByTagName(document, '*');
      listLength := xmlparser.getLength(nodeList);

      -- loop through elements
      FOR elements IN 0..listLength-1 LOOP
         node := xmlparser.item(nodeList, elements);
         DBMS_OUTPUT.PUT(xmlparser.getNodeName(node) || ' ');
      END LOOP;
```

```
      DBMS_OUTPUT.PUT_LINE('');
   END;

-- prints the attributes of each element in a document

   PROCEDURE printElementAttributeValues(document
            xmlparser.DOMDocument) IS

     nodeList        xmlparser.DOMNodeList;
     lengthList      NUMBER;
     lengthChild     NUMBER;
     lengthAttr      NUMBER;
     node            xmlparser.DOMNode;
     childNode       xmlparser.DOMNode;
     childNodeList   xmlparser.DOMNodeList;
     nodeElement     xmlparser.DOMElement;
     data            xmlparser.DOMCharacterData;
     namedNodeMap    xmlparser.DOMNamedNodeMap;
     attrname        VARCHAR2(100);
     attrval         VARCHAR2(100);
   BEGIN

      -- get all elements
      nodeList   := xmlparser.getElementsByTagName(document, '*');
      lengthList := xmlparser.getLength(nodelist);

      -- loop through elements
      FOR element IN 0..lengthList-1 LOOP
         node          := xmlparser.item(nodeList, element);
         nodeElement   := xmlparser.makeElement(node);
         dbms_output.put(xmlparser.getTagName(nodeElement) || ':
             ');

         -- get value of elements

         childNodeList :=
         xmlparser.getChildNodes(xmlparser.makeNode(nodeElement));

         IF(xmlparser.isNull(childNodeList)=FALSE) THEN

           lengthChild := xmlparser.getLength(childNodeList);

           FOR childElement IN 0..lengthChild-1 LOOP
             childNode :=
               xmlparser.item(childNodeList,childElement);
             IF xmlparser.getNodeValue(childNode) IS NOT NULL THEN
```

```
dbms_output.put_line(xmlparser.getNodeValue(childNode));
             END IF;
           END LOOP;
         END IF;

         -- get all attributes of element
         namedNodeMap := xmlparser.getAttributes(node);
        IF (xmlparser.isNull(namedNodeMap) = FALSE) THEN
           lengthAttr := xmlparser.getLength(namedNodeMap);

           -- loop through attributes
           FOR attribute in 0..lengthAttr-1 LOOP
              node := xmlparser.item(namedNodeMap, attribute);
              attrname := xmlparser.getNodeName(node);
              attrval := xmlparser.getNodeValue(node);
              dbms_output.put(' ' || attrname || ' = ' ||
                 attrval);
           END LOOP;
           dbms_output.put_line('');
        END IF;
      END LOOP;
   END;

   BEGIN

   -- new parser
      parser := xmlparser.newParser;

   -- set some characteristics
      xmlparser.setValidationMode(parser, FALSE);
      xmlparser.setErrorLog(parser, directory || '\' ||
       errorfile);
      xmlparser.setBaseDir(parser, directory);

   -- parse input file
      xmlparser.parse(parser, directory || '\' || inputFile);

   -- get document
      document := xmlparser.getDocument(parser);

   -- Print document elements
      dbms_output.put('The elements are: ');
      printElements(document);

   -- Print document element attributes
      dbms_output.put_line('The attributes of each element are:
       ');
```

```
      printElementAttributeValues(document);

   -- handle exceptions
   EXCEPTION

      WHEN xmlparser.INDEX_SIZE_ERR THEN
         raise_application_error(-20120, 'Index Size error');

      WHEN xmlparser.DOMSTRING_SIZE_ERR THEN
         raise_application_error(-20120, 'String Size error');

      WHEN xmlparser.HIERARCHY_REQUEST_ERR THEN
         raise_application_error(-20120, 'Hierarchy request
          error');

      WHEN xmlparser.WRONG_DOCUMENT_ERR THEN
         raise_application_error(-20120, 'Wrong doc error');

      WHEN xmlparser.INVALID_CHARACTER_ERR THEN
         raise_application_error(-20120, 'Invalid Char error');

      WHEN xmlparser.NO_DATA_ALLOWED_ERR THEN
        raise_application_error(-20120, 'Nod data allowed error');

      WHEN xmlparser.NO_MODIFICATION_ALLOWED_ERR THEN
        raise_application_error(-20120, 'No mod allowed error');

      WHEN xmlparser.NOT_FOUND_ERR THEN
        raise_application_error(-20120, 'Not found error');

      WHEN xmlparser.NOT_SUPPORTED_ERR THEN
        raise_application_error(-20120, 'Not supported error');

      WHEN xmlparser.INUSE_ATTRIBUTE_ERR THEN
        raise_application_error(-20120, 'In use attr error');

   END;
/
show errors;
```

To execute the preceding procedure against the suspect.xml defined in the preceding section, you would execute the following command from SQL*Plus:

```
SQL> exec plsqlxml('c:\xml\demo','suspect.xml','err.txt');
```

The elements are suspect name, first, last, demographics age, height, weight, address, street, comms, and phone (areacode prefix suffix). The attributes of each element are included in the following example:

```
suspect:
id = S1
name:
first: Joe
last: Jackson
demographics:
gender = male race = white hair = blond eyes = blue
age: 32
height: 6ft
weight: 175
address:
type = home
street: 821 ELM
comms:
phone:
type = residential
areacode: 704
prefix: 333
suffix: 1234

PL/SQL procedure successfully completed.
```

Obtaining the Oracle XML Parser Utility

The Oracle XML Parser is currently available for download on the Oracle Technology Network at http://technet.oracle.com/.

Examining the Oracle XML Class Generator

The Oracle XML Class Generator generates a set of Java source files based on an existing DTD. The generated Java source files can be used to construct, validate, and print an XML document that conforms to the specified DTD. The Oracle XML Class Generator is written in Java and requires the Oracle XML Parser.

Implementing the Oracle XML Class Generator

The following Java application, which is borrowed from the sample provided with the Oracle XML Class Generator, will create an XML document and create a .java file for each element in the document:

```
import java.io.*;
import java.net.*;
import oracle.xml.parser.*;
import oracle.xml.classgen.*;
import org.w3c.dom.Element;

public class xmlClassGen {

  public static void main(String[] args) {
        // validate arguments
      if (args.length < 1)
      {
         System.out.println("Usage: java SampleMain "+
                           "[-root <rootName>] <fileName>");
         System.out.println("fileName\t   Input file, XML document
          or " + "external DTD file");
         System.out.println("-root <rootName>   Name of the root
          Element " + "(required if the input file is an external
          DTD)");
         return ;
      }
      try // to open the XML File/ External DTD File
      {
         // instantiate the parser
         XMLParser parser = new XMLParser();

         if (args.length == 3)
            parser.parseDTD(fileToURL(args[2]), args[1]);
         else
            parser.parse(fileToURL(args[0]));

         XMLDocument doc = parser.getDocument();
         DTD dtd = (DTD)doc.getDoctype();
         String doctype_name = null;

         if (args.length == 3)
         {
            doctype_name = args[1];
         }
         else

         {
            /* get the Root Element name from the XMLDocument*/
            doctype_name = doc.getDocumentElement().getTagName();
         }

         // generate the Java files...
         ClassGenerator generator = new ClassGenerator();
```

```
            // set generate comments to true
            generator.setGenerateComments(true);
            // set output directory
            generator.setOutputDirectory(".");
            // set validating mode to true
            generator.setValidationMode(true);

            // generate java src
            generator.generate(dtd, doctype_name);

         }
         catch (Exception e)
         {
            System.out.println ("XML Class Generator: Error " +
             e.toString());
             e.printStackTrace();
         }
      }

      static public URL fileToURL(String sfile)
      {
         File file = new File(sfile);
         String path = file.getAbsolutePath();
         String fSep = System.getProperty("file.separator");
         if (fSep != null && fSep.length() == 1)
            path = path.replace(fSep.charAt(0), '/');
         if (path.length() > 0 && path.charAt(0) != '/')
            path = '/' + path;
         try
         {
            return new URL("file", null, path);
         }
         catch (java.net.MalformedURLException e)
         {
            /* According to the spec this could only happen if the */
            /* file protocol were not recognized. */
            throw new Error("unexpected MalformedURLException");
         }
     }
  }
```

If the application is run for the following XML document, the Java source located following this XML document will be created:

```
<?xml version="1.0" ?>
<!DOCTYPE team[
```

```
<!ELEMENT team (member*)>
<!ATTLIST team name CDATA #REQUIRED>
<!ELEMENT member (#PCDATA)>
]>
<team name="Eagles">
  <member>Joe Smith</member>
</team>
```

Here is the resulting Java source that is generated from the above XML code for the top element team:

```
import java.io.*;
import java.net.*;

import oracle.xml.classgen.CGNode;
import oracle.xml.classgen.CGDocument;
import oracle.xml.classgen.InvalidContentException;
import oracle.xml.parser.*;

/**
 * The Document Class (for the root element Team)
 */
public class Team extends CGDocument
{

    public static DTD globalDTD = null;

    static
    {
        String dtdFile = "Team_dtd.txt";

        XMLParser parser = new XMLParser();

        try
        {
            File file = new File(dtdFile);
            String path = file.getAbsolutePath();
            String fSep = System.getProperty("file.separator");
            if (fSep != null && fSep.length() == 1)
                path = path.replace(fSep.charAt(0), '/');
            if (path.length() > 0 && path.charAt(0) != '/')
                path = '/' + path;
            parser.parseDTD(new URL("file", null, path), "team");
            globalDTD = (DTD)parser.getDocument().getDoctype();
        }
        catch (Exception e)
        {
```

```
            System.out.println("Unexpected error opening DTD
            file");
        }
    }


    /**
     * Constructor with the required Attributes
     * @param varName for the Attribute name
     * @exception InvalidContentException  if invalid value is
     * specified for an attribute
     */
    public Team(String varName) throws InvalidContentException
    {
        super("team", globalDTD);
        try
        {
            setName(varName);
        }
        catch (IllegalArgumentException e) {
            throw new InvalidContentException("Invalid Attribute
            value specified"); }
        isValidating = true;
    }

    /**
     * Prints the document to the specified OutputStream
     * @param out Java outputstream.
     * @exception InvalidContentException  if the document is not
     * valid
     */
    public void print(OutputStream out) throws
      InvalidContentException
    {
        super.print(out);
    }

    /**
     * Prints the document to the specified OutputStream
     * in the given encoding
     * @param out Java outputstream.
     * @exception InvalidContentException  if the document is not
     * valid
     */
    public void print(OutputStream out, String enc) throws
          InvalidContentException
    {
```

```
            super.print(out, enc);
        }

        /**
         * Add <code>Member</code> to <code>Team</code>
         * @param M Node of type <code>Member</code>
         * @exception InvalidContentException  if node cannot be added
         * as per the Content model of the element.
         */
        public void addNode(Member M) throws InvalidContentException
        {
            super.addNode(M);
            M.setDocument(this);
        }

        /**
         * Sets the value of attribute <code>name</code>
         * @param theData value of the attribute
         */
        public void setName(String theData)
        {
            setAttribute("name", theData);
        }

        /**
         * Returns the Team DTD.
         * @return the DTD
         * @see oracle.xml.parser.DTD
         */
        public DTD getDTDNode()
        {
            return globalDTD;
        }

        /**
         * Validate contents of element <code>Team</code>
         * @return true if valid contents, else false
         */
        public boolean validateContent()
        {
            return super.validateContent();
        }
    }
```

The following example is the resulting Java source for the element member:

```
import java.io.*;
import java.net.*;
```

```
import oracle.xml.classgen.CGNode;
import oracle.xml.classgen.CGDocument;
import oracle.xml.classgen.InvalidContentException;
import oracle.xml.parser.*;

/**
 * The Node Class (for the root element Member)
 */
public class Member extends CGNode
{


    /**
     * Default Constructor
     */

    public Member()
    {
        super("member");
        isValidating = true;
    }

    /**
     * Constructor taking <code>#PCDATA</code>
     * @param theData  text for the Element
     * @exception InvalidContentException  <code>theData</code> is
     * invalid
     */
    public Member(String theData) throws InvalidContentException
    {
        this();
        super.addData(theData);
        isValidating = true;
    }

    /**
     * Add  a text node to <code>member</code>
     * @param theData value of the text node
     * @exception InvalidContentException  if the value of the
     * text node is invalid
     */
    public void addData(String theData) throws
       InvalidContentException
    {
        super.addData(theData);
    }
```

```
    /**
     * Returns the Team DTD.
     * @return the DTD
     * @see oracle.xml.parser.DTD
     */
    public DTD getDTDNode()
    {
        return Team.globalDTD;
    }
    /**
     * Validate contents of element <code>Member</code>
     * @return true if valid contents, else false
     */
    public boolean validateContent()
    {
        return super.validateContent();
    }

    /**
     * Get Document Class <code>Team</code>
     * @return <code>Team</code> class
     */
    public Team getDocument()
    {
       return (Team)super.getCGDocument();
    }
}
```

Obtaining the Oracle XML Class Generator

The Oracle XML Class Generator is currently available for download on the Oracle Technology Network at http://technet.oracle.com/.

Examining the Oracle XML SQL Utility

The Oracle XML SQL utility is comprised of a set of Java classes that perform the following tasks:

- Generate an XML document given a SQL query or JDBC ResultSet
- Load data from an XML document into a database table

The Oracle XML SQL utility includes five components. Four components are Java classes: OracleXML class, OracleXMLStore class, OracleXMLQuery class, and

OracleXMLSave class. The fifth component is a PL/SQL wrapper around the OracleXMLStore class called xmlgen.

Defining the OracleXML Class

The OracleXML class is the client-side front-end to the utility. The utility is a command-line application that contains the following two components:

- **getXML** Generates an XML document based on a query
- **putXML** Loads data from an XML document into the database

Each of the preceding methods has a unique set of command-line parameters. Running Java OracleXML at the command-line produces the following list of command-line parameters:

```
OracleXML getXML
 [-withDTD]                  -- include the DTD in the output
 [-user "username/password"]-- the user name and password
 [-maxRows <maxRows>]        -- maximum number of rows in output
 [-skipRows <skipRows>]      -- number of rows to skip in output
 [-rowsetTag <rowsetTag>]    -- the name for the document root
 [-noRowTag | -rowTag <rowTagName>] -- the name for row elements
 [-errorTag <errorTagName>]-- the name for the error tag
 [-stylesheet <stylesheetURI>]       -- the URI for the stylesheet
 [-raiseNoRowsException]     -- raise exceptions when no rows are
                                output
 [-useLowerCase| -useUpperCase]-- the case for tag names
 [-raiseException]           -- raise exceptions when error occurs
 [-useDOMDoc]                -- use DOMParser to create the doc
 [-useNullAttrId]            -- use null attribute to indicate null
                                values
 <sql_string>                -- the query string

 -- OR --
OracleXML putXML
 [-user "username/password"] -- the user name and password
 [-fileName fileName | -URL url | -xmlDoc <XMLDocumentString>]
                              -- the file name containing the XML doc
                                 or a URL or the XML string
 <tableName>                  -- the table name to put into
```

Entering **java OracleXML getXML -user scott/tiger "select * from emp"** at the command-line would produce a DTD for the EMP table and an XML document containing the data in the EMP table. The table columns become tags.

Defining the OracleXMLStore Class

The OracleXML Store class is a noncommand-line executable utility. The utility is intended to be loaded into the database and wrapped by PL/SQL, but it may also be called by other Java functions. The OracleXML Store utility is the Java portion of the server-side front-end of the Oracle XML SQL utility.

Defining the OracleXMLQuery Class

The OracleXMLQuery class is the API used to generate XML documents from a query or JDBC ResultSet. The OracleXMLQuery class enables the user to set the markup tags enclosing a record, as well as setting the case of the tags. The API will return an XML string, or a DOM object. The DOM object can either be attached to a node passed to the API or it can be stand-alone.

Defining the OracleXMLSave Class

The OracleXMLSave class is the API used to load data from an XML document into the database. The OracleXMLSave class maps the tag names in the XML document to the column names of the specified table. The OracleXMLSave utility is limited to mapping only the XML document elements to table columns.

Defining the xmlgen PL/SQL Package

The xmlgen package wraps the OracleXMLStore class. The OracleXMLStore class is the PL/SQL front end to the class. The functions in the xmlgen package can be executed from SQL and PL/SQL.

```
SQL> desc employee
 Name                            Null?    Type
 ------------------------------- -------- ----
 EMPLOYEE_ID                     NOT NULL NUMBER(4)
 LAST_NAME                                VARCHAR2(15)
 FIRST_NAME                               VARCHAR2(15)
 MIDDLE_INITIAL                           VARCHAR2(1)
 JOB_ID                                   NUMBER(3)
 MANAGER_ID                               NUMBER(4)
 HIRE_DATE                                DATE
 SALARY                                   NUMBER(7,2)
 COMMISSION                               NUMBER(7,2)
 DEPARTMENT_ID                            NUMBER(2)

SQL> select xmlgen.getXML('select * from employee where rownum <
3') from dual
```

```
XMLGEN.GETXML('SELECT*FROMEMPLOYEEWHEREROWNUM<3')
------------------------------------------------------------------
<?xml version="1.0"?>
<ROWSET>
 <ROW num="1">
  <EMPLOYEE_ID>7369</EMPLOYEE_ID>
  <LAST_NAME>SMITH</LAST_NAME>
  <FIRST_NAME>JOHN</FIRST_NAME>
  <MIDDLE_INITIAL>Q</MIDDLE_INITIAL>
  <JOB_ID>667</JOB_ID>
  <MANAGER_ID>7902</MANAGER_ID>
  <HIRE_DATE>1984-12-17 00:00:00.0</HIRE_DATE>
  <SALARY>800</SALARY>
  <DEPARTMENT_ID>20</DEPARTMENT_ID>
 </ROW>
 <ROW num="2">
  <EMPLOYEE_ID>7499</EMPLOYEE_ID>
  <LAST_NAME>ALLEN</LAST_NAME>
  <FIRST_NAME>KEVIN</FIRST_NAME>
  <MIDDLE_INITIAL>J</MIDDLE_INITIAL>
  <JOB_ID>670</JOB_ID>
  <MANAGER_ID>7698</MANAGER_ID>
  <HIRE_DATE>1985-02-20 00:00:00.0</HIRE_DATE>
  <SALARY>1600</SALARY>
  <COMMISSION>300</COMMISSION>
  <DEPARTMENT_ID>30</DEPARTMENT_ID>
 </ROW>
</ROWSET>
```

Executing the following PL/SQL procedure from SQL Plus will create the XSQLDemo procedure:

```
CREATE OR REPLACE PROCEDURE XSQLDemo AS
        xmlString CLOB;
        amount integer:= 255;
        position integer := 1;
        charString varchar2(255);
        i binary_integer;
        inclDTD number := 0;
BEGIN

       xmlString := xmlgen.getXML('select * from employee where
                              rownum < 3');

        dbms_lob.open(xmlString,DBMS_LOB.LOB_READONLY);
        loop
           dbms_lob.read(xmlString,amount,position,charString);
```

```
            dbms_output.put_line(charString);
            position := position + amount;
        end loop;

EXCEPTION
    when no_data_found then
        dbms_lob.close(xmlString);
        dbms_lob.freetemporary(xmlString);
END;
/
```

Executing the preceding example will yield the following results:

```
SQL> exec xsqldemo
<?xml version="1.0"?>
<ROWSET>
 <ROW num="1">
  <EMPLOYEE_ID>7369</EMPLOYEE_ID>

<LAST_NAME>SMITH</LAST_NAME>
 <FIRST_NAME>JOHN</FIRST_NAME>
  <MIDDLE_INITIAL>Q</MIDDLE_INITIAL>

<JOB_ID>667</JOB_ID>
  <MANAGER_ID>7902</MANAGER_ID>
  <HIRE_DATE>1984-12-17 00:00:00.0</HIRE_DATE>
  <SALARY>800</SALARY>
  <DEPARTMENT_ID>20</DEPARTMENT_ID>
 </ROW>
 <ROW num="2">
  <EMPLOYEE_ID>7499</EMPLOYEE_ID>
  <LAST_NAME>ALLEN</LAST_NAME>

<FIRST_NAME>KEVIN</FIRST_NAME>
  <MIDDLE_INITIAL>J</MIDDLE_INITIAL>
  <JOB_ID>670</JOB_ID>
  <MANAGER_ID>7698</MANAGER_ID>
  <HIRE_DATE>1985-02-20 00:00:00.0</HIRE_DATE>

<SALARY>1600</SALARY>
  <COMMISSION>300</COMMISSION>
  <DEPARTMENT_ID>30</DEPARTMENT_ID>

</ROW>
</ROWSET>

PL/SQL procedure successfully completed.
```

Obtaining the Oracle XML SQL Utility

The Oracle XML SQL utility is currently available for download on the Oracle Technology Network at http://technet.oracle.com/.

Examining the Oracle XSQL Servlet

The Oracle XSQL Servlet is a Java Servlet. The Oracle XSQL Servlet enables the user to easily create dynamic XML documents based on queries. The Oracle XSQL Servlet also enables the user to transform the resulting XML document using XSLT. Neither Oracle8i release 8.1.5 nor Oracle Application Server release 4.0.7 supports the use of Java Servlets. Support for Java Servlets will emerge in Oracle8i release 8.1.6 and Oracle Application Server release 4.0.8. The examples in the following sections were executed using Apache Web Server and Apache JServ.

Examining Oracle XSQL Servlet Dependencies and Requirements

Let's take a quick look at the Oracle XSQL Servlet dependencies and requirements.

Defining XSQL Servlet Dependencies

The Oracle XSQL Servlet depends on the following components:

- The Oracle XML Parser for Java V2
- The Oracle XML SQL utilities for Java
- A Web server that supports Java Servlets
- A JDBC driver

Installing the XSQL Servlet

The Oracle XSQL Servlet classes are located in a .jar file named oraclexsql.jar. The .jar file must be added to the CLASSPATH of the Web server executing the Servlet.

Setting Up the Connection Document

For the Servlet to connect to the database, it needs to have connection data. The Servlet obtains connection data through an XML document called XSQLConnections.xml. The following example illustrates the structure and content of the XSQLConnections.xml file:

```
<?xml version="1.0" ?>
<connectiondefs>
  <connection name="demo">
    <username>scott</username>
    <password>tiger</password>
    <dburl>jdbc:oracle:thin:@your-server-machine:your-port:your-
     SID</dburl>
  </connection>
  <connection name="xmldemo">
    <username>xmldemo</username>
    <password>xmldemo</password>
    <dburl>jdbc:oracle:thin:@localhost:1521:ORCL</dburl>
  </connection>
</connectiondefs>
```

The connection document needs to be in the root directory of the Web server.

Generating a Dynamic XML Document

The following example demonstrates how the Oracle XSQL Servlet generates a dynamic XML document based on a query. We are executing the query from a Web environment, and therefore the query must be submitted in the following XML document format:

```
<?xml version="1.0"?>
<query connection  = "demo"
       doc-element = "employee-list"
       row-element = "employee"
       tag-case    = "lower">
      SELECT first_name,last_name FROM employee WHERE rownum
        BETWEEN 1 and 6
</query>
```

The preceding document would be saved as file employeelist.xsql. Executing the file from an XML-enabled Web browser will produce an XML document based on the query given between <query> tags. Figure 13-4 illustrates the resulting document in MS Internet Explorer 5.

Obtaining the Oracle XSQL Servlet

The Oracle XSQL Servlet is currently available for download on the Oracle Technology Network at http://technet.oracle.com/.

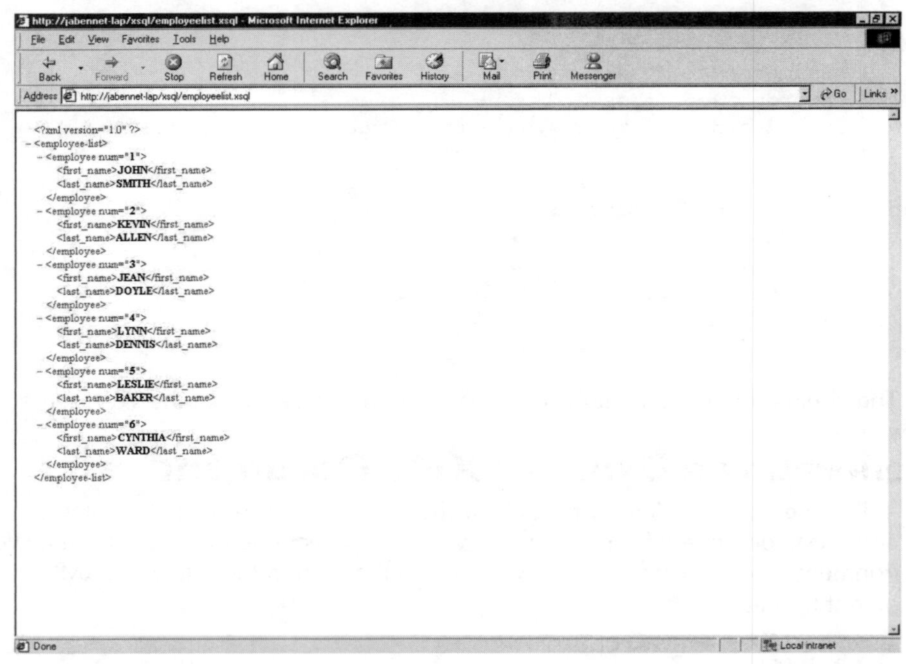

FIGURE 13-4. *XML document based on a query generated by the XSQL Servlet*

Summary

XML is fast becoming the standard for electronic data interchange (EDI). XML has powerful applications in e-business. Because of XML's simplicity and flexibility, it may revolutionize the way we exchange information in a global environment. Oracle's strategy for XML is to "deliver the best platform for developers to productively and cost effectively deploy reliable and scalable Internet applications exploiting XML." Starting with version 8.1.6 of Oracle8i, a set of core XML support features will be available to help developers marry the power of the Oracle database with the power of XML.

CHAPTER 14

PL/SQL Cartridge

At every Oracle conference that I speak at, I poll the audience about their expertise. What is the most common skill across all sectors of Oracle developers? They all know PL/SQL. When I ask people if they know how to develop Web applications, quite often they do not. When I ask if they know any HTML, they usually know some HTML. I then tell them they actually do know how to develop Web applications. It's difficult for them to believe at first, but when I walk them through a little exercise to develop a Web page, they get excited. You can quickly see the fire in their eyes. If this scenario describes you, you can develop on the Web using the OAS PL/SQL Cartridge—you just didn't know it. The first part of this chapter will provide a little exercise that I go through with my students. This will help you to understand how to move from knowing PL/SQL and HTML into knowing how to use the PL/SQL Cartridge to develop Web applications. This chapter assumes you know both HTML and PL/SQL. Refer to Chapter 11 for further information about HTML. I recommend *Oracle PL/SQL Tips and Techniques* by Joe Trezzo (Oracle Press, 1999) as an excellent reference on PL/SQL.

This chapter will not cover each of the Toolkit commands. My prior book, *Oracle Application Server Web Toolkit Reference* (Oracle Press, 1998), covers the Toolkit in detail. This chapter includes the following topics:

- Going from PL/SQL and HTML to Web development
  - Understanding the PL/SQL Web Toolkit
  - Using your HTML knowledge
  - Using WebAlchemy
  - Performing magic
  - Adding your PL/SQL logic
- Calling your Web procedure
- Passing parameters to your PL/SQL procedures
- Retrieving CGI environment variables
- Maintaining source code history
- Storing cookies
- Referring to pseudocolumns
- Calculating time to the hundredth of a second
- Making external calls

- Wrapping or securing your procedures from source viewing
- Redirecting users to another URL
- Sending mail using UTL_FILE
- Extracting and viewing a BLOB
- Querying multiple selects from a listbox
- Wrapping text without using <PRE>
- Generating a PDF report from PL/SQL
- Clearing the buffer
- Improving PL/SQL error messages
- New ROWID format
- Debugging PL/SQL
- Disappearing sessions
- Encrypting key information
- Ordering data based on user requests
- Editing PL/SQL code
- Receiving an authorization check failure after upgrading
- Catching the domain name from an IP
- Missing radio buttons
- Submitting a form, the hard way
- Overdefining actions
- Converting numbers to words—literally
- Enhancing client sessions
- Using Transaction Services
- Getting information about your users
- PL/SQL XML utilities
- Understanding why htp.linkrel is now useful
- OAS 4.0 Toolkit additions

Going from PL/SQL and HTML to Web Development

In this section, the information presented will be centered on what it takes to go from knowing a little HTML and PL/SQL to turning that into Web development knowledge.

Understanding the PL/SQL Web Toolkit

OAS comes with a group of PL/SQL packages called the PL/SQL Web Toolkit. This Toolkit generates HTML sent to the user's browser. For most every HTML command, there is a corresponding Toolkit command. By using the Toolkit, you can generate Web pages. You can also pull data stored in an Oracle database and display that information in your Web page. Using PL/SQL logic, you can dynamically calculate the contents of the Web pages. The Toolkit PL/SQL packages enable you to create your own customized PL/SQL program units (packages and procedures) to access and process the Oracle data you wish to place on the Web. From within your customized program units, you can call the PL/SQL Web Toolkit packaged procedures and functions to create the HTML (and any other client-side code) composing your Web page. The procedures you write are stored in the database, just as other PL/SQL procedures are stored.

While the PL/SQL Web Toolkit minimizes your need to know HTML syntax, you are required to have a working knowledge of HTML. For example, you will need to understand hyperlinks and that they are created with the anchor tag, but you will not need to know the exact sequence of characters needed to generate an HTML anchor tag. By using the Web Toolkit, you will not have to hardcode the exact HTML syntax for the HTML tags. You will, however, need to know the parameters to pass the Toolkit's procedures and function.

The main package that generates HTML to send to the browser is the HTP package. HTP stands for HyperText Procedures. There is a corresponding package, HTF (HyperText Functions), which contains functions generating HTML as their output. Most HTML tags have matching HTP and HTF program units. For example, the HTML <TITLE> tag's matching HTP procedure is called title. The title procedure is referenced as htp.title. There is one input parameter to the htp.title procedure, which is ctitle. The "c" stands for character; this is a varchar2 input parameter. The word "title" is the actual title of the HTML document. The htp.title syntax is as follows:

```
htp.title('My First Page Title');
```

The preceding syntax generates the following HTML code sent back to the user's browser:

```
<TITLE>My First Page Title</TITLE>
```

Calling the htf.title function will return the preceding HTML code as a varchar2 variable. You can store that value in a PL/SQL variable. For example:

```
title := htf.title('My First Page Title');
```

Or, you can nest the call to the HTF functions within an HTP procedure. Let's build an example. First, to print an HTML header (level 1), the code might appear identical to the following:

```
htp.header(1, 'My First HTML Header - Level 1');
```

The preceding line of syntax would generate the following output:

```
<H1>My First HTML Header - Level 1</H1>
```

To center the heading in the browser, we would need to nest the call to the heading procedure inside the center procedure. You cannot nest a procedure in a procedure, but you can nest a function inside a procedure. To center the heading, the syntax might appear identical to the following:

```
htp.center(htf.header(1, 'My First HTML Header - Level 1'));
```

The preceding syntax would generate the following output:

```
<CENTER><H1>My First HTML Header - Level 1</H1></CENTER>
```

A catch-all procedure called print in the HTP package (for example, htp.print) will send whatever is placed inside the quotation marks back to the user's browser. For example:

```
htp.print ('<span class=major>This is a major division</span>');
```

The preceding PL/SQL command will send the following text to the user's browser:

```
<span class=major>This is a major division</span>
```

Even though I would not recommend bypassing all of the HyperText Procedures (HTP) and HyperText Functions (HTF), some developers choose to do so. In my opinion, the code becomes fragmented and difficult to read because all of the information is concatenated together. Therefore, you must know the specific HTML syntax to embed within your PL/SQL code. You must also run the PL/SQL code through a browser to verify the HTML is generated properly (for example, you did not forget a space or another character). Consider the future compatibility of HTML, XML, or whatever new standards come out. If you have embedded HTML in htp.print statements, you will need to go back and revisit your code when new standards are published. If you use the Toolkit, as the Toolkit is upgraded, you will be able to take advantage of new HTML versions with little effort, thereby eliminating the need to be intimately familiar with World Wide Web technology and syntax. Some programmers consider the choice to be a personal preference. Whatever path you choose, it is important to pick a standard and adhere to it.

If you find a specific HTML tag is not in the Toolkit, you can build your own procedure using the htp.print tag to build the HTML command that will be sent back to the user's browser. For example, there is not a span procedure in HTP or HTF. You can modify the HTP and HTF packages to add the new procedures and functions, as the following illustrates.

Changes to the HTP package—the HTP procedures use the p or print procedure to call the embedded HTF function:

```
procedure spanOpen (cclass varchar2)
is
begin
  p(htf.spanOpen(cclass));
end;

procedure spanClose
is
begin
  p(htf.spanClose);
end;
```

Changes to the HTF package—the functions use the ifnotnull function, similar to a DECODE statement, to determine if the value is NULL. If the value is not NULL, additional HTML attributes are included; otherwise, the attributes are not included, as the following illustrates:

```
function spanOpen (cclass varchar2)
returns varchar2
is
begin
  return ('<span'||
          ifnotnull(cclass,' class="'||cclass||'"')||
          '>');
end;

function spanClose
returns varchar2
is
begin
  return ('</span>');
end;
```

You will also need to modify the package specifications to include the new procedures and functions.

TIP
Oracle provides a free quick reference guide for the PL/SQL Web Toolkit along with each copy of OAS. If you would like to purchase additional copies of the quick reference guide, or you cannot find the copy that came with OAS, the part number is A60119-02.

Using Your HTML Knowledge

You may be wondering if an easier solution exists to using the Toolkit. For example, let's assume you have already created the following HTML file using a GUI HTML editor such as FrontPage or Dreamweaver:

```
<html>
<head>
<title>Employee List</title>
</head>
<body bgcolor="#FFFFFF">
<p>Here is a list of our employees:</p>
<table border="1" width="75%">
  <tr>
    <th>Employee Name</th>
    <th>Manager's Name</th>
    <th>Salary</th>
  </tr>
  <tr>
    <td>ename</td>
    <td>mgrname</td>
    <td>sal</td>
  </tr>
</table>
<p>Total salary for all employees $totsal</p>
</body>
</html>
```

The preceding HTML would appear identical to Figure 14-1 in the browser.

In the preceding HTML file, I have included a table containing employee information and a total salary figure at the end of the page. This is not static information; therefore, this information needs to be dynamically pulled from my database.

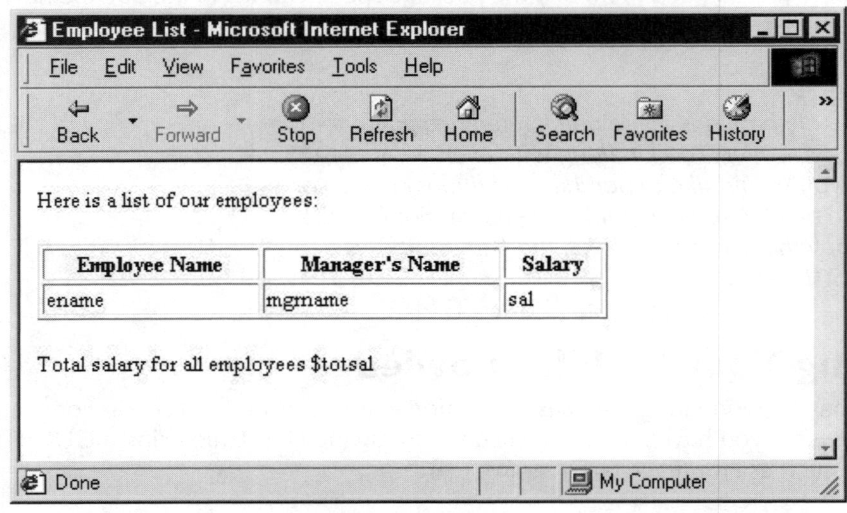

FIGURE 14-1. *Simple HTML file in a browser*

Using WebAlchemy

WebAlchemy is a GUI tool written in Microsoft Visual C++ to reverse engineer HTML pages to PL/SQL procedures (containing HTP and HTF commands). An Oracle consultant in Australia created WebAlchemy. It is free from your Oracle representative. WebAlchemy converts HTML into PL/SQL Toolkit code. For further information on WebAlchemy, refer to Chapter 6. Figure 14-2 displays the WebAlchemy GUI interface after opening the preceding HTML example. By clicking the Generate PL/SQL icon (the beaker shown here), WebAlchemy generates the code in the following subsection.

Performing Magic

By clicking on the Generate PL/SQL icon, WebAlchemy generated the following PL/SQL code. Now that's magic!

```
------------------------------------------------------------
--
--  fig14_01
--  ========
--
--  Author: Bradley D. Brown
--  Date:   03 September 2000
--
--  Copyright (C) Oracle Services
--
------------------------------------------------------------
CREATE OR REPLACE PROCEDURE fig14_01 AS
BEGIN
    htp.htmlOpen;
    htp.headOpen;
    htp.title( 'Employee List');
    htp.headClose;
    htp.bodyOpen(  cattributes => ' bgcolor="#FFFFFF"' );
    htp.para;
    htp.print( 'Here is a list of our employees:' );
    htp.tableOpen(  cattributes => ' border="1" width="75%"' );
    htp.tableRowOpen;
    htp.tableHeader( 'Employee Name');
    htp.tableHeader( 'Manager''s Name');
    htp.tableHeader( 'Salary');
    htp.tableRowClose;
    htp.tableRowOpen;
    htp.tableData( 'ename');
    htp.tableData( 'mgrname');
    htp.tableData( 'sal');
    htp.tableRowClose;
    htp.tableClose;
    htp.para;
    htp.print( 'Total salary for all employees $totsal' );
    htp.bodyClose;
    htp.htmlClose;
END;
/
```

Adding Your PL/SQL Logic

With the preceding procedure, you can modify the PL/SQL code to add your cursors (to select data from the database) and a for loop (to extract individual records from

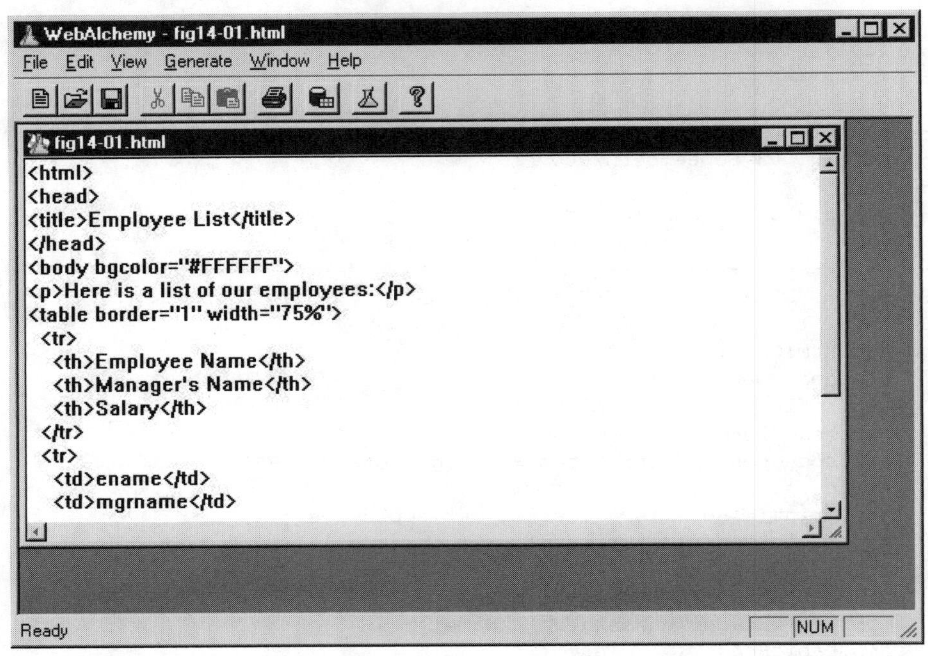

FIGURE 14-2. *WebAlchemy interface*

the database), then change the hardcoded text to field names (from your cursors). The following code represents the changed code:

```
CREATE OR REPLACE PROCEDURE fig14_01 AS
  cursor emp_cur is
  select a.ename, b.ename mgrname, a.sal
    from emp a, emp b
   where a.mgr = b.empno(+);
  tot_sal number(10,2) := 0;
BEGIN
    htp.htmlOpen;
    htp.headOpen;
    htp.title( 'Employee List');
    htp.headClose;
    htp.bodyOpen(  cattributes => ' bgcolor="#FFFFFF"' );
    htp.para;
    htp.print( 'Here is a list of our employees:' );
    htp.tableOpen(  cattributes => ' border="1" width="75%"' );
```

```
    htp.tableRowOpen;
    htp.tableHeader( 'Employee Name');
    htp.tableHeader( 'Manager''s Name');
    htp.tableHeader( 'Salary');
    htp.tableRowClose;
    for emp_rec in emp_cur loop
        htp.tableRowOpen;
        htp.tableData(emp_rec.ename);
        htp.tableData(emp_rec.mgrname);
        htp.tableData(to_char(emp_rec.sal,'999,999,999.99'),'RIGHT');
        htp.tableRowClose;
tot_sal := tot_sal + emp_rec.sal;
end loop;
htp.tableClose;
    htp.para;
    htp.print( 'Total salary for all employees $'
||to_char(tot_sal,'999,999,999.99'));
    htp.bodyClose;
    htp.htmlClose;
END;
/
```

The preceding bolded text represents the changed code. As you can see, the changes in the procedure were minimal.

Calling Your Web Procedure

Upon the completion of the preceding steps, the procedure is ready to be called from the browser. After establishing the DAD (to log into the database—discussed in Chapter 4) and a virtual path to the PL/SQL Cartridge (also discussed in Chapter 4), the procedure should be executed. For example, if the virtual path to the PL/SQL Cartridge is /plsql/, and your host name is tuscco_db1, your URL might appear identical to the following:

```
http://tuscco_db1/plsql/fig14_01
```

That's it! By calling the preceding URL, your first dynamically created PL/SQL procedure using the PL/SQL Web Toolkit would appear, as illustrated in Figure 14-3.

The PL/SQL Cartridge calls stored procedures and passes the appropriate values. The PL/SQL code facilitates the generation of HTML, which is sent back to the browser. Having your code executed within the database has performance, security, and portability benefits. These benefits are the main reason why you should design your dynamically generated Web pages to produce URLs that call PL/SQL procedures in response to user actions.

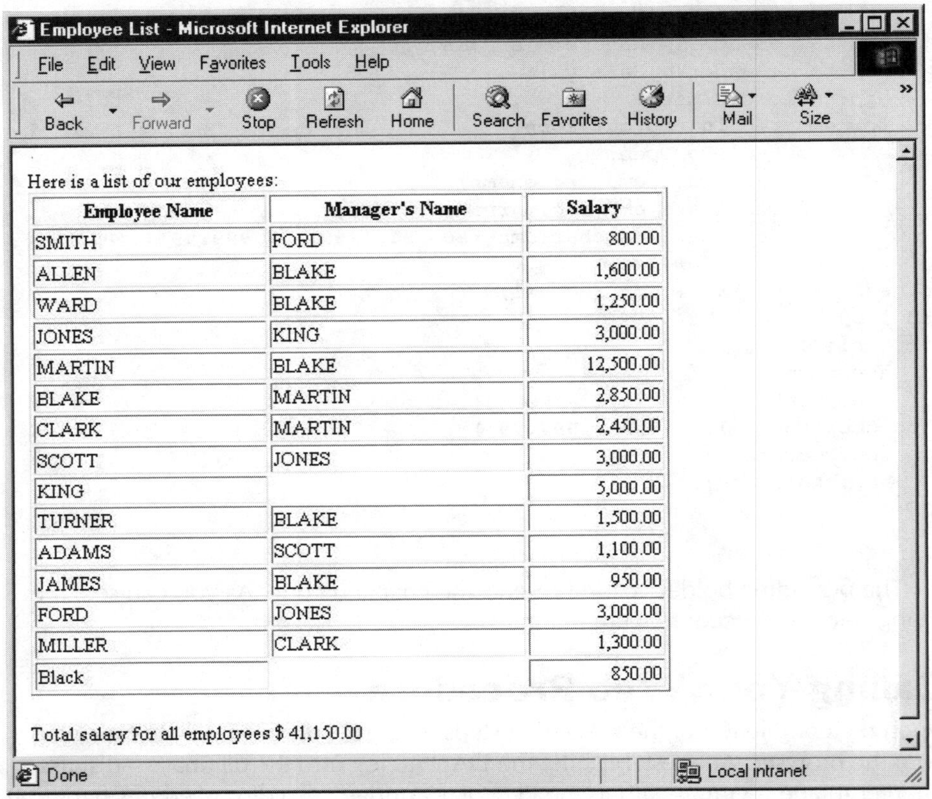
Employee List - Microsoft Internet Explorer
File Edit View Favorites Tools Help
Back Forward Stop Refresh Home Search Favorites History Mail Size
Here is a list of our employees:
Employee Name | Manager's Name | Salary
SMITH | FORD | 800.00
ALLEN | BLAKE | 1,600.00
WARD | BLAKE | 1,250.00
JONES | KING | 3,000.00
MARTIN | BLAKE | 12,500.00
BLAKE | MARTIN | 2,850.00
CLARK | MARTIN | 2,450.00
SCOTT | JONES | 3,000.00
KING | | 5,000.00
TURNER | BLAKE | 1,500.00
ADAMS | SCOTT | 1,100.00
JAMES | BLAKE | 950.00
FORD | JONES | 3,000.00
MILLER | CLARK | 1,300.00
Black | | 850.00
Total salary for all employees $ 41,150.00
Done
Local intranet

FIGURE 14-3. *Execution of Figure 14-1 procedure from the browser*

Passing Parameters to Your PL/SQL Procedures

Passing parameters to a PL/SQL procedure is easier than it might first appear. If you know how HTML forms work, you will understand the GET and POST methods. Any anchor (or hyperlink) implicitly uses the GET method of sending information to a Web server. The POST method is only used by HTML forms. However, for every HTML form that you create, you can choose the GET or POST method. To understand parameter passing, you must first understand a standard

URL and its composition. First, let's break down the following URL to get a better understanding of this information:

```
http://host:port_no/virtual_path/program?param1=value1&param2=value2
```

The preceding URL is broken down into the following components:

- **host** The host name
- **port_no** The number of the TCP/IP port that the Web Listener is on
- **virtual_path** The virtual path of the CGI program or (for this chapter) a PL/SQL Cartridge
- **program** The name of the CGI program or (for this chapter) a procedure name
- **param1** and **param2** The names of the parameters to pass
- **value1** and **value2** Respective values for param1 and param2

To be more specific, look at an actual URL used to call a procedure to login that passes a username (brad) and password (brown) to the procedure (login):

```
http://tuscco_db1/plsql/login?username=brad&password=brown
```

When using the GET method, the parameters of an HTML form show up on the address line in the browser (unless the form is in a frame, but by viewing the properties for the frame, the user can view the full URL). Therefore, with sensitive data, such as the username and password, it is suggested that you use the POST method. The POST method sends the data through standard input, so the information is not displayed in the address line or in the URL. A user cannot bookmark a POSTed form's data, because the information does not appear in the URL. But since GET passes the parameter as a part of the URL, users could bookmark those pages. This can be an effective security measure.

TIP
Using the GET method builds a visible URL, so it can be useful for testing and debugging.

In the preceding example, the PL/SQL procedure's input variables must match the name of the preceding variables used exactly—specifically, username and password, as the following syntax illustrates:

```
create or replace procedure login
(username varchar2,
 password varchar2)
is
begin
...code here...
end;
```

If the information was not passed through an anchor, but rather using an HTML form, the HTML would appear identical to the following:

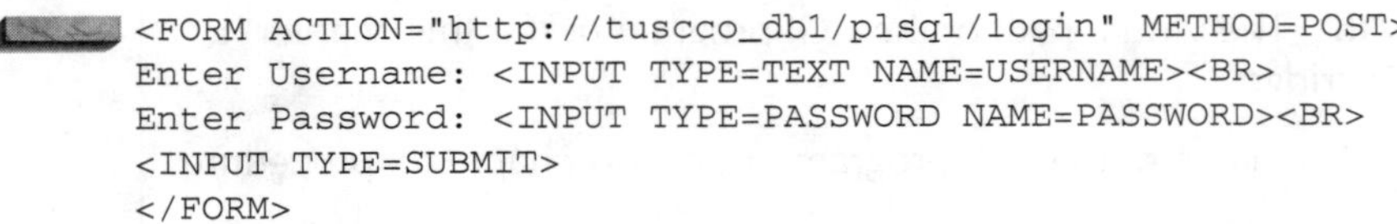

```
<FORM ACTION="http://tuscco_db1/plsql/login" METHOD=POST>
Enter Username: <INPUT TYPE=TEXT NAME=USERNAME><BR>
Enter Password: <INPUT TYPE=PASSWORD NAME=PASSWORD><BR>
<INPUT TYPE=SUBMIT>
</FORM>
```

The preceding attribute METHOD can be GET or POST:

- **GET method** Through the QUERY_STRING environment variable. If the GET method is used by the Web browser, the Web Listener passes the parameters to the PL/SQL Cartridge in this environment variable.
- **POST method** Through standard input (STDIN). If the POST method is used, the Web Listener passes the parameters to the PL/SQL Agent using standard input.

TIP
HTML's default form method is GET, whereas the PL/SQL Web Toolkit's default method is POST.

To create the preceding form dynamically using PL/SQL code, your code would appear identical to the following:

```
htp.formOpen( curl => 'http://tuscco_db1/plsql/login', cmethod =>
'POST');
htp.print( 'Enter Username: ' );
htp.formText( cname => 'USERNAME');
htp.br;
htp.print( 'Enter Password: ' );
htp.formPassword( cname => 'PASSWORD');
htp.br;
htp.formSubmit;
htp.formClose;
```

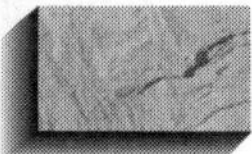

TIP

Web Listeners typically experience difficulty and crash when URLs exceed roughly 1,000 characters. When creating HTML forms to accept a large number of fields, remember that when using the GET method, the URL is composed of the host name, virtual path, program name, each parameter name, and the corresponding parameter values. This can quickly lead to URLs over 1,000 characters in length. For this reason, unless you specifically need to use the GET method, it is recommended that you use the POST method.

Whether your HTML form uses the GET or POST method does not matter to your PL/SQL procedure because the PL/SQL Cartridge handles the translation from the QUERY_STRING or standard input automatically. The PL/SQL procedure is actually unaware of the method used to pass the parameters from the Web Listener to the PL/SQL Cartridge. This is an important feature of the Oracle PL/SQL Cartridge because the PL/SQL programmer does not need to know whether GET or POST is used, nor does the programmer have to be concerned with parsing either the QUERY_STRING environment variable or standard input. The PL/SQL programmer can concentrate on what he or she knows best—developing the logic to extract data from the Oracle database based on previously parsed parameters passed by the Oracle PL/SQL Cartridge.

Retrieving CGI Environment Variables

All Common Gateway Interface (CGI) environment variables conforming to the CGI 1.1 specifications are passed from the Web Listener to the PL/SQL Cartridge.

Table 14-1 contains the available CGI environment variables. These environment variables can be accessed from within PL/SQL using the OWA_UTIL.GET_CGI_ENV function, which is defined as

```
owa_util.get_cgi_env( param_name in varchar2) return varchar2;
```

where param_name is the name of the CGI environment variable as defined in Table 14-1. For example, the following code would retrieve the IP address of the remote node (the client's PC):

```
remote_ip := owa_util.get_cgi_env('REMOTE_ADDR');
```

Variable	Variable Meaning
AUTH_TYPE	Method used to validate user
GATEWAY_INTERFACE	The revision of the CGI specification to which the server complies; for example, CGI/1.1
HTTP_USER_AGENT	The browser the client is using to send the request; for example, Mozilla/4.0 (compatible; MSIE 5.0; Windows NT; DigExt)
PATH_INFO	Extra path information given by the client; for example, /test_cgi
PATH_TRANSLATED	Translated version of PATH_INFO provided by server for mapping; for example, c:\orant\ows\4.0\bin\test_cgi
REMOTE_HOST	Host name making the request if it can be determined; for example, tuscco_fs1
REMOTE_ADDR	IP address of the remote host making the request; for example, 206.214.152.190
REMOTE_USER	Used to authenticate user
REMOTE_IDENT	Set to the remote username retrieved from the server
SERVER_PROTOCOL	Name and revision of the information protocol used in the request; for example, HTTP/1.1
SERVER_SOFTWARE	Name and version of information server software answering the request; for example, Oracle_Web_Listener/4.0.7.1.0EnterpriseEdition
SERVER_NAME	The server's host name, or IP address; for example, tuscco_db1
SERVER_PORT	Port number on which the server is running; for example, 80
SCRIPT_NAME	Virtual path to the script being executed, used for self-referencing URL; for example, /condo/plsql
HTTP_ACCEPT	The types of HTTP that will be accepted; for example: image/gif, image/x-xbitmap, and so forth
HTTP_REFERER	Contains the URL that called this URL
HTTP_COOKIE	All of the raw cookie values

TABLE 14-1. *CGI Environment Variables*

Maintaining Source Code History

Maintaining a history of the source code will enable you to roll back a change at any point. By extending this example, you could build an entire source code control application within the database. This trigger only works as of the release of Oracle8i. This statement will assist in placing a trigger on the source$ table.

Oracle8i gives you the capability to create triggers on database events and on complex views. The following is an example of a trigger on the CREATE event. This trigger fires for all CREATE or REPLACE statements for tables, triggers, procedures, and so forth. Because the trigger written queries the dba_source view, it will only track the history of packages, functions, and procedures.

Each time a procedure is created or modified, a snapshot of its source code will be saved and time-stamped in the source_history table.

The following example's current implementation does not store trigger source, type source, or method source; however, you can enhance it to the desired levels. First, create your source_history table, which will store our prior source code versions:

```
create table source_history
(change_dt date          not null,
 owner     varchar2(30) not null,
 name      varchar2(30) not null,
 type      varchar2(20),
 line      number        not null,
 text      varchar2(4000))
```

Once the preceding source_history tables has been created, use a DBA-authorized account and execute the following syntax to create the source_history trigger:

```
create or replace trigger source_history
after  create on database
/* Maintain history of source code */
declare
v_sysdate date := sysdate;
begin
insert into source_history
       (change_dt,    owner,    name,    type,    line,    text)
(select v_sysdate, ds.owner, ds.name, ds.type, ds.line, ds.text
 from   dba_source ds
 where  sys.dictionary_obj_owner = ds.owner
 and    sys.dictionary_obj_name  = ds.name
 and    sys.dictionary_obj_type  = ds.type)
;
end source_history;
/
```

Storing Cookies

Cookies enable any site to store information on a Web browser's hard disk for semipermanent storage (cookie.txt file) or in the browser's memory for short-term use. This information is sent back to the originating site whenever your application requests it.

To set a cookie on the browser, your PL/SQL code might appear identical to the following:

```
owa_util.mime_header ('text/html', FALSE);
owa_cookie.send ('cookie_name', cookie_value, sysdate+5);
owa_util.http_header_close;
```

Cookies must be set in the MIME header of the HTTP request. The preceding PL/SQL code opens the MIME header sent to the browser defining the HTTP request as text/html MIME type. The mime_header procedure does not close the MIME header yet (False). The cookie is sent to the browser—the cookie's name is cookie_name and the value is set to the value of the PL/SQL variable named cookie_value. The expiration date for this cookie is today plus five days. Until that time, the cookie will remain "alive," or active, even if the user closes their browser and opens it later for a five-day period (down to the second).

To retrieve the preceding cookie from a browser, you would include the following code in your PL/SQL procedure. The owa_cookie.get function does not need to be called as part of the HTTP header.

```
read_cookie_value := owa_cookie.get('cookie_name');
```

Referring to Pseudocolumns

Oracle provides a number of potential pseudocolumns used to pull information from the database. For example, if you want to know the username currently executing the procedure, retrieve the user pseudocolumn. The psuedocolumn sysdate returns the current date and time down to the second. If your application uses database authentication, user will contain the Oracle username of the person who logged into OAS. Another valuable psuedocolumn is ROWID, which will contain a value that uniquely identifies a single row in a table. The ROWNUM psuedocolumn returns the relative position of the current row.

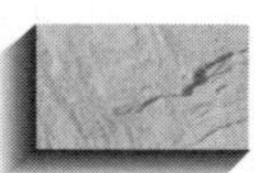

TIP

rownum is assigned at selection time, prior to an order by clause.

To retrieve psuedocolumns within PL/SQL, select the information in your SELECT statement (for example, ROWID and ROWNUM). If the information is not related to the data in the table (for example, sysdate and user), select the information from the dual table. For example:

```
Select ename, sal, emp.rowid
into   nbt_ename, nbt_sale, nbt_rowid
from   emp
```

The following is another example of the preceding syntax, using the dual table:

```
Select sysdate, user
into   todays_date, current_user
from   dual
```

Calculating Time to the Hundredth of a Second

To calculate time down to the hundredth of a second, use the dbms_utility.get_time function. This function returns a reference number. By retrieving this number at the beginning of your timer and again at the end, then subtracting the two numbers, you can effectively calculate execution time. For example:

```
start_time := dbms_utility.get_time;
for emp_rec in emp_cur loop
  ...logic here...
end loop;
end_time := dbms_utility.get_time;
htp.print('Time to run this procedure and select all employees: '||
   to_char((end_time - start_time)/100, '99999.999')||
   ' seconds. ');
```

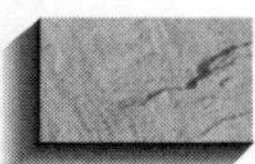

TIP
Chapter 9 discusses additional DBMS_UTILITY procedures and function.

Making External Calls from PL/SQL

Have you ever needed to make a call to external routine from PL/SQL? For example, what if you would like to call a C program from PL/SQL? In Chapter 9, the PL/SQL UTL_HTTP package is covered in depth. One of the suggested uses is to make calls to CGI programs, such as a C program.

Wrapping or Securing Your Procedures from Source Viewing

Are there times when you do not want other developers to view the source code in your packages, procedures, or functions? Oracle provides the capability to offer PL/SQL code to someone, yet not allow them to see what is in it. This technique is called *wrapping*. To wrap a procedure within Oracle8, use the following wrap80 program:

```
wrap80 iname=input_file.sql [oname=output_file.sql]
```

For example, to wrap send_mail.sql into send_mail.plb:

```
wrap80 iname=send_mail.sql oname=send_mail.plb
```

If you leave the oname parameter off of the command execution, the default output filename will be the input filename (minus the extension) with an extension of plb. The following command produces the same results as the preceding command:

```
wrap80 iname=send_mail.sql oname=send_mail.plb
```

Once a procedure is wrapped, the wrapped output file is readable only by the Oracle database engine. If you look at (open in an editor) the plb file, you will notice that the text within the file is ASCII text but is not decipherable into any meaningful information. However, you can execute the following script in SQL*Plus just as you would have executed the SQL script:

```
Sqlplus> @send_mail.plb
```

Anyone who attempts to view the source from a tool, such as TOAD (discussed in Chapter 23), will receive the following message (instead of viewing the source code):

```
package body exa12a wrapped
```

This method will enable you to secure your PL/SQL code from being viewed by other developers.

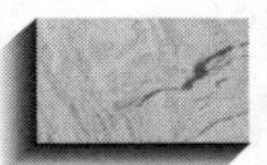

TIP
Be sure to secure the source code by placing it into a directory that other developers do not have access to.

Redirecting Users to Another URL

If you are unfamiliar with the PL/SQL language and are wondering if it is possible to perform redirection like in Perl, it is. For example, to redirect the user to www.somewhere.com in Perl, the code would appear identical to the following:

```
print "Location: http://www.somewhere.com\n\n";
```

Redirection is possible with PL/SQL using the owa_util.redirect_url procedure as follows:

```
owa_util.redirect_url('http://www.somewhere.com');
```

However, you need to be careful using this command with some of the prior OAS versions. For example, some versions of the Oracle Web Server 2 and 3 have problems with this command. The problem will cause the WRB to no longer respond until it is bounced—it hangs! The hanging problem was logged as bug 590392, and a patch is available from Oracle Support. Rather than using the owa_util.redirect_url procedure, you could write your own procedure using the refresh Meta tag, as the following illustrates:

```
procedure my_redirect(clocation in varchar2) is
begin
   htp.htmlOpen;
   htp.headOpen;
   htp.print('<meta http-equiv="refresh" content="0;url=' ||
             clocation || '">');
   htp.headClose;
   htp.htmlClose;
end;
```

Test to make sure the owa_util.redirect_url procedure works on your platform with the following procedures. The first procedure, test_redirect, will test the redirect procedure. The second procedure, redirected_url, will be called if the redirect is successful. If your WRB hangs, you know you have the bug. The following example illustrates the test_redirect procedure:

```
create or replace procedure test_redirect as
begin
   owa_util.redirect_url('http://machine.domain.com/plsql/redirected_url');
end;

create or replace procedure redirected_url as
begin
  htp.print('Redirect worked just fine.');
end;
```

To perform your test to see if OAS hangs upon redirect, follow these steps:

1. Go to your browser, type the URL to invoke redirected_url to verify that it works fine before trying the redirect; for example, http://tuscco_db1/plsql/redirected_url.
2. Change the URL to execute test_redirect (http://tuscco_db1/plsql/test_redirect) and press RETURN.
3. Repeat the test two to ten times. You cannot click the Refresh button because the URL in the address location will have changed to redirected_url. You must move the mouse pointer to the URL in the address section and change the URL back to test_redirect.

If the WRB stops responding, the browser will just wait until it times out and the bug will become apparent. You will need to reload the Listener.

Another example of a similar requirement is as follows. The following procedure will verify the user is logged in (by checking a cookie). If the user is not currently logged in, they will be sent to another procedure, start_login, passing that procedure the name of the procedure that it needs to branch to once the user is logged in. If the user is already logged in, then branch the user directly to the URL passed, in_url.

```
create or replace procedure check_logged_in
(in_url varchar2 default '/index.html')
is
user_no owa_cookie.cookie;
begin
   user_no := owa_cookie.get('user_no');
   -- If the user is logged in, branch to in_url
   if user_no.num_vals != 0 then
      htp.htmlopen;
      htp.headopen;
      htp.meta('refresh',null,'0;url='||in_url);
      htp.headclose;
      htp.bodyopen;
      htp.bodyclose;
      htp.htmlclose;
   else
      -- Otherwise call start_login
      start_login(in_url);
   end if;
end;
```

Sending Mail Using UTL_FILE

The following method of sending email from PL/SQL uses the UTL_FILE package. This solution *only* uses:

- /usr/ucb/mail and a few shell-commands
- crontab
- Sequence number
- UTL_FILE package

Oracle provides a method of producing unique integers across all users. This method is called a sequence number. You will need to create a sequence number for this procedure to work. The sequence seq_mail would be created in the following way:

```
create    sequence seq_mail
increment by       1
start     with     1;
```

UTL_FILE makes it is possible to write a file to a specific directory. The init.ora UTL_FILE_DIR parameter defines the directory. The PL/SQL procedure, send_mail, accepts five parameters and in the background your email is sent. The following is the send_mail procedure:

```
procedure send_mail (in_password in varchar2,  -- Password protected
                     in_reply    in varchar2,  -- Sending email addr
                     in_address  in varchar2,  -- Send email to addr
                     in_subject  in varchar2,  -- Subject of message
                     in_message  in varchar2)  -- Full message
is
  nbt_message_no number;
  nbt_out_file   utl_file.file_type;
begin
  if in_password = 'tiger' then
     select seq_mail.nextval
     into   nbt_message_no
     from   dual;
     out_file := utl_file.fopen(
          '{utl_file_dir}',
          '{utl_file_dir}' || nbt_message_no || '.mail', 'w');
     utl_file.put(out_file, in_message);
     utl_file.fclose(out_file);
     out_file := utl_file.fopen(
```

```
          '{utl_file_dir}',
          '{utl_file_dir}' || 'mailqueue', 'a');
     utl_file.put_line(out_file,
          'cat {utl_file_dir}' || nbt_message_no ||
          '.mail | /usr/ucb/mail -s "' || in_subject ||
          '" ' || in_address || ' ' || in_reply);
     utl_file.put_line(out_file,
          '{utl_file_dir}' || nbt_message_no || '.mail');
     utl_file.fclose(out_file);
     htp.print('Sent Mail Successfully');
     -- You may want to log each email sent to a table
     -- which could be done here.
  else
     htp.print('Unauthorized email attempt');
     -- You may want to log these attempts to a table or you
     -- could send yourself an email recursively
  end if;
exception
  when others then
     htp.print( 'An error occurred in send_mail: ' || sqlerrm );
end;
```

The preceding procedure performs the following steps, assuming the correct password is passed:

1. Retrieves a number from the seq_mail sequence number and places the number into a variable called nbt_message_no.
2. Write the in_message variable to a file called nbt_message_no.mail.
3. Appends a command file (mailqueue) with the two lines (the command and the input file).

The in_password is hardcoded; however, it provides a slight bit of added security. You could take security beyond this measure if desired. The concept is that not just anyone who figures out the name of the send_mail procedure and the parameters will be able to send anonymous mails. To secure this further, the package should be wrapped as previously described. Remember, the calling procedures will have a hardcoded reference to this password, too. Use the encrypt function, as described in Chapter 15, or another method of securing such procedures.

Once this information is written to a file, the second part begins its work. A small shell script, plsqlmailer.sh, is invoked every 10 minutes (you can set the frequency as desired) by the crontab job. The following script uses the input from the command file (mailqueue). If the shell script finds a mailqueue file, it moves this file into an execution directory, sets the privileges to execute, executes the file, deletes the file, and logs the transactions to a file. The email messages will not be sent at the moment the send_mail is invoked, but rather messages will be sent at the frequency established by your crontab job. Words in asterisks (***) must be replaced with an appropriate value for your system.

```
#!/usr/bin/sh
# plsqlmailer.sh
# (c) by Christian Bergler
# cbergler@wst.edvz.sbg.ac.at
# system-command-level-part of send_mail procedure
# files: mailqueue, logfile.plsqlmailer
# executed by crontab
FILERDIR=*** Directory where this script is located ***
CMDFILELOC=*** UTL_FILE_DIR ***
CMDFILENAME=mailqueue
LOGFILE=logfile.plsqlmailer

if [ -f ${CMDFILELOC}/${CMDFILENAME} ] then
  # Move the file to a directory to execute file
  mv ${CMDFILELOC}/${CMDFILENAME} ${CMDFILELOC}/ToBeExecuted
  # Change the privs to execute the file
  chmod 750 ${CMDFILELOC}/ToBeExecuted
  # Execute the program
  ${CMDFILELOC}/ToBeExecuted
  # Remove the file
  rm ${CMDFILELOC}/ToBeExecuted
  echo PLSQLMAILER: Message sent [ `date` ]  >> ${FILERDIR}/{LOGFILE}
fi
```

The next step is to add an entry similar to the following to your crontab file. This entry calls the plsqlmailer.sh script every 10 minutes, every day:

```
1,11,21,31,41,51 * * * * /your_path/plsqlmailer.sh
```

Another fine example of a similar approach can be found at http://www.cetis.hvu.nl/~koos/oraclemail.html. This example provided by Koos van den Hout includes the entire source code for you to implement an email strategy for your company.

Extracting and Viewing a BLOB

When extracting images from Oracle8, the dbms_lob package, as discussed in Chapter 9, will help you accomplish this. However, if you are still using Oracle7, working with blobs in the database is a little more work.

If your images in the database are stored in a long column, you can fetch the image into a varchar2(32760) variable and print it with htp.prn after setting the MIME header accordingly. For example:

```
owa_util.mime_header('image/jpeg');
htp.prn(v_long);
```

If your images are stored in the database as a long raw column, you must first convert the data to a varchar2 variable with the utility utl_raw that comes with the Oracle database. For example:

```
owa_util.mime_header('image/jpeg');
htp.prn(sys.utl_raw.cast_to_varchar2(v_long_raw));
```

If you wish to reference multiple images in a browser page, or you wish to include text with your image, you will need to first write the information to a file using utl_file, as is also discussed in Chapter 9.

Querying Multiple Selects from Listbox

First, let's define the issue. Let's say that you build an HTML form that displays a listbox of departments. When the user selects a department, then clicks the Execute Query (Submit) button on the form, you call a routine returning information about the employees in that department. For example, the HTML to display the list of departments might appear identical to the following:

```
<form action=/plsql/query_department>
<select name=in_dept_no>
<option value=10>Sales
<option value=20>Consulting
<option value=30>Training
<option value=40>Administration
</select>
</form>
```

The query in the procedure, query_department, returning the information may appear identical to the following:

```
create or replace procedure query_department (in_dept_no varchar2)
is
cursor dept_cursor is
       select emp_no, ename, mgr, sal, comm
```

```
        from    emp
        where   dept_no = in_dept_no;
begin
 ...
end;
```

The problem is that when you wish to expand the functionality of the HTML form to enable you to report on multiple departments, you run into a problem. When you alter the listbox to enable the return of multiple values, you must pass that information to PL/SQL, too. PL/SQL supports this functionality via a PL/SQL table (an array of values). The only change to the HTML is to the SELECT tag as follows:

```
<select multiple name=in_dept_no>
```

Now, you need to change the declaration within PL/SQL to a PL/SQL table as follows:

```
create or replace procedure query_department (in_dept_no owa_util.ident_arr)
```

If you leave the cursor defined as previously illustrated, it will not work. If you change the query to an IN clause, it will still not work. You could use dynamic SQL, but that would be a lot of work. One option is to change the query to loop through each of the departments as follows:

```
create or replace procedure query_department (in_dept_no owa_util.ident_arr)
is
cursor dept_cursor (nbt_dept_no) is
       select emp_no, ename, mgr, sal, comm
       from   emp
       where  dept_no = nbt_dept_no;
begin
  for x in 1 .. in_dept_no.count loop
      for dept_rec in dept_cursor(in_dept_no (x)) loop
       ...
      end loop;
  end loop;
end;
```

However, if you need to sort the information by anything other than department and a value (for example, salaries across all selected departments), this method will not work. If you need to sort by another value, you will need to use the dbms_sql package, as defined in Chapter 9, or you could insert the PL/SQL table values into a table and then use a subquery, as shown here:

```
create or replace procedure query_department (in_dept_no owa_util.ident_arr)
is
cursor dept_cursor is
```

```
        select emp_no, ename, mgr, sal, comm
        from   emp
        where  dept_no in (select dept_no
                           from   temp_dept_no
                           where  userid = uid)
        order  by sal desc;
begin
  -- Purge prior uses of this Unique ID (uid)
  delete temp_dept_no
  where  userid = uid;
  -- Now insert the values into a temp table
  for x in 1 .. in_dept_no.count loop
      insert into temp_dept_no
      (dept_no,userid)
      values (in_dept_no (x),uid);
      end loop;
  -- Now select the data
  for dept_rec in dept_cursor loop
      ...
  end loop;
end;
```

Wrapping Text Without Using <PRE>

You may have formatted text in a column of an Oracle table. By formatted, I mean the text is stored in the database with embedded carriage returns. Within your Web application, you may then desire to show the data in that text column in an HTML table on a Web page. However, HTML ignores all special characters (including a carriage return) unless you embed the text within the <PRE> tag (using htp.preOpen and htp.preClose in PL/SQL) so the users can see the carriage returns. However, some lines of the text may be too long for the user to see them. Also, the <PRE> tag makes the text look rather boring. You might have even attempted to use the WIDTH attribute in htp.tableData and the COLSPEC attribute in the htp.table command; however, nothing happens.

This problem is best solved with PL/SQL rather than with HTML by replacing carriage returns with the break tag (<BR>) as follows:

```
htp.tableData(replace(text_field,chr(13), '<BR>'));
```

Using this method, you will not be forced to use the <PRE> tag. By replacing the carriage returns with a <BR> tag, the browser will wrap on words as you desire. Another option would be to use the <WBR> tag, if it is optional to break at that point.

Generating a PDF Report from PL/SQL

Perl routines are available to generate output in a PDF format, but I have yet to see such a solution for PL/SQL. However, many techniques can be used to accomplish this from PL/SQL. For example, you could use utl_http to call a Perl (or other) program that generates the PDF file for your PL/SQL program. Another approach would use a technique similar to the preceding approach for sending email by using a crontab job to convert your output to PDF. You could build the PDF file in the background and then email it to your user. As is noted in Chapter 23, Gymnast will convert ASCII text files to PDF files. The best solution for generating PDF output from Oracle is by using Developer Reports as is discussed in Chapter 18.

Clearing the Buffer

Have you ever been in the middle of your PL/SQL procedure (for example, writing HTML) and then wanted to clear the buffer of HTML commands (so you could write a clean error page)? A command does not exist that is specifically designed to clear the buffer. However, the owa_util.showpage procedure will do the trick by moving any previous commands from the HTML buffer (a PL/SQL table) into the dbms_output PL/SQL table. In effect, this will clear the HTML buffer, as the following syntax illustrates:

```
...
htp.htmlClose;
exception
  when no_data_found then
     owa_util.showpage;
     htp.htmlOpen;
     ...
     htp.print('Go back and make a selection');
end;
```

Improving PL/SQL Error Messages

By default, when the PL/SQL Cartridge fails, it will display a rather cryptic message—Request Failed. To provide further information back to the browser, as to the specific Oracle error message, set the PL/SQL error level to Advanced or, in versions prior to OAS 4, use an error level of 2. The error level parameter is set in the configuration for the PL/SQL Cartridge under PL/SQL Parameters, as illustrated in Figure 14-4.

New ROWID Format

As you are probably aware by now, one of the best-kept secrets about Oracle8 was the change to the format of ROWID. ROWID is a unique value that references an absolute location of a record in a table. The new format is discussed in "New ROWID Format in Oracle8," document ID 10352679.6 from Oracle. As explained in the report, this information will be of importance to those who rely on ROWID or use ROWID-type columns in their applications.

Oracle8 introduced a new format for ROWIDs. This change was primarily driven by the introduction of partitioned objects and tablespace-relative data block

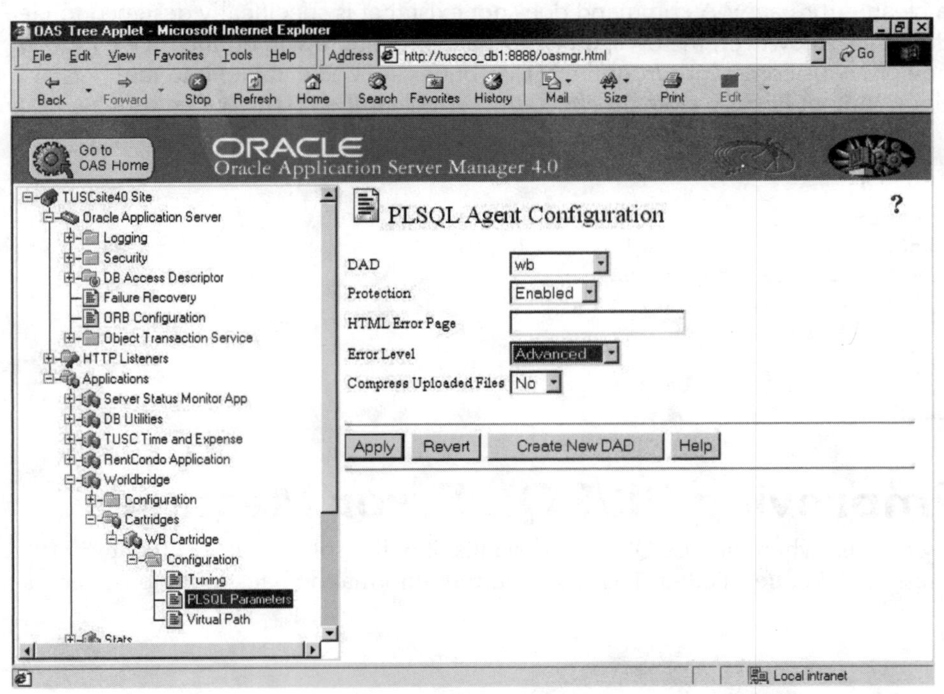

FIGURE 14-4. *Setting the PL/SQL error level*

addresses (DBAs). In Oracle7 and prior releases, the ROWID had the format BBBBBBBB.RRRR.FFFF where BBBBBBBB was the block number, RRRR was the slot (row) number, and FFFF was a file number. The new Oracle8 ROWID is 10 bytes long (compared to the existing ROWID of 6 bytes) and contains the data object number, the DBA (data block address) and the row number of the row. For backward compatibility, Oracle has provided functions that return the file number, block number, and so forth, which is supplied in the package dbms_rowid and can be used for interpreting ROWID contents. If an Oracle8 database is being accessed from a pre-V8 client, the server will return the ROWID in the extended format. Therefore, you will be unable to interpret the ROWID contents or store ROWIDs in a user column of ROWID type without using the dbms_rowid package.

Oracle7 snapshots store master ROWIDs as type ROWID at the snapshot site. An Oracle7 snapshot is unable to reference an Oracle8 master. Therefore, Oracle8 snapshot compatibility is restricted to 7.1.3 and subsequent releases. Furthermore, when a master site is upgraded, the upgrade script will have to invalidate the logs, so the snapshots are forced to do a complete refresh next time.

Two migration issues are related to the new ROWID format:

- **Application migration** Applications that do not attempt to manually assemble or disassemble ROWIDs will not have to be changed or recompiled because the new ROWIDs will fit the current storage requirements for host variables. Applications that attempt to manufacture ROWIDs will have to use the new package dbms_rowid.
- **Data migration** This will have to be performed for columns containing ROWID values (either in ROWID or in character format) if these tables are to be migrated to Oracle8. Otherwise, it will not be possible to retrieve any rows using their stored values. However, if these ROWID values point to a pre-Oracle8 table, migration is not needed because the value points to an existing pre-Oracle8 table that uses the restricted ROWID. Column definitions will automatically adjust during Oracle7 to Oracle8 dictionary migration.

Debugging PL/SQL

If you go back about five years, the number (and type) of tools was *very* limited for debugging PL/SQL. However, today a number of firms sell PL/SQL debuggers. For example, the following companies provide PL/SQL debuggers:

Company	Web Site	PL/SQL Debugger
Sylvain Faust	http://www.sfi-software.com	SQL-Programmer
Qwest Software	http://www.qwest.com/	TOAD
Compuware	http://www.compuware.com/	XPEDITER/SQL

Disappearing Sessions

If you look in the v$session table, sessions will appear, then disappear. The following is an excerpt from an email about this issue:

> "Here is something interesting. The other day we, the people in IT, were debating about the connection to the database from OAS. Does the Web server maintain the connection to the database for a user's session? Or does it disconnect once it sent the dynamic page back the browser and then re-connect again when the user needs more info from database. How can you test this? Even though the v$session table has the records regarding active/inactive sessions, there is no record for our Web user in the v$session table. Does that mean OAS is no longer connected to the database?"

The individual who asked this question obviously has their database on a fast processor. Sessions will show up in the v$session table for at least the life of the session. The default behavior of the OAS PL/SQL Cartridge (unless you use Transaction Services) is that when a procedure is executed (through a URL), the PL/SQL Cartridge will:

- Log in to Oracle (using the username/password in the DAD or the username/password specified through database authentication)
- Execute the procedure
- Log the user out

Even though the life of the session may be short, it appears in the v$session table for a period of time. You may notice the session in the table and then watch it disappear shortly thereafter. The next session may use the same session number, which may give the impression a session is appearing, then disappearing—when it's two different sessions.

Encrypting Key Information

When it comes to sensitive information, encrypt the information in PL/SQL and, more importantly, in the database. If you are storing credit card numbers in the database, you would not want a user to be able to query those numbers (and expiration dates) directly from an Oracle table. Multiple approaches can encrypt key information. For example, you could take the spy decoder ring approach and use the TRANSLATE statement to turn A's to Z's, B's to G's, and so forth. You could also use an external program, such as a C program, to convert values through utl_http as described in Chapter 9. Going through dbms_pipe, also described in Chapter 9, you could execute an external program. Another approach is to use the encrypt and decrypt functions as described in Chapter 15.

Ordering Data Based on User Requests

When developing Web applications that report information to the user, a requirement might be to sort the data retrieved based on the user's desired order by column. For example, let's say that your page displays a list of orders that your customer has in progress at the current time. The current_orders procedure displays the priority of the order, the date the order was placed, the total order value, the current status of the order, and so forth. By default, you might choose to order this information by the priority, order date, and dollar value, or you pull the default order by from your user's profile record. After you accomplish the default order by, maybe the user should be able to change the sorting order. At the top of each column in the table, provide a link that enables the user to click the column heading to order by. There are many ways that you could handle the underlying PL/SQL logic, as described below.

First, you could use dbms_sql (discussed in Chapter 9) to dynamically build your query. This is the least preferred method because the execution plan is not stored in the pcode (binary compiled PL/SQL code) and DBAs typically frown upon dynamic SQL. For example:

```
create or replace procedure current_orders
  (in_customer_no varchar2,
   in_order_by    number default 1)
is
begin
  sql_string = 'select priority, order_date, order_total, status' ||
               'from   order_header order by ';
  if in_order_by = 1 then
     sql_order_by = 'priority, order_date, order_total';
  elsif in_order_by = 2 then
     sql_order_by = 'order_date, priority, order_total';
  ...
  end if;
  sql_string := sql_string || sql_order_by;
  -- dbms_sql calls belong here
  ...
end;
```

Second, you could define the cursor with *n* variations (one per sort order method) and then by passing in the sort order using the corresponding order by clause. DBAs typically prefer this method because the execution plans are stored and this method does not use dynamic SQL.

The final method is by using a DECODE statement on the order by. This method is the easiest to implement. However, if you have multiple datatypes to order by (numbers, characters, and dates), this method will not be as efficient as the second method because all values will need to be converted to the least common denominator (character date) prior to the order by. If you are retrieving a large number of rows, this could be an issue. Otherwise, this is not an issue. Another issue is regarding the sorting of data in descending order. Dates and numbers are easier than character data in this case. For dates, you can subtract the date from 10,000. For example:

```
to_char(10000 - order_date, 'yymmddhh24miss');
```

With the following syntax, you can multiply by -1. For example:

```
to_char(order_total * -1, '099999999.99'));
```

With the following syntax convert character values, you will need to use the TRANSLATE statement to turn an A to a Z, a B to a Y, and so forth:

```
translate(last_name, 'ABCDE…', 'ZYXWV…');
```

The following code is a complete example:

```
create or replace procedure current_orders
  (in_customer_no varchar2,
   in_order_by    number default 1)
is
  cursor order_cur is
        select priority, order_date, order_total, status
        from   order_header
        order  by decode(in_order_by,
                         1, priority,
                         2, to_char(order_date, 'yymmddhh24miss'),
                            status),
                   decode(in_order_by,
                         1, to_char(order_date, 'yymmddhh24miss'),
                         2, priority,
                            to_char(order_total, '099999999.99')),
                   decode(in_order_by,
                         1, to_char(order_total, '099999999.99')),
                         2, to_char(order_total, '099999999.99')),
                            priority);
begin
  -- opening of cursor, etc here
  …
end;
```

Editing PL/SQL Code

When editing PL/SQL code, you can certainly use good old Windows' Notepad or UNIX's vi. However, a number of excellent PL/SQL editors exist, some of which have context-sensitive editors. For example, TOAD by Quest Software, Procedure Builder from Oracle, and several others are excellent PL/SQL editors. You can also use an editor such as TextPad (www.textpad.com) by Helios Software Solutions. On the TUSC Web site (www.tusc.com), we have placed a number of add-ons for the TextPad editor. These include a script that sets up the registry to use TextPad as the default editor in Forms.

To make TextPad your default editor in SQL*Plus, execute the following line into the glogin.sql in $oracle_home\Plus33 or $oracle_home\Plus80 directory (depending on which version you are using):

```
define _editor="C:\Program Files\TextPad 4\TextPad.exe"
```

The macros and add-ins available (from the TUSC site) for download make TextPad easier to use with PL/SQL code. These were put together by a developer at Resorts Computer Corporation in Denver, Colorado. These scripts will only work with TextPad version 4.0.

One macro will change SQL keywords in selected text blocks to uppercase. You will want to save the macro files in the c:\Program Files\TextPad 4\User directory. In TextPad 4, under Configure | Preferences | Macros select Upper Selected SQL from the list and add it to the menu.

If you want the same kind of syntax coloring SQL code found in the Forms 6.0 editor, perform the following steps:

1. Copy the file into C:\Program Files\TextPad 4\Samples (It contains the syntax information for the SQL document class).
2. Double-click on the registry script.
3. Choose open (this tells your registry about the PL*SQL document class).

The .syn file contains the keywords for PL/SQL and for Forms; therefore, it can be used as a default editor for Forms.

Receiving an Authorization Check Failure After Upgrading

After upgrading from a prior OAS version, such as OWAS 3.0, you may receive the following error message:

```
An error occurred while the cartridge performed authorization check.
```

This error indicates a problem with the authentication for the server. In OWS 2.1, no authentication package existed. OWAS 3.0 added authentication to the OWA_INIT package. OAS 4.0 changed the authentication package to OWA_CUSTOM. Therefore, if you upgraded versions of OAS without upgrading the Toolkit (and removing the old instances), you will receive the preceding error.

Catching the Domain Name from an IP

If you ever need to retrieve the domain name that your user is originating from, you can first attempt to obtain this using the following syntax:

```
remote_host_name := owa_util.get_cgi_env('remote_host');
```

However, quite often this will only return the IP address of the remote host. If you need to perform a reverse domain name lookup, you can perform this using the operating system command traceroute (abbreviated as tracert on NT). Traceroute is discussed in detail in Chapter 23.

Missing Radio Buttons

Have you ever attempted to display a form containing some radio buttons, but nothing displayed in the browser? For example, to display two radio buttons, you might have written the following code:

```
htp.print('<TD>');
htp.formRadio(cname=>'summdet',cvalue=>'YES',cchecked=>'TRUE');
htp.print( 'Summary' );
htp.formRadio(cname=>'summdet', cvalue=>'NO');
htp.print( 'Detail' );
htp.p('</TD>');
```

Do you notice anything missing from the preceding HTML? What about the <FORM> tag? Without the <FORM> tag, the radio buttons will be MIA.

TIP

Similar ghostly issues will occur if you inadvertently forget the </table> tag.

Submitting a Form, the Hard Way

After creating an HTML form and submitting the data to an Oracle procedure, OAS sometimes appears unable to find the procedure. The error typically received is OWS-05101 (no procedure matches this call). Check the procedure and your HTML file to make sure your variable names match up. The PL/SQL error message will also show you the name of the parameters you passed. Then, you should attempt to explicitly call the procedure by specifying parameter values (http://server/plsql/projects?in_supplier=a&in_password=b) and the procedure will work. Are you confused? Is OAS senile? Not likely. Here's what is commonly the problem. The following procedure is suppose to access two fields from our HTML form:

```
create or replace procedure projects
(in_supplier varchar2,
 in_password varchar2)
```

The following is the commonly flawed HTML file (the <Form> tag only):

```
<form action="http://tuscco_db1/plsql/projects">
Supplier Login:
<input type="text" name="in_supplier" size="20" maxlength="20"><br>
Password:
<input type="password" name="in_password" size="10" maxlength="10">
<input type="submit" name="submit" value="Submit">
<input type="reset" name="clear" value="Clear">
</form>
```

The problem is that the Submit button is named. The advantage to this feature is that you can have multiple Submit buttons on a form, all providing different actions within a resulting PL/SQL procedure. However, when you name a Submit button, the name of the button is passed as a parameter to the procedure. The solution to the problem is that you should not name your Submit button. Change the highlighted line to read like this and your procedure will work:

```
<input type="submit" value="Submit">
```

The OWS-05101 error message indicates the procedure was found; however, the procedure was not found with the parameters you passed. This error could indicate a typo in a (input) variable or it can also indicate a missing or extra parameter that was passed to the procedure. You could also change the declaration of your procedure to read:

```
projects(in_supplier varchar2, in_password varchar2, submit varchar2)
```

If you learned this the hard way, you will remember it!

Overdefining Actions

What's wrong with the following HTML form's action clause?

```
<form action="http://tuscco_db1/plsql/projects?in_hidden_action=3>
...
</form>
```

When you call your HTML routine, the same OWS-05101 error will appear as previously discussed if the in_hidden_action field does not have a default value (if it has a default value, the value of the field will always be equal to the default value). This error will occur because the browser will actually strip off all of the information past the question mark (?) to build its own URL with parameters. To pass a value like in_hidden_action, you need to define a hidden field identical to the following:

```
<input type=hidden name=in_hidden_action value="3">
```

Hidden fields will be placed into the URL by the browser.

Converting Numbers to Words—Literally

When it comes to printing checks or other documents, such as a letter, it becomes necessary to convert some numbers into the words that represent the numbers—for example, turning 100 into one hundred or 402 into four hundred and two. The following function will automatically perform this task. You must pass the function a value, and it will return the number as words:

```
create or replace function number_to_words (p_number number)
return varchar2
is
  t_char_number  varchar2(64) := to_char(p_number);
  t_integer      varchar2(8);
  t_mantissa     varchar2(128)  := ' point';
  t_return_value varchar2(128);
```

```
function digit_to_word(p_digit varchar2)
return varchar2
is
  t_return_value varchar2(8);
begin
   if     p_digit = '1' then t_return_value := ' one';
    elsif p_digit = '2' then t_return_value := ' two';
    elsif p_digit = '3' then t_return_value := ' three';
    elsif p_digit = '4' then t_return_value := ' four';
    elsif p_digit = '5' then t_return_value := ' five';
    elsif p_digit = '6' then t_return_value := ' six';
    elsif p_digit = '7' then t_return_value := ' seven';
    elsif p_digit = '8' then t_return_value := ' eight';
    elsif p_digit = '9' then t_return_value := ' nine';
    elsif p_digit = '0' then t_return_value := ' zero';
   end if;
   return t_return_value;
end digit_to_word;

begin
  if instr(t_char_number, '.') <> 0 then
   t_integer     := substr(t_char_number, 1, instr(t_char_number, '.') -1);
   t_char_number := substr(t_char_number, instr(t_char_number, '.') +1);
   while t_char_number is not null loop
     t_mantissa    := t_mantissa ||
                      digit_to_word(substr(t_char_number, 1, 1));
     t_char_number := substr(t_char_number, 2);
   end loop;
   t_return_value := to_char(to_date(t_integer, 'j'), 'jsp') || t_mantissa;
  else
    t_return_value := to_char(to_date(p_number, 'j'), 'jsp');
  end if;
  return t_return_value;
end;
```

The following example illustrates the use of functions in a SELECT statement. For example:

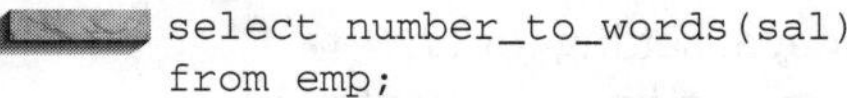

```
select number_to_words(sal)
from emp;
```

Enhancing Client Sessions

If you experiment with the configuration of your OAS cartridges, you may find the Client Sessions setting. As you can see in Figure 14-5, the setting can be easily changed from its default setting of Disabled to Enabled without understanding the full effect. When you enable client sessions, you are making every client's session into a transaction. OAS will maintain state (know who you are and keep you logged

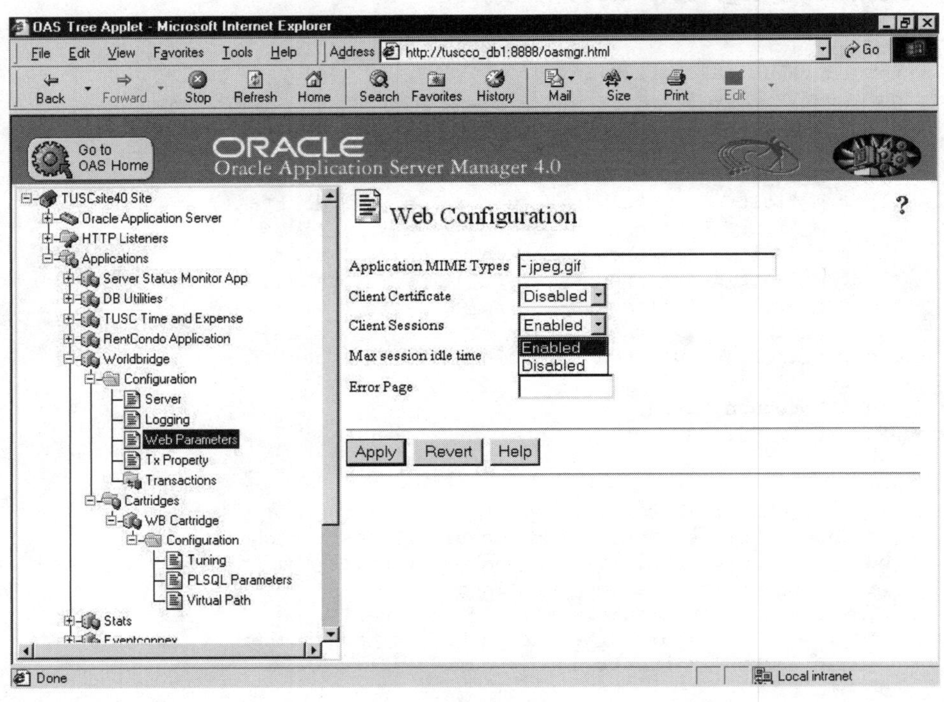

FIGURE 14-5. *Web configuration for client sessions*

in to the Oracle RDBMS) between each call to OAS. The cartridge will generate cookies that link a particular client browser to an instance of the cartridge. You can set the timeout period as well. This would not be a practical setting for an Internet-based application, but for an intranet application or a known quantity of users this could be a significant performance enhancement. However, issues occur when a session times out. The cartridge will then generate a message, "Session Expired," back to the user. This might be confusing (if not frustrating) to your users. Subsequent requests start an entirely new session.

Knowing the timeout period, place a refresh Meta tag into all of your pages (you could go so far as to modify OWA_CUSTOM to automatically include this) that would branch the user to a friendly page explaining that they were logged out and provide a link to start a new session. You could also handle this with a JavaScript timer.

Using Transaction Services

Transaction Services provide the capability to start and end transactions, demarcate the transaction boundaries, and make the decision whether to commit or roll back each transaction. This is a zero-code implementation. OAS handles the transaction for you (using cookies, just like client sessions). To add a transaction, click on the Add icon illustrated in Figure 14-6.

The Web Declarative Transactions: Add form, shown in Figure 14-7, enables you to configure transaction services for OAS.

The Transactions page contains the fields described in Table 14-2.

Between the begin and the commit or rollback URL, the user would invoke other URLs that call procedures to perform actions on the database. These procedures might or might not be within the transaction boundary. If the URL is within the transaction boundary, the actions performed by that procedure would be

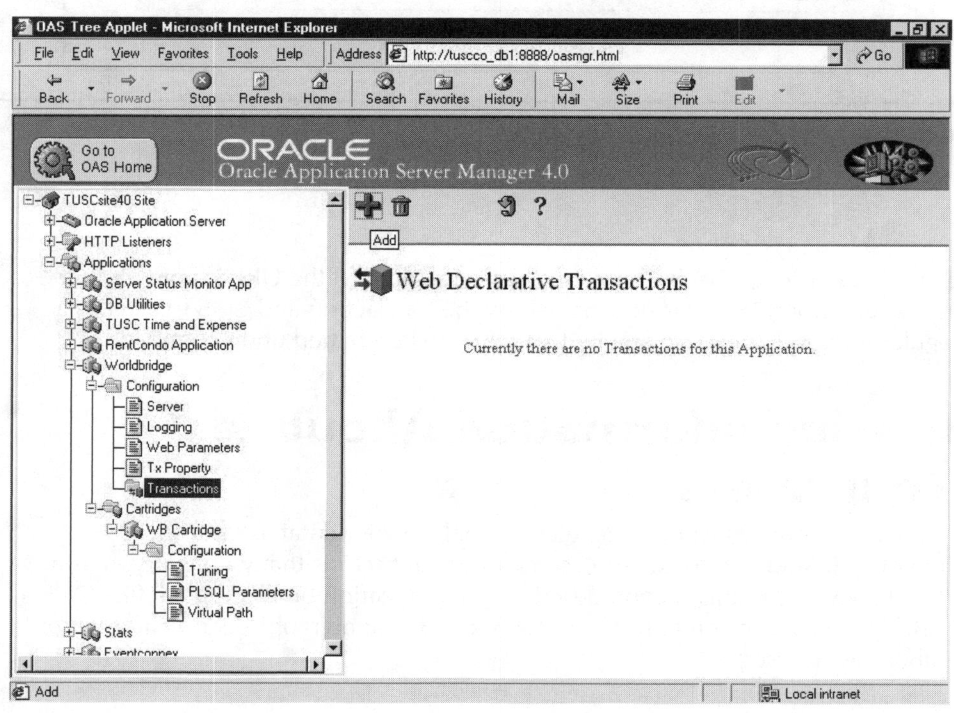

FIGURE 14-6. *Adding Web declarative transactions*

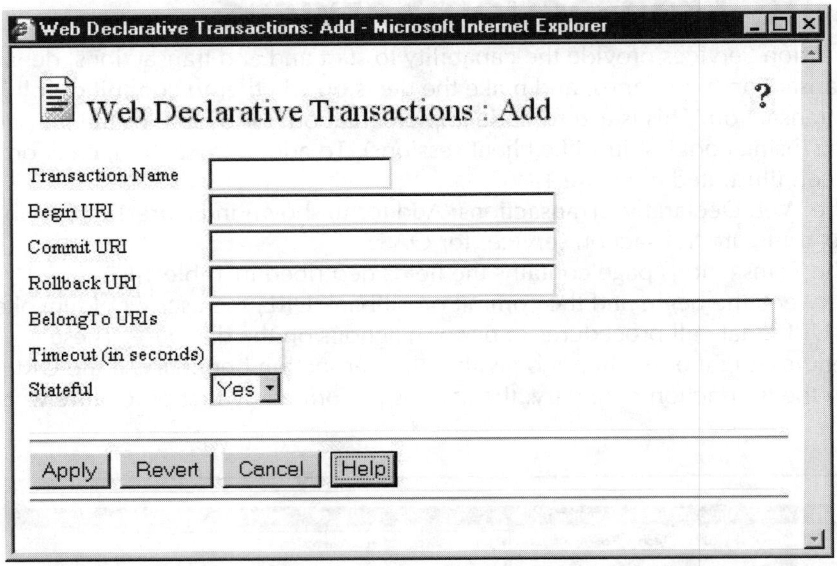

FIGURE 14-7. *Defining a Transaction*

committed or rolled back when the transaction ends. If the URL is not within the transaction boundary, it is not affected by the transaction and OAS treats it as a regular request (changes made by that URL are committed upon completion).

Getting Information About Your Users

A number of queries can be executed to analyze your database statistics. However, in addition to covering some important scripts that will help you as a PL/SQL developer, this section describes an application built using the PL/SQL Cartridge, enabling you to run any SQL statement and graph specific information within the browser.

Field	Description
Transaction Name	The name of the transaction to use—this is a logical name for the transaction; for example, txn_order
Begin URI	The URI to enable the transaction; for example, /plsql/txn_order.start_order, where plsql is the virtual path of the PL/SQL Cartridge, txn_order is the package name, and start_order is the name of the procedure that begins the transaction.
Commit URI	The URI to commit or finish an on-going transaction; for example, /plsql/txn_order.commit_order.
Rollback URI	The URI to roll back an ongoing transaction. A rollback can be performed by the user, or when the transaction times out, OAS automatically executes this URI; for example, /plsql/txn_order.rollback_order.
BelongTo URIs	The list of URIs that belong to the transaction; for example, /plsql/txn_order.*.
Timeout (in seconds)	The time elapsed (measured in seconds) before a transaction is terminated and rolled back; for example, 90 means in 90 seconds.
Stateful	Cartridges using the Transaction Service can be stateful or stateless. Possible values are as follows: **Yes** Make the transaction stateful. This is the default. In a stateful cartridge, requests from the same client are directed to the same cartridge instance. You can think of stateful cartridges as being similar to a session-enabled cartridge. The difference is that a client is associated with a cartridge instance only for the duration of a transaction. You set a cartridge to be stateful if you want to keep track of database operations invoked by a specific client. **No** Do not make the transaction stateful. In a stateless cartridge, requests from the same client can be directed to any free cartridge instance.

TABLE 14-2. *Add Transaction Form Fields*

Before addressing the application, create a table containing each of your key analysis SQL scripts. You can add records to the table as desired. The following syntax is the table creation:

```
create table www_dba.top_dba_scripts (
  script_no      number(10)      not null ,
  short_desc     varchar2(4000),
  long_desc      varchar2(4000),
  cat_no         number(10),
  text_script    varchar2(4000),
  graph_script   varchar2(4000),
  header_sql     varchar2(4000),
  refresh_rate   number          default 0);
```

The following script inserts SQL statements—more can be added at any time. This example only includes one SQL statement for an example. You can download the entire script from the TUSC Web site.

```
insert into www_dba.top_dba_scripts
(script_no, short_desc,
 long_desc,
 cat_no,
 text_script,
 graph_script,
 header_sql,
 refresh_rate)
values (
 10, 'Users Logged On',
 'This query will return a listing of users that are
  currently logged into the Database.',
 1,
 'SELECT username, count(*) FROM v$session
  WHERE username NOT IN (''SYS'', ''SYSTEM'')
  GROUP BY username ORDER BY count(*) DESC',
 'SELECT null, username, count(*)
  FROM v$session
  WHERE username NOT IN (''SYS'', ''SYSTEM'')
  GROUP BY username ORDER BY count(*) DESC',
 'select ''<B>Username</B>'',
         ''<B>Number of Times Logged On</B>''
  from dual',
 10);
```

The following procedure is called from your browser, enabling you to pick a script from the top_dba_script table:

```
create or replace procedure pick_top_dba_script
as
   cursor script_cur is
       select *
       from   www_dba.top_dba_scripts
       order  by script_no;
    refresh_it varchar2(2000) := '';
begin
    htp.htmlopen;
    htp.headopen;
    htp.title('Top DBA Scripts for Web Developers');
    htp.print('<style type="text/css">');
    htp.print('body {font-family: arial; margin-left: 100px;}');
    htp.print('h1 {background-color: blue; color: white;
                   font-size: 28pt; font-family: arial;}');
    htp.print('</style>');
    htp.headclose;
    htp.bodyopen('/img/ivybackground.gif');
    htp.header(1,'Top DBA Scripts for Web Developers');
    htp.tableopen('border=2');
    htp.tablerowopen;
    htp.tableheader('Short Description');
    htp.tableheader('Long Description');
    htp.tablerowclose;
    for script_rec in script_cur loop
        htp.tablerowopen;
        if script_rec.refresh_rate > 0 then
           refresh_it := '&in_refresh_at=' ||
                               to_char(script_rec.refresh_rate);
        else
           refresh_it := null;
        end if;
        htp.tabledata(htf.anchor(
         'run_top_dba_script?in_script_no='||
          script_rec.script_no||
          refresh_it,script_rec.short_desc));
        htp.tabledata(script_rec.long_desc);
        htp.tablerowclose;
    end loop;
    htp.tableclose;
    htp.bodyclose;
    htp.htmlclose;
end;
```

The preceding procedure displays a page as illustrated in Figure 14-8, containing links to run any of the reports in the top_dba_scripts table. The link runs a specific query by executing the run_top_dba_script procedure, as illustrated in the following example. Rather than using dbms_sql to execute the query, this procedures uses cellsprint to display the information, as illustrated in Figure 14-9. To graph this information, use the owa_chart package, which Oracle says your representative will provide for free.

```
create or replace procedure run_top_dba_script
  (in_script_no      varchar2,
   in_start_at       number   default 0,
   in_refresh_at     number   default 0)
as
   cursor script_cur is
   select *
     from www_dba.top_dba_scripts
    where script_no = in_script_no;
   more_records boolean;
   max_rows     number(10) := 100;
begin
   htp.htmlopen;
   htp.headopen;
   htp.title('display script results' );
   if in_refresh_at > 0 then
      htp.print('<meta http-equiv="refresh" ' ||
                'content="' || in_refresh_at ||
';URL=run_top_dba_script' ||
                '?in_script_no='  || in_script_no  ||
                '&in_start_at='   || in_start_at   ||
                '&in_refresh_at=' || in_refresh_at || '">');
   end if;
   htp.print('<style type="text/css">');
   htp.print('body {font-family: arial; margin-left: 100px;}');
   htp.print('h1 {background-color: blue; color: white; ' ||
             'font-size: 28pt; font-family: arial;}');
   htp.print('</style>');
   htp.headclose;
   htp.bodyopen('/img/ivybackground.gif');
   for script_rec in script_cur loop
      htp.header(1,script_rec.short_desc);
      htp.tableopen('border=2');
      owa_util.cellsprint(script_rec.header_sql);
      owa_util.cellsprint(script_rec.text_script, max_rows,
                          null, in_start_at, more_records);
      if in_start_at > 0 then
         htp.anchor('run_top_dba_script'
                    '?in_script_no='  || in_script_no ||
                    '&in_start_at='   ||
                     to_char(in_start_at - max_rows) ||
```

```
                '&in_refresh_at=' || to_char(in_refresh_at),
                htf.img('/img/previous.gif', null, 'previous ' ||
                       to_char(max_rows) || ' records'));
   end if;
   if more_records then
      htp.anchor('run_top_dba_script' ||
                '?in_script_no='  || in_script_no ||
                '&in_start_at='   ||
                  to_char(in_start_at + max_rows) ||
                '&in_refresh_at=' || to_char(in_refresh_at),
                htf.img('/img/next.gif', null, 'next ' ||
                       to_char(max_rows) || ' records'));
   end if;
   htp.tableclose;
   -- display arrows top and bottom
   if in_start_at > 0 then
      htp.anchor('run_top_dba_script' ||
                '?in_script_no='  || in_script_no ||
                '&in_start_at='   ||
                  to_char(in_start_at - max_rows) ||
                '&in_refresh_at=' || to_char(in_refresh_at),
                htf.img('/img/previous.gif', null, 'previous ' ||
                       to_char(max_rows) || ' records'));
   end if;
   if more_records then
      htp.anchor('run_top_dba_script'
                '?in_script_no='  || in_script_no ||
                '&in_start_at='   ||
                  to_char(in_start_at + max_rows) ||
                '&in_refresh_at=' || to_char(in_refresh_at),
                htf.img('/img/next.gif', null, 'next ' ||
                       to_char(max_rows) || ' records'));
   end if;
   if script_rec.graph_script is not null then
      htp.br;
      htp.br;
      htp.hr;
      owa_chart.show_chart(
         q            => script_rec.graph_script,
         chart_type   => 'hbar',
         bar_image    => 'multi',
         image_locat  => '/img/',
         chart_title  => script_rec.short_desc,
         font_size    => '-2',
         show_summary => 'camxvs');
   end if;
end loop;
htp.formopen('run_top_dba_script', 'get');
```

```
   htp.formhidden('in_script_no', in_script_no);
   htp.formhidden('in_start_at', in_start_at);
   htp.print('refresh data every ');
   htp.formtext('in_refresh_at', 4, 4, in_refresh_at);
   htp.print(' seconds');
   htp.formsubmit(null, 'change refresh rate');
   htp.formclose;
   htp.bodyclose;
   htp.htmlclose;
end;
```

PL/SQL XML Utilities

XML is here to stay! Read all about Oracle's vision for XML on their site at http://www.oracle.com/xml. Read the information to satisfy your curiosity about Oracle's thoughts about XML. Chapter 13 covers XML in further detail. With respect

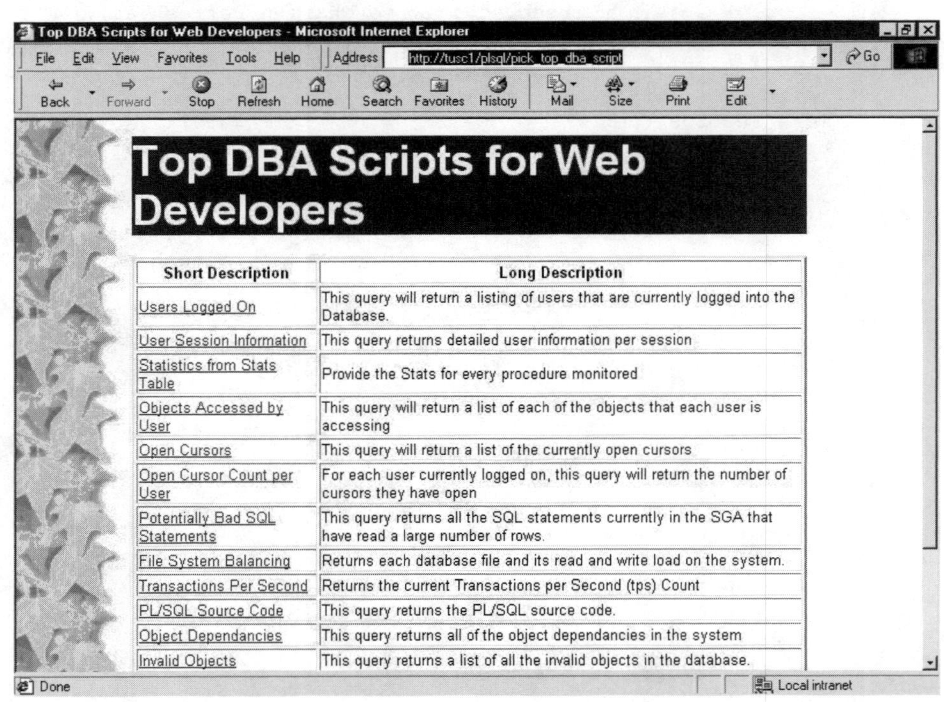

FIGURE 14-8. *Pick a top DBA script to execute*

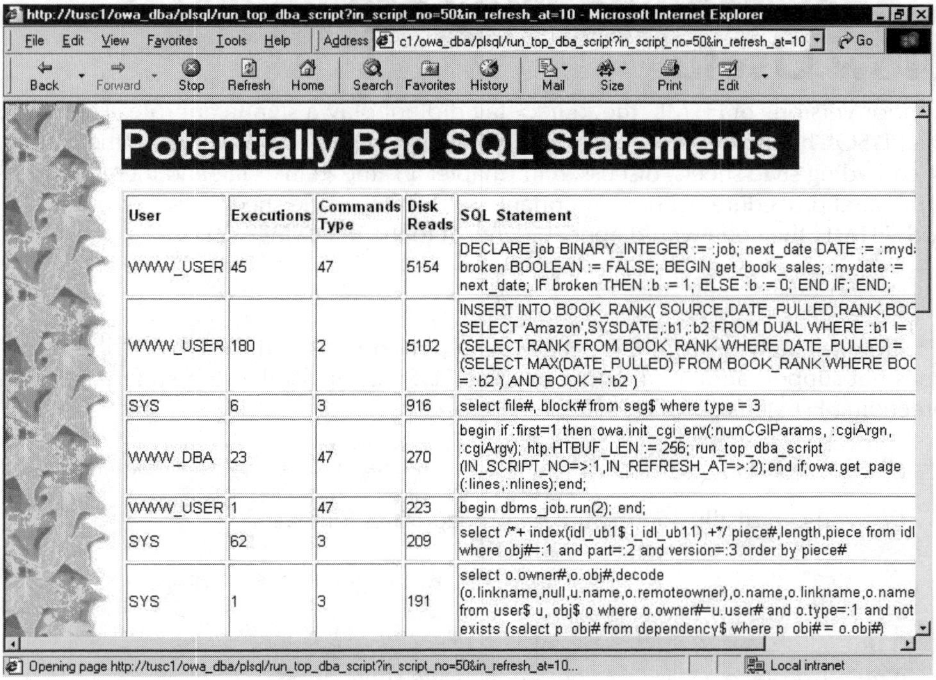

http://tusc1/owa_dba/plsql/run_top_dba_script?in_script_no=50&in_refresh_at=10 - Microsoft Internet Explorer

Potentially Bad SQL Statements

User	Executions	Commands Type	Disk Reads	SQL Statement
WWW_USER	45	47	5154	DECLARE job BINARY_INTEGER := :job; next_date DATE := :myd broken BOOLEAN := FALSE; BEGIN get_book_sales; :mydate := next_date; IF broken THEN :b := 1; ELSE :b := 0; END IF; END;
WWW_USER	180	2	5102	INSERT INTO BOOK_RANK(SOURCE,DATE_PULLED,RANK,BOO SELECT 'Amazon',SYSDATE,:b1,:b2 FROM DUAL WHERE :b1 != (SELECT RANK FROM BOOK_RANK WHERE DATE_PULLED = (SELECT MAX(DATE_PULLED) FROM BOOK_RANK WHERE BOO = :b2) AND BOOK = :b2)
SYS	6	3	916	select file#, block# from seg$ where type = 3
WWW_DBA	23	47	270	begin if :first=1 then owa.init_cgi_env(:numCGIParams, :cgiArgn, :cgiArgv); htp.HTBUF_LEN := 256; run_top_dba_script (IN_SCRIPT_NO=>:1,IN_REFRESH_AT=>:2);end if;owa.get_page (:lines,:nlines);end;
WWW_USER	1	47	223	begin dbms_job.run(2); end;
SYS	62	3	209	select /*+ index(idl_ub1$ i_idl_ub11) +*/ piece#,length,piece from idl where obj#=:1 and part=:2 and version=:3 order by piece#
SYS	1	3	191	select o.owner#,o.obj#,decode (o.linkname,null,u.name,o.remoteowner),o.name,o.linkname,o.name from user$ u, obj$ o where o.owner#=u.user# and o.type=:1 and not exists (select p_obj# from dependency$ where p_obj# = o.obj#)

Opening page http://tusc1/owa_dba/plsql/run_top_dba_script?in_script_no=50&in_refresh_at=10...

FIGURE 14-9. *Execution of a DBA script*

to the PL/SQL Cartridge, Oracle has provided the PLSXML Utilities. Downloads and instructions for installing packages are located at http://www.oracle.com/xml/plsxml/index.html.

PLSXML is a set of PL/SQL-based XML utilities and demonstrations. The PLSXML suite consists of:

- **DBXML** For generating rich, nested XML documents from SQL queries.
- **DBDOM** For creating, parsing, traversing, and searching XML documents using the Document Object Model API.
- **DBXSL** For generating a database-driven XSL style sheet for a tree-rendering of data.

Understanding Why htp.linkrel Is Now Useful

In prior versions of HTML, the <Link> tag did not play a significant role. Therefore, the PL/SQL htp.linkrel procedure did not have an impact. However, with the creation of cascading style sheets, discussed in Chapter 11, the <Link> tag and therefore the htp.linkrel procedure become important. To refer to a style sheet called navdata.css with HTML, the code would appear identical to the following syntax:

```
<link rel=stylesheet href="navdata.css" type="text/css">
```

Unfortunately the htp.linkrel command does not support the type attribute and it does not support additional attributes. The PL/SQL call for the same reference as the preceding HTML is as follows:

```
htp.print('<link rel=stylesheet href="navdata.css" type="text/css">');
```

Or, you can disillusion the linkrel procedure as follows:

```
htp.linkrel(crel=>'stylesheet', curl=>'/navdata.css' type='text/css');
```

TIP
You must place a slash (/) before the style sheet name or the file will be assumed to come from the same virtual path as your PL/SQL procedure, likely causing a file not found error.

You could also modify the underlying linkrel procedure in the htp and htf packages, but it's not typically wise to modify the vendor's packages. Another option would be to create a linkrel procedure of your own.

OAS PL/SQL 4.0 Web Toolkit Additions

The OAS Web Toolkit has not changed very much over the versions of the product. Version 4.0 provided no exception to this rule. Surprisingly, no DHTML or HTML 4.0 packages or procedures were added. Even procedures like htp.linkrel, as discussed in the preceding section, were not refined to accommodate the type attribute. However, the following packaged procedures were added as of OAS 4.0:

- htp procedures:
  - htp.download_file
  - htp.get_download_files_list

- htf functions:
    - htf.escape_url
    - htf.format_cell
- Entire owa_content package (as discussed in Chapter 10)

Summary

In this chapter we covered topics regarding the PL/SQL Cartridge. The chapter began by helping you understand the simplicity of developing Web code using the PL/SQL Cartridge. The rest of this chapter was dedicated to helpful tips for using the PL/SQL Cartridge. Is PL/SQL going to go away? Certainly not any time in the near future. A number of applications exist today using PL/SQL as their core language, including the Oracle applications, which contain more than four million lines of PL/SQL code. Invest the time to understand the PL/SQL Cartridge and the power it will provide to your existing (and new) applications—you will be amazed.

CHAPTER 15

Security

ecurity is a broad topic. This chapter will discuss security as it relates to your Web application development. Specifically, this chapter addresses five types of security and the following topics:

- OAS built-in security
  - Setting up security for a virtual path
  - Configuring authentication services
  - Considering OAS authentication schemes
  - Comparing in-memory to ORB communication
- Application-level security
  - Requesting authentication upon each request
  - Passing authentication along
  - Combining database authentication
  - Combining Basic or Digest authentication
  - Using owa_custom
  - Baking cookies
- Network security
  - SSL Basics
  - SSL Setup
  - Protecting digital certificates
  - Securing email with digital IDs
  - Securing credit card transactions
- RDBMS security
  - Encrypting with PL/SQL
  - PL/SQL interface to Oracle Cryptographic Toolkit
  - Setting up a secure schema plan
- Physical security

OAS Built-In Security

OAS Manager enables you to configure security for OAS virtual paths. You can configure the security of OAS with several authentication schemes to protect specific files and virtual directories. When a file or virtual directory is protected by an authentication scheme, a client requesting access to it must provide a username and password.

OAS uses the authentication server for Web security. The authentication server is an object that encapsulates the authorization performed against cartridges. It consists of three parts: client, broker, and providers:

- **Client** The portion that sends authorization requests.
- **Broke** The portion that receives the authorization requests from the dispatcher or a cartridge, then sends back the message specifying whether authorization was successful, and optionally provides a specific failure message if it was not successful. Each authorization request is associated with a protect string that specifies one or more realms and their associated schemes. For each scheme to be used (generally, no more than one realm from a given scheme is used), the broker invokes the authorization provider associated with that scheme, and lets the authorization provider determine whether the protection for that scheme is satisfactory. When it has received responses from all providers, the broker applies the AND/OR logic specified in the protect string and sends a message back to the dispatcher or cartridge that invoked it, stating whether authorization is granted.
- **Providers** Objects called by the broker to implement authorization schemes. For each scheme the broker recognizes, there is one and only one provider.

Setting Up Security for a Virtual Path

After adding and configuring several parameters for your Listener, as discussed in Chapter 4, you can assign security mechanisms to protect access to individual files or entire virtual directories.

Configuring Authentication Services

OAS Authentication Services provide for the authentication of client requests based on a specific virtual path request. The client communicates with the Listener, which in turn communicates with the Web Request Broker (WRB), and the WRB communicates with the OAS cartridges. Based on the virtual path requested, authentication may not be required. When you perform the installation and configuration, specify the authentication requirements for each path.

The Security forms enable you to use several authentication schemes to protect specific files and directories. In addition, OAS also provides authentication for OAS cartridges to authenticate users before they can use a cartridge.

Depending on the authorization scheme, when a file or directory is protected, a client requesting access to it must provide a username and password, be a member of the appropriate domain, and/or have an authorized IP address. The Basic and Digest authentication schemes enable you to define named groups of username/password combinations, and named realm groups of these groups. Then, you can assign user, group, and realm names to virtual files and directories, requiring any client requesting access to input one of the specified username/password combinations.

Five authentication methods are available under each of the Listener and security options:

- **Basic Authentication** Uses an unencrypted username and password prompt to authenticate the user.
- **Digest Authentication** Same as Basic Authentication, except that the password is slightly encrypted.
- **Database Authentication** Uses the Oracle DBMS schemas (users) to authenticate the user.
- **Domain-based Restriction** Based on a specific domain group. You may instruct the authentication to include or exclude specific domain groups; for example: +*.tusc.com or -*.microsoft.com.
- **IP-based Restriction** Based on a specific IP class level. You may instruct the authentication to include or exclude specific IP groups; for example: +205.204.102.* or -24.3.*.

Considering OAS Authentication Schemes

OAS provides three ways to require requestors to authenticate themselves prior to accessing certain files and directories, as described in the sections below.

DEFINING BASIC AUTHENTICATION Basic Authentication enables you to assign passwords to users, assign users to groups, and define groups of users, called "realms." Then, you can assign the realms to specific files and virtual paths, requiring requestors to provide a username and password to gain access. Figure 15-1 illustrates the Basic Authentication form for a listener. Basic Authentication sends unencrypted passwords across the network, making this method subject to subversion. Basic Authentication is not recommended when security is critical.

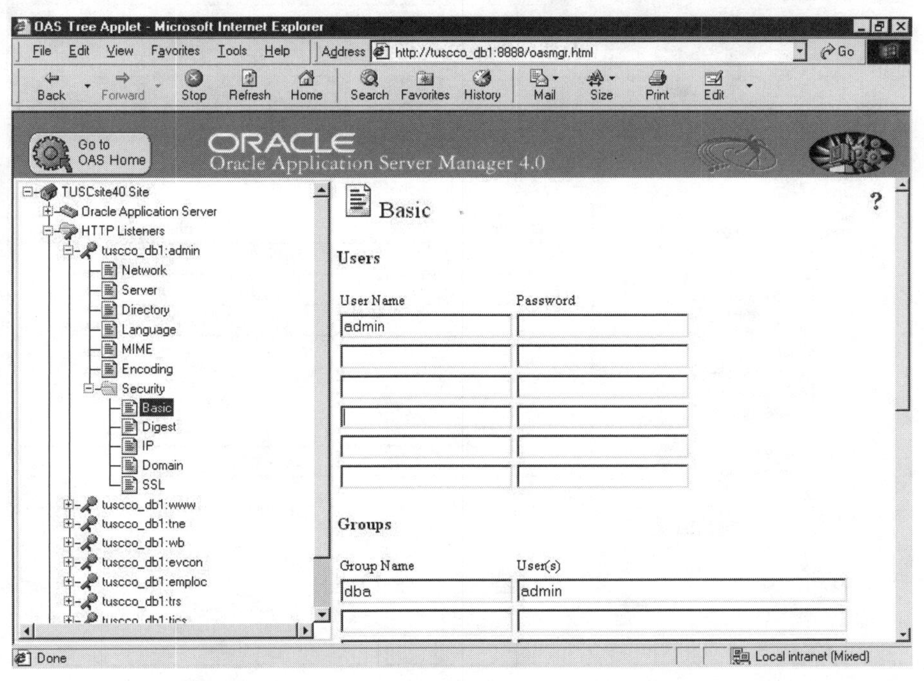

FIGURE 15-1. *Basic Authentication form*

When Basic Authentication is assigned to a specific virtual path, the browser prompts the user for a username and password when an attempt is made to access the protected page or application.

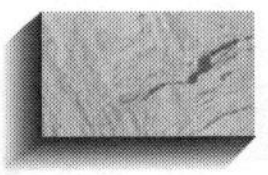

TIP
As illustrated in Figure 15-2, you can use Basic Authentication to protect cartridges, such as PL/SQL.

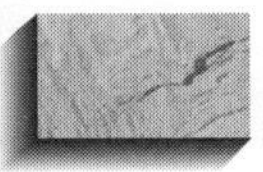

TIP
Basic Authentication used with SSL provides encrypted password security.

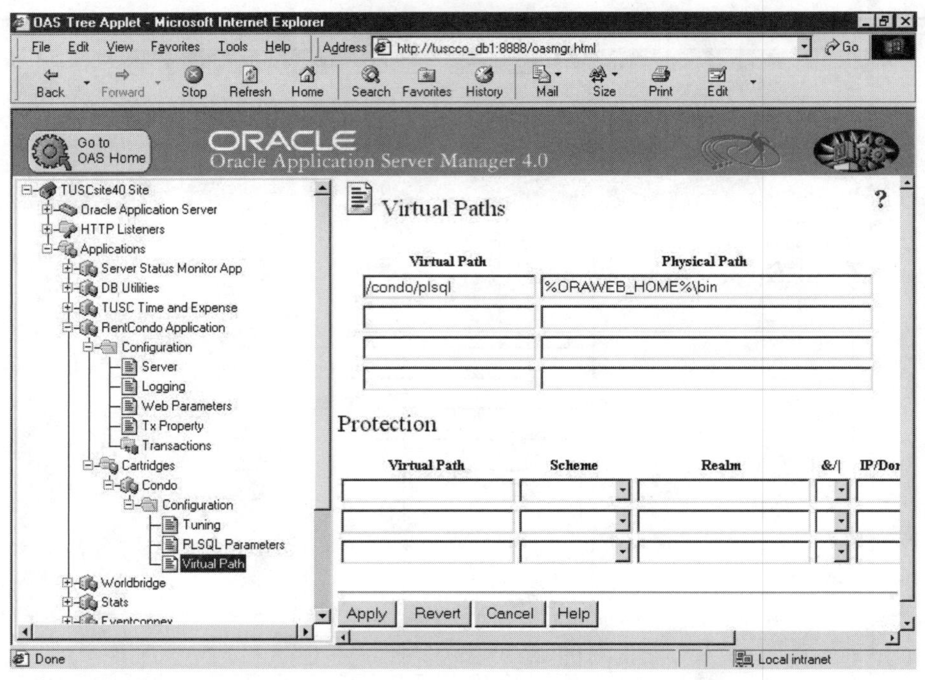

FIGURE 15-2. *Cartridge virtual path protection form*

CONSIDERING DIGEST AUTHENTICATION OVER BASIC Digest Authentication is similar to Basic Authentication except it sends passwords unencrypted across the network in the form of a cryptographic checksum, also called a "digest." You should use this scheme whenever authentication is required. Figure 15-3 illustrates the Digest Authentication form for a Listener.

The Digest Authentication protocol is part of HTTP 1.1. If Digest Authentication is specified for a page and a user with a browser that does not support Digest Authentication tries to access that page, the Listener automatically reverts to Basic Authentication. You should treat digest as effectively equivalent to basic for the minority of users, but take precautions accordingly. Using SSL and Digest Authentication will assure an encrypted password is transmitted end to end. Within the OAS authentication server, both the username and password are stored locally in an unencrypted format.

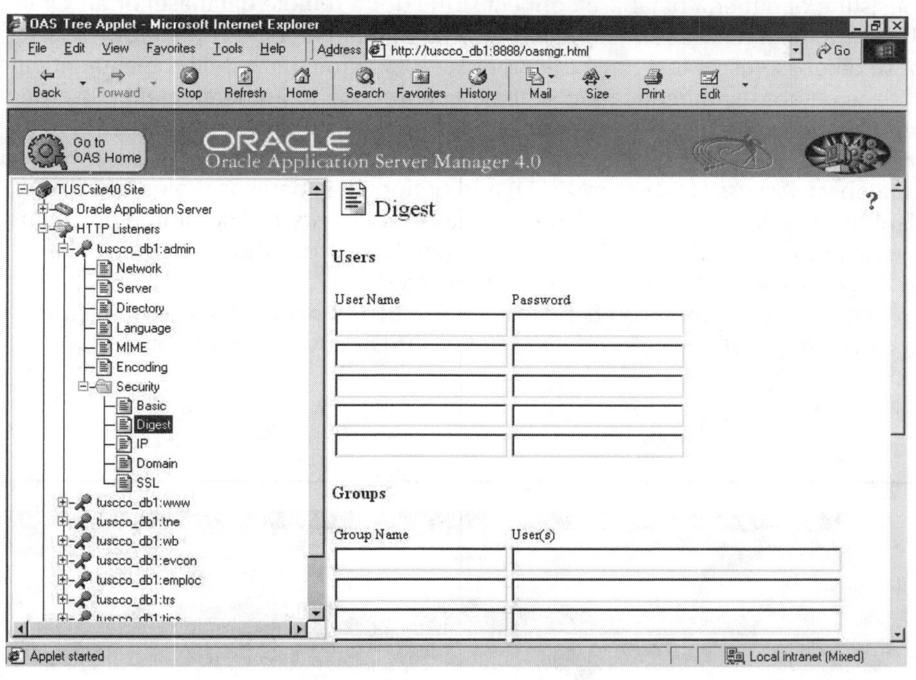

FIGURE 15-3. *Digest Authentication form*

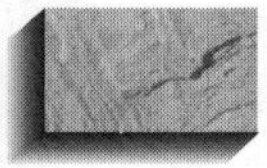

TIP
You can also use Digest Authentication to protect cartridges, such as PL/SQL.

USING DATABASE AUTHENTICATION Database authentication is only available through the authentication server, not the Listener. Database authentication, also called BASIC_ORACLE authentication, illustrated in Figure 15-4, stores the usernames and passwords in an Oracle database instead of an operating system file as in the basic and Digest Authentication schemes. For an intranet, this simplifies the work of the administrator; only one set of usernames and passwords needs to be managed for both Web and database access. Database authentication also enhances security because the Oracle Database Server provides more granular access control than the operating systems. The administrator configures a realm, consisting of either a database connect string (for a remote database) or an Oracle SID (for a local database). The realm may contain a database role, allowing only those database users that have the privilege to assume that role to be authenticated.

The database authentication scheme enables you to authenticate the username and password pair against a database by using the username and password to log on to an Oracle RDBMS. The realm of database authentication consists of two parts: a Database Access Descriptor (DAD) and optionally a database role. The DAD identifies the database to check the username and password combination against. The database role allows only a subset of database users (those who have the privilege to assume the role) to be authenticated.

Database authentication can also be used by not storing the username and password in a Database Access Descriptor (DAD), covered in Chapter 4.

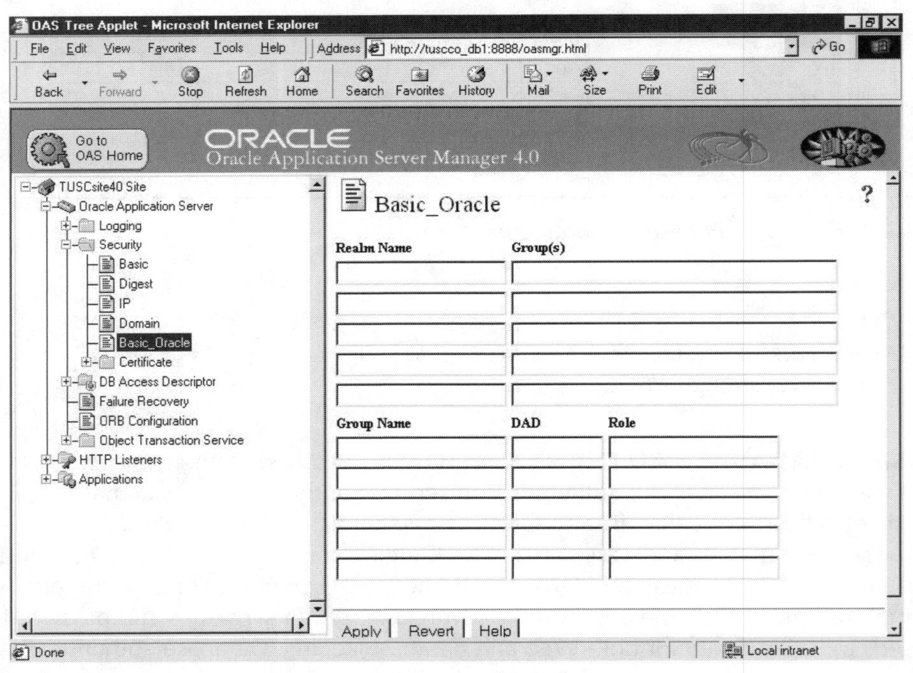

FIGURE 15-4. *Basic_Oracle authentication form*

Understanding Restriction Schemes

OAS provides two methods of restricting access to certain files and virtual directories: IP-based restriction and domain-based restriction. The preceding authentication schemes either allow or disallow a user to access a specific virtual path based on knowing a username and password. Restriction schemes protect virtual paths based on physical information about the user.

CONSIDERING IP-BASED RESTRICTION Under IP-based restriction, requestors must issue requests for the protected files and virtual directories from specified IP addresses or groups of IP addresses. IP-based restriction is a more convenient security scheme than basic or Digest Authentication because it does not require password files to be maintained, but it is consequently less secure as clever intruders can falsify their IP addresses (commonly called *spoofing*). Figure 15-5 illustrates the IP-based restriction form for a Listener.

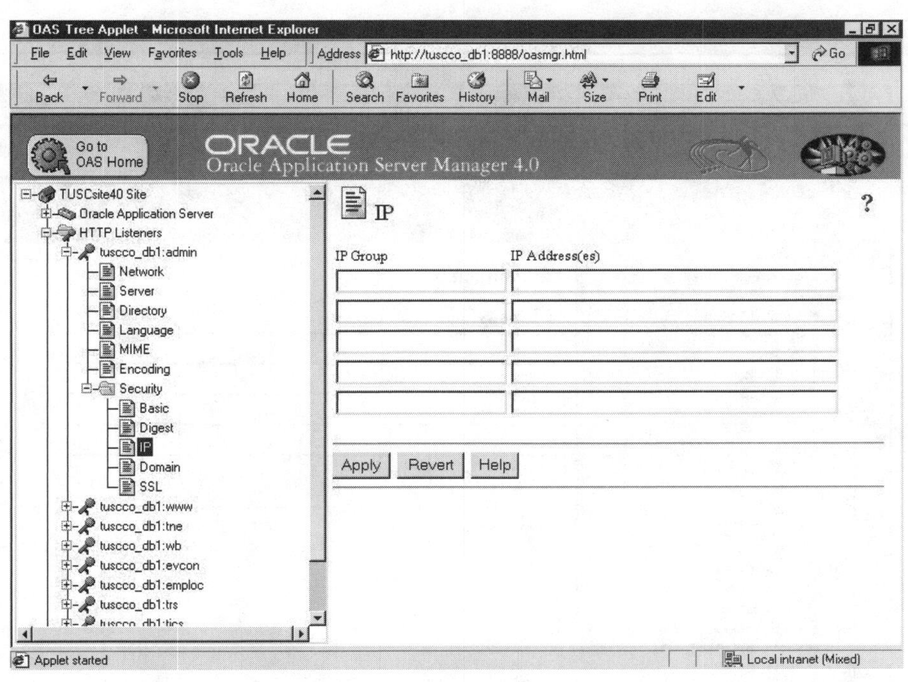

FIGURE 15-5. *IP-based restriction form*

The administrator can either enable or deny access to specified IP addresses. IP addresses are organized hierarchically; this mechanism enables entire subtrees to be specifically included or excluded (class A, B, or C), as in the example +130.*.

To use the IP-based restriction scheme to grant access to users who go through a proxy server to get outside a firewall, you must grant access to the firewall machine itself, which nonselectively grants access to all users who use that proxy server.

DOMAIN-BASED RESTRICTION Domain-based restriction works the same as IP-based restriction except domain-based restriction uses symbolic Domain Name Service (DNS) host names and domain names rather than the numeric IP addresses. This scheme has an advantage over IP-based restriction—the symbolic names are insulated from underlying changes in IP addresses. It's more difficult to spoof a domain name than an IP address, but not impossible. Figure 15-6 illustrates the domain-based restriction form for a Listener.

Instead of enabling or restricting access through IP addresses, the administrator can allow or restrict access through domain names. Portions of the domain name

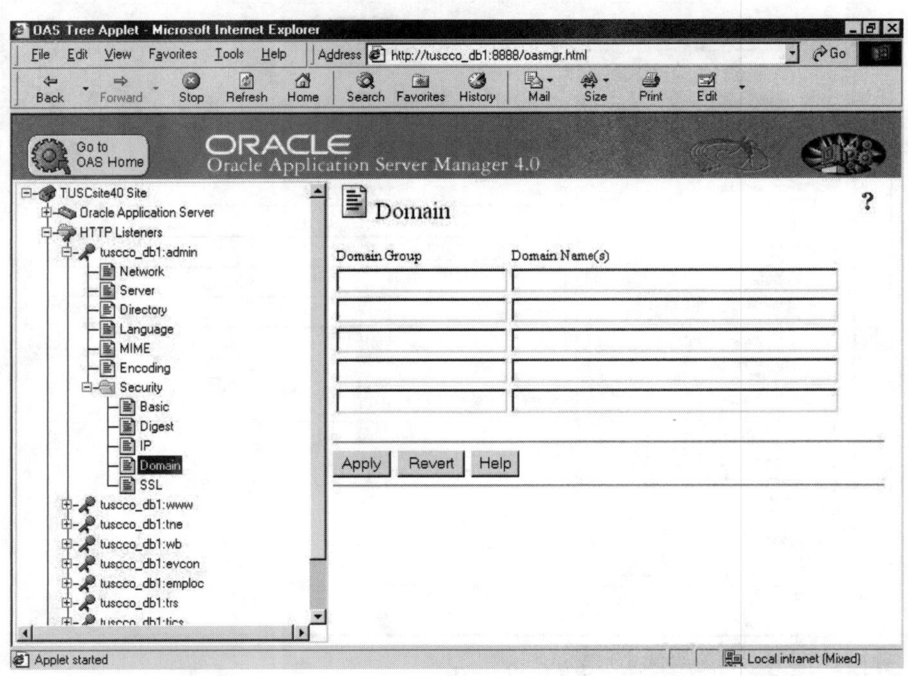

FIGURE 15-6. *Domain-based restriction form*

can be wildcards, so that restricted strings such as *.xyz.com deny access to all clients coming from the xyz.com domain. Domain names are a more convenient expression of IP addresses because one company may own many IP groups.

Comparing In-Memory to ORB Communication

As illustrated in Figure 15-7, within OAS you can also specify the operation mode for your authentication server to control the interface (in-memory or ORB) between the client and the broker. The Security form enables you to configure your authentication service (broker) and schemes (providers) to run in either of the two available modes:

- **In-memory** The broker and/or providers communicate using simple APIs instead of across the ORB to transfer information.
- **Object Request Broker (ORB)** The broker and/or providers communicate with each other through a CORBA-compliant ORB.

I recommend using in-memory for a single node OAS implementation and ORB for a multi-node OAS implementation.

You can also configure virtual paths so users requesting access to the paths are verified against a directory server. Directory servers are used by organizations to define a hierarchical view of the organization's employees, units, and other resources. OAS can read the contents of directory servers that support Lightweight Directory Access Protocol (LDAP) v3.

Application-Level Security

If your application is available on the Internet and provides unrestricted access by anyone, you do not need application-level security. However, if you intend to track who your users are and you plan to require your users to log in to your application, you will need application-level security.

Many methods can be deployed to authenticate users. The following subsections will discuss six different methods of providing application authentication (or security):

- Upon each request
- Passing through the URL (or standard input)
- Database authentication
- Basic or Digest authentication
- Using owa_custom
- Using a cookie

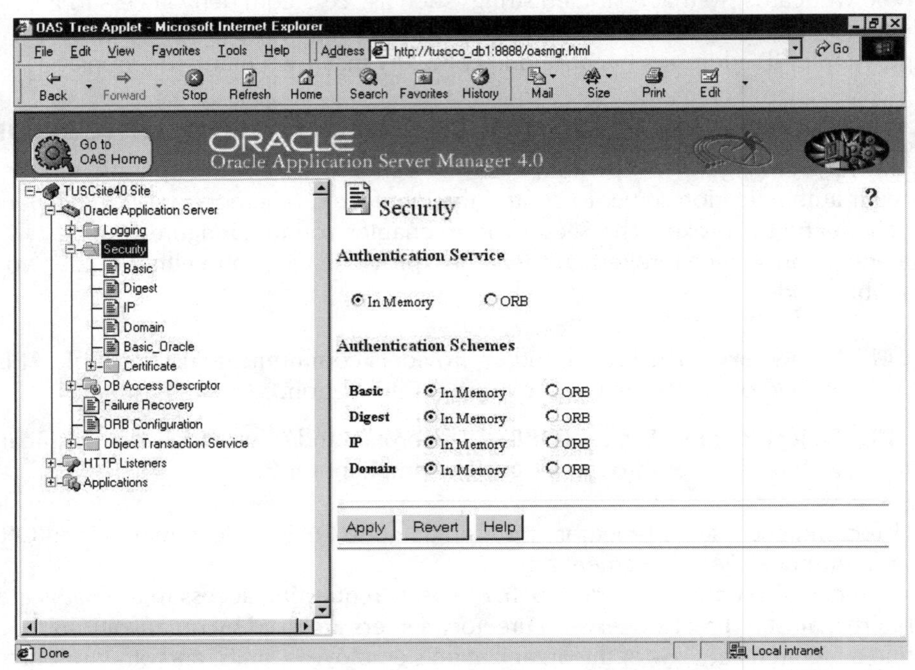

FIGURE 15-7. *Security – in-memory or ORB*

Beyond the previously listed methods, countless methods can be used for your application-level security. Feel free to construct your own authentication method, but hopefully these suggestions will spark an idea to improve your own method.

Requesting Authentication upon Each Request

If you rarely require authentication, you could authenticate the user upon each request. Otherwise, you will frustrate your users. Prior to calling the page requiring authentication, you would display a page containing an HTML form requesting the authentication information. Upon submission of the form the authentication information (for example, username and password) would be passed to the request (procedure).

Passing Authentication Along

Similar to preceding approach, you could use an HTML form to prompt for the authentication information. After prompting for this information and passing the information on to your page routine (procedure), the information can be passed from page to page as a part of the URL (using the implicit GET method) or through standard input (using a hidden HTML form and the POST method). Rather than passing specific authentication information (for example, username and password), you would want to pass less sensitive information, such as a session ID. The session ID can be decoded back into the username/password on the back end. If the information being passed is not secure information (for example, a ZIP code), your application can pass this information directly from routine to routine. This method is not considered a secure authentication scheme.

Combining Database Authentication

Database authentication is a valid authentication method. Database authentication uses a database schema (for example, username and password) to authenticate users. By combining database authentication with logic in your application, you can provide application-level authentication. By using the user pseudocolumn, your application logic can use database roles or table-based roles to determine a user's level of functionality. Build packages to support the level of application authentication you wish to provide for your users.

Combining Basic or Digest Authentication

Basic or Digest authentication, as previously described, is essentially an all or none type of authentication. If you do or do not know a valid username and password, you can or cannot access the virtual path. By combining Basic or Digest authentication with application logic that retrieves the username specified (using owa_sec.get_user_id), you have a powerful application authentication mechanism.

Using owa_custom

As discussed in detail in Chapter 10, you can implement application authentication using the owa_custom authentication function. As of the release of version 3.0 of OWAS, the packaged function was named owa_init.authorize.

Baking Cookies

The preferred method of application authentication is to ask for the information once and store a session (or user ID) in a cookie. By applying the cookie method, your application can retrieve the session ID from the cookie, then decode the session ID into other information from a database table. It is recommended to store state information in a session table. Your application can apply rules based on the users' privileges (also stored in a table) to provide for application authentication and logic.

Using Cookies to Store User Information

The following example demonstrates one method to handle application authentication using a cookie to store the information and a generic authentication routine. In this example, if the user is not logged on to the application, the user is provided generic information throughout the site and is only permitted to see limited application components. Therefore, when users enter the application, they can choose whether to log in. When logging in, users are also permitted to choose whether they wish to store the cookie beyond the life of the session. Retrieving the user's profile information is performed with one line of code, as demonstrated in the following script:

```
profile_rec tusc_util.profile_cur%rowtype :=
            tusc_util.get_profile_info;
```

The preceding statement will define a PL/SQL record based on the profile cursor's rowtype. Each of the fields selected from the user's profile record will be placed into each respective profile_rec variable. For example, the last name of the user will be placed into the profile_rec.last_name variable. Each of the columns shown in the following *profile* table can be referenced as profile_rec.{column_name}. The get_profile_info function in the tusc_util package returns the record if one is available for the current user.

REVIEWING THE USER PROFILE TABLE Before we get into the underlying code, an example of the user profile table is provided. This table is used to store profile information for a company in the airline business. As discussed in Chapter 3, for your site you will need to ask your marketing team what demographics are important to your application. The following statement creates the profile table for a sample application:

```
create table profile
( user_no           number,             -- Unique id for user
  username          varchar2(50),       -- User's specified username
  password          varchar2(2000),     -- User's password (encrypted)
  first_name        varchar2(50),       -- User's first name
  last_name         varchar2(50),       -- User's last name
  company           varchar2(50),       -- Company user works for
  flying_club       varchar2(50),       -- Flying club they are member in
  address_1         varchar2(50),       -- First address line
  address_2         varchar2(50),       -- Second address line
  city              varchar2(50),       -- City they live in
  state             varchar2(10),       -- State they live in
  zip               varchar2(10),       -- Zip code for address
  country           varchar2(50),       -- Their country
  mail_flag         varchar2(1),        -- Do we own them an email?
  phone             varchar2(15),       -- User's phone number
  fax               varchar2(15),       -- User's fax number
  custnumber        varchar2(10),       -- Cust no in corporate systems
  email             varchar2(50),       -- email address
  email_flag        varchar2(1),        -- Can we send email?
  email_freq        varchar2(1),        -- How often?
```

```
  gender          varchar2(1),    -- Gender of user
  age             varchar2(2),    -- Age bracket of user
  hours           varchar2(10),   -- Hours of flying time
  ordercat_flag   varchar2(1),    -- Do we own them a catalog?
  airline_no      number,         -- What is favorite airline?
  plane_no        number,         -- What is favorite plane?
  ics_no          number          -- User id in Commerce Server
);
```

In following examples, we will reference the airline_no and plane_no columns joining them to their foreign key reference tables, airline and plane. The following CREATE statements create the airline and plane tables. In addition, these tables only contain a full description for the item and image locations. The pilot_type, position, and ratings tables and the intersection entities (creating a many-to-many relationship between the profile table and each of these tables) are also created.

```
create table airline (
  airline_no  number,
  airline     varchar2(50),
  image_file  varchar2(200));

 create table plane (
  plane_no    number,
  plane       varchar2(50),
  image_file  varchar2(200));

create table pilot_type (
  pilot_type_no  number   ,
  pilot_type  varchar2(50));

create table position (
  position_no  number   ,
  position  varchar2(50));

create table rating (
  rating_no  number   ,
  rating  varchar2(50));

create table user_profile_pilot_type (
  user_no  number   ,
  pilot_type_no  number);

create table user_profile_position (
  user_no  number   ,
  position_no  number);

create table user_profile_rating (
  user_no  number   ,
  rating_no  number);
```

RETRIEVING THE USER'S INFORMATION The get_profile_info function is illustrated in the following example. The cursor is defined in the package specification and the meat of the routine is in the package body itself. The get_profile_info function first reads the value of the cookie to determine the user information, then extracts the user information from the profile table. The fundecryption (and funencryption) functions are shown in the following example titled "Another Cookie Example."

```
create or replace package tusc_util
as
   cursor profile_cur (in_user_no number, in_orig_user_no varchar2) is
   select profile.*,
          airline.airline airline,
          decode(airline.image_file,NULL, '/IMGS/hom-top-right.jpg',
                 '/IMGS/' || airline.image_file) airline_image,
           plane.plane plane,
           decode(plane.image_file, NULL, '/IMGS/hom-middle-tile.jpg',
                  '/IMGS/' || plane.image_file) plane_image,
           in_orig_user_no funencrypted_user_no
    from   profile, airline, plane
    where  profile.airline_no    = airline.airline_no (+)
    and    profile.plane_no      = plane.plane_no (+)
    and    profile.user_no       = in_user_no;

    profile_rec profile_cur%rowtype;

    function get_profile_info return profile_cur%rowtype;
end;

create or replace package body tusc_util
as
   function get_profile_info return profile_cur%rowtype is
      user_no     owa_cookie.cookie;
      nbt_user_no varchar2(2000);
   begin
      -- Retrieve the cookie
      user_no := owa_cookie.get('user_no');

      -- If the cookie is found, calculate the unencrypted
      -- value of the user id in the cookie
      if user_no.num_vals != 0 then
         nbt_user_no := fundecrypt(user_no.vals(1));
      end if;

      -- Fetch the profile record and return it
      open tusc_util.profile_cur(to_number(nbt_user_no));
      fetch tusc_util.profile_cur into tusc_util.profile_rec;
      close tusc_util.profile_cur;
```

```
      return tusc_util.profile_rec;
    end;
 end;
```

LOGGING IN TO THE APPLICATION When the user enters the application, you need to verify whether they are already logged in to the application. Other checkpoints also exist within the application where you will wish to determine whether the user is already logged in. If the user is logged in already, you will want to branch to a specific URL. If they are not logged in, you will want to take them to the login page. The following code is an example of such a routine. By calling this procedure and passing it a URL, it will determine whether the user is already logged in. If they are, the routine will use a refresh Meta tag to call the URL passed to it. If the user is not logged in, the routine will call the start_login procedure, passing the requested URL on to the start_login routine; so, after logging in, the user will be taken directly to the page you were originally directing them to. This routine also takes the protocol (http or https) into consideration based on the Listener port being used. If a URL is not passed to the check_logged_in routine, the user will be directed to the main index.html page.

```
create or replace procedure check_logged_in
   (in_url   varchar2    default '/index.html')
as
   user_no  owa_cookie.cookie;
   protocol varchar2(100);
begin
   user_no := owa_cookie.get('user_no');
   htp.htmlopen;
   htp.headopen;
   calc_meta_data;
   if user_no.num_vals != 0 then
      htp.meta('refresh', null, '0;url=' || in_url);
   else
      if owa_util.get_cgi_env('server_port') = '443' then
         protocol := 'https';
      else
        protocol := 'http';
      end if;
      htp.meta('refresh', null, '0;url=' || protocol ||
               '://' || owa_util.get_cgi_env('server_name') ||
               owa_util.get_owa_service_path || 'start_login?in_url=' ||
               in_url);
   end if;
   htp.headclose;
   htp.bodyopen;
   htp.bodyclose;
   htp.htmlclose;
end;
```

In the preceding example, the calc_meta_data routine was called. This routine pulled Meta data (for example, keywords) for the page from the Wisebot tables. Wisebot is covered in Chapter 23. The calc_meta_data routine is shown in the following example for completeness:

```
create or replace procedure calc_meta_data
   (in_url varchar2 default null)
as
   nbt_url  varchar2(2000) := in_url;
   nbt_meta varchar2(2000);
   dummy    varchar2(2000);
   dummy_no number;
   /* Note that the "tet" tables are generated
      and maintained by Wisebot */
   cursor meta_cur is
   select distinct phrase
     from tet_keyphrase a,
          tet_url_keyphrase c,
          tet_url_canonical d
    where a.id                 = c.keyid
      and c.urlid              = d.id
      and upper(canonical) like upper(nbt_url) || '%'
      and lower(phrase)  not in ('none', 'color', 'text-decoration')
    order by length(phrase) desc;
begin
  -- If a URL wasn't passed to this routine, figure out who
  -- called the routine to build data about that routine
  if in_url is null then
     owa_util.who_called_me(dummy,nbt_url, dummy_no, dummy);
  end if;

  nbt_url := 'http://' || owa_util.get_cgi_env('server_name') ||
             owa_util.get_owa_service_path || nbt_url;

  for meta_rec in meta_cur loop
     nbt_meta := nbt_meta || meta_rec.phrase || '; ';
  end loop;

  htp.meta(null, 'keywords', lower(nbt_meta));
end;
```

STARTING THE LOGIN PROCESS The following procedure is called to help the user log in to the application. The start_login routine displays the prompts for the username and password, but also enables the user to indicate that they forgot their password or that they would like to create a new account.

```
create or replace procedure start_login
   (in_url        varchar2 default '/index.html',
    in_type       varchar2 default 'e',
    in_target     varchar2 default '_top')
as
   nbt_url        varchar2(2000) := in_url;
begin
   htp.htmlopen;
   htp.headopen;
   calc_meta_data;
   -- Check to see if this is an actual first time login or
   -- post account creation login, meaning that the user was
   -- on the login page, clicked to create a new account,
   -- created the new account and are now back to login after
   -- their account was created.
   if in_type = 'n' then
      htp.title( 'Post Account Creation Login');
   else
      htp.title( 'Login');
   end if;
   htp.headclose;
   -- Change the background based on the login type
   if in_type = 'n' then
      htp.bodyopen('/imgs/lgn-bg-tile4.jpg',
                   cattributes => ' vlink="#ffffff"' );
   else
      htp.bodyopen('/imgs/lgn-bg-tile.jpg',
                   cattributes => ' vlink="#ffffff"' );
   end if;
   htp.centeropen;
   -- If this was a post account creation, we need to let them
   -- know their account was saved so they don't get confused
   -- about why they are back here again.
   if in_type = 'n' then
      htp.img('/imgs/lgn-yps-b.gif',
              calt => 'Your profile has been saved.');
   end if;
   htp.br;
   htp.print( htf.fontopen( csize => '3' ) ||
              'Please enter your username and password' ||
              htf.fontclose );
   htp.formopen( curl => 'login', cmethod => 'post',
                 cattributes => ' name="login"');
   htp.formhidden('in_url', nbt_url);
   htp.formhidden('in_target', in_target);
   htp.tableopen( cattributes => ' border="0" width="45%"' );
   htp.tablerowopen;
```

```
   htp.tabledata( htf.fontopen( csize => '3' ) ||
                  'username:' || htf.fontclose,
                   cattributes => ' width="25%"');
   htp.tabledata( '<div align="center">' ||
                  htf.formtext( cname => 'in_username',
                  csize => '30') ||
                  '</div>', cattributes => ' width="45%"');
   htp.tablerowclose;
   htp.tablerowopen;
   htp.tabledata( htf.fontopen( csize => '3' ) ||
                 'password:' || htf.fontclose,
                  cattributes => ' width="25%"');
   htp.tabledata( '<div align="center">' ||
                  htf.formpassword( cname => 'in_password',
                  csize => '30') ||
                  '</div>', cattributes => ' width="45%"');
   htp.tablerowclose;
   if in_type != 'n' then
      htp.tablerowopen;
      htp.tabledata( htf.anchor2( owa_util.get_owa_service_path ||
         'home_edit?in_type=n&in_url=' ||
         nbt_url, htf.img( '/imgs/lgn-cnp.gif',
         calt => 'Create new profile',
         cattributes => 'border="0"'),
         ctarget => 'home',
         cattributes => 'window.status = "create new login"'),
         ccolspan => '2', calign => 'center');
      htp.tablerowclose;
   end if;
   htp.tableclose;
   htp.formcheckbox( cname => 'in_save_password', cvalue => 'y');
   htp.print( htf.fontopen( csize => '3' ) ||
            'Save password in browser' || htf.fontclose);
   htp.br;
   htp.formcheckbox( cname => 'in_send_password', cvalue => 'n');
   htp.print( htf.fontopen( csize => '3' ) ||
        'I forgot my password, please send it to me' ||
        htf.fontclose);
   htp.para;
   htp.formsubmit( cvalue => 'submit');
   htp.centerclose;
   htp.formclose;
   htp.bodyclose;
   htp.htmlclose;
end;
```

ACTUALLY LOGGING IN After the user specifies a username and password, make sure the username and password specified are stored in the profile table. The following login procedure will perform this validation and set the user's cookie accordingly:

```
create or replace procedure login
   (in_user_no          varchar2 default null,
    in_username         varchar2 default null,
    in_password         varchar2 default null,
    in_save_password    varchar2 default null,
    in_send_password    varchar2 default null,
    in_url              varchar2 default '/index.html',
    in_target           varchar2 default '_top')
as
   cursor profile_cur is
   select *
     from profile
    where (username = in_username
      and fundecrypt(password) = in_password)
       or (user_no             = in_user_no);
   profile_rec  profile_cur%rowtype;
   profile_rec2 tusc_util.profile_cur%rowtype;
   expires      date;
begin
   if in_username is null and in_send_password is not null then
      htp.htmlopen;
      htp.headopen;
      calc_meta_data;
      htp.meta('refresh',null,'2;url=start_login');
      htp.headclose;
      htp.bodyopen('/imgs/lgn-bg-tile.jpg',
                   cattributes => ' bgcolor="#ffffff"' );
      htp.print('Please enter your username and try again.');
      start_login;
      htp.bodyclose;
      htp.htmlclose;
   else
      if  in_username      is not null
      and in_password      is     null
      and in_send_password is not null then
         send_password(in_username);
      else
         open profile_cur;
         fetch profile_cur into profile_rec;
         if profile_cur%notfound then
            htp.htmlopen;
            htp.headopen;
```

```
            calc_meta_data;
            htp.title( 'Login');
            htp.headclose;
            htp.bodyopen('/imgs/lgn-bg-tile.jpg',
                         cattributes => ' bgcolor="#ffffff"' );
            htp.tableopen(cborder => '0',
                          cattributes => 'width="629" height=165"');
            htp.tablerowopen;
            htp.tabledata( htf.img('/imgs/lgn-iun.jpg'),
                           calign => 'middle',
                           cattributes => 'valign="middle"');
            htp.tablerowclose;
            htp.tableclose;
            start_login;
            htp.bodyclose;
            htp.htmlclose;
         else
            if in_save_password is null then
               expires := null;
            else
               expires := sysdate+365;
            end if;
            owa_util.mime_header ('text/html',false);
            owa_cookie.send('user_no',
                            funencrypt(profile_rec.user_no),
                            expires);
            owa_util.http_header_close;
            profile_rec2 := tusc_util.get_profile_info;
            -- After setting the cookie, try to read it now
            -- if it's not set, cookie wasn't accepted.
            if profile_rec2.user_no is null then
               htp.comment('Cookie not accepted');
            end if;
            htp.htmlopen;
            htp.headopen;
            calc_meta_data;
            htp.meta('refresh',null,'2;url='||in_url ||
                     ';target='||in_target ||' ');
            htp.headclose;
            htp.bodyopen(profile_rec2.plane_image);
            htp.center(
               htf.header(1, 'Please wait... login in progress'));
            htp.bodyclose;
            htp.htmlclose;
         end if;
      end if;
   end if;
end;
```

EDITING THE ACCOUNT From the application, your user's may wish to edit their profile accounts. The following routine displays the information for editing:

```
create or replace procedure edit_profile
   (in_type                varchar2 default 'n',
    in_user_no             varchar2 default null,
    in_username            varchar2 default null,
    in_password            varchar2 default null,
    in_url                 varchar2 default '/index.html')
as
   nbt_username varchar2(2000);
   cursor profile_cur is
   select *
     from profile
    where (username              = in_username
      and fundecrypt(password) = in_password)
       or (user_no  = fundecrypt(in_user_no));
   profile_rec profile_cur%rowtype;

   -- note how we build our select list containing selected and
   -- non selected items with the selected items at the top.
   cursor airline_cur is
   select airline_no, airline, 'selected' selected
     from airline
    where airline_no = nvl(profile_rec.airline_no, -1)
   union
   select airline_no, airline, null selected
     from airline
    where airline_no != nvl(profile_rec.airline_no, -1);

   cursor position_cur is
   select x.position_no, x.position,
          decode(y.user_no, null, null, 'checked') checked
     from position x, user_profile_position y
    where x.position_no = y.position_no (+)
      and y.user_no (+) = fundecrypt(in_user_no);

   cursor rating_cur is
   select x.rating_no, x.rating,
          decode(y.user_no, null, null, 'checked') checked
     from rating x, user_profile_rating y
    where x.rating_no    = y.rating_no (+)
      and y.user_no (+) = fundecrypt(in_user_no);

   cursor flight_time_cur is
   select x.flight_time_no, x.flight_time,
          decode(y.user_no, null, null, 'checked') checked
```

```
     from flight_time x, user_profile_flight_time y
    where x.flight_time_no = y.flight_time_no (+)
      and y.user_no (+)     = fundecrypt(in_user_no);

   cursor pilot_type_cur is
   select x.pilot_type_no, x.pilot_type,
          decode(y.user_no, null, null, 'checked') checked
     from pilot_type x, user_profile_pilot_type y
    where x.pilot_type_no = y.pilot_type_no (+)
      and y.user_no (+)   = fundecrypt(in_user_no);

   cursor plane_cur is
   select plane_no, plane, 'selected' selected
     from plane
    where plane_no = nvl(profile_rec.plane_no, -1)
   union
   select plane_no, plane, null selected
     from plane
    where plane_no != nvl(profile_rec.plane_no, -1);
begin
   -- If we are attempting to edit an existing account, then
   -- we need to get the account information.
   if in_type = 'e' then
      open  profile_cur;
      fetch profile_cur into profile_rec;
      if profile_cur%notfound then
         htp.centeropen;
         htp.print('*** Unknown User ***');
         htp.centerclose;
      end if;
   end if;
   htp.htmlopen;
   htp.headopen;
   calc_meta_data;
   htp.title( 'TUSC User Profile Maintenance');

   -- JavaScript to check the user fields
   htp.print( '<script language="javascript">');
   htp.print( 'function alertuser( name, passwd, vpasswd ){');
   htp.print( '   // check the form');
   htp.print( '   founderror = false;');
   htp.print( '   if (isempty(name)) {');
   htp.print( '      alert("please enter a username. thank you.");');
   htp.print( '      document.profile.in_username.focus();');
   htp.print( '      founderror = true;');
   htp.print( '   }');
   htp.print( '   if (top.indexcenter.home.hidden.document.profile.'||
              'in_unique.value == ''n'') {');
```

```
htp.print( '      alert("Username is already in use,'||
                    'please pick a new username." );');
htp.print( '      document.profile.in_username.focus();');
htp.print( '      founderror = true;');
htp.print( '   }');
htp.print( '   if (isempty(passwd)) {');
htp.print( '      alert("Please enter a password. thank you.");');
htp.print( '      document.profile.in_password.focus();');
htp.print( '      founderror = true;');
htp.print( '   }');
htp.print( '   if (isempty(vpasswd)) {');
htp.print( '      alert("Please enter password verification. '||
                    'thank you." );');
htp.print( '      document.profile.in_verify_password.focus();');
htp.print( '      founderror = true;');
htp.print( '   }');
htp.print( '   if (passwd != vpasswd) {');
htp.print( '      alert("Please correct your password '||
                    'verification. thank you." );');
htp.print( '      document.profile.in_verify_password.focus();');
htp.print( '      founderror = true;');
htp.print( '   }');
htp.print( '   if (founderror == false)');
htp.print( '      return true;');
htp.print( '   else');
htp.print( '      return false;');
htp.print( '}');
htp.print( 'function isempty(inputstr) {');
htp.print( '   if ( inputstr == null || inputstr == "") {');
htp.print( '      return true');
htp.print( '   }');
htp.print( '   return false');
htp.print( '}');
htp.print( '</script>');
htp.headclose;
htp.bodyopen( '/imgs/lgn-bg-tile.jpg',
              cattributes => ' bgcolor="#ffffff"' );
htp.formopen( curl => 'save_profile',
              cmethod => 'post',
              cattributes=>'name="profile" onsubmit="return ' ||
              'alertuser(this.in_username.value,
                          this.in_password.' ||
              'value, this.in_verify_password.value)"');
htp.formhidden('in_url', in_url);
htp.para;
htp.centeropen;
htp.big( ctext => 'TUSC User Profile' );
htp.br;
```

```
htp.fontopen( csize => '2');
htp.anchor2( curl => '/privacy_policy.html',
             cname => 'priv',
             ctarget => 'homecenter',
             ctext => '** Privacy Policy **');
htp.para;
htp.print(htf.italic('Fields marked with an ' ||
   'asterisk(*) must be entered.'));
htp.fontclose;
htp.formhidden( cname => 'in_type', cvalue => in_type);
htp.formhidden( cname => 'in_user_no', cvalue => in_user_no);
htp.formhidden( cname => 'in_position', cvalue => '');
htp.formhidden( cname => 'in_rating', cvalue => '');
htp.formhidden( cname => 'in_pilot_type', cvalue => '');
htp.formhidden( cname => 'in_flight_time', cvalue => '');
htp.tableopen(  cattributes => 'border="0" width="400"' );
htp.tablerowopen;
htp.tabledata( htf.fontopen( csize => '2') || 'username' ||
    htf.fontclose, calign => 'right',
    cattributes => 'width="30%"');
htp.tabledata( htf.formtext( cname => 'in_username',
   cvalue => profile_rec.username, csize => '25',
   cattributes => 'onchange=''top.indexcenter.home.hidden.' ||
      'location.href="check_dup_profile?in_username=' ||
      '"+this.value+"&in_orig_username="+' ||
      'this.defaultvalue''') || '  *');
htp.tablerowclose;
htp.tablerowopen;
htp.tabledata( htf.fontopen( csize => '2') ||
   'password' || htf.fontclose, calign => 'right',
   cattributes => ' width="30%"');
htp.tabledata( htf.formpassword( cname => 'in_password',
   cvalue => fundecrypt(profile_rec.password),
   csize => '25') || '  *');
htp.tablerowclose;
htp.tablerowopen;
htp.tabledata( htf.fontopen( csize => '2') ||
   'verify password' || htf.fontclose,
   calign => 'right', cattributes => ' width="30%"');
htp.tabledata( htf.formpassword( cname => 'in_verify_password',
   cvalue => fundecrypt(profile_rec.password),
   csize => '25') || '  *');
htp.tablerowclose;
htp.tablerowopen;
htp.tabledata( htf.fontopen( csize => '2') || 'first name' ||
   htf.fontclose,
    calign => 'right', cattributes => ' width="30%"');
```

```
http.tabledata( htf.formtext( cname => 'in_first_name',
   cvalue => profile_rec.first_name, csize => '25'));
http.tablerowclose;
http.tablerowopen;
http.tabledata( htf.fontopen( csize => '2') ||'last name'||
   htf.fontclose, calign => 'right',
   cattributes => ' width="30%"');
http.tabledata( htf.formtext( cname => 'in_last_name',
   cvalue => profile_rec.last_name, csize => '25'));
http.tablerowclose;
http.tablerowopen;
http.tabledata( htf.fontopen( csize => '2') ||'company'||
   htf.fontclose, calign => 'right',
   cattributes => ' width="30%"');
http.tabledata( htf.formtext( cname => 'in_company',
   cvalue => profile_rec.company, csize => '25'));
http.tablerowclose;
http.tablerowopen;
http.tabledata( htf.fontopen( csize => '2') || 'address line 1' ||
   htf.fontclose,
    calign => 'right', cattributes => ' width="30%"');
http.tabledata( htf.formtext( cname => 'in_address_1',
   cvalue => profile_rec.address_1, csize => '25'));
http.tablerowclose;
http.tablerowopen;
http.tabledata( htf.fontopen( csize => '2') || 'address line 2' ||
   htf.fontclose,
    calign => 'right', cattributes => ' width="30%"');
http.tabledata( htf.formtext( cname => 'in_address_2',
   cvalue => profile_rec.address_2, csize => '25'));
http.tablerowclose;
http.tablerowopen;
http.tabledata( htf.fontopen( csize => '2') || 'city' ||
   htf.fontclose,
    calign => 'right', cattributes => ' width="30%"');
http.tabledata( htf.formtext( cname => 'in_city', csize => '25',
   cvalue => profile_rec.city));
http.tablerowclose;
http.tablerowopen;
http.tabledata( htf.fontopen( csize => '2') || 'state/province' ||
   htf.fontclose,
    calign => 'right', cattributes => ' width="30%"');
http.tabledata( htf.formtext( cname => 'in_state',
   csize => '15', cvalue => profile_rec.state));
http.tablerowclose;
http.tablerowopen;
http.tabledata( htf.fontopen( csize => '2') ||'zip'||
   htf.fontclose, calign => 'right',
   cattributes => ' width="30%"');
```

```
htp.tabledata( htf.formtext( cname => 'in_zip',
   cvalue => profile_rec.zip, csize => '25'));
htp.tablerowclose;
htp.tablerowopen;
htp.tabledata( htf.fontopen( csize => '2') || 'country ' ||
   htf.fontclose,
    calign => 'right', cattributes => ' width="30%"');
htp.print('<td>');
owa_util.listprint('select code, name, decode(''' ||
   profile_rec.country ||
   ''',null,decode(code,''us'',''selected'', null),
   code, ''selected'',null) from sdosjep1.ec_cntry',
   'in_country', 1);
htp.print('</td>');
htp.tablerowclose;
htp.tablerowopen;
htp.tabledata( htf.fontopen( csize => '2') ||
  'Daytime telephone' || htf.fontclose,
   calign => 'right', cattributes => ' width="30%"');
htp.tabledata( htf.formtext( cname => 'in_phone',
   cvalue => profile_rec.phone, csize => '25'));
htp.tablerowclose;
htp.tablerowopen;
htp.tabledata( htf.fontopen( csize => '2') ||
   'Fax number' || htf.fontclose,
   calign => 'right', cattributes => ' width="30%"');
htp.tabledata( htf.formtext( cname => 'in_fax',
   cvalue => profile_rec.fax, csize => '25'));
htp.tablerowclose;
htp.tablerowopen;
htp.tabledata( htf.fontopen( csize => '2') ||
   'Customer number' || htf.fontclose,
   calign => 'right', cattributes => ' width="30%"');
htp.tabledata( htf.formtext( cname => 'in_custnumber',
   cvalue => profile_rec.custnumber, csize => '25'));
htp.tablerowclose;
htp.tablerowopen( cvalign => 'top' );
htp.tabledata( htf.fontopen( csize => '2') ||
   'e-mail address' || htf.fontclose,
   calign => 'right', cattributes => 'width="30%"');
htp.tabledata( htf.formtext( cname => 'in_email',
   cvalue => profile_rec.email, csize => '25'));
htp.tablerowclose;
htp.tablerowopen;
htp.tabledata( htf.fontopen( csize => '2') ||
   'Gender'|| htf.fontclose,
   calign => 'right', cattributes => ' width="30%"');
```

```
htp.tabledata( htf.formselectopen( cname => 'in_gender' ) ||
   htf.formselectoption( 'Male',
      cselected => decode_it(profile_rec.gender,
         'm', 'selected', null),
      cattributes => ' value="m"') ||
   htf.formselectoption( 'female',
      cselected =>decode_it(profile_rec.gender,
         'f', 'selected', null),
      cattributes => ' value="f"') ||
   htf.formselectclose);
htp.tablerowclose;
htp.tablerowopen;
htp.tabledata( htf.fontopen( csize => '2') ||
   'Age'|| htf.fontclose, calign => 'right',
   cattributes => ' width="30%"');
htp.tabledata( htf.formselectopen( cname => 'in_age' ) ||
   htf.formselectoption( '10-20',
      cselected => decode_it(profile_rec.age,
         '1', 'selected', null),
      cattributes => ' value="1"') ||
   htf.formselectoption( '20-30',
      cselected => decode_it(profile_rec.age,
         '2', 'selected', null),
      cattributes => ' value="2"') ||
   htf.formselectoption( '31-40',
      cselected => decode_it(profile_rec.age,
         '3', 'selected', null),
      cattributes => ' value="3"') ||
   htf.formselectoption( '41-50',
      cselected => decode_it(profile_rec.age,
         '4', 'selected', null),
      cattributes => ' value="4"') ||
    htf.formselectoption( '51-60',
      cselected => decode_it(profile_rec.age,
         '5', 'selected', null),
      cattributes => ' value="5"') ||
    htf.formselectoption( '61+',
      cselected => decode_it(profile_rec.age,
         '6', 'selected', null),
      cattributes => ' value="6"') ||
    htf.formselectclose);
htp.tablerowclose;
htp.tablerowopen;
htp.tabledata( htf.fontopen( csize => '2') ||
   'Please check all that apply:' || htf.fontclose,
   calign => 'middle', ccolspan => '2',
   cattributes => ' width="30%"');
htp.tablerowclose;
```

```
htp.tableclose;
htp.tableopen(cattributes => 'border="0", width="500"');
htp.tablerowopen(cvalign=>'top');
htp.print('<td width=33%>' || htf.para ||
   htf.fontopen( csize => '2') || 'Are you a licensed pilot?' ||
   htf.fontclose || htf.br);
for pilot_type_rec in pilot_type_cur loop
   htp.formcheckbox( cname => 'in_pilot_type',
      cvalue => pilot_type_rec.pilot_type_no,
      cchecked => pilot_type_rec.checked);
   htp.print (htf.fontopen( csize => '2') ||
      pilot_type_rec.pilot_type || htf.fontclose || htf.br);
end loop;
htp.para;
htp.print(htf.fontopen( csize => '2') ||
   'Flight time' || htf.fontclose || htf.br);
for flight_time_rec in flight_time_cur loop
   htp.formcheckbox( cname => 'in_flight_time',
      cvalue => flight_time_rec.flight_time_no,
      cchecked => flight_time_rec.checked);
   htp.print (htf.fontopen( csize => '2') ||
      flight_time_rec.flight_time || htf.fontclose || htf.br);
end loop;
htp.print( '<font size=2>tt hours</font>');
htp.formtext( cname => 'in_hours',
   csize => '5', cvalue =>profile_rec.hours);
htp.print('</td>');
htp.print('<td width=33%>' || htf.para ||
   htf.fontopen( csize => '2') ||
   'Are you an aviation professional?' || htf.fontclose || htf.br);
for position_rec in position_cur loop
   htp.formcheckbox( cname => 'in_position',
      cvalue => position_rec.position_no,
      cchecked => position_rec.checked);
   htp.print (htf.fontopen( csize => '2') ||
      position_rec.position || htf.fontclose || htf.br);
end loop;
htp.print('</td>');
htp.print('<td width=33%>' || htf.para ||
         htf.fontopen( csize => '2') || 'ratings' ||
         htf.fontclose || htf.br);
for rating_rec in rating_cur loop
   htp.formcheckbox( cname => 'in_rating',
      cvalue => rating_rec.rating_no,
      cchecked => rating_rec.checked);
   htp.print (htf.fontopen( csize => '2') ||
      rating_rec.rating || htf.fontclose || htf.br);
end loop;
```

```
htp.print('</td>');
htp.tablerowclose;
htp.tableclose;
htp.tableopen( cattributes => 'border="0"');
htp.tablerowopen;
htp.tabledata(
   htf.anchor2(curl => 'send_me_acat',
               cname => 'in_ordercat', ctarget => 'homecenter',
               ctext => '** Send me a tusc catalog **'),
   cattributes => 'colspan=2', calign => 'center');
htp.tablerowclose;
htp.tablerowopen;
htp.tabledata( htf.fontopen( csize =>'2') ||
   'Customize your browser...'|| htf.fontclose,
   calign => 'left', ccolspan => '2');
htp.tablerowclose;
htp.tablerowopen;
htp.tabledata( htf.fontopen( csize => '2') ||
    'Airline of choice'|| htf.fontclose, calign => 'right');
htp.print('<td>');
htp.formselectopen( cname => 'in_airline' );
for airline_rec in airline_cur loop
   htp.formselectoption(
      airline_rec.airline, cselected => airline_rec.selected,
      cattributes => 'value="' || airline_rec.airline_no || '"');
end loop;
htp.formselectclose;
htp.print('</td>');
htp.tablerowclose;
htp.tablerowopen;
htp.tabledata( htf.fontopen( csize => '2') ||
   'Favorite plane' || htf.fontclose, calign => 'right',
   cattributes => ' width="35%"');
htp.print('<td>');
htp.formselectopen( cname => 'in_plane' );
for plane_rec in plane_cur loop
   htp.formselectoption(
     plane_rec.plane, cselected => plane_rec.selected,
     cattributes => 'value="' || plane_rec.plane_no || '"');
end loop;
htp.formselectclose;
htp.print('</td>');
htp.tablerowclose;
htp.tablerowopen;
htp.tabledata;
htp.tabledata(htf.formsubmit( cvalue => 'submit'));
htp.tablerowclose;
htp.tableclose;
htp.formclose;
```

```
   htp.centerclose;

   htp.print('<script language=javascript>');
   htp.print('top.indexcenter.home.hidden.location.href=' ||
             '"check_dup_profile?in_username="+' ||
             'document.profile.in_username.value+' ||
             '"&in_orig_username="+' ||
             'document.profile.in_username.defaultvalue;');
   htp.print( '</script>');
   htp.bodyclose;
   htp.htmlclose;
end;
```

DECODING IT In the preceding edit_profile procedure, the decode_it function is referenced. Oracle's decode statement is a powerful feature for the select statement. Unfortunately, within a PL/SQL assignment statement, the decode statement cannot be used. Therefore, create your own decode_it function, as the following illustrates:

```
create or replace function decode_it
   (in_column     varchar2,
    in_condition1 varchar2,
    in_result1    varchar2,
    in_else1      varchar2)
return varchar2
is
begin
   if in_column = in_condition1 then
      return in_result1;
   else
      return in_else1;
   end if;
end;
```

This generic function can be used for just about all data scenarios. If necessary, convert input parameters using TO_CHAR before calling the function and/or convert the output datatype after the function completes. For example:

```
nValue := to_number(decode_it(to_char(profile_rec.age),
                              '10', '100',
                              '1');
```

DETERMINING WHETHER THE USERNAME ALREADY EXISTS In the preceding edit_profile routine, a JavaScript routine (for example, check_dup_profile) has been placed on the in_username field's onChange event. The check_dup_profile routine is illustrated in the following example. In the preceding edit_profile procedure, the results of the check_dup_profile procedure are directed to a hidden (nondisplayed) frame on the page, which pushes JavaScript code to pop up an alert box for a duplicate username.

```
create or replace procedure check_dup_profile
   (in_username            varchar2,
    in_orig_username       varchar2)
as
   cursor profile_cur is
   select *
     from profile
    where username = in_username;
   profile_rec profile_cur%rowtype;
begin
   open profile_cur;
   fetch profile_cur into profile_rec;
   if profile_cur%notfound or in_username = in_orig_username then
      htp.htmlopen;
      htp.headopen;
      htp.title('Check duplicate profile');
      htp.headclose;
      htp.bodyopen;
      htp.print('Profile ' || in_username || ' is unique');
      htp.formopen('#', cattributes => 'name=profile');
      htp.formhidden('in_unique', 'y');
      htp.formclose;
      htp.bodyclose;
      htp.htmlclose;
   else
      htp.htmlopen;
      htp.headopen;
      htp.title('Check duplicate profile');
      htp.print('<script language=javascript>');
      htp.print('alert ("This username is already used, please ' ||
                'select another username.");');
      htp.print('top.indexcenter.home.homecenter.document. ' ||
                'profile.in_username.focus()');
      htp.print('</script>');
      htp.headclose;
      htp.bodyopen;
      htp.print('Profile ' || in_username || ' is not unique');
      htp.formopen('#', cattributes => 'name=profile');
      htp.formhidden('in_unique', 'n');
      htp.formclose;
      htp.bodyclose;
      htp.htmlclose;
   end if;
   close profile_cur;
end;
```

SAVING THE PROFILE When the user has finished editing their profile, store the information in the profile table (and other profile support tables). If this is a new user, their profile information needs to be inserted, whereas an existing user's information needs to be updated. The following routine performs the save (insert or update) and routes the user to the proper page thereafter:

```
create or replace procedure save_profile
   (in_type                  varchar2    default null,
    in_user_no               varchar2    default null,
    in_username              varchar2    default null,
    in_password              varchar2    default null,
    in_verify_password       varchar2    default null,
    in_first_name            varchar2    default null,
    in_last_name             varchar2    default null,
    in_company               varchar2    default null,
    in_flying_club           varchar2    default null,
    in_address_1             varchar2    default null,
    in_address_2             varchar2    default null,
    in_city                  varchar2    default null,
    in_state                 varchar2    default null,
    in_zip                   varchar2    default null,
    in_country               varchar2    default null,
    in_mail_flag             varchar2    default null,
    in_phone                 varchar2    default null,
    in_fax                   varchar2    default null,
    in_custnumber            varchar2    default null,
    in_email                 varchar2    default null,
    in_email_flag            varchar2    default 'n',
    in_email_freq            varchar2    default 'n',
    in_gender                varchar2    default null,
    in_age                   varchar2    default null,
    in_position              owa_util.ident_arr,
    in_rating                owa_util.ident_arr,
    in_flight_time           owa_util.ident_arr,
    in_pilot_type            owa_util.ident_arr,
    in_hours                 varchar2    default null,
    in_ordercat_flag         varchar2    default null,
    in_airline               varchar2    default null,
    in_plane                 varchar2    default null,
    in_url                   varchar2    default '/index.html',
    in_target                varchar2    default '_top')
is
   nbt_user_no            number(10) :=
      to_number(fundecrypt(in_user_no));
   new_ics_no             number(10);
```

```
   -- Mail Parameters
   cr                     varchar2(5);
   mailto                 varchar2(30);
   itbmail_to             varchar2(30);
   itbmail_from           varchar2(30);
   itbmail_smtp_server    varchar2(20);
   itbmail_subject        varchar2(40);
   itbmail_body           varchar2(2000);
   itbmail_url            varchar2(2000);

begin
   if in_type = 'n' then
      -- Get the next user number
      select nvl(max(user_no), 0) + 1
        into nbt_user_no
        from profile;

     -- Create the profile record
     insert into profile
        (user_no, username, password, first_name,
         last_name, company, flying_club, address_1,
         address_2, city, state, zip, country,
         mail_flag, phone, fax, custnumber, email,
         email_flag, email_freq, gender, age, hours,
         ordercat_flag, airline_no, plane_no, ics_no)
     values
        (nbt_user_no, in_username,
         funencrypt(in_password), in_first_name,
         in_last_name,in_company, in_flying_club, in_address_1,
         in_address_2, in_city,in_state, in_zip, in_country,
         in_mail_flag, in_phone, in_fax, in_custnumber, in_email,
         in_email_flag, in_email_freq, in_gender, in_age, in_hours,
         in_ordercat_flag,in_airline,in_plane, new_ics_no);
   else
     update profile
     set    username        = in_username,
            password        = funencrypt(in_password),
            first_name      = in_first_name,
            last_name       = in_last_name,
            company         = in_company,
            flying_club     = in_flying_club,
            address_1       = in_address_1,
            address_2       = in_address_2,
            city            = in_city,
            state           = in_state,
            zip             = in_zip,
            country         = in_country,
            mail_flag       = in_mail_flag,
```

```
         phone          = in_phone,
         fax            = in_fax,
         custnumber     = in_custnumber,
         email          = in_email,
         email_flag     = in_email_flag,
         email_freq     = in_email_freq,
         gender         = in_gender,
         age            = in_age,
         hours          = in_hours,
         airline_no     = in_airline,
         plane_no       = in_plane
         where user_no  = fundecrypt(in_user_no);
end if;

-- It's easier to delete and recreate these records
delete user_profile_position
 where user_no = nbt_user_no;

for x in 1 .. in_position.count loop
   insert into user_profile_position
      (user_no, position_no)
   values
      (nbt_user_no, in_position(x));
end loop;

delete user_profile_rating
 where user_no = nbt_user_no;
for x in 1 .. in_rating.count loop
   insert into user_profile_rating
      (user_no, rating_no)
   values
      (nbt_user_no, in_rating(x));
end loop;

delete user_profile_flight_time
 where user_no = nbt_user_no;
for x in 1 .. in_flight_time.count loop
   insert into user_profile_flight_time
      (user_no, flight_time_no)
   values
      (nbt_user_no, in_flight_time(x));
end loop;

delete user_profile_pilot_type
 where user_no = nbt_user_no;
for x in 1 .. in_pilot_type.count loop
   insert into user_profile_pilot_type
      (user_no, pilot_type_no)
```

```
      values
         (nbt_user_no, in_pilot_type(x));
   end loop;

   -- If this is a new profile record, ask the user to log
   -- in using their new username and password now
   if in_type = 'n' then
      start_login (in_url, in_type);
   else
      htp.htmlopen;
      htp.headopen;
      calc_meta_data;
      htp.meta('refresh', null, '0;url=' || in_url ||
               ';target=' || in_target);
      htp.headclose;
      htp.bodyopen;
      htp.bodyclose;
      htp.htmlclose;
   end if;
end;
```

SENDING A USER THEIR PASSWORD In the event that a user forgets their password (assuming they remember their username—if not, you could key the application off of the email address instead of the user ID), the following send_password routine will send an email to the user:

```
create or replace procedure send_password
   (in_username        varchar2,
    in_email           varchar2 default null)
is
   cursor profile_cur is
   select *
     from profile
    where username = in_username;
   profile_rec          profile_cur%rowtype;
   itbmail_url          varchar2(2000);
   nbt_username         varchar2(2000);
begin
   open profile_cur;
   fetch profile_cur into profile_rec;
   if profile_cur%notfound then
      htp.centeropen;
      htp.print('*** This is not a valid username ***');
      htp.centerclose;
   else
      if nvl(profile_rec.email, in_email) is null then
         htp.htmlopen;
```

```
      htp.headopen;
      calc_meta_data;
      htp.title( 'Email my tusc profile password');
      htp.headclose;
      htp.bodyopen( '/imgs/lgn-bg-tile.jpg',
                    cattributes => ' vlink="#ffffff"' );
      htp.para;
      htp.print( '  ' );
      htp.para;
      htp.print( '  ' );
      htp.br;
      htp.centeropen;
      htp.br;
      htp.fontopen( csize => '3');
      htp.print( 'Your profile does not contain an email ' ||
                 'address.  please enter the email to send ' ||
                 'your password to.' );
      htp.fontclose;
      htp.formopen( curl => 'send_password', cmethod => 'post',
                    cattributes => ' name="password"');
      htp.tableopen(  cattributes => ' border="0" width="45%"' );
      htp.tablerowopen;
      htp.tabledata( htf.fontopen( csize => '3') ||
                    'username:' ||
      htf.fontclose, cattributes => ' width="25%"');
      htp.tabledata( htf.div( calign => 'left') ||
      htf.formhidden( 'in_username', in_username) || in_username);
      htp.tablerowclose;
      htp.tablerowopen;
      htp.tabledata( htf.fontopen( csize => '3') ||
                     'email address:' ||
      htf.fontclose, cattributes => ' width="25%"');
      htp.tabledata( htf.div( calign => 'center') ||
         htf.formtext( cname => 'in_email', csize => '30') ||
         '</div>', cattributes => ' width="45%"');
      htp.tablerowclose;
      htp.tableclose;
      htp.para;
      htp.formsubmit( cvalue => 'submit');
      htp.formclose;
      htp.centerclose;
      htp.bodyclose;
      htp.htmlclose;
   else
      htp.htmlopen;
      htp.headopen;
      calc_meta_data;
      htp.title( 'Email username and password');
```

```
        htp.headclose;
        htp.bodyopen( '/imgs/lgn-bg-tile.jpg',
                      cattributes => ' bgcolor="#ffffff"' );
        itbmail_url := 'http://' ||
                       owa_util.get_cgi_env('server_name') ||
                       '/java/itbmail?itbmail_to=' ||
                        nvl(profile_rec.email,in_email) ||
                       '&' ||
                       'itbmail_from=web_admin@tusc.com' ||
                       '&' ||
                       'itbmail_smtp_server=mail.co.verio.net' ||
                       '&' ||
                       'itbmail_subject=tusc+profile+password' ||
                       '&' || 'itbmail_body=' ||
                       'Your+password+for+the+tusc+web+site+' ||
                       '(www.tusc.com)+is+' ||
                       replace(fundecrypt(profile_rec.password),
                               ' ', '+');
        htp.print(utl_http.request(itbmail_url));
        htp.br;
        htp.br;
        htp.centeropen;
        htp.header(3, 'Your password has been emailed to ' ||
                   nvl(profile_rec.email,in_email));
        htp.centerclose;
        htp.bodyclose;
        htp.htmlclose;
     end if;
  end if;
end;
```

Another Cookie Example

The following example contains its own set of security tables: web_sessions, users, and user_roles. These tables control the login process, facilitate the drop-down menu creation, and specify which screens the person is allowed to view and/or make changes to. To save space, I have not included all of the tables and functions below, but I did include all of the important routines. The security for the application will encompass the following features that will be discussed in detail:

- Determining whether the user exists (logging in to the application)
- Validating cookie on user's local machine
- PL/SQL encryption
- Setting the JavaScript script timer

There are many approaches for application authentication. The method that you use will depend on the flow of your application. For example, users might bookmark pages deep within your site. If the user attempts to access a page but is not authenticated, you need to determine the flow within your site. Will you immediately prompt the user to log in? Will you direct them to the index page within your site? How will you handle this situation? In most cases, once a user logs in to your application, you should enable them to continue to access application components without relogging in and without passing information from procedure to procedure. You may want your users to log in once and store their username and password for a day, week, month, year, or indefinitely. You can store information such as a user ID in a cookie. Because a user ID is likely to be a secure piece of information, you probably will unencrypt this information stored in the cookie.

The code in the following section is meant to be an example. The code that you use should take your application flow into account.

DETERMINE WHETHER THE USER EXISTS (LOGGING IN TO THE APPLICATION) The first security check in the code below will ensure the person exists in the users table. The username and fundecrypted password are validated against the users table. If the person exists, then the next step of security is performed. If the person's user ID does not exist in the table, an error page is created stating they are not a valid user for the system. Successful or not, the user's information is updated (or inserted) into the web_sessions table. If a record for the user already exists in the web_sessions table, the created_time column, logout_time column, and various other information are updated for the record. If the user is new (does not exist in the user table), this information is inserted into the web_sessions table.

Prior to storing sensitive information in a table (for example, password, credit card numbers, and so forth), we funencrypt this information so it is unreadable by selecting the information directly from the column. It is highly recommended that you funencrypt information that needs to be secure in the database. You can create a routine as complex or simple as deemed appropriate. For example, I call the simplest of them the "spy decoder ring" funencrypt and fundecrypt routine. The spy decoder ring funencrypt routine uses the translate function to convert A's to F's, B's to X's, C's to G's and so forth. The spy decoder ring fundecrypt routine uses the translate function to convert F's to A's, X's to B's, G's to C's, and so forth. The following routines are examples of more complex funencryption and fundecryption functions. Be creative and develop your own routine. It is also recommended that you wrap these routines in a package.

```
-----------------------------------------------------
-- This procedure validates the user and updates the
-- web_sessions table if the user is granted access
-----------------------------------------------------
procedure provalidateuser
   (vbadge     in varchar2,
```

```
     vpassword  in varchar2,
     vpid       in varchar2,
     voperation in varchar2 default null,
     vappname   in varchar2 default null,
     vattrib    in varchar2 default null)
is
   brevalidate         boolean;
   btest               boolean;
   vtempuser           varchar2(50);
   vtempbadge          varchar2(50);
   vthisprocorfuncname varchar2(30) := 'provalidateuser';
   cursor c_user (p_badge in varchar2) is
   select user_id
     from users
    where user_id = p_badge;

   cursor c_revalidate_user (p_pid in varchar2) is
   select v.user_id, fundecrypt(l.user_id)
     from users v,  web_sessions l
    where v.user_id = fundecrypt(l.user_id)
      and l.pid     = p_pid;
begin
   --validate pid
   if (voperation != 'revalidate') then
      open c_user(vbadge);
      fetch c_user into vtempuser;
      if (c_user%notfound) then
         close c_user;
         proprolog(vpid,null);
         htp.print('<center>');
         htp.print ('Access denied. please try again.');
         htp.print('</center>');
         prostartpage;
         return;
      end if;
      close c_user;
      brevalidate := false;
      vtempbadge := vbadge;
   else
      open c_revalidate_user(vpid);
      fetch c_revalidate_user into vtempuser,vtempbadge;
      close c_revalidate_user;
      brevalidate := true;
   end if;
   if ((not funloginok(vtempuser,vpassword)) or
       (brevalidate)) then
      update web_sessions
         set user_id      =  funencrypt(vtempuser),
             access_level = 'denied',
             active_flag  = 'f'
```

```
         where pid          = vpid;
        htp.nl;
        prologin(vappname,'retry');
     else
        update web_sessions
           set user_id       = funencrypt(vtempuser),
               access_level = 'granted'
         where pid          = vpid;
        btest := funcheckcookie(vtempuser);

        --------------------------------------------------------
        htp.p('<font color=' || vbackgroundcolor || '> </font>');
        --------------------------------------------------------
        --return to calling package
        if (((voperation = 'login')   and
              (not funchangepw(vpid))) or
             (brevalidate)) then
           htp.htmlopen;
           if (vattrib is not null) then
              htp.p('<meta http-equiv="refresh" content="2;' ||
                     'url=../plsql/' || 'pkglogin'|| '.' ||
                     'prostartpage' || '?vpid=' || vpid || '&' ||
                     vattrib||'">');
           else
              htp.p('<meta http-equiv="refresh" content="2;'||
                     'url=../plsql/' || 'pkglogin'|| '.' ||
                     'prostartpage' || '?vpid=' || vpid || '">');
           end if;
           htp.print('<body bgcolor="'||vbackgroundcolor||'">');
           htp.nl;
           htp.nl;
           htp.nl;
           htp.nl;
           htp.print('<h2><strong><center>authenticating user ' ||
                      'privileges... one moment please... ' ||
                      '</center></strong></h2>');
           htp.print('</body>');
           htp.htmlclose;
        end if;
        if ((funchangepw(vpid)) or
             (voperation='change password')) then
           progetnewpw(vpid,vattrib);
        end if;
     end if;
exception
     when others then
        proshowerror(vthispackagename, vthisprocorfuncname, 0,
                       sqlerrm, 'nothing', true);
end provalidateuser;
```

```
----------------------------------------------------
-- This function checks the users login for validity
----------------------------------------------------
function funloginok
   (vuser          in varchar2,
    vpassword      in varchar2)
return boolean
is
   bresult                  boolean;
   vtemp                    varchar2(1);
   vthisprocorfuncname      varchar2(30) := 'funloginok';
   cursor c_login(p_user in varchar2, p_pass in varchar2) is
   select '1'
     from users
    where user_id  = p_user
      and p_pass   = fundecrypt(vpassword);
begin
   open c_login (vuser, vpassword);
   fetch c_login into vtemp;
   if (c_login%notfound) then
      bresult := false;
   else
      bresult := true;
   end if;
   close  c_login;
   return bresult;
exception
   when others then
      proshowerror(vthispackagename, vthisprocorfuncname, 0,
                   sqlerrm, 'nothing', true);
end funloginok;

----------------------------------------------------------------------
-- This function is used to funencrypt the userid in the web_sessions
-- table, the password in the users table, the cookie, and other
-- information requiring security
----------------------------------------------------------------------
function funencrypt
   (vstring in varchar2)
return varchar2
is
   nseconds           number(3);
   vtranslateto       varchar2(2000);
   vtranslatefrom     varchar2(2000);
   vbyte1             varchar2(1);
   vrandom            varchar2(2000);
   vlength            varchar2(1);
   vtranslateshifted varchar2(2000);
```

```
   vfinalstring      varchar2(2000);
   dthedate          date;
begin
   /*
     1. Calc current number of "seconds" (1-60) - e.g. 20
     2. Look at the 20th character of the translation string
     3. Byte #1 = value of 20th byte in translation string (e.g. "x")
     4. Make up 19 characters for bytes 2-19 from random string
     5. Byte #20 - length of string - e.g. 5 bytes, set byte 20 to
        the character in translation string position 5 - e.g. "b"
     6. Change translation string to substr(ts, seconds) ||
        substr(ts, 1, seconds-1)
     7. Translate string
     8. Byte #21 - 25 - translated string
     9. Bytes #26 - 52 + length of string = more random filler
   */

   nseconds        := to_number(to_char(dthedate,'ss')) + 2;
   vtranslateto    := '0987654321)(*&^%$#@!-_=+\|]}[{pPoOiIuU' ||
                      'yYtTrReEwWqQAasSdDfFgGhHjJkKlL;:''"zZx' ||
                      'cvbnm,./?><M NBVCX`~';
   vtranslatefrom := 'abcdefghijklmnopqrstuvwxyzABCDEFGHIJ' ||
                      'KLMNOPQRSTUVWXYZ1234567890-=!@#$%^&' ||
                      '*()_+[]\{}|;'':",./ ?~`';
   vbyte1          := substr(vtranslateto,nseconds,1);
   vrandom         :=  '4r98437yriu56r675elgljkhxfcvjk78dfshreoite' ||
                       'jhoi90retgujoitdgjis56dfjlkdfgjlkr''egjrtl' ||
                       'g34ekjroigrtjo787ifcxv34mnfkjenwkjw2543457' ||
                       '5tre89rtu8dutfgdfdlrdjsftgrflkesdroe0tu5te';
   vlength         := substr(vtranslateto,length(vstring),1);
   vtranslateshifted := substr(vtranslateto, nseconds + 1) ||
                              substr(vtranslateto, 1, nseconds);
   vfinalstring := vbyte1 ||
                   substr(vrandom,nseconds,nseconds - 1) ||
                   vlength ||
                   translate(vstring, vtranslatefrom,
                             vtranslateshifted);
   vfinalstring := vfinalstring ||
                   substr(vrandom, nseconds, length(vfinalstring));
   return vfinalstring;
end funencrypt;

------------------------------------------------------
-- The following function is used to fundecrypt values
------------------------------------------------------
function fundecrypt
   (vstring in varchar2)
```

```
return varchar2
is
   noffset           number(3);
   nlength           number(3);
   vtranslateto      varchar2(2000);
   vtranslatefrom    varchar2(2000);
   vtranslateshifted varchar2(2000);
   vfinalstring      varchar2(2000);
   dthedate          date;
begin
   /*
      1. Look at byte 1 ("x"), figure out which position in
         translation string is equal to "x" - e.g. 20 (equals offset)
      2. Ignore bytes 1-19
      3. Look at byte 20 ("b", figure out which position in
         translation string is equal to "b" - e.g. 5 (equals
         length of string)
      4. Extract bytes 21 - 25 (5 bytes), ignore everything else
      5. Untranslate string - this is the result
   */
   vtranslatefrom := '0987654321)(*&^%$#@!_=+\|]}[{pPoOiIu' ||
                     'UyYtTrReEwWqQAasSdDfFgGhHjJkKlL;:''"' ||
                     'zZxcvbnm,./?><M NBVCX`~';
   vtranslateto   := 'abcdefghijklmnopqrstuvwxyzABCDEFGHIJ' ||
                     'KLMNOPQRSTUVWXYZ1234567890-=!@#$%^&*' ||
                     '()_+[]\{}|;'':",./ ?~`';
   noffset        := instr(vtranslatefrom, substr(vstring, 1, 1));
   nlength        := instr(vtranslatefrom, substr(vstring,
                     noffset + 1, 1));
   vtranslateshifted := substr(vtranslatefrom, noffset + 1) ||
                              substr(vtranslatefrom, 1, noffset);
   vfinalstring   := translate(substr(vstring, noffset + 2, nlength),
                              vtranslateshifted, vtranslateto);
   return vfinalstring;
end fundecrypt;
```

VALIDATE COOKIE ON USER'S LOCAL MACHINE After logging in to the application, make sure the user ID cookie is present on the user's system. If the cookie is not there, one is created. You might ask yourself, why store information in a cookie at all? That is a good question. In this example, the cookie is used for validation, coupled with the web_sessions table, throughout the application. In this example, a session's IP address is stored in the web_sessions table. This way, if someone attempts to spoof another machine's cookie, the validation will fail because the IP address is stored in the web_session table—the addresses will not match. The "spoofing" user would also have to know the IP address of the session they are hoping to spoof. Because the information in the cookie is funencrypted, it would be nearly impossible for anyone to break the secret.

The following code shows an example of a cookie validation, a creation process, and the function to validate a user. This example uses the owa_cookie.get_all procedure, which when retrieving multiple cookies is an efficient method of quickly retrieving all of the cookies at one time. To retrieve only one cookie, use owa_cookie.get, as is demonstrated in the function funisvalid, following the funcheckcookie.

```
-------------------------------------------------------------
-- This function checks for a cookie on the users machine. If it
-- does not exist, one is created.
-------------------------------------------------------------
function funcheckcookie
   (vstring in varchar2)
return boolean
is
   kcookie      owa_cookie.cookie;
   knames       owa_cookie.vc_arr;
   kvals        owa_cookie.vc_arr;
   dthedate     date    := sysdate + 10;
   icount       integer := 0;
   nloopcnt     boolean := false;
begin
   owa_cookie.get_all(knames, kvals, icount);
   for i in 1 .. icount loop
      if (kvals(i) = 'user_id'
      and vstring = fundecrypt(kvals(i))) then
         nloopcnt := true;
         exit;
      end if;
   end loop;
   if nloopcnt then
      owa_util.mime_header('text/html', false);
      owa_cookie.send('user_id', funencrypt(vstring),
                       dthedate+.5, '/',
                      null, null);
      owa_util.http_header_close;
   end if;
   return true;
end;

------------------------------------------------------------------
-- This function checks to see that the screen the user is requesting
-- can be viewed by them based on the combination of the cookie on
-- their machine and the ip address stored in the web_sessions table.
------------------------------------------------------------------
```

```
function funisvalid
return boolean
is
   kcookie                      owa_cookie.cookie;
   bresult                      boolean;
   vtemp                        varchar2(1);
   vnamehold                    varchar2(50) := null;
   vexpire_time                 number(10)   := 10;
   vthisprocorfuncname          varchar2(30) := 'funisvalid';
   cursor get_user_info(p_user in varchar2, p_addr in varchar2) is
   select 'x'
     from web_sessions
    where user_id              = p_user
      and remote_addr          = p_addr
      and active_flag          = 't'
      and session_expire_time >= sysdate;
begin
   kcookie := owa_cookie.get('user_id');
   if kcookie.num_vals = 0 then
      bresult := false;
   else
      vnamehold := fundecrypt(kcookie.vals(1));
      open get_user_info(vnamehold,
                         owa_util.get_cgi_env('remote_addr'));
      fetch get_user_info into vtemp;
      if get_user_info%notfound then
         bresult := false;
      else
         update web_sessions
            set session_expire_time = sysdate + vexpiretime,
                session_update_time = sysdate
          where user_id = vnamehold;
         commit;
         bresult := true;
      end if;
      close get_user_info;
   end if;
   return (bresult);
exception
   when others then
      proshowerror(vthispackagename, vthisprocorfuncname, 0,
                   sqlerrm, 'nothing', true);
end funisvalid;
```

SET JAVASCRIPT SCRIPT TIMER Once the user has entered the application, a JavaScript timer is set to track how long they are on a page. The following JavaScript timer will automatically log the user off if the user does not perform an OAS activity within 20 minutes:

```
// These functions are used for timing to let the person know that
// their session is about to expire
var bAlertCount = false;
function jsDisplay() {
   nRunTime = nExpTime - nCurrTime;
   if (nRunTime > 60)
      m = parseInt(nRunTime / 60);
   else
      m = 0;
   s = parseInt(nRunTime - (m * 60));
   if (s < 10)
      s = "0" + s
   window.status = "Time Remaining :  "+m+":" + s
   window.setTimeout("jsCheckTime()",1000)
}

function jsSetTimes() {
   var vTime = new Date();
   vHours = vTime.getHours();
   vMins = vTime.getMinutes();
   vSecs = vTime.getSeconds();
   nExpTime = vHours * 3600 + vMins * 60 + vSecs;
   nAlertTime = vHours * 3600 + vMins * 60 + vSecs;
   nExpTime += 1200;
   /* You can change the value of 1200 according to how much
      time you wish to set the timer. Where 1200 is time in secs
      (1200 = 20 mins * 60 secs/min). Max time is 60 mins (3600secs)
   */
   /* This is the time variable representing when the alert will
      come up telling them that they need to save
   */
   nAlertTime += 900;
   jsCheckTime();
}

function jsCheckTime() {
   var vTime = new Date();
   vHours = vTime.getHours();
   vMins = vTime.getMinutes();
   vSecs = vTime.getSeconds();
```

```
   nCurrTime = vHours * 3600 + vMins * 60 + vSecs
   if ((nCurrTime >= nAlertTime) && (!bAlertCount))
      jsAlertTime();
   else {
    if (nCurrTime >= nExpTime)
       jsExpired();
    else
       jsDisplay();
    }
}

function jsExpired() {
   alert("Your Session has expired. Please do not make " +
         "any changes as you will need to login again.");
   location.href = "nextpage.html";  //Put here the next page
   window.status = "Time Remaining :  0:00"
}

function jsAlertTime() {
   alert("Your Session will expire in 5 minutes. " +
         "Please save your work.");
   bAlertCount = true;
   jsDisplay();
   location.href = "nextpage.html";  //Put here the next page
}
```

Network Security

When it comes to protecting the data that is transferred on your network, Secure Sockets Layer (SSL) is the answer for OAS. SSL encrypts the data from end to end, but not on the ends. SSL protects the data that is transferred from the client to the server and vice versa. This protects the data from being "sniffed" by someone else. Is data on the Internet insecure? Not really. The security issues primarily exist at the networks on the ends of the network that the client is connected to and the network that the server is connected to. At these ends, a sophisticated network specialist can read unencrypted data. They will not be able to read encrypted data.

If the data you are transferring is sensitive, valuable, or confidential, use SSL!

Basics of SSL

This section explains how to impose public key cryptography on the communication between the Listener and the browser. SSL is a protocol on top of HTTP that encrypts all messages sent between the browser and the Web server.

URLs that require SSL use https in place of http. The Listener must be configured to accept an SSL connection, and the system administrator must have a certificate for the Listener (usually obtained from VeriSign).

In addition to providing for encryption, SSL also provides for authentication. When the browser connects to the server, the server presents its certificate. The browser then either accepts that certificate (if it is included in the site certificates in the browser) or prompts the user to decide whether to accept the certificate. The certificate allows the user to be sure that the server is what it is claiming to be. However, the simple fact that a server has a certificate does not mean the user must or should permit access.

In addition to the server being authenticated, it can request that the client be authenticated. The client must have obtained its own certificate and present that certificate to the server when prompted. Client authentication is not required as part of the SSL protocol, and most Listeners enable this to be configured.

SSL encryption and authentication can be used for static HTML pages, CGI programs, and cartridges. If a request for a cartridge uses SSL, then the resulting HTML page generated by the cartridge is encrypted. Application programmers do not have to know anything about SSL and its associated encryption methods in order to develop an application.

Setting Up SSL

The instructions within the online documentation and those listed in my prior book will help you configure SSL. When referring to the online documentation, you may find enough ambiguity that it will be difficult to make SSL work with OAS. The following tips will help you through this process. The process of registering and obtaining a certificate is performed online and you receive your trial certificate immediately (no more waiting).

Tips for Setting Up SSL

The following list contains a number of tips that you may wish to consider when setting up SSL:

- Do not abbreviate. For example, you must specify the exact state (the state your business is in, such as Illinois). For the most secure keys, use a file and random keys.
- Use filenames that make sense (for example, privkey.der).

- Previously, the genreq utility generated the key files on the server. You may need to do a system-level file find to locate the files.
- The genreq utility will ask for the distinguished name, which is somewhat confusing as to what that might be. The distinguished name is the fully qualified domain name (fqdn) registered on the Internet. Thus, only boxes that have a domain name that is "publicly" shared can use SSL. You cannot register SSL to an IP address. You could use an internal domain name, if that is your intent.
- The security entries requested want exact paths leading to the key files, such as "c:\orant\owa\bin\cert.der."
- Be careful what you do with the key file. VeriSign sends back the file in email. We had a situation once where somebody had forwarded the file to somebody else. Exchange (email) added a greater than (>) character to every line that was forwarded, but this was not obvious to the person implementing the key file because it was their first time implementing SSL. The file (and SSL) was unusable until the alterations were removed from the file.
- Prior to OAS 4.0, when a new port was added for SSL, you needed to alter the PL/SQL cartridge so it could use the new port.
- Netscape handles cookies differently than Microsoft Internet Explorer. In an application, we had a session cookie that suddenly became unavailable to the SSL portion in Netscape Navigator 4.0, whereas within Explorer it works just fine. After further research, we discovered the Netscape cookie file in C:\Program Files\Netscape\User\Default\cookies.txt; Explorer's cookies live in C:\Windows\cookies in several different files. After further examination of the Netscape cookie file, we found that Netscape included a port number with the cookie information, suggesting that Netscape cookies are port-dependent.
- Cookies can be marked as secure, which means that they are only accessible if the user is using the HTTPS protocol. Otherwise, the cookie will not be available to the server.
- Set up SSL on port 443 (it's the default https port, just as port 80 is the default http port), and proxy servers are likely to limit your remote (Internet-based) clients to these ports.
- OAS 4.0 supports certificates issued from other certificate authorities (CAs), such as Netscape.

Protecting Digital Certificates

Due to sensitivity of your certificate files for SSL, it is extremely important to protect the digital certificate (for example, a VeriSign certificate). The method of protection is determined by your system administrator's philosophy on physical file protection. All VeriSign files are stored in a single directory. The Listener account needs read and write access to the files in that directory. You should not enable other access to that directory by other users. The password to the Listener account should be secure, so only your operating system Web administrator knows the password. If the VeriSign certificate was stolen or altered, it would result in security ramifications. Outside of protecting file access to this directory, further steps are not available. On UNIX, the security level for these files should be set to 700 permissions (read, write, execute by the owner only) on your system.

Securing Email with Digital IDs

Many popular email packages support secure email using digital IDs. To protect your email, check out http://www.verisign.com/securemail/guide to walk you through VeriSign's step-by-step Secure E-mail Guide.

Securing Credit Card Transactions

To secure credit card transactions on the Web, one name comes to my mind—CyberCash (http://www.CyberCash.com). CyberCash is a provider of e-commerce solutions. CyberCash has provided secure Internet credit card services since 1995. CyberCash's secure credit card service is used by thousands of merchants to process millions of transactions per month. The CyberCash solution provides a complete set of features and functionality available, including:

- Automation that supports lights-out, continuous commerce.
- Security that stores transactions in encrypted form.
- Support for card-not-present transactions through the Administration Server interface, so you do not have to buy another point-of-sale device to enter non-Internet transactions.
- Support for all major payment cards (Visa, MasterCard, American Express, Diners Club, Discover, and JCB).
- A full complement of credit card payment capabilities, including authorization requests/captures, voids and returns, AVS, automarking and autosettlement options, on-demand transaction searching capabilities, and reporting through the administration server interface.
- SET standard compliant capabilities that are preintegrated into their solution, so you can add SET capability to your existing SSL credit card service without needing to integrate a "new" piece of software.

For further information about securing your credit card transactions with CyberCash, check out http://www.CyberCash.com/cybercash/merchants/. CyberCash uses SSL for encrypting the end-to-end transactions. Typically, the longest lead time and most headaches are related to the interaction with your bank, not CyberCash.

RDBMS Security

As previously discussed, it's important to secure the data moving around your network. However, it's equally important to secure information stored in your database. For example, if you collect information such as credit cards and expiration dates, then store this information in the database unprotected, you are likely treading on thin legal waters.

Encrypting with PL/SQL

As is shown in a preceding example, you can write your own packaged procedure to encrypt and decrypt data. When storing confidential data into the database, you can use these procedures to make the data unreadable. The preceding example functions—funencrypt and fundecrypt—demonstrate how this is accomplished with PL/SQL. A function can be used in a SELECT statement. For example, the following query could quickly expose confidential information:

```
select fundecrypt(password)
from profile;
```

The preceding query assumes the user has access to the fundecrypt function. It is critical that you secure access to this function. The data is secure to a user who does not have access to the fundecrypt function (or users that are not aware the function exists). For added security, you could add a password to the function. Another option would be to build additional logic into the routine using the user pseudocolumn (or the program column in the v$session value to determine source of call), restricting access to a hardcoded set of users based on a table or database roles. Many options are available for providing additional security within this function.

PL/SQL Interface to Oracle Cryptographic Toolkit

The Oracle Cryptographic Toolkit (OCT) is an interface to the cryptographic services provided by the Oracle Security Server (part of Oracle's Advanced Security Option). OCT is intended to unify all cryptographic services, including the use, storage, retrieval, import, and export of credentials. This interface is used by both internal and external Oracle customers to add security enhancements to their applications. External customers can use either OCI or PL/SQL to access the Oracle Cryptographic Toolkit. One set of OCT functions contains procedures for data encryption (encryption and decryption).

Setting Up a Secure Schema Plan

OAS automatically places the PL/SQL Web Toolkit in an independent schema. It is important that your application's procedures and data be secure. An OAS DAD references a specific schema in the database. From a URL, users will be able to execute all procedures in the DAD's schema. It is important to separate the following components, each into their own schema:

- **Web Toolkit** Automatically placed into oas_public schema by the OAS installation.
- **Public application procedures** All procedures in the DAD's schema can be executed directly from a URL. These procedures should not physically reside in this schema, but access should explicitly be granted to this schema (for example, www_application) by the application schema manager.
- **Application procedures** The application itself (procedures and functions that make up the application) should be in this schema (for example, application_app).
- **Application data** For security reasons (to protect the application data from the application developers), the data for the application should reside in a separate schema from the application procedures (for example, application_data).

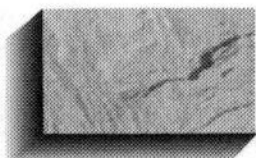

TIP

In a development environment, if you use database authentication (don't store the password in the DAD) each developer can log in to the application, effectively using their own objects (procedures, functions, tables, etc.) without affecting other developers or the "main" path into the application.

TIP

To enhance the preceding four schema separations, you could also create developer schemas and DADs. The developer schemas could contain a copy of the procedures in the application procedure schema or they could be granted access to them. Procedures and tables stored in the developer schema will override the application and application data schema's procedures and data.

Physical Security

For your OAS server to be secure, you must make sure no unauthorized person has access to your OAS host machine. The following are some suggestions:

- Place the machine in a locked server room.
- Limit distribution of keys or combinations to the server room to a few trusted individuals.
- Set up a secure area of the machine's file system that can be accessed only by the root user. This is the location to store your private key and your certificate when you receive it. Do not use a location that is accessible through FTP, NFS, or other network protocols.
- Set a secure root password on the machine, using at least six characters and mixing numbers, legal punctuation marks, and mixed-case letters. Try not to use a character string that is a proper name or a word in any language. Change passwords frequently, and never write a password on paper.
- Strictly limit the programs installed and allowed to run on the machine.
- Limit TCP/IP connections to the machine to port 443, the default SSL port for secure connections. Disable all other ports.

Summary

Security is a complex and multifaceted subject. Many books have been written on the subject. In this chapter, we covered OAS built-in security, application-level security, network, RDBMS, and physical security.

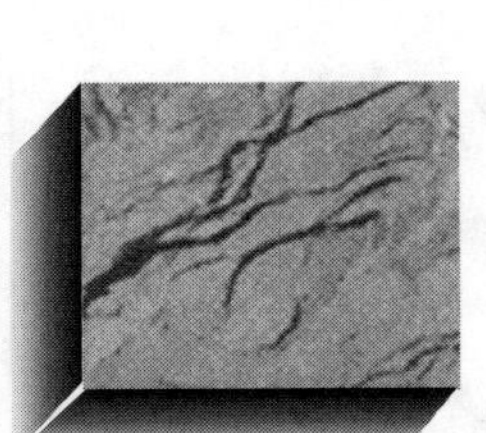

PART III

Oracle Tools

CHAPTER 16

Using Designer to Develop Web Code

f you're familiar with Oracle's toolset, you probably have a number of questions about Oracle Designer and how it fits into Web development. You might be wondering just what the Oracle Designer Web Server Generator is? Why would I use it over the Web Developer's PL/SQL Toolkit? Is one better than the other? This chapter hopes to answer these questions for you. The learning curve for Oracle Designer is steep. Therefore, to take full advantage of Oracle Designer, you must be committed to investing in yourself and learning the entire tool. This typically requires training from an Oracle Designer training provider like TUSC or Oracle Education.

Oracle Designer Web Server Generator creates fully functional Web applications that enable users to query, update, enter, and delete information in an Oracle database over the World Wide Web. These generated applications are based on module and database design specifications recorded in the Oracle Designer Repository.

The main input to the generation process is a module design specification created by using the Oracle Designer Design Editor. This records the tables and columns used by the module, the links between them, and detailed information on how the module uses data.

Other inputs to the generation process include module links and preferences. Module links define the navigation between modules (in a multiple-module application) and are created by using the Design Editor. Preferences determine the general appearance and behavior of the generated application; the preferences can be customized to suit your particular requirements. In Figure 16-1, we see the component of a Web Server Generator module from design to implementation.

During generation, Web Server Generator creates a set of PL/SQL packages, which are then compiled into the database to enable the application to be executed via OAS. Any HTML browser can be used to execute generated applications.

For data manipulation, generated OAS applications make use of PL/SQL API packages providing insert, update, delete, and lock procedures for each application table. These packages may be generated and installed once the table design is complete and prior to generating the Web application.

The Web Server Generator makes complete use of the Web Developers PL/SQL Toolkit. The Web Server Generator offers several advantages over using the Web Developers Toolkit by itself. The primary advantage is that the Web Server Generator generates significant amounts of code for you. This minimizes the amount of manual coding required for each module. Web Server Generator generates all GUI elements, such as tables, buttons, checkboxes, and pop-up lists. Other advantages include centralized code, a database object repository, and common application appearance and behavior. On the other hand, the Web Developers PL/SQL Toolkit offers the advantage of complete control over the appearance and behavior of your application. When you manually develop all of your code using the PL/SQL Toolkit, the developer has more flexibility in methods used for data retrieval and manipulation. The PL/SQL Toolkit's advantages are

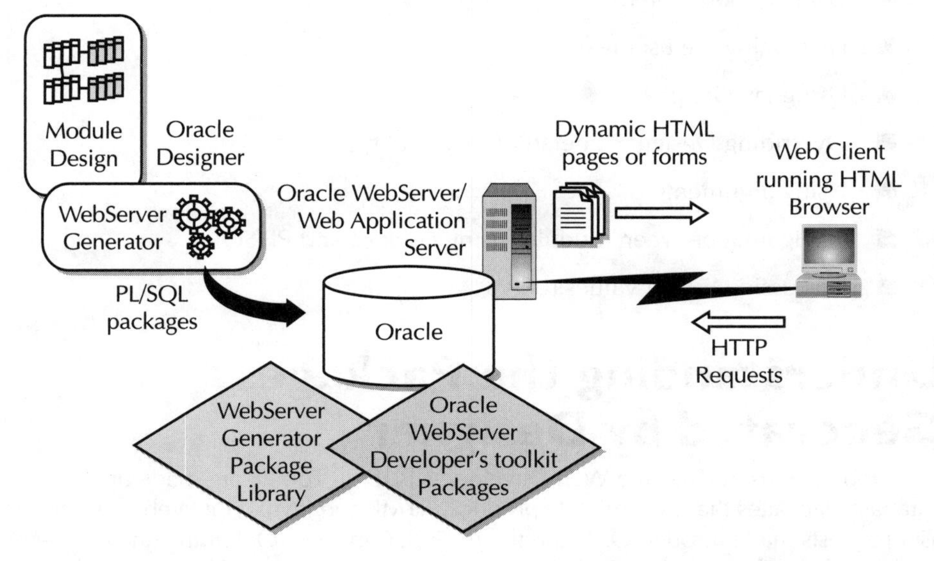

FIGURE 16-1. *Designer WebServer Generator Module design and implementation process.*

sacrificed to some degree with the Web Server Generator. In other words, you lose some flexibility when generating applications with a tool. Editing the generated code is not a good option either. The generated code is complex and difficult to manipulate. The other disadvantage of the Web Server Generator is the learning curve, as mentioned above. Reading this chapter before you understand Designer may provide you with good background material, but some parts may also be confusing to you. Reading this chapter after you have experienced Designer will give an even better understanding.

The following topics are covered in this chapter:

- Understanding the packages generated by Designer
- Incorporating views into generated modules
- Building an effective database security scheme when using generated modules
- Using events and named routines
- Leveraging key Web Server Generator preferences and attributes
- Using frames and style sheets

- Using unbound items
- Leveraging the user text area
- Using JavaScript
- Overriding Designer's default functionality
- Using arguments
- Navigating between modules using cookies and PL/SQL
- Discussing lists of values (LOVs)

Understanding the Packages Generated by Designer

OAS applications that use the Web Developers PL/SQL Toolkit are made up of database packages that dynamically produce HTML and JavaScript Web pages from user requests made through OAS and the PL/SQL Cartridge. Obtaining knowledge of the procedures, functions, record structures, and parameters used in these packages enables the developer to enhance applications through the various means described later in this chapter. This knowledge is also necessary before attempting any of the postgeneration changes often needed to develop polished Web applications. The PL/SQL Cartridge is discussed in detail in Chapter 14 as well as in numerous other examples that can be found throughout this book. This section describes the procedures, record structures, and parameters entailed in the Oracle Designer Web Generator's generated package. It is also important to understand how Designer handles named routines, events, and user text areas to embrace the primary means of enhancing applications.

Understanding Module Package Procedures

During module generation, Designer creates a database package using the module name with a dollar sign ($) concatenated to the end. This serves as a starting point for the module. For example, if the module name was myModule, then the package name would be myModule$. In addition, it creates a package for each module component using the module component concatenated to the end of the module name with a dollar sign ($) between them. Extending the preceding example by adding a module component myModuleComponent would produce the package myModule$myModuleComponent. For ease of reference, the former package will be referred to as the module$ package and the latter as the module$moduleComponent package. The key functions and procedures contained in these packages are described in the following tables.

The procedures found in the module$ package are listed in the following table:

Procedure Name	Description
Startup	Entry point for the module
FirstPage	Creates the first page of the module
ShowAbout	Shows the about page for the module

The procedures and functions comprising the module$moduleComponent package can be classified into four groups:

- **Screen form procedures** Build each of the screens that comprise the module
- **Action submit procedures** Called when a particular HTML form is submitted
- **Event functions** Functions that serve as place holders for PL/SQL code to be entered into the module component events
- **Miscellaneous procedures and functions**

The following table outlines the screen form procedures.

Procedure Name	Description
Startup	Entry point for the module component
FormQuery	Builds an HTML form for entering query criteria
FormInsert	Builds an HTML form for inserting data
FormView	Builds an HTML form for viewing/updating a record
QueryList	Builds the record list screen resulting from a query
FormDelete	Builds the form to confirm deleting a record

The following table outlines the action submit procedures.

Procedure Name	Description
ActionQuery	Called when the query form is submitted
ActionView	Called when the view form is submitted
ActionInsert	Called when the insert form is submitted
QueryList	Builds the record list screen resulting from a query

The following table outlines the event functions.

Function Name	Description
PreUpdate	Contains the code entered for the module component PreUpdate event
PostUpdate	Contains the code entered for the module component PostUpdate event
PreInsert	Contains the code entered for the module component PreInsert event
PostInsert	Contains the code entered for the module component PostInsert event
PreDelete	Contains the code entered for the module component PreDelete event
PostDelete	Contains the code entered for the module component PostDelete event
PreQuery	Contains the code entered for the module component PreQuery event
PostQuery	Contains the code entered for the module component PostQuery event

The following table outlines the other important functions.

Procedure Name	Description
ActionDelete	Called when the delete confirmation form is submitted
ActionUpdate	Called from the ActionView procedure when a record update is requested
QueryView	Selects the appropriate record and calls FormView to build the screen to display the record
QueryHits	Returns the number of records matching a specific query; called by QueryList to display the number of records the record list screen displays
BuildSQL	Called by QueryList and QueryHits to build the SELECT statement for a particular query

Procedure Name	Description
Validate	Validates the items of a module component before they are saved to the database; performs case conversion, number conversion, validation against domains, and so forth
CreateQueryJavaScript	Creates JavaScript necessary for the Query form
CreateListJavaScript	Creates JavaScript necessary for the Record List form
CreateViewJavaScript	Creates JavaScript necessary for the View form
CreateInsertJavaScript	Creates JavaScript necessary for the Insert form

Understanding How Named Routines Are Handled

Designer's named routines can be defined at the module level, module component level, and item level. They can be either PL/SQL routines or JavaScript routines. The PL/SQL routines can be either public or private, and the JavaScript routines must have a target location defined. How the named routine is defined dictates the location in which the generated package will be handled.

All public PL/SQL named routines are declared in the appropriate package specification. A module-level PL/SQL named routine is declared in the module$ package specification. Public module-component-level and item-level PL/SQL named routines are declared in the appropriate module$moduleComponent package specification. All private PL/SQL named routines are declared within the appropriate package body.

Each PL/SQL named routine is defined in the appropriate package body. A module-level PL/SQL named routine is defined in the module$ package body. Module-component-level and item-level PL/SQL named routines are defined in the appropriate module$moduleComponent package body.

Designer enables JavaScript named routines to be defined at the module level, module component level, and item level. The generator places the defined JavaScript code in the module$moduleComponent package based on the defined target location. The following table lists the specific procedures for each target location:

Target Location	Specific Procedure
Insert/view	CreateViewJavaScript and CreateInsertJavaScript
Record list	CreateListJavaScript
Query form	CreateQueryJavaScript

Understanding How Events Are Handled

Designer's events can be defined at the module level, module component level, and item level. At the module level and module component level, Designer will only enable PL/SQL code to be used. At the item level, all events must be defined as one of the provided JavaScript events. Table 16-1 lists the location Designer will place the event code for each type of event.

Understanding How User Text Is Handled

Table 16-2 indicates which module$moduleComponent procedure handles the text entered into the user text areas. The text is simply wrapped in an htp.print at the top or bottom of the appropriate screen form procedure. Refer to Table 16-2 for a listing of procedures handling each of the user text locations.

Understanding Procedure Parameters

Each of the screens that make up a generated module is produced as an HTML form. When the user requests a form, the values of all the HTML input items are passed to the action submit procedure. The action submit procedures, ActionInsert, ActionView, ActionQuery, and QueryList, have parameters to receive these values. The P_, O_, U_, and Z_ parameters are the four types of parameters passed to the procedures.

The P_ parameters contain the current values of the HTML input items on the screen.

Event Type	**Specific Procedure**
Module-level event - Private Declarations	module$ package body
Module-level event - Public Declarations	module$ package specification
Module component - PreUpdate	module$moduleComponent.PreUpdate
Module component - PostUpdate	module$moduleComponent.PostUpdate
Module component - PreInsert	module$moduleComponent.PreInsert
Module component - PostInsert	module$moduleComponent.PostInsert
Module component - PreDelete	module$moduleComponent.PreDelete
Module component - PostDelete	module$moduleComponent.PostDelete
Module component - PreQuery	module$moduleComponent.PreQuery
Module component - PostQuery	module$moduleComponent.PostQuery

TABLE 16-1. *Event Code Procedures*

User Text Area	Procedure Handling User Text
Top of record list	QueryList
Bottom of record list	QueryList
Top of Query form	FormQuery
Bottom of Query form	FormQuery
Top of View form	FormView
Bottom of View form	FormView
Top of Insert form	FormInsert
Bottom of Insert form	FormInsert
Top of Delete form	FormDelete
Bottom of Delete form	FormDelete

TABLE 16-2. *Procedures Handling User Text*

The O_ parameters are used on updates to hold the previous values of the HTML input items. The previous values are needed to verify that no other user has updated the record because it was queried into the HTML form.

The U_ parameters are used in procedures performing queries with date items. The upper bounds of the date range query are contained in these parameters.

The Z_ parameters pass mode information to procedures, such as which action was requested by the user.

The developer can add parameters to the module$moduleComponent.startup procedure by creating module arguments and defining the argument item usage. This enables the passing of arguments to the startup procedure as part of the URL.

Understanding the Package-Defined Record Types

The module$moduleComponent package declares several record types, including FORM_REC, CURR_REC, PREV_REC, and NBT_REC. For each of these types, a variable is declared global to the package with the corresponding names of FORM_VAL, CURR_VAL, PREV_VAL, and NBT_VAL. These record variables are global to the package; therefore, they can be referenced by named routines and in user text.

The FORM_VAL record variable holds all the items passed from the HTML form to the action submit procedures. Its structure maps to the bound items in the module. The CURR_VAL record is used to pass values to the appropriate Table API. This record maps to the actual structure of the module component base table. The FORM_VAL values are moved into the CURR_VAL record by the Validate procedure, performing all the necessary validation and conversion. The PREV_VAL record variable is used for updates. Identical to the CURR_VAL record variable, its structure maps to the structure of the module component base table. This record holds the previous values of an update and verifies that another user has not made changes to the record between the time the record was selected and an update issued. The NBT_REC maps to nonbase table values passed to the action submit, including unbound items and items displayed from a lookup table usage type.

Incorporating Views into Generated Modules

Using views as base tables in generated modules is a logical method in providing needed functionality. However, using views with generated modules is not as straightforward as one might think because of dependencies that the generated modules have with using the Designer-generated Table API. All base tables must contain the Table API package for proper execution. Therein lies the problem. Designer does not generate Table APIs for views—at least, not from a simple click of a toolbar button or pull-down menu selection.

To "fool" Designer to generate the desired view API is to first create a temporary table in the Designer Repository with the same name and structure of the view. Next, generate the temporary table into the target database, making sure the name and structure exactly match the view ultimately desired. Once the table is created, generate the Table API, drop the table from the target database, rename the table in the Designer Repository (for future modifications, if necessary), create the view in the Designer Repository, and, finally, generate the view to the target database. Magically, you fooled Designer!

TIP

By creating a Table API on a table with the same name and structure as our desired view, you are effectively creating the view API. This does increase maintenance effort and may cause some confusion; however, it may be smart to avoid using views as base tables.

Building an Effective Database Security Scheme when Using Generated Modules

Database security is always a primary concern when developing any application. For Oracle applications, security is typically handled by assigning a user to specific roles, which have been granted certain privileges on a set of database objects. By providing direct privileges on database objects, a database administrator may unintentionally provide access to data the user should not have. While possibly not the best design, often security rules are embedded in the application logic, perhaps due to their complexity. A user connecting to the database with one of many data-browsing tools available could circumvent these rules. The best method to ensure that application users cannot gain undesired access to database objects is to not grant privileges to them.

With OAS applications, ensuring that users cannot gain undesired access to database objects can be achieved easily. The key is to understand two facts. First, OAS PL/SQL Cartridge applications execute database packages accessing database objects through DML for SELECT operations and through the Table API packages for all other operations. Second, a user can access a database object by executing a stored procedure owned by a user that has direct privileges on the database object. Using these facts, a recommended security scheme is presented in Table 16-3 giving application users access to database objects through the use of the OAS applications, without providing any privileges to database objects themselves.

By limiting access to the data owner and application owner accounts to database administrators, the capability of application users to gain direct access to database objects is eliminated.

Database User	**Database Objects Owned**	**Privileges Granted**
Data owner	All tables, views, sequences, and indexes	Resource
Application owner	OAS application packages and Table API packages	All privileges on the database objects owned by data owner
Application user	None	Execute on specific application owner packages

TABLE 16-3. *OAS Application Security Scheme*

Using Events and Named Routines

Events and named routines in Web Server Generator modules serve the same purpose as triggers and program units serve in Oracle Forms modules. Events and named routines are defined at the module level, module component level, and bound item level (refer to Figure 16-2 for the hierarchical structure). Events are generally used for controlling navigation or performing validation. Named routines have a general purpose; they are used for coding routines that can be used in multiple locations throughout a module.

Using Named Routines

Named routines can be coded in either JavaScript or PL/SQL. JavaScript routines are executed on the client side, and the PL/SQL routines are executed on the server

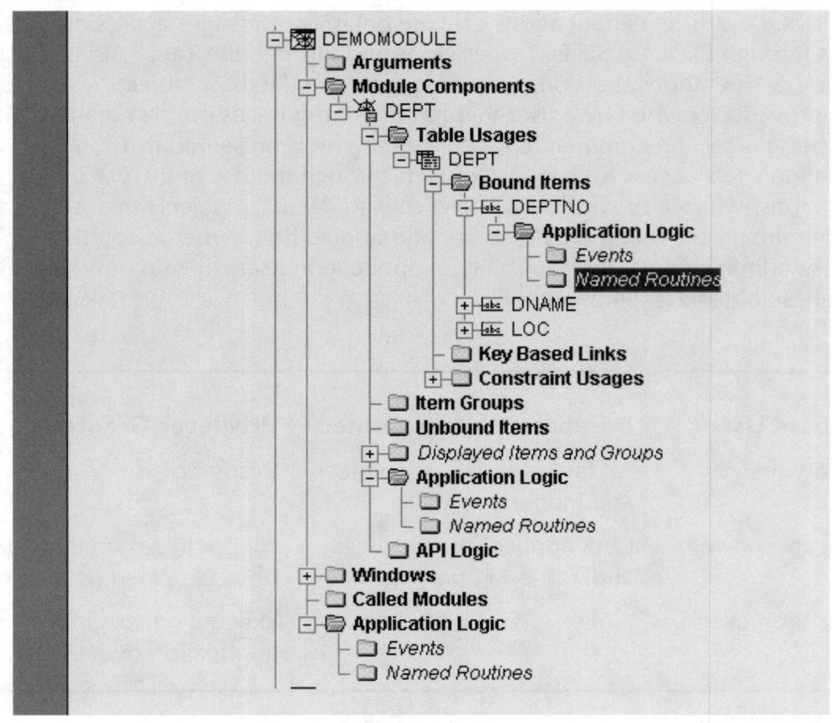

FIGURE 16-2. *Module event hierarchy*

side. As of the release of Designer 2.1.2, the only choice offered for a PL/SQL routine type by the Named Routine Wizard is Procedure. To change the named routine to a function, with the Code Editor, simply change Procedure to Function and add the Return clause.

Using Events

Events follow a different set of rules than do named routines. Table 16-4 details the types of events supported at each level.

Event Scope Level	Event Name	Implementation Language
Module, module component	Public declarations	PL/SQL
Module, module component	Private declarations	PL/SQL
Module component	PreQuery	PL/SQL
Module component	PostQuery	PL/SQL
Module component	PreInsert	PL/SQL
Module component	PostInsert	PL/SQL
Module component	PreUpdate	PL/SQL
Module component	PostUpdate	PL/SQL
Module component	PreDelete	PL/SQL
Module component	PostDelete	PL/SQL
Module component	ServerValidate	PL/SQL
Module component	Validate	PL/SQL
Bound item	OnBlur	JavaScript
Bound item	OnChange	JavaScript
Bound item	OnClick	JavaScript
Bound item	OnFocus	JavaScript
Bound item	OnSelect	JavaScript

TABLE 16-4. *Module-Level Event Support*

Leveraging Key Web Server Generator Preferences and Attributes

As with all Designer generators, the Web Server Generator contains a multitude of generator preferences enabling a developer to influence the appearance and behavior of a generated application. Preferences can be set at the application level or the individual module level.

In Table 16-5, the OAS preferences are grouped into categories.

Category	Description
DBA	To reference database objects
Document Attributes	To add color and background images to OAS applications
Document Templates	Define style templates for generated HTML documents
Frames	Options affecting the appearance and behavior of pages containing HTML frames
Frames - Custom	Define custom frameset templates
Frames - Default	Define the relative sizes of frames in the default frameset
General Layout	Options governing various aspects of the user interface
Headers and Footers	Define page headers and footers
Insert Form	Options determining the appearance of the Insert form
Links	Options determining the appearance of hyperlinks
List of Values	Options determining the appearance of lookup LOVs
Query Form	Options determining the appearance of the Query form
Record List	Options determining the content and appearance of the record list
Security	To add security features
Startup Page	Options determining the content and appearance of the startup page
Text Handling	Options determining how to process user text
View Form	Options determining the appearance of the View form

TABLE 16-5. *Web Server Generator Module Preference*

Each preceding category contains a set of preferences. The following subsections will only focus on a few key preferences in some of the preceding categories. The key preferences address the use of custom HTML in modules, registering PL/SQL packages external to the module, integrating frames into a module, and setting up security features.

Using HTML Tags in Module Components

When it is necessary to add custom HTML tags to a Designer-generated module, two obvious methods exist. The first is to alter the PL/SQL packages generated by Designer; this is considered to be a postgeneration change and may cause version control headaches. Additionally, the code is difficult to maintain, because it is generated code, not handwritten code. The second, and the preferred method, is to add the HTML directly to the module component through the user text areas. The user text areas are the artist's palettes for generated module design, and will be covered in a later section. If the module's preferences are not set correctly, the HTML tags will be manifested as plaintext on the Web page. Specifically, the MODSUB or substitute HTML reserved characters preference in the Text Handling category must be set to No at the module level, as shown here.

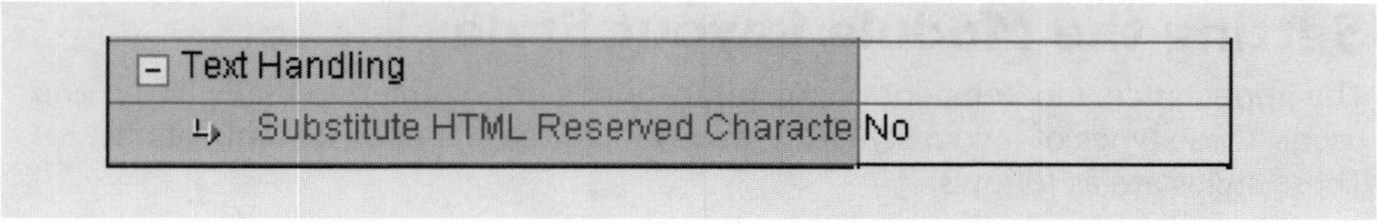

Text Handling	
Substitute HTML Reserved Characte	No

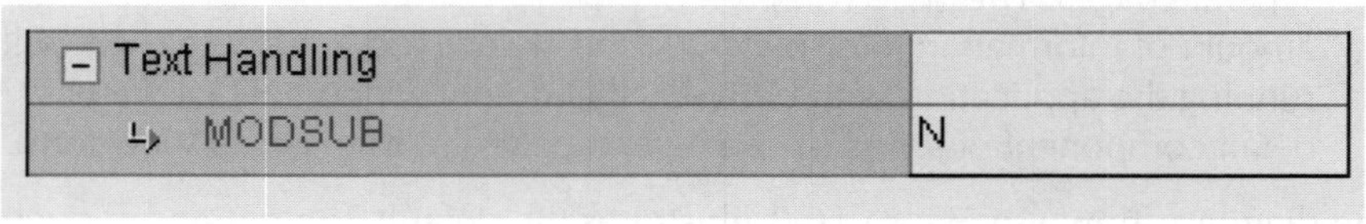

Text Handling	
MODSUB	N

Registering and Using External PL/SQL Packages in User Text

PL/SQL packages are an effective method to implement libraries of reusable code over a large application. A single code change propagates itself over the entire application. If you plan on using PL/SQL packages in your user text area, they must be registered with the module through the PKGLST or PL/SQL package list preference in the Text Handling category, as shown here.

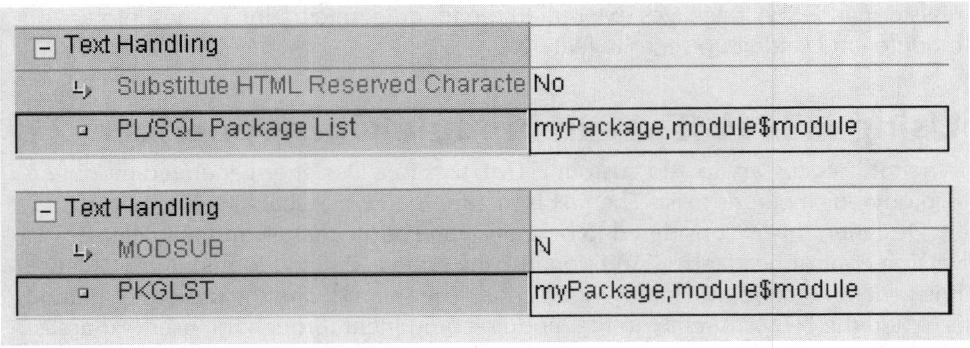

Text Handling	
Substitute HTML Reserved Characte	No
PL/SQL Package List	myPackage,module$module

Text Handling	
MODSUB	N
PKGLST	myPackage,module$module

The package with the name module$module, refers to the package that actually defines a module component. If you want to reference a PL/SQL named routine, defined in the module component, the module component's package must be added to the PL/SQL package list.

Setting the Module Layout Style

The appearance and behavior of an application is important, especially to the end users. Three types of layout styles are available for Designer OAS applications. These styles are as follows:

- **List** The Query form, record list, View form, and Insert form appear on separate pages. This style will present module components having a large amount of information to display. Use this style if you anticipate users will be running the application with browsers that do not support HTML frames. A detail component of style List can be embedded in its master's View form.

The diagram shown in Figure 16-3 illustrates the default content and sequence of pages generated from a module component where the layout style is set to List.

Each HTML document appears on a separate page. When you select a record from the record list, the details are displayed within a View form on a new page.

- **List/Form** The Query form, record list, View form, and Insert form appear within HTML frames on the same page. Choose this style if the browsers used to run the application support HTML frames and the content of each frame can be displayed effectively within a smaller area.

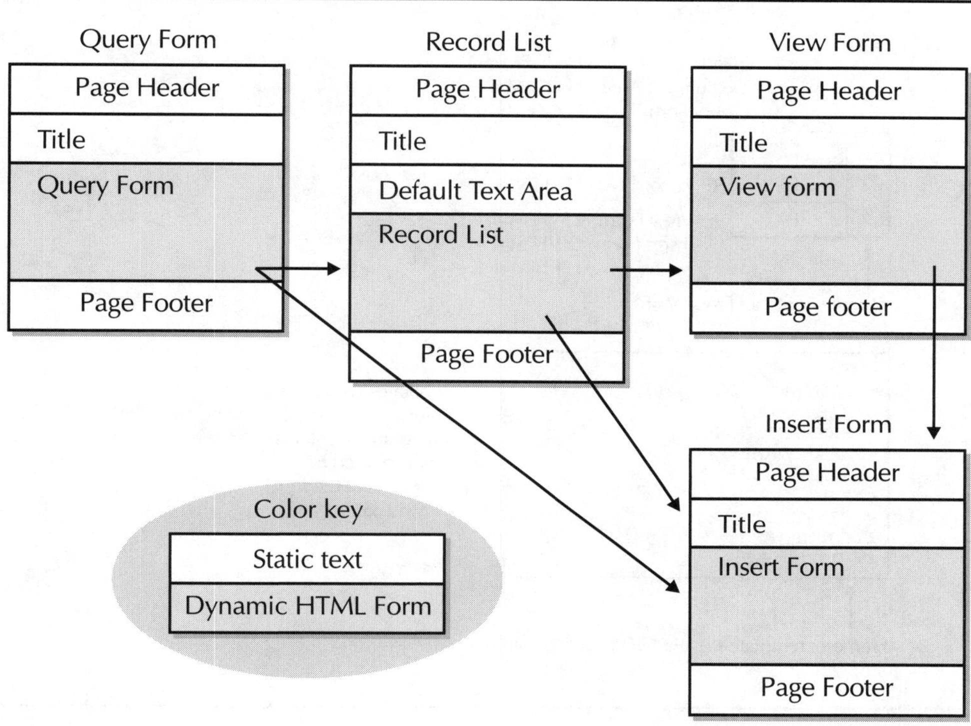

FIGURE 16-3. *List layout*

- **Form** No record list is created. A View form is displayed with a set of navigation buttons for navigating through record details one at a time. Choose this style to present read-only information. For example, the entire module component must be query only.

Using Frames and Style Sheets

A Web Server Generator module consists of several Web pages, including a page for inserting records, a page for updating, and a record list page. By default, these pages appear singularly. What if you wanted to show the record list at the top of the page and the update screen on the bottom, using two frames? How would you do it? All you need is a frame template (see Figure 16-4) and the correct generator preferences.

Designer provides a number of preferences to enable the implementation of frames in a module, represented in Table 16-6.

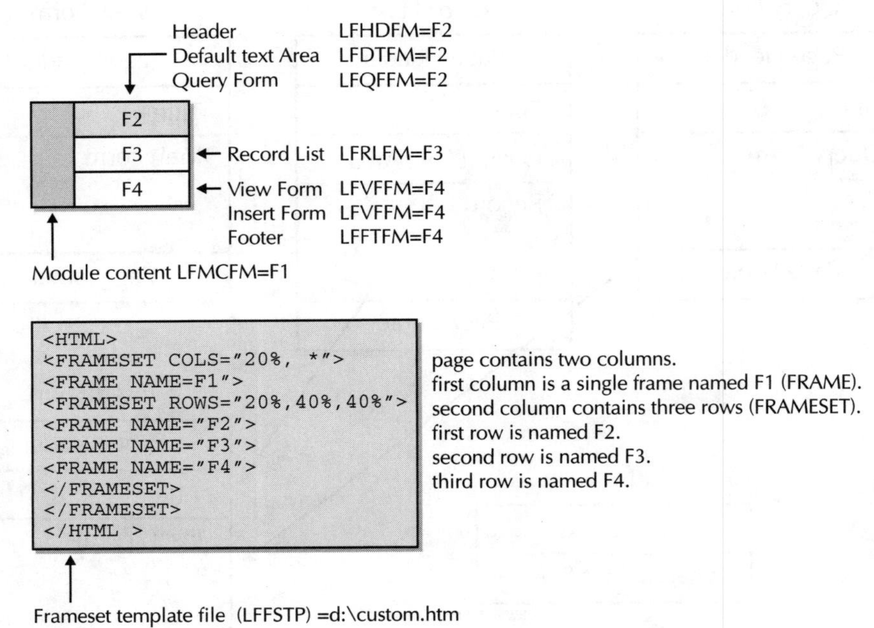

FIGURE 16-4. *Custom frame layout diagram*

Using Style Sheets

Style sheets contain HTML formatting information. They can be coded directly into the source of the Web page using the <STYLE> tag or they can be called externally with the <LINK> tag. More than one style sheet can be used in a single Web page. Including a style sheet in a Web Server Generator application is simple. We can include them through the use of templates or a global generator preference, or simply code them in the user text areas. The following is a simple example of a style sheet.

```
H1     {font-size:   20px;
        color:       red;}
BODY   {color:       blue;
        background:  white;
        font-size:   12px;}
```

```
TABLE  {border:      4;}
H2,B,TH,TR,TD,SELECT:OPTION,INPUT:type  {font-size:12px}
BIG,UL,LI{font-size:15px}
```

The preceding code can exist within an external file, a PL/SQL procedure, or a <STYLE> tag. The following sections detail the different methods of deployment.

Preference Set	Preference and Usage
Frames	<u>**Use Custom Frameset (LFCUST)**</u> Use this preference to define whether you want to use a custom frameset for pages containing HTML frames. **Default:** No **Values:** Yes, No **Levels:** Application, table, module, and module component **Value Definitions:** **Yes** The custom frameset template is used (defined using the template filename (LFFSTP)). **No** The default frameset is used.
Frames	<u>**Place Query Form on Separate Page (LFQOSP)**</u> Use this preference to define whether the Query form appears on the same page as the record list and View form (in a frame). This preference is only relevant if the layout style of the module component is List/Form. **Default:** Yes **Values:** Yes, No **Levels:** Application, table, module, and module component **Value Definitions:** **Yes** A separate page is created for the Query form. **No** The Query form, record list, and View form appear within frames on the same page. The contents of the View form will not change if the record list is requeried, because HTML frame functionality enables multiple frames to be populated only at the point when the page is originally created.

TABLE 16-6. *Designer WebServer Generator Preferences for Using Frames*

Preference Set	Preference and Usage
Frames	**Auto Query View Form (LFVFAQ)** Use this preference to choose whether the View form frame displays the details of the first record when the page is initially opened (or created). This preference is only relevant if the layout style of the module component is List/Form. This preference only determines the behavior of pages when they are first opened (or created). If the page contains a Query form (Place Query Form on separate page in Frames (LFQOSP) is set to No) and the record list is requeried, the contents of the View form will not change. **Default:** Yes **Values:** Yes, No **Levels:** Application, table, module, module component **Value Definitions:** **Yes** When the page is first opened, the View form frame displays the details of the first entry in the record list. **No** The first record is not automatically queried. The View form frame is empty when the page is first opened.
Frames	**Align Center Text Frame (ZONTAC)** Use this preference to determine whether the content of a frame containing just text is aligned to the center of the frame. **Default:** No **Values:** Yes, No **Levels:** Application, table, module, and module component
Frames - Custom	**Template Filename (LFFSTP)** Use this preference to specify the name and file extension of the ASCII file where the custom frameset is defined. The full pathname must also be specified. The template file is only read during generation; it is not required when the application is executed. Refer to Figure 16-4. **Default:** None **Values:** Up to 100 characters **Levels:** Application, table, module, and module component

TABLE 16-6. *Designer WebServer Generator Preferences for Using Frames* (continued)

Preference Set	Preference and Usage
Frames - Custom	**Module Content Frame (LFMCFM)** Use this preference to identify which frame displays the module content. If a custom frameset is used and this preference is left blank, or does not specify a frame in the frameset definition, the module content is placed in the first (top) frame. Refer to Figure 16-4. **Default:** None **Values:** Up to 20 characters **Levels:** Application and module
Frames - Custom	**Default Text Area Frame (LFDTFM)** Use this preference to identify which frame is used for the default text area. If a custom frameset is used and this preference is left blank, or does not specify a frame in the frameset definition, the record list frame is used as the default text area. Refer to Figure 16-4. **Default:** None **Values:** Up to 20 characters **Levels:** Application, table, module, and module component
Frames - Custom	**Record List Frame (LFRLFM)** Use this preference to identify which frame displays the record list. If a custom frameset is used and this preference is left blank, or does not specify a frame in the frameset definition, the record list is placed in the first (top) frame. Refer to Figure 16-4. **Default:** None **Values:** Up to 20 characters **Levels:** Application, table, module, and module component

TABLE 16-6. *Designer WebServer Generator Preferences for Using Frames* (continued)

Preference Set	Preference and Usage
Frames - Custom	**Query Form Frame (LFQFFM)** Use this preference to identify which frame displays the Query form. This preference only takes effect if the Query form is not being displayed on a separate page (Place Query Form on separate page (LFQOSP) = No). If a custom frameset is used and this preference is left blank, or does not specify a frame in the frameset definition, the Query form is placed in the record list frame. Refer to Figure 16-4. **Default:** None **Values:** Up to 20 characters **Levels:** Application, table, module, and module component
Frames - Custom	**View/Insert Form Frame (LFVFFM)** Use this preference to identify which frame displays the View form, Insert form, and Delete Confirmation form. If a custom frameset is used and this preference is left blank, or does not specify a frame in the frameset definition, these forms are placed in the frame after the record list (if one exists). If the record list appears in the last frame, all three forms will be displayed in the same frame (but not at the same time). Refer to Figure 16-4. **Default:** None **Values:** Up to 20 characters **Levels:** Application, table, module, and module component
Frames - Custom	**List of Values Frame (LFLVFM)** Use this preference to identify which frame displays the list of values. This preference only takes effect if LOVs are being placed in frames rather than windows (LOV style (LOVSTL) = FRAME). If a custom frameset is used and this preference is left blank, or does not specify a frame in the frameset definition, the frame following the View/Insert form frame is used. **Default:** None **Values:** Up to 20 characters **Levels:** Application, table, module, and module component

TABLE 16-6. *Designer WebServer Generator Preferences for Using Frames* (continued)

Preference Set	Preference and Usage
Frames - Custom	**Header Frame (LFHDFM)** Use this preference to identify which frame displays the page header (MODSHD). The frame name you specify must appear in the frameset definition. If a custom frameset is used and if this preference is left blank, or does not specify a frame in the frameset definition, the page header is placed in the first (top) frame. **Default:** None **Values:** Up to 20 characters **Levels:** Application, table, module, and module component
Frames - Custom	**Footer Frame (LFFTFM)** Use this preference to identify which frame displays the page footer (MODSFT). The frame name you specify must appear in the frameset definition. If a custom frameset is used and if this preference is left blank, or does not specify a frame in the frameset definition, the page footer is placed in the last frame. **Default:** None **Values:** Up to 20 characters **Levels:** Application, table, module, and module component
Frames - Default	**Column Widths (LFCOLS)** Use this preference to specify the width (or relative width) of frame 2 and frame 3, shown in Figure 16-5. If the module component contains any enterable foreign key lookup columns and the style of the LOV window is set to FRAME, an additional frame will be created. If this is the case, you should consider the width required for the LOV frame when choosing a width for frames 2 and 3. **Default:** None **Values:** Any valid COLS attribute for the HTML <FRAMESET> tag, up to 20 characters in length (<Width of Frame 2>,<Width of Frame 3>) **Levels:** Application, table, module, module component **Examples:** *,2% 100,* 25%,75%

TABLE 16-6. *Designer WebServer Generator Preferences for Using Frames* (continued)

Preference Set	Preference and Usage
Frames - Default	**Row Heights (LFROWS)** Use this preference to specify the height (or relative height) of frames 1, 2, and 3, shown in Figure 16-5. **Default:** None **Values:** Any valid ROWS attribute for the HTML <FRAMESET> tag, up to 20 characters in length (<Height of Frame 1>,<Height of Frame 2 & 3>) **Levels:** Application, table, module, module component **Examples:** *,2% 100,* 25%,75%
Frames - Default	**Standard Footer Frame Height (MODSFH)** Use this preference to define the height of the footer frame, in pixels. This preference is only used if the standard footer must be placed on a page containing frames. Refer to Figure 16-5. **Default:** 50 **Values:** 1 to 1,000 **Levels:** Application, module

TABLE 16-6. *Designer WebServer Generator Preferences for Using Frames* (continued)

Including a Style Sheet Using the <STYLE> Tag

Including a style sheet using the <STYLE> tag is simple. In the user text area, or in a template, include the following:

```
<STYLE>
H1     {font-size:   20px;
        color:       red;}
BODY   {color:       blue;
        background:  white;
        font-size:   12px;}
TABLE  {border:      4;}
H2,B,TH,TR,TD,SELECT:OPTION,INPUT:type  {font-size:12px}
BIG,UL,LI{font-size:15px}
</STYLE>
```

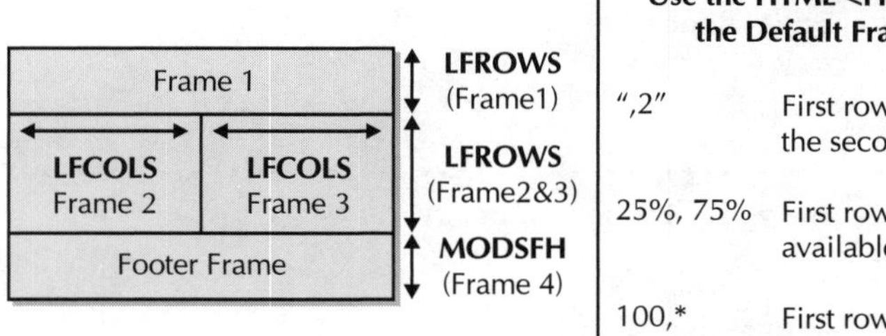

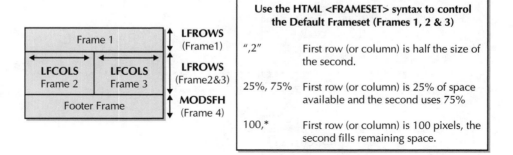

Use the HTML <FRAMESET> syntax to control the Default Frameset (Frames 1, 2 & 3)

",2"	First row (or column) is half the size of the second.
25%, 75%	First row (or column) is 25% of space available and the second uses 75%
100,*	First row (or column) is 100 pixels, the second fills remaining space.

FIGURE 16-5. *Default frame layout diagram*

The new formatting characteristics will be applied to any of the referenced tags, followed by the <STYLE> tag. This method is simple; however, it is not a practical method for application-wide deployment. Therefore, the following method, external style sheets, is preferable.

Referencing External Style Sheets

Using external style sheets is the preferred method for including a style sheet in an OAS application. They can be stored as files with a .css extension or coded in a PL/SQL package procedure. The latter method can also be referred to as a dynamic style sheet library. The package should contain a public procedure called css. The reference to the packaged procedure, package_name.css, will be interpreted by the Web server as an external file reference. Ensure that OAS is configured to recognize .css as mime type text/css. The following code illustrates both constructs:

The following code illustrates a Cascading Style Sheet as it would be coded in a physical file. The file would reside in a directory on some server.

```
H1     {font-size:   20px;
        color:       red;}
BODY   {color:       blue;
        background:  white;
        font-size:   12px;}
TABLE  {border:      4;}
H2,B,TH,TR,TD,SELECT:OPTION,INPUT:type  {font-size:12px}
BIG,UL,LI{font-size:15px}
```

The code below represents a Cascading Style Sheet which is coded into a PL/SQL package and stored in the database.

```
create or replace package styleSheet as
      procedure css(p_library varchar2 := null);
end;
/
/*******************************************************************/
create or replace package body styleSheetLibrary as
     procedure generalModule is
     begin
        htp.print('H1     {font-size:   20px;
                           color:        red;}
                 BODY   {color:        blue;
                         background:   white;
                         font-size:    12px;}
                 TABLE  {border:       4;}
                 H2,B,TH,TR,TD,SELECT:OPTION,INPUT:type {font-
                                                          size:12px}
                 BIG,UL,LI{font-size:15px}');
     end;
/********************************************************************/
     procedure css(p_library varchar2 := null) is
     begin
        generalModule;
     end;
end;
/
```

External style sheets are referenced with the <LINK> tag, which is included within the <HEAD> tag (see Figure 16-6). Two preferred methods can be implemented to include external style sheets in an OAS application. The first

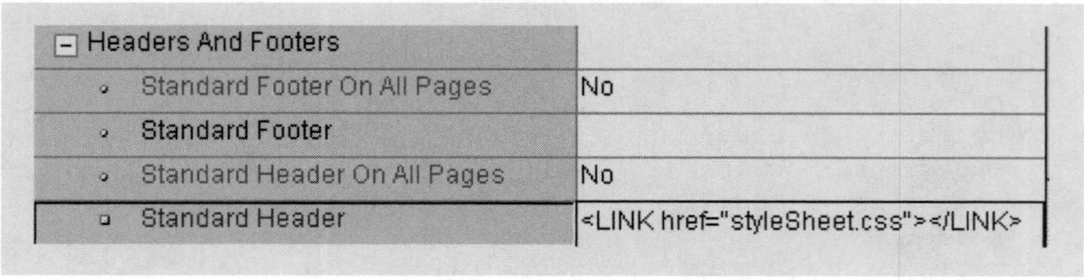

⊟ Headers And Footers	
Standard Footer On All Pages	No
Standard Footer	
Standard Header On All Pages	No
Standard Header	<LINK href="styleSheet.css"></LINK>

FIGURE 16-6. *Generator preference for standard header*

method is through the MODSHD, or standard header generator preference. The second method is to simply include the code in a template.

Using Unbound Items

Unbound items are module component items not directly tied to a column in a table. Unbound items can be used by the developer to manipulate data, as well as control screen layout. This enables the developer to employ creativity in module design by providing additional flexibility that is not available using bound items alone.

The following are four types of unbound items:

- **Client-side function** An unbound item, used to generate an HTML form element that derives its value from a function held on the client browser.
- **Server-side function** An unbound item, used to generate an HTML form element deriving its value from a function held on the server. The derivation calculation can only take place on the server; the changes to derived fields are displayed only after a record is refreshed.
- **SQL expression** An unbound item, used to generate an HTML form element that derives its value from a SQL expression.
- **Custom** A custom unbound item provides you with the capability to create an item totally under your control. Using the events defined on the client side and/or the server side, you can process the value of the item in the appropriate manner.

In addition to using unbound items as a means to perform calculations and display summary information, such as totals, unbound items can also be used in other useful methods. For example, unbound items can be used to insert HTML in a form by calling either client-side JavaScript named routines or server-side PL/SQL named routines. The usage sequence can then be changed to insert the unbound item between bound items on the form. This is useful because while the user text areas can also be used to insert HTML in a Web page, it can only place the HTML at either the top or bottom of the page. Unbound items enable control over the appearance and behavior of generated Web pages.

Leveraging the User Text Area

The user text area is the artist's palette for generated module design. Not only does it enable creativity and flexibility during module design without making postgeneration changes, it also serves as the glue for most of the advanced techniques presented in this chapter. It is essential to obtain a solid understanding of what it is and how it works.

Despite the powerful capabilities of user text areas, they are easy to understand and easy to use. It is simply a method of using Designer to add custom HTML to generated pages. While the custom HTML can take the form of plaintext, it can also be created using named routines and PL/SQL functions as long as they return valid HTML syntax. Similarly, the text can be formatted directly with HTML syntax, as long as the Designer preference MODSUB (substitute HTML reserved characters) is set correctly. By using these methods, any structure that can be rendered using HTML can be added to your application.

User text can be added at both the module level and module component level. Module-level user text can be placed on the first page and/or the about page. Module-component-level user text can be placed on any of the HTML documents generated for a module component, such as a Query form, a record list, a View form, an Insert form, and a Delete form. If a location is not specified, the user text is placed in the default area. The default area is the top of the first page for module-level user text and the top of the record list for module-component-level user text.

In addition, you can specify whether the user text is inserted at the top or the bottom of the particular page. At first glance, this may appear straightforward; however, there are subtle yet important implications in where you place user text. If it is placed at the top of a page, be careful not to reference items that will be defined in the lower half of the HTML document (unless the reference is within a JavaScript function definition). HTML pages are interpreted line by line, top to bottom. Most Designer-generated items (forms, bound items, unbound items, and so forth) will not exist. In most cases, this will not raise concerns. Many of the advanced techniques, such as overriding Designer's default functionality, will not work because they manipulate items on the Web page after it is created but before it is displayed to the user. It is important to keep this in mind when working with cookies and server-side JavaScript libraries.

The following two sections are excerpts from Designer's Help feature on formatting user text with PL/SQL and HTML.

Formatting Text with PL/SQL Functions

Within user text, you may reference any PL/SQL function defined in the HyperText Functions (HTF) package within the Oracle Web Developers PL/SQL Toolkit, the Web Server Generator Library package (WSGL and WSGFL), or any custom packages specified within the PL/SQL package list (PKGLST) preference returning valid HTML.

During generation, user text is scanned for function calls and the appropriate PL/SQL is generated to combine the HTML generated by the Web Toolkit function calls with the rest of the static text. For example:

- **Sample user text:** Welcome to the htf.bold('ACME Corporation') home page. Send comments on this page to htf.MailTo('jbloggs@acme.com','Joe Bloggs').
- **Generated PL/SQL:** htp.print('Welcome to the '||htf.bold ('ACME Corporation')||' home page. Send comments on this page to '||htf.MailTo('jbloggs@acme.com','Joe Bloggs'))
- **Generated output:** Welcome to the **ACME Corporation** home page. Send comments on this page to Joe Bloggs.

Formatting Text with HTML

Normally, HTML reserved characters (**< > " &**) within user text are replaced with escape characters (< > " &). This behavior ensures there are no formatting problems with generated Web pages.

If you have HTML experience, you may prefer to use the HTML syntax to directly format user text. Two methods of deployment exist with the Design Editor:

- Add HTML syntax to user text
- Add entire HTML documents in their native format, through an HTML editor

Adding HTML Syntax to User Text

Add HTML syntax to user text for simple formatting requirements; the assistance of an HTML editor is not required to create or view the formatted text. During generation, the user text is placed between the <BODY></BODY> tags of the appropriate HTML document.

If you use this method, set the substitute HTML reserved characters (MODSUB) preference to No, as the following output illustrates:

```
Welcome to the <b>ACME Corporation</b> home page.
```

Generated output:

```
Welcome to the ACME Corporation home page.
```

You must take care to use escape characters where they are appropriate. For example:

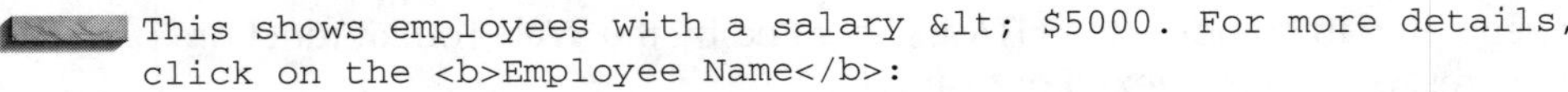

```
This shows employees with a salary &lt; $5000. For more details,
click on the <b>Employee Name</b>:
```

Generated output:

```
This shows employees with a salary < $5000. For more details, click
on the Employee Name:
```

The substitute HTML reserved characters (MODSUB) preference affects all the pages generated from a particular module, not just an individual HTML document.

Adding Entire HTML Documents via an HTML Editor

You can add an entire HTML document by using an HTML editor when more complex formatting is required. Sometimes the assistance of an HTML editor to create or view the formatted text is extremely beneficial.

Your preferred HTML editor can be invoked from the user text property in the Design Editor. Then, you can create, view, and test the required content. Save the entire source of the HTML document back to the Repository as User/Help Text.

When using an external HTML editor, an HTML document is treated as text containing the following strings: "<HTML>", "<BODY>", "</BODY>", and "</HTML>." The Design Editor is not case sensitive for these tags, but does require they be in the correct order.

If modifications are required, the entire HTML document can be loaded back into the HTML editor and the changes made in a native HTML editing environment. The following code is generated if MODSUB=NO:

```
<html>
<head>
  <title></title>
</head>
<body>
Welcome to the <b>ACME Corporation</b> home page.
</body>
</html>
```

During generation, the Web Server Generator will extract the user text between the <BODY> and </BODY> tags and place it into the appropriate HTML document. In the preceding case, the value of MODSUB is ignored and assumed to be No.

The following are several examples of methods used in user text areas.

Example 1: Loading a Server-Side JavaScript Library

```
<SCRIPT SRC="javaScriptLibrary.js">
</SCRIPT>
```

Example 2: Using Server-Side PL/SQL Functions (Oracle Web Developers PL/SQL Toolkit)

```
htf.hr
htf.tableopen
htf.tablerowopen
htf.tabledata(htf.big('Row 1, Column 1'))
htf.tabledata(htf.big('Row 1, Column 2'))
htf.tablerowclose
htf.tableclose
```

Example 3: Using Server-Side PL/SQL Functions (Custom)

```
myPackage.myFunction
```

Example 4: Using HTML Formatted Text

```
<TABLE>
<TR>
<TD>Row 1, Column 1</TD>
<TD>Row 1, Column 2</TD>
</TR>
</TABLE>
```

Example 5: Calling Named Routines

```
<SCRIPT>
   myNamedRoutine();
</SCRIPT>
```

Example 6: Adding JavaScript

```
<SCRIPT>
   function doNothing() {
      return true;
   }
</SCRIPT>
```

Using JavaScript

JavaScript is to Web development as PL/SQL is to Oracle Forms development. See Chapter 12 for plenty of OAS JavaScript examples. As with PL/SQL, JavaScript is used to handle or control events behind the scenes. It should also be noted that JavaScript is not Java, even though the name implies it. Microsoft browsers use their own form of JavaScript called JScript. JavaScript and JScript are not always compatible; having some proprietary quirks. This section discusses methods of avoiding proprietary pitfalls, loading external JavaScript libraries, and creating and loading Oracle dynamic server-side JavaScript libraries. It will also cover several Designer-specific topics, including the Web Server Generator JavaScript object and parameter naming conventions. We are only going to cover some specific points concerning the use of JavaScript in OAS applications. Designer's built-in help covers this subject in greater depth.

Avoiding the Proprietary Pitfall

As previously discussed, two versions of JavaScript exist. JavaScript is the original version, created by Netscape and supported by Netscape browsers. The other widely implemented version is called JScript, created by Microsoft and supported by Internet Explorer browsers. With many of the same features, the subtle differences can become cumbersome. Some of these differences include array index referencing of form elements, the default value of an undefined variable, and proprietary features among commonly named objects. How do we avoid these pitfalls? The easiest method is to choose a particular browser as the standard for deployment. While that is acceptable for an intranet application, what about an application designed for Internet deployment? The application must determine what browser has initiated the call. The following code segment checks the browser type:

```
function checkNavigator(nav){
   var returnVal  = false;
   if (navigator.appName == "Netscape" &&
      av.toUpperCase() == "NS4") {
      returnVal = true;
   }
   else if (navigator.appVersion.indexOf("MSIE") != 1 &&
            nav.toUpperCase() == "IE4"){
      returnVal = true;
   }
   return returnVal;
}
```

The preceding function will return True for NS4 (Netscape) or if IE4 (Internet Explorer). Otherwise, all other browsers will return False. The following code segment illustrates how to apply this function:

```
function setFocus(itemName,form) {
   var undefined;
   if(form==null || form==undefined) {
      form = 0;
   }
   var itemIndex = getItemIndex(itemName,form);
   if (itemIndex != -1) {
      if (checkNavigator("NS4")){
         document.forms[form].elements[itemIndex].focus();
      }
      else {
         document.forms[form].elements(itemIndex).focus();
      }
   }
   return true;
};
```

In the preceding code, if the browser is Netscape Navigator, the elements array is referenced using square brackets; otherwise, we reference it using parentheses. The code assumes the other browser is Internet Explorer. The same method can be applied where other implementation discrepancies occur.

Using External JavaScript Libraries

External JavaScript libraries are loaded into a Web-based application through the SRC attribute of the <SCRIPT> tag. The following code illustrates how this is accomplished:

```
<SCRIPT SRC="javaScriptLibrary.js"></SCRIPT>
```

In a Web Server Generator application, this tag can be placed in the user text area of the module component, or in the standard header generator preference. In most cases, javaScriptLibrary.js would be a file. It can also be a packaged procedure, with the help of the OAS. Once the library is loaded, any of its functions can be used in events, such as onBlur, or in module-specific JavaScript routines. The library's functions are not visible to the user if the page source is displayed.

Creating Oracle Server-Side JavaScript Libraries

Using the Oracle Application Server's PL/SQL Cartridge makes it possible to fool the browser into seeing a packaged PL/SQL procedure as a regular file. If this concept is applied to creating JavaScript libraries, we can control the content of the library at runtime based on parameters such as the user's role, the date, or a number of other factors. It makes the libraries dynamic. The following steps outline the process to complete this task.

Step 1: Configure Your Web Listener

Ensure your Web listener is configured to map files with the extension of .js, to MIME type application/x-javascript. Otherwise, the reference loading the library will appear in your Web page as plaintext. If you are using the Oracle Application Server v4.0, this setting can be added through the OAS Manager utility, under HTTP Listeners. See Chapter 4 for more configuration information.

Step 2: Create the Library

Create a PL/SQL package with any name and include only one public procedure called js. The procedure js is to an Oracle package what the file extension .js is to a browser. Optional parameters may be added to the procedure. The actual library routines should be coded in private procedures accessed through the js procedure, as illustrated in the following example:

```
create or replace package javaScriptLibrary as
   procedure js;
end;
/
create or replace package body javaScriptLibrary as
   procedure generalModules is
   begin
      htp.p('function  .........'); /* Some set of functions . */
      htp.p('function  .........');
      …
   end;

   procedure js is
   begin
      generalModules;
   end;
/
```

Step 3: Add the JavaScript Library in Your Module

In the user text area of the module component, include the following line of code:

```
<SCRIPT SRC="javaScriptLibrary.js"></SCRIPT>
```

Understanding Web Server Generator Naming Conventions

The Web Server Generator uses specific naming conventions when creating JavaScript functions that handle item-level events or perform application-level validation.

Naming Convention for Event Handlers

Events in a Web application are comparable to triggers in a Forms application. A displayed item or document form element on a Web page can have the following events: onBlur, onChange, onClick, onFocus, and onSelect—which are the only item-level events supported by the Web Server Generator.

Designer uses a simple naming convention for JavaScript functions that are assigned to handle events. The convention is P_<item name>_<event name>(this). For example:

```
P_MY_ITEM_onBlur(this)
```

Understanding the ctl Parameter

As we start digging through code that the Web Server Generator generates, we frequently encounter references such as ctl.name, or just ctl, in the parameter list. The ctl (control) parameter is the standard parameter for all JavaScript generated by Designer. In a Form element, ctl.name refers to document.forms[0].element(<index>).

Overriding Designer's Default Functionality

Designer provides basic capabilities by enabling custom code to be added through named routines and events at the module, module component, and item levels. Sometimes it is necessary to add functionality that cannot be implemented using these methods. For example, Designer does not provide a method to add code behind the buttons that are automatically generated for inserting, updating, and deleting. The following section provides the procedures to override Designer's default functionality.

Even though Designer does not provide a means to add custom code to every aspect of a generated form, experienced programmers can manipulate them. The following technique is powerful and can be expanded to provide additional capabilities.

To override Designer's default functionality/actions with your own, use the user text area to manipulate a Web page, after it is built and before it is displayed. This can only be performed at the bottom of the appropriate user text area, because the form will not have been built yet at the top of the form. However, after the form is built, using the standard HTML and JavaScript, the page can be manipulated before it is displayed. This is accomplished by simply traversing the document and form elements and making the desired modifications.

To better understand how this is accomplished, consider the following procedure, which overrides the routine behind the Submit button with custom code.

Step 1: Create a JavaScript Routine

```
function customRoutine() {
   <custom code>
   document.forms[0].submit();
   return true;
}
```

Step 2: Create a JavaScript Routine to Override Designer's Routine

This function defined below searches all elements on the form until it finds the Submit button. Then, it sets the onClick method to call your function instead of the function originally assigned to the Submit button by the WebServer Generator.

```
function setFormValidation {
  for (var i=0; i < document.forms[0].elements.length; i++) {
     if (checkNavigator("NS4")) {
        e = document.forms[0].elements[i];
     } else {
       e = document.forms[0].elements(i);
     }
     if (e.type == "button" && e.value == "Submit") {
        e.onclick = new Function("customRoutine();");
         break;
     }
  }
  return true;
}
```

Step 3: Call the setFormValidation function at the bottom of the module form that will use your validation routine (e.g., bottom of View form)

```
<SCRIPT>
   setFormValidation();
</SCRIPT>
```

Step 4: Generate the module

When you access the View form Web page, the JavaScript library will load, the page will load, and then your validation function will override Designer's default routine for the Submit button with the routine you created.

Using Arguments

Arguments can be used to pass parameters between modules. These arguments can then be bound to items on a form to automatically populate when the form is loaded. One useful technique is to create a master-detail relationship between modules without using Designer's key-based links. This offers the programmer a greater degree of control over both the appearance and behavior and the navigation between modules than that afforded by Designer's key-based links. In addition, it enables a module to be used as a detail module by more than one master module simply by passing the arguments that are specific to the relationship between the master and the detail.

To use arguments in the creation of a master-detail relationship between modules, the underlying base tables must contain the appropriate foreign key relationships. Then, it is simply a matter of adding arguments to the detail module and binding them to the foreign key items on the form. When the master module calls the detail module, it passes the appropriate parameter as an argument creating the relationship. Any arguments not used will default to NULL, effectively enabling a detail module to be used by more than one master module.

To better understand how this works. Suppose you want to capture address information for people and businesses. Your database is normalized, so the address table contains foreign keys to the person and business tables. You create three modules: one to capture person information, one to capture business information, and one to capture address information. Two master-detail relationships with the address module will serve as the detail module for both the person and business modules. To accomplish this task, simply create two arguments in the address module and bind them to the foreign keys of the person and business tables as argument item usages. When the person and business modules call the address module, they will simply pass a parameter as an argument to the address module. When the address information is saved, the parameter is saved along with the address information creating the appropriate relationship.

Assuming that "per" and "bus" are the names of the arguments in the address module, the following syntax calls to the address module (where xx is the value of the parameter) would be (from the person module):

```
addressModule$addressModuleComponent.queryview?p_per=xx
```

and (from the business module):

```
addressModule$addressModuleComponent.queryview?p_bus=xx
```

Navigating Between Modules Using Cookies and PL/SQL

The Web Server Generator, by default, contains hyperlinks for navigating based on the specified key-based links and called modules. In most cases, these default hyperlinks will provide sufficient navigation; however, more flexible dynamic hyperlinks are possible using HTML, PL/SQL, and cookies. These techniques enable total control over navigation and some control over the hyperlink screen location.

Creating Custom Hyperlinks with PL/SQL and HTML

Using PL/SQL and HTML is the most straightforward method of creating hyperlinks in a Web Server Generator application. In the user text area of a module component, use the htf.anchor to generate a link to another module or static Web page. We can also create a PL/SQL function, which must be contained in a package, creating hyperlinks based on application specifications. These links may differ from standard links generated by Designer. Finally, we can create hyperlinks by using standard HTML tags in the user text area. A PL/SQL function may also be placed between tags. The function will be interpreted at runtime, prior to the page loading.

Creating Dynamic Hyperlinks Between Modules Using Cookies

Navigating between two modules in an HTML-based environment is not a problem. Each module contains a link to the other. Consider the situation of a single module accessed by more than one module. In such a situation, how would we create a link back to the calling module? We cannot create static hyperlinks, because we do not know which module performs the call. Some people might say, "Just hit the Back button." The Back button solution is sufficient if no data dependency exists between the modules. The Back button does not perform a refresh; it merely loads the last document cached in the browser's history buffer. Sometimes we need to identify the calling page and how to return to it. How do we maintain the calling module's information (URL and parameters) between pages of a Web-based application? Traditional applications, such as Oracle Forms, used global variables or other forms of intermodule communication. Since Web-based modules are static, they do not have access to common data or structures. How can we maintain key data between HTML-based modules? Simple—the answer is by using cookies.

Defining Cookies

Cookies are a means of maintaining persistent data on a client's browser. The browser maintains a file called cookies.txt containing this data. Cookies are composed of three parts: name, value, and expiration date. A Web page's document object contains a cookie property. We use this property to read from and write to a cookie.

Creating a Cookie

The code below is an example of a JavaScript function that sets the value of a cookie. The cookieName parameter will become the name of the cookie. The parameter data is the data stored in the cookie. We did not specify an expiration date; therefore, this cookie will be deleted (expire) when the browser closes:

```
<SCRIPT>
   function setCookie(cookieName,data){
      document.cookie = cookieName + "=" + data;
   }
</SCRIPT>
```

Reading a Cookie

The following is a sample JavaScript function that reads a cookie. It scans through the browser's cookie file looking for the cookie matching the parameter cookieName. Cookies in the cookie file are separated by a semicolon (;).

```
function getCookieData(cookieName) {
   var nameLen      = cookieName.length;
   var cookieLen    = document.cookie.length;
   var start_pos    = 0;
   var end_pos      = 0;
   var cookieEnd;
   var cookieData;

   while (start_pos < cookieLen) {
      end_pos = start_pos + nameLen;
      if (document.cookie.substring(start_pos, end_pos)
          == cookieName) {
         cookieEnd = document.cookie.indexOf(";", end_pos);
         if (cookieEnd == -1) {
            cookieEnd = cookieLen;
         }
         cookieData = document.cookie.substring(end_pos + 1,
                      cookieEnd));
```

```
            return unescape(cookieData);
        }
        start_pos++;
    }
    return "";
}
```

Using Cookies to Create Links

In the bottom of View form, bottom of Insert form, and bottom of record list user text sections of the calling module, moduleOne, create a cookie with a name like moduleThreeCaller. Then, moduleOne calls moduleThree. The data section of this cookie will contain the URL for moduleOne. Repeat the same procedure for moduleTwo, which also calls moduleThree. In the user text sections of moduleThree, read the cookie named moduleThreeCaller. Use the URL from moduleThreeCaller to create a hyperlink back to the calling module, which was either moduleOne or moduleTwo. A cookie like moduleThreeCaller could be created for every module, which is called by more than one module. For example:

The following code in moduleOne sets a cookie named 'moduleThreeCaller' which provides moduleThree with return link information to moduleOne:

```
<SCRIPT>
   setCookie("moduleThreeCaller",
             "moduleOne$moduleOne.queryview?p_id=5");
</SCRIPT>
```

The following code in moduleTwo sets a cookie named 'moduleThreeCaller' which provides moduleThree with return link information to moduleTwo:

```
<SCRIPT>
   setCookie("moduleThreeCaller",
             "moduleTwo$moduleTwo.queryview?p_id=8");
</SCRIPT>
```

The following code in moduleThree reads the cookie named 'moduleThreeCaller' and creates a return link to the calling module:

```
<SCRIPT>
   var href = getCookie("moduleThreeCaller");
   //Creates a hyperlink back to calling module based on URL
   //from Cookie
   document.write("<A HREF="+href+">Return to Calling
                  Module</A>");
/SCRIPT>
```

Limitations of Multiple Cookies

The method previously described works when applied to an application that requires only a few cookies, but falls short if your applications require the use of more than 20 cookies. Currently, a browser will not accept more than 20 cookies from a single Web server. After 20 cookies, the browser simply overwrites existing entries in the cookie file. This could cause serious side effects, such as erratic or unpredictable navigation.

Overcoming the 20-Cookie Limit with Logical Cookies

A logical cookie (sometimes called a chip) is a single cookie masquerading as multiple cookies. This method enables the storing of multiple labels referencing multiple URLs in a single cookie of up to 4KB. A logical cookie consists of several constructs, such as data storage, data structure, and data manipulation constructs. The data storage construct is the cookie itself. This cookie is used throughout the entire application. The data structure is a multidimensional JavaScript array. The array is constructed each time a module is instantiated. The data from the cookie populates the array. The structure of the array elements are label, link text, url, and url target. The data manipulation constructs consist of functions initializing the array, loading existing data from the cookie to the array, populating the array with new data, removing array elements, and generating hyperlinks based on the data in the array elements. The following code represents an implementation of this model:

```
//**************************************************************
//* This is the array which will store the navigational data
//* passed by the cookie.
//**************************************************************
var cookieArray = new Array();
//**************************************************************
//* This is the structure that makes up the array's cells.
//*************************************************************
function cookieData(moduleName,linkTitle,url,winTarget){
   this.moduleName = moduleName;
   this.linkTitle  = linkTitle;
   this.url        = url;
   this.winTarget  = winTarget;
}

//**********************************************************
//* This function reads the data string from the cookie.
//**********************************************************
```

```
function getNavCookieData(label){
   var labelLen = label.length;
   var cLen     = document.cookie.length;
   var i        = 0;

   while (i < cLen) {
      var j = i + labelLen;
      if (document.cookie.substring(i,j) == label) {
         cEnd = document.cookie.indexOf(";",j);
         if (cEnd == -1) {
            cEnd = document.cookie.length;
         }
         return unescape(document.cookie.substring(j+1, cEnd));
      }
      i++;
   }
   return "";
}

//*******************************************************
//* This function populates the cookie array with data
//* from the data string read from the cookie.
//* Note the use of the cookieData structure
//* in simulating a multidimentional array.
//*******************************************************
function populateCookieArray(){
   var dataString  = new String(getNavCookieData("NAVCOOKIE"));
   var dataSets    = dataString.split("<c>");
   var loadLength  = dataSets.length;

   for (var iteration = 0; iteration < loadLength; iteration ++){
      var cookieDataSet = dataSets[iteration].split("<,>");
      if (cookieDataSet[0].length != 0) {
         cookieArray[iteration] = new cookieData(
            cookieDataSet[0], cookieDataSet[1],
            cookieDataSet[2], cookieDataSet[3]);
      }
   }
}

//***************************************************************
//* This function adds a new element to the cookie array or
//* updates an existing element.
//***************************************************************
```

```
function updateCookieArray(moduleName_in,
                           linkTitle_in,
                           url_in,
                           winTarget_in) {
   var loopstop    = false;
   var updated     = false;
   var arrayindex  = cookieArray.length;
   var undefined;

   if (winTarget_in == null || winTarget_in == undefined) {
      winTarget_in = "notarget";
   }
   while (!loopstop) {
      arrayindex = arrayindex - 1;
      if (arrayindex < 0) {
         loopstop = true;
      }
      else if (cookieArray[arrayindex].moduleName ==
               moduleName_in) {

         if (cookieArray[arrayindex].linkTitle != linkTitle_in) {
            cookieArray[arrayindex] = new
              cookieData(cookieArray[arrayindex].moduleName,
                         linkTitle_in,
                         cookieArray[arrayindex].url,
                         cookieArray[arrayindex].winTarget_in);
         }
         if (cookieArray[arrayindex].url != url_in) {
           cookieArray[arrayindex] = new
              cookieData(cookieArray[arrayindex].moduleName,
              cookieArray[arrayindex].linkTitle, url_in,
              cookieArray[arrayindex].winTarget_in);
         }
         if (cookieArray[arrayindex].winTarget != winTarget_in) {
            cookieArray[arrayindex] = new
               cookieData(cookieArray[arrayindex].moduleName,
               cookieArray[arrayindex].linkTitle,
               cookieArray[arrayindex].url, winTarget_in);
         }
         loopstop = true;
         updated  = true;
      }
   }
```

```
   if (!updated) {
      if (cookieArray.length == 0) {
         cookieArray[0] = new cookieData(moduleName_in,
            linkTitle_in, url_in, winTarget_in);
      }
      else {
         cookieArray[cookieArray.length] = new
            cookieData(moduleName_in, linkTitle_in, url_in,
                       winTarget_in);
      }
   }
   setNavCookie();
}

//***************************************************************
//* This function, given the module/label name, will build the
//* navlink based on data in the associated array element.
//***************************************************************

function returnToCaller(moduleName_in,winTarget_in) {
   var moduleName  = new String("undefined");
   var linkTitle   = new String("undefined");
   var url         = new String("undefined");
   var newUrl      = new String();
   var target      = new String("undefined");
   var returnVal   = new String("undefined");
   var loopstop    = false;
   var arrayindex  = cookieArray.length;

   if (winTarget_in == null || winTarget_in == undefined) {
      target = "notarget";
   }
   else {
      target = winTarget_in;
   }
   while (!loopstop) {
      arrayindex = arrayindex - 1;
      if (arrayindex < 0) {
         loopstop = true;
      }
      else if (cookieArray[arrayindex].moduleName ==
                        moduleName_in) {
         moduleName = cookieArray[arrayindex].moduleName;
         linkTitle  = cookieArray[arrayindex].linkTitle;
         url        = cookieArray[arrayindex].url;
         if (target == "notarget") {
            target = cookieArray[arrayindex].winTarget;
         }
         newUrl = "javascript:checkDataChanges('"+url+"')";
```

```
         if (target == "notarget") {
            returnVal  = "<BIG><UL><LI><A HREF=" + newUrl +
               ">" + linkTitle + "</A></UL></BIG>";
         }
         else {
            returnVal = "<BIG><UL><LI><A TARGET=" + target +
               " HREF=" + newUrl + ">" + linkTitle +
               "</A></UL></BIG>";
         }
         loopstop   = true;
      }
   }
   if (returnVal != "undefined") {
      document.write(returnVal);
   }
}

//**************************************************************
//* This function allows the user to retrieve individual elements
//* of the logical cookie.
//**************************************************************
function getCookieValue(moduleName_in,component_in){
   var moduleName  = new String("undefined");
   var linkTitle   = new String("undefined");
   var url         = new String("undefined");
   var target      = new String("undefined");
   var returnVal   = new String("undefined");
   var loopstop    = false;
   var arrayindex  = cookieArray.length;

   while (!loopstop) {
      arrayindex = arrayindex - 1;
      if (arrayindex < 0) {
         loopstop = true;
      }
      else if (cookieArray[arrayindex].moduleName ==
               moduleName_in) {
         if (component_in.toUpperCase() == "NAME") {
            returnVal = cookieArray[arrayindex].moduleName;
         }
         else if (component_in.toUpperCase() == "TITLE") {
            returnVal = cookieArray[arrayindex].linkTitle;
         }
         else if (component_in.toUpperCase() == "URL") {
            returnVal = cookieArray[arrayindex].url;
         }
         else if (component_in.toUpperCase() == "TARGET"){
            returnVal= cookieArray[arrayindex].winTarget;

         }
```

```
            loopstop   = true;
         }
      }
      return returnVal;
   }

   //**********************************************************
   //* This function allows the user to remove individual elements
   //* of the logical cookie.
   //**********************************************************
   function removeCookieValue(moduleName_in) {
      var loopstop    = false;
      var arrayindex  = cookieArray.length;

      while (!loopstop) {
         arrayindex = arrayindex - 1;
         if (arrayindex < 0) {
            loopstop = true;
         }
         else if (cookieArray[arrayindex].moduleName ==
                  moduleName_in) {
            cookieArray[arrayindex].moduleName = "<REMOVE>";
            setNavCookie();
            loopstop = true;
         }
      }
   }

   //**********************************************************
   //* This function compiles the data from the cookie
   //* array and loads it into the cookie.
   //**********************************************************
   function setNavCookie() {
      var dataString  = new String();
      var arrayLength = cookieArray.length;
      for (var loopIndex = 0; loopIndex<arrayLength;
           loopIndex ++) {
         if (cookieArray[loopIndex].moduleName != "<REMOVE>") {
            dataString = dataString +
               cookieArray[loopIndex].moduleName + "<,>" +
               cookieArray[loopIndex].linkTitle + "<,>" +
               cookieArray[loopIndex].url + "<,>" +
               cookieArray[loopIndex].winTarget + "<c>";
         }
      }
      document.cookie = "KBCOPSNAVCOOKIE"+"="+dataString+";PATH=/";
      return true;
   }
```

Applying Logical Cookies to a Web Server Generator Module

The following code demonstrates the application of the logical cookie in a module, which will call other modules. In the following examples, moduleOne calls moduleTwo and moduleThree. The JavaScript functions for the logical cookie must be included in the page/module before calling the functions.

This is the user text area's top of View form section for moduleOne:

```
<SCRIPT>
   //This line of code populates the array with the cookie
   //data string.
   populateCookieArray();
   //This line of code updates the array and reloads the cookie
   UpdateCookieArray("moduleTwoCaller", "Back to moduleOne",
      "moduleOne$moduleOne.queryView?p_id=5");

   UpdateCookieArray("moduleThreeCaller","Back to moduleOne",
      "moduleOne$moduleOne.queryView?p_id=5");
</SCRIPT>
```

This is the user text area's top of View form section for moduleTwo:

```
<SCRIPT>
   populateCookieArray():
   // This line of code creates a hyperlink back to moduleOne
   returnToCaller("moduleTwoCaller");
</SCRIPT>
```

This is the user text area's top of View form section for moduleThree:

```
<SCRIPT>
   populateCookieArray():
   // This line of code creates a hyperlink back to moduleOne
   returnToCaller("moduleThreeCaller");

</SCRIPT>
```

Discussing Lists of Values (LOVs)

LOVs in a Web Server Generator module are similar to LOVs in a Forms module. They enable the user to choose a value for a foreign key lookup. They can be displayed in a separate window if the browser supports JavaScript (see Figure 16-7), or in a separate frame. The following subsections focus on the JavaScript implementation.

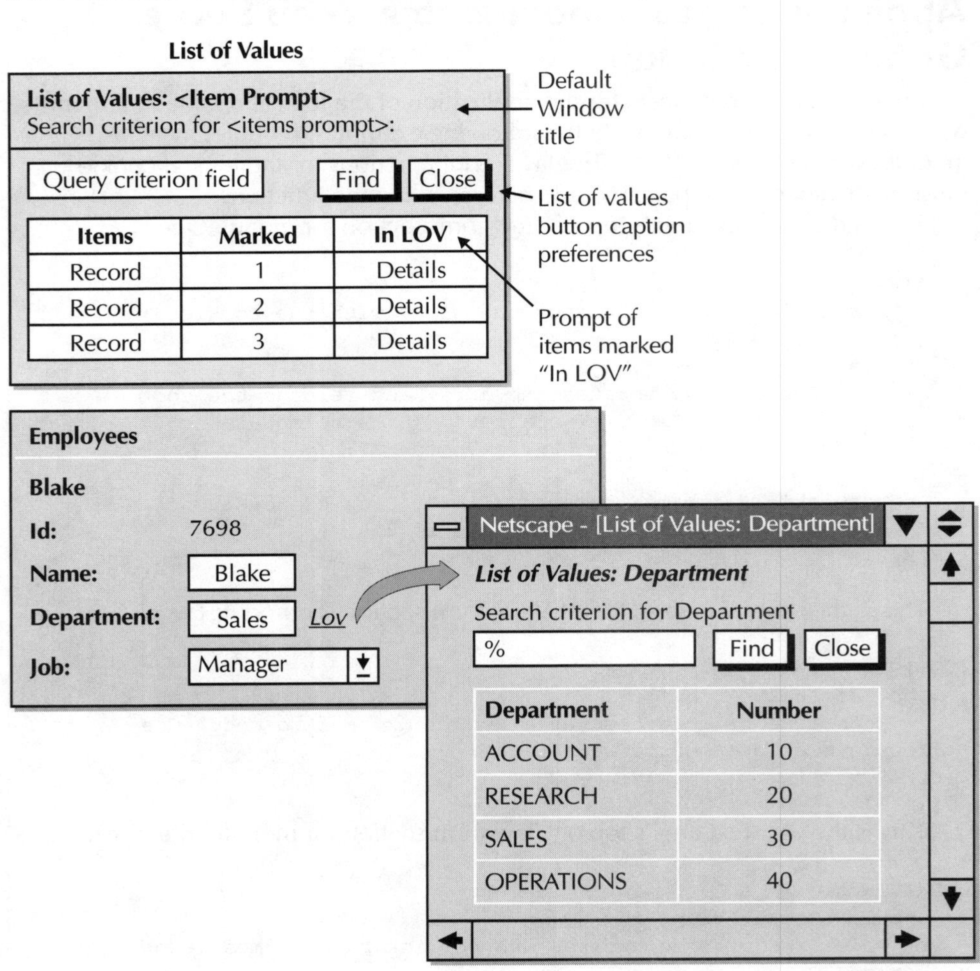

FIGURE 16-7. *LOV generated by Web Server Generator*

Looking at Web Server Generator's Flavor of LOV

The LOV generated by the Web Server Generator is based on a single lookup table associated with a module component's table. LOVs are defined using the Edit Lookup Table Usage Wizard (see Figure 16-8). The developer can choose which columns of the LOV to display. These columns appear on the Web page and are populated by the LOV at runtime. The LOVs are limited to single table lookups. The return values are limited to items or columns in the lookup table. Complex or multiple table queries are not allowed. Be sure to include the primary key or other unique identifier for the lookup table in the LOV. If the unique identifier is left out and two of the data selections are the same, then the reference to the first of the two items will be returned. This will also occur if the user chooses the second item instead of the first. It is also important to note that the Display, Insert, and Update properties of foreign key items on the base table must all be set to No.

The user's method of accessing an LOV is a hyperlink located to the right of the item, indicating a lookup column. The text of the hyperlink can be modified using the LOVBUT generator preference. The hyperlink is anchored to a JavaScript script function, which launches the LOV. The JavaScript function uses the naming convention <item_name>_LOV.

Creating a Custom LOV Using Oracle8 Objects

We can base an LOV on a query containing a multiple table join or include more than one limiting parameter in our where clause. One method is to change the PL/SQL code generated by Designer; however, this is not the recommended solution. Oracle8 provides us with a method to define our own objects or abstract

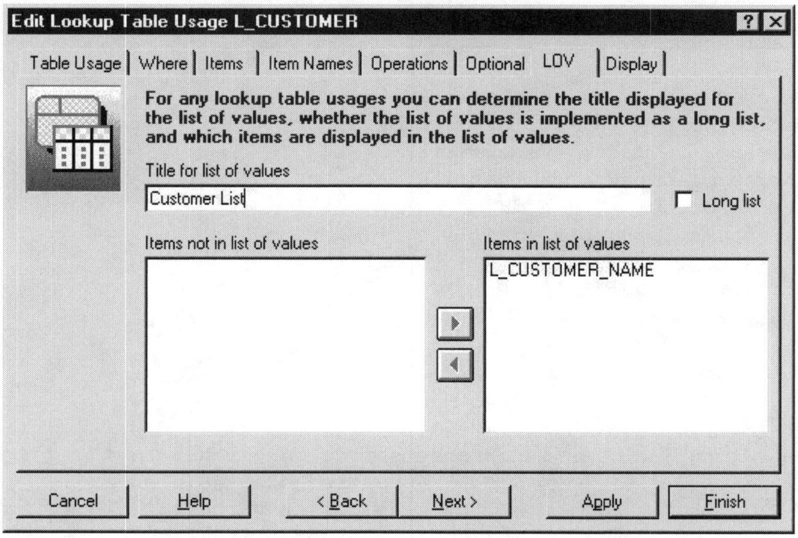

FIGURE 16-8. *Edit Lookup Table Wizard*

datatypes (ADTs). This powerful capability gives us the means to create an object that mimics and extends the Web Server Generators LOV. The following sections detail the procedures to create an LOV object.

Coding the LOV Object

The following Oracle object definitions represent an implementation of a custom LOV:

```
create or replace type t_charArray100
as varray(100) of varchar2(500);
/
create or replace type t_lovColumn AS object(
   position       number(3),
   name           varchar2(100),
   form           varchar2(3));
/
create or replace type t_lovColArray100
as VARRAY(100) of t_lovColumn;
/
create or replace type lovType as object(
   lovObjectName        varchar2(100),
   title                varchar2(100),
   lovHandler           varchar2(500),
   selectStatement      varchar2(2000),
   executeStatement     varchar2(2000),
   lovCallingForm       varchar2(3),
   headings             t_lovColArray100,
   limiter              t_charArray100,
   returnColumns        t_lovColArray100,
   debugFlag            varchar2(1),
   member procedure     initarrays,
   member procedure     addHeading(
        column_in number,
        value_in varchar2 := 'None Defined',
        form_in  varchar2 := '0'),
   member procedure     addLimiter(value_in varchar2),
   member procedure     addReturnColumn(
        column_in number,
        value_in   varchar2 := 'None Defined',
        form_in    varchar2 := '0'),
   member function      quickParse(string_in varchar2,
                                   desired_element number,
                                   delimiter varchar2,
                                   safe_parse in varchar2 := 'Y')
   return varchar2,
   pragma restrict_references (quickParse,
```

```
                                WNDS, RNDS, WNPS, RNPS),
   member function countSelectColumns (select_in varchar2)
   return number,
   pragma restrict_references (countSelectColumns,
                                WNDS, RNDS, WNPS, RNPS),
   member procedure     replaceValues,
   member procedure     setLimiters(limiter_string varchar2),
   member function      lovJscript(
      function_name  varchar2, parameter_list varchar2 := null,
                                ctlValue boolean         := true,
                                w_width number           := 400,
                                w_height number          := 400
   ) return varchar2,
   pragma restrict_references (lovJscript,WNDS,RNDS,WNPS,RNPS),
   member procedure     lovJscript(
       function_name  varchar2, parameter_list varchar2 := null,
                                 ctlValue boolean         := true,
                                 w_width        number    := 400,
                                 w_height       number    := 400
   ),
   member procedure     executeLov(callingUrl     varchar2,
                                    limiter_string varchar2,
                                    displayOnly boolean := false,
                                    returnFocus varchar2 := null)
   );
/
show errors

create or replace type body lovType as
   /*************************************************/
   /* Procedure: initarrays                         */
   /* initializes the attributes defined by varrays */
   /*************************************************/
   member procedure initarrays is
   begin
      begin
         if self.headings.count = 0 then
           self.headings := t_lovColArray100();
         end if;
      exception
         when others then self.headings := t_lovColArray100();
      end;
      begin
         if self.limiter.count = 0 then
            self.limiter        := t_charArray100();
         end if;
      exception
         when others then
```

```
          self.limiter := t_charArray100();
      end;
      begin
         if self.returncolumns.count = 0 then
            self.returncolumns   := t_lovColArray100();
         end if;
      exception
         when others then
            self.returncolumns := t_lovColArray100();
      end;
   end;

   /**************************************************/
   /* Procedure: addHeading                          */
   /* Add a value to the headings attribute          */
   /**************************************************/
   member procedure addHeading (
       column_in number,
       value_in  varchar2 := 'None Defined' ,
       form_in varchar2 := '0') is
   begin
      if self.headings.count < self.headings.limit then
         self.headings.extend;
         self.headings(headings.count) :=
            t_lovColumn(column_in, value_in, form_in);
      end if;
   end;

   /**************************************************/
   /* Procedure: addLimiter                          */
   /* Add a value to the limiter attribute           */
   /**************************************************/
   member procedure addLimiter(value_in varchar2) is
   begin
      if self.limiter.count < self.limiter.limit then
         self.limiter.extend;
         self.limiter(limiter.count) := ltrim(rtrim(value_in));
      end if;
   end;

   /**************************************************/
   /* Procedure: addReturnColumn                     */
   /* Add a value to the addReturnColumn attribute   */
   /**************************************************/
   member procedure addReturnColumn(
       column_in number,
       value_in varchar2 := 'None Defined',
       form_in varchar2 := '0') is
```

```
begin
   if self.returncolumns.count < self.returncolumns.limit then
      self.returncolumns.extend;
      self.returncolumns(returncolumns.count) :=
         t_lovColumn(column_in, value_in, form_in);
   end if;
end;

/*******************************************************/
/* Function: quickParse                                */
/* Returns the requested element in a delimited string, */
/* provided there are not leading delimiters, or multiple */
/* delimiters in a row.                                */
/*******************************************************/
member function quickParse(string_in        varchar2,
                           desired_element number,
                           delimiter       varchar2,
                           safe_parse   in varchar2 := 'Y')
return varchar2 is
   edit_string        varchar2(2000);
   temp_string        varchar2(2000);
   current_grab       varchar2(2000);
   last_grab          varchar2(2000);
   position           number(4) := 1;
   fall_back_pos      number(4) := 0;
   delimiter_count    number(4) := 0;
   element_count      number(4) := 0;
   del_length         number(4) := length(delimiter);
   start_position     number(4);
   end_position       number(4);
   end_process   exception;
begin
   /* handle null string */
   edit_string := string_in;
   if string_in is null then
      raise end_process;
   end if;
   /* remove leading delimiters */
   loop
      if delimiter =
         substr(string_in, position, del_length) then
         edit_string:=substr(string_in,
            (position+(del_length)));
         position := position + del_length;
      else
         exit;
      end if;
   end loop;
```

```
element_count := trunc(length(edit_string) /
                 length(delimiter)) + 1;
/* remove extra delimiters between elements */
if upper(safe_parse) = 'Y' then
   element_count := 0;
   position      := 1;
   temp_string   := edit_string;
   edit_string   := null;
   current_grab  := substr(temp_string, position,
                    del_length);
   fall_back_pos := position;
   loop
      if position >= (length(temp_string) + del_length)
      then
         edit_string := edit_string ||
           substr(temp_string, fall_back_pos,
           ((position+del_length) - fall_back_pos));
      end if;
      exit when (position >=
                (length(temp_string) + del_length));
      last_grab := current_grab;
      current_grab := substr(temp_string, position,
                      del_length);
      if (current_grab=last_grab) and
         (current_grab=delimiter) then
         position      := (position + del_length);
         fall_back_pos := position;
      elsif (current_grab=delimiter) and
            (current_grab!= last_grab) then
         delimiter_count := delimiter_count + 1;
         edit_string := edit_string || substr(temp_string,
           fall_back_pos, ((position+del_length) -
           fall_back_pos));
         position      := (position + del_length);
         fall_back_pos := position;
         element_count := delimiter_count + 1;
      else
         position := position + 1;
      end if;
   end loop;
   /*****************/
   /* SPECIAL CASES */
   /*****************/
   /* If delimiter count is 0 return the entire string */
   if (delimiter_count = 0) and (desired_element = 1) then
      raise end_process;
   end if;
```

```
         /* Disqualify bogus requests for elements */
         if (desired_element > element_count) or
            (desired_element < 1) then
            edit_string := null;
            raise end_process;
         end if;
      end if; /* safe parsing */
      /*******************************/
      /* Isolate the desired element. */
      /*******************************/
      /* Find starting position of desired element */
      if (desired_element = 1) then
         start_position := 1;
      else
         start_position := (instr(edit_string, delimiter, 1,
            desired_element - 1) + length(delimiter));
      end if;
      /* Find ending position of desired element */
      if (desired_element = element_count) then
         end_position := length(edit_string);
      else
         end_position := (instr(edit_string, delimiter,
           start_position, 1) - start_position);
      end if;
      /* get requested element */
      edit_string := substr(edit_string, start_position,
                     end_position);
      return edit_string;
   exception
      when end_process then
         return edit_string;
   end;

/*************************************************************/
/* Function: countSelectColumns                              */
/* Function used to count number of columns in select clause   */
/*************************************************************/
member function countSelectColumns (select_in varchar2)
return number is
   columnlist varchar2(2000);
   parenOpen   number(3) := 0;
   parenClose  number(3) := 0;
   parenCount  number(3) := 0;
   location    number(3) := 0;
   colcount    NUMBER(3) := 0;
begin
   columnlist := self.quickParse(upper(select_in),1,'FROM');
```

```
   /*---------------------------------------------------------*/
   /* Locate Functions with parenthesis in the SELECT clause */
   /*---------------------------------------------------------*/
   loop
        parenOpen  := instr(columnlist, '(', 1, 1);
        parenClose := instr(columnlist, ')', 1, 1);

        exit when parenOpen + parenClose = 0;
        columnlist := replace(columnlist,
                      substr(columnlist,parenOpen,
                            (parenClose-parenOpen)+2),
                             '<sqlfunc>');
   end loop;

   loop
      colcount := colcount + 1;
      location := instr(columnlist, ',', 1, colcount);
      exit when location = 0;
   end loop;
   return colcount;
end;

/**************************************************************/
/* Procedure: replaceValues                                   */
/* Replace references to limiter array elements with actual   */
/* element. This is necessary because of Javascript to PL/SQL */
/* data transition.                                           */
/**************************************************************/
member procedure replaceValues is
begin
   self.executeStatement := self.selectStatement;
   for loop_var in 1 .. self.limiter.last loop
      self.executeStatement := replace(self.executeStatement,
         'limiter(' || to_char(loop_var) || ')',
         self.limiter(loop_var));
   end loop;
end;

   /**************************************************/
   /* Procedure: setLimiters                         */
   /* Populates limiter VARRAY with values passed in */
   /* the form of a <,> delimited text string.       */
   /**************************************************/
   member procedure setLimiters(limiter_string varchar2) is
      position_cnt     number(3)       := 1;
      delimiter_cnt    number(3)       := 0;
      element          varchar2(500);
```

```
      element_cnt      number(3)        := 0;
      limiter_vals     varchar2(2000)   := limiter_string;
      done             boolean          := false;

    begin
      if instr(limiter_string,'<,>',1) = 1 then
         limiter_vals := ' '||limiter_vals;
      end if;

     /* Count the number of delimiters present.  */
     /* Number of elements will = delimiters + 1 */
     loop
        exit when done;
        if (instr(limiter_vals,'<,>',1,position_cnt) != 0) then
           position_cnt   := position_cnt + 1;
           delimiter_cnt := delimiter_cnt + 1;
        else
           element_cnt := delimiter_cnt + 1;
           done := true;
        end if;
     end loop;
     /* Load the values into the limiter VARRAY */
     for loop_var in 1.. element_cnt loop
        element :=  quickParse(limiter_vals,loop_var,'<,>');
        if self.limiter.exists(loop_var) then
           self.limiter(loop_var) := replace(
              replace(element,'<p>','%'), '<s>',' ');
        else
           addLimiter(replace(replace(element, '<p>', '%'),
              '<s>', ' '));
        end if;
      end loop;
   end;

/**********************************************************/
/* Function: lovJscript                                   */
/* This function creates the JavaScript function which    */
/* launches the LOV from the calling Web page.            */
/* This method is specifically designed to be coded into a */
/* Designer 2000 Web module component. Specifically in the */
/* TOP OF INSERT/VIEW FORMS. The function_name parameter   */
/* should take the same name as the JavaScript script     */
/* function generated by Designer. The new function will  */
/* override the old. It uses the object's lovHandler      */
/* attribute as a reference which external procedure will */
/* call and execute the LOV.                              */
/**********************************************************/
```

```
member function lovJscript(function_name  varchar2,
                           parameter_list varchar2 := null,
                           ctlValue boolean        := true,
                           w_width        number   := 400,
                           w_height       number   := 400 )
return varchar2 is
   j_script_top     varchar2(2000);
   j_script_bottom  varchar2(2000);
   j_script         varchar2(4000);
begin
   /*******************************************************/
   /* The parameter list can contain values which represent */
   /* JavaScript function calls. The function is evaluated  */
   /* and placed into the limiter string at runtime. The    */
   /* entire parameter list is split into an array. Each    */
   /* element of the array is passed through an anonymous   */
   /* function for evaluation. If the element is a function */
   /* call, then the value of that function is assigned to  */
   /* the limiter string. Otherwise, the value in the       */
   /* element is returned.                                  */
   /*******************************************************/

   if ctlvalue then
      j_script_top := '<SCRIPT> function ' || function_name ||
        '(ctl) { var reppct   = "%";
                 var repspc   = " ";
                 var pList    = new
                   String(" ' || parameter_list || '");
                 var pTranslate   = new String("");
                 if (pList.length > 0){
                    pTranslate   = pList.split("<,>");
                 }
                 if (pTranslate.length == 0){
                   limiters = new String(ctl.value);
                 } else {
                   for (var limiternum = 0;
                       limiternum < pTranslate.length;
                       limiternum ++) {
                       var val = new Function("limiterval",
                         "return " + pTranslate[limiternum]);
                         if (limiternum == 0) {
                           limiters = val(pTranslate[limiternum]);
                         } else {
                            limiters = limiters + "<,>" +
```

```
                                val(pTranslate[limiternum]);
                          }
                       }
                       limiters = new String(ctl.value +
                                           "<,>" + limiters);
                    }';
else
   j_script_top := '<SCRIPT> function ' || function_name ||
     '() { var the_pathname = location.pathname;
           var reppct = "%";
           var repspc = " ";
           var pList  = new string("'||parameter_list||'");
           var pTranslate   = pList.split("<,>");
           for (var limiternum = 0;
                limiternum < pTranslate.length;
                limiternum ++) {
               var val = new Function("x", "return " +
                  pTranslate[limiternum]);
               if (limiternum == 0) {
                  limiters = val(pTranslate[limiternum]);
               } else {
                 limiters = limiters + "<,>" +
                    val(pTranslate[limiternum]);
               }
           }
           limiters = new String(limiters);';
end if;
j_script_bottom := 'while (limiters.search("%") != -1) {
                      limiters = limiters.replace(reppct,
                      "<p>"); };
                    while (limiters.search(" ") != -1){
                      limiters = limiters.replace(repspc,
                      "<s>"); };
                frmLOV = open("'||SELF.lovHandler||'" +
                    "?CALLINGURL=" + escape(location.protocol +
                    "//" + location.host + location.pathname +
                    location.search) + "&LIMITER_STRING=" +
                    limiters,"winLOV", "scrollbars=yes,
                    resizable=yes, width=' || w_width ||
                    ',height=' || w_height || '");
                    if (frmLOV.opener == null) {
                     frmLOV.opener = self;
                    }
                } </SCRIPT>';
   j_script := j_script_top || j_script_bottom;
```

```
      return j_script;
   end;

/***************************************************************/
/* Procedure: lovJscript                                       */
/* This procedure is designed for use in traditional non-      */
/* Designer 2K Web development.                                */
/***************************************************************/

member procedure lovJscript(function_name  varchar2,
                            parameter_list varchar2 := null,
                            ctlValue       boolean  := true,
                            w_width        number   := 400,
                            w_height       number   := 400 )
is begin
  htp.p(lovJscript (function_name, parameter_list, ctlValue,
                    w_width, w_height));
end;

/***************************************************************/
/* Procedure: executeLov                                       */
/* This procedure builds the LOV Web page. All of the object's */
/* attributes are geared toward this procedure.                */
/***************************************************************/

member procedure executeLov(callingUrl     varchar2,
                            limiter_string varchar2,
                            displayOnly    boolean  := false,
                            returnFocus    varchar2 := null) is
   type t_valueArray IS varray(100) of varchar2(500);
   return_data_string  varchar2(2000);
   lastlimiters        varchar2(500);
   limiter_string_init varchar2(500);
   formNum             varchar2(30) :=
     nvl(self.lovCallingForm, '0');
   valueArray          t_valueArray := t_valueArray();
   v_Cursor            integer;
   v_num_rows          integer;
   v_columns           number(3):=
     self.countSelectColumns(self.executeStatement);
   valString           varchar2(500);
   displayStringFront  varchar2(500);
   displayString       varchar2(500);
begin
   /* initialize array */
   for loop_var in 1 .. v_columns loop
      valueArray.extend;
      valueArray(loop_var) := null;
   end loop;
```

```
htp.htmlOpen;
htp.headOpen;
   htp.title(self.title);
   if self.returncolumns.count > 0 then
     for loop_var in 1 .. v_columns loop
        for inner_loop in 1 .. self.returnColumns.count loop
          if (self.returnColumns(inner_loop).position =
              loop_var) then
             if return_data_string is null then
                return_data_string :=
                  upper(self.returnColumns(inner_loop).Name);
             else
                return_data_string := return_data_string ||
                   ',' ||
                   upper(self.returnColumns(inner_loop).Name);
             end if;
          end if;
        end loop;
     end loop;
   end if;
   /* Returns to calling page and sets specified values. */
   for loop_var in 2..self.limiter.count loop
      lastlimiters := lastlimiters || '<,>' ||
         self.limiter(loop_var);
   end loop;
   htp.p('<SCRIPT>
            var lastlimiters = new String("' || lastlimiters
               || '");
            function ReturnData(' || return_data_string||'){
               if (opener.location.href != document.forms[' ||
                 formNum || '].callingUrl.value){
                  alert("Lov out of context.");
                  return;
               }');

   for loop_var in 1 .. v_columns loop
      for inner_loop in 1 .. self.returnColumns.count loop
         if (self.returnColumns(inner_loop).position =
              loop_var) then
            http.p('opener.document.forms['||
                  self.returnColumns(inner_loop).Form ||
                  '].' ||
                  upper(self.returnColumns(inner_loop).Name)||
                  '.value = '||
                  upper(SELF.returnColumns(inner_loop).Name)||
                  '.replace("<sq>","''");');
         end if;
      end loop;
   end loop;
```

```
if self.returnColumns.count > 0 then
   for loop_var in 1 .. self.returncolumns.count loop
     if self.returnColumns(loop_var).position = 1 then
         if returnFocus is null then
            htp.p('opener.document.forms['||
            self.returnColumns(loop_var).Form||'].'||
            upper(self.returnColumns(loop_var).Name)||
            '.focus();');
         else
            htp.p('opener.document.forms['||
            SELF.returnColumns(loop_var).Form||'].'||
            upper(returnFocus)||'.focus();');
         end if;
     end if;
   end loop;
end if;
htp.p('close(); }');
if not displayOnly then
   htp.p('function Find_OnClick() {
            var limiters = new String(document.forms[' ||
                 formNum||'].LIMITER_STRING.value +
                 lastlimiters);
            if (lastlimiters.length != 0) {
               document.forms[' || formNum ||
               '].LIMITER_STRING.value = limiters.replace("
               ",""); }
              document.forms[' || formNum || '].submit();
           }');
end if;
htp.p('function Close_OnClick(){
          close();
      }');
htp.p('</SCRIPT>');
htp.p('<LINK REL=StyleSheet HREF="styleSheetLibrary.css">
      </LINK>');
htp.headClose;
htp.bodyOpen(cattributes=>'BGCOLOR=C0C0C0');
htp.header(1,htf.italic(SELF.title));

/* lovHandler is the procedure which accepts this  */
/* object and generates the call to the LOV. It is */
/* defined by the programmer.                      */

htp.formOpen(lovHandler);
htp.formHidden('callingUrl',callingUrl);

if not displayOnly then
   htp.para;
```

```
    htp.p('Search criteria for '||SELF.headings(1).Name);
    htp.para;

    /* This code will place the value from the calling */
    /* screen's control in the search string text      */
    /* area of the LOV on it's opening.                */
    IF self.limiter(1) = '%' then
       limiter_string_init := ltrim(
       replace(self.limiter(1),'%','')||'%');
    else
       limiter_string_init := self.limiter(1);
    end if;

    htp.formText('LIMITER_STRING',
                 cvalue=>limiter_string_init);
    htp.p('<input type = "button" value="Find" onclick =
           "Find_OnClick()">');
 end if;
 htp.p('<input type = "button" value="Close" onclick =
        "Close_OnClick()">');
 htp.formClose;

 /* This is where we use the cursor variable and build */
 /* the table of return values.                         */
 htp.tableOpen(cborder=>'BORDER');
 htp.tableRowOpen;

 for loop_var in 1..self.headings.count loop
    for inner_loop in 1..self.headings.count loop
       if(self.headings(inner_loop).position = loop_var)
       then
          htp.tableHeader(calign=>'LEFT',
             cvalue=>SELF.headings(inner_loop).Name);
       end if;
    end loop;
 end loop;
 htp.tableRowClose;

 /* Building the data */
 v_Cursor := dbms_sql.open_cursor;
 if self.debugFlag = 'Y' then
    htp.p(self.executeStatement);
 end if;

dbms_sql.parse(v_Cursor, self.executeStatement,
               dbms_sql.native);
for loop_var in 1 .. v_columns  loop
   dbms_sql.define_column(v_Cursor,loop_var,
```

```
                                valueArray(loop_var),500);
        end loop;
        v_num_rows := dbms_sql.execute(v_Cursor);

         /**********************************/
         /* LOOP to fetch and populate LOV */
         /**********************************/
         loop
            exit when dbms_sql.fetch_rows(v_Cursor) = 0;
            for loop_var in 1 .. v_columns loop
               dbms_sql.column_value(v_Cursor, loop_var,
                                     valueArray(loop_var));
            end loop;

            for loop_var in 1 .. v_columns loop
              /****************************************/
              /* This loop builds the data string     */
              /* displayed in the LOV.                */
              /****************************************/
              for headvar in 1 .. self.headings.count loop
                 if self.headings(headvar).position = loop_var then
                 /**********************************************/
                 /* Checks to see if this is first column in    */
                 /* display list. The first column item is      */
                 /* hyper-linked unless the LOV is display only.*/
                 /**********************************************/
                 if headvar = 1 then
                    for inner_loop in 1 .. self.headings.count loop
                       if self.headings(inner_loop).position = 1
                       then
                          displayStringFront :=
                      valueArray(SELF.headings(inner_loop).position)
                            || '</a></td>';
                          displayString := displayStringFront ||
                                           displayString;
                      end if;
                   end loop;
                else
                   for inner_loop in 1 .. self.headings.count loop
                      if self.headings(inner_loop).position =headvar
                      then
                         displayString := displayString || '<td>' ||
                      valueArray(SELF.headings(inner_loop).position)
                           ||'</td>';
                      end if;
                   end loop;
                end if;
             end if;
```

```
      end loop; /* display column loop */
    end loop; /* column loop */

    /************************************************/
    /* This loop builds the list of data that will be */
    /* passed back to the calling form.              */
    /************************************************/
    for retvar in 1 .. v_columns loop
      for inner_loop in 1 .. self.returncolumns.count loop
        if self.returnColumns(inner_loop).position =
          retvar then
          if valString is null then
            valString := '''' || replace( valueArray(
              self.returnColumns(inner_loop).position), '''',
              '<sq>') || '''';
          else
            valString := valString || ',' || '''' || replace(
              valueArray(
              SELF.returnColumns(inner_loop).position), '''',
              '<sq>') || '''';
          end if;
        end if;
      end loop;
    end loop; /* return column loop */

    if not displayOnly then
      htp.p('<TR VALIGN="TOP"><TD ALIGN="LEFT">
        <a href="javascript:ReturnData(' || valString ||
        ')">' || displayString || '</TR>';
    else
      htp.p('<TR VALIGN="TOP">
            <TD ALIGN="LEFT">' || displayString || '</TR>');
    end if;

    displayStringFront  := null;
    displayString       := null;
    valString           := null;
  end loop; /* row loop */

  dbms_sql.close_cursor(v_Cursor);
  htp.tableClose;

  if not displayOnly then
    htp.p('<SCRIPT>
            document.forms[' || formNum ||
              '].LIMITER_STRING.focus();
          </SCRIPT>');
  end if;
```

```
   htp.bodyClose;

   htp.htmlClose;

exception
   when others then
      dbms_sql.close_cursor(v_Cursor);
      htp.print(SQLERRM);
      htp.bodyClose;
      htp.htmlClose;
end;
end;
/
show errors
```

Implementing the LOV Object

Implementing the LOV object in a generated module component is simple; however, it requires several steps. Our new LOV has to override the existing LOV. This piece of code must bridge the PL/SQL, HTML, and JavaScript gap. The LOV contains components of all three languages. Follow these outlined steps to implement a LOV object.

The example LOV is a list of customers for an order entry module. The tables, customer and sales_order, come from the demo schema, which can be installed as part of Oracle8i.

Step 1

Under the Events heading of the Application Logic section under the module component, create the private declarations event. This is where the LOV object types are declared. For example:

```
customerLov  lovType :=
     lovType(NULL,NULL,NULL,NULL,NULL,NULL,NULL,NULL,NULL,'N');
```

Each NULL represents the initialization of one of the object's attributes. The last attribute is the debug attribute. If it is set to Y, then the SELECT statement defined for the LOV will be displayed in the LOV window.

Step 2

Create a public named routine under the module component to act as the LOV setup procedure, as the following code illustrates:

```
procedure customerLovSetup is
begin
   customerLov.initArrays;
   customerLov.lovObjectName    := 'customerLov';
   customerLov.title            := 'Customer Listing';
```

```
   customerLov.lovHandler       := 'orders$orders.customerLovRun';
   customerLov.selectStatement :=
      'SELECT name, TO_CHAR(credit_limit),
              first_name || '' '' || last_name
         FROM customer, employee
        WHERE (name LIKE ''limiter(1)%'' OR
              ''limiter(1)'' = '' '')
          AND salesperson_id = employee_id';

   customerLov.addHeading(1,'Customer');
   customerLov.addHeading(2,'Credit');
   customerLov.addHeading(3,'Sales Rep.');

   customerLov.addReturnColumn(1,'P_L_CUSTOMER_NAME');
end;
In the preceding select statement, 'limiter(n)' is used to specify
limiting/replacement values.
```

In the addHeading and addReturnColumn methods, the first parameter indicates which column in the select clause, associated with the heading or return column. The second parameter in addHeading specifies the column heading to be displayed in the LOV. The second parameter in the addReturnColumn specifies which item in the calling Web page will receive the data value of the specified column. The addReturnColumn method takes a third parameter enabling the developer to specify which form the Web parameter resides.

The lovHandler attribute names the PL/SQL procedure, which is referenced by the JavaScript function that launches the LOV.

Step 3

Create a public routine for the JavaScript function that executes the LOV:

```
function customerLovJscript() return varchar2 is
begin
   customerLovSetup;
   return customerLov.lovJscript('P_L_CUSTOMER_NAME');
end;
```

The lovJscript method creates the JavaScript function launching the LOV. The first parameter identifies the JavaScript function that will be created in the Web page. In the current instance, it is given the name of the JavaScript function generated by Designer 2000's Web generator. This enables the developer to override the original function and insert his or her own function. The second parameter is the parameter list. The items in this parameter (list) will replace the limiter(*n*) values in the SELECT statement. LovJscript method takes a third parameter called ctlValue. ctlValue is a Boolean parameter that specifies whether the new function will be associated with a ctl value. If so, then limiter(1) will always be replaced by the value of ctl. Otherwise, limiter(1) will be replaced by the first item in the passed parameter list.

Step 4

Create a public routine to act as the LOV handler. For example:

```
procedure customerLovRun(callingurl varchar2,
                         limiter_string varchar2) is
begin
   customerLovSetup;
   customerLov.setLimiters(limiter_string);
   customerLov.replaceValues;
   customerLov.executeLov(callingurl, limiter_string);
exception
   when others then
      htp.print(SQLERRM);
end;
```

The setLimiters method loads the replacement values passed through the JavaScript function created by lovJscript.

The replaceValues method replaces the instances limiter(*n*) in the user-defined SELECT statement.

The executeLov method constructs, displays, and manages the actual LOV. This method takes an optional third Boolean parameter called displayOnly. If displayOnly is False, then a normal LOV will be displayed. If displayOnly is True, then an LOV is displayed without a search line, Find button, or hyperlinks in the return list.

Step 5

Call the routine creating the LOV JavaScript function from the top of View/Insert form, as the following syntax illustrates:

```
orders$orders.customerLovJscript;
```

Be sure to register the module package name (i.e., orders$orders) in the Text Handling section of the module's generator options. If the package name is not registered, then the call to the PL/SQL function creating the LOV JavaScript function will fail to execute and be displayed as plaintext in the Web page.

As illustrated in Figure 16-9, the custom LOV previously defined has the identical appearance and behavior as Web Server Generator's LOV—however, with a little more flexibility.

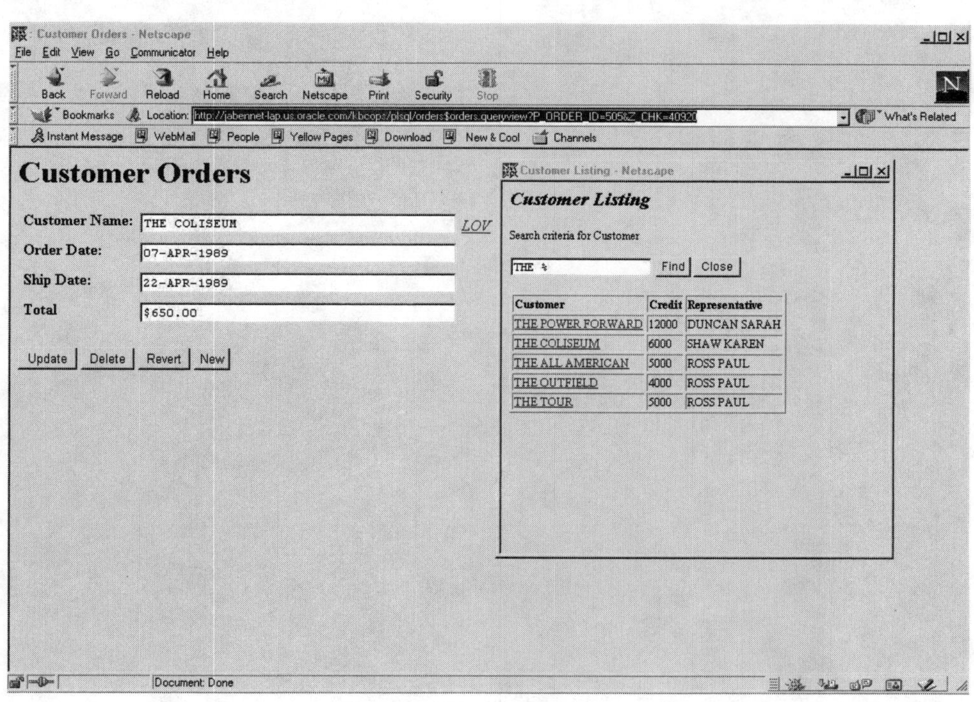

FIGURE 16-9. *Example of a custom LOV*

Summary

This chapter has covered a number of valuable topics for using Designer to generate Web applications. At this point, if you're not familiar with Designer, you should have a good understanding of Designer's capabilities. If you are familiar with Designer, you now have a number of tips and techniques that you can implement for your applications.

CHAPTER 17

Oracle Developer - Forms

ne of the most powerful features that Oracle Developer contains is its capability to be ported to many different platforms. The most popular deployment platform today is the Internet. Is anyone developing new client/server applications anymore? Is client/server deployment dead? The process of deploying Oracle Forms on the Web is a little more complex than deploying in a client/server environment. However, the results of this type of implementation are tremendous. Just think, you can take a form or report and deploy it to your corporate client/server users and then take the same form and make it available to employees over the corporate intranet, an extranet, or even the Internet—code modifications are not even necessary!

If you've followed the Oracle product line like I have over the past 12+ years, you've probably noticed that Oracle continues to support Developer time and time again. You may remember products like OraCard or PowerObjects (refer to the introduction to Chapter 5 for further information). Each of these products generated a lot of hype and confusion about Developer's direction, but in the end these products came and went in a matter of years. I have been using Oracle Forms since version 1, back when it was called IAG. The product has certainly come a long way since then. The Internet architecture and platform further extends your Oracle Forms platform choices.

This chapter will cover the following topics:

- Deciding to use Oracle Forms
- Installing Oracle Forms
- Making sure your icons appear on the Web
- Configuring Oracle Forms as a CGI (noncartridge)
- Configuring Oracle Forms 6.0 as a cartridge
- Configuring Oracle Forms 5.0 as a cartridge
- Creating the Generic Cartridge HTML file
- Understanding the Cartridge URL
- Using a non-Oracle Web server
- Generating and placing your FMX files
- Setting up Forms Server as Windows NT service
- Starting, and stopping the Forms Server Listener
- Configuring the Forms client
- Setting up load-balancing

- Designing Web applications
- What to do when memory requirements are too high for comfort
- Understanding feature restrictions for Forms on the Web
- Finding good papers on Web-enabled Forms
- Analyzing sysdate issues with Oracle8 and Forms 5.0 PL/SQL
- Resolving FRM-40735 messages

Deciding to Use Oracle Forms (Or Not)

Oracle Forms is a tool used for developing interactive GUI screens with robust data validation capabilities. With Oracle Forms, you can quickly develop a form that automatically manages the inserting, updating, and deleting of the underlying data through SQL. If you are already using Oracle Forms, you may be considering deploying these forms on the Web.

What's the alternative to deploying Oracle Forms on the Web? The other options may involve considerably more coding to match the graphical user interface (GUI), powerful data validation capabilities, and automated data manipulation language (DML, which includes insert, update, and delete) management built into Oracle Forms. One alternative is to use HTML Forms and a scripting language (such as JavaScript) for the client side validation and a CGI or cartridge to manipulate the data accordingly. To create forms functionality without using Oracle Forms, your HTML forms will need to be dynamically created with a CGI or cartridge (for example, PL/SQL, Perl, and so forth). You can also develop such code with WebDB, as described in Chapter 5. Another alternative would be to develop a Java applet that provides this capability, developed using a tool like JDeveloper. However, neither method is nearly as easy as developing a form with Oracle Forms.

How It Works

A common misconception is that you create the form in the Oracle Forms Developer module and then you run it through a converter to generate a Java applet. This actually seems like a logical solution—and one that might involve a smaller footprint as well as provide many other advantages—but this is not how it works. The Web deployment of Oracle Forms is a bit more complex than that. The client requests a URL, which points to a virtual path that identifies the Forms cartridge—at which point, an applet is downloaded to the client. This Java applet is capable of painting the form canvas, performing data validation, and communicating with the Forms Server. The Forms Server is a program on the server (the program is a DLL on NT and a shared library on UNIX) that reads and understands a standard FMX file (Oracle Forms executable file format—a platform-specific object-like file format). After reading the FMX file, the cartridge determines how the form should appear and sends this information to the client's Java applet. In turn, the client browser paints the page as it would look if you were running this application in a client/server model. The client's Java applet and the Forms cartridge stay in an open dialog through TCP/IP, similar to a client/server user session communicating over SQL*Net. Therefore, you could say that the Application Server becomes what was traditionally known as the client in the client/server world.

State, Licensing, and Memory

Assuming that you plan to decide between using Oracle Forms or HTML Forms, there are some basic questions that need to be answered before you can make an informed decision. As previously mentioned, similar to a client/server session, Oracle Forms actually maintains state (an active connection throughout the life of the session) over the Web. By using another cartridge, such as the PL/SQL cartridge, a connection to the database is only open upon each request from the time that the requested procedure starts until it ends. However, you must maintain state on your own. This will result in a significant difference in the concurrent user count between using Oracle Forms and the PL/SQL cartridge. Because of the scalability requirements of a typical application, my general rule for PL/SQL cartridge applications is that absolutely no procedure should take longer than one second to run or you (as the developer) need to talk to the resident tuning expert. Refer to Chapter 14 for further information on PL/SQL performance. In general, the average procedure time should be subsecond. Remember that a Forms-based application will connect users to the database from the beginning of the session to the end, nonstop. This will result in significant concurrent user count differences which, in turn, will result in higher RDBMS licensing differences (Oracle likes this). Selecting Oracle Forms over PL/SQL also results in considerably heavier server memory requirements (your hardware vendor likes this). You may respond with something like "we already have an unlimited user license and memory's cheap." Then again, you may not. The memory requirements are obviously higher because the concurrent user count is higher, but the footprint of the Forms cartridge is about 3-12MB per user and the PL/SQL cartridge footprint is about 6MB, yet another thing to consider. However, each version of Developer is improving the memory requirements per user. I have heard that Developer 6.0 has brought this footprint to as low as 1.5MB per user. Each version shares memory more effectively as well.

Existing Forms?

Beyond memory and RDBMS licensing, other factors must be considered when making the decision whether to use Oracle Forms on the Web or write your own HTML Forms and logic. What if you have hundreds of existing Oracle Forms that have been developed and you want to deploy your application on the Web? You certainly would not want to rewrite all of this code, would you? Overnight, Oracle was able to Web-enable their entire suite of products, including Oracle Financials. If this is similar to your situation, take this into consideration.

Browser and Bandwidth

Assuming that you do not have hundreds of forms to convert, numerous browser and bandwidth options must be investigated. Do you have any control over the user's browser? Can you instruct the users that they must run on a specific browser version? Can you inform the users that they must install a plug-in? If the answer to any of these questions is no, Oracle Forms is probably not a candidate for your Web solution. Specifically, Oracle Forms requires Java 1.1 Virtual Machine or subsequent releases be loaded on the client (browser). Java 1.1.is not found in the early browsers. In fact, you must be running Navigator 4.04 with the Java 1.1 patch, Netscape 4.06+, IE 4.0 and Service Patch 1, or IE 4.01 with Service Patch 1. Internet Explorer 5.0 includes Java 1.1. Sun has a plug-in called Java Activator (http://www.javasoft.com/products/plugin/), which is similar to JInitator, Oracle's plug-in that will run the Java 1.1 Virtual Machine on the older browsers. JInitator also includes some other benefits over the standard Java 1.1, most notably that it caches the class files on the client. Consequently, by running JInitiator, your application will run considerably faster than a standard noncached method. Depending on the form, the Java class files range from 300K to 1M in total size. That's a lot of Java to download over a 56K dial-up connection. The second benefit of using JInitiator is that it resolves a number of the bugs in the browser's virtual machine. For example, in Internet Explorer, the status line for your forms does not appear—however, it does if you use JInitiator. If you choose not to use JInitiator, other bugs may cause some major headaches for your users, such as:

1. The server may disconnect from the client after so much free time (5-10 minutes)
2. After executing a number of call_form statements, executing the close_form statement will not close the currently open form
3. Not all items on canvas may display

All of the above items are browser specific issues.

Decision Time

The following questions are instrumental in your decision-making process. Do you have control of the browser? Can your users download an 8-10M program and install it—specifically JInitiator? Do you have *enough* bandwidth? Do you have a number of existing forms? Do you have heavy/intensive user interface requirements? Is it OK if everything does not work, such as a missing status line? Is the concurrent user count a concern? Is total memory usage a concern? After reviewing your options, it may appear as though the decision is almost an intranet versus Internet decision. The other options are numerous, but the most obvious option, in my opinion, is to develop your application (from scratch or using WebDB to generate your code) using the PL/SQL cartridge that dynamically creates HTML and JavaScript code. The footprint of the PL/SQL cartridge is considerably lighter, but so is the robustness and client/server-like functionality.

The bottom line is that, based on the current status of Java in browsers, unless you are planning to run Oracle Forms on your intranet or a special extranet, I would recommend finding another solution. If you have the right fit for Oracle Forms, please continue forward.

Installing Oracle Forms

After making the difficult decision to use Oracle Forms, it's time to perform the installation. It's a very standard and easy Oracle installation process. You must purchase and install Developer Server. You will want to install Patch 4 for Developer 6. However, at the end of the installation, if your new cartridges are not configured correctly, Developer will not work (therefore, the installation is not complete). For each of the Developer cartridges (Forms and Reports), you can elect to install them as a CGI or as a full-blown cartridge. For testing, it's easier to configure and run the CGI versions of each. However, for a production system with higher performance requirements, run the cartridge version of each. To systematically perform the configuration, I would recommend doing the CGI configuration first, progressing to the cartridge version. Be sure to install Developer Server in its own Oracle home director (i.e., separate from OAS).

TIP

Forms 5.0 will work with OWAS 3.0 both as a cartridge and using the CGI method. Under OAS 4.0, Forms 5.0 will only work using the CGI method. However, Forms 6.0 works as a cartridge (or CGI method) under OAS 4.0.

Creating the Virtual Directories

Whether you choose to run your forms using the CGI or cartridge method, virtual directories need to be created on your Web server to be used by the Forms Server. These virtual directories are maintained at a Listener level. Since the Java applet code is in the same physical directory as the Java archive code (JAR files), you can elect to create only one virtual directory for the Java code. However, if you separate the applet files from the JAR files, two virtual directories need to be created. In addition to a virtual directory for the applet and JAR files, a virtual directory will need to be created containing the HTML file that your browser will reference. This could be an existing HTML virtual directory. However, it is preferable to keep the Forms Server HTML files separate from your other HTML files to maintain a clean system. As noted in the following tip, another directory will contain your Forms icon images. The virtual directories that need to be created are as follows:

Virtual Directory Path	Physical Directory	Example
/java_code/	$ORACLE_HOME/forms60/java/	c:\orant\forms60\java\
/forms_html/	An application directory for your Forms HTML files	c:\apps\forms\html\

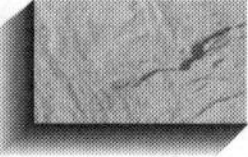

TIP
If you are using Forms 5.0, when you see references to forms60 directories, use forms50 instead.

Making Sure Your Icons Appear on the Web

If Forms applications are deployed on the Web, the icons will not be displayed unless you inform the Forms Server of the location. To view the icons, either put the icons into a directory that currently has a virtual mapping or create a new virtually mapped directory. In addition, create a temporary directory for the boilerplate images and to use run_product. For this example, add a new directory mapping, which will be for a virtual directory called forms_icons:

Virtual Directory Path	Physical Directory	Example
/forms_icons/	Any application directory for the icons will be fine.	C:\orant\forms60\oracle\forms\handler\icons\
/forms_temp/	Any temporary directory will be fine.	c:\apps\temp\

The following environmental parameters need to be established. For Windows NT, the NT system registry needs to be modified. Back up the registry prior to modification. The following four parameters need to be added to

HKEY_LOCAL_MACHINE, SOFTWARE, ORACLE. The first three are new string values, the last is a DWORD value:

Parameter	Parameter Value
FORMS60_MAPPING	/forms_temp/
FORMS60_OUTPUT	c:\apps\temp\
FORMS60_REPFORMAT	HTML
FORMS60_TIMEOUT	3 (minutes before a timeout occurs—3 to 1,440)

Then, edit the registry.dat file; this is not the Windows registry. On NT, this file is located in the $ORACLE_HOME\forms60\java\oracle\forms\registry directory and is called registry.dat. You cannot edit this file with Notepad (Notepad will not wrap the lines properly)—you will need to use another tool, like Wordpad. In this file, you need to change the following line:

```
default.icons.iconpath=
```

to read as follows:

```
default.icons.iconpath=/forms_icons/
```

where /forms_icons/ is a virtual directory pointing to the location of the GIF files. As an alternative, put all the GIF files in the same location as the HTML files.

Configuring Oracle Forms as a CGI (Noncartridge)

To run Oracle Forms as a CGI program, you need to configure the virtual directory mappings, previously noted, and create a static HTML file pointing to each form that can be accessed through a URL. Since the noncartridge implementation requires that each form have a static HTML file pointing to the Oracle Forms for the Web, the initial form is typically the main menu that branches to all of the other forms.

The easiest way to create the static HTML file for each application deployed on the Web is to modify the "static" (noncartridge) HTML file template provided by Oracle. This static.html file is located in the $ORACLE_HOME/tools/devdem60/web directory. Make a copy of this file, placing the copy in the physical location that is equivalent to the virtual /forms_html/ directory. Rename this file to a name relating to your application's name. For example, if your application is a call processing application, you might choose to name the HTML file callproc.html. Next, edit this file in a standard text editor (for example, vi on UNIX or Notepad on Windows).

Based on the virtual directories previously described and assuming the runtime form file (FMX) is in the physical directory of c:\apps\forms\fmx\, the callproc.html would be identical to the following (if you compare this file to the standard file that Oracle provides, the primary differences you will note have to do with the modification of the text and applet tags):

```
<HTML>
<!-- FILE: Callproc.html -->
<HEAD><TITLE>ACME Call Processing Application for the Web</TITLE></HEAD>
<BODY><BR>Please wait while the Forms Client class files download and run.
     <BR>This will take a little while...<P>
<APPLET CODEBASE="/java_code/"
        CODE="oracle.forms.engine.Main"
        ARCHIVE="/java_code/f60all.jar"
        HEIGHT=20
        WIDTH=20>
<PARAM NAME="serverPort"
       VALUE="9000">
<PARAM NAME="serverArgs"
       VALUE="module=c:\apps\forms\fmx\main_menu.fmx">
<PARAM NAME="serverApp"
       VALUE="ACME">
</APPLET>
</BODY>
</HTML>
```

Noncartridge (CGI) URL

The URL that you will provide to your end users simply points to the page we have previously defined. For example, to announce the availability of our new call processing application, the company ACME would broadcast the following URL:

http://www.acme.com/forms_html/callproc.html

ACME's URL consists of the following components:

- Protocol: http
- Domain: www.acme.com
- HTML files virtual directory: /forms_html
- Static HTML file: callproc.html

Configuring Oracle Forms 6.0 as a Cartridge

In a production environment, you will want to configure and use the Forms cartridge to enhance performance. Cartridge servers are persistent—they stay loaded in memory and they can share memory between them like forms. This leads to better performance and lower overall memory requirements. Whereas a CGI program is loaded every time a user makes a request for that program, the cartridge is persistent. Considering that the Forms CGI is roughly 12MB, this is a big CGI program to be loading with each new request. Performance will be enhanced using the cartridge implementation versus CGI. However, it is more difficult to set up the cartridge than noncartridge method. If you elect not to use OAS, you can't use cartridges.

Up to this point, other than minor directory changes, the Forms 5.0 and Forms 6.0 installations are pretty much the same. Forms 5.0 will not work (as a cartridge) with OAS 4.0, but Forms 6.0 will. After setting up your OAS 4.0 server, to create a Forms Web cartridge, follow these steps. From the OAS Welcome page, click OAS Manager. In the OAS Manager navigational tree, click the + icon beside the Web site icon, then click the Applications icon. Click the Add icon to display the Add Application form. In the Add Application form's Application Type field, specify CWEB and click Apply. In the Add form's Application Name field, specify the name of your application—for example, forms. In the Display Name field, specify the display name—for example, My application forms. In the Application Version field, specify a version number, such as 1.0, and then click Apply. In the Success dialog box, click "Add Cartridge to this Application." In the Add CWEB Cartridge form, enter the appropriate information into the following fields and then click Apply:

Field	**Value to specify**
Cartridge	Forms60Cartridge
Display Name	Forms60Cartridge
Cartridge Shared Object	d:\orant\bin\ifwebc60.dll
Entry Point (Shared Object)	form_entry
Virtual Path	/forms

Next, prior to OAS 4.0.8, you need to refresh the navigational tree. This is accomplished by pressing the SHIFT key, then clicking Reload in your browser; this will update the navigational tree. Now it's time to set the (Forms) application configuration properties. First, navigate to your application's Configuration folder by expanding the appropriate tree nodes in the Navigator. Within the Configuration folder, click Web Parameters. In the Listener List field, specify a Listener and click Apply. Next click on Cartridge Parameters, then enter the parameters and values and click Apply when you are finished:

Field	Description	Value
Code	The starting point for your Forms cartridge.	oracle.forms.engine.Main
Codebase	The name of the virtual directory you defined to point to the physical directory for $ORACLE_HOME\forms60\java\.	/java_code/
BaseHTML	The physical directory path and filename for the base HTML file accessed by your cartridge at runtime. Do not specify a virtual directory location when defining the baseHTML parameter. At runtime, the Forms Server uses the baseHTML file, along with the application's cartridge settings and URL, to dynamically create a new HTML file.	c:\apps\forms\html\forms.html (Refer to the notes on creating this file.)
HTMLdelimiter	The one-character delimiter used to denote parameter values in the application's cartridge HTML file. The delimiter can be any character. The default is % (percent symbol).	^

There are a number of optional cartridge parameters that you can elect to set. These include the following:

Field	Description	Value
archive	The virtual directory path and filename of any JAR files you want downloaded to the end-user's browser at application startup.	c:\orant\forms60\java\f60web.jar
ServerApp	The name of the application class you want to apply to the application. Use application classes for creating application-specific font mapping and icon path settings.	Acme
MetricsServerHost, MetricsServerPort, MetricsServerErrorURL, MetricsDomainName, and MetricsTimeout	Load-balancing parameters that allow you to dynamically balance the load of multiple Forms Servers across systems.	

Configuring Oracle Forms 5.0 as a Cartridge

Even though Forms 5.0 will not run on OAS 4.0 (as a cartridge), you may be running OWAS 3.0 and be curious about the setup. To run Oracle Forms as a cartridge, configure the virtual directory mappings as previously noted, create a generic cartridge HTML file, and create the cartridge in OWAS 3.0.

Assuming OWAS 3.0 is already installed and running, go the cartridge administration page and click on Add New Cartridge, where you will manually configure the new cartridge. The OAS will prompt for a number of new fields. The following is what is to be specified for each of the values:

Field	Example	Explanation
Cartridge Name	`Forms50`	The cartridge name

Field	Example	Explanation
Object Path	NT: `%ORACLE_HOME%\bin\f50webc.dll` UNIX: `$ORACLE_HOME/lib/f50webc.so`	The directory path and filename of the Forms Cartridge Handler
Entry Point	`form_entry`	form_entry is the name of the entry point routine in the cartridge shared library. This is the required value.
Minimum # of Instances	`5`	The minimum number of users that can simultaneously connect to the Forms cartridge.
Maximum # of Instances	`100`	The maximum number of users that can simultaneously connect to the Forms cartridge.
Virtual Path	`/forms`	At runtime, end users pass URLs (HTTP requests) to your Web server. If a request contains the virtual directory associated with your cartridge, the Web server automatically transfers the request to the Web Request Broker (WRB). Then, the Web Request Broker starts the cartridge associated with the virtual directory. When defining the virtual path, do not include a trailing slash.
Physical Path	NT: `%ORACLE_HOME%\bin\` UNIX: `$ORACLE_HOME/lib/`	The directory path for the Forms Cartridge Handler.

Once the information has been entered in the preceding fields, you can click Register New Cartridge. OAS will register the cartridge and create a link to your cartridge in the OAS home page. Click on your cartridge link (forms) to display the Cartridge Configuration page. Click on Cartridge Specific Parameters, then enter the following parameters and parameter values (it is important to remember that these cartridge parameters and parameter values are case sensitive):

Parameter	Example	Explanation
BaseHTML	`C:\apps\forms\html\forms.html` (see notes below on creating this file)	Enter the physical directory path and filename for the base cartridge HTML file (created above) accessed by the Forms cartridge at runtime.
HTMLdelimiter	^	Enter the one-character delimiter used to denote parameter values in the application's cartridge HTML file. The delimiter can be any character. The default is % (percent sign). Note that we used a carat (^) in the forms.html file shown above.

A number of optional cartridge parameters should be specified, including the following:

Parameter	Example	Explanation
Archive	`/java_code/f50web.jar`	Provide the virtual directory path and filename of any JAR file(s) you want downloaded to end-users' Web browsers at application startup.
Code	`oracle.forms.uiClient.v1_4.engine.Main`	This is the starting code applet for the forms engine.
Codebase	`%ORACLE_HOME%\forms50\java\`	Enter the name of the virtual directory you defined to point to the physical directory.
serverApp	`ACME`	Enter the name of the application class you wish to apply to the application. Use application classes for creating application-specific font mapping and icon path settings.

Parameter	Example	Explanation
serverPort	`9000`	Enter the number of the port on which the Forms Server Listener process was started. In most cases, the port is 9000 (the default).
<forms_param>	`Module=^modname^`	Enter valid Forms command-line parameters (such as module) and corresponding values.
<user_param>	`Userid=^userval^`	Enter valid user-defined parameters and corresponding values.

After modifying these parameters, click Modify Cartridge Configuration. Cartridges fall into the WRB; then, to deploy the changes all of the Listeners and the WRB must be stopped and restarted.

Creating the Generic Cartridge HTML File

The easiest way to create the generic cartridge HTML file for applications you deploy on the Web is to modify the cartridge HTML file template provided by Oracle. This file is located in the $ORACLE_HOME/tools/devdem60/web physical directory. Make a copy of the cartridge.html file, placing the copy in the physical location that is equivalent to the virtual /forms_html/ directory. Rename this file to a name that makes sense to you. For example, you could name the HTML file forms.html. Next, you will edit this file in a standard text editor (for example, vi on UNIX or Notepad on Windows). Based on the virtual directories previously described, the forms.html would appear identical to the following. If you compare this file to the standard file that Oracle provides, the primary differences to be noted pertain to the modification of the text and applet tags. You will also notice the HTML file shown here (forms.html) is similar to the static file above (Callproc.html)—a significant addition to the following routine over the preceding routine is the handling of JInitiator:

```
<HTML>
<!-- FILE: forms.html -->
<!-- This html assumes the following: -->
<!--  You are using JInitiator version 1.1.5.3-->
<!--  You want to use both Internet Explorer and Netscape as Browsers-->
<!--  You have the jinit_download.html file located at forms_html -->
```

```
<!--  You have set up your web server with the following virtual directories: -->
<!--  java_code/ maps to the physical directory oracle_home\forms60\java -->
<!--  /forms_html/ maps to the physical directory where html and the -->
<!--        j-initiator executable is located -->
<HEAD><TITLE>ACME Web Applications</TITLE></HEAD>
<BODY>
<P><OBJECT classid="clsid:9F77a997-F0F3-11d1-9195-00C04FC990DC"
        WIDTH=800
        HEIGHT=600
        codebase="http://www.acme.com/forms_html/jinit11711.exe">
<PARAM NAME="CODE"          VALUE="oracle.forms.engine.Main" >
<PARAM NAME="CODEBASE"      VALUE="/java_code/" >
<PARAM NAME="ARCHIVE"       VALUE="/java_code/f60all.jar" >
<PARAM NAME="type"
VALUE="application/x-jinit-applet;version=1.1.7.1">
<PARAM NAME="serverPort" VALUE="9000">
<PARAM NAME="serverArgs" VALUE="module=^modname^ userid=^usrval^">
<PARAM NAME="serverApp"  VALUE="ACME">
<COMMENT>
<EMBED type="application/x-jinit-applet;version=1.1.7.1"
       java_CODE="oracle.forms.engine.Main"
       java_CODEBASE="/java_code/"
       java_ARCHIVE="/java_code/f60all.jar"
       WIDTH=800
       HEIGHT=600
       serverPort="9000"
       serverArgs="module=^modname^ userid=^usrval^"
       serverApp="ACME"
       pluginspage="http://www.acme.com/forms_html/jinit_download.html">
  <NOEMBED>
</COMMENT>
</NOEMBED></EMBED>
</OBJECT>
</BODY>
</HTML>
```

The preceding example references the page jinit_download.html. If the user does not have JInitiator loaded, this page will instruct them how to retrieve JInitiator. The file appears identical to the following example:

```
<HTML>
<HEAD>
   <TITLE>Oracle JInitiator 1.1.7.1 Download Page</TITLE>
</HEAD>

<h1>Oracle JInitiator 1.1.7.1 Download Page</h1>

<hr size="3" noshade>
```

```
<br>

<BODY>
This page requires Oracle's JInitiator plug-in or ActiveX
component.  If you have already configured your browser
to use Oracle JInitiator, please wait while your browser
loads it and downloads your Oracle Developer application.

<P>If your browser has not been configured to use Oracle
JInitiator, this page will allow you to download it now.
Save the file (jinit1171.exe) when you are prompted. When
it finishes downloading, go to the location you saved it in
Explorer and double-click the executable. When the installation
has finished, exit your browser session, then restart it and
return to this page. The browser will then load Oracle JInitiator
and download your Oracle Developer application.
<BR> 

<P><A HREF="jinit1171.exe">
Download the Oracle JInitiator 1.1.7.1 plug-in.</A>

<BR> 
<P><B>System Requirements</B><BR>

<P>The Oracle JInitiator supports the following configurations:
<BR> 
<TABLE>

<TR VALIGN=TOP>
<TD>Platform</TD>
<TD>Internet Explorer 3.0.2 </TD>
<TD>Internet Explorer 4.0 </TD>
<TD>Navigator 3.0 </TD>
<TD>Navigator 4.0** </TD>
</TR>

<TR VALIGN=TOP>
<TD>Windows 95* </TD>
<TD></TD>
<TD>X </TD>
<TD>X </TD>
<TD>X </TD>
</TR>

<TR VALIGN=TOP>
<TD>Windows NT* </TD>
<TD>X </TD>
<TD>X </TD>
<TD>X </TD>
<TD>X </TD>
```

```
</TR>
</TABLE>

<BR>
* Oracle JInitiator 1.1.7.1 does not currently support
  Microsoft's Active Desktop.

<BR><BR>
** Oracle JInitiator 1.1.7.1 does not currently support
Netscape Navigator 4.04 with the JDK 1.1 Smart Update, due to
a bug in Netscape's Smart Update. Please use Netscape Navigator
4.04 without the Smart Update, or use other versions
of Netscape Navigator.

<BR>
<BR>Other minimum system requirements for the Oracle JInitiator on
<BR>Win32 are as follows:
<BR>
<BR>- Pentium 90 MHz or better processor
<BR>- 12 MB free hard disk space (recommended 20 MB)
<BR>- 16 MB system RAM (recommended 24 MB)

<P><B>Note:</B> Oracle JInitiator works
best over direct LAN (Ethernet)
<BR>connections. It will also function properly over dial-up modem
<BR>(28.8 or better).

<p><hr size="3" noshade>
<table border="0" width="100%">
    <tr>
        <td valign="top"><font size="1">Copyright )1998 <a
        href="http://www.oracle.com/">Oracle Corporation
        </font></a><font size="1"> All Rights Reserved. <br>
        Last update: 9/16/98.<br>
        Questions, comments, etc: Please contact your local
        Oracle support representative.
            </td>
    </tr>
</table>
<p>  </p>

</BODY>
</HTML>
```

Understanding the Cartridge URL

The cartridge URL to be provided to your end users simply points to the virtual host of the cartridge as previously defined. If you did not hardcode the form name into the cartridge file (forms.html), then specify the name of the form that you wish to run. For example, to announce the availability of our new call processing application, the company ACME would broadcast the following URL:

http://www.acme.com/forms?modname=main_menu

ACME's URL consists of the following components:

- Protocol: http
- Domain: www.acme.com
- Forms cartridge virtual directory: /forms
- Forms module to start: main_menu.fmx

Using a Non-Oracle Web Server

You may elect to use a Web server other than OAS (or OWAS), in which case you have a few different choices when using Developer Server. First, if you purchase the Developer Server, it comes with OAS. If you desire, you could install and use OAS. If you are using Microsoft IIS, Netscape Enterprise, or an Apache Listener, you will be able to register OAS as an external Listener (covered in Chapter 8). If you are using a Listener other than those previously listed, you could install OAS on another port (e.g., 8080) and run all of your Developer requests through that port, or you could elect to simply run the CGI versions of each of the Developer programs.

Generating and Placing Your FMX Files

To run a form through a browser, you must first generate a form into a runtime executable. This file will have an extension of FMX and is commonly referred to as an FMX file. You *must* generate the FMX on the platform that OAS is running on. After creating a form, Oracle Forms will automatically create a forms definition file with an extension of FMB. To generate the runtime executable, Forms provides you with the option that allows you to generate the runtime executable using File | Administration | Compile File or CTRL-T. Place the FMX file into a directory that your Forms Server will be able to access (any OAS directory). Specify the exact placement of the FMX file when referring to the Form. The Forms Server itself will search the $ORACLE_HOME/bin directory first, then the $FORMS60_PATH directory. If you do not wish to specify the exact directory location of your runtime executable, place your form into one of the two previously named directories.

Developer 6.0 on NT also enables you to run a form directly from the Form Builder using Run Form Web on the toolbar. This displays the form as it would appear in a browser window without having to deploy the executables to a server during development.

Setting Up Forms Server as Windows NT Service

On Windows NT, the Forms Server is best run as an NT service, even though you can also run the Forms Server as a nonservice as noted below. As with any other NT service, you can configure the Forms Server service to be started manually or automatically when the system is brought up. After the installation of Oracle Forms to set up the Forms Server as an NT service, execute the following at the command line:

```
ifsrv60 -install fsrv60
```

At this point, your Forms Server is now registered as an NT service. You can now go into the Control Panel's Services page and look for the entry "Forms Server60 for fsrv60." Click Startup. *This next step is critical.* From the Startup dialog box, select This Account on the Log On As section and type in your operating system username and password. This specifies that the Forms Server is being run under a specific operating system account (this account can be the administrator, but you simply need a valid account that also has a default printer established). In addition, you can also set the service to be started automatically (when the system is booted up) or manually. If you want the Forms Server to start after each system boot, set this to Automatic.

Starting and Stopping the Forms Server Listener

The Forms Server runs on an individual port. The communication from the browser to the Web Server is made through the standard HTTP port (usually the standard HTTP port is port 80). The Web Server will communicate with the Forms Server through the Forms Server's port (port 9000 is the default port number that the Forms Server uses). The Forms Server is in the $ORACLE_HOME/bin directory and is named ifsrv60 (Forms 5.0 is f50srv32) on NT, and ifsrvm60 (Forms 5.0 is f60srvm) on UNIX. This process accepts a parameter of "port," which specifies the port that the Forms Server is listening on. To start this process on NT, from the NT taskbar select Start | Programs | Oracle Developer R6.0, then run the Forms Server Listener. Under UNIX, ensure that the process is executed as a background process. The command from a shell prompt would be (assuming $ORACLE_HOME/bin is in your path) ifsrv60 -listen &. You may want to consider using nohup (no hangup) for the startup of the UNIX processes. The default port number is 9000. If you do not specify the port parameter, the Forms Server Listener will start on port 9000. You only need to change this port number if it is conflicting with another process using port 9000 on your system. I leave this set to 9000.

To check the status of the Forms Server Listener under NT, go to the Process tab in the Task Manager and find the IFSRV60 processes. Each active connection will have a Forms Server running. Under UNIX, at a shell prompt type **ps -ef | grep ifrunw60**, which should display an ifrunw60 process for each active connection. There will also be one ifsrvm60 process running.

To stop the process on NT, after viewing the status of the process, click End Process. Under UNIX, kill each of the ifrun60w processes and the ifsrvm60 process as listed when you viewed the process status.

Configuring the Forms Client

When an end user starts up a Web-enabled Form Builder application, the Forms Client (and related Java class files) downloads from the Application Server to the user's browser. As the user continues interacting with the application, additional Java class files are downloaded on an as-needed basis. However, you can control how class files are downloaded to the user's browser. There are two methods: 1)*incremental* (the default), in which only those class files required to render the initial state of the application are downloaded at startup, and 2) *bundled*, where one or more "bundles" of class files are downloaded to the client machine at application startup. The advantage of the bundled option is that each bundle downloads in a single network roundtrip. The disadvantage is the initial download may take longer than under the incremental method. You explicitly specify each of the Java class files that should be loaded rather than referencing a JAR file. To figure out how to create your own JAR files or bundles, you can read about it in the Oracle documentation as well as on Javasoft's Web site at www.javasoft.com.

Setting Up Load Balancing

The load-balancing feature enables you to dynamically balance the load of multiple Forms Servers across systems. Load-balancing directs a Forms Client to connect to a Forms Server running on the least loaded system available. Which system is least loaded is determined by a count of the total number of processes running on that system. The "Performance & Tuning" chapter of the OAS 4.0 online documentation contains a considerable amount of information on configuring a system for maximum performance and good load-balancing techniques. OAS 4.0 offers many more options for load-balancing than does OWAS 3.0. Chapter 4 also discusses load balancing.

Designing Web Applications

Are Web applications different than client/server applications? Yes, primarily with regard to bandwidth etiquette. Keep in mind that Web applications imply a "thin client." Not only should the requirements on the client be thin, but the bandwidth requirements should be even thinner. When developing Web applications, seriously consider network factors that could affect the performance of your Web applications. Consider how your application will interact with a security firewall or what will happen under heavy user loads. When developing client/server applications, you should be concerned about frequent network roundtrips from the client to the server. For Web applications, the same level of conscientiousness for roundtrips from the application to the database servers would be ideal. It's also important to limit the number of images (page and background) included in your forms and reports. This increases bandwidth requirements, and each time an image is required, it must be downloaded from the Application Server. This could burden the Application Server during heavy loads. To display a company logo, for example, include the image in the HTML page that downloads at application startup instead of retrieving it from the database. You should always optimize your network connections where possible. Further essential information can be found regarding SQL*Net in the SQL*Net documentation.

As with any Oracle application, you should always design your queries to execute as efficiently as possible and ensure PL/SQL program units are compiled. For further information regarding PL/SQL, refer to *Oracle PL/SQL Tips and Techniques* by Joseph Trezzo (Oracle Press). Bad SQL code can pull down the entire performance of your database server and, in turn, your entire Web application. For more information on performance tuning, refer to *Oracle Performance Tuning Tips and Techniques* by Richard Niemiec (Oracle Press).

Reducing Network Traffic

To cut down on the number of network roundtrips required for users to operate your Forms application, consider reducing or eliminating the following features in your applications:

- **Mouse triggers** Including When-Mouse-Click, When-Mouse-DoubleClick, When-Mouse-Down, and When-Mouse-Up triggers in your forms will impact speed and performance; the Forms Client must communicate with the Forms Server (necessitating a network roundtrip) each time one of these triggers fires. The When-Mouse-Move trigger is not supported due to the high number of network roundtrips required each time that it fires.
- **Timers** If your form includes a timer that fires every 1/100th of a second, end users face the performance ramifications of 6,000 network roundtrips every minute. Either reduce the number of timers in your forms or change the timing interval on which your timers fire.

Selecting Fonts

Most fonts are not supported across all platforms. For example, Sans Serif is a commonly used font in Microsoft Windows applications. However, Sans Serif is not available in UNIX. When a font is not available on a platform, Forms will attempt to use a similar font.

At runtime, the Forms Server maps a form's fonts into their Java equivalents. Then, Java renders the font in a font predefined for the deployment platform. To convert your form's fonts into Java equivalents, Java uses an alias list located in the registry.dat file, which is discussed earlier in this chapter.

The following table lists the Java fonts and their equivalents on the major deployment platforms:

Java Font	Windows Font	X Windows Font	Macintosh Font
Courier	Courier New	adobe-courier	Courier
Dialog	MS Sans Serif	b&h-lucida	Geneva
DialogInput	MS Sans Serif	b&h-lucidatypewriter	Geneva
Helvetica	Arial	adobe-helvetica	Helvetica
Symbol	WingDings	itc-zapfdingbats	Symbol
TimesRoman	Times New Roman	adobe-times	Times Roman

If a font from your form does not map to a Java font (through the Form Builder font alias table), Java automatically assigns a Java font to the unmapped application font. To change the Java font alias scheme, edit registry.dat as previously noted. As a result, when designing forms to deploy on the Web, be sure to follow the font guidelines, discussed in the online documentation.

Memory Requirements Too High for Comfort?

When I first read the Forms memory requirements, I was a bit concerned. The requirements are about 12MB per user session. However, when I have shared this concern with hundreds of companies, their response has been "memory is cheap" every time. It has never once been an issue with anyone, because the form is actually running on the server. Since the client is only screen painting, it is a very server-heavy process. However, the more complex the form, the more memory it will consume per user. Remember that the more users you have, the more memory will be shared across forms.

Understanding Feature Restrictions for Forms on the Web

When designing forms to eventually be deployed on the Web, remember that certain Form Builder features behave differently or not at all when a form is deployed on the Web. The following table lists Form Builder features, whether the feature is supported on the Web, and provides notes or guidelines about the feature:

Feature	Supported?	Guidelines and Notes
ActiveX, OCX, OLE, VBX	No	Third-party controls that display screen output on the Application Server are not supported because end users cannot view the output.
Combo boxes	Yes	Available in Developer/2000 release 2.1, pending Java implementation of combination box widget.
Console	Yes	To display the console (includes the status and message lines) to end users, set the form-level property Console Window to the window in which you wish to display the console.
Firewall	Yes	To deploy Form Builder applications on the Internet, you must run the Forms Server outside a security firewall (if any), and you must have a tunnel (through the firewall) that supports SQL*Net.
HOST_COMMAND, ORA_FFI, USER_EXIT	Yes	Calls to these functions often display visual output or GUI elements on end-users' machines in client/server mode. In a Web implementation, the same calls will display the output and GUI elements on the Application Server (where end users cannot see or interact with them).
Iconic buttons	Yes	Icon image files must be in GIF format (and not in ICO format), and must reside in the same directory as the HTML page or Web cartridge.

Feature	Supported?	Guidelines and Notes
MDI (window and toolbars)	No	If the console or any toolbars are assigned to the Multiple Document Interface (MDI) window, you must reassign them to another window in your Form Builder application.
NLS, BIDI	Yes	Supported for 8-bit languages only.
When-Mouse-Enter/ Leave/Move triggers	No	Each execution of the trigger requires a network roundtrip, creating a negative impact in performance.
Sound Items (5.0 and 6.0)	No	Sound items are not supported in Web deployment.

Finding Good Papers on Web-Enabled Forms

As of the release of this book, three white papers are available on the Oracle site (www.oracle.com) providing additional reference for reviewing Oracle's capabilities to support Web-enabled Forms and Oracle's approach to Web-enabling Oracle Forms. The first is titled "Developer/2000: Project Java Activator and Browser Support." This paper addresses the use of the Java Activator (JInitiator) and how it makes Web applications, using Forms, browser independent. Basically, by adopting this front end for running your Java Applets, you can be platform and browser independent. Another paper is called "Tuning Developer/2000 Application Performance on the Web", a little older (11/97) but informative. It speaks to the use of applets and optimizing the deployment of applets to the user's browser. The third document is called "Building Database Applications for the Web." This white paper includes further information on graphics and Web fundamentals.

Analyzing sysdate Issues with Oracle8 and Forms 5.0 PL/SQL

A bug exists with a Forms 5.0 bug in the built-in PL/SQL Engine that does not interpret parameters defaulted to SYSDATE or USER for stored program units within an Oracle8 database. If a program unit has been stored with parameters using SYSDATE or USER functions as defaults, any attempt to compile a reference to this procedure from within Forms will fail if all of the parameters are not being sent. For example:

```
create or replace procedure test1 ( p1 DATE := sysdate )
is
begin
  null;
end;
```

Files that were previously compiled, *.FMX files, do seemingly still work, but any recompilation would fail.

The Forms 5.0 bug was discovered when we upgraded to Oracle8. As a result, we issued a tar (#11435816.600) for this bug, of which Oracle was unaware. The workarounds that we came up with include not implementing defaulted parameters, creating your own function that returns SYSDATE or USER as values and referencing this function in your procedure headers, or implementing package variables that are defaulted to these built-ins and referencing these variables in your procedure headers.

A second workaround is as follows:

```
-- New function
create or replace function sys_date
   return date is
begin
   return (sysdate);
end;

-- Modified procedure header
create or replace procedure test1 (p1 date := sys_date )
is
begin
   null;
end;
```

The following syntax is another workaround:

```
-- New global package header
create or replace package generic is
   sys_date DATE := SYSDATE;
end;

-- Modified procedure header
create or replace procedure test1 (p1 date := generic.sys_date )
is
begin
   null;
end;
```

Resolving FRM-40735 Messages

The FRM-40735 error is raised from an ON-INSERT trigger unhandled exception, ORA-01400. If you look at the line following the error message after the ORA-01400 statement, it will reveal the procedure causing the problem. It could be a setup issue or a possible bug. However, this error typically occurs when you have invalid objects in the Oracle database. In Oracle Applications, this commonly occurs after patches have been applied and when changes have been made to your procedures. Therefore, consider establishing a standing requirement for the DBA to check for invalid objects and disabled triggers. You can also recompile the entire schema's packages and procedures.

This could be the result of a recompilation of a PL/SQL package specification, which is typically due to the remote_dependencies_mode parameter. You don't want recompile package specifications unless something actually changed in the specification. Some graphic editors (such as T.O.A.D., www.toadsoft.com) automatically recompile the package specification if you edit the package contents, so be careful.

Summary

As of version 6.0, the Forms Server component of Oracle Developer is not ready for prime-time general Internet deployment. However, the section labeled "Deciding to Use Oracle Forms (Or Not)" will help you to determine whether the Oracle Forms cartridge is right for your project. The best news of all is that with each new version of Developer, the restrictions, limitations, and problems lessen, so if it's not a fit for your project today, keep an eye out for the future.

CHAPTER 18

Oracle Developer – Reports

ven though Oracle Forms may not be ready for prime-time Internet deployment, Oracle Reports certainly is ready. Oracle Reports enables you to generate files for display on the Web in the following formats:

- HTML can be displayed in an HTML 3.0-compliant Web browser, such as Netscape version 2.2 or subsequent releases.
- HTML with cascading style sheets (HTMLCSS) can be displayed by an HTML 3.0-compliant Web browser that supports cascading style sheets, such as Microsoft Internet Explorer 3.01 or subsequent releases.
- Portable Document Format (PDF) can be displayed in a standalone or plug-in PDF viewer, such as Adobe Acrobat Reader. The *huge* advantage of PDF over every other format is that PDF output is a "what you see is what you get" format. In other words, the pages break where you expect them to break and pages can contain headers and footers. Other advantages would include the capability to zoom in and out of a page and the capability to view the output in an outline format that enables hyperlinks to additional information.

While it is possible to generate HTML or PDF output without changing your report definition, the report is often more useful on the Web if you add Web functionality to it (for example, bookmarks and hypertext links). The Web Wizard in Report Builder is the quickest way to deploy a static report to the Web. It enables you to add basic Web functionality and generate HTML or PDF output immediately. If you want to add further Web functionality or tweak what the Web Wizard has done, you can use the Report Editor and/or the Object Navigator.

Web functionality in a report is ignored when you are not generating HTML or PDF. Adding Web functionality will not interfere with your capability to run the report to more traditional destination types (printers, ASCII files, and so forth).

In this chapter, the following topics will be covered:

- Deploying reports on the Web
- Setting up the Reports Server – general information
- Configuring Oracle Reports as a CGI

- Configuring Oracle Reports 6.0 as a cartridge
- Configuring Oracle Reports 3.0 as a cartridge
- Setting optional Reports parameters
- Specifying URL run requests for Reports
- Adding Web functionality
- Prompting for the parameter form
- Configuring the default printer for Oracle Reports on UNIX
- Identifying Reports Server errors
- Running multiple reports concurrently
- Using MetaLink to figure out why RUN_PRODUCT fails
- Creating headers, footers, and page breaks for Web pages
- Resolving the PDF issue in IE (and AOL)
- Suggesting Oracle Reports performance tips
- Developing data to generate Acrobat PDF files

Deploying Reports on the Web

If you want to develop reports that pull information from your Oracle database and report it on the Web, Oracle Reports for the Web Developer Server is your answer. As with the Oracle Forms implementation, you have a similar choice for implementation of Reports—CGI or cartridge method. The CGI method is easier to set up. While the cartridge method is more difficult to set up, it is considerably more robust and scalable. Because the cartridge method is more difficult to set up, if you are going to use this method I would highly recommend setting up the CGI Reports first. The benefit of the Oracle cartridge technology is that cartridges are persistent, or in other words, they stay loaded in memory. On a UNIX system we noticed as much as a ten-second load time for the CGI versus virtually no load time for the cartridge method.

Reports deployed on the Web are created in the same way you create them in any other environment, using the Report Wizard and the Report Editor. The Web

Wizard enables you to quickly add basic Web functionality, such as bookmarks, and deploy the report to the Web in a static form. The Report Editor enables you to add more advanced functionality, such as custom report escapes and URLs, for running the report dynamically on the Web (in real-time).

After the reports you want to deploy on the Web are ready, generate them and copy the RDF files to the appropriate directory on the Oracle Application Server file system. Be sure to generate the RDF files on the same platform as the Oracle Application Server on which you will deploy them.

Setting Up the Reports Server – General Information

Whether you plan to use the CGI or the cartridge method to run your reports, you will need to set up a Reports Server. The setup of the Reports Server varies between platforms. The following sections describe the setup on each major platform. The online documentation, found in the Oracle Developer Online Manuals on the Oracle Developer R6.0 Docs menu, also contains information on setting up and using the Reports Server.

TIP
Reports 3.0 will work with OWAS 3.0 both as a cartridge and using the CGI method. Under OAS 4.0, Reports 3.0 will only work using the CGI method. However, Reports 6.0 works as a cartridge (or CGI method) under OAS 4.0.

TIP
The online documentation for Reports 3.0 can be found in the r30mtsus.htm file.

Setting Up Reports on OAS

Reports 6.0 is best suited for OAS 4.0. This section will cover the setup requirements for Reports 6.0, and also the setup of Reports 3.0 on OWAS 3.0. Reports 3.0 is best suited for OWAS 3.0.

Setting Up Reports Server for Windows NT as a Service

On Windows NT, the Reports Server is best run as an NT service, although you can also run the Reports Server as a nonservice. Setting up the Reports Server as a nonservice is well described in manuals and because I am not sure why you would want to do this, I will not cover it in this section. As with any other service, you can configure the Reports Server service to be started manually or automatically when the system is brought up. After the installation of Oracle Reports from the Developer Server CD, a few steps need to be taken to ensure the Reports Server is an NT service.

The first step may seem odd—to edit (with Notepad or your favorite text editor) your tnsnames.ora file. This seems like an odd place to register the Reports Server to me, but this is how you make it work. On Windows platforms, people typically edit their tnsnames.ora file with the SQL*Net Easy Configuration tool. Remember that once you modify the TNSNAMES.ora file manually, you will not be able to edit the file with the Easy Configuration tool there after. You will find your tnsnames.ora file in the $ORACLE_HOME\network\admin\ directory for SQL*Net 2.1 and in $ORACLE_HOME\net80\admin\ directory for Net8. Edit the file and add the following line:

```
<tnsname> = (ADDRESS=(PROTOCOL=tcp)(HOST=<hostname>)(PORT=<portnum>))
```

where <tnsname> is the name of the Reports Server instance, <hostname> is the IP address or domain name of the Reports Server, and <portnum> is the port number to which the Reports Server is listening. Below is an example entry in tnsnames.ora:

```
rptsrv.world=(ADDRESS=(PROTOCOL=tcp)(HOST=www.acme.com)(PORT=1949))
```

Using the preceding example, your Reports Server will be named rptsrv, will be placed on the www.acme.com host, will use TCP/IP for the protocol, and will communicate on port 1949 (a random number, but it cannot conflict with another TCP/IP service's port).

Next, you need to install the Reports Server as an NT service by running the following command line (depending on the Reports version):

Reports 6.0

```
rwmts60 -install rptsrv tcpip
```

Reports 3.0

```
r30mts32 -install rptsrv tcpip
```

If you did not call your Reports Server rptsrv, you will need to replace this accordingly. At this point, your Reports Server is now registered as an NT service. Go into the Control Panel's Services page and look for the entry "Reports Server60 for rptsrv" for Reports 6.0 or "Developer/2000 Reports Multi-tier Server for rptsrv" for Reports 3.0. Click Startup. *This next step is critical.* From the Startup dialog box, select This Account on the Log On As section and type in your operating system username and password. This specifies that the Reports Server is being run as you (it can be the administrator, but you need a valid account that also has a default printer established). In addition, you can also set the service to be started automatically (when the system is booted up) or manually. If you want the Reports Server to start after each system boot, set this to Automatic.

Start the service from the Control Panel by selecting the service and clicking Start. Once the service has started for the first time, a configuration file is created. The file is in the $ORACLE_HOME\report60\server\ directory (report30 for Reports 3.0) and in this example is named rptsrv.ora (the name it was registered with in the tnsnames file). Several parameters in this file can be edited. If you edit the file and change any parameters, the Reports Server does not pick up the changes until you shut it down and restart it (just like any listener). Refer to the list, presented in the section " Reports Server Configuration File," of parameters in this file that can be changed.

You can run multiple Reports Servers on one machine. If you do this, make sure that you specify different port numbers for each Reports Server.

Starting the Reports Server Under UNIX

On UNIX, after you have installed Oracle Reports from the Developer Server CD, a few steps must be taken to ensure the Reports Server is running in the background on UNIX.

As described in the preceding NT section, the first step is to edit the tnsnames.ora file. This step is identical between platforms. Set tns_admin to the location of tnsnames.ora (for example, $ORACLE_HOME/network/admin), then run the following command line to the background to start the Reports Server on UNIX:

Reports 6.0

```
rwmts60m name=rptsrv &
```

Reports 3.0

```
r30mtsm name=rptsrv &
```

Place the preceding command into your .rc script for the UNIX system to automatically start every time the system is rebooted.

Reports Server Configuration File

The Reports Server configuration file (as previously mentioned—the file is located in the $ORACLE_HOME\report60\server\ directory and is named rptsrv.ora) specifies the parameters for the Reports Server. When the Reports Server is started, it retrieves a tns name to listen to from the installation or the command line. The server then identifies the configuration file with the tns name as its filename and .ora as its file extension in $ORACLE_HOME\report60\server directory. If the configuration file is not present, a default one is created.

The following are formats of the configuration file:

```
identifier=string
maxconnect=number
sourcedir=path
cachedir=directory
tempdir=directory
cachesize=number
minengine=number
maxengine=number
initengine=number
maxidle=number
security=number
englife=number
```

A few things are worthwhile to note. If two servers are running on the same Windows machine, they will have to share the same $ORACLE_HOME, $REPORTS60_PATH, and $REPORTS60_TMP logical directories. However, each server listens to a different tns name and has a unique configuration file, which can specify different sourcedir, cachedir, and tempdir settings, optionally on different drives.

The minengine, maxengine, maxidle, and cachesize settings can be viewed and changed from the Reports Queue Manager. The queue administrator user ID and password can also be changed from the Queue Manager. The server process can overwrite the configuration file when these settings change or when it needs to be overwritten. Additionally, any optional arguments on the command line override the settings in the configuration file. If you want to include strings in a parameter, they must be in quotes if they contain spaces. Do not put spaces around the equal sign. Table 18-1 describes the reports server configuration file parameters in detail.

Parameter	Example	Explanation
identifier		An internal setting that contains the encrypted queue administrator user ID and password. You should not attempt to modify it. If an identifier is not specified or is deleted, or the configuration file is not present, anyone can supply any user ID and password from the Reports Queue Manager to log on as the queue administrator. Once someone has logged on in this way, the user ID and password specified become the queue administrator's user ID and password until changed from the Queue Manager.
maxconnect	100	The maximum number of processes that can communicate with the server process at any one time. This setting is the sum of the number of engines and clients and must be greater than two (at least one engine and one client).
sourcedir	c:\apps\ reports\	A path to be searched before $REPORTS60_PATH when searching for reports and other runtime files. This setting is useful when you have more than one Reports Server sharing the same $ORACLE_HOME because each Reports Server can search different directories.
cachedir	c:\orant\ report60\ server\cache\	The cache for the Reports Server. The cachedir parameter can be set to any directory or logical drive on the machine. If it is not specified, the default is $ORACLE_HOME/report60/server/cache. Assuming the Reports Server and OAS are on the same physical server, this parameter should be set to the physical equivalent of the REPORT60_WEBLOC directory.
tempdir	c:\temp\	A directory that will be used instead of $REPORTS60_TMP when creating temporary files. The tempdir parameter can be set to any directory or logical drive on the machine.

TABLE 18-1. *Reports Server Configuration File Parameters*

Parameter	Example	Explanation
cachesize	100	The size of the cache in megabytes. If you expect to store the output of many of your reports in the Reports Server cache, you may want to increase this setting. If you do not expect to store a lot of output in the cache and have limited system resources, you may want to reduce it.
minengine	5	The minimum number of runtime engines the Reports Server should have available to run reports. The server process will attempt to keep at least this many engines active. Ensure that you have sufficient memory and resources available to accommodate the number of the engines specified.
maxengine	100	The maximum number of runtime engines available to the Reports Server to run reports. The server process will attempt to keep no more than this many engines active. Ensure that you have sufficient memory and resources available to accommodate the number of the engines specified.
initengine	5	The initial number of runtime engines started by the Reports Server. The server process will spawn this many engines when it is started. It will wait two minutes for these engines to connect to it and will shut itself down if they fail to do so. If the engines cannot connect in this amount of time, there is usually some setup problem.
maxidle	5	The maximum amount of time an engine is allowed to be idle before being shut down. The Reports Server will not shut down the engine if doing so would reduce the number of available engines to less than minengine.

TABLE 18-1. *Reports Server Configuration File Parameters* (continued)

Parameter	Example	Explanation
security	1	The security level (0, 1, 2, or 3) for accessing cached output files through the Reports Queue Manager. The default level of security is 1. This setting only controls access through the Queue Manager. Accessing output files via other methods (for example, opening an output file in a browser or an editor) is controlled by the security you have in place for your file system. For example, if a job writes an ASCII output file to a particular directory, any user who has privileges on that directory will be able to look at the output in a text editor or viewer: 0 means that anyone can access a job's cached output 1 means that only a user whose user ID is identical to that of the user who ran the job can access the job's cached output 2 means that only the same process that sent the job can access the job's cached output 3 means that the cached output cannot be accessed Note: When someone uses the Reports Queue Manager to access output, the output is not encrypted when being moved across the network. In addition, with security level 1, anyone who has administrator privileges on any machine can fake the user ID to retrieve someone else's output.
englife	20	The maximum number of reports that an engine will run before shutting itself down. The Reports Server will then bring up fresh engines for new requests.

TABLE 18-1. *Reports Server Configuration File Parameters* (continued)

The preceding references to report60 are for Reports 6.0. These references should be changed to report30 for Reports 3.0.

Configuring Oracle Reports as a CGI

To set up Oracle Reports to run as a CGI, you must have the CGI executable in the Oracle bin directory and you must establish several environmental parameters.

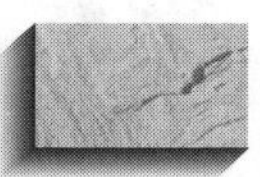

TIP
Setting up Reports as CGI is non-Web server specific, so this configuration will work for any Web server including OWAS 3.0 or OAS 4.0.

Setting Up Reports as a CGI Under NT

For Windows NT, after Oracle Reports is installed from the Developer Server CD, ensure the rwcgi60.exe (r30cgi32.exe for Reports 3.0) file located in the $ORACLE_HOME\bin directory is copied into your Web server script directory. The NT system registry will need to be modified. It may seem as though the installation should handle this for you, but it doesn't. Remember to back up the registry file prior to modification. You need to add two parameters to HKEY_LOCAL_MACHINE> SOFTWARE>ORACLE. Both are new string values:

Parameter	Parameter Value
REPORTS60_WEBLOC	/reports_cache
REPORTS60_WEBLOC_TRANSLATED	c:\orant\report60\server\cache\

The REPORTS60_WEBLOC variable means that a Web listener is using /reports_cache as a virtual directory path. Do not set REPORTS60_WEBLOC_TRANSLATED unless the Web Server and Reports Server are on different physical machines. A number of optional parameters can be set, too. You will find these listed in the following tip.

Setting Up Reports as a CGI Under UNIX

For UNIX, after you have installed Oracle Reports, ensure the rwcgim60 file located in the $ORACLE_HOME/bin directory is copied into your Web server script directory.

Then, set up a shell script in a Web Server script (CGI) directory to define the following environment variables listed and invoke rwcgim60:

```
#!/bin/sh

# cgi-specific variables
REPORTS60_WEBLOC=/reports_cache/
REPORTS60_WEBLOC_TRANSLATED=/oracle/report60/server/cache

# Other required variables
DISPLAY=mymachine:0.0; export DISPLAY
ORACLE_HOME=/oracle/; export ORACLE_HOME
PATH=.:${ORACLE_HOME}/bin; export PATH
TNS_ADMIN=${ORACLE_HOME}/network/admin; export TNS_ADMIN
TWO_TASK=acme; export TWO_TASK
LD_LIBRARY_PATH=${ORACLE_HOME}/lib; export LD_LIBRARY_PATH

# Here's the call to the cgi executable
./rwcgim60
```

Configuring Oracle Reports 6.0 as a Cartridge

After setting up your OAS 4.0 server, to create a Reports Web cartridge, start from the OAS Welcome page, then click OAS Manager. In the OAS Manager navigational tree, click the + icon beside the Web site icon. Click the Applications icon, then click the Add icon to display the Add Application form. In the Add Application form, fill in the Application Type field, specify D2KWEB, and click Apply. In the Add form, fill in the Application Name field, specify the name of your application (e.g., MyApp). In the Display Name field, specify the display name (e.g., This is my application). In the Application Version field, specify a version number (e.g., 1.0), then click Apply. In the Success dialog box, click "Add Cartridge to this Application." In the Add D2KWEB Cartridge form, fill in the Cartridge field, then type **Reports60Cartridge** and in the Display Name field, type **Reports60Cartridge**. For the Cartridge Shared Object field, type **C:\ORANT\BIN\RWOWS60.DLL** and in the Entry Point (Shared Object) field, type **rwows_start**, and then click Apply. Press the SHIFT key, then click Reload to update the navigational tree. Set application configuration properties by first navigating to your application's Configuration folder by expanding the appropriate tree nodes in the Navigator. Then, within the Configuration folder, click Web Parameters. In the Listener List field, specify a listener and click Apply. Next, set the cartridge configuration properties by navigating to your application's Cartridge Configuration folder by expanding the appropriate tree nodes in the Navigator and, within the Cartridge Configuration folder, click Cartridge Parameters. Enter the parameters and values shown in the following table and click Apply.

Field	**Description**	**Value**
REPORTS60_WEBLOC	The physical directory path and filename for the base HTML file accessed by the Reports cartridge at runtime.	/reports_cache/
REPORTS60_WEBLOC_ TRANSLATED	The one character delimiter used to denote parameter values in the application's cartridge HTML file. The delimited can be any character. The default is % (percent symbol). Do not set unless the Reports server and Web server are on different machines.	On Microsoft Windows NT: c:\orant\ report60\ server\cache\
Minimum # of instances	The minimum number of users that can simultaneously connect to the cartridge.	5
Maximum # of instances	The maximum number of users that can simultaneously connect to the cartridge.	100

Configuring Oracle Reports 3.0 as a Cartridge

Assuming the OWAS 3.0 is already installed and running, go to the Cartridge Administration page and click on Add New Cartridge to manually configure the new cartridge. To configure a new cartridge, OAS prompts for a number of new fields. The following are the values to be specified in each field as decribed in Table 18-2.

Once you have entered the following fields, you can click Register New Cartridge. The Web Application Server will register the Reports cartridge and create a link for the cartridge in the Web Application Server Home page (It will be the server:8888 page—where server is the name of your OAS server and 8888 is your administrative port). Click on your cartridge link (Reports) to display the Cartridge Configuration page. Click on "Cartridge specific parameters," then enter the following parameters and

Field	Example	Explanation
Cartridge Name	Reports	The cartridge name.
Object Path	NT: %ORACLE_HOME%\bin\r30ows32.dll UNIX: $ORACLE_HOME/r30owsm.so	The directory path and filename of the Reports Web cartridge.
Entry Point	r30ows_start	r30ows_start is the name of the entry point routine in the cartridge shared library. r30ows_start is the required value for the enter point parameter.
Minimum # of Instances	5	The minimum number of users that can simultaneously connect to the Reports cartridge.
Maximum # of Instances	100	The maximum number of users that can simultaneously connect to the Reports cartridge.
Virtual Path	/reports	At runtime, end users pass URLs (HTTP requests) to your Web server. If a request contains the virtual directory associated with your cartridge, the Web server automatically transfers the request to the Web Request Broker. The Web Request Broker in turn starts the cartridge associated with the virtual directory. Do not include a trailing slash.
Physical Path	NT: %ORACLE_HOME%\bin UNIX: $ORACLE_HOME/bin	The directory path for the Reports Web cartridge.

TABLE 18-2. *Reports Cartridge Fields*

parameter values (it's important to note that these cartridge parameters and parameter values are case sensitive):

Parameter	Example	Explanation
REPORTS30_WEBLOC	/reports_cache/	Specifies where the Web Server looks for the Reports Server output (file cache). It is a virtual directory, as defined in the Web Server configuration file. This is the directory that the Reports Server will redirect (location) the browser to.
REPORTS30_WEBLOC_ TRANSLATED	c:\orant\report30\ server\cache\	Specifies which directory the report output will be transferred to on the Web Server machine only if the Reports Server and Web Server do not share file systems. If the value of this variable would be the same as the cachedir setting in the Reports Server configuration file, *you should not* specify a value for it.

After modifying these parameters, click Modify Cartridge Configuration. Cartridges are a part of the WRB. For your changes to take effect, stop and restart all listeners and the WRB.

Setting Optional Reports Parameters

A number of optional cartridge parameters can be specified (for both the CGI and cartridge methods) as described in Table 18-3.

Parameter	Example	Explanation
ORACLE_HOME	C:\orant\	Specifies the file directory location of all the Oracle software. The location of Oracle shared libraries and NLS resource and message files is derived from this variable.
LD_LIBRARY_PATH	/shared_library/	Specifies the directory path to search for shared libraries—UNIX only.
REPORTS60_OWSHELP	http://www.acme.com/ myhelpfile.html	For the Reports Web cartridge; defines URL/URI of the r60ows help file, which will be navigated to when r60ows is invoked with the empty request: http://your_webserver/r60ows? If this parameter is not defined, a default help screen will be displayed.
REPORTS60_OWSMAP	C:\orant\report60\ mymap.dat	The Reports Web cartridge defines fully qualified filename/location of the r60ows map file (if map file configuration is used).
REPORTS60_ OWSDIAGBODYTAGS	BACKGROUND= testing.jpg	For the Reports Web cartridge; specifies HTML tags, which will be inserted as a <BODY> tag in the r60ows diagnostic/debugging output. For instance, you may want to use this environment to set up text/background color, image, and so forth.

TABLE 18-3. *Optional Reports Parameters*

Parameter	Example	Explanation
REPORTS60_ OWSDIAGHEADTAGS	<TITLE>Testing ACME Site</TITLE>	For the Reports Web cartridge; specifies HTML tags that will be inserted between <HEAD> </HEAD> tags in the r60ows diagnostic/debugging output. For instance, you may want to use this environment to set up <TITLE> or <META> tags, and so forth.
REPORTS60_ OWSPATHONLYURL	Y	For the Reports Web cartridge; when defined (the value does not matter), it causes r60ows to use path-only URLs (for example, /rscache/... instead of http://mywebsrv.com:1550/rscache/...) in HTTP redirection to report output and in the r60ows-generated diagnostic output.
REPORTS60_ OWSNODIAG	Y	For the Reports Web cartridge; when defined, disables all debugging/diagnostic output from r60ows: http://your_webserver/r60ows/help? will not work when REPORTS60_OWSNODIAG is defined.
REPORTS60_CGIHLP	http://www.acme.com/myhelpfile.html	For the Reports Web CGI; defines URL/URI of the r60cgi help file, which will be navigated to when r60cgi is invoked with the empty request: http://your_webserver/your_virtual_cgi_dir/rwcgi60.exe? If this variable is not defined, a default help screen will be displayed.

TABLE 18-3. *Optional Reports Parameters* (continued)

Parameter	Example	Explanation
REPORTS60_CGIMAP	c:\orant\report60\acmemap.dat	For the Reports Web CGI; defines fully qualified filename/location of the r60cgi map file, if map file configuration is used.
REPORTS60_CGIDIAGBODYTAGS	BACKGROUND=testing.jpg	For the Reports Web CGI; specifies the HTML tags that will be inserted as <BODY> tags in the r60cgi diagnostic/debugging output. For example, you can use this environment variable to set up text/background color and image.
REPORTS60_CGIDIAGHEADTAGS	<TITLE>Testing ACME Site</TITLE>	For the Reports Web CGI; specifies HTML tags that will be inserted between <HEAD> </HEAD> tags in the r60cgi diagnostic/debugging output. For example, you may want to use this environment to set up <TITLE> or <META> tags.
REPORTS60_CGINODIAG	Y	For the Reports Web CGI; when defined, disables all debugging/diagnostic output from r60cgi: Http://your_webserver/cgi-bin/rwcgi60.exe/help? will not work when REPORTS60_CGINODIAG is defined.

TABLE 18-3. *Optional Reports Parameters* (continued)

Parameter	Example	Explanation
REPORTS60_ CGIPATHONLYURL	Y	For the Reports Web CGI; when defined (the value does not matter), forces r60cgi to return any URLs to the browser as partial, path-only URLs; i.e., instead of returning: Location: http://your_webserver:port/path it will return only: Location: /path This variable can be used to resolve problems with Web server setups that use multiple ports, including a default port.
USER_NLS_LANG or NLS_LANG	American_America. WE8ISO8859P1	Defines NLS Language used in your URL request as well as HTML/PDF output (using Oracle NLSRTL language IDs).

TABLE 18-3. *Optional Reports Parameters* (continued)

Specifying URL Run Requests for Reports

When specifying URL run requests to the Reports Web cartridge or CGI, you should:

- Ensure all of the report filenames and connection strings are valid on the Reports Server's file system.
- Specify at least three parameters: SERVER, REPORT, and USERID.
- Use rwcgi60.exe (case insensitive) if you are using the Reports Web CGI on Windows. On UNIX, use rwcgim60 (case sensitive) unless you use a shell script to invoke CGI runtime, in which case you should use the name of the script that calls rwcgim60.

The examples shown below are equivalent to the following command line:

```
R60CLI SERVER=rptsrv REPORT=acmesales.rdf USERID=acme/roadrunner@sales
DESTYPE=CACHE DESFORMAT=HTML
```

TIP
The online documentation for Reports 6.0 can easily be found through the menus, whereas the online documents for Reports 3.0 can be found in the files r30ows.htm and r30cgi.htm, which contain information about URL run requests. The online document r30mtsus.htm and the Reports Runtime help system contain a complete description of the command-line parameters and semantics.

URL for a Cartridge Request

```
http://www.acme.com/reports?server=rptsrv&report=acmesales&userid=acme/
roadrunner@sales&destype=cache&desformat=HTML
```

URL for a CGI Request on NT

```
http://www.acme.com/orabin/runt60.exe?server=rptsrv&report=acmesales&us
erid=acme/roadrunner@sales&destype=cache&desformat=HTML
```

URL for a CGI Request on UNIX

```
http://www.acme.com/orabin/rwcgim60?server=rptsrv&report=acmesales&user
id=acme/roadrunner@sales&destype=cache&desformat=HTML
```

Adding Web Functionality

To make your report more useful on the Web, Report Builder provides the capability to add Web functionality to it. You can add Web functionality to a report in any of the following ways:

- **Web Wizard** Specify bookmarks and HTML files to insert at the beginning and end of the report.
- **Property palette** In the Property palette for the report, you can enter report escapes that define HTML to be inserted at the beginning and end

of the report, and at the beginning and end of pages. In the Property palette for layout objects, you can specify Web link properties that make the object a hyperlink destination or hyperlink, or execute a PDF application command line.

- **SRW package** The SRW package provides procedures that set Web properties programmatically in triggers. For example, you could use a procedure from the SRW package in the format trigger of a layout object to make it a hyperlink.

Hyperlinks

You can add hyperlink (or hypertext link) functionality into your reports, enabling users to navigate to different sections of a report or other documents on the Web. To create a hyperlink, first create a target (or hyperlink destination), which is a unique identifier for the current location. Then, create a hyperlink elsewhere in the same or a different document that points to the target. When users click on the hyperlink, they will be taken to the target to which it points.

A hyperlink can take you to the following:

- Another document on the same machine—for example:
  `file:/c_drive/mynewdoc.pdf`
- Another document on a different machine—for example:
  http://www2.acme.com/newdoc.pdf
- A destination within the current document—for example:
  #introduction
- A destination within a local document—for example:
  file:/c_drive/mynewerdoc.pdf#summary
- A destination within a remote document—for example:
  http://www2.acme.com/newdoc.pdf#chapter_2
- Any URL—for example:
  http://www.tusc.com/training.html
  ftp://www.oracle.com/oracle8i.exe
  http://search.acme.com/search/plsql/search.start

Hardcoded Hyperlink PL/SQL Example

The format trigger below defines a hypertext link to a destination (chapter_2) in another document (mynewerdoc.pdf) for the boilerplate object B_2.

If the target were in the same document, you would omit http://www.acme.com/mynewerdoc.pdf.

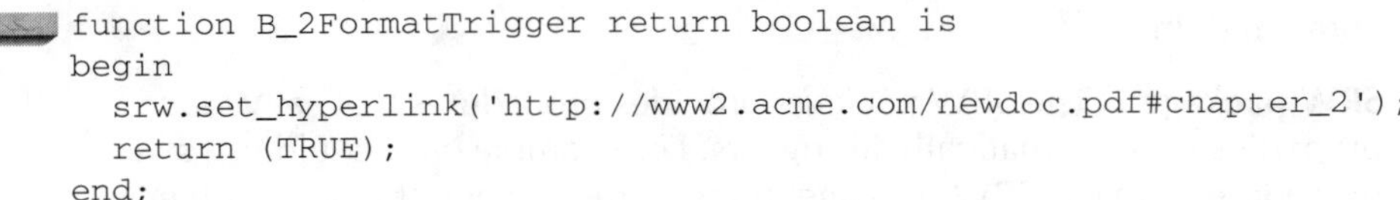

```
function B_2FormatTrigger return boolean is
begin
  srw.set_hyperlink('http://www2.acme.com/newdoc.pdf#chapter_2');
  return (TRUE);
end;
```

Dynamic Hyperlink PL/SQL Example

The following format trigger defines a hypertext link for the boilerplate object B_3. The destination of the link is determined dynamically based on the values of SRCDIR and CF_PICKVIDEO. For example, if the value of SRCDIR is http://www.acme.com, and the value of CF_PICKVIDEO is good.avi, this function would assign the following hypertext link to the object:

```
http://www.acme.com/webdemo/src/good.avi
```

The following code would be included into your report to generate the above hyperlink:

```
function B_3FormatTrigger return boolean is
begin
  srw.set_hyperlink(:srcdir||:cf_pickvideo);
  if ( upper(:cf_pickvideo) like '%GOOD%' ) then
    srw.set_foreground_bordercolor('green');
    srw.set_background_border_color('green')
  end if;
  return (TRUE);
end;
/* SRCDIR is a parameter whose value is determined at
** runtime by the following After Parameter Form Trigger
*/
function AfterPForm return boolean is
begin
  :srcdir := :web_server || '/webdemo/src/';
  :docsdir := :web_server || '/webdemo/docs/';
  return (TRUE);
end;
/* CF_PICKVIDEO is a formula column whose value is
** determined by the following function
*/
function CF_pickvideoFormula return Char is
begin
  if ( :avg_h_div < .80 )
    then return ('bad.avi');
    else return ('good.avi');
  end if;
end;
```

Creating Bookmarks

A bookmark is a string that will appear in a frame of the master HTML document or in the PDF viewer if you open the bookmark area. Clicking on the bookmark displays the associated object at the top of the window. A list of bookmarks can serve as an outline or table of contents for your report.

For reports with master/detail relationships, the Web Wizard can create bookmarks for you automatically. You can also create bookmarks by specifying the Bookmark property through the Property palette or SRW.SET_ATTR in a format trigger.

Example of a Bookmark Report

By default, the order in which bookmarks appear in the list is determined when Oracle Reports renders the objects when you generate the report. You can hierarchically order bookmarks by embedding ordering information in the bookmark definition string. A string with explicit ordering information takes the form:

```
x#book_mark_name
```

where x is an outline number. The pound sign (#) and outline number do not appear in the bookmark area but are used to determine order and indentation—for example:

```
1#TUSC Expense Summary Section
2#TUSC Expense Detail Section
2.1#TUSC Expenses for the Administration Department
2.2#TUSC Expenses for the DBA Consulting Division
2.3#TUSC Expenses for the Sales Department
2.3.1#Expenses for the Chicago Sales Region
2.3.2#Expenses for the Denver Sales Region
2.3.3#Expenses for the Detroit Sales Region
```

Example of a Bookmark when Ordering Information

The following format trigger defines a bookmark for the boilerplate object B_2. Note the use of explicit ordering information (1#) in this example. If you did not want the ordering information, you could omit 1#.

```
function B_2FormatTrigger return boolean is
begin
  srw.set_bookmark('1#TUSC Expense Summary Section');
  return (TRUE);
end;
```

Example of a Dynamic Bookmark

The following format trigger defines a bookmark for the boilerplate object B_2. In this example, the name of the bookmark is dynamic. *Category* is a column value that is concatenated with the string Expense Summary Section for each execution of the Format Trigger. In this case, *category* could contain ordering information (for example, 1#) or perhaps a string that makes the bookmark unique within the report.

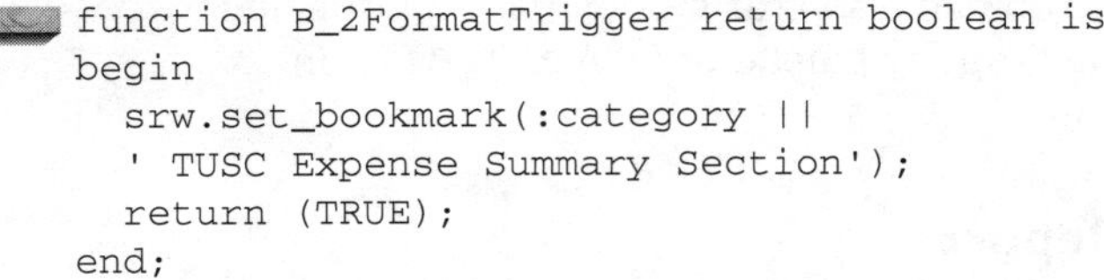

```
function B_2FormatTrigger return boolean is
begin
  srw.set_bookmark(:category ||
  ' TUSC Expense Summary Section');
  return (TRUE);
end;
```

Prompting for the Parameter Form

If a report has been written to prompt the user with the parameter screen, on that screen the user will pick a specific value that is based on a list of values (LOV). When you run your report in client/server mode, everything works just fine—it will prompt you with the drop-down LOV box. However, when you run it over the Web, it does not prompt you with your Parameter page. In fact, it will consider the value to be equal to the default value for each parameter (NULL-if none are defined). If you experiment, you can pass the parameter into the report on the URL. If you wanted to implement the report this way, it would require that you build a Web-based parameter screen too—in Oracle or HTML Forms.

When running a report in client/server mode, the parameter form comes up automatically. However, when running the report through the Web, the parameter form does not come up by default. If you add the following text onto the URL, Reports will prompt the user with your parameter form:

```
&paramform=yes
```

The following is a complete example:

```
http://www.acme.com/reports?server=rptsrv&report=sales&userid=acme/road
runner@sales&destype=cache&desformat=html&paramform=yes
```

Magically, your parameter form will appear.

Configuring the Default Printer for Oracle Reports on UNIX

If you do not have a default printer defined for Oracle Reports, you will receive an error message that Reports is unable to initialize the printer (error REP-3002) in Reports 6.0 or a REP-1800: Formatter error in Reports 3.0. This error indicates that you do not have a default printer defined. Therefore, after installing Oracle Reports on UNIX platforms, you must perform some postinstallation tasks.

First, you must gen a PostScript print queue on your UNIX machine to the operating system. Even if you do not have a physical printer, you still need to gen this queue. Reports uses the presence or absence of a PostScript print queue to determine whether your UNIX box is capable of handling graphical (bitmapped) output. In this example, the queue name is lp1.

Edit the uiprint.txt file in the guicommon2/tk21/admin directory (under the $ORACLE_HOME directory) and change the last line to include the queue name from the preceding step.

The following is a sample uiprint.txt line that works:

```
"lp1:PostScript:1:LNO printer on np3:default.ppd:"
|    |           | |                 |
|    says it's a| +- cosmetic name   |
|    Postscript  |     for the queue   is the Name of the PPD
|    Printer     |                     (Postscript Printer Definition)
|                says it's a           file which gives details about
Operating        Postscript Level 1    the fonts available on this
System Print     Printer               printer. Don't change this unless
queue name                             you know what you're doing.
```

When Oracle Reports starts up, the toolkit layer of the product reads the uiprint.txt file, finds the line for each print queue, and gives it a print queue name and PPD file name. It then interrogates the operating system to ensure that each queue really exists and determines if it is a PostScript print queue. Reports loads the list of fonts in each PPD file (from 1) for each print queue and for each font (from 3), then loads the corresponding Adobe Font Metric (AFM) file to obtain sizing information.

If this process does not happen as described, or if no PostScript print queues are found, then Reports only produces character mode output and refuses to run in bitmapped mode when forced (giving the previously mentioned error messages).

The easiest way to test this is to run a report from the demo directory under reports and try to get postscript output. You can verify if the output file is a flat ASCII or PostScript file by running the report. The following command runs the report:

```
r30runm module=test.rdf userid=scott/tiger destype=file
desname=test.lis  batch=yes
```

Remember that this command must be entered on one line (no carriage returns). You can view the output file using the command:

```
more test.lis
```

The beginning of a PostScript file appears similar to the following:

```
%!PS-Adobe-3.0
%%Creator: Oracle Toolkit 2 for Motif 2.1.5.6.2 PRODUCTION
%%Version: 2.1 5
%%CreationDate: (Fri May 24 15:46:29 1996)
%%For: Brad Brown (brownb@tusc2))
%%Routing: (Brad Brown,RPS,x6889)
%%Title: 'TEST.LIS' (Oracle Toolkit Application)
%%LanguageLevel: 2
%%Requirements: numcopies(1)
%%DocumentData: Clean7Bit
%%PageOrder: Ascend
%%Pages: (atend)
%%Orientation: Landscape
% NOTE: This file was generated with the PPD file default.ppd
```

Identifying Reports Server Errors

If you attempt to start the Reports Server and you receive the infamous 186 error, start by checking the Reports Server log file for more information. This file can be found in the $ORACLE_HOME/report60/server/ directory and will be named rptsrv.log (or the name your server's report service). In the case of the 186 error, you will discover that your tnsname entry has a problem. When you look at your tnsnames.ora file, you will probably find that your Reports Server entry is gone. If someone used the SQL*Net Easy Configuration tool, they may have accidentally removed the Reports Server entry in the file.

Running Multiple Reports Concurrently

After installing the Reports Server, you might notice that reports are cueing up and running in succession, not concurrently. In other words, whoever got to the Reports

Server first got their report first, and whoever was second waited for the first to complete, and so on. This is the long road to running reports. Unless you configure the Reports Server to do otherwise, that is the default functionality. It would seem as though you should just have to set the minimum and maximum number of cartridge instances and that would do the trick (as it does for PL/SQL, Java, LiveHTML, and other cartridges). However, you need to set the MIN cartridge instance parameter to the average number of reports that you expect users to be running at any point in time (concurrently), and you need to set the Reports Server parameter respectively. To do this, you will need to edit the Reports Server configuration file, which is discussed in detail above. The specific parameters to be modified are minengine and maxengine—these parameters should be set the same as your min and max instances for the Report cartridge. Initengine should typically be set to the same setting as minengine. The default settings are as follows:

```
minengine=0
maxengine=1
initengine=1
```

These settings indicate only 1 (concurrent) engine is running. If your min and instance parameters were set to 5 and 100, you would want to set the parameters as follows:

```
minengine=5
maxengine=100
initengine=5
```

After you change this setting, bounce (stop and start) the Developer 2000 service. This is done from the Control Panel on NT.

On UNIX, go to a UNIX prompt and find the r30mtsm process. Kill that process and then restart the process as previously described.

Using MetaLink to Figure Out Why RUN_PRODUCT Fails

An unusual problem was encountered while running reports out of Oracle Forms. By using the Forms RUN_PRODUCT command to launch a varying number of reports (1 to 10) asynchronously in batch, the form launched the reports, then put them into the Reports Server queue and moved on. Every time the process was executed, an FRM-41211 error occurred, indicating a problem with the RUN_PRODUCT command. The error occurred after a third report had been sent to the Reports Server. After acknowledging the error, the next report ran and the error reoccured. All of the reports printed correctly, and their output went to the correct destinations.

The RUN_PRODUCT command would not accept more than three report launches at a time without the error. It did not make a difference which reports were selected, or in which order they were executed.
We tried using the runtime/batch and asynchronous/synchronous setting in RUN_PRODUCT. We tried the BATCH, BACKGROUND, PRINTJOB, and so forth, command-line parameters for R25RUN, and tried passing them in a parameter list, also.

So, we began the search on MetaLink (support.oracle.com). We found out that the error was an SSL failure in the Reports Server. This error is normally caused by the Web server, or secure Oracle interfacing to the Reports Server, as it involves encryption of the data being passed. The error simply stopped the process so it could be acknowledged, and once acknowledged, the rest of the reports printed.

The workaround was to build an on_error trigger at the form-level to trap that specific FRM error. This worked since the error was a bogus error and should not have been sent anyway. Rather than calling Oracle Support, you may want to first go to MetaLink to attempt to find your solution.

Creating Headers, Footers and Page Breaks for Web Pages

In our paperless dream world, we only view reports in a browser. However, in reality, we often desire to print these reports on paper. In HTML, there is not a page break facility and no functionality to put headers and footers on an HTML page. How do you print out Web pages with the correct page breaks, headers with your company logo, and footers in the right place on the printout?

By using a PDF file for your output, you can get these results. This format provides a what you see is what you get (WYSIWYG) output format. You can purchase Adobe's Distiller to convert other file formats into PDF. However, if you want reports from an Oracle database, the easiest way to get the desired result is to use Oracle Reports since it produces PDF files automatically for you.

Resolving the PDF Issue in IE (and AOL)

A bug may creep up on you if your browser is Internet Explorer v4. The longer a report takes to run (on the server), the more likely it is that IE will have problems processing the PDF file. However, there is a patch for OAS and Oracle Reports that fixes the IE PDF issue. Several workarounds exist, too. You could always upgrade to IE v5 or use a Netscape browser. A workaround for IE v4 is to place the actual report into a small (1 pixel big—I call this an invisible frame) frame and use a JavaScript routine to check the href or location of the invisible frame. When it contains the letters PDF, you can set your visible frame equal to the href or location of the invisible frame. This will work for IE 4. The code for this workaround is shown below. Oracle Support tells me that the problem is fixed in 3.0.1.1 of OAS, but the patch will work up through that version. It is a patch for bug number 720074, and it replaces 2 files—wwwlsnr30.exe and wwwlsnr30.dll. I installed a great many patches and it never seemed to work for me. The following code is from the www.esports-net.com Web site. This first code segment shows the source code for the main page (note the hidden1 frame that is 1 pixel big):

```
<html>
<head>
<title>ESports-net Softball Stat Keeper</title>
<META name="description" content="The first interactive statistics
keeper on the Internet and it is free.  Advertise or lookup
tournament info., track rosters, keep player statistics and much more.">
<META name="keywords" content="ESports, Esports-net, Softball,
Baseball, Bat, Ball, Glove, Statistics, Stats, Tourn, Tournament,
Tournaments, Slow Pitch, Fast Pitch, Reports, Leagues, Rosters,
Teams, Players">
</head>

<frameset rows="101,*" frameborder="NO" border="0"
framespacing="0" bordercolor="003300" noresize="YES">
<frameset cols="1,*" frameborder="NO" border="0"
framespacing="0" bordercolor="003300" noresize="YES">
<frame src="hidden1.htm" scrolling="NO" name="hidden1"
marginwidth="0" marginheight="0" yes>
<frame src="Titlebar.htm" name="TitleBar" scrolling="NO"
marginwidth="0" marginheight="0" yes>
</frameset>
<frameset cols="104,40,*" frameborder="NO" border="0"
framespacing="0" bordercolor="003300" noresize="YES">
<frame src="NavBar.htm" scrolling="AUTO" name="navbar"
marginwidth="0" marginheight="10" yes>
<frame src="BatPage.htm" scrolling="NO" name="batpage"
marginwidth="0" marginheight="0" yes>
<frame src="start.htm" scrolling="AUTO" name="main"
marginwidth="0" marginheight="8" yes>
</frameset>
</frameset>
<noframes><body bgcolor="#FFFFFF">
This site requires a browser that supports frames.
</body></noframes>
</html>
```

The following segment of code is the HTML that is used to prompt the user for the report parameters. At the beginning of this code, you will notice two important JavaScript routines and two input parameters with important JavaScript onClick events. These routines are highlighted below. The first routine, submit_report, is called when the form is actually submitted. The submit_report routine simply checks to ensure that the user did not already submit this report. When users run reports, they might get impatient waiting for the report and wonder if clicking on Submit Again will speed up the report. However, in a Web environment, such a request will actually duplicate the efforts and submit the report again (and again). Therefore, if the user already submitted the report, this routine just pops up an alert message stating that the report is already running. The second routine, check_report is the workaround for the bug. Notice the timer that falls inline (outside of any function). This causes the check_report routine to be executed every second. The routine takes a look at the hidden1 frame to see if the hidden1.htm file is still the hypertext reference (href) in that frame. If so, it does nothing. If not, that means that the PDF file is now in the hidden1 frame. At that point, the main frame's href is set equal to the href of the hidden1 frame (hidden1.htm is placed back into the hidden1 frame and the timer is turned off). This causes the browser to go back to the server to download the PDF file and place it into the main frame. You will also notice two input radio buttons further down in the HTML. Each radio button has an onClick event that sets the target frame. HTML files are targeted to the main frame and PDF files are directed to the hidden1 frame. Goofy, but easy enough—and it works!

```
<HTML>
<HEAD>
<TITLE>On Deck Softball Stat Keeper - Reports</TITLE>
<SCRIPT language="javascript">

function submit_form()
{
if (x == 0)
 {document.run_report.submit();x=1}
else
 {alert("Report is Running");}
}

timerID = setInterval(''check_report()'',1000);

function check_report () {
   hrefID = top.frames[0].hidden1.location.href;
   hrefID = top.hidden1.location.href;
   pos = hrefID.indexOf("hidden1");
```

```
   if (pos < 0) {
       top.hidden1.location.href = "/hidden1.htm"
       top.main.location.href = hrefID
       clearInterval(timerID)
       x=0;
  }
}
</SCRIPT>
</HEAD>

<BODY  bgcolor="#003300", link="#DEC621", alink="#DEC621",
       vlink="#FF9933">
<CENTER>
<B><DIV CLASS="Heading1">Report Design - Criteria Form for:
</DIV></B>
<BR>
<P ALIGN="center">
<FONT COLOR="#FF9933" FACE="Tahoma, Arial, Helvetica">
Individual Statistics Grouped by Season - Team
</FONT>
<FORM ACTION="PCK_REPORT_CRIT.RUN_REPORT" METHOD="post"
TARGET="hidden1" NAME=run_report onSubmit="submit_form()">
<P>
<INPUT TYPE="hidden" NAME="IN_RPT_GROUP" VALUE="PLAYER">
<INPUT TYPE="hidden" NAME="IN_RPT_NAME" VALUE="P_SEAS_TEAM">
<INPUT TYPE="hidden" NAME="IN_SEASON_ID" VALUE="">
<INPUT TYPE="hidden" NAME="IN_TEAM_ID" VALUE="">
<INPUT TYPE="hidden" NAME="IN_PLAYER_ID" VALUE="">
<P ALIGN="center">
<TABLE   CELLSPACING="2" CELLPADDING="2" BORDER="0" WIDTH="75%">
<TR>
<TD ALIGN="RIGHT"  width="15%" BGCOLOR="#006000"><B>Season: </B></TD>
<TD  width="45%" BGCOLOR="#608060">All Seasons</TD>
<TD  width="6%" BGCOLOR="#006000"><DIV align="center">
<A HREF="PCK_REPORT_CRIT.CHOOSE_SEASON?IN_DISPLAY_START=1
&IN_DISPLAY_LETTER=&IN_RPT_GROUP=PLAYER&IN_RPT_NAME=P_SEAS_TEAM
&IN_SEASON_ID=&IN_YEAR=&IN_CITY=&IN_STATE=&IN_TOURN=
&IN_TEAM_ID=&IN_PLAYER_ID="  TITLE="Select a season" litup1>
[Select]</A></DIV></TD>
</TR>
<TR>
<TD ALIGN="RIGHT"  width="15%" BGCOLOR="#006000"><B>Year: </B></TD>
<TD WIDTH="45%" BGCOLOR="#608060">
<SELECT NAME="V_YEAR" SIZE="1">
<OPTION SELECTED value="">All Years
```

```
<OPTION value="1999">1999
<OPTION value="1998">1998
<OPTION value="1997">1997
</SELECT>
</TD>
</TR>
<TR>
<TD ALIGN="RIGHT"  width="15%" BGCOLOR="#006000"><B>City: </B></TD>
<TD  width="57%" BGCOLOR="#608060">
<INPUT TYPE="text" NAME="V_CITY" SIZE="20" MAXLENGTH="20"></TD>
</TR>
<TR>
<TD ALIGN="RIGHT"  width="15%" BGCOLOR="#006000"><B>State: </B></TD>
<TD WIDTH="45%" BGCOLOR="#608060">
<SELECT NAME="V_STATE" SIZE="1">
<OPTION value="CO">CO
<OPTION value="WY">WY
<OPTION SELECTED value="">All States
</SELECT>
</TD>
</TR>
<TR>
<TD ALIGN="RIGHT"  width="15%" BGCOLOR="#006000">
<B>Tournament?: </B></TD>
<TD WIDTH="45%" BGCOLOR="#608060">
<SELECT NAME="V_TOURN" SIZE="1">
<OPTION value="N">Leagues
<OPTION value="Y">Tournaments
<OPTION SELECTED value="">Tournaments & Leagues
</SELECT>
</TD>
</TR>
<TR>
<TD ALIGN="RIGHT"  width="15%" BGCOLOR="#006000"><B>Team: </B></TD>
<TD  width="45%" BGCOLOR="#608060">All Teams</TD>
<TD  width="6%" BGCOLOR="#006000"><DIV align="center">
<A HREF="PCK_REPORT_CRIT.CHOOSE_TEAM?IN_DISPLAY_START=1
&IN_DISPLAY_LETTER=&IN_RPT_GROUP=PLAYER&IN_RPT_NAME=P_SEAS_TEAM
&IN_SEASON_ID=&IN_YEAR=&IN_CITY=&IN_STATE=&IN_TOURN=
&IN_TEAM_ID=&IN_PLAYER_ID="  TITLE="Select a team" litup1>
[Select]</A></DIV></TD>
</TR>
<TR>
<TD ALIGN="RIGHT"  width="15%" BGCOLOR="#006000"><B>Player: </B></TD>
<TD  width="45%" BGCOLOR="#608060">All Players</TD>
```

```
<TD  width="6%" BGCOLOR="#006000"><DIV align="center">
<A HREF="PCK_REPORT_CRIT.CHOOSE_PLAYER?IN_DISPLAY_START=1
&IN_DISPLAY_LETTER=&IN_RPT_GROUP=PLAYER&IN_RPT_NAME=P_SEAS_TEAM
&IN_SEASON_ID=&IN_YEAR=&IN_CITY=&IN_STATE=&IN_TOURN=&IN_TEAM_ID=
&IN_PLAYER_ID="  TITLE="Select a player" litup1>[Select]</A>
</DIV></TD></TR>
<TR>
<TD ALIGN="RIGHT"  width="12%" BGCOLOR="#006000"><B>Format: </B></TD>
<TD  width="45%" BGCOLOR="#608060">
<INPUT TYPE="radio" NAME="FORMAT" VALUE="PDF" CHECKED
onClick="javascript:run_report.target='hidden1'">
:PDF -
<a href="http://www.adobe.com/prodindex/acrobat/readstep.html"
target=x><img src="/images/getacro.gif" border="0"
align="middle"></a><br>
<INPUT TYPE="radio" NAME="FORMAT" VALUE="HTML"
onClick="javascript:run_report.target=''">
:HTML </TD>
</TR>
</TABLE>
<BR>
<TABLE >
<TR>
<CENTER>
<TD ALIGN="center">
<INPUT TYPE="submit" NAME="ACTION" VALUE="Execute" align="center">
</TD>
</TR>
<TR>
<TD ALIGN="center">
<A HREF="PCK_REPORT_CRIT.RPT_CRITERIA?IN_RPT_GROUP=PLAYER
&IN_RPT_NAME=P_SEAS_TEAM&IN_SEASON_ID=&IN_YEAR=&IN_CITY=
&IN_STATE=&IN_TOURN=&IN_TEAM_ID=&IN_PLAYER_ID="
TITLE="Reset Report Criteria Form">[Reset Report Criteria Form]
</A></TD>
</CENTER>
</TR>
</TABLE>
<HR  width="90%">
<CENTER>
<FONT face="Tahoma, Arial, Helvetica" size="-1">
<FONT COLOR="#FFFFFF">
<A HREF="/start.htm"
  TARGET="main" TITLE="Back to Main Page" litup1>[Home]</A>
-
```

```
<A HREF="/stats/stats/PCK_SEASON.DISPLAY_SEASONS?DISPLAY_START=1"
   target="main" TITLE="Goto Statistics Entry"
   litup1>[Statistics Entry]</A>
<BR>
<A HREF="/stats/stats/PCK_SEASON.DISPLAY_SEASONS?DISPLAY_START=1"
   target="main" TITLE="Goto Season Maintenance"
   litup1>[Season Maintenance]</A>
-
<A HREF="/stats/stats/PCK_TEAMS.DISPLAY_TEAM_INFO?DISPLAY_START=1"
   target="main" TITLE="Goto Team Maintenance"
   litup1>[Team Maintenance]</A>
-
<A HREF="/stats/stats/PCK_PLAYERS.DISPLAY_PLAYER_INFO?DISPLAY_START=1"
   target="main"
   TITLE="Goto Player Maintenance"
   litup1>[Player Maintenance]</A>
<BR>
<A HREF="/stats/stats/PCK_CALENDAR.DISPLAY_CALENDAR"
target="main" TITLE="Goto Reports Design" litup1>[Calendar]</A>
-
<A HREF="/stats_rpt/plsql/PCK_REPORT_CRIT.CHOOSE_REPORT"
target="main" TITLE="Goto Reports Design" litup1>[Reports]</A>
-
<A HREF="/stats/stats/PCK_LOGIN.START_LOGIN?in_type=E"
target="main" TITLE="Log on to the Stat Keeper" litup1>[Login]</A>
<BR>
<A HREF="advertising.htm"  TARGET="main"
TITLE="View Advertising Information" litup1>[Advertising]</A>
-
<A HREF="/Help.htm"  TARGET="main"
   TITLE="ESports-net Help" litup1>[Help]</A>
-
<A HREF="mailto:scottl@tusc.com"
TITLE="E-mail Comments & Suggestions" litup1>[E-mail]</A>
</FONT>
</FONT>
<BR>
<HR  width="50%">
<DIV align="center">
<FONT COLOR="#FFFFFF" SIZE="1">
Copyright 1999 ESports-net.    All rights reserved.
</FONT>
</DIV>
</BODY>
</HTML>
```

Even though the workaround will work for any browser (that supports frames and JavaScript), you really only need the check_report logic and a target of hidden1 if the browser version is IE 4.0. If your routine (identical to the preceding code) is a static routine, you can determine the browser within your JavaScript. If your report submission routine is created with PL/SQL, you can determine the browser by retrieving the CGI environmental parameter named HTTP_USER_AGENT as follows:

```
if (instr(owa_util.get_cgi_env('HTTP_USER_AGENT'),'MSIE 4.')     > 0 or
    instr(owa_util.get_cgi_env('HTTP_USER_AGENT'),'AOL-IWENG')   > 0)
    then
    htp.print( '    timerID = setInterval(''check_report()'',1000);');
    htp.print( '    function check_report () {');
    htp.print( '     hrefID = top.hidden1.location.href;');
    htp.print( '     pos = hrefID.indexOf("hidden1");');
    htp.print( '     if (pos < 0) {');
    htp.print( '        top.hidden1.location.href = "/hidden1.htm"');
    htp.print( '        top.main.location.href = hrefID');
    htp.print( '        clearInterval(timerID)');
    htp.print( '        x=0;');
    htp.print( '    }');
    htp.print( '}');
end if;
```

Suggesting Oracle Reports Performance Tips

Performing operations in SQL may be faster than performing them in Oracle Reports or PL/SQL. The list below explains the most common cases where using SQL would improve performance:

- Perform calculations directly in your query rather than in a formula or summary column
- Use a WHERE clause instead of a group filter or format trigger to exclude records
- Use the SUBSTR function to truncate character strings instead of truncating in Oracle Reports

SQL can perform calculations more quickly than a summary or formula. The WHERE clause and the SUBSTR function can reduce unnecessary fetching, because they operate on the data during, rather than after, data retrieval.

SRW.DO_SQL Statements

SRW.DO_SQL enables you to add DDL or DML operations to your report. This functionality is very valuable, but it can also be very expensive if used unwisely.

Only use SRW.DO_SQL when necessary. SRW.DO_SQL statements are parsed, a cursor is opened to the database, and then the statement is executed. Unlike queries, an SRW.DO_SQL statement will do those things each time its owner (a group) fetches data. For example, if your SRW.DO_SQL statement is owned by a group that fetches 10 records, the statement will be parsed 10 times, 10 cursors will be opened, and the statement will be executed 10 times. Instead, perform computations within the query or PL/SQL.

Using CDE_MM.GET_REF

Only use the CDE_MM.GET_REF packaged procedure when necessary. It is intended to reduce the amount of temporary space used by Oracle Reports. Oracle Reports will not cache a column retrieved through the CDE_MM.GET_REF in a temporary file. While this reduces the need for temporary space, it slows performance because the column's values must always be retrieved from the database.

When You Should Use Multiquery Data Models

Reduce the number of queries in your report as much as possible. The fewer queries, the faster your report will run. Multiquery data models are easier to understand, but single-query data models tend to execute more quickly.

Use multiquery data models only when:

- You are fetching several large columns from the parent and only a few small columns from the child
- You are trying to do queries that SELECT does not support directly (multiway outer join)
- You have complex views (distributed queries or GROUP BY queries)
- You need but do not have or want to use a view

For a one-query report, only one cursor is opened to fetch all the master and detail records. For a two-query report, Oracle Reports opens two cursors (one for each query) after appending the detail query's link to the WHERE clause of the detail query. For each master record fetched, Oracle must rebind, execute, and fetch data from the detail query.

Indexes

Evaluate the use of indexes on columns used in the SELECT statements, WHERE clauses, on database key columns, and on the table(s) in the detail queries. Indexes have little impact on master queries, for those queries access the database only once. Indexes significantly improve performance of master/detail reports. The lower the ratio of master to detail records, the more important the indexes on the detail query become for two-query reports.

Indexes are recommended for tables in the detail queries, because Oracle Reports implicitly creates a WHERE clause from the parent/child relationships and adds it to the detail query.

Modifications

Oracle Reports modifies your queries in the following cases:

1. For each link you create, Oracle Reports will append a clause to the child query as specified in the link.
   For example:

   ```
   select   deptno, ename, sal
   from     emp
   where    sal > 1000
   ```

   If you create a link to this query using DEPTNO as the child column, a SQL clause of WHERE, and a condition of equal to, then your query will be modified as follows:

   ```
   select   deptno, ename, sal
   from     emp
   where    (sal > 1000) AND (deptno = :deptno)
   ```

   This is not true for multiquery matrix report data models.

2. For each database column with *break order* set, Oracle Reports will prepend an ORDER BY clause to the query. For example:

   ```
   select    deptno, ename, sal
   from      emp
   order by  sal
   ```

If you create a break group with DEPTNO as the break column, then your query will be modified as follows:

```
select    deptno, ename, sal
from      emp
order by  1, sal
```

These SQL statements will be sent to the database, then the SQL Optimizer will determine the optimal way to get the data from the database and return it to Oracle Reports. The optimizer will determine whether to use indexes, which table to use as the driving table, and so forth.

Break Columns

When you create a break group, place as few columns as possible in the group. Try to keep a 1:1 ratio of break columns to break groups, and try to ensure that the break column is as small as possible. A break column that is shorter in length will typically give better performance than a break column that is longer. For larger break columns, it may help performance to use the SUBSTR function to reduce the length of the column.

For each break group, Oracle Reports prepends its break columns to the ORDER BY clause of the query. (The only exception to the rule is when the break column is a formula column.) By minimizing the number of break columns in your break groups, you minimize the number of columns that are added to the ORDER BY clause. The fewer the columns added to the ORDER BY clause, the less processing that needs to be done when the query runs. The size of the key that Oracle Reports uses internally to build indexes will also be smaller, resulting in better performance.

Maximum Rows and Group Filters

Use the Maximum Rows property in the Query property sheet to reduce the number of records retrieved by the report's queries. When designing a report that accesses large amounts of data, you may want to restrict the amount of data retrieved so the report will run more quickly during testing.

Maximum Rows in the Query property sheet restricts the number of records fetched by the query. A group filter determines which records to include and which records to exclude. Since Maximum Rows actually restricts the amount of data retrieved, it is faster than a group filter in most cases.

If you use a group filter of Last or Conditional, Oracle Reports must retrieve all of the records in the group before applying the filter criteria. Maximum Rows or a Filter of First is faster. Typically, Maximum Rows is faster than a Filter of First because it only retrieves as many records as needed. The performance difference may vary depending upon the ARRAYSIZE you have specified.

Unused Data Model Objects

Make sure that you remove or suppress any data model objects that are not actually used in your report. If your data model includes a query that is only used in certain cases (when a parameter is set to a certain value), you can conditionally suppress the query with the SRW.SET_MAXROW packaged procedure from within a before report trigger. SRW.SET_MAXROW (queryname, 0) will cause the query to fetch no records.

Unused Frames

Remove any unnecessary frames from the layout. When Oracle Reports creates a default layout, it puts frames around virtually everything. This is performed to protect the objects in the frames from being overwritten by other objects in the output. If you know that the objects in the frames are not in danger of being overwritten, you can eliminate the frame without adversely affecting your report output. Be very careful to save a working copy of your report before deleting frames.

The fewer objects in the layout, the fewer objects Oracle Reports must format at runtime. As a result, performance is better when you reduce the number of objects in the layout.

Total Number of Pages

Limit your use of total number of pages as the source of fields (total logical pages)—for example, displaying the boilerplate Page 1 of 6. When you use a total number of pages as a field source, Oracle Reports must save all of the pages in temporary storage in order to determine the total number of pages. This can significantly increase the amount of temporary disk space used by Reports and the additional writing to files can slow performance.

Format Triggers

Place PL/SQL in the format trigger of the object with the lowest frequency possible. PL/SQL in the format trigger of a frame instead of a field typically makes the report run faster.

PL/SQL in format triggers is executed for each instance of its object. The lower the frequency of the object, the fewer times the PL/SQL will be executed and the faster the report will run.

Oracle Graphics Integration

If an Oracle Graphics display referenced by a report uses some or all of the same data as the report, pass the data from the report to the display. If the report and the display use the same data, passing the data reduces the amount of fetching that needs to be performed. If you do not pass the data from the report to the display, the data is actually fetched twice—once for the report and once for the display.

Developing Data to Generate Acrobat PDF Files

If you would like to output a report into an Adobe Acrobat PDF file, what are your options? The easiest option is to use Oracle Reports because it handles this for you automatically. However, if you are developing a report with the PL/SQL cartridge, it cannot write directly to a PDF. Adobe makes a product called Distiller that can convert files to a PDF file. By using this technique, you could have the PL/SQL cartridge write its data to a file (with UTL_FILE), run the file through the distiller, and then redirect the user to the PDF file. There are several other ways to accomplish this goal. For example, there is a Perl library that writes a PDF file directly.

Summary

The Oracle Reports functionality for Web-enabling reports is certainly ready for prime-time Internet deployment. If you are deploying reports on an intranet or on the Internet, you will certainly want to consider using Oracle Developer to create these reports.

PART IV

Other Cartridge Options

CHAPTER 19

Java and OAS

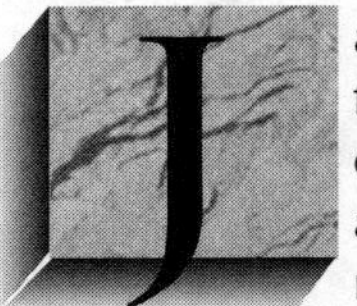

ava is currently the premier application development language for the Internet, and for the immediate future, this will not likely change. If you are familiar with Java and the myriad of class libraries and standards emerging from this language, you know why Java retains this position. If you are unfamiliar with Java, all the hype in the professional magazines can be daunting. The stream of new acronyms can be overwhelming—EJB, RMI, JSP, JDBC, SQLJ, JCORBA, JWeb, and JServlets. What are these new acronyms all about and how do you know which of these should be implemented into your environment?

If you work in an Oracle IT organization (aka Oracle shop), you need to know how committed Oracle is to supporting Java. You cannot afford to jump into any technology without knowing that Oracle will support you through the long haul. What about deployment and scalability of Java-based applications? If Java has a future in your organization, it had better be for justifiable reasons, so let's identify potential reasoning for your organization. The topics covered in this chapter include:

- Understanding Oracle's commitment to Java
- Why you should use Java
- Client-side Java
- Server-side Java
- Java technologies in OAS

Understanding Oracle's Commitment to Java

Oracle is 300 percent committed to Java! Good reasons exist for Oracle's devotion and commitment to Java. These reasons include:

- 300 percent Java—Oracle foresees Java's place on the client in applets and applications (100 percent), on Application Servers (another 100 percent), and in the database as Java stored procedures (the final 100 percent, totaling 300 percent).
- Java is gaining acceptance and significant market share. Over 70 percent of Global 1000 companies are either currently implementing or have specific plans to implement Java solutions to business problems within the next year.
- There is a growing base of Java developers, and a corresponding growth in demand for Java developers.

- Standards within Java are Servlets, Java Server Pages (JSP), Enterprise Java Beans (EJB), Remote Method Invocation (RMI), Java Database Connectivity (JDBC), Swing, and so forth. These are well-established standards used in the industry and have proven themselves in production environments.
- Availability of design and development tools. A plethora of mature development environments execute on multiple platforms: Oracle offers JDeveloper, Inprise offers JBuilder; Semantec offers Visual Café, IBM sells Visual Age, and Microsoft offers Visual J++, and the list continues. The major players in the development community are spending fortunes building tools, enabling you to immerse yourself in Java.

Determining If You Should Use Java

Oracle is committed to using Java, but why should you? If you already use Java for application development, you have probably found numerous ways to use this language. However, if your are a novice Java developer, or you are considering moving to Java development, consider the following:

- Java is a modern, object-oriented programming language. The designers of Java carefully avoided the pitfalls of other languages. For example, memory leaks are virtually eliminated. You can allocate memory by creating instances of classes, but you do not have to free that memory when you are finished with it. Java's built-in garbage collector frees the memory automatically. C and C++ developers often had trouble with memory pointers, so Java does not support pointers. C++ enables you to redefine operators such as the plus sign (+) to be useful with complex classes. While this is powerful, it is responsible for countless software bugs. Java does not support the use of the plus sign in this way.
- The developers of Java included some powerful concepts directly into the language. For example, a semaphore is built into the root class (object), which means all classes support semaphores for coordinating changes. Java also supports synchronized methods to eliminate thread contention problems. The language supports introspection, so a class can reveal its capabilities.
- You can be productive quickly. Because you can create specialized classes by inheriting from existing ones, you only build the code that makes it different from its parent into your derived class.
- Java is portable across operating systems and hardware. Compile your Java classes on a Windows 98 machine and run it on a Sun Solaris computer. All hardware-specific parts of Java are constrained to the Java Virtual Machine (JVM); therefore, you do not need to recompile for every possible platform and operating environment.

- An amazing number of new technologies are arising around Java, including Java Cartridges in OAS, Servlets, EJB, CORBA, RMI, JDBC, SQLJ, and JSP. These can be used in conjunction with each other.
- In addition to new technologies, hundreds of classes are built into the class libraries that accompany Java. Additionally, countless classes are available for free or commercially; therefore, you do not have to build all the classes yourself.
- OAS is an enterprise environment. Java is an important part of this environment. However, Java will also run on equipment as small as a cell phone or a 3Com Palm Pilot. Java is the most universal programming language in existence.
- Using Java means you are not limited to a single vendor's architecture or price structure. It means your site and code are not tied to a particular Web server, database, or operating system; therefore, you have control.
- Java supports threads. It lets you develop threaded software whether the underlying operating system supports native threads or not. Therefore, you can build efficient multithreaded applications.
- Java reduces expenses. Porting costs are no longer an issue. *Polymorphism* means you can specialize an existing class by deriving from it, but you only have to build the parts that differ from its parent class.

Client-Side Java

Your first encounter with Java was probably in the form of an Applet. An Applet is a Java program that runs within a Web page in your browser. Java has not achieved significant acceptance in this arena. Applets require a long time to download and they are not preserved in your browser between sessions. Your browser must download the Applet for every applicable session. Plug-ins are available to address this problem, but distributing and maintaining them is problematic for corporations because someone has to support them. The browser has a sandbox, which is a security manager that prevents applets from doing anything harmful to your computer. Therefore, an Applet cannot obtain environment variables, write anything to your disk drive (except for cookies), execute another program on your computer, or establish a connection with any computer except the one that executed the applet. These rules limit the usefulness of Applets. The Netscape and Microsoft browsers support the sandbox concept but some others do not. The sandbox rules are in the browser, and not in Applets. It is possible to give a digitally signed applet permission to bypass the sandbox rules; however, you have to trust the site sending you the

Applet. Some companies have firewall rules preventing Applets that originate in the Internet from running behind the firewall.

An example of Applet use is the OAS 4.0 tool used to configure your Web site, the OAS Manager. The configuration Applet will not work if your browser uses a version less than Java 1.2, and problems with fonts can occur in some browsers.

Applets are one form of client-side Java, and another is an application. Applications do not have a sandbox because they do not run in a browser. Java applications have to be installed on your computer, identical to other software. You have to maintain the correct version of the application and the Java VM, which can be a hassle. Even though Java is a fully developed application development language, it has not enjoyed widespread acceptance for building client applications.

Making the Most of Server-Side Java

In contrast with client-side Java, server-side Java has gained wide acceptance. Most application (Web) servers support various forms of Java. Some are written entirely in Java. OAS includes JServlets, JWeb cartridges, JCORBA, and Enterprise Java Beans, and the Oracle8i database supports Java stored procedures. A thumbnail sketch of these technologies will be presented in this section, and they will be covered in detail later in this chapter.

The Java Cartridge (JWeb)

OAS uses cartridges to build applications. The cartridge that supports the Java language, the Java Cartridge, is JWeb. Applications built for the JWeb cartridge have independent main functions, which are called when requests are sent from a browser to be executed by this cartridge. The JWeb Toolkit is available to build HTML documents and access databases from JWeb. Identical to all cartridges, JWeb takes advantage of features built into OAS, such as load-balancing, logging, and built-in monitoring.

Servlets

Servlets are currently the most popular Java technology for building dynamically generated Web pages. They are easy to build because all Servlets have the same life cycle characteristics and provide a standard set of method calls. Servlets support user authentication and can normally call other Servlets in an unlimited chain fashion, even though OAS does not currently support servlet chaining.

Java Server Pages (JSP)

As of the release of this book, OAS does not support JSP, however the beta JSP is available on www.olab.com so it looks like it won't be long! Essentially, JSP is a template document consisting of HTML with embedded Java. The HTML is static within each page, and the Java is executed to produce the HTML that will be placed in the document before passing it back to the browser. Other similar technologies exist, such as Oracle's LiveHTML (HTML with embedded Perl scripts) and Microsoft's Active Server Pages (HTML with embedded Visual Basic scripts).

Enterprise Java Beans (EJB)

EJB is an exciting new Java technology aimed at bringing Java to the enterprise. EJB is actually a specification originating with Sun Microsystems. EJB is a specification; therefore, any software vendor may build EJB support into their product, as Oracle has decided to do. At the time this book was written, the specification was still changing, even though implementations are commercially available. So what is an EJB? Basically, it is a well-behaved class written in Java that complies with the EJB specification. EJB includes methods to retrieve and set all of its attributes. It also includes a *home* interface providing a separate class to find and create instances of this bean. Whether you find an existing bean or create one, you obtain a *handle* to the bean. A handle is essentially a reference to the bean; the bean can be physically located on a remote computer or it may be local.

Two kinds of Enterprise Java Beans exist, *Session Beans* and *Entity Beans*. They both follow all of the EJB rules, but only Entity Beans are persistently stored. OAS only includes support for *Session Enterprise Java Beans*. The container-managed persistence is the constantly changing part of the EJB specification, which applies to Entity Beans. Oracle decided to wait on the specification before implementing Entity Beans. Technically, Session Beans may be stateful or stateless. Stateful Beans maintain state information between calls, implying that they write their state to a persistent store in case they need to be recovered from a failure.

From this extremely simplified explanation of EJB, it is evident that beans are powerful but somewhat complicated. You can develop effective enterprise applications using Java, and choose to use simpler technologies such as JWeb cartridges, or more technically challenging technologies such as JServlets, or complex EJBs.

Using Java Technologies in OAS

The best way to introduce a technology is with an example. We present a simple Web application below performing an HTTP GET and an HTTP POST operation. Your application presents a form for prospective clients to provide personal information and request that a company representative contact them. After submitting the form, the application adds a record to a database table and sends the appropriate regional representative an email. The following example sends email through the UNIX sendmail server. In this section, two methods of adding a record to the database will be demonstrated below—JDBC, and calling a PL/SQL procedure.

JWeb - The Java Cartridge

OAS provides a variety of cartridges supporting different languages (PL/SQL, C, and Java) and standards (CORBA and SQL). The Java Cartridge, JWeb, is one of three components of OAS enabling you to build your Internet application using the Java programming language. The other possibilities are JServlets and Enterprise Java Beans. See Figure 19-1 for a diagram of the path through OAS to this cartridge.

OAS includes a complete set of online documentation to help you exploit Java's rich development and deployment environment. This chapter provides an introduction to the Java technology, but when you need the complete set of JWeb and Toolkit details, have the online documents readily available. They are invaluable.

Advantages and Disadvantages of JWeb Cartridges

A number of advantages become apparent when using the JWeb cartridges rather than traditional CGI applications:

- A single Java Virtual Machine (JVM) is started for each Application Server instead of for each request. The JVM remains active for the life of the Application Server.
- Multiple cartridge instances are run in a single JVM, saving memory.
- JWeb cartridges take advantage of many of OAS's advanced features, such as load-balancing, scalability, built-in monitoring, logging, and sessions.
- While JWeb cartridges do not support multiple threads per cartridge instance, you can create and use your own threads within cartridge instances.

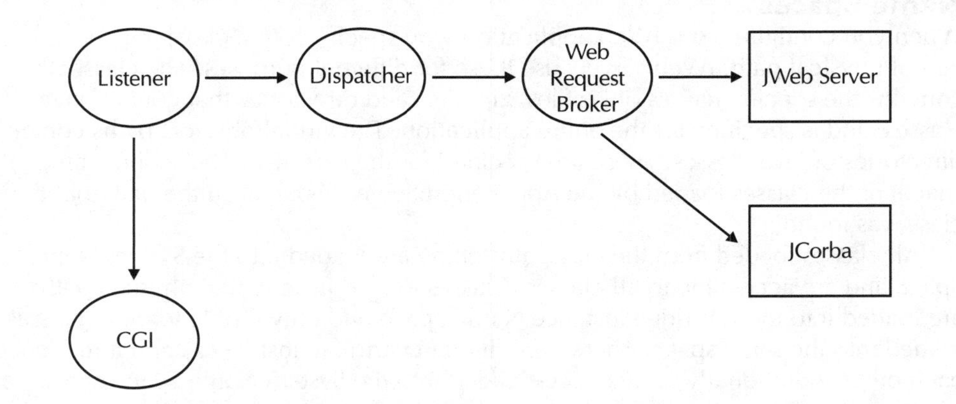

FIGURE 19-1. *Path to the Java cartridges*

The following are disadvantages to JWeb application development:

- Built-in debuggers do not exist.
- JWeb cartridges do not support multithreading in cartridge instances; therefore, you must start a separate cartridge instance to service each concurrent client.
- JWeb cartridges lack the convenience of a standard interface, such as those JServlets provide, or the consistent framework of Enterprise Java Beans (EJB).

How JWeb Works

When you configure your site, you must declare the virtual path to use to find JWeb cartridge instances, the minimum number of Cartridge Servers you want started, and the maximum number of concurrent Cartridge Servers to meet demand. You also specify the number of cartridge instances each server will manage and the number of threads associated with each cartridge instance. JWeb cartridge instances can manage state for their clients; therefore, each JWeb cartridge instance can handle exactly one thread. So, the minimum number of threads and cartridge instances must be the same. This is true for the maximum number as well.

The JWeb Cartridge Server contains a single JVM, compliant with Sun's Java Development Kit. See Figure 19-2 for the components of the JWeb cartridge. The Cartridge Server also contains the set of class libraries specified in the CLASSPATH environment variable, configuration information, a thread pool, and a database connection pool. The JVM executes the instances of JWeb cartridges by assigning a thread and a context from the WRB to a cartridge instance for each request. The context is only valid for the duration of the request.

Name Spaces

When you configure your JWeb application, you specify both a classpath and virtual/physical path. JWeb servers use these for different purposes. The classpath contains the specific names of jar files, zip files, and directories that contain Java classes, and is specified for the entire application. The virtual/physical paths contain directories of Java classes. These are specified for the cartridge. The scope (name space) of the classes loaded by the Application Server depends on the path that the class was found.

All classes loaded from the classpath setting are loaded into the System Name Space and are accessible to all classes. Classes loaded from virtual/physical paths are loaded into the Cartridge Instance Name Space and only visible to other classes loaded into the same space. Therefore, different cartridge instances cannot reference each other. Additionally, only classes loaded into the System Name Space can implement native methods. For these reasons, you may choose to load your classes through the classpath environment variable.

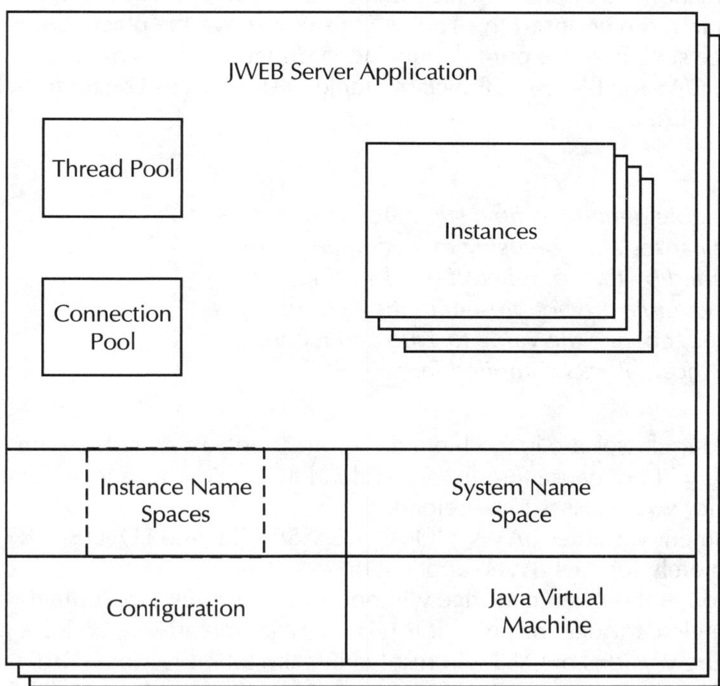

FIGURE 19-2. *JWeb server application*

If your classes are loaded from virtual/physical paths, each cartridge instance receives an independent copy. This is essentially equivalent to running your application in multiple processes because static variables are not shared between cartridge instances. As an example, it is common to use a static attribute to keep track of the number of instances of a class in memory. If a particular class is loaded from virtual/physical paths, the count is incorrect, because each instance has its own copy of the class, and therefore its own copy of the static attributes. Cartridge instances access the System Name Space classes as a thread. It is important that these classes be thread-safe. If your classes are not thread-safe, ensure they run in the cartridge instance name space.

Additional Important Points for Developers

A built-in debugger for the JWeb cartridge does not exist. You must debug your code before executing it within the cartridge. The JWeb Toolkit can only be used within an Application Server; therefore, you need to avoid using the Toolkit or provide placeholders for the Toolkit classes. Once you are ready to run your application in a server, insert the Toolkit calls or remove the placeholder classes. Include trace statements to print debugging information to standard output, or write to the OAS log file using the class oracle.OAS.Services.Logger to help debug your application.

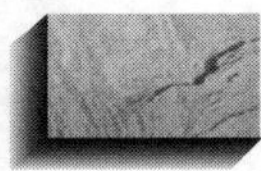

TIP
Any variable defined as final static Boolean and set to False causes all code using that variable to be disregarded by the compiler. If blocks using this type of variable are not present in the byte code generated, change the value to True and recompile to have those blocks compiled in.

Once your classes are loaded into an Application Server, recompiling your source code will not cause the server to reload them. You have to stop and restart the servers for your classes to be reloaded.

Environment variables (JAVA_HOME, CLASSPATH, and LD_LIBRARY_PATH) are set separately for each JWeb application.

Even though the JWeb cartridge will not support running multiple threads against a single cartridge instance, it is wise to write thread-safe code. A guarantee that the future versions of OAS will resolve this limitation is premature.

The JWeb Toolkit

JWeb includes a Toolkit you can use to generate HTML dynamically from JWeb applications. The JWeb Toolkit is actually a library of classes enabling you to communicate with the world outside your application. This includes generating the HTML sent back to the requesting browser, accessing databases, accessing WRB services, and logging runtime information. Rather than list the entire contents of the Toolkit in this section, an overview is provided to enable you to get comfortable with using the JWeb Toolkit.

Using the JWeb Toolkit to generate HTML involves learning a large class library. Basically, each element of HTML is generated with a call to one of these classes. For example, consider adding a row to an HTML table. The HTML appears as <TABLE COLS=2><TR>. Using the Toolkit, your Java code would appear identical to the following:

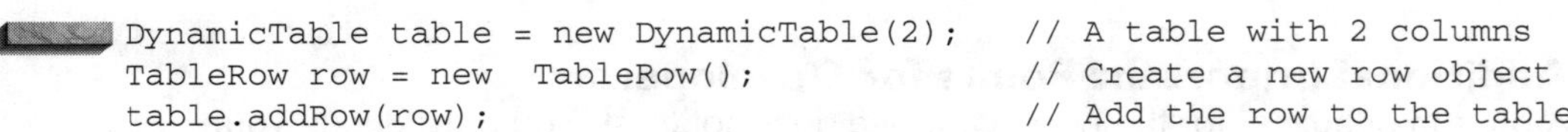

```
DynamicTable table = new DynamicTable(2);    // A table with 2 columns
TableRow row = new  TableRow();              // Create a new row object
table.addRow(row);                           // Add the row to the table
```

If you are unfamiliar with HTML syntax, but are familiar with Java, you may prefer the following style of generating HTML. However, if you prefer to write HTML directly, you can use System.out.println(...). In this case, your code would look like the following:

```
System.out.println ("<TABLE COLS=2>");
System.out.println("<TR>");
```

The problem with the preceding example is that it is not thread-safe. It is also more difficult to maintain this code. If your application is single-threaded, this fact will not be problematic. If you need to support threads, another advisable approach is similar to using System.out, as illustrated in the following example:

```
import oracle.html.*;
HtmlStream out = HtmlStream.theStream();
out.println ("<TABLE COLS=2>");
out.println("<TR>");
```

The style you use is a matter of preference. The JWeb Toolkit contains eleven packages stored in two jar files, and they are described in Tables 19-1 and 19-2.

To become comfortable with using the JWeb Toolkit, a few basics are described below. First, you need to access HTTP request information, such as header information, CGI environment variables, and parameters. Then, you need to create an HTTP response.

HTTP REQUESTS The JWeb Toolkit provides an HTTP class giving you a request object from which you can get all the details of the request you need. For example, if you want to get the identity of the type of browser that made the request, the IP address of the requesting host, and the value of the input field named

Package Name	Purpose
Oracle.OAS.Services	Provides access to configuration settings
Oracle.OAS.Services.ICX	Provides intercartridge communication (ICX)
Oracle.OAS.Services.Logger	Provides access to log runtime information

TABLE 19-1. *$ORAWEB_HOME/classes/services.jar*

Package Name	Purpose
Oracle.html	Dynamically generates HTML. You will become familiar with these classes if you create significant amounts of HTML code.
Oracle.owas.nls	Provides natural language support (NLS), which means using different character sets for different languages.
Oracle.owas.wrb	Accesses the WRB environment to obtain client context for the current request.
Oracle.owas.wrb. services.http	Provides details of requests.
Oracle.plsql	Translates between Java datatypes and PL/SQL datatypes.
Oracle.rdbms	Provides access to Oracle databases.

TABLE 19-2. *$ORAWEB_HOME/classes/jWeb.jar*

"name" from the form being submitted, your code would be identical to the following example:

```
HTTP request = HTTP.getRequest();  // get the request object
String agent = request.getHeader("User-Agent"); //identify the browser
// IP address
String remoteHost = request.getCGIEnvironment("REMOTE_HOST")
String name =  request.getURLParameter("name");  // value of "name"
```

HTTP RESPONSES Similar to above example, the output stream to write your HTML will appear as the following:

```
HtmlStream out = HtmlStream.theStream();
out.println ("HTML Goes Here");
```

The JWeb Application Example

After completing the preceding steps, you are ready to build a JWeb application. For this example, you need four classes: a dispatcher, an emailer, a database writer, and a technician finder. The dispatcher provides the main() method. All JWeb applications must provide their own main() method. Main instantiates the dispatcher and calls its dispatch() method. The dispatch() method obtains the field values from the request object and constructs a vector containing the parameters. It instantiates the emailer and uses it to send an email message to the appropriate technician. Then, it creates a database writer to add a record to the database table. When dispatch() returns, the main() method generates the HTML output to send back to the browser.

The following example retrieves the User-Agent field (the client's browser and platform) from the HTTP header and the REMOTE_HOST CGI environment variable (the client's IP address). This example does not need them, but they are included as an example of retrieving this type of information.

For the sake of brevity, the sample code below does not provide robust error handling. Try-catch blocks are included where the compiler requires them, and when you catch an error, the program writes the error to system.out. Obviously, this example does not contain production-quality error handling. Ideally, you would add an application-specific error to the calling method. Because the sample code would be harder to follow, I elected to omit it.

DISPATCHER.JAVA As previously mentioned, the dispatch() method will retrieve the field values from the request object and construct a vector containing these parameters. It instantiates the emailer and uses it to send an email message to the appropriate technician. Then, it creates a database writer to add a record to the database table.

```
package JavaChapter;

import java.util.*;
import oracle.html.*;
import oracle.owas.wrb.services.http.*;

public class Dispatcher {
   /** The Main. **/
   public static void main(String inArgs[]) {

      Dispatcher dispatcher = new Dispatcher();
      dispatcher.dispatch();

      // Build the page to be returned to the browser
      HtmlStream out = HtmlStream.theStream();
      out.println("<HTML>");
      out.println("<HEAD><TITLE>Recieved</TITLE></HEAD>");
      out.println("<BODY>");
      out.println("<H2>Thank you for your business!</H2>");
      out.println("A Technician will contact you soon.");
      out.println("</BODY>");
      out.println("</HTML>");
   }
```

```
   public void dispatch() {
      // Obtain the current request object
      HTTP request = HTTP.getRequest();

      // Although this application doesn't need any information from
      // the Header or the CGI Environment, the following code lines
      // illustrate how to retrieve information from them.
      String agent = request.getHeader("User-Agent");
      String remoteHost = request.getCGIEnvironment("REMOTE_HOST");

      // The information needed is in the URL parameters.
      // Retrieve this information and put it in the Client Info Vector
      Vector clientInfo = new Vector();

      clientInfo.addElement(request.getURLParameter("name"));
      clientInfo.addElement(request.getURLParameter("address"));
      clientInfo.addElement(request.getURLParameter("city"));
      clientInfo.addElement(request.getURLParameter("state"));
      clientInfo.addElement(request.getURLParameter("zip"));
      clientInfo.addElement(request.getURLParameter("phone"));
      clientInfo.addElement(request.getURLParameter("request"));

      // Email the Technician.
      Emailer emailer = new Emailer();
      emailer.sendEmail(clientInfo);

      // Enter the client's information into your database
      DatabaseWriter dbwriter = new DatabaseWriter();
      dbwriter.enterClientInfo(clientInfo);
   }
}
```

EMAILER.JAVA The emailer class demonstrates how to create and send an email message from a JWeb application. The Runtime class used in the following code demonstrates the process to send commands to the operating system. You can send the spawned process additional instructions, as shown in the example, and you may receive information that is not included in this example. The emailer also instantiates and calls a TechnicianFinder, calling a PL/SQL stored procedure to get the email address for a technician.

```
package JavaChapter;

import java.util.*;
import java.io.*;

public class Emailer {
   /** This method sends the client information to the email address
   *  of the technician.
   *
   *  @param inContents   Vector   Information about the client.
```

```
    **/
    public void sendEmail(Vector inClientInfo) {

       // Get the email address of the next available repair person by calling
       // a method that gets the next repair person in line.
       TechnicianFinder technicianFinder = new TechnicianFinder();
       String techToEmail = technicianFinder.getTechnician(
                            (String)inClientInfo.elementAt(Client.ZIP));
       try {
          // Get the Runtime Object
          Runtime runtime = Runtime.getRuntime();

          // Get a Process Thread from the Operating System and run the
          // execute sendmail.
          Process process = runtime.exec("/usr/lib/sendmail -t");

          // Establish a PrintWriter to write to the output stream obtained
          // from the process object.  Then send the contents of your email
          // to sendmail.
          PrintWriter printWriter =
             new PrintWriter( process.getOutputStream() );
          printWriter.println("From:AutomatedDispatchSystem");
          printWriter.println("To:" + techToEmail);
          printWriter.println("Please visit the following client...");
          printWriter.println((String)inClientInfo.elementAt(Client.NAME));
          printWriter.println((String)inClientInfo.elementAt(Client.ADDRESS));
          printWriter.println((String)inClientInfo.elementAt(Client.CITY));
          printWriter.println((String)inClientInfo.elementAt(Client.STATE));
          printWriter.println((String)inClientInfo.elementAt(Client.ZIP));
          printWriter.println((String)inClientInfo.elementAt(Client.PHONE));

          printWriter.println("The Client's Request is: ");
          printWriter.println((String)inClientInfo.elementAt(Client.REQUEST));
          printWriter.close();
       }

       catch (IOException ioe) {
          System.out.println("Error sending email: " + ioe);
       }
    }
 }
```

TECHNICIANFINDER.JAVA The TechnicianFinder class finds the email address of the technician that represents your customer's geographic area. First, several methods can be used to connect to the database. You can use JDBC or call a PL/SQL stored procedure. For this class, I chose to demonstrate calling a PL/SQL stored procedure. You can call stored procedures using JDBC or using Oracle's pl2java program to create a Java class wrapping a PL/SQL package. By default, the name of the class is the name of the package. The class' methods are the procedures found in the wrapped package. The details of using pl2java are included later in this chapter.

Because environment variables, such as ORACLE_HOME, are defined for each application, you cannot set them once for OAS and use these environmental variables in your JWeb application. You must set the environment variable in your session from the configuration information you provided when you created the application.

To call the stored procedure, first instantiate the wrapper class (RegionalTech). Your stored procedure takes a varchar2(30) for the geographic region and returns a varchar2(30) containing the appropriate email address. Java does not support varchar2 datatypes; therefore, you need to convert between Oracle datatypes and Java datatypes. Fortunately, Oracle provides classes for this purpose. Each conversion datatype starts with a capital "P". The PstringBuffer datatype encapsulates the varchar2 datatype. Create two variables of PstringBuffer—assignedTech and pRegion. Calling the stored procedure is a matter of calling a method on your wrapper class: regTech.getRegionalTech(pRegion). OAS includes thorough documentation for all the datatype conversion classes. The following example illustrates what we have discussed in detail above:

```
package JavaChapter;

import oracle.rdbms.*;
import oracle.plsql.*;

public class TechnicianFinder {
   /** This method gets the email address of the next technician.  This
   *  method illustrates how to invoke a stored procedure and return its
   *  results.
   *
   *  @return assignedTech String   The next technician in line.
   **/
   public String getTechnician(String inRegion) {

      PstringBuffer assignedTech = null;
      try {
         // Define ORACLE_HOME
         Session.setProperty("ORACLE_HOME",
                             System.getProperty("oracleHome"));

         // Create a new session and logon
         Session session = new Session();
         session.logon("user", "password", "technician_db");

         // Instantiate the wrapper class for the stored procedure
         RegionalTech regTech = new RegionalTech();
```

```
            // Instantiate a PstringBuffer to pass a string to the
            // PL/SQL procedure. The PstringBuffer is an ORACLE specific
            // type of StringBuffer class you need to use for passing to
            // a stored procedure Wrapper class.
            PstringBuffer pRegion = new PstringBuffer(30);
            pRegion.setValue(inRegion);

            // Invoke the PL/SQL procedure
            assignedTech = regTech.getRegionalTech(pRegion);
         }
         catch (ServerException se) {
            System.out.println("Exception thrown from the database: " + se);
         }
         return assignedTech.toString();
      }
   }
```

DATABASEWRITER.JAVA The DatabaseWriter class connects to the database. In this class, you are adding a new record to the customer table, using JDBC. The first thing you must do is get a connection to the database using a JDBC Driver Manager. Then, use the connection's prepareStatement() method to construct a SQL statement to be executed in the database. Question marks act as placeholders for variables. These variables are inserted at the question marks using the PreparedStatement class' setString. Use the PreparedStatement class' executeUpdate() method to execute the insert. In the finally block, close the statement and connection. This should be completed in the finally block to ensure it is performed even if an error occurred earlier.

```
package JavaChapter;

import java.util.*;
import java.sql.*;

public class DatabaseWriter {
   /** This method enters the client information into the CUSTOMER table in
    *   the database.
    *
    *  @param inInfo   Vector   Information about the client.
    **/
   public void enterClientInfo(Vector inInfo) {

        Connection con = null;
        PreparedStatement ps = null;
        try {
          // Get connected to the Database
          System.out.println("Getting connection...");
          con = DriverManager.getConnection("jdbc:oracle@fri",
```

```
                                                    "user","password");

         System.out.println("Got connection.");

         // Prepare the statement to be executed through JDBC.
         ps = con.prepareStatement("insert into customer(name, " +
                                   "address, " + "city, " + "state, " +
                                   "zip, " + "phone, " + "problem) " +
                                   "values (?, ?, ?, ?, ?, ?, ?)");

         /* Set the JDBC hooks with the information passed in
          * to the function.
          * REMEMBER: All elements returned from a vector are of
          * type "Object" and must be cast to a String. */
         ps.setString(1, (String)inInfo.elementAt(Client.NAME));
         ps.setString(2, (String)inInfo.elementAt(Client.ADDRESS));
         ps.setString(3, (String)inInfo.elementAt(Client.CITY));
         ps.setString(4, (String)inInfo.elementAt(Client.STATE));
         ps.setString(5, (String)inInfo.elementAt(Client.ZIP));
         ps.setString(6, (String)inInfo.elementAt(Client.PHONE));
         ps.setString(7, (String)inInfo.elementAt(Client.REQUEST));

         // Execute the query
         if (ps.executeUpdate() != 1) {
            System.out.println("JDBC did not create any row");
            throw new SQLException ("JDBC did not create any row");
         }
      }
      catch (SQLException sqe) {
         System.out.println("SQL Exception ... " + sqe);
      }
      finally {
         try {
            ps.close();
            System.out.println("Closing connection...");
            con.close();
         }
         catch (Exception e){
            System.out.println("Unable to close the connection! " + e);
         }
      }
   } //end of enterClientInfo()
} //end of DatabaseWriter
```

PL2JAVA OAS provides the pl2java utility to create Java wrapper classes for your PL/SQL packages. Each procedure and function in the package becomes a method in the class. This utility depends on the dbms_package package provided with OAS. Oracle includes a set of datatype classes to convert between Java and PL/SQL datatypes. Table 19-3, from the JWeb Cartridge documentation, lists the supported datatypes.

PL/SQL Datatype	Java Wrapper Class
BINARY_INTEGER (+ NATURAL, POSITIVE)	Pinteger
NUMBER (+ DEC, DECIMAL, DOUBLE PRECISION, FLOAT, INTEGER, INT, NUMERIC, REAL, SMALLINT)	Pdouble
CHAR(n) (+ CHARACTER, STRING)	PstringBuffer
VARCHAR2(n) (+ VARCHAR)	PstringBuffer
LONG	PstringBuffer
RAW (n)	PbyteArray
LONG RAW	PbyteArray
BOOLEAN	Pboolean
DATE	Pdate
PL/SQL table	Java array

TABLE 19-3. *JWeb Supported Datatypes*

Table 19-4 covers the equally important unsupported datatypes, also from Oracle's documentation.

Disallowed PL/SQL Datatypes	Substitute PL/SQL Datatypes
POSITIVE	BINARY INTEGER
PL/SQL table of BINARY INTEGER, NATURAL or POSITIVE	PL/SQL table of NUMBER
PL/SQL table of LONG	PL/SQL table of CHAR or VARCHAR2
PL/SQL table of BOOLEAN	PL/SQL table of NUMBER, treat 0 as False and 1 as True
ROWID	None
MSLABEL	None
PL/SQL table of ROWID	None
PL/SQL table of MSLABEL	None

TABLE 19-4. *JWeb Unsupported Datatypes*

The RegionalTech PL/SQL package demonstrates the use of pl2java to create a wrapper class, also named RegionalTech. In the following example, a fixed address is returned. Use the region input variable as a unique key in a SELECT statement to find the appropriate email address.

```
create or replace package RegionalTech as
   procedure getRegionalTech(region in varchar2,
                             technician_email out varchar2);
end RegionalTech;
/
create or replace package body RegionalTech is
   procedure getRegionalTech(region in varchar2,
                             technician_email out varchar2) as
    begin
       -- This is where your selection code would reside. In this
       -- example, return a fixed address.
       technician_email := 'Technician@fri.com';
    end getRegionalTech;
end RegionalTech;
/
```

The following command line executes the pl2java utility for the RegionalTech package. Pl2Java creates the compiled file RegionalTech.class. The Oracle documentation suggests Java source is generated, but in practice only a class file is created. The following is not source code:

```
OSprompt> pl2java user/password@technician_db RegionalTech
```

Servlets

One of the latest additions to OAS is servlet support; Oracle refers to them as JServlets. Servlets must support the methods they inherit from HttpServlet, and support the lifecycle defined for that class. For example, the init() method is called once per servlet when it is first loaded into memory. Servlets support threads and a single instance of a servlet can support all client requests for its services.

DispatcherServlet.java

You can convert the preceding Dispatcher class from a JWeb cartridge to a servlet by having it extend HttpServlet. First, import the new classes (javax.servlet.* and javax.servlet.http.*), and eliminate the main() method. Servlets do not need a main() method. Instead, they are initialized by the init() method. Init takes ServletConfig as its argument. If you specified any servlet configuration settings, you can use ServletConfig to retrieve the values, as the following example illustrates:

```
String user = cfg.getInitParameter("run_as");
```

The preceding syntax would return the value of the initialization parameter run_as, assuming your configuration set that parameter.

When an HTTP POST request is called for a servlet, the doPost() method is invoked. The doPost() and doGet() (for HTTP GET requests) methods receive an HttpServletRequest and an HttpServletResponse object. The name-value pair arguments from the URL are available from the request object, and you can write HTML to the response object. The response object has a PrintWriter containing a println() method. When the dispatch() is called, pass the request object along so the method can retrieve parameter values. The values are passed back as an array of strings. This is true even if your HTML form presented a text-input field for that value containing only a single string.

```
package JavaChapter;

import java.util.*;
import java.io.* ;
import javax.servlet.* ;
import javax.servlet.http.* ;

public class DispatcherServlet extends HttpServlet {

   public void init (ServletConfig cfg) throws ServletException {
   }

   public void doPost (HttpServletRequest req, HttpServletResponse res)
                throws ServletException, IOException {

      // generate the MIME type and character set header
      res.setContentType("text/html; charset=us-ascii");

      dispatch(req);

      // generate the HTML page
      PrintWriter out = res.getWriter();
      out.println("<HTML>");
      out.println("<HEAD><TITLE>Recieved</TITLE></HEAD>");
      out.println("<BODY>");
      out.println("<H2>Thank you for your business!</H2>");
      out.println("A Technician will be with you shortly.");
      out.println("</BODY>");
      out.println("</HTML>");
   }

   public void dispatch(HttpServletRequest req) {

      // The information needed is in the URL parameters.
      // Retrieve this information and put it in the Client Info Vector
```

```
        Vector clientInfo = new Vector();
        clientInfo.addElement(req.getParameterValues("name")[0]);
        clientInfo.addElement(req.getParameterValues("address")[0]);
        clientInfo.addElement(req.getParameterValues("city")[0]);
        clientInfo.addElement(req.getParameterValues("state")[0]);
        clientInfo.addElement(req.getParameterValues("zip")[0]);
        clientInfo.addElement(req.getParameterValues("phone")[0]);
        clientInfo.addElement(req.getParameterValues("request")[0]);

        // Email the Technician .
        Emailer emailer = new Emailer();
        emailer.sendEmail(clientInfo);

        // Enter the client's information into your database
        DatabaseWriter dbwriter = new DatabaseWriter();
        dbwriter.enterClientInfo(clientInfo);
    }
}
```

Enterprise Java Beans (EJB)

Enterprise Java Beans is a component architecture. You can build some components and buy others. For example, you can buy the container component and build the business logic components. OAS's EJB implementation is built on an Object Request Broker (ORB). Therefore, it can communicate with remote CORBA classes.

DispatcherServletEJB

To convert your sample application to use EJB, change the Dispatcher Servlet to get an initial context, then look up the home interfaces for the emailer (a Session Bean) and the DatabaseWriter (another Session Bean). The home interface provides the method to create new instances of beans (Session or Entity) and find existing beans. Define the method lookupHomeInterfaces() to find the interfaces using Java Naming and Directory Interface (JNDI). After finding the home interface, call the create() method to instantiate a bean. If the call fails, the home interface activates a CreateException.

The create() method returns a remote interface to the bean. The remote interface is a handle to the bean, which is assumed to be located on a remote host. Next, call the sendEmail() method on the bean to send the email message. If the bean is unavailable for any reason, the request will activate a RemoteException.

```
package JavaChapter;

import java.util.*;
import java.io.* ;
import java.rmi.*;
import javax.naming.*;
```

```
import javax.servlet.* ;
import javax.servlet.http.* ;
import oracle.oas.eco.*;

public class DispatcherServletEJB extends HttpServlet {

   private final String EMAILERHOME                  =
              "oas://host/ejb/JavaChapter/EmailerHome";
   private final String DATABASEWRITERHOME           =
              "oas://host/ejb/JavaChapter/DatabaseWriterHome";
   private javax.naming.Context aInitialContext    = null;
   private EmailerHome aEmailerHome                 = null;
   private DatabaseWriterHome aDatabaseWriterHome = null;

   public void doPost (HttpServletRequest req,
                       HttpServletResponse res)
                      throws ServletException, IOException {
      // If the home interfaces have not been found yet, find them
      if (aEmailerHome == null) {
         lookupHomeInterfaces();
      }

      // generate the MIME type and character set header
      res.setContentType("text/html; charset=us-ascii");

      // execute the dispatch method
      dispatch(req);

      // generate the HTML page to thank the user
      PrintWriter out = res.getWriter();
      out.println("<HTML>");
      out.println("<HEAD><TITLE>Recieved</TITLE></HEAD>");
      out.println("<BODY>");
      out.println("<H2>Thank you for your business!</H2>");
      out.println("A Technician will be with you shortly.");
      out.println("</BODY>");
      out.println("</HTML>");
   }

   public void dispatch(HttpServletRequest req) {
      // The information needed is in the URL parameters.
      // Retrieve this information and put it in the
      // Client Info Vector
      Vector clientInfo = new Vector();
      clientInfo.addElement(req.getParameterValues("name")[0]);
      clientInfo.addElement(req.getParameterValues("address")[0]);
      clientInfo.addElement(req.getParameterValues("city")[0]);
      clientInfo.addElement(req.getParameterValues("state")[0]);
      clientInfo.addElement(req.getParameterValues("zip")[0]);
```

```
        clientInfo.addElement(req.getParameterValues("phone")[0]);
        clientInfo.addElement(req.getParameterValues("request")[0]);

        // Email the Technician and enter the client's information into
        // your database.
        try {
           // Create a remote handle to the bean through the create()
           // method on the home interface.
           EmailerRemote eRemote = aEmailerHome.create();
           DatabaseWriterRemote dbRemote = aDatabaseWriterHome.create();

           // Execute methods on the remote interface handles.
           eRemote.sendEmail(clientInfo);
           dbRemote.enterClientInfo(clientInfo);
       }
        catch (javax.ejb.CreateException ce) {
           System.out.println("Unable to create a bean: " + ce);
        }
        catch (RemoteException re) {
           System.out.println("Error executing method on
               remote bean: " + re);
        }
     }

     private synchronized void lookupHomeInterfaces() {
        // Set up the environment hashtable
        Hashtable env = new Hashtable();
        env.put(javax.naming.Context.URL_PKG_PREFIXES,
                "oracle.oas.naming.jndi");

        try {
           // get the initial context without specifying an environment
            aInitialContext = new InitialContext(env);

           // get the EmailerHome
            aEmailerHome = (EmailerHome)PortableRemoteObject.narrow(
                                  aInitialContext.lookup(EMAILERHOME),
                                  EmailerHome.class);
           // get the DatabaseWriterHome
            aDatabaseWriterHome = (DatabaseWriterHome)
                           PortableRemoteObject.narrow(
                           aInitialContext.lookup(DATABASEWRITERHOME),
                           DatabaseWriterHome.class);
        }
        catch (NamingException ne) {
           System.out.println("Unable to establish
               a naming context: " + ne);
        }
     }
  }
```

EmailerBean.java

The Emailer EJB implements SessionBean and contains a SessionContext as an attribute. The session context is needed to obtain information and services from the container. All EJB classes must provide methods to support the EJB life cycle. These include ejbCreate, ejbActivate, ejbPassivate, ejbRemote, and so forth. The dispatch() method does not need to be changed to support EJB.

```
package JavaChapter;

import java.util.*;
import java.io.*;
import javax.ejb.*;
import java.util.Properties;
import javax.naming.*;

public class EmailerBean implements javax.ejb.SessionBean {

   private SessionContext aSessionContext = null;

   // the bean.
   public void setSessionContext(SessionContext inCtx) {
      // save the session context for any future information needs
      aSessionContext = inCtx;
   }

   // implement ejbCreate, which is called by the container when the
   // Home create is invoked by the client.
   public void ejbCreate() throws CreateException {
   }

   // implement the activation routine. anything that needs to be
   // done to the bean upon activation should be included here.
   public void ejbActivate() {
   }

   // implement anything that needs to be done before the
   // bean is passivated. this would include closing any open
   // resources. however, for this example, no open resources need
   // to be closed. thus, the method is empty.
   public void ejbPassivate() {
   }

   // implement anything that needs to be done before the
   // bean is destroyed. this would include closing any open
   // resources. however, for this example, no open resources need
   // to be closed. thus, the method is empty.
   public void ejbRemove() {
   }
```

```
/**  This method sends the client information to the Email address
*  of the technician.
*
*  @param inContents   Vector   Information about the client.
**/
public void sendEmail(Vector inClientInfo) {
   // Get the email address of the next available
   // repair person by calling a method that gets
   // the next repair man in line.
   TechnicianFinder technicianFinder = new TechnicianFinder();
   String techToEmail = technicianFinder.getTechnician(
                        (String)inClientInfo.elementAt(Client.ZIP));
   try {
      // Get the Runtime Object
      Runtime runtime = Runtime.getRuntime();

      // Get a Process Thread from the Operating System and run the
      // execute sendmail.
      Process process = runtime.exec("/usr/lib/sendmail -t");

      // Establish a PrintWriter to write to the output
      // stream obtained from the process object.  Then
      // Send the contents of your Email to sendmail.
      PrintWriter printWriter =
           new PrintWriter(process.getOutputStream());
      printWriter.println("From:AutomatedDispatchSystem");
      printWriter.println("To:" + techToEmail);
      printWriter.println("Please visit the following client...");
      printWriter.println(
           (String)inClientInfo.elementAt(Client.NAME));
      printWriter.println(
           (String)inClientInfo.elementAt(Client.ADDRESS));
      printWriter.println(
           (String)inClientInfo.elementAt(Client.CITY));
      printWriter.println(
           (String)inClientInfo.elementAt(Client.STATE));
      printWriter.println(
           (String)inClientInfo.elementAt(Client.ZIP));
      printWriter.println(
           (String)inClientInfo.elementAt(Client.PHONE));

      printWriter.println("The Client's Request is: ");
      printWriter.println(
           (String)inClientInfo.elementAt(Client.REQUEST));
      printWriter.close();
   }
```

```
        catch (IOException ioe) {
           System.out.println("Error sending Email: " + ioe);
        }
     }
  }
```

EmailerHome.java

The following Home and Remote interfaces illustrate the appearances of these classes. The Home interfaces provide the create method and the Remote interfaces provide the methods supplying the business services for these beans.

```
package JavaChapter;

public interface EmailerHome extends javax.ejb.EJBHome {
   public EmailerRemote create() throws javax.ejb.CreateException;
}

EmailerRemote.java
package JavaChapter;

import java.util.*;
import java.rmi.*;

public interface EmailerRemote extends javax.ejb.EJBObject {
   public void sendEmail(Vector inClientInfo) throws RemoteException;
}

DatabaseWriterBean.java
package JavaChapter;

import java.sql.*;
import javax.ejb.*;
import java.util.*;

import oracle.rdbms.*;
import oracle.plsql.*;

public class DatabaseWriterBean implements javax.ejb.SessionBean {

   private SessionContext aSessionContext = null;

   // the bean.
   public void setSessionContext(SessionContext inCtx)
   {
      // save the session context for any future information needs
      aSessionContext = inCtx;
   }
```

```
// implement ejbCreate, which is called by the container when the
// Home create is invoked by the client.
public void ejbCreate() throws CreateException {
}

// implement the activation routine. anything that needs to be
// done to the bean upon activation should be included here.
public void ejbActivate() {
}

// implement anything that needs to be done before the
// bean is passivated. this would include closing any open
// resources. however, for this example, no open resources need
// to be closed. thus, the method is empty.
public void ejbPassivate() {
}

// implement anything that needs to be done before the
// bean is destroyed. this would include closing any open
// resources. however, for this example, no open resources need
// to be closed. thus, the method is empty.
public void ejbRemove() {
}

/**  This method enters the client information into the
*    CUSTOMER table in the database.
*
*  @param inInfo   Vector   Information about the client.
**/
public void enterClientInfo(Vector inInfo) {

    Connection con = null;
    PreparedStatement ps = null;
    try {
      // Get connected to the Database
      System.out.println("Getting connection...");
      con = DriverManager.getConnection(
                            "jdbc:oracle@fri","user","password");

      System.out.println("Got connection.");

      // Prepare the statement to be executed through JDBC.
      ps = con.prepareStatement("insert into customer(name, " +
                            "address, " + "city, " + "state, " +
                            "zip, " + "phone, " + "problem) " +
                            "values (?, ?, ?, ?, ?, ?, ?)");

       /* Set the JDBC hooks with the information passed in to
       * the function.
```

```
        * REMEMBER: All elements returned from a vector are of type
        * "Object" and must be cast to a String. */
        ps.setString(1, (String)inInfo.elementAt(Client.NAME));
        ps.setString(2, (String)inInfo.elementAt(Client.ADDRESS));
        ps.setString(3, (String)inInfo.elementAt(Client.CITY));
        ps.setString(4, (String)inInfo.elementAt(Client.STATE));
        ps.setString(5, (String)inInfo.elementAt(Client.ZIP));
        ps.setString(6, (String)inInfo.elementAt(Client.PHONE));
        ps.setString(7, (String)inInfo.elementAt(Client.REQUEST));

        // Execute the query
        if (ps.executeUpdate() != 1) {
           System.out.println("JDBC did not create any row");
           throw new SQLException ("JDBC did not create any row");
        }
     }
     catch (SQLException sqe) {
        System.out.println("SQL Exception ... " + sqe);
     }
     finally {
        try {
           ps.close();
           System.out.println("Closing connection...");
           con.close();
        }
        catch (Exception e){
        System.out.println("Unable to close the connection! " + e);
        }
     }
  }  // end of enterClientInfo(
}

DatabaseWriterHome.java
package JavaChapter;

public interface DatabaseWriterHome extends javax.ejb.EJBHome {
  public DatabaseWriterRemote create()
        throws javax.ejb.CreateException;
}

DatabaseWriterRemote.java
package JavaChapter;

import java.util.*;
import java.rmi.*;

public interface DatabaseWriterRemote extends javax.ejb.EJBObject {
  public void enterClientInfo(Vector inInfo) throws RemoteException;
}
```

Summary

This chapter provided an introduction to Java. It suggested reasons for using Java and touched on Oracle's commitment to Java within OAS. It introduced an overview of the JWeb Cartridges and advances being made on Servlets and concludes with the support for EJB. This progression reflects the increasing complexity, power, and scalability. It is important to consider the advantages and disadvantages of each before proceeding with your development project.

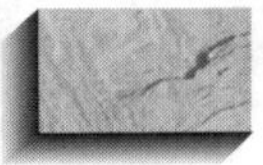

TIP
Thorough Java documentation is provided with OAS and available from Sun Microsystems.

CHAPTER 20

Perl and the Perl Cartridge

If you are looking for an interpretive programming language that optimizes the scanning of arbitrary text files to extract information for printing reports, or if you are looking for a good language to handle file operations or system management tasks, then Practical Extraction and Report Language (Perl) might just be the tool for you. Perl is a powerful, portable, interpretive scripting language. While an interpretive language is slower than a compiled language (such as C), interpretive languages such as Perl, Java, JavaScript, and so forth are easily ported across platforms. Because Perl is an interpretive language, you can use a simple text editor (for example, Notepad, vi, Write, or Word) for code development, but you will also need a Perl interpreter to run your Perl scripts. Perl is similar to C, but it has less restrictive specifications (for example, you are not required to declare or initialize variables). If you already know C, the concepts and intricacies of Perl can be obtained effortlessly. If you lack the knowledge of C, you will be delighted to know that Perl is easier to learn than C. For example, string manipulation and arrays are nearly effortless in Perl. Perl combines the best features of Korne shell scripting, C programming, and the UNIX utilities (sed, awk, and grep) to make a powerful programming language.

Perl is often called a Common Gateway Interface (CGI) for Web development. Perl was developed long before the Web became popular. While people seem to mention Perl in association with Web development, it is also a powerful server-side tool. Perl is truly a portable language that runs on a variety of platforms. The OAS Perl cartridge will also support direct access to the Oracle database. Perl is available on UNIX and Win32 environments. Best of all, it's free. Larry Wall, the author of Perl, still holds the copyright.

In this chapter, the following tips and techniques will be covered:

- Learning Perl
- Testing and debugging Perl
- Using the Perl cartridge
- Getting CGI Perl to work with OAS
- Using Perl with other listeners
- Simulating a cartridge on NT
- Installing and configuring the Perl cartridge in OWAS version 3
- Fixing the OWAS version 3 Perl demo
- Installing and configuring the Perl cartridge in OAS version 4
- Using a standard CGI library

- Avoiding the *Save As* dialog box
- Displaying a list of files
- Determining if a file exists
- Creating or appending a file
- Invoking a PL/SQL procedure from Perl
- Byteserving with Perl
- Emulating a browser from the command line
- Emulating a post request from the command line
- Cleaning up your HTML
- Getting access to Perl documentation
- Looking at the environmental parameters
- Sending mail from Perl
- Determining the client browser and acting accordingly
- Including site components
- Resolving OraPerl references in OWAS 3.0 documentation
- Resolving OraPerl references in OAS 4.0 documentation
- Using Perl in the LiveHTML cartridge
- Understanding OraPerl versus DBD and DBI
- Using OraPerl (DBD and DBI)
- Reviewing sample OraPerl code
- Understanding the "use OraPerl" statement
- Making database connections persistent
- Reviewing production OraPerl code

Learning Perl

You might wonder, why bother learning Perl? If you are developing applications using OAS, PL/SQL may provide all the flexibility you need to develop powerful, robust, dynamic Web applications. While this is probably true 95 percent of the time, it is that other 5 percent you need to consider. If you are not using OAS, Perl is free, works well for Web development, and can access the Oracle database (and others), so Perl may be the answer for a Web CGI.

If you are using OAS, the following might be an example of a situation falling into that 5 percent previously mentioned. In a typical production configuration, the Web server resides outside of the firewall and the database is inside the firewall. If your database resides on one server and your Web server resides on another, the Oracle database engine would be able to access files on the database server using PL/SQL, but not on the Web server. Given the same situation, with Perl you can access the Web server's file system but not the database server's file system. The capability to interact with a file system to read password files or compare directory trees can be useful when developing secure applications. Which server you need to access flat files from will dictate which tool will serve your needs.

Perl can also fill the PL/SQL gap when running an operating system program (for example, Sendmail) from your application. Perl can call operating system commands and programs, while PL/SQL cannot.

To learn Perl, many great books are available to review the Perl language in detail. However, unless you are developing 100 percent of your code with the Perl cartridge, you will probably want to select one or two developers that can code you right through the situations where Perl is required.

Testing and Debugging Perl

If you are running your OAS on NT with the software straight out of the box, there is no easy way to debug your Perl scripts. Therefore, consider installing a standalone version of Perl, to test your code outside of OAS. You can download the standard distribution of Perl for NT (Win32) from www.perl.com or the ActivePerl distribution from www.activestate.com. If OAS is running on UNIX, a program called persistperl is already installed and enabling the testing of Perl code from the command line. The UNIX version also comes with all of the man pages (i.e., help pages on UNIX) for Perl. On OWAS version 3, STDERR (standard error output) that results from Perl scripts is written to the Perl.log file, which can be found in the $ORAWEB_HOME/cartx/perl/log directory on UNIX or NT. On OAS version 4, you must turn logging on, and define the directory and filename where errors should be written. The xlf.log file contains a consolidated error log as well.

To debug any Perl script from the command line, add the debug mode parameter (-d). A cryptic debugger is available under standard Perl. You may wish to consider purchasing a Perl debugger. ActiveState has developed a Perl debugger for the NT environment, along with a number of programs that enhance Perl. ActiveState's Perl debugger enables you to visually debug Perl code by showing watches, variables, and registers. The tool also makes it simple to jump to statements, edit source, step through code, insert breakpoints, and so forth. If you are developing a considerable amount of Perl code, consider getting a debugging tool.

Using the Perl Cartridge

If Perl is going to be developed to run with the OAS, use the Perl cartridge shipped with the software. The purpose of using cartridges over any standard CGI program is performance. Remember that cartridges are persistent. Not only is the Perl cartridge persistent, but the executed Perl scripts are also cached. This persistence and caching leads to serious performance benefits over a standard CGI program. As of OAS version 4.0.7, Perl version 5.003 is compiled into the cartridge. However, as described in Chapter 19, the LiveHTML cartridge uses Perl version 5.004. OAS 4.0.8 uses Perl version 5.004_01 for both Perl and LiveHTML. If you plan to use Perl to access your database, be sure to install OAS 4.0.8.

Getting CGI Perl to Work with OAS

After installing Perl on the Web server, as long as you map the source directory for the Perl programs as a CGI directory, most platforms will execute the Perl script as a CGI without any further modification. However, on NT, CGIs are either executables (i.e., an extension of EXE) or batch scripts (i.e., an extension of BAT). For the NT version of Perl, you should find a program called pl2bat. This program will convert a Perl script into a batch script, a valid executable CGI program for NT. You must convert your Perl script to a BAT script using pl2bat—once this has been completed, your script will execute on NT.

Using Perl with Other Listeners

If a Web server other than OAS (or OWAS) is selected to be used, a few different choices exist when using the Perl cartridge. First, if you buy OWAS or OAS, install and use OAS in conjunction with your existing listener in one of two ways. If you are using Microsoft IIS, Netscape Enterprise, or an Apache listener, you will be able to register the listener (covered in Chapter 8) to OAS as an external listener. If you are using a listener other than these listeners, install OAS on another port (for example, 8080) and execute the Perl cartridge requests through that port. Another option is to execute the CGI versions of each of the Perl scripts. Another option is explained in the following section.

Simulating a Cartridge on NT

As previously discussed, the primary benefit of the Oracle cartridges is that they are a persistent process. In other words, it stays in memory. Additionally, the Perl cartridge also caches the Perl script. This leads to performance benefits that can seriously enhance the speed of your site. However, if you are running Perl on NT (as a CGI), ActiveState makes a cartridge-like version of Perl. It is called PerlEx. The performance gains are similar to those of the Perl cartridge—from 4 to 24 times faster than Perl executing as a traditional CGI. A benefit of PerlEx over the Oracle Perl cartridge is that PerlEx can use the Perl CGI with DBI and DBD (or any other library) compiled into it. Unfortunately, you cannot compile additional libraries into the Oracle Perl cartridge.

Installing and Configuring the Perl Cartridge in OWAS Version 3

When you install Oracle Web Application Server version 3, the Perl cartridge is automatically installed. A separate option to install the Perl cartridge does not exist. However, a couple of tasks must be performed to set up the Perl cartridge, even though the documentation suggests the Perl cartridge is already set up. These steps include the following:

1. At an operating system–level prompt, create a new physical directory for your Perl scripts (for example, c:\apps\perl)
2. Place your Perl scripts into the above directory
3. Through the WRB configuration, configure the Perl cartridge by setting the physical path for the cartridge to be equal to the preceding directory (c:\apps\perl), and set the virtual path as desired (for example, /perl). Make sure you change the minimum number of processes to one or more (otherwise, you will be operating Perl like a CGI).

After configuring the Perl cartridge, bounce (stop and start) the WRB and all of the listeners. Remember, when you modify cartridge parameters you must bounce the WRB.

Fixing the OWAS Version 3 Perl Demo

After installing Oracle Web Application Server version 3, a Perl directory is created under ORAWEB_HOME (for example, c:\orant\ows\3.0\perl). The WRB contains a virtual path (/perl) pointing to this physical path. However, in the listener configuration, it also contains a virtual path (/perl) pointing to this physical path. So, who wins? Well, the listener is contacted first. If a virtual path is requested that does not exist in the listener, the request goes to the WRB to verify if it has such a virtual path. Technically, the listener is contacted first, so the listener "wins." In the listener, the /perl virtual path is configured as a NR (Normal Recursive directory). The listener will send the files in that directory to the browser (not execute them). Therefore, if you attempt to use any of the Perl scripts in the /perl directory, you will quickly discover that your browser does not know what to do with a file with an extension of pl. Your browser will display a Save As dialog box. Obviously, this is not the desired result. To fix this problem, delete the /perl virtual path from the listener directory list.

Installing and Configuring the Perl Cartridge in OAS Version 4

When installing OAS version 4, the Perl cartridge is only installed if you install it during product installation for version 4.0.7 if you perform a "typical" installation, even though most cartridges are installed automatically, Perl is not. Version 4 offers the "complete" installation, which will install the Perl cartridge. If the Perl cartridge has not been installed, the Perl cartridge will not be in the list of available cartridge types. If at some point you want to install new Perl applications, go back through the installation as explained in Chapter 2 and add the Perl cartridge component. In OAS version 4, the installation does not automatically configure the cartridges. Therefore, a few things must be completed to set up the Perl cartridge for your use. These steps include the following:

1. Create a new physical directory for your Perl scripts (for example, c:\apps\perl)
2. Place your Perl scripts into the new physical directory
3. In the OAS Manager, through the Node Manager port, add an application as discussed in Chapter 4. For debugging purposes, be sure to turn logging on for your new Perl cartridge. Initially, I prefer to set the severity level to 15, to view detailed error messages. For performance reasons, ensure the minimum instances and thread parameters are set according to the recommendations in Chapter 4. It is recommended to set each of these parameters to a minimum of 1; otherwise, you are effectively using the Perl cartridge as a CGI. Your virtual path should be set to identical to /perl, and your physical path should be set to your newly created physical directory as previously noted (for example, c:\apps\perl). It is important to set the Perl parameters PRIVLIB and SITELIB to %ORAWEB_HOME\..\cartx\perl\lib and %ORAWEB_HOME\..\cartx\common\perl\lib\site, respectively. OAS 4.0.8 will set this up for you automatically.

After reconfiguring the Perl cartridge, then reload the site. Remember, when you modify any cartridge parameters, you must bounce the entire site.

Using a Standard CGI Library

Rather than writing your own routines to obtain information from standard input (STDIN) and writing standard headers and other HTML output, use a standard Perl CGI library. Several such libraries are available on the Web. However, mycgi-lib.pl comes with OAS and provides a standard CGI library for GET/POST operations. Include this library in your Perl scripts as follows:

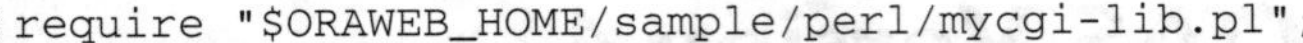

```
require "$ORAWEB_HOME/sample/perl/mycgi-lib.pl";
```

Avoiding the Save As Dialog Box

If a Perl script is executed and it fails because of a runtime or compilation failure, the user will not receive an error message. Instead, the browser will display a *Save As* dialog box. This occurs when Perl sends across error codes and the browser does not receive the MIME type in the HTTP header. It cannot recognize the type of the file; therefore, the browser prompts the user to download and save the file. When the *Save As* dialog box appears in the browser, try executing the Perl script from the command line to make sure it is working correctly. In other words, debug your Perl script at the command line first; however, examine the Perl log to find the detailed error information. On commands that could fail, consider using the *die* command to print the desired error page for the user and exit the Perl program more gracefully.

Displaying a List of Files

Let's say that you want to display a directory listing the files on the Web server itself. The following example shows a Perl script that reads through a directory (that is passed in or it defaults to the root directory on the d: drive). This script uses the CGI library previously described. The following script includes links that recursively calls itself as the user drills into the directory listings:

```
# Dirlist.pl
# Include the standard cgi library that comes with Application Server
require "c:\apps\perl\mycgi-lib.pl";

# Read in all the variables set by the form
  &ReadParse(*input);

# Print the HTTP header (Content-type: text/html)
  print &PrintHeader;
```

```
# Get the directory passed in
  $dir = $in{"dir"};

# If no directory ($dir) was received, set it to the root directory on the d drive
  if    ($dir eq "" || $dir eq "d:/") {
      $dir = "d://";
      $dir2 = $dir;
      chop($dir2);
  }
  else {
      $dir2 = $dir;
  }

# Start the HTML file off with the standard HTML tag, then the
# HEAD tag. Put the window title up - that includes the
# dynamic directory passed in

# Close the head and start the body.
print "<html>";
print "<head>";
print "<title>Directory Listing on Server for Folder $dir</title>";
print "</head>";
print "<body>";

# Print a header level 2 with the directory name that we are currently reviewing
print "<h2>Folder $dir</h2>";

# Set the flag to N(o) that we haven't seen the table header yet.
$flag = "N";

# Open the directory that was set above
opendir (DIR,$dir);

# Read the directory, sorting the file names and for each value
# in the array returned, loop with a foreach loop

foreach $name (sort readdir(DIR)) {
      # If the table header flag is set to N(o), then we need to start the table
    # and print the headings at the top of the table

      if ($flag eq "N") {
            print "<table border=1>";
            print "<tr>";
            print "<td><b>Profile</b></td>";
            print "<td><b>Created</b></td>";
            print "<td><b>Operations</b></td>";
            print "</tr>";
            $flag = "Y";
     }

     # Concatenate the directory and the file name (that we are working on)
        $file = $dir2 . $name;

     # Collect each of the components about the file we are working with
      ($dev,$inode,$perm,$hardl,$userid,$groupid,$devtype,$size,$atime,
        $mtime,$sts,$block,$bsize) = stat($file);

     # Convert the mtime (last modified time) to the localtime zone's time
```

```
        ($sec,$min,$hour,$mday,$mon,$year,$wday,$yday,$isdst) = localtime($mtime);

        # Since month is 0-11, need to add 1 to it for printing
        $mon++;

        # Format the minutes to left pad with a 0
        $min = sprintf("%02.0f",$min);

        # Start a new table row, print the modified date in a cell
        print "<tr>";
        print "<td>$name</td><td>$mon/$mday/$year $hour:$min</td>";

        # If the file size is 0, we are assuming this is a directory,
        # which in this case, print an anchor that allows the user to
        # drill into that directory. Then end the table row.
        if ($size eq "0" || $size eq "") {
           print "<td><a href=\"dirlist.pl?dir=$dir2$name\/\">Go to Folder</a>";
        };
        print "</tr>";
}

# Close up the directory
closedir(DIR);

# If the flag didn't get set, if never saw a file in the directory, then say so
if ($flag eq "N") {
      print "<p><h3>There are no files in this folder $dir</h3></p>";
}

# End the HTML table, the body and the HTML file.
print "</table>";
print "</body>";
print "</html>";
```

Determining If a File Exists

If you want to determine whether an operating system flat file exists, the following script will be of assistance. In this example, $filename is passed into this routine. If the file already exists, one action should be presented and if it does not exist, another action should be taken.

```
if(-T $filename) {
     # text file exists so take action here
     print "Text file ($filename) was found.";
} else {
     # text file doesn't exist so take another action
     print "Text file ($filename) was not found.";
}
```

-T will return True if the file exists and is a text file.

Creating or Appending a File

To always create a new file (overwrite an existing file and create a new file) execute the following syntax.

```
open(FILE, ">$filename") ||
die("Couldn't open $filename for writing \n");
```

To append to an existing file or create a new file if the file does not exist, the syntax would be identical to the following:

```
open(FILE, ">>$filename") ||  die("Can't append to $filename \n");
```

In other words, when one greater than sign (>) precedes the filename, Perl will open the file for writing, overwrite the existing file, and create a new file. If two greater than signs (>>) precede the filename, Perl will append to the existing file or create a new one if the file does not exist. Opening the file with less than (<) or nothing opens the file read-only. The *die* clause traps runtime errors to control the flow and is *very* important in CGI programming. A well-behaved routine that will not abort with an unaccounted-for condition is the desired result. Otherwise, the user will receive the *Save As* dialog box as previously described.

You must also be aware of the process or account opening the file (do they have access rights to create/write to files). Remember, you are running in a multithreaded environment, and should ensure that the filenames are unique or concurrency locked to prevent multiple writes happening at the same time to a single file. Opening a file in append mode does not guarantee that your data will be in the file if other processes can access/write to it while you think you are writing to it.

Invoking a PL/SQL Procedure from Perl

If you have a Perl script that needs to access the PL/SQL cartridge—or for that matter, you may have a need to access any URL from Perl—this section will explore the solution. For example, a Perl script may exist that performs authentication, and if the entered data is valid, place the data into your Oracle database. From PL/SQL, branch to any other URL using the owa_util.redirect_url (new_location) command. This command outputs a "location: {new_location}" HTTP header. To call another URL, instead of printing the content-type: header, use the location: header as illustrated in the following syntax:

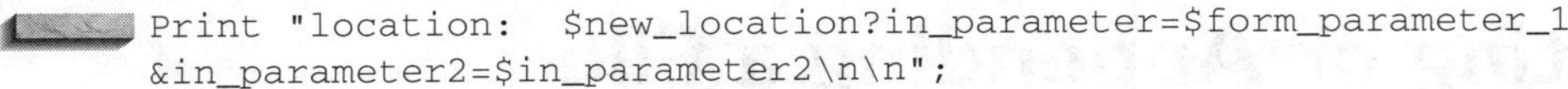

```
Print "location:  $new_location?in_parameter=$form_parameter_1
&in_parameter2=$in_parameter2\n\n";
```

If your desire is to embed the results of the PL/SQL script into your Perl output, this can be accomplished by using the utl_http.request command as described in Chapter 6.

Byteserving with Perl

It would appear that as of version 3.0.1.8 of OWAS, the product may support byteserving of files. However, I cannot confirm this from anyone at Oracle. Byteserving is part of the HTTP 1.1 specification and is a feature of optimized pdf files. Oracle may have put part, but not all, of HTTP 1.1 in this release. However, if you wish to perform your own byteserving, there is a Perl script available from Adobe that will actually perform complete byteserving. This Perl script (byteserve.pl) is available at:

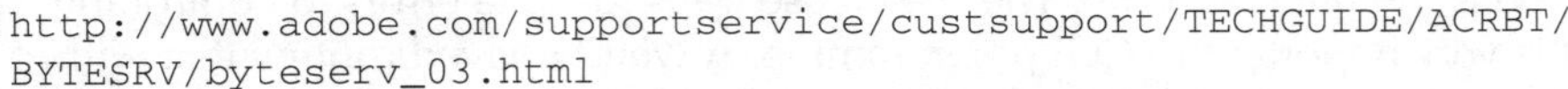

```
http://www.adobe.com/supportservice/custsupport/TECHGUIDE/ACRBT/
BYTESRV/byteserv_03.html
```

Emulating a Browser from the Command Line

If you are experiencing difficulties debugging a Perl script from the browser, emulate a browser from the server by setting the HTTP_USER_AGENT environment variable manually. For example, for csh (C Shell):

```
setenv HTTP_USER_AGENT "Mozilla/4.05"
```

For ksh (Korne Shell):

```
export HTTP_USER_AGENT = "Mozilla/4.05"
```

Emulating a POST Request from the Command Line

If the HTML form is passing the information to your Perl script through the POST method, you can also emulate this functionality from the command line. Emulate a

POST request by placing the data in a file and piping it to your Perl script, as illustrated in the following syntax:

```
cat mypost.file | my_perl_script.pl
```

Cleaning Up your HTML

What if you have HTML code that was generated (FrontPage) or came from another source (Word, PowerPoint) and the HTML is not clean (in other words, it does not follow the de facto standards of HTML development)? A great Perl script can be used for the exact purpose of cleaning up HTML code. Weblint is available at:

```
http://www.weblint.org/
```

This Perl script could be executed through the Perl cartridge or from the command line. The output can be redirected and executed against a tree structure to evaluate more than one file.

Another tool, called the demoroniser (you have to love the name), performs a similar function. In the documentation, its stated purpose is as follows: "The **demoroniser** keeps you from looking dumber than a bag of dirt when your Web page is viewed by a user on a non-Microsoft platform." The author is John Walker, who founded AutoDesk and was the original author of AutoCAD. The demoroniser utility can be found at:

```
http://www.fourmilab.ch/webtools/demoroniser/
```

The following are some errors the demoroniser fixes.

- Missing semicolons at the end of numeric character escapes (=) are supplied
- Numeric renderings of special characters (< > &) are replaced with readable equivalents
- Unquoted <table> tags containing nonalphanumeric characters are quoted
- PowerPoint's misnesting of <font> and <strong> tags is corrected
- PowerPoint's use of <ul> and </ul> tags to accomplish paragraph breaks is corrected and the proper <p> tags are inserted
- Missing <tr> tags in text-only slides are inserted
- Nugatory </p> tags are removed

- Unmatched <li> tags in headings are removed
- Idiot "paragraph-long lines" are broken into something suitable for editing with a normal text editor

Another good source for an HTML validator that is more strict than Weblint can be found at:

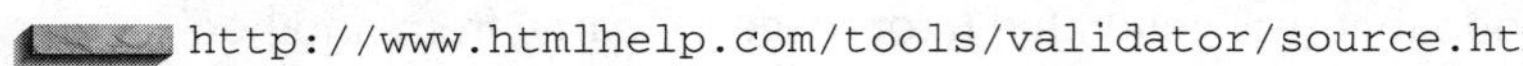

```
http://www.htmlhelp.com/tools/validator/source.html
```

It is Open Source with the Perl Artistic License. It is useful and includes a CSS validator and CGI test suite, found in the Tools section of this site.

Getting Access to Perl Documentation

The Perl documentation is included along with the Perl distribution. However, the complete Perl documentation can be found on the www.perl.com site at:

```
http://www.perl.com/pub/v/documentation
```

Additional tutorial information is available at:

```
http://www.perl.com/reference/query.cgi?tutorials
```

Looking at the Environmental Parameters

To view all of the environmental variables, Perl provides an associative array named %ENV. The following is a script segment that dumps out all of the environment variables (sorted):

```
foreach $key (sort keys %ENV) {
    print $key, " = ", $ENV{$key}, "\n";
}
```

The preceding code provides the same basic functionality as the owa_util.print_cgi_env packaged PL/SQL procedure.

Sending Mail from Perl

To send electronic mail from a Perl script is actually easier than it might sound. The following code segment assumes that you passed in the following variables: $from, $name, $to, $subject, and $message. This script uses Sendmail (www.Sendmail.org) to send the email from the server:

```
open (SENDMAIL, "| c:\sendmail\sendmail.exe -t -n");
print SENDMAIL <<End_of_Mail;
From: $from <$name>
To: $to
Reply-To: $from
Subject: $subject
$message
End_of_Mail
```

For additional sophistication, a Perl script can be called Formmail to simplify the process. It is simple to work with, and you can find it at:

```
http://www.worldwidemart.com/scripts/formmail.shtml
```

Determining the Client Browser and Acting Accordingly

The following segment of code queries the environmental variable containing specific browser information. Using this information, your Perl script can adjust to the browser accordingly.

```
$browser = $ENV{'HTTP_USER_AGENT'};
if ($browser =~ /Mozilla/) {
    # Netscape actions here
} else {
    # Non Netscape actions here
}
```

Including Site Components

Have you ever wanted to include another HTML page (maybe a template or other information) into your current page? Or include a snippet of information from another site into your current page? The previously-mentioned library (libwww-perl) is the source of a number of such utilities, such as WWW::Search, WebMirror, WebPluck, and WebFetch. These utilities and more can be found at:

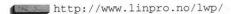

http://www.linpro.no/lwp/

Resolving OraPerl Reference in OWAS 3.0 Documentation

In OWAS version 3, an example of the online documentation illustrates OraPerl code. OWAS does not include the OraPerl.pm—it is not linked into the cartridge at all. The Perl cartridge is a beta cartridge in OWAS version 3. It is a production cartridge in OAS version 4. To use OraPerl with OWAS, you cannot use the Perl cartridge; you must use standalone Perl and compile OraPerl into it.

Resolving OraPerl Reference in OAS 4.0 Documentation

Perl is now a production cartridge; however, OAS 4.0.7 under NT the Perl cartridge does not yet contain the OraPerl capabilities. The LiveHTML cartridge supports OraPerl. Along with OAS version 4.0.7, you will find the OraPerl.pm file. I worked countless hours trying to get this working, and have come close. The only thing stopping me was that the works process died when I attempted to execute the OraPerl code. Specifically, I am referring to version 4.0.7 on NT. Version 4.0.8 fully supports the access of the Oracle database.

Specifically, according to Oracle support, "We understand that you wish to use Perl DBI/DBD along with Oracle Application Server (OAS) Perl cartridge (on NT). According to page 33-6 in the "Oracle Application Server Developer's Guide and OAS Online Documentation," you should be able to run the scott.pl sample as presented in Online Docs. The Online Docs pertain to UNIX use and configuration and not how to configure it for OAS residing on a Microsoft NT Server." The problem description is defined as "Perl DBI/DBD does not work with OAS 4.0.6.4 or 4.0.7. The online documentation is incorrect in stating it will work." Their explanation for this is "Support for Perl DDI/DBD has not been incorporated into OAS 4.0.6.4 or OAS 4.0.7. This feature may be available in OAS 4.0.8." Their solution to this problem is "There is no fix for this problem other than possibly upgrading to OAS 4.0.8 when available." My fingers were crossed for version 4.0.8 and Oracle delivered.

Using Perl in the LiveHTML Cartridge

OAS version 4 includes Perl and all of its built-in features. As previously mentioned, even though OraPerl does not work in the Perl cartridge under 4.0.7, it works in the LiveHTML cartridge. Refer to Chapter 21 for further information regarding the LiveHTML cartridge. This new capability (adding Perl to LiveHTML) extends its capabilities. If you prefer to use an HTML-based tool and embed Perl within your HTML, then LiveHTML is for you.

Understanding OraPerl versus DBD and DBI

Even though most people still refer to the capability as OraPerl, the capabilities were split into two components to make the capabilities more generic. The first component, DBI, stands for Database Interface. DBI provides for a common database interface, so no matter what database you wish to access, you can call the database in the same manner. DBI is essentially ODBC for Perl. DBI defines the functions, variables, and conventions providing a consistent database interface independent of the actual database being used. The second component, DBD (Database Driver), is an interface between the drivers and the applications. Therefore, there is only one DBI interface, but there are multiple DBD interfaces—one for each database that has been developed. The term *OraPerl* refers to DBI and DBD:Oracle. (DBI and DBD:Oracle provide complete OraPerl emulation.)

If you wish to download and install DBI and DBD:Oracle, you can find them at these locations:

ftp://ftp.demon.co.uk/pub/perl/db/DBD
http://www.symbolstone.org/technology/perl/DBI/index.html

DBD interfaces exist for a number of databases, including Adabas, Altera, CSV, DB2, Fulcum, Illustra, and Informix. You can find all of the DBD interfaces at the preceding locations. This method of running Perl will not function as a cartridge, but merely as a CGI. However, ActiveState sells a product called PerlEx (http://www.activestate.com/plex/) enabling Perl to operate identically to the Oracle cartridges, assisting in the performance you expect.

Using OraPerl (DBD and DBI)

As previously mentioned, OraPerl interfaces for the Perl cartridge are promised in future OAS versions. However, if you wish to use OraPerl prior to the capability being available in the cartridge, you can download DBD and DBI, and compile them into a standalone version of Perl. Even though you will not be able to use the Perl cartridge for your OraPerl access, you will still be able to use the OAS Perl cartridge for non-OraPerl scripts.

Reviewing Sample OraPerl Code

The following example will log on to a database, make a query, and display the output. This is a standard structure. The complete OraPerl documentation is available on the Web.

```
# Loads the DBI module. Loading the DBI module consists of
# reading in the Perl module script (DBI.pm) and the shared
# object (DBI.so). These files extend the Perl language by
# defining calls that enable Perl scripts to connect to
# Oracle databases. Once the module is loaded, the shared
# object is dynamically linked with the cartridge, the
# .pm Perl scripts are read in, compiled, and stored in
# the package namespace. Scripts can then make calls defined
# in the .pm file. The example calls the connect(), prepare(),
# execute(), rows(), fetchrow(), finish(), and disconnect()
# methods in the DBI module.
use DBI;

# Prints the HTTP header for this HTML page
print "Content-type: text/plain\n\n";

# Logs into the Oracle database using SQL*Net connect string
# of sales.
$dbh = DBI->connect("sales", "scott", "tiger", "Oracle") ||
       die $DBI::errstr;

# Prepares the SQL statement (parses the cursor)
$stmt = $dbh->prepare("select * from emp order by empno") ||
        die $DBI::errstr;

# Executes the above SQL statement
$rc = $stmt->execute() || die $DBI::errstr;

# Retrieve the number of fields returned from the above statement
$nfields = $stmt->rows();

# Prints a message to the user, showing how many fields can be
```

```
returned print "Query will return up to $nfields fields\n\n";

# Each relative column (field) returned from the SQL statement are
# placed into each of the relative field names in the while statement.
# In other words, the first field is placed into a variable called
# $empno and the second is placed into a field called $name.
while (($empno, $name) = $stmt->fetchrow()) { print "$empno $name\n"; }

# Display error messages if we get an error
warn $DBI::errstr if $DBI::err;
die "fetch error: " . $DBI::errstr if $DBI::err;

# Close up the cursor and disconnect from the DB
$stmt->finish() || die "can't close cursor";
$dbh->disconnect() || die "can't log off Oracle";
```

Understanding the *use OraPerl* Statement

When you include *use OraPerl,* this tells Perl to read in the Perl module scripts (OraPerl.pm and DBI.pm) along with the shared objects (DBI.so and Oracle.so). These files enhance the Perl language by defining calls that enable Perl scripts to connect to Oracle databases. Once the module is loaded, the shared object is dynamically linked with the cartridge and the .pm Perl scripts are read in, compiled, and stored in the package namespace. Scripts can then make calls defined in the .pm files.

Making Database Connections Persistent

To change the preceding example so it preloads the DBI module and logs into the database, thus making the connection to the Oracle database persistent, you need to define packages in perlinit.pl and perlshut.pl. This feature will be available when OraPerl is supported in OAS. The following code would exist in perlinit.pl:

```
package Scott;

# Setup for calling the Oracle database
use DBI;

# Logs into the Oracle database using SQL*Net connect string
# of sales.
$dbh = DBI->connect("sales", "scott", "tiger", "Oracle") || die $DBI::errstr;;
```

To close the database connection when the cartridge is shut down, the following code needs to be in the perlshut.pl script:

```
package Scott;

# Log off of Oracle
$dbh->disconnect() || die "can't log off Oracle";
```

The preceding script would be modified to appear identical to the following example.

```
package Scott;

# Prints the HTTP header for this HTML page
print "Content-type: text/plain\n\n";

# Prepares the SQL statement (parses the cursor)
$stmt = $dbh->prepare("select * from emp order by empno") || die $DBI::errstr;

# Executes the above SQL statement
$rc = $stmt->execute() || die $DBI::errstr;

# Retrieve the number of fields returned from the above statement
$nfields = $stmt->rows();

# Prints a message to the user, showing how many fields can be returned
print "Query will return up to $nfields fields\n\n";

# Each relative column (field) returned from the SQL statement are
# placed into each of the relative field names in the while statement.
# In other words, the first field is placed into a variable called
# $empno and the second is placed into a field called $name.
while (($empno, $name) = $stmt->fetchrow()) { print "$empno $name\n"; }

# Display error messages if we get an error
warn $DBI::errstr if $DBI::err;
die "fetch error: " . $DBI::errstr if $DBI::err;

# Close up the cursor and disconnect from the DB
$stmt->finish() || die "can't close cursor";
```

The logging on and off functions, and the use OraPerl statements, are not needed in the scripts any more.

Reviewing Production OraPerl Code

It is nice to see a short example of code to gain an understanding of how the code appears, but it is more effective to take a look at production code for a comprehensive example. The following code uses Perl as a CGI with DBI and DBD:Oracle compiled into the Perl code.

```
#Set up to use DBI and DBD
use DBI;
use DBI::DBD;

$dbh = DBI->connect('dbi:Oracle:',$vcd_user, $vcd_password) ||
       die "Unable to connect to Oracle: $DBI::errstr";
$test = length($key);

if ($test == 1){
   $csr = $dbh->prepare("
              SELECT DESCRP,
              COMMON_NAME,
              BOTANICAL_NAME,
              LOCATION,
              HARV_BLOOM_PER,
              CHEMICAL_CONTROL,
              ORGANIC_CONTROL,
              CULTURAL_CONTROL,
              MED_FILE,
              SOURCE
            FROM    tx_plants
            WHERE  (UPPER(COMMON_NAME) like '$key%'
            OR      UPPER(BOTANICAL_NAME) like '$key%')
            AND     gard_type = 'WEED'
            AND     UPPER(BOTANICAL_NAME) > UPPER('$last')
              ORDER BY BOTANICAL_NAME
          ");
}else{
          $csr = $dbh->prepare("
            SELECT DESCRP,
              COMMON_NAME,
              BOTANICAL_NAME,
              LOCATION,
              HARV_BLOOM_PER,
              CHEMICAL_CONTROL,
              ORGANIC_CONTROL,
              CULTURAL_CONTROL,
              MED_FILE,
              SOURCE
            FROM    tx_plants
            WHERE  (UPPER(COMMON_NAME) like '%$key%'
            OR      UPPER(BOTANICAL_NAME) like '%$key%')
            AND     gard_type = 'WEED'
            AND     UPPER(BOTANICAL_NAME) > UPPER('$last')
            ORDER BY BOTANICAL_NAME
         ");
}

$count = 0;
```

```
if ( defined $csr ) {
  $csr->execute;
  $count = 0;
  while ((( $descrp, $common_name, $botanical_name, $location, $harv_bloom,
            $chemical_control, $organic_control, $cultural_control,
            $med_file, $source ) =  $csr->fetchrow())
            && ($count < 20){
     $count = $count + 1;
      $last = $botanical_name;
print <<"DETAIL1"
      <TR>
     DETAIL1
;
    $med_test = length $med_file;
      if ($med_test > 0) {
         print <<"DETAIL2"
           <TD VALIGN="TOP"><IMG SRC=$med_file WIDTH="120"
               HEIGHT="120" ALIGN="BOTTOM" BORDER="0"></TD>
         DETAIL2
;
    }else{
         print <<"DETAIL3"
            <TD VALIGN="TOP" WIDTH="120" ALIGN="BOTTOM" BORDER="0"></TD>
DETAIL3
;
                        }

print <<"DETAIL4"
      <TD WIDTH="120" VALIGN="TOP"><B>Common Name:</B></TD>
      <TD WIDTH="296" VALIGN="TOP"><B><FONT SIZE="5"
        FACE="Helvetica, arial">$common_name</FONT></B></TD>
      </TR>
       <TR>
      <TD VALIGN="TOP" WIDTH="120" ALIGN="BOTTOM" BORDER="0"></TD>
      <TD WIDTH="120" VALIGN="TOP"><B>Scientific Name:</B></TD>
      <TD WIDTH="296">$botanical_name</TD>
      </TR>
      <TR>
      <TD VALIGN="TOP" WIDTH="120" ALIGN="BOTTOM" BORDER="0"></TD>
      <TD WIDTH="120" VALIGN="TOP"><B>Description</B></TD>
      <TD WIDTH="296">$descrp</TD>
      </TR>
      <TR>
      <TD VALIGN="TOP" WIDTH="120" ALIGN="BOTTOM" BORDER="0"></TD>
      <TD WIDTH="120" VALIGN="TOP"><B>Location:</B></TD>
      <TD WIDTH="296">$location</TD>
      </TR>
      <TR>
      <TD VALIGN="TOP" WIDTH="120" ALIGN="BOTTOM" BORDER="0"></TD>
      <TD WIDTH="120" VALIGN="TOP"><B>Life Cycle:</B></TD>
      <TD WIDTH="296">$harv_bloom</TD>
      </TR>
      <TR>
```

```
      <TD VALIGN="TOP" WIDTH="120" ALIGN="BOTTOM" BORDER="0"></TD>
      <TD WIDTH="120" VALIGN="TOP"><B>Organic Control:</B></TD>
      <TD WIDTH="296">$organic_control</TD>
      </TR>
      <TR>
      <TD VALIGN="TOP" WIDTH="120" ALIGN="BOTTOM" BORDER="0"></TD>
      <TD WIDTH="120" VALIGN="TOP"><B>Cultural Control:</B></TD>
      <TD WIDTH="296">$cultural_control</TD>
      </TR>
      <TR>
      <TD VALIGN="TOP" WIDTH="120" ALIGN="BOTTOM" BORDER="0"></TD>
      <TD WIDTH="120" VALIGN="TOP"><B>Chemical Control:</B></TD>
      <TD WIDTH="296">$chemical_control</TD>
      </TR>
      <TR>
      <TD VALIGN="TOP" WIDTH="120" ALIGN="BOTTOM" BORDER="0"></TD>
      <TD WIDTH="120" VALIGN="TOP"><B>Where to Buy:</B></TD>
      <TD WIDTH="296"><A HREF="../supply/supply.htm"
                                  target="_parent">$source</A></TD>
      </TR>
DETAIL4
;
  }
  $csr->finish;
}

$dbh->disconnect;
```

Example with a Procedure Call

The following code will log into the database and execute a procedure called get_journal_note.

```
use DBI;
use DBI::DBD;

 $desc;
$ret_error;

$dbh = DBI->connect('dbi:Oracle:',$vcd_user, $vcd_password) || die
"Unable to connect to Oracle:
$DBI::errstr";

$dbh->{RaiseError} = 1;
$csr = $dbh->prepare(q{
                     BEGIN
                         GET_JOURNAL_NOTE(:name,:desc, :ret_error);
                     END;
                     });
    $csr->bind_param(":name",$key);
    $csr->bind_param_inout(":desc",\$desc, 500);
    $csr->bind_param_inout(":ret_error",\$ret_error, 1500);
```

```
$csr->execute;
$error_out = $ret_error;
$dbh->disconnect;
```

Summary

Perl is a powerful tool for programming robust, dynamic Web applications. It is an excellent way to make otherwise static HTML documents "come alive." When used with the Oracle Application Server, Perl is best for file system reads and running operating system programs. Another great advantage of Perl is the countless number of public domain Perl scripts available on the Web.

Sites that Provide Perl Information

ftp://ftp.cis.ufl.edu/pub/perl	University of Florida; largest FTP site for Perl interpreter and Perl scripts
http://www.perl.com	Perl site maintained by Tom Christiansen with over 14,000 files and over 300MB of Perl information
http://www.perl.org	Perl Institutes site dedicated to making Perl more useful
http://www.oasis.leo.org	An extensive archive of Perl scripts, extensions, documentation, platform-specific issues, and so forth
http://www.worldwidemart.com/scripts	A good collection of scripts that do generic tasks. Matt Wright's Web site is fun to visit.
http://www.stars.com	Wal-Mart of Web development
http://www.perl.com/cgi-bin/cpan_mod?module=dbd::oracle	To download DBD for Oracle
http://post.sunyit.edu/perl5/	Perl 5 on NT documentation
http://www.symbolstone.org/technology/perl/DBI/index.html	Perl and DBD
http://www.apache.org/httpd.html	Apache home page
www.oasis.leo.org/cgi-bin/search-perl	Perl search site
www.activestate.com	Download Perl for Win32
http://www.4images.com/ntperl/	Perl on NT hints, tips and techniques

CHAPTER 21

LiveHTML Cartridge

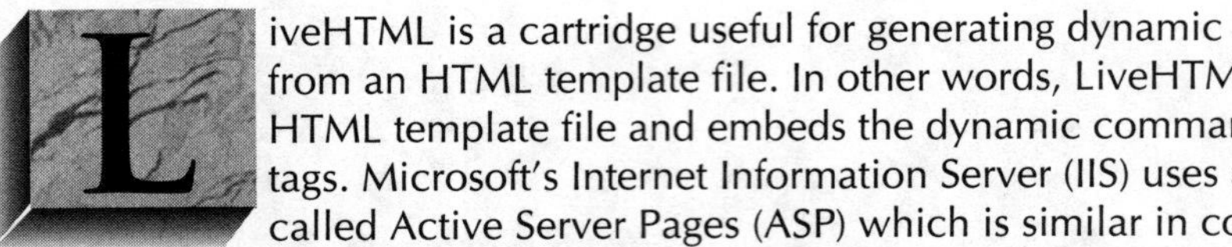

LiveHTML is a cartridge useful for generating dynamic HTML pages from an HTML template file. In other words, LiveHTML uses an HTML template file and embeds the dynamic commands within tags. Microsoft's Internet Information Server (IIS) uses a language called Active Server Pages (ASP) which is similar in concept to LiveHTML, except ASP uses Visual Basic as the underlying language, whereas Oracle's LiveHTML now uses Perl. LiveHTML also follows an industry standard syntax known as Server-Side Includes (SSI). SSI is available with most Web servers. SSI enables you to perform operations, such as including other files in the current file, reading CGI environmental variables, retrieving the current date and time, reading the size or last modification date of a file, running scripts (Perl) that can access the Oracle database, and sending requests to other cartridges. Microsoft, Netscape, Apache, and other Web servers also support the industry standard SSI.

In this chapter, the following topics will be covered:

- Finding good help
- Setting up the LiveHTML cartridge
- Using Perl in LiveHTML
- Creating a counter
- Including a page within a page
- Calling Oracle from LiveHTML

Finding Good Help

A tremendous amount of information about Server-Side Includes is accessible through list servers and newsgroups on the Web. One that I have found to be particularly useful for SSI is DejaNews, which can be found at www.dejanews.com. Just be sure to include *Server Side Includ*es in your search criteria.

Setting Up the LiveHTML Cartridge

After installing the LiveHTML cartridge (similar to other cartridge installations as defined in Chapter 2 and Chapter 4), set certain parameters, as noted in the following subsections.

Enable LiveHTML

Enable LiveHTML indicates whether the LiveHTML cartridge is enabled. Ensure the cartridge is enabled, or SSI commands, scripting commands, and Web application objects will not be interpreted and will be ignored in the browser. If you want to enable only some features of the cartridge, enable the LiveHTML cartridge and disable the features you do not want active.

Parse LiveHTML Extensions Only

Parse LiveHTML Extensions Only indicates whether the cartridge should only parse files with the extensions specified in the *LiveHTML Extensions* field. If this parameter is enabled, the cartridge will parse files with only those extensions listed in the *LiveHTML Extensions* field. If it is not enabled, the cartridge will parse all files in the cartridge's virtual path, regardless of the extension.

LiveHTML Extensions

LiveHTML Extensions contains the list of file extensions handled by the cartridge. This field is used only if you have enabled the *Parse LiveHTML Extensions Only* field. The default SSI extensions are html, shtml, and lhtml. If you have files with other extensions that should be considered SSI files, add those extensions in the Live HTML extensions field. You can also configure the cartridge to process all HTML files (set the extension list to include html). However, unless all your HTML files actually use SSI, this will downgrade the performance.

Enable Exec Tag

If you wish to disable the exec command, accomplish the task by disabling *Enable Exec Tag.* If you disable this parameter, the cartridge will ignore all exec commands. You might disable this command for security purposes—so no LiveHTML script can execute programs.

Enable ICX Tag

You can also disable the *request* command from being interpreted by the cartridge. If you do not intend to use Inter Cartridge Exchange (ICX), disable this feature, with security in mind.

Check for <BODY> Tag in ICX

The *Check for <BODY> tag in ICX* section indicates whether the cartridge checks for the <BODY> tag inside the response to an ICX request. (ICX requests are sent using the *request* command.) If this parameter is enabled, only data in the <BODY> section of the ICX response is included in the page that sent the *request* command. If no <BODY> section is found in the ICX response, the cartridge raises an error. If this parameter is not enabled, the entire ICX response is included in the page, which means you may have multiple <HEAD> sections within your resulting page.

Default Page

The *Default page* section contains the URL of the page that is returned to the client if the URL does not specify a file along with the LiveHTML virtual directory. The default page is index.html.

Enable Script Execution

Enabling or disabling *Enable Scripts Execution* dictates whether the cartridge interprets embedded scripts in the files. If you will never embed scripts, the LiveHTML cartridge will process scripts faster because it will not have to identify the embedded scripts to process. So, if you will never embed scripts, disable *Enable Scripts Execution.*

Script Page Extension

By default, LiveHTML will check the following extensions for embedded scripts: hsp, has, asp, and asa. If you want to add more extensions, add the extensions in the *Script Page Extension* field.

Default Scripting Language

The Default Scripting Language section contains the default scripting language that will be used in the LiveHTML scripts. Currently, Perl is the only language supported. You can specify a different language for the scope of a page or script block. The default parameter for this parameter is Perl. Because Perl is currently the only language supported by LiveHTML, this parameter is designed for future use.

Max Requests

The *Max Requests* field indicates the number of requests that a cartridge server handles before it terminates. This field can be useful while you are developing LiveHTML applications. If your page calls a Perl library, the Perl interpreter caches the Perl library and uses the cached version for subsequent requests. If you modify the library, the interpreter should load the new version. To accomplish this task, you must terminate the cartridge server process, so a new cartridge server process (with a new Perl interpreter) would handle the request. A way to avoid those troubles is to set the *Max Requests* value to 1 during testing, meaning that the LiveHTML cartridge server will handle one request, then terminate. No default exists for this parameter; if you do not set the parameter to a specific value, the cartridge server will handle an unlimited number of requests.

Perl Application Library Paths

The *Perl Application Library Paths* option indicates the directories the Perl interpreter searches for Perl libraries. If you add paths to this option, you should use full pathnames. If specifying multiple directories, use **:** to delimit each directory. The default for this parameter is **.** (the current working directory of the cartridge server process).

Using Perl in LiveHTML

As of OAS version 4, the online documentation bundles the *LiveHTML and Perl cartridges*, so they are obviously closely tied cartridges. LiveHTML includes the Perl version 5.004 as the default scripting language. However, the Perl cartridge has bundled version 5.003 of Perl. Numerous modules are available for download on the www.perl.com site. Select *The Module List* from http://www.perl.com/CPAN/modules/index.html to view a list of modules available for download.

The `<%...%>` tag encloses scripts in the language specified by the `<% @Language = language %>` tag of each LiveHTML page. If the language tag is not present in a page, the default scripting language specified in the cartridge configuration form is applied to the scripts. By default, the language will be Perl—as previously noted, Perl is currently the only supported language of the LiveHTML cartridge. Interweave the standard HTML tags with this tag using control structures to determine which HTML tags will be sent to the client. You can also embed these tags within other HTML tags. This can be useful for dynamically generated links (for example, the HREF attribute of the Anchor tag).

The following example prints out the text "LiveHTML is cool" in incremental font sizes ranging from 3 to 7; the following code is actually Perl code:

```
<%
    $str = "LiveHTML is cool";
    for ($fontsize = 3; $fontsize < 8; $fontsize++) {
%>
    <font size =
<%
    $Response->write($fontsize)
%>
    ><p>
<%
    $Response->write($str)
%>
    </font>
<%
    }
%>
```

In the preceding example, the scope of variables is not limited to just one script block. Variables persist for script blocks over the entire page.

Creating a Counter

If you wanted to include a counter on your HTML page, as illustrated in the preceding example, use Perl within your LiveHTML file. However, by searching www.perl.com, you will find countless numbers of Perl counter scripts available for download. The following script executes a Perl script generating a counter and returns this information back to the LiveHTML file (assuming you have downloaded the Perl script count.pl into your cgi-bin directory):

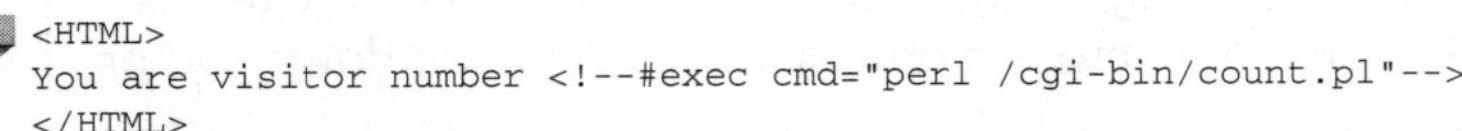

```
<HTML>
You are visitor number <!--#exec cmd="perl /cgi-bin/count.pl"-->!
</HTML>
```

Including a Page Within a Page

At some point, you may wish to include one piece of HTML code into another HTML page. This is useful if you have standard headers or footers that you want to include on each page—thus, modularizing your code. The syntax is as follows:

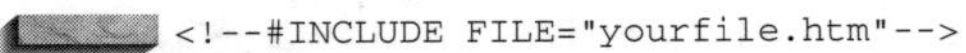

```
<!--#INCLUDE FILE="yourfile.htm"-->
```

Calling Oracle from LiveHTML

The capability to write HTML, use Perl as a scripting language, and call the Oracle database using DBI and DBD:Oracle reveals the extensive power of LiveHTML. LiveHTML is extremely fast. The following syntax is an example segment of code that works properly as of OAS 4.0.7 and beyond.

```
<HTML>
<HEAD>
<TITLE>LiveHTML Example that Calls Oracle</TITLE>
</HEAD>

<BODY BGCOLOR=#FFFFFF>
<H1>LiveHTML Script Sample calling Oracle Database</H1>
<HR>
<!-- Script block -->
<%
use DBI;
```

```
# Connects to the Oracle database using the SQL*Net connect string
# of sales for the Scott user.  Displays an error message if it fails.
$dbh = DBI->connect("sales", "scott", "tiger", "Oracle") ||
       die $DBI::errstr."Error logging in";

# Prepare (parse) the SQL statement into a cursor
$stmt = $dbh->prepare("select * from emp order by ename") || die $DBI::errstr;

# Execute the SQL statement
$rc = $stmt->execute() || die $DBI::errstr;

# Figure out how many fields can be retrieved from this query
$nfields = $stmt->rows();

# Send the number of fields returned to the users browser
# and set up a table to print the information.
$Response->write( "Query will return up to $nfields fields<br><br><table border=1>");

# Each respective field is placed into each respective field name
# listed.  Specifically field 1 is placed into $empno, 2 into $ename
# and field 3 into $job.  This information is printed in a table row.
while (($empno, $ename, $job) = $stmt->fetchrow()) {
   $Response->write( <tr><td>$empno</td><td>$ename</td><td>$job</td></tr>" ); }

# Close up the HTML table
$Response->write( "</table>" );

# Print any error messages
warn $DBI::errstr if $DBI::err;
die "fetch error: " . $DBI::errstr if $DBI::err;

# Close up the cursor
$stmt->finish() || die "can't close cursor";

# Log off of the Oracle DB
$dbh->disconnect() || die "cant't log off Oracle";
%>

</BODY>
</HTML>
```

Summary

Perl can be embedded into LiveHTML. LiveHTML provides a extensive flexibility in conjunction with Perl, and also provides the capability to execute other scripts (Perl or otherwise) and include headers and footers on the page.

CHAPTER 22

Oracle Internet Commerce Server

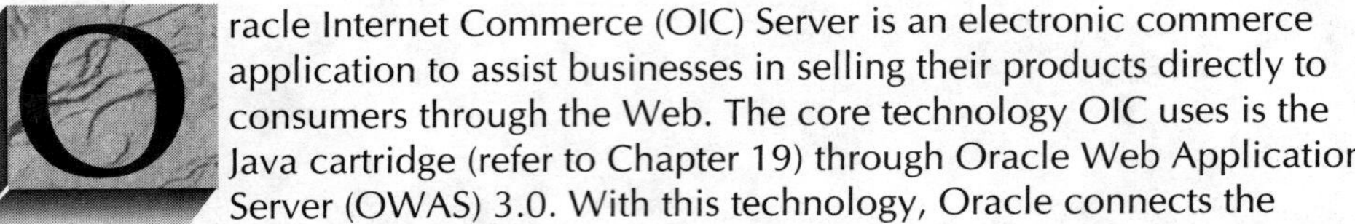

Oracle Internet Commerce (OIC) Server is an electronic commerce application to assist businesses in selling their products directly to consumers through the Web. The core technology OIC uses is the Java cartridge (refer to Chapter 19) through Oracle Web Application Server (OWAS) 3.0. With this technology, Oracle connects the database and Java technology to a Web server that reaches the entire Internet. This configuration gives OIC its strength, but is also the source of its complexity. This chapter covers OIC 1.1.0.7.5, with enhancements in version 2.0 discussed at the end. The following topics will be covered in this chapter:

- Considering who should use OIC
- Installing OIC
- Uninstalling OIC
- Third-party products
- Discussing the features of the store
- The object hierarchy
- Designing your store conceptually
- Creating the store—batch-loading
- Maintaining the store
- Customizing the store
- Looking at what's new in version 2.0

Considering Who Should Use OIC

When it comes to developing an electronic commerce (e-commerce) site, you can either build your site from the ground up or buy an application, such as OIC, that you can customize for your particular needs. The advantages as well as the disadvantages must be explored for both options. Table 22-1 illustrates some of the suggestions on the decision to build or buy. The suggestions are not established rules, but issues to be considered when determining the best solution for your business needs.

OIC is designed for businesses already invested in Oracle and its products. It's not a stand-alone product—it is an add-on. OIC is good for businesses that do not want to spend a lot of money to get their products on the Web, but want the basic functionality of a Web store. For these situations, OIC is a viable solution.

Criteria	Buy OIC	Build from scratch
Appearance and behavior	If you are willing to accept the appearance and behavior of OIC out-of-the-box. Some customization possible	You cannot live with an out-of-the-box look. Completely customizable
Programming staff	Limited programming staff	Will need a larger programmer staff
Time	Relatively short period of time to implement than building from scratch	Will take longer to develop and get online (than to accept packaged solution as is)
E-commerce mission	Simple site to take orders over the Web	More complex site serving a broad range of Internet/ e-commerce needs
Product lines	Best for standard product hierarchy with distinct product lines	Can be developed to support a highly complex product line
Price structures	Simple pricing structures	Complex pricing structures

TABLE 22-1. *Suggestions on Buying OIC or Developing from Scratch*

Installing OIC

Installation of OIC is straightforward, assuming all the required pieces are in place. OIC is an OWAS cartridge; therefore, it relies on many other pieces to provide the full functionality of an Internet store. Individually, each piece is simple to install. All of the products must work together to produce the desired end product.

Getting All the Pieces Installed

OIC has several software dependencies, such as the Oracle database, several other Oracle products, Java, and your browser. Third-party "optional" requirements, include CyberCash (or some method to handle online payments), Taxware (or a method to calculate taxes), and TanData (or another method to handle shipping and handling).

For the Oracle database installation, you need at least the following pieces:

- Oracle Database 7.3.3/8.0.3 or higher
- ConText Cartridge 2.0.4.0.0 or higher
- Replication Manager
- SQL*Net and optionally Net8
- SQL*Plus 3.3.0
- PL/SQL

You do not need to install Parallel Server options, the spatial cartridge, the image cartridge, or the visual information retrieval cartridge.

Before installing OIC, these other products must be installed. First, install the database, and include the options previously listed. Because of the high number of initial database transactions you will be performing during the installation and to increase performance, disable the archive log until the installation is complete. Discuss archive logging with your DBA. After installing the database, create the OIC tablespace—make sure you use the following sizing recommendations. I recommend you let the OIC installation perform this task for you automatically.

During the OIC installation, you will be prompted for the relative size of the database you want to create: small, medium, or large. The size of database/tablespace created will depend on whether you are installing for a single-node system or a two-node system. "Single node" means *staging* (for example, development) and *deployment* (for example, production) will be on the same physical machine but in separate physical directories. Multinode means staging will be on one physical machine and deployment on another. For a single-node configuration, a small installation will need a 150MB tablespace, a medium installation will need a 175MB tablespace, and a large installation will need a 1GB tablespace. In the two-node system, the space is split between the staging and deployment databases. For the staging area, a small installation needs 85MB, a medium installation needs 100MB, and a large installation needs 550MB. For the corresponding deployment database, a small installation needs 55MB, a medium installation needs 85MB, and a large installation needs 400MB. After ensuring the database is properly installed, created, and configured correctly, verify Oracle ConText Server starts.

TIP
*When configuring the tnsnames.ora file, be sure to update the tnsnames.ora file located in the network directory of ORACLE_HOME, because OIC uses SQL*Plus 3.3.*

Next, install OWAS 3.0.1, which is included on the OIC CD. Follow the installation instructions included with OIC. After installation, exit Oracle Installer and reboot the system. If you try to access OWAS without first rebooting, errors will occur. After rebooting, OWAS should automatically start. On NT, you can verify auto restart by ensuring the following services have been started: OracleWRBPrimaryService, OracleWWWListener30Admin, and OracleListener30www. Connect to the administration port of OWAS by typing **http://hostname:portnumber/** in your browser. OWAS will prompt you for the administrative login. Once you specify the login information (provided during installation), the administrative interface will appear. Next, you will want to confirm that the default www port works by typing **http://hostname/** in your browser.

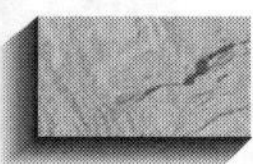

TIP
You must install the OWAS and Oracle Reports versions located on the OIC CD, or OIC is unlikely to work. Unfortunately, OIC may appear to work with other versions but cause problems later. Be sure to verify with Oracle Support that the version you plan to run works with OIC.

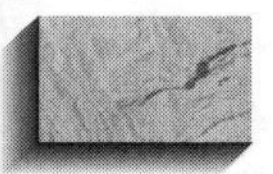

TIP
The OIC machine will reside on the Internet; therefore, it would be advisable to specify a port other than 8888 for the default administration port.

The following instructions relate to the directories for OIC template storage. Two directories need to be created: a staging directory and a deployment directory. These two directories hold all the HTML templates, as well as any associated media content. One set of files is for the staging directory and one set for the deployment directory. The single-node installation creates both directories under the same parent directory. For example, on NT you might create a directory called C:\OICStore and within that directory create a staging directory and a deployed directory. In a two-node installation, create the respective directories on their respective machines.

TIP
Creating directories prior to installation may seem like an odd step. However, the HTML template directories must be created prior to OIC installation or the installation will fail.

Once the preliminary pieces are in place, installing OIC is straightforward and follows the Oracle installation convention. Follow the instructions included with OIC. Near the end of the installation, you will receive a notification informing you the installer has attempted to create all the necessary listeners and cartridges. If it discovers a listener or cartridge already exists, the OIC installation will display an error message and the installation will fail. This error generally occurs on subsequent installations of OIC. If this happens, you must first uninstall OIC, then verify all OIC listeners and cartridges have been deleted from OWAS, all of which is accomplished through the administrative interface for OWAS.

If the listeners are created successfully, the installer will create the OIC database objects. If the tablespace has been created, specify its name here. If not, you may choose to create the tablespace at this time. After the tablespace has been created, execution of the SQL scripts to populate the database will begin.

TIP

The script execution is not a trivial step as the impact on the database is significant, including approximately 160 tables, 350 indexes, more than 100 sequences, nearly 80 views, 100 packages, and more than 200 triggers. If the step executes quickly, something is wrong (or you have a really fast machine).

If all the scripts execute successfully, a success notification will display. When the scripts are finished executing, check the appropriate .lst file that exists within the $ORACLE_HOME\oec\Admin directory containing the error messages. If errors have been logged, you must identify and correct the problem, uninstall OIC, and install it again.

After installing OIC, more products need to be installed. First, you need a Java Development Kit (JDK). Even though the documentation recommends version 1.0.2, JDK 1.1.x also works well. You need a Java-enabled browser. I recommend at least Netscape Navigator 4.5 or Internet Explorer 5.0. Finally, Oracle Reports 3.0 will need to be installed to enable the Store Manager reports.

Checking that the Installation Worked

Once the software is installed and everything appears to work, how can you make sure the installation was successful? Check the following areas:

- **Database** Six database accounts should have been created: sdos, tdos, sdod, tdod, oectps, and oectpd. Make sure all these accounts contain objects, such as tables, synonyms, views, indexes, and packages.

- **OIC configuration files** These files are located in $ORACLE_HOME/oec/config. Verify that no parameters in these files contain values of the form %<variable_name>%—this would indicate an incomplete installation.
- **OWAS** Log in to the administrative port on the OWAS and make sure the OIC listeners and cartridges are present. Four listeners should be present: mstage for the Store Manager utility, cstage for the staging area of the store, cdeploy for the deployment area of the store, and the Web Store Listener that you named in the installation. Confirm mstage, cstage, and cdeploy each have a corresponding Java cartridge, then start all listeners.
- **Store directories** Make sure a multimedia directory structure was created and templates have been copied to the directories. Both staging and deployment folders should have the same content and structure.
- **Store Manager** Using your browser (with the caching turned off), try the Store Manager URL: http://hostname:portnumber. A page identical to Figure 22-1 should appear.

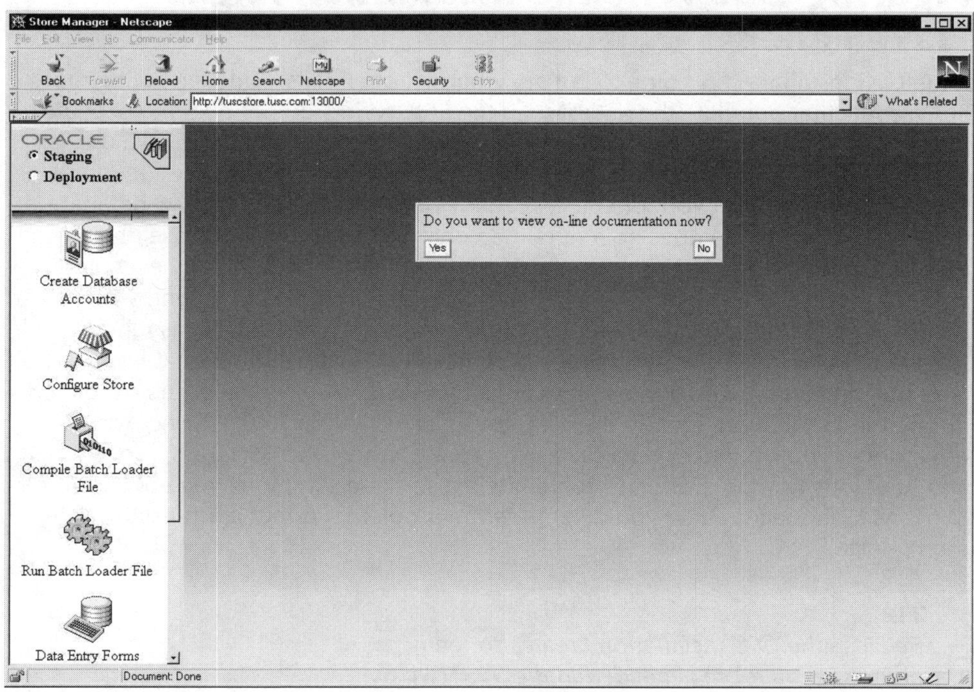

FIGURE 22-1. *Store Manager utility first page*

TIP
When using the Store Manager, it is recommended that you turn off browser caching.

- **Data Entry Forms** Click on the Data Entry Forms icon in the left-side toolbar. This loads the utility for creating and modifying the store and its products. It is a Java applet; therefore, this is a good test to verify the JDK is installed and configured properly. Try accessing other functions from the toolbar. They may not all be applicable, but you should see appropriate prompts.
- **Staging and deployment** Try the staging (for example, http://hostname:portnumber) and the deployment (for example, http://hostname:80) URLs. The appearance and behavior should be identical between staging and deployment. A store does not yet exist; therefore, you cannot test all the functionality—but make sure you can maneuver to the different store features without receiving Java errors. If everything functions properly at this point, the installation was successful.

Figuring Out Why the Installation Might Have Failed

If the OIC installation is going to fail anywhere, it often fails while executing the SQL scripts that populate the database. If the SQL scripts do not begin to execute, the problem may be that OIC was unable to connect to the database. OIC uses SQL*Plus 3.3, which means that you must configure the tnsnames.ora file in the $ORACLE_HOME/Network directory, even if you are using an Oracle8 database. If the tnsnames.ora file does not contain an entry for your OIC database, the installation fails while trying to invoke SQL*Plus. If the scripts initially execute without errors, then suddenly start generating errors on every statement, you may have run out of tablespace. If your tablespace does not have at least as much free space as Oracle recommends, the scripts will still execute, but once tablespace runs out, any attempt to create a new object will fail. To view the errors generated during the installation, look in the .lst files in the $ORACLE_HOME/oec/Admin directory. If you run out of data dictionary space (where the packages, procedures, and functions reside), a similar problem with the same symptoms may occur in the SYSTEM tablespace. Once you determine the problem, correct it, uninstall OIC, then reinstall OIC.

TIP
Because the OIC installation creates so many objects, extra room is needed in the SYSTEM tablespace. The manual recommends 100MB of free space in the SYSTEM tablespace, but this may not be enough; I highly recommend at least 150MB.

Uninstalling OIC

If the installation of OIC failed, you need to identify and correct the problem. This often means reinstalling OIC. You cannot reinstall OIC over an existing installation. Instead, perform the following steps:

1. Delete all six of the OIC database accounts. This can be accomplished from SQL*Plus by typing **DROP USER username CASCADE**.
2. Uninstall the Oracle OIC product through the Oracle Installer.
3. Delete the $ORACLE_HOME/oec directory.
4. Delete the OIC listeners using the OWAS Administrative facility.
5. Delete the cartridges using the OWAS Administrative facility.
6. Reboot.

If subsequent installations (after deinstallation) do not solve the problem, you may also have to uninstall the OWAS. Uninstalling both OIC and OWAS will give you a clean slate to reperform the installation. First, uninstall OIC as previously described; then, follow these steps to uninstall OWAS:

1. Uninstall OWAS using the Oracle Installer.
2. Delete $ORACLE_HOME/owa directory.
3. Reboot.

Thinking About Third-Party Products

A topic that should not be overlooked is a discussion about third-party products. This is software that "plugs into" OIC and provides a necessary function in the operation of your store. Because the store deals primarily with in-store functions like tracking customers, keeping shopping carts, and creating invoices, functions, such as calculating shipping and handling fees, calculating taxes, and online customer payment are left undefined by the out-of-the-box OIC. Oracle has designed OIC so functions can be easily integrated into the store's operations. Even though the functions could be implemented with custom code (as discussed later in this chapter), more often they are implemented with commercial products.

Typically, the third-party vender provides a product *and* a service. For example, TanData's Progistics product provides you with the software containing shipping and handling costs for the major carriers, but you are required to pay for the service to have this information updated on a regular basis.

As part of any Internet store implementation, shipping and handling, taxation, and payment functionality must be supplied. In OIC, this is provided in two ways. First, Oracle has exposed Java abstract classes for integration of these functions into OIC. By exposing the integration information, you can write custom code, integrate with existing systems, or integrate with a third-party product. Second, taking the Java classes one step further and adding the logic for a third-party product can provide this functionality. OIC includes Java logic for the integration of Taxware's Internet Tax Systems, TanData's Progistics, and CyberCash's Cash Register. Other third-party products will perform similar services, but Oracle does not provide the Java code for other products.

Discussing the Features of the Store

OIC has several notable features. Some of these are unique to OIC (for example, coupons). Others are more common to Internet stores in general. It is worth describing these features as they exist in OIC:

- **Sales** Products may be put on sale for an established period of time. OIC automatically displays the sale price during the specified date range and reverts back to the regular price at the end of the sale period.
- **Coupons** Account customers may be given the opportunity to "clip" coupons and apply them towards their purchases as discounts.
- **User Preferences** Account customers can customize which store departments (sections) and products they want to view on entry to the store. This does not prevent them from viewing all the other departments and products; rather, it enables the customers to view only the desired sections.
- **Searching** Customers can search for products in the store by product attributes or by keywords that apply to the product name and description. The search results are displayed in a list of products containing links to the product's detailed display area. Customers can add the item to their shopping cart, if desired.
- **Customer feedback** When a customer has a question or complaint with the store, this feature provides a mechanism for them to contact the Store Manager, a Webmaster or site administrator.
- **Order status** Once the customer places the order, the customer can come back to the store to check the status of the order(s) at any time.

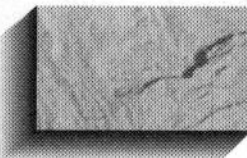

TIP

For users to be able to use OIC, they must allow cookies to be stored in their browser. If they have cookies turned off, they will experience errors from the site indicating a message similar to "The requested action could not be executed due to the following error(s): OEC-11507: NULL arguments passed while calling lstPrdItmsByPrd." To prevent this issue, develop a front-end page that verifies that the user supports cookie storage before allowing them into OIC.

The following sections offer development tips for implementing OIC store features.

Holding a Sale

To put a specific item on sale, you must navigate to the Details portion of the product in the store hierarchy. This is the same place you defined the price for the product. To provide a sale price, you must add a new row to the table, specifying "sale" as the price type, provide the sale price for this item, then select the start and end dates for the sale.

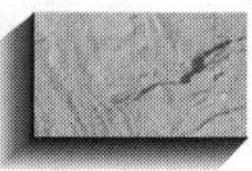

TIP

If you want to show a "permanent" sale, like discount stores do, omit the end date. The sale is effective forever.

TIP

If you are starting a sale today, set the begin date to yesterday. This ensures that the sale will show up in the store today.

Using the default product display template, customers can only see that an item is on sale; they cannot see the effective dates of the sale. However, this HTML template could easily be modified to display the additional information, if desired.

Setting Up Coupons

OIC enables the Store Manager to offer coupons to the customers to be "clipped" and applied to their purchases. When creating the coupon, you can set the applicable Account Category. You can also designate that customers with predefined accounts (ACCOUNT) and/or walk-in customers (WALKIN) can use the coupon. However, the default behavior of the store does not allow the walk-in customers to use coupons.

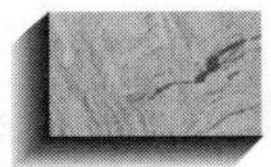

TIP
If you want walk-in customers to be able to use coupons, you can easily modify the "walk-in" HTML templates, adding the appropriate coupon images (GIF files) and links to enable the customer to view, clip, and apply the coupons.

Creating User Preferences

OIC refers to user preferences as PersComs, or Personal Commerce Attributes. Store configuration can be performed in the Store Manager utility or through batch-loading—configuring user preferences, or creating themes or topics that represent your products. In an online bookstore, topics might include business, cooking, computers, classical literature, and so forth. These are your preference categories. After you have created the categories, you need to designate sections and products to the appropriate topics. To extend the example, suppose that the bookstore separates computer books into three sections: Java, HTML, and Oracle. You would first set the preference of these three sections (Java, HTML, and Oracle) to the "computer" preference. Products are assigned to a specific section. Then, in the store, if the customer chose "computer" as a preference, they would see the Java, HTML, and Oracle sections on the directory page, but not any other sections.

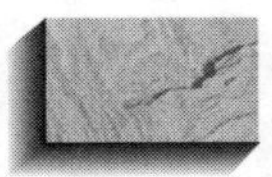

TIP
User preferences are not automatically available to account (nonwalk-in) customers; account customer preferences must be configured through the Store Manager.

Searching

OIC uses Oracle's ConText server for searching. While the search is completed in real time, the ConText index tables searched must be updated when a product changes in the store. Two different types of searches exist. The first search type is accessed by clicking on the Search icon on the toolbar and is known as a store-level search. When using this search mechanism, the user enters keywords to search, and the ConText server searches the product names and descriptions for words that meet the criteria. By default, the ConText server performs an "AND" search when multiple keywords are specified. Because this search only looks at product names and descriptions, during store setup make sure you phrase your product names and descriptions carefully and use terms the customer might use.

The second type of search is a section-level search and involves searching for products in a given section based on product attributes. The customer is given a display with all the attributes and corresponding values for the products in a particular section, and is prompted to choose what values to search. For example, if the product is T-shirts and the store sells T-shirts in small, medium, and large sizes, a section-level search in the T-shirt section of the store would give the customer the choice of searching for products that have a size of small, medium, or large. If the customer chooses small, a list is returned of all products in a size small.

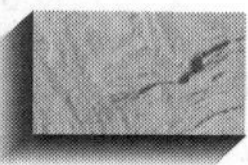

TIP
To maximize the effectiveness of section-level searches, you want to make sure you create attributes that make sense to your customers for the product, and where the cardinality is more than one.

Receiving Customer Feedback

After the OIC installation, customer feedback is not "plugged in." You must add this functionality on your own. The HTML page template exists to ask customers to submit their questions and comments, but displaying the page itself does nothing. Several options exist once the user hits the Submit button. For example, the comments could be emailed using the mailto URL for the FORM tag action, or the comments could be sent back to the database using a call to a PL/SQL procedure through the PL/SQL cartridge.

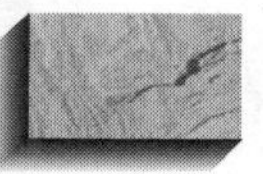

TIP
To make the customer feature functional, you will need to add code to the ECASSISTANT.EN.HTM template.

Checking Order Status

After the OIC installation, the Order Status function is displayed on the same page as the Customer Feedback page. To give customers the capability to check the status of their order, the customer needs to provide both an order number and a password.

TIP

Because customers need their order number and password to retrieve the order information, the trick is to ensure the customer notices the order number when making a purchase. The order number is placed in the middle of the invoice page in a small font and is easy for the customer to overlook. At a minimum, you should change the template to draw the customer's attention to the order number. A more effective approach is to send them an email with the order number and other information as a confirmation. The email could contain a complete invoice, as well as a link to check on their order status.

You may wish to repeat the order number after they finish the purchase. If the customer has an account, they should know their password. If the customer is a walk-in customer, they will be prompted for a password when asked for their address. Again, this information is in the middle of the page and may be easily missed by the customer. It is advisable to modify this template so the customer sees and clearly understands the need for a password. Finally, you need to consider the actual status of the order. If you are maintaining the status of the order through the Store Manager, the customer will see that status. If you are using the store to take orders, but are processing them offline, you need to get the status information back to the store orders so the customer can see it. This will require that you develop a custom external interface.

The Object Hierarchy

A picture is worth a thousand words. If coupons are defined at the Product-level only, show Coupon as an attribute of Product.

When creating the store, strict hierarchy constraints exist. The objects are obviously related to each other, but they are not all intuitive. The following is a list of some relationships to observe:

- A store contains a list of top-level sections
- Sections do *not* contain a list of their subsections, but contain a reference to their parent sections instead
- Sections contain a list of products

- Products do *not* contain any reference to the section where they are located
- Products do *not* contain a list of the product items
- Product items contain a reference to the product where they reside

The preceding constraints can be elusive when creating batch-loading expressions. For example, when you are adding a product to a section, you must remember to update the section with that new product. If you do not add the product to the section, the product will exist, but because it does not belong to a section, customers will not be able to see (or order) the product.

TIP
A good way to view all of the products is to look up the product list in the Store Manager utility, looking under Data Entry Forms, under Store Components, and finally under Products. This will show all products that exist in the store, and whether they are associated with a section.

You can create all of your product objects then come back and add each product to its appropriate section. However, it is best to create the store from the top down.

Designing Your Store Conceptually

Whether you are building a store from scratch or using OIC, conceptual design is one of the first steps. The more specific you are in how you want to sell your products, the faster you will be up and running. If you are using OIC, you will want to understand OIC's simple hierarchical structure before you begin to design an elaborate store. Regardless, decisions must be made. The following is a list of questions to consider when designing the store layout and its products:

- What do you want to sell?
- How much will each product cost?
- How do you want to present the products?
- Will there be pictures of the products?
- What kind of descriptions, if any, will there be for the products?
- How will products be arranged or grouped?

- How will the store be broken down into departments and sections?
- What attributes do each of the products have?
- How will the store and its inventory be maintained?
- Who will maintain this information?

An important item to establish is the appearance of the store. One of the best ways to get ideas for your store is to visit existing e-commerce sites. This will help you establish what you do and do not like. Consider hiring an outside design team for this task.

Beyond products, decisions must be made on how the store will function at a high-level view. These decisions focus primarily on the functionality that will be available to the customers. The following are some relevant questions that need to be addressed relating to the high-level design of the store:

- Will there be customer accounts?
- Will there be walk-in customers?
- Will there be sales? Other discounts?
- Will we offer coupons for customers to "clip" and apply?
- Will we offer customer preferences?
- Will we restrict where the customer can go?

Once your store is created in OIC, it stands alone from the rest of your business. If this is not what you want, you have integration decisions to make. The following questions should be considered:

- How will orders be filled?
- Will order processing from the store be integrated with current order processing systems?
- Do I need to link my inventory into the store?
- How will the customers pay for the products?
- Do I need to calculate shipping, handling, and tax? If I perform this in my current system, will I integrate these systems with the store? If not, will I use third-party products or will I write my own?

If the store will be small(for example, less than 25 products), it is not as important to make all of these decisions up front because things can be moved around and changed easily. If the store stocks hundreds or thousands of products, moving and changing the location of the products in the hierarchy can be a big project. The design requires a considerable amount of forethought to get the store up and running.

TIP
To maximize your time and efforts, I highly advise first creating a "throwaway" store using a small subset of data to represent your store structure and products. Set up your store manually and use this small subset for testing. You could propose your throwaway store to your customers or business analysts and request feedback. This may help indicate what improvements (structural, design, graphics, help, and so forth) need to be made.

Creating the Store – Batch-Loading

Creating a store is basically adding the appropriate data to the database, whether using the Store Manager interface or batch-loading the data. To this end, OIC offers Data Entry Forms in the Store Manager utility. Use the interface to add a few simple products, to define an initial scheme, or to update a store object. However, when a store is complex or large, this method of adding data is too slow. For those cases, you will want to create the store by batch-loading it. Batch-loading uses OIC expressions (their own batch-loading or scripting language) to create, delete, or update store objects. These expressions are compiled into SQL scripts, which are then applied to the database. For convenience, multiple expressions can be grouped together in one source file. The file should have a .bl extension. The following is an example of a batch-loading file to add, change, or delete information to and from the store:

```
CREATE PrdItm
   SKU: 'C1-bk-xsm'
   prdItmName: 'TUSC T-shirts'
   dscr: 'Extra small, black TUSC T-shirt'
   prd: Prd{ partNum = 'C1' }
   mfr: 'TUSC'
   prdItmDlvrType: 'STANDARD'
END
UPDATE Sect { name = 'Clothes'}
   ctntLst +
      Img { name = 't-shirt_display_section' }
END
DELETE Prd  { partnum ~ 'ED%' } END
```

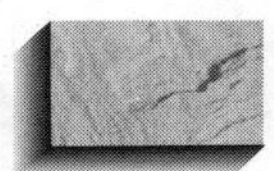

TIP
Another advantage to batch-loading is the capability to uninstall and reinstall OIC without having to manually re-create every store object.

The preceding file contains three OIC expressions. The first expression creates a product item. It's a T-shirt that belongs to the product with part number C1. The expression specifies the SKU, name, description, manufacturer, and delivery type. The second expression updates a section. Because the Clothes section already exists, it was modified with an update statement. In the preceding example, I have indicated I want a certain image displayed on the section pages where appropriate. The third expression deletes all the products where the part number begins with ED. The expressions do not have to be related to be in the same file, even though they typically are related.

Once the .bl file is created, it must be compiled. You can compile through the Store Manager utility or from an operating system prompt.

TIP
The easiest method of creating a batch-loading script is to dynamically extract the script from another source. For example, if you were able to pull product information from another corporate database, you could use SQL to dynamically create the batch-loading script.

TIP
Compiling batch-loading scripts from the system prompt is faster than using the Store Manager utility because it does not have to redraw the windows. It also provides you with more verbose error messages.

To compile at the command line, use the following syntax:

```
$ORACLE_HOME\bin\batchload option inputfile.bl outputfile.sql
     where: option is -r for rollback; -c for commit
            input_file.bl is the file containing the OIC expressions
                        to be compiled
            output_file.sql is the compiled output.
```

If the compiled file is omitted, the compiled code will be sent to standard output (for example, the screen). The compiled file is a normal SQL script and can be executed at the SQL*Plus command line. Execute these scripts in the SDOS schema, which is the staging account. To deploy the store, you can synchronize the deployment account through the Store Manager utility. Using the preceding example expressions, the following SQL code shows the output or compiled file after executing it through the batch-load program:

```
WHENEVER SQLERROR EXIT ROLLBACK
SET SERVEROUTPUT ON SIZE 1000000
SET DEFINE OFF
PROMPT Executing CREATE PRDITM from source ...
DECLARE
   PRDITM_0v NUMBER;
   PRD_7v NUMBER;
   PRD_6v NUMBER;
   PRD_1v NUMBER;
BEGIN
   SELECT PRD_7.PRDID
     INTO PRD_1v
     FROM EC_PRD PRD_7
    WHERE PRD_7.dbsts = 'A'
      AND PRD_7.PARTNUM = 'C1';
   PRDITM_0v:= EC_PRDITMDB.make(PRDITMDLVRTYPEv=>'STANDARD',
                      MFRv=>'TUSC',
                      PRDPRSTIDv=>PRD_1v,
                      DSCRv=>' Extra small, black TUSC T-shirt ',
                      PRDITMNAMEv=>'TUSC T-shirts',
                      SKUv=>'C1-bk-xsm');
   EC_PRDDB.PrdItmLst_add(PRD_1v,PRDITM_0v,'PrdItm');
END;
/
PROMPT Executing UPDATE SECT from source ...
DECLARE
   IMG_11v NUMBER;
   SECT_9v NUMBER;
   SECT_0v NUMBER;
BEGIN
   SELECT SECT_9.SECTID
     INTO SECT_0v
     FROM EC_SECT SECT_9
    WHERE SECT_9.dbsts = 'A'
      AND SECT_9.NAME = 'clothes_section';
   DECLARE
      CURSOR c IS
         SELECT IMG_11.IMGID
           FROM EC_IMG IMG_11, EC_Ctnt CTNT_12
          WHERE IMG_11.dbsts = 'A'
            AND IMG_11.Ctntid = CTNT_12.CTNTID
```

```
            AND CTNT_12.dbsts = 'A'
            AND CTNT_12.NAME = 't-shirt_display_section';
      FLAG NUMBER := 0;
   BEGIN
      FOR i IN c LOOP
         FLAG := 1;
         EC_SECTDB.CtntLst_add(SECT_0v,i.IMGID,'Img');
      END LOOP;
      IF (FLAG = 0) THEN
         dbms_output.put_line('***WARNING: No objects found.');
      END IF;
   END;
END;
/
PROMPT Executing DELETE PRD from source ...
DECLARE
   PRD_1v NUMBER;
   PRD_0v NUMBER;
BEGIN
   DECLARE
      CURSOR c IS
         SELECT PRD_1.PRDID
           FROM EC_PRD PRD_1
          WHERE PRD_1.dbsts = 'A'
            AND PRD_1.PARTNUM LIKE 'ED%';
      FLAG NUMBER := 0;
   BEGIN
      FOR i IN c LOOP
         FLAG := 1;
         EC_PrdDB.dbdelete(i.PRDID);
      END LOOP;
      IF (FLAG = 0) THEN
         dbms_output.put_line('***WARNING: No objects found.');
      END IF;
   END;
END;
/
COMMIT;
PROMPT Execution succeeded!
EXIT;
```

A store can be created manually, fully batch-loaded, or any combination thereof. No matter what approach you take, remember the order you load the items is critical, because many objects depend on other objects. Even though objects are not directly related to each other, all objects become attributes of sections and products, so you must create the objects before you create the store. Then, you can reference the required objects when creating sections and products. In many cases, a valid value (foreign key) is required, such as product type and units of measure, so the object must exist beforehand. In most cases, these attributes can be added afterwards, but it is common to add them at the time of creation.

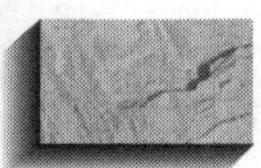

TIP
Certain objects must be created before the main store hierarchy is created. These include product types, units of measure, user preference categories, media content, and product attributes.

Maintaining the Store

Once your store has been created and customized, you must maintain it. Both the staging and deployment areas of the store require upkeep. This maintenance applies to the back-end of the store as well as the store's contents. Two main tools are used to perform maintenance. One tool, as previously mentioned, is the Store Manager utility, which is used to update store objects and to ensure the integrity of the underlying data. The second tool is the Batch-Loader and is only used to create and maintain store objects. The Batch-Loader provides enough functionality that the loading process can be automated. Between these two tools, all of the store maintenance can be performed.

Looking at the Store Manager Utility

The Store Manager utility is a Web-based administrative tool. This tool will not only be used for store and product creation during store startup, but it will also be used after the store is up and running for store maintenance. Store maintenance functions include updating the store objects, synchronizing the staging area to the deployment area, cleaning up the database, and filling orders.

After updating some products in the store, you may opt to refresh the search tables through the Maintain Store search option. For maintenance, this means repopulating the ConText tables.

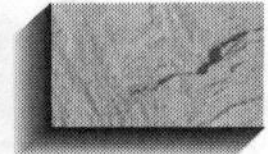

TIP
Maintaining the search capabilities in the staging area does not automatically maintain them in the deployment area, nor does synchronizing the two areas. Maintaining search capabilities in the staging area must be done separately through the deployment interface of the Store Manager utility.

The option used most often is the Data Entry Forms module. This is the core of the store, with all of the store's products and attributes. This module is written in Java and is a large client-side application. It is slow to download. This can be a nuisance if you are trying to maintain the store remotely, but it is ideal over a LAN or directly on the server. The documentation states that the Data Entry Forms requires Netscape Navigator to run this piece. However, both browsers have come a long way with Java capabilities and the latest versions of both Netscape Navigator and Internet Explorer will work satisfactorily. With either browser, Oracle recommends that caching be turned off. Within this Java application, the interface is intuitive and it is easy to maneuver through the functions.

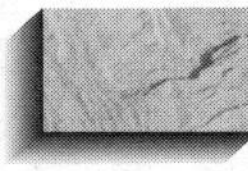

TIP
When it comes to entering object descriptions (a property of almost every object) be careful. Because these descriptions are displayed in HTML, you should not use special characters (ampersand - &) in the descriptions; instead, use the HTML equivalent (&). You can embed other HTML tags in the description, if desired.

TIP
The Data Entry Forms Java application enforces a description length of 255 characters, but the underlying database table has the corresponding column defined with a width of 512 characters. The constraint is enforced at the Java level and not the database level; therefore, you can get around it (exceed the 255 character restriction) by directly updating the description column in the given table. Unfortunately, after this has occurred, you will no longer be able to modify that object through the Store Manager utility. If you attempt to modify the description through the utility, the Java application will halt, displaying a message indicating the description field is too long.

Feel free to use this work around technique on objects that do not often change, or objects that are always updated from the database and not from the Store Manager utility. Because the descriptions are displayed in HTML text, for sections, products, or other descriptions, you can add HTML tags to customize the appearance of a particular description. If you want the customized HTML tag(s) to be applied to all products or all sections, you should modify the template. However, modifying the description enables you to break out of the templates temporarily to highlight a specific part of the description or draw the customer's attention.

If you have made changes to the store in the Data Entry Forms option, the changes may not be consistent with the transaction data the customers will generate. To synchronize the databases, execute the Synchronize Transactions Database option. Synchronize the staging static data to the staging transaction data. Then, synchronize the staging data to the deployment data. No facility exists for synchronizing the deployment static data with the deployment transaction data.

The deployment area within the Store Manager utility has several options that may be used for regular maintenance of the store. Identical to the staging area, the deployment area has a Maintain Store Search option. This is used to repopulate the ConText tables used for customer searches.

Any changes made on the staging area must be synchronized in the deployment area before they will be visible to the customers. When using the Deploy Static Data option, two components must be deployed: the static templates and the database data. For the deployment of the static templates, enter the staging and deployment directory paths and click on the Deploy button. Executing this command will copy all HTML templates as well as the contents of the multimedia directory from the staging directory to the deployment directory. For this to work, the staging and deployment listeners must be shut down, because OWAS will cache the pages and lock them until the listener has shut down. If the command encounters files that it cannot overwrite because they are locked, it will abort the command without any indication of what went wrong. If the command is successful, a list of all the files copied from the staging directory to the deployment directory will appear and a message will be displayed stating that the command was successful. The second part of synchronizing staging with deployment involves copying database data. To accomplish this task, specify the requested usernames and passwords and click the Deploy button. Be careful when entering the password, because if you supply the wrong password, the application spins (cycles indefinitely) and does not inform you of the incorrect password attempt.

Once the store has been running, periodically clean up the unneeded data with the Cleanup Walk-ins and Delete Tracking Data options. The Cleanup Walk-ins option clears out the user tables populated by walk-in customers. These user tables contain information such as shopping carts and system-generated user login IDs. Do not delete all data because current data might be in use. The Cleanup Walk-ins option enables a cutoff date to be selected. The data up to the specified date, but not past it, will be deleted.

TIP
A customer's path through the store is recorded in a URL history table. Every page the customer visits is recorded in the history table. Depending on the number of customers you attract, and the size of your store, you will need to watch the size of this table. Either adjust the tablespace to enable the growth of the table in the database, or use the Delete Tracking Data option to periodically delete data from the table.

To clear out the customer-tracking table, use the Delete Tracking Data option. This also enables you to choose a range of dates where the data is deleted. No method currently exists to turn off customer tracking.

After a customer has confirmed a purchase and payment has been authorized, the order must be retrieved and filled. In OIC, this step has to be performed manually (or through the batch interface). If you are manually updating the orders through the Store Manager utility, as opposed to pushing the orders into an existing system outside of OIC, use the Maintain Order option. Through this option, you can retrieve orders and set the status of the order accordingly. The Maintain Order screen is the same page the customer sees when checking the status of their order.

Maximizing Batch-Loading

If your product line changes frequently, you can automate the constant updates to the products. If you keep your current catalog in an Oracle database, batch-loading is an ideal method to perform these updates. As described previously in the "Creating the Store – Batch-Loading" section, batch-loading can be used to add, update, and delete specific objects in the store. By taking advantage of the complexity batch-loading offers, you can create sophisticated scripts to pull data from one part of your database and dynamically determine what needs to be changed in the store database.

Adding power behind batch-loading scripts requires supplementing them with PL/SQL code in and around the batch-loading expressions. By indicating the location of the batch-loading expressions, you can add PL/SQL code to your .bl file. Upon compilation, the PL/SQL code will be preserved and the batch-loading scripts will be compiled.

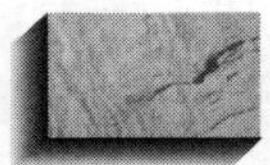

TIP
The advantage of adding PL/SQL to the batch-loading scripts is you can use PL/SQL to access existing data elsewhere in the database and then use this data to populate fields in the batch-loading expressions.

The following .bl file illustrates a cursor pulling data from an existing table and populating a CREATE expression:

```
// product defaults

default Prd
   mfr : 'TUSC'
   prdType : 'EDOCS'
   UOM : 'EACH'
   bgnDate : ##sysdate##
end
// price defaults
default Prc
   bgnDate : ##sysdate-1##
   value_currCode : 'USD'
   value_value : 0.00
   PrcType : 'REGULAR'
end
// product item defaults
default PrdItm
   mfr : 'TUSC'
   prdItmDlvrType : 'DOWNLOADABLE'
end
BLOCKBEGIN
##
// get title, file name, create the desc field for the prod item,
// trunc the abstract field, generate the part number (and sku)
DECLARE
   CURSOR documents IS
      SELECT title,
             file_name,
             title || ' (' || file_size || ') ' ||
                          presentation_date prditm_desc,
             substr(abstract, 1, 255) abstract,
             'ED' || decode(category,'appdev', 'AD',
                    'cs'    , 'CS', 'dba'   , 'DB',
                    'inet'  , 'IN', 'misc.' , 'MS') part_num_sku
       FROM Website_documents_tab;
   next_num INTEGER;
   part_num_sku VARCHAR(10);
BEGIN
   FOR rec IN documents LOOP
##
##
      SELECT misc_seq.nextval INTO next_num FROM dual;
      – append the sequence number to the partnum to generate
      – a unique number
```

```
        part_num_sku := rec.part_num_sku || next_num;
##
        // create a product item
        create PrdItm
           SKU : ##part_num_sku##
           prdItmName : ##rec.file_name##
           dscr : ##rec.prditm_desc##
           prd :
              Prd.new {partNum: ##part_num_sku##
                       name : ##rec.title##
                       dscr : ##rec.abstract## }
           // create price entries
           prcLst :
              Prc.new { prcCat : 'WALKIN' },
              Prc.new { prcCat : 'ACCOUNT' }
        end
##
    END LOOP;
END;
##
BLOCKEND
```

In the preceding example, the double pound sign (**##**) is used to delineate the PL/SQL code from the batch-loading expressions. Within the product item creation, the corresponding product is created at the same time. You can create complex batch-loading scripts by nesting object creation within the batch-loading expressions, then adding PL/SQL to these compound expressions. In the following compiled file, the PL/SQL was preserved from the .bl file while the batch-loading expressions were converted to PL/SQL:

```
WHENEVER SLQERROR EXIT ROLLBACK
SET SERVEROUTPUT ON SIZE 1000000
SET DEFINE OFF
// get title, file name, create the desc field for the prod item,
// trunc the abstract field, generate the part number (and sku)
DECLARE
   CURSOR documents IS
      SELECT title,
             file_name,
             title || ' (' || file_size || ') ' ||
                                  presentation_date prditm_desc,
             substr(abstract, 1, 255) abstract,
             'ED' || decode(category,'appdev', 'AD',
                    'cs'    , 'CS', 'dba'   , 'DB',
                    'inet'  , 'IN', 'misc.' , 'MS') part_num_sku
         FROM Website_documents_tab;
```

```
next_num INTEGER;
   part_num_sku VARCHAR(10);
BEGIN
FOR rec IN documents LOOP
select misc_seq.nextval into next_num from dual;
-- append the sequence number to the partnum to generate
      -- a unique number
      part_num_sku := rec.part_num_sku || next_num;
DECLARE
          PRDITM_0v NUMBER;
          PRC_3v NUMBER;
          PRC_2v NUMBER;
          PRD_1v NUMBER;
      BEGIN
          PRD_1v:= EC_PRDDB.make(DSCRv=>rec.abstract,
                   NAMEv=>rec.title, PARTNUMv=>part_num_sku,
                   BGNDATEv=>sysdate, UOMv=>'EACH',
                   PRDTYPEv=>'EDOCS', MFRv=>'TUSC');

          PRC_2v:= EC_PRCDB.make(PRCCATv=>'WALKIN',
                   PRCTYPEv=>'REGULAR', VALUE_VALUEv=>0,
                   VALUE_CURRCODEv=>'USD', BGNDATEv=>sysdate-1);

          PRC_3v:= EC_PRCDB.make(PRCCATv=>'ACCOUNT',
                   PRCTYPEv=>'REGULAR', VALUE_VALUEv=>0,
                   VALUE_CURRCODEv=>'USD', BGNDATEv=>sysdate-1);

          PRDITM_0v:= EC_PRDITMDB.make(PRDPRSTIDv=>PRD_1v,
                   DSCRv=>rec.prditm_desc, PRDITMNAMEv=>rec.file_name,
                   SKUv=>part_num_sku, PRDITMDLVRTYPEv=>'DOWNLOADABLE',
                   MFRv=>'TUSC');

          EC_PRDDB.PrdItmLst_add(PRD_1v,PRDITM_0v,'PrdItm');
          EC_PRDITMDB.PrcLst_clean(PRDITM_0v);
          EC_PRDITMDB.PrcLst_add(PRDITM_0v,PRC_2v,'Prc');
          EC_PRDITMDB.PrcLst_add(PRDITM_0v,PRC_3v,'Prc');
      END;
   END LOOP;
END;
/
COMMIT;
PROMPT Execution succeeded!
EXIT;
```

With a complex set of batch-loading scripts and by combining batch-loading expressions with PL/SQL, it is possible to automate routine changes to your store's product line. This will ensure consistency between your store and other business systems.

Customizing the Store

OIC has a simple appearance and behavior that you can customize. But what and how can customization be achieved? The types of customization range from making simple modifications to the HTML templates to overriding Java methods or writing your own code outside the OIC cartridges.

Modifying the HTML Templates

The easiest, and probably the most frequent, customization will be to the HTML templates. This is the location to define the overall appearance of your store. Typical customizations include adding company logos, changing background colors, changing fonts, rearranging objects, and perhaps adding some JavaScript. Usually, you start customizing at the beginning, or the login page. The following is the default HTML template for the login page:

```
<HTML>
<HEAD></HEAD>
<BODY BGCOLOR="#FFFFFF">
<CENTER>
<FORM METHOD="POST" ACTION="/cust/cdeploy">
   <INPUT TYPE="HIDDEN" NAME="ecaction" VALUE="ecacctauth">
   <INPUT TYPE="HIDDEN" NAME="template" VALUE="account1.en.htm">
   <TABLE BORDER="0" WIDTH="80%">
      <TR><TD ALIGN="CENTER"><IMG SRC="/multimedia/icon/shopper.gif">
          </TD></TR>
      <TR><TD>
         <TABLE BORDER="0" WIDTH="100%">
            <TR>
               <TD ALIGN="CENTER">Welcome to Oracle Shopper</TD>
            </TR>
         </TABLE>
         </TD>
      </TR>
      <TR><TD>
         <TABLE BORDER="0" WIDTH="100%">
            <TR><TD WIDTH="50%"></TD>
                <TD ALIGN="RIGHT" WIDTH="25%">Username:</TD>
                <TD WIDTH="25%"><INPUT TYPE="TEXT" NAME="username">
                </TD></TR>
            <TR><TD WIDTH="50%"></TD>
                <TD ALIGN="RIGHT" WIDTH="25%">Password:</TD>
                <TD WIDTH="25%">
                  <INPUT TYPE="PASSWORD" NAME="password"></TD>
            </TR>
            <TR><TD WIDTH="25%">
```

```
   <A HREF="/cust/cdeploy?ecaction=ecwalkin&template=walkin1.en.htm">
   <IMG SRC="/multimedia/icon/walkin.gif" BORDER="0"></A></TD>
                <TD WIDTH="50%"></TD>
                <TD WIDTH="25%"><INPUT TYPE="IMAGE" BORDER="0"
                           SRC="/multimedia/icon/login.gif">
                </TD>
            </TR>
         </TABLE></TD>
      </TR>
   </TABLE>
</FORM>
</CENTER>
</BODY>
</HTML>
```

The following example is the same HTML page as the preceding example, with some modifications. Objects were moved, a new title was added, along with a company logo, a background, and explanatory text. JavaScript was added to control focus on the page and to pop up a message when the customer first accesses the page. The following is the resulting HTML template:

```
<HTML>
<HEAD>
<TITLE>TUSC Technology Store</TITLE>
<SCRIPT LANGUAGE = "JavaScript">
   function setFocus() {
      document.DummyLogin.username.select();
      document.DummyLogin.username.focus();
      return true;
   }
   function setFocusNext() {
      document.UserLogin.password.focus();
      return false;
   }
   function getUserName() {
      document.UserLogin.username.value =
           document.DummyLogin.username.value;
      return true;
   }
   function newForm() {
      document.writeln("<FORM NAME='DummyLogin' METHOD='POST'
                         onSubmit='return setFocusNext()'>");    }
   function switchForms() {
      document.writeln("</FORM>");
      document.writeln("<FORM NAME='UserLogin' METHOD='POST'
                       ACTION='/cust/cdeploy'
                       onSubmit='return getUserName()'>");
```

```
        document.writeln("<INPUT TYPE='HIDDEN' NAME='username'
                          SIZE=20 MAXLENGTH=20>");
     }
</SCRIPT>
</HEAD>
<BODY BACKGROUND="/multimedia/icon/tusc_bg4.jpg">
<CENTER>
<TABLE BORDER=0 WIDTH="80%">
  <TR><TD ALIGN=CENTER>
        <IMG SRC="/multimedia/icon/logo_dblue1.gif"></TD>
      <TD ALIGN=CENTER><B><I><FONT COLOR="#000066" SIZE=+3>
           Welcome to the TUSC Technology Store</FONT></I></B></TD>
  </TR>
  <TR><TD><FONT=1><em>
     You may enter your username/password that you have
     previously created, then the Login button, or click
     the Walk In button and create one.
     </em></FONT></TD>
  </TR>
  <TR><BR></TR>
  <SCRIPT LANGUAGE = "JavaScript">    newForm();    </SCRIPT>
  <TR><TD ALIGN="right">
      <B>User Name</B><BR>
      <INPUT TYPE=TEXT NAME="username" SIZE=20 MAXLENGTH=20></TD>
  </TR>
  <TR></TR>
  <SCRIPT LANGUAGE="JavaScript">     switchForms();     </SCRIPT>
  <TR><TD align="right">
      <B>Password</B><BR>
      <INPUT TYPE="PASSWORD" NAME="password" SIZE=20 MAXLENGTH=20>
      <INPUT TYPE="HIDDEN" NAME="ecaction" VALUE="ecacctauth">
      <INPUT TYPE="HIDDEN" NAME="template" VALUE="account1.en.htm">
      </TD>
  </TR>
  <TR>
   <TD ALIGN=RIGHT><INPUT TYPE="image" BORDER="0"
                          SRC="/multimedia/icon/login.gif"></TD>
   <TD><SPACER TYPE=horizontal size=50>
   <A HREF="/cust/cdeploy?ecaction=ecwalkin&template=walkin1.en.htm">
   <IMG SRC="/multimedia/icon/walkin.gif" BORDER=0></A> </TD>
  </TR>
</FORM>
</TABLE>
</CENTER>
<TABLE BORDER=0 WIDTH="100%" >
   <TR><TD>
         <IMG SRC="/multimedia/icon/ics_flash.gif"
              ALT="TUSC Technology Store" BORDER="0"></A><BR></TD>
```

```
        <TD>
        <FONT=1><em>This electronic store uses the Oracle Internet
          Commerce Server(ICS)from
    <A HREF="http://www.oracle.com/products/ics/html/ics_nest.htm"
    target="Main">Oracle Corporation</A>. Please contact
    <A HREF="mailto:emrgtech@tusc.com?subject=Emerging Technologies
    Information Request"><B>TUSC</B></A> for more information about
    implementing ICS.</em></font></TD>
    </TR>
</TABLE>
<SCRIPT LANGUAGE="JavaScript">
    setFocus();
    alert("Note: Currently, the TUSC store only ships to
           Canada and the U.S.");
</SCRIPT>
</BODY>
</HTML>
```

Figure 22-2 illustrates the appearance of the preceding page after modification.

Along with modifying the HTML template with standard Web modifications, such as HTML and JavaScript, OIC offers other methods to customize the HTML templates.

Imbedding Static Variables

The static variable OIC component enables you to store a value in a separate file and reference it through the use of a static variable in the HTML template. For example, you may have the following HTML code in your template:

```
<H1><B>There are no clipped coupons in the account</B></H1>
```

Instead of hardcoding the text, you could use a static variable. Given the preceding example, an entry to the cnls.en.msg file containing a variable name and its value has been added, identical to the following:

```
couponsavailablemsg=No coupons available to apply.
```

Next, delete the hardcoded text from the preceding template and replace it with the static variable name surrounded by at-signs (@). The following code fragment illustrates this process:

```
<H1><B>@couponsavailablemsg@</B></H1>
```

At runtime, OIC parses the templates. When the parser encounters a static variable, it performs a lookup in the cnls.en.msg file and replaces the variable with the designated text.

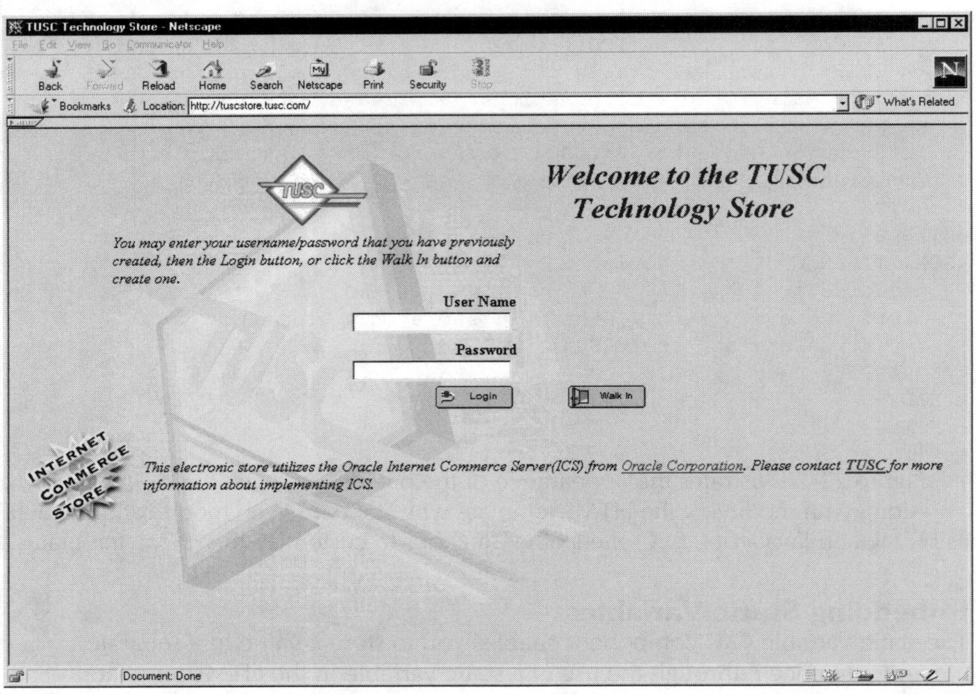

FIGURE 22-2. *Opening page of the TUSC store after customization*

One use for static variables is text that might change frequently, such as an announcement of the latest product. Another use is supporting stores in multiple languages. You can use the same templates but, depending on the language, use a different cnls.*xx*.msg file, where *xx* is the language definition.

One variable often used is the eccookie variable, which is always surrounded by at-signs (i.e. @) but is only static during a customer session. This variable is an encrypted cookie that is present on every page and is sent to the Java programs with any other data from the current page. The eccookie variable is not stored in the cnls.en.msg file, rather it is the electronic commerce (ec) cookie containing state information for the session.

Using Dynamic Variables

A second type of OIC component is the dynamic variable. The variables are considered dynamic because their values come from the database and not from a static file. A good example of a dynamic variable use can be found in the taddress.en.htm file. This page displays address information of a customer. For walk-in customers, the address will be blank. For account customers (who entered their address on a previous visit), the Address page retrieves your information from the database to populate this page, as shown in the following example:

```
<!-- taddress.en.htm -->
<INPUT TYPE="HIDDEN" NAME="AddrInfo.%%n%%.addrType"
      VALUE="%%addresscode%%">
<TR>
   <TD ALIGN="LEFT" COLSPAN="4" WIDTH="100%" BGCOLOR="#303080">
   <FONT SIZE="+1" COLOR="#FFFFFF">%%addresstype%%</FONT></TD>
</TR>
<TR>
   <TD ALIGN="RIGHT" WIDTH="20%" BGCOLOR="#94AAD6">*@address1@</TD>
   <TD COLSPAN="3" WIDTH="75%" BGCOLOR="#94AAD6">
      <INPUT TYPE="TEXT" NAME="AddrInfo.%%n%%.addr1"
            VALUE="%%AddrInfo.addr1%%" SIZE="60"></TD>
</TR>
<TR>
   <TD ALIGN="RIGHT" WIDTH="20%" BGCOLOR="#94AAD6">@address2@</TD>
   <TD COLSPAN="3" WIDTH="75%" BGCOLOR="#94AAD6">
      <INPUT TYPE="TEXT" NAME="AddrInfo.%%n%%.addr2"
            VALUE="%%AddrInfo.addr2%%" SIZE="60"></TD>
</TR>
<TR>
   <TD ALIGN="RIGHT" WIDTH="20%" BGCOLOR="#94AAD6">@address3@</TD>
   <TD COLSPAN="3" WIDTH="75%" BGCOLOR="#94AAD6">
      <INPUT TYPE="TEXT" NAME="AddrInfo.%%n%%.addr3"
            VALUE="%%AddrInfo.addr3%%" SIZE="60"></TD>
</TR>
<TR>
   <TD ALIGN="RIGHT" WIDTH="20%" BGCOLOR="#94AAD6">*@city@</TD>
   <TD WIDTH="25%" BGCOLOR="#94AAD6">
      <INPUT TYPE="TEXT" NAME="AddrInfo.%%n%%.city"
            VALUE="%%AddrInfo.city%%" SIZE="15"></TD>
   <TD ALIGN="RIGHT" WIDTH="25%" BGCOLOR="#94AAD6">@county@</TD>
   <TD WIDTH="25%" BGCOLOR="#94AAD6">
      <INPUT TYPE="TEXT" NAME="AddrInfo.%%n%%.cnty"
            VALUE="%%AddrInfo.cnty%%" SIZE="15"></TD>
</TR>
<TR>
   <TD ALIGN="RIGHT" WIDTH="20%" BGCOLOR="#94AAD6">@state@</TD>
   <TD WIDTH="25%" BGCOLOR="#94AAD6">
      <INPUT TYPE="TEXT" NAME="AddrInfo.%%n%%.state"
            VALUE="%%AddrInfo.state%%" SIZE="15"></TD>
   <TD ALIGN="RIGHT" WIDTH="20%" BGCOLOR="#94AAD6">@postalcode@</TD>
   <TD WIDTH="25%" BGCOLOR="#94AAD6">
```

```
    <INPUT TYPE="TEXT" NAME="AddrInfo.%%n%%.postCode"
           VALUE="%%AddrInfo.postCode%%" SIZE="15"></TD>
</TR>
<TR>
    <TD ALIGN="RIGHT" WIDTH="20%" BGCOLOR="#94AAD6">@country@</TD>
    <TD COLSPAN="3" WIDTH="25%" BGCOLOR="#94AAD6">
       <OEC NAME=viewSelectedList( name="AddrInfo.%%n%%.cntryCode"
            nlist="countrynames" vlist="countrycodes"
            select="AddrInfo.%%n%%.cntryCode")
         DEFAULT=viewNotImplemented()></TD>
</TR>
```

In the preceding example, the dynamic variables are denoted by two percent signs (for example, **%%**) on either side of the variable. At runtime, the HTML template is parsed and any dynamic variables are resolved through lookups in the database. The exact data element to retrieve from the database is defined by the Info Class field that is referenced in the HTML template. In the preceding example, the Info class is AddrInfo. The Info classes and their fields are defined in the OIC documentation. The dynamic variables in the previously listed file include AddrInfo.addr1, AddrInfo.addr2, AddrInfo.addr3, AddrInfo.city, AddrInfo.cnty, AddrInfo.state, AddrInfo.postCode, and so forth. Using dynamic variables to modify your HTML templates is a powerful method of pulling information from the database to display additional information.

Breaking Down the OEC Tag

A third type of OIC component is the OEC tag (for example, <OEC>), used to display data. OEC tags are similar to dynamic variables because their source for data is the database. They differ from dynamic variables in that they combine a predefined function, called a view method, and an HTML template that defines the layout of the page for the results of the view method. View methods accept various parameters, but most of them accept the parameter that specifies a template name to display the data. These templates contain static and dynamic variables dictating what information will be displayed. The following code demonstrates the use of two view methods:

```
<!-- dtprodview.en.htm -->
<TABLE BORDER="0" WIDTH="90%">
   <TR><TD>
      <TABLE BORDER="0" WIDTH="100%">
         <TR>
            <OEC NAME=viewFile(template  = "prdlinklbl.en.htm"
                               alternate = "prdlbl.en.htm")
```

```
                DEFAULT=viewNotImplemented()>
         </TR>
         <TR><TD WIDTH="20%">
      <OEC NAME=viewContent(template="timgthmbctnt.en.htm" index="0"
               content="thumbnail" format="imginfo"
               type="prdCtntInfoLst" alternate="tdimgthmbctnt.en.htm")
                   DEFAULT=viewNotImplemented()></TD>
               <TD WIDTH="80%">%%PrdInfo.dscr%%</TD>
         </TR>
      </TABLE></TD>
   </TR>
</TABLE>
```

The viewFile() method is used in the preceding example to insert a partial template—the product label displayed as a link. The viewContent() method is used to display a graphic. In both cases, the specified templates are partial templates dictating how the data should be displayed on the page. Changing the HTML templates used by the view methods is an easy way to quickly change the appearance of a page.

Calling Action Methods

The last OIC component used in HTML templates is called an action method. Action methods are procedures that use an HTML form (POST) or an anchor (HREF) to invoke an action. Just like view methods, action methods often require various parameters. These methods require the eccookie value. Once decrypted, the eccookie uniquely identifies the customer. The following HREF tag is calling the eccheckout action to check out a customer. Eccookie is the encrypted customer cookie and ecroot is the Java cartridge name of cstage or cdeploy, depending on the area of the store you are accessing.

```
<A HREF="@ecroot@?eccookie=@eccookie@&ecaction=eccheckout"
   TARGET="main"><IMG SRC=/multimedia/icon/jcheckout.gif
                       WIDTH=80 HEIGHT=24 BORDER=0> </A>
```

The following code fragment illustrates equivalent functionality using an HTML form:

```
<FORM METHOD="POST" ACTION="@ecroot@">
   <INPUT TYPE="HIDDEN" NAME="eccookie" VALUE="@eccookie@">
   <INPUT TYPE="HIDDEN" NAME="ecaction" VALUE="eccheckout">
```

When the form is submitted, the appropriate Java cartridge is called, the cookie is sent, and the action method is specified.

Creating Your Own Templates

OIC comes with all of the HTML templates for you to get your store up and running quickly. As discussed in the previous section, you can modify these templates. OIC encourages modifications by providing many different ways to customize the templates through the use of static variables, dynamic variables, view methods, and action methods. Oracle provides several ways to modify an HTML template; therefore, you are not limited to modifying the provided templates. Using functionality including HTML, JavaScript, and OIC's additions, you can essentially redesign the store. For example, you could implement a JavaScript pull-down menu instead of a side toolbar.

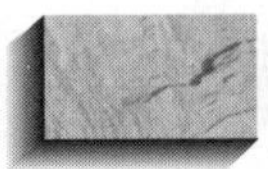

TIP
For the view and action methods you must have the correct arguments and you must include the hidden input, eccookie, in all of your pages, as this identifies the user.

Before you undertake writing new templates, it's a good idea to be familiar with OIC's templates and the general structure. Even though many of the templates are common across the board, several templates are specific to a particular piece of the application. Two login templates exist, one for the staging area and another for the deployment area. The login templates are essentially the same except on login, one calls the staging cartridge and the other calls the deployment cartridge. Some templates are specific to walk-in customers and others are specific for account customers. Templates are often embedded into other templates; therefore, you will often find the walk-in versus account customers templates used to display menu options, such as the toolbar or buttons appearing at the bottom of a page. Take the time to investigate each template and it will become apparent that they are not full HTML pages, but they are partial templates embedded within other templates. These partial templates are often tables, or even a single row of a table. The partial templates are usually used in the view methods where the method returns multiple rows of data that need to be displayed. At runtime, the call to the view method is replaced by the retrieved data applied to the named template. For example, the following piece of HTML code is one OIC template:

```
<!-- prdlinklbl.en.htm -->
<TD COLSPAN="2">
   <A HREF="%%eclink%%&eccookie=@eccookie@">
      <FONT color="#000000" SIZE=+1>
      <I><B>%%PrdInfo.name%%</B></I></FONT></A>
</TD>
```

The preceding template is only a table data item displaying the product name as a link. This template is called as a result of several view methods ultimately displaying all the products for a section on a single page. The preceding template is used once for each product on the page. When the section view template page is processed at runtime, the preceding HTML fragment will replace the view method that executed the call. OIC replaces the view method with the specified HTML template for each view method that it encounters while parsing the page. As a result, all of the replaced view methods will create one whole page.

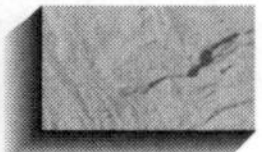

TIP

Whether using the default templates or creating your own, you may want to use a technique illustrated in this section. For example, we added a comment at the top of each HTML file stating the name of the file. The technique of adding the filename is particularly useful when viewing the source of a page that is a combination of several partial templates. You can also identify which templates generate a particular part of the page.

The templates provided with OIC should not be seen as an end product, but as a starting point to creating your unique store. Be creative!

Extending the Java Classes

OIC's main functionality presents a store interface to an end user and collects needed information for the customer to make an online purchase. Once this information has been collected, OIC's role ceases. From there, your company needs to provide the remaining logic. Additional logic may be needed to include tax calculation and payment authorization. While OIC cannot provide all the code and logic to deal with such areas, it provides the developer with a way to easily integrate this logic into OIC.

OIC has defined abstract Java classes in the eight areas described in Table 22-2. An abstract Java class lists the methods that belong in the class—a template of a different sort. Because abstract classes cannot be instantiated, subclasses must be created defining the behavior within the methods. OIC has provided sample subclasses for all eight areas. You can get the store up and running first, then deal with each of these areas one at a time. In some areas, the sample subclasses may be adequate—such as the Account Number Generation subclass, generating account numbers from a sequence.

Abstract Java Subclass	Functionality Provided
Account Number Generation	Generates unique IDs for new accounts
Soft Delivery	To "soft deliver" ordered items
Inventory	Keep track of inventory
Order Processing	To process orders in a system external to OIC
Order Number Generation	Generate unique order numbers
Payment	Payment preparation and authorization for an order
Shipping and Handling Calculation	Calculate shipping and handling fees for an order
Tax Calculation	Calculate taxes for an order

TABLE 22-2. *OIC's Exposed Abstract Java Subclasses and What Function They Provide*

Typically, you will either be integrating third-party applications, integrating your business' existing systems, or defining the behavior in the class itself. In some cases, OIC is enabled to easily integrate with third-party products (for example, TanData for shipping and handling, CyberCash for payments, and Taxware for tax calculation). For areas where third-party classes are in place, install the software and configure both the product and OIC to work together. For integrating existing systems or defining the behavior explicitly, you must write Java code. In integration, you are using the Java class as a link to your other system.

Creating a New Java Subclass

The easiest way to create a new subclass is to copy the sample class, rename it appropriately, then perform modifications within a file. The sample classes are located in the /OEC/TPI directory. With each sample class there will be a corresponding TP*.java file. This file is the abstract class for that area. Your new subclass must extend this TP*.class file. The following syntax is an example of subclassing the Shipping and Handling class:

```
/**
  Copyright © TUSC 1999. All rights reserved.
  NAME:         Class MyShpHdlg.java
  Dated:        Apr. 1997.
```

```
  DESCRIPTION: This class calculates shipping and
               handling charges for orders.
**/
import java.util.*;
import java.io.* ;
import oracle.rdbms.*;
import oracle.plsql.*;

public  class  TuscstoreShpHdlg  extends TPShpHdlg
{
  public static final String ClassName = "TuscstoreShpHdlg";

  // US  (except AK and HI) - UPS Ground 1st item
  private static final double p_UPSGroundInit = 5.95;
  // US (except AK and HI) - UPS Ground 2nd+ item
  private static final double p_UPSGroundNext = 2.00;
  // Alaska and Hawaii - USPS 3 Day 1st item
  private static final double p_USPS3DayInit = 10.00;
  // Alaska and Hawaii - USPS 3 Day 2nd+ item
  private static final double p_USPS3DayNext = 2.00;
  // Canada - UPS Ground  1st item
  private static final double p_CaUPSGroundInit = 10.00;
  // Canada - UPS Ground 2nd+ item
  private static final double p_CaUPSGroundNext = 2.00;

  public void init(Ctx ctx) throws TPException
  { return; }

  public void calcShpHdlg(Ctx ctx, OrdShpInfo ordShp)
        throws TPException
  {    calcShpHdlg(ctx, ordShp, true);  }

  public void calcShpHdlg(Ctx ctx,OrdShpInfo ordShp,boolean confirm)
        throws TPException
{
  String  mthdName       = ClassName + "::calcShpHdlg()";
  Session s              = (Session) ctx.get(Ctx.Session);

  // check if there are items or shipment methods in the order
  if ((ordShp.ordItmInfoLst == null) ||
       ordShp.ordItmInfoLst.size() == 0) ||
      (ordShp.shpMthdInfo    == null) ||
      (ordShp.shpMthdInfo.name      == null))
   return;

  String      shpMthd     = ordShp.shpMthdInfo.name;
  String      shpSvc      = ordShp.shpMthdInfo.shpSvcInfo.name;
  CurrDefInfo cd          =
```

```
              ordShp.ordItmInfoLst.elemAt(0).unitPrc.currDefInfo;
int           prec          = Integer.valueOf(cd.prec).intValue();
double        shpFee        = 0.0;
double        hdlFee        = 0.0;
int           totQty        = 0;
int           numOrdItms    = ordShp.ordItmInfoLst.size();

// Get the total number of order items
for (int i = 0; i < numOrdItms; i++)
  totQty +=
   Integer.valueOf(ordShp.ordItmInfoLst.elemAt(i).qty).intValue();

// Calculate the shipping and handling fee.
if (shpSvc.equalsIgnoreCase("TuscstoreShpHdlg"))
{
boolean        shipLocal;
boolean        FirstPosterItem = true;
OrdItmInfoLst ordItmInfoLst    = ordShp.ordItmInfoLst;
  if (ordShp.sndrAddrInfo.cntryCode.equals
     (ordShp.recvAddrInfo.cntryCode))
    shipLocal = true;
  else
    shipLocal = false;
  for (int i = 0; i < ordItmInfoLst.size(); i++)
  {
  OrdItmInfo ordItmInfo     = ordItmInfoLst.elemAt(i);
  CurrInfo   currShp        = new CurrInfo();
  CurrInfo   currHdl        = new CurrInfo();
  currShp.currDefInfo       = cd;
  currHdl.currDefInfo       = cd;
    if (FirstPosterItem==true)
    {
      if(shpMthd.indexOf("US (not AK and HI)-UPS Ground")!=-1)
        shpFee = p_UPSGroundInit + (p_UPSGroundNext *
            (Integer.valueOf(ordShp.ordItmInfoLst.elemAt(i).qty)
              .intValue()-1));
      else if(shpMthd.indexOf("AK and HI - USPS 3 Day")!=-1)
        shpFee = p_USPS3DayInit + (p_USPS3DayNext *
            (Integer.valueOf(ordShp.ordItmInfoLst.elemAt(i).qty)
              .intValue()-1));
      else if (shpMthd.indexOf("Canada - UPS Ground")!=-1)
        shpFee = p_CaUPSGroundInit +(p_CaUPSGroundNext *
            (Integer.valueOf(ordShp.ordItmInfoLst.elemAt(i).qty)
              .intValue()-1));
        FirstPosterItem = false;
    }   else  {
```

```
        if (shpMthd.indexOf("US(not AK and HI)-UPS Ground")!=-1)
          shpFee = p_UPSGroundNext * integer.valueOf(ordShp.
                   ordItmInfoLst.elemAt(i).qty).intValue();
        else if (shpMthd.indexOf("AK and HI - USPS 3 Day")!=-1)
          shpFee = p_USPS3DayNext * Integer.valueOf(ordShp.
                   ordItmInfoLst.elemAt(i).qty).intValue();
        else if (shpMthd.indexOf("Canada - UPS Ground") != -1)
          shpFee = p_CaUPSGroundNext *  Integer.valueOf(ordShp.
                   ordItmInfoLst.elemAt(i).qty).intValue();
      }
      currShp.value =ECMath.doubleToString(shpFee,prec,cd.sep);
      if (shipLocal)
        ordItmInfo.shpFeeLoc = currShp;
      else
        ordItmInfo.shpFeeFor = currShp;
        currHdl.value = ECMath.doubleToString(0.0,prec,cd.sep);
      if (shipLocal)
        ordItmInfo.hdlFeeLoc = currHdl;
      else
        ordItmInfo.hdlFeeFor = currHdl;
    }
  }

  public void cleanup(Ctx ctx) throws TPException
  { return;  }
}
```

After you create your subclass you must compile and install it. Located in the /OEC/JAVA directory is a file named oec.zip. This file contains all the OIC Java classes. Unzip this file into a directory. Once successfully compiled, place the new class into the /OEC/JAVA/TPI directory.

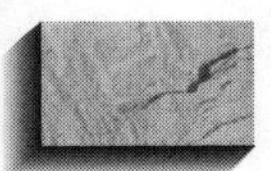

TIP
Create a directory for the unzipped OIC Java classes under the /OEC/JAVA directory. Make sure the Java compiler is configured to find all these classes, as it will need some of them to resolve class references.

Adding Subclasses to OIC

Once the new subclass has been created, OIC must be configured accordingly. For all classes except Shipping & Handling and Payments, add the name of the subclass to the appropriate store attribute as shown in Table 22-3.

Subclass Area	Store Attribute to Modify
Account Number Generation	COAcctNumSW
Soft Delivery	CODownloadSW
Inventory	COInvItmSW
Order Processing	COOrdSW
Order Number Generation	COOrdNumSW
Tax Calculation	COTaxSW

TABLE 22-3. *Store Attributes for Java Classes*

For the Shipping and Handling subclass, add a new entry under Shipping Services in the Store Manager's Data Entry Forms and remove the sample entry. Completing this form will modify the list box for shipment methods on the Invoice page. For the Payment subclasses, add a new entry under Payment Services in the Store Manager. Adding a new entry will modify the list box for payment methods on the Invoice page.

"Stepping Out" – Customization Beyond OIC

At some point you will need to "step outside" the OIC "box." Add functionality or present your store in a way that is unique, or perform business requirements that OIC has not anticipated. From here, your options are limitless. This section gives a few examples of what can be accomplished.

Directing Customer's Views

Have you noticed the Amazon.com image that appears on many sites which says, "Search for ______"? If you click on it, you are brought to the search results page based on your search criteria. This accomplishes two things: it gets the customer into the store and directs the customer's attention to a place where they have interest. Using OIC, similar customer directing can be implemented. The following HTML file automatically logs a customer into the store, and directs the customer to a specific page within the store:

```
<HTML>
<HEAD></HEAD>
<BODY BGCOLOR="#94AAD6">
<SCRIPT language = "JavaScript">
   top.document.location.href ="http://tuscstore.tusc.com/cust
         /cdeploy?ecaction=ecwalkin&template=walkin5.en.htm";
</SCRIPT>
</BODY>
</HTML>
```

In the following example, the customer is directed to a specific section view, the results of which can be seen in Figure 22-3.

```
<!-- walkin5.en.htm -->
<HTML>
<HEAD>
   <TITLE>TUSC Technology Store</TITLE>
</HEAD>
<FRAMESET FRAMEBORDER=0 BORDER=0 FRAMESPACING=0 COLS="125,*">
   <FRAME NAME="common" MARGINWIDTH=0 MARGINHEIGHT=0
    SRC="@ecroot@?eccookie=@eccookie@&template=walkincommon1.en.htm">
   <FRAME NAME="main" MARGINWIDTH=0 MARGINHEIGHT=0
         SRC="http://tuscstore.tusc.com/cust/cdeploy
         ?ecaction=ecsectview&ecsid=1041&eccookie=@eccookie@">
</FRAMESET>
<BODY BGCOLOR="#94AAD6" TEXT="#000000">
</BODY>
</HTML>
```

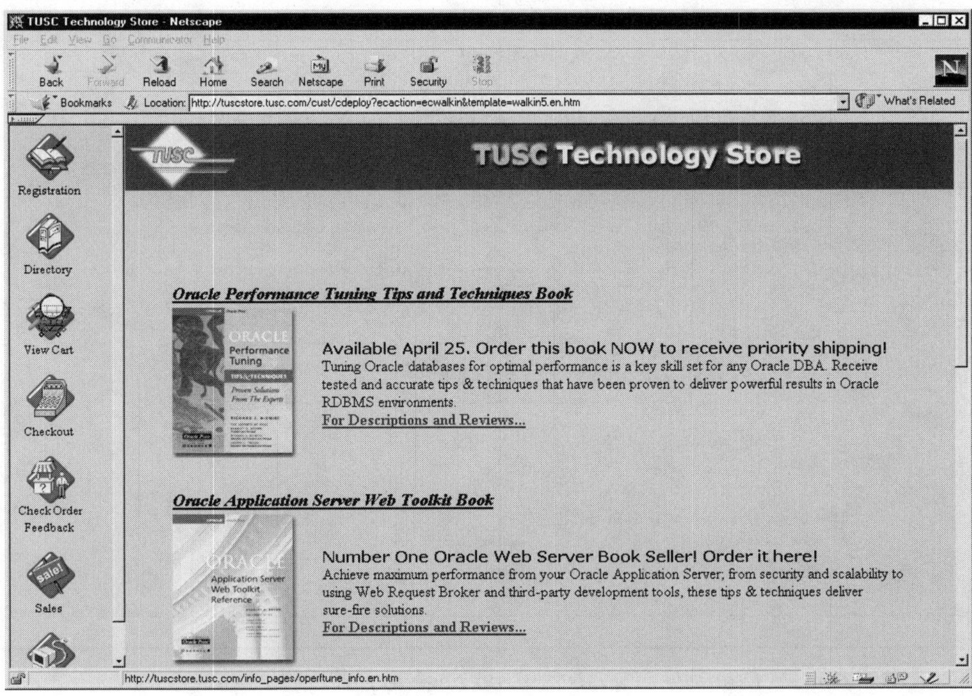

FIGURE 22-3. *Results of the direct link to the TUSC store*

In the preceding example you are stepping out of OIC because you are circumventing the login page. You do not have to leave OIC because you use some of its action methods to log in the customer and produce the desired page. Once you have directed the customer to where you want them to go, the customization ends and the customer is back in the OIC box.

Collecting Credit Card Information

Numerous ways exist to take credit card orders directly on the Web. You can automate the transaction all the way to the bank or you can collect this information and have an administrative person manually process the credit card transactions. If you choose the latter, you must prompt the customer for the needed information, such as a credit card number or an account number containing billing information.

The following PL/SQL procedure takes an order number and searches to identify if the customer has an account. Then, it displays a page prompting the customer for their credit card information, an example of the output is shown in Figure 22-4.

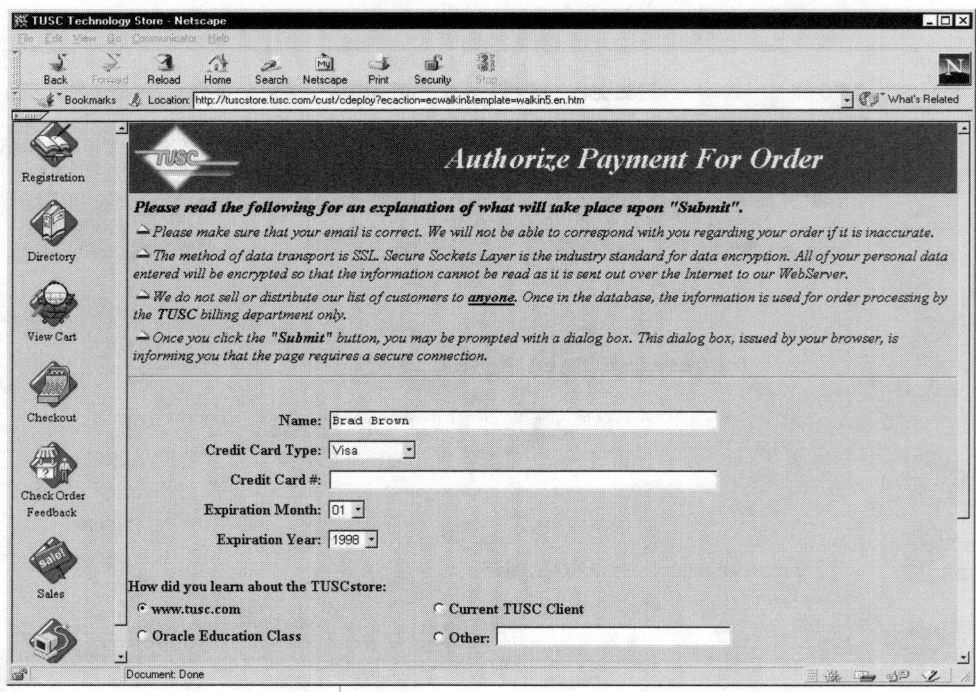

FIGURE 22-4. *Example of a customized page to prompt customers for their credit card number*

```
procedure get_default_info(pordnum number) is
  cursor   get_name is
    select ecuserid, billname
    from   ec_ord, ec_ecord
    where  ec_ord.ordnum = pordnum
    and    ec_ord.ordid = ec_ecord.ordid;
  billname                varchar2(100);
  userid                  number;
  cursor   get_email is
    select distinct emailaddr
    from   ec_ecuser_emaillst, ec_email
    where  ec_ecuser_emaillst.ecuserid = userid
    and    ec_ecuser_emaillst.emailid = ec_email.emailid;
  cursor   get_phone is
    select phonenum
    from   ec_ecuser_phonelst_v
    where  ec_ecuser_phonelst_v.ecuserid = userid;
  emailhold               varchar2(80) := null;
  selecthold              boolean := false;
begin
  open  get_name;
  fetch get_name into userid, billname;
  close get_name;
  htp.htmlOpen;
  htp.headOpen;
  htp.headClose;
  htp.bodyOpen(cattributes =>' BGCOLOR="#94AAD6"' );
  htp.tableOpen(calign => 'CENTER',
              cattributes => ' BORDER=0 WIDTH="100%"');
  htp.tableRowOpen(calign => 'CENTER',
                 cattributes => ' BGCOLOR="#303080"');
    htp.tableData(htf.img('/logo_dblue1.gif', calign => 'LEFT'));
    htp.tableData('<FONT COLOR="#FFFFFF" SIZE=+3><B><I>' ||
                'Authorize Payment For Order '|| '</I></B></FONT>');
  htp.tableRowClose;
  htp.tableClose;
  htp.tableOpen(calign=>'CENTER', cattributes=> ' WIDTH="100%"');
  htp.tableRowOpen;
    htp.print('<td>');
    htp.print('<FONT SIZE=4><B><I>Please read the following for an' ||
           'explanation of what will take place upon Submit".'  ||
           '</I></B></FONT>');
    htp.print('</td>');
  htp.tableRowClose;
  htp.tableRowOpen;
    htp.print('<td>');
```

```
  htp.print('<IMG ALIGN="LEFT" SRC="/bullet_white.gif" BORDER=0>');
  htp.print('<I>Please make sure that your email is correct. ' ||
        'We will not be able to correspond with you ' ||
        'regarding your order if it is inaccurate.</i>');
  htp.print('</td>');
htp.tableRowClose;
htp.tableRowOpen;
  htp.print('<td>');
  htp.print('<IMG ALIGN="LEFT" SRC="/bullet_white.gif" BORDER=0>');
  htp.print('<I>The method of data transport is SSL. Secure Sockets ' ||
        'Layer is the industry standard for data encryption. '    ||
        'All of your personal data entered will be encrypted '    ||
        'so that the information cannot be read as it is sent '   ||
        'out over the Internet to our WebServer.</I>');
  htp.print('</td>');
htp.tableRowClose;
htp.tableRowOpen;
  htp.print('<td>');
  htp.print('<IMG ALIGN="LEFT" SRC="/bullet_white.gif" BORDER=0>');
  htp.print('<I>We do not sell or distribute our list of customers ' ||
        'to  <B><U>anyone</U></B>. Once in the database, the '   ||
        'information is used for order processing by the '       ||
        '<B>TUSC</B> billing department only.</I>');
  htp.print('</td>');
htp.tableRowClose;
htp.tableRowOpen;
  htp.print('<td>');
  htp.print('<IMG ALIGN="LEFT" SRC="/bullet_white.gif" BORDER=0>');
  htp.print('<I>Once you click the <B>"Submit"</B> button, you ');
  htp.print('may be prompted with a dialog box. This dialog ');
  htp.print('box, issued by your browser, is informing you  ');
  htp.print('that the page requires a secure connection.</I>');
  htp.print('</td>');
htp.tableRowClose;
htp.tableClose;
htp.hr;
htp.tableOpen(cattributes => ' width="100%"' );
htp.formOpen(curl => '/inet/owa/Credit_Processing.Insert_Card_Info',
             cmethod => 'POST');
htp.formHidden( cname => 'OrdNum', cvalue => pOrdNum);
htp.tableRowOpen;
  htp.tableData(htf.bold('Name:'), calign => 'RIGHT');
  htp.tableData(htf.formText(cname => 'Name',  csize => '50',
                    cmaxlength => '80', cvalue => billName));
htp.tableRowClose;
htp.tableRowOpen;
```

```
    http.tableData('<B>Credit Card Type:</B>', calign=> 'RIGHT');
    http.print('<td>');
      http.formSelectOpen(cname => 'CCType', nsize => '1' );
      http.formSelectOption('Visa',cattributes=>' VALUE="VISA"');
      http.formSelectOption('MasterCard',
                            cattributes => ' VALUE="MASTERCARD"');
      http.formSelectClose;
    http.print('</td>');
  http.tableRowClose;
  http.tableRowOpen;
    http.tableData(htf.bold('Credit Card #:'), calign => 'RIGHT');
    http.tableData(htf.formText(cname => 'CCNo', csize => '50',
                               cmaxlength => '50', cvalue => ''));
  http.tableRowClose;
  http.tableRowOpen;
    http.tableData('<B>Expiration Month:</B>', calign => 'RIGHT');
    http.print('<td>');
      http.formSelectOpen( cname => 'CCExpMon', nsize => '1' );
      http.formSelectOption( '01', cattributes => ' VALUE="JAN"');
      http.formSelectOption( '02', cattributes => ' VALUE="FEB"');
      http.formSelectOption( '03', cattributes => ' VALUE="MAR"');
      http.formSelectOption( '04', cattributes => ' VALUE="APR"');
      http.formSelectOption( '05', cattributes => ' VALUE="MAY"');
      http.formSelectOption( '06', cattributes => ' VALUE="JUN"');
      http.formSelectOption( '07', cattributes => ' VALUE="JUL"');
      http.formSelectOption( '08', cattributes => ' VALUE="AUG"');
      http.formSelectOption( '09', cattributes => ' VALUE="SEP"');
      http.formSelectOption( '10', cattributes => ' VALUE="OCT"');
      http.formSelectOption( '11', cattributes => ' VALUE="NOV"');
      http.formSelectOption( '12', cattributes => ' VALUE="DEC"');
      http.formSelectClose;
    http.print('</td>');
  http.tableRowClose;
  http.tableRowOpen;
    http.tableData(htf.bold('Expiration Year:'), calign=>'RIGHT');
    http.print('<td>');
      http.formSelectOpen( cname => 'CCExpYr', nsize => '1' );
      http.formSelectOption('1998', cattributes=>' VALUE="1998"');
      http.formSelectOption('1999', cattributes=>' VALUE="1999"');
      http.formSelectOption('2000', cattributes=>' VALUE="2000"');
      http.formSelectOption('2001', cattributes=>' VALUE="2001"');
      http.formSelectOption('2002', cattributes=>' VALUE="2002"');
      http.formSelectOption('2003', cattributes=>' VALUE="2003"');
      http.formSelectOption('2004', cattributes=>' VALUE="2004"');
      http.formSelectOption('2005', cattributes=>' VALUE="2005"');
      http.formSelectClose;
```

```
  htp.print('</td>');
htp.tableRowClose;
htp.tableRowOpen;
htp.tableClose;
htp.br;
htp.print('<p align=leftt>');
htp.bold('How did you learn about the TUSCstore:');
htp.tableOpen(calign=>'CENTER', cattributes=>' width="100%"');
htp.tableRowOpen;
  htp.tableData(htf.formRadio(cname => 'v_user_got_here',
         cvalue => 'TUSC.COM',
         cchecked => 'TRUE') || htf.bold('www.tusc.com'));
  htp.tableData(htf.formRadio(cname => 'v_user_got_here',
         cvalue => 'CURRENT CLIENT')||
                    htf.bold('Current TUSC Client'));
htp.tableRowClose;
htp.tableRowOpen;
  htp.tableData(htf.formRadio(cname => 'v_user_got_here',
           cvalue => 'ORACLE EDUCATION') ||
                      htf.bold('Oracle Education Class'));
  htp.tableData (htf.formRadio(cname => 'v_user_got_here',
                               cvalue => 'OTHER') ||
            htf.bold('Other: ') || htf.formText(cname => 'v_other',
            csize=>'30', cmaxlength=>'30', cvalue=>' '));
htp.tableRowClose;
htp.tableClose;
htp.br;
htp.bold('Please provide the following to be used to ' ||
          'contact you regarding your order:');
htp.tableOpen(calign=>'CENTER', cattributes=>' width="100%"');
htp.tableRowOpen;
  htp.tableData(htf.bold('Phone:'), calign => 'RIGHT');
  htp.print('<td>');
    htp.formSelectOpen( cname => 'Phone', nsize => '1' );
    FOR Get_Phone_Rec IN Get_Phone LOOP
     selectHold := TRUE;
      htp.formSelectOption( Get_Phone_Rec.phonenum,
           cattributes=>' VALUE="'||Get_Phone_Rec.phonenum||'"');
    end loop;
    if (not (selectHold)) then
      htp.formSelectOption('None', cattributes=>' VALUE="None"');
  end if;
    htp.formSelectClose;
  htp.print('</td>');
htp.tableRowClose;
htp.tableRowOpen;
```

```
    htp.tableData(htf.bold('Use Other Phone:'), calign=>'RIGHT');
    htp.tableData(htf.formText(cname=> 'PhoneOtr', csize => '50',
                               cmaxlength => '80', cvalue => ''));
  htp.tableRowClose;
  open  get_email;
  fetch get_email into emailhold;
  close get_email;
  htp.tableRowOpen;
    htp.tableData(htf.bold('Email:'), calign => 'RIGHT');
    htp.tableData(htf.formText(cname => 'Email', csize => '50',
                  cmaxlength => '80', cvalue => emailHold));
  htp.tableRowClose;
  htp.tableClose;
  htp.tableOpen(calign=> 'CENTER', cattributes=>' width="100%"');
  htp.tableRowOpen;
    htp.print('<td align=center>');
      htp.formSubmit( cvalue => 'Submit');
      htp.formReset( cvalue => 'Clear');
    htp.print('</td>');
  htp.tableRowClose;
  htp.hr;
  htp.tableClose;
  htp.formClose;
  htp.bodyClose;
  htp.htmlClose;
end;
```

After the customer enters the appropriate information and submits the page, the information is securely sent back and stored in a table. A final page is displayed informing the customer the order has been received and will be processed.

Once you collect and store the customer's order and other information, you can manually authorize the customer's account, fulfill the order, or move the order information to an existing payment authorization system and fulfill it there. The preceding example stepped out of the store by leaving the deployment Java cartridge and calling our own PL/SQL procedure using the PL/SQL cartridge. I did not reenter the store because the process did not return to the deployment cartridge.

Viewing the Orders

OIC provides a method to view orders and updates the status, one at a time. If you want different views of the pending orders, write your own applications to retrieve the order information from the OIC database. You can use Java, PL/SQL, Oracle Reports, Oracle Forms, or another appropriate tool to retrieve and display data from the database.

When the following PL/SQL procedure is invoked, it sends a page to the Web browser listing all the orders, their current processing status, and a link to display detail order information:

```
procedure getorderslist is
  cursor orderslistcur is
  select ordnum, card_holder_name, status, ord_date
    from tusc_ccard
   order by ord_date, ordnum;
begin
  htp.htmlOpen;
  htp.headOpen;
  htp.title('Current Order List');
  htp.headClose;
  htp.bodyOpen(cattributes => 'BGCOLOR="#94AAD6"');
  htp.formOpen('/inet/owa/Order_Interface_Pkg.UpdateStatus', 'POST');
  htp.tableOpen(calign => 'CENTER',
                cattributes => 'BORDER=0 WIDTH="100%"');
  -- add in table headers
  htp.tableHeader('Order Number');
  htp.tableHeader('Customer Name');
  htp.tableHeader('Order Date');
  htp.tableHeader('Status');
  -- loop through and retrieve each order and it's info
  for orderslistrec in orderslistcur loop
    htp.tableRowOpen(calign => 'CENTER',
                     cattributes => 'BORDER=0 WIDTH="100%"');
    htp.formHidden(cname => 'pOrdStatusBefore',
                   cvalue => ordersListRec.status);
    htp.formHidden(cname => 'pOrdNum',
                   cvalue =>ordersListRec.ordnum);
    htp.tableData(htf.anchor(
        'Order_Interface_Pkg.GetOrders?pOrdNum=' ||
        ordersListRec.ordnum, ordersListRec.ordnum));
    htp.tableData(ordersListRec.card_holder_name);
    htp.tableData(ordersListRec.ord_date);
    -- create a list box for the valid status choices
    htp.print('<TD>');
    htp.formSelectOpen(cname => 'pOrdStatusAfter', nsize=> '1');
    if (ordersListRec.status = 'ORDERED') then
      htp.formSelectOption('ORDERED', 'Selected', 'VALUE="ORDERED"');
      htp.formSelectOption( 'SHIPPED',  NULL, 'VALUE="SHIPPED"');
      htp.formSelectOption( 'ON HOLD',  NULL, 'VALUE="ON HOLD"');
    elsif (ordersListRec.status = 'SHIPPED') then
      htp.formSelectOption( 'ORDERED', NULL,'VALUE="ORDERED"');
```

```
        htp.formSelectOption( 'SHIPPED', 'Selected', 'VALUE="SHIPPED"');
        htp.formSelectOption( 'ON HOLD',  NULL, 'VALUE="ON HOLD"');
      elsif (ordersListRec.status = 'ON HOLD') then
        htp.formSelectOption( 'ORDERED', NULL,'VALUE="ORDERED"');
        htp.formSelectOption( 'SHIPPED', NULL, 'VALUE="SHIPPED"');
        htp.formSelectOption( 'ON HOLD', 'Selected', 'VALUE="ON HOLD"');
      else
        htp.formSelectOption( ordersListRec.status, 'Selected',
                             'VALUE=' || ordersListRec.status);
        htp.formSelectOption( 'ORDERED', NULL,'VALUE="ORDERED"');
        htp.formSelectOption( 'SHIPPED', NULL, 'VALUE="SHIPPED"');
        htp.formSelectOption( 'ON HOLD',  NULL, 'VALUE="ON HOLD"');
      end if;
      htp.formSelectClose;
      htp.print('</TD>');
      htp.tableRowClose;
    end loop;
    -- add a submit button and close up the page
    htp.tableClose;
    htp.para;
    htp.center(htf.formSubmit);
    htp.formClose;
    htp.bodyClose;
    htp.htmlClose;
  end;
```

Clicking on the link generated by the preceding procedure (to view the details of an order) invokes the following PL/SQL procedure. The following GetOrders procedure takes an order number and retrieves the following information: order date, order status, shipping address, itemized list of order, shipping and handling fees, taxes, and the order total. The GetOrders procedure could easily be modified to display further order information, such as the email address and phone number.

```
procedure      getorders(pordnum number) is
  cursor ordidcur is
  select ordid
    from ec_ord
   where ordnum = pordnum;
  orderid      number;

  cursor statuscur is
  select status, ord_date
    from tusc_ccard
   where ordnum = pordnum;
  orderstatus  varchar2(30);
  orderdate    date;
```

```
  cursor shiptoaddrcur is
  select shiptoname,addr1,addr2,addr3,city,state,postcode,cntry
    from ec_ord, ec_addr
   where ec_ord.ordnum       = pordnum
     and ec_ord.shiptoaddrid = ec_addr.addrid;
  shiptoname   varchar2(160);
  addr1        varchar2(80);
  addr2        varchar2(80);
  addr3        varchar2(80);
  city         varchar2(80);
  state        varchar2(40);
  zip          varchar2(20);
  cntry        varchar2(40);

  cursor orderitemscur is
  select sku, prditmname, qty, value, (qty*value) sub_total
    from tusc_ec_orditm_v
   where ordid = orderid;

  cursor ordertotalscur is
  select sum(qty*value) sub_total,
         sum(tax_value) tax,
               sum(shfee_value) shfee,
              (sum(qty*value)+sum(tax_value)+sum(shfee_value)) total
    from tusc_ec_orditm_v
   where ordid = orderid;
  sub_total    number;
  tax          number;
  shfee        number;
  total        number;
begin
  open  ordidcur;
  fetch ordidcur into orderid;
  close ordidcur;
  open  statuscur;
  fetch statuscur into orderstatus, orderdate;
  close statuscur;
  htp.htmlOpen;
  htp.headOpen;
  htp.headClose;
  htp.bodyOpen(cattributes => 'BGCOLOR="#94AAD6"');
  -- add page headers
  htp.header(2, 'Order Invoice for Order #' || pOrdNum,
                cattributes=>'ALIGN="CENTER"');
  htp.header(3, orderDate, cattributes=>'ALIGN="CENTER"');
  htp.tableOpen(calign => 'RIGHT',
               cattributes => ' BORDER=1 WIDTH="35%"');
```

```
htp.tableRowOpen(cattributes => 'BORDER=1');
  htp.tableData('Status: ' || orderStatus);
htp.tableRowClose;
htp.tableClose;
-- get shipping info
open  shiptoaddrcur;
fetch shiptoaddrcur
 into shiptoname,addr1,addr2,addr3,city,state,zip,cntry;
close shiptoaddrcur;
htp.header(3, 'Ship To Information');
htp.tableOpen(cattributes => 'BORDER="0" WIDTH="50%"');
htp.tableRowOpen(calign => 'LEFT', cattributes => 'BORDER=0');
  htp.tableData('Name: ');
  htp.tableData(shipToName);
htp.tableRowClose;
htp.tableRowOpen(calign => 'LEFT', cattributes => 'BORDER=0');
  htp.tableData('Address(1): ');
  htp.tableData(Addr1);
htp.tableRowClose;
if (addr2 is not null) then
  htp.tableRowOpen(calign =>'LEFT', cattributes =>'BORDER=0');
    htp.tableData('Address(2): ');
    htp.tableData(Addr2);
  htp.tableRowClose;
end if;
if (addr3 is not null) then
  htp.tableRowOpen(calign =>'LEFT', cattributes =>'BORDER=0');
    htp.tableData('Address(3): ');
    htp.tableData(Addr3);
  htp.tableRowClose;
end if;
htp.tableRowOpen(calign => 'LEFT', cattributes => 'BORDER=0');
  htp.tableData('City: ');
  htp.tableData(City);
htp.tableRowClose;
htp.tableRowOpen(calign => 'LEFT', cattributes => 'BORDER=0');
  htp.tableData('State/Province: ');
  htp.tableData(State);
htp.tableRowClose;
htp.tableRowOpen(calign => 'LEFT', cattributes => 'BORDER=0');
  htp.tableData('Zip: ');
  htp.tableData(Zip);
htp.tableRowClose;
htp.tableRowOpen(calign => 'LEFT', cattributes => 'BORDER=0');
  htp.tableData('Country: ');
  htp.tableData(Cntry);
htp.tableRowClose;
```

```
htp.tableClose;
htp.nl;  htp.nl;  htp.nl;
-- order items
htp.tableOpen(calign => 'CENTER',
              cattributes => 'BORDER=0 WIDTH="100%"');
htp.tableRowOpen(calign =>'CENTER', cattributes =>'BORDER=0');
  htp.tableHeader('SKU');
  htp.tableHeader('Product Item Name');
  htp.tableHeader('Qty');
  htp.tableHeader('Price');
  htp.tableHeader('Sub-total');
htp.tableRowClose;
for orderitemsrec in orderitemscur loop
  htp.tableRowOpen(calign=>'CENTER', cattributes=>'BORDER=0');
    htp.tableData(orderItemsRec.sku);
    htp.tableData(orderItemsRec.prditmname);
    htp.tableData(orderItemsRec.qty);
    htp.tableData(orderItemsRec.value);
    htp.tableData(orderItemsRec.sub_total);
    htp.tableRowClose;
end loop;
htp.tableClose;
htp.nl;   htp.nl;   htp.nl;
-- order totals
open  ordertotalscur;
fetch ordertotalscur into sub_total, tax, shfee, total;
close ordertotalscur;
htp.tableOpen(calign => 'CENTER',
              cattributes => 'BORDER="0" WIDTH="100%"');
htp.tableRowOpen(calign =>'CENTER', cattributes=>'BORDER=0');
  htp.tableHeader('Sub_total');
  htp.tableHeader('Tax');
  htp.tableHeader('Shipping and Handling Fee');
  htp.tableHeader('Total');
htp.tableRowClose;
htp.tableRowOpen(calign =>'CENTER', cattributes =>'BORDER=0');
  htp.tableData(sub_total);
  htp.tableData(tax);
  htp.tableData(shfee);
  htp.tableData(total);
htp.tableRowClose;
htp.tableClose;
htp.nl;   htp.nl;   htp.nl;
-- add a back button
htp.print('<FORM>');
htp.print('<CENTER><INPUT TYPE="Button" VALUE="Back"
           onClick="history.go(-1)"></CENTER>');
```

```
  -- close the page
  htp.formClose;
  htp.bodyClose;
  htp.htmlClose;
end;
```

The preceding SQL procedure retrieves information at the database level and produces a report. It also steps out of OIC, because it does not interact with any OIC procedures.

Looking at What's New in Version 2.0

Version 2.0 has new features that make customizing easier. Among the additions are expansion of batch-loading capabilities, more fields in the Info classes, and more Java abstract class exposure.

Using the Enhanced Batch-Loader for Flat Files

The batch-loading capabilities in OIC 2.0 include a program, called flat2bl.exe, to convert flat data files to Batch-Loader files. This program uses a control file and a data file. The control file sets options and can define default values. The data file contains the data that needs to be loaded; it can be fixed-length fields or field-delimited. If no errors are generated from the flat2bl conversion, the .bl file is compiled into the associated .sql file and the resulting file is executed.

Enhancing Your Java Capabilities

OIC provides access to data through Info classes. The fields in the classes can be accessed through the use of dynamic variables in the HTML templates and through overriding the exposed Java classes. In OIC 2.0, several of the Info classes contain additional fields, such as InvPageInfo, OrdShpInfo, PayPageInfo, PmtInfo, PmtSvcInfo, PrdItmInfo, and UpdtPageInfo. The CfgOptInfo class has also been added, giving the developer access to all the values affecting global configuration, such as which currency will be displayed, the maximum monetary amount allowed per order, and the maximum allowed per line item.

OIC 2.0 includes more exposure to Java classes and the integration of more Oracle products. The Account Java class enables the developer to override the default behavior on several account functions. Specifically, you can override the behavior on creating walk-in and account customers when they enter your store. After the customer enters the store, several customer properties can be modified, including the password, phone lists, email lists, address lists, and account category.

Another new Java class is the Telephone Number Validation class. Using this class, the developer can add appropriate logic to validate phone numbers entered by customers. The default logic for this class validates and formats U.S. phone numbers, which can then be sent to Oracle's Call Center—a product integrated with OIC 2.0.

Bettering Your Pricing Structures

In the version 1.0 of ICS, an account customer was assigned ACCOUNT for the account category and a walk-in customer was assigned an account category of WALK-IN. This functionality eliminated the capability to have several different pricing categories, grouped by the account category. The enhancement in OIC 2.0 added considerable flexibility to the system. For example, the customer could be looked up in a customer profile table and assigned an account category based on how they have spent their money in the store over the last six months. The assigned account category might provide larger discounts or more sales.

TIP
Account category is an important property to be able to modify, enabling a customer to be put into different price categories based on something other than how they entered the store.

Using the Payment Cartridge

OIC 2.0 has integrated Oracle's Payment Server through the Payment class. This enhances your payment capabilities beyond the CyberCash option.

Looking at Other E-Commerce Solutions

The Table 22-4 contains a number of e-commerce solutions available on the market today. A Fortune 500 company that shall remain nameless developed this chart. This company was looking for a solution to handle business to business (B2B) e-commerce with hundreds of thousands of customers. As the following table illustrates, Oracle does not provide a solution in this ballpark. ICS is not this type of solution. This table should be used to help you develop your own product comparison when purchasing an e-commerce (EC) solution that is beyond the scope of ICS.

Vendor	Company Description	Offering Description	Product Analysis	Architecture	Integration	Price	RFP Analysis
ATG	Self described as a company founded, built, and run by engineers. They have a small sales/marketing force. They are a privately held company, started in 1991, with about 180 employees. Historically, they have relied on their product to basically sell itself, but they are expanding their sales force. Financially, they have a ways to go. They have a $4M net worth.	ATG's EC offering is best described as a toolset. There is limited out-of-the-box functionality. The product is not touted as a strong B2B offering and the company has not made a clear business to business (B2B) versus business to consumer (B2C).	Extremely flexible, open environment, excellent personalization. Beyond that, it's truly a strong toolset, but nothing more. If we were looking for a good technical architecture and a development environment, this would be our choice, hands down. They also seem to be one of the ones that just doesn't get B2B.	100% Java, distributed, EJB compliant. Comes with load-balancing and failover capability that includes the ability to do geographic failover for maximum uptime. Session information is cached and replicated across servers using RMI. Database independent through JDBC. The techies love this solution. Login or cookie authentication. We would need to add support for certificates.	Real-time integration through Java and EJB. Uses "Order Pipeline" metaphor to add custom hooks at any point in the order process. No batch loading tools available.	We stopped short of talking dollars.	Did an outstanding job of presenting their services group and their technology—we were hooked. Then when it came to the demo, they fell apart. They were not prepared to show their product. We were disappointed.

TABLE 22-4. *ECommerce Solutions*

Vendor	Company Description	Offering Description	Product Analysis	Architecture	Integration	Price	RFP Analysis
BroadVision	Started in 1993, IPO in '96. Last five quarters profitable. One of the market share leaders in electronic commerce. 317 customers, 115 live sites. Company has $80M net worth.	Strong emphasis on B2B. Out-of-the-box functionality is robust.	Integration story is strong and deep, but not a differentiator. Uses third-party text search engine Verity (separate licensing). Personalization is excellent. Would need to customize product to handle multiple shopping baskets per user.	C++/COBRA, distributed. Comes with load-balancing and failover capability. Session failover is accomplished through DB. Supports login, cookie, and certificate-based authentication. Rich caching mechanism increasing overall performance.	Real-time integration through C++/COBRA implementing BV's IDL. Batch load tools available that ensure referential integrity.	Software: $1M for 1 million users. Services: $680K.	Responded extremely well. Thoroughly covered the RFP requirements. Functionally, it would require minor customization for approval routing. Technically also strong. Well-established company. Definitely our leader.
Digital River	Strong company and growing rapidly.	Outsourcing, but almost exclusively B2C.	Pretty good offering, but severely hampered by B2C focus.	OAS		We stopped short of talking dollars.	They tried to convince us to take their outsourced solution and bring it in-house. No way.

TABLE 22-4. *ECommerce Solutions* (continued)

Vendor	Company Description	Offering Description	Product Analysis	Architecture	Integration	Price	RFP Analysis
IBM	Implementing some of the largest sties on the Web. Incredible stock growth lately based on EC growth.	Net.Commerce is their EC package. It has basic out-of-the-box functionality. Most of their work is in services.	Net.Commerce is not very impressive. Out-of-the-box it offers base functionality, but not much more. They really didn't even push it—they were clearly pushing the services side.	CGI based. Next version will be based on WebSphere.		Software: $20K per user server. Services: $1M-1.5M.	BroadVision and InterWorld came in with third-party integrators, but IBM came across as a much stronger player in this role. They would make a strong partner, as long as they bring people who have done installs in our chosen package.
Intershop	German company with strong presence in B2C market. Huge install base and 350+ employees.	Robust out-of-the-box functionality, but with almost exclusive emphasis on B2C.	Great product for B2C.	Application servers written in Perl.	Real-time integration through custom Perl modules	Software: $80K. Services: $350K.	Great presentation and preparation, but no functionality suited for B2B EC.

TABLE 22-4. *ECommerce Solutions* (continued)

Vendor	Company Description	Offering Description	Product Analysis	Architecture	Integration	Price	RFP Analysis
InterWorld	Privately held, founded in '95. Filed for IPO July '98, withdrew in November '98 due to "market conditions." They are clearly losing money by their own admission and will continue to do so in the short term. Financial analysis that we have obtained looks rather negative.	Similar to BroadVision. Robust out-of-the-box functionality, with little need for customization. Strong emphasis on B2B.		C++/distributed. Have written their own distributed layer on top of TCP/IP. This is a bit riskier than the other two winners because it's not standards-based. Load-balancing and failover capabilities are included using their WebBroker application. Currently does login and cookie based authentication. Next version may support certificates.	Real-time integration through DLLs or using their Java cartridge. Uses "Order Pipeline" metaphor to add custom hooks at any point in the order process. No known batch loading tools.	Software: $764.5K. Services: $1.8M–2.3M.	Excellent job of preparing for specific needs. Definitely at the same level as BroadVision, maybe even a little better in terms of functionality. But the financial issues they have may be a deal-breaker.

TABLE 22-4. *ECommerce Solutions* (continued)

Vendor	Company Description	Offering Description	Product Analysis	Architecture	Integration	Price	RFP Analysis
Netscape	Complicated company picture. They have moved from being the browser guys to being the EC guys, been purchased by AOL, and now they are in the alliance with Sun. It appears that the dust is far from settled on these mergers and that their product offerings may not be settled yet either. Their install base is also shallow.	Their EC line of products is extremely broad, but not real deep: BuyerExpert for buy-side, SellerExpert for sell-side, BillerExpert and PublishExpert, etc., plus all the infrastructure to run it on; Netscape App Server (Kiva), portal service (NetCenter), Directory (LDAP) and security services, etc.	Good B2B focus through SellerExpert, but out-of-box functionality is shallow; many of our requirements would be custom. They also provide the best approach for training and implementation of their products, but using their products is a key component of using them.	Moving to Netscape Application Server platform with EJB compliance.		We stopped short of talking dollars.	Because they are so broad, they provide an excellent solution in terms of scaling and providing for our future needs. But the out-of-the-box features threw the group off.

TABLE 22-4. *ECommerce Solutions* (continued)

Vendor	Company Description	Offering Description	Product Analysis	Architecture	Integration	Price	RFP Analysis
Oracle	Although they bill themselves as the engine behind the Internet, they are really more of the database behind the Internet. Almost every vendor we talked to was Oracle compliant or had an Oracle version of their software. But the only vendor we talked to using Oracle Application Server was Digital River.	They came in with a best-of-breed approach: RTI for search engine, NetPreceptions for personalization, NetGravity for ad server, Oracle workflow for approval routing Kiva (Netscape) or WebObjects for app server, Vignette for front end.	If we thought we needed to be best of breed in every area, this may be an attractive solution, but since we are looking for robust out-of-the-box functionality, it's not very attractive, and in fact quite complicated.	Would need to create architectural framework on chosen app server platform. Way too much to write and maintain.		Products and services: $1.5M–2.25M.	We have no desire to manage seven different vendors for our EC solution, and they have never implemented this best of breed solution elsewhere.

TABLE 22-4. *ECommerce Solutions* (continued)

Vendor	Company Description	Offering Description	Product Analysis	Architecture	Integration	Price	RFP Analysis
Trilogy	Interesting company. Started in '89, 1,000 employees, average age of 26. Young up and coming company. They started out as an enterprise procurement vendor but have been in B2B EC for several years. Still, install base is moderate.	Their products are broad, including the entire procurement chain. Since they have always been an enterprise company, they see the big picture and really seem to get it.	The out-of-the-box of their B2B product is good. They have some of the features others are missing, like approval routing. But their install base is light. They have only one customer running on the application and architecture they proposed to us. But they are an attractive solution because of their by-side solution, positioning us to expand and have an integrated EC procurement solution.	100% Java. Runs on JWS. Load-balancing through third-party products from F5, Cisco, etc. Not sure what their failover story is. No search engine integration.	Real-time integration through EJB. No known batch load capabilities.	They were vague at the presentation: \$1M–\$10M.	The lack of install base was the deal-breaker on this one. We just couldn't see selling it to upper management.

TABLE 22-4. *ECommerce Solutions* (continued)

Vendor	Company Description	Offering Description	Product Analysis	Architecture	Integration	Price	RFP Analysis
Vignette	Company started in Dec '95, first release in Jan '97. Really didn't present a clear history message, so kind of vague. They seem to have a significant install base and some major customers.	Vignette StoryServer is an offering that provides the front-end component of what they call Internet Relationship Mgmt. but there is no back end for transaction processing. Their approach is that the back end should be your ERP system.	Although Vingette would be a strong contender for content management and personalization, we would have built it on top of our existing database. They want to hook directly into our database for transaction processing, but we need so much more, and because of our lack of integration with legacy systems we need a component of transaction.	C++. Template language uses TCL.	Unknown.	We stopped short of talking dollars.	Despite plenty of discussions with us leading up to the presentation, they were not prepared and some members of the presenting team had not even read the RFP. This, combined with comments at left, eliminated them as a solution.

TABLE 22-4. *ECommerce Solutions* (continued)

Comparison of BroadVision and InterWorld

The Table 22-5 contains an analysis of the BroadVision (BV) and InterWorld (IW) e-commerce solutions available on the market today. This table reflects the results of an independent study by the same company as above. This company limited their final analysis down to these two vendors. It's recommended that you perform your own study when selecting an e-commerce solution, but this table could be used as a guide for your research.

Area of Evaluation	BroadVision	InterWorld	Edge?	Notes
Scalability	4.5	4	BV	Although we did no internal testing, our scalability evaluation is based on DocuLabs and Home Depot. According to DocuLabs, the two are almost even, and both will potentially scale very well. Home Depot actually did the load testing and found that BroadVision "scaled elegantly."
Architecture	4	3.5	BV	No clear winner here. Both have competent architectural approaches and very strong individuals within their technical architecture organizations. If anything, BroadVision has a slight advantage because of many more Solaris installations. InterWorld was originally designed for NT.
Development environment and tools	3	4	IW	InterWorld has definitely invested more time and thought into their developers' toolkit. This includes tools for development and debugging. BroadVision is a strong product, but it is not simple to use and requires depth on the development team.
Ease of integration	3	3	—	No clear differentiator here. In testing, found that both worked well in doing external calls. Neither has anything special

TABLE 22-5. *BroadVision vs. InterWorld*

Area of Evaluation	BroadVision	InterWorld	Edge?	Notes
Customizing the application	4	3	—	Again, neither product clearly differentiated in this area, but the robustness of BroadVision gives it the edge because we'll probably have to customize less.
Company fundamentals	4.5	2.5	BV	There was a big difference here. BroadVision is publicly traded and has shown a profit for five consecutive quarters. InterWorld is losing money and has stated that they will continue to lose money for some time. They filed their S1 (to go public) last year, withdrew it, and resubmitted in late June. We are confident in InterWorld's management team and financial plan, but given the number of players in this market and the likely consolidation that will occur, BroadVision is a safer bet.
Out-of-box functionality	3.5	3	BV	InterWorld's next release is a tremendous improvement on their current offering and bridges the gap between the two. It is in Beta right now and the release is set for the fall of 1999, but is not yet scheduled.
Personalization	3.5	3	BV	BroadVision's personalization is much more mature.

TABLE 22-5. *BroadVision vs. InterWorld* (continued)

Area of Evaluation	BroadVision	InterWorld	Edge?	Notes
Future Direction	3	4	IW	We felt that InterWorld got the nod here. They spoke about their future and emphasized their need to concentrate on the sell-side solution and building partnerships into other areas (buy-side, personalization, etc.) BroadVision is going the opposite direction and is looking to build an enterprise solution, like Trilogy. Covering the whole enterprise is an attractive offering, but may affect their depth in any one area, like sell-side B2B (business to business).
Best Partner	3	4.5	IW	We definitely felt that we were extremely important to InterWorld, both in a general sense and in a very specific financial sense. We felt that we would get a high level of attention from InterWorld. BroadVision can most accurately be described as exploding. Their growth is awesome and they are having a tough time keeping up in terms of personalized attention and responsiveness in their level of support. Our reference calls confirmed this. If BroadVision is chosen, we must either get a strong integrator with deep BroadVision skills, or get a BroadVision person on our implementation team.

TABLE 22-5. *BroadVision vs. InterWorld* (continued)

Area of Evaluation	BroadVision	InterWorld	Edge?	Notes
Choice of Integrator	2	2	—	It's a wash. Based on the reference calls, we decided that regardless of which we go with, the vendor had to lead the implementation, not the third party.
References	4.5	2	BV	The Home Depot reference was the deal-maker for BroadVision. Their testing was exhaustive, and they were clear on their decision to go with BroadVision. InterWorld's reference was useless to helpful.
Internationalization	3.5	3	BV	Slight edge goes to BroadVision in this category. This is not a huge decision point, but is worth considering. BroadVision has had Baan implemented for some time now. This site is translated into five languages, and the language can be changed based on the user making that choice in the first screen. They have several other translated sites. InterWorld has done some work in this area, but not quite as much. In terms of tools, they are about equal, but BroadVision's expansion into Europe is faster than InterWorld's right now.
Total	45.5	41.5	BV	

TABLE 22-5. *BroadVision vs. InterWorld* (continued)

Summary

OIC is your virtual storefront. By plugging the Java cartridge into OWAS, a store can be up and running in a few months (or maybe less). In addition to being integrated with several Oracle products, OIC is integrated with several third-party products. OIC supports customization, so you can create a storefront that uniquely announces your store. Customizations run from simple HTML alterations to Java class creations that encapsulate your business rules and bind the store to existing business systems. Oracle Internet Commerce Server connects your business with the Internet world.

PART V

Miscellaneous

CHAPTER 23

Utilities to Help Web Development

Thousands of tools and utilities promise to help your Web development. As you have noticed throughout the rest of this book, including Chapter 6, Oracle has contributed their share to the list of utilities. This chapter will cover some non-Oracle tools to assist in your Web development. This chapter is a small sampling compared to the vast numbers available today. In this chapter, the following topics are covered:

- Looking closer at Graphics Tools
  - Reviewing Paint Shop Pro (PSP)
  - Using Animation Shop
  - Creating image maps with MapEdit
  - Making the most of the GIF Construction Set
- Considering development tools
  - Determining whether you need a Programmers File Editor (PFE)
  - Making the most of TOAD
  - Using SynEdit
  - NetObjects ScriptBuilder 3.0
  - Understanding the power behind Dreamweaver
  - Thinking about HomeSite
  - Making the most of SnadBoy Revelation
- Reviewing other tools
  - Understanding WS_FTP
  - Realizing the value of WinZip
  - Using Traceroute
  - Automating content creation
- Converting Access RDBMS to Oracle RDBMS
  - Migrating Access to Oracle Tables
  - Creating/modifying an ODBC connection

- Directory Toolkit
    - Comparison between directories
    - Comparison of files
    - Concatenation of files (combining files)
- Anawave WebSnake
    - Snaking 101
    - Creating a new project

Looking Closer at Graphics Tools

Graphics may be the single most important component of any Web site. Having the right tools to do the job is half the battle. At times, I need to edit and convert images, so I need a graphics tool to help me. The following sections outline some of these phenomenal tools.

Reviewing Paint Shop Pro (PSP)

Paint Shop Pro is an inexpensive shareware graphics program that enables you to create and/or manipulate graphic images of most any type. The primary benefit of Paint Shop Pro is that it has a small footprint compared to the other, more powerful, graphic editors.

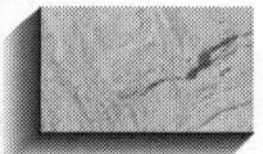

TIP
If you use CTRL-V to paste an image, it will create a new image. If you want to add the image to your existing image, go to the Edit menu, choose Paste, then select the "As New Selection" option.

Using the Paint Shop Pro Browser

To use the Paint Shop Pro (PSP) browser, run the pspbrwse.exe executable. You may wish to establish a Windows shortcut on your desktop that branches to the browser. Once started, you can pick the directory holding the images you wish to view. The images will be displayed in 2×2 inch squares. Once you have located the image you want to view or edit, double-click the image. The image will come up in PSP, ready for editing.

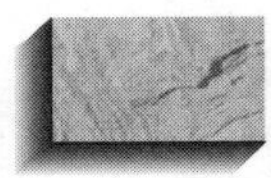

TIP

One of the least-known executables that comes with PSP is the pspbrwse.exe program enabling you to view your image directories. From the pspbrwse.exe program, you can easily go straight into the PSP program to do your image editing.

Filling Specific Shapes in an Image

To describe filling specific shapes in an image, we will use Figure 23-1 as a reference.

Say you want to cut out the fill color of the "S" in "TUSC". This would be hard to do if you were using the Eraser tool—the letter would be difficult and tedious to remove. Fortunately, PSP provides a tool for this job. Click the Magic Wand icon.

This tool will enable you to select any distinct part of the image. That is, it will select just the "S" because it is not part of the "U" or the "C". Once selected, you can perform another operation on the selected object. For example, if you press the DEL key, the object will be deleted, which will result in the image shown in Figure 23-2.

FIGURE 23-1. *Logo prior to editing*

FIGURE 23-2. *Logo after editing*

Converting Images in Bulk

Choose Batch Conversion from the File menu. When the Batch Conversion dialog box opens, select the images you want to convert from the correct directory (located under Look In). Under Output Settings, choose the desired graphic type. Finally, pick the output folder/directory where you want to send the converted files. When you are ready to convert the images, press the Start button.

Using Animation Shop

Jasc Software's Animation Shop is user friendly and replaces the need for the shareware GIF Construction Set. Animation Shop enables you to compose or edit animated GIF images (sometimes referred to as GIFa images). The tool enables you to see each frame in the animation sequence, set timing and add graphic transitions between frames, add text transitions—and, of course, you can view the animation. The Animation Wizard will prompt you through steps to assist in building an animation frame set and save the finished product. Animation Shop is bundled with Paint Shop Pro 5.0.

Creating a Transparent Image

When you have a finished product, to save the file for Web deployment, you must first convert the image to *indexed color* (for example, 256 colors). Indexed color means a color that is indexed somewhere between 0 and 255. To accomplish this task, go to the *Image* menu and select *Mode*, then select Indexed Color from the submenu. The Indexed Color dialog box will appear. Because the defaults for this dialog box are sufficient as is, click OK. To make the image transparent, go to the File menu and select Export, then select GIF98a Export. The GIF Export dialog box will appear. Use the Eyedropper tool to select the color(s) you want to appear as transparent. When finished, click OK.

Creating Image Maps with MapEdit

MapEdit is a shareware what-you-see-is-what-you-get (WYSIWYG) GUI image map editor. You can use MapEdit to create unique areas of an image that have distinct target URLs for each area. This is all accomplished by using your mouse. MapEdit will export an HTML map file for you to use within your HTML page.

Using MapEdit

Start the MapEdit application and open an image file. Once you have chosen an image to work on, the MapEdit window will appear as shown in Figure 23-3.

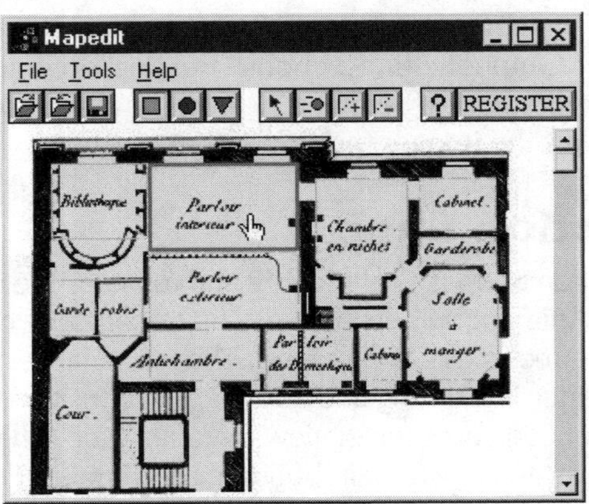

FIGURE 23-3. *MapEdit main window*

A number of iconic images or buttons exist within this page. These buttons enable you to select the type of mapping image you would like to draw. The description of these images is shown the following table.

Image	Description of use
	This button draws an outline in the shape of a rectangle.
	This button draws an outline in the shape of a circle.
	This button draws an outline in the shape of a polygon.

After selecting a shape (rectangle, circle, or polygon), outline the part of the image that you want to attach to a URL. After selecting and sizing a shape, a dialog box pops up prompting you for further information about your newly selected shape. In this box, enter the appropriate fields that you wish to include into your generated HTML. The fields include the following:

- **URL for clicks on this object** The destination URL that is called when the selected shape of the image is selected by the user.
- **Alternate text** Used when the user has graphics turned off on their browser, until the image downloads (for a slow loading HTML page).
- **Mouse-over** The text that pops up when the user's mouse pointer goes over the specific shape on the image.
- **Target** The destination frame for the URL being called. This is left blank unless you are using frames. If you do not have frames on your page, or if you reference a frame that does not exist, a new window will open.
- **OnMouseOver & onMouseOut** Contains JavaScript functions that will be called when the user's mouse pointer goes over (or out of) a specific image.

After you have mapped all of the objects within your image, save the image map. After saving the image map, include the image map and image definition in your HTML file. What was once a single image transforms into one image with many destination URLs.

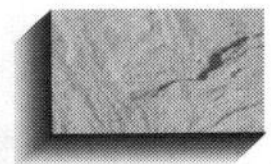

TIP
If you make a mistake and need to add points to your polygon, click the Polygon icon (shown earlier). If you need to take points away, click the Remove Points icon.

Making the Most of the GIF Construction Set

GIF Construction Set is shareware software used for creating animated GIF images for your Web pages—for example, creating a spinning globe or a ball that bounces. It will enable you to assemble GIF files containing image blocks, plaintext blocks, comment blocks, and control blocks. It includes facilities to manage palettes and merge multiple GIF files together. Even though the GIF Construction Set is not as friendly as Animation Studio, this shareware package will do the job.

Using GIF Construction Set

The Insert Object dialog box is illustrated next.

Insert Object
Image
Control
Comment
Plain Text
Loop
Cancel

New objects can be added to the animated image using this option. The HEADER parameter in the work area contains the animation image's action list. The HEADER parameter is used to set up the screen width, depth, background color, and global color palette.

Clicking Image in the Insert Object dialog box will bring up a dialog box enabling you to choose an image to be used in your animation. If you click Control, a dialog box will enable you to set control parameters for your animation, such as setting the entire image to be transparent, setting the animation to wait for user input, or setting the delay time of the animation. The HEADER for an image is shown in Figure 23-4.

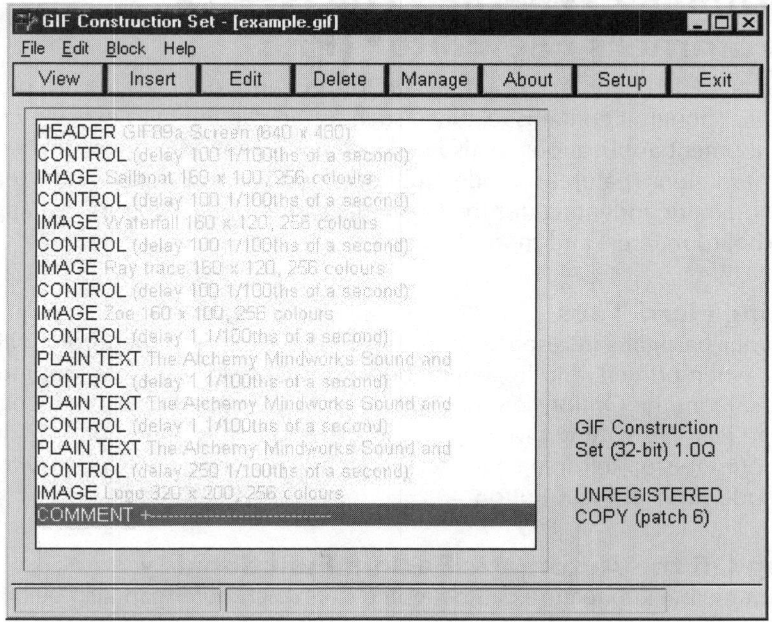

FIGURE 23-4. *GIF Construction Set HEADER*

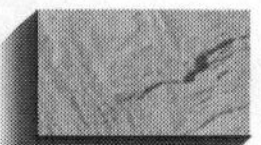

TIP
To make a spinning image quickly, go to the Edit menu and pick the Spin option. When the dialog box appears, press the Select button, then choose the image that you wish to make spin. Press OK, then press View to see your image in action.

Considering Development Tools

When it comes to developing Web applications, your team will need good development tools. Even though the following lists a few of my favorite tools, you are entitled to your own favorites.

Determining Whether You Need a Programmers File Editor (PFE)

Programmer's File Editor is a 32-bit text editor primarily oriented toward program developers. Though it contains features, such as the capability to execute compilers and development applications, it also makes a good general-purpose text editor for any other function. Features include multilevel undo, active buttons on a tear-off toolbar, automatic indenting (for the C language), UNIX file support, remappable keys, keyboard macros, and more.

Replacing Hard Tabs

Turning your hard tabs into spaces makes your code easier to read from within the database, when printed, and in general because spaces take up less room than tab characters. From the Options menu choose Current Modes. From the dialog box, choose the Text Formatting Mode type. Click the Soft Tabs radio button. You can also set your tab stop to three characters, which is my preference for easy to read PL/SQL code. Click the OK button.

Turning Off the Automatic Backup Functionality

The automatic backup feature can be a nice safety net, but it can also be annoying to have a number of files with an extension of bak hanging around on your hard drive. From the Options menu, choose Current Modes. From the dialog box, choose the Saving Mode type. Select the "Make backup of original file" checkbox. You can also set this off when you save a document, but setting it as described will turn this option off globally. The checkbox when saving individual files is located in the lower left-hand corner of the Save dialog box.

Using the Automatic Backup and Sending the Files to a Different Directory

If you like the safety of the automatic backups but dislike the files cluttering up your source directory, this setup is the best of both worlds. To validate that you are backing up the original file, go to the Options menu and choose Current Modes. In the dialog box, choose the Saving Mode type. Make sure the "Make backup of original file" checkbox is checked. Then, go to the Options menu and choose Preferences. Select the category entitled Backup. Click the Into Subdirectory radio button. In the text box, specify the directory to back up the file. Press the OK button.

Setting the Different Parameters Permanently

The changes in both of the preceding examples will set your parameter changes for the current session only. If you want to set the parameters permanently, then go to the Options menu and choose Default Modes. In the dialog box, click the "Files whose name is not in any mode group" checkbox and click the Edit Modes button that is in the lower left-hand corner of the dialog box. The following Mode Types are displayed:

- **Display** Checkbox to show line numbers
- **File Properties** File is read-only parameter
- **Input** Input parameters when typing new lines
- **Language Awareness** Checkbox to show line numbers
- **Loading** File opening parameters based on what type of file you are editing
- **Print Defaults** What default values should be used when printing
- **Saving** Saving parameters based on what type of file you are editing
- **Text Colors** What colors should be used by default when displaying the file
- **Text Formatting** Text formatting relating to tabs, tab stop, and text wrapping

After setting the Mode Types, parameters will be permanent.

Using Macros

Macros are text inputs or key commands strung together to perform a certain task. For example, in the following code snippet, you can see a file that has 15 lines of code. If you wanted to strip off the first seven characters and the last three characters, which would convert this script from a PL/SQL script to an HTML script, this could be accomplished with a macro, as the following example illustrates:

```
htp.print('<HTML>');
htp.print('<HEAD>');
htp.print('<TITLE>PFE macro example </TITLE>');
htp.print('</HEAD>');
htp.print('<BODY>');
htp.print('<H1>Macros</H1>');
htp.print('<TABLE>');
htp.print('<TR>');
htp.print('<TD>');
htp.print('What are macros? ');
htp.print('</TD>');
htp.print('</TR>');
htp.print('</TABLE>');
htp.print('</BODY>');
htp.print('</HTML>');
```

Even though it may seem easier to edit this file without a macro, imagine if 2,000 lines of code needed editing—a macro will suddenly look more attractive. A macro is easy to build by performing the following steps:

1. Click the macro recorder, shown below. This will start recording your events.
2. Highlight the first seven spaces of the first line by holding the SHIFT key down and pressing the RIGHT ARROW key seven times.
3. Then, press the BACKSPACE key.
4. To delete the last three characters, press the END key, which will move the cursor to the end of the line and backspace three spaces.
5. Next, press the DOWN ARROW key and then the HOME key, which will take you to the beginning of the next line.

This is exactly what we want to occur for every single line in the file, so our macro is complete. Once your macro is finished, click the Macro Stop icon, which will stop the macro recording. Now you are ready to use your macro. You can choose Play Recording from the Macro menu, or you can press the F7 key.

Mapping a Keystroke to an Action

In the following example, we will make CTRL-U cause the selected text to be uppercase. Verify that the key sequence you want to use is not already mapped by pressing it to make sure that no action occurs. From the Options menu, choose Key Mapping. Click the CTRL + checkbox and select the letter you want to map with the CTRL key. In the following example, we will use the character "U". Below the drop-down box, you will see a number of options. If the key mapping is not used, the option will read, "Currently mapped to (nothing)". If the option does not appear in this manner, you must choose another combination of keys or choose to overwrite the existing definition. Once you have a valid key combination, choose the function to map from the Functions drop-down list. For this example, we chose EditTextUppercaseSelection. If the function is already mapped, the "Currently mapped from" box will be filled in with the current key combination. Upon completion, click Add, Save, then Close.

TIP
The Numbering icon will turn line numbers on and off.

Making the Most of TOAD

TOAD is a Windows 95/NT tool for Oracle Application developers—hence, the name TOAD. TOAD assists in developing queries, performing Explain Plans, browsing and editing database objects, editing table data, and editing and debugging PL/SQL. TOAD also has script-driven configurable syntax highlighting, direct OCI access to Oracle, optimizing statistics, sharing pool recall, AutoTrace, and reports. A powerful function of TOAD is the capability to color-code and automatically uppercase specific input. No matter who's PL/SQL coding standards you choose, the editor is a must.

Automatically Uppercasing Specific Input

You can download the PL/SQL reserved keywords file from the download section on the TUSC Web site (www.tusc.com). The document file name is PL/SQL_reserved.txt. Perform the following steps to automatically capitalize PL/SQL reserved words:

1. Make sure TOAD is not currently running. After downloading the file, make a backup copy of the toadsub.txt file located in the temps directory under TOAD's home directory.
2. Copy the PL/SQL_reserved.txt file to be the new toadsub.txt file. The toadsub.txt file contains all the PL/SQL reserved words.
3. Start TOAD and when you edit a package, procedure, function, or trigger, the words in the toadsub.txt file will automatically be capitalized for you.

The file will also transform text inputted as (tm) into the trademark character (™), text inputted as (r) into the registered character ®, plus many others. You can also add more words to this file through TOAD, as described later in this chapter.

TIP
The words are only capitalized when you type them. Case conversion will not happen if you cut and paste words from another application.

Changing the PL/SQL Editor Options

As illustrated in Figure 23-5, from Editor Properties located on the Edit menu, the Options tab is the first tab in the Editor Options dialog box.

FIGURE 23-5. *TOAD Editor Options window, Options tab*

TIP
You can navigate through your open windows in TOAD by pressing the CTRL *and* TAB *keys in unison.*

The Editor Option window is used for the general format of the text while editing or inputting new information. The checked boxes and settings in the text boxes in Figure 23-5 are the options that I have found to be the best for me. Experiment with what works best for you. Notice the "Tab stop" property is set to 3, which is what I prefer for my PL/SQL code. As discussed in the preceding PFE section, this is space indentation.

As illustrated in Figure 23-6, the next Editor Options tab—Highlighting—is used for the color-coding of your inputted text.

From the Highlighting tab, you can set your text to be bold, italic, and underlined. You can also change the foreground and background color, font style, and font size. Just select the element that you want to have changed, then set the

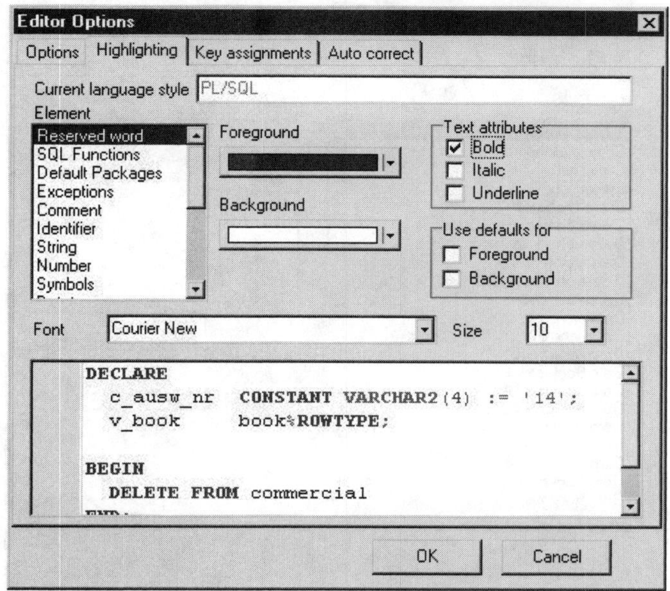

FIGURE 23-6. *TOAD Editor Options window, Highlighting tab*

attributes to add your desired settings. Be sure to observe the text's appearance once the attributes have been enforced.

As illustrated in Figure 23-7, the Key Assignments tab is used to assign keys to actions, identical to PFE.

As illustrated in Figure 23-8, the Auto Correct tab is meant to replace commonly typed words and phrases with the associated text.

To capitalize words or establish other autocorrect rules, type what you want replaced, along with what should replace it. For example, to add a comment, type the characters **xxx**, which would automatically replace xxx with the phrase "-- This code was created by TUSC."

TIP
Code templates are a convenient method to ensure coding standards, especially when coding an exception block.

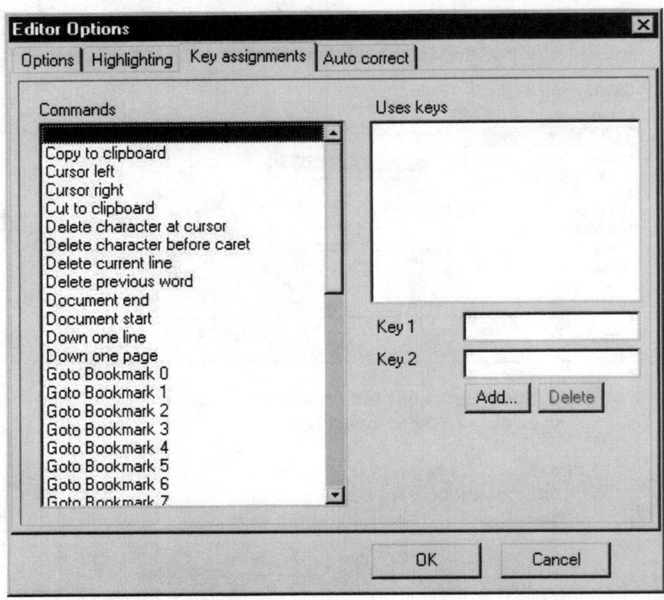

FIGURE 23-7. *TOAD Editor Options window, Key Assignments tab*

The final tab in the Editor Options window is used for code templates. Code templates expand upon the autoreplace substitution concept, but a manual keystroke (CTRL-SPACE) is required to perform the substitution. Code templates are more than a single phrase and can contain line feeds. If a vertical pipe character is in the code template, the cursor will be placed at that point in the template. Code templates are loaded from the text file toad.dci in the temps directory.

TIP

A number of great GUI PL/SQL editors are available on the market. TOAD offers a free version. However, before you purchase a tool, take the time to review the tools available and choose the tool that best fits your business requirements. It's all a matter of personal preference.

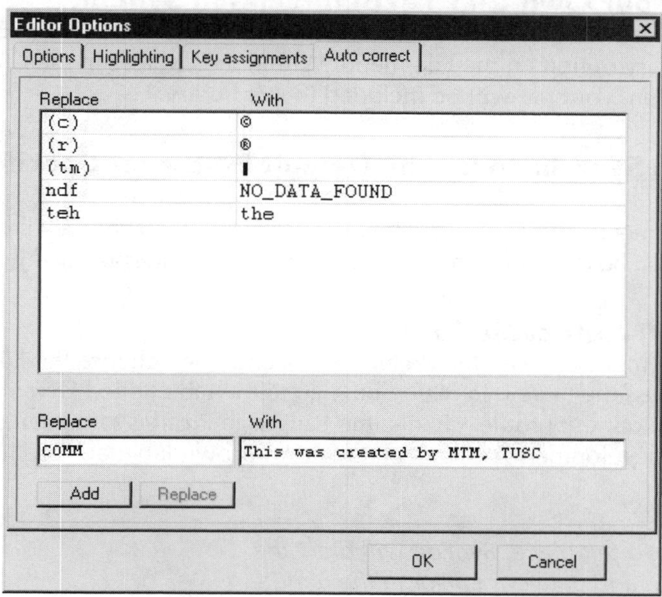

FIGURE 23-8. *TOAD Editor Options window, Auto Correct tab*

Using SynEdit

SynEdit is a 32-bit freeware text editor for Windows. It provides drag-and-drop editing, opens files of nearly unlimited size, and enables you to open over 255 files simultaneously in a tabbed workspace. Other features include a Clip Text window for commonly used keywords and phrases, autocorrect functionality, and a convenient file browser for quick navigation through the directory tree. SynEdit contains "double-click and drop" functionality for keywords in the following languages: Ada, ASM, BATCH, C/C++, Clipper 5, COBOL, Common Special Characters, DataFlex, Eiffel, HTML, Java, Limbo, LISP, Modula 2, Object Pascal, Paradox Objects, QBASIC, REXX, SQL, VDHL, Visual Basic Functions, Methods and Statements, and Perl 5.

Creating Your Own Clip Text Libraries in SynEdit

Open the file you want to convert into a Clip Text library. Choose the Export as Clip Text Library option on the File menu. Within the choices in the Clip Text Libraries section, your file will be included in this library.

Setting Up SynEdit to Be the Default Editor for Specific File Extensions

Go to the File menu, and choose the Preferences menu, then choose File Associations. Once the dialog box appears, check the file types you want associated with SynEdit.

Turning Off Autocapitalization

Go to the File menu, choose the Preferences menu, then choose the Editor Setup, or you can press the F4 key. In dialog box, go to the tab entitled Default Profiles. To change the current profile, change the Language Profiles to the language you are using for development, or you can create your own language profile.

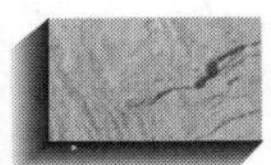

TIP
If you type a left brace, SynEdit will draw the right brace and put your cursor in the middle.

NetObjects ScriptBuilder 3.0

ScriptBuilder (formerly Acadia Infuse) is a fast and effective means to develop client and server-side code. It enhances productivity and reduces errors during development. It has built-in references for the following languages: Cold Fusion, ECMASript, HTML, Java 1.0, Java 1.1, JavaSoft Java, Lotus Script, Microsoft Active Server Pages (ASP), Microsoft Channel Definition Format, Microsoft DOM 1.0, Microsoft JScript 3.0, Microsoft VBScript, Netscape JavaScript 1.1, Netscape JavaScript 1.2, Netscape Server-Side JavaScript, and Perl 5.0. It also contains drag-and-drop functionality for all syntax and keywords. It also comes with over ten useful examples of ASP, JavaScript, LiveWire, Lotus, Perl, and VBScript—plus a full GUI HTML editor for under $150.00!

Previewing Your HTML

To preview your HTML, open your HTML document and click the Preview icon. This will preview the HTML as if it were in a browser window.

Using AutoCorrect

Identical to SynEdit and TOAD, ScriptBuilder supports an autocorrect feature. In ScriptBuilder, choose AutoScripting from the Tools menu. A dialog box will appear consisting of keywords and their associated replacement text. NetObject's AutoScripting feature is similar to TOAD's code templates in that they both support multiple lines of autoreplace text. For example, say you are developing in PL/SQL. Replace the characters "crloop" with the following text—the keyword crloop stands for Cursor Loop.

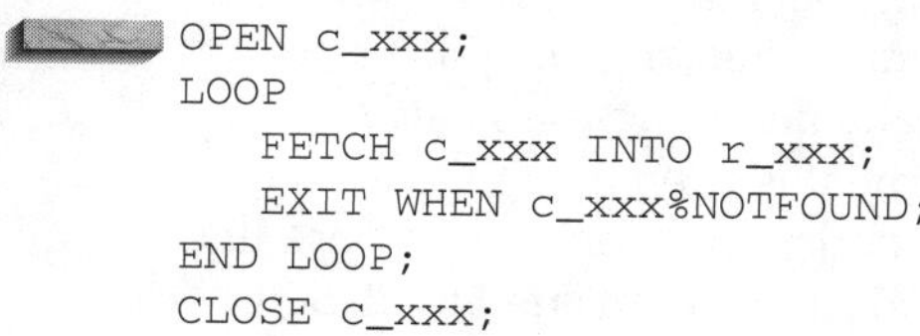

```
OPEN c_xxx;
LOOP
   FETCH c_xxx INTO r_xxx;
   EXIT WHEN c_xxx%NOTFOUND;
END LOOP;
CLOSE c_xxx;
```

To create your own AutoScripting keywords, as in the preceding example, click the Add button and a dialog box will appear. In the Keyword field, type your keyword—for example, **crloop**. In the Text to Insert box, type the code to be automatically scripted.

Using Smart File Searching

From the Edit menu, choose the Find in Files option and a dialog box will appear. Choose the appropriate search options and type the files you are looking for into the "Find what" text box. In the "File types" text box, input the files to be searched. In the "In folder" text box, pick the directory to be searched. Pick the options you want to use and then click the Find button. When the filenames display in the Results view, you can double-click any file to automatically open the file, which is then ready for editing.

TIP
You can merge a file from a directory into another open file. Choose the Insert option on the File menu. It will insert the file into the location of the cursor.

Understanding the Power Behind Dreamweaver

Dreamweaver is a visual Web page layout tool and an HTML and Dynamic HTML text editor wrapped into one package. Features include roundtrips between graphical editing mode and your favorite source editor, absolute positioning, cascading style sheets, a Dynamic HTML animation timeline, a JavaScript behavior library, visual table and frame design, a client-side image map editor, and a repeating element library. Dreamweaver includes a global search-and-replace function and the capability to view and test the site as you design.

Combining the Power of Dreamweaver and WebAlchemy

Dreamweaver generates static HTML files. The OAS PL/SQL cartridge pulls data from your database to create HTML pages dynamically. The skill set required to develop HTML code using Dreamweaver is low compared to the skill set required to write PL/SQL code. Learning to develop static HTML pages with Dreamweaver is similar to learning a word processing package—it's a GUI interface that outputs HTML, whereas learning PL/SQL is identical to learning any other programming language. Because Dreamweaver is easy to learn, with little training, visually designing Web pages and turning them over to an administrator for development is often much easier. WebAlchemy converts static HTML code into PL/SQL code. Therefore, a page visually designed and created in Dreamweaver (as a static page) can be converted to PL/SQL using WebAlchemy. From there, a programmer can add the SQL statements (for example, cursors) and record extraction (for example, cursor for loops) to dynamically pull data from the database. See Chapter 14 for an example.

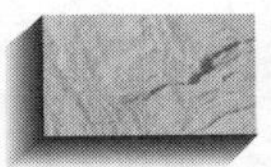

TIP

By adding input parameters to PL/SQL code, the procedure can build an HTML page with customized output.

Changing the Case of Your HTML

If you want to develop HTML in uppercase, change your preferences. To accomplish this task, choose Preferences on the Edit menu, or press CTRL-U, then choose the Source Format category. Lastly, choose either Case for Tags or Case for Attributes to specify how your HTML page is displayed.

Changing Browser Preferences

To change browser preferences, choose Preferences on the Edit menu, then choose the Preview in Browser category and click the Add button. In the dialog box, input a name for your browser in the Name text box, then type in the path where the browser is located. If you do not know the exact location, click the Browse button and find the directory on your file system. Finally, click the checkbox indicating which browser you wish to use as the default choice when previewing your work.

Changing the Color of Your HTML Output

To change the color of your HTML output, choose Preferences on the Edit menu, select the HTML Tag Colors category, then choose the Tag Specific colors that your HTML will display.

Checking Spelling in HTML

To check the spelling in your HTML document, choose Check Spelling on the Text menu, or press SHIFT-F7. A dialog box will display with the misspellings in your HTML.

Checking JavaScript Events for Browser Compliance

To check JavaScript events for browser compliance, choose Behaviors in the Window menu or press F8. Click an HTML attribute that supports JavaScript events, such as an HTML form input field. In the Behaviors dialog box, check different browser versions for JavaScript syntax availability. Choose the browser version you are planning to support with your application. Click the Events icon and make sure your JavaScript event is listed.

TIP
If you want to edit the HTML manually, click the HTML icon; or, press F10 at any time. Whether you edit the HTML directly or edit the page through the GUI, they update each other.

Thinking About HomeSite

HomeSite is an HTML design tool for professional Web developers. HomeSite is less feature-intensive and less expensive than Dreamweaver, but it is a functional, feature-rich tool. Features in HomeSite 4.0 include high-end language support (JavaScript, ASP, Perl, and DHTML); a style editor to create and edit cascading style sheets; a JavaScript wizard; a Tag Inspector to display properties in a single sheet; a Tag Tree for easy visualization of a page's tag structure and user interface features, such as FTP, link verification, spell check, and color-coding; an Expression Builder; color-coding for Java server pages; new HTML and VTML tag editors; and Dreamweaver integration.

Understanding why HomeSite is a Perfect Choice if You Are New to Web Development

Many of the features included in HomeSite were designed for the beginner. The examples include the following:

- HTML tag validation. If you type a tag that is not supported or understood, a message will be displayed.
- HTML tag completion. If you type **<td>**, it will input <td>< /td> with your cursor in the middle.

- You can browse and test your completed HTML. Just click the Browse tab.
- You can work in a design mode that has a GUI interface.

Using HomeSite's Special Character Reference

If you click the Special Character icon, HomeSite will open a reference section at the bottom of the page. From the reference section, you can double-click any character and the appropriate text will be transferred to your HTML. For example, if you double-click the ampersand symbol, HomeSite will place & on your page.

Using Style Sheets Supported in HomeSite

HomeSite is not just for the beginner. HomeSite includes a complete style sheet (SS) editor that is easy to customize. Click the Design Style Sheets icon, and a dialog box will appear, enabling you to create and edit style sheets. HomeSite will begin with a few HTML tags to help you create your own style sheets. If you want to create a new SS, click the Add Style Sheet icon. A dialog box for you to associate an HTML tag, or to create a user-named SS, will appear. Once you have picked the name you wish to use for this style sheet, choose the options you want to apply. For example, pick the font size, text alignment, and background color.

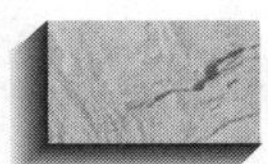

TIP

Right-click the mouse and choose the Insert Tag menu option to insert any supported HTML tags and many other attributes.

Making the Most with SnadBoy Revelation

SnadBoy is the ultimate tool if you have forgotten a password. Maybe, like me, you work with as many as five or ten clients at one time. How are you supposed to remember all those passwords? Should you write them down? Not really, because that breaks the security rules. In a Windows environment, most of us take the easy route and check the Save Password box. But what if someone needs to know what that password is? SnadBoy can help you with your password dilemmas.

Using SnadBoy

As shown in the following illustration, after starting the SnadBoy application, you can left-click and drag the Password Field Selector crosshairs onto the password field that you are trying to resolve. The password will be displayed in the Password field on the SnadBoy dialog box. If you highlight the password in this textbox, you can right-click and pick the Copy menu choice to copy it to your application. Pretty cool, huh!

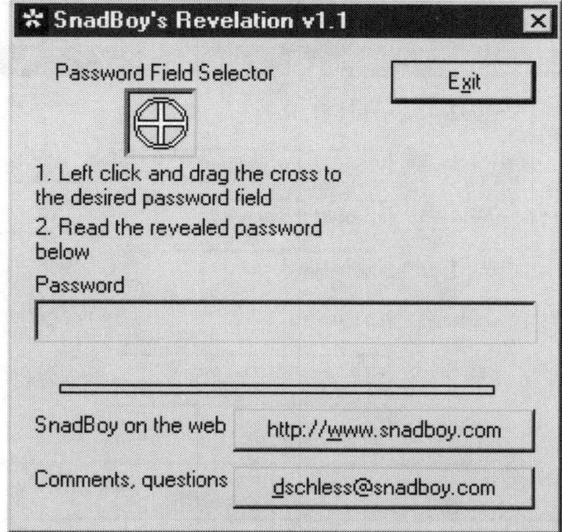

Reviewing Other Tools

Beyond graphics and development tools, you are sure to find other tools that you need to get your job done. This section will discuss those tools.

Understanding WS_FTP

WS_FTP is a standard FTP client for Winsock, but you must download the graphical version of WS_FTP for the full functionality discussed in the following subsections. The graphical interface was designed with the novice FTP user in mind, but advanced features exist for power users. It's easy to set up profiles so you can easily toggle between commonly visited FTP sites.

Using WS_FTP

To use WS_FTP, you must first set the session properties. As illustrated in Figure 23-11, you will want to set the properties as shown in Table 23-1.

After you have entered the information, click the OK button, which will log you in and connect you to the root directory of the specified host.

Starting Automatically in a Different Directory

Once you have drilled into the desired directory, you can set that directory as the default directory that will always appear upon logging in to the current host. At the bottom of the screen, a group of buttons will appear. Click the Options button, which will bring you to the Properties dialog box. Click the Save Current Directories

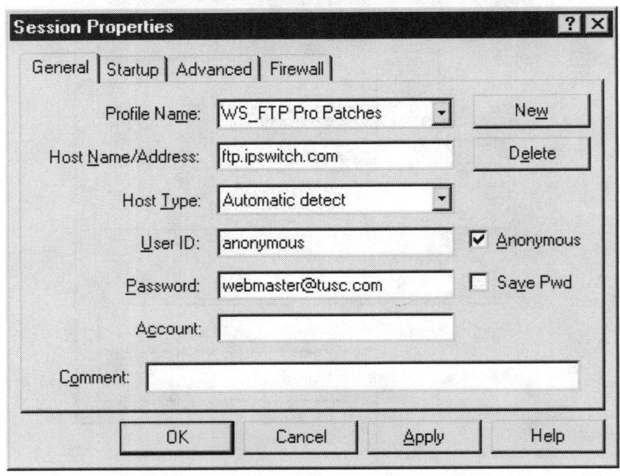

FIGURE 23-9. *WS_FTP session properties*

Property	**Set to**
Profile Name	Word or phrase describing the connection.
Host Name/Address	Either a fully qualified Internet host name or an IP address.
Host Type	If you know the host type, select it from the drop-down list. If not, choose the "Automatic detect" choice.
User ID	Enter the user ID for this configuration.
Password	Enter the password for the user ID entered.
Account	Enter the account for the user ID entered, if the remote host requires an account.
Comment	Enter any comments you want to include with this session profile.

TABLE 23-1. *WS_FTP Session Properties*

as Connection Directories button. This will save the directory you are currently in as the default for future startups.

TIP
You can sort files by name, date, or size. Just click the header on the column you want to order by. Click it once for ascending and click it again for descending order.

Realizing the Value of WinZip

Nico Mak Computing's WinZip software is a user-friendly zipping (file compression) and unzipping (file decompression) utility that includes built-in support for popular Internet file formats, such as TAR, ZIP, UUencode, XXencode, BinHex, MIME, and UNIX-compressed files. ARJ, LZH, and ARC files are supported through external programs. An optional wizard simplifies unzipping and installing software in ZIP files.

Using Drag and Drop from the Main WinZip Window

To extract a file from the main WinZip window, drag a file (or set of files) to a directory listed in any open Windows Explorer window. To view a file from the main WinZip window, drag a file (or set of files) to the appropriate application window or to a shortcut to the application. For example, you can open a text file for viewing in PFE. To print a file from the main WinZip window, drag a file to a Printer icon or a printer shortcut.

Using WinZip Functionality from the Windows Explorer

From Windows Explorer, you can extract all the files in a zip file by clicking on the right mouse button, then choose "Extract to" from the context menu. You can unzip the contents directly to a folder by dragging the zip file to a directory, but be sure to use the right mouse button while dragging.

To add files to a zip file without leaving the Windows Explorer, just select one or more files in Windows Explorer and drag and drop them on an existing zip file in the active Windows Explorer window, in another Windows Explorer window, or to a zip file on the desktop. To create new zip files in Windows Explorer, click the right mouse button, then select New->WinZip File from Windows Explorer.

Another way to add files to a zip file directly from Windows Explorer is to right-click any file (or selected group of files) in the Windows Explorer and choose Add to Zip from the context menu. For example, if you right-click on a document named dev.doc, Windows Explorer will display an option "Add to dev.zip". Click on this option and your file will be zipped automatically.

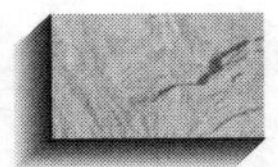

TIP
You can order the toolbar buttons as desired. Just right-click the mouse and choose Select Buttons. Once the dialog box appears, you can customize the buttons.

Using Traceroute

Traceroute is a program that performs the tasks as the name implies—it traces the route of a TCP/IP connection from the specified host to another machine's IP address. On UNIX, the command is fully spelled out (for example, traceroute), whereas on Windows platforms, the command is abbreviated as tracert. You can trace the route using a specific IP address or the machine's domain name. Traceroute will work its way through the network to find the remote host and will report the time it took to hit each hop (aka leg) of the route. Each hop is hit three times and the time is reported for each hit. Tracing the route and each of the hops can help you to debug whether network performance issues are a factor at all, at a specific hop, or throughout your connection. In the following example, we are tracing the route to a specific IP address. The first hop to 207.225.97.65 is the hop from the host the command was typed on through our intranet (or LAN) to our Denver office Internet router. The next hop is from our Internet router to our ISP's local (Denver, CO) router. The next hop is from our ISP's Denver router to the Chicago, Illinois router, then to the ISP's router in Downers Grove, Illinois, then to our router in our Lombard (near Downers Grove) office's Internet router, and finally to the host (for example, 209.108.212.207). In the following example, the connection from the ISP in Downers Grove to our Lombard office's Internet router and then to the final machine took roughly 110ms (milliseconds) each. This may indicate a problem in the two locations.

```
tracert 209.108.212.207

Tracing route to tuscil_ws1 [209.108.212.207] over a maximum of 30 hops:
  1   <10 ms   <10 ms   <10 ms  207.225.97.65
  2    40 ms    81 ms   120 ms  den-co-gw1.netcom.net [163.179.16.1]
  3    80 ms    80 ms    80 ms  h9-0-chw-il-gw1.netcom.net [163.179.232.146]
  4    80 ms    80 ms    90 ms  h2-0-dgr-il-gw1.netcom.net [165.236.192.254]
  5   100 ms   110 ms   101 ms  209.108.212.129
  6   111 ms   110 ms   110 ms  tuscil_ws1 [209.108.212.207]

Trace complete.
```

After your network administration team reconfigures your routers, use traceroute to verify the configuration. For example, we had purchased a fast (T1) leased line connecting us directly to a client. After reconfiguring the routers, the speed did not appear to be notably faster. By running traceroute, we were able to quickly determine that the connection was going through the Internet, not through the direct leased line connection. After taking this information back to the router configuration experts, they were able to reconfigure the routers correctly, which fixed the problem and resulted in great performance. Another example of how we resolved an issue using traceroute was when we determined that performance of a client's Web site was poor because of the number of hops their ISP had in their network. We were able to provide this information back to the ISP, which they quickly resolved.

Automating Content Creation

In a Web site, a considerable amount of information can be extracted automatically just by traversing through the site. For example, what's new on the site can be determined by looking at the file modification dates, a search engine can be built by reading the words on every page, and a site map can be generated from the links on each page. Develop your own auto content creation tool by dynamically reading through the site (for example, using UTL_HTTP, as discussed in Chapter 9), but why? Tools are available to effectively perform this task. Technet Software's Wisebot is a tool that reads through your site and creates content automatically. A distinct advantage of using Wisebot is that it will save this information into tables in an Oracle database. The benefit of having the data stored in an Oracle database is that you can write your own routines to extract and use this information however desired.

Wisebot is a Web development tool that scans your Web site(s) to automatically create a site map, an index, a What's New page, and a push channel. The benefits of having these features automatically generated for you are that they will make your site easier to navigate, the information helps visitors locate information on your site, and it keeps visitors informed about updates to your site. The keyword index generated by Wisebot automatically extracts the keywords from your site's pages and publishes them in an interactive index or to your Oracle database tables. Your visitors can use the index to locate the pages relevant to the information they are seeking. The Explorer-like style site map publishes an interactive map for your site that will automatically update itself when your site changes. Wisebot creates and publishes the content for a CDF-compliant channel receiver, such as Internet Explorer or PointCast Network. The channel content is automatically created and always remains current. Wisebot will publish a What's New page that always remains current. As updates are applied to your side, the headlines on the page change automatically.

By storing this information in the Oracle database, you can make use of the information as desired. You can build and display your own site map, enabling queries against the keyword index, or display a What's New This Hour page—the control is completely in your hands.

Converting Access RDBMS to Oracle RDBMS

If your application was developed using the Access database, you may wish to convert the application to an Oracle database application. To help you with this process, you can use the Oracle Migration Assistant provided by Oracle. This utility can be found on the Technet site (technet.oracle.com) or on TUSC's site (www.tusc.com).

To convert your application, perform the following steps:

1. Start the Oracle Migration Assistant for MS Access application.
2. The first screen is the Welcome screen. If you do not want to see this screen again, click the checkbox. To proceed to the next screen, click the Begin button.
3. On the Select Database screen, click the Add Database button and the Add Database dialog box will appear.
4. Locate the Microsoft Access database file that you would like to convert. The file type that you want to convert will be an .mdb file. You can select multiple databases to convert. If you would like to remove one, click it in the grid, and click the Remove Database button. After you are satisfied with your database selection(s), click the Next button.
5. The next screen enables you to customize the datatype conversion. In most cases, you can accept the defaults, but if you want to change the way a datatype is converted, click the Customize button. When you are ready to continue to the Scan Databases screen, click Next button. The databases you selected will be scanned for table and relationship information.
6. The following screen is the location to customize your database object names. You can change table, column, or index names, username, and tablespace name. Once you are finished customizing your objects, click the Next button.
7. On the Generate Schema Instructions screen, your new database schema will be generated. If you need to make changes to your database objects,

click the Back button. Otherwise, click the Next button to begin the generation.

8. On the Customize Migration Options screen, you can choose not to migrate certain objects of the Access database: indexes, relationships, default values, and validation rules. All the checkboxes are checked by default. Once you have chosen your migration settings, click the Next button.
9. The next screen is for Migration Type selection. Two choices exist on this screen: only migrate the database structure, or migrate both the database structure and the data. Or, you also can choose to modify the Access database to use the Oracle tables instead of the Access tables. If you have checked the Modify Microsoft Access database(s) checkbox, refer to the Migrate Access to Oracle Tables section. If you have not checked the Modify Microsoft Access database(s) checkbox, refer to the Proceed with Oracle Migration section.

Migrate Access to Oracle Tables

If you have checked the Modify Microsoft Access database(s) checkbox, you will need to enter the ODBC driver information. The ODBC administration page is the location to enter the database connection information. Enter the ODBC data source name and the administrative user's username and password, then click the Next button.

If the error shown next occurs, the ODBC is configured properly but the combination of the ODBC connection source and the username/password combination is incorrect.

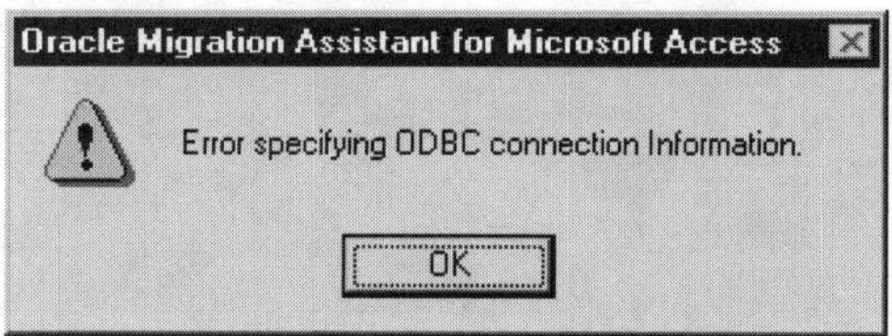

Check with your database administrator to ensure the username and password you are using are valid and/or correct. If the username/password combination is correct, you may have to create a new ODBC connection to the schema you are attempting to use. If this is the case, refer to the following instructions to create/modify an ODBC connection.

Create/Modify an ODBC Connection

To create or modify an ODBC connection, perform the following steps:

1. Start the Microsoft ODBC Administrator application.
2. To modify an existing ODBC connection, click the data source you wish to modify and click the Configure button. The dialog box shown in Figure 23-10 will appear.
3. Make sure the SQL*Net Connect String entry matches your entry in your tnsnames.ora file located in the C:\ORAWIN95\NET80\ADMIN directory. If a User ID entry is present, validate that it is correct. The Data Source Name box represents the name of the ODBC connection you are modifying. The Description box is for a short clause describing the data source name. After you are satisfied with the input, click the OK button.
4. To add an ODBC connection, click the Add button. The dialog box will appear, as illustrated in Figure 23-11.

   The preceding dialog box enables you to pick the appropriate driver for the Oracle database that you are connecting to.
5. Choose the driver you want to use and click the Finish button. The dialog box will appear, as illustrated in Figure 23-12.

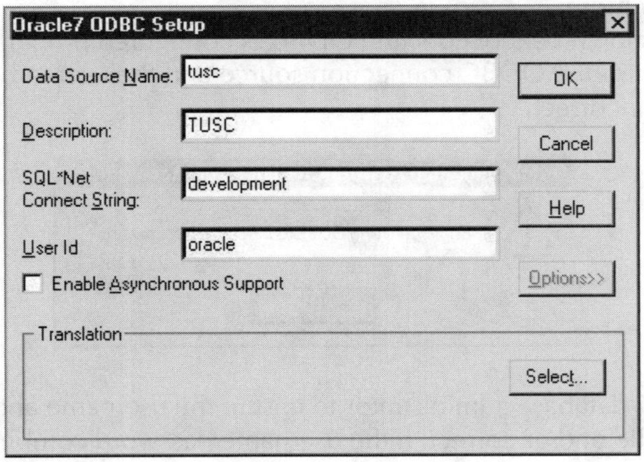

Oracle7 ODBC Setup
Data Source Name: tusc
Description: TUSC
SQL*Net Connect String: development
User Id oracle
Enable Asynchronous Support
Translation
OK
Cancel
Help
Options>>
Select...

FIGURE 23-10. *Adding a new connection*

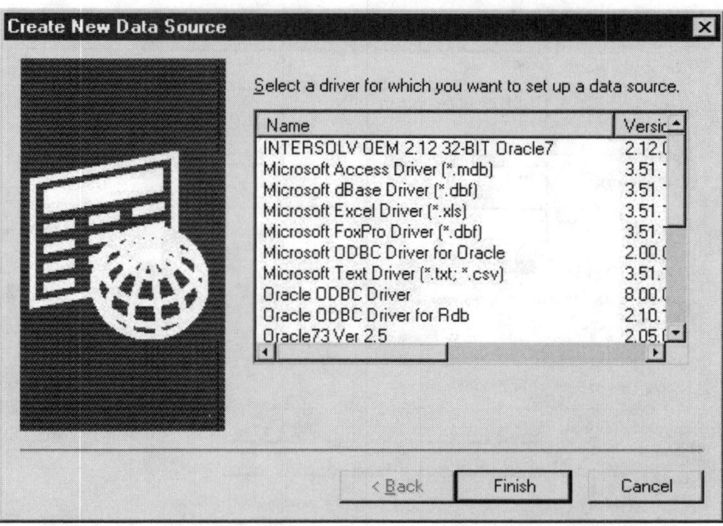

FIGURE 23-11. *Selecting a driver*

6. At a minimum, you need to enter the data source name, the service name, and the user ID. In the Data Source Name text box, input the name of your new ODBC connection. In the Description field, enter a short sentence describing the data source. For the Service Name input box, enter in the connect string from your tnsnames.ora file of the database schema you wish to connect to (for example, ORCL). Finally, enter the appropriate user ID of the database in the UserID box. Once this is completed, click the OK button. Now you are ready to use your ODBC connection, so click the OK button within the ODBC administrator. To test the connection, start the 32-bit ODBC TEST utility, which comes with Oracle's ODBC driver. In the top text area, type **SELECT sysdate FROM dual**. Depending on the creation of the data source, you may be required to input a username and/or password. If you are ready to test, click the Execute button.

7. If the driver is working properly and all the information was entered correctly, you should see the query results in the box below where you entered the query. If the test worked successfully, go to the Proceed with Oracle Migration section.

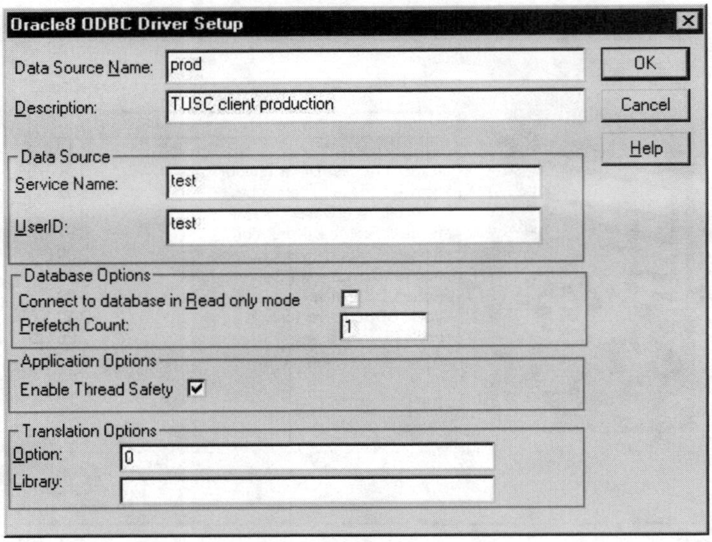

FIGURE 23-12. *Configuring the driver*

Proceed with Oracle Migration

To proceed with the Oracle migration, perform the following steps:

1. The next screen will migrate the Access database to Oracle. Click the Next button and watch the migration progress.
2. Once the migration has completed, you will be able to verify that it went smoothly. On this screen, you can view the migration status and migration reports. If you click the Summary button, it will show you a summary report that gives you the status of the migration. The report tells whether the object creation was successful or failed.
3. By clicking the Reports button, the dialog box will appear, as illustrated in Figure 23-13.

You can generate four types of reports: Migration Log, SQL Scripts, Tables, and Relations. The Migration Log report is a history of all the SQL instructions that were issued during the migration process. The SQL Scripts report enables you to save to a file to regenerate the schema at a later date to re-create it on another database.

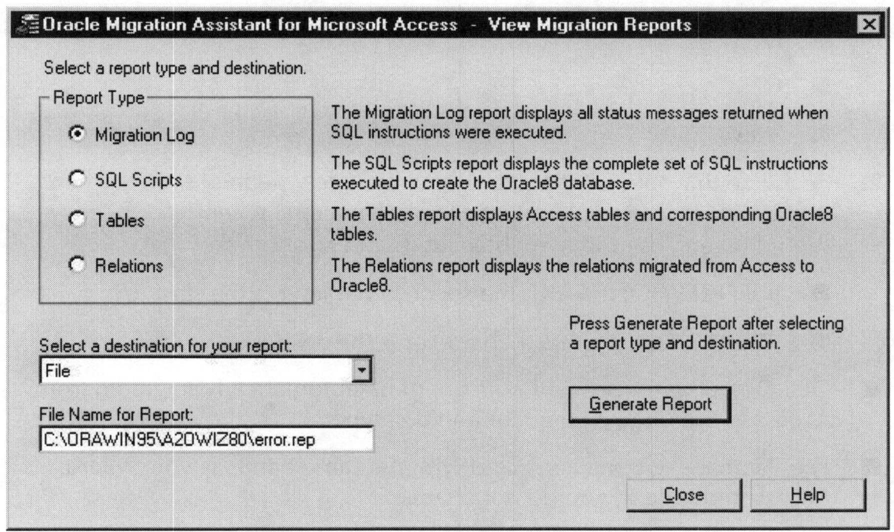

FIGURE 23-13. *Generating reports*

Detailed data about the tables that were created, the columns in the tables, and a comparison between Microsoft Access tables and Oracle tables is what you will find in the Tables report. Finally, the Relations report details all the referential links created between columns in your new Oracle database user. You also can generate the report types in three different ways: window, printer, and file. When you generate the report to a file, you are able to save it to your file system. After you have saved or viewed the appropriate reports, click the Close button to exit the Oracle Migration Assistant.

The following are some notes on the conversion process.

- Beware of using, or the use of, reserved words for column names. They include the following:
  - NOTE
  - START
  - CREATE
  - ORDER

- COMMENT
- DATE
- DESC
- VIEW

- Be aware that special characters have uniquely defined syntax when structured in queries or code. Special characters, when referenced, should be enclosed in a left bracket ([) and right bracket (]):
  - [OFFICEPHONE/FAX]; the special character is the slash (/).
  - [BOX15-1]; the special character is the dash (-).
- OLE Object datatypes will not/cannot be automatically migrated from Access to the Oracle Long column datatype.
- The database schema is created with the same name as your Microsoft Access .mdb file, if you do not change it.
- The password is oracle.
- Macros and modules are not converted.
- A datatype of AutoNumber in Microsoft Access on a column is automatically converted to a sequence and a trigger is created on the table for the column.

Gymnast

Gymnast will convert ASCII text files to PDF files for viewing with the Adobe Acrobat reader. To convert ASCII files to PDF, perform the following steps:

1. Start the Gymnast application. The long box on the left is the files that are in the directory that you are viewing.
2. Pick the directory you would like to work in from the box to the right of this box. Choose the directory you are viewing, just like you would in Windows Explorer. The PDF will be created in this directory. If you need to change the drive you are working in, click the drop-down box and make your selection. Once you have found the appropriate directory, the files in that directory will appear in the leftmost box. Not all files can be converted to PDF format with this utility. You can also change the font size, font name, page color, page size, page orientation, and page rotation. Once the file to be converted has been selected, choose Make PDF from the File menu.

Directory Toolkit

Directory Toolkit is an application to perform comparisons and concatenations between files, touches to files, and normal file operations, to split files over multiple disks, and for comparing directories. To use Directory Toolkit, perform the following steps based on your desired results. Due to the multiple uses for Directory Toolkit, in the following subsections the comparisons between directories, comparisons and concatenations between files, and touches to files will be covered.

Comparison Between Directories

To compare two directories, perform the following steps:

1. Click the Compare Directories icon, shown here, or select Compare Directories on the View menu.
2. The comparison will be done in a split frame, as shown in Figure 23-14. Files that appear with a green check next to them are in both directories. Files that have a red slash through a circle are either newer than their corresponding file in the other directory or they are not in the other directory. Finally, files that have a blue slash through a circle are older than the corresponding file in the other directory. For further information, refer to the Directory Toolkit Help page.

Comparison of Files

To compare two files, perform the following steps:

1. Click the Compare Files icon or select Compare Files on the File menu.
2. The comparison will be accomplished in a new window. Click the top Select (or Drop) File button. This will bring up a File Open dialog box.
3. Pick the appropriate file and click the Open button.
4. Click the lower Select (or Drop) File button.
5. When the dialog box appears, choose the second file to compare and click the Open button. Once you have your files chosen, click the Compare button in the upper left-hand corner of the screen.
6. After the files have been compared, the results will be displayed below the Compare button. A red note page means that the expression is missing in one of the files. The expression will be highlighted in red in the file that

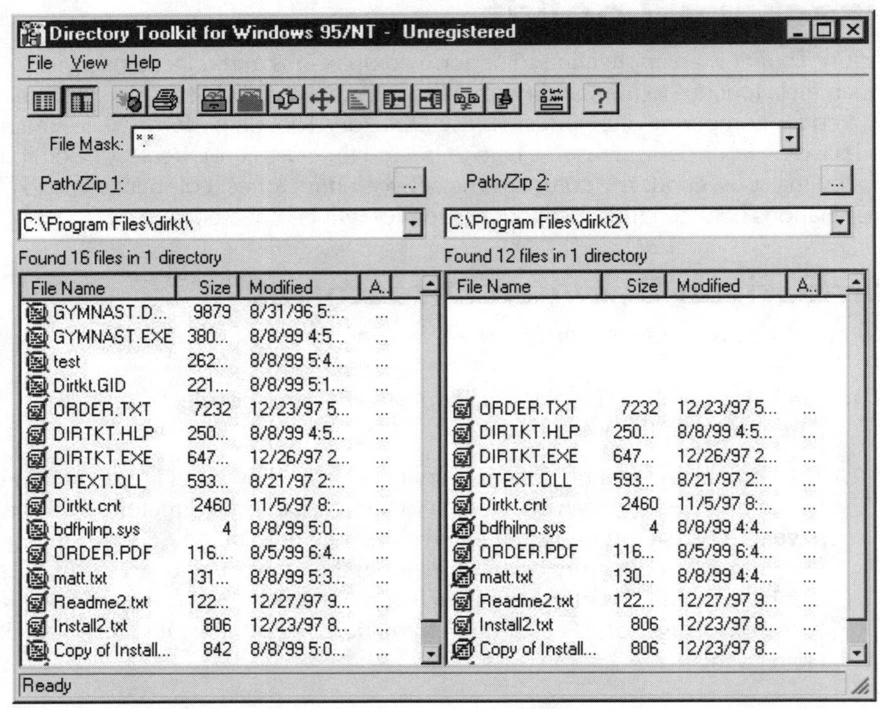

FIGURE 23-14. *Directory Toolkit split frame*

the text resides in. A green note page means that the text is the same for the lines listed.

Concatenation of Files (Combining Files)

To concatenate two files, perform the following steps:

1. Click the Concatenate Files icon, or select Concatenate Files on the File menu.
2. The dialog box shown next will appear. You must assign a filename and be sure to assign an extension, as one will not be added automatically.

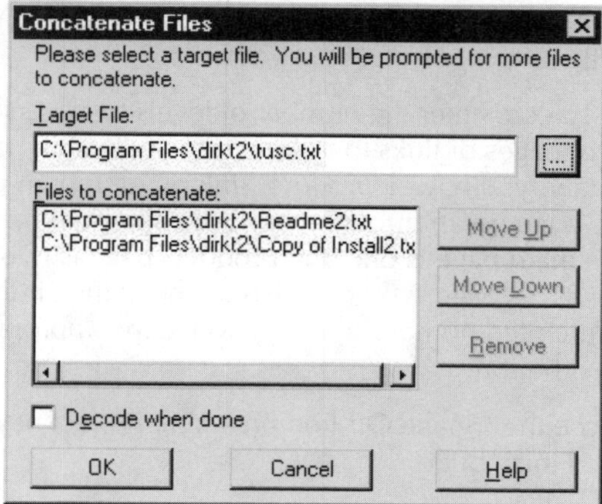

3. You can concatenate any number of files. To change the order of the concatenation, click the Move Up or the Move Down button on the file you wish to move. You can also remove a file by clicking the Remove button. When you are satisfied with the files you have selected, click the OK button to begin the concatenation process.

Anawave WebSnake

Anawave WebSnake is a tool that enables you to capture information from Web sites onto your hard drive. This is handy because you can view a site offline. For example, if you can use a browser to connect to a site, but only temporarily during a demo, you could snake (capture) that session for later review. Previously, there were offline browsers, and now there is WebSnake.

Snaking 101

If you wish to capture a Web site to your hard drive, perform the following steps:

1. Start the WebSnake application. The first page displayed is the Main WebSnake Wizard page.
2. Choose the "Snake a copy of a Web site for offline browsing" radio button and click the Next button.
3. On the next screen, enter the URL that you want to snake, and a project name for the Web site that you are downloading. Click the Next button.

4. If the Web site requires a username/password, click the Yes checkbox. Then, enter the username and password.
5. On the next screen, enter the number of levels to traverse—in other words, the number of pages of links to follow from your main page. If you choose three levels, and you have a products link of your main page, the snake will go one more page down through your Web site from the products link—for example, the main page is one, the products page is two, and one more followed link to its page. You can also uncheck the Limit checkbox and it will do an unlimited number of levels. Make the appropriate changes and click the Next button.
6. Finally, choose the "Snake Off-line Browsing Project now" radio button and click the Finish button.

Creating a New Project

To start a new Snake project follow these steps:

1. Within the screen, illustrated in Figure 23-15, click the New button and everything will be cleared out. Make sure you save any work that you do not want to lose.
2. Then click the Add button. The dialog box, just like in the first example in the preceding section, will appear.
3. Choose the "Snake a copy of a Web site for offline browsing" radio button and click the Next button.
4. On the next screen, enter the URL that you want to snake, and a project name of the Web site you are downloading. Click the Next button.
5. If the Web site requires a username/password, click the Yes checkbox. Then, enter the username and password.
6. On the next screen, you enter the number of levels that you want to traverse—in other words, the number of pages of links that you want to follow from your main page. If you chose three levels, and you have a products link of your main page, the snake will go one more page down through your Web site from the products link—the main page is one, the products page is two, and one more followed link to its page. You can also uncheck the Limit checkbox and it will do an unlimited number of levels. Make your changes and click the Next button.

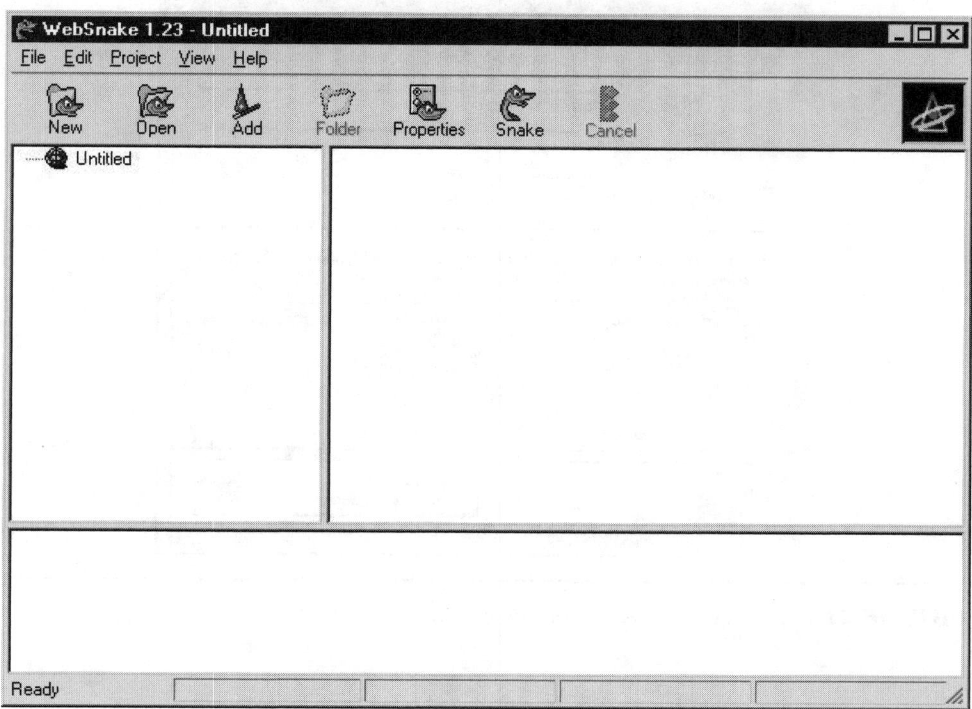

FIGURE 23-15. *New WebSnake project*

7. Finally, choose the "Setup advanced settings" radio button and click the Finish button. A dialog box will appear.
8. Enter the name and the location of your WebSnake project and click the Save button.
9. The next dialog box enables you to set project properties.

If you ever want to change the properties, just click the Properties button on the main WebSnake screen and the following dialog box will appear, as illustrated in Figure 23-16.

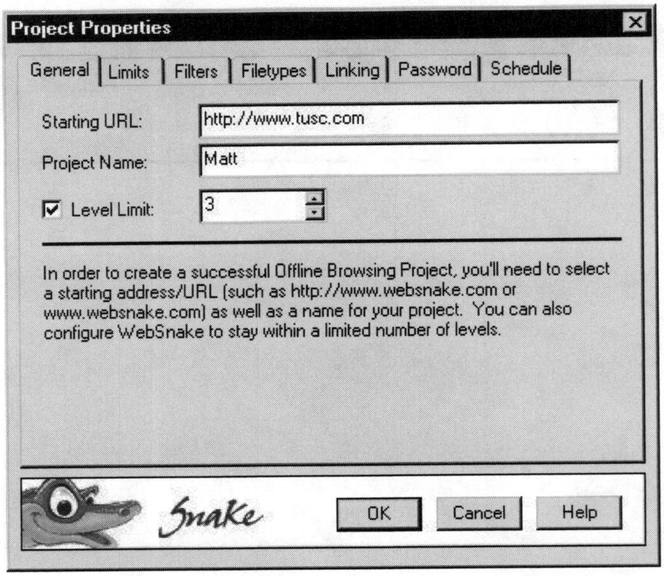

FIGURE 23-16. *WebSnake Project Properties screen*

Project Properties

The Project Properties dialog box consists of seven tabs: General, Limits, Filters, Filetypes, Linking, Password, and Schedule.

The General tab enables you to enter data pertaining to your WebSnake project. If you want to change something, this is the location.

The next tab is Limits, illustrated in Figure 23-17.

On this tab, you choose if you want your WebSnake project to go into other domains or stay just in your domain. The following bullet points provide a brief description of each radio button:

- **Stay within qualified domain (i.e., tusc.com)** For example, if I have a link to tuscstore.tusc.com and this radio button is clicked, it would traverse this site because it is within our domain.
- **Stay within current server (i.e., www.tusc.com)** For example, if I have a link to TUSC's RemoteDBA program on this site, as long as it is on this server it would traverse the RDBA pages, too.

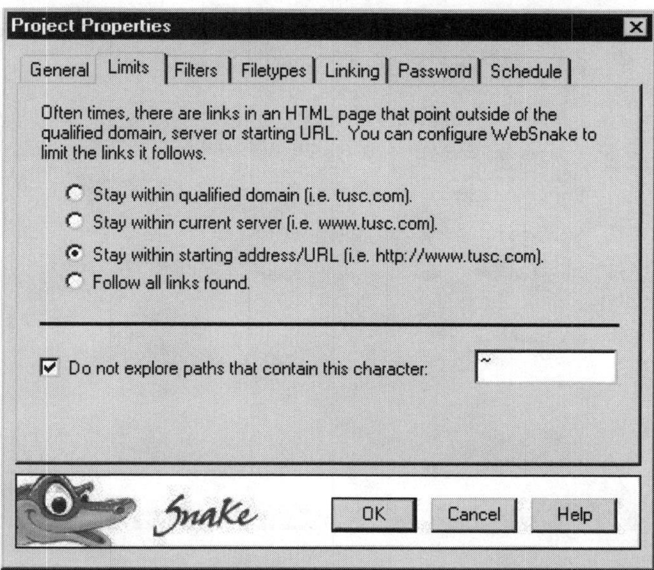

FIGURE 23-17. *WebSnake project Limits tab*

- **Stay within starting address (i.e., http://www.tusc.com)** For example, if I have a link to the TUSC intranet and its URL is http://ilnet.tusc.com/, it would not traverse through it.
- **Follow all links found** For example, if I have a link to Oracle's site and this radio button is clicked, it would traverse their site also.

The next tab is Filters, as illustrated in Figure 23-18.

On this tab, you can set limits to your downloading. The limits that you can set are downloaded files size, space on the drive, number of downloaded files, number of HTML files, and files greater than a certain size.

On the Filetypes tab, you can select which file types you want to download and which ones you do not wish to download. The dialog box is illustrated in Figure 23-19.

The Filetypes tab contains the following categories: Images, Text Files, Video, Audio, Other, and User-Defined. In each of the categories, the major file types are represented. Just check or uncheck the appropriate box. You can also add or remove file types.

The next tab is for HTML links. The dialog box is illustrated in Figure 23-20.

Project Properties

General | Limits | Filters | Filetypes | Linking | Password | Schedule

Stop project if downloaded files exceed: 100 MB

Stop project if space left on drive is less than: 10 MB

Stop project if number of downloaded files exceed: 500

Stop project if number of HTML files exceed: 50

Do not download files whose size exceeds: 500 KB

Snake

OK Cancel Help

FIGURE 23-18. *WebSnake project Filters tab*

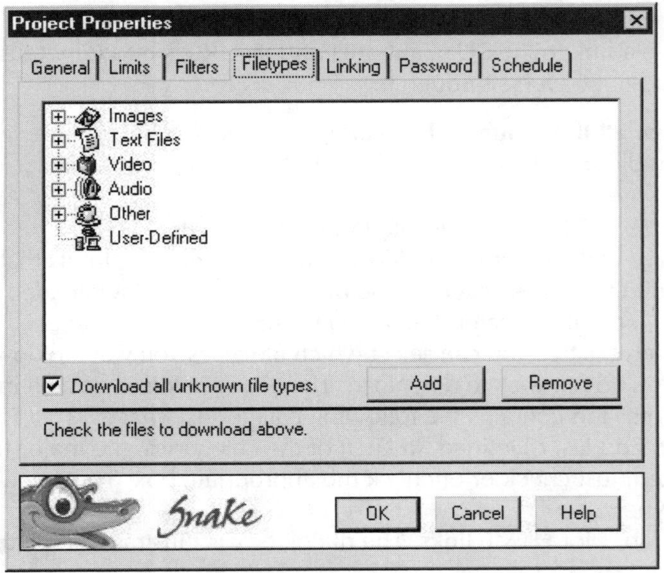

FIGURE 23-19. *WebSnake project Filetypes tab*

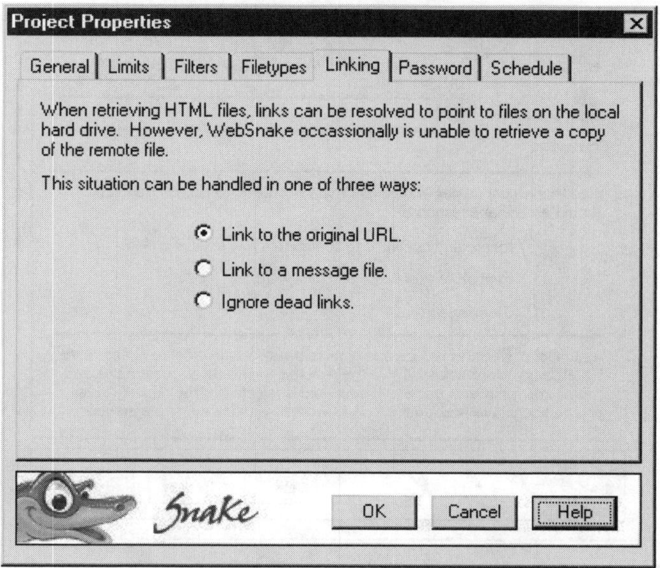

FIGURE 23-20. *WebSnake project Linking tab*

By clicking the appropriate radio button, you decide what happens if a link cannot be resolved. In other words, it is no longer available. The following choices are available:

- **Link to the original URL** If selected, it will link to the URL of the file, even if it no longer exists.
- **Link to a message file** If selected, it will link to a message HTML page stating that the file is no longer available.
- **Ignore dead links** If selected, it will skip over links that it cannot resolve.

The next tab, Password, enables you to change the username/password that you already entered. You can also decide on what happens if the need for your username/password combination should arise. The three choices are self-descriptive: Ignore and continue to search for other matching files, Prompt for username and password, or Stop project, as illustrated in Figure 23-21.

In the last tab, Scheduling, you can schedule your snaking to take place in off-hours or whenever you wish, as illustrated in Figure 23-22.

You can choose at what intervals the snaking process should take place, what time it should start, and on which days it should be performed. When you have

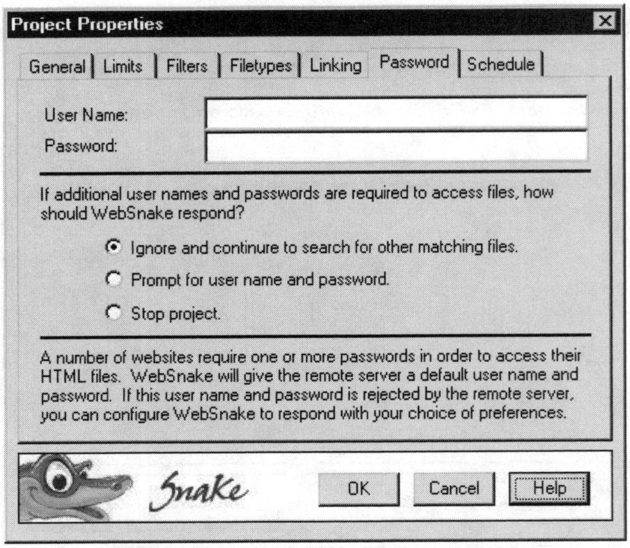

FIGURE 23-21. *Password tab*

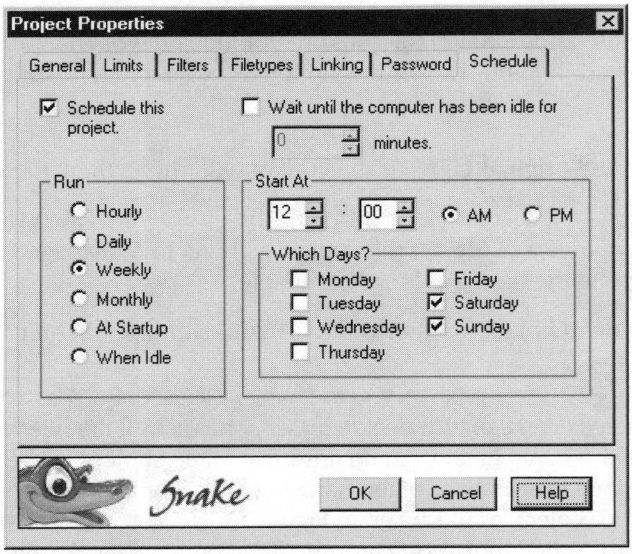

FIGURE 23-22. *Scheduling tab*

completed all your changes on each of the tabs, click the OK button to continue. If you chose not to schedule WebSnake to run automatically, you can click the Snake button to start the process immediately.

Summary

A number of tools are available to help you with Web development. Many of the tools are inexpensive and well worth the cost. Tools are even available to help you register your site to the search engines, such as TrafficBuilder. So, before you pay for a service to perform a task, make sure software is not already available to perform the task. Before you create custom functionality in your application, conduct research and take some time to make sure you are not reinventing the wheel.

CHAPTER 24

Troubleshooting

any questions need to be answered when troubleshooting your application. What is the problem? How do you fix it? Where do you start? Is there an easy way to approach the problem?

The simplest technique combines basic knowledge with common sense. If you can identify the possible problem, the rest will fall into place.

When you are developing an application and an error occurs, a number of thought-process paths can be taken to solve your problem. You need to know where to begin to discover the solution. What steps should you take down the troubleshooting stairway? The following four scenarios suggest how you might deal with problems in general, not just problems in your code. Hopefully, one of the following scenarios will occur when you encounter an obstacle:

- You know the answer
- You know how to find the answer
- You know who knows the answer
- You know when to ask for help

You Know the Answer

You may already know why your application will not work. If not, you may know how to resolve the problem. Review your prior knowledge base. More than likely, you have had some formal education on problem solving. It is possible you learned the answer at school, or maybe even at an adult education course you have taken since school. Remember, on-the-job-experience is an invaluable tool that is at your disposal. Even life's experiences can assist you as you search for the answer. Sometimes mundane solutions hold the key to make the impossible possible. This includes soft skills picked up along the way.

You Know How to Find the Answer

Maybe you do not know why an error has occurred. With the rapid changes in technology, it is possible this problem is one you have never faced before. Knowing where to find the answer is just as good as knowing the answer. At your disposal is a wealth of information and resources, which are explained in detail in the following subsections.

Log Files

Located in your OAS log directories, the log files can be of great assistance in identifying the problem. The Logger is discussed in further detail in Chapter 26. The wrb.log file (Web Request Broker or "system" log) will state the type of error that has occurred. It will also list the variables passed to the program unit that you were calling upon submit. Double-check the variables are named correctly and that they are all present. In addition to the WRB log, you can check the attrib.log (attribute log), xlf.log (extended log file), sv{listener}.err (Listener's log), and {cartridge}.log (cartridge log file, for example, plsql.log). Severe system errors are logged by the operating system, such as the Event Viewer in an NT environment.

Exception Handling

Exception handling in your code is similar to performing the job of the WRB log file, except the information provided is more accessible. In fact, you can provide the error handling directly back to the browser. Refer to Chapter 25 for further information about debugging your code.

If you are on a LAN, WAN, or the Internet, you might not have access to the OAS log files. If you write the errors to a table that you have insert and select privileges on, you will be able to mimic the logging of errors. It is easier to obtain the last error that occurred in a system_errors table than it would be to look through a 3MB log file. You can also pinpoint the exact location (line number) in your code where the error occurred. The log files do not provide information that is nearly as detailed as your own exception logic can provide.

Books and Other Media

You should establish an arsenal of books you can reference for your Web applications. Remember, other forms of media, including magazines, documentation, theoretical material, and technical support, can provide valuable information. Books in your library should include each of the topics that your application is composed of—for example, books on OAS, HTML, JavaScript, PL/SQL programming, database and application tuning, and so forth.

Oracle Support

Oracle offers many technical avenues to explore in your search for answers. They offer online iSeminars, video tapes (many of which are free), and Oracle Support (including MetaLink). The following are some of our favorite Oracle Web sites:

- technet.oracle.com - Technet
- http://metalink.oracle.com (explained in further detail in the following sections)
- www.oracle.com/support or support.oracle.com - Oracle Support
- www.olab.com - Oracle Application Server Division
- alliance.oracle.com - Oracle Alliance
- www.tusc.com - The Ultimate Software Consultants

- www.rmoug.org - Rocky Mountain Oracle Users Group
- www.ioug.org - International Oracle Users Group
- www.orafans.com - Orafans
- www.orafaq.org/faqmain.htm - Oracle Underground FAQ
- www.geocities.com/SiliconValley/Peaks/9111/ - Unofficial Oracle WebServer site

Oracle Support - MetaLink

With MetaLink, you can search for prior issues that were submitted online or through the phone. You can also submit a TAR online. Go to the MetaLink Web site. It is located at http://metalink.oracle.com/. If you are a frequent visitor, you can click the Login link. If this is the first time at MetaLink, or you if you have not visited in a while (since version 1), you will need to register.

To register perform the following steps:

1. Click the Registration link.
2. When you join Oracle Support, they give you a support identifier, such as a CSI number, a SAC, or an access code. Enter your Support Identifier and choose the appropriate country. Click the Proceed button.
3. On the next screen, enter your pertinent personal information. Once you have entered the appropriate fields, click the Proceed button.
4. The subsequent screen enables you to choose a username and password. Once you have selected a username and password, click the Proceed button.
5. The next screen contains the legal disclaimer. After you have read the text, click the Accept button.
6. When the registration is complete, click on the "Oracle's Web-based support services" link to enter MetaLink. A dialog box will appear. Enter the username and password that you chose in previous steps.

If you are looking for information on upgrading OAS, or any other Oracle-related topic, perform the following steps.

1. In the search text box, input the phrase you want to search for. As an example, I entered "upgrading Webserver."

2. The results will be listed in the Query Result section just below the search box.
3. If you see an entry that is of interest, click that entry's title link. The document will appear in the browser's current active window.
4. If you would like to search for a specific word, press CTRL-F within the browser and enter what you are looking for in the text box that appears.

Search Engines and Web Sites

Search engines and Web sites provide valuable sources of information when you are troubleshooting a problem. Appendix A contains a list of Web sites (including several search engines) that can help you find the information you are searching for. Many sites include their own internal search engine, similar to the search engine previously described within MetaLink. Deja (www.deja.com) also provides a search engine that will help you by searching list server documents.

You Know Who Knows the Answer

You probably know someone who knows the answer. Maybe a friend at work knows the answer, or they may have an idea of who would. Use all the resources (including coworkers, contacts, and consultants) you can before you move to the next step. As you are probably aware, if you call Oracle Support, it could be hours, days, or weeks before a resolution to your problem is offered. They are not going to say, "John Smith needs help, so let's create a patch today to solve his specific dilemma." At the same time, you need to know when to say when. If it truly is an Oracle bug, Oracle Support should work on solving the problem.

You Know When to Ask for Help

You have an error and you do not know how to resolve it. You are not sure who to ask for help or where to begin looking. Now is the time to ask for help. You are on the clock and cannot waste time spinning your wheels, because time is money. You need to act. There is an escalation path I use when I ask for help. First, I will ask a specific person(s). Next, I will query our local office, then TUSC's various offices around the country through an email, asking if anyone has encountered the problem, knows how to fix it, or knows where I can find the answer. If that fails to return a response, I turn to Oracle Support. Take a little time to establish an escalation policy for your company.

Summary

Troubleshooting is not as difficult as it first appears. Remember the four scenarios that can occur when developing Oracle applications (or any of life's problems). Once you pinpoint the problem area, all you need to know is when you need help, where to look for help, and when to ask for help.

The most effective troubleshooting is done proactively. Do not let problems and error messages paralyze you. Consider ongoing education (for example, learn before you need to know). Join a "knowledge network," such as your local Oracle user's group, so you have a resource you can always turn to for help. Keep proven Web sites and resources handy, so when you need them they are available.

CHAPTER 25

Debugging Your Code

Debugging is a necessary evil in all software development. The capabilities and complexities of modern development tools almost guarantee that something will not work correctly the first time. To many people, debugging and tweaking code to make sure it runs properly is what makes software development interesting and challenging. However, once a piece of code moves into production, most of these same people would prefer that it run without problems—indefinitely. Look at our Y2K problems. It's obvious that none of us expected the programs written 20 or more years ago to be in operation today, but they are.

This chapter will focus on development and coding techniques to decrease the total life-cycle cost of an application by guaranteeing robustness and reducing the time needed to recover from production problems.

In this chapter, the following topics will be covered:

- Reviewing general debugging techniques
- Painting complete screens with PL/SQL application
- Determining who holds the lock on a row
- Buying PL/SQL debugging tools
- Debugging without interfering with user's view
- Looking up general Oracle errors
- Providing further information than "Request Failed"
- Reviewing the log files
- Using proper error-handling techniques to decrease bug recovery time
- Sending error messages to a user interface using raise_application_error
- Preparing for production problems by designing enhanced debugging/tracing logic into application
- Presenting all validation errors simultaneously using an error array
- Confirming proper codes using version reporting package

Reviewing General Debugging Techniques

If you are experiencing any "interesting" issues regarding the compilation of stored procedures, beyond checking the log files, try the following steps for additional debugging techniques. Maybe you have experienced a situation where you have changed the PL/SQL, recompiled it, opened a new browser window to load that page—yet the change is not reflected in the newly generated HTML source. After clearing the memory cache and the disk cache, then turning off caching all together, still nothing works.

From the browser, hold down the SHIFT key and click Reload. V4.0 of the major browsers have a caching issue that makes Reload not quite the Reload you might expect. If this is your issue and you are doing a lot of development, use the no cache meta tag, as illustrated in the following syntax.

```
<meta http-equiv='pragma' content='no-cache'>
```

Use the preceding syntax in the head section of your HTML pages. Remember to remove it when that page is stable, unless you never want this page to be cached.

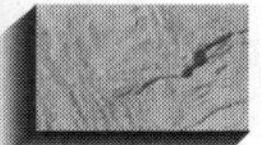

TIP
Somewhere in the process of changing PL/SQL code, recompiling, and reloading the browser, the OAS 4.0.7 architecture has been known to cache dynamic pages on the server. I have seen this happen on Sun 2.6 and on NT 4.0 SP3. An OAS listener flag (on NT) indicates whether the listener should cache static pages, but nowhere on any platform is there an option for the server to cache dynamic pages. Nonetheless, the bug exists. To flush the OAS's cache, use the following code:

```
$ owsctl reload -w all
```

Make sure you are actually compiling the PL/SQL code into the correct schema. Trace this information from the PL/SQL logical path to the agent, to the DAD, then the schema and database SID. If you are using a SQL*Net connect string, check your tnsnames.ora file. If all of the above criteria match up, confirm that the stored procedure is actually generating the desired code (select text from user_source where name='XXXXX' order by type, line). If all of this fails, log in (using SQL*Plus) as the schema user and enter the following syntax:

```
SQL> set serveroutput on
SQL> execute your_web_procedure
SQL> execute owa_util.show_page
```

Does the preceding syntax display the HTML code that you expect? Confirm your DAD is not pointing to an alternate schema and/or you do not have a synonym defined overriding what you think is being called (select * from all_objects where object_name = 'XXXXX').

TIP

*The owa_util.show_page procedure can produce misleading errors. The Web pages you develop are assumed to be called from a Web browser. When called from a SQL*Plus prompt, commands, such as owa_util.get_cgi_env (amongst others), have no meaning and will return a fatal error.*

Painting the Complete Screen with PL/SQL Application

If you ever run into a situation where the browser only paints part or none of the screen, first take a look at the HTML source. Is it there? Most likely it is, and you probably forgot an ending tag, such as the end of an HTML table (for example, </TABLE>). Newer browsers, such as Netscape v4.x, color-code the underlying HTML syntax—identify the inconsistencies in colors.

The issue may also be less predictable. You may have a network issue that is losing a portion of your HTTP transmission, or it could be as simple as an IP address conflict. If not, resolving this is more involved. You can set up a sniffing program (like Snoop) and capture the packets being sent to and from a test machine to your Web server. Just try one request/response session or you will get lost in the packet information and encapsulation. Then take the log of your request/response test and identify the last packet being sent from your Web server to your test machine. If the packet is not there, then modify htp.htmlClose in the Toolkit, pad the end of the tag with spaces equivalent to the packet size on your network, and recompile the Toolkit.

Determining Who Holds the Lock on a Row

If two users are locking rows in the database, you can execute the following script to identify who's locking who:

```
rem locks.sql - shows all locks in the database.
set linesize 132
set pagesize 60

column object          heading 'Database|Object' format a15 truncate
column lock_type       heading 'Lock|Type'       format a4 truncate
column mode_held       heading 'Mode|Held'       format a15 truncate
column mode_requested  heading 'Mode|Requested'  format a15 truncate
column sid             heading 'Session|ID'
column username        heading 'Username'        format a20 truncate
column image           heading 'Active Image'    format a20 truncate

spool locks.lis

select c.sid,
       substr(object_name,1,20) OBJECT,
       c.username,
       substr(c.program,length(c.program)-20,length(c.program)) image,
       decode(b.type,
              'MR', 'Media Recovery',
              'RT', 'Redo Thread',
              'UN', 'User Name',
              'TX', 'Transaction',
              'TM', 'DML',
              'UL', 'PL/SQL User Lock',
              'DX', 'Distributed Xaction',
              'CF', 'Control File',
              'IS', 'Instance State',
              'FS', 'File Set',
              'IR', 'Instance Recovery',
              'ST', 'Disk Space Transaction',
              'TS', 'Temp Segment',
              'IV', 'Library Cache Invalidation',
              'LS', 'Log Start or Switch',
              'RW', 'Row Wait',
              'SQ', 'Sequence Number',
```

```
                'TE', 'Extend Table',
                'TT', 'Temp Table',
                 b.type) lock_type,
        decode(b.lmode,
                 0, 'None',           /* Mon Lock equivalent */
                 1, 'Null',           /* NOT */
                 2, 'Row-SELECT (SS)',     /* LIKE */
                 3, 'Row-X (SX)',     /* R */
                 4, 'Share',          /* SELECT */
                 5, 'SELECT/Row-X (SSX)',  /* C */
                 6, 'Exclusive',      /* X */
                 to_char(b.lmode)) mode_held,
        decode(b.request,
                 0, 'None',           /* Mon Lock equivalent */
                 1, 'Null',           /* NOT */
                 2, 'Row-SELECT (SS)',     /* LIKE */
                 3, 'Row-X (SX)',     /* R */
                 4, 'Share',          /* SELECT */
                 5, 'SELECT/Row-X (SSX)',  /* C */
                 6, 'Exclusive',      /* X */
                 to_char(b.request)) mode_requested
from    sys.dba_objects a, sys.v_$lock b, sys.v_$session c
where   a.object_id = b.id1 and b.sid = c.sid
and     owner not in ('SYS','SYSTEM');
```

Buying PL/SQL Debugging Tools

A number of tools are available to debug PL/SQL code. You might find such tools on Oracle's Web site; at a local, regional, or international conference; or in a magazine. Oracle's Procedure Builder product includes a debugger.

Though not line-by-line, GUI products can also assist in the debugging process by color-coding your syntax; thereby helping to identify basic errors early in the coding process. An example of a GUI tool is TOAD (Tool for Oracle Application Developers) by Quest Software.

Debugging Without Interfering with User's View

Occasionally, you may need to track certain information from your site to debug your code. To avoid interfering with the users who are using the system, put your debug write statements in as HTML comments so the system will still run visually. This way, you can view the HTML source to see the "I got here" flags and values while still testing changes.

Looking Up General Oracle Errors

If you have access to a UNIX server and you receive an Oracle error and you do not have an error manual handy, Oracle provides an Oracle Error (oerr) utility to assist in identifying the symptom, cause, and recommended solution. To execute oerr, you need the name of the product and the specific error number, as the following syntax illustrates:

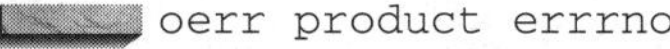

```
oerr product errrno
```

For example:

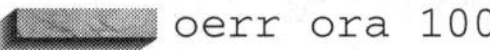

```
oerr ora 100
```

Providing Further Information than "Request Failed"

As mentioned in Chapter 4, set the PL/SQL agent's error level to Advanced (2) for OWAS 3.0 was the default Basic (0), which means to display the "Request Failed, Try Again Later" message. For debugging, it would be advisable to set this to a value of Advanced. Production systems can leave this set to Basic.

Reviewing the Log Files

Do not forget to review *all* of the logs files for errors that may occur. OAS provides consolidated error information in the XLF file.

Using Proper Error-Handling Techniques to Decrease Bug Recovery Time

One of the largest frustrations of debugging a production problem is figuring out what went wrong and why. Once the problem has been identified, the resolution is not far behind. Before the resolution can be implemented, a few basic questions must be answered:

- What procedure was running?
- Who executed it?
- What browser (and version) were they using?

- What platform are they on?
- What (virtual) host did they come in on?
- When did they run it?
- What record was being processed?
- What error was generated?

Though the list of questions to be answered is relatively small, in an error-handling deficient system, the time it takes to answer these questions can be quite lengthy. We have all spent hours tracing simple bugs, like a primary key violation, which in the end was being caused by something simple, like the use of an incorrect sequence number. Many applications are not written with problem resolution in mind. Therefore, to resolve bugs, you would naturally start by working through the user interface until the error occurs again just to identify the troublesome module. After you identify the module, you typically gut the entire module components to identify the source of the problem.

Users are not the best at describing the problem. When it comes to Internet applications, you are likely to get considerably less information from your users. For example, if a user cannot place an order on your site, they might send you an email (if you are lucky) saying "Here's my order that I could not place on your Web site—please fix your site."

It stands to reason that the overall time and frustration spent solving a production problem can be greatly reduced if the time it takes to identify the problem can be reduced—if not completely eliminated. This may sound like a major undertaking, but it is quite simple if sound error handling is used throughout the application.

Two simple rules can be applied to accomplish this:

1. Use exception handlers in every program unit
2. Record *all* abnormal errors—those that a program unit is not specifically written to handle

The following sections describe two rules individually to understand how they come into play in a total error-handling solution.

Using Exception Handlers in Every Program Unit

An active exception handler is the *only* way to programmatically respond to a runtime error. Without an active exception handler, the program unit terminates abnormally and immediately. If the PL/SQL Agent's error level is set to Basic, the user will receive a "try again later" message. If the error level is set to Advanced, the user will receive the "try again later" message and the Oracle error number and message—not likely the desired result. By using exception handlers, the program unit can remain in control when problems arise, thereby, being able to wrap things up gracefully—displaying a user-friendly message, logging the error, and continuing the user's session. Is it necessary to include exception handlers in *every* program unit? Absolutely!

Consider the following function that computes the line item total of an order—to the nearest, but lowest, whole dollar—and records it in the order header table:

```
create or replace function web_total (in_order in integer)
return integer
is
  nbt_running_total integer := 0;
  cursor order_detail_cur (in_id in integer) is
    select qty, amount
    from   order_detail
    where  order_id = in_id;
begin
  for order_detail_rec in order_detail_cur(in_order) loop
    nbt_running_total := nbt_running_total +
                         floor(order_detail_rec.qty *
                         order_detail_rec.amount);
  end loop;
  update order_header
  set    order_total = nbt_running_total
  where  order_id    = in_order;
  return nbt_running_total;
end web_total;
```

The preceding function is so basic and short that there does not seem to be a need for exception handling. Unfortunately, this function will generate a runtime error once the order total exceeds the precision of the integer data type.

Rewriting the preceding function to accommodate this potential problem yields the following program unit:

```
create or replace function web_total (in_order in integer)
return integer
is
  nbt_running_total integer := 0;
  cursor order_detail_cur (in_id in integer) is
    select qty, amount
    from   order_detail
    where  order_id = in_id;
```

```
begin
  for order_detail_rec in order_detail_cur(in_order) loop
    nbt_running_total := nbt_running_total +
                         floor(order_detail_rec.qty *
                         order_detail_rec.amount);
  end loop;
  update order_header
  set    order_total = nbt_running_total
  where  order_id    = in_order;
  return nbt_running_total;
exception
  when value_error then
    raise_application_error(-20000, 'Max order total exceeded.');
end web_total;
```

With the addition of the exception handler, the preceding function can now remain in control during the identified possible problem—a calculated value that exceeds the precision of the result variable. But…is this the only error that needs to be accommodated?

Absolutely not! Many other potential problems could generate a runtime error. For example:

- The precision of the order_total column could be less than the integer data—an error will occur if the calculated total is near the maximum value of the integer data type.
- The UPDATE statement may require another database extent be added to the database for the table to continue to grow—a problem will arise if the tablespace contains insufficient room for the new extent required.
- The UPDATE statement may violate a table constraint.
- A database trigger may reject the update.
- A database or hardware error may be encountered during the table update.

It is imperative the function be protected against *any* possible runtime problems, not just the ones that we have identified so far in our error routine. The resolution of any possible runtime problem can be accomplished using the OTHERS exception. The OTHERS exception enables the exception handler to accommodate all other errors not specifically handled.

Rewriting the preceding function to accommodate all potential problems yields the following program unit:

```
create or replace function web_total (in_order in integer)
return integer
is
```

```
  nbt_ora_error     varchar2(4000);
  nbt_running_total integer        := 0;
  cursor order_detail_cur (in_id in integer) is
    select qty, amount
    from   order_detail
    where  order_id = in_id;
begin
  for order_detail_rec in order_detail_cur(in_order) loop
    nbt_running_total := nbt_running_total +
        floor(order_detail_rec.qty * order_detail_rec.amount);
  end loop;
  update order_header
  set    order_total = nbt_running_total
  where  order_id    = in_order;
  return nbt_running_total;
exception
  when value_error then
    raise_application_error(-20000, 'Max order total exceeded.');
  when others then
    nbt_ora_error := sqlerrm;
    raise_application_error(-20000, nbt_ora_error);
end web_total;
```

While the preceding function can compensate for all possible runtime errors, it still has a severe limitation—it relies on the user to scribble the error onto a piece of paper and deliver it to the proper authority. If it is an end-user Web-based procedure, the user will see the Request Failed page, containing gibberish to the end user. The calling procedure would need to process the error and display a user-friendly error message. Rather than raise an exception, call your generic error display page. The generic page could be as simple as the following procedure, displaying a message providing the phone number of the support personnel for unexpected errors and displaying the passed message for expected errors (data entry type errors):

```
Create or replace procedure user_error_message
  (in_type    number,
   in_message varchar2) is
begin
  htp.htmlOpen;
  if in_type = 'U' then
    htp.title('Support Required - Unexpected Error');
    htp.header(1,'Unexpected Error, Please Call Support');
    htp.header(3,'Please contact I.T. support at extension 2043');
  else
    htp.title(in_message);
    htp.header(1,in_message);
    htp.print('Please press the BACK button and fix the problem');
```

```
  end if;
end user_error_message;
```

To call our newly created user_error_message routine, our web_total procedure would be changed as follows:

```
create or replace function web_total (in_order in integer)
return integer
is
  nbt_ora_error      varchar2(4000);
  nbt_running_total integer          := 0;
  cursor order_detail_cur (in_id in integer) is
    select qty, amount
    from   order_detail
    where  order_id = in_id;
begin
  for order_detail_rec in order_detail_cur(in_order) loop
    nbt_running_total := nbt_running_total +
      floor(order_detail_rec.qty * order_detail_rec.amount);
  end loop;
  update order_header
  set    order_total = nbt_running_total
  where  order_id    = in_order;
  return nbt_running_total;
exception
  when value_error then
    user_error_message('E', 'Max order total exceeded.');
  when others then
    nbt_ora_error := sqlerrm;
    user_error_message('U', nbt_ora_error);
end web_total;
```

Recording of All Abnormal Errors

The second rule of effective error handling is we must record all abnormal errors. Rather than writing the same generic error-logging logic in every routine, write a procedure geared to handle and record these abnormal errors. This approach not only ensures the error is recorded, but that the error is recorded accurately. In addition, a program unit that records all runtime errors offers the following key advantages:

- The arguments passed to the program unit can be recorded, identifying errors caused by logically invalid arguments.
- The database record being processed can be recorded, identifying errors caused by data anomalies.

- The current settings of any environmental variables can be recorded. This item is especially important when dealing with Web applications, as capturing the environment (system) variables can provide a wealth of knowledge regarding the interface at the time of the error.
- The call stack (dbms_utility.format_call_stack) can be recorded, identifying the chain of events that led to the calling of the subject program unit.
- The error stack (dbms_utility.format_error_stack) can be recorded, providing a complete error list that was automatically generated by the problem.
- The section of code in which the failure occurred can be recorded. When dealing with large program units, it is beneficial to break your code into small, logical, uniquely identified sections. A section should be roughly one to thirty lines in length. By recording the section identifier in the error log, the time spent finding the troublesome statement in a large program unit can be reduced.

To support our generic error-logging routine, the system_error table, system_error_id sequence number, and log_error procedure need to be created. To minimize the potential problems when writing to our system_error table, the table should not contain constraints or triggers. Also, by sizing the table relatively large, the possibility of taking out a new extent during inserts is reduced. The following is an example to create the system_error table:

```
-- DDL creates the system_error table.
create table system_error(
    system_error_id        number(10),
    program_unit_name      varchar2(4000),
    unit_type              varchar2(4000),
    unit_owner             varchar2(4000),
    execution_location     varchar2(4000),
    browser                varchar2(4000),
    server_software        varchar2(4000),
    server_name            varchar2(4000),
    server_port            varchar2(4000),
    remote_host            varchar2(4000),
    remote_addr            varchar2(4000),
    path                   varchar2(4000),
    script_name            varchar2(4000),
    oracle_error_text      varchar2(4000),
    additional_information varchar2(4000),
    call_stack             varchar2(4000),
    error_stack            varchar2(4000),
    insert_time            date,
```

```
    insert_user              varchar2(30))
tablespace any_big_one
storage   (initial 1M next 100K pctincrease 0);
```

The following example creates the system_error_id sequence number:

```
-- This DDL creates the sequence number for the primary key
-- values for the system_error table
create sequence system_error_id
       increment by 1
       start     with 1
       maxvalue  100000
       minvalue  1
       cycle
       cache     100
       order;
```

The following script creates the log_error procedure to record the errors to the system_error table:

```
-- Name: log_error
-- Description: Records an error in the error logging table.
-- Syntax: log_error (in_location,
--                    in_error,
--                    in_text,
--                    in_commit)
--
-- Where: in_location   = The reference to a physical location within
--                          the procedure/function in which the error
--                          occurred.
--        in_error      = The Oracle error message.
--        in_text       = Any additional information provided by the
--                          developer to aid in identifying the problem.
--                          For example, this might be a rowid/account
--                          number.
--        in_commit     = Boolean flag to determine if this procedure
--                          should perform a commit after writing to the
--                          error table.
create or replace procedure log_error (
                     in_location in varchar2 default NULL,
                     in_error    in varchar2 default NULL,
                     in_text     in varchar2 default NULL,
                     in_commit   in boolean  default TRUE)
is
  pu_failure          exception;
  pragma              exception_init (pu_failure, -20000);
  nbt_ora_error       varchar2(4000);
```

```
  nbt_id               number;
  nbt_program_unit     varchar2(4000);
  nbt_unit_type        varchar2(4000);
  nbt_unit_owner       varchar2(4000);
  nbt_unit_line        number;
  nbt_call_stack       varchar2(4000) :=
                       substr(dbms_utility.format_call_stack, 1, 4000);
  nbt_error_stack      varchar2(4000) :=
                       substr(dbms_utility.format_error_stack, 1, 4000);
  nbt_browser          varchar2(4000) :=
                       owa_util.get_cgi_env('HTTP_USER_AGENT');
  nbt_server_software varchar2(4000) :=
                       owa_util.get_cgi_env('SERVER_SOFTWARE');
  nbt_server_name      varchar2(4000) :=
                       owa_util.get_cgi_env('SERVER_NAME');
  nbt_server_port      varchar2(4000) :=
                       owa_util.get_cgi_env('REMOTE_HOST');
  nbt_remote_host      varchar2(4000) :=
                       owa_util.get_cgi_env('REMOTE_ADDR');
  nbt_remote_addr      varchar2(4000) :=
                       owa_util.get_cgi_env('SERVER_PORT');
  nbt_script_name      varchar2(4000) :=
                       owa_util.get_cgi_env('SCRIPT_NAME');
  nbt_path             varchar2(4000) :=
                       owa_util.get_owa_service_path;

  cursor sys_err_id_cur is
    select system_error_id.nextval
    from   dual;

begin
  open  sys_err_id_cur;
  fetch sys_err_id_cur into nbt_id;
  close sys_err_id_cur;

  owa_util.who_called_me(nbt_unit_owner, nbt_program_unit,
                         nbt_unit_line, nbt_unit_type);

  -- If the pseudo column user isn't the "user" that you want, you can
  -- retrieve the correct user now. For example, if your application
  -- is using a cookie to store the real user or if you're using basic
  -- or digest authentication, you could retrieve the username
  -- at this point.

  insert into system_error
  (   system_error_id, program_unit_name, unit_type, unit_owner,
      execution_location, browser, server_software, server_name,
    server_port, remote_host, remote_addr, path,
```

```
    script_name, oracle_error_text, additional_information,
    call_stack, error_stack, insert_time, insert_user)
  values
(     nbt_id, nbt_program_unit, nbt_unit_type, nbt_unit_owner,
      in_location, nbt_browser, nbt_server_software, nbt_server_name,
    nbt_server_port, nbt_remote_host, nbt_remote_addr, nbt_path,
    nbt_script_name, in_error, in_text,
    nbt_call_stack, nbt_error_stack, sysdate, user);

  if in_commit then
    commit;
  end if;

  -- Display a message to the user now - we could send an email to
  -- someone, page an administrator, send a message through DBMS_PIPE
  nbt_ora_error := sqlerrm;
  user_error_message('U', nbt_ora_error);

exception
  when others then
    raise pu_failure;
end log_error;
```

Once the log_error creating procedure (creating our supporting tables and sequence numbers) has been implemented, identify the impacts to the web_total function. Note that the code_section variable was added and set accordingly throughout the function:

```
create or replace function web_total (in_order in integer)
return integer
is
  nbt_code_section  varchar2(4000);
  nbt_ora_error     varchar2(4000);
  nbt_running_total integer;
  cursor order_detail_cur (in_id in integer) is
    select qty, amount
    from   order_detail
    where  order_id = in_id;
begin
  nbt_code_section := 'Beginning';
  nbt_running_total   := 0;
  for order_detail_rec in order_detail_cur(in_order) loop
    nbt_code_section  := 'In cursor loop';
    nbt_running_total := nbt_running_total +
                         floor(order_detail_rec.qty *
                         order_detail_rec.amount);
  end loop;
```

```
  nbt_code_section    := 'Before update';
  update order_header
  set    order_total = nbt_running_total
  where  order_id    = in_order;
  nbt_code_section    := 'After update';
  return nbt_running_total;
exception
  when value_error then
    user_error_message('E', 'Max order total exceeded.');
  when others then
    rollback;
    log_error (nbt_code_section,
               sqlerrm,
               'Runtime error calculating total for Order '||
                  to_char(in_order),
               true);
end web_total;
```

Sending Error Messages to a User Interface Using raise_application_error

When writing stored program units to support a user interface written for the Web, you may need to send error messages back to the user interface. For example, validation errors that are within the user's capability to correct. Errors originating from system problems or logic errors should always be written to an error log to assist in problem resolution.

Using either the return value of a function or an OUT parameter of a procedure to communicate validation error messages back to the interface can solve error handling to the user level. These techniques rely on properly constructed front-end logic to make the interface "aware" of the validation error; this could result in numerous problems. In the following code snippet, the conditional statement returns the execution from this routine to the stored program unit performing the user interface. It is likely that you have seen code similar to the following:

```
create or replace procedure web_payroll_calc(in_emp     in number,
                                          out_gross  out number,
                                          out_ded    out number,
                                          out_net    out number,
                                          out_error  out varchar2) is
  nbt_timesheet_found boolean       := false;
  nbt_code_section    varchar2(4000);
```

```
  cursor timesheet_cur (in_id in number) is
    select *
      from  web_timesheet
      where emp_id          = in_id
      and   processed_flag = 'N';
begin
  --Access all outstanding timesheet entries for the employee
  --and process.
  nbt_code_section := 'Before timesheet_rec loop';
  for timesheet_rec in timesheet_cur(in_emp) loop
    nbt_code_section := 'In timesheet_rec loop';
    nbt_timesheet_found := true;
    --Call incremental payroll logic here…
    …
  end loop;
  nbt_code_section := 'After timesheet_rec loop';

  --Prevent check creation if no timesheet records were found.
  if not nbt_timesheet_found then
    out_error := 'Check not created - no timesheet records found.';
  end if;
exception
  when others then
    rollback;
    log_error (nbt_code_section,
               sqlerrm,
               'Runtime error doing payroll calculation for emp
#'||to_char(in_emp),
               true);
end web_payroll_calc;
```

The preceding code will perform payroll calculations for a specific employee, setting the error code, if necessary. The following code is the Web procedure called from another procedure to gather the employees to be processed. The accept_emp_info program unit is the procedure that would be called from the user's browser displaying the employee information:

```
create or replace procedure accept_emp_info
  (in_emp varchar2) is
nbt_gross_amt    number(10,2);
nbt_ded_amt      number(10,2);
nbt_net_amt      number(10,2);
nbt_error_msg    varchar2(4000);
nbt_code_section varchar2(4000);
```

```
begin

   -- Perform payroll calculations and populate the payroll tables.
   -- The gross, deduction, and net check amounts will be returned.
   -- Use these to complete the payroll check record and display
   -- to the browser
   web_payroll_calc(to_number(in_emp), nbt_gross_amt,
                    nbt_ded_amt, nbt_net_amt, nbt_error_msg);

   --Check for errors in the called package.
   if nbt_error_msg is not null then
      user_error_message('E', nbt_error_msg);
      return;  -- Stops the procedure here
   end if;

   htp.htmlOpen;
   -- This is where we would display all the information we calculated
   -- back to the browser. This would simply use htp.prints,
   -- tableOpen,…
   …
   htp.htmlClose;

   --Commit transaction
   commit;

exception
  when others then
    rollback;
    log_error (nbt_code_section,
               sqlerrm,
               'Runtime error doing payroll calculation for emp
#'||in_emp,
               true);
end accept_emp_info;
```

Technically, the preceding code would work, but it is seriously flawed because it relies on programming logic to maintain the error condition identified in the stored program unit. A preferred approach would be to use the error propagation mechanism at the foundation of PL/SQL—the exception. Rewriting the preceding code using raise_application_error provides a mechanism for returning custom error messages to the user's browser, which removes the dependency on logic to maintain the error condition identified in the stored program unit. The following example illustrates the web_payroll_calc routine with exception logic instead of just setting an error message.

```
create or replace procedure web_payroll_calc(in_emp      in number,
                                             out_gross  out number,
                                             out_ded    out number,
                                             out_net    out number,
                                             out_error  out varchar2) is
  no_timesheet        exception;
  nbt_timesheet_found boolean        := false;
  nbt_code_section    varchar2(4000);

  cursor timesheet_cur (in_id in number) is
    select *
      from  web_timesheet
      where emp_id         = in_id
      and   processed_flag = 'N';
begin
  --Access all outstanding timesheet entries for the employee
  --and process.
  nbt_code_section := 'Before timesheet_rec loop';
  for timesheet_rec in timesheet_cur(in_emp) loop
    nbt_code_section := 'In timesheet_rec loop';
    nbt_timesheet_found := true;
    --Call incremental payroll logic here…
    …
  end loop;
  nbt_code_section := 'After timesheet_rec loop';

  --Prevent check creation if no timesheet records were found.
  if not nbt_timesheet_found then
    raise no_timesheet;
  end if;
exception
  when no_timesheet then
    raise_application_error(-20000, 'Check not created - no timesheet
                                     records found.');
  when others then
    rollback;
    log_error (nbt_code_section,
               sqlerrm,
               'Runtime error doing payroll calculation for emp #'||to_char(in_emp),
               true);
end web_payroll_calc;
```

Notice the effect on the accept_emp_info routine—an obligation no longer exists to check the error text to verify if it's NULL (or empty), and user-defined exceptions have been implemented to process accordingly:

```
create or replace procedure accept_emp_info
(in_emp number) is
-- User-defined exception to prevent exception raised in
-- stored program units (by raise_application_error) from being
-- handled by others clause.
pu_failure        exception;
pragma            exception_init(pu_failure, -20000);
nbt_gross_amt     number(10,2);
nbt_ded_amt       number(10,2);
nbt_net_amt       number(10,2);
```

```
nbt_error_msg    varchar2(4000);
nbt_code_section varchar2(4000);
begin

  -- Perform payroll calculations and populate the payroll tables.
  -- The gross, deduction, and net check amounts will be returned.
  -- Use these to complete the payroll check record and display
  --  to the browser
  web_payroll_calc(in_emp, nbt_gross_amt, nbt_ded_amt, nbt_net_amt, nbt_error_msg);

  -- This is where we would display all the information we calculated
  -- back to the browser. This would simply use htp.prints, tableOpen
  htp.htmlOpen;
  …
  htp.htmlClose;

  --Commit transaction
  commit;

exception
  when PU_FAILURE then
    user_error_message('E', sqlerrm);
  when others then
    rollback;
    log_error (nbt_code_section,
               sqlerrm,
               'Runtime error doing payroll calculation for emp #'||to_char(in_emp),
               true);
end accept_emp_info;
```

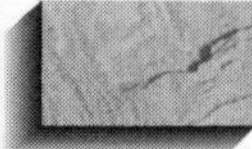

TIP

Remember, if you do not handle the exception, the PL/SQL Agent will display a cryptic request failed message to the user's browser. If you do not set the PL/SQL Agent's error level to Advanced, the user will only see "Request Failed, Try Again Later."

Preparing for Production Problems by Designing Enhanced Debugging/Tracing Logic into Application

Debugging is often thought of as a task that occurs only during an application's development phase. Code in the development phase is littered with htp.comment, dbms_output, text_io, and file_io commands for the sole purpose of tracing bugs and logic errors. It seems unfortunate these debugging statements are removed from the production code, as they will likely be needed should the subject code begin to encounter runtime problems, such as abnormal terminations, excessive execution times, or undesired output.

Logically removing the debugging statements—through comments—from the code is a good compromise, but this technique requires the code be edited (to restore the statements) before debugging can begin.

An ideal solution would be to design debugging statements into the application and enable them dynamically with a Debug Control option. If the setting for the debug control variable (or column data) is stored within a table as data, then the application can be placed into a debugging/tracing mode without touching a single line of code. The other option is to set the variable in the package body's init procedure.

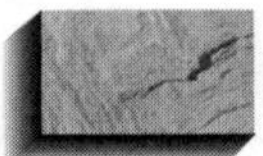

TIP
Package body units can be recompiled without invalidating the procedures dependent on the package. When a package specification is recompiled, every program unit referencing this package will become invalid. If you use this procedure throughout your application, a blunder like that (recompiling the package specification when it is unnecessary) could invalidate your entire application! Oracle will attempt to revalidate (recompile) an invalid procedure (or function) upon the next execution. For deeply nested procedures, the first Web user to access a page will have to wait several extra seconds for all invalid stored modules to be recompiled.

The following explains a couple of immediate advantages to an application that supports dynamic debugging/tracing:

- The application can be debugged/traced while executing without interfering with the actual execution. Thus, debugging can be performed in the environment where the problem is occurring. This can help those "it worked on the development server" types of problems, and the intermittent types of problems that only the user community seems to be able to generate.

- The application can be debugged without spending time and money hacking the code to insert debugging statements. This will eliminate that feel of "it seems like we were here before (during development) and now we are expecting someone to pay us to duplicate earlier work."

- If the debugging log includes time information (identical to the web_debug procedure, illustrated in the following example) then the log can be used to trace slow-running routines. The right combination of debugging statements can help identify the exact statement affecting performance.
- If you wish to further extend the debug mode power, rather than debug_mode being a Boolean variable, you could set it to a number. This would enable you to turn on different levels of debug messaging.
- The log could be written to a file or table. The following script directs logging information to a table:

```
create or replace package web_debug is
  debug_mode boolean;
  start_time integer;
  procedure init;
  procedure write_log(in_location varchar2,in_debug_text in varchar2);
  procedure really_write_log(in_location varchar2,
                             in_debug_text in varchar2);
end web_debug;
/

create or replace package body web_debug is
  procedure init is
    -- We could store the debug value in a table, but for this
    -- example, to shorten the code, we're just going to hardcode
    -- this. It's important to put this in the package body
    -- so that the value can be changed, the package body
    -- recompiled without invalidating all referencing procedures.
  begin
    web_debug.debug_mode := true;
    if web_debug.start_time is NULL then
       web_debug.start_time := dbms_utility.get_time;
    end if;
  end init;

  procedure write_log
    (in_location varchar2,
     in_debug_text in varchar2) is
  begin
    -- Only write the log, if we are in debug mode
    web_debug.init;
    if web_debug.debug_mode then
       really_write_log(in_location, in_debug_text);
    end if;
  end write_log;

  procedure really_write_log
    (in_location varchar2,
     in_debug_text in varchar2) is
```

```
    nbt_log_time        date            := sysdate;
    nbt_start_time      integer         := dbms_utility.get_time;
    nbt_program_unit    varchar2(4000);
    nbt_unit_type       varchar2(4000);
    nbt_unit_owner      varchar2(4000);
    nbt_unit_line       number;
    nbt_browser         varchar2(4000) :=
                        owa_util.get_cgi_env('HTTP_USER_AGENT');
    nbt_server_software varchar2(4000) :=
                        owa_util.get_cgi_env('SERVER_SOFTWARE');
    nbt_server_name     varchar2(4000) :=
                        owa_util.get_cgi_env('SERVER_NAME');
    nbt_server_port     varchar2(4000) :=
                        owa_util.get_cgi_env('REMOTE_HOST');
    nbt_remote_host     varchar2(4000) :=
                        owa_util.get_cgi_env('REMOTE_ADDR');
    nbt_remote_addr     varchar2(4000) :=
                        owa_util.get_cgi_env('SERVER_PORT');
    nbt_script_name     varchar2(4000) :=
                        owa_util.get_cgi_env('SCRIPT_NAME');
    nbt_path            varchar2(4000) := owa_util.get_owa_service_path;
    begin
      owa_util.who_called_me(nbt_unit_owner, nbt_program_unit,
                             nbt_unit_line, nbt_unit_type);

      -- Insert the date and time of the log entry, the time the
      -- grand (the one called from the user's browser) procedure
      -- started (in 100ths of a second), the time this call was made
      -- (in 100ths of a second) and the debug text.
      insert into debug_log
        (log_time, grand_start_time, debug_start_time,
         debug_text, program_unit_name, unit_type, unit_owner,
         execution_location, browser, server_software, server_name,
         server_port, remote_host, remote_addr, path,
         script_name, log_user)
      values
        (nbt_log_time, web_debug.start_time, nbt_start_time,
         in_debug_text, nbt_program_unit, nbt_unit_type, nbt_unit_owner,
         in_location, nbt_browser, nbt_server_software, nbt_server_name,
         nbt_server_port, nbt_remote_host, nbt_remote_addr, nbt_path,
         nbt_script_name, user);
    exception
      when others then
        raise_application_error(-20000, 'Error in write_log procedure');
    end really_write_log;
  end web_debug;
```

The preceding package will assist in debugging your code at any time. You can log as much or as little debugging information as deemed necessary. In the preceding example, we captured a significant amount of information. An important piece of information captured is the time the Web procedure started and the time that each debug statement was captured. By subtracting these two numbers, you are able to track execution speed down to the hundredth of a second. The following procedure is an example of a procedure using the preceding web_debug package.

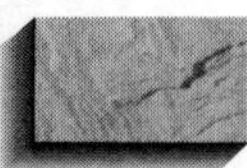

TIP
Using dbms_utility.get_time, you can retrieve time down to the hundredth of a second.

```
create or replace procedure web_submit
  (in_emp_no    integer,
   in_name      varchar2,
   in_address   varchar2,
   in_address_2 varchar2,
   … ) is
  insert_counter integer;
  update_counter integer;
  nbt_code_section varchar2(4000);
begin
  nbt_code_section := 'Procedure web_submit starting';
  web_debug.write_log(nbt_code_section, 'Incoming Args - Emp No: '||
                      in_emp_no||…);

  nbt_code_section := 'Validation';
  web_debug.write_log(nbt_code_section,'Starting');
  web_validate(in_emp_no, …);

  --Begin calculation routines.
  nbt_code_section := 'Calculation';
  web_debug.write_log(nbt_code_section,'Starting');
  web_calc(in_emp_no, …);

  --Create transaction records.
  nbt_code_section := 'Transaction Creation';
  web_debug.write_log(nbt_code_section,'Starting');

  insert into order_header...
  web_debug.write_log(nbt_code_section,'Order Header: '||
     sql%rowcount||' records inserted.');

  insert into order_detail...
  web_debug.write_log(nbt_code_section,'Order Detail: '||
     sql%rowcount||' records inserted.');

  update inventory...
  web_debug.write_log(nbt_code_section,' Inventory: '||
     sql%rowcount||' records inserted.');

  nbt_code_section := 'Procedure web_submit ending normally';
```

```
  web_debug.write_log(nbt_code_section,NULL);
exception
  when others then
    rollback;
    log_error (nbt_code_section,
               sqlerrm,
               'Processing emp #'||to_char(in_emp_no),
               true);
end web_submit;
```

Presenting All Validation Errors Simultaneously Using an Error Array

Most Web applications rely on server-side code to validate user input to some extent. While it is customary to perform as much validation as possible within the Web page (with JavaScript), certain types of validations, such as checking stock quantities, can only be performed on the server. When performing these server-side validations, a couple of key advantages are apparent when performing a complete validation and returning a complete list of problems to the user.

Most users seem to prefer an all-inclusive list of errors prior to attempting another submit. An application that forces the user to fix one validation error only to warn of another can quickly affect the user's patience. Add a slow Internet connection to this type of validation logic and the user will quickly become frustrated.

By providing an exhaustive list of errors to the user, network communication can be reduced. The user can work from the error list to correct all identified errors prior to performing subsequent commits. If the user has properly corrected all error conditions, then the next submission will most likely succeed. Compare this to a piecemeal validation routine that requires repeated submits for the user to be warned of all data validation errors. If validation can be performed on the client, it should. Client-side validation is usually accomplished with JavaScript. For further information about using JavaScript for your client-side validation, refer to Chapter 12.

Our all-inclusive validation can be implemented using a simple PL/SQL table (similar to an array in most languages) serving as an error stack that the validation routines can push messages into. The algorithm is as follows:

- The server-side submission procedure receives a submission from the Web application
- It calls validation/processing routines
- These routines will push messages into the array as problems are encountered

- Upon completion of the validation/processing routines, the array is checked for contents (using the count property)
    - If the error array is empty, then no errors were encountered and the transaction can be finalized
    - If the array contains any data, then the transaction may need to be rolled back and the array contents sent back to the user as a Web page

The following sample code demonstrates the technique. The following web_validation package contains the validation routines. Notice the io_error_array is declared at the package level and is passed in and out of each of the other procedures—all of which build on the error messages:

```
create or replace package web_validation is
  type error_type is table of varchar2(4000) index by binary_integer;
  io_error_array web_validation.error_type;
  procedure check_customer (
            in_cust        in     number,
            in_total       in     number,
            io_error_array in out web_validation.error_type);
  procedure check_stock (
            in_item        in owa_util.ident_arr,
            in_qty_wanted  in owa_util.ident_arr,
            io_error_array in out web_validation.error_type);
end web_validation;
/

create or replace package body web_validation is
  -- This procedure validates the customer account.
  procedure check_customer (
    in_cust        in     number,
    in_total       in     number,
    io_error_array in out web_validation.error_type) is
    nbt_cust_found boolean := false;
    cursor cust_cur(in_id in number) is
      select credit_amt
      from   web_cust
      where  cust_id = in_id;
  begin
    for cust_rec in cust_cur (in_cust) loop
      nbt_cust_found := true;
      if cust_rec.credit_amt < in_total then
        io_error_array(io_error_array.count + 1) :=
            'Your credit limit ('||cust_rec.credit_amt||
            ') is insufficient to complete order - '||
            'please reduce items and/or quantities.';
```

```
      end if;
    end loop;
    if not nbt_cust_found then
      io_error_array(io_error_array.count + 1) :=
           'Incorrect account number - please re-enter.';
    end if;
  exception
    when others then
      io_error_array(io_error_array.count + 1) :=
       'Unable to access your account. Please call customer service.';
  end check_customer;

  --This procedure verifies that the item is still available.
  procedure check_stock (
    in_item        in owa_util.ident_arr,
    in_qty_wanted  in owa_util.ident_arr,
    io_error_array in out web_validation.error_type) is
    nbt_item_found boolean;
    cursor stock_cur(in_id in number) is
      select on_hand
      from   web_stock
      where  item_id = in_id;
  begin
    for nbt_item_no in 1 .. in_item.count loop
      nbt_item_found := false;
      for stock_rec in stock_cur (in_item(nbt_item_no)) loop
        nbt_item_found := true;
        if stock_rec.on_hand < in_qty_wanted(nbt_item_no) then
          io_error_array(io_error_array.count + 1) :=
               'Only '||stock_rec.on_hand||' units of item '||
               in_item(nbt_item_no)||
               'are available - please re-enter quantity.';
        end if;
      end loop;
      if not nbt_item_found then
        io_error_array(io_error_array.count + 1) :=
             'Incorrect item number - please re-enter.';
      end if;
    end loop;
  exception
    when others then
      io_error_array(io_error_array.count + 1) :=
       'Unable to verify inventory. Please call customer service.';
  end check_stock;
end web_validation;
```

The preceding package performs the data validation. The following is an example of a procedure called from the user's browser, calling each of the validation routines to build the error array:

```
create or replace procedure web_process_order
  (in_cust  number,
   in_total number,
   in_item  owa_util.ident_arr,
   in_qty   owa_util.ident_arr) is
  done              exception;
  io_error_array    web_validation.error_type;
  nbt_code_section varchar2(4000);
begin
  --Validate the customer.
  nbt_code_section := 'Validate customer';
  web_validation.check_customer(in_cust, in_total, io_error_array);

  --Validate the selected items.
  nbt_code_section := 'Checking Stock';
  web_validation.check_stock(in_item, in_qty, io_error_array);

  --If any of the validation procedures encountered errors then
  --put all error messages in a Web page and send back to the user.
  --Otherwise, process the order.
  if io_error_array.count > 0 then
    for loopctr in 1 .. io_error_array.count loop
      user_error_message('E', io_error_array(loopctr));
    end loop;
    raise done;
  end if;

  --Code to actually process order should be placed here.
  --The same error array should be used to record processing errors
  --and present them to the user.
  …
exception
  when done then
    null;
  when others then
    rollback;
    log_error (nbt_code_section,
               sqlerrm,
               'Runtime error processing order for cust #' ||
                 to_char(in_cust)…,
               true);
end web_process_order;
```

Confirming Proper Codes Using Version Reporting Package

It may become difficult to determine if the changes made to a package's source code were ever installed into the database. In addition, stored program units undergo minor formatting changes as source code is moved into the database, thus making it impossible to check the installed code by extracting it and comparing it to the source script. The simple solution is to add a versioning variable to the package specification and updating it to the current date whenever the source code is changed. This versioning can provide the first line of offense to tackle a production problem by verifying that the installed versions of program units are the correct versions.

```
create or replace package my_package is
  -- Always maintain version when making coding changes
  version varchar2(4000) := '19991230.1';
  ...
end my_package;
```

A decimal addition to the timestamp value enable multiple changes within the same day to be traced. The variable should be highlighted with a comment and kept near the top of the package body, or the developers may forget to update it. A simple query against the user_source table will yield the version of a package installed into the database. The SELECT statement would appear identical to the following snippet of code:

```
select text
from   user_source
where  name = 'MY_PACKAGE'
and    type = 'PACKAGE'
and    upper(text) like '%VERSION%';
```

The results of the preceding query are not very user friendly, nor terribly effective:

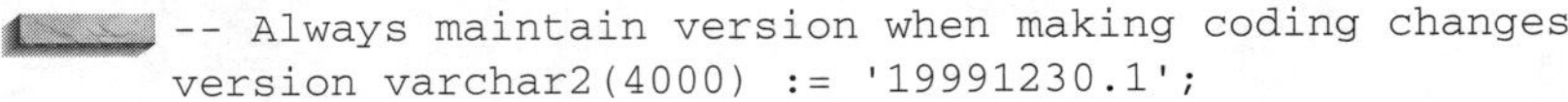

```
-- Always maintain version when making coding changes
version varchar2(4000) := '19991230.1';
```

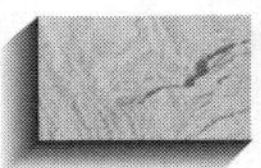

TIP
Never recompile the package specification unless you are making a change to the definition of the program units (procedures or functions) therein.

Taking this tip along with our versioning approach one step further, a simple what_version function can be added to the package to set and return the contents of the version variable:

```
create or replace package my_package is
  version varchar2(4000);
  function what_version return varchar2;
  pragma restrict_references (what_version, WNDS);
  …
end my_package;

create or replace package body my_package is
  function what_version return varchar2 is
  begin
    — Always maintain version when making coding changes
    my_package.version := '19991230.1';
    return version;
  end what_version;
end my_package;
```

The packages can be probed individually to return the version string, or a simple PL/SQL block, such as the following check_versions procedure, can be used to probe all packages at once. The user_objects table contains two important columns—created and last_ddl_time. The last_ddl_time column identifies the date and time that the program unit was last recompiled. In the following procedure, the last_ddl_time column is converted to the character format of yyyymmdd (same format as our version number) and compared with our version variable to provide the developer with further information:

```
create or replace procedure check_versions
  (in_program_unit      varchar2 default '%') is
   nbt_dml_statement   varchar2(4000);
   nbt_package_version varchar2(4000);
   nbt_record_count    integer;
   nbt_version_cursor  integer;
  cursor source_cur is
    select distinct name
    from   user_source
    where  type    = 'PACKAGE'
    and    name like in_program_unit;
cursor object_cur (in_object varchar2) is
    select to_char(last_ddl_time, 'YYYYMMDD') last_ddl_time
    from   user_objects
    where  object_name = in_object
    and    object_type = 'PACKAGE';
begin
```

```
htp.htmlOpen;
htp.headOpen;
htp.title('View Program Unit Versions');
htp.headClose;
htp.bodyOpen;
htp.tableOpen('BORDER=1');
htp.tableRowOpen;
htp.tableHeader('Program Unit');
htp.tableHeader('Version');
htp.tableHeader('Last DDL Date');
htp.tableHeader('Notes');
htp.tableRowClose;
for source_rec in source_cur loop
  nbt_version_cursor := dbms_sql.open_cursor;
  nbt_dml_statement := 'select '||source_rec.name||
                       '.what_version from dual';
  begin
    dbms_sql.parse(nbt_version_cursor, nbt_dml_statement,
                   dbms_sql.native);
    dbms_sql.define_column(nbt_version_cursor, 1,
                   nbt_package_version, 100);
    nbt_record_count := dbms_sql.execute(nbt_version_cursor);
    if dbms_sql.fetch_rows(nbt_version_cursor) > 0 then
       dbms_sql.column_value(nbt_version_cursor, 1,
                   nbt_package_version);
    else
      nbt_package_version := 'Version Reporting Failed';
    end if;
  exception
    when others then
      nbt_package_version := 'Version Reporting Not Supported';
  end;
  htp.tableRowOpen;
  htp.tableData(lower(source_rec.name));
  htp.tableData(nbt_package_version);
  for object_rec in object_cur (source_rec.name) loop
    htp.tableData(object_rec.last_ddl_time);
    if substr(nbt_package_version,1,8) !=
             object_rec.last_ddl_time then
       htp.tableData('*** Versions do not match ***');
    else
       htp.tableData;
    end if;
  end loop;
  htp.tableRowClose;
  dbms_sql.close_cursor(nbt_version_cursor);
end loop;
htp.tableClose;
```

```
  htp.bodyClose;
  htp.htmlClose;
end check_versions;
```

The results of the check_versions package are shown next.

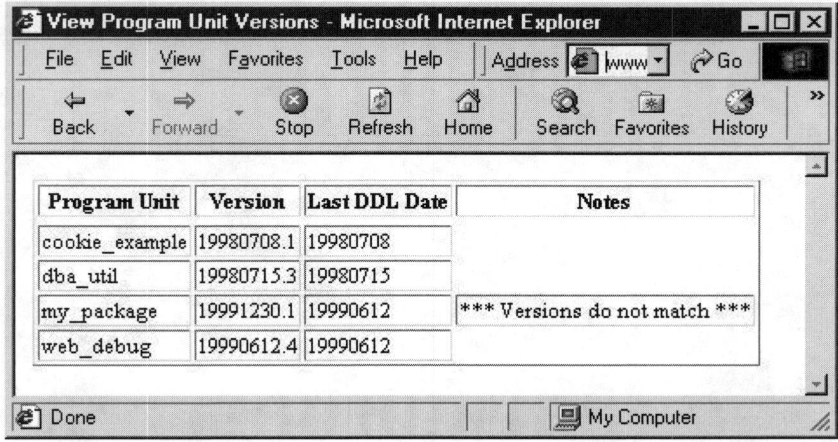

Program Unit	Version	Last DDL Date	Notes
cookie_example	19980708.1	19980708	
dba_util	19980715.3	19980715	
my_package	19991230.1	19990612	*** Versions do not match ***
web_debug	19990612.4	19990612	

Summary

In this chapter, we have covered numerous debugging tips for your Web applications. Topics included general debugging techniques, determining table/row locks, debugging tools, debugging without interfering with a users' view, how to look up general Oracle errors, reviewing the log files, and heavier topics. The heavier topics included the following:

- Discussions on using proper error-handling techniques to decrease bug recovery time
- Sending error messages to a user interface using raise_application_error
- Preparing for production problems by designing enhanced debugging/tracing logic into an application
- Presenting all validation errors simultaneously using an error array
- Confirming proper codes using a version reporting package

CHAPTER 26

Logging and Site Analysis

When it comes to developing Web sites, it's important to understand your customers. Who are they? What are their personalities? What is the best way to communicate with them? How can I tell them more about my company? How can I offer them more services?

Who they are can typically be answered by *demographics* type questions, such as gender, race, age, education, home value, family size, income level, and so forth. *Pyschographics* measures their self-concept, attitude, interests, opinions, beliefs, preferences, and personality traits. *Communigraphics* information, such as understanding their communication skills, cooperation, and participation, is another component that needs to be understood. These traits (*demographics, pyschographics,* and *communigraphics*) are strategic components you need to build into your application.

The final component to understanding your customers could be called *clickographics,* which is their attention span, focus, appetite, impulsiveness, judgment, and analytical skills. Web logs can help you understand this customer component.

Understanding all of these components will result in predictive marketing. You will know which customers you should cross-sell, versus up-sell. For your company, your sales group will no longer use assumptive marketing techniques. It's a one-on-one sales method for every unique customer. When you are successful at understanding your customers and how they find you, you will see more page hits, increased editorial exposure, feedback received, shortened sales cycle, increased sales, and decreased lead costs.

All Web servers generate log files recording requests made to the Web server. The OAS is no exception. OAS performs three types of logging:

- System logging
- Web server usage logging
- Client-defined attribute logging

Measuring the success of your Web site can primarily be attributed to the visitors it receives. Web server usage logs will be the main focus of this chapter. Adequate analysis of the value and impact of your site requires monitoring and accumulating user activity. Most HTTP listeners, including the OAS SpyGlass HTTP Listener, provide activity logs to support your analysis requirements. The HTTP Listener accepts HTTP requests, forwarding them to the OAS back-end. OAS processes the request in a cartridge server and generates a result to be redirected back to the client. With most Web server installations, the capability exists to writelog information about requests to standard text files. Interpreting the data within the accumulated log files to represent your Web server's activity involves creating programs (perhaps in PERL or C). Alternatively, you could purchase a program specifically designed to do this. I highly recommend the latter. Why reinvent the wheel when low-cost (and even no-cost shareware) solutions are available? The information in the log files is parsed and subjected to programmatic analysis. The data is presented in a specific text or graphic report format. Typically, this analysis process is completed as a batch operation with little capability of ad hoc query operations on the data. A good tool will also enable you to query the data.

Most Web servers do not possess an integrated (usage/errors/warning) logging environment for the listener or the server programs invoked by the Web Listener. Site managers who wish to adequately monitor their Web sites may be relegated to review many logs and error files derived from different components.

OAS addresses these issues by enabling all log information to be written to either a standard log file or to an Oracle database in real-time. OAS also implements utilities to batch-load log files or records (100 at a time) into the database for further analysis (if real-time database logging is not enabled). Capturing log information in the database enables the site manager to perform ad hoc reporting, functionality provided with the Log Analyzer component of OAS. Log Analyzer's reports can run against either real-time or archived activity in the database, depending on the logging configuration.

OAS supports an integrated application error and warning log system enabling all components (both Oracle branded and user-written) to write error messages, warnings, or debugging information to a single log destination. Components can be configured to log to their own files, even though integrated logging makes monitoring the site easier.

What is all the hype over log files? The log files contain the information providing factual answers to business questions, such as:

- Who is hitting my Web site?
- Which pages are requested the most?
- What are the top paths through the site?
- Which files are downloaded the most?
- What is the activity of my site by day?
- What is the activity level by day of the week/hour?
- What is my best advertising source?

Beyond marketing, advertising, and sales, log information can be used to tune the server properly, identify a timeframe when your site can afford to be down, forecast the adding of new machines, and perhaps justify expanding Web-based services. Some of the newer analysis reports promise to analyze how users are actually using your site. For example, are users stuck in Web page jail (an infinte loop on the site) or are they pogo-sticking (going up and down the site's structure) to find information?

This chapter will cover the following topics:

- Getting a basic understanding of Web server usage logging
- Retrieving further information on log file formats
- Looking at Web site management tools
- Reviewing the iLux solutions
- Comparing WebTrends solutions
- Defining the WRB log and listener log
- Adjusting the severity settings for the PL/SQL cartridge
- Understanding the Logger
- Logging usage to the database
- Developing your own reports from the Logger tables
- Reviewing the XLF logging parameters
- Getting the most out of the Log Analyzer
- Uploading log files into the database to create user-defined log reports

Getting a Basic Understanding of Web Server Usage Logging

The OAS Log Server collects data specific to who is hitting the Web server and how it is being used. Every time an HTTP request is made, information is collected about the connection. With all Web servers generating log files that record requests made to the Web server, listener log files will contain the time of the request, the source IP address of the request, the URL requested, the response code, and the size of the response block.

Web servers typically perform logging of an HTTP request in either the Common Log File (CLF) format or the Extended Log File (XLF) format. XLF is a superset of CLF because XLF includes logging of HTTP request and response headers. The CLF log file format was developed by the National Center for Supercomputing Applications (NCSA) and has become the standard logging format for most Web servers. The XLF format is not yet a recognized standard. Rather than use a proposed standard, each vendor (including Oracle) has its own proprietary XLF format.

Getting Further Information on Log File Formats

For technical information on log file formats, consult the World Wide Web Consortium Web site at www.w3.org. The working draft (it's been in a working draft status since 1996) for the Extended Log File format can be found at the following URL: http://www.w3.org/pub/WWW/TR/WD-logfile.html.

Looking at Web Site Management Tools

Site management (SM) tools are used to gather and report statistical data regarding activity on your Web server. This is accomplished through swift analysis of the raw data stored by the OAS Logger. In today's competitive marketplace, any information that can be learned about a customer visiting your Web site can be of great worth. Essentially, the SM user can learn what people are looking for on a Web site, how the contents of a Web site are being accessed, who the most common visitors are, and which links are repeatedly accessed. Armed with this information, you can organize a Web site more efficiently.

In today's highly competitive electronic commerce and dot com information technology market, any information collected about your public audience can serve invaluably for strategizing a solid marketing campaign. Because the largest portion of most Internet-based business' budget is advertising, the analysis of this information can prove to be of exceptionally high value.

SM tools have even found their place within our criminal justice system. Investigators have revealed that Web management tools have helped them to quickly identify perpetrators of electronic viruses (for example, the Melissa virus in 1999). The power driving these tools comes from their capability to crunch data stored within the Web server's log files. Furthermore, sophisticated graphical reports are generated from these tools, offering an array of choices for customizing output. Features common to the leading SM tools include multilanguage reporting, scheduled reporting, and several reporting platform options: Excel, Word, HTML, text file format, and email.

Too many SM vendors exist to list within this chapter. However, when shopping for a SM tool, narrow the selection by comparing the business needs (for example, volume of log files, frequency of reporting, and OS platform) to the core features offered by SM tools. Particular mention will be given later in this chapter to Oracle's SM tool of choice, WebTrends Log Analyzer, shipped on the OAS partner CD in a trial format. If you would like to find these tools through a search engine, type **Site Management**. The original feature of the SM tools is rooted in an advanced Web server log analysis capability. SM vendors are extending the product scope to merge technology with consumer demand. These tools have become strong and dependable for advanced reporting on the activity of your Web server. iLux and WebTrends are two examples of a SM product with feature offerings that continue to grow.

Reviewing the iLux Solutions

The iLux Suite 2000 (www.ilux.com) consists of five components to fulfill your entire research and marketing needs, as shown in Table 26-1.

Product Name	Product Description
iLux Enterprise 2000	The foundation product gathering data from multiple sources (Web servers, corporate databases, and call center databases) to develop comprehensive market research analyses and reports.
iLux Focus 2000	An in-depth market segment identification and reporting tool that yields additional personalization and segmentation functions for comprehensive e-marketing campaigns.
iLux Campaign Manager 2000	One-stop marketing manager, providing a single console to define, set up, schedule, and monitor all e-marketing campaigns for all channels: Web, mail, phone, and store. For real-time e-commerce sites, iLux Campaign Manager 2000 enables marketers to deliver marketing messages through online dynamic banners, personalized pop-billboards, email, and offline direct mail.
iLux Commerce Center 2000	An integrated marketing facility for call centers and corporate sales personnel. Telemarketers and order fulfillment personnel can use a single interface to leverage outbound and inbound phone calls with information gathered by the iLux Enterprise 2000.
iLux InStore E-Pilot 2000	From a kiosk located inside the retail store, shoppers have access to personalized purchase recommendations. This electronic sales associate provides individual customer service without the need for hiring additional store personnel.

TABLE 26-1. *iLux Product Line*

The biggest advantage of the iLux product line is that it is Java-based. Therefore, it is platform-independent. Another advantage of the iLux suite is it tends to be more geared towards marketing than many other products. iLux understands and can interpret the Oracle XLF format. The downside to the iLux tools, compared to others, is their complexity.

Comparing WebTrends Solutions

Once you have determined you want to create reports based on the data coming from your Web server's log files, you can create a profile in WebTrends and away you go. The product is truly that simple. A WebTrends profile points to where your log files are stored. WebTrends supports analysis of access, referrer, and agent log files. You can also specify how you want these log files analyzed and whether you want any filters applied to the data. The profile settings are reflected in the generated output in the form of a Web log analysis report.

WebTrends provides a number of key features and products to help you analyze your Web logs. These tools and features are listed in Table 26-2. The log analysis of WebTrends provides roughly 100 reports for your review. Even though WebTrends comes on Oracle's partner CD, it cannot read the Oracle Logger Tables, nor can it read the Oracle XLF files. WebTrends can only read CLF files. Despite the number of calls, this issue remains unresolved.

However, WebTrends produces a number of valuable reports, including the following:

- **General statistics reports** Introduction, general statistics, server statistics
- **Resources accessed** Most requested pages, most requested content groups, least requested pages, entry pages, exit pages, single access pages, most accessed directories, paths through site, most downloaded file, most uploaded file, submitted forms, and dynamic page parameters
- **Dynamic page details** Downloaded file types
- **Advertising** Top advertising, advertising views, and clicks
- **Visitors and demographics** Visits per user, new versus returning users, authenticated users, users most active, countries, North American states and provinces, most active cities, most active organizations, and organization breakdown
- **Activity statistics** Summary of activity for report, period summary of activity by time, increment activity level by day of week, activity level by hour, and bandwidth

- **Technical statistics** Web server/technical information, server cluster load-balance (server cluster add-on), forms submitted by users, browser/client errors, page not found (404) errors, and server errors
- **Referrers and keywords** Referring sites, referring URLs, search engines, search phrases, search phrases by engine, search keywords, search keywords by engine, search keywords, and phrases by engine
- **Browsers and platforms** All browsers, Netscape browsers by version, Microsoft browsers by version, visiting spiders, most-used platforms, and operating systems

Do you want to reinvent all of these reports? Table 26-2 contains a list of reports that analysis tools, such as WebTrends, will provide.

As previously mentioned, WebTrends communicates an overall focus on delivering finite statistics and advanced reporting on every component of your Web server. On the other hand, iLux has placed great emphasis on how their total product can help you to better strategize a marketing campaign.

WebTrends Log Analysis

With a brief overview of how WebTrends acts as a reporting mechanism for your Web logs, let us analyze Web Server log extracts from actual access, referrer, and agent file reports. Web servers typically generate an access log automatically. The Web server records information, such as the user and the URL they requested.

Access Log: Activity Level by Hour of the Day

The Activity Level by Hour of the Day report shows the most and the least active hours of the day for the report period. The report also includes a table that breaks down activity to show the average for each individual hour of the day. If several days exist within the report period, the value presented is the sum of all hits during that period of time for all days. This information will determine whether the Web site is being hit 24 hours a day and if there is a pattern of downtime (for backups and so forth). It also provides you with insight into how "globally" your site is accessed. If peak hours tend to be obvious and pretty close to your hours of business, then your site is probably not "global."

Access Log: Most Active Organizations

The Most Active Organizations report identifies the companies or organizations that access your Web site most often. Without the use of this report, we would have never known that Oracle was the number one company hitting our Web site. It can also help you judge what you want to include on the next revision of your Web site. Based on the domain, you can direct people to a specific portion of your site. For

Component Name	Component Description
Web Server Traffic Analysis	Provide detailed Web site analysis and traffic reporting to others in your organization
Streaming Media Server Analysis	Understand the details of streaming media usage on your site, including the most popular clips, stops, starts, replays, and so forth
Proxy Server Analysis	Track the usage trends of your intranet and better understand your users' productivity
Link Analysis and Quality Control	Improve the quality, performance, and integrity of your Web site
Site Manager	Gain a visual understanding of your Web site's structure and layout
Monitoring, Alerting, and Recovery	Keep your Web site up and running at all times
ClusterTrends Server Cluster Add-On (Optional)	Accurately analyze Web site traffic and technical performance across clusters of local or geographically dispersed servers
DBTrends technology	Correlate information from existing ODBC databases with results from WebTrends data analysis
FastTrends ODBC technology	Export results from WebTrends FastTrends database to high-end Oracle, Microsoft SQL, Sybase, Informix, and other ODBC-compliant databases for further data analysis

TABLE 26-2. *WebTrends Features and Functionality*

example, a major hardware vendor once directed every request coming from their competitors' domain to their job listings.

Access Log: Most Downloaded Files

The Most Downloaded Files report identifies the most popular file downloads from your Web site. If an error occurred during the transfer, that transfer is not counted. TUSC has hundreds of documents available for download on our site. It is helpful for us to understand which papers and presentations people are downloading, so we can plan future presentations on the key topics people want to hear. Our mission is to make a difference, and this report helps us measure just how effective we are in making a difference for people's companies.

Access Log: Bandwidth

The Bandwidth report helps you understand the bandwidth requirements of your site by indicating the volume of activity as Kbytes transferred. This is useful information for judging your telecommunications requirements if you host your site internally. It is also useful for determining your ISP bandwidth requirements.

Referrer Log Analysis

Referrer is defined as the URL of an HTML page from which a visitor clicks to access your site. A referrer log file is generated by the Web server. The data contained within this log file is used to identify who is accessing your Web site. What sites are people coming from to access your site (referring URLs)? What are they searching for? What search engines are they using to hit your site?

Referrer Log: Top Referring Sites

The Top Referring Sites report identifies the domain names or numeric IP addresses with links to your site. This information will only be displayed if your server is logging this information. The data is useful for determining how effectively your advertising dollars are spent and who you should thank for providing a link to your site.

Referrerer Log: Top Search Engines By Keyword

How about finding out what search engines are returning your Web site as the result of a keyword search? This information will provide you with valuable information for your Meta tags and keywords when submitting to the search engines.

Agent Log Analysis

The Web server can generate an agent log that maintains information on the operating system and browser used by visitors to your Web site. The following subsections are a few reporting samples from this particular log file.

Agent Log: Most Used Browsers

The Most Used Browsers report identifies the most popular WWW browsers used by visitors to your site. This information will only be displayed if your server is logging the browser/platform information. With this knowledge, you can take measures to ensure your Web site is compliant with these browsers. WebTrends will break down each of the browser versions that visitors are using to access your site.

Agent Log: Most Used Platforms

The Most Used Platforms report identifies the operating systems most used by the visitors to your Web site. This information is useful for determining compliance with these platforms.

Link Analysis

WebTrends can crawl through your site and offer suggestions for repairing and optimizing your site. As you add more links, the task of testing your site may become time-consuming. A Web site analysis tool can save you time by automating the task. Within your link analysis profile, you indicate to WebTrends the location of the Web site you want to analyze and how you want the site checked. WebTrends locates the starting URL and walks through the site, checking all internal and external links according to your profile settings.

The following subsections are sample extracts from a WebTrends Link Analysis report. Information from these reports will prove helpful in debugging and improving your site.

Link Analysis: Broken Pages

The Link Analysis: Broken Pages report will provide information similar to the following: "2 pages (.01%) contain broken links. Refer to the Broken Pages section for further details."

Link Analysis: Suggestions for Improvements

The Link Analysis: Suggestions for Improvements report will provide you with a number of suggestions for how to improve your Web site. For example: "Of the 90 pages on this site, 5 could be improved by adding titles, and ALT attributes, or height and width attributes to images. ALT attributes give a description of the image for visitors who view the page in text mode (this description is also displayed while the page loads, and before the image appears). Height and width attributes enable browsers to load images faster." Tip: Always use height/width attributes for images embedded within HTML tables. A browser will not display an HTML table until it knows how to size its borders. Without the height/width tag attributes, the browser will wait until all images are completely downloaded before displaying the table.

Link Analysis: Site Statistics by Link Types

The Link Analysis: Site Statistics by Link Types report will provide you with analysis of your link types, for example: "Of the 5268 total links on this site, 95 percent are HTTP, 0 percent are FTP, and the remaining are of email, news, gopher, or other types."

Link Analysis: Oldest and Newest Pages

The Link Analysis: Oldest and Newest Pages report provides information about the oldest and newest pages on your Web site. For example, "The oldest HTML page was last modified on Wed Nov 30 19:02:52 1999. The most recent change was made on Tue Nov 24 17:54:15 2000 at page: http://www.tusc.com/consulting/emrgtech.html."

Link Analysis: Biggest (Slowest) Pages

The Link Analysis: Biggest (Slowest) Pages report will provide statistics about the slowest pages throughout your site. For example: "This site contains 90 HTML pages, with a combined total size of 5021 kilobytes (including all graphics and other linked files). The bigger the pages, the slower they load, which may be a problem if the majority of your visitors use dial-up connections. Refer to the Biggest Pages section for further details."

Defining the WRB Log and Listener Log

Logging can be captured at two levels within OAS: the Web Request Broker (WRB) and the listener. The OAS logging services provide a centralized location for collecting and examining alert, warning, and error messages from all components of an OAS application. At the WRB level, activities on every listener port on the Web server are logged under the same file in Extended Log File (XLF) format. You can turn the logging on/off, set the destination (FS – file system or DB – database), set the directory and file, and set the archive size and the directory.

The Logger is the primary component of the Log Server. Log Analyzer is another available component. Together, they provide the capability to collect and analyze information about people visiting your Web sites, all from a centralized location. The listeners can write their own (decentralized) log files, if you prefer. Visitors automatically identify themselves to the Logger, which captures this key data. Data, such as the visitor's IP address, domain name, OS platform, and browser type, are collected and stored by the Logger. With this type of information, you can identify where the visitor went when he or she arrived at your site; each distinct date, time, and URL requested; how long they stayed at your site, and so forth.

The Common Log Format (CLF) and Extended Log Format (XLF) logs contain information logged by the Web Listener. CLF is an industry standard logging format. Every SM tool can process the CLF logs. The XLF logs contain further information than a CLF log. XLF is a vendor-specific file format. If you purchase an SM tool and plan to process XLF logs, be sure the tool you are planning to purchase supports the Oracle XLF logs. OAS provides you with the option to write the logs in either XLF or CLF.

The second type of logging is system message logging. The system message log contains information logged by the WRB, through its cartridges, components, and third-party developed cartridges. The messages in the system message log will enable you to trace or debug a specific component that is providing information to the logger.

The final WRB log contains client-defined name-value pairs for use with logging performance statistics and debugging information. You can use this information to monitor a specific component, such as CPU load and queue length. For example, a cartridge can log specific name-value pairs in the Cartridge Parameters form under the Applications folder, which the Logger uses to generate component specific components. As another example, queue length=5 is a name-value pair which the Logger would log.

As previously mentioned, logging can also occur from the OAS Listener. The listener cannot log requests to the database; rather, log files are written to the file system. Whether you use the OAS Spyglass Listener or another listener (for example, Apache), they all write file-based log files. As detailed in Chapter 2, the OAS Utilities function provides tools to enable certain HTTP Listeners to work with OAS. The NT release of the OAS will detect the presence of third-party HTTP Listeners during the installation process and will ask the administrator which of the listeners they would like to use as the default HTTP. At the listener level, logging occurs for only one listener. You may specify the rollover parameter to define how often you want to roll over the log files. Valid values are daily, weekly, monthly, and never. For most sites, monthly should be adequate. Time styles, which instruct the way time stamps should be written in log files, may also be specified. Possible values for the report format are local time (default) and Greenwich Mean Time (GMT). Local time is typically preferred over Greenwich Mean Time (GMT). Common Log File format (CLF) or the Extended Log File (XLF) format may be specified.

Another logging level is for each OAS cartridge. Identical to listener logs, listener logs are only written to the file system, not to the database. The cartridge logs can provide you with information specific to the cartridge.

Adjusting the Severity Settings for the PL/SQL Cartridge

As previously mentioned, OAS cartridges can write logs. The PL/SQL cartridge is no exception. For the PL/SQL cartridge, you can turn logging on or off, specify the log directory, the filename, and the severity level. The PL/SQL cartridge severity levels are defined in Table 26-3.

Error Type	Severity Level	Recommended Uses
Fatal errors	0	Indicates a core failure occurred
Soft errors	1–3	Use 1 for a file or resource access failure
Warning	4–6	Use 4 for a configuration error
Tracing	7–10	Use 7 to indicate entry into the initialization, termination, or reloading states Use 8 to indicate entry into the authentication or execution states Use 9 or 10 to indicate messages defined by a cartridge or the WRB
Debugging	11–15	Use 11 for printing debugging variables

TABLE 26-3. *Conventional Use of Logging Severity*

Understanding the Logger

The Logger has three main functions. First, the Logger generates different statistics concerning incoming HTTP requests. The different requests from the HTTP Listener that the Logger is able to record include the IP address of clients, methods of the HTTP requests, and the URL. The Logger also logs HTTP requests and response headers, such as user agent. Second, the Logger can log system messages of each individual component of OAS. These components may include a cartridge, dispatcher, adapter, and any other component of OAS. The messages are used for debugging, tracing, and monitoring purposes. A severity level is associated with each message. The severity level indicates the significance of each message. For example, when the severity level is 7, the Logger logs all messages with a severity level below or equal to 7. More detailed logging messages will be retrieved when you use a higher number. Table 26-4 describes the severity levels.

Thirdly, the Logger can record client-defined attributes for each component in the form of name-value pairs. You can use the information provided to monitor a specific component. CPU load and/or queue lengths are examples of possible attributes. Each component decides what attributes to log; therefore, total logging flexibility is given to each component.

Severity Level	Description	Comments
0	Fatal errors	A core init, malloc, or any other error that is fatal such that the process has to exit.
1–3	General errors	An error writing to a file or database or accessing a resource in general.
4–6	Warnings	A missing directory, file, service, or section in a configuration file. These will not kill the process.
7–8	Tracing information	7—Any messages that occur in ini, shutdown, and reload stages for the cartridges; for example, SSI has been initialized. For the WRB, messages indicating a service has been loaded successfully, terminated successfully, or reloaded. 8—Any messages that occur in authentication and execution stages for the cartridges; for example, request foo has been executed. For the WRB, messages indicating a request for a particular service, or any messages that occur in the execution path of carrying out the request for a service.
9–10	Tracing information (continued)	Messages defined by a cartridge or the WRB.
11–15	Debugging information	Logging of certain variables or arguments; for example, foo=5.

TABLE 26-4. *Web Request Broker Logging File (wrb.log) Severity Levels*

Logging Usage to the Database

To store the Logger information in the database, you must first create (or install) the Logger Tables. This operation is performed by selecting OAS Utilities from the OAS Node Manager's Main Menu. Next, open the Utilities folder, then the Install folder, and click on Logger Tables. To create the Logger Tables, you must first establish a DAD for the Logger Tables. If you click on Create New DAD, a page identical to Figure 26-1 will appear. The DAD identifies the database schema

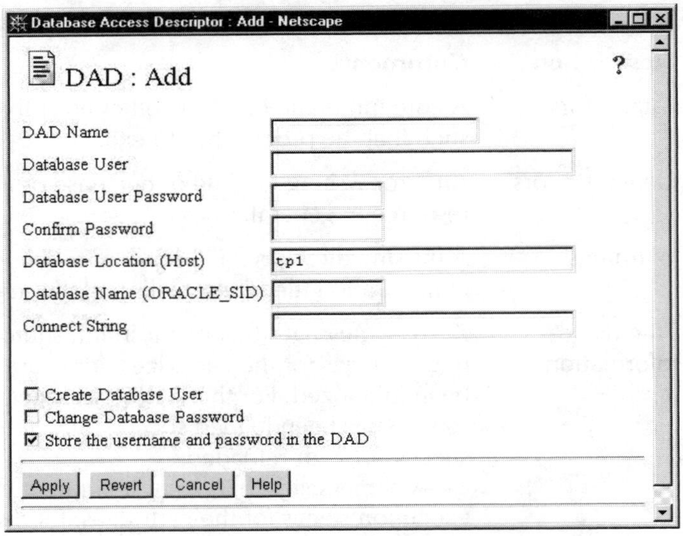

FIGURE 26-1. *Create a new DAD*

under which to install all required Logger Tables. You can also select an existing DAD. If you must first create a DAD, follow the instructions in Chapter 4 for this operation. Once you select a DAD, click Apply. The Logger Tables will be created in the corresponding schema.

The database tables listed in Table 26-5 are created to store log information:

Logxlf	Stores all XLF information, except the HTTP headers
Logxlfheader	Stores all HTTP response and request headers
Logsysmsg	Stores system messages for each individual component of the OAS
Logattrib	Stores client-defined attributes for each component

TABLE 26-5. *Logger Tables*

A sequence called XLFSEQ is created to match up an entry in the Logxlf table with the entries in the Logxlfheader table. For further information about these tables, refer to the fields in Tables 26-6 and 26-7.

If you wish to use the Log Analyzer, after installing the Logger Tables click on Log Analyzer under the Utilities/Install folder as previously described. First, choose the DAD used by the Log Analyzer. The DAD will be the same DAD you stored the tables within. The next tip discusses the Log Analyzer in further detail.

Developing Your Own Reports from the Logger Tables

The Logxlf and Logxlfheader tables contain valuable information that can be mined. You may elect to purchase a tool, such as WebTrends or iLux, but maybe your log query needs are not as extensive. Tables 26-6 and 26-7 illustrate the columns for each of the tables.

Column	Information in Table
ENTRY_DATE	Date and time of entry was recorded
USEC	
WRB	
COMPONENT	
ID	
XLFSEQ	Link to the Logxlfheader
TIME_TAKEN	Time taken to complete the transaction
BYTES	Content-length of the transferred document
CACHED	Was the cache hit for the results?
C_IP	Client's IP address and port
C_DNS	Client's DNS name

TABLE 26-6. *Logxlf Table's Columns*

Column	Information in Table
S_IP	Server's IP address and port
S_DNS	Server's DNS name
SC_STATUS	Server-to-client status code
C_AUTH_ID	Client username for authentication
SC_COMMENT	Status code comment
CS_METHOD	Client method (GET and POST)
CS_URI_STEM	Client-to-server stem portion of URI, omitting the query
CS_URI_QUERY	Client-to-server query portion of URI, omitting the stem
CS_PROTOCOL	HTTP protocol version

TABLE 26-6. *Logxlf Table's Columns* (continued)

The data in the Logxlfheader table comes from the HTTP header of the request, such as Cookie, User-Agent, Accept-Language, or Client-ip information. The following is an example of a record from this table:

```
Hname = User-Agent

Hvalue = Mozilla/4.0 (compatible; MSIE 4.0; Windows 95)
```

Column	Information in Table
XLFSEQ	Link to Logxlf
PREFIX	cs for request header record and sc for response header record
HNAME	Name of the HTTP header
HVALUE	Value of the HTTP header

TABLE 26-7. *Logxlfheader Table's Columns*

The following procedure extracts, displays, and graphs key information from the Logger Tables:

```
PROCEDURE LOG_SUMMARY (refresh number default 600)
is
  cursor distinct_dates is
  select distinct trunc(entry_date) dedate
    from logxlf
   order by trunc(entry_date) desc;

  cursor distinct_ips is
  select count(distinct c_ip) dip
    from logxlf
   group by trunc(entry_date)
   order by trunc(entry_date) desc;

  cursor distinct_dns is
  select count(distinct c_dns) ddns
    from logxlf
   group by trunc(entry_date)
   order by trunc(entry_date) desc;

  cursor distinct_uri is
  select count(distinct cs_uri_query) duri
    from logxlf
   group by trunc(entry_date)
   order by trunc(entry_date) desc;

  server  varchar2(100) := owa_util.get_cgi_env('SERVER_NAME');
begin
htp.htmlOpen;
htp.headOpen;
htp.meta('Refresh',NULL,refresh);
htp.title('Summary Statistics for '||server||' Web Server');
htp.headClose;
htp.bodyOpen;
htp.header(1,'Summary Statistics for '||server||' Web Server');
htp.tableOpen('BORDER=2');
htp.tableRowOpen;
htp.tableHeader('Distinct');
for dates_rec in distinct_dates loop
  htp.tableHeader(dates_rec.dedate);
end loop;
htp.tableRowClose;
htp.tableRowOpen;
htp.tableHeader('IPs');
for ip_rec in distinct_ips loop
  htp.tableData(ip_rec.dip);
end loop;
htp.tableRowClose;
htp.tableRowOpen;
htp.tableHeader('DNSs');
```

```
for dns_rec in distinct_dns loop
  htp.tableData(dns_rec.ddns);
end loop;
htp.tableRowClose;
htp.tableRowOpen;
htp.tableHeader('URIs');
for uri_rec in distinct_uri loop
  htp.tableData(uri_rec.duri);
end loop;
htp.tablerowClose;
htp.tableClose;
htp.formOpen('log_summary','GET');
htp.tableOpen('BORDER=5');
htp.tableRowOpen;
htp.tableData('Last Refresh');
htp.tableData('Refresh in ');
htp.tableData('Next Refresh');
htp.tableRowClose;
htp.tableRowOpen;
htp.tableData(to_char(sysdate,'mm/dd/yy hh24:mi:ss'));
htp.tableData(htf.formText('refresh',5,5,refresh)||' seconds'||htf.formSubmit);
htp.tableData(to_char(sysdate+refresh/86400,'mm/dd/yy hh24:mi:ss'));
htp.tableRowClose;
htp.tableClose;
htp.formClose;
owa_chart.show_chart(
  q => 'select  null the_link, ' ||
       '      trunc(entry_date) the_text, ' ||
       '      count(distinct cs_uri_query) the_value ' ||
       'from   logxlf '||
       'group  by trunc(entry_date) '||
       'order  by trunc(entry_date) desc',
   chart_type  => 'HBAR',
   bar_image   => 'MULTI',
   image_locat  => '/img/',
   chart_title  => 'Distinct URIs by Day',
   font_size   => '-2',
   show_summary => 'CAMXVS');
owa_chart.show_chart(
  q => 'select  null the_link, ' ||
       '      to_char(entry_date,''hh24'') the_text, ' ||
       '      count(distinct cs_uri_query) the_value ' ||
       'from   logxlf '||
       'group  by to_char(entry_date,''hh24'') '||
       'order  by to_char(entry_date,''hh24'')',
   chart_type  => 'HBAR',
   bar_image   => 'MULTI',
   image_locat  => '/img/',
   chart_title  => 'Distinct URIs by Hour of the Day',
   font_size   => '-2',
   show_summary => 'CAMXVS');
owa_chart.show_chart(
```

```
  q => 'select  to_char(entry_date,''D'') the_link, ' ||
       '       to_char(entry_date,''Day'') the_text, ' ||
       '       count(distinct cs_uri_query) the_value ' ||
       'from   logxlf '||
       'group  by to_char(entry_date,''D''),to_char(entry_date,''Day'') '||
       'order  by to_char(entry_date,''D'')',
   chart_type   => 'VBAR',
   bar_image    => 'MULTI',
   image_locat  => '/img/',
   chart_title  => 'Distinct URIs by Day of Week',
   font_size    => '-2',
   show_summary => 'CAMXVS');
htp.bodyClose;
htp.htmlClose;
end;
```

Reviewing the XLF Logging Parameters

This chapter has introduced the two main components of the Log Server: Logger and Log Analyzer. These Log Server components enable you to write log files to the database as an alternative to storing them on the file system.

By default, the OAS Logger captures the clf, cs (User-Agent), and cs(Referrer) fields. These constitute XLF logging (because user agent and referrer data are collected in addition to the clf data).

The text box labeled XLF fields in Figure 26-2 is the location to define the specific fields to log. To specify the values, enter the fields separated by spaces. Table 26-8 describes the values available.

Getting the Most Out of the Log Analyzer

The Log Analyzer is a set of packages whose purpose is to analyze the Logger information. Log Analyzer functions can be categorized into three main areas:

- Analyze OAS activity and provide reports
- Enable reports that indicate which Web sites are being accessed
- Enable viewing of performance statistics

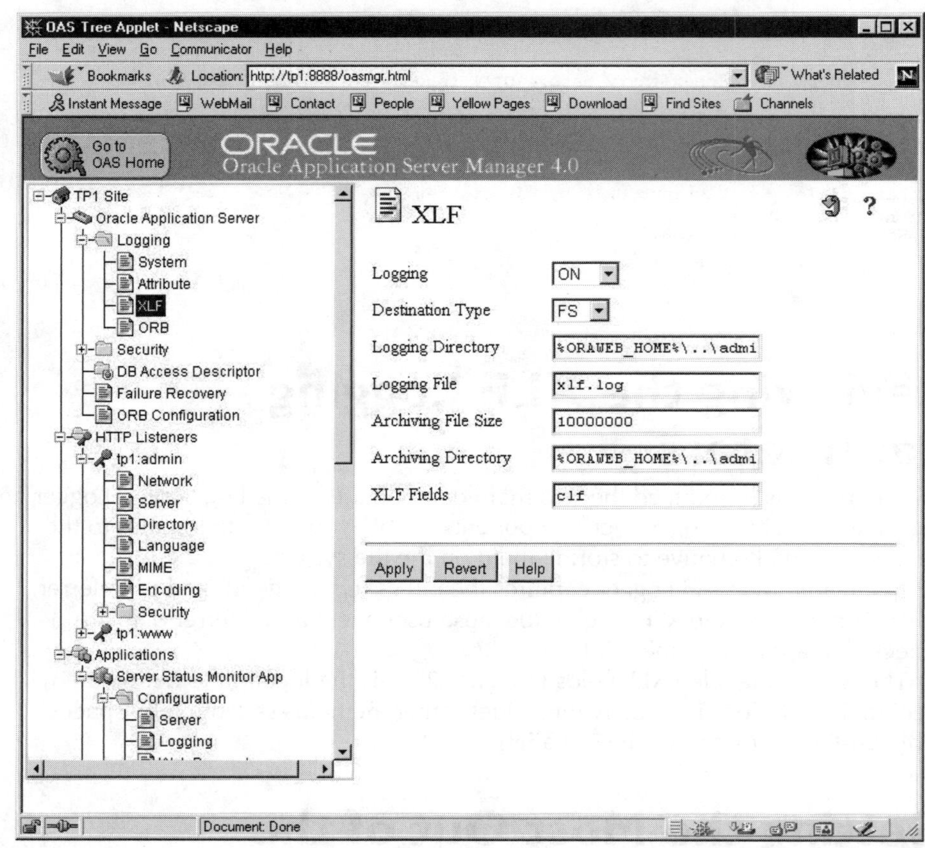

FIGURE 26-2. *XLF logging parameters*

Value	Description
Clf	Fields that would normally be written to a Common Log File (CLF) format file. Those include cauth-id, [clf-date], "request line," and sc-status bytes
cs (User-Agent)	Information about the user agent originating the request

TABLE 26-8. *XLF Logging Parameters*

Value	Description
cs (Referrer)	Allows the client to specify the address (URI) of the resource from which the Request-URL was obtained
clf-date	Date and time of the request in the same format as used in the CLF: [dd/mm/yyyy:hour:minutes:seconds GMT_offset]
c-auth-id	Username if the request contained an attempt to authenticate
Bytes	Content-length of the transferred document
date	Date at which the transaction completed
time	Time at which the transaction completed
time-taken	Amount of time taken (in seconds) for transaction to complete
c-ip	Client's IP address and port
s-ip	Server's IP address and port
c-dns	Client's DNS name
s-dns	Server's DNS name
sc-status	Server-to-client status code
sc-comment	Server-to-client comment returned with the status code
cs-method	Server-to-client method (GET, POST, or others)
cs-protocol	HTTP protocol version
cs-uri	Client-to-server URI
cs-uri-stem	Client-to-server stem portion of URI, omitting the query
cs-uri-query	Client-to-server query portion of URI, omitting the stem
prefix (header):	Header is an HTTP header field and prefix is one of the following: c: client s: server r: remote cs: client-to-server sc: server-to-client

TABLE 26-8. *XLF Logging Parameters* (continued)

The main purpose of Log Analyzer is to provide reports using the raw data stored by the Logger. After installing the Log Analyzer as previously described, you can access the Log Analyzer through the OAS Manager, under Applications.

The XLF reporting of the Log Analyzer, shown in Figure 26-3, includes predefined reports, including the following:

- Average bytes per day
- Average bytes per hour
- Average requests per hour
- Average requests per day
- Top client by byte count
- Top client by URL count
- Top URL
- Total requests

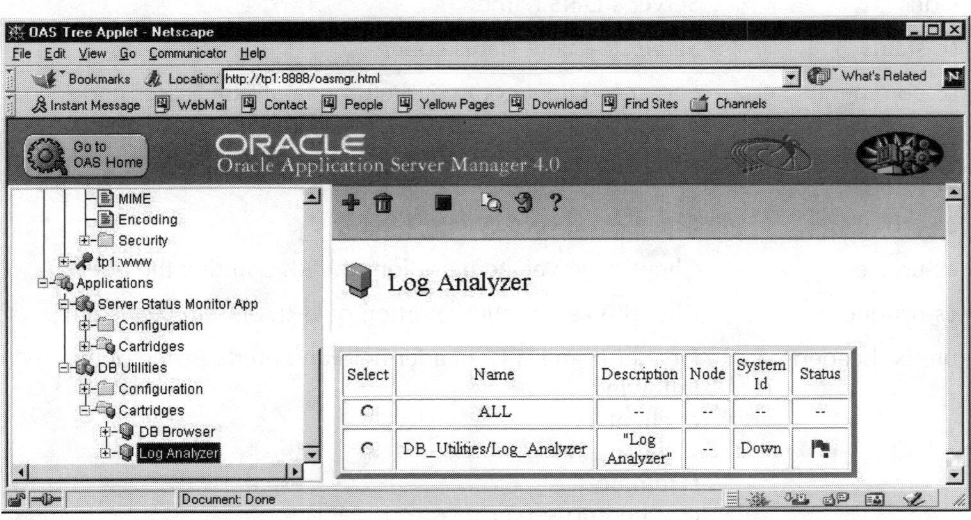

FIGURE 26-3. *Log Analyzer Selection*

These predefined reports are available directly from the Log Analyzer. Custom reports are easily created using Log Analyzer or using your own PL/SQL code. The information from the log reports can help you with scalability, performance, and load-balancing issues.

The information the Log Analyzer provides is important to determine how the contents of a Web site are being accessed, who the most common visitors are, or which links are repeatedly accessed. This information can help you organize the Web site information more efficiently. For example, if your reports indicated that over 20 percent of your visitors requested a particular page, consider putting a hyperlink to that page directly from your home page.

The Log Analyzer can also determine which times are peak hours, so you can evaluate the performance characteristics of the servers at those times. Overall, the Log Analyzer generates meaningful but not extensive information about the activities of a Web site. Consider purchasing one of the previously mentioned products for in-depth site analysis.

Reporting Usage from the Database – Default XLF Reports

A number of XLF Log Reports are provided with the Log Analyzer. These can be found under the Utilities/Log Analyzer folder. Use the XLF Log Reports form to create, delete, or run reports. To run a default report, select the required report, choose Run to run the report, then interpret the results.

Setting the Log Analyzer Parameters for User-Defined XLF Reports

You can use the Add/Modify XLF Report form to create your own statistics or modify an existing XLF report. You can define your queries to determine information, such as how the contents of a Web site are being accessed or which links are repeatedly accessed. This information can help you with performance, scalability, and load-balancing issues. The available field names for user-defined XLF reports include the following: client IP address, client host, URL, bytes, status, method, domain, country, auth id, server IP address, server host, date, and time. Report modifiers specify the ways to modify the generated report:

- **Dimension** Enables you to display a fixed number of rows.
- **Sort by** Sorts a particular operation or report field. It is not allowed to sort a field when Display = No and Operation = NULL.

- **Sort Order** Specifies the order to sort the results: ascending (lowest number at the top of the report) or descending (highest number at the top of the report).

Setting Log Analyzer Parameters for User-Defined System Message Reports

Use the Submit System Messages Report form to create your own system messages report. You can create your own set of queries to trace a specific component providing information to the Logger. The Severity Level field indicates the severity of the system message. It has three operator choices: =, >, and <. Therefore, you can generate statistics, such as all the severity levels > 8. The possible values are 0–15 (refer to Table 26-3).

Uploading Log Files into the Database to Create User-Defined Log Reports

Once the Log Analyzer has been configured for logging to the database, you can upload log files into the database and create user-defined log reports. Navigate to the OAS Utilities (OAS 4.0) or the Log Analyzer Administration page (OWAS 3.0) to upload a log file into the Logger database tables using a generated log file.

Summary

OAS provides a comprehensive solution for fully monitoring activity on your Web server. Whether it is logging information about the visitors to your Web site(s) or individual OAS component logging, the capability to capture this information is integrated into the OAS full-scale Web solution product.

PART VI

Appendix

APPENDIX A

Good Sites

he Web contains thousands of sites that provide valuable information on Oracle's Application Server and related topics. As this information is constantly being added to and updated, you are encouraged to make use of the Internet search engines in the following table to get an updated list of sites that relate to this subject. This appendix attempts to list numerous sites relating to this technology, but this list is meant only as a starting point.

Note regarding comments: Many of the comments were directly copied from the Web sites. They have been placed here to assist you in finding the Web sites that may be of particular interest to you, in the unlikely case that the URLs have changed since this book was published.

Site Type	Site Address	Comments
CGI	http://scriptsearch.internet.com	World's largest CGI library for developers.
CGI	http://www.boutell.com/cgic/	cgic: an ANSI C library for CGI programming.
CGI	http://www.olab.com/cdk/content/samples/cdk/cdg/cdg6.htm	Migrating CGI programs to cartridges.
Cold Fusion	http://webnet-global.com/cold_fusion_wng.html	Cold Fusion hosting.
Cold Fusion	http://www.bo.uiowa.edu/~home/coldf.htm	Information on Cold Fusion, including documentation, utilities, and examples.
Cold Fusion	http://www.futuresystems.com/coldfusion.htm	Discusses the features of Cold Fusion's latest release; this site contains several examples.
Cold Fusion	http://www-a.developer.com/directories/pages/dir.cfm.development.hosting.html	Very complete site. Contains information on ActiveX, C++, Case and Modeling, Cold Fusion, CGI, Delphi, HTML and DHTML, Java, JavaScript, Middleware, Perl, Security, Visual Basic, VRML, XML, and Year 2000.
Cold Fusion for Solaris	http://143.54.5.204/cfdocs/aboutdocs.htm	Documentation for Solaris and Windows.
Cold Fusion for Solaris	http://www.target4.com/cfassolarisfaq.htm	Offers an overview of Cold Fusion on Solaris platforms and answers to frequently asked questions.

Site Type	**Site Address**	**Comments**
Color, use of on Web site	http://lightsphere.com/dev/	Kira's Web Toolbox. A good collection of tools for the Web developer, including color tools.
Color, use of on Web site	http://webdeveloper.com/design/design_choosing_colors.html	An excellent article on choosing colors for Web sites.
Color, use of on Web site	http://www.maximized.com/shareware/colorbrowser/	Color Browser 2.0 is a useful program to help pick colors when designing Web pages (or any other graphics work, for that matter). Color Browser can help you to pick browser-friendly colors, and copy the color string to the Clipboard so you can paste it into your HTML editor. The special Color Pick-Me-Up tool lets you pick up a color from anywhere on the screen!
Color, use of on Web site	http://www.phoenix.net/~jacobson/rgb.html	RGB color chart with HEX codes.
Cool site	http://www.efax.com	Receive faxes using email.
Cool site	http://www.esports-net.com	Well done site for tracking statistics for your team and/or league, tracking teams and rosters, running reports for statistics grouped by season, team, player, city, state, etc.
Cool site	http://www.evite.com	Electronic invitations on the Web, very well done.
Cool site	http://www.wisen.com	Well done OAS site for the service industry and households needing services.
Developer/2000	http://www.oracle.com/support/products/dev2k/win/html/doc.html	Documentation for Developer/2000.

Site Type	Site Address	Comments
Developer/2000	http://www.orafans.com/bbs/forms/bbs.htm	ORACLE User Forum: ORACLE Forms & Designer/2000 Conference.
Developer's guide and Web development sites	http://awsd.com/scripts/index.shtml	Contains a large number of valuable scripts pooled from a variety of sources.
Developer's guide and Web development sites	http://pinpub.com/oracle/home.htm	Oracle Developer site containing several useful tips including deploying Oracle WebForms, calling JavaScript effectively from PL/SQL, guidelines for defining domains in Developer 2000, three useful locking strategies, setting properties in Forms 4.5 for things that cannot be changed, and using owa_util.get_cgi_env to get the IP address.
Developer's guide and Web development sites	http://tinman.cs.gsu.edu:9001/ows-doc/books/runtimes.htm	Contains information on applications in general, including PL/SQL cartridge, JWeb cartridge, LiveHTML cartridge, Perl cartridge, C cartridge, JCOBRA, Enterprise JavaBeans, pl2Java, wrbjidl, and ODBC. There is also a valuable link for Cartridge Management Framework (CMF).
Developer's guide and Web development sites	http://webdeveloper.com/tutorials.html	Another excellent tool for all issues related to Web development. You will find tutorials on HTML, advanced HTML, CGI-Perl, design graphics, Java, JavaScript, multimedia, and site management. There is a wealth of information at this site, which will prove helpful for beginners and advanced Web developers.

Site Type	**Site Address**	**Comments**
Developer's guide and Web development sites	http://www.asis.com/meganm/links.html	Contains valuable information on HTML, Web graphics, CGI + Perl, counters and logs, frames, tables, Java and JavaScript, Server, and miscellaneous tips.
Developer's guide and Web development sites	http://www.dogtech.com/webcenter/	A comprehensive site offering excellent tutorials and tools for CGI, HTML and Dynamic HTML, JavaScript, images, audio, and more!
DHTML	http://www.insidedhtml.com	A comprehensive site for DHTML.
Flexible parameter passing	http://www.olab.com/doc/books/plsql/pl_invk.htm	Describes how to add PL/SQL applications to Oracle Application Server and how to invoke them from browsers.
Flexible parameter passing	http://www.olab.com/doc/books/plsql/plsqlix.htm	Index for the OAS online documentation.
Flexible parameter passing	http://www.rmoug.org/training.htm	A presentation by Bradley D. Brown & Scott Heaton highlights the differences between version 3 of Oracle Web Application Server and version 4 of Oracle Application Server. Participants will become familiar with some of the new features, including Oracle Application Server Java-based management tool, flexible parameter passing, executing SQL from disk, the monitor tool, and more.
	http://www.rmoug.org/pres/td9904sb.zip	Contains the above RMOUG presentation for download.
Glossary of Internet terms	http://www.matisse.net/files/glossary.html	Contains a very extensive glossary of terms used in Web Development. Highly recommended!

Site Type	Site Address	Comments
HTML	http://www.cnet.com/Content/Builder/Authoring/Htmltips/ss06.html	BUILDER.COM—Web authoring, HTML tips and tricks, all HTML tips.
HTML	http://www.cosy.sbg.ac.at/~lendl/tags.html	Tags with explanations for usage.
HTML	http://www.cs.cmu.edu/~tilt/cgh	Style guide and recommendations.
HTML	http://www.jmarshall.com/easy/html	HTML made easy.
HTML	http://www.liberate.com/	Liberate Technologies home page—formerly Oracle's Network Computing (NC).
HTML	http://www.olab.com/doc/books/plsql/pl_tut.htm	Displaying Oracle table as HTML.
HTML	http://www.w3.org/MarkUp/	Excellent overview.
HTML	http://www-pcd.stanford.edu/mogens/intro/tutorial.html	Overview and tutorial.
Internet browsers	http://www.sni.net/~duffy/browsers/	Rick Duffy's excellent browser usage report.
Internet commerce	http://gmccomb.com/commerce/	Web commerce cookbook.
Internet commerce	http://survey.com/onoracle.html	Top 50 E-Business ISV Challenge Sponsored by Oracle, Oracle Venture Fund, and CMP publications, this competition will recognize the top 50 e-business vendors and provide the opportunity for a select few to present to the Oracle Venture Fund.
Internet commerce	http://webreview.com/	Web Review – eCommerce Suites.
Internet commerce	http://www.greatcircle.com/	Great Circle Associates.

Site Type	Site Address	Comments
Internet usage	http://www.snopes.com/	Another good site for tracking down info about those bogus emails you get, most of which are hoaxes.
Internet usage	http://www.statmarket.com/	Statistics on Internet usage.
Java	http://Javaboutique.internet.com	The Java Boutique: The Ultimate Java Resource. Free Java applets.
Java	http://www.javaworld.com	They have a monthly email that contains good information about Java, XML, and so forth. Presentations focus especially on Web development under UNIX. The URL to subscribe is http://www.javaworld.com/common/jw-subscribe.html.
Java	http://library.advanced.org/13947/Java/jvariables.html	Variables.
Java	http://library.advanced.org/17862/jintro.htm	General information.
Java	http://library.advanced.org/17862/jvar.htm	Variables.
Java	http://ragnar.spinweb.net/programming/index.shtml	Collections of scripts and "how-to" advice.
Java	http://technet.oracle.com/software	Java Stored Procedures—How to write Java stored procedures, functions, triggers, and advanced topics. Look for the following features: JDBC and SQLJ, JDeveloper 2.0 free download, Oracle's JDeveloper, and Stored procedures

Site Type	Site Address	Comments
Java	http://technet.oracle.com/tech/Java/access/info/jdbcperf.pdf	ORACLE8i, JDBC performance. This technical paper describes how Oracle's JDBC drivers, optimized and tuned for the Oracle8i release, have been shown to outperform their strongest competitors.
Java	http://technet.oracle.com/tech/Java/info/otn.htm	Architecting Applications on OTN. This white paper discusses one of the major software components of OTN: its registration system. The paper shows how OTN, enabling new users to register online, and it describes the different modules that make up the registration system. **Note:** Requires OTN Login.
Java	http://www.cgi-Java.com	Collections of scripts and "how-to" advice.
Java	http://www.gamelan.com/	Java downloads.
Java	http://www.inf.fu-berlin.de/~bokowski/pmgJava/proposals.html	Variables: Includes new proposals.
Java	http://www.javasoft.com	General information.
Java	http://www.kacweb.com/Java/Javaticker/tickfeat.html	A server-push ticker applet for sale.
JavaScript	http://developer.netscape.com	Netscape's resource to help you build Web applications.
JavaScript	http://developer.netscape.com/library/documentation/communicator/jsguide4/index.htm	JavaScript guide.
JavaScript	http://developer.netscape.com/one/Javascript/resources.html	JavaScript resource sites that feature JavaScript resources and examples.

Site Type	Site Address	Comments
JavaScript	http://Javascript.internet.com	The JavaScript Source is an excellent JavaScript resource with tons of "cut & paste" JavaScript examples for your Web pages. All for free! We have put together a collection of hundreds of free JavaScripts that are available to you for use on your Web pages. These scripts are available via a user-friendly interface—including a working demo of all the scripts and a text box with the complete actual JavaScript coding used. To start, just select a JavaScript category from the Navigation menu on the right, browse our site contents, use 'Our Newest JavaScripts' pull-down menu (below), or check out our 'What's New?' page to view the latest scripts on our site.
JavaScript	http://Javascriptsource.internet.com	Hundreds of free JavaScripts for Web.
JavaScript	http://members.tripod.com/JavaScriptForum/	The JavaScript forum.
JavaScript	http://w3.one.net/ronlwzz/JavaScript.htm	Ron's JavaScript resources.
JavaScript	http://www.developer.com/directories/pages/dir.Javascript.html	JavaScript information provided by Developer.com.
JavaScript	http://www.dowebpages.com	Links for fun and/or exceptional utility programs. Review pages to see different features for development.
JavaScript	http://www.dummies.com	"Dummy" tips, newsletter, tips for JavaScript.
JavaScript	http://www.freqgrafx.com/411/	JavaScript 411 home page.

Site Type	**Site Address**	**Comments**
JavaScript	http://www.geocities.com/SiliconValley/7116/	The JavaScript Planet—Collection with 367 FREE examples!
JavaScript	http://www.hwg.org/resources/newtech/Javascript.html	JavaScript resources.
JavaScript	http://www.infohiway.com/Javascript/indexf.htm	Cut-n-Paste JavaScript.
JavaScript	http://www.intricate.com/Javascript/	JavaScript Planet v3.0.
JavaScript	http://www.javascripts.com/	Read all about this Web site: FAQ's, recommended browsers, support, and more! Enter Javascripts.com and access 2,717 free JavaScripts, tutorials, and more! Subscribe to OnFocus!, the JavaScripts.com weekly newsletter!
JavaScript	http://www.livesoftware.com/jrc/index.html	Live Software: JavaScript resource center.
JavaScript	http://www.serve.com/hotsyte/	HotSyte- The JavaScript resource.
JavaScript	http://www.webreference.com/js	Doc JavaScript (SM)—webreference.com.
JDBC & SQLJ	http://technet.oracle.com/software	JDBC & SQLJ—Connecting to single or multiple databases, using DML and various datatypes, and accessing PL/SQL and Java stored procedures. Large objects (LOBs), binary files (BFILEs), collections, streams, objects, datatype mapping, Oracle performance extensions, dynamic SQL, and programming with threads.

Site Type	Site Address	Comments
JDeveloper	http://technet.oracle.com/software	JDEVELOPER 2.0 free download Oracle JDeveloper 2.0 shifts balance of power in the Java Development tools arena. Get a free download or subscribe to the Internet Tools CD track. See how to build Internet-based business applications using JDBC and Oracle Application Server's JWeb and Java CORBA Object technologies.
Liquid Motion	http://webdeveloper.com/design/design_review_liquid-motion.html	Review of Liquid Motion.
Meta-Search search engines	http://www.askjeeves.com/ a.k.a. http://www.ask.com	Jeeves answers millions of questions. Just type a question and click "Ask!"
Meta-Search search engines	http://www.dogpile.com/	A search engine that allows you to search a number of other search engines and sources, including the Web, Usenet, Ftp, Newswires, BizNews, Stock Quotes, Weather, Yellow Pages, White Pages and Maps.
Meta-Search search engines	http://www.thebidhub.com/	The final destination for everything... megasearch, commerce, services, news, content, community, chat, auction, and beyond.
Multithreaded search engines	http://www.go2net.com/search.html	Searches a number of search engines, and provides valuable information about how people are querying the search engines. You can even view searches in real time.

Site Type	Site Address	Comments
Multithreaded search engines	http://www.highway61.com/	Highway 61 is a "metasearch" site. Your search will be sent to a number of Internet search engines and the results will be compiled into a single page.
Multithreaded search engines	http://www.savvysearch.com/	Enter your query to metasearch the major search engines and guides, or select one of the specialized metasearch or metashop categories.
Online Web development guides	http://pbs.mcp.com/	Contains online reference books on many subjects pertaining to Web development.
Oracle Application Server/Node Manager	http://Osprey7.Npac.Syr.Edu:3768/Reference-Docs/Cwou/Database/Ows/Ows.Html	An excellent overview of Oracle's Web Server.
Oracle Application Server/Node Manager	http://tinman.cs.gsu.edu:9001/ows-doc/books/inst_nt/post.htm	Explains how to get Oracle Application Server started and how to connect to the Node Manager and Administration Utilities listeners.
Oracle Application Server/Node Manager	http://www.dites.com.tr/oas.htm	A very complete presentation on Oracle's Web Server and its features.
Oracle Application Server/Node Manager	http://www.geocities.com/SiliconValley/Peaks/9111/	The Unofficial Oracle Web Server site.
Oracle Application Server/Node Manager	http://www.olab.com/doc/books/admin/adminix.htm	OAS Administration documentation online.

Site Type	Site Address	Comments
Oracle Application Server/Node Manager	http://www.olab.com/doc/books/admin/overview.htm	Oracle Application Server 4.0. Introduces the Oracle Application Server Manager, a new tool for the configuration and management of Oracle Application Server. This new interface uses both HTML forms and Java navigational applets to allow an administrator to maintain an Oracle Application Server site.
Oracle in general	http://gserver.grads.vt.edu/	RGS Oracle-PL/SQL-WWW interface.
Oracle in general	http://iseminar.oracle.com/iccdocs/seminarDesc.shtml	Extending The Oracle Enterprise to Mobile Users with Oracle8i. Joining this interactive online seminar will describe how to build and deploy low-TCO mobile applications to mobile users on Windows 95/NT, Windows CE, and Palm OS platforms. To register, visit the Web site.
Oracle in general	http://technet.oracle.com	ORACLE on NT CONTENT zone. Learn the technical details of the best development and deployment platform on Windows NT and download the Oracle Application Wizard for Microsoft Visual InterDev (Beta), Oracle AppWizard for Microsoft Visual C++, the Oracle8i COM Automation feature, and Oracle Objects for OLE.
Oracle in general	http://www.dejanews.com/~oracleappserver	Tired of sifting through hundreds of irrelevant database-related messages looking for that rare post about Oracle's Application Server family? Me too! So I took it upon myself to create a discussion forum just for Oracle Application Server developers and managers. (From the site's creator).

Site Type	Site Address	Comments
Oracle in general	http://www.olab.com/	Topics relating to OAS development.
Oracle in general	http://www.oracle.com/	Oracle Corporation's home page.
Oracle in general	http://www.technosolutions.com/oracle.html	Oracle Resources Center at TechnoSolutions.
Oracle in general	http://www.webring.org/cgi-bin/webring?ring=oracleweb;list	Good Web sites for Oracle.
Oracle Magazine	http://www.oraclemagazine.com/	Oracle Magazine online.
Oracle Proxy Server 2.0	http://www.olab.com/proxy/html/ds_20.html	General information about Oracle Proxy Server.
Oracle user groups	http://www.ioug.org	International Oracle Users Group—your link to all of the regional Oracle Users Groups.
Oracle Web cartridges	http://www.olab.com/cdk/content/samples/cdk/bluestone/oracarts.htm	Creating Oracle cartridges.
Oracle Web cartridges	http://www.olab.com/cdk/content/samples/cdk/cdg/cdg1.htm	Introduction to Oracle cartridges.
Oracle Web cartridges	http://www.olab.com/cdk/content/samples/cdk/sampcart.htm	Cartridge samples from Oracle.
OWA_SEC	http://oac1.oac.tju.edu:8888/ows-adoc/ap2dvtkt.htm#406009	The PL/SQL Web Toolkit Reference online, including information on OWA_SEC.
OWA_SEC	http://teku.pspt.fi/ows-adoc/psqlwtlk.htm	The PL/SQL Web Toolkit Reference online.
OWA_SEC	http://www.mpimg-berlin-dahlem.mpg.de/~kramer/	Documentation compiled by an Oracle user.

Site Type	Site Address	Comments
OWA_SEC	http://www.olab.com/doc/books/plsql/pssec.htm	The owa_sec documentation online.
PDF files	http://www.adobe.com/prodindex/acrobat/readstep.html	Free reader 4.0 now available.
PDF files	http://www.adobe.com/supportservice/custsupport/database.html	Support database.
PDF files	http://www.adobe.com/supportservice/custsupport/download.html	Files for downloading.
PDF files	http://www.adobe.com/supportservice/custsupport/techguide.html	Technical guides.
PERL	http://www.cis.ufl.edu:80/perl/	Perl archive.
PERL	http://www.cpan.org	A comprehensive site for material on Perl. Highly recommended!
PERL sources	http://ftp.cis.ufl.edu	Directory /pub/perl/scr/5.0.
PERL sources	http://ftp.netlabs.com	Directory /pub/outgoing/perl5.0.
PERL sources	http://www.activestate.com	Active Perl 5.15 available for Windows platforms.
PERL sources	http://www.iupui.edu/npi/intro2perl	Online introduction to Perl.
PERL sources	http://www.microsoft.com/com/dcom/dcom95/download.asp	Dcom 1.3 available for Windows 95. This is necessary to run Active Perl 5.15.
PERL sources	http://www.rexswain.com/perl5.html	Rex Swain's HTMLified Perl 5 Reference Guide.
PL/SQL	http://oac1.oac.tju.edu:8888/ows-adoc/ap2dvtkt.htm#406009	Web toolkit.

Site Type	Site Address	Comments
PL/SQL	http://technet.oracle.com/public/spotlite/nca/csn.htm	Technical spotlight: cartridge developer resources.
PL/SQL	http://www.columbia.edu/~nv49/qc2203/plsql01.htm	Series of excellent lectures on PL/SQL.
PL/SQL Cartridge	http://www.icarus.at/ows-adoc/docs/cart/plaguse.htm	An excellent series of tutorials on using PL/SQL cartridges.
PL/SQL Cartridge	http://www.olab.com/doc/books/plsql/pl_intro.htm	PL/SQL cartridge documentation online.
PL/SQL Cartridge	http://www.tusc.com/software/posters.html	TUSC offers a poster showing the PL/SQL language for a nominal fee. Highly recommended for both beginner and advanced PL/SQL programmers.
PL/SQL cartridge	http://www.webresource.net/database/articles/owas_plsqlcart/	Article on PL/SQL cartridge that looks at one of the most popular methods of building applications with Oracle's Application Server: the PL/SQL Cartridge.
Popular search engines	http://galaxy.einet.net/search-pages.html	The Galaxy directory links to thousands of sites around the Internet. Galaxy makes it possible to search these sites in various ways to help you find the information you're looking for.
Popular search engines	http://infoseek.go.com/	Infoseek search engine.
Popular search engines	http://magellan.excite.com/	Magellan Internet Guide search engine.
Popular search engines	http://webcrawler.com/	Webcrawler search engine.
Popular search engines	http://www.altavista.com/	AltaVista search engine.
Popular search engines	http://www.excite.com/	Excite search engine.

Site Type	Site Address	Comments
Popular search engines	http://www.google.com/	Google search engine. Uses a complicated mathematical analysis, calculated on more than a billion hyperlinks on the Web, to return high-quality search results so you don't have to sift through junk.
Popular search engines	http://www.hotbot.com/	Hotbot search engine.
Popular search engines	http://www.looksmart.com/	Looksmart search engine. Looksmart live is similar to Ask Jeeves, except you receive an e-mail with an answer to your question.
Popular search engines	http://www.lycos.com/	Lycos search engine.
Popular search engines	http://www.miningco.com/	About.com search engine. a.k.a. About.com
Popular search engines	http://www.northernlight.com/	Northern Light search engine.
Popular search engines	http://www.thunderstone.com/	Thunderstone is an independent R&D company that has been providing state-of-the-art solutions to intelligent information retrieval and management problems for over 18 years.
Popular search engines	http://www.yahoo.com/	Yahoo search engine that is a directory search engine that breaks Web sites into 25,000 categories.
Search engines	http://www.browserwatch.com	Leading site for information on browsers and plug-ins.
Search engines	http://www.rankthis.com	RankThis! is a free online tool to help you determine your "ranking" on different keyword sets in 10 of the major search engines.

Site Type	**Site Address**	**Comments**
SQL*Plus Plus	http://www.msw.com.au/sqlpp/sqlpp.htm	SQL++ is a tool to manipulate and execute SQL commands and PL/SQL programs. It is designed to be compatible with Oracle's SQL*Plus and encompasses most of its features in addition to a number of enhancements.
SSL	http://oac1.oac.tju.edu:8888/ows-adoc/concept3.htm#534251	Oracle SSL documentation online.
Thin client	http://www.compstar.com/newsst4.htm	An excellent article on thin client.
Thin client	http://www.news.com/News/Item/0,4,26041,00.html	Article: "First CE-based thin client ships."
Thin client	http://www.news.com/SpecialFeatures/0,5,16480,00.html	Article: "What exactly is a thin client?"
Thin client	http://www.state.fl.us/stp/project/ThinsClient.htm	Thin Client Libraries project.
Thin client	http://www.taylorcenter.com/entprise.htm	The Taylor Center for Thin Client Computing has been involved in architecting some of the largest thin client deployments in existence.
Thin client	http://www.wyse.com/sitemap/thin.htm	Wyse thin client information.
Thin client	http://www.zdnet.com/pcweek/reviews/0330/30thin.html	Article about how tricky measuring thin client savings can be.
TOAD	http://www.alphaworks.ibm.com/formula/toad	A review of TOAD.
TOAD	http://www.quests.com/	Information about TOAD directly from the owners of the product.

Site Type	Site Address	Comments
TOAD	http://www.toadsoft.com/	The original TOAD site.
TUSC	http://www.tusc.com/	Free downloads of scripts, PowerPoint presentations, tips and techniques, and more. Contains items of interest for DBA's, developers, and so forth.
Using Web Server Generator	http://www.oracle-korea.com/oeds/html/collater.htm	Contains Quick Tours and white papers on Oracle's Enterprise Developer Suite. Allows you to take the Designer and Developer Quick Tour.
UTL_FILE	http://apoug.oracle.com.sg/techtips/400-2.htm	Data and File I/O using PL/SQL.
UTL_FILE	http://dingo.vut.edu.au/voug/news97/news25/utl_file.html	Oracle 7.3 comes with a utility called UTL_FILE for performing file I/O in PL/SQL. It is very similar to the C programming language's file I/O facility where a file is opened, read from, written to, and closed in the end. This package may be found in $ORACLE_HOME/ rdbms/admin/utlfile.sql. Its accompanying documentation is covered in Chapter 8 of the Application Developers' Guide Release 7.3. This article elaborates on UTL_FILE's finer features, and demonstrate its usefulness through an example.
UTL_FILE	http://www.columbia.edu/~nv49/qc2203/plsql14.htm	A valuable presentation on using UTL_FILE presented as a lecture in a series of fine presentations on PL/SQL.

Site Type	Site Address	Comments
UTL_FILE	http://www.nxt-wave.com/techtalk/art1017.html	The following procedure will export package body, specification, and procedures to a given directory (idir). The objects like the supplied iLikeObject string will be exported. The directory specified has to be added to the ora[instance] parameter file. If this is not done, a file access error will result. The files are written to the database servers directory structure.
Visual Café	http://www.beasys.com/action/press/press136.htm	Article: "BEA Bundles Symantec Visual Café with BEA WebLogic Application Server, Symantec Offers BEA WebLogic to Java Tools Customers."
Visual Café	http://www.devdaily.com/Java/edu/vc/	Visual Cafe Education Center, where you'll find "how-to" articles, tips, techniques, and free source code that we've developed using Visual Cafe, from Symantec.
Visual Café	http://www.symantec.com/vcafe/guide/overview.html	Symantec's excellent site on Visual Café. Among its contents are a discussion of new features, a visual walkthrough of the product, a closer look at the components of the product, and a discussion of the integrated Just In Time compiler.
Visual Café	http://www.zdnet.com/pcweek/stories/news/0,4153,363870,00.html	Article: "Visual Cafe for Java: Have It Your Way."
Web development in general	file:////Tuscil_tcdb1/WebPages/Tcdb1/Tips/Index.htm	MOUG Oracle WebServer mini-session.

Site Type	Site Address	Comments
Web development in general	http://browserwatch.internet.com/plug-in.html	Downloads BrowserWatch—Plug-In Plaza.
Web development in general	http://filepile.com/nc/start	FilePile—Over 1,000,000 FREE Files!
Web development in general	http://home.netscape.com/bookmark/40/download.html	Files to download.
Web development in general	http://infolab.webdevelop.com/	Welcome to infolab by Atif Ghaffar (courtesy of www.webdevelop.com and www.cyberlab.ch).
Web development in general	http://software.infoseek.com/download/ultra_hostname_nt.htm	Ultraseek Server Download Key Request—NT.
Web development in general	http://webcoder.com/index_real.html	WebCoder.com—Your home for JavaScript and Dynamic HTML on the Web.
Web development in general	http://webreview.com/wr/pub/webtools/	A complete list of Web tools.
Web development in general	http://worldwidemart.com/scripts/	Matt's script archive.
Web development in general	http://www.Adeveloper.com/links.html	Web site development links.
Web development in general	http://www.builder.com	An excellent, very comprehensive site dealing with a wide variety of subjects pertaining to Web development. Highly recommended!

Site Type	Site Address	Comments
Web development in general	http://www.cast.org/bobby/	Checks your code for you.
Web development in general	http://www.cpuniverse.com/archives/1999/guide/ratesurvey.html	Contract Professional universe—Pay rates for Computer professionals.
Web development in general	http://www.crevier.org/	A Webmaster's resource from Scott Crevier.
Web development in general	http://www.danworld.com/	The Danworld Network.
Web development in general	http://www.delorie.com/web/wpbcv.html	Checks your code for you.
Web development in general	http://www.download.com/PC/Result/TitleList/0,2,0-d-37-51,00.html	Files to download.
Web development in general	http://www.webtrends.net	As for styles, you can run your site through http://www.webtrends.net—they will analyze your site (backward compatibility).
Web development in general	http://www.fccc.edu/users/muquit/Count.html	WWW homepage access counter.
Web development in general	http://www.freecode.com/	FreeCode—free programming source code.
Web development in general	http://www.freesoft97.com/	Extensive freeware downloads! Well-maintained and comprehensive.

Site Type	**Site Address**	**Comments**
Web development in general	http://www.inetu.net	Internet consulting Web site development and design.
Web development in general	http://www.inquiry.com	Ask the professional Web developers related questions.
Web development in general	http://www.internet.com	Web developers channel.
Web development in general	http://www.jumbo.com/	The JUMBO! Download Network.
Web development in general	http://www.newapps.com/	NewApps.com...Web software releases as they happen.
Web development in general	http://www.projectcool.com/developer/	Project Cool Developer Zone: tutorials + reference on HTML, design, acrobat, and more.
Web development in general	http://www.shareware.com/	shareware.com—The way to find shareware on the Internet.
Web development in general	http://www.stars.com/Vlib/Software/Tools.html	Developer tools.
Web development in general	http://www.sunworld.com	The URL to subscribe to the regular e-mail newsletter(about three times per month) is http://www.Sunworld.com/sunworldonline/subscribe.html.
Web development in general	http://www.uwsuper.edu/	University of Wisconsin—Superior's site: has some good links for Internet developers.

Site Type	Site Address	Comments
Web development in general	http://www.wdvl.com	Web developers virtual library.
Web development in general	http://www.webdeveloper.com	Resources and technical information on Web development. WebDeveloper.com home page.
Web development in general	http://www.webreference.com	Information about the Web and Web development.
Web development in general	http://www.winfiles.com	Of particular interest for Windows development.
Web development in general	http://www.yotta.com/magazine/freecomp.htm	Free computer magazines.
Web development in general	http://www.xoom.com/clips/website	Xoom clip art.
Web development in general	www.developer.com	A very comprehensive site offering free code and discussions of almost every subject pertaining to Web development. This is a highly recommended site for both the beginner and advanced Web developer.
Web development in general	www.htmlgoodies.com	An EarthWeb site offering comprehensive treatment of HTML. Includes free code, tutorials, how-tos, and much more. Highly recommended!
Web development in general	www.web-developer.com	One of the most comprehensive Web sites for developers. If it pertains to Web development, you will find it here!

Site Type	Site Address	Comments
Web development in general	www.webreference.com	An excellent starting place for Web development. Contains information on HTML, Java, etc.
Web development in general	http://cws.internet.com/	Stroud's Consummate Internet Apps List.
Web graphics	http://www.graphxkingdom.com/	The graphics kingdom.
Web graphics	http://www.webplaces.com	Webplaces Internet search guide.
Web graphics	http://www.xanthviper.com	Custom design and cool graphics, and cyber cam.
Web graphics	http://www.yuengling.com	Containing moving graphics for Web pages.
Web graphics	www.clipart.com	Clipart for your Web site and more.
Web graphics	www.coolarchive.com	Fonts, icons, clipart, animations, backgrounds, bullets, bars, arrows, sounds, and more.
Web graphics	www.iconbazaar.com	A large collection of graphics for your Web page.
Web graphics	www.infinitefish.com	Screen saver bitmaps.
Web graphics	www.mediabuilder.com	Great graphics; make buttons too!
Web security	http://www.spirit.com/CSI/firewall.html	CSI's Free Firewall Resource.
Web security	http://www.zdnet.com/	Web security and Internet commerce.
WEB Server	http://www.dulcian.com/papers/webpaper.html	Migrating from previous versions.
WEB Server	http://www.olab.com/doc/books/inst_sol/upgrade.htm	Online documentation for migrating from prior OAS versions.

Site Type	Site Address	Comments
Web: selected company profiles	http://www.broadvision.com	BroadVision, Inc. develops, markets, and supports fully integrated application software solutions. The company's solutions manage one-to-one relationships for the extended enterprise. BroadVision's software is used by financial services, retail, distribution, high technology, telecommunications, and travel industries.
Web: selected company profiles	http://www.netperceptions.com	Net Perceptions, Inc. provides real-time relationship marketing solutions that enable Internet retailers to market to customers on a personalized, one-to-one basis. The Company's customers include barnesandnoble.com inc; CDnow, Inc.; Egghead.com, Inc.; Preview Travel, Inc.; Ticketmaster Online-CitySearch, Inc.; and Value America, Inc.
WebAlchemy	http://www.olab.com/cdk/content/samples/cdk/webalch/readme1.htm	Information on WebAlchemy from OLAB.
XML	http://technet.oracle.com/tech/xml/info/indus/iEMPAC.htm	XML and Oracle8i case study. Learn how Indus International, an Oracle partner company, rearchitected its application for the Internet using Oracle8i and XML.
XML	http://www.informationweek.com/725/xml.htm	Links to a .pdf file with some helps for xml.
XML	http://www.jclark.com/xml/	Includes a test suite, some software, and so forth.

Site Type	Site Address	Comments
XML	http://www.oasis-open.org/cover/	This SGML/XML Web page is a comprehensive online database containing reference information and software pertaining to the Standard Generalized Markup Language (SGML) and its subset, the Extensible Markup Language (XML). The database features an SGML/XML news column "What's New?" and a cumulative annotated bibliography with over 2,000 entries. The collection contains over 2,500 documents explaining and illustrating the application of the SGML/XML family of standards, including HyTime, DSSSL, XSL, XLL, XLink, XPointer, SPDL, CGM, ISO-HTML, and several others. These documents are accessible from a condensed topical overview or from the fully expanded contents listing (Site Index) in a separate document. An extended introduction to the Web site is provided in the site description. The SGML/XML Web page is currently sponsored by OASIS (Organization for the Advancement of Structured Information Standards) and four OASIS Members: GCA (Graphic Communications Association), ISOGEN International Corp, Inso Corporation, and Sun Microsystems.
XML	http://www.oracle.com/xml/	Learn how your business can benefit from an XML-enabled infrastructure.

Site Type	Site Address	Comments
XML	http://www.schema.net/	SCHEMA.NET, along with sister sites XMLINFO (http://www.xmlinfo.com/) and XMLSOFTWARE (http://www.xmlsoftware.com/), aim to provide well-organized information and resources on the Extensible Markup Language (XML), one of the most significant developments on the World Wide Web and in electronic publishing and electronic commerce.
XML	http://www.sciam.com/1999/0599issue/0599bosak.html	XML and the Second-Generation Web. The combination of hypertext and a global Internet started a revolution. A new ingredient, XML, is poised to finish the job. By Jon Bosak and Tim Bray for Scientific American.
XML	http://www.sgmlsource.com/8879rev/	This archive contains the latest revisions of the key documents that are considered to govern the Project Editor's review of ISO 8879.
XML	http://www.stg.brown.edu/~sjd/xlinkintro.html	An excellent article on XML linking edited by Steve DeRose.
XML	http://www.w3.org/XML/	W3C's official XML page. This is a very comprehensive site for XML.
XML	http://www.xml.com/xml/pub	This two-part tutorial demonstrates how XML can be used to improve how search engines work. It shows how to automate retrieval of search results and when those results are available in XML, instead of HTML, how much more easily they can be organized and displayed for users. This demo requires IE 5 because the XML processing is done on the client side

Index

A

B

C

D

F

G

H

I

J

K

L

M

N

O

P

Q

R

S

T

U

V

W

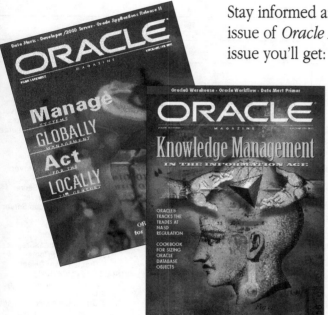